Springer Texts in Business and Economics

Springer Texts in Business and Economics (STBE) delivers high-quality instructional content for undergraduates and graduates in all areas of Business/Management Science and Economics. The series is comprised of self-contained books with a broad and comprehensive coverage that are suitable for class as well as for individual self-study. All texts are authored by established experts in their fields and offer a solid methodological background, often accompanied by problems and exercises.

Pasquale De Luca

Corporate Finance

Fundamentals of Value and Price

Springer

Pasquale De Luca
Faculty of Economics
University of Rome Sapienza
Rome, Italy

ISSN 2192-4333 ISSN 2192-4341 (electronic)
Springer Texts in Business and Economics
ISBN 978-3-031-18299-0 ISBN 978-3-031-18300-3 (eBook)
https://doi.org/10.1007/978-3-031-18300-3

This Springer imprint is published by the registered company Springer Nature Switzerland AG
The registered company address is: Gewerbestrasse 11, 6330 Cham, Switzerland

GPSR Compliance

The European Union's (EU) General Product Safety Regulation (GPSR) is a set of rules that requires consumer products to be safe and our obligations to ensure this.

If you have any concerns about our products, you can contact us on ProductSafety@springernature.com

In case Publisher is established outside the EU, the EU authorized representative is:

Springer Nature Customer Service Center GmbH
Europaplatz 3
69115 Heidelberg, Germany

Batch number: 10844661

Printed by Printforce, the Netherlands

Advances in Intelligent Systems and Computing

Volume 928

The series "Advances in Intelligent Systems and Computing" contains publications on theory, applications, and design methods of Intelligent Systems and Intelligent Computing. Virtually all disciplines such as engineering, natural sciences, computer and information science, ICT, economics, business, e-commerce, environment, healthcare, life science are covered. The list of topics spans all the areas of modern intelligent systems and computing such as: computational intelligence, soft computing including neural networks, fuzzy systems, evolutionary computing and the fusion of these paradigms, social intelligence, ambient intelligence, computational neuroscience, artificial life, virtual worlds and society, cognitive science and systems, Perception and Vision, DNA and immune based systems, self-organizing and adaptive systems, e-Learning and teaching, human-centered and human-centric computing, recommender systems, intelligent control, robotics and mechatronics including human-machine teaming, knowledge-based paradigms, learning paradigms, machine ethics, intelligent data analysis, knowledge management, intelligent agents, intelligent decision making and support, intelligent network security, trust management, interactive entertainment, Web intelligence and multimedia.

The publications within "Advances in Intelligent Systems and Computing" are primarily proceedings of important conferences, symposia and congresses. They cover significant recent developments in the field, both of a foundational and applicable character. An important characteristic feature of the series is the short publication time and world-wide distribution. This permits a rapid and broad dissemination of research results.

**** Indexing: The books of this series are submitted to ISI Proceedings, EI-Compendex, DBLP, SCOPUS, Google Scholar and Springerlink ****

More information about this series at http://www.springer.com/series/11156

Zheng Xu · Kim-Kwang Raymond Choo ·
Ali Dehghantanha · Reza Parizi ·
Mohammad Hammoudeh
Editors

Cyber Security Intelligence and Analytics

Set 2

Springer

Editors
Zheng Xu
Shanghai University
Shanghai, China

Kim-Kwang Raymond Choo
University of Texas at San Antonio
San Antonio, TX, USA

Ali Dehghantanha
University of Guelph
Guelph, ON, Canada

Reza Parizi
Kennesaw State University
Marietta, GA, USA

Mohammad Hammoudeh
Manchester Metropolitan University
Stockport, UK

ISSN 2194-5357 ISSN 2194-5365 (electronic)
Advances in Intelligent Systems and Computing
ISBN 978-3-030-15234-5 ISBN 978-3-030-15235-2 (eBook)
https://doi.org/10.1007/978-3-030-15235-2

Library of Congress Control Number: 2019933893

This Springer imprint is published by the registered company Springer Nature Switzerland AG
The registered company address is: Gewerbestrasse 11, 6330 Cham, Switzerland

Preface

The 2019 International Conference on Cyber Security Intelligence and Analytics (CSIA 2019) is an international conference dedicated to promoting novel theoretical and applied research advances in the interdisciplinary agenda of cyber security, particularly focusing on threat intelligence and analytics and countering cybercrime. Cyber security experts, including those in data analytics, incident response, and digital forensics, need to be able to rapidly detect, analyze, and defend against a diverse range of cyber threats in near real-time conditions. For example, when a significant amount of data is collected from or generated by different security monitoring solutions, intelligent and next-generation big data analytical techniques are necessary to mine, interpret, and extract knowledge of this (big) data. Cyber threat intelligence and analytics are among the fastest-growing interdisciplinary fields of research bringing together researchers from different fields such as digital forensics, political and security studies, criminology, cyber security, big data analytics, and machine learning to detect, contain, and mitigate advanced persistent threats and fight against organized cybercrimes.

Each paper was reviewed by at least three independent experts, and the acceptance rate was 45%. The conference would not have been possible without the contributions of the authors. We sincerely thank all the authors for their valuable contributions. We would like to express our appreciation to all members of the Program Committee for their valuable efforts in the review process that helped us to guarantee the highest quality of the selected papers for the conference.

We would like to express our thanks to Prof. Shunxiang Zhang, Anhui University of Science and Technology, and Prof. Xiangfeng Luo, Shanghai University, for being the keynote speakers at the conference. We would also thank the Steering Committee, General Chairs, Program Committee Chairs, Organizing Chairs, and Workshop Chairs. The local organizers' and the students' help is highly appreciated.

Our special thanks are due also to the editors for publishing the proceedings in Advances in Intelligent Systems and Computing of Springer.

Zheng Xu
Kim-Kwang Raymond Choo
Ali Dehghantanha
Reza Parizi
Mohammad Hammoudeh

Organization

General Chair

Zheng Xu	TRIMS, China

Program Committee Chairs

Ali Dehghantanha	University of Guelph, Canada
Mohammad Hammoudeh	Manchester Metropolitan University, UK
Reza M. Parizi	Kennesaw State University, USA

Publication Chairs

Shuai Ding	Hefei University of Science and Technology, China
Kun Gao	Zhejiang Wanli University, China

Publicity Chairs

Xianchao Wang	Fuyang Normal University, China
Jemal Abawajy	Deakin University, Australia

Local Organizing Chairs

Xueping Liu	Anhui Polytechnic University, China
Qingjun Wang	Anhui Polytechnic University, China

Program Committee Members

William Bradley Glisson	Sam Houston State University, USA
George Grispos	University of Nebraska Omaha, USA
V. Vijayakumar	VIT Chennai, India
Aniello Castiglione	Universit di Salerno, Italy
Neil Yen	University of Aizu, Japan
Shunxiang Zhang	Anhui University of Science and Technology, China
Guangli Zhu	Anhui University of Science and Technology, China
Tao Liao	Anhui University of Science and Technology, China
Xiaobo Yin	Anhui University of Science and Technology, China
Kelei Sun	Anhui University of Science and Technology, China
Xiangfeng Luo	Shanghai University, China
Xiao Wei	Shanghai University, China
Huan Du	Shanghai University, China
Zhiguo Yan	Fudan University, China
Abdulbasit Darem	Northern Border University, Saudi Arabia
Hairulnizam Mahdin	Universiti Tun Hussein Onn Malaysia
Anil Kumar K. M.	JSS Science & Technology University, Mysore, Karnataka, India
Haruna Chiroma	Abubakar Tafawa Balewa University, Bauchi, Nigeria
Yong Ge	University of North Carolina at Charlotte, USA
Yi Liu	Tsinghua University, China
Foluso Ladeinde	SUNY Korea
Kuien Liu	Pivotal Inc., USA
Feng Lu	Institute of Geographic Science and Natural Resources Research, Chinese Academy of Sciences
Ricardo J. Soares Magalhaes	University of Queensland, Australia
Alan Murray	Drexel University, USA
Yasuhide Okuyama	University of Kitakyushu, Japan
Wei Xu	Renmin University of China
Chaowei Phil Yang	George Mason University, USA
Hengshu Zhu	Baidu Inc., China
Morshed Chowdhury	Deakin University, Australia
Elfizar	University of Riau, Indonesia
Rohaya Latip	Universiti Putra Malaysia

Contents

Short Papers

An Improved Load Balancing Algorithm Based on Neural Network

Rui Song and Hongqiong Huang(✉)

Shanghai Maritime University, Shanghai 201306, China
2369654285@qq.com

Abstract. The rapid growth of Internet technology makes our life more convenient and exciting. However, the number of Internet users is also increasing rapidly. More and more data requests make large-scale concurrent access to network resources. All kinds of faults appear in network services. For example, the time delay of network service and the collapse of network system are all kinds of phenomena. How to solve these problems has become a hotspot of current research. Generally speaking, the combination of neural network and cluster equalization is a more appropriate method. The combination of Neural Network and Cluster Equilibrium can make it possess some characteristics of high precision. Such as availability, feasibility, reliability and manageability. At the same time, it can improve the system throughput CPU efficiency tasks, request rate and so on. This topic is based on server cluster architecture and common classics. The classical balancing algorithm has a good effect on load balancing, but they also have some shortcomings, for example, the weight cannot be adaptively changed. For some users, the performance of request service and cluster equilibrium cannot be accurately reflected. Based on the shortcomings of existing neural networks and load balancing, an improved scheme and algorithm are proposed.

Keywords: Neural network · Load balancing · Server cluster

1 Introduction

In today's world, with the rapid development of the Internet, network access is also increasing rapidly, the demand for various services is diverse, results in a sharp increase in network load, the difficulty of dealing with transactions is greatly enhanced [1–5]. Because the server loads data too slowly, the problem of not serving a large number of users at the same time also arises. Clusters can be connected through high-speed network and managed in a single-system mode by independent Web servers [6–12]. Clustering enables servers to load-balance tasks reasonably and improve the quality of service of servers [13, 14].

In the current situation, there are two kinds of load balancing: dynamic and static. Static load balancing algorithm distributes tasks in a fixed proportion, such as polling algorithm (RR) and weighted polling algorithm (WRR); dynamic load balancing algorithm distributes tasks according to the status of the current server, such as minimum number of connections algorithm (LC) and weighted minimum number of

Z. Xu et al. (Eds.): CSIA 2019, AISC 928, pp. 730–736, 2020.
https://doi.org/10.1007/978-3-030-15235-2_100

connections algorithm (WLC) [19, 20]. However, in practice, the performance of servers is uneven, and it is difficult to get a more accurate value to reflect the current running situation. In the case of large server load balancer, the dynamic load balancing algorithm is not necessarily accurate to express the current running situation. Based on the traditional load balancing algorithm, this paper proposes an improved weighted minimum number of connections algorithm (IWLC) based on neural network feedback mechanism, which can improve CPU utilization, reduce service delay and reduce the time required for task request rate.

2 Necessity Analysis of Load Balancing

G The main traffic scheduling algorithms designed according to the current network conditions have lag effect. They can't allocate the available resources in advance and can't realize the real-time transfer of network traffic. Especially when new services occur frequently, they cannot cope with the sudden negative carrier movement. In cognitive networks, its pre-learning ability enables the network to allocate available resources in advance according to the changing trend of network traffic, to ensure the service's quality of service, and to improve the efficiency of network resource utilization. Therefore, it is very necessary to design a dynamic traffic scheduling algorithm to allocate the available network resources in advance according to the load changes, to achieve real-time and dynamic scheduling of network traffic, so as to make the traffic uniformly distributed in the whole network and reduce network congestion, on the premise of guaranteeing users' QoS requirements.

In the realization of load balancing, scheduling algorithm is the core content. In the current network, the existing traffic scheduling algorithms mainly include: round-call scheduling algorithm, weighted round-call scheduling algorithm, minimum connection scheduling algorithm, weighted minimum connection method, destination address hash scheduling, source address hash scheduling and so on. It can be divided into static traffic scheduling algorithm and dynamic traffic scheduling algorithm. With the expansion of network scale and the increase of user demand, static traffic scheduling algorithm can no longer meet the needs of load balancing. A dynamic adaptive traffic scheduling algorithm is more suitable for today's network applications.

2.1 Round-Call Scheduling Algorithm

This algorithm does not consider the current number of connections and response speed of server. The requirement for servers is that all servers have the same processing performance. Because its algorithm is relatively simple, it is not suitable for different processing performance in server groups. And once the request service time changes greatly, the cyclic scheduling algorithm can easily cause the load imbalance of the server.

2.2 Weighted Round Call Scheduling Algorithms

The advantage of this algorithm is simple and efficient. It considers the difference of processing performance between different servers, but it also has disadvantages. Weighted round-call scheduling algorithm is a stateless scheduling algorithm. When the request service time changes greatly, a single weighted round-call scheduling algorithm may lead to load imbalance between servers.

2.3 Minimum Connection Scheduling Algorithms

This algorithm assigns new connection requests to the server with the smallest number of connections. This refers to a dynamic scheduling algorithm, the minimum connection scheduling algorithm estimates the load of the server by the number of currently active connections of the server. The scheduler needs to record the number of connections established by each server. When a request is scheduled to a server, the number of connections is added, and when the connection terminates or times out, the number of connections is reduced by one. If we assume that each server has the same processing performance, the minimum connection scheduling algorithm sends load changes to the same server.

3 Improved Adaptive BP Neural Network Algorithm

Artificial neural network (ANN) is a new intelligent learning system of biomimetic system, which is developing rapidly at present. It is realized by simulating the structure and function of biological neural network and establishing similar mathematical and computational models. Its basic unit is a single neuron. Neural network has the characteristics of multi-input and multi-output, and has a strong advantage in dealing with the non-linearity of the system. The basic idea of BP neural network is to calculate the inverse propagation of errors by least square method, and to reduce the error between the actual output and the expected output by using the derivative of errors when each weight changes. In addition to forward propagation, it also needs to calculate back propagation. The information of each layer of neurons is only affected by the former layer of neurons. If the expected error of the output layer satisfies the given requirements, the learning will be completed. Otherwise, the error signal will be back-propagated, and the weights of neurons will be revised to reduce the network error.

Although BP neural network has the ability of realizing complex non-linear mapping and generalization, it can solve many complex internal problems, and has been applied in many fields. But it still inevitably has some shortcomings, as follows:

(1) Because the traditional BP network calculation model is based on gradient descent method, the gradient cannot descend too fast, otherwise the network calculation will fluctuate greatly, which limits the convergence speed of the network.
(2) The choice of learning rate, too large or too small initial learning rate will cause deviation in network learning and affect the performance of the algorithm. In addition, only by changing the initial value and network parameters several times can the network cross the local minimum and obtain the global optimal solution.

For the shortcomings of traditional BP and the characteristics of load balancing, we add momentum BP algorithm to the traditional BP neural network, and propose an adaptive neural network algorithm.

Aiming at the over-fitting problem of the wavelet neural network, an improved strategy is proposed. On the basis of the prediction model of the wavelet neural network, the least square method (LMS) is introduced to process the input samples, that is, to fuzzify the input samples. Then the processed samples are used as input samples of the following WNN prediction model. The least squares method can be used to process a set of data and to find the dependence between variables from a set of measured data. This functional relationship is called empirical formula. Firstly, the input samples are processed by LMS, and the predicted results are used as the input of wavelet transform. Then, the scaling coefficient series and the wavelet coefficient series obtained by wavelet transform are used as the input of linear neural network and ELman neural network respectively. The original time series is used as the output to train the network. Finally, BP network simulation and data are used to output the predicted network traffic value.

Proportional factors are introduced to speed up learning. Dynamic ξ regulation can make the learning efficiency of traditional BP inefficient, because the neural network is based on the idea of negative gradient. At the beginning, it is hoped that ξ become larger, so the error will decrease rapidly, and when approaching convergence, it is hoped that ξ will become smaller and avoid over-regulation. Next, we introduce a dynamic regulation of ξ aspect, which includes $\xi_1 \in (0, 1]$ regulate ξ and introduce a ξ to control the area of action of ξ. The formula is as follows:

$$\xi = \begin{cases} \frac{1}{\xi_1}\xi, \frac{E(K+1)}{E(K)} < \xi_2 \\ \xi_1\xi, \frac{E(K+1)}{E(K)} < \xi_2 \end{cases}$$

From the above formula, we can see that E (k + 1) and E (k) have current error and step-up error respectively. Take $\xi_2 = 1$ as an example, when E (k, 1) is smaller than E (k), it means that the learning direction is correct, ξ_2 dividing by less than 1 of 1 to improve the learning rate and accelerate convergence. On the contrary, it means that the learning direction is wrong, ξ is multiplied by less than 1 of ξ to reduce the learning rate and correct it in time. This lightweight change improves the convergence speed and stability of the algorithm, and improves the correctness of the algorithm. At the same time, a "momentum factor" is added to enable the network to cross the local minimum. The inertia is used to make the network pass these local minimum values when it converges. The weights of the output layer and the hidden layer obtained by this method can improve the performance of the network to a certain extent. The increase of learning rate improves the fitting and generalization ability of the network to a certain extent, thus avoiding the illusion of iteration entering local minimum.

4 An Improved Load Balancing Algorithm Based on Neural Network

Although the weighted minimum number of connections algorithm takes into account the performance of the service node and the number of connections currently active, it is easy to cause load imbalance when the weight of the request connection changes greatly. Based on this, an improved weighted minimum number of connections (IWLC) algorithm based on neural network feedback mechanism is proposed. Based on the WLC algorithm, this algorithm obtains the optimal load weight by observing the real-time load of the server.

(1) Design Ideas of Improved Algorithms

The load of the server node is equal to the product of the utilization ratio of the node in the server and the corresponding weight. The idea of improved IWLC algorithm: The parameter values of server nodes are collected within a certain period of time, and then the load ratio R (Si) of the nodes is obtained by comparing the collected parameter values with the initialization threshold values, and the load distribution of the server nodes is determined by the load ratio. When the load ratio is not greater than the initial load ratio threshold, the weight of the current node is recalculated and compared with the weight of the initialized node, so as to get the weight ratio of a node, and finally redistribute the load for each node of the server according to this ratio.

Load ratio represents the processing capacity of the server, and the smaller the value, the better the server node can handle most of the capacity, so it can receive more processing load. The larger the value, the weaker the server can handle, the less the load it can receive and process. When the load ratio reaches 0.95, it shows that the load of this server has reached the edge of the load. During the current dynamic weight distribution period, the load balancer will no longer assign tasks to the server.

According to the principle of load balancing technology, the client consisting of a subnet will send requests to the server using remote IPNetwork, and the requests will be sent to the router first. After router arrives at LoadBalancer, LoadBalancer monitors and adjusts the load of the cluster node composed of Web servers, and then sends the request back to the client. The improved load balancing algorithm model is shown in Fig. 1.

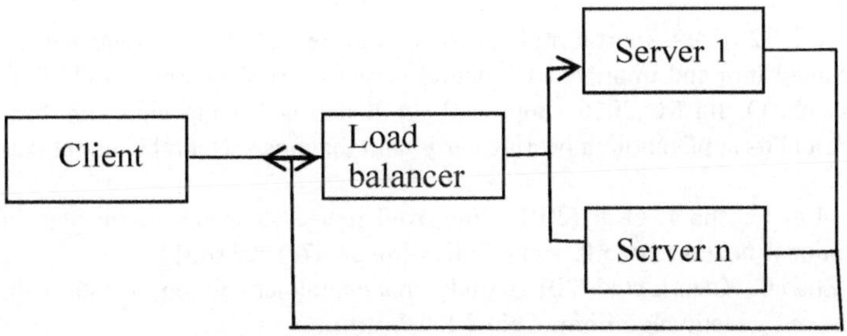

Fig. 1. An improved load balancing algorithm model

(2) Flow Chart of Improved Algorithm

The first step is to collect the parameters of the server node within a period of time.

In the second step, the collected CPU utilization L (Ci) and network utilization L (Ni) are compared with the threshold set at initialization (CPU utilization threshold is M (Ci), and network utilization threshold is M (Ni). If L (Ci) > M (Ci) or L (Ni) > M (Ni), the real-time load ratio R (Si) = 0.95, is set. Thus, during the current dynamic weight distribution load period, the server is no longer assigned tasks.

The third step is to calculate the load ratio R (Si) of the Web server node. The fourth step is to compare the calculated load ratio R (Si) of the Web server node with the load threshold set at the initial time. If the load ratio is greater than the threshold set at the initial time, the server cluster node will no longer be allocated.

In the improved IWLC algorithm, server CPU utilization, task request rate and service delay time are better than WLC algorithm and WRR algorithm. This shows that IWLC load balancing algorithm can better achieve the purpose of load balancing compared with the common traditional load balancing algorithm, so as to solve the problem of serving a large number of users on a large scale at the same time in the business.

5 Summary

Aiming at the disadvantage that the system cannot dynamically reflect the real-time load of the server, an improved load balancing algorithm based on neural network feedback mechanism is proposed. Compared with common load balancing algorithms and considering the impact of cluster real-time load on load balancing, BP neural network feedback mechanism is introduced to feedback load status in real-time. According to the load status of real-time feedback, the data is transmitted to the improved WLC algorithm to judge the connection requests accepted by the server. According to OPNET simulation results, IWLC algorithm can well reflect the load status of servers, which can more effectively realize the problem of serving a large number of users at the same time, reduce response time, and balance the utilization of each server according to IWLC algorithm.

References

1. Yu F, Xu X (2014) A short-term load forecasting model of natural gas based on optimized genetic algorithm and improved BP neural network. Appl Energy 134(134):102–113
2. Zhao Z, Xu Q, Jia M (2016) Improved shuffled frog leaping algorithm-based BP neural network and its application in bearing early fault diagnosis. Neural Comput Appl 27(2):375–385
3. Xiao J, Liu E, Zhu L et al (2017) Improved image super-resolution algorithm based on convolutional neural network. Acta Optica Sinica 37(3):0318011
4. Liu H, Zhao C, Xuan L et al (2016) Study on a neural network optimization algorithm based on improved genetic algorithm. Chin J Sci Instrum

5. Ya-Li ER, Wang QS (2014) Load balancing strategy based on improved ant colony algorithm in cloud network. Comput Eng Des
6. Du JH (2017) Automatic text classification algorithm based on Gauss improved convolutional neural network. J Comput Sci
7. Liu F, Liu T, Fu Y (2016) An improved SoC estimation algorithm based on artificial neural network. In: International symposium on computational intelligence and design. IEEE, pp 152–155
8. Zhu Y, Zhao D, Wang W et al (2016) A novel load balancing algorithm based on improved particle swarm optimization in cloud computing environment. In: Revised selected papers of the second international conference on human centered computing. Springer, New York, pp 634–645
9. Zhou Y, Wang XR (2016) Image compression algorithm based on improved wavelet neural network. J Xian Univ
10. Pan D, Cao J (2015) An improved neural network algorithm based on artificial bee colony algorithm and its application in sewage treatment. In: International conference on behavioral, economic and socio-cultural computing. IEEE, pp 83–88
11. Duan P, Li H (2014) The radar target recognition research based on improved neural network algorithm. In: Fifth international conference on intelligent systems design and engineering applications. IEEE Computer Society, pp 1074–1077
12. Zheng MQ, Yang F (2017) Face recognition based on improved NMF and neural network. Chin J Liq Cryst Disp 32(3):213–218
13. Zhu H, Cui Y, Xiong H (2016) Power network load forecasting based on improved BP neural network. Mod Electron Tech
14. Sun M, Liu J (2017) Improved Garson algorithm based on neural network model. In: Control and decision conference. IEEE
15. Nan SP, Guo ZJ, Cheng C et al (2017) Improved competitive classification algorithm based on neural networks. Comput Knowl Technol
16. Li D, Zheng Z, Li Y et al (2017) Design and implementation of load balancing strategy in Openstack cloud platform. In: IEEE international conference on computational science and engineering. IEEE, pp 428–435
17. Wei Q, Yang M (2017) Short term load forecasting based on improved neural network algorithm. J Harbin Univ Sci Technol
18. Yu W, Xu Z-M, Yi Y-F et al (2016) Network load balancing algorithm based on feedback cycle. Comput Eng Des
19. Sun M, Zhang Q, Cao W (2015) An improved QoS multicast routing algorithm based on chaotic neural network. In: International conference on intelligent human-machine systems and cybernetics. IEEE, pp 139–143
20. Gu N-J, Zhao Z, Lv Y-F et al (2015) Algorithm of depth neural network training based on multi-GPU. J Chin Comput Syst

Research on International Logistics Supply Chain Management Mode from the Perspective of Cross-border E-commerce

HaiLan Pan[1,2,3](✉)

[1] School of Computer Engineering and Science, Shanghai University, No. 99, Shangda Rd, Baoshan District, Shanghai, China
panhailan@sspu.edu.cn
[2] Research Center of Resource Recycling Science and Engineering, Shanghai Polytechnic University, No. 2360, Jinhai Rd, Pudong New District, Shanghai, China
[3] School of Economics and Management, Shanghai Polytechnic University, No. 2360, Jinhai Rd, Pudong New District, Shanghai, China

Abstract. Under the background of global economic integration and rapid development of information technology, the international foreign trade market has further expanded, and cross-border e-commerce has begun to rise. The rise of cross-border e-commerce has had an impact on the past logistics supply chain management model, and it is urgent for enterprises to create a new management model and keep pace with the times. From the perspective of cross-border e-commerce, the international logistics supply chain management model is in line with the needs of the times, and can ensure that the core competitiveness of enterprises is continuously improved, and thus promote the long-term development of enterprises. Based on this, this paper introduces the relationship between the various components of the logistics supply chain, and proposes the construction strategy of the logistics supply chain management model from the perspective of international e-commerce, in order to provide a theoretical basis for enterprise development.

Keywords: Cross-border e-commerce · Logistics supply chain · Supply chain management · Mode · Global

1 Introduction

In recent years, with the further expansion of global economic integration and informatization, a new type of foreign trade with a combination of logistics, finance, and electricity business is a new feature of cross-border e-commerce. The emergence of cross-border e-commerce is increasingly demanding the management of the relationship between enterprises and customers, and enterprises need to improve their competitiveness in the international market and strive to occupy a certain position in the international market. Now the relationship between enterprises and customers has been digitalized and information management. Enterprises can use computers to collect and organize customer information, analyze customer information, and adjust the

Z. Xu et al. (Eds.): CSIA 2019, AISC 928, pp. 737–744, 2020.
https://doi.org/10.1007/978-3-030-15235-2_101

production and sales process of the company to provide customers with More quality services to increase partnerships and promote business development [1]. The relevant departments of the enterprise manage the information, capital and logistics involved in the operation of the enterprise, strengthen the joint development of the internal and external enterprises, and improve their economic benefits. In enterprise management, supply chain management is the most important link. To promote supply chain management to international standards and ensure long-term development of enterprises, it is necessary to conduct in-depth research on the international logistics supply chain management model. This paper introduces the relationship between the various components of the logistics supply chain, and proposes the construction strategy of the logistics supply chain management model from the perspective of international e-commerce, in order to provide a theoretical basis for enterprise development [2, 3].

2 Defines the Concept of Cross-border Electricity Supplier

Cross-border e-commerce refers to an international business activity that is divided into transaction entities of different customs, through transactions through e-commerce platforms, payment settlement, and delivery of goods through cross-border logistics. Cross-border e-commerce is a global, paperless and direct international trade activity. Transaction entities with different customs clearances can reach a transaction agreement on the e-commerce platform, and payment settlement through various financial payment institutions at home and abroad. The goods are delivered to the consumers through international logistics to finally complete the transaction. Cross-border e-commerce is a new type of trade that relies on the Internet and cross-border logistics [4–6]. Compared with traditional e-commerce, it can meet customer needs more quickly and conveniently. It has the following characteristics:

2.1 Open, Global

The network itself is a medium with no clear boundaries. It is characterized by openness, globality, compensatoryness, and decentralization. Therefore, cross-border e-commerce that is attached to the online trading platform is also open, global, and compensatory (Features such as compensation for offline transactions) and decentralization [7].

2.2 Immediacy

For enterprises, the information in the supply chain can be shared in a timely and effective manner. The information exchange methods under the traditional transaction mode, such as letters, telegrams, faxes, etc., exist between the sending and receiving of information. Time error. Cross-border e-commerce is immediacy because it uses online transactions, payment methods, and data exchange using the network [8, 9].

2.3 Direct

Cross-border e-commerce companies can display the specific information of products through the network service platform and update them at any time. Customers can directly query the products they need on the network service platform, conduct commodity transactions through the service platform, complete the printing and sales contract, and cross-border [10]. The directness of e-commerce is significantly different from traditional foreign trade.

2.4 Low Cost

Online trading activities conducted by cross-border e-commerce companies are carried out on their own web pages or online service platforms, which greatly reduces the time and labor costs of buying and selling, while improving work efficiency. On the other hand, e-commerce itself is a paperless operation. The information recording and storage of computers in the transaction process can basically replace the traditional paper transaction files. Users only need to simply send and receive electronic information [12, 13]. Since the electronic information is transmitted in the form of bits, the process of transmitting and receiving the information is completely paperless, and thus the paperless transaction undoubtedly saves a lot of cost.

3 The Development of International Logistics and Supply Chain Management Issues

3.1 Distribution Costs

The cross-border logistics model directly affects the user experience of the consumption of overseas e-commerce products. Since the development of the cross-border logistics industry requires various expenses, such as cross-border taxes and fees, network technology construction fees, and courier fees, if these costs are too high, the user's consumption experience will be bad [14]. At the same time, the problem of product return for cross-border trade has an impact on money and time cost. Once a return occurs, it will inevitably lead to a large loss of cost.

3.2 Delivery Time Problem

In the process of cross-border trade product distribution, the time period is an uncontrollable factor. Because international express delivery is mostly centralized delivery, this type of delivery is used to reduce the cost of the seller. This form has a great security risk. It is not only time-consuming, but also the fact that the goods are concentrated together and the goods are lost. The rise and development of the cross-border logistics industry, logistics routes in Europe and the United States and other places are relatively smooth, compared to Brazil, Africa and other countries or regions, the time is short, if the time is too long will seriously affect the user's consumption experience [15, 16]. Once the user experience is not working well, the user will request a refund service. The processing of refund services is not only time consuming but also increases costs.

3.3 Logistics System Imperfect

With the development of e-commerce, people's consumption patterns have also changed. E-commerce has gradually become the main way people buy goods. However, the cross-border e-commerce trade logistics system is imperfect, and the cross-border payment method has not achieved international unification [17]. This problem limits the e-commerce barrier-free development of cross-border trade.

3.4 Customs Issues Under Cross-border Trade

Cross-border distribution of products is subject to two-way audits of domestic and foreign customs, but in the face of interests, some e-commerce sellers will evade the state's regulatory system, in order to reduce the actual value of goods to reduce the cost of shipping products [18]. However, there will also be a phenomenon of reporting low prices and misreporting product prices and being detained by customs, which affects the transportation of products. If the customs detains the goods, the products cannot be delivered within the specified time, which will cause dissatisfaction of the customers, which is not conducive to the development of the enterprise.

4 Study Management at the International Logistics Supply Chain to Build Cross-border E-commerce

4.1 Transit Logistics Management Mode

The so-called transit type cross-border logistics mode is that the overseas product suppliers transport the goods to the designated distribution center of the domestic e-commerce enterprise, and then the local warehousing center carries out unified warehousing management and distribution management. When the consumers place orders on the e-commerce platform, Distribution and delivery by the distribution center to provide courier services [19]. This involves the integration of the receiving place and the individual parcels of different countries. The center will transfer the parcels through the international logistics company in batches, and the whole batch of the logistics centers of the overseas transit countries will be single-united into a single piece. The form is distributed and distributed by the international express delivery company. The specific process is as shown in Fig. 1:

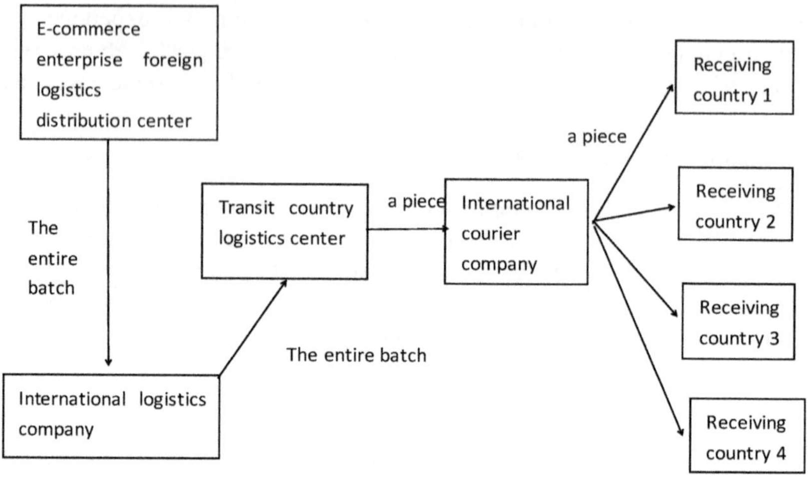

Fig. 1. Two-stage transit cross-border e-commerce logistics model

The whole transportation process is divided into two sections. The goods need to be transferred in the transit country for distribution, and the resources are integrated and delivered in the local logistics center, which greatly saves the logistics cost and reduces the cumbersome process of cooperation with the local express delivery. This logistics model integrates parcels from different countries and regions to effectively save logistics efficiency.

4.2 Two-Stage Receipt Logistics Management Mode

Overseas suppliers distribute the goods to e-commerce companies for stocking at the country's logistics center. When the consumer places an order on the platform, the local logistics center carries out the parcel sorting and packaging according to the different delivery place of the parcel. The goods will be integrated according to the destination, and then sent to different destinations by international logistics companies in the form of whole goods. The entire batch of goods is then split into individual packages by the destination logistics center and distributed to the consumers by the courier company [20].

Because the transportation route carries two sections of transportation and the transit type transportation, it has more integration advantages in cost control. The goods are integrated from the logistics center of the sending country and sent in batches according to different destinations. However, this mode of transportation is more suitable for customers with a large number of customers and destinations. Since the goods need to be integrated in batches, at the delivery time. There may be a problem of lag, and the efficiency of logistics centers and courier companies in different countries and regions is different, and there is a certain discrepancy in the supervision and progress of goods.

The optimized transportation method is much faster than the previous method. The comparison between the traditional transportation method and this paper is shown in Fig. 2:

Fig. 2. Comparison of traditional transportation mode and existing mode transportation time

4.3 The Management of the Supply Chain Should Have Certain Planning

Regarding the issue of constructing an international trade logistics supply chain in cross-border trade in e-commerce, the core of the problem is the construction of the basic database. The development of an enterprise must have an independent and basic database, and its role is to provide basic support for the logistics supply chain of international trade. The underlying database can guide the planning of the supply chain and reduce the material cost of the e-commerce logistics supply chain. The information and data contained in the basic database can also improve the efficiency of the enterprise and its related cooperative enterprises to ensure cooperation between enterprises and promote the development of the enterprise. Based on the management of the logistics supply chain of cross-border trade based on the basic database, the improvement of the basic database must be started as soon as possible.

4.4 Increase the Number of Business Entities Under the International Logistics Supply Chain, and Carry Out the Horizontal Extension of the International Logistics Supply Chain

First of all, with the continuous development of China's economy, the number of domestic enterprises participating in international trade is increasing, and the share in the international logistics supply chain is also increasing, but it is not in the main position of the international logistics supply chain. Chinese enterprises must recognize this realistic problem and improve their position in the international logistics supply chain through the improvement of production, sales and transportation channels. Only when the company's development strength is improved can it have a voice in international trade and establish its own logistics supply chain in international trade. Second, the horizontal extension of the international logistics supply chain. With the internationalization of business operations under the Internet trade, companies have begun to pay attention to the global market. When the management of domestic logistics supply chain is becoming more mature and the domestic e-commerce trade volume has become more stable, enterprises must begin to turn their attention to the international market and realize the global trade of e-commerce through the establishment of an international trade logistics supply chain.

5 Conclusion

In the 20th century, logistics supply chain management is at a disadvantage in economic development, and its impact on enterprise development is lower than that of the present. The emergence of e-commerce highlights the role of logistics supply chain and proposes a new management model to achieve cross-border trade. The number of Chinese companies entering the international market has increased in recent years, so it is particularly urgent to improve their competitiveness in the international market. In summary, although cross-border e-commerce has appeared late in China, its development speed is rapid, and the development of small and medium-sized cross-border e-commerce is particularly striking, which shows a trend of geometric growth, and provides experience for the transformation of traditional foreign trade enterprises. Logistics is an important link to support the development of cross-border e-commerce. Therefore, the exploration of the construction and operation mode of modern logistics system has strong practical significance, but at the same time, the development of cross-border e-commerce industry has also promoted the development of cross-border logistics. From the research of this paper, the establishment of a new international logistics supply chain management model can bring great convenience to the transformation and upgrading of enterprises, and at the same time, it can enhance the core competitiveness of enterprises, and promote the internationalization of corporate products, and then win the right to speak in international trade.

Acknowledgments. This research was supported in part by Gaoyuan Discipline of Shanghai–Environmental Science and Engineering (Resource Recycling Science and Engineering), Discipline of Management Science and Engineering of Shanghai Polytechnic University (Grant No. XXKPY1606).

References

1. Baik B, Cho K, Choi W et al (2015) The role of institutional environments in cross-border mergers: a perspective from Bidders' earnings management behavior. Manag Int Rev 55 (5):615–646
2. Nie CT, He Z-Y (2016) Influencing factors of consumers' purchase decision in cross-border e-commerce: from the perspective of negative online review text. J Fujian Commerc Coll (in Chinese)
3. Mao M (2016) On the Cross-border e-commerce based on micro economic perspective in china. Reform Strateg

4. Lu X (2016) Third-party logistics construction of oversea location based on cross-border supply chain integration. China Bus Market
5. Wang H (2017) Research on the construction of international logistics supply chain management model from the perspective of cross-border ecommerce. Reform Strateg
6. Wang J, Zheng H (2017) Research on integration of customs clearance in "the Belt and Road" region based on perspective of cross-border e-commerce. J Beijing Technol Bus Univ (in Chinese)
7. Sui B (2016) Research on optimization of cross-border agri-food supply chains between Guangxi and ASEAN—based on double perspective of relationship stability and alliance performance. Agric Econ Manag
8. Wang JX, Tian JY (2016) On the performance evaluation of cross-border electricity supplier in Ningbo based on TOE model. J Zhejiang Wanli Univ (in Chinese)
9. Zhang A, Hui SL, Thai VV (2015) Impacts of global manufacturing trends on port development: the case of Hong Kong. Asian J Ship Logist 31(1):135–159
10. Xia J, Jiang MS, Li S et al (2014) Practice standardization in cross-border activities of multinational corporations: a resource dependence perspective. Manag Int Rev 54(5):707–734
11. Avelar-Sosa L, García-Alcaraz JL, Vergara-Villegas OO et al (2015) Impact of traditional and international logistic policies in supply chain performance. Int J Adv Manuf Technol 76 (5–8):913–925
12. Buciuni G, Mola L (2014) How do entrepreneurial firms establish cross-border relationships? A global value chain perspective. J Int Entrepreneurship 12(1):67–84
13. Jones G, Pitelis C (2015) Entrepreneurial imagination and a demand and supply-side perspective on the MNE and cross-border organization. J Int Manag 21(4):309–321
14. Wang X, Li L (2018) Business model innovation and policy system design of cross-border e-commerce under the new normal. Contemp Econ Manag
15. Cao C (2018) Logistics mode and risk analysis of China's cross-border electronic business platform on the perspective of supply chain resilience. J Wuxi Inst Technol (in Chinese)
16. Zhang X (2018) Endogenous mechanism and development path of synergism of cross-border e-commerce and cross-border logistics from the perspective of global value chain. Contemp Econ Manag
17. Wu Y-J (2018) The improving path of cross-border E-commerce marketing from the perspective of "The Belt and Road Initiative". J Changchun Inst Technol (in Chinese)
18. Davarzani H, Norrman A (2015) Toward a relevant agenda for warehousing research: literature review and practitioners' input. Logist Res 8(1):1
19. Arasteh A (2016) Combination of real options and game-theoretic approach in investment analysis. J Ind Eng Int 12(3):361–375
20. Zheng HM (2016) An analysis on the impact of cross-border e-commerce on China's import and export trade based on the perspective of industrial chain. Prices Mon

Optimization of Logistics Warehouse Location Based on Genetic Algorithm

Xu Wang[1] and Qing Xia[2(✉)]

[1] Institute of Data Science, City University of Macau, Macao, China
[2] School of Management, Guangdong University of Education, Guangzhou, China
xiaqing@gdei.edu.cn

Abstract. With the continuous progress and development of the global economy, our requirements for the quality of goods and services provided by service providers and suppliers are becoming higher and higher. In order to meet the needs of our customers, many enterprises expand their market share. We need to evolve to respond and adjust quickly to a highly changeable market. Nowadays, social competition is no longer just product competition between enterprises in simple industries, but gradually evolved into joint competition between social supply chains and supply chains. Logistics has always been a crucial link in the development of supply chain, so warehousing management, as the core part of logistics, especially logistics warehousing center, has attracted more and more attention from the public. In many logistics enterprises, how to effectively improve the warehouse location optimization rate is regarded as the top priority. Nowadays, in the logistics warehouse center, it is an effective way to improve the efficiency of warehouse location optimization to optimize its original warehouse location effectively. Whether the warehouse location is allocated reasonably will affect the efficiency of the overall warehousing operation of the logistics warehouse center, and then affect the rate of profits for enterprises.

Keywords: Genetic · Repository optimization · Warehouse management

1 Brief Introduction

Genetics algorithm is a new optimization algorithm, which originates from bio-genetics and the natural law of survival of the fittest. It was developed by Professor Holland of Michigan University and his students. Logistics system is developing in the direction of large-scale and mufti-function. The complexity of controlled objects is getting higher and higher, and the difficulty of precise control is getting more and more difficult. The complexity and control precision of logistics system form a contradiction [5–10]. In order to improve the control precision decline caused by complex logistics system, adaptive control algorithm is a common method. As a common adaptive control and adaptive search algorithm, genetic algorithm has obvious advantages in the control and parameter optimization of non-linear systems, and is widely used in logistics warehouse location system [14–20]. This paper systematically introduces the mechanism of genetic algorithm, the meaning of genetic operator and the method of parameter

Z. Xu et al. (Eds.): CSIA 2019, AISC 928, pp. 745–752, 2020.
https://doi.org/10.1007/978-3-030-15235-2_102

optimization. On this basis, the logistics warehouse location optimization based on genetic algorithm is designed. Through transformation of genetic operators and controller parameters, we optimize the design of logistics warehouse location.

2 Genetic Algorithm and Cargo Optimization

2.1 Genetic Algorithm

As a new optimization algorithm, genetic algorithm is developing rapidly in recent years. With its high efficiency and practical characteristics, genetic algorithm has been applied in various fields, and has achieved good results, and has attracted more and more attention from academia. Genetics algorithm has been applied in many fields. Genetic algorithm is applied to solve the shortest path problem in graph theory. Some methods of solving this problem are put forward, and a set of shortest path sets can be obtained quickly. Genetic algorithm is applied to solve the vehicle routing problem with time windows to obtain its approximate or optimal solution. It can effectively solve complex optimization problems. The mathematical model of master-slave hierarchical decision-making problem has a nested structure, which is characterized by that part of the variables of each level planning problem are determined by its lower level planning problem, so it is also called Multilevel Programming Problems (MLPP). If the problem has only two decision levels, it is called Bi-level Programming Problems (BLPP). Any multilevel programming problem can be decomposed into multiple bi-level programming.

The variables that the upper level decision-makers control are $x = (x_1, x_2, \ldots, x_n)^T \in X \subset R^n$, the variables controlled by the lower level decision-makers are $y = (y_1, y_2, \ldots, y_m)^T \in y \subset R^m$. The general mathematical model of bi-level programming problem can be described as:

$$\min_{x \in X} F(x, y)$$

S.t. G(x,y) ≤ 0
among them, y solution from lower level planning:

$$\min_{y \in Y} f(x, y)$$

S.t. $g(x, y) \leq 0$

Among them, $F, f : R^n \times R^m \to R$ they are called the objective function of the upper level planning and the lower level planning respectively. $\mathrm{G} : R^n \times R^m \to R'$ and $g : R^n \times R^m \to R''$ They are called the constraints of upper level planning and lower level planning respectively. Set X and Y contain non negativity or integer requirement constraints of variables.

2.2 Cargo Location Optimization

Location optimization refers to a more reasonable allocation of goods on the basis of the original arrangement of goods. Usually, in order to optimize the storage location, we need to take into account the storage center's location, shelf, goods, labor, equipment, cost and other factors. In order to achieve a better location layout, so as to effectively improve the efficiency of the storage center, while reducing storage costs. Therefore, the optimization of goods location is based on the analysis of existing goods location based on certain optimization rules and more rational distribution of goods location than before, in order to make each category and each commodity can be arranged into a more reasonable and effective storage area.

3 Logistics Storage Center Cargo Location Management Analysis

The main tasks of the warehousing and logistics management center are warehousing, outgoing and inventory operations. In the process of commodity storage, the warehousing of commodities is the unloading, inspection, input information, storage and so on when the commodities arrive at the warehousing logistics management center. If there is a fixed storage space in the system of information center when the goods arrive at the storage center where they need to be stored, the information can be input directly and then added to the corresponding storage space.

3.1 Warehousing of Commodities

After the goods arrive at the warehouse logistics management center, after the quantity and quality inspection, logistics staff are required to store them in the storage box of login information. Additional commodity information should be allocated according to the objective conditions of the commodity itself such as quality and volume specifications, and taking into account the space of its storage area and other storage items. Then, the information is input, and the goods are stored on a reasonable allocation of specific goods by logistics operators with the help of equipment and facilities. This process is the warehousing of goods.

3.2 Goods Out of Stock

According to the requirement of sales order, some goods are selected from the fixed shelves in the storage center, and the process of checking and discharging is the operation of goods discharging from the warehouse. Logistics operators will distribute, verify the quantity and package after acceptance of the goods according to the rules of distribution range and order, and then place them in the waiting area for loading and distribution.

3.3 Inventory Check Work

Inventory checking mainly checks whether the data of this type of commodity in the login information center are the same as the actual data of the storage area. If the actual quantity of storage is larger than the number of registered information centers, then the inventory record of the commodity is surplus; if the actual quantity is less than the login information, the inventory record of the commodity is shortage.

3.4 Inventory Management

Goods are stored in and out of warehouse according to the needs of storage and sales orders. The flow speed of each kind of goods is different, which leads to the storage center can be divided into storage golden area, slow flow area and even dark part. Therefore, storage area needs to be sorted out in fixed or non-fixed period of time. For example, if the frequency of a commodity entering and leaving the warehouse is low in a quarter, it is considered to be placed in the storage compartment of a relatively slow flow area.

4 Cargo Location Optimization Parameter Analysis

The objective of this optimization is to improve the efficiency of warehouse entry and exit and to minimize the total amount of logistics. First, setting parameter variables is the foundation of building models. If the total amount of logistics is set as the product of the distance between goods stored on the shelf of the logistics warehouse and the frequencies of goods entering and leaving the warehouse, two variables, i.e. the frequencies F of goods entering and leaving the warehouse and the distance L of each warehouse to the warehouse platform, need to be defined. So, let's first calculate the distance from each container to the warehouse platform through the actual situation of the logistics center. The principle of "first in, first out" is guaranteed for goods stored on shelves in order to prevent some goods from long-term accumulation and detention in the shelves. As far as the whole storage area is concerned, the storage platform is located in the southwest corner of the storage area, the storage platform is located in the southeast corner of the storage area, and the goods are placed perpendicular to the connection line of the storage platform. Therefore, all the goods stored in the storage area follow the principle of "west-in-east-out". For example, the distance between a certain type of goods in the storage area from the storage platform to the specified p-tier q-row shelf is the sum of the following sections:

(1) The vertical distance between the cargo layer P and the first level of the shelf.
(2) Section q lists the horizontal distance between the cargo compartment and the first column of the shelf.
(3) The horizontal distance between the first t shelf and the first row shelf.
(4) The distance from the storage platform to the first row shelf in the storage area.

5 The Principle of Cargo Location Optimization

5.1 Basic Rules for Turnover Rate

Here, the concepts of inventory turnover rate and financial awareness turnover rate are different. For warehouse management centers, the optimization of inventory turnover rate, i.e. the frequency of goods entering and leaving warehouses, usually means that every commodity stored in warehouse management centers has the frequency of operations in a certain period. We can specify that the circulation of the quantity of goods in a year, or a quarter of a month, is a standard time. Then we can specify how to arrange these product numbers according to the quantity or specifications, and then we can set up several sub-standards. For example, it could be 75%, 50% or 25% of the standard segments, and each segment in the storage area could be allocated with their characteristics. At the same time, the rules of "golden lots" can also be combined. For example, the first quarter of commodities, i.e. the high turnover section of commodities, can be allocated to the calculated golden lots. Frequency of goods entering and exiting warehouses in storage centers can usually be studied and obtained by order information during commodity trading. One case is that when a new kind of commodity enters the market, due to trial production, the market reaction has relatively irregular characteristics, resulting in the irregularity of the inventory status of new commodities, which also results in the irregularity of data research.

5.2 Commodity Density Flow Rule

Product density flow refers to a commodity transaction occurring once in a specific volume and can be understood as a single shipment or purchase of a product in large quantities. Some commodities may have a low turnover rate, but each shipment and transport volume is huge, so these products may usually be stored in the gold area in conjunction with the "golden area" rule. Full storage management center's overall requirements, in the spatial layout, need to first analyze the same or similar unit size and specifications of the commodity category, when allocation, it is best to store it in a large storage area; from the visual effect, this is also for the sake of a more holistic understanding. In addition, when designing the overall form of storage centers, we should not only include the unit specifications of goods, but also take into account the other unit volumes of bulk goods packaged in the same shape. In order to provide enough space to meet all unit volume specific requirements.

5.3 Rule of "Golden Lot"

The preceding basic turnover rules and density flow rules are all about the "golden section" stored in the warehouse management center. Now let's talk about the so-called "golden section" rule. Generally speaking, there is a certain area or scope in the warehouse management center. These areas are easy to operate, easy to enter and exit warehouses, and easy to access, so they are called gold area. For general warehouse management centers, the distance value of the comprehensive path from the warehouse to the warehouse platform can be sorted by ascending order rule, and the first fifth of the sorting can be divided into the golden area of the storage area. This method can divide the walking distance of operators into standard methods. This method is suitable for large storage centers with many kinds of goods and large storage areas, which need to frequently use equipment and facilities. In some smaller storage areas, the location of the area near the waist that is accessible to the operator can also be defined as the gold waist area in the first fifth of the order.

5.4 Commodity Association Rules

Typical analysis shows that some aspects of certain commodities or commodities may be correlated, resulting in that they are often listed in the same market sales order. Obviously, these commodities may have similar characteristics of use, or these commodities need to be combined with each other. That is to say, there are some correlations between these commodities. Analyzing the relationship and relationship between commodities, orders can be based on historical information, which is determined to be related to the same production in the same order, or because complementary functions are part of the related other commodity types. After determining the interaction or similarity of certain commodities, when they need to be stored in a designated storage area, such commodities should be allocated by managers to more convenient units of common access. Thus, when receiving the information of goods entering and leaving the warehouse, the walking distance of required operations is reduced, thus improving operational efficiency.

5.5 Weight Characteristics Rules

The weight of goods stored in different shelves is used to determine the weight of rule characteristics and determine the location of storage height of goods. When choosing the height of the shelf, the location of the cargo layer near the waist is usually determined, based on the waist of the operator. Then move to the upper and lower levels of the shelves one by one, because under normal conditions, the unit weight of goods in the storage area may play a contact role in the status of the warehouse management center staff. Therefore, on the basis of safety protection, in order to minimize unnecessary labor consumption, slightly larger goods should be kept near the floor or lower shelves, while lighter goods can be stored in higher shelves.

5.6 Commodity Identification Rules

The so-called principle of identity refers to the same type of goods stored in a fixed storage area. When distributing certain products of the same or similar type, according to the same principle of goods, operators can reduce time to find products. Otherwise, if the goods in an order are selected for warehousing operation, the selection of the same type of goods may require multiple equipment or multiple operators to select the goods at multiple locations at the same time. The same type of goods are dispersed in different locations of multiple storage areas, which will take extra time and increase unnecessary path distances for operators, thus reducing the efficiency of sorting and warehousing.

6 Conclusion

In this paper, genetic algorithm is used to analyze the current situation of logistics warehousing management. Although the results obtained by this optimization are applied to the sample space to verify its validity, it also gains some practical significance. However, due to my limited academic level and relative lack of practical experience, I still know little about all aspects of modern logistics enterprises and warehouse management centers, so this study still has relative limitations. At this stage, the warehouse management center has discussed and decided to optimize the sample space in an orderly manner, and track the actual test results of the analysis. If the monitoring period after real-time operation shows that the scheme is feasible and effective, the research can be extended to other storage areas optimized for the whole logistics warehouse location on the basis of the actual situation of each storage center.

References

1. Li F (2012) Discussion on PID parameter optimization method based on genetic algorithm. Heilongjiang Sci Technol Inf 16:89
2. Jiang Q, Zou Z, Cao J (2006) Multi-machine power system UPFC controller based on immune genetic algorithm. Trans China Electrotech Soc 21(7):60–68
3. Dai T (2012) Study on the optimization of three-dimensional warehouse location based on classified stochastic strategy. Techs Method
4. Cai J, Li H (1999) Robot pose control method based on biogenetics. J Appl Sci 2:216–220
5. Zhao W, Weng C, Zhou Q (2010) Dynamic determination and application of standby position of stacker in stereoscopic warehouse. J Shanghai Railw Univ 12:05–08
6. Su Q, Wu W (2011) Application of linear programming based on path, turnover rate and picking cost coefficient in location optimization (13):87–105
7. Ma T, Guo Y (2013) Research on location optimization based on minimum time algorithm. Packag Eng 12(1):45–92
8. Jiang Y, Zhang M (2010) Multi-attribute decision making method and its application. J Beijing Inst Graph Commun 4:11–16
9. Ma Q (2015) Research on the optimization method of cargo storage location in enterprise storage center. Tianjin, Tianjin University
10. Liu C (2013) Selection and design of picking and selection system for logistics distribution center. Beijing, Mechanical Industry Press
11. Zheng L (2014) Optimization of warehouse location in automated warehouses. Mod Shop Malls (235):125–184
12. Wang Y (2014) Discussion on China's warehousing logistics management. Chin Inf
13. Chen D (2014) Research on optimization of automated warehouse location and path optimization of stacker. Shenyang, Shenyang University
14. Zhu D, Gong G, Luo Q (2013) Logistics and supply chain management. Fudan University Press
15. Zheng H (2012) Research on path optimization problem of automated warehouse. Changchun, Jilin University
16. Chen L (2011) Research on warehouse location optimization system in logistics pulling manufacturing service platform. Sichuan, Department of Computer, Southwest Jiaotong University

17. Song H, Hu Z (2014) Modern logistics and supply Chain management. Beijing, Economic Management Press, pp 140–193
18. Chen W (2013) E-commerce logistics. Beijing, Mechanical Industry Press, pp 61–88
19. Huo Y, Liu H, Sun Y (2011) Design principles of modern logistics solutions. Beijing, China Communications Press
20. Zheng L, Yong H, Chen J (2012) Logistics center warehouse slotting optimization system research. J Logist Technol

Application of Intelligent Algorithms in System Integration Design

Hequn Wu(✉)

Network Management Center, Hohhot Vocational College, Hohhot, China
wuhequn53@163.com

Abstract. System integration has been the fastest growing industry in the international information service industry. The essence of system integration is optimum integrated design with a large-scale integrated computer network system. System integration includes the integration of computer software, hardware, operating system technology, database technology, network communication technology, as well as the integration of product selection, collocation and system integration of different manufacturers. The goal-overall performance is the best, that is, all components can work together, and the whole system is a low-cost, efficient, symmetrical, scalable and maintainable system. In order to achieve this goal, the merits and demerits of system integrators are crucial. However, the traditional models can not provide sufficient considerations on the system integration, so the actual computation has a larger error and reliability of system integration formula is greatly limited. In this paper, a new method applied to system integration is proposed combining Grey Relational Analysis (GRA) and BP Neural Network Technology (BPNN).

Keywords: System integration · Grey relational analysis · BP neural network · Difference matrix

1 Introduction

Information system integration refers to the integration of computer software, hardware, network communication technology and products into an information system that can meet the specific needs of users, including overall planning, design, development, implementation, service and reporting barriers [1, 2]. System integration should adopt many integration technologies [3], such as function integration, BSV LCD splicing integration, integrated wiring. Information system integration is a basic starting point to satisfy users' needs. It is a high-tech engineering process and provides users with comprehensive solutions. The final delivery is a complete information system rather than a separate product, including technology, management and commerce, systematic engineering of conformity. Technology is the core, and management and business are the guarantee of project success [4].

Z. Xu et al. (Eds.): CSIA 2019, AISC 928, pp. 753–759, 2020.
https://doi.org/10.1007/978-3-030-15235-2_103

2 Grey Relational Analysis Method

Grey Relational Analysis (GRA) is a statistical analysis method for multiple factors [5, 6]. It can analyze the main relationship between various factors in a giving system and find out the key factors which have great influence on the target value, so that the system's main features can be characterized with those factors. In general, GRA is a quantitative description and comparative method of a system [7] which can describe system's current situation and predict its future development. This method is based on the sample data of different factors, and grey correlation degree is used to describe the relationship among various factors, like strength, size and order. A higher degree indicates a strong correlation between two factors, conversely, a small degree indicates a weak correlation.

2.1 Determination of Serial

An analysis serial and reference serial should be determined at first in GRA process. The analysis serial X_0 in this model is the reliability of system integration, and the influential factors compose the reference serial X_1, X_2, ..., X_n. Their relations can be described by formulas (1).

$$\left(X_0', X_1', \ldots, X_n'\right) = \begin{bmatrix} x_{01} & x_{11} & \cdots & x_{n1} \\ x_{02} & x_{12} & \cdots & x_{n2} \\ \vdots & \vdots & & \vdots \\ x_{0m} & x_{1m} & \cdots & x_{nm} \end{bmatrix}_{m\times(n+1)} \tag{1}$$

2.2 Dimensionless Transformation on Analysis and Reference Serial

The new dimensionless matrix could be obtained as following formula (2)

$$(Y_0, Y_1, \ldots, Y_n) = \begin{bmatrix} y_{01} & y_{11} & \cdots & y_{n1} \\ y_{02} & y_{12} & \cdots & y_{n2} \\ \vdots & \vdots & & \vdots \\ y_{0m} & y_{1m} & \cdots & y_{nm} \end{bmatrix}_{m\times(n+1)} \tag{2}$$

The formula (3) is average method and the formula (4) is the divided method. They are the most common dimensionless methods.

$$y_{ik} = \frac{x_{ik}}{\sum_{k=1}^{m} x_{ik}/m} (i = 0, 1, 2, \ldots, n; k = 1, 2, \ldots, m) \tag{3}$$

$$y_{ik} = \frac{x_{ik}}{x_{0k}}(i = 0, 1, 2, \ldots, n; k = 1, 2, \ldots, m) \tag{4}$$

2.3 Calculation of Difference Serial

Calculate corresponding absolute difference value between reference sequence and compare sequence to form difference sequence, as shown in formulas (5) and (6)

$$\begin{bmatrix} \Delta_{01} & \Delta_{11} & \cdots & \Delta_{n1} \\ \Delta_{02} & \Delta_{12} & \cdots & \Delta_{n2} \\ \vdots & \vdots & & \vdots \\ \Delta_{0m} & \Delta_{1m} & \cdots & \Delta_{nm} \end{bmatrix}_{m\times(n+1)} \tag{5}$$

$$\Delta_{0i}(k) = |y_0(k) - y_i(k)| \tag{6}$$

The minimum and maximum difference matrix are as shown in formulas (7) and (8)

$$\max_{1\leq i\leq n, 1\leq k\leq m}(\Delta_{ik}) = \Delta(\max) \tag{7}$$

$$\min_{1\leq i\leq n, 1\leq k\leq m}(\Delta_{ik}) = \Delta(\min) \tag{8}$$

The correlation coefficient can be obtained by formula (9).

$$\xi_{ik} = \frac{\Delta(\min) + \rho \cdot \Delta(\max)}{\Delta_{ik} + \rho \cdot \Delta(\max)} \tag{9}$$

In which, $\rho \in (0, 1)$, usually the value of ρ is 0.5, the smaller the valve is, the more different between the relation coefficient is.

The relation coefficient matrix could be formed as shown in formula (10).

$$\begin{bmatrix} \xi_{01} & \xi_{11} & \cdots & \xi_{n1} \\ \xi_{02} & \xi_{12} & \cdots & \xi_{n2} \\ \vdots & \vdots & & \vdots \\ \xi_{0m} & \xi_{1m} & \cdots & \xi_{nm} \end{bmatrix}_{m\times(n+1)} \tag{10}$$

3 BP Neural Network Technology

There are dozens of Neural Network models, and Back-Propagation Neural Network is the most famous and most widely used model among those models, which is called BP network for short [8]. BP network is a typical multi-layer neural network and composed of input layer, middle layer and output layer [9]. Since middle layer is invisible for input and output layer, it is also called hidden layer [10]. There are full connections between layers and no connection between different neurons in the same layer. The statistic of input layer reflects the characteristics change of sample data. In order to enhance the convergence rate of network and reduce error, normalization of sample data is needed before the input process. Nodes quantity of hidden layer decides the quality of the model and it can be determined approximately by Kolmogorov theorem. Through the calculation and normalization of input data, a final result can be achieved in the output layer. The process is shown in Fig. 1.

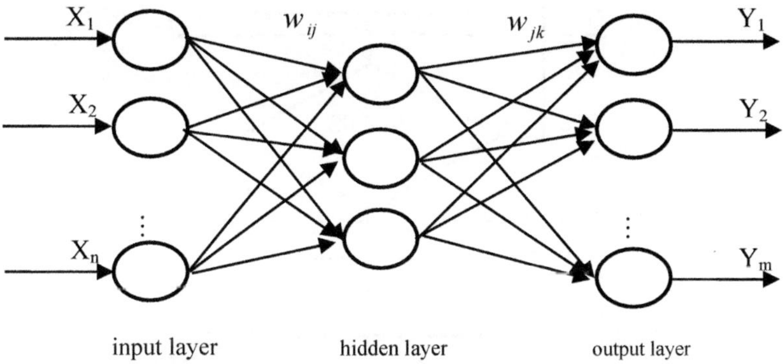

Fig. 1. BP neural network structure

Sigmoid function is often used as transfer function for hidden layer in BP-ANN, because its output is close to the signal output of biological neurons and it can simulate the nonlinear characteristic of biological neurons, which can also strengthen network's nonlinear reflecting capability at the same time. The input node n and the output node m reflect the mapping between the independent variables n and the dependent variables m. The prediction steps based on BP neural network include network architecture components, training and prediction. The basic work flow is shown in Fig. 2.

The construction phase of BP neural network model is primarily based primarily on system model and design goal to value assignment of the network parameters, which include the input nodes n, the output nodes m, and the hidden nodes l. The hidden layer threshold and output layer threshold are initialized according to the network forms and the learning rate and neuronal activation function are set.

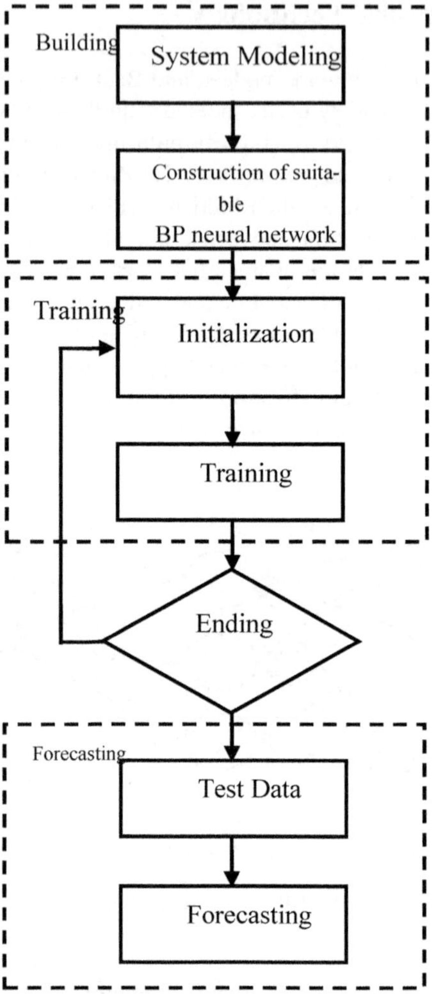

Fig. 2. BPNN flow chart

4 Simulation

The parameters of BP neural network weights and threshold are optimized. The change of genetic algorithms fitness value in the optimization is process shown in Fig. 3.

BP neural network training is a process of multiple cycles. Firstly, enter the training sample and calculate the output layers, then adjust the weights of each layer based on the output error and error in each layer which generate by the output error feedback, repeat this process until the end of the training.

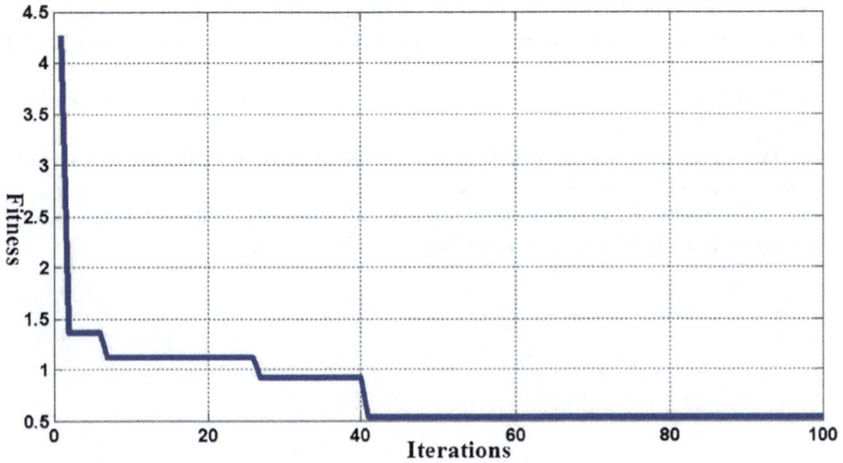

Fig. 3. Fitness value curve

5 Conclusion

This method is adopted to train the BPNN model and this paper establishes a model based on BPNN. The experimental results show that the whole target identification system has good generalization ability and has higher prediction accuracy rate. Thus, the proposed method can play a role in the system integration design.

Acknowledgments. This research was supported by the Key Projects of Natural Science Research in Inner Mongolia Higher Education Institutions (Grant No. NJZZ17647), and the Project of Humanities and Social Sciences Research in Inner Mongolia higher Education Institutions (Grant No. NJSY17149).

References

1. Mullineux AW, Murinde V (2014) Financial sector policies for enterprise development in Africa. Rev Dev Finance 4(2):66–72
2. Akin S (2016) Mathematical modeling of steam-assisted gravity drainage. Comput Geosci 32(2):240–246
3. Nukhaev MT, Pimenov VP (2010) Grey relational analysis method for multiple attribute decision making in intuitionistic fuzzy setting. J Converg Inf Technol 5(10):194–199
4. Pradhan MK (2013) Estimating the effect of process parameters on surface integrity of EDMed AISI D2 tool steel by response surface methodology coupled with grey relational analysis. Int J Adv Manuf Technol 67(12):2051–2062
5. Zain AM, Haron H (2010) Prediction of surface roughness in the end milling machining using artificial neural network. Expert Syst Appl 37(2):1755–1768
6. Ongenae F, Looy SV (2016) Time series classification for the prediction of dialysis in critically ill patients using echo state networks. Eng Appl Artif Intell 26(3):984–996

7. Ren C, An N (2014) Optimal parameters selection for BP neural network based on particle swarm optimization: a case study of wind speed forecasting. Knowl-Based Syst 56:226–239 (in Chinese)
8. Basu JK, Bhattacharyya D (2010) Use of artificial neural network in pattern recognition. Int J Soft Eng Appl 4(2):371–377
9. Wakelam M (1998) Intelligent hybrid system for integration in design and manufacture. J Mater Process Technol 76(1–3):23–28
10. Wakelam M (2000) Evolutionary optimization within an intelligent hybrid system for design integration. Artif Intell Eng Des Anal Manuf 13(5):351–363

Research on Obstacle Avoidance of Mobile Robot Based on Multi-sensor Fusion

Ting Wang(✉) and Xiaoqing Guan

Beijing Polytechnic, Beijing, China
13693541961@163.com

Abstract. This paper studies the obstacle avoidance and navigation of mobile robots in unstructured environments. Because of the shortcomings of one single sensor, the system integrates the stereo vision sensor blumblebee2 with the lidar sensor to detect the information surrounding the mobile robot's surroundings. And then through data fusion to get a more complete, more accurate scene distribution. Then use the improved system of ant colony optimization to increase the convergence speed and precision of the algorithm in robot path planning. Finally, the simulation experiment is carried out in the environment of Matlab and Visual Studio, and the physical experiment is carried out under the ROS platform. The experimental results show the feasibility and effectiveness of the proposed method.

Keywords: Stereo vision · Laser radar · Ant colony algorithm · 3D reconstruction · Path planning

1 Introduction

Autonomous mobile machines move in an unstructured environment and need to obtain environmental information through sensors. Then the information is processed and fed back to the mobile robot to realize map reconstruction, path planning, navigation and obstacle avoidance. How to ensure that mobile robots work stably in complex environments and effectively understand the surrounding scenes is one of the key links [1]. Since mobile machines are highly mobile, they have higher requirements on the cognition and adaptability of the environment. Therefore, a single sensor can no longer meet the work needs of mobile robots in complex scenes [2].

With the development of computer vision technology, binocular stereo vision sensor plays a more and more important role in navigation control of mobile robot. The image has rich information, high-speed sampling and other characteristics [3, 4]. At the same time, it is also affected by light more, and it is difficult to match areas with weak texture and other shortcomings. And laser radar may through independently lasers to detect the surrounding environment, it has high precision, high speed, affected by the external environment change the advantages of small, but it also had a disadvantage of low data sparse, sweep frequency [5], so this article will stereo vision and laser radar data fusion, to make up for their respective faults [6], to realize the obstacle avoidance and navigation of mobile robot.

Z. Xu et al. (Eds.): CSIA 2019, AISC 928, pp. 760–770, 2020.
https://doi.org/10.1007/978-3-030-15235-2_104

In the aspect of path planning algorithm, it mainly includes Dijkstra algorithm, configuration space method, generalized cone method, vertex image method and ant colony algorithm. As the most basic path planning algorithm, the traditional Dijkstra algorithm often has unsatisfactory results due to its limited factors. Ant colony algorithm (aco) has been widely used in the path planning research of wheeled robots due to its advantages of good robustness, parallel distributed computing, and easy to be improved by combining other algorithms. Literature [7] simulates and studies path planning with improved ant colony algorithm, which introduces the principle of Wolf pack allocation to update pheromones locally to prevent local optimal solutions. Literature [8] improved ant colony algorithm with immune calculation, extracted useful domain knowledge, analyzed the problem, and then combined the domain knowledge with the specific situation of the problem to obtain the solution scheme. In this paper, the improved ant colony optimization algorithm is used to solve the problem that the whole algorithm may be stuck in the deadlock state, which increases the convergence speed and reliability of the algorithm in robot path planning.

2 Modeling the Environment Around the Robot

2.1 Acquisition of Sensor Data

The scanning point of lidar is almost on the same geometric plane, and the scanned environmental data is mapped to the three-dimensional coordinate system with the mobile robot as the center and the plane where the robot is located as the reference plane. The environment data is converted to 3d coordinates in the coordinate system centered on the robot through calculation. All scanning points of the single-line lidar are on the same geometric plane, and the scanning points are projected onto the coordinate plane and coordinate axis, as shown in Fig. 1, so as to obtain the coordinates of the scanning points in the robot coordinate system:

$$c = \begin{bmatrix} X_i \\ Y_i \\ Z_i \end{bmatrix} = \begin{bmatrix} \rho \cos\theta \cos\alpha \\ \rho \sin\theta \\ h_0 - \rho \cos\theta \sin\alpha \end{bmatrix} \tag{1}$$

Where ρ is the distance from the scanning point to the lidar, the scanning angle, the installation pitch angle, and the installation height.

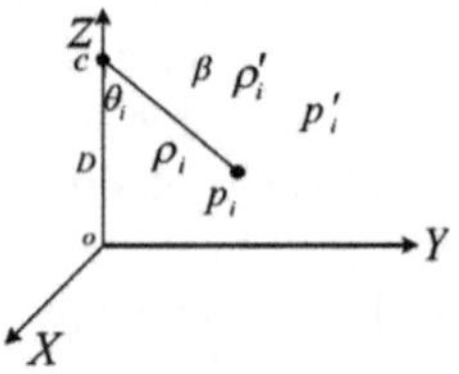

Fig. 1. Principle of the lidar.

Considering the change of the attitude of the robot on the three-dimensional terrain plane, the scanned environmental data is mapped to the global coordinate system where the starting point of the mobile robot is the origin. The current pose of the mobile robot in the global coordinate system is obtained from the odometer calculation and can be represented by the status. After the above coordinate transformation, the three-dimensional coordinates in the world global coordinate system are obtained: Considering the change of the attitude of the robot on the three-dimensional terrain plane, the scanned environmental data is mapped to the global coordinate system where the starting point of the mobile robot is the origin. The current pose of the mobile robot in the global coordinate system is obtained from the odometer calculation and can be represented by the status (P_{Xi}, P_{Yi}, P_{Zi}). After the above coordinate transformation, the three-dimensional coordinates in the world global coordinate system are obtained (x_r, y_r, z_r):

$$\begin{cases} x_r = X_i \cos P_{\theta i} - Y_i \sin P_{\theta i} + P_{Xi} \\ y_r = X_i \sin P_{\theta i} + Y_i \cos P_{\theta i} + P_{Yi} \\ z_r = Z_i \end{cases} \tag{2}$$

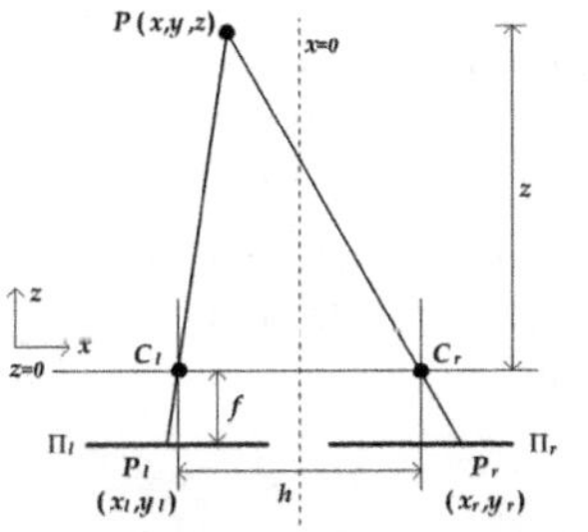

Fig. 2. Principle of stereo vision

Figure 2 is a top plan view of a binocular stereo vision system. f is the focal length for the two cameras. P is the object point in the scene where the three-dimensional coordinates are (x, y, z), the projections on the left and right camera images are point p_l and point p_r, respectively. The z axis of the coordinate system represents the distance from the object point to the camera, x axis represents the "horizontal" direction (y axis vertical page). $x = 0$ is the midpoint position of the polar line, x_l and x_r are the horizontal coordinate of the imaging point on the left and right camera image planes. The three-dimensional coordinates of the spatial point can be obtained according to the triangulation geometry:

$$\begin{cases} x = -\frac{h}{x_r - x_l} x_l \\ y = -\frac{h}{x_r - x_l} y_l \\ z = \frac{hf}{x_r - x_l} \end{cases} \tag{3}$$

2.2 Create a 2.5D Grid Map

After getting the coordinates of each point in the space, you need to represent these points in the same map. Traditional 2D raster maps typically use obstacle or free space to mark the state of each grid in the map and are therefore typically used to model indoor or flat ground. Although the 3D raster map can accurately describe the spatial information of the stereo, for the mobile robot, it will greatly increase the space consumption of saving the 3D raster map data and the idleness of the storage space while improving the height resolution, so this paper adopts 2.5D. A raster map form to store stereoscopic spatial information. In the 2.5D raster map creation process, the environment 3D point cloud description obtained by the stereo vision sensor is first converted from the camera coordinate system (CCS) to the robot coordinate system (RCS), thereby forming a local environment description. Then, using the robot's autonomous positioning information, the local environment description is transformed into the world coordinate system (WCS) according to the pose of the robot, thereby creating a global environmental map [9]. The initial position of the robot is the zero point of the world coordinate system, and the direction of each coordinate axis is determined by the posture of the robot. In this paper, the forward direction of the robot is taken as the y axis, and the direction perpendicular to the y axis of the robot in the same horizontal plane is taken as the x axis, and the z axis is determined by the right-hand rule. Assume that the horizontal distance between the right camera and the center pole is w, the vertical distance between the stereo vision sensor and the base is h, the horizontal distance between the support rod and the center of the robot is l, and the angle between the camera and the horizontal plane is ω, then based on the camera coordinate system. The corresponding transformation $P_w(x_w, y_w, z_w)$ to $P_C(x_c, y_c, z_c)$ the robot coordinates is shown as:

$$\begin{bmatrix} x_R \\ y_R \\ z_R \\ 1 \end{bmatrix} = \begin{bmatrix} 1 & 0 & 0 & -\omega \\ 0 & \cos w & \sin w & -\frac{l}{2} \\ 0 & -\sin w & \cos w & -h \\ 0 & 0 & 0 & 0 \end{bmatrix} \begin{bmatrix} x_c \\ y_c \\ z_c \\ 1 \end{bmatrix} \tag{4}$$

When it is necessary to convert the coordinates of the three-dimensional point from the robot coordinate system into the global coordinate system, the robot self-positioning function is required to provide the position and posture information of the robot, such as considering only the plane motion (x_0, y_0, θ). If the position and orientation of the robot are defined as the origin of the global coordinate system at the beginning of the task, the conversion of the point $P_C(x_c, y_c, z_c)$ in the robot coordinate system to the corresponding point $P_w(x_w, y_w, z_w)$ in the global coordinate system is as shown in the equation.

$$\begin{bmatrix} x_w \\ y_w \\ z_w \\ 1 \end{bmatrix} = \begin{bmatrix} \cos\theta & -\sin\theta & 0 & x_0 \\ \sin\theta & \cos\theta & 0 & y_0 \\ 0 & 0 & 1 & 0 \\ 0 & 0 & 0 & 1 \end{bmatrix} \begin{bmatrix} x_R \\ y_R \\ z_R \\ 1 \end{bmatrix} \tag{5}$$

After getting $P_w(x_w, y_w, z_w)$, According to the plane projection of each 3D point, the grid containing the point can be determined as $P_{ij} = \{p(x_{(i,j)} \leq x \leq x_{(i+1,j)}, y_{(i,j)} \leq y \leq y_{(i,j+1)})\}$, By counting the average height of the 3D points within the grid, you can get the grid height in the 2.5D raster map [10]. Finally, a grid map is constructed, as shown in Fig. 3.

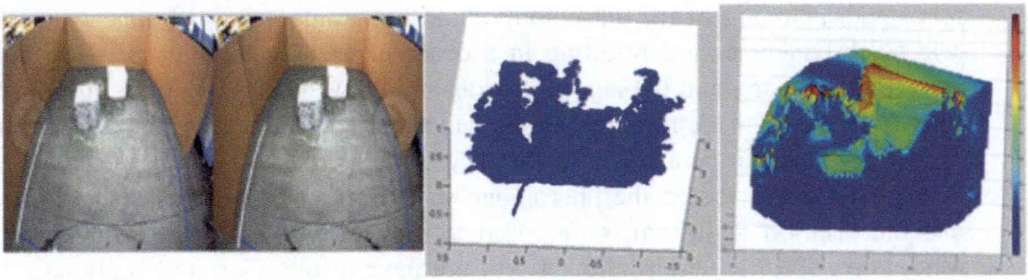

Fig. 3. The 2.5D grid

3 Obstacle Avoidance Navigation Algorithm for Mobile Robots

3.1 Ant Colony Obstacle Avoidance Navigation Algorithm

Ant colony algorithm is a heuristic search algorithm with strong robustness, distributed computing, etc. It is easy to combine with other algorithms. Finding the best path is a common behavior of ant colony. In the process of finding the optimal path, the ant will leave a pheromone on the path. The concentration of the pheromone is inversely proportional to the length of the path. The higher the pheromone concentration, the higher the pheromone concentration, which means the corresponding path distance is shorter. Usually, ants will preferentially select a path with a higher concentration of pheromone with a higher probability, and continue to release a certain amount of pheromone to enhance the concentration of pheromone on the path, so as to form a positive feedback. Eventually, the latter ants can find the best path from the nest to the food source along the pheromone, the shortest distance [11, 12]. In the application of obstacle avoidance and navigation for mobile robots, the calculation steps are as follows:

(1) The transition probability of an ant individual moving from a grid i to an adjacent grid j according to the state is

$$p_{ij}^{k}(t) = \frac{t_{ij}^{a}(t) h_{ij}^{b}(t)}{\sum\limits_{s \in C} t_{is}^{a}(t) h_{is}^{b}(t)} \tag{6}$$

$$C = D - B_K, \; \eta_{ij}(t) = \frac{1}{d_{ij}}.$$

d_{ij} The distance from the grid i where the mobile robot is located to the grid j, the degree of enlightenment from which the η_{ij} mobile robot is transferred from i to j, and the pheromone which is the trajectory strength. That the τ_{ij}^{α} mobile robot moves from i to j.

(2) Revise B_k: Every time ant P is transferred, add the node j to the taboo table B_k.

(3) Repeat the above steps until all ants that have not exited the loop reach the end point, calculate the path length of each ant reaching the end point and save. In the robot path planning of the ant colony algorithm, some ants may appear but not select subsequent nodes, resulting in a deadlock state, which makes the whole algorithm stagnant, and the algorithm does not converge fast enough. In order to further improve the efficiency of the algorithm, two improved strategies are proposed: the main parameters of the algorithm such as the number of ants, the expected stimulus factor, the pheromone volatilization coefficient are optimized, and the back-off algorithm is proposed to prevent entry and save convergence time. For a specific terrain, the ant will not have a follow-up node optional, the optional grid is adjacent to zero, and a deadlock situation occurs, so the algorithm is called ant trapping. For that, we propose another method: intelligent fallback algorithm, which can quit the trap for ants, new path to find, and prevent the algorithm from stalling.

3.2 Improved Ant Colony Algorithm-Regression Algorithm

In the ant colony algorithm of the above robot path planning, some ants may have a situation in which no subsequent nodes are selectable, resulting in a deadlock state, which causes the entire algorithm to stagnate and affect the reliability of the entire algorithm, in order to further improve the algorithm speed of operation and propose the optimization strategy of the fallback algorithm.

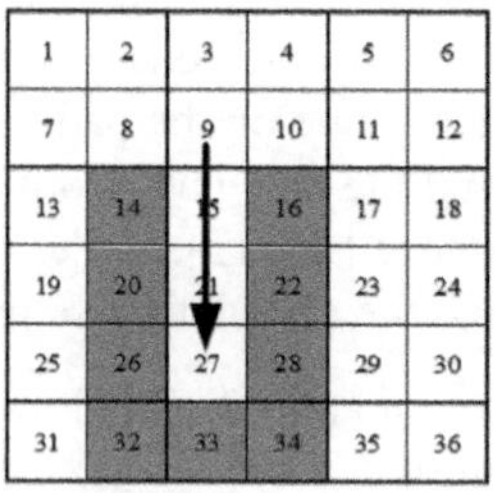

Fig. 4. The ant colony grid trap

As shown in Fig. 4, when a concave map appears, the ants can enter the terrain without any subsequent nodes to choose, and the algorithm appears to be dead. This situation is called falling into the trap. When the ant falls into the trap, if there is no good treatment, the ant will be judged as invalid ant, and the whole algorithm will be in a stagnant state, making the algorithm less robust to the complexity of the environment. The current common solution is to fill the concave obstacle into a solid convex obstacle. The consequence of this is that the deadlock problem can be solved locally, but it does not eliminate the traps and the traps of the entire environment edge, indicating that this method has a very big limitations. Therefore, this paper proposes a regression algorithm. When the ant enters the trap, it retreats along the original path, and while deleting the grid in the trap, and knows that there are other paths to choose, the process of the previous chapter is performed. Complete the regression algorithm. This algorithm ensures that every ant can reach the destination safely, greatly enhancing the robustness and adaptability of the algorithm.

4 Experimental Result

4.1 Environmental Detection and Reconstruction

4.1.1 Stereo Vision Inspection Environment

First, the experiment is carried out in an indoor experiment, as shown in Fig. 5, which makes it easier to control the experiment, and it is convenient to set the corresponding scene according to the experiment.

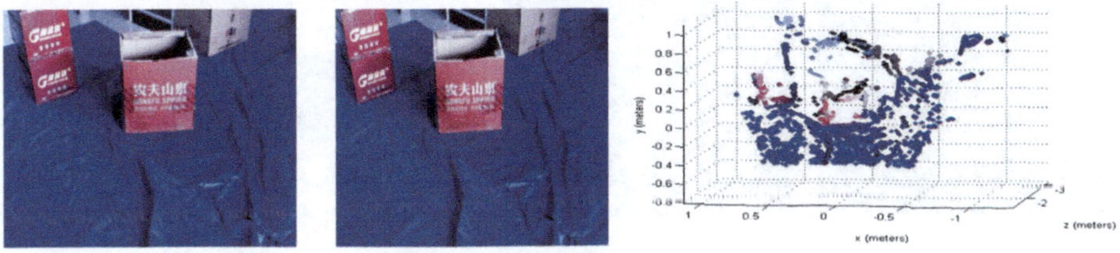

Fig. 5. Indoor environment

The left and middle images in the table are the left and right images acquired by the binocular vision system, and the right is the result of the 3D reconstruction. Table 1 is a comparison of the actual distance and reconstruction of the two cartons. We can find that the measurement deviation in the direction perpendicular to the plane is 4–6 cm, and the precision is higher in the direction parallel to the image plane, which is basically consistent with the actual distance.

Table 1. Comparison of actual size and reconstructed size

	Distance from camera/cm		Size (width × height)/cm	
Object	Actual	Reconstruction	Actual	Reconstruction
Nongfu Spring	170	166	30 × 32	30 × 32
Gao Pinle	200	206	22 × 44	22 × 44

Because the system is applied to the outdoor environment of mobile robots, we need to conduct outdoor experiments after verifying the correctness and accuracy of the algorithm. The results are shown in Figs. 6 and 7. Figure 6 shows the environment of the cement floor, and Fig. 7 shows the environment of the land. It can be seen that the results of the reconstruction are consistent with the environment.

Fig. 6. Outdoor environment 1

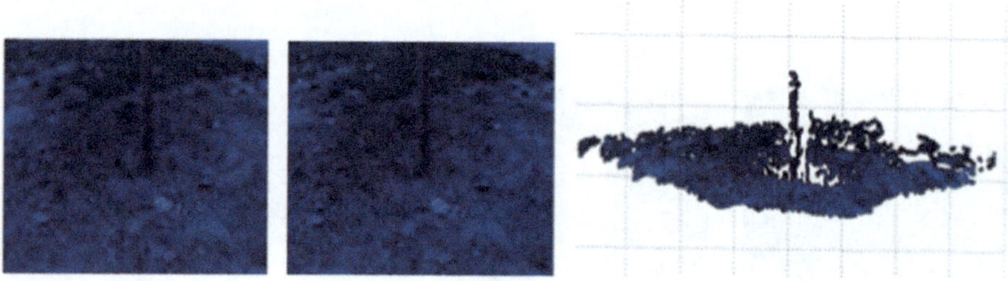

Fig. 7. Outdoor environment 2

4.1.2 Lidar Detection Environment

We use lidar to detect the environment. I verified the accuracy of the lidar in a structured environment in the lab, as shown in Fig. 8. On the left is the environment for lidar scanning, where the distance between the two tables is about 1 m. The picture on the right shows the data we obtained using a lidar scan. It can be seen that the width of the channel is approximately 1 m. So the distance obtained by laser scanning is consistent with the actual object. Therefore, we can use Lidar for the next experiment.

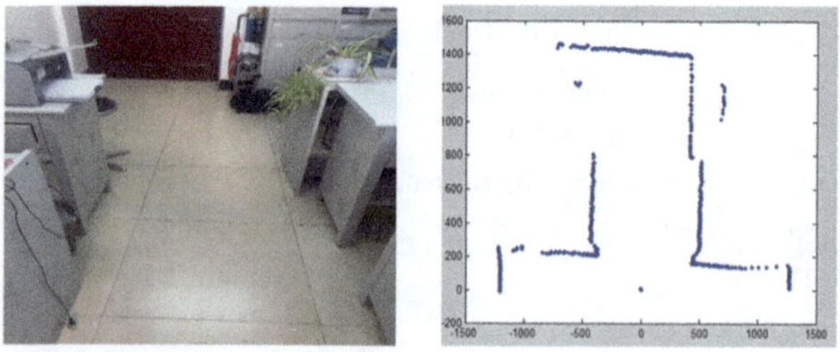

Fig. 8. Lidar experiment

4.2 Simulation of Ant Colony Algorithm

In the last section, the 2.5D grid map of the environment in which the robot is located and the grid map after the dimension reduction are obtained. The environment model of the ant colony algorithm is based on the grid map, and the path planning operation is performed, as well as the grid structure is simple. Through programming operations, we reduce the dimensionality of the 2.5D grid map, and turn all the grid heights beyond the height of the robot into obstacles, which are displayed as black grids. Grid below the height of the climb, we call it free grid. As shown in the figure, the ant colony algorithm is used to find a collision-free optimal path from the starting point (0.0) to the ending point (20.20). The simulation in the program and the real object is as follows.

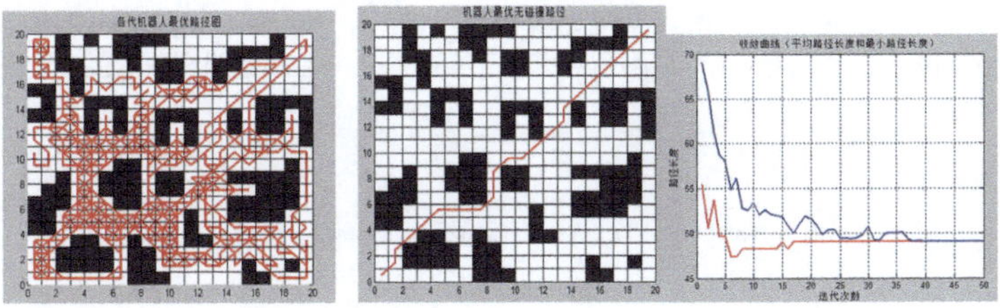

Fig. 9. Ant colony algorithm simulation and convergence curve

After releasing a number of ants, the ant colony algorithm will automatically converge to find the final path as shown in the figure. The convergence speed meets the mobile robot path planning requirements and reaches convergence when about 40 ants are released. At the same time, it is found from Fig. 9 that the optimized ant colony algorithm has obvious regression algorithm. The retreat strategy enhances the reliability of the ant and the robustness of the entire algorithm. The programming simulation verifies that the whole ant colony algorithm is well understood and feasible. The latter section will use the real robot to verify the ant colony algorithm path planning.

4.3 Physical Verification

In this paper, the flexible and flexible robot platform is used fluently to verify the feasibility and accuracy of the whole scheme. The whole mobile robot consists of four parts: the sensing layer, the decision control layer, the execution control layer and the user layer (as shown in Fig. 10). The sensing layer is the robot interfaces with the outside world, and the external environment is sensed by various sensors to obtain environmental information. The odometer formed by the combination of the inertial measurement unit and the encoder can calculate the current pose of the mobile robot; while the binocular camera and the 2D laser radar through scanning the surrounding environment of the robot to sense and describe the unknown environment, so that it can give its absolute pose under its own reference coordinate system; the decision control layer is the master control system of the robot, based on the data transmitted by the sensory layer. The corresponding motion strategy is formulated for the mobile robot, mainly to complete the positioning, path control and mapping of the environment map to the mobile robot; the execution control layer is the execution mechanism, which processes the actions of the decision control layer, including moving speed, adjusting the pose, etc.; The user layer is mainly composed of the PC of the host computer and the data transmitted by PC carried through the wireless Ethernet receiver to completes the synchronous monitoring of the path planning process of the ant colony algorithm.

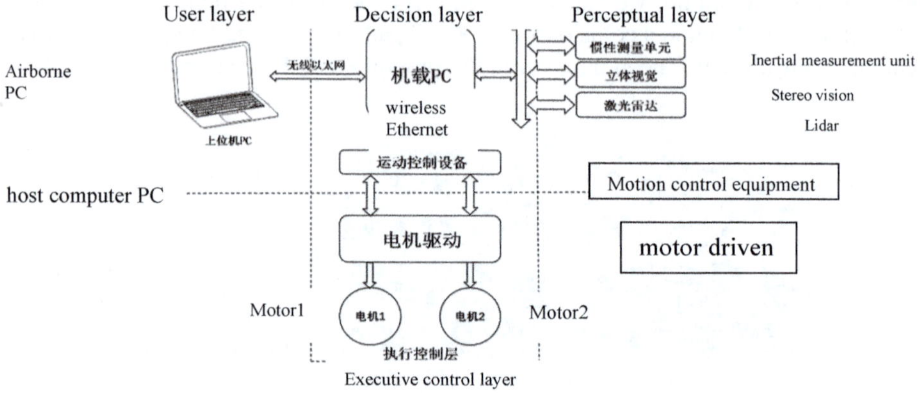

Fig. 10. The composition of mobile robot

In the above four levels, the sensor data of the sensing layer is transmitted to the decision layer through the serial port, and the decision layer constructs a map based on the data and formulates a navigation strategy (Fig. 11).

Fig. 11. The overall structure of the mobile robot platform

In the course of the experiment, we used the binocular camera of the sensory layer and 2D lidar and odometer for data acquisition, and then transmitted to the decision control layer for our data processing, including: stereo vision detection, lidar detection, 2.5D Map generation and improved ant colony algorithm for obstacle avoidance navigation. The generated navigation control information is then transmitted to the execution control layer to control the mobile robot to move. And display and interact at the user level.

It can be seen from the experimental results that the robot can find a collision-free optimal path and has an anti-deadlock retreat strategy optimization algorithm. The convergence speed satisfies the robot path planning requirements, indicating that the algorithm can guide the mobile robot to trajectory planning.

5 Conclusion

This paper presents a multi-sensor fusion obstacle avoidance and navigation system. The system integrates a stereo camera and lidar to detect surrounding scenes and model the surrounding environment through data fusion. Then the ant colony algorithm is optimized by using the regression algorithm, which increases the convergence speed and accuracy of the algorithm in the robot path planning. Finally, the feasibility and effectiveness of the proposed method are proved by simulation and physical experiments.

References

1. Yuan C, Zhimin Z, Zhen C (2008) The improvement of extrinsic calibration of laser rangefinder with CCD and its applications. Appl Laser 3:011
2. Zhang K, Xu B, Tang L et al (2006) Modeling of binocular vision system for 3D reconstruction with improved genetic algorithms. Int J Adv Manuf Technol 29(7–8):722–728
3. Zhao Y, Li W (2014) Self-calibration of a binocular vision system based on a one-dimensional target. J Mod Opt 61(18):1529–1537
4. Dong C (2009) Joint calibration and data fusion between 3D laser and monocular vision. Dalian University of Technology
5. Lian X (2010) 3D model reconstruction technology of mobile robot and indoor environment. National Defense Industry Press
6. Liu T, Carlberg M, Chen G et al (2010) Indoor localization and visualization using a human-operated backpack system. In: 2010 International Conference on Indoor Positioning and Indoor Navigation (IPIN). IEEE, pp 1–10
7. Zhang P, Xu XX (2013) Simulation study on global path planning of improved ant colony algorithm. Aeronaut Comput Technol (6):1–4 (in Chinese)
8. Qiu L, Zheng J (2015) Robot path planning based on improved ant colony algorithm. Inf Technol (6):150–152
9. Pavlou M, Acheson J, Nicolaou D et al (2015) Effect of developmental binocular vision abnormalities on visual vertigo symptoms and treatment outcome. J Neurol Phys Ther 39 (4):215–224
10. Hess RF, Thompson B, Baker DH (2014) Binocular vision in amblyopia: structure, suppression and plasticity. Ophthalmic Physiol Opt 34(2):146–162
11. Anwar S, Shoaib TI, Mansoor MS et al (2007) Depth measurement and 3-D reconstruction of multilayered surfaces by binocular stereo vision with parallel axis symmetry using fuzzy. Lecture Notes in Engineering and Computer Science, p 21671
12. Chen CL, Tai CL, Lio YF (2007) Virtual binocular vision systems to solid model reconstruction. Int J Adv Manuf Technol 35(3–4):379–384

Interaction Steady State Transportation Network and Planning Optimization Model

Baiyu Chen[1], Da Fu[2(✉)], and Yuanyuan Yang[1,2]

[1] College of Engineering, University of California Berkeley, Berkeley, CA 94720, USA
baiyu@berkeley.edu
[2] Business School, Sichuan University, Chengdu 610064, People's Republic of China
fuda1213@outlook.com

Abstract. This paper studies the relationship among flow, density and speed of steady-state traffic network. Taking the inner ring road in Shanghai as an example, the relationship model of three parameters of traffic flow is verified, and the evaluation criteria of traffic conditions are given by three parameters. Based on the three-parameter relationship model of traffic flow, combined with the law of vehicle conservation, the macroscopic steady flow is derived. In addition, the service traffic volume and traffic resistance are selected as the objective function to establish the optimal planning model to achieve the maximum service traffic volume or the minimum traffic resistance. The establishment of the above model provides a new statistical reference value for the driverless car sharing road with private cars and the emotional interaction between the human and the automobile in the era of intelligent Internet of things.

Keywords: Traffic flow · Current divider coefficient · Service traffic volume · Traffic resistance · Linear combination

1 Background of the Study

At present, traditional auto companies realize unmanned driving by developing vehicle networking and ADAS system technology, while Internet companies are making breakthroughs in GPS navigation, artificial intelligence and system security [1–6]. The technologies require integrated sensing components installed in the car to perceive all kinds of information about the road environment during driving [7–13]. At this time, it is very important whether the perceived road condition information can be effectively acquired and accurately processed.

The driverless system is divided into three levels: the perception layer, the decision layer, and the execution layer. The radar and camera of driverless cars belong to the category of perception layer, through which the system realizes the perceptual recognition of the surrounding environment of the vehicle. [14–21], and supports decision-making activities such as driver action planning and route planning. In the case of obtaining effective information and having a high-performance database architecture, the acquisition of traffic signs, traffic police gestures, license plates, models and other

Z. Xu et al. (Eds.): CSIA 2019, AISC 928, pp. 771–780, 2020.
https://doi.org/10.1007/978-3-030-15235-2_105

information in various situations ensures that the traffic management strategy is safe and effective [22–26]. At present, driverless cars are the integration of high-intelligence AI technology, which combines speech recognition, face recognition, 3D slam and other technologies to cover the frontier fields of robot interaction, perception, motion control and so on [27–35]. It brings not only technology but also emotion to smart cities. The car can analyze human facial expressions, driving habits, adjust the seat [36–38] to calm them down [39–47] when the drivers are anxious, or shake them to remind them when they doze off [48–56], or may propose parking in complex road conditions, even through the computer vision algorithm for the driver's facial expression health diagnosis [57–61], or biological sampling at any time for health tracking analysis [62–68], give a treatment plan, conduct intimate communication between humans and mobile devices, and realize the protection and mutual help of human beings in the era of intelligent IOT.

2 Macro Steady State Traffic Model

Steady-state traffic flow refers that traffic flow, speed and traffic density on a road within a certain period (e.g., rush hour) only are related to the spatial coordinates of the target road segment, and have nothing to do with time T. Figure 1 is a schematic diagram of the section of the north-south viaduct in Shanghai.

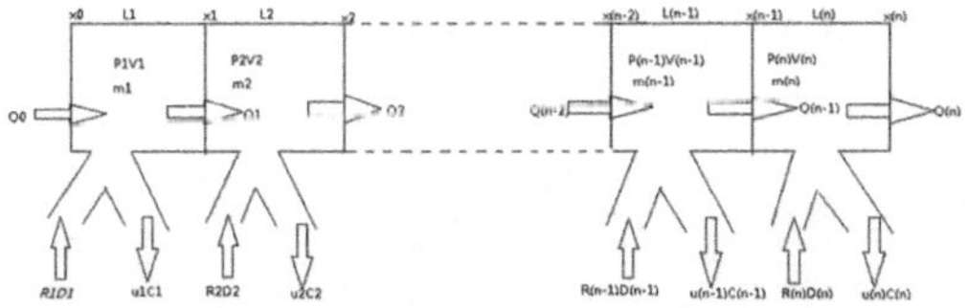

Fig. 1. Sub-diagram of the north and South Viaduct in Shanghai

V_i is the average running speed on the i_{th} segment of the elevated road, unit is m/s. K_i is the average traffic density on the i_{th} segment of the elevated road, unit is veh/km. R_i is the inflow into the i_{th} segment of elevated road entrance, unit is veh/h. D_i is the traffic demand on the i_{th} segment of elevated road entrance, unit is veh/h. C_i is the outflow of the i_{th} segment of elevated road exit, unit is veh/h, A_i is the traffic capacity of the i_{th} segment of elevated road. L_i is the length of the i_{th} segment of elevated road, the unit is km and U_i is the current divider coefficient of the i_{th} segment of elevated road. $u_i \in [0, 1]$, $i = 1, \cdots, N$.

Select the direction of traffic flow in the positive direction, traffic flow from x_0 goes into the 1st section of the elevated road. At this time the speed and traffic floware known, respectively, $V_0(km/h)$ and $Q_0(veh/h)$; On the 1st section of the elevated road, traffic volume can flow out of the 1th exit ramp, the outflow volume is C_1, and the current divider coefficient of the outlet is u_1. At the same time, there will be other traffic flowing from the 1th inlet ramp, the inflow volume is R_1, the traffic capacity of the entrance is D_1, so the traffic flow on the elevated road in the 1st section is

$Q_1(veh/h) = Q_0 + R_1 - C_1$; Next, traffic will enter the 2nd section of the elevated road from x_1. At this time the traffic and speed are respectively $Q_1(veh/h), (V_1, km/h)$; on the 2nd elevated road, traffic flow can flow out of the 2nd exit ramp with an outflow of C_2, the current divider coefficient of the outlet is u_2. At the same time, there will be other traffic flowing out of the 2th inlet ramp, the inflow volume is R_2, the traffic capacity of the entrance is D_2, so the traffic flow on the 2nd section of the elevated road is $Q_2(veh/h) = Q_1 + R_2 - C_2 \ldots$. By analogy, the traffic finally exits the elevated road from x_N, with an outflow of $Q_N(veh/h)$ and a speed of $V_N(km/h)$. Therefore, according to the basic relationship between the three parameters of traffic flow we canget: $Q_i = K_i V_i$, $C_i = u_i Q_{i-1}$.

It is also equal to the sum of all the outflows of the section, that is, the traffic flow obeys the law of vehicle conservation: $Q_i = Q_{i-1} + R_i - C_i = (1 - u_i)\, Q_{i-1} + R_i$. So, there are:

$$K_i V_i = (1 - u_i)\, Q_{i-1} + R_i \tag{1}$$

This is the macroscopic steady-state traffic model.

3 Planning Optimization Model

3.1 Maximum Service Traffic Volume Planning Models

Suppose M is the total service traffic volume of the target elevated road. To maximize M, it can establish the following objective function:

$$\max M = \sum_{i=1}^{N} K_i V_i$$

$$s.t. \begin{cases} K_i V_i = (1 - u_i)\, Q_{i-1} + R_i,\ i = 1, 2, \cdots, N \\ 0 \le Q_i \le A_i,\ 0 \le R_i \le D_i,\ Q_0 = K_0 V_0 \end{cases} \tag{2}$$

Select a coordinate origin in the target section, recorded as X = 0, with a positive direction to the right. Assuming that on the section $[x_1, x_2]$ the total number of vehicles passing by at T moment was i, the rate of increase on T is $\frac{d}{dt}\int_{x_1}^{x_2} K(x,t)\,dx$, so there are: $Q(x_2,t) - Q(x_1,t) = \frac{d}{dt}\int_{x_1}^{x_2} K(x,t)dx$. Let this formula bring into formula (2), it can get: $K_i V_i = (1 - u_i)\, K_{i-1} V_{i-1} + R_i$, $i = 1 \ldots N$.

So the optimal planning model can simplify as a linear programming model:

$$\max M = \alpha + \sum_{i=1}^{N} \beta_i R_i$$

$$s.t. \begin{cases} 0 \le R_i \le D_i \\ \eta_{i1} R_1 + \eta_{i2} R_2 + \cdots + \eta_{ij} R_j \le A_i - \eta, i > j, i, j = 1, \cdots, N \end{cases} \tag{3}$$

Solving the Eq. (3) by the simplex method it can obtain $R_1^*, R_2^*, \cdots, R_N^*$, and then the corresponding optimal solution K_i^*, V_i^*, $i = 1, 2, \cdots N$ can be obtained according to the macroscopic steady traffic model and the relationship between velocity and density.

3.2 Minimal Traffic Impedance Planning Model

The traffic resistance on the selected elevated road is selected as the objective function, setting to Q, and the unit is: hour (h). Obtain BPR functions $V = \frac{V_M}{1+a(\frac{Q}{A})^b}$; $b = b_1 + b_2 \frac{Q}{A}$ and the urban road traffic resistance model: $T = \frac{L}{V}$.

An optimal planning model for traffic resistance can be established:

$$\min T = \sum_{i=1}^{N} T_i$$

$$s.t. \begin{cases} T_i = \frac{L_i}{V_i},\ i = 1, 2, \cdots, N \\ V_i = \frac{V_M}{1+a(\frac{Q_i}{A_i})^b} \end{cases},\ 0 \le Q_i \le A_i \quad (4)$$

a, b, b_1, b_2 is the undetermined parameter. Generally, V_M is taken as the maximum designed vehicle speed, and the unit is: km/h. At this time, $a = 0.15, b = 4.0$. Similar to the planning model (3), from the macroscopic steady-state traffic model, $R_1^*, R_2^*, \cdots, R_N^*$ are obtained by the simplex method, and the corresponding optimal solution K_i^*, V_i^*, $i = 1, 2, \cdots N$ can be obtained.

3.3 Maximum Programming Model of Interaction Combination of Service Traffic Volume and Traffic Resistance

Service traffic volume and traffic impedance are two important indicator parameters. In reality, these two goals are not always consistent. Therefore, an optimal planning model that takes into account the roles of both is given.

The linear combination of traffic resistance and service traffic is selected as the objective function to establish an optimal planning model:

$$\max W = \sum_{i=1}^{N} (\lambda - 1)T_i + \lambda M_i$$

$$s.t. \begin{cases} Q_i = K_i V_i = (1-u_i)K_{i-1}V_{i-1} + R_i,\ Q_0 = K_0 V_0,\ i = 1, 2, \cdots, N \\ T_i = \frac{L_i}{V_M}(1 + a(\frac{Q_i}{A_i})^b,\ 0 \le Q_i \le A_i, 0 \le R_i \le D_i;\ \lambda \in [0, 1] \end{cases} \quad (5)$$

Function (5) is a 2N-dimensional nonlinear programming problem. MATLAB can be used to find R_i^*, $i = 1, 2, \cdots, N$ under different λ values. In the process of searching solution, the traffic density K can be used to represent the driving speed V. According to the value range of the traffic density, the optimal problem (5) can be divided into three different optimal problems. The optimal solution to this problem varies with the value of λ. When $\lambda = 1$, this plan is the optimal model with the maximum service traffic as the objective function (2). When $\lambda = 0$, the above formula becomes the special case with the minimum traffic resistance as the objective function. Therefore, the new optimal planning model (5) covers the first two optimal planning models and is an improvement of the single optimal planning problem.

4 Macro-steady State Traffic Model of Shanghai North and South Viaduct Example Calculation and Analysis

The total length of the elevated section is 8.45 km. There are 18 upper and lower ramps in the whole line, 6 lanes in both directions, and the width is 25.5 m. The single lane design capacity of the main line is 1800 vehicles/h. The single-lane design has a capacity of 1,600 vehicles/h and a design speed of 60 km/h. Select the traffic flow data measured on the south side of the Xinzha Road on the north-south elevated road in the downtown area of Shanghai, close to Beijing Road, and the measurement time is 11:00–12:30 on a sunny day. The time interval is 5 s. Drawing a scatter plot, the analysis shows that the maximum flow is $Q_m = 5400$ veh/h, the critical speed is $V_m = 25$ m/s $= 90$ km/h, the smooth speed is $V_f = 15$ m/s $= 54$ km/h, the optimal density is $K_m = 60$ veh/km, and the blocking density is $K_j = 120$ veh/km (one-way traffic is positive), see Fig. 2.

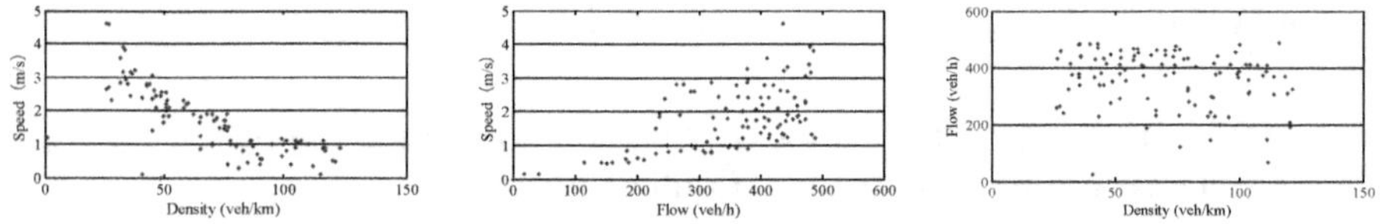

Fig. 2. Density-velocity, flow-velocity and density-flow distribution of North and South Viaduct

$V_0 = 16.67$ m/s $= 40$ km/h, $K_0 = 38.5975$ veh/km, $Q_0 = 2315.85$ veh/h, $u_1 = 0.13$, $u_2 = 0.30$, $u_3 = 0.33$, $u_4 = 0.37$, $u_5 = 0.52$, $u_6 = 0.18$, $u_7 = 0.27$, $u_8 = 0.75$, $u_9 = 0.22$ can be obtained by optimizing the data. The length of the take-up section is $L_i = 1$ km, i = 1, 2, $\cdots$, 9, and the maximum design speed is $V_M = 120$ km/h. When the one-way traffic is in the positive direction, the number of lanes in the main line of the elevated road is 3, the number of lanes in other ramps is 1, the traffic capacity is $A_i = 5400$ veh/h, $i = 1, 2, \cdots, 9$, and the traffic demand of the exit is $D_i = 1600$ veh/h, $i = 1, 2, \ldots, 9$. Select the value of λ as: $\lambda_1 = 0$, $\lambda_2 = 0.25$, $\lambda_2 = 0.5$, $\lambda_2 = 0.75$, $\lambda_3 = 1$. Solutions for optimal programming problems at different F values can be obtained.

From the inflow amount R_i^*, $i = 1, 2, \cdots, 9$ of each section inlet, the optimal density K_i^* and the optimal speed V_i^* of each section are obtained according to the macro steady state traffic model formula (1). From formula (5), the optimal problem of minimizing the linear combination of traffic resistance and service traffic on the north-south elevated can be obtained. The calculation results by means of MATLAB are shown in Table 1: (R_i^* : Veh/h, K_i^* : Veh/KM, V_i^* : km/h, $i = 1, 2, \cdots, 9$).

Table 1. North and South Viaduct Optimal Planning

	R_1^*	K_1^*	V_1^*	R_3^*	K_3^*	V_3^*	R_6^*	K_6^*	V_6^*	R_9^*	K_9^*	V_9^*
$\lambda = 0$	0.2089	119.9759	0.0109	1.7961	0.101	53.9092	0.7729	0.0796	53.9284	0.2181	0.0184	53.9835
$\lambda = 0.5$	0.0301	100.7499	8.6625	83.3233	21.1487	37.959	97.1657	62.6825	25.7929	119.139	60.0000	27.0000

It can be available from the table above:

(1) When $\lambda = 0$, the linear combination of service traffic and traffic resistance is the largest, the traffic resistance is minimized, and the travel time through the elevated part is 0.075 h, and the optimal speed V^* is about 53.98 km/h, which is equal to the speed V_f, the optimal density C is about 0.03 veh/km. This means that the current traffic density is small, there are fewer vehicles, and traffic flow is free.
(2) When $\lambda = 0.5$, the linear combination of service traffic and traffic resistance is the largest, 1227.45, the optimal speed V^* is between 8–60 km/h, and the optimal density K^* is between 3–70 veh/km. The range of variation of optimal density and optimal speed increase, the current traffic flow distribution is uneven, the restricted factors of vehicle traffic increase, and the vehicle speed begins to decrease.
(3) The optimal solution has a certain relationship with the value of λ. With the gradual increase of λ, the optimal density is getting larger and larger, and the optimal speed is getting lower and lower.

5 Summary

At present, the research on steady-state traffic network is still lacking. This paper studies the relationship between flow, density and speed of steady-state traffic network. The conclusions make up for the limitations of traditional traffic model and the constraints of over-optimal constraints. And get the following results:

1. Taking the inner ring road in Shanghai as an example, the traffic flow data on the elevated road is processed and analyzed. The relationship model of three parameters of traffic flow is verified, and the characteristics of traffic flow are analyzed. And the three parameters to determine the traffic conditions.
2. Considering the uniformly divided traffic flow as a whole, based on the three-parameter relationship model of traffic flow, combined with the law of vehicle conservation, the macro-steady traffic flow is derived, which lays a foundation for the establishment of subsequent optimal problems.

3. Select the service traffic volume and traffic resistance as the objective function, and propose the optimal problem of reaching the maximum service traffic volume or minimizing traffic resistance. Then, based on the actual situation, further improve the optimal problem.

References

1. Zhou Y, Wang X, Chen Y, Wang Z (2014) Armlock: hardware-based fault isolation for arm. In: Proceedings of the 2014 ACM SIGSAC conference on computer and communications security, November 3. ACM, pp 558–569
2. Chen Y, Wang Z, Whalley D, Lu L (2016) Remix: on-demand live randomization. In: Proceedings of the sixth ACM conference on data and application security and privacy, 9 March. ACM, pp 50–61
3. Chen Y, Khandaker M, Wang Z (2017) Pinpointing vulnerabilities. In: Proceedings of the 2017 ACM on Asia conference on computer and communications security, 2 April. ACM, pp 334–345
4. Wang X, Chen Y, Wang Z, Qi Y, Zhou Y (2015) SecPod: a framework for virtualization-based security systems. In: USENIX annual technical conference, 8 July, pp 347–360
5. Chen Y, Zhang Y, Wang Z, Wei T (2017) Downgrade attack on TrustZone, 17 July. arXiv preprint arXiv:1707.05082
6. Chen Y, Zhang Y, Wang Z, Xia L, Bao C, Wei T (2017) Adaptive android Kernel live patching. In: Proceedings of the 26th USENIX security symposium, August (USENIX Security 2017)
7. Chen B, Yang Z, Huang S, Du X, Cui Z, Bhimani J et al (2017) Cyber-physical system enabled nearby traffic flow modelling for autonomous vehicles. In: 36th IEEE international performance computing and communications conference, special session on cyber physical systems: security, computing, and performance (IPCCC-CPS). IEEE
8. Escalante HJ, Ponce-López V, Wan J et al (2016) Chalearn joint contest on multimedia challenges beyond visual analysis: an overview. In: 2016 23rd international conference on pattern recognition (ICPR), pp 67–73
9. Barrs A, Baiyu C How emerging technologies could transform infrastructure. http://www.governing.com/gov-institute/voices/col-hyperlane-emerging-technologies-transform-infrastructure.html
10. Chen B, Escalera S, Guyon I et al (2016) Overcoming calibration problems in pattern labeling with pairwise ratings: application to personality Traits. In: Computer vision–ECCV 2016 workshops. Springer, Cham, pp 419–432
11. Ponce-López V, Chen B, Oliu M et al (2016) Chalearn LAP 2016: first Round Challenge on first impressions-dataset and results. In: Computer vision–ECCV 2016 workshops. Springer, Cham, pp 400–418
12. Zhang SF, Shen W, Li DS, Zhang XW, Chen B (2018) Nondestructive ultrasonic testing in rod structure with a novel numerical laplace based wavelet finite element method. Lat Am J Solids Struct E48(7):1–17
13. Chen B, Wang B (2017) Location selection of logistics center in e-commerce network environments. Am J Neural Netw Appl 3(4):40–48 Science Publishing Group
14. Deng ZQ, Tian Y, Tang DW, Jiang S, Quan Q, Xiao H (2013) Research on the new structure coring ly for extraterrestrial bodies exploration. Chin J Mech Eng 49:104–110

15. Tian Y, Deng ZQ (2016) Coring bit with enhanced structural parameters to improved Lunar Soil Sampling and reduced mechanical disturbance. J Aerosp Eng Am Soc Civ Eng 29:04016015
16. Tian Y, Deng Z-Q, Tang D-W, Chen J-K (2017) Drilling power consumption analysis of coring bit in lunar sample mission. J Aerosp Eng Am Soc Civ Eng 30:04017055
17. Tian Y, Sun E, Zhang L (2012) Analysis of structural parameters of flexible spiral conveyor and blades of its study N power. Ammonia Plant Saf Relat Facil 200:455–458
18. Tian Y, Tang D, Deng Z, Jiang S, Quan Q (2015) Drilling power consumption and soil conveying volume performances of lunar sampling Auger. Chin J Mech Eng 28:451–459 Chinese Mechanical Engineering Society
19. Tian Y, Deng Z, Tang D, Jiang S, Hou X (2012) Structure parameters optimization and simulation experiment of auger in lunar soil Drill-sampling device. Chin J Mech Eng 48:10–15
20. Tian Y, Yuan P, Yang F, Gu J, Chen M, Tang J et al (2018) Research on the principle of a new flexible screw conveyor and its power consumption. NATO Adv Sci Inst Ser E Appl Sci 8:1038 Multidisciplinary Digital Publishing Institute
21. Tian, Y, Deng ZQ, Tang, DW et al (2016) Power consumption of lunar subsurface coring driller and earth environment stimulant experiments. J Jilin Univ Eng Technol Ed. http://www.airitilibrary.com/Publication/alDetailedMesh?docid=jlgydxzrkxxb201601025
22. Wang L, Liu G, Chen B et al (2010) Typhoon influence considered method for calculating combined return period of ocean extreme value: China INA, ZL 10595807.6. Patent 2013-03-20
23. Liu G, Zheng Z, Wang L et al (2015) Power-type wave absorbing device and using method Thereof: China, ZL 10575336.5. Patent 2017-11-03
24. Wang L, Guilin L, Chen, B et al (2010) Typhoon based on the principle of maximum entropy waters affect the design wave height calculation method: China, ZL 10595815.0[p]. Patent 2015-08-19
25. Liu G, Chen B, Wang L et al (2018) Wave height statistical characteristic analysis. J Oceanol Limnol 36(4):1123–1136
26. Zeng Y, Xie Z, Yu Y, Liu S, Wang L, Jia B et al (2016) Ecohydrological effects of stream–aquifer-interaction: a case study of the Heihe river basin, Northwestern. Hydrol Earth Syst Sci 20:2333–2352 Copernicus GmbH
27. Zeng Y, Xie Z, Liu S (2017) Seasonal effects of irrigation on land–atmosphere latent heat, sensible heat, and carbon fluxes in Semiarid BAS. Earth Syst Dyn 8:113–127 Copernicus GmbH
28. Zeng Y, Xie Z, Zou J (2016) Hydrologic and climatic responses to global anthropogenic groundwater extraction. J Clim Am Meteorol Soc 30:71–90
29. Zeng Y, Xie Z, Yu Y, Liu S, Wang L, Zou J et al (2016) Effects of anthropogenic-regulation and groundwater lateral flow on land proc Esses. J Adv Model Earth Syst 8:1106–1131
30. Zeng Y, Xie Z, Liu S, Xie J, Jia B, Qin P et al (2018) Global land surface modeling including lateral groundwater flow. J Adv Model Earth Syst 10:1882–1900
31. Xie Z, Liu S, Zeng Y, Gao J, Qin P, Jia B et al (2018) A high-resolution land model with groundwater lateral flow, the soil, and the freeze-thaw front dynamics and their applications in an endorheic Basin. J Geophys Res Atmos. https://doi.org/10.1029/2018jd028369
32. Xie Z-H, Zeng Y-J, Xia J, Qin P-H, Jia B-H, Zou J et al (2017) Coupled modeling of land hydrology–regional climate including Carbon emission and exploitation. Adv Clim Res 8:68–79
33. Liu S, Xie Z, Zeng Y (2016) Discharge estimation for a ungauged Inland river at an Arid/Related to Anthropogenic activities: a case study of Heihe River Basin, Northwestern. Adv Meteorol. Hindawi. https://doi.org/10.1155/2016/6716501

34. Jia B, Xie Z, Zeng Y, Wang L, Wang Y, Xie J et al (2015) Diurnal and seasonal variations of CO2 fluxes and their climate controlling factors to a subtropical forest in Ningxiang. Adv Atmos Sci 32:553–564 Science Press
35. Chen B, Liu G, Wang L, Zhang K, Zhang S (2018) Determination of by-a-estuarine City. J Oceanol Limnol 37(1):20–29
36. Liu X, He Y, Fu H, Chen B, Wang M, Wang Z (2018) How environmental the motivation influences on residents recycled, reuse behaviors: a case study in Xian city. Water 10:1282
37. Liu X, He Y, Fu H, Chen B, Wang M Scientometric of nearly zero energy building research: a systematic review from the perspective of co-citation analysis. J Therm Sci
38. Gasper R, Shi H, Ramasubramaniam A (2017) Adsorption of CO on low-energy, low-symmetry PT nanoparticles: energy decomposition analysis and prediction via machine-learning models. J Phys Chem C. Am Soc 121:5612–5619
39. Shi H, Koskinen P, Ramasubramaniam A (2017) Self-consistent charge density-functional tight-binding parametrization for PT-RU alloys. J Phys Chem A 121:2497–2502
40. Shi H, Auerbach SM, Ramasubramaniam A (2016) First-principles predictions of structure–function relationships of graphene-supported platinum nanoclusters. J Phys Chem C Am Soc 120:11899–11909
41. Shi H, Migues AN, Auerbach SM (2014) Ab initio and classical simulations of the temperature dependence of zeolite pore sizes. Green Chem. 16:875–884 The Royal Society of Chemistry
42. Chen J, Gomez JA, Höffner K, Barton PI, Henson MA (2015) Metabolic modeling of synthesis gas Fermentation in bubble column reactors. Biotechnol Biofuels 8:89
43. Chen J, Gomez JA, Höffner K, Phalak P, Barton PI, Henson MA (2016) Spatiotemporal modeling of microbial metabolism. BMC Syst Biol 10:21
44. Phalak P, Chen J, Carlson RP, Henson MA (2016) Metabolic modeling of a chronic wound biofilm consortium predicts spatial partitioning of bacterial species. BMC Syst Biol 10:90
45. Chen J, Henson MA (2016) In silico metabolic engineering of Clostridium Ljungdahlii for synthesis gas fermentation. Metab Eng 38:389–400
46. Chen J, Daniel J, Griffin D, Li X, Henson MA (2018) Experimental testing of a spatiotemporal metabolic model for carbon monoxide fermentation with Clostridium autoethanogenum. Biochem Eng J 129:64–73
47. Kou Y, Koag MC, Cheun A, Lee S, Cheun Y (2012) Application of hypoiodite-mediated aminyl radical cyclization to synthesis of solasodine Acetate. Steroids 77:1069–1074
48. Chen B, Zhang K, Wang L, Jiang S, Liu S (2019) Generalized extreme value - pareto distribution function and its applications in ocean engineering. Chin Ocean Eng, 2
49. Kou Y, Cheun Y, Koag MC, Lee S (2013) Synthesis of 14′, 15′-dehydro-Ritterazine Y via reductive and oxidative Functionalizations of Hecogenin acetate. Steroids 78:304–311
50. Lei X, Kou Y, Fu Y, Rajashekar N, Shi H, Wu F et al (2018) The cancer mutation d83v induces an α-helix to β-strand conformation switch in MEF2B. J Mol Biol https://doi.org/10.1016/j.jmb.2018.02.012
51. Lei X, Shi H, Kou Y, Rajashekar N, Wu F, Sen C et al (2018) Crystal structure of Apo MEF2B reveals new Insights in DNA binding and cofactor interaction. Biochemistry 57:4047–4051
52. Kou Y, Koag MC, Lee S (2018) Structural and kinetic studies of the effect of guanine N7 alkylation and metal cofactors on DNA replication. Biochemistry 57:5105–5116
53. Koag M-C, Kou Y, Ouzon-shubeita H, Lee S (2014) Transition-state destabilization reveals how the DNA polymerase β proceeds across the chemically unstable lesion n7-methylguanine. Nucleic Acids Res 42:8755–8766
54. Yang Y, Chen L, Pan H-Z, Kou Y, Xu CM (2009) Glycosylation modification of prion protein provokes apoptosis in HeLa cells in vitro. BMB Rep 42:331–337

55. Chen B, Liu G, Zhagn J et al (2016) A calculation method of design wave height under the three factors of typhoon: China, ZL 10972118.X. Patent 2016-10-31
56. Kou Y, Koag M-C, Lee S (2015) N7 methylation alters hydrogen-bonding patterns of Guanine in Duplex DNA. J Am Chem Soc 137:14067–14070
57. Cheun Y, Koag MC, Kou Y, Warnken Z, Lee S (2012) Transetherification-mediated e-ring opening and stereoselective "Red-Ox" Modification of Furostan. Steroids 77:276–281
58. Koag MC, Cheun Y, Kou Y, Ouzon-shubeita H, Min K, Monzingo AF et al (2013) Synthesis and structure of 16, 22-diketocholesterol bound to oxysterol-binding protein Osh4. Steroids 78:938–944
59. Cheun Y, Kou Y, Stevenson B, Kim H-K, Koag MC, Lee S (2013) Synthesis of C17-OH-north unit of Ritterazine G via "Red-Ox" modifications of hecogenin acetate. Steroids 78:639–643
60. Kou Y, Lee S (2013) Unexpected opening of steroidal e-ring during hypoiodite-mediated oxidation. Tetrahedron Lett 54:4106–4109
61. Kou Y et al (2015) Structural and kinetic Study of N7-methyl, N7-benzyl and C8-chloro guanine/lesions using the DNA polymerase β[Internet]. https://repositories.lib.utexas.edu/handle/2152/46815
62. Lee S, Kou Y, Koag M Mechanism of alkylation and platination-induced mutagenesis. Environ Mol Mutagen 59:107
63. Wang L-P, Chen B-Y, Chen C, Chen Z-S, Liu G-L (2016) Application of Linear-mean-square estimation in ocean engineering. China Ocean Eng 30:149–160 Chinese Ocean Engineering Society
64. Wang L-P, Chen B, Zhang J-F, Chen Z (2013) A New model for calculating the design wave height in typhoon-affected sea areas. Nat Hazards 67:129–143 Springer, Netherlands
65. Chen B, Liu G, Wang L (2017) Predicting joint return period under ocean extremes based on a maximum entropy compound distribution model. Int J Energy Environ Sci 2(6):117–126
66. Wang L, Xu X, Liu G, Chen B, Chen Z (2017) A new method to estimate wave height of specified return period. Chin J Oceanol Limnol 35:1002–1009 Science Press
67. Jiang S, Lian M, Lu C, Ruan S, Wang Z, Chen B SVM-DS fusion based soft fault detection and diagnosis in solar water heaters. Energy Explor Exploit https://doi.org/10.1177/014459871881660
68. Chen B, Liu G, Wang L, Zhang K, Zhang S (2019) Determination of water level design for an Estuarine city. J Oceanol Limnol. https://doi.org/10.1007/s00343-019-8107-z

Fatigue Damage and Creep Modeling of Combined Rotor and Its Application

Lijun Guo(✉)

Weifang University, No. 5147 Dongfeng East Street, Weifang, Shandong, China
wfxyglj@163.com

Abstract. With the improvement of low cycle fatigue Basic test technology, the main failure modes of engine turbine blades have changed from static strength failure to vibration fatigue failure. In order to determine the vibration stress level of turbine blade in working state, it is necessary to measure the vibration stress of turbine blade on the basis of numerical calculation. In this paper, the theory and technology of Aero-engine Turbine blade dynamic stress measurement are studied and applied to a certain type of engine. Three vibration signal processing methods, namely, amplitude domain analysis method, Fourier analysis method and order analysis method, are mainly studied for turbine blade dynamic stress measurement. Based on the resonance theory and the working characteristics of turbine blades, the natural frequencies, modes, exciting forces and resonances of turbine blades are analyzed. Under low-cycle fatigue load, the increase of strain amplitude or temperature shortens the low-cycle fatigue life of rotor steel. Based on the plastic strain-cycle cycle curve of the specimen after experiment, the low-cycle fatigue life model of rotor steel is obtained by linear fitting and formula derivation. Through the calculation and verification of the model, the model can predict the low cycle fatigue life of rotor steel more accurately.

Keywords: Aeroengine · Turbine blade · Fatigue damage · Creep life

1 Brief Introduction

Turbine blade is one of the most important parts of aeroengine. When it works in the harsh environment of high temperature, high pressure and high speed, fatigue damage will lead to extremely serious consequences. Therefore, it is of great significance to study the fatigue problem of turbine blades. The main failure modes of turbine blades are external damage, deformation and elongation, and fatigue fracture. The probability of fatigue fracture failure is the highest and the most harmful, which poses a great threat to the safety of the engine [1–4]. At the same time, due to the limitation of working environment, it is not easy to detect cracks on turbine blades in work, and there is no sign, which seriously threatens the safety of use [5, 6]. Therefore, it is urgent to strengthen the research on the fatigue life of turbine blades in terms of scientific and technological research. Chen et al. [7, 8] studied the influence of centrifugal force and aerodynamic force on the low cycle fatigue life of the whole turbine blade when the blade was working, and carried out finite element elastoplastic analysis of the blade, but

Z. Xu et al. (Eds.): CSIA 2019, AISC 928, pp. 781–787, 2020.
https://doi.org/10.1007/978-3-030-15235-2_106

did not consider the temperature load. Song et al. [9–13] mainly considered the influence of centrifugal force and thermal stress on the fatigue life of turbine blades, but did not consider the effect of stress on creep life, because the fatigue failure of turbine blades often accompanied by creep failure, creep damage occupies a large part of the total damage of turbine blades [13–19].

In this paper, the method of thermo-mechanical coupling calculation is used to predict the life of turbine blades, taking fully into account the three major loads on the blades: centrifugal load, temperature load and aerodynamic load, and considering the creep damage caused by high temperature. The location of dangerous points of turbine blades is accurately pointed out. This is of great significance to the optimization design of turbine blade structure, the improvement of fatigue strength, the accurate prediction of blade life and the guarantee of aeroengine safety. Turbine blades include turbine stator blades (i.e. turbine guide blades) and turbine rotor blades. Because the working conditions of turbine stator blades are not complicated and harsh, the turbine blades studied in this paper refer to turbine rotor blades.

2 Fatigue Characteristics of Engine Turbine Blades

Fatigue is the initiation and propagation of cracks and damage to materials under alternating loads. In order to clarify the effect of fatigue damage on materials, it is necessary to understand the fracture morphology characteristics of three stages of fatigue crack fracture, because fatigue fracture records all mechanical processes throughout the life cycle of materials. The three stages of crack are crack initiation, crack propagation and specimen fracture.

(1) Crack initiation stage. Most of the fatigue cracks are formed at the residence slip zone, metallurgical defects and process defects. When the metal is subjected to alternating stress, the grains on the surface slip parallel to the maximum shear stress plane, which makes the surface of the specimen rough, and the fatigue cracks are easy to form. The second phase defects, such as particles, inclusions and pore, are prone to stress concentration and crack initiation under high temperature and low cycle fatigue conditions, which are also closely related to the stress state, micro-structure and environmental factors. Under high temperature, creep damage and creep voids will occur under tensile stress, so crack initiation is also related to temperature and oxidation.

(2) Crack propagation stage. The fatigue crack growth is affected by the slip characteristics of the material, the characteristic scale of the microstructure, the stress level and the size of the plastic zone near the top. The crack propagation can be divided into two stages: in the first stage, the crack mainly propagates in pure shear along the direction of the main slip system, and the crack path is "Z-shaped". In this stage, the crack length has little relation with the grain size, mainly with the plastic zone near the top of the crack. As long as the plastic zone near the top is smaller than the grain size, this kind of propagation will occur. In the second stage, under the action of higher stress, the plastic zone of the crack can cross many grains. Cracks occur simultaneously or alternately along two slip

systems, showing a plane crack path perpendicular to the axis of the specimen. The number of fatigue striations is large and parallel. The spacing of the striations corresponds to the average propagation distance of the cracks measured by experiments in each cycle.

(3) Specimen fracture stage. Fatigue fracture occurs at the later stage of the second stage of crack growth. With the increase of stress and crack growth, the residual bearing area decreases continuously until the bearing area cannot bear alternating load, the specimen will undergo instantaneous fracture.

The stress life curve (S-N curve) is obtained through extensive tests. In constant stress amplitude fatigue test, stress amplitude ($\sigma_a = \Delta\sigma/2$) is described, the expression of the relationship between the number of times of the load and the number $2N_f$ of times of the reverse of the load (Basquin formula) is:

$$\frac{\Delta\sigma}{2} = \sigma_a = \sigma_f'(sN_f)^b \tag{1}$$

In Formula σ_f' is fatigue strength factor, b is fatigue strength index or Basquin index. Because the average stress has a great influence on fatigue life, but the Basquin formula only applies to the case where the average stress is zero. Morrow takes the influence of the average stress into account and proposes a modified formula:

$$\sigma_a = \left(\sigma_f' - \sigma_m\right)(2N_f)^b \tag{2}$$

Among them: σ_m is mean stress. The stress fatigue description method is only applicable to constant amplitude fatigue load, and it is difficult to conform to the variation of cyclic stress amplitude, average stress and frequency in engineering fatigue. Therefore, Palmgren-Miner cumulative damage rule is used to describe the fatigue produced by different stress amplitudes.

$$\sum \frac{n_i}{N_i} = 1 \tag{3}$$

In each load cycle, the load is completely symmetrical, and the size and direction of the load are the same, each time the damage is the same. It can be concluded that Miner's linear damage accumulation theory does not take into account not only the characteristics of the material itself, but also the environmental factors in which the material is located, nor even the loading sequence and the loading condition of the previous load. All these factors will have an important impact on the damage condition of the material.

3 Creep Theory and Characteristic Law

Creep is the damage caused by the decrease of fracture toughness and permanent plastic deformation of materials under high temperature and constant load. The essence of creep is the interaction process between stress induced plastic deformation and temperature induced recovery. The difference between creep is that the nucleation and propagation of cracks are related to events. Creep damage is unavoidable for supercritical steam turbine rotors. Static loads such as centrifugal force, steam pressure and self-weight always accompany the whole life cycle of the rotors, leading to creep damage of the rotor materials. At present, 9–12% Cr heat-resistant steel is mostly used in steam turbine rotors. It is theoretically believed that creep must be considered when the working temperature reaches 30% of the melting point of the material. The main steam temperature of supercritical steam turbines can reach 600 °C, which has already reached the Creep Range theoretically considered. When the temperature changes, the creep sensitivity of the material is very high. A slight increase in the temperature will cause a significant change in its creep properties and lead to a decrease in the creep resistance of the material. Therefore, the durable strength and creep of supercritical steam turbine rotor under high temperature and static load must be paid attention to.

There are three main theories of creep deformation: dislocation slip theory, diffusion creep theory and grain boundary sliding theory. According to the theory of dislocation slip, dislocations encounter various obstacles in crystal motion. Under the action of high temperature thermal activation, dislocations can overcome some obstacles and continue to move, so deformation results in creep. The edge dislocation at high temperature can also be resolved by atomic diffusion to the direction perpendicular to the slip plane. In the stable stage of creep, the recovery creep theory is involved. The stacking of dislocations in the process of slip increases the dislocation density, while the stacking of dislocations can annihilate each other by climbing.

Diffusion creep theory holds that the creep rate increases with the increase of stress value when the temperature is high and the stress is very low. At this time, the creep is not affected by dislocation. The creep deformation is mainly caused by the diffusion of stress from high potential energy point to low potential energy point, which is diffusion creep. The thermal activation atoms and vacancies at high temperatures are generated by external forces, and the grain boundary sliding theory holds that the plastic deformation caused by the relative sliding of grain boundaries at high temperatures is the main cause of creep.

At lower temperatures, dislocation slip is the main form of creep deformation; with the increase of temperature and the decrease of stress, atomic diffusion and grain boundary slip become more and more important for creep deformation. The evolution of microstructures has an effect on creep fatigue properties of materials at high temperatures, involving the micro-mechanism or model of interaction between dislocations and various crystal defects. From the analysis of dislocation movement to the appearance and growth of creep voids to the initiation and propagation of cracks, many theories and models are involved. The creep fatigue damage mechanism at high temperature can be summarized as follows: (1) dislocation movement (2) grain boundary sliding and the occurrence of grain boundary voids (3) nucleation and growth of voids in inclusions and precipitates.

4 Creep Life Model and Life Consumption Factor

According to the flight statistics of the engine, it is found that the flight altitude of the engine is mainly at the middle and low altitudes of 7 km, the ambient temperature varies from – 5 °C to 35 °C according to the season of flight, the Mach number of flight is below 0.7, and the working condition of the engine is dominated by the most continuous and cruising conditions. And the rotor speed of high pressure has a lot of small changes. When the engine runs in the main state of maximum and cruise, its control law is to keep the speed of the high-pressure rotor constant. In cruise state, the speed of high-pressure rotor is kept at the speed of low fuel consumption; in maximum state, the speed of high-pressure rotor is kept at the maximum speed, and the thrust of engine is close to the maximum.

When the engine operating conditions (high-pressure rotor speed) remain unchanged, the change of operating conditions mainly changes the performance parameters of the engine cross-section by changing the engine inlet conditions. Figure 1 shows the calculated values of engine performance parameters when the relative speed of engine high-pressure rotor is 95%, when the flight altitude, Mach number and ambient temperature change individually and comprehensively. RE indicates the relative error between the calculated results when the operating conditions change comprehensively and individually.

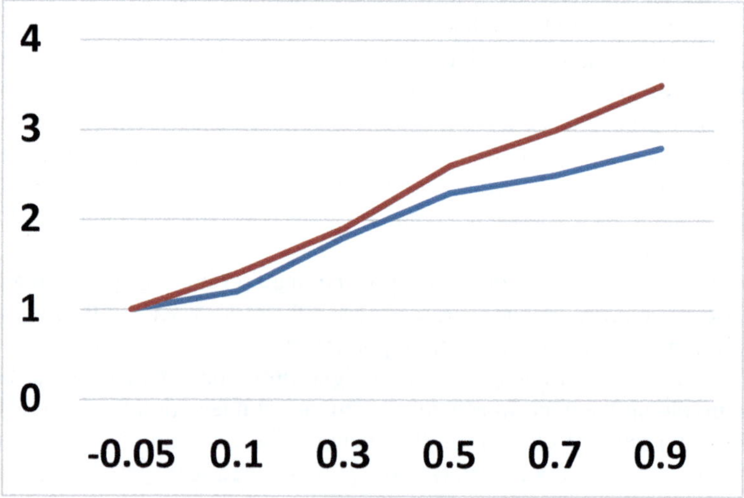

Fig. 1. Variation of flight height and flight Maher number

Figure 1 shows that the effects of various operating conditions on engine inlet conditions and engine performance parameters are independent and can be linearly superimposed. Similar conclusions are obtained under other conditions of engine. Therefore, in the actual use of the engine, the comprehensive effect of each operating condition on the life expenditure of the engine turbine blade can be simplified into the influence of each operating condition changing independently. Therefore, this paper only considers the influence of each condition on turbine blade life consumption. At the same time, other operating conditions remain unchanged while studying the single effect of a certain operating condition on the life expenditure of turbine blades.

Fatigue creep tests were carried out at four different typical temperatures (600, 550, 500, 300). After different low cycle cycles, the tests were interrupted and the specimens were removed for metallographic analysis. Considering that the cyclic softening property of the steel under fatigue creep load changes rapidly in the first 10% Ni (the number of low cycle fatigue cycles at the time of crack initiation), the process of microstructural change is analyzed at this stage. During the whole fatigue loading process, the specimens were taken off for metallographic analysis when the cycle times were about 2%, 5%, 10%, 50%, 80% and 100% Ni, respectively. The above work requires a number of samples for long-term experimental research, but due to the relationship between time and funding, the cycle number at 600 °C after 50% Ni is chosen as the experimental research content at constant temperature.

5 Summary

Through the research in this paper, it is concluded that the crack propagation is a typical transgranular mode in the creep fatigue process under high temperature without holding time by analyzing the fatigue crack and fatigue fracture morphology. Due to creep, the main mode of crack propagation is transgranular fracture in the period of strain holding, and there is a part of intergranular mixed fracture in the later stage of crack. Combining with the fatigue life of specimens, temperature and holding time will aggravate the crack growth. The higher the temperature or holding time, the faster the crack growth is. This is because the introduction of creep further accelerates the crack growth and growth rate. From the fracture scanning, it can be seen that the fatigue crack originates from the surface of the rotor, the propagation area is relatively flat, the instantaneous fracture area is rough and has obvious slip shear trace, and the fracture oxidation is serious. The embrittlement effect of the oxide layer aggravates the crack propagation, and the crack growth rate of the specimen is higher at high temperature.

References

1. He J-F, Tang T, Wang CS (2017) Thermal cycling creep research of combined rotor turbine disc under alternating temperature field. Comput Simul
2. Zhang HB, Wang AL (2016) Research on performance degradation characteristic of combined rotor considering turbine discs creep. Chin J Eng Des
3. Liu Q, He J, Zhao L (2017) Research on creep relaxation non-uniformity and effect on performance of combined rotor. In: Materials science and engineering conference series
4. Liu Q, Wang AL, Luo Z (2016) Study on analytical modeling and performance degradation induced by rod relaxation of combined rotors. Noise Vib Control
5. Qiang L, Ailun W (2017) Research on creep damage and life forecast of rod fastening rotor based on damage mechanics. In: Materials science and engineering conference series, p 012031

6. Abikoff W (2014) Research on performance degradation of combined rotor considering the fatigue crack in the rod. Chin J Eng Des, 7–11
7. Zhao N, Wang W, Jiang J et al (2017) Study of creep-fatigue behavior in a 1000 MW rotor using a phenomenological lifetime model. J Mech Sci Technol 31(2):605–614
8. Appalanaidu Y, Gupta S (2014) Probabilistic damage estimation in piping components against thermal creep and fatigue. Nucl Eng Des 273(101):202–214
9. Sun Y, Pang C (2014) Research on rotor creep properties under bending residual stress. J Mech Eng 50(18):162
10. Jensen EM, Fertig RS (2015) Physics-based multiscale creep strain and creep rupture modeling for composite materials. In: Scitech, pp 703–711
11. Semenov AS, Semenov SG, Getsov LB (2015) Methods of computational determination of growth rates of fatigue, creep, and thermal fatigue cracks in poly- and monocrystalline blades of gas turbine units. Strength Mater 47(2):1–23
12. Li S-M, Wang AL (2018) Research on propagation rules of cracks of combined rotor considering centrifugal force and thermal stress. Comput Simul
13. Li X-P, Wang AL (2015) Research on performance degradation of combined rotor considering the microcrack on the rod caused by frequent start-up and stop-down. Chin J Eng Des
14. Wang WZ, Buhl P, Klenk A et al (2016) The effect of in-service steam temperature transients on the damage behavior of a steam turbine rotor. Int J Fatigue 87:471–483
15. Paweł B, Dominik G, Agnieszka N et al (2016) Fe analysis of a steam turbine HP rotor blade stage concerning material effort, dynamic properties and creep damage assessment. Arch Mech Eng 63(1):163–185
16. Cui L, Wang P (2014) Two lifetime estimation models for steam turbine components under thermomechanical creep–fatigue loading. Int J Fatigue 59(2):129–136
17. Zhang Y, Ji D, Chen J et al (2015) Comparison of two steam turbine rotor steel creep-fatigue cracks propagation characteristics. J Shanghai Univ Electr Power
18. Holdsworth S (2016) Creep ductility of 1CrMoV rotor steel. High Temp Technol 34(2):99–108
19. Xu H, Zhang WW, Maile K (2014) Life prediction of two rotor steels under creep-fatigue interaction at elevated temperature. Appl Mech Mater 470:581–584

Electromagnetic Force of Power Transformer with Different Short Circuit Current Based on FEM

Yan Wu[1], Lingyun Gu[1], Xue Zhang[2], and Jinyu Wang[3(✉)]

[1] Beijing Key Laboratory for Energy Saving of Distribution Transformer, Beijing, China
[2] State Grid Beijing Electric Power Company, Beijing, China
[3] School of Electrical and Electronic Engineering, North China Electric Power University, Beijing 102206, China
wangjinyu_1993@163.com

Abstract. Transformer winding deformation may cause security incidents of power systems, the main reason basically derives from short-circuit impulse current and switching inrush current. In order to study the influence of different inrushing current stress on winding, the 2-D finite element method (FEM) is adopted to research the stress of high and low voltage winding in a 2 kVA transformer. It reveals that, as to the axial force, the compression force occurs in both the high and the low voltage windings with the increasing of short circuit current. However, as to the radial force, the contraction force mainly exists in the low voltage winding and the expansion force mainly exists in high voltage winding, respectively. Meanwhile, the quadratic relationship between force and current is also obtained by FE analysis. Finally, the short-circuit test of an isolated transformer in the laboratory verifies that the reactance has changed obviously after the transformer winding has been deformed by axial and radial forces.

Keywords: Electromagnetic force · Transformer · Short circuit test · FEM

1 Introduction

Transformers are one of the most important electrical equipment in power system [1], which is of great significance to ensure the safe operation of the whole power grid. If a hub transformer fails, it may cause a large area of power grid blackout, and seriously affects the safe operation of the power grid.

According to the statistical data of transformer accidents over the past years, 35 kV and above power transformers have been damaged by short-circuit faults, which accounts for 50% of the total number of accidents. According to the maintenance, accidents can cause most of the transformer windings to be deformed by different degrees and insulation damage [2, 3], such as radial and axial size change, insulation damage, body displacement, twisting and broken windings. In power systems, the electromagnetic force generated by fault and impulse currents may act directly on the windings [4], and the winding deformation has cumulative effects under multiple

Z. Xu et al. (Eds.): CSIA 2019, AISC 928, pp. 788–797, 2020.
https://doi.org/10.1007/978-3-030-15235-2_107

electromagnetic forces. The slight deformation of the winding may cause partial insulation damage and discharge, which can further aggravate the insulation aging [5]. Moreover, the winding deformation is a gradual process, at the beginning of winding deformation, it may not significantly affect the operation of transformer, and so the monitoring of transformer winding deformation is easy to overlook [6]. Though with the winding deformation and insulation aging, once serious external short-circuit occur, it may cause sever deformation, damage and stop of transformer, resulting in a large area blackout [7]. At present, after the short circuit, People usually open the transformer to check whether the winding deformation has happened, but this method requires a lot of manpower and resources. The deformation defects of power transformer windings have certain concealment, and the deformation of winding is destructive to transformers itself and harmful to the safe operation of power grid.

With the rapid development of power grids, the capacity of a power grid is increasing day by day, which leads to the increase of system short circuit capacity. The statistic of transformer damage caused by short circuit fault is also increasing year by year [8], The winding deformation fault has become one of the main reasons for the failure of transformer fault and power system [9]; therefore it is necessary to explore causes of deformation of transformer winding. It is significant to reduce the cause of accidents in transformers and ensure the safe operation of the power grid. In this paper, a 2-D finite element model is established to analyze the electromagnetic force of winding in transformers. Also the variation of electromagnetic force of transformer windings is also revealed.

2 Theoretical Analyses

Finite element method is one of the widely used numerical methods at present. It has the characteristics of high efficiency and strong mathematical foundation. In the field of scientific computing research, it needs to solve many kinds of differential equations, and many analytical solutions of many equations are difficult to obtain. However, by using the finite element method many equations can be solved after discretized and programmed by a computer. The finite element method was developed from variation principle in the early days, so it is widely used in the physics field described by Laplace equation and Poisson equation (usually, this kind of field is closely related to the extremum problem of function).

Maxwell equations can be expressed in two forms: one is integral form, and the other is differential form, and the finite element method uses differential equation method. The unique solution of the system of equations can be obtained by the selection of the potential function and the application of the boundary conditions. The differential form of the Maxwell equations is shown in (1):

$$\begin{aligned} &\nabla \times \vec{H} = \vec{J} + \frac{\partial \vec{D}}{\partial t} \\ &\nabla \times \vec{E} = -\frac{\partial \vec{B}}{\partial t} \\ &\nabla \cdot \vec{\mathrm{D}} = \rho \\ &\nabla \cdot \vec{B} = 0 \end{aligned} \tag{1}$$

Where H is the magnetic field strength (A/m); J is conduction current density (A/m^2); B(T) is flux density and ρ(C/m^3) is charge density.

According to the Maxwell equation, the differential equation of the potential function for the electromagnetic field distribution in the transformer can be obtained:

$$\nabla \times \frac{1}{\mu}(\nabla \times \vec{A}) = \vec{J} - \sigma \frac{\partial \vec{A}}{\partial t} \tag{2}$$

Where μ(H/m) is the permeability, A (Wb/m) is the magnetic vector potential; σ is conductivity (S/m).

In a transformer, the boundary condition of the non-air electromagnetic region satisfies the continuity:

$$n \times (\vec{H}_1 - \vec{H}_2) = 0 \tag{3}$$

The air region of the transformer meets the boundary conditions:

$$n \times \vec{A} = 0 \tag{4}$$

After the magnetic vector potential A is calculated, the flux density B can be obtained, and the electromagnetic force can then be obtained according to formula [10] (5):

$$\vec{F}(t) = F_m[\frac{1}{2} + e^{-\frac{2R}{L}} - 2e^{-\frac{R}{L}} \cos wt + \frac{1}{2} \cos 2wt] \tag{5}$$

Where Fm(N) is the maximum value of short-circuit electromagnetic force, R(Ω) and L(H) are the equivalent resistance and equivalent inductance of transformer.

Through the electromagnetic theory analysis, the leakage flux density and the winding force of the transformer is shown in Fig. 1. The axial electromagnetic force of

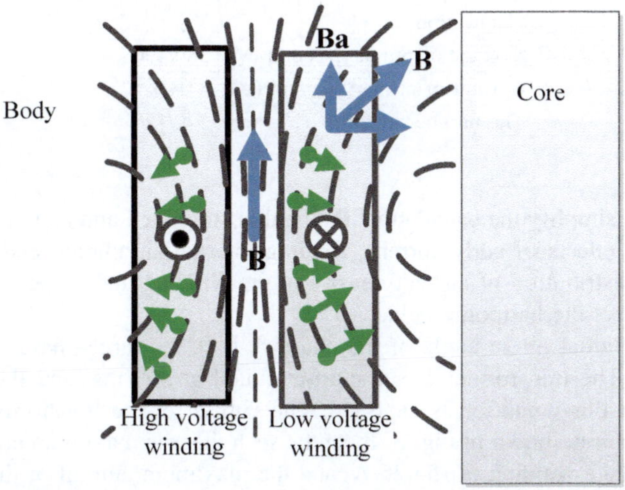

Fig. 1. Lectromagnetic force and leakage flux distribution density in concentric windings of a power transformer

low-voltage and high-voltage winding lead the winding to be axially squeezed from the top and bottom to the middle. In addition, radial force of low voltage winding is inward compression force, with reduction effect of winding diameter. On the contrary, the radial force of high voltage winding is outward expansion force, with tensile effect of winding diameter. Therefore, the radial force of winding may cause insulation damage between winding and core or winding layer.

3 2-D FE Model of Transformer

Short circuit tests are necessary for transformers before they are put into operation, but serious irreversible damage to the transformer can be caused by general short-circuit test. So the finite element method is suitable for transformer short-circuit test, not only can it accurately test the winding force, but also can save manpower and reduce economic cost.

A 2-D model of a three-phase transformer is established by using the ANSYS Maxwell software. The parameters of the transformer are shown in Table 1. The 2-D FE model of the transformer is shown in Fig. 2. High- and low-voltage windings are placed according to the actual conditions, and they are divided into 30 segments, the windings near the core are low voltage windings, and the high-voltage windings are far from the core.

Table 1. The specifications of the transformer

Item	Parameter
Phase	3
Structure	Core type
f_n (Hz)	50
Sn (vA)	2000
Connection	Y_N, y_n
Voltage of primary/second (V)	380/190
Current of primary/second (A)	3.04/1.52
The number of turns	240/120

In order to simplify the calculation, the field is simplified and assumed reasonably: (1) ignore the effects of eddy current, winding internal circulation and the vortex in core; (2) the distribution of current density in the winding and ampere turns are uniform; (3) neglect the harmonic field.

When the initial phase angle of the phase A is 0, the three-phase short circuit is most serious. The transformer is set short-circuited at 500 ms, and the force of the winding under this condition is analysed. The current of the transformer before and after short circuit is shown in Fig. 3. It can be seen that the maximum current of phase A of high voltage winding is 154.25 A, and the maximum current of the low voltage winding is 308.56 A.

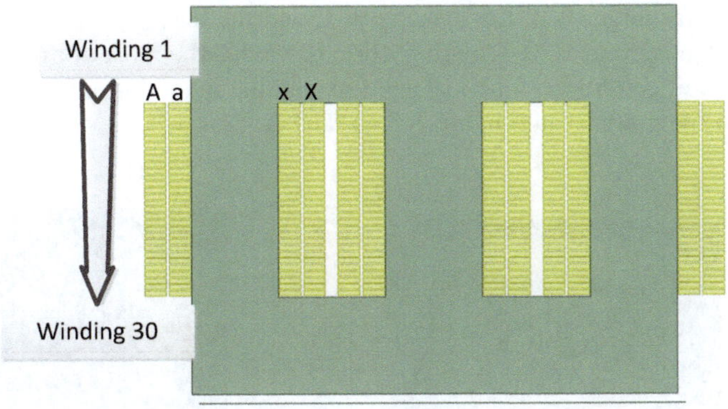

Fig. 2. The 2-D FE model of the three-phase transformer

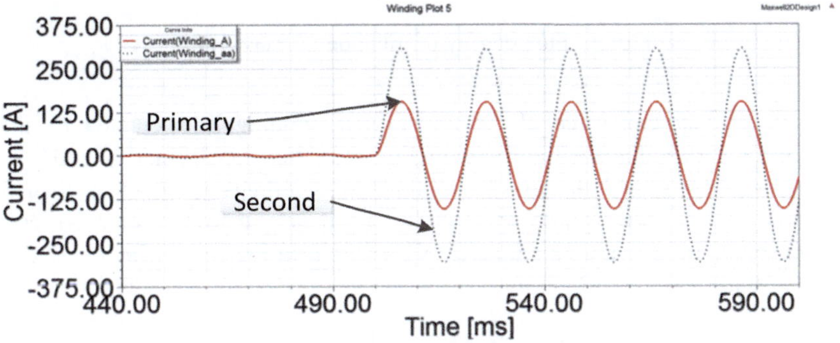

Fig. 3. Comparison of current before and after short circuit

The simulated and theoretical value of maximum shorted-circuit current of phase A is shown in Table 2, which indicates finite element analysis is reasonable.

Table 2. The simulated and theoretical current value of HV and LV winding in phase A

	Simulated value (A)	Theoretical value (A)
HV winding	154.25	154.48
LV winding	308.56	309.67

4 Calculation Results

With ANSYS Maxwell software, the normal operation and the three-phase short-circuit of the transformer are simulated, the normal and short-circuit flux density distribution diagram are respectively given in Fig. 4. It can be found that in normal operation, the mutual flux is far larger than the leakage flux, and the leakage flux is very small, the maximum value is up to 1.90 T. Figure 4(b) shows that the most of flux in transformer with short-circuit condition is the leakage flux and the mutual flux is very small in this case, and the maximum value is up to 4.51 T (Fig. 5).

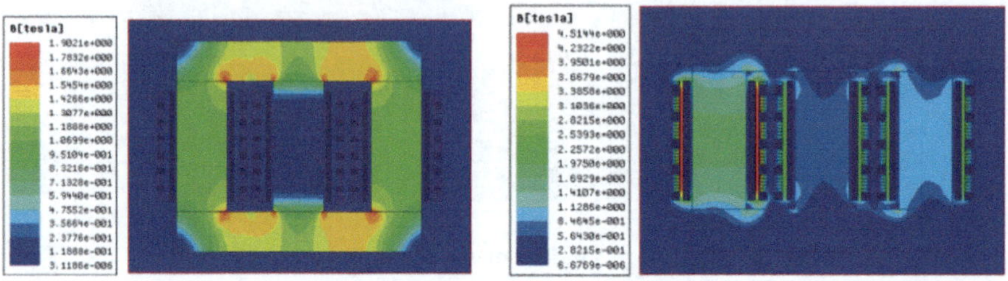

(a) normal state of transformer (b) three-phase short circuit state of transformer

Fig. 4. Flux density distribution in transformer

The electromagnetic force of the transformer winding is calculated by the flux density and the instantaneous current. In Fig. 6(a), the transformer is under normal operating conditions, and the maximum force of windings is no more than 5 mN, However at 500 ms three-phase short circuit happened in low voltage winding, the force whose maximum value is up to 18 N as shown in Fig. 6(b) which is 3600 times larger than that before short-circuit.

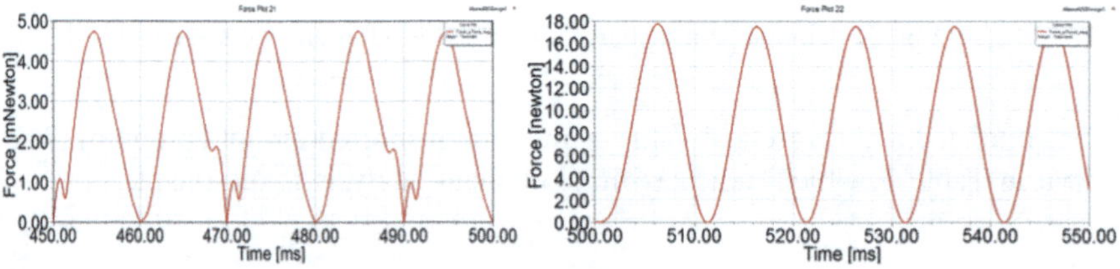

(a) Electromagnetic force before short circuit (b) Electromagnetic force after short circuit

Fig. 5. The electromagnetic force on winding before and after short circuit

The electromagnetic force is divided into axial and radial force, which is calculated by finite element method. Figure 6 shows the axial force distribution of high-voltage and low-voltage winding, the axial force is determined by radial flux density and instantaneous current, in which this paper define upward as positive, and downward as negative. It can be seen from Fig. 6 that the axial force exerted on the winding is the extrusion force, and that the winding segment with the maximum value of the axial force is located at both ends of the winding, and the central force is less than that of top and bottom.

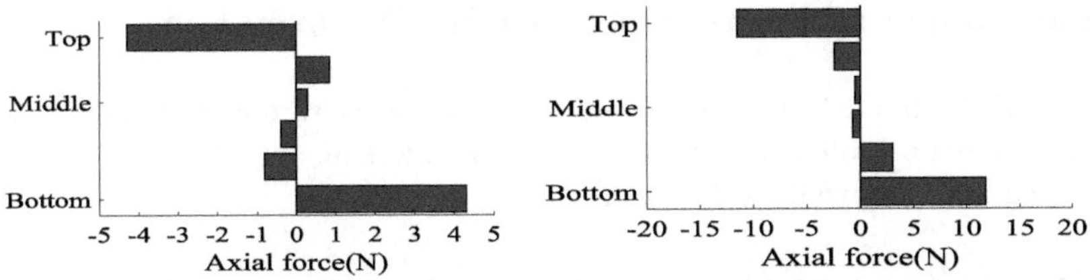

(a) Force of HV (b) Force of LV

Fig. 6. The axial forces on HV and LV winding of phase A

The distribution of radial force exerted on windings is given in Fig. 7, which is decided by axial magnetic flux density and instantaneous current. Outward is defined as negative and inward is defined as positive. The radial force of the HV (high voltage) winding is negative, so the HV winding is expanded. The radial force of the LV (low voltage) winding is positive, so the low voltage winding is subjected to the extrusion force. As seen in Fig. 7, the winding segments in the middle of the winding are affected by the radial force which is greater than that of the two ends.

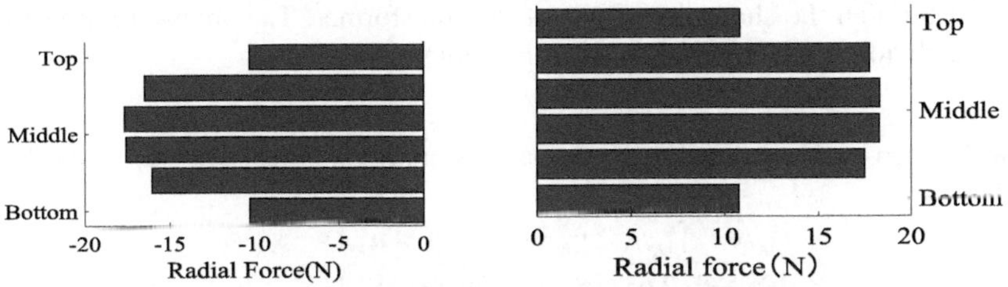

(a) HV winding (b) LV winding

Fig. 7. The radial forces on HV and LV winding of phase A

On the basis of above, the force of high voltage winding is compared under the condition of different short-circuit current. As shown in Fig. 8, the solid line represents force of winding segment 1, dash line represents force of winding segment 16, the force of different positions of the winding vary with the square of current approximately. So the greater the current is, the greater the force is.

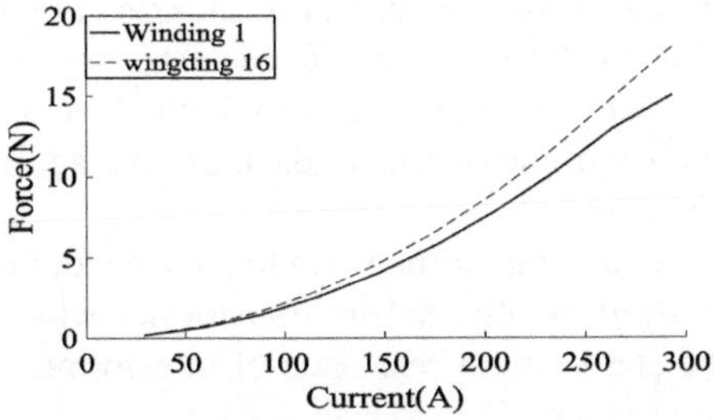

Fig. 8. Electromagnetic force with different current

5 Experiment of Transformer Winding Deformation

Because of the limited laboratory condition, a three-phase double winding isolation transformer with 1000 VA capacity is used to measure the short-circuit reactance before and after the winding deformation.

5.1 Measurement of Initial Value of Short Circuit Reactance of Transformer

The transformer used in laboratory test is shown in Table 3, and its nameplate is:

Table 3. Nameplate of transformer

Term	Single phase transformer	Output voltage	380
Model	DK-1 kVA	Rated capacity	1000 VA
input voltage	380 V	Winding mode	Double winding

In this test, the initial value of the short-circuit reactance of the transformer is obtained through the short-circuit test of the transformer. The short-circuit test results of this isolation transformer are shown in Table 4.

Table 4. Short-circuit test results of isolation transformer (temperature 20 °C, relative humidity 50%)

U_K/V	I_K/A	P_K/W	Z_K/Ω	R_K/Ω	X_K/Ω
106.580	2.632	86.573	40.494	12.497	38.517

It can be seen from Table 4 that the initial value of the short-circuit reactance of the isolation transformer is 38.517, that is to say, the short-circuit reactance value of the isolated transformer.

5.2 On Line Detection of Short Circuit Reactance of Transformer

After the initial value of the short-circuit reactance of the isolation transformer is determined, the on-line state is simulated, that is, the operation state of the transformer, and the on-line detection of the short-circuit reactance after the transformer winding deformation is made by using the experimental schematic diagram shown in Fig. 9. In order to ensure the accuracy of measurement data, the average value method is adopted to get the average value (Table 5).

It can be seen that after the transformer winding changed, the short-circuit reactance of transformer was changed greatly, so the transformer winding deformation can be judged according to the short-circuit reactance of transformer.

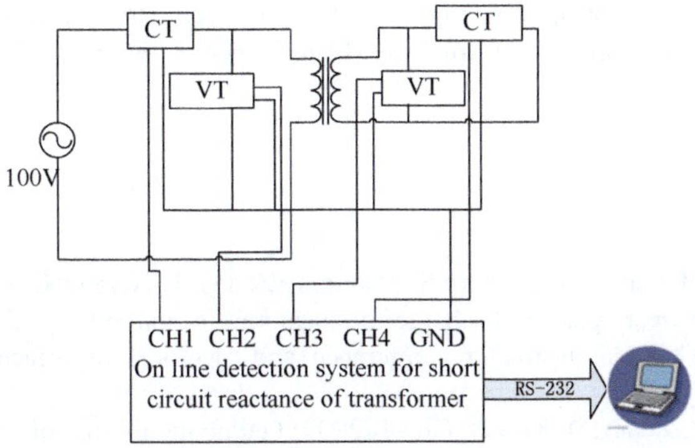

Fig. 9. Wiring diagram of on line detection principle of transformer short circuit reactance

Table 5. Online test results of winding reactance of isolated transformer

Items	Short-circuit impedance (Ω)	Comparison with initial value of short circuit reactance (%)
1	40.366	4.8
2	40.520	5.2
3	40.404	4.9
Average value	40.430	5.0

6 Conclusions

In this paper, the force law of power transformer winding under the action of short circuit current is studied by the finite element method. Firstly, the force of winding under short circuit condition is analysed theoretically and then a two-dimensional model of the power transformer is established by using ANSYS Maxwell software. Secondly, the short circuit current, field distribution and short-circuit force are presented using FEM and it shows that the winding is under axial extrusion pressure, and the maximum axial force is located at the top and bottom of windings, the force in the middle of winding is smaller. Moreover, the high-voltage winding is expanded and low-voltage winding shrink, and at the end of the winding radial force is greater than that of both ends; finally, by comparison of the force of different winding a conclusion can be made that when the current increases, the winding force also increases in square relation. However, this paper neglects the influence of winding deformation on the transformer's short circuit reactance parameters, and then leads to the change of the force of the transformer. Therefore, coupling analysis of electromagnetic field and structure field will be more accurate for the analysis of the force of the transformer winding.

Acknowledgments. This project is supported by Key Laboratory Opening Fund Project of Energy Saving Technology for Distribution Transformer in Beijing (China Electric Power Research Institute).

References

1. Naderi MS, Vakilian M, Blackburn T, Phung T, Zhang T, Nam OH, Naderi MS (2005) A comparison between partial discharge propagation in multiple- and single-transformer winding. In: Electrical insulation conference and electrical manufacturing expo. IEEE, pp 108–111
2. Zhang S, Cai Z, Zhang D, Kou H, Guo J (2009) Online monitoring of winding deformation of power transformer based on ARM and FPGA. In: 2009 ICMTMA measuring technology and mechatronics automation. IEEE, pp 657–659
3. Yan HY (1996) Discussion on short circuit capacity of domestic power transformer. Transformer 33(9):2–7
4. Hashemnia N, Abu-Siada A, Islam S (2015) Improved power transformer winding fault detection using FRA diagnostics – part 2: radial deformation simulation. IEEE Trans Dielectr Electr Insul 22(1):564–570
5. Zhang HJ, Wang SH, Wang S (2015) Cumulative deformation analysis of transformer winding under short-circuit fault using 3-D FEM. In: IEEE international conference on applied superconductivity and electromagnetic devices (ASEMD), pp 370–371
6. Zhang JF (2003) Transformer accident analysis and preventive measures for short circuit damage. Fujian Electr Power Electrotech 23(1):1–4
7. Ziomek W, Vijayan K, Boyd D, Kuby K, Franchek M (2011) High voltage power transformer insulation design. In: 2011 EIC electrical insulation conference. IEEE, pp 211–215
8. Lv WY (2002) Development of electric power industry and adjustment of industrial structure in China. China Power 35(1):1–7
9. Zhao ZY, Yao CG, Li CX, Dong SL (2015) Application of short time Fourier transform to obtain impulse frequency response curves of transformer winding deformation. In: IEEE conference on electrical insulation and dielectric phenomena, CEIDP 2015, pp 314–317
10. Li ZY, Hao ZG, Yan CG, Dang YQ, Xu HX, Zhang BH (2016) Deformation simulation and analysis of power transformer windings. In: Asia-Pacific power and energy engineering conference, APPEEC, pp 1445–1449

Analysis and Research of Dynamic Data Path Selection Algorithm in Heterogeneous Networks

Zaiyi Pu(✉)

Network and Information Management Center, China West Normal University,
Nanchong 637009, Sichuan, China
Zaiyipu1@126.com

Abstract. The continuous development of wireless communication theory and engineering practice technology has led to the heterogeneous wireless network situation represented by 4G and wireless technology. At the same time, with the rapid development of wireless services based on mobile internet, its complex business types and high traffic demand pose a huge challenge to the resource scheduling of operators. In this paper, the current status of research and application of heterogeneous wireless networks in China is reviewed, the key technologies and promotion schemes are analyzed, the impact of existing network planning concepts is discussed, and the relevant issues are given strategic suggestions. In order to better study the resource consumption of user service models in different access networks under heterogeneous networks, a multi-QoS traffic algorithm for mixed services under heterogeneous networks is proposed. This algorithm is based on the mixed services in various access networks, and takes the guarantee of the mixed services in different access networks of heterogeneous networks as the premise to accurately evaluate the traffic from the perspective of business identification. According to the number of active users, the bandwidth requirements of different user sizes are assessed, and the network planning is guided to expand reasonably.

Keywords: Heterogeneous network · Four network convergence · Access network · Data traffic channel

1 Brief Introduction

In recent years, with the dual impetus of application demand and technological innovation, the rapid development of mobile Internet and the rapid rise of multimedia services, the data traffic of user demand is increasing day by day. In order to alleviate the contradiction between user demand and the limited capacity of macro cellular network and the low indoor coverage [1–5], Introducing different kinds of low-power base station nodes into Macro-cellular network can effectively solve the coverage problem in Macro-cellular network, and improve the network capacity and spectrum efficiency. In order to deal with heterogeneous multi network, multi business and multi-user complex resource management scenario, [6–11]. From the perspective of resource optimization, how to optimize the allocation of network resources becomes the key to

Z. Xu et al. (Eds.): CSIA 2019, AISC 928, pp. 798–805, 2020.
https://doi.org/10.1007/978-3-030-15235-2_108

guarantee the service quality of users [12, 13]. The resource allocation strategies of GPRS/EDGE hybrid service network are studied, which are static channel allocation strategy and dynamic channel allocation strategy [14–17]. It includes three algorithms: voice service priority allocation algorithm, long-term statistical allocation strategy and short-term adjustment strategy based on service attributes and their applications [17–19].

In order to better study the resource consumption of user service models in different access networks under heterogeneous networks, this paper proposes a multi-QoS traffic algorithm for mixed services under heterogeneous networks. This algorithm is based on the mixed services in various access networks, and takes the guarantee of the mixed services in different access networks of heterogeneous networks as the premise to accurately evaluate the traffic from the perspective of business identification. According to the number of active users, the bandwidth requirements of different user sizes are assessed, and the network planning is guided to expand reasonably.

2 Convergence of Heterogeneous Wireless Networks

Wireless resources in wireless communication networks mainly include wireless spectrum, transmission time, transmission power and transmission space. Wireless resources are scarce resources in wireless heterogeneous networks. Especially in the future ultra-dense network environment, how to use the limited wireless resources to meet the growing needs of users is the key problem to be solved in the resource optimization technology of wireless heterogeneous networks. Resource optimization technology is the appropriate management and allocation of limited resources in wireless heterogeneous networks. While guaranteeing users' quality of service, it can improve network spectrum efficiency and energy efficiency. According to the different types of resources, resource optimization of wireless heterogeneous networks can be divided into three basic aspects: wireless access selection, spectrum allocation and power control.

With the summary of operational experience and continuous feedback of customer needs, the industry has gradually realized that the gradual integration of WLAN and cellular network is an irreversible trend. Technological innovation is the inevitable choice. In the initial stage, this change may be based on the innovation and upgrading of equipment capability at the present stage. In the later stage, a comprehensive technological revolution will be formed from protocol framework, hardware structure to covering switching capability. Finally, a new type of base station WLAN equipment system is formed, which meets the needs of large granular data services, such as cellular handover, large traffic carrying and telecommunication level management, so as to fully undertake the task of mobile Internet services in the new era. At present, WLAN aims at carrying data services. The industry is trying to distribute data traffic in WLAN cellular network. From the initial reminder of customers through hot SMS to achieve manual shunt collaboration, to the later stage, through the cooperation of network and terminal software, WLAN hot spot automatic discovery and shunt are realized.

For the general heterogeneous network traffic diversion problem, the graph is its basic scenario and architecture diagram. As can be seen from Fig. 1, the shunt system needs modules such as service source, shunt server, heterogeneous subnet, terminal and so on.

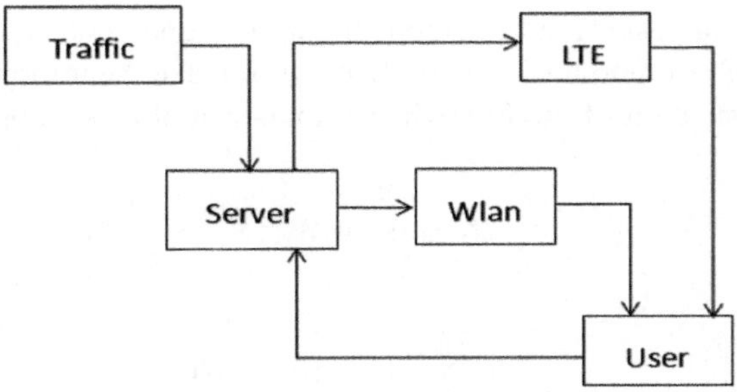

Fig. 1. Diffluence transmission structure of heterogeneous network

The business source is responsible for sending the business to the shunt server. It should be pointed out here that the modules shown in the figure are only logically meaningful and not physically meaningful. For example, business source and diffluence server can be implemented on the same physical entity. The shunt server is the core module of the shunt system, which is responsible for the realization of shunt schemes (including various shunt algorithms and mechanisms, access to network information, receiving end-user business applications and feedback information, etc.). The interface design between this module and other modules is the core part of the whole shunt system architecture. In the fifth chapter, the shunt server architecture designed in this paper will be introduced in detail.

3 Aggregation of Multiple Isomorphic Networks

For the multiple isomorphic networks obtained in the previous section, they depict the interconnection of target types in different ways. Therefore, each isomorphic network plays an important role. Therefore, we must integrate them equally. However, for different relationships depicted by different metapaths, quantified relationships have different metrics. Therefore, before we polymerized, we first need to unify the scale of each network. Therefore, this paper first performs normalization operations on every isomorphic network. Finally, all the isomorphic networks are aggregated into an effective isomorphic network. Assuming that from the known bar paths, we obtain several isomorphic networks of the associated target type, whose adjacency weight matrices are W_{ct}^{i} and $i \in \{1, 2, ..., M\}$ respectively. For $\forall W_{t}^{i}$, $W_{t}^{i,norm}$ represents the adjacency weighting matrix after normalization. The adjacency weight matrix H_t of the aggregated isomorphic network is:

$$H_t = \sum_{i=1}^{M} W_t^{i,norm} \tag{1}$$

Of course, the aggregation process of isomorphic networks can not only adopt the direct summation method mentioned above. In fact, the aggregation method in this paper has a certain loss of information, because it does not consider the different importance of each isomorphic network. In order to make the information loss smaller, the weighted summation of the following formula can also be adopted.

$$H_t = \sum_{i=1}^{M} w_i W_t^{i,norm} \tag{2}$$

$$s.t. \sum_{i=1}^{M} w_i = 1, \ w_i \geq 0 \tag{3}$$

After the aggregation of isomorphic networks, we can capture information from heterogeneous networks in metric space. However, isomorphic networks are usually high-dimensional and sparse, so the time and space complexity of detecting communities in such networks will be enormous. Therefore, in order to cluster graphs better, we introduce non-negative matrix factorization (NMF) to find a low-dimensional representation to approximate the original isomorphic network. Because all the elements in the non-negative matrix are non-negative, this fits well with the practical significance of our network.

Synchronization is a common phenomenon in nature. A typical example of natural synchronization is the synchronous flashing of fireflies observed in South Asian forests. Recently, inspired by the phenomenon of natural synchronization, many synchronization-based clustering algorithms have been proposed. Compared with many existing clustering algorithms, these algorithms show many excellent characteristics, such as the ability to maintain the local structure of the data itself. The key idea of synchronous clustering is to use each data object as a phase oscillator, and the eigenvector of the object as its phase, and to simulate the dynamic behavior of the object over time. By interacting with similar objects, driven by local cluster structure and non-linear interactive motion, the phase of the object is aligned with its neighborhood gradually. Finally, the objects in the cluster are synchronized and have the same phase (eigenvector).

4 Multi QoS Traffic Evaluation Algorithm for Hybrid Services Under Heterogeneous Networks

To overcome the shortcomings of existing traffic algorithms, a multi-QoS traffic algorithm for mixed services in heterogeneous networks is studied. Starting from the unified service carrier EPC in heterogeneous networks, the algorithm starts with the access networks in heterogeneous networks. This paper identifies the types and proportion of services carried by each access network through signaling feature field, analyses the service demand and service activation time of various services, and establishes a refined traffic algorithm model based on hybrid service identification and multi-QoS guarantee to guide network planning and operation. The new algorithm mainly solves the following technical problems:

1. Based on the mixed service identification and multi-QoS guarantee evaluation traffic in heterogeneous networks, it can meet the needs of various kinds of services and enhance the service perception of mixed services in heterogeneous networks.
2. Identifying the service type, service proportion, service demand and service activation time of each access network under heterogeneous network can accurately evaluate the impact of new service promotion, guide expansion and avoid network congestion.
3. Implement multi-QoS traffic assessment of mixed services in heterogeneous networks, and ensure the load balance of entities in EPC from the dimension of traffic.

In order to better study the resource consumption of user service models in different access networks under heterogeneous networks and evaluate the actual user traffic situation and changing trend in heterogeneous networks, we propose a multi-QoS traffic algorithm for mixed services under heterogeneous networks. Based on the mixed services in different access networks of heterogeneous networks, the algorithm starts with the evaluation parameters of service type identification, service proportion, QoS requirements and service activation time. A traffic algorithm model based on heterogeneous network hybrid service identification and multi-QoS guarantees is established. The algorithm is based on the premise of guaranteeing the mixed service required by heterogeneous network access networks. The traffic is accurately evaluated from the perspective of business identification. The bandwidth requirement of each service user is calculated by extracting the algorithm parameters, and then the bandwidth requirement of different user sizes is evaluated according to the number of service active users.

The deduction process of traffic assessment algorithm based on hybrid service identification and multiple QoS guarantees: Bw per service user refers to the bandwidth required for each user to use various services in an access network of heterogeneous networks. According to the service model of different access networks (4G/WLAN) in heterogeneous networks, the throughput and traffic proportion of each service user are calculated, and then the bandwidth of each service user is calculated by weighting:

$$Bw = \sum_{i=1,j=1}^{n} \mathrm{s_i} * p_j \tag{4}$$

Among them, Bw represents the bandwidth of each business user, S1, S2... Sn represents the throughput, P1 and P2 of each business user in each network of a heterogeneous network, pn represents the traffic ratio of each type of traffic in an access network of heterogeneous networks.

5 Four Network Collaborative Cellular Network Optimization and Preparation

The coverage probability of each layer network is expressed as the probability that a random user in the layer receives the SINR value of Huang's base station signal to reach its target threshold T. This channeling considers the non-public access strategy, that is, Macro-cellular users are not allowed to access the microcellular network. Because Macro-cellular network and micro-cellular network may overlap in a certain geographical location, it is difficult to determine whether an emerging user is a Macro-cellular user or a micro-cellular user. Therefore, this chapter considers both cases when evaluating base station coverage probability. According to the fairness principle of network, the coverage probability of the whole heterogeneous network is defined as a smaller value of the coverage probability of Macro-cellular layer and micro-cellular layer, namely:

$$P_{total}(T) = \min\{P_M(T), P_m(T)\} \tag{5}$$

Improve the efficiency of network resources and maintain the wireless utilization rate between 70–75%. Improve the accuracy of planning, scientifically and reasonably carry out frequency and site planning; strictly carry out the management of new stations, accurately build stations, improve the planning rate. In hot business areas, around the three indicators of average station distance, service density and frequency multiplexing coefficient, full 900 MHz frequency and good 1800 MHz frequency are used; combined with the construction of macro base stations, indoor coverage, Street stations and other micro-cell construction are strengthened to effectively absorb traffic; network structure is optimized, frequency interference is reduced, and network quality is improved. The average carrier frequency allocation of a single cluster in GSM900M network is more than 7 or 1800M network is more than 9 and 7 high-configuration cells with 25 MHz and 20 MHz bandwidth respectively. The carrier frequency allocation should be reduced by cell splitting, service shunting and traffic sinking.

For outdoor high-rise stations with over-coverage affecting more than 20 residential areas, when the site resources are limited and the high-rise stations cannot be removed or reduced, the influence of over-coverage and interference of the high-rise stations should be weakened by reducing power, downward pressure dip and configuration. In urban areas, except for special scenarios such as underground garage and elevator, repeaters should not be used as the source of information in the newly built room subsystem in principle. For those repeaters which are not covered by repeaters in the above areas, priority should be given to those repeaters with high background noise, serious system interference and long network operation time, which should be gradually replaced by micro-cellular, Macro-cellular or distributed base stations. By optimizing the parameter allocation, we can promote the dynamic allocation of wireless resources for sub-services and sub-users, and continuously improve the carrying efficiency of single PDCH. Pay attention to business development and diversion, distinguish between key cities and prefecture level cities. To distinguish different scenarios, such as urban, county and rural areas, determine the strategy of network construction, strengthen the monitoring of network operation, and timely adjust network planning and construction.

6 Conclusion

With the development of mobile communication technology and wireless access technology, the next generation mobile communication network presents a trend of heterogeneity. This brings new challenges to the implementation and effectiveness of mobility management mechanism in traditional wireless networks. Heterogeneous wireless network convergence is a relatively new research direction in recent years. There is still a lack of prior theory and algorithm mechanism that can be used for reference, and a lack of mathematical analysis to quantify network model, service model and processing resources. In this paper, the key technologies of heterogeneous interconnection and mobility management are studied, and some attempts are made on the basic theory of location management and handoff management in heterogeneous wireless networks. Several algorithmic schemes are proposed to optimize the system performance, which provides new ideas and schemes for the research of the next generation mobile communication network architecture. At the same time, some theoretical results have been applied to the development and research of the "mobile communication" wireless multimedia communication system, and good results have been achieved.

Acknowledgement. This research was supported by Excellent Talents Foundation of China West Normal University (No: 17YC497).

References

1. Nguyen N, Sato T (2014) A proposal for dynamic WLAN selection for mobile data offloading in heterogeneous network. In: Vehicular technology conference. IEEE, pp 1–5
2. Yeryomin Y, Seitz J (2016) Enhanced multi-criteria-based path selection algorithm for heterogeneous networks. In: Eighth international conference on ubiquitous and future networks. IEEE, pp 804–809
3. Jian P, Biao XU, Sun YQ et al (2014) Data transmission algorithm based on path-fixed sink in heterogeneous delay tolerant mobile sensor networks. J Beijing Univ Posts Telecommun 2014(3):53–57
4. Obayiuwana E, Falowo O (2016) A new network selection algorithm for group calls over heterogeneous wireless networks with dynamic multi-criteria. In: Consumer communications & networking conference. IEEE, pp 491–494
5. Haddad M, Wiecek P, Sidi H et al (2016) An automated dynamic offset for network selection in heterogeneous networks. IEEE Trans Mob Comput 15(9):2151–2164
6. Xiang M, Qu Q, Chen C et al (2017) Access selection algorithm of heterogeneous wireless networks for smart distribution grid based on entropy-weight and rough set. Int J Emerg Electr Power Syst 18(6):81–93

7. Ma Y, Zhu J, Liu L et al (2016) A dynamic affinity propagation clustering algorithm based on MDT in self-healing heterogeneous networks. In: International symposium on communications and information technologies. IEEE, pp 318–323
8. Yu HW, Zhang B (2018) A heterogeneous network selection algorithm based on network attribute and user preference. Ad Hoc Netw 72:68–80
9. Li X, Zhang X (2017) A concurrent multi-path transmission of data allocation algorithm based on heterogeneous networks. In: International conference on systems and informatics. IEEE, pp 487–491
10. Kumari PA, Prabha IS (2015) Optimum network selection in heterogeneous wireless environment using gravitational search algorithm. In: International conference on signal processing and communication engineering systems. IEEE, pp 464–467
11. Zalghout M, Crussiere M, Abdul-Nabi S et al (2017) Context-aware network selection algorithm for heterogeneous wireless networks. In: Sensors networks smart and emerging technologies. IEEE, pp 1–4
12. Wu H, Wen X, Lu Z et al (2015) Multi-access selection with attractor selection algorithm in heterogeneous network. In: IEEE/CIC international conference on communications in China. IEEE, pp 1–5
13. Zhe J, Pan Z, Nan L et al (2015) Dynamic pico switch on/off algorithm for energy saving in heterogeneous networks. In: Vehicular technology conference. IEEE, pp 1–5
14. Wang L, Wang Y, Ding Z et al (2015) Cell selection game for densely-deployed sensor and mobile devices. In: 5G networks integrating heterogeneous cells and the internet of things. Sensors 15(9):24230–24256
15. Luo C, Guan R, Wang Z et al (2014) HetPathMine: a novel transductive classification algorithm on heterogeneous information networks. In: European conference on information retrieval. Springer, Cham, pp 210–221
16. Wu H, Wen X, Lu Z et al (2017) Mobile data offloading under attractor selection in heterogeneous networks. In: International symposium on wireless communication systems. IEEE, pp 164–169
17. Lu F, Pu Y, Dong R et al (2016) Research on data mining based on shared local algorithm in heterogeneous networks. Autom Instrum 2016(9):181–183
18. Orimolade J, Ventura N (2015) Intelligent access network selection for data offloading in heterogeneous networks. In: Africon. IEEE, pp 1–5
19. Euchi J, Yassine A, Chabchoub H (2015) The dynamic vehicle routing problem: solution with hybrid metaheuristic approach. Swarm Evol Comput 21:41–53

Contribution Title Graphical Language Transmission Mechanism in Visual Communication Design Based on Data Abstraction

Rui Li[1(✉)], Chunyan Li[1], and Meiyan Tian[2]

[1] HongHe University, Honghe, Yunnan, China
lirui_honghe@126.com
[2] Meng Qiao Middle School of Jinping County in Yunnan Province, Honghe, Yunnan, China

Abstract. In visual communication design, the coding and decoding of graphics is an inseparable whole, the coding is for the vividness of information transmission, and the decoding is for the complete release of graphics information. The process of graphic coding is also the process of visualization and fusion of images, and the audience reads out concepts or information from creative graphics. The interpretation process of graphical language is also the process of generating and deepening ideas. The visual participation and existing experiences of the viewers have enhanced the effectiveness of the transfer of information in the graphic language.

Keywords: Data abstraction method · Visual communication design · Graphical language transfer

1 Introduction

Visual communication design mainly uses graphics to effectively convey the information the designer wants to express to the viewer, enabling the viewer to interact or resonate psychologically or ideologically, and obtain a clear concept, so as to achieve the purpose of propaganda and education [1]. Therefore, in the process of coding and decoding of graphics, images and ideas are in the middle of the conversion from text concept to graphic language, which is the key in the process of thinking [2–5]. It is also the way of thinking or the material in thinking. They belong to two different thinking subjects—designers and audiences, and therefore have different thinking purposes. The designer creates a graphic modeling structure that conveys information from the concept of words. The audience is to interpret the concept or information from the graphic model [6]. In the field of visual thinking, people's understanding of abstract concepts such as writing originally originated from some images produced by the brain when reading [1]. These images are formed in the initial perception of the text, just as people in the reading of a literary works, some of the images or images flashed in the brain. Similarly, the process of creating a graphic language is also the processing of the image by the brain [7]. Because the image at this time is vague, flashing, and changeable, the

Z. Xu et al. (Eds.): CSIA 2019, AISC 928, pp. 806–815, 2020.
https://doi.org/10.1007/978-3-030-15235-2_109

image at this time is also called imagery. Therefore, this process can also be called the process of imagery, or the combination of images. Imagery and ideas are a pair of psychological concepts, and often appear in the field of artistic thinking. Creative thinking is achieved through the fusion of imagery. Most of these images are instinctively presented in an unconscious state. From this point of view, imagery is a simplified image of a specific visual object. It is a "fuzzy" thinking illusion that appears in the brain, and it is a flash of local typical characteristics of the object image in thinking. However, it points to the essential characteristics of things with the greatest accuracy [5]. It is an intuitive instinct. Imagery is different from figuration. Its fundamental difference lies in the fuzziness and typicality of the image. It abandons the insignificant components of the original object, and only captures the local impression of the typical features of the object [8].

In visual communication design, the purpose of a good picture or graphic design is not just how beautiful the visual experience is, but to attract people's attention. At the same time, attention should also be paid to the selection of typical images. According to the characteristics of images, in the coding process of the graphic language, attention is paid to the prominent parts of the psychological image in the visual experience, and the insignificant parts are discarded and appropriate corrections are made. This is also a process of fusion and refinement of imagery [6]. Its purpose is to improve the expressiveness and visual tension of the graphic itself. In the process of the coding of the graphic language, the visual image is mainly embodied in five forms of image combination [9]. Each of these is also the organization and construction of the imagery in creative thinking, or the product of the fusion of visual images. In the process of the transfer of the graphic language, images interact with the viewer's visual experience and existing cognition through coding and decoding to generate ideas together [8]. In the interpretation process from the graphic to the concept, the audience will first decompose the image into multiple relatively independent images, and generate its relatively independent ideas under the influence of thinking. Each idea unit is a molecule that constitutes the concept of graphics. Multiple images present multiple ideas. When multiple ideas merge with each other, they form the concept of the source of graphic communication [10]. The generation of ideas in the process of decoding graphics is mainly due to the direct guidance of graphic images. An image is a smaller, fuzzy image unit, and an idea is a unit of information of a smaller movement; one destination is a graphic, and the other destination is a concept, but the two are not completely separated [9]. An idea is different from a concept, the concept is clear and can be accurately described in words, and ideas are smaller units of information in the interpretation of graphical information.

2 Visual Communication Definition

2.1 The Development Process of Visual Communication Design

These information units are the result of the intuitive intuition of the brain to the graph and the interpretation of the experience consciousness. It is the direct direction of the semantics of the image and the starting point for the generation of specific concepts.

Therefore, whether the accuracy of the graphic image presentation directly relates to the clarity of the audience's idea acquisition, or whether the graphic can be effectively extracted and released by the audience, and also relates to the clarity and accuracy of the concept conveyed by the designer. In addition, ideas are dynamic representations of graphical semantics. In the decoding process of the graphic language, each imagery has the presentation of ideas, and the images have times and times. Therefore, the fusion of ideas is complicated and dynamic, and it has dynamic characteristics. The idea is dynamic because it is not a figurative object in the objective world, but a creative figure that is reorganized through the imagery of thought. It is a product of multiple images and overlapping ideas (Zamzow and Losey 2012). Therefore, it has strong metaphor and symbolism. The text description can sometimes be used to add a touch or supplementary meaning to the graphic, which can partially eliminate the lack of image. Sometimes, even if we do not use words to read images, we can clearly and accurately interpret the information the designers want to convey by relying on the display of scenes. We need to mobilize our brains to actively judge and analyze various kinds of information. In this process, the audience becomes the main body of the decoding of the graphic language. The idea is directly guided by the graphic image and combined with the audience's existing experience and understanding to generate the concept.

2.2 The Difference Between Visual Design and Information Design

From this, we can know that in visual communication design, images and ideas as elements of graphic creative design have always existed in the designer's thinking process. However, if the Fig. 1 cannot clearly and accurately draw ideas, then a beautiful shape is meaningless in vain. In the process of the transfer of graphic language, graphics and concepts are two components of a problem, and less of them cannot complete the effective transmission of information. Therefore, graphic creativity is more a model process under the dual effects of images and ideas. The cultural symbol is an abstract concept.

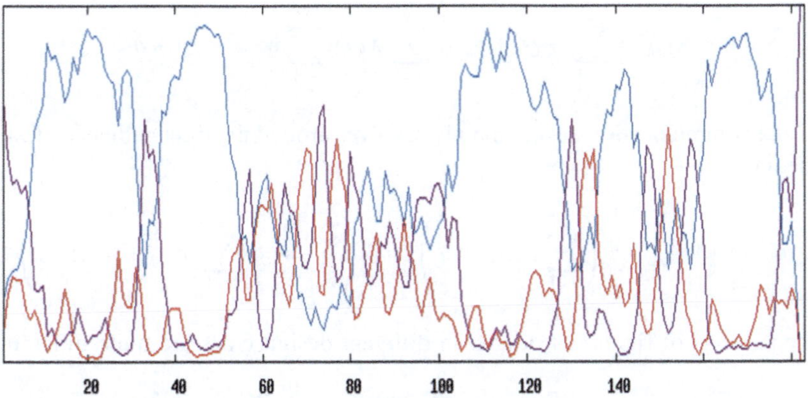

Fig. 1. Ethnic language

3 Design Rights

3.1 The Difference Between Visual Design and Information Design

The visual design is mainly based on graphic design. Therefore, the carrier of its information is mainly traditional paper media such as newspapers, periodicals, etc. The use of graphics and image symbols to obtain visual effects, with the characteristics of instant clarity and completeness of information. Information design is more dependent on modern digital imaging technology. Through the connotation of three-dimensional dynamic image transmission information, it uses the Internet, television and other media as the means of dissemination of product information. It is mainly based on the accuracy of information, visual impact effect as a means of product information display. At the same time, the model of human development, to understand the relationship between education and human development is the core of the education idea, namely respect individual and individual differences, teaching students in accordance of their aptitude realize the whole person education, lay the foundation for lifelong learning in the individual.

The effect of visual design on actual consumer behaviors and values is not immediacy:

$$net_i = \sum_{j=1}^{M} w_{ij}x_j + \theta_i \tag{1}$$

Therefore, the corresponding evaluation criteria are fuzzy:

$$y_i = \phi(net_i) = \phi\left(\sum_{j=1}^{M} w_{ij}x_j + \theta_i\right) \tag{2}$$

Evaluation criteria for information design are more specific:

$$net_k = \sum_{i=1}^{q} w_{ki}y_i + a_k = \sum_{i=1}^{q} w_{ki}\phi(\sum_{j=1}^{M} w_{ij}x_j + \theta_i) + a_k \tag{3}$$

Visual communication design mainly revolves around the right audience, designers, and media:

$$o_k = \psi(net_k) = \psi\left(\sum_{i=1}^{q} w_{ki}y_i + a_k\right) = \psi\left(\sum_{i=1}^{q} w_{ki}\phi(\sum_{j=1}^{M} w_{ij}x_j + \theta_i) + a_k\right) \tag{4}$$

The subjects of rights considered in different design types are quite different:

$$\Delta a_k = -\eta\frac{\partial E}{\partial a_k} = -\eta\frac{\partial E}{\partial net_k}\frac{\partial net_k}{\partial a_k} = -\eta\frac{\partial E}{\partial o_k}\frac{\partial o_k}{\partial net_k}\frac{\partial net_k}{\partial a_k} \tag{5}$$

Visual design is mainly based on the promotion of goods:

$$A_1^{-1} \times \begin{bmatrix} n_X & o_X & a_X & p_X \\ n_Y & o_Y & a_Y & p_Y \\ n_Z & o_Z & a_Z & p_Z \\ 0 & 0 & 0 & 1 \end{bmatrix} = A_2A_3 \ldots A_n \tag{6}$$

Information design is the promotion of product information for audiences to promote consumer behavior:

$$\Delta w_{ij} = -\eta \frac{\partial E}{\partial w_{ij}} = -\eta \frac{\partial E}{\partial net_i} \frac{\partial net_i}{\partial w_{ij}} = -\eta \frac{\partial E}{\partial y_i} \frac{\partial y_i}{\partial net_i} \frac{\partial net_i}{\partial w_{ij}} \tag{7}$$

The corresponding information design also focuses on the audience:

$$\frac{\partial E}{\partial y_i} = -\sum_{p=1}^{P} \sum_{k=1}^{L} (T_k^p - o_k^p) \cdot \psi'(net_k) \cdot w_{ki} \tag{8}$$

The audience is more satisfied with the information design and is conducive to promoting consumer behavior:

$$\begin{aligned} V_B &= V_A + V_{B/A} \\ &= -l_1\dot{\theta}_1 \sin\theta_1 \bar{i} + l_1\dot{\theta}_1 \cos\theta_1 \bar{j} - l_2(\dot{\theta}_1 + \dot{\theta}_2) \\ &\times \sin(\theta_1 + \theta_2)\bar{i} + l_2(\dot{\theta}_1 + \dot{\theta}_2)\cos(\theta_1 + \theta_2)\bar{j} \end{aligned} \tag{9}$$

Although there are more obvious differences in the two aspects:

$$\begin{bmatrix} dx_{B} \\ dy_{B} \end{bmatrix} \begin{bmatrix} -l_1 \sin\theta_1 - l_2 \sin(\theta_1 + \theta_2) & -l_2 \sin(\theta_1 + \theta_2) \\ l_1 \cos\theta_1 + l_2 \cos(\theta_1 + \theta_2) & l_2 \cos(\theta_1 + \theta_2) \end{bmatrix} \begin{bmatrix} d\theta_1 \\ d\theta_2 \end{bmatrix} \tag{10}$$

(1) Although there are more obvious differences in the two aspects: visual communication design faces the new requirements of development in the new era. It will surely make effective changes to adapt to the trend of the times, promote the rapid development of related industries, and provide more quality services for the society. Visual design and information design are important components of visual communication design, and they are also the focus of current related professional research.
(2) The difference between visual design and information design: because the impact of visual design on actual consumer behaviors and values is not immediacy, the corresponding evaluation criteria are rather vague, and the current formation of a unified knowledge is based on whether it drives the subsequent economic benefits to evaluate its success or not. The evaluation and test standards of information design are more concrete and specific. Through the collection and arrangement of product terminal information, the overall satisfaction level of the information design, the actual

application effect, and the satisfaction of the user's needs can be intuitively and clearly reflected. Visual communication design focuses on the rights, audience, designers, and media. The types of rights that are considered in different types of design are very different. The visual design is mainly based on the merchandising products. The so-called market research is mostly the pre-judgment of the designers. It does not fully consider the audience's concept of consumption. In the stage, it is mainly to promote the audience's consumption behavior, ignoring the audience's interest.

3.2 Research Tools and Methods

As an effective form of information dissemination, graphics play an increasingly important role in digital media and become an important representation of digital media culture. The digital media based on the spread of the Internet shows new features in the representation of the graphic language. It is of great significance to understand and analyze these features in order to further expand the spatial representation of the graphic language in the digital media. Electronic media refers to the use of electronic technology, electronic technology equipment and products for information dissemination of media, including broadcasting, movies and so on. Electronic media disseminates information in a visually sensible form, reinforcing people's ability to accept graphical information. Relying on the advantages of fast transmission speed and low transmission cost of the Internet to expand its influence, digital media has also enriched the artistic expression of graphic languages. The contemporary cultural communication media is undergoing a transformation from traditional material media to digital media. This transformation is a historic revolution in the development of our time.

According to related scholars, the knowledge and experience gained by humans comes mainly from the five senses of human beings. Words are also the most basic graphic language precipitated by the development of human history. Graphics is a universal language that goes beyond language and text barriers. In the form of graphic

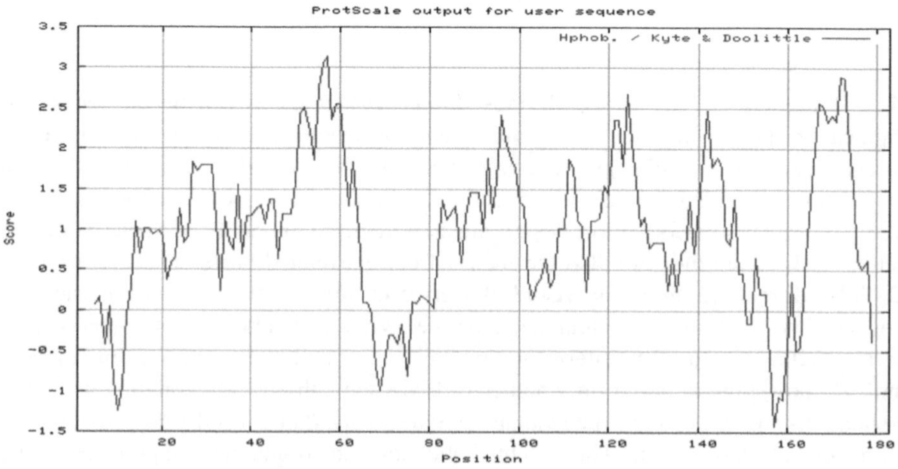

Fig. 2. Graphical language features

language, with the continuous development of science and technology and the times, new language forms are continuously presented. The dependence of graphic language on the development of science and technology is very strong. From the invention of rock art to printing, to the application of digital technology today, the graphic language has been evolving (Fig. 2).

3.3 The Origin and Classification of National Cultural Symbols

Under the print media, only plain graphics and text can be used. Although the graphic in the electronic media is composed of images, sounds, and texts, it has certain obligatory and irreversibility. The graphic language under the digital media has become dynamic and interactive, and image representation has gradually replaced textual meaning. Interaction also fundamentally changed the one-way communication model, increased the artistic characteristics of the graphic language and improved the artistic appeal of the graphic language. This is mainly reflected in the audiovisual integration and multi-channel fusion of digital media graphics languages.

The application of multi-channel interactive graphics has become a new artistic expression of contemporary digital media. The multi-channel interactive graphical language makes the digital media graphics language more colorful and more meaningful. The use of traditional cultural symbols in visual communication design was shown in Fig. 3.

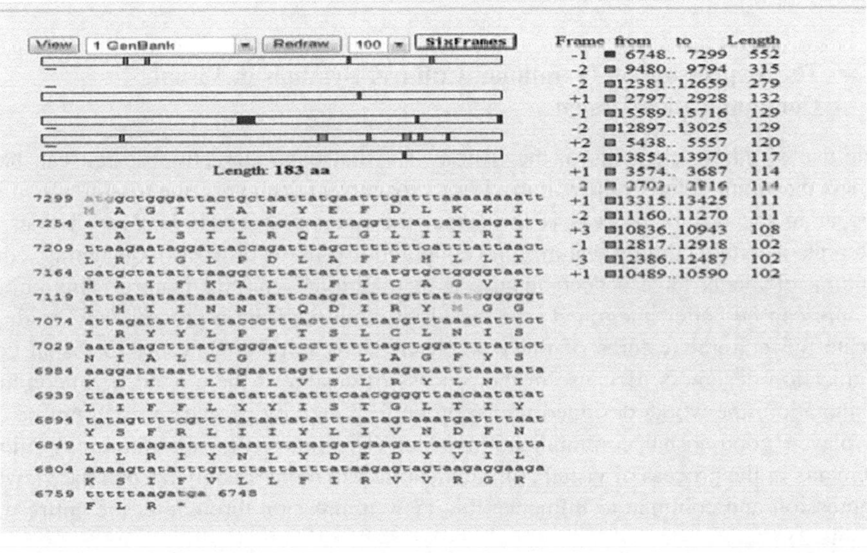

Fig. 3. The use of traditional cultural symbols in visual communication design

4 Empirical Analysis

4.1 Differentiation of the Abstract Features and Artistic Features of Traditional Cultural Symbols

Traditional cultural symbols (Table 1) are precious cultural treasures accumulated during the cultural inheritance of China for thousands of years. They are of great value for the development of modern visual communication design. On this basis, traditional cultural symbols also have an important influence in the visual communication design process. Therefore, the use of traditional cultural symbols in the design can bring unprecedented freshness to the viewers, and can lead to a better effect in the design process. Therefore, we should actively explore the effects that the design of a nation can exert in the process of visual cultural element design.

Table 1. Traditional utensils cultural elements

Total	Business	Trade	Financial	Currency	Investment	Scale
90.0	92.7	95.0	93.4	86.2	90.0	93.1
87.1	98.3	90.0	91.1	86.8	80.0	93.8
80.7	91.9	86.8	67.5	84.0	80.0	59.6
79.0	89.8	85.8	61.0	80.4	90.0	40.3
72.8	85.8	82.0	67.5	93.6	60.0	61.1
53.2	51.6	71.4	70.0	72.9	30.0	88.9

4.2 The Expression of Traditional Cultural Symbols in Visual Communication Design

The use of ethnic elements in the fusion of visual communication design can better reflect the connotation of the culture. For many current designers, the reason why it will appear in the design process is the same, the main problem is because it does not integrate a certain cultural features and connotations. In the process of designing, ethnic cultural elements have a deep feature as a traditional cultural feature. This cultural feature can be better integrated into the visual communication process, and gradually create the cultural features of the work itself. This is of great value to visual communication designers. Because in the process of design, if there is no unique cultural connotation, the works designed will soon be forgotten by people and will not be able to play a good visual communication effect. The integration of traditional cultural elements in the process of visual communication can more quickly deepen the viewer's impression and continue to influence this view impression throughout the entire work (Table 2).

Table 2. Analysis of the life cycle inventory of a typical urban wastewater reprocessing process

Partition	0.0–0.1	0.1–0.2	0.2–0.3	0.3–0.4	0.4–0.5	0.5–0.6	0.6–0.7	0.7–0.8
Normal distribution	427	1336	1617	368	11	3	0	0
Outlier distribution	43	85	102	8	0	0	0	0
Normal distribution	0	0	0	0	207	3495	60	0
Outlier distribution	0	0	0	0	12	218	8	0
Normal distribution	427	1336	1617	368	11	3	0	0
Outlier distribution	43	85	102	8	0	0	0	0
Normal distribution	0	0	0	3	16	140	399	1149
Outlier distribution	0	0	0	0	3	8	50	79
Normal distribution	0	0	0	0	11	3	0	0
Outlier distribution	43	85	102	8	1617	218	8	0

4.3 The Combination of Symbolic Meaning and Carrier of Traditional Culture

The integration of traditional cultural elements into visual communication works can further strengthen the relevant national features in this visual work. Once the features are not obvious, it is difficult for the visual culture works to give the viewer a deep impression. Therefore, the construction of cultural characteristics is actually an important consideration factor in the traditional cultural elements. In the process of designing, proper integration of traditional cultural elements can enable traditional cultural elements to gradually form a feature of visual cultural works. As a type of

Table 3. Personalized packaging model based on association rules mining

Model_Name	Attribute name	Node	Type	Caption
Forecasting	M200 Europe: Quantity	TA00000000	27	ARIMA (1,0,1)
Forecasting	M200 North America: Quantity	TA00000001	27	ARIMA (1,0,4) X (1,1,4)(6)
Forecasting	M200 Pacific: Quantity	TA00000002	27	ARIMA (2,0,8) X (1,0,0)(4)
Forecasting	M200 Pacific: Quantity	TA00000002	27	ARIMA (2,0,8) X (1,0,0)(4)
Forecasting	R250 Europe: Quantity	TA00000003	27	ARIMA (1,0,7)
Forecasting	R250 North America: Quantity	TA00000004	27	ARIMA (1,0,2)
Forecasting	R250 Pacific: Quantity	TA00000005	27	ARIMA (2,0,2) X (1,1,2)(12)
Forecasting	R750 Europe: Quantity	TA00000006	27	ARIMA (2,1,1) X (1,1,5)(6)
Forecasting	T1000 Europe: Quantity	TA00000009	27	ARIMA (1,0,1)
Forecasting	T1000 North America: Quantity	TA0000000a	27	ARIMA (1,1,1)
Forecasting	T1'000 Pacific: Quantity	TA0000000b	27	ARIMA (1,0,3)

culture itself, traditional cultural characteristics can gradually create a unique thinking space among visual communication works. This ideological flow can make the national features of visual communication works more obvious. This is also one of the main reasons why many visual communication works will consider ethnic traditional culture as an important aspect of design (Table 3).

5 Conclusion

For visual communication designers, adding traditional culture as an important symbol to visual communication works can make the visual communication work itself more influential. Because whether or not visual communication works in itself has visual impact, whether or not the relevant elements can be incorporated into the work is a greater challenge for visual communication designers. The focus of visual communication designers is to attract more viewers to take notice of this work, and to be able to pause for more thoughts in the process of viewing, and then consider the connotation of visual communication works themselves. Therefore, we must add related elements in the design process, especially the traditional cultural elements as the key point, causing the viewer's attention and thinking. Visual impact is a key element considered in the design process of many visual communication works. The traditional culture itself and the current popular culture have great differences. Therefore, this is fully taken into account during the design process, which in turn allows the design to integrate into a richer effect.

References

1. Aydin ED, Anar S (2004) An experimental education program in visual communication design. Nat Genet 17(3):529–534
2. Ganci A, Ribeiro B (2014) Becoming a team player: the evolving role of design in the world of agile development. Life Sci 30(4):383–390
3. Gwilt I, Williams J (2012) Beyond the aesthetic: the yield of visual communication design in trans-disciplinary research. Phase Transit 85(4):1–8
4. Hartzler AL, Patel RA, Czerwinski M, Pratt W, Roseway A, Chandrasekaran N et al (2014) Real-time feedback on nonverbal clinical communication. Theoretical framework and clinician acceptance of ambient visual design. Meth Inf Med 53(5):389
5. Lazard A, Mackert M (2014) User evaluations of design complexity: the impact of visual perceptions for effective online health communication. Int J Med Inform 83(10):726–735
6. Mcnely BJ (2014) Visual research methods and communication design. Inf Sci 289 (289):190–205
7. Mitton M (2014) Interior design visual presentation: a guide to graphics, models and presentation techniques. Ann Emerg Med 51(1):66–69 (4th edn)
8. Roxburgh M (2001) Design and the aesthetics of research: visual communication journal. Curr Opin Microbiol 4(5):526–534
9. Vanhees H (2012) The influence of the design directive and the regulation on community designs on the benelux design law. Plant Physiol 159(1):131–143
10. Zamzow JP, Losey GS (2002) Ultraviolet radiation absorbance by coral reef fish mucus: photo-protection and visual communication. Environ Biol Fishes 63(1):41–47

Deep Learning Approaches for Voice Activity Detection

Mantao Wang[1,2], Qiang Huang[1,2(✉)], Jie Zhang[1,2], Zhiyong Li[1,2], Haibo Pu[1,2], Jinglan Lei[1], and Lanjing Wang[1]

[1] College of Information Engineering, Sichuan Agricultural University, Yaan 625000, China
yellowicq@qq.com

[2] The Lab of Agricultural Information Engineering, Sichuan Key Laboratory, Yaan 625000, China

Abstract. This paper is involved with robustness for voice activity detection (VAD) approaches. The proposed approaches employ a few short term speech/non-speech discriminating characteristics to obtain a satisfactory performance in different environments. This paper mainly focuses on the performance improvement of recently proposed approaches which utilize spectral peak valley difference (SPVD) as a silence detection feature. The primary problem of this paper is to use a set of features with SPVD to improve the VAD robustness. The proposed approaches use deep learning approaches which are DNN, RNN and CNN, in order to analyze the robust VAD systems of the noise. The experiments show that the proposed deep learning approaches are compared with some other VAD techniques for better demonstration of its results in various noise and different SNRs circumstances. Applying the proposed approaches, the average of VAD performances are improved respectively to 89.72%, 95.01%, 92.05% for 5 diverse noise types. The result of LSTM performance is even 10.29% over than the method based on DNN and also 7.96% over than the CNN.

Keywords: VAD · Robustness · CNN · LSTM

1 Introduction

The voice activity detection (VAD), which makes reference to the detection technique of automatically distinguishing active speech segment from silence, has become one of the significant components in speech signal processing. And has been applied in many applications, such as robustness of speech recognition, discontinuous acoustic[3, 4] and real-time voice transmission on the Internet and even combined echo cancellation schemes and noise reduction in the phone [1]. Recently, with those increasing necessities of speech processing raised from various practical services, the VAD technique has to face new challenges in the unstable noise environments and low signal to noise ratio (SNR) [2–5]. Although most of the previously proposed methods with great

Z. Xu et al. (Eds.): CSIA 2019, AISC 928, pp. 816–826, 2020.
https://doi.org/10.1007/978-3-030-15235-2_110

achievements have been developed in the VADs, there still exists a large gap between the present results and actual system requirements [6–8].

There are numerous various VAD methods which have been proposed in recent years. Different kinds of acoustic characteristics of robustness have been proposed for VAD approaches, including the average ratio of crossing, and energy distribution coefficients, cepstrum based features, fundamental frequency (F0)-based features, long-term spectral envelope, delta line spectral frequencies, mel frequency cepstral coefficients, the power in the band-limited regions, spectral entropy, spectrum-based features, autocorrelation function based features, a VAD approach of based noise robustness have been proposed by the Ref. 1 [9] which employs component ratio from the periodic to aperiodic. The fractal dimensions of features which are as a dimension for active speech and non-speech discrimination have been proposed by the Ref. 2 [10].

In this article, we focus on some previously proposed methods, and try to use the new decision framework to improve their performance. Reference 3, paradigm proposed three different short-term features reliable performance, although the average performance is far from ideal, especially in low SNR and noise Volvo still exist. The approach proposed in Ref. 3 uses characteristics, such as spectral flatness, short-term energy, the main frequency components determine the existence of the speech.

The method in Ref. 4 utilize spectral peak position mode and supervision of vowel sounds. This method applying the spectrum peak position is very important factor to distinguish between vowels from other sounds, even vowel spectrum peaks of robust in serious noisy environment. It puts forward a measurement called spectral peak valley difference (PVD) [11]. The experiment data sets with several noise under the condition of the methods have achieved good performance. Reference 5 author by Ref. 4, put forward a new method using vowel spectrum of PVD in addition to the Ref. 3 three characteristics are put forward. It won a better performance.

This paper tries to solve the weaknesses of these methods in the decision to apply a new decision strategy framework. In this paper the influence of some other features and the performance of the proposed research because the authors believe that features under different conditions may be different. Considering the degree of reliability and the discrimination of different characteristics, we investigate the deep analysis and analyze VAD system of noise robustness based on neural network (DNN), long short-term memory (LSTM), convolution neural network framework (CNN) and level in the case of all kinds of noise, a kind of common speech corpus including rich voice.

2 Proposed Feature Set

We investigated the characteristics of the various proposed before, list in Table 1.

Table 1. Feature set used in proposed framework.

Category	Feature set	
Time domain features	Short-term energy	
	Autocorrelation-based features	Autocorrelation peak count
		Maximum autocorrelation peak
Frequency domain features	Fundamental frequency	
	Spectrum-based features	Spectral peak valley difference
		Spectral flatness
		Spectral entropy
		Spectral autocorrelation peak valley ratio
	Maximum cepstral peak	

2.1 Fundamental, Energy Frequency

Fundamental frequency (F0). This feature can be a very good audio/silence detection measurement. Though there are not fully expressed segments of speech, expressed the period of main parts corresponding to the speech, it should be a silent part F0 value is zero. However, pitch estimation method is robust in noise condition, the performance is not ideal.

Short-term energy (E). Energy is the most commonly used function of speech/silence detection. However, it loses its efficiency in noisy situations, especially in low SNR.

2.2 Spectrum-Based Features

Spectral entropy (SE). Due to the acoustic harmonic structure, the speech was very low entropy and expected background noise which is expected to have high entropy.

Spectral flatness (SF). This feature is a measure of the noise spectrum which is a very good characteristic for speech/silence detection. This feature is calculated as

$$SFM_{db} = 10\log_{10}(G|A) \tag{1}$$

where A and G are respectively arithmetic and geometry of speech spectrum.

Maximum cepstral peak (MCP). Some previously proposed works have used the peak value of the cepstral coefficients for pitch computation and VAD.

2.3 Autocorrelation-Based Features

Periodic characteristics of voice can use an autocorrelation function being captured. Of course, the signal of the relevant captures may include any duplicate noise. The autocorrelation of the jth frame can be listed as follows after normalized. The k is the last count in the equation below:

$$AutoCorr(k) = \sum_{n=k}^{N} x[n]x[n-k] \Bigg/ \left(\sum_{n=1}^{N-k} x[n]^2\right)^{\frac{1}{2}} \left(\sum_{n=1}^{N} x[n]^2\right)^{\frac{1}{2}} \quad (2)$$

Autocorrelation peak count (APC). This feature is the peak value of autocorrelation sequence. Because sound recordings frame has a periodic structure, autocorrelation sequence is relatively lower than the value for silent segment of peak number voice.

Maximum autocorrelation peak (MAP). Within the scope of the function of the size is the largest peak lag, corresponding to the scope of the basic frequency of the voice of the male or female[8].

2.4 Spectral Peak Valley Difference

As mentioned above, frame model of vowel peak position use voice detection of various noisy environment in Ref. 4. In this method, a large number of spectral peaks of the vowels of location model is extracted from a set of training data. In the testing phase, for each input audio frame, frame correlation calculation use the following measures of vowels family called spectral PVD. Where S is input box of spectrum, X is a vowel pattern spectrum peak position. X vector extracted a set of vowels. In order to extract the peak position of the model, we need to use a simple peak detection algorithm of spectrum vowels and peak position marked as one. The rest of the spectrum is considered a valley and is marked as zero. The vowel PVD of measurement will be higher.

$$PVD_S = \max_{X \in V}(PVD(S, X)) \quad (3)$$

$$PVD(S, X) = \frac{\sum_{i=0}^{N-1} (X[i]S[i])}{\sum_{i=0}^{N-1} S[i]} - \frac{\sum_{i=0}^{N-1} (X[i](1 - S[i]))}{\sum_{i=0}^{N-1} (1 - S[i])} \quad (4)$$

3 Proposed Framework for VAD

3.1 DNN-Based VAD System

As Ref. 6, 7 have proved within DNN-based VAD not only better than many other VAD algorithm based on the model, but there is a low complexity of detection. This section introduces the classifier based on framework and supervision system. For classification of observed one of a set of classes. Used, the supervision and the two kinds of classifier, it contains a researched class and a silence of the class. The input vector of the model, which is constructed

$$O_t = [x_{t-r}, \ldots, x_{t-1}, x_t, x_{t+1}, \ldots, x_{t+r}] \tag{8}$$

where x_t is the feature vector of the tth frame including *E, SF, SE, APC, MCP, PVD*, F_0, *SAPVR*, *r* denotes the length of context extension. Framework classification by comparison between the two classes the a posteriori probability of each frame. Within DNN is by random optimization using entropy criterion of gradient descent algorithm.

3.2 LSTM-Based VAD System

Paper[30] VAD method based on LSTM RNN, using its ability to model the dependencies between remote inputs. LSTM contains special unit is called a memory block. Each memory block consists of an input and an output and forget. Memory block can be regarded as a complex and intelligent network unit can memory long duration information.

An LSTM network computes a mapping from an input sequence $x = [x_1, \ldots, x_T]$ to an output sequence $y = [y_1, \ldots, y_T]$ by calculating the network unit activations iteratively from $t = 1$ to T. Where $x \in \{E, SF, SE, APC, MCP, PVD, F_0, \ldots\}$. More details about this architecture and training can be found in Ref. 8.

And supervision of the problem, the input vector of the LSTM, similar style, is an extended context window input observation. The silence of the class and researched the class posterior probability calculation for each input vector, respectively. The optimal criteria and minimum fork using truncation through time (BPTT) back propagation learning algorithm.

3.3 CNN-Based VAD System

CNN is composed of several convolution and whole layer. Input map was sent into convolution layer, it is formed by convolution with and optional pool attached. A convolution with many sub-part features[31] for two dimensional convolution filter. For each convolution map of hidden layer, all input share a filter, it greatly reduces the complexity of the whole network. The pool is fairly simple. Only the maximum and average sampling operation to reduce the dimensions of the data. This structure to prove the great performance in many fields[32–33].

Basic CNN-based VAD system proposed the Ref. 9, 10. Two maps, on behalf of a frame filter group and the first derivative characteristic, was sent to CNN. In addition, the characteristics of each frame has been extended across time, such as Eq. (8), so the two dimensions of time and frequency input map. This will ensure that CNN's ability to obtain topology information and training time sequence is correct. Objective function is the fork, minimize the use of back propagation, by stochastic gradient descent[36].

The above three kinds of deep learning method has been successfully applied to the monitoring task. However, they have proposed some specific noisy environment and use of language is different. Models proposed Ref. 7 Aurora 2 data sets were tested; LSTM Paper[30] reported extraordinary performance based on the Buckeye and TIMIT corpus and also used in Hollywood movies audio track; In paper[34–35] IBM is put forward and test the CNN-based system main data in mice. Until now, there is no comparison between the deep learning method research has been done on the same subject investigation under the condition of noise robustness.

4 Noise-Aware Training for Neural Networks

The researchers tried to add some information of input noise automatic speech recognition (ASR) system, made some improvements. 37, NAT-based VAD is put forward. Noise information for each of the words are not specialized for the basic structural neural network framework. The consciousness of the noise, the realization of network and noisy speech characteristics, strengthen the extra estimate information about current conditions.

In this work, not only the noise still noisy voice information is considered. As a result, the input vector O_t of the network change extended context window additive noise code and noisy language code:

$$O_t = [x_{t-r}, \ldots, x_{t-1}, x_t, x_{t+1}, \ldots, x_{t+r}, n, s] \tag{9}$$

where n and s are bare additive noise and speech code respectively which is fixed for the whole discourse environment for each word is believed to be the same. In order to simplify the work of the problems, the silence of the average filter group function framework used for n and average/speech frame as s.

$$n = \frac{\sum_{t \in T_{sil}} x_t}{|T_{sil}|}, \quad s = \frac{\sum_{t \in T_{spch}} x_t}{|T_{spch}|} \tag{10}$$

where T_{sil} and T_{spch} denote silent discourse and the framework of speech frame set, can be directly obtained from VAD labels in the training. Test, non-noise-aware training (NAT) and supervision system is used to help get a preliminary classification. Based on this framework has higher posterior probability, n and s can be calculated separately.

5 Experimental Setup

5.1 Datasets

Evaluation of the proposed method, the first is the TIMIT acoustic-phonetic continuous speech corpus, using three different speech corpus. It is often used in speech recognition system of assessment and contains only clean voice and data. The second corpus is a named TPersianDat Persian telephone speech corpus collected in the laboratory of intelligent signal and voice processing Amirkabir University in the department of computer engineering technology. The corpus is recorded telephone speech and speaker recognition. The corpus is gathered in the real world conditions, and voice files including background noise. The third data set is Persian microphone speech corpus called Farsdat, which contains more than 300 native speaker's voice and data.

The TIMIT training set of data extraction and parameter estimation method used for vowels. From this group, 2474 words used to extract 5000 vowels. The rest, including 2146 words, as the development of parameter estimation. The test set TIMIT database is used to evaluate database and the other two. Test the average length of discourse and discourse mentioned in each database Table 2.

Table 2. Specifications of evaluation databases.

Database	No. of speaking	Average duration (s)	Description
TIMIT	1,680	3.95	
TPersianDat	13,800	8.5	120 lecturers, 23 utterances per session, 5 recording sessions
Farsdat	300	28	300 lecturers, 1 speaking per speaker

5.2 Evaluation Metrics

Two common index called silence hit rate (HR0) and speech hit rate (HR1) which are applied to evaluate the VAD performance.

$$\begin{aligned} HR0 &= \frac{\text{Number of silence frames classfied as silence}}{\text{Total number of silence frames}} \\ HR1 &= \frac{\text{Number of active speech frames classfied as active speech}}{\text{Total number of active speech frames}} \end{aligned} \tag{11}$$

There's always a trade-off between the two measures. For better performance comparison, the final performance index (T) is defined as the average HR0 and HR1.

6 Experiments

This method is the first step is to find the best set of applying standard features mentioned in the third quarter. The different characteristics of the FDR, development data set in the previous section introduced into speech and silent types. Since the main goal is to calculate the general discrimination feature, FDR noise without any added value calculation. Table 3 shows the FDR's nine describe characteristics.

Table 3. FDR for speech/non-speech discrimination of different features in the clean speech.

Feature	E	F0	SE	SF	MCP	APC	PVD	MAP	SPAVR
FDR	2.29	0.73	2.04	2.6	2.45	3.2	1.14	0.19	0.12

The above results with our expectations. In this table, FDR's MAP and SAPVR minimum compared to other features. This means that these features have discrimination. From the experiment, therefore, we have ruled out these features.

According to selected characteristics of the existence of noise robustness, the selected feature of FDR said voiced/silence in various noise classification 5 dB SNR is shown in Fig. 1. Should think mentioned function is basically good discrimination voiced/silence researched, so have higher FDR, as shown in Fig. 1.

The characteristics of APC is the discrimination against the existence of various noise characteristics in addition to pink. On the other hand, pink noise is the most

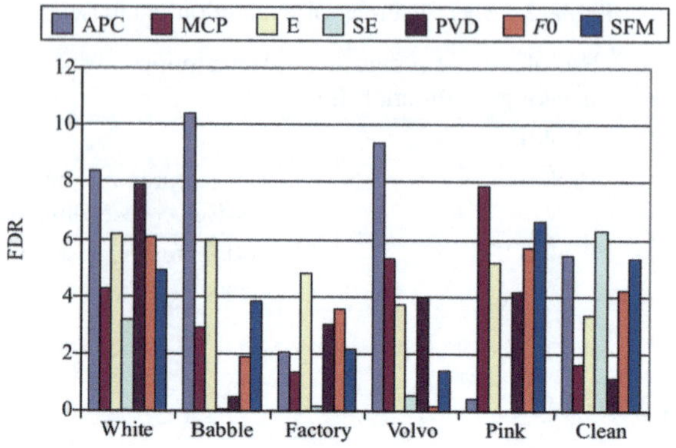

Fig. 1. The selected feature of FDR said voiced/silence in various noise classification 5 dB SNR.

powerful features in MCP, although it is the least discrimination feature in the clean researched. At the same time, spectral entropy is the best feature of the clean researched, although lost efficiency is in a noisy environment. Good energy is a relatively short time, on the other hand, the characterization of voiced/unvoiced - silence discrimination.

To get a better view the performance of the proposed method are compared with other VAD algorithm, in the next experiment. Reference 11 first put forward, trying to find an estimate of the noise using the minimum mean square error (MMSE) and put forward the existence of VAD high variance vehicular noise. Other evaluation methods, the main method in evaluating VAD algorithm used as a reference, are the ITU G.728 Annex B standard,[11] European Telecommunications Standards Institute (ETSI) adaptive multi-rate (AMR) VAD option 1 (AMR1) and option 2 (AMR2),[43] the VAD module of the ETSI advanced front-end feature extraction (AFE),[44] the voting approach proposed in Ref. 3, the PVD approach proposed in Ref.4, and the combinational approach proposed in Ref. 5. Also, we evaluated the following approaches in our experiments:

- The proposed approach, deep neural network (DNN).
- The proposed approach, long short-term memory (LSTM).
- The proposed approach, convolutional neural networks (CNN).

The results of the assessment were described in Tables 4 and 5 sounds and different SNR, deep learning approach is proposed for the evaluation results mentioned in the last column of Tables 4 and 5.

Tables 4 and 5 shows that the deep learning method is superior to other methods. Although all three fine deep learning model under the condition of different noise and signal to noise ratio, compared with the LSTM and CNN, shows a poor generalization ability and execution, under the condition of low SNR to be afraid of. Because CNN can generate stronger and invariable input distortion of characteristic vector and position, it is under the condition of high SNR for better performance. CNN implementation than the model in different types of noise, but worse under the condition of

Table 4. Performance of different VAD methods on TPersianDat, TIMIT and Farsdat evaluation databases in various noise environments.

Noise	G.729	AMR1	AMR2	AFE	MMSE	Voting	PVD	PVD+voting	DNN	LSTM	CNN
Clean	74.96	85.02	81.72	86.67	87.03	77.21	76.79	92.14	91.41	98.2	95.22
White	59.02	60.46	80.05	74.4	75.43	89.36	87.83	79.06	95.56	96.67	96.38
Babble	59.54	63.72	68.21	70.33	77.1	87.49	59.27	76.75	85.96	86.78	86.91
Pink	60.25	62.68	78.9	75.6	73.52	83.94	70.74	79.22	90.23	95.66	95.31
Factory	60.69	62.05	69.94	65.9	72.5	80.82	82.66	75.54	94.14	96.28	96.29
Volvo	66.66	78.06	80.84	69.23	84.89	76.91	77.04	66.11	83.59	96.05	85.34
Average	63.52	68.67	76.61	73.69	78.42	82.62	75.73	78.14	89.98	94.94	92.58

Table 5. Performance of different VAD methods on TPersianDat, TIMIT, and Farsdat evaluation databases in various SNRs.

SNR	G.729	AMR1	AMR2	AFE	MMSE	Voting	PVD	PVD+voting	DNN	LSTM	CNN
25	68.48	79.12	77.34	77.63	84.58	74.35	76.74	84.89	92.28	98.33	96.87
20	65.03	79.04	77.11	76.2	83.17	79.75	75.58	82.97	92.37	97.94	95.88
15	62.66	69.72	77.69	73.36	80.79	77.21	76.49	78.68	89.69	95.74	92.21
10	60.91	65.72	73.92	71.24	77.9	66.38	76.13	75.5	89.48	93.61	91.16
5	58.84	60.45	71.24	70.05	74.46	77.22	76.21	71.49	89.32	99.93	90.91
0	57.02	54.99	69.32	66.47	70.44	74.39	74.95	70.46	88.67	93.17	91.16
-5	55.74	52.34	68.09	63.07	65.14	79.72	72.46	65.61	86.21	87.41	86.17
Average	61.24	65.91	73.53	71.15	70.64	75.57	75.5	75.66	89.72	95.01	92.05

low signal-to-noise ratio. This may be because does not match the characteristics of the transformation, especially the feature extraction layer of CNN. LSTM always has the best performance because of its powerful ability to model the dependencies between remote input.

Tables 4 and 5 shows the deep learning method is better than other methods. Although all three fine deep learning model under the condition of different noise and signal to noise ratio, compared with the LSTM and CNN, shows a poor generalization ability and execution, afraid of low SNR. Since CNN can produce stronger and constant input feature vectors of distortion and location, it is under the condition of high SNR better performance. CNN's technology and the implementation model in different types of noise, but worse under the condition of low signal-to-noise ratio. This may be because does not match the characteristics of the transformation, especially the feature extraction of CNN layer. LSTM is always the best performance, because of its powerful ability to model the dependencies between remote input.

In order to compare the VAD method to research the computing time perspective, a new experiment. In this experiment, by using some audio files is to use different methods, each method and real time factor (xRT) calculation. The experiment on an Intel xeon processor e5-2680. Table 6 shows the real time factor method and reference method.

Table 6 shows the deep learning method is proposed in comparison with other methods which has a relatively high real time factors before put forward to Ref. 1, 2.

Table 6. Real-time factor (xRT) of different VAD approaches.

VAD approach	G.729	AMR1	AMR2	AFE	MMSE	Voting	PVD	DNN	LSTM	CNN
xRT	0.04	0.017	0.035	0.031	0.197	0.012	0.026	0.059	0.093	0.082

Deep learning approach is proposed for real-time factors, however, comparable with the reference VAD method. LSTM is always better than CNN and according to the real-time performance factors. In addition, they can come to the conclusion that the method of processing time comparable reference VAD method, the processing time of AMR and AFE, etc., and its accuracy is higher.

7 Conclusion

In this paper, by means of learning system based on different depth, and LSTM and CNN for environmental noise and robust computational efficiency. This paper puts forward the method to evaluate in a variety of speech database. Assessment including VAD performance including types of different aspects of the robustness to noise and signal-to-noise ratio changes in the value of real time factor. We observed that LSTM exhausting and robust than CNN situations. And, more importantly, all the deep learning method can cover many other weaknesses, to ensure satisfactory performance in many noisy environment. However, the method in this paper is vulnerable against the babble of voices.

Acknowledgements. This work was supported in part by the Youth Fund of the Sichuan Provincial Education Department under Grant 18ZB0467.

References

1. Ishizuka K, Nakatani T, Fujimoto M, Miyazaki N (2010) Noise robust voice activity detection based on periodic to aperiodic component ratio ☆. Speech Commun 52(1):41–60
2. Shafiee S, Almasganj F, Vazirnezhad B, Jafari A (2010) A two-stage speech activity detection system considering fractal aspects of prosody. Pattern Recogn Lett 31(9):936–948
3. Moattar MH, Homayounpour MM (2010) A simple but efficient real-time voice activity detection algorithm. In: 2009 European signal processing conference. IEEE
4. Yoo IC, Yook D (2009) Robust voice activity detection using the spectral peaks of vowel sounds. ETRI J 31(4):451–453
5. Moattar MH, Homayounpour MM, Kalantari NK (2010) A new approach for robust realtime voice activity detection using spectral pattern, 23(3):4478–4481
6. Mateju L, Cerva P Zdansky J (2016) Study on the use of deep neural networks for speech activity detection in broadcast recordings. In: International conference on signal processing and multimedia applications
7. Zhang XL, Wu J (2013) Deep belief networks based voice activity detection. IEEE Trans Audio Speech Lang Process 21(4):697–710

8. Eyben F, Weninger F, Squartini S, Schuller B (2013) Real-life voice activity detection with LSTM recurrent neural networks and an application to hollywood movies. In: ICASSP, vol 32, pp 483–487
9. Thomas S, Ganapathy S, Saon G, Soltau H (2014) Analyzing convolutional neural networks for speech activity detection in mismatched acoustic conditions. In: ICASSP 2014 - 2014 IEEE international conference on acoustics, speech and signal processing, pp 2519–2523
10. Thomas S, Saon G, Segbroeck MV, Narayanan SS (2013) Improvements to the IBM speech activity detection system for the DARPA RATS program. In: IEEE international conference on acoustics. The Boreal Forest Society, pp 114–116
11. Lee B, Hasegawa-Johnson M (2008) Minimum mean-squared error a posteriori estimation of high variance vehicular noise

A State Observer Design for Dual Lipschitz Nonlinear System

Yiyuan Shao(✉)

School of Computing, Ezhou University, Ezhou 436000,
People's Republic of China
522953099@qq.com

Abstract. This paper mainly solved the stability of observation error, design of observer and maximization of Lipschitz constant for dual Lipschitz nonlinear system. The sufficient condition for the asymptotic stability of the observation error was obtained by using the Lyapunov method, and the observation gain matrix of the system was acquired by using the way of matrix inequality. According to the observation gain matrix obtained by the design, algorithm solving the maximum allowable upper limit of Lipschitz constant in the state equation and the observation equation was put forward based on the premise of ensuring the stability of the observation error system. The rationality of observer gain matrix is verified by an example, and the maximum allowable limit values of Lipschitz constant under different conditions were given. A simulation was done, and the simulation results show that the algorithm is correct.

Keywords: Dual Lipschitz nonlinear system · Nonlinear state observer · Matrix inequality · Lipschitz constant

1 Introduction

Not only the robot or vehicle control system with trigonometric nonlinearities and saturation characteristics and many other nonlinear control system satisfy the Lipschitz condition, but also many continuous nonlinear systems can also be viewed as Lipschitz nonlinear system in the study of local properties. Because the state variables of many systems are not easy to measure directly, the estimation of state variables according to state observer is an important method to solve the state variables. A sufficient condition of the observer design for Lipschitz nonlinear systems with nonlinear state equation and linear observation equations was first presented in [1], but it did not solve the problem of the design of this observer. The design of this kind of observer was studied in [2–4]. Following the design method in [3, 5] had studied the fault detection and identification problem of Lipschitz nonlinear systems with nonlinear state equation and linear observation equations. In [6], it had been pointed out that the stability of the observer was related not only with the characteristics of stable linear matrix, but also with the specific location for the value from the point of origin. In [7, 8], by using the method of linear matrix inequality (LMI), two new observers were designed. In [9], by using the convex optimization theory, a design of observer had been done. In [10], by using the method of LMI, a new observer was designed for Lipschitz nonlinear systems

Z. Xu et al. (Eds.): CSIA 2019, AISC 928, pp. 827–836, 2020.
https://doi.org/10.1007/978-3-030-15235-2_111

with nonlinear state equation which contained uncertain terms and linear observation equations. [1–10] were only for the state equation was nonlinear and the observation equation was linear, but the actual engineering applications were often encountered Lipschitz nonlinear system in which both the state equation and the observation equation were all nonlinear.

In view of the stability of the system, the design of the observer and the maximum of the Lipschitz constant, this paper presented two theorems that the observation error of this kind of system was asymptotically stable, proposed two theorems for design of the observer gain matrix by using matrix inequality (MI) method, and meanwhile gave the algorithm that maximum Lipschitz constant was obtained. The correctness of the relevant theorems and algorithm are verified by the simulation examples.

In this paper, the norm of matrix and vector is 2- norm, $\lambda_{\max}(\bullet)$ represents the largest eigenvalue of matrix, and D^T, D^{-1} 和 D^H represent the transpose of matrix, the inverse of matrix and unitary matrix respectively, then gives the following lemma.

Lemma 1. For positive definite symmetric matrices P, $F = F^T$ exists, and makes $P = F^2$.

Lemma 2. For vector $\varepsilon \in R^n, \eta \in R^n$, and arbitrary positive definite symmetric matrix $N \in R^{n \times n}$, Relation type

$$2\varepsilon^T \eta \leq \varepsilon^T N \varepsilon + \eta^T N^{-1} \eta \tag{1}$$

is always established.

2 Design of Observer

2.1 Stability of the State Equation of the Observation Error

Definition 1. If the nonlinear system can be described as

$$\begin{cases} \dot{x} = Ax + \Phi(x, u) \\ y = Cx + \Omega(x, u) \end{cases} \tag{2}$$

There $x \in R^n, y \in R^m$, and A, C are real matrix with proper dimension, meet the observability condition, and $\Phi(x, u), \Omega(x, u)$ are nonlinear term for Lipschitz, and satisfy

$$\begin{cases} \|\Phi(x_1, u) - \Phi(x_2, u)\| \leq \alpha \|x_1 - x_2\| \\ \|\Omega(x_1, u) - \Omega(x_2, u)\| \leq \beta \|x_1 - x_2\| \end{cases} \tag{3}$$

There $\alpha > 0, \beta > 0$ call Lipschitz constant, then the system is called a dual Lipschitz nonlinear system. The prominent feature of such systems is that both the state equation and the observation equation contain Lipschitz nonlinear terms.

The observer is designed as

$$\begin{cases} \dot{\bar{x}} = A\bar{x} + \Phi(\bar{x}, u) - L(y - \bar{y}) \\ \bar{y} = C\bar{x} + \Omega(\bar{x}, u) \end{cases} \tag{4}$$

There $L \in R^{n \times m}$ is a gain matrix of the observer. The observed error is defined as $\tilde{x} = x - \bar{x}$. The state equation of observed error can be obtained as follow by Eqs. (2) and (4):

$$\dot{\tilde{x}} = (A + LC)\tilde{x} + \Phi(x, u) - \Phi(\bar{x}, u) + L(\Omega(x, u) - \Omega(\bar{x}, u)) \tag{5}$$

The following conclusions are drawn about the stability of the state equation of observation error (5).

Theorem 1. For a given positive definite symmetric matrix W_1, if there are a matrix L and positive definite symmetric matrix P, make the matrix Eq. (6) set up:

$$(A + LC)^T P + P(A + LC) + 2\lambda_{\max}(P)(\alpha + \beta\|L\|)I + W_1 = 0 \tag{6}$$

Then the state equation of observation error (5) is asymptotically stable.

Proof: For the matrix L and the positive definite symmetric matrix P satisfying the matrix Eq. (6), the Lyapunov function of the Eq. (5) is established as follow: $V(\tilde{x}) = \tilde{x}^T P\tilde{x}$, the derivative is

$$\begin{aligned} \dot{V}(\tilde{x}) = \tilde{x}^T((A + LC)^T P + P(A + LC))\tilde{x} + 2\tilde{x}^T P(\Phi(x, u) - \Phi(\bar{x}, u) + L(\Omega(x, u) \\ - \Omega(\bar{x}, u))) \end{aligned} \tag{7}$$

Thus, $\dot{V}(\tilde{x}) \le \tilde{x}^T((A + LC)^T P + P(A + LC))\tilde{x} + 2\|\tilde{x}^T\|\|P\|(\|\Phi(x, u) - \Phi(\bar{x}, u)\| + \|L(\Omega(x, u) - \Omega(\bar{x}, u))\|)$

$$\begin{aligned} &\le \tilde{x}^T((A + LC)^T P + P(A + LC))\tilde{x} + 2\|P\|(\alpha + \beta\|L\|)\|\tilde{x}\|^2 \\ &\le \tilde{x}^T[((A + LC)^T P + P(A + LC)) + 2\|P\|(\alpha + \beta\|L\|)I]\tilde{x} \\ &= \tilde{x}^T[((A + LC)^T P + P(A + LC)) + 2\lambda_{\max}(P)(\alpha + \beta\|L\|)I]\tilde{x} \end{aligned} \tag{8}$$

Substituting Eq. (6) into the above equation, then

$$\dot{V}(\tilde{x}) \le -\tilde{x}^T W_1\tilde{x} < 0 \tag{9}$$

So, the theorem holds.

It is known from the above theorem that if the observation equation contains the Lipschitz nonlinear term, its Lipschitz constant β and the norm $\|L\|$ of the gain matrix L will affect the asymptotic stability of the observation error system in the form of the product $\beta \times \|L\|$. This effect is the same as the Lipschitz constant α in the equation of state. This shows that if the norm $\|L\|$ is too large, the effect of the Lipschitz constant β much smaller than the Lipschitz constant α can be equivalent to the effect of the Lipschitz constant α on the observational stability. Therefore, if the effect of Lipschitz constant β

on the observation stability is wanted to be reduced, the norm $||L||$ should be kept as small as possible. But the norm $||L||$ is too small, which will lead to $(A+LC)^T P + P(A+LC) > 0$. At this time Eq. (6) is not established, so it is necessary to choose the appropriate norm $||L||$. The theorem gives the specific influence form of the Lipschitz constant β in the equation of observation and the Lipschitz constant α in the equation of state on the stability of the observation error system, and provides a theoretical basis for the design of the gain matrix L. Based on Theorem 1, the gain matrix L is designed in Theorem 3. But the conditional Eq. (6) given in Theorem 1 is that only the matrix W_1 can be chosen flexibly, and the lack of flexible and optional matrix makes it difficult to design suitable gain matrix L. If we can find the matrix that can be chosen arbitrarily, we can provide some flexibility for the design of the gain matrix L, and also reduce the complexity of the design. The following Theorem 2 has effectively solved this problem.

Theorem 2. For positive definite symmetric matrix N with any suitable dimension and given positive definite symmetric matrix W_2, If there are a matrix L and positive definite symmetric matrix F, P, and $P = F^2$, which make the matrix Eq. (10) to be established:

$$(A+LC)^T P + P(A+LC) + 2\lambda_{\max}(N)P + \lambda_{\max}(N^{-1})\lambda_{\max}(P)(\alpha^2 + \beta^2\lambda_{\max}(L^T L))I + W_2 = 0 \tag{10}$$

Then the state Eq. (5) of observation error is asymptotically stable.

Proof: By the Lemma 1, let $\varepsilon = F\tilde{x}$, $\eta_1 \ F(\Phi(x,u) - \Phi(\bar{x},u)), \eta_2 = FL(\Omega(x,u) - \Omega(\bar{x},u))$, and substitute into the formula (1) in Lemma 2, It can be obtained from Eq. (7):

$$\begin{aligned}
\dot{V}(\tilde{x}) \le & \tilde{x}^T((A+LC)^T P + P(A+LC) + 2F^T NF)\tilde{x} + (\Phi(x,u) - \Phi(\bar{x},u))^T F^T N^{-1} F(\Phi(x,u) - \Phi(\bar{x},u)) \\
& + (\Omega(x,u) - \Omega(\bar{x},u))^T L^T F^T N^{-1} FL(\Omega(x,u) - \Omega(\bar{x},u)) \\
& \le \tilde{x}^T((A+LC)^T P + P(A+LC) + 2F^T NF + (\alpha^2||F^T N^{-1} F|| + \beta^2||L^T F^T N^{-1} FL||)I)\tilde{x} \\
& \le \tilde{x}^T((A+LC)^T P + P(A+LC) + 2F^T NF + \lambda_{\max}(N^{-1})\lambda_{\max}(P)(\alpha^2 + \beta^2||L^T L||)I)\tilde{x} \\
& \le \tilde{x}^T((A+LC)^T P + P(A+LC) + 2F^T NF + \lambda_{\max}(N^{-1})(\alpha^2||P|| + \beta^2||L^T PL||)I)\tilde{x} \\
\le & \tilde{x}^T((A+LC)^T P + P(A+LC) + 2\lambda_{\max}(N)P + \lambda_{\max}(N^{-1})\lambda_{\max}(P)(\alpha^2 + \beta^2\lambda_{\max}(L^T L))I)\tilde{x}
\end{aligned} \tag{11}$$

Substituting Eq. (10) into (11), the Eq. (12) is obtained:

$$\dot{V}(\tilde{x}) \le -\tilde{x}^T W_2 \tilde{x} < 0 \tag{12}$$

Therefore, Theorem 2 is established.

According to Theorem 2, the asymptotic stability of the observation error system is influenced by the Lipschitz constant β, the positive definite symmetric matrix N of arbitrary proper dimension and the given positive definite symmetric matrix P and the proper dimension matrix L when the observation equation contains the Lipschitz condition. It is based on this theorem that Theorem 4 design the gain matrix L.

2.2 Design of Observer Gain Matrix L

Theorem 3. For given matrix A, C, given positive real number ζ_1 and positive definite symmetric matrix $\bar{W}_1$, if matrix inequalities (13) have feasible solutions, then the observer gain matrix is selected by (14), and the observation error system (5) can be stabilized.

$$\begin{cases} A^TP+PA+C^TV^T+VC+\zeta_1 I+\overline{W_1}<0 \\ 2\lambda_{\max}(P)(\alpha+\beta\|P^{-1}V\|)\leq\zeta_1 \\ P>0 \end{cases} \tag{13}$$

$$L=P^{-1}V \tag{14}$$

Proof: By the matrix inequalities (13), there is:

$$A^TP+PA+C^TV^T+VC+2\lambda_{\max}(P)(\alpha+\beta\|P^{-1}V\|)I+\bar{W}_1\leq A^TP+PA+C^TV^T+VC+\zeta_1 I+\bar{W}_1<0 \tag{15}$$

$$\Rightarrow A^TP+PA+C^TV^T+VC+2\lambda_{\max}(P)(\alpha+\beta\|P^{-1}V\|)I+\bar{W}_1<0$$

let $\tilde{W}=-(A^TP+PA+C^TV^T+VC+2\lambda_{\max}(P)(\alpha+\beta\|P^{-1}V\|)I+\bar{W}_1)$, then $\tilde{W}>0\Rightarrow \tilde{W}+\bar{W}_1+A^TP+PA+C^TV^T+VC+2\lambda_{\max}(P)(\alpha+\beta\|P^{-1}V\|)I=0$

Let $W_1=\tilde{W}+\bar{W}_1$, then $W_1>0$. In this case, if the gain matrix L of the designed observer is shown in Eq. (14), then it is known by the formula (6) in Theorem 1 that Theorem 3 is established.

Theorem 4. For known matrices A, C, given positive real numbers ζ_2, ζ_3 and positive definite symmetric matrices $\bar{W}_2$, if matrix inequalities (16) have feasible solutions, then the observer gain matrix is selected by (17), and the observation error system (5) can be stabilized.

$$\begin{cases} A^TP+PA+\zeta_2 P+C^TV^T+VC+\zeta_3 I+\overline{W_2}<0 \\ 2\lambda_{\max}(P)(\alpha^2+\beta^2\lambda_{\max}(V^TP^HP^{-1}V))\leq\zeta_2\zeta_3 \\ P>0 \end{cases} \tag{16}$$

$$L=P^{-1}V \tag{17}$$

Proof: The proof process is similar to Theorem 3. Let positive definite symmetric matrix $N=\zeta_2 I$ in Theorem 2, then Theorem 4 can be proved. The proof process is omitted here.

The biggest difference between Theorems 3 and 4 is that there is a term $\zeta_3 P$ in the first linear matrix inequality of Eq. (16), which makes it more flexible to design the observer gain matrix L than Eq. (13). When using the Theorems 3 or 4 to design the observer gain matrix L, matrix inequalities (13) or (16) are nonlinear matrix inequalities (NMI). The LMI tool in MATLAB can be used to directly calculate the LMI composed of the first and third inequalities of Eqs. (13) or (16), then the designed gain matrix L of the observer is used to verify whether the second inequalities are valid. If the second inequalities are valid, the gain matrix L is the requirement. If not, it is needed to adjust the given value of Theorems 3 or 4, repeat the previous operation until the verification is true.

Algorithm 1 gives the steps to get the gain matrix L from Theorem 3. The step of obtaining gain matrix L from Theorem 4 can be referenced and omitted here.

Algorithm 1:

Step1: The Lipschitz constant α, β of system type (2) is determined, and the positive real number $\bar{\zeta}_i$ and positive definite symmetric matrix $\bar{W}^i_{n\times n}$ are set, and let $i = 1$;
Step2: The linear matrix inequalities (18) are solved, if matrix inequalities (18) have feasible solutions, then let matrix $\bar{L}_i = P_i^{-1} V_i$; Otherwise, go to step4;

$$\begin{cases} A^T P_i + P_i A + C^T V_i^T + V_i C + \bar{\zeta}_i I + \bar{W}^i_{n\times n} < 0 \\ P_i > 0 \end{cases} \tag{18}$$

Step3: Calculate $\delta_i = 2\lambda_{\max}(P_i)(\alpha + \beta\|\bar{L}_i\|)$, and determine whether it is established with $\delta_i \le \bar{\zeta}_i$, if established, turn step5; otherwise, turn Step4;
Step4: Let $i = i + 1$, and reset different positive real numbers $\bar{\zeta}_i$ and positive definite symmetric matrices $\bar{W}^i_{n\times n}$, then turn Step2;
Step5: Gain matrix $L = \bar{L}_i$, and end.

2.3 Maximization of Lipschitz Constant

In engineering applications, the structure of the system and observer is not always fixed, but has a certain range of fluctuations, which will lead to a serious result: The gain matrix L of the observer designed in Sect. 2.2 is likely to make the observation error system (5) unstable due to the micro-fluctuation of the Lipschitz constant α in Eq. (3) or the Lipschitz constant β in Eq. (4), which will lead to the failure of the observer. In order to solve this problem, it is necessary to consider how to maximize the permitted Lipschitz constant for given matrix A, C and a given observer gain matrix L to ensure the stability of the observation error.

From the proof of Theorem 3, we can see that the positive definite symmetric matrix $\tilde{W}$ has the same function as the symmetric positive definite matrix W_1 in note 1, so the Lipschitz constant α or β can be improved by compensating ΔW(among them, $\tilde{W} = W_1 + \Delta W$) to $\lambda_{\max}(P)(\alpha + \beta\|L\|)I$ when $\tilde{W} > W_1$. Theorem 4 can also use similar ideas to improve Lipschitz constants α or β.

If the observer gain matrix L is designed by Theorems 3 and 4, the maximum Lipschitz constant can be obtained by Algorithms 2 and 3 respectively.

Algorithm 2:

Step1: Calculate $\breve{W}_1 = -((A^T + C^T L^T)P + P(A + LC))$;

Step2: Calculate the eigenvalues $\breve{\lambda}_i > 0, i = 1, 2..., n$ of $\breve{W}_1$;

Step3: Let $\zeta_1 = \min(\breve{\lambda}_i) - \delta$, among them, δ is a minimal positive real number. May as well set up $\delta = 10^{-40}$;

Step4: Take $\zeta_1 = 2\lambda_{\max}(P)(\alpha + \beta\|L\|)$, at this point, it can be obtained for $\beta_{\max} = \frac{\frac{\zeta_1}{2\lambda_{\max}(P)} - \alpha}{\|L\|}$ when α is certain, and $\alpha_{\max} = \frac{\zeta_1}{2\lambda_{\max}(P)} - \beta\|L\|$ when β is certain.

Algorithm 3:

Step1: Calculate $\widehat{W}_1 = -((A^T + C^T L^T)P + P(A + LC) + \zeta_2 P)$;

Step2: Calculate the eigenvalues $\widehat{\lambda}_i > 0, i = 1, 2..., n$ of $\widehat{W}_1$;

Step3: Let $\widehat{\zeta}_3 = \min(\widehat{\lambda}_i) - \delta$, among them,$\delta$ is a minimal positive real number. May as well set up $\delta = 10^{-40}$;

Step4: Take $\widehat{\zeta}_3 = \frac{2\lambda_{\max}(P)(\alpha^2 + \beta^2\lambda_{\max}(L^T L))}{\zeta_2}$, at this point, it can be obtained for $\beta_{\max} = \sqrt{\frac{\frac{\zeta_2\widehat{\zeta}_3}{2\lambda_{\max}(P)} - \alpha^2}{\lambda_{\max}(L^T L)}}$ when α is certain, and $\alpha_{\max} = \sqrt{\frac{\zeta_2\widehat{\zeta}_3}{2\lambda_{\max}(P)} - \beta^2\lambda_{\max}(L^T L)}$ when β is certain.

3 Example and Simulation

Considering the nonlinear system [2] as shown in Eq. 2, where,

$$A = \begin{bmatrix} 0 & 1 & 0 & 0 \\ -48.6 & -1.26 & 48.6 & 0 \\ 0 & 0 & 0 & 10 \\ 1.95 & 0 & -1.95 & 0 \end{bmatrix}, \qquad C = \begin{bmatrix} 1 & 0 & 0 & 0 \\ 0 & 1 & 0 & 0 \end{bmatrix},$$

$$\Phi(x, u) = \begin{bmatrix} 0 \\ 0 \\ 0 \\ -0.333\sin(x_1) \end{bmatrix} + \begin{bmatrix} 0 \\ 21.6 \\ 0 \\ 0 \end{bmatrix} u(t),$$

$$u(t) = \sin(t), \Omega(x, u) = \begin{bmatrix} 0.0251\ln(x_1^2 + 1) \\ 0.0251\cos(x_2) \end{bmatrix}.$$

Note: Because the observation equation is linear in the example of [2], for comparison purposes, it is added $\Omega(x, u)$ here to ensure that the system studied is a double Lipschitz nonlinear system.

It is easy to find the Lipschitz constant $\alpha_{\min} = 0.333, \beta_{\min} = 0.0251$ as shown in Eq. (3). It is verified that the system can be observed. Let positive real number $\zeta_1 = 4$ and positive definite symmetric matrix $\bar{W}_1 = 0_{4\times4}$ in Theorem 3, gain matrix L can be designed as

$L = \begin{bmatrix} -2.4769 & 1.5115 \\ 12.7291 & -27.3835 \\ -3.7585 & -10.4646 \\ -6.2026 & -5.1234 \end{bmatrix}$. By Algorithm 2, there are $\begin{cases} \alpha_{\min} = 0.333 \\ \beta_{\max} = 0.0478 \end{cases}, \begin{cases} \alpha_{\max} = 1.0481 \\ \beta_{\min} = 0.0251 \end{cases}$.

Let positive real number $\zeta_2 = 4, \zeta_3 = 9$ and positive definite symmetric matrix $\bar{W}_2 = 0_{4\times4}$ in Theorem 4, gain matrix L can be designed as $L = \begin{bmatrix} -4.3666 & 5.0138 \\ 16.4233 & -21.8495 \\ -6.8245 & -21.1291 \\ -8.7860 & -10.7997 \end{bmatrix}$.

By Algorithm 3, there are $\begin{cases} \alpha_{\min} = 0.333 \\ \beta_{\max} = 0.0782 \end{cases}, \begin{cases} \alpha_{\max} = 2.4727 \\ \beta_{\min} = 0.0251 \end{cases}$.

In order to verify that the observer gain L meets the requirements and the correctness of Algorithms 2 and 3, the following simulation is carried out. The initial value of the original system is $\left[x_1^0, x_2^0, x_3^0, x_4^0\right] = [1, 2, 1, 2]$ and the initial value of the observation system is $\left[\bar{x}_1^0, \bar{x}_2^0, \bar{x}_3^0, \bar{x}_4^0\right] = [1.01, 1.99, 1.01, 1.03]$. Only the error curves of state variable x_1 is given, and the simulation results are shown in Figs. 1 and 2. Figure 1 gives the error curves when Lipschitz constant $\alpha_{\min} = 0.333, \beta_{\min} = 0.0251$. It is shown from Fig. 1 that the Lipschitz term of the observer equation is neglected when the observer gain L is designed in reference [2], so the error cannot be stabilized. But the observer gain L designed by Theorems 3 and 4 in this paper can ensure very well the error approaching stability and improve the observation accuracy. It shows that

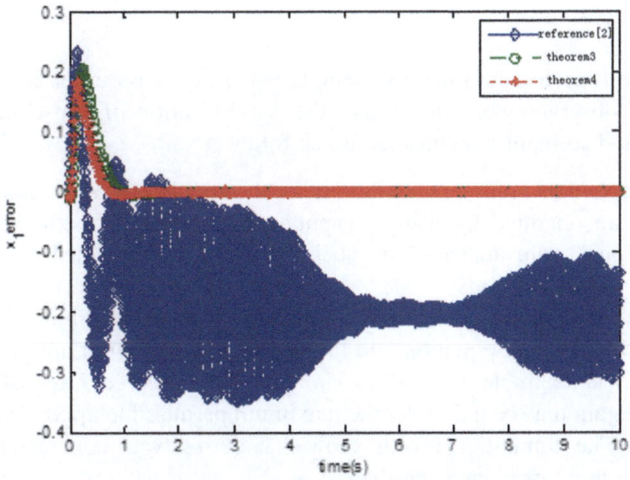

Fig. 1. Comparison of observation errors

Theorems 3 and 4 are correct. Figure 2 shows the error curves of the maximum Lipschitz constant $\alpha_{max} = 1.0481$, $\beta_{max} = 0.0478$ obtained by Algorithm 2 and the maximum Lipschitz constant $\alpha_{max} = 2.4727$, $\beta_{max} = 0.0782$ obtained by Algorithm 3. It is shown from Fig. 2 that the errors in these four cases tend to be stable, indicating that Algorithms 2 and 3 are reliable.

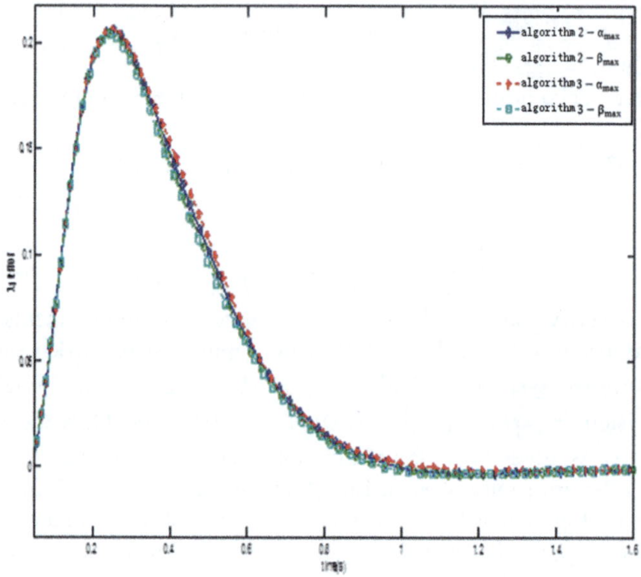

Fig. 2. Comparison of observation errors under the largest Lipschitz constant

4 Conclusion

For the double Lipschitz nonlinear system, the stability of observer error state system, the design of observer gain matrix and the maximization of Lipschitz constant are mainly solved. The main conclusions are as follows:

(1) Two independent sufficient conditions for the stability of observational error state systems are obtained by using Lyapunov method. Two methods for designing observational gain matrices of such systems are obtained by using matrix inequality (MI) method.
(2) Algorithms for solving the maximum allowable upper limit of the Lipschitz constant of the state equation and the observation equation are proposed.
(3) A numerical example is used to simulate the observed error of the designed observed gain matrix and under the maximum permissible upper limit of Lipschitz constant. The simulation results show that the relevant conclusions obtained in this paper are correct and feasible.

(4) Because observer design method is an important method in the field of robust fault diagnosis, these results can be applied to the field of robust fault diagnosis.

Acknowledgments. This work was supported by science and technology research project of Ezhou University in China (Project No. 2018YB09).

References

1. Thau FE (1973) Observing the state of nonlinear dynamic systems. Int J Control 17(3):471–479
2. Zhang W, Su HS, Liang Y, Han ZZ (2012) Full-order and reduced-order observers for one-sided Lipschitz nonlinear systems using Riccati equations. Commun Nonlinear Sci Numer Simul 17:4968–4977
3. Raghavan S, Hedrick J (1994) Observer design for a class of nonlinear systems. Int J Control 59(2):515–528
4. Phanomchoeng G, Rajamani R (2010) Observer design for Lipschitz nonlinear systems using Riccati equations. In: American control conference (ACC), pp 6060–6065
5. Garg V, Hedrick J (1996) Fault detection filters for a class of nonlinear systems. In: Proceedings of American control conference, Seattle, Washington, pp 1647–1651
6. Rajamani R (1998) Observers for Lipschitz nonlinear systems. IEEE Trans Autom Control 43(3):397–401
7. Zemouche A, Boutayeb M (2012) Observers for continuous-time Lipschitz nonlinear systems. Analysis and comparisons. In: 51st IEEE conference on decision and control, Maui, Hawaii, USA, pp 10–13
8. Zhang W, Su HS, Liang Y, Han ZZ (2012) Non-linear observer design for one-sided Lipschitz systems: an linear matrix inequality approach. IET Control Theory Appl 6 (9):1297–1303
9. Song B, Hedrick K (2011) Nonlinear observer design for Lipschitz nonlinear systems. In: 2011 American control conference on O'Farrell Street, San Francisco, CA, USA, pp 2578–2583
10. Abbaszadeh M, Marquez HJ (2006) A robust observer design method for continuous time Lipschitz. In: Proceedings of the 45th IEEE conference on decision & control Manchester Grand Hyatt Hotel San Diego, CA, USA, pp 3895–3900

Research on Speech Enhancement Algorithms Based on Blind Source Separation in Outdoor Environment

Chunli Wang(✉) and Quanyu Wang

Department of Electronics and Information Engineering, Lanzhou Jiaotong University, Lanzhou, Gansu, China
wcl@mail.lzjtu.cn

Abstract. Aiming at the complex environmental noise, unknown channel parameters and dynamic changes of the receiver position with the mobile phone communication outdoors, a blind source separation algorithm based on microphone arrays is adopted, and the combined algorithms of the fast ICA and spectral subtraction are used to ensure the intelligibility. The maximum noise suppression is achieved. The simulation results show that the residual music noise is basically eliminated, the signal-to-noise ratio is improved, and the enhanced speech waveform is smoother.

Keywords: Microphone array · Blind source separation · Fast ICA · Spectral subtraction · Intelligibility

1 Introduction

In daily life, outdoor mobile phone voice communication often encounters noise interference problems, such as whistling cars, high-profile passers-by, all kinds of machine running sounds will be collected into the mobile phone microphone, if not processed, such signals will be carried out after being encoded and transmitted to the other end, the speech signal and the noise signal are interlaced and aliased, and it is difficult for the receiving end to hear the speech content and affect the normal voice communication. Therefore, obtaining a high-quality voice signal in an outdoor noise environment is an urgent problem to be solved by the voice enhancement technology.

2 Fast ICA Algorithm

The fast ICA algorithm, Fast ICA algorithm, also known as fixed-point recursive algorithm, is a fast optimization iterative algorithm proposed in the late 1990s [1, 2]. It uses batch processing to process signal data, and each iteration has more signal data involved in the operation. Among them, the negative entropy-based Fast ICA search target is to maximize negative entropy [3]. It can be known from the central limit theorem that the Gaussian property of linear combination of multiple independent signal sources is stronger than that of each signal source, that is, the non-Gaussian property of each source signal is stronger than that of the mixed signal [4, 5].

Z. Xu et al. (Eds.): CSIA 2019, AISC 928, pp. 837–842, 2020.
https://doi.org/10.1007/978-3-030-15235-2_112

Therefore, in all random signals with equal variance, the entropy of the Gaussian variable is smaller, that is, the larger the negative entropy, the stronger the non-Gaussian property [6, 7]. Using this mechanism, the independence of the separated signals can be judged by measuring the non-Gaussian of the separation results in the blind source separation process: when the non-Gaussian metric reaches the maximum, it indicates that the individual components have been separated [8, 9].

3 Implementation of Outdoor Speech Enhancement Algorithm Based on Fast ICA Algorithm

The fast ICA algorithm is not very high in hardware processing capacity, and it occupies less memory. It converges faster than the traditional ICA algorithm, and its performance can be optimized by a nonlinear function [10, 11]. Compared with indoors, the outdoor voice environment is more complicated in noise environment, more interference signals, and more obvious noise. The signal-to-noise ratio of the mixed signals received by each array element of the microphone array is different. In the simulation experiment based on MATLAB, the white noise white.wav is selected as the background noise, and the sa1.wav in the standard speech library is the speech signal, where Mixi represents the speech signal received by the i-th microphone, and noisei and Noisei respectively indicate The pure speech signal component and the noise component of the mixed signal received by the microphone i. The signal construction process is as follows:

a1 = audioread('E:\sa1.wav') noise1 = audioread('E:\white.wav')
Noise1 = audioread('E:\Noise1.wav');% Read in noise signal
Noise2 = Noise1 = Noise3 noise1 = noise2 = noise3
Signal received by microphone a: Mix1 = a1 + 0.5 * noise1 + 0.2 * Noise1. The signal to noise ratio is 5.104 dB;

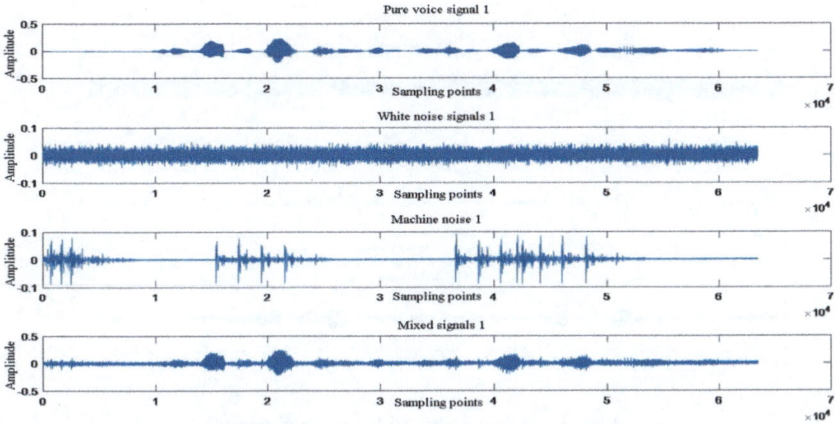

Fig. 1. Mixed signal received by microphone a

Signal received by microphone b: Mix2 = a2 + 0.4 * noise2 + 0.6 * Noise2. The signal to noise ratio is −2.9562 dB;
Signal received by microphone c: Mix3 = a3 + 0.8*noise3 + 0.8 * Noise3. The signal to noise ratio is −5.6215 dB.

The above three microphone array elements receive a mixed signal of a speech signal and a noise signal, and the speech signal to noise ratios of the microphones b and c are all less than 0, and the simulation result is shown in Figs. 1, 2 and 3.

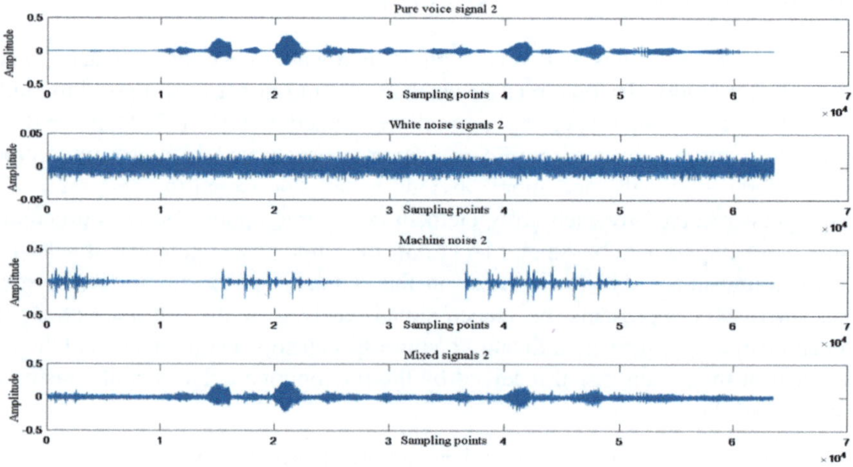

Fig. 2. Mixed signal received by microphone b

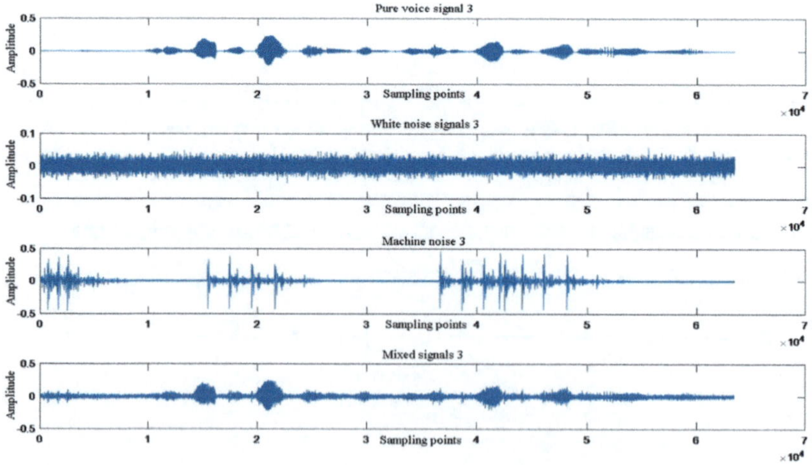

Fig. 3. Signal received by microphone c

4 Fast ICA Algorithm Combined with Spectral Subtraction for Speech Enhancement

Under the condition of strong outdoor noise, the ICA demixing is first carried out. According to the ICA separation result, the three signal components separated by ICA are not pure speech signals, and the two signals are mixed with noise signal components, and the other is It is a noise signal component, and the second separation signal is the best estimate of the original speech signal, and then the separated signal is spectrally subtracted to achieve further noise suppression. Before the enhancement, the signal-to-noise ratio of the signals received by the three elements is: 5.1004 dB, −2.9562 dB, −5.6215 dB. After ICA separation, the signal-to-noise ratio is 40.5769 dB after the spectral reduction is further reduced. As shown in Figs. 4, 5 and 6, the signal-to-noise ratio of the speech signal is improved and significantly enhanced.

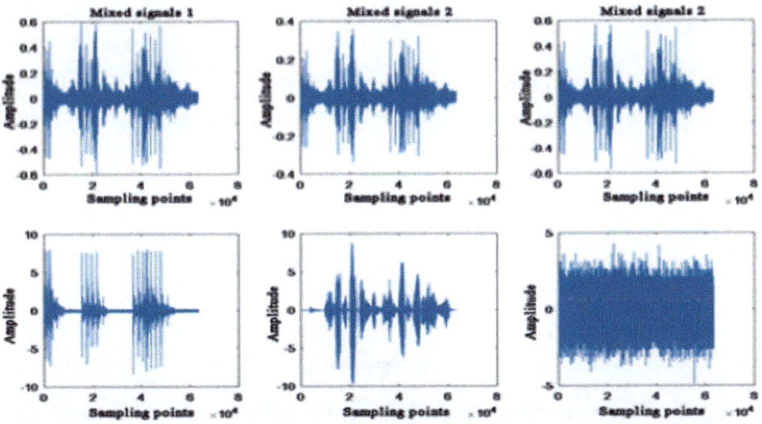

Fig. 4. ICA separation results

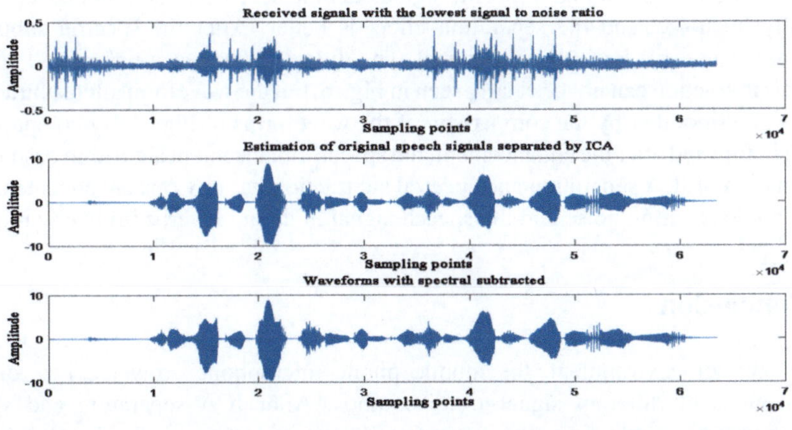

Fig. 5. Microphone array element receiving signal, ICA separated speech signal, spectrum subtracted signal waveform

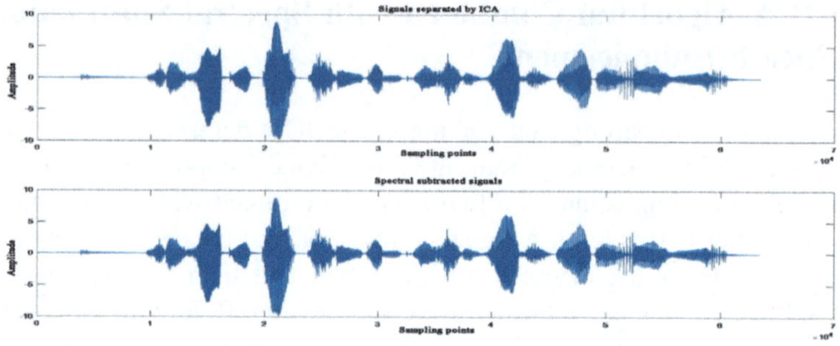

Fig. 6. Waveform signal waveform before and after spectral subtraction

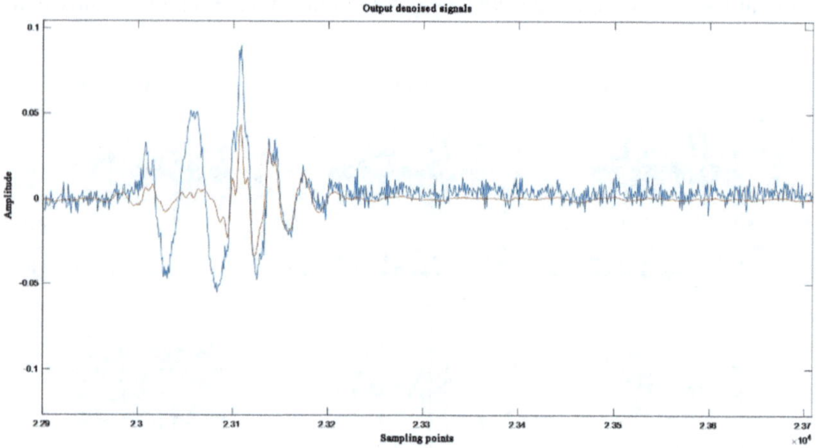

Fig. 7. Waveform comparison chart before and after spectral subtraction

From the analysis of the waveform before and after the spectrum subtraction, it can be seen from the analysis of Fig. 7 that the signal after the ICA separation (orange curve) has basically no noise, and the separation effect is better. After the spectral subtraction method, the noise is basically eliminated. The difference between before and after the spectral subtraction can not be clearly seen in Fig. 6, but the waveform after subtraction is found to be smoother by the comparison of the waveforms of Fig. 7. By comparing the speech before and after the enhancement, the speech enhancement algorithm based on the combination of ICA separation and spectral subtraction has obvious enhancement effect on the outdoor strong noise and the speech signal in the no reverberation environment.

5 Conclusion

In the outdoor environment, the mobile phone microphone array receives different voice signals of different signal-to-noise ratios. After ICA separation and spectral subtraction noise reduction, the background noise of the source signal is greatly reduced, and the voice quality is significantly improved. The feasibility of the speech enhancement algorithm combining fast ICA algorithm and spectral subtraction in speech enhancement technology based on mobile phone microphone array. The algorithm also has some shortcomings. The external noise set by the experiment is relatively simple, the sound source is less, and the signal-to-noise ratio is not accurate enough. In addition, because the ICA algorithm has the problem of unmixed signal amplitude and sorting uncertainty, when using the spectral subtraction method for noise reduction, the artificial selection signal is needed, and the algorithm should be further improved by the algorithm of automatic selection property.

References

1. Yan H (2013) Research on speech enhancement algorithm based on microphone array. Yanshan University, Qinhuangdao (in Chinese)
2. Li H (2011) Digital signal processing and MATLAB implementation. Mechanical Industry Press, Beijing (in Chinese)
3. Zhou S, Song Y, Wu G (2012) Research on speech enhancement based on microphone array. Comput Technol Dev 22(7):204–210 (in Chinese)
4. Kuo SM, Lee BH, Tian W (2017) Principle, implementation and application of digital signal processing. Tsinghua University Press, Beijing (in Chinese)
5. Yu L (2015) Research on speech enhancement method based on mobile phone microphone array. University of Electronic Science and Technology of China, Beijing (in Chinese)
6. Zhang X, Chen H, Qiu X (2015) Array signal processing and MATLAB implementation. Publishing House of Electronics Industry, Beijing (in Chinese)
7. Zhang X (2015) Modern signal processing. Tsinghua University Press, Beijing (in Chinese)
8. Ma Z, Xu Y, Ni Z (2017) Speech enhancement of microphone array based on CTF-GSC and post filtering. J Northwest Univ 47(6):829–837 (in Chinese)
9. Wang Z (2015) Research and implementation of microphone array speech processing based on beamforming algorithm. Harbin Institute of Technology, Harbin (in Chinese)
10. Song G (2016) Research on indoor speech localization algorithm based on microphone array. Nanjing University of Information Science and Technology, Nanjing (in Chinese)
11. Yu C, Su L (2015) Speech enhancement method of microphone array Based on GSC and spectral subtraction method. J Shenyang Aerosp Univ 32(5):80–85 (in Chinese)

An Improved Apriori Algorithm Research in Massive Data Environment

Yu Xu, Ranzhi Zhan, Gang Tan, Lu Chen(✉), and BoJin Tian

State Grid Chongqing Electric Power Company
Information Communication Branch, Chongqing 400000, China
zyc_hd@sina.com

Abstract. Smart grid computing environment is an information platform that has lots of production data, data management, and the real-time and non real-time data. Under such massive data environment, the classic Apriori algorithm of mining association rules has a significant performance bottleneck. After analyzing the Apriori algorithm, the MapReduce programming model is used to realize the parallel Apriori algorithm. In order to improve the mining efficiency further, auxiliary tables and attribute columns are added and parallel strategy is improved in the process of candidate itemsets generation. Simulation experiments show that the improved Apriori algorithm can effectively reduce the algorithm execution time and improve the efficiency of data mining under the massive data environment.

Keywords: Data mining · Apriori algorithm · MapReduce · Smart grid

1 Introduction

In recent years, with the rapid development of computer and Internet technology, people's activity in the network world is increasingly frequent, and the data in Internet show explosive growth. In this information age, many enterprises or individuals hope to mine valuable information and patterns from these massive complex data to help them find rules and make policy decision.

Data mining is using the specific technologies to extract the implicit and potentially valuable information from massive data stored in the database [1]. Association rule mining is an important branch of data mining, and it collects a great deal of the transaction records in the database to analyze and find the relationship between huge amounts of data. In the smart grid, analyze power users' behavior, to help power grid enterprises to make policy decision, to realize intelligent services, to construct smart grid system and meet the diverse needs of users.

Apriori algorithm is one of the most famous in the association rules algorithm. However, the traditional Apriori algorithm has obvious performance bottlenecks. Although there are many improved algorithms, but many of the algorithms are used to approximate the algorithm [2]. With the rapid development of computer technology, cloud computing has become the direction of the future development of distributed computing. Google's MapReduce programming framework is representative of cloud computing technology. It is suitable for the distributed processing of large data

Z. Xu et al. (Eds.): CSIA 2019, AISC 928, pp. 843–851, 2020.
https://doi.org/10.1007/978-3-030-15235-2_113

sets and has a high computational efficiency. Using MapReduce to realize the parallelization of Apriori algorithm can effectively improve the operation efficiency of Apriori algorithm [3].

2 Association Rules

2.1 Association Rules Description

Association rules, that is, to reflect the interdependence and interconnectedness between one thing and other things. If there is an association between two or more things, it can be predicted from the known things to other unknown things.

In the various methods of data mining, association rules analysis is most commonly used. Analysis of association rules launches certain regularity by mining hidden relationships between properties from large complex data set. A typical example is the shopping cart problem. By finding the connection between the different goods in the shopping cart, analyze customer buying habits further, and then develop marketing strategy for the enterprise [4].

2.2 Association Rules Definition

In the transaction database D, set $I = \{i_1, i_2, \ldots, i_d\}$ as the collection of all items, set $T = \{t_1, t_2, \ldots, t_n\}$ as the collection of all transactions, and each item in transaction t_i is a subset of I [5].

In the analysis of association rules, a collection of multiple items is called itemsets. For example, an itemsets contains k items, so this itemsets is called k-itemsets. Association rules expression $\mathrm{A} \Rightarrow \mathrm{B}$, in which A and B is a non empty subset of I, and $\mathrm{A} \cap \mathrm{B} = \emptyset$.

Association rules $\mathrm{A} \Rightarrow \mathrm{B}$ in database D also need to meet two important thresholds: the support and confidence.

Support is the percentage of transaction which contains both A and B, that is, $\mathrm{support}(\mathrm{A} \Rightarrow \mathrm{B}) = \mathrm{P}(\mathrm{A} \cup \mathrm{B})$.

Confidence is the percentage of transaction which contains both A and B account for the transaction only containing A, that is, $\mathrm{confidence}(\mathrm{A} \Rightarrow \mathrm{B}) = \mathrm{P}(\mathrm{B}|\mathrm{A})$.

2.3 Association Rules Mining

The problem of mining association rules is to find the association rule which meet the user's specified minimum support min_sup and minimum confidence min_conf in database D. Association rule mining is generally divided into the following two steps [6]: (1) Find all frequent itemsets in D according to the minimum support. That is, if $\mathrm{support(A)} \geq \mathrm{min\_sup}$, then A is called frequent itemsets. This is the core of the association rules mining process, and also a measure standard of the algorithm efficiency. (2) Use frequent itemsets to generate association rules. The generated rules must satisfy the minimum support and minimum confidence.

3 Apriori Algorithm

3.1 Apriori Algorithm Description

Apriori algorithm proposed by Agrawal et al. in 1994 is the most influential association rules analysis algorithm. The algorithm using iterative method of layered search, scanning database repeatedly, find all frequent itemsets [7]. In the process of getting higher frequent itemsets, the following two properties of association rules are used: (1) A subset of frequent itemsets is also frequent itemsets. (2) A superset of non frequent itemsets is also non frequent itemsets.

3.2 The Principle of Apriori Algorithm

Apriori algorithm steps are as follows [8]:

(1) Set the minimum support min_sup and minimum confidence min_conf.
(2) Read in all transactions from database, each item in the transaction is considered as candidate 1-itemsets; record the set of candidate 1-itemsets as C1.
(3) Calculate the support of each item in C1, select the items which support is no less than min_sup, they are frequent 1-itemsets, recorded as L1.
(4) L1 connect itself to generate C2, the set of candidate itemsets which contain two data items; Count the support of each item in C2 in the database, then get the frequent 2-itemsets L2.
(5) The k ($k \geq 3$) cycles, divided into three steps.
Connect: Frequent ($k - 1$)-itemsets L($k - 1$) connect itself to generate Ck, the set of candidate k-itemsets. Prune: If subset ($k - 1$) of one itemsets in Ck is not in L ($k - 1$), then remove the itemsets from Ck. Get frequent itemsets: Count the support of each candidate itemsets in Ck, then get the frequent k-itemsets Lk.
(6) Repeat scanning database, until there is no new frequent itemsets.

3.3 The Shortage of the Apriori Algorithm

From the implementation steps of the Apriori algorithm, it has obvious problems [9].

The generation of candidate itemsets involves a large amount of calculation. When the database is in large scale, it will become the bottleneck of algorithm performance.

Repeat scanning database, causing huge consumption of time and memory space, increase the burden on the I/O.

4 Parallel Apriori Algorithm in Massive Data Environment

Under the environment of massive data, cloud computing has characteristics of distributed parallel, and support parallel execution of algorithm, thus to improve the mining efficiency. Cloud computing use the MapReduce programming model, and include two steps Map and Reduce to achieve tasks scheduling and allocation in large-scale computing nodes.

Map and Reduce are the core functions of MapReduce. First, simply process the Map function of user, take the input data for operation, and then get the generation of key/value pairs. Second, the data of same key are collected into the MapReduce library, and passed to the Reduce function. Third, Reduce function obtains these data of same key, and merges them into a smaller set of values. Programs that use such functions can be automatically distributed to a large cluster composed of ordinary machines. This model allows programmers to deal with the resource of large distributed systems without the need for any concurrent processing or distributed systems experience [10].

The basic idea of traditional Apriori algorithm is assigning computing tasks to N nodes, and each node using the Apriori algorithm to calculate. Operation Steps are just as shown in Fig. 1:

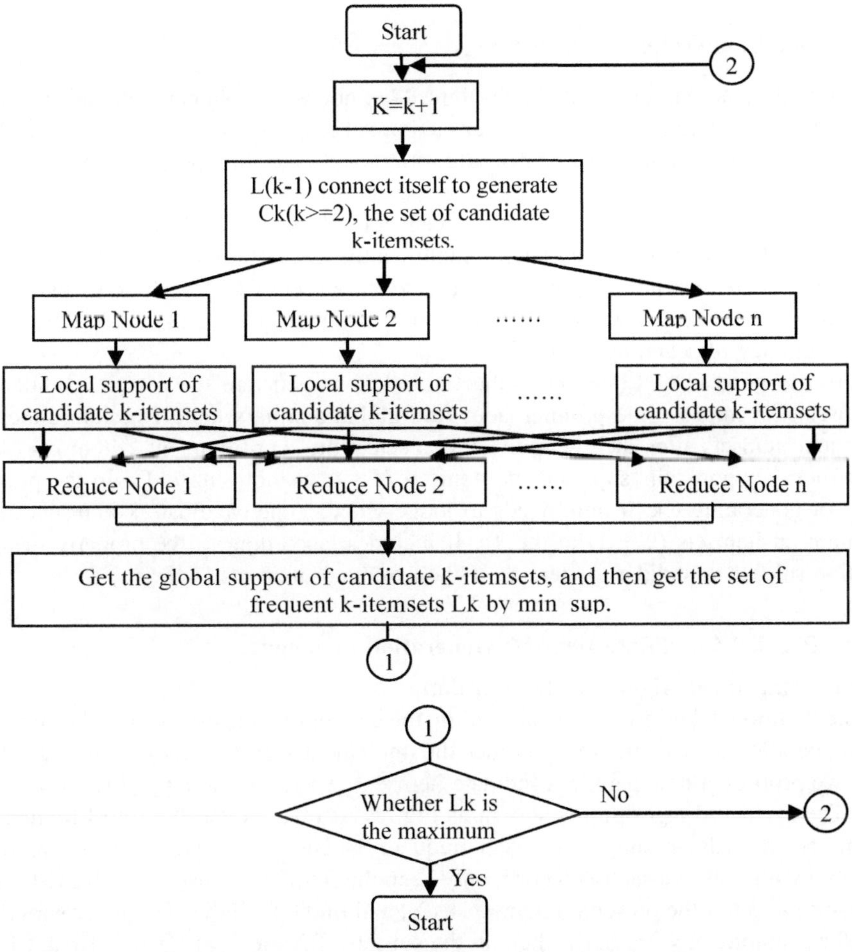

Fig. 1. Operation steps of parallel Apriori algorithm.

(1) Divide the database into N equal size sub databases, and send them to N different Map nodes.
(2) Use the MapReduce model to get the set of frequent 1-itemsets L1.
(3) L(k − 1) connect itself to generate Ck(k ≥ 2), the set of candidate k-itemsets, and send Ck to each Map node.
(4) Map node calculates the support of each itemsets of Ck in the sub database.
(5) Use hash function to send the same itemsets and support of N Map nodes to Reduce nodes.
(6) The Reduce nodes count the support of candidate itemsets in Ck, and then get the global support of candidate k-itemsets.
(7) Select the set of frequent k-itemsets Lk by the minimum support min_sup.

5 The Improved Apriori Algorithm Parallel Strategy

5.1 Database Optimization Strategy

In the traditional Apriori parallel algorithm, Map nodes work in parallel, and each Map task process different sub database transaction set respectively. In terms of each Map node, it still perform iterative Apriori algorithm, and algorithm performance is still not high [11].

In each Map node, execute pre-treatment for sub database. Back up sub database, and then add an attribute "transaction length" in the transaction table. When a Map task requires computing the support of candidate k-itemsets Ck (length is k) in the sub database, do not need to scan the transaction of which length is less than k, thus reduce the frequency of scanning data [12].

In the process of L(k − 1) connecting itself to generate the set of candidate k-itemsets Ck, improve the pruning step. Add global auxiliary table Ts to store the non frequent itemsets after each iteration. When select the set of frequent k-itemsets Lk by minimum support min_sup, add the itemsets less than min_sup to Ts. In the pruning step of generating Ck, it only needs to judge whether the candidate k-itemsets of Ck contain an itemsets (k − 1) in the Ts. If includes, according to the property of association rule, the candidate k-itemsets is non frequent itemsets [13].

5.2 Parallel Candidate Itemsets Generation Strategy

5.2.1 Improved Algorithm Description

In the traditional Apriori parallel algorithm, the generation process of candidate itemsets is not parallel, which will greatly reduce the implementation efficiency of the algorithm. So, we propose a new parallel candidate itemsets generation strategy [14, 15].

The improved algorithm is shown as Fig. 2. At first, we get the set of frequent 1-itemsets L1 and the support of each frequent 1-itemsets. In each Map node, when dealing with each transaction record, only keep the frequent itemsets which exist in L1. Record the set of the preserved itemsets as X, and find out all the non empty subsets of X (for example, X = {a, b, c}, then all the subsets of X are {{a}, {b}, {c}, {a, b}, {b, c}, {a, c}, {a, b, c}}), and then record the set of them as G. Each itemsets in G can be used as a candidate itemsets, and set support of each candidate itemsets as 1. After all the transactions are processed, count the support of the same candidate itemsets, and then send <candidate itemsets, support> to Reduce nodes as <key, value>. In each Reduce node, count candidate itemsets and its support of each Map node, and compared with the minimum support min_sup, then get the frequent itemsets Lk.

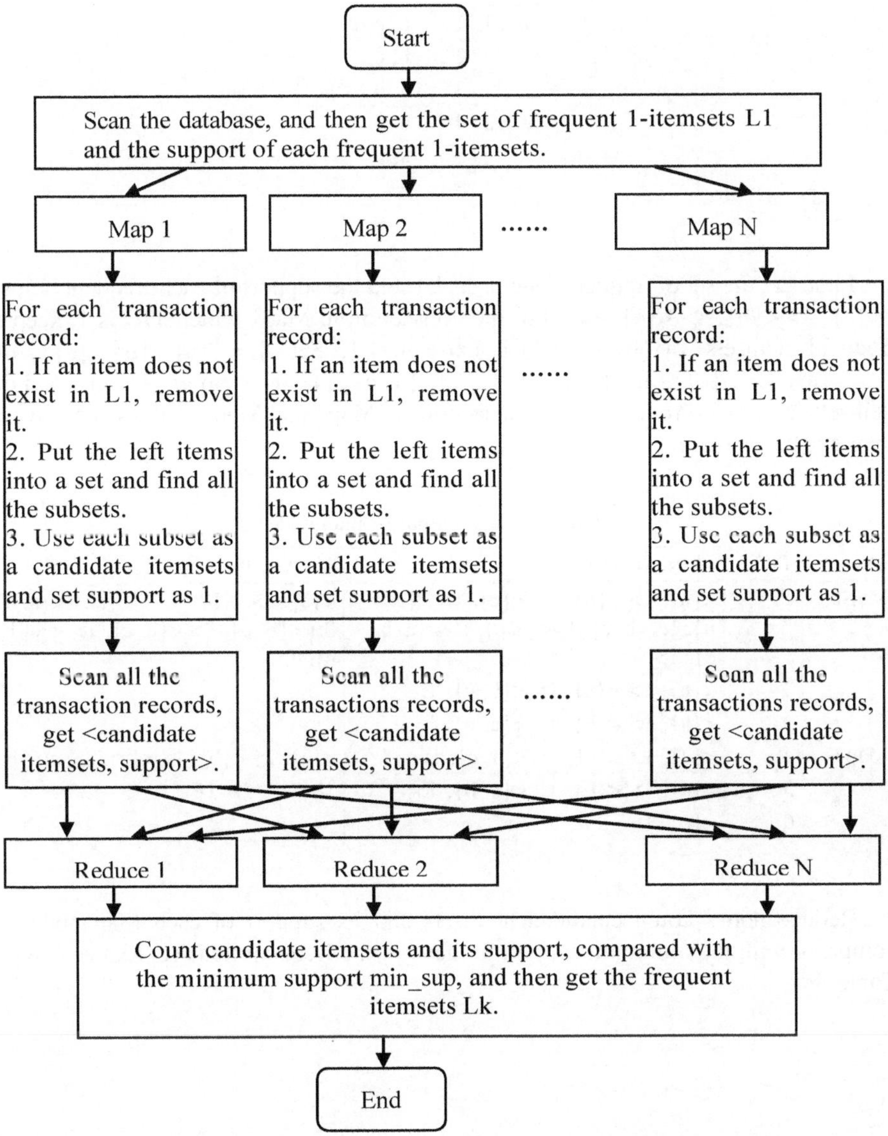

Fig. 2. Operation steps of the improved algorithm

5.2.2 Algorithm Example

The following example is to illustrate the algorithm implementation process.

Database is divided into two sub databases, each sub database has 3 transaction records, and the minimum support is 3, as shown in Table 1.

Table 1. Transaction records in the database.

Map	TID	Item list
Map1	1	a, b, c
	2	b, c
	3	a, b
Map2	4	a, c
	5	a, b
	6	c

First, get the set of frequent 1-itemsets L1 and the support of each frequent itemsets {<{a}, 4> <{b}, 4> <{c}, 4>}. For the transaction in Map1 which TID is 1, keep the frequent itemsets {a}{b}{c} which exist in L1. Set X = {{a}, {b}, {c}}, then G = {{a}, {b}, {c}, {a, b}, {b, c}, {a, c}, {a, b, c}}. Set support of each candidate itemsets in G as 1. Process all the transactions in Map1 and Map2 in the same way, and then get the Table 2.

Table 2. The output of map node.

Map	TID	<key, value>	<key, value> by map
Map1	1	<{a}, 1> <{b}, 1> <{c}, 1> <{a, b}, 1> <b, c}, 1><{a, c}, 1> <{a, b, c}, 1>	<{a}, 2> <{b}, 3> <{c}, 2> <{a, b}, 2> <{b, c}, 2> <{a, c}, 1> <{a, b, c}, 1>
	2	<{b}, 1> <{c}, 1> <{b, c}, 1>	
	3	<{a}, 1> <{b}, 1> <{a, b}, 1>	
Map2	4	<{a}, 1> <{c}, 1> <{a, c}, 1>	<{a}, 2> <{b}, 1> <{c}, 2> <{a, b}, 1> <{a, c}, 1>
	5	<{a}, 1> <{b}, 1> <{a, b}, 1>	
	6	<{c}, 1>	

Reduce nodes count candidate itemsets and its support of each Map node, and compared with the minimum support 3, then get the frequent itemsets Lk, as shown in Table 3.

Table 3. Get the frequent itemsets Lk.

Candidate itemsets	Support	Frequent itemsets Lk
{a}	4	{{a}, {b}, {c}, {a, b}}
{b}	4	
{c}	4	{{a}, {b}, {c}, {a, b}}
{a, b}	3	
{b, c}	2	
{a, c}	2	
{a, b, c}	1	

6 The Experiment and Analysis

In order to verify the improved Apriori algorithm can effectively improve the mining efficiency under the environment of massive data, now we compare improved Apriori algorithm and the classical Apriori algorithm under the same experimental conditions.

Experiment preparation: Built a Hadoop platform with 3 machines, the machines are configured as: Intel(R) Core(TM) i5-2400 4-core CPU@2.60 GHz, 4 GB RAM. Hadoop version is 2.2.0. Operation system is Linux. The experiment data uses the user basic electricity data of simulation grid, and the number of transaction records is 897200.

The experimental results of classic Apriori algorithm, parallel Apriori algorithm and the improved parallel algorithm are shown in Fig. 3. With the increase of the minimum support, the number of frequent itemsets is reduced, and the algorithm running time is greatly reduced. The experimental results show that compared with the classical Apriori algorithm, the execution time of parallel Apriori algorithm is greatly reduced, and compared with the former two algorithms, the improved parallel algorithm improve the efficiency of data mining further.

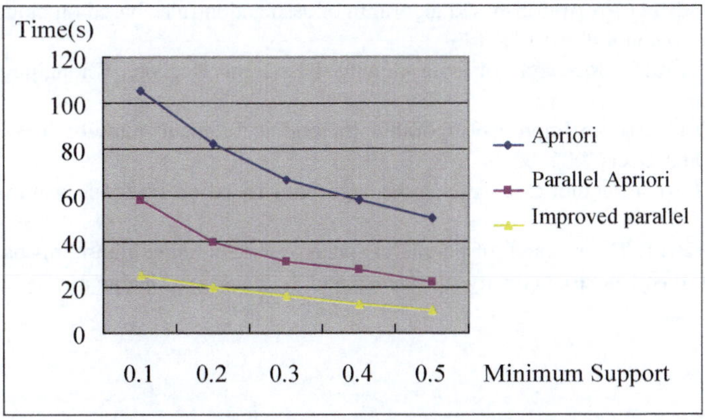

Fig. 3. The comparison of the different algorithms.

7 Summary

Aiming at massive user basic electricity data in the smart grid, an improved strategy is proposed on the basis of the classic Apriori algorithm. According to the distributed environment of cloud computing, the MapReduce programming model is used for implementing parallel Apriori algorithm. Based on the parallel Apriori algorithm, execute pre-treatment for the database to reduce scan frequency of database transaction, and then improve efficiency of mining frequent itemsets. Finally, according to the shortage that the parallel Apriori algorithm remains, new parallel strategy is proposed. The improved parallel strategy only needs to scan global database twice. Under the environment of massive data, data mining performance will be improved significantly.

References

1. Zhu M (2002) Data mining. Hefei, University of Science and Technology of China Press
2. Yang X (2014) Improvement and application of association rules algorithm for big data. Comput Modern 12:23–26
3. Zhu A (2012) Study on improvement and transplantation of Apriori algorithm based on Hadoop. Huazhong University of Science and Technology, Wuhan
4. Li L, Zhang M (2011) Research on algorithms of mining association rule under cloud computing environment. Comput Technol Dev 21(2):43–46
5. Chen Y (2011) Data mining technology and application. Tsinghua University Press, Beijing
6. Xu Z, Liu M, Zhang S, Lu J, Ou Y (2004) Three kinds of optimization methods of Apriori algorithm. Comput Eng Appl 40(36):190–192
7. Xie G, Luo S (2010) Research based on the application of Hadoop MapReduce model. Microcomput Appl 29(8):4–7
8. Che B (2013) Key technology research-based the Hadoop of massive data processing. University of Electronic Science and Technology of China, Chengdu
9. Qian G, Jia R, Zhang R, Li L (2008) One optimized method of Apriori algorithm. Comput Eng 34(23):196–198
10. Liu H, Guo R, Jiang H (2009) Research and improvement of Apriori algorithm for mining association rules. Comput Appl Softw 26(1):146–149
11. Zhang S (2011) An Apriori-based algorithm of association rules based on cloud computing. Commun Technol 44(6):141–143
12. Yang C (2010) Research of data mining based on Hadoop. Chongqing University, Chongqing
13. Zhang Q (2015) An improved algorithm for finding frequent itemsets in association rule mining. Stat Decis 4:32–35
14. Chen L (2012) Parallel association rules algorithm based on Hadoop. Nanjing University, Nanjing
15. Mao W (2014) The research of parallel association rules mining algorithms based on cloud platform. East China University of Science and Technology, Shanghai

Research on the Development Trend of Online Education Industry Considering the Influence of Big Data and Artificial Intelligence

Yong Fu(✉)

Sichuan Agricultural University,
Ya'an 625014, Sichuan, People's Republic of China
fuyonga6666@163.com

Abstract. With the concept of lifelong education being widely recognized, people's demand for education and training is growing, and online education has gradually become one of the important ways for people to meet the needs of education and training. Through analysis, it is found that online education also faces the development bottleneck of the lack of on-site teaching sense, systemic needs to be improved, the course completion rate is low, the quality of the course is difficult to guarantee, the teacher's teaching pressure is high, and lack of social recognition, which restricts the further development. With the help of current technology hotspots – big data and artificial intelligence, we can effectively break through the above bottlenecks and make the online education industry maintain rapid development. This paper analyzes the root causes of the problems in the current online education and discusses the solutions to improve online education.

Keywords: Online education industry · Big data · Artificial intelligence · Online education development trend

1 Introduction

Online education is a network-based approach to teaching, through the application of information technology and Internet technology for content dissemination and rapid learning methods, the development of online education, while being influenced by the development of information technology and mobile Internet technology, and also by the development of education and training itself. Impact [1–3]. Traditional education and training has relied heavily on the professional level and teaching skills of the instructors. Especially in the school education stage, the education is centered on the teacher, and the teaching teacher decides the teaching arrangement, implements the teaching, and corrects the assignment. As the research on adult education and training continues to mature, the student-centered view is increasingly recognized [4–7]. With the explosive development of information technology and mobile Internet technology, the integration of big data and education and training industry can help educators to more accurately understand the information, skill level, learning habits and other information of the educated, so as to improve the teaching in a targeted manner. Link

Z. Xu et al. (Eds.): CSIA 2019, AISC 928, pp. 852–859, 2020.
https://doi.org/10.1007/978-3-030-15235-2_114

and ultimately improve the quality of teaching [8–12]. At the same time, the rapid development of artificial intelligence technology has also emerged in recent years. The deep integration of artificial intelligence and education and training is not limited to examination robots. Examination robots are actually a kind of complex with deep learning, expert system and natural language understanding. The system, for further research and development of this complex system, will have a profound impact on the entire education and training industry [12–15]. The online education industry, as the educational industry of mobile Internet with integrated information technology, will be affected by the impact of big data and artificial intelligence technology, and will generate new growth points [16–20].

2 Status Quo of Online Education Industry Development

2.1 Status of the Development of Foreign Online Education Industry

2.1.1 United States

The United States has been at the forefront of research in information technology. The online education industry has also blossomed with the support of its advanced information technology. At the same time, the US government is also very supportive of the online education industry, and revised a series of policies to promote the development of online education. In such a favorable environment, the online education industry in the United States has developed rapidly. After the "first year of online education" in 2012, the three online education platforms (Coursera, Udacity, Edx) grew rapidly by MOOC, and they integrated a large number of high-quality educational resources in a short period of time and implemented them on the Internet. And sharing, breaking the boundaries of higher education. This model has swept the world and has received a lot of attention and reference from higher education worldwide. At the same time, some American colleges have also launched their own online education courses to meet the needs of different students. Although MOOC brings a lot of conveniences, it also exposes many problems, mainly in the quality of the courses, the low recognition of teachers on online education, the low completion rate of the courses, and the problem of regionalization. Although MOOC is very popular among students, its non-certified, non-mandatory and non-degree qualifications restrict its further development. Therefore, how to make up for the above shortcomings is a difficult problem to be solved in the current US online education.

2.1.2 India

India is the same country as China, and it is also a populous country, also a developing country. Therefore, the development of online education industry in India can be used as a reference for the development of China's online education industry. India's lack of resources for higher education has led many Indian youth to focus on acquiring knowledge through online learning. According to statistics, the proportion of Indian students registered in the US online education platform is as high as 10%. India's online educational resources are concentrated in several national universities in the country, including the Indira Gandhi National Open University, which has transplanted the UK's open education model and some courses. However, in the process of transplantation, problems such as dissatisfaction with water and soil have also arisen, including professional settings that are inconsistent with market demand, unresolved educational equity issues, and difficult to guarantee course quality. Although there are many problems in online education in India, it is worthwhile to learn from the degree of recognition of online education. For students who have passed the online education, those who pass the test can obtain the qualification certificate issued by the university.

2.1.3 Japan

Japan and China have a long history of exchanges and learning. The two countries are not only geographically similar, but also have similarities in population density, cultural cognition, and living habits. Therefore, online education in Japan is also very useful for China. Online education in Japan is mainly based on academic education. Unlike online education in other countries, Japan's online education and credits are more closely integrated, even more demanding than school education. Not only are online education courses strictly produced and reviewed. After completing the online education course, you also need to take a written test at the prescribed test center. It can be seen that Japan attaches great importance to the quality of education in online education. At the same time, Japan also emphasized that the homogenization of online education not only led the development of unified specifications of electronic textbooks, but also developed a unified education cloud platform. Although the development of online education in Japan has begun to take shape and has good development opportunities, it is still difficult to face many problems such as shortage of funds, shortage of teachers, and ineffective teaching effects. How to further utilize existing advantages to absorb funds and train more teachers Accurate evaluation and improvement of teaching effects are the focus of current online education development in Japan.

2.2 Bottlenecks in the Development of Online Education Industry in China

Due to the uneven distribution of educational resources in China, high-quality educational resources are often concentrated in first-tier cities. Therefore, the demand for quality education resources in second- and third-tier cities is very large. At the same time, first-tier cities are not only K12 (mainly refers to primary schools) because of their faster pace. In the three stages of junior high school and high school, the increasing learning pressure, the working population is experiencing a spurt of growth in the demand for learning and growth under the increasing pressure of competition. The rise of online education just meets these strong educational needs. Therefore, when online education sprouted in China, it has received extensive attention. Many traditional educational institutions have quickly completed the Internet transformation and absorbed a large amount of investment in the short term. A group of people who eat crabs have achieved leapfrog development. As shown in Fig. 1, from 2012 to 2018, the market size of China's online education industry and the growth rate of users have remained above 20%, and has doubled in just four years. In 2018, China's online education industry market has exceeded 650 billion yuan, and its user scale has reached

20 million. This shows that its development is rapid. It can be seen that the online interest education market has strong potential and needs to be explored.

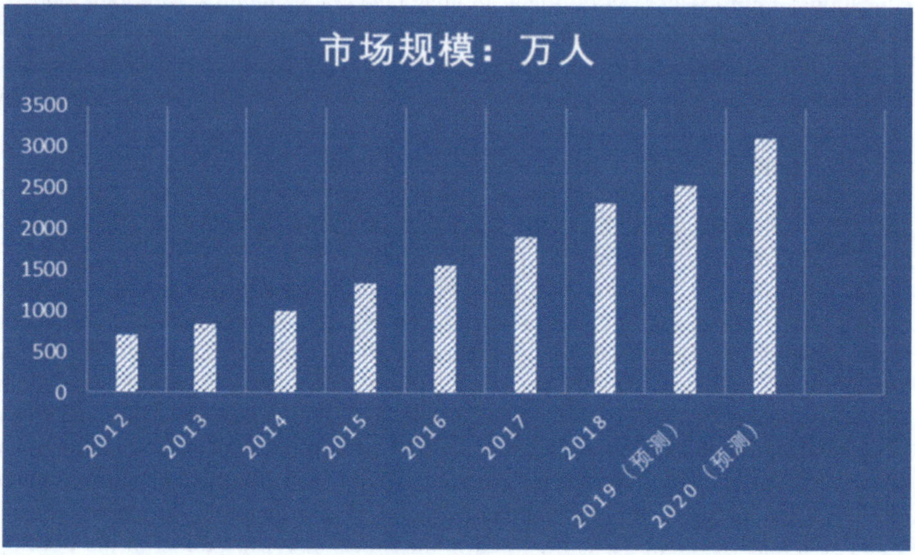

Fig. 1. China online education industry market population chart

3 The Development Trend of Online Education Industry

3.1 Diversification of Educational Resources

In the future, online education will surely present a diversified educational resources, including recording and live courses, a large number of lecturer resources, artificial intelligence teachers, etc. The diversification of these educational resources will give educational objects more choices. Due to the diversification of educational resources, there will be a trend of "three-person must have my teacher". More and more people are becoming training targets for online education, and more and more people have become providers of educational resources. No matter in which field, one's knowledge, skills, practical insights, experience and experience will be collected by big data and provided to others to learn. Everyone has something to learn from others, and the future online education can really To achieve "three people must have me a teacher". At the same time, due to the diversification of educational resources, people will find that sometimes our learning teachers are often younger than them, but because these teachers "specialize in the profession", their professional level in the field they teach is relatively high. "The situation of learning no young and old, capable as a teacher". Therefore, in the future online education, everyone can become a teacher, while on the other hand, they become students. Everyone is a teacher, and everyone is a student. From childhood to old age, the concept of lifelong learning will be fully achieve.

3.2 Online Education Is Expected to Become a Buyer's Market

At present, online education is still at a stage where demand is greater than supply. It belongs to the seller's market. The scarcity of quality education resources makes it difficult for users to truly select the educational resources that are suitable for them. The initiative of the market is controlled by the seller. However, as the potential needs of users are deeply explored and the educational resources are diversified, more and more course providers will flood into the online education market, and the market will quickly return to the balance of supply and demand, and the supply will be greater due to the increasing supply. Seek to enter the buyer's market stage. In the buyer's market stage, users have the initiative in the market, and can choose the course that suits them best according to their own needs and with the help of big data and course evaluation system. For educational resource providers, the online education market will become a completely competitive market and will no longer be the seller's market for products and services. Therefore, the future online education companies can only keep abreast of their needs and change their positions in time to gain a place in the future buyer's market.

3.3 Perfect Teaching Quality Evaluation System

At present, online education obviously lacks a scientific and effective evaluation system for teaching quality, which is also the main reason for the current unevenness of online educational products. The reason why online education courses are difficult to have a sound quality evaluation system is mainly due to the lack of a large number of deep and multi-faceted data support. With the upgrade of big data and artificial intelligence technology, a perfect evaluation system for online education and teaching quality will be realized soon. With the analysis of the historical data of the educational object, learning ability, learning attitude and other aspects of the big data analysis, it is possible to accurately assess the level of scholastic ability of the educational subject in the learning field before, during and after the online education course, and then Accurately analyze the degree of improvement of the educational level of the educational object, and combine the subjective feedback of the educational object intercepted by the artificial intelligence technology on the online course to scientifically evaluate the quality of the online course. Therefore, the future online education will apply a perfect teaching quality evaluation system, on the one hand to promote the standardization of the industry as a whole, on the other hand, it can also serve as an important reference for online education enterprises to improve teaching quality, thus ensuring the sustainable development of the online education industry.

4 The Impact of Big Data and Artificial Intelligence on the Online Education Industry

4.1 The Development Trend of Online Education Industry

In addition to the new classroom model of the online education industry, the future of online education has also shown a trend of development, making the potential demand for online education fully explored, along with the growing demand for online education, according to the theory of industrial economics, online education Supply will also grow, and the overall size of the online education industry is bound to accelerate. How to firmly follow the demand and create higher user value in this new round of high-speed growth is the key to whether online education companies can maintain rapid development. By comparing the high-speed development experiences of many well-known online education companies, we will find that one of the core factors of their success is to be able to accurately mine the potential needs of customers and to provide products and services to these needs. To achieve this, the prerequisite is to be able to accurately judge the new trends in the development of the online education industry, and to explore customer needs around this. For example, VIPKID fully judges the trend of online education across regions, and fully exploits the needs of users for language-based foreign teachers, and quickly becomes an industry unicorn. It can be seen that grasping the development trend of online education is one of the driving forces for the rapid development of online education enterprises.

4.2 Big Data and Artificial Intelligence Help Break Through the Bottleneck of Online Education

The main reason for the lack of online education system is that the online course pays more attention to fragmented learning and it is easy to ignore the overall systemicity, or there are more related content courses. It is difficult for students to choose the most suitable course that suits their actual level and needs. By applying big data and artificial intelligence, students can learn the interest of students' learning interest, study habits, knowledge and skill mastery, knowledge and skill mastery in real-time, and conduct in-depth mining and analysis to accurately grasp the learning needs of students. And automatically match the most suitable related courses according to their learning ability and status quo. Thereby, it helps students to stay away from the difficulty of selection, realize the seamless connection of knowledge upgrade, save students time for screening courses, and improve learning efficiency. Therefore, by applying big data and artificial intelligence, it can effectively improve the pertinence of online education and help students to achieve accurate matching with the course providers, which not only improves the learning efficiency of students, but also enhances the satisfaction of students' courses as a whole. The degree of social recognition of online education.

4.3 Big Data and Artificial Intelligence Help Change the Concept of Online Education

In the past, the concept of online education was still in a transitional phase from teacher-centered to student-centered. The concept of online education in the era of big data and artificial intelligence will be completely transformed into a student-centered approach. Just as big data and artificial intelligence have caused huge changes in the concept of other industries, the changes brought about by big data and artificial intelligence are also subversive for the online education industry. In the traditional educational concept, it is often emphasized that the teacher is the center, and the teacher decides the content of the lecture, the learning method, the study plan, and the test content. In the big student-centered education philosophy of the era of big data and artificial intelligence, these will be decided by students, and big data and artificial intelligence will accurately analyze the needs of students and carry out various Teaching work.

5 The Future Trend of China's Online Education Industry

The future trend of China's online education industry China is a country with a large population. Due to the imbalance of educational resources and information asymmetry, there is a huge demand for quality education resources. Although the scale of the online education industry has maintained an average annual growth rate of 20%, it is not rapid, but it is only due to the strong demand for online education. The market is automatically adjusted in terms of "quantity". Obviously, such rapid growth has short-term Sex. In the long run, the core factor in the growth of the entire online education industry is the upgrading of educational concepts, the optimization of educational quality, and the innovation of mobile Internet technologies. Moreover, the development of the online education industry in the future is not only the growth of scale, but with the deep integration of mobile Internet technology and education industry, there will be a new classroom model, which can not only achieve high-quality educational resources sharing across regions, but also bring Give teachers and students a new educational experience. The future of China's online education industry, under the guidance of the new model of the classroom, will have great potential and will gradually turn these potentials into reality. The future of online education in China is bright.

6 Summary

In the future, with the overall development of the online education industry, the concept of lifelong learning will be fully implemented in everyone's life. Through future online education, people can learn anytime and anywhere, with the help of big data and artificial intelligence. High learning efficiency for learning, and the ability to learn in a personalized way, everyone can use the learning method, learning strategy, learning mode that suits them best. Learning and development will truly become an indispensable activity in people's lives. Although big data and artificial intelligence, especially artificial intelligence, are still at an embarrassing stage of development and require constant investment, exploration and experimentation, how these two technologies can further influence the development of the online education industry and help online education companies. Breaking through the bottleneck of development also requires practice to test. It is believed that through the test of practice, we will further grasp the help of big data and artificial intelligence technology on the development of online education enterprises, and truly promote the healthy, orderly and efficient breakthrough development of online education industry.

References

1. Niu X (2015) Research on the development characteristics and trend of the smart terminal industry in Henan province. In: International conference on economics
2. Huang T (2011) The research on income effect of service industry development in Northeast China. In: Education and management
3. Liu H, Liu X (2017) A novel research on the influence of enterprise culture on internal control in big data and Internet of Things. Mob Netw Appl 1–10
4. Ban J (2016) Research on the development direction and trend of interior design education under the green building background (2), 91–93
5. Luo X, Xie L (2018) Research on artificial intelligence-based sharing education in the era of Internet+
6. Sun T, Zhang J, Yang Y (2017) Review on the development and future trend of the intrusion detection system (IDS). In: International conference on communication & electronics systems
7. Alfred R (2017) The rise of machine learning for big data analytics. In: International conference on science in information technology
8. Del Río S, López V, Benítez JM et al (2014) On the use of MapReduce for imbalanced big data using Random Forest. Inf Sci Int J 285(C):112–137
9. Ma B, Wang X, Li Q (2012) The research on physical education teaching in sino-foreign cooperation in running schools. In: Knowledge discovery and data mining
10. Bara JE (2013) Considering the basis of accounting for CO2 mole fractions in ionic liquids and its influence on the interpretation of solution nonideality. Ind Eng Chem Res 52 (9):3522–3529
11. de Carvalho SM (1996) Effect of sublethal concentrations of Azadirachtin on the development of Spodoptera littoralis. Arch Dis Child 27(131):10–33
12. Manjula P, Saraswathi G, Prakash P et al (2009) Involvement of parents in the education of children with reading and writing difficulties–impact of an intervention. Educ Res Rev 4 (4):208–212
13. Blauw SL, Franses PH (2011) The impact of mobile telephone use on economic development of households in Uganda. Social Science Electronic Publishing, pp 1–48
14. Plesch PH, Austin JC (2010) Some effects of the initiator on the cationic polymerization of alkenes. J Polym Sci Part A Polym Chem 46(13):4265–4284
15. Okurberberoglu E (2015) The effect of ecopodagogy-based environmental education on environmental attitude of in-service teachers. Int Electron J Environ Educ 5(2):86–110
16. Walker LR, Wardle DA, Bardgett RD et al (2010) The use of chronosequences in studies of ecological succession and soil development. J Ecol 98(4):725–736
17. Maunder MN, Sibert JR, Fonteneau A et al (2006) Interpreting catch per unit effort data to assess the status of individual stocks and communities. ICES J Mar Sci 63(8):1373–1385
18. Blustein DL, Walbridge MM, Friedlander ML et al (1991) Contributions of psychological separation and parental attachment to the career development process. J Couns Psychol 38 (1):39–50
19. Kohn MJ (2008) P-T-t data from central Nepal support critical taper and repudiate large-scale channel flow of the greater Himalayan sequence. Geol Soc Am Bull 120(3–4):259–273
20. Ishii T (1984) Future trend of technological research and development and its potential impact on society. Problems of advanced economies

Feature Analysis and Selection in Acoustic Events Detection

Mantao Wang[1,2], Jie Zhang[1,2(✉)], Haitao Tang[3], Zhiyong Li[1,2], Jun Li[1,2], and Yuchen Wang[1]

[1] College of Information Engineering, Sichuan Agricultural University, Yaan 625000, China
12340@sicau.edu.cn
[2] The Lab of Agricultural Information Engineering, Sichuan Key Laboratory, Yaan 625000, China
[3] Speech Processing Laboratory, Harbin Institute of Technology, Harbin 150001, China
HaitaoTang.Ape@gmail.com

Abstract. This study aimed at demonstrating the AED derived feature component significantly outperforming MFCC features or log frequency filter parameters. This is effectively achieved without increasing the number of parameters in acoustic events detection under the speech and other audio sounds recognition. This has been made possible and suitable for the use of AdaBoost approach as discussed in the paper.

Keywords: Acoustic Events Detection · MFCC · AdaBoost

1 Introduction

Growing interest has been observed in research of Acoustic Events Detection (AED) [1]. Despite the fact that speech is one of the auditory sources known to be a great provider of information, such useful information can also be carried by other types of sounds. Specifically, this refers to information provided by non-speech sounds and those related to the sense and the ear as the organ of hearing as related to all events that reveal social and human activities. For instance, the sound of moving chairs and the creaking of a door at the commencement of a meeting [2], audience cheering during a game say soccer [3], the gunshot sounds in the street [4] and quick or hurried steps heard in a nursing room. All these are sounds that rely on crucial information but are not speech in the actual sense. However, there is always a relative difference in the events of these sounds, some salient while others being consistent. Consistency can be noted in the cheering squad of the team, while the sounds made keys of a laptop keyboard when one is typing, the wrapping of a paper and the steps heard in a carpeted room are all subtle.

Reported research on detection of acoustic events have been done on several papers for varying databases and areas for various scholarly reasons [5, 6]. One major study is the Acoustic Events Detection (EAD), which was an undertaking done in the year 2006 [7] for CLEAR assessment. This task was seen to accomplishment by three participant

Z. Xu et al. (Eds.): CSIA 2019, AISC 928, pp. 860–868, 2020.
https://doi.org/10.1007/978-3-030-15235-2_115

members from a project known as CHIL [8]. The Support Vector Machine (SVM) [9] distinguishing approach forms the basis for the UPC system which uses four different kinds of acuity features and logs Frequency Filter (FF) bank measurements. Both of these two systems: ITC and CMU are created using the Hidden Markov Model (HMM). This uses same features that are used as for the Mel-Frequency Cepstral Coefficients (MFCC) [10].

It can be observed from these aspects that Automatic Speech Recognition (ASR) structure that was based on the Hidden Markov approach operated better for the task of detection. Another approach called the Support Vector Machine (SVM) was well adaptive and succeeded for classification works. Complete speech cognition sets i.e. the censorious band restoration as simulated by the easy log frequency and the Mel/Bark filter bank measurements are the major features known for acoustic event detection. Also, these have been studied and proven as a clear representation of spectral framework of speech.

However, the same characteristics have been noted to be suitable for Acoustic Events Detection (AED) for various reasons. The first reason is that insufficient work has been done on research and studies concerning the spectral framework of acoustic events. This means that the characteristics of speech designed based on its ghostly framework might not correlate to the optimum features for Acoustic Events Detection. The second reason may be that when the indistinct and overlapping aspects of speech are perceived as noise, the ratio of Signal-to-Noise has been proven to be low for Acoustic Events Detection (EAD).

Therefore, this study proposes a pristine selection method for Acoustic Events Detection. From the observed different distinguishable capabilities of each of the EAD's task feature components, this study hypothesizes a method to create a distinct aspect from a huge characteristic pool. The experiments for acoustic detection have shown that distinguishable aspect set, as obtained from the data-driven approaches significantly override the Coefficients called Mel-Frequency Cepstral. It performs well but without raising the number of parameters.

2 Spectral Correlates of Acoustic Events Detection

Today, the use of vocalizations to communicate features is created based on the perception and production properties of the same. Founded on knowledge gathered from the human auditory structures and organs, the enclosure of the spectrogram which is referred to as the formant structure is thought to have the empirical evidence that it hold to a great extent knowledge of speech. However, the human auditory system works in line with several other sense organs including the brain in the human body. It is a fact that both log and Mel-Frequency sieve storage arguments use triangular band filter passages when refining out the spectrogram's harmonic framework [11]. Also, to simulate the diversified coherent resolution seen in the perceptive function undertaken by the human auditory system, the communication vocalization sets manipulate bandwidths framed on the essence of the perceptual fastidious band. However, as shown in Fig. 1 below, the spectral frame of acoustic events is not the same as that of speech. This leads to uncertainty of specifically using characteristic of a speech as set for Acoustic Events Detection (EAD).

To make a feasible and clear analysis for the spectral framework of the auditory speech, and have the ability to design relevant features for Acoustic Events Detection, this study performs the KLD founded feature discriminant capability experiment. This would aid in understanding the subtle characteristic feature component of vocalizations to communicate as set in the Acoustic Events Detection work. Spontaneously, such as discriminative feature aspect is expected to make a difference between acoustic and other audio events including sounds and noises. Based on a statistical point of view, smaller Bayesian rates of error resulting from a huge difference between acoustic events distributions and other sound parts can be observed. The distinct distance between the acoustic distributions and other audio components shows the distinguishing events. This is the basic reason that makes the study to propose a KLD based approach of analysis to quantification the discriminant capability of characteristic aspects.

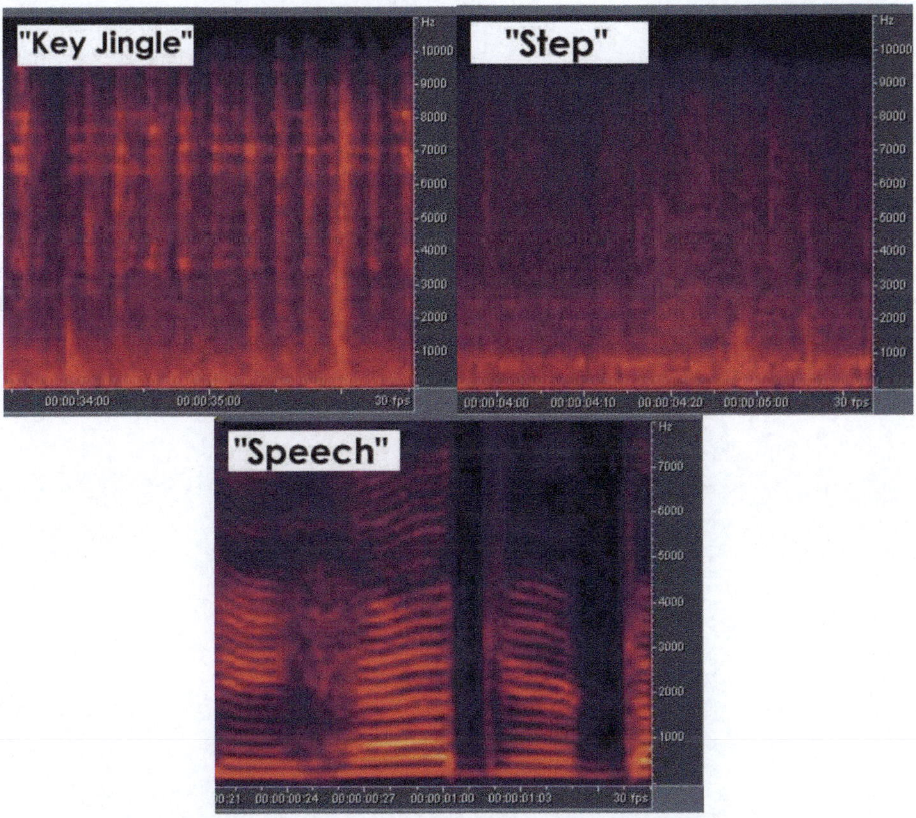

Fig. 1. Spectrograms of the acoustic events and human speech

KLD, i.e. KL Divergent, is denoted by $D(p||q)$ and it is a parameter that represents a measure of "distance" in a problem-solving sense. This is done distinctively between the two variables p and q which is defined as the transverse measure of the level of information and noise contained in the signal between p and q less the self-entropy of the variable p. This can be represented mathematically as shown below:

$$D(p||q) = \int p(x) \log \frac{p(x)}{q(x)} \tag{1}$$

This study uses the KLD to quantify the distinguishable capability of every characteristic component for each acoustic event. Let $d_{ij} = D(p_{ij}||q_i)$ stand for the disparity between the distribution of the *ith* characteristic aspect of the *jth* event and the universal arrangement of the *ith* feature aspect for all other audio sounds.

The universal discriminative capability of the ith characteristic component is given by:

$$d_i = \sum_j p_j d_{ij} \tag{2}$$

where p_j refers to the initial likelihood of the *jth* acoustic event.

Argumentatively, a huge universal KL distance d_i indicates that the distributions in the *ith* aspect have a bigger disparity between diverse acoustic events, therefore having equally huge discriminant capabilities. Figure 2 below shows the universal KL distances for diverse log frequency sieve bank measurements for AED are diverse from the for speech numeric recognition. The KL distances for speech numeric recognition are measured in a similar way as in the above description. This calculation is based on replacing acoustic events with speech digits and normalizing the means for all universal KL distances.

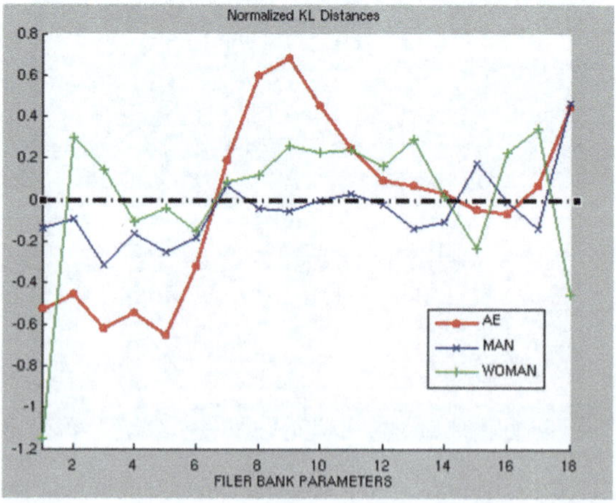

Fig. 2. Men and women speech digit recognition and acoustic event detection global KL distances.

3 Feature Selection Based on AdaBoost Approach

A two class arrangement problem is the base for the general Adaboost algorithm [12]. It is achieved by iteratively selecting and combining various effective classifiers among several other weak classifiers. For all iterations, single weak classifiers are selected from the pool of weak classifiers where the rate of error should not be more than 0.5.

Adaboost method follows various steps:

(1) Frames labeled $x_1, x_2, \cdots, x_m$ and their corresponding $y_1, y_2, \cdots, y_m$ labels are prepared.
(2) The weights $D_1 = \frac{1}{m}, i \in \{1, \ldots, m\}$ with m being the total number of labeled examples are initiated.
(3) Erect $t = 1, \ldots, T$ where T refers to the total sum of features:
(a) Look for the characteristic F_t that reduces the error ε_t. The weights D_t above. The iteration error is denoted by:

$$\varepsilon_t = \sum_{i=1}^{m} D_t(t)[LLR_{F_t}(x_i) \leq 1] \tag{3}$$

where $LLR_{F_t}(x_i)$ is the likelihood ratio of characteristic F_t in frame x_i which corresponds to its correlating y_i label against the universal distribution.
(b) Select $\alpha_t \in R$, and form $\alpha_t = \frac{1}{2}\ln\frac{1-\varepsilon_t}{\varepsilon_t}$
(c) Bring the weights D_t to current problem:

$$D_{t+1}(i) = D_t(i)\frac{\exp\{-\alpha_t \cdot sign(LLR_{F_t}(x_i) - 1)\}}{Z_t} \tag{4}$$

where the constant of normalization is Z_t such that

$$\sum_{i=1}^{m} D_{t+1}(i) = 1 \tag{5}$$

(4) Get the final output for the classifier:

$$H(x) = sign(\sum_{t=1}^{T} \alpha_t h_t(x)) \tag{6}$$

In the paper [13, 14] can find the details about AdaBoost algorithm.

4 AED System Design Based on the HMM

The implementation of a Markov model is applied to show and classify acoustic events as shown in the AdaBoost approach. The study goal of acoustic event detection is formulated. Then the event sequence that maximizes the posterior likelihood of the acoustic event is $W = (w_1, w_2, ..., w_M)$ and the corresponding observation being $O = (o_1, o_2, ..., o_T)$. Therefore,

$$\hat{W} = \arg\max_{W} P(W|O) = \arg\max_{W} P(O|W)P(W) \tag{7}$$

$P(O|W)$ acoustic model represents one HMM for every event that consists of three output joined using self-loop to all directions. The observation arrangements of the states refer to incrementally-directed Gaussian mixtures. The bigram langsuage model was then used to represent $W = (w_1, w_2, ..., w_M)$, the likelihood of an event label sequence so as to get short-term factors on the sequence of acoustic events. This is shown by:

$$P(w_1, w_2, ..., w_m) = P(w_1) \prod_{i=2}^{m} P(w_i|w_{i-1}) \tag{8}$$

In AED, a bigram model favors observed event sequences with statistical data on sequences similar to the ones obtained for the training data. The bigram language model improves performance, even though it does not use similar linguistic implications as those used in recognition of speech. A major reason for this is that it can suppress prolonged arrangements of similar acoustic event labels during the decoding process. Also, this is satisfying since it makes the HMMs to fit the internal temporal framework of the audio segments that corresponds to the acoustic events more suitable.

Upper part of the HMM-based EAD System Design above produces a speech recognition stimulus which is a solid indicator of N-best results. Language and acoustic models scores are then annotated on each edge of the lattice. The components used to train HMMs for the stimulus are made up of 26 frequency-filtered log sieve storage measurements of 26 MFCCs, acceleration and delta, and their total energy calculated on a 25 ms Hamming window in 10 ms intervals.

The lower part of the design chosen the most discriminative characteristic set based on the Adaboost method explained earlier. New acoustic values are assigned to each arc in the recognition stimulus by the new HMMs trained in this characteristic set. The most suitable route in the updated stimulus results as the understood event arrangements.

5 Experiments

Metric and Dataset. This study's AED experiments utilizes about 3-hour development data consisting of labels and event stages to direct the designs and test them on a 2-hour data testing period. This is according to the CLEAR 2007 AED Evaluation, the universally agreed lapse for data testing [15]. The evaluation data consists of 1454 cases of target events. These target events included in the acoustic event detection were: knocking (kn), key jingle (kj), chair moving (cm), laughter (la), coughing (co), applause (ap). Keyboard typing (kt), cup jingle (cj), phone ringing (pr), footsteps (st), paper rustling (pw) and door slam (ds). The Fig. 3 below represents the evaluation data for these acoustic events.

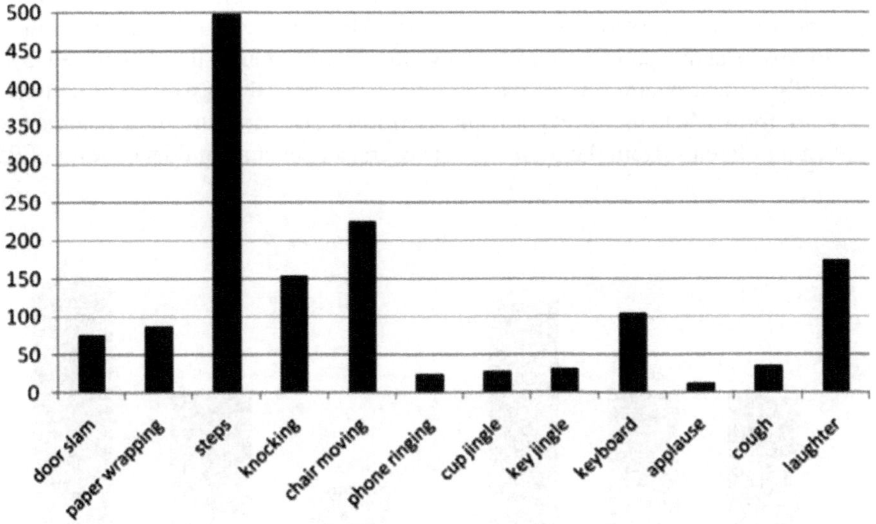

Fig. 3. Histogram showing twelve acoustic events in the evaluation data

Most of these events have low SNR and are salient as compared to speech or the background noise. Speech and unknown event labels were used as control variables for this experiment. Both speeches labeled and unlabeled frames were treated as background class.

Experiment Set-Up. Such an experiment set-up is used to investigate and demonstrate the performance of the derived characteristics. This makes a comparison between the performances of the AED designs as based on HMMs and manipulates either the baseline set MFCC or the derived EAD characteristic. Both of them are currently widely used in other audio applications as well as speech recognition systems. The initial baseline characteristic set is made up of 26 MFCCs calculated in the 0–11,000 Hz frame along with acceleration and delta as the second and first coefficients respectively. The 2nd baseline characteristic component is made up of 26 log frequency sieve bank measurements, their acceleration and delta factors on the same frequency lag. The EAD characteristic set is derived from utilization if the AdaBoost method, as discussed earlier. Each of the features set in the test contains a similar number of trainable measurements as wells as 78 character components. When the measurements are obtained, the designs are retained with all the evaluation data again.

Experimental Results. The Fig. 4 below represents the EAD feature set performance as obtained using the AdaBoost approach and the log frequency measurements. EAD-ACC score of detection accuracy is indicated in Fig. 4a below. It can clearly be seen that the both MFCC and log frequency sieve storage characters have been outperformed by the EAD character component without an increase in the dimension.

Performing experiments based on statistics on the detection metric is complex. To conclude that the obtained EAD feature excellently performs differently, a classification experiment in Fig. 4b below is carried out. HMMs contained in the EAD designs are used to group audio parts into various events. These include those obtained by the universally agreed parameters of data testing. Also, Fig. 4b classification outputs are borrowed from McNemar's experiment. Performances of both frequencies show a significant difference from the derived AED character set at a confidence level of 95%.

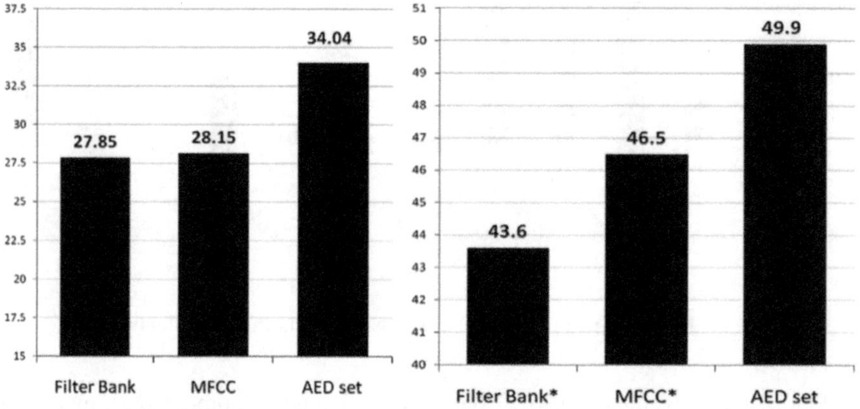

(a) AED-ACC scores %

(b) Classification accuracy % (* indicates meaningfully difference from AED set (McNemar's test, p=0.05))

Fig. 4. Performance obtained from using diverse feature sets

Table 1. Tabulation of effectiveness of each aspects of the studies framework (AED-ACC (%)).

Frequency	ap 13	cl 28	co 36	cm 226	ds 76	kn 153	kj 32	kt 105	pr 25	pw 88	la 174	st 498	ave 121
MFCC	79.2	25.8	23.1	30.6	55.2	8.8	38.8	0.0	36.3	13.1	38.0	29.8	28.15
FB	33.6	20.9	23.8	26.5	37.8	19.8	26.1	0.0	14.9	10.6	48.1	29.2	27.85
Boosted	44.5	26.6	30.1	32.4	56.2	14.6	32.1	1.7	37.8	16.5	50.2	37.9	34.04

The values in Table 1 demonstrate the best performance about the EAD character set. Hence, the EAD system based on HMM is above 7.19% increase from bottom character and model (MFCC + HMM as 28.15% or HMM + filter bank as 27.85%). These outperform previous results termed as best performance on CLEARED AED work.

6 Conclusion

This paper has presented both system designs and discriminative characters framed for better AED. The AdaBoost approach was proposed to determine the most distinct character set for AED from a character pool of both frequencies. There is an indication by the CLEAR AED Evaluation that the presented models and characters all contribute towards enhanced results as compared with best results obtained in previous studies.

Acknowledgements. This work was supported in part by the Youth Fund of the Sichuan Provincial Education Department under Grant 18ZB0467.

References

1. Novell A, Arena CB, Oralkan O (2006) J Acoust Soc Am 139(6):3193–3198
2. SaNakanishi AB, Soares AA, Natali MR (2014) J Acoust Soc Am 19(11):590–603
3. Raventos A, Quijada R (2014) International multi-conference on systems, 8–10 May 2014, vol 3, pp 1–6
4. Transfeld P, Martens U, Binder H (2015) IEEE international conference on acoustics, speech and signal processing, 15–18 October 2015, vol 2, pp 2629–2633
5. Parviainen M, Pertila P, Hamalainen MS (2014) Joint workshop on hands-free speech communication and microphone arrays, 3–5 March 2014, vol 4, pp 152–156
6. Holt DE, Johnston CE (2015) Biol Conserv 11(87):27–33
7. Plinge A, Grzeszick R, Fink GA (2006) Acoustics, speech and signal processing, 12–14 August 2014, vol 2, pp 3704–3708. http://chil.server.de/
8. Scardapane S, Comminiello D, Scarpiniti M (2015) IEEE Trans Neural Netw Learn Syst 26 (9):2212–2220
9. Fux, T, Jouvet D (2015) Signal processing conference, 18–22 November 2015, vol 3, pp 1416–1420
10. Fukumori T, Nakayama M, Nishiura T (2016) J Acoust Soc Am 3(23):140–144
11. Hu W, Gao J, Wang Y (2014) IEEE Trans Cybern 44(1):66–82
12. Yuan F, Fang Z, Wu S (2015) IET Image Process 9(10):849–856
13. Chen Q, Hui Z, Zhao J (2014) LWT: J Acoust Soc Am 57(2):502–507. http://isl.ira.uka.de/clear07, 2007

Prediction of Dollar Exchange Rate Based on Wavelet Neural Network

Chen Liu[1,2], Hongyan Wu[1,2], and Wenbin Liu[3,4](✉)

[1] School of Economics and Business Foreign Languages, Wuhan Technology and Business University, Wuhan 430065, China
[2] Hubei Province Commerce and Service Development Research Center, Wuhan 430065, China
[3] Department of Public Course, Wuhan Technology and Business University, Wuhan 430065, China
812926096@qq.com
[4] College of Information Engineering, Wuchang Institute of Technology, Wuhan 430065, China

Abstract. In order to predict the trend of the exchange rate between USD and RMB in the financial world, a method for predicting the exchange rate between USD and RMB based on wavelet neural network and grey relational analysis was proposed. The grey relational analysis was used to calculate the correlation degree between the influencing factors and the exchange rate of USD, and several parameters with high correlation degree were optimized. The wavelet neural network was used to find the mapping relationship between the influencing factors and the exchange rate of USD. The method was tested by selecting the data related to the exchange rate of USD in the third quarter of 2018. The experimental results showed that the average relative error of the calculated exchange rate of USD was 1.43%. After the gray correlation analysis method was used, the experimental convergence speed and calculation accuracy were also improved. Therefore, the wavelet neural network method can use the known data of dollar exchange rate to predict the change trend of USD exchange rate, which has a high reliability, practicality and application prospect in the field of financial research.

Keywords: USD exchange rate · Wavelet neural network · Gray relational analysis

1 Introduction

USD has been falling steadily since 2002. Weighted against a basket of currencies, USD has lost 37% of its value since 2001. After September 2007, affected by the subprime mortgage crisis, USD showed a sharp decline, with the exchange rate against all 16 major currencies declining. In 2008, the direction of USD exchange rate was full of uncertainty. As the US economy may decline or even decline, the subprime mortgage crisis may continue to deteriorate, and investors' confidence in holding USD assets is affected, central Banks around the world have reduced their holdings of US treasury bonds, USD may continue to decline in 2008. But with US current account deficit

Z. Xu et al. (Eds.): CSIA 2019, AISC 928, pp. 869–876, 2020.
https://doi.org/10.1007/978-3-030-15235-2_116

somewhat smaller, the economy is likely to continue to shrink after a brief downturn. The long-term current account deficit and fiscal deficit in US are the fundamental reasons for the depreciation of the dollar. The subprime crisis that broke out in 2007 dealt a huge blow to US financial system and the real estate market, further exacerbating the depreciation trend of USD. The change of USD exchange rate has an important impact on China's economy: the increase in the cost of imports leads to the increase in the cost of goods using imported parts, and thus the price of sales. Therefore, even if imported parts are used in domestic goods, the cost and price will be affected. Of course, a change in the exchange rate would also boost exports, since it would be cheaper to sell abroad. Nowadays, with the increasing degree of internationalization, the change of exchange rate has an omnipresent impact on people's lives [1].

Therefore, it is important to study that change of us dollar exchange rate to financial and economic development, and many scholars have carried out relevant studies. Cai studies the allocation of foreign exchange assets between USD and euro from the perspective of investors' management of exchange rate risk [2]. Wang proposed that NDF is an important factor that can be used as the prediction of RMB exchange rate [3]. Xiao used time series analysis methods such as co-integration and Granger causality test to make an empirical analysis of the relationship between the foreign exchange reserves and the exchange rate of RMB against major foreign currencies [4]. Wang constructed a currency prediction model based on support vector machine regression [5]. Qiu used USD index as an object, collects monthly index data and builds an estimation model, and studies quantitatively the changing trend of dollar index [6]. Liu conducted research on RMB exchange rate prediction based on ARMA model [7]. Zhang combined different single models by using co-integration relations and the nonlinear characteristics of neural networks [8].

Based on the research results of the above scholars, there is still room for discussion on the study of USD exchange rate. It is still of research significance to analyze the influencing factors more effectively and how to apply the time series of the changes of the exchange rate of USD to the analysis. Since there are many factors influencing the exchange rate of USD, the grey relational analysis method can effectively reduce the impact of various factors on the target result. Wavelet neural network can effectively predict and analyze the sequential and can be used in the study of the change of USD exchange rate. Therefore, this paper proposes a research on the prediction of the exchange rate of USD based on gray relational analysis and wavelet neural network.

2 Influencing Factors of USD Exchange Rate

USD exchange rate is closely related to the dollar index. The index of USD is a measure of the strength of the dollar, which indirectly reflects the changes in the competitiveness of American exports and the cost of imports. In a deeper strategic level, the rise and fall trend of the USD index is the layout of the global economic and financial strategy of US. The calculation of USD index is based on the trade balance between US and several major global trading partners. The dollar's overall strength is measured in a weighted exchange rate against the currencies of these countries, with 100 points as the border between strength and weakness. After the launch of the Euro on January 1, 1999, the basket of currencies was adjusted from 10 countries to six, including the Euro (EUR), Yen (JPY), Pound (GBP), Canadian dollar (CAD), Swedish krona (SEK) and Swiss franc (CHF). The USD index is defined as the weighted geometric average of the exchange rate of this blue sub-currency against the USD. Based on the above, this paper selects the exchange rate between USD and the above six countries as the influencing factor of the exchange rate between USD and RMB [9].

3 Grey Relational Analysis

For the factors between the two systems, the measurement of the degree of correlation, which varies from time to time or from different objects, is called the degree of correlation. Grey relational analysis is a method to measure the degree of correlation between the factors according to the degree of similarity or divergence of the development trends among the factors. The grey system theory puts forward the concept of grey relational degree analysis for each subsystem to seek the numerical relationship between the various factors in the system [10]. Therefore, GRA provides a quantitative measurement for the development and change of the system. The calculation steps are as follows.

Step 1: A reference sequence that reflects the behavior characteristics of the system and a comparison sequence that affects the behavior of the system are determined.

Step 2: Dimensionless processing of each sequence.

Step 3: Calculate the gray correlation coefficient $\xi(xi)$. There are several comparison columns x1, x2, …, xn for a reference x0, the correlation coefficient $\xi(xi)$ of the correlation and reference series at each point can be calculated using the following formula, ρ is the differentiation coefficient, and it usually take 0.5.

$$\xi_{0i} = \frac{\Delta(\min) + \rho\Delta(\max)}{\Delta_{0i}(k) + \rho\Delta(\max)} \tag{1}$$

In the formula, Δmin and Δmax is the difference in two levels of minimum and maximum difference respectively. Δ0i(k) is the sequence of the xi each point on the curve and the reference sequence x0 curve of each point on the absolute difference value.

Step 4: The correlation is calculated. The average of the correlation coefficients was calculated. The formula of correlation degree r_i is as follows. The closer the r_i value is to 1, the better the correlation is.

$$r_i = \frac{1}{N}\sum_{k=1}^{N} \xi_i(k) \tag{2}$$

Step 5: Rank of correlation degree. The correlation between each factor is described in the order of correlation.

4 Wavelet Neural Networks

The wavelet transform is similar to the Fourier transform, and the Fourier transform is the projection of the signal in the space of a set of fundamental functions. It is that classical Fourier transform to express the arbitrary function as a linear superposition of the harmonic function of different frequencies base on the triangular sine cosine base spread signal. It's a good way to describe the frequency signatures of the signal, but there's no resolution in the time or airspace, and you can't do a local analysis. This has brought a lot of inadequacies in theory and application. In order to overcome this drawback, a window Fourier transform is proposed. By introducing the "window function" of the time domain, the Fourier transform has been improved, but the size and shape of the window is fixed, and it doesn't fundamentally make up for the deficiency of the Fourier transform. Wavelet transform has good time domain and frequency domain localization performance, with a flexible time-frequency window, has important significance in theory and practice.

The wavelet transform has the time and the local characteristics and the focus characteristics, and the neural net has self-learning, adaptive, robustness, fault-tolerance, and generalization ability. How to combine the advantages of the two has always been a concern. Wavelet space is used as the feature space of pattern recognition to extract signal features. The extracted feature vectors are then fed into the neural network for processing. Another method is called a wavelet neural network, or WN. It was propose by Zhang et al., that IRLSA of the famous information science research institute of France, that the wavelet neural network was first proposed in 1992. The little wave neural network is a neural network model based on little waves, and it uses nonlinear little boobs to replace the usual non-linear neurons incentive functions, like the sigmoid function, to integrate the small wave transform into the neural network, and to get the best of both. In comparison with the forward neural network, the wavelet neural network has obvious advantages: firstly, the basic elements and the whole structure of the wavelet neural network are determined according to the wavelet analysis theory, which avoids the blindness of the BP neural network structure design. Secondly, the small wave neural network has a strong learning ability, rapid convergence rate and higher precision [11]. The structure diagram of wavelet neural network is shown below (Fig. 1).

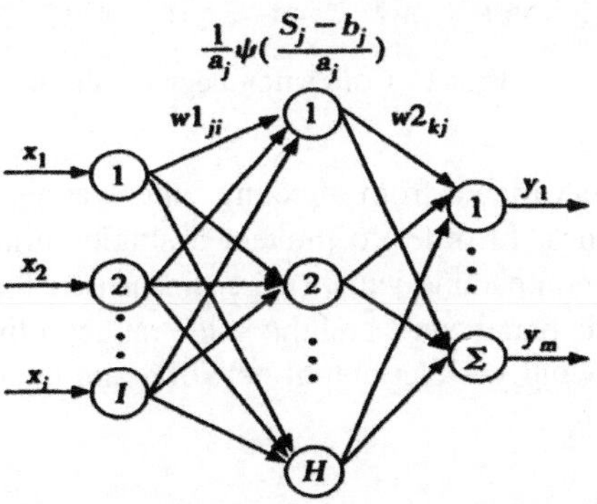

Fig. 1. Structure of wavelet neural network

5 Experimental Analyses

In the experiment, the influence factors of the exchange rate of USD were analyzed by using the grey correlation analysis method first, and several parameters related to the exchange rate of USD were selected. The grey associated analyzed data is then trained and calculated using wavelet neural network and the results are analyzed and compared.

5.1 Grey Relational Analysis

The experiment used 90 sets of data from the bank of China on the exchange rate of USD to RMB in the third quarter of 2018 for testing. As mentioned above, each sample data has 6 influencing parameters related to the exchange rate USD. The influencing parameters are input into the wavelet neural network for training to calculate the corresponding exchange rate of USD.

Firstly, GRA was used to analyze the correlation degree of six influencing parameters and the exchange rate of USD in the sample data group. Three different no dimensional methods (initialization, averaging, and interval relative value) were used respectively to obtain the average correlation degree values of these three methods to represent the correlation degree between each influencing parameter and USD exchange rate. According to the curve shown in the figure below, three influencing parameters with a correlation degree of more than 0.9 are selected as the input data of wavelet neural network. These three influencing parameters are GBP, GPY and EUR respectively (Fig. 2).

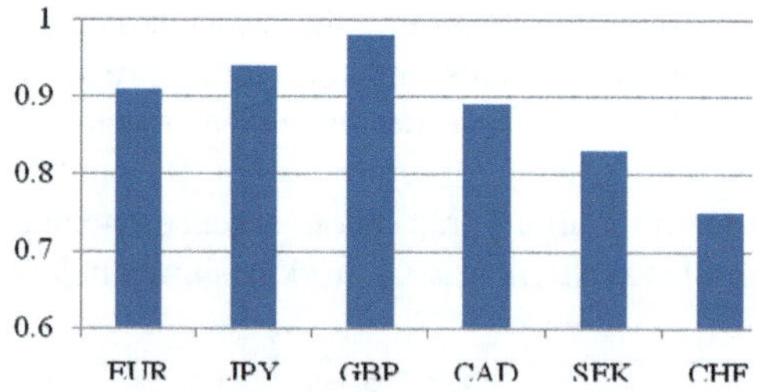

Fig. 2. Correlation degree value

To prevent a single variable from affecting other variables and to obtain a corresponding range of values, In order to prevent a single variable from affecting other variables and obtain a comparable value range, linear transformation is carried out on these three characteristic parameters, and the value range of the transformed variable is [0.01, 0.99]. The following wavelet neural networks are then trained and tested.

5.2 Establishment of Wavelet Neural Network Model

According to the input and output data of the nonlinear function, the structure of wavelet neural network is 3-6-1, that is, three input neurons represent the above three influencing factors, the number of the hidden layer neurons is set to 6, and one output neuron corresponds to the exchange rate of USD to be calculated.

The experimental data was composed of 90 groups of preprocessed data, each group of data has three input values and a corresponding output value. The training set and test set of wavelet neural network are randomly divided into 70 groups and 20 groups. The data of wavelet neural network were used to train 70 pairs of training sets. As the error of the network is decreasing, after over 1,500 practices, the training error tends to stabilize (Fig. 3).

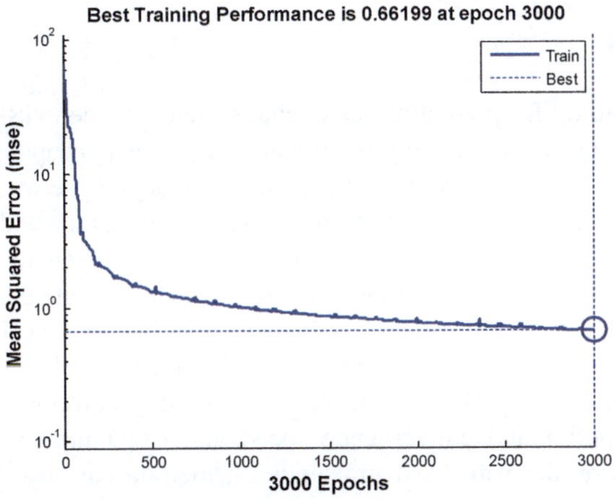

Fig. 3. Training error

5.3 Result Analysis

By using wavelet neural network to the trained 20 did not attend the test set of training data to make predictions. The predicted output and expected output of the wavelet neural network are shown below (Fig. 4).

It can be seen from that figure that the predicted output of the wavelet neural network and the exchange rate of the actual dollar value of the game, and the average relative error of the 20 test sets are 1.43%, indicating that the accuracy of the prediction of the wavelet neural network is still high. A few there still exists certain error of the test data, it also suggests that the dollar exchange rate prediction based on wavelet neural network there are still some problems. For example, in order to constantly improve the precision of neural network training, need a lot of training data.

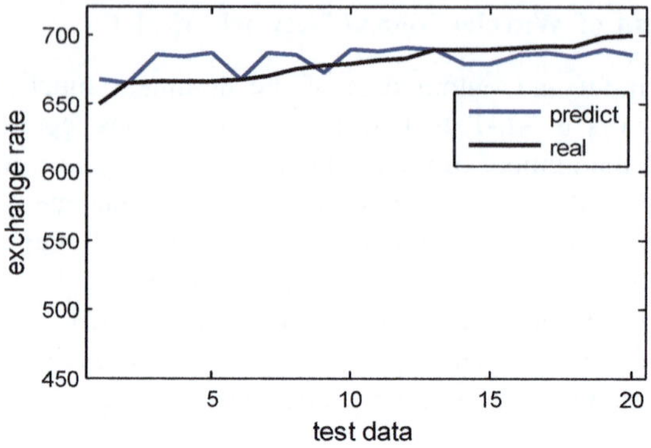

Fig. 4. Prediction of wavelet neural network

6 Conclusion

In this paper, a method for predicting the exchange rate between USD and RMB based on wavelet neural network and grey relational analysis was proposed. The grey relational analysis was used to calculate the correlation degree between the influencing factors and the exchange rate of USD, and several parameters with high correlation degree were optimized. The wavelet neural network was used to find the mapping relationship between the influencing factors and the exchange rate of USD. The method was tested by selecting the data related to the exchange rate of USD in the third quarter of 2018. The experimental results showed that the average relative error of the calculated exchange rate of USD was 1.43%. After the gray correlation analysis method was used, the experimental convergence speed and calculation accuracy were also improved. Therefore, the wavelet neural network method can use the known data of dollar exchange rate to predict the change trend of USD exchange rate, which has a high reliability, practicality and application prospect in the field of financial research. At the same time, the wavelet neural network and the gray relational analysis method still have some shortcomings, such as the convergence of the mean square error is still a certain error, and the prediction of USD exchange rate is partial error, which may be due to the number of samples is insufficient. Future work is to collect a large amount of data associated with the dollar for subsequent tests, so as to improve the accuracy of the wavelet neural network computing.

Acknowledgments. This research was supported by Humanities and Social Sciences Project of Hubei Provincial Department of Education (Project No. 15G156), Funded Project of Hubei Business Service Development Center (Project No. 2017Y009), and Funded Project of Wuhan Technology and Business University (Project No. A2014002).

References

1. Cai C, Li X (2005) USD exchange rate change and its impact on China economy. Heilongjiang Foreign Econ Relat Trade 27(10):26–27 (in Chinese)
2. Cai W, Tang Q (2012) Analysis of the currency allocation of foreign exchange assets based on exchange rate predictability. Int Econ Trade Res 23(8):80–90 (in Chinese)
3. Wang N, Hou T (2013) Research on forecasting of NDF and the RMB exchange rate. J Shenyang Inst Eng: Soc Sci 9(2):11–15 (in Chinese)
4. Xiao H, Wang Z (2009) The empirical research between China's foreign exchange reserves and the exchange rates. Econ Manag 23(7):65–68 (in Chinese)
5. Wang D (2010) USD exchange rate of RMB forecasting based on re-constructed phase space and SVM. J ABC Wuhan Manag Inst 20(4):9–13 (in Chinese)
6. Qiu M (2018) Quantitative method of exchange rate prediction: a case study of USD index. J Finance Econ 18(6):13–20 (in Chinese)
7. Liu Y (2016) Research on RMB exchange rate prediction based on ARMA model – taking RMB exchange rate against USD as an example. J Lang Fang Norm Univ (Nat Sci Ed) 16 (2):53–58 (in Chinese)
8. Zhang Y (2014) A combined prediction model of RMB/USD exchange rate based on artificial intelligence. J Shaanxi Univ Sci Technol (Nat Sci Ed) 30(4):74–78 (in Chinese)
9. Ma Y, Pan H (2018) DB wavelet neural network model and empirical study of dollar index prediction. J Zhengzhou Univ (Philos Soc Sci Ed) 51(5):60–66 (in Chinese)
10. Wang H, Liu L, Liu L (2007) Application research of BP neural network based on GRA and PCA. Manag Rev 19(10):50–54 (in Chinese)
11. Shi F, Wang X, Yu L et al (2013) MATLAB neural network analysis of 30 cases. Beijing University of Aeronautics and Astronautics Press, Beijing (in Chinese)

Computer Performance Determination System Based on Big Data Distributed File

Kong Lu(✉)

Jiangxi Modern Polytechnic College, Nanchang 330095, Jiangxi, China
79364652@qq.com

Abstract. The high concurrency, high scalability, high performance, high availability, and large capacity of the distributed file system make it an ideal choice for storing large amounts of data. To determine the performance of the distributed computer in big data analysis, it is necessary to compare the performance test of different distributed file systems. This paper compares the different distributed file systems, analyzes the computer performance characteristics of distributed files, and summarizes the rules of different characteristics.

Keywords: Big data · Distributed file system · Performance decision

1 Introduction

The era of big data has arrived, and it will set off waves of change in many fields. But we must calmly see that the core of big data lies in mining the value hidden in the data for customers, rather than the accumulation of hardware and software [1–4]. Distributed file system performance testing tools provide limited coverage, and most focus on specific functional testing, lacking a unified performance testing framework, and implementing an ideal distributed file system performance testing framework faces many difficulties and challenges [5–7]. First, the framework must be universally scalable to test performance across different distributed file systems easily; second, it needs to provide flexible, customizable test cases to meet different user needs and application characteristics; The test framework should be able to adapt to different distributed environments, and can not significantly affect the performance of the distributed file system itself, in order to obtain accurate and reliable test results [8–11]. The strategic significance of big data technology is not to master tremendous data information, but to professionalize these meaningful data [12]. In other words, if big data is likened to an industry, the key to profitability in this industry is to increase the "processing power" of the data and "add value" of the data through "processing" [13–16]. In a distributed system, each computer shares a common distributed operating system. A distributed operating system consists of a kernel and modules and processes that provide various system functions [17–19]. Every computer in the system must maintain the kernel of the distributed operating system to achieve basic control of the computer system [20].

Z. Xu et al. (Eds.): CSIA 2019, AISC 928, pp. 877–884, 2020.
https://doi.org/10.1007/978-3-030-15235-2_117

2 The Meaning of Big Data

2.1 The Connotation of Big Data

When it is challenging to measure, collect and record the data with the help of conventional tools in the given time frame, then "Big Data" is used to solve the problem. New state of the art decision-making techniques is requiring to process the data and optimization of the process. Big Data deals with diverse information and have capabilities for high growth. According to the deification of Gartner, the "Big Data" research organization, Big Data has capabilities of dealing with diverse information, capable of precise and correct decision, accommodate big data for the optimization purpose. Big Data enhance the capabilities of traditional software to measure, compute, process, analyze, and store data with different scale and dimension. In addition, Big data also possess great features, in the form of fast data flow, handling diverse data.

2.2 The Composition of Big Data

Recently, with the advancements in the Cloud technology, more attention has been paid to Big Data. In the past, it was difficult for a company to manage and analyze the structured and unstructured data. However, now, Big Data has capabilities to manage it quickly and accurately with spending a lot of time and money. Big Data needs a distributed computing system (DCS) to distribute the given data to different servers, sometimes these severe exceeds up to thousands. So, sometimes Big Data is also associated with Cloud computing technologies. There is a narrow difference between the technical definition of the Big Data and Cloud computing. They are considered as close as the two different sides of the coin. A distributed architecture is necessary and fundamental need to process Big data, and it cannot be managed by a single computer or server. "Big Data" rely on the DCS system, distributed and efficient cloud storages, and virtual technologies. To handle with a real-time big data, exclusive and new techniques are required.

Development Trends of Big Data

Resourceization

Resourceization can also be as the essential strategic resources which are dealt with by the big data, and this new trend has become the focus of many companies of these days as everyone is competing for it. Therefore, it is a dire need for an all companies to develop their Cloud computing technologies based on big data to grab the market opportunities. As defined before, big data has very less difference from cloud processing technologies. Cloud computing is a platform for generating big data, and it also provides a platform to process flexible data. In the start, cloud computing technology integrated the diverse data and optimization algorithms. Researcher thought that, in the near future, cloud computing and the Big Data would have no difference. Mobile Data and Internet of things IoT is also responsible for the fast advancements in the cloud computing. This makes data handling marketing more efficient and reliable.

Financial performance is directly affected by the data management, and it is a core competency of the company. Importance of the data management can be realized from the saying, "data assets are the core assets of enterprises". It is responsible for sustainable development, core competitiveness, and strategic and industrial application.

The Core of Management
The benefits of the data management are associated with the main business high growth rate, and the big sale revenue. In addition, the data handling, storage and competitiveness is 36.8% with the help of Internet of thinking. This data management also significantly affect the performance and the cost benefits of the companies.

In addition, for enterprises with Internet thinking, the proportion of data asset competitiveness is 36.8%, and the management effectiveness of data assets will directly affect the financial performance of the company.

3 Distributed File System

3.1 The Goal of a Distributed File System

A distributed file system is a system for providing reliable file storage and sharing services in a distributed environment. They distribute file data across different storage nodes and manage and maintain ever-expanding amounts of data in a node-extensible manner. The distributed file system exposes a unified namespace to the user and upper-layer applications. Through the file operation interface provided by the distributed file system, the upper-layer application can perform files and directories in the distributed file system in a manner similar to operating a single file system. Add, delete, modify, query and other operations.

3.2 Advantages of a Distributed File System

A distributed computer system is a new type of computer system that interconnects multiple small microcomputers. It breaks through the traditional centralized stand-alone situation, organizes computer systems from the concept of decentralized processing, has a high performance-price ratio, flexible system scalability, good real-time, reliability and fault tolerance. It is a new type of computer system that has received considerable attention in the field of computer science and technology in recent years, and has now become a new direction of rapid development. The read rate of the data includes the response to the user's request to read the data file, the node where the data file is located, the time of reading the data file in the actual hard disk, the data transmission time between different nodes, and the processing time of a part of the processor. The distributed network storage system adopts a scalable system structure, uses multiple storage servers to share the storage load, and uses the location server to locate the storage information, which not only improves the reliability, availability and access efficiency of the system, but also is easy to expand. Various factors determine the user experience of a distributed file system. That is, the read rate of data in the distributed file system cannot be too different from the real rate of data in the local file system. Otherwise, it takes 2 s to open a file in the local file system, and various factors in the distributed file system. More than 10 s of impact will seriously affect the user experience. The data security mechanism, because the data is dispersed in each node, must be redundant, backup, mirroring, etc. to ensure that the node fails, data recovery can be performed to ensure data security.

3.3 The Overall Architecture of the Distributed File System

Centralized and decentralized are two common architectural approaches in distributed systems. For distributed file systems, the centralized architecture can easily monitor and manage the entire cluster. Users and system administrators can understand the running status of different nodes in time as shown in Fig. 1. However, a distributed file system with a centralized architecture must withstand the risk of a single point of failure and require additional modules or components to ensure system reliability. The distributed file system of the decentralized architecture has good load balancing characteristics. However, it needs to synchronize data between each node, which increases the network burden of the entire cluster.

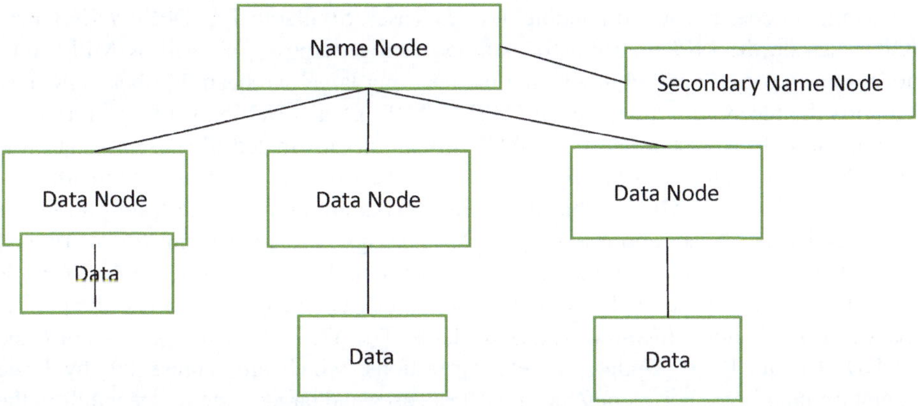

Fig. 1. HDFS architecture diagram

3.4 Type of Distributed File System

Common distributed file systems are GFS, HDFS, Lustre, Ceph, GridFS, mogileFS, TFS, FastDFS, and so on. Each applies to a different field. They are not system-level distributed file systems, but application-level distributed file storage services. The file system is an abstraction layer between physical storage and file operations, making file management and storage management more convenient. The distributed file system makes the file system accessible to expand, easy to configure, and easy to share and manage. Of course, the specific explanation is that the physical storage resources managed by the file system are not necessarily directly connected to the local node, but are connected to the node through the computer network, that is, the cluster file system, which can support a large number of nodes and PB level data storage.

4 Distributed File System Performance Testing Process

4.1 The Importance of Performance Testing

In the face of such a diverse distributed file system and its features, performance testing is essential. On the one hand, existing performance testing efforts are mostly optimized for a single performance problem and bottleneck, and the coverage of existing performance testing tools is limited. On the other hand, other performance testing tools in the distributed storage world cannot be used well for distributed file systems. Therefore, there is a need for a unified distributed file system performance testing framework.

4.2 IOR

IOR is a performance testing tool for testing the underlying distributed file system in an MPI computing environment. IOR supports basic file read and write operations, and can configure the specific operation sequence and the data size of test cases by scripting, but does not support adding new test cases. Similar to Test DFSIO/NNBench, IOR relies on the MPI platform for parallel testing purposes, as well as MPI multi-node, multi-process parallel mode, and the resulting large overhead. Further, IOR only supports the file system interfaces of POSLX, MIP-IO, and HDF5, that is, performance testing can only be performed on POSIX-compatible distributed file systems, and it is difficult to cover more test targets.3.3 YCSB and AMP Lab big data benchmark

The YCSB and AMP Lab big data benchmarks are performance testing tools for distributed data storage and query systems. Although their goal is not for distributed file systems, there is some similarity with the above performance testing tools. YCSB is a test framework for key-value storage systems that is widely used to test the performance of distributed structured storage systems. The YCSB test case consists of basic CRUD (Create, Read, Update, Delete) operations, which are represented by basic operation interfaces such as put/get. It has test cases and target system extensibility, the ability to add custom test cases by combining different operations, and the ability to add target test systems by implementing new key-value storage system access interfaces. YCSB does not depend on the existing computing platform. It can run in a multi-threaded manner on a single machine. It can also launch multiple YCSBs on multiple nodes for distributed deployment, but still cannot flexibly support different parallel modes. The AMP Lab Big Data Benchmark is a performance testing tool for big data query systems that test the processing and response performance of the underlying system by performing data table related operations. In this tool, test cases are SQL query statements or user-defined query requests. The AMP Lab Big Data benchmark is scalable in test cases, providing both typical SQL queries for real-world applications as test cases and new queries. At the same time, it does not rely on the computing platform, playing a role in initiating requests and collecting results during performance testing. The underlying query engine determines the specific platform, so its parallel mode is also limited.

5 Computer Performance Determination of Distributed Files

5.1 Distributed File System

The distributed system refers to the problem of computing, storage, etc. that cannot be solved by a single computer by using multiple computers. There are two types of distributed systems: distributed storage and distributed computing. Distributed storage mainly has distributed file systems and distributed databases. The distributed file system is mainly used for file storage. All resources on the Internet will eventually be stored as files on the storage device of the specific physical machine. It is undoubtedly impossible to store, read, and manage these massive files by relying on a single machine, so distributed file systems have emerged.

5.2 Characteristics of Computer Performance of Distributed Test Files

The performance of a distributed file computer generally includes two major aspects: first, availability (see computer system reliability); and second, workability, that is, the ability of the system under normal working conditions. There are many performance indicators for characterizing workability, which generally varies with the system and targets evaluated. They are the main research objects of system performance evaluation. The time when the computer system can work normally, the indicator can be the length of time that can continue to work, such as the average time between failures, or the percentage of time that can normally work in a period of time. Another aspect is its processing power or efficiency.

5.3 Ways to Test File System Performance

One common way to measure the performance of an online file system is: How much time does it take to complete a service request? In a traditional system, the time required to complete a request includes the actual hard disk access time, and a small portion of the CPU processing time. However, in an online file system, due to the distributed architecture, remote access actions create additional recurring burdens, including: the time to send a request from the client to the server, the time the response is sent back from the server to the client, and the central processing time used to run the online transport protocol during these two transmissions. The performance of an online file system can be seen as a dimension to assess its transparency and to make a full comparison with local disks.

6 Summary

Nowadays, a wide variety of distributed file systems have different design goals and characteristics. These features have a significant impact on the performance of big data applications. It is essential to understand the performance characteristics of distributed file systems fully. On the one hand, users need performance test results to select the most suitable distributed file system for the target application; on the other hand, developers need a performance test tool to optimize the distributed file system; further, performance judgment can be excellent reflects the bottleneck of distributed file system, computer performance judgment based on big data distributed files. The distributed file system extends the service to the entire network. Not only has it changed the way data is stored and managed, but it also has the advantages of data backup and data security that the local file system cannot.

References

1. Min C, Mao S, Liu Y (2014) Big data: a survey. Mob Netw Appl 19(2):171–209
2. Varian HR (2014) Big data: new tricks for econometrics. J Econ Perspect 28(2):3–27
3. Hashem IAT, Yaqoob I, Anuar NB et al (2015) The rise of "big data" on cloud computing: review and open research issues. Inf Syst 47(C):98–115
4. Jagadish HV, Gehrke J, Labrinidis A et al (2014) Big data and its technical challenges. Commun ACM 57(7):86–94
5. Lazer D, Kennedy R, King G et al (2014) Big data. The parable of Google Flu: traps in big data analysis. Science 343(6176):1203
6. Shan S (2016) Distributed file system
7. Shahabinejad M, Khabbazian M, Ardakani M (2014) An efficient binary locally repairable code for hadoop distributed file system. IEEE Commun Lett 18(8):1287–1290
8. Hua X, Hao W, Ren S (2014) Enhancing throughput of Hadoop distributed file system for interaction-intensive tasks. J Parallel Distrib Comput 74(8):2770–2779
9. Sivaraman E, Manickachezian R (2014) High performance and fault tolerant distributed file system for big data storage and processing using Hadoop. In: International conference on intelligent computing applications
10. Zhang Y, Yang H, Maoqing YE (2014) A data management scheme for massive power quality monitoring data based on distributed file system. Autom Electr Power Syst 38 (2):102–108
11. Zhou J, Wang W, Meng D et al (2014) Key technology in distributed file system towards big data analysis. J Comput Res Dev 51(2):382–394
12. Wang Y, Wang W, Ma C et al (2014) Zput: a speedy data uploading approach for the Hadoop distributed file system. In: IEEE international conference on cluster computing
13. Chiwande VN, Tayal AR (2014) An approach to balance the load with security for distributed file system in cloud. In: International conference on electronic systems
14. Krishna TLSR, Ragunathan T, Battula SK (2014) Performance evaluation of read and write operations in Hadoop distributed file system. In: Sixth international symposium on parallel architectures
15. Zhang X, Gaddam S, Chronopoulos AT (2016) Ceph distributed file system benchmarks on an openstack cloud. In: IEEE international conference on cloud computing in emerging markets
16. Aishwarya K, Arvind RA, Sreevatson MC et al (2014) Efficient prefetching technique for storage of heterogeneous small files in Hadoop distributed file system federation. In: Fifth international conference on advanced computing
17. Mukhopadhyay D, Agrawal C, Maru D et al (2014) Addressing name node scalability issue in Hadoop distributed file system using cache approach. In: International conference on information technology

18. Jeong YS, Kim YT (2015) A token-based authentication security scheme for Hadoop distributed file system using elliptic curve cryptography. J Comput Virol Hacking Tech 11 (3):137–142
19. Sharma N, Irwin D, Shenoy P (2015) BlinkFS: a distributed file system for intermittent power. Sustain Comput Inform Syst 6(Complete):69–80
20. Nishanth S, Radhikaa B, Ragavendar TJ et al (2014) CoHadoop++: a load balanced data co-location in Hadoop Distributed File System. In: Fifth international conference on advanced computing

Research and Application of Bipartite Graph Optimal-Matching Algorithm on Task-Driven Teaching Method

Mei-shan Li, Jia-mei Xue(✉), and Yue Liu

College of Information Science and Electronic Technique, Jiamusi University, Jiamusi 154007, China
xuejiameixzy@sina.com

Abstract. With the continuous improvement of people's education level, the quality of higher education has received much attention. The country has introduced policies to create "golden courses", and advanced teaching concepts are constantly emerging in the teaching of basic computer courses in universities. This paper adopts the "task-driven" teaching method, in which tasks are the main line in class and the roles between teachers and students are truly exchanged, making students become the main part in class and improving their interest in learning and innovation ability. In research, it is found that the establishment and distribution of tasks are particularly important. In this paper, the bipartite graph optimal-matching algorithm is adopted in the distribution of tasks, which enables different levels of students to be assigned to their best tasks and greatly improves the class effect of "task-driven" teaching method. Through the data analysis of the experimental class and the comparison class, it is concluded that the method in this paper is more efficient.

Keywords: Bipartite graph · Task-driven · Optimal-matching

1 Introduction

Driven by the rapid development of the times, the contents and teaching methods of basic computer courses are also constantly improving. Through the continuous exploration of teaching methods, the "task-driven" teaching method has entered into the classes of basic computer courses in universities. The computer courses have strong practicality and operability. "Task-driven" mainly runs through the teaching by taking the tasks as the main line, achieves the learning of knowledge points by completing the tasks, and stimulates students' learning ability, learning interest and innovation ability with tasks, which improves the students' hands-on ability and has developed high-level talents with strong operational ability for the society.

In the student group, each student has different personal qualities and learning levels and the workload that they complete within the same time and the difficulty of their work are different. Then, how to assign different tasks according to the characteristics of students is also the difficult part in the implementation of "task-driven" teaching method. The bipartite graph optimal-matching algorithm is used to assign different tasks to each student in order to achieve better learning results.

Z. Xu et al. (Eds.): CSIA 2019, AISC 928, pp. 885–892, 2020.
https://doi.org/10.1007/978-3-030-15235-2_118

2 Bipartite Graph Algorithm

2.1 Optimal Distribution of Bipartite Graph

Consider a weighted complete bipartite graph named G with a bipartite graph named (x, y). Here $X = \{x_1, x_2, \ldots\ldots x_n\}$, $Y = \{y_{1,}y_2, \ldots\ldots y_n\}$ the edge x_iy_j has the weight w_{ij}, representing the working efficiency of the workers x_i for job y_j. The optimal distribution is obviously equivalent to finding a perfect match with the greatest weight in this weight drawing, which is called the optimal match [1, 2].

If a real-valued function l is determined on the vertex set $V = X \cup Y$ to meet the following conditions: all $x_i \in X, y_j \in Y$

$$l(x_i) + l(y_j) \geq w_{ij} \tag{1}$$

That have such l are called a feasible vertex label of bipartite graph G, or called label of vertex x_i or y_j, command

$$\begin{cases} l(x_i) = \max\{w_{ij}\}, & x_i \in X \\ l(y_j) = 0, & y_j \in Y \end{cases} \tag{2}$$

Then l is a feasible label of the given weighted complete bipartite graph, command

$$E_l = \{x_i | l(x_i) + l(y_j) = w_{ij}\} \tag{3}$$

The sub-graph of G with the edge set E_l is called the equivalent sub-graph corresponding to the feasible vertex label l, marked as G_l. The relation between the equivalent sub-graph and the optimal match is given by the following theorem.

2.2 Kuhn-Munkras Algorithm Thought

The Kuhn-Munkras (KM) algorithm was independently proposed by Kuhn and Munkras in 1955 and 1957 respectively, which is the classical algorithm for solving the optimal matching of bipartite graphs. The basic idea of the algorithm that finds the optimal matching in the weighted complete bipartite graph is as follows: First, a feasible vertex label l is given, then an equivalent sub-graph G_l is constructed, and the Hungarian algorithm G_l is applied accordingly. If a perfect match M^* is found in G_l, then according to the theorem, M' is an optimal match of G_l; otherwise, the Hungarian algorithm ends with aim perfect match M' and an alternating tree T that does not contain M' – the increasing road, nor can it grow in G_l. Subsequently, l is modified to another feasible vertex label l : that has the following properties M' and T are included in G_l and T can be increased and grow in G_l. Such modification of the feasible vertex label is repeated until [3].

2.3 Basic Steps of Kuhn-Munkras Algorithm [4]

(1) A feasible vertex label of G is given randomly to determine G_l, and a match M is randomly selected in M.
(2) If all the vertexes of X are M–the saturating points, then because of $|X| = |Y|$, M is a perfect match of G_l, so that it is the optimal match of G, and the algorithm ends; otherwise, u is assumed as M–the non-saturating point in x, command.
(3) If $N_{G_l}(S) \supset J$, then turn to Step (4); otherwise, $N_{Gl}(S) = J$, calculate

$$a_l = \min_{x_i \in S, y_j \in J}\left\{ |l(x_i) + l\left(y_j\right) - w_{ij} \right\} \tag{4}$$

$$\text{And}\,\bar{l}(v) = \begin{cases} l(v) - a_l, & v \in S, \\ l(v) + a_l, & v \in J, \\ l(v), & \text{other}. \end{cases} \tag{5}$$

(4) A vertex y is selected from $N_{G_l}(S) \supset J$, and if y is M – the saturating point, and $yz \in M$, $S \cup \{z\}$ is replaced by S, and J is replaced by $J \cup \{y\}$, then turn to Step (3); otherwise, find a M–the increasing P in G_l, and M is replaced by $\bar{M} = M \oplus E(P)$, then turn to Step (2).

3 "Task-Driven" Teaching Method

3.1 Summary of "Task-Driven"

The "task-driven" teaching method [5] is established on the basis of teaching theories of constructivism. The learning theories of constructivism believe that knowledge is not obtained through teachers' instruction, but is obtained by learners, in a certain situation and with the help of others, through using necessary learning materials and the meaning construction. The so-called "task-driven" teaching method is that teachers design the teaching contents into one or more specific tasks and make students master the contents of courses by completing specific tasks to achieve the teaching objectives. It is a teaching method that students are active to learn with teachers' guidance. It breaks the old pattern of traditional teaching methods which pays attention to step-by-step learning and accumulation of learning, and it drives the teaching through the completion of tasks to complete the teaching tasks, instead of following the order of teaching contents which is from easy to difficult.

3.2 Teaching Process of "Task-Driven" Teaching Method

The "task-driven" teaching method can be roughly divided into five stages [6, 7].

Stage I, the teacher guiding period. The teachers mainly propose a specific task and requirements, and give some explanations of methods on how to accomplish such task.

Stage II, the period for students' operation and application. Based on the specific operation of the students, many students have been eager to try after the teachers' guidance. At this time, the teachers should leave sufficient time for the students to operation, let them be brave to try and enable them to experience, feel and comprehend in application.

Stage III, the exchange and discussion period. Entering into the exchange and discussion period, the teachers check and supplement the omission of knowledge, explain some common difficult and key points, give a lot of application examples through comprehending by analogy, and further deepen the students' understanding of the knowledge they have learned.

Stage IV, entering into the period of consolidation and innovation. After seeing others' works or methods, students will pick up their desire to try again. At this stage, students will further consolidate their knowledge, and at the same time, they will make some adjustments and innovations after being enlightened to further apply the knowledge that they have mastered while improving the level of creation.

Stage V, the conclusion period. Since the teachers mainly provide guidance on the methods when adopting the "task-driven" teaching method, the students spend most of their time on hands-on exploration. Thus, students with different learning abilities will master different knowledge in the same class. Regarding these problems, teachers should strengthen the class summary and the review of knowledge points so that all students at different levels can keep up with the teaching progress of teachers.

4 Case Analysis on "Task-Driven"

4.1 Setting of Teaching Tasks

This paper adopts the basic computer courses in universities as the research object. The basic computer culture courses include the application of office software, computer introductory theory and the five parts of network. When designing a task, the teachers should first consider the characteristics of each student and the differences of their basic knowledge, cognitive ability and interest. Each task should be designed from the perspective of students, and different levels of tasks are set for different students to enable all of them to complete the tasks smoothly. This paper designs five tasks and gives five word documents in terms of the knowledge of integrating graphs and texts. Each document has different levels of difficulty and materials, and students are required to design the corresponding effects of integrating graphs and texts according to the requirements of the questions. The bipartite graph optimal-matching algorithm is used to complete the assignment of students' tasks to obtain the tasks that are most suitable for each student and achieve better teaching results.

4.2 Assignment of Teaching Tasks

The assignment of tasks is an important part of the "task-driven" teaching method [8, 9]. During implementation, we divided the experimental class into groups of 5 students, and the matching between groups should be basically balanced. The 5 students completed different tasks respectively and conducted representations to each other after the completion of the tasks to find out the deficiencies from the works of their companions, and then improved them to complete the display and communication of tasks. In this paper, the bipartite graph optimal-matching algorithm was used in the assignment of tasks, and the students and teachers were abstracted into a matching graph of bipartite graph with weights [10]. As shown in Fig. 1, the weights in the bipartite graph were determined by the completion of tasks that had been conducted by the students and the weights were sorted and ordered, with a range of 0–5. Then each student was assigned with a most suitable task through the optimal-matching algorithm, and the best teaching effect was finally achieved.

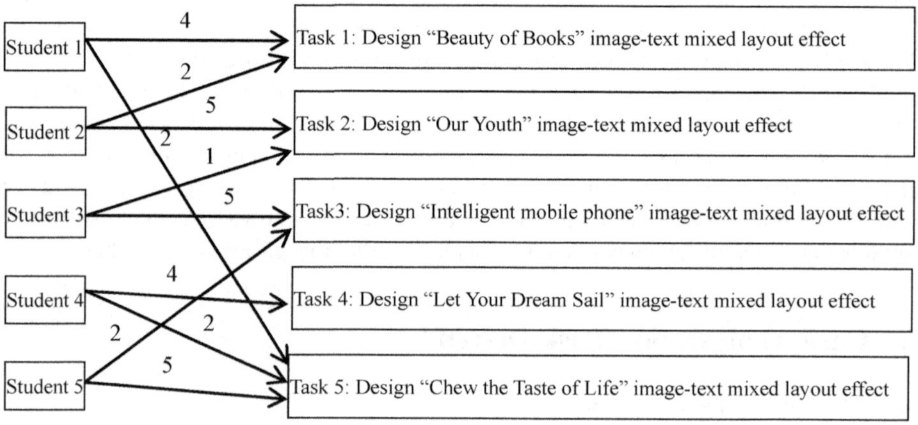

Fig. 1. Bipartite graph matching algorithm with weights

4.3 Evaluation of Teaching Tasks

1. Comparative Analysis of Performance

In order to clearly compare the teaching effects after adopting the "task-driven" teaching method, before the adoption of this teaching method, a placement test of performance was carried out between the experimental class (Class 1 of Property Management) and the comparison class (Class 2 of Property Management). Both the experimental class and the comparison class took the same test paper, and the results of the experimental test are shown in Table 1. The "task-driven" teaching method using the bipartite graph optimal algorithm to assign tasks was adopted in the experimental class, and the results of the experimental test after one semester are as shown in Table 2. The mode of answering questions via computer was adopted and the operation of the Office software, mastery of basic knowledge and network architecture knowledge were tested separately.

Table 1. Comparison of computer scores before experiment

Classes	Average score (office)	Average score (basic knowledge)	Average score (network system)
Experimental class	71.6	68.9	72.3
Comparison Class 1	70.2	70.3	69.8

Table 2. Comparison of computer scores after using "Tasks Driving" teaching

Classes	Average score (office)	Average score (basic knowledge)	Average score (network system)
Experimental class	89.2	83.7	82.3
Comparison Class 1	75.5	71.5	73.8

2. Analysis on the Improvement of Students' Ability

The questionnaire survey method is used to investigate the improvement of students' ability in five aspects, including the ability to search, process, and handle information, the analysis and problem-solving ability, the self-learning and inquiry ability, the innovation ability, and the communication and cooperation ability. There are a total of 34 questionnaires issued, and 34 questionnaires collected, of which 32 questionnaires are valid. Statistical analysis is performed on the valid questionnaires, and the data obtained is as shown in Fig. 2.

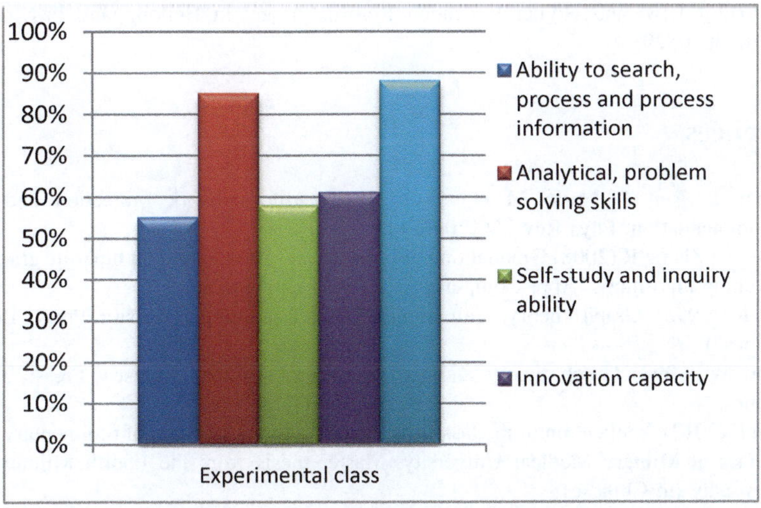

Fig. 2. Statistics of improvement of students' ability

According to the data analysis of Tables 1 and 2, for the office software, the average score of the experimental class is increased by 17.6 points, while that of the comparison class is only increased by 5.3 points; the average score of the basic knowledge of the experimental class is increased by 14.8 points, while that of the comparison class is increased by 1.2 points; the average score of the network of the experimental class is increased by 10 points, while that of the comparison class is only increased by 4 points. From the analysis of Fig. 2, it is concluded that the improvement of students' ability is also relatively obvious; especially the analysis and problem-solving ability and the communication and cooperation ability have been greatly improved. More than 80% of students choose these two abilities.

5 Conclusion

Through the analysis on the practical feedback and teaching effect of the "task-driven" teaching method adopted in the basic computer courses in universities, this paper uses the bipartite graph optimal-matching algorithm to assign tasks, which can find the tasks that are best suitable for each student, unify the progress of them, enable the knowledge points to be fully covered and the students' satisfaction will be the best. Assigning different tasks to each student can also obtain different works from them, and enable them to be inspired through watching others' works during the display and communication of works, as well as continuously improving their works and stimulating their creative desires. Meanwhile, students' collaborate, exchange, communicate and problem-solving abilities will also be improved.

Acknowledgments. This research was financially supported by Heilongjiang Province "Thirteenth Five-Year" Planning Record Subject (Grant No. GBD1317136), Education and Teaching Research Project of Jiamusi University (Grant No. 2018JYXB-041, Grant No. 2017LGL-011) and Education and Teaching Research Project of Jiamusi University (Grant No. 2017LGL-018) and Higher Education Reform Project in Heilongjiang Province (Grant No. JG2013010529).

References

1. Zhou T, Ren J, Medo M et al (2007) Bipartite network projection and personal recommendation. Phys Rev 76(4):046–115
2. Yang C, Zhang R (2008) Graduation thesis selection system based on bipartite graph optimal matching algorithms. Appl Comput Syst 7:14–34 (in Chinese)
3. Lu K (1995) Graph theory with applications. Tsinghua University Press, Beijing (in Chinese)
4. Xiao W (1993) Graph theory and its algorithms. Aviation Industry Press, Beijing (in Chinese)
5. Ren F (2012) Application of the task driven method to the teaching of rudimentary computer courses at Military Medical University. Master thesis from the Fourth Military Medical University (in Chinese)

6. Fang H-F (2012) Application and study on the task driven method to the teaching of rudimentary computer courses at Military Medical University. Master thesis from Northeast Normal University (in Chinese)
7. Zang J (2010) Application of the task driven method to college information technology courses. Master thesis from Hebei University (in Chinese)
8. Liu Y (2014) The application research of "task-driven" network curriculum based on moodle. Master thesis from Bohai University (in Chinese)
9. Gallagher SA, Stepien WJ, Sher BJ, Workman D (1995) Implementing problem based learning in science classrooms. Sch Sci Math 9:136–146
10. Wang B (2012) The applications of bipartite graph optimal-matching algorithm in task-driving instructional effect analysis. J Hefei Univ 22(1):36–40

Research on Hybrid Quantum Genetic Algorithm Based on Cross-Docking Delivery Vehicle Scheduling

Yue Yang(✉)

Shenyang Institute of Technology, Fushun 113122, Liaoning, China
Yangyue801202@163.com

Abstract. Quantum genetic algorithm (QGA) is a new algorithm to solve the optimal problem by applying classical quantum theory to genetic algorithm and introducing quantum states into the traditional bit model. Cross-docking delivery vehicle scheduling is a classical combinatorial optimization problem. Based on QGA, in order to improve the speed and efficiency of logistics distribution process, this paper studies a hybrid QGA framework, proposes a new idea to solve the distribution optimization scheme in traditional logistics scheduling, and studies new strategies of quantum updating and probability adjustment, so as to make the method more suitable for the actual problems of logistics distribution.

Keywords: Vehicle scheduling · Combinatorial optimization · Hybrid quantum genetic algorithm

1 Introduction

Logistics distribution is closely related to consumers in the process of consumption activities [1]. In the whole logistics process, efficient distribution has always been one of the core issues in the logistics industry [2]. Whether the distribution scheduling is efficient and reasonable has a vital impact on the company's costs and benefits [3]. Therefore, vehicle scheduling optimization is a key part of logistics [4]. The theoretical analysis and research of vehicle scheduling optimization is an important basis for modern logistics intensification [5], development of functional transportation system and establishment of a new era of intelligent e-commerce system [6].

In 1959, Dantzig and Ramser first put forward the related problems of logistics distribution and vehicle optimized scheduling [7]. The vehicle scheduling optimization has become a hot research topic for a time. In this paper, a hybrid QGA algorithm is used to solve this problem. The experimental results show that the hybrid QGA is an effective solution to this problem [8].

2 Overview of QGA

2.1 Quantum Computing and Genetic Algorithms

Quantum information processing and its calculation process are a new concept based on quantum bits [9]. Quantum bits are often treated as a very abstract mathematical

Z. Xu et al. (Eds.): CSIA 2019, AISC 928, pp. 893–900, 2020.
https://doi.org/10.1007/978-3-030-15235-2_119

object by scientists. In the classical bit framework, there are only two states, 0 and 1, but in quantum science, quantum bits can be in the third superposition state other than 0 and 1, which are two eigenstates, as shown in the following formula.

$$|\psi> = \alpha|0> + \beta|1> \tag{1}$$

Among them, α and β are the magnitudes of left vector and right vector respectively. In the actual operation of quantum bits, there should be the following constraints.

$$|\alpha|^2 + |\beta|^2 = 1 \tag{2}$$

The coherence of quantum states means that the amplitudes of the two states can interfere with each other [10]. If this coherence is applied to the problem of vehicle distribution, it can be regarded as two different trends affecting the distribution volume. Once the probabilistic magnitude of α, β changes, the probability of quantum bits $|\alpha|^2$ and $|\beta|^2$ at 0 and 1 will also change. Mapping to the actual problem, the distribution volume changes, which can indicate whether the distribution center has full or incomplete possession, and can be in any of the two states, which can greatly expand the information search space.

In traditional QGA, the function of quantum gates is to mutate the population. The renewal process is as follows.

$$\left[\alpha_i' \beta_i'\right]^T = U \cdot [\alpha_i \beta_i]^T \tag{3}$$

The rotating quantum gate U is:

$$U - \begin{bmatrix} cos\theta_i & -sin\theta_i \\ sin\theta_i & cos\theta_i \end{bmatrix} \tag{4}$$

According to the designed adjustment strategy, the size and symbol of rotation angle θ are given.

Genetic algorithm is a new parallel computing optimization algorithm. The main steps are as follows: firstly, chromosomes satisfying certain constraints are constructed and data are coded. The main purpose of this process is to make the solution form of the optimization problem suitable for the operation of genetic algorithm. In the actual coding process, the constraints that conform to the problem should be selected as far as possible, otherwise the computational efficiency of genetic algorithm will be greatly affected. The encoding process is as follows:

$$\text{output y} = \text{Encoding}(input\, x) \tag{5}$$

x is the input data, and the encoding output y is obtained after encoding in a certain way.

The second step is to generate the initial population and select the number of the initial population. Then, the fitness function is selected and constructed according to the objective function of the actual problem. By calculating the fitness of each chromosome, the advantages and disadvantages of the chromosome are reflected.

Assuming that f is the objective function and F is the relative fitness, if the objective function is the maximization problem, then there is

$$\mathrm{F}(x) = f(x) \tag{6}$$

$$F(x) = \begin{cases} f(x) - C_{min} & f(x) > C_{min} \\ 0 & others \end{cases} \tag{7}$$

Among them, C_{min} is the minimum estimate of $f(x)$.

When the fitness function is determined, the future replication process is to determine which chromosomes in the next generation are "adapted to survive" or are "not adapted to survive and then are eliminated" based on the probability distribution of fitness. Chromosome crossover is also an important step in inheritance. Genes inherited from offspring are generated by cross-merging between the chromosomes of the paternal generation. Generation of offspring is not only a process of production, but also a process of mutation. After the generation of new solutions, with the occurrence of gene mutation, quantum rotation gate U changes the coding of some chromosomes.

$$\left[\alpha_i' \beta_i'\right]^T = U \cdot [\alpha_i \beta_i]^T \tag{8}$$

Therefore, the new solution will have more possibilities and more ergodicity.

2.2 Implementation Process of Hybrid QGA

In application, both quantum algorithms and genetic algorithms are implemented for quantum bits, so the conversion to binary strings is only to calculate individual fitness values, but there are a lot of operations for binary direct coding in function optimization, so traditional genetic algorithms and quantum algorithms are considered for mixing.

The traditional binary coding BGA and real coding RGA are considered to be mixed to obtain the BQGA encoding mode. The first generation population is initialized randomly.

$$G_i(0) = randominit() \tag{9}$$

Iterative QGA searches are carried out continuously for $G_i(0)$ in the longitudinal direction by the hybrid algorithm, and single-point crossover and arithmetic crossover are adopted to retain the dominant population.

$$G_i(n+1) = QGA\,search(G_i(n)) \tag{10}$$

The population of each generation is transformed transversely.

$$G_i'(n) = Transform(G_i(n)) \tag{11}$$

$G_i'(n)$ is the population after the transformation of the same generation. After selecting the best population, the dominant population can be obtained. Horizontal search can also be done by multi-generation search.

3 Modeling of Vehicle Scheduling Optimization Problem

For the optimization of the optimal logistics path, we can use the model to summarize it. Figure 1 is a schematic diagram of the traditional logistics distribution mode. The new logistics scheduling model is shown in Fig. 2.

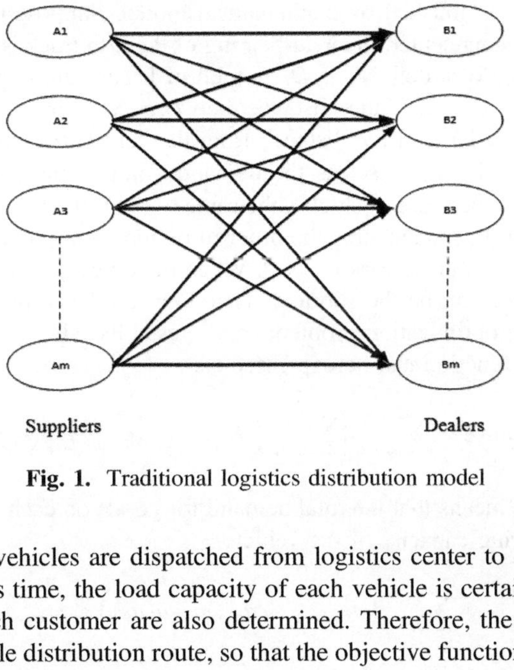

Fig. 1. Traditional logistics distribution model

First, multiple vehicles are dispatched from logistics center to different customers for delivery. At this time, the load capacity of each vehicle is certain, and the location and demand of each customer are also determined. Therefore, the problem is to efficiently plan a vehicle distribution route, so that the objective function can be optimized. At this time, the total load capacity of vehicles on each route is larger than the total demand of customers, and the length of each route is smaller than the maximum driving distance of vehicle distribution. The most critical point is that all customers' needs should be met, and there are only one or two vehicles in the delivery process.

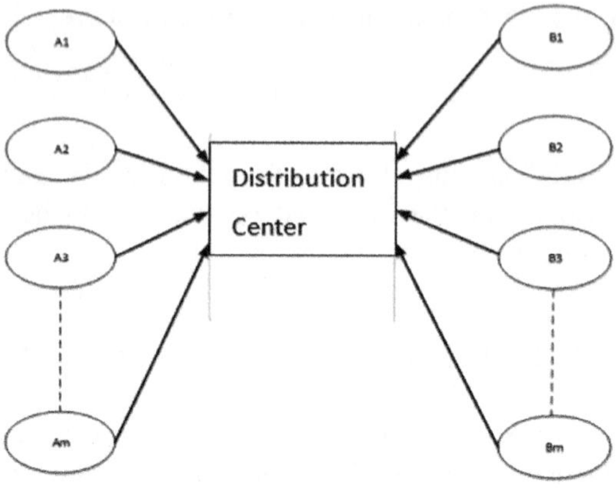

Fig. 2. New logistics distribution model

The process is established by mathematical model. Suppose there are C trucks in the general dispatching center, the load-bearing of the k-th truck is $Q_k(1, 2, 3 \ldots\ldots \mathrm{C})$, the farthest distance of a delivery is D_k, a total of L sites are required, with each site requiring $q_i(1, 2, 3 \ldots\ldots \mathrm{L})$, the distance between two sites can be expressed as $d_{ij}(\mathrm{i}, \mathrm{j} = 1, 2, 3 \ldots\ldots \mathrm{L})$, and the distance from the center to each site is expressed as $d_{0j}(\mathrm{i}, \mathrm{j} = 1{,}2{,}3 \ldots\ldots \mathrm{L})$. n_k is set as the demand point of the k-th truck distribution ($n_k = 0$ means the k-th unused vehicle), the route of the k-th vehicle is expressed as R_k, and the elements in R_k indicate that the order of requirement point r_{ki} in the route R_k is i. Logistics center is expressed as $r_{k0} = 0$. When the objective function is optimal, the distribution distance can be the shortest. Therefore, the basic mathematical model of vehicle scheduling optimization problem can be established.

The objective function can be expressed as:

$$\mathrm{minZ} = \sum_{k=1}^{C} \left[\sum_{i=1}^{n_k} \left(d_{r_{k(i-1)} r_{ki}} + d_{r_{kn} r_{k0}} sign(n_k) \right) \right] \tag{12}$$

$\sum_{i=1}^{n_k} q_{r_{ki}} \leq Q_k$ means that the total demand for goods on each road will not exceed the total load-bearing capacity of the vehicle.

$$\sum_{i=1}^{n_k} \left(d_{r_{k(i-1)} r_{ki}} + d_{r_{kn} r_{k0}} sign(n_k) \right) \leq D_k \tag{13}$$

It is stipulated that the total length of each path shall not be greater than the maximum distance of a truck travelling at one time. $0 \leq n_k \leq L$ constrains the total number of customers on each driving path to be less than or equal to the total number of customers.

$$\sum_{k=1}^{C} n_k = L \tag{14}$$

It shows that every site will get the distribution of goods. A single customer can only have one truck for delivery, rather than multiple trucks for delivery.

$$sign(n_k) = \begin{cases} 1 & n_k \geq 1 \\ 0 & \text{Others} \end{cases} \tag{15}$$

The above formula shows that when the number of sites served by a truck is greater than or equal to 1, the truck has already made the act of distribution.

4 Hybrid QGA Based on Routing Optimization

4.1 Research on Coding Method and Fitness

As previously mentioned, the smallest unit for storing information in quantum computation is a quantum bit. Quantum bits may be in different states 0 or 1, or they may be linear superposition of two states.

In hybrid QGA, an individual of quantum bits with M-bit length in the m-th generation population Q(m) can be represented by the following formula:

$$q_j^m = \begin{pmatrix} \alpha_1^m & \alpha_2^m & \wedge & \alpha_M^m \\ \beta_1^m & \beta_2^m & \wedge & \beta_M^m \end{pmatrix} \mathrm{j} = 1, 2, 3, \wedge, \mathrm{N} \tag{16}$$

N in the formula represents the size of the population, B is the number of generations of population evolution. For all i values, there are

$$|\alpha_i|^2 + |\beta_i|^2 = 1 \tag{17}$$

QGA uses the form of quantum bits to represent chromosomes, so a chromosome can be represented by multiple state information at the same time. When the number of digits is M, the quantum chromosome can represent 2^M states that can occur, so it can effectively maintain the diversity of the population. In application, it shows more possibilities of vehicle scheduling optimization, and can overcome the result of falling into local convergence.

For a specific distribution plan of a vehicle, if we need to judge whether it is good or not, we should first make it meet certain constraints, and secondly, we should correctly calculate the objective function of the problem. This paper tries to use the encoding method of direct arrangement of customers to determine their distribution scheme, so that each customer can get the delivery service. In addition, it is assumed that each customer has only one vehicle to distribute the goods. This scheme also satisfies that the demand of each site on each route will be less than or equal to the maximum freight volume per vehicle for one delivery, but it can not limit the number of distribution routes to less than the number of delivery vehicles.

Individual fitness can be expressed as:

$$F = 1/(Z + K \times P_w) \tag{18}$$

For a single individual, assuming that the difference between the number of delivery routes and the number of delivery trucks is K, the value of the objective function is Z, and K is regarded as the number of unreasonable routes corresponding to the individual, there is a penalty factor P_w for each infeasible route, and the penalty factor is determined according to the objective function.

4.2 Hybrid QGA Flow Based on Routing Optimization

Firstly, the quantum bit population is initialized. Then the binary population is generated through the initial quantum bit population. For the infeasible solution, we modify it with repair function to make it solvable. After decoding the obtained binary data, the routes generated by each vehicle are obtained. After obtaining the routes, immune factors are added to optimize them. After selecting better routes, each route is evaluated, and the best individual (driving path) is selected. Then the quantum rotation gate is updated to determine whether the stopping condition is satisfied, and the algorithm is iterated or terminated.

5 Experimental Results

For the vehicle scheduling optimization problem, it can generally be summarized as follows: There are many vehicle unloading points and vehicle loading points; Vehicle scheduling center chooses and organizes efficient driving routes, so that freight vehicles can successfully pass through different nodes in turn, and meanwhile, they can achieve a series of goals, such as the shortest driving distance, the lowest cost, and the use of as few vehicles as possible when meeting a series of requirements, such as goods demand, delivery time, vehicle capacity, etc.

Taking vehicle scheduling as the model, this paper analyzes and discusses the goods distribution by dispatching trucks of distribution centers, and simplifies and analyzes complex problems by establishing simple and clear mathematical models. In this experiment, a hybrid QGA with immune operator which is used to solve optimal vehicle routing is used to optimize the traditional QGA. Compared with the actual experiments, the improved hybrid QGA has better performance under the same parameters, which is a more effective algorithm to solve the vehicle routing optimization problem.

This algorithm can not only solve the problem of goods distribution in the dispatching center, but also can be applied to solve the corresponding combinatorial optimization problem in other backgrounds. It has great reference value for the management of the supply chain and the dispatching of goods. The hybrid QGA presented in this paper has a broad development prospect in solving the optimization problem and is worth further study.

Acknowledgement. Fund Project: Research on Key Technologies of Intelligent Logistics System Based on Multi-Agent(SIT-i5201801).

References

1. Wang L, Hao W, Tang F et al (2005) Analysis of hybrid quantum genetic algorithms and their performance analysis. Control Decis 20(2):156–160
2. Yang Y, Wang X, Xiao J. Research on distribution optimization of logistics distribution center based on QGA. In: Proceedings of the annual conference of the China's control and decision-making
3. Cai B, Zhang X (2010) Hybrid quantum genetic algorithms and their application in VRP 27 (7):267–270
4. Dijkstra EW (1959) An appraisal of some shortest path algorithms. Oper Res (17):395–412
5. Hammond G (1986) AGVS at work: automated guided vehicle systems. Springer, Berlin
6. Gintner V, Kliewer N, Suhl L (2005) Solving large multiple-depot multiple-vehicle-type bus scheduling problems in practice (27):507–523
7. Chow WM (1986) Development of an automated storage and retrieval system for manufacturing assembly Lines (1):490–495
8. Koo PH, Jang VJ (2002) Vehicle travel time models for AGV systems under various dispatching rules. Int J Flex Manuf Syst 14:249–261
9. Joon ML (2000) Genetic algorithm for determining the optimal operating policies in an Integrated-automated manufacturing system. Procedia Eng 3(4):291–299
10. Corréa A, Langevin A, Rousseau LM (2007) Scheduling and routing of automated guided vehicles: a hybrid approach. Comput Oper Res 34(1):1688–1707

Optimization and Improvement of Lucene Index Algorithm

Ya Tao Su(✉)

Bozhou College, Bozhou, Anhui, China
bzszxcbsyt@163.com

Abstract. Lucene has a wide range of applications in text retrieval and search. The similarity scoring algorithm is one of the core parts of its search engine. In the question and answer system, the retrieval function is also used. The similarity scoring algorithm is also one of its core parts. This paper introduces the analysis of Lucene's system structure, and proposes a search engine optimization method and index algorithm improvement.

Keywords: Lucene · Indexing algorithm · Search engine optimization · Improvement

1 Introduction

Lucene is a full-featured, open source and freely modifiable full-text search engine toolkit implemented in the Java language. Lucene is not a true search engine. It is just a toolkit for further development and creation. This toolkit provides. The search engine's necessary query and indexing capabilities, as well as the English and German full-text search engine architecture [1–3]. The motivation for developing the Lucene Engine Toolkit is mainly to facilitate the use of software developers. It can be used by developers for full-text search, and the toolkit is embedded in the developed full-text search service, and then adds some basic class functions to the system. Finally, an open source, secondary development search engine [4–8] is implemented. At present, the Internet has developed rapidly, the information resources of the Internet are becoming more and more abundant, and the amount of information is increasing, showing an exponential growth [9, 10]. People are increasingly dependent on the Internet, and access to information resources on 7the Internet is becoming more frequent [11]. The information resources of the Internet are so huge that it is necessary to use good search engine tools [12–15] in order to quickly and accurately find the required resources in a massive information resource library. The search engine provides an information retrieval service for network users, which belongs to the Internet application software. The system provides information retrieval services for users according to certain retrieval strategies, and ranks the retrieval results into user-provided Internet information inquiry services [16–18]. At present, with the development of search engine technology, more and more organizations and personnel regard search engines as research hotspots [19, 20].

Z. Xu et al. (Eds.): CSIA 2019, AISC 928, pp. 901–907, 2020.
https://doi.org/10.1007/978-3-030-15235-2_120

2 Lucene Index System Structure Theory

2.1 Basic Algorithm Based on Lucene

Any system is made up of code, and the data structure determines the pros and cons of code efficiency. The design of the data structure has a direct impact on the secondary development of the Lucene toolkit. The direct feeling brought to the user is the speed and accuracy of the search engine query. A software system consists of a program and a data structure. For a search engine that processes large amounts of data, the quality of the program is second and foremost. It is important to optimize the data structure of the program. In order to be able to process large data volumes of documents, search engines are implemented using indexing techniques. Currently, there are three commonly used indexing techniques: inversion, suffix arrays, and signatures. The data processing of the suffix array is very efficient, but it is not suitable as the main technology of the search engine, because maintaining this indexing technology requires a high price; although the signature technology is suitable for search engine technology, the first indexing technology - Inverted, which is already faster than signature technology in terms of speed and efficiency. Inverted files are a way of indexing that is used primarily in major search engines and it is also a core technology in search engines.

2.2 Lucene Inverted Index Overview

One of the keys to search engine technology is inverted technology, which is very important. Because the algorithm and implementation of the system will directly affect the efficiency and accuracy of the search engine. If the keyword order is used to match such an algorithm, it matches the content of the document in order. In the matching process, if there is keyword information, the index is sent to the system, and if not, the document will continue to be searched. This type of search is very primitive. When the matching documents are not large, the speed is not slow, but if you encounter a document with a large amount of data, the retrieval time will be very long. For documents with a large amount of data, inverted technology can help search engines achieve better and more accurate retrieval performance. But maintaining inverted indexing is difficult. However, the inverted index has its irreplaceable advantage. Because it sends out a query, it can traverse the place where the search data has search keywords. Therefore, in the case of high response time requirements, many use the inverted index technology.

2.3 Fast Suffix Sorting Algorithm

Now let's introduce the suffix. The suffix sorting is to arrange all the suffixes of the initial string S according to certain setting rules. For example, the result of suffixing the original string S (that is, sorting S0, S1, S2, S3, S4, and S5) is: S1, S4, S2, S5, S0, S3. Let S denote the character string in the character queue. If the serial number of the string is smaller than the serial number of any character in the character queue, add a mark at the end of the string to obtain a new string. The format of the elements in the suffix array is all integer. The subscript index is stored in the lexicographic order of each suffix of S, which is called the suffix array corresponding to the string s, and is recorded as SA. According to the sequence number of the suffix array SA in the above example, {1, 4, 2, 5, 0, 3} can be obtained.

When constructing the index directory of the library file, we need to solve the efficiency problem of the retrieval, if we can find the index directory faster. This requires solving the suffix sorting. In the actual search engine search work, the amount of text data is very large, the general sorting algorithm is not enough to solve the fast search, we designed an algorithm to solve the fast search through the suffix array.

3 Lucene Index Algorithm Analysis

3.1 Preliminary Analysis of the Algorithm

We analyze the algorithm, sorting the elements into larger and smaller than the algorithm, and equalizing the algorithm as a new case analysis, thus obtaining three different element arrays. The algorithm of our team has adopted different treatments, and the specific analysis method has really improved the efficiency of the algorithm. We make full use of the results of the previous sorting algorithm, compare the complex algorithm with the simple algorithm, and multiply the K value in the recursive sorting process. It is also possible to determine whether the group of elements has been sorted by the symbol values in the array, and if the judgment is already sorted, it can be skipped. This way is more efficient.

3.2 Suffix Tree Index Performance and Function Analysis

The construction time complexity of the suffix tree is O(n), where n is the length of the text. The word segmentation operation is not required when establishing the suffix tree index, so the suffix tree index can be well adapted to the word boundary undetermined language and well supported phrase query. The longest suffix of document d is d itself, so the suffix tree contains enough information to generate the original document is a self-indexing. The suffix tree can only query where the string appears in the document collection and does not support sorting queries. The space complexity is too high and the sorting query is not supported, which limits the application of the suffix tree in information retrieval. The suffix array, like the suffix tree, is a self-index that fits well with the word boundary undetermined language and supports the phrase query very well. And query time performance and storage space performance is more effective than the suffix tree. The suffix array does not contain topology information like a suffix tree, and the hierarchical relationship between suffixes cannot be displayed. Like the suffix tree, the suffix array itself does not support sorted queries.

4 Search Engine Optimization

4.1 Search Engine Optimization System Structure

Search engine optimization is to improve the search engine's search results page ranking by searching the search engine's search and ranking rules, and using search engine search and ranking rules. It is to optimize and update the website through special methods. The keywords of the website are ranked relatively high in the search engine to compete for the clicks of the search users, thereby increasing the user traffic of the website. The main work is divided into internal optimization and external optimization. Internal optimization refers to the adjustment of the basic elements of the webpage. External optimization refers to how to increase the external links of the website. The ultimate goal of optimization is to improve the visit volume of the website and enhance the propaganda ability of the website.

4.2 Optimization of Website Domain Name

Website domain name. The domain name itself is also weighted. Generally, non-profit organization-type websites such as edu, gov, org, etc. have higher suffix domain names than com, cn, etc., and com domain names are more important than cn domain names. The impact of the choice of website name on the search results is mainly reflected in two points. The relevance of the domain name to the content of the website and the name of the domain name are recognized by the search engine. The relevance of the domain name to the content of the website is mainly reflected in whether the content of the website can be reflected in the website name. Then there is no need to buy domain names that have been punished by search engines.

4.3 Keyword Optimization

It can also be seen that in the whole process of search engine optimization, the positioning and analysis of keywords is the most important and at the core. If you choose too popular keywords, you may waste a lot of manpower, time and promotion costs, and it is not easy to get a good ranking; if you choose an unpopular keyword, even if you get a good ranking, you can bring the website A certain amount of traffic, but it is difficult to increase the conversion rate of potential customers; if you choose inaccurate keywords, it may bring some garbage traffic to the website, and even increase the burden on the website server, affect the browsing speed, and will seriously affect the follow-up All SEO promotion work. Therefore, the research on keywords has become the top priority of search engine optimization. If the keyword selection is appropriate, the search engine optimization work will be much easier, and naturally it will work quickly.

4.4 Optimization of Website Structure

The website structure refers to the hierarchical relationship between the pages in the website, which can be divided into logical structure and physical structure according to the nature. The structure of the website plays a very important role in determining the weight of the page, which directly affects the search engine's inclusion of the page. A reasonable website structure can effectively guide the search engine to capture more and more valuable pages. The optimization of the structure of the website refers to the reasonable adjustment of the physical structure of the website page and the internal link relationship, so as to reduce the depth of the page directory and the depth of the link with the important page. At the same time, the link entry of important pages is increased, thereby increasing the records and weights of these pages that are included in the search engine.

5 Index Algorithm Improvement

5.1 Semantic Improvement

Although the above Lucene internal similarity scoring algorithm works well in practical applications, it fails to capture the semantic information of the text. In the automatic response system, the questions asked by the user are relatively short, and the information that can be captured is relatively small. If the semantic information is not considered, the accuracy of the answer returned to the user can be imagined. For example, the user asks questions about the computer, and the computer is also called the computer. If only Lucene considers the word frequency without considering the semantic method, only the answer with the word "computer" can be found, and only the "computer" is used. The answer to the word is not found. If the semantic information of the term is considered, the retrieval information of the user can be obtained more accurately.

5.2 Terminology Improvement

The positional relationship of the term also plays a very important position in the question and answer system. For the question that the amount of information is relatively small, the influence of the positional relationship feature of the term on the answer accuracy may be crucial. The positional relationship characteristics of the term are not only related to the frequency of occurrence of the term, but also related to the relationship of the position of the word. The location relationship between terms is shown in Table 1.

Table 1. The location relationship between terms

Distance value	Adjacency
=1	Direct adjacency
>0 and <1	Adjacent
=0	Non adjacent

In this paper, the relationship characteristics of the position of the term are divided into three types: when the distance is 1, the two words are directly adjacent; when the distance is greater than 0 and less than 1, the word is adjacent after the stop word is removed; When the distance is equal to 0, the two words are not adjacent. Therefore, the positional relationship feature of the term can be further expressed as the distance relationship between the terms. In order to better reflect this relationship, "term position adjacent similarity" is introduced to reflect the degree of similarity between the query term and the term in the search document.

6 Summary

The Lucene full-text search mechanism works primarily in the indexing and retrieval phases of search engines. The results of this paper show that the proposed method is feasible and effective. Although the algorithm has some improvements, it still has some shortcomings; in this algorithm, the imported external dictionary needs to organize the synonyms and other things in advance, which is more troublesome. There is a need to find a simpler and more efficient way for the automatic response system to automatically recognize synonyms without external introduction, which will be the next stage of research considerations. It can be seen that Lucene's application in the field of search engines has great development prospects.

Acknowledgments. This research is supported by the key scientific research project of Anhui Provincial Department of Education (approval number: KJ2018A0819).

References

1. Ben-Porath DD, Federici A, Wisniewski L et al (2014) Dialectical behavior therapy: does it bring about improvements in affect regulation in individuals with eating disorders? J Contemp Psychother 44(4):245–251
2. Kelly AC, Wisniewski L, Martin-Wagar C et al (2017) Group-based compassion-focused therapy as an adjunct to outpatient treatment for eating disorders: a pilot randomized controlled trial. Clin Psychol Psychother 24(2):475–487
3. Stalnaker D, Zanibbi R (2015) Math expression retrieval using an inverted index over symbol pairs. In: Document recognition & retrieval XXII
4. Rane DD, Ghorpade VR (2015) Multi-user multi-keyword privacy preserving ranked based search over encrypted cloud data. In: International conference on pervasive computing
5. Patalia TP (2016) SearchAutomaton: searching mechanism for multi-format data by combining indexing tools and techniques. In: International conference on advances in information communication technology & computing
6. Tuarob S, Bhatia S, Mitra P et al (2016) AlgorithmSeer: a system for extracting and searching for algorithms in scholarly big data. IEEE Trans Big Data 2(1):3–17
7. Durumeric Z, Adrian D, Mirian A et al (2015) A search engine backed by internet-wide scanning. In: ACM SIGSAC conference on computer & communications security
8. Wei MK, Mycroft A, Anderson R (2013) Rendezvous: a search engine for binary code. In: Mining software repositories
9. Jeong JW, Morris MR, Teevan J et al (2013) A crowd-powered socially embedded search engine. Proc ICWSM
10. Xin Y, Pan B, Evans JA et al (2015) Forecasting Chinese tourist volume with search engine data. Tourism Manag 46:386–397
11. Evans MP (2013) Analysing Google rankings through search engine optimization data. Internet Res 17(1):21–37
12. Ghose A, Ipeirotis PG, Li B (2014) Examining the impact of ranking on consumer behavior and search engine revenue
13. Zhang S, Cabage N (2016) Search engine optimization: comparison of link building and social sharing. Data Processor Better Bus Educ 57(2):148–159

14. Gasparotto M (2014) Search engine optimization for the research librarian: a case study using the bibliography of U.S. Latina Lesbian history and culture. Acad Div Spec Libr Assoc
15. Giomelakis D, Veglis A (2016) Investigating search engine optimization factors in media websites. Digit Journalism 4(3):379–400
16. Sarlis AS, Drivas IC, Sakas DP (2017) Implementation and dynamic simulation modeling of search engine optimization processes. Improv Website Ranking
17. Moreno L, Martinez P (2013) Overlapping factors in search engine optimization and web accessibility. Online Inf Rev 37(4):564–580
18. Kritzinger WT, Weideman M (2013) Search engine optimization and pay-per-click marketing strategies. J Organ Comput Electron Commer 23(3):273–286
19. Gudivada VN, Rao D, Paris J (2015) Understanding search-engine optimization. Computer 48(10):43–52
20. Jindal M, Kharb N (2014) Data mining in web search engine optimization and user assisted rank results. Int J Comput Appl 95(8):1–5

Social Public Safety Investigation and Prevention Based on Big Data

Qing Lu[1(✉)], Jun Lu[2], and Xin Chen[3]

[1] Hunan Police Academy, Changsha 410100, Hunan, China
hn_luqing@126.com
[2] China Academy of Launch Vehicle Technology, Beijing, China
[3] Yueyang Housing Fund Management Center, Yueyang, China

Abstract. When social security has shifted from traditional security threats to the coexistence of traditional and non-traditional, the "rationality" of public security is no longer "management" but "governance". This paper first analyzes the definition of social public security based on big data, and compares the status quo of public security management at home and abroad, and puts forward the necessity of adopting early warning of social public safety. Provide technical support for social public safety investigation and prevention.

Keywords: Big data · Social public safety · Public safety management

1 Introduction

With the rapid development of the Internet and information technology, big data is slowly infiltrating into various fields of society, and people have gradually entered a "big data era" [1]. Big data can bring new thinking and new technologies to urban public safety warnings. In the context of big data, to achieve early warning of public security incidents is no longer a simple one-sidedness under traditional thinking, and based on some natural signs, it is not only required to collect, process, and transmit such huge information. It can be massively mined and intelligently processed [2–6]. Social public security is a prerequisite for social development and civilized progress [7]. In today's era, various crisis events triggered by rapid social changes have brought human society into a real "risk society" [3, 5, 8–10]. The essential feature of a risk society is "uncertainty", which means that it is difficult to effectively predict and control risks. In view of this, the improvement of government managers and the public's risk perception ability has become the key to improving the effectiveness of public safety governance [11–13]. The development of information technology in recent years, especially the advent of the era of "big data", has brought about fundamental changes in the way data and information are processed, which has brought new opportunities and challenges to traditional public security governance practices [11, 13, 14]. Fundamentally, the biggest feature of the big data era is the deep excavation of the value of various types of data, which is the high degree of scientific and technological rationality in the information society [15, 16].

Z. Xu et al. (Eds.): CSIA 2019, AISC 928, pp. 908–915, 2020.
https://doi.org/10.1007/978-3-030-15235-2_121

2 Definition of Social Public Safety Under Big Data

2.1 Big Data

Big data is frequently displayed in public cognition and applied by every industry. However, its analysis and exploration are still not perfect at this stage. There are many different opinions on the connotation of big data in the world. From the meaning, big data is a huge amount of information, but the analysis of the emergence of this term and its application, the meaning is far more than that. According to Wikipedia's overview, big data refers to a large, complex, and diverse information pool that cannot be collected, stored, extracted, analyzed, and transformed using systems that exist at this stage. In fact, the academic community has not reached an agreement on what constitutes big data. The widely cited concept is that "big data refers to data sets that are larger than conventional database tool acquisition, storage, management, and analysis capabilities". The use of big data not only requires the support of material technology, but also the change of the concept of the relevant subject. Unlike data in the usual sense, big data has its own uniqueness. Big data looks cumbersome from an individual perspective, but because the total amount of information included is extremely large, it can often lead to very critical and thought-provoking conclusions.

2.2 Social Public Safety

Public security mostly refers to citizen public safety, including a safe social environment and conditions that people need in their daily research, shopping, travel, and entertainment. From the perspective of government departments, public safety is the most useful service provided by the national public security department to citizens. Maintaining social security and stability, and building harmonious and stable living conditions for the people is an important task of the state's public security organs. At present, the core work of the service-oriented public sector is to provide citizens with public goods and perfect services, especially to protect their public safety, and to ensure that citizens' lives and property are not coerced and lost. Public security is a prerequisite for national development and social harmony. As a guarantee of a sound public security system, the country's talents can be stabilized, the economy can take off, and citizens can live and work in peace. Therefore, the quality of public security is closely related to national stability, social harmony, and people's happiness. It is an important part of national security management and public security prevention and control. It is an important condition for government departments to improve public management, build a country with science and technology, and people's happiness and well-being. Affecting the direction of the national economy, the public security situation, and the stability of the people are public hotspots that are of great concern to the public administration and the people.

2.3 Public Safety Management

Public safety management means that the state has comprehensive supervision and perfect legislative control. There are specialized institutions in the government departments, and there is a set of standard operating procedures and a theoretical system. The goal is to build a safe society and ensure the people. The safety and stability of the masses. In addition, in addition to the government, the government can also establish relevant laws and regulations, use relevant technical means, establish relevant government departments, improve relevant institutional systems, and advocate civil society organizations to participate in public safety management, such as various charitable foundations. Red Cross and volunteer organizations. Public safety management is the cornerstone and fundamental requirement of government governance, and it is a scientific, systematic and humanized governance project. Public safety management work has both the attributes of government administrative governance and legal attributes.

3 Comparison of Domestic and International Situation

3.1 Analysis of Current Situation Abroad

There are many international big data practices, and the United States is the leader in big data practice research. In many public security fields, there are specific practices of big data. National government departments use big data technology to improve public safety management. Significant results; use of big data to enhance its ability to oppose international terrorism. The United States has established a "prism" big data platform. By using big data mining technology, big data extraction technology and analysis tools, the US national security agencies can acquire and study a variety of data to discover the relationship between actions. And then predict the next action trend of criminals. This has added strong technical support and effective evidence for national security agencies to defend against terrorists and other acts that harm national interests; the ability to use big data to protect social security. In addition to the anti-terrorism work carried out by government departments at all times, the involvement of private enterprises and social welfare organizations in public security is also the essential work of the state to safeguard public safety and social security. Use big data to reduce the ability of criminal cases to occur. The emergence of crime prevention cases, especially large-scale crimes, is an important task in safeguarding public safety. Using big data technology as a means, it is possible to extract and analyze effective information from huge data, so as to find similarities of cases and predict crime cases, which can effectively reduce the occurrence of cases.

3.2 Analysis of Domestic Situation

The research on the construction of public security prevention and control system under the background of big data at home and abroad is constantly improved and developed by countries and regions based on their actual conditions and the actual exploration process of comprehensive police work. Through research and review, it can be clarified from multiple angles. Under the background of big data, the current basic theory of social security prevention and control system construction research field, grasp the development trend of this research. The public security big data application platform built at this stage is a comprehensive platform based on cloud computing and big data technology, such as centralized collection, data synchronization, resource sharing, and information release. It ensures social stability, safeguards people's safety, and prevents and controls. Unknown disasters are an important support platform for smart policing. With the increasing investment in the informationization construction of the public security department, the data resources of the public security departments are increasing, and the breadth and depth of their data are qualitatively improved. The demand for big data by police officers at all levels is increasing. Bigger data customization requirements are also more detailed, and big data plays a valuable role in police work. The government's public security governance based on big data has an obvious effect on improving the efficiency of the public security department. It is a powerful weapon for public security departments at all levels to provide high-quality services to the people.

4 Social Public Safety Prevention

The early warning of urban public safety management has played an effective role. It can play a preventive role in the face of unexpected situations and reduce the threats and losses brought to society. In recent years, the early warning system has been continuously optimized, and social public safety has also reached the corresponding Feedback, as shown in Fig. 1, when the entire emergency warning system can not operate effectively, and ultimately pay a painful price because of the defense. Optimizing the urban public security early warning mechanism in the era of big data is an important guarantee for improving the city's emergency management capabilities, and it can also greatly improve the public security governance level of modern cities.

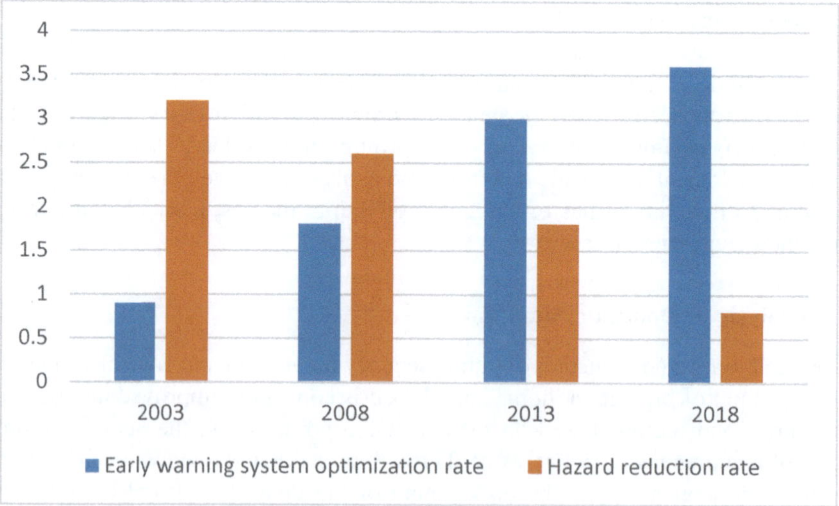

Fig. 1. Optimization feedback map of early warning system

4.1 Precision Warning

The most important and important function of the urban public safety early warning mechanism is the pre-forecasting of public safety incidents. The focus of the early warning work is to be able to predict public crisis events within a certain period of time, that is, to accurately and refine various types of information and data. The prediction and research, anti-micro-duration, to get the time and opportunity for early preparations for various precautions. The concept of precision warning is to require the early warning mechanism to accurately and comprehensively monitor the abnormal situation, and to carry out scientific grading according to the scope and degree of impact of the crisis event, and issue alarms according to different levels to guide the relevant government departments to formulate science, Reasonable grading plan, take appropriate measures to prevent and control the crisis.

4.2 Collaborative Warning

The urban public security early warning mechanism is a highly complex system that requires the participation and cooperation of departments and departments, governments and multiple entities to achieve efficient operation of the early warning mechanism. The concept of coordinated early warning first requires strengthening the coordination and sharing of early warning data, early warning information, early warning technology, early warning funds, and early warning personnel in the era of big data. Secondly, it is necessary to build an urban public security early warning unified command and coordination organization to realize various resources and Timely dispatching and sharing of information, clarifying the responsibilities and authorities of various departments, and preventing the phenomenon of multiple outs of government and mutual suspicion affecting resource utilization efficiency.

4.3 Rapid Warning

The outbreak of public safety events in most cities is very rapid, and early warning mechanisms need to be able to respond quickly. This requires us to use the concept of rapid warning to guide the optimization of urban public safety early warning mechanism, adhere to the concept of rapid warning, and to establish the concept of time first. Ensure that public safety incidents are controlled in a timely manner, to minimize or reduce the economic and personnel losses caused by the outbreak of public security incidents, to maintain the stability of social order, to protect the public from harm, and to promote the orderly development of security measures. Second, we must uphold the concept of decisive decision. When urban public safety incidents occur, decisions must be made decisively and the warplanes must not be delayed. Ensure that all departments work together, communicate effectively, and respond promptly and accurately.

4.4 Specification Warning

To realize the optimization of urban public security early warning mechanism in the era of big data, the opening and sharing of data is indispensable, and to realize the opening of all kinds of public big data, it is necessary to have laws to follow, to achieve openness and evidence, and to share effectively. The harmonious situation. In addition, the construction of urban public security early warning mechanism is a comprehensive system involving government, society, citizens and other subjects. Without a unified standard and normative regulations, all kinds of information will be disordered, and public security management will develop in an orderly manner. To this end, it is necessary to use laws and regulations as a guide to improve the relevant rules and regulations of the urban public safety early warning mechanism from the national and individual levels, clarify the responsibility of each department, and standardize the operation of various information and processes.

5 Optimization of Public Safety Governance Under the Participation of Big Data

5.1 System Sound Guarantee

It is necessary to strengthen the top-level design and overall planning to promote the construction of the social security prevention and control system from top to bottom. After the unified construction plan has been formulated, the task of subdivision construction will be promoted in the form of special classes. "Based on the current, planning long-term, close to actual combat", the design of a scientific and complete public security prevention and control system construction overall plan in line with the actual situation of local public security. It is necessary to strengthen the top-level design and overall planning to promote the construction of the social security prevention and control system from top to bottom. After the unified construction plan has been formulated, the task of subdivision construction will be promoted in the form of special classes. "Based on the current, planning long-term, close to actual combat", the design of a scientific and complete public security prevention and control system construction overall plan in line with the actual situation of local public security.

5.2 Platform Basic System Construction

The construction of public security prevention and control system urgently needs to introduce new technologies such as big data, cloud computing, Internet+, and Internet of Things. It is necessary to increase efforts to promote big data platforms, cloud computing centers, mobile police systems and other related basic platforms on the basis of overall planning. System construction, the formation of backbone support for information applications. In the era of big data, the most important and most important object of public security informationization and big data application is data. It is necessary to attach great importance to the collection and integration of basic data, and use the techniques of face recognition, RFID radio frequency chip, two-dimensional code, etc. to build a comprehensive information collection network covering the whole range, and comprehensively collect basic security data such as the residential vehicle yard network in real time. At the same time, strengthen data integration and sharing, open up the data circulation channels of the whole society, and provide the source of living water.

5.3 Cultivation of Technical Talents

The purpose of the public security prevention and control system is to realize a series of systems, platforms and mechanisms that can be applied continuously, extensively and deeply, and the ultimate goal is to serve the actual situation. Actively use information technology to serve police and actual combat, close to practical practice, focus on police actual combat, deepen police-enterprise, police-institutional cooperation, not only attach importance to independent innovation, but also make good use of external wisdom and make full use of various types of New technology and new technology innovations are in actual combat, and existing problems are solved. It is necessary to pay attention to cooperation with high-end technology companies in different fields, especially some enterprises have unique resources and unique technologies, such as Tencent's leading position in the social field. It is necessary to actively introduce and cultivate the government's professional data talents. In-depth cooperation with companies, institutions and universities to ensure that the staff, whether at the leadership, management, executive and supervisor levels, have the necessary expertise and skills.

6 Summary

Improving the city's public safety risk management and control capabilities and improving the urban public safety system have become the top priority for solving "urban diseases". Using big data thinking and means to build a city public safety big data platform is an important starting point for solving urban public security problems. Of course, in addition to the conceptual change, the real implementation of smart governance requires the improvement of the system of institutional rules and the support of advanced technology tools. These changes and developments will bring new prospects for the realization of public security governance and social stability and harmony.

Acknowledgments. This research was supported by Ministry of Public Security Applied Innovation Project (No. 2018YYCXHNST048), and Science and Technology Project of Hunan Provincial Public Security Department.

References

1. Nan Z, Hong H (2013) Social vulnerability for public safety: a case study of Beijing, China. Chin Sci Bull 58(19):2387–2394
2. Vries AD (2013) Project X: impact of social media on public safety. Proj X Impact Soc Media Pub Saf Tno Repository
3. Wu S, Ell K, Grossschulman SG et al (2014) Technology-facilitated depression care management among predominantly Latino diabetes patients within a public safety net care system: comparative effectiveness trial design. Contemp Clin Trials 37(2):342–354
4. Hendriks T, Laar PVD (2013) METIS: dependable cooperative systems for public safety. Proc Comput Sci 16(1):542–551

5. Bartoli G, Fantacci R, Gei F et al (2013) A novel emergency management platform for smart public safety. Int J Commun Syst 28(5):928–943
6. Yu D, Fang C, Dan X et al (2014) assessing urban public safety via indicator-based evaluating method: a systemic view of shanghai. Soc Indic Res. 117(1):89–104
7. Lin J, Petersilia J (2014) Follow the money: How California counties are spending their public safety realignment funds. Social Science Electronic Publishing
8. Kennedy DM, Sherker S, Brighton B et al (2013) Rocky coast hazards and public safety: moving beyond the beach in coastal risk management. Ocean Coast Manag 82(Sept):85–94
9. Surobhi NA, Jamalipour A (2014) A MANET-based semantic traffic management framework for ubiquitous public safety networks. Wirel Commun Mob Comput 14 (12):1127–1142
10. Kożuch B, Sienkiewicz-Małyjurek K (2015) Information sharing in complex systems: a case study on public safety management. Proc - Soc Behav Sci 213:722–727
11. Dunaway M, Murphy R, Venkatasubramanian N et al (2017) Research agenda in intelligent infrastructure to enhance disaster management, community resilience and public safety
12. Morris R (2015) Public safety from a management perspective. RSM Discov Mag Collect
13. Lee S, Chen L, Duan S et al (2017) URBAN-NET: a network-based infrastructure monitoring and analysis system for emergency management and public safety. In: IEEE International conference on big data
14. Nguyen TT, Bonnet C (2016) 5 – IP mobility management for future public safety networks. Wirel Pub Saf Netw, 127–172
15. Wu S, Ell K, Grossschulman SG et al (2014) Technology-facilitated depression care management among predominantly Latino diabetes patients within a public safety net care system: comparative effectiveness trial design. Contemp Clin Trials 37(2):342–354
16. Ball DJ, Ballking L (2013) Safety management and public spaces: restoring balance. Risk Anal 33(5):763–771

Intelligent Diagnosis of Middle and Low Voltage Distribution Network Fault Based on Big Data

Jing Hua[1,2], Yan-Ping Zhou[1,2], Wei Xiong[1,2(✉)], Lin Niu[1,2], and Xu Zhao[1,2]

[1] Honghe University, Mengzi 661100, YunNan, China
459353359@qq.com
[2] Kunming Power Supply Company, Yunnan Power Gird Co., Ltd., Kunming 650011, China

Abstract. At present, the fault diagnosis information of the middle and low voltage distribution network is insufficient and scattered, and the fault diagnosis and positioning of the low and low pressure synthesis is urgently needed for the comprehensive utilization of power distribution automation, metering automation and 95598 customer service report. This paper carried out based on the large data of low voltage intelligent fault diagnosis and positioning analysis, further enhance the fault of the distribution and grab the dispatcher commander and people with disabilities positioning analysis efficiency, improve the level of fault disposal of the lean management.

Keywords: Big data · Middle and low voltage distribution network · Intelligent diagnosis

1 Introduction

Under the background of speeding up the construction of distribution network during the 13th Five-Year Plan and a new round of upgrading and transformation of rural power network, based on the "customer-centered" theory, Kunming Bureau seized the opportunity of rapid construction of distribution automation system, taking the lead in practicality and reforming the command and management system of distribution network emergency repair, initially established the command level of distribution automation and distribution network emergency repair and other systems [1, 2]. The construction of distribution automation master station realizes the integration of distribution network regulation and control, effectively integrates dispatching, control and monitoring services, establishes a safe and efficient dispatching operation mechanism, and forms a three-in-one centralized operation mode of distribution network dispatching, control and monitoring. The establishment of distribution network emergency repair command center and the pilot development and application of Kunming distribution network platform have initially realized the unified command of distribution network fault handling system [3, 4].

Z. Xu et al. (Eds.): CSIA 2019, AISC 928, pp. 916–922, 2020.
https://doi.org/10.1007/978-3-030-15235-2_122

At present, the main station of distribution automation mainly realizes the three remote functions of distribution automation switch, and the command platform of distribution network emergency repair mainly realizes the management and control of medium and low voltage emergency repair operation flow and resource dispatch command. In the comprehensive use of distribution automation, metering automation, 95598 customer service work order for low-voltage integrated fault diagnosis and location is blank area, it is urgent to improve through information technology [5].

In this paper, intelligent fault diagnosis and location analysis of medium and low voltage based on large data is carried out to further improve the efficiency of fault location analysis of distribution dispatchers and distribution preemption commanders, improve the level of lean fault management [6, 7].

2 The Status of Fault Diagnosis in Kunming Middle Low Voltage Distribution Network System

Medium and low voltage distribution network refers to the voltage level of 10 kV and below. Kunming Power Supply Bureau 10 kV ring network cabinet, post switch and distribution station are connected to distribution automation main station system. The system was built in 2012 and put into SCADA function application. The DA function of distribution automation in 2017 was tested and put into operation. The fault diagnosis of distribution automation line is through distribution. Automation system DA function, to achieve fast fault location, fault isolation and restoration of power supply in non-fault areas. The main station system has realized the information integration with GIS and EMS of dispatching automation. It collects the operation data of distribution network of Kunming power grid centrally. According to the fault alarm detected by each distribution terminal, and combines the relay protection signal of substation, switch station, switch tripping and other fault information, it starts the fault processing program. Determine the type and location of the fault. The fault section is clearly shown on the automatic single-line diagram of distribution network by dynamic topology colouring. According to the need, the main station can provide one or more operation plans for accident isolation and restoration of power supply, assist the management personnel of distribution network to carry out remote control operation, quickly isolate fault and restore power supply [8].

For non-distribution automation lines, the distribution network fault information comes from the provincial customer service fault report sheet, the distribution and preemption command platform for fault diagnosis and analysis, and according to the line fault area, voltage level distribution to the District Power Supply Bureau emergency repair class, low-voltage emergency repair station for processing. The problem is that there is no information exchange between the command platform and distribution automation system, dispatching automation system EMS, metrology "four in one" system, marketing system PMS and other systems, so it is impossible to make intelligent diagnosis of distribution network by using multi-source information such as customer fault reporting, distribution line tripping, distribution data, PMS and so on [9].

In the existing CSGII system, dispatching automation, distribution automation, metering automation systems have information data support, but each system does not have multi-source information integration, for distribution network dispatchers and distribution network emergency repair commanders in the low and medium-voltage fault diagnosis and analysis function. For example, the GIS platform provides graphic and topological relationships between medium and low-voltage distribution networks. The marketing system provides station line to user relationship. The dispatching automation system provides SOE signals for switch trip and protective action in substations. Distribution automation system provides SOE signal of distribution automation switch tripping and protection action in distribution lines and stations. The metering "four in one" system provides telemetry data such as distribution and alarm, power and voltage [10].

3 Intelligent Diagnosis of Low Voltage Fault in Distribution Network Based on Big Data

Centralized dispatching automation EMS, distribution automation system, metering automation system and marketing system and other sources of information to form a data center to achieve intelligent diagnosis of low-voltage faults in distribution network, including automatic system alarm intelligent diagnosis [10], distribution and transformer terminal power loss alarm push-back switch tripping, low-voltage barrier back-push medium-voltage fault and so on (Fig. 1).

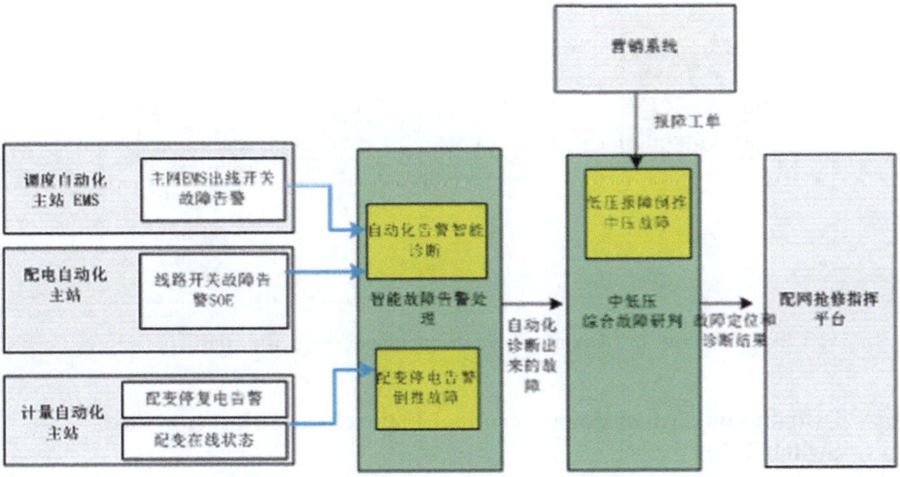

Fig. 1. Intelligent diagnosis architecture of low voltage fault in distribution network based on big data

3.1 Automatic System Fault Alarm Processing, Automatic Start up

By visiting the three-zone event database of dispatching automation and distribution automation, the SOE signals of switching and protection actions of substation and line automation switches are read, and several SOE events such as switching and closing, protective action and reclosing action of the same line are merged automatically, which are automatically diagnosed as normal switching and permanent switching of the switch and line. The conclusions of switch tripping caused by long-term faults and switch tripping caused by instantaneous faults of transmission lines make it possible for dispatchers to quickly identify critical events from a large number of alarms and improve the processing efficiency of a large number of alarms under extreme weather conditions [11].

For the diagnosis of line tripping fault automatic generation work order, transmission to the fault repair command platform, for permanent fault automatic generation fault order, for instantaneous fault automatic generation patrol order, sent to the distribution network repair command and production system, reduce the 10 kV switch tripping after the single dispatch time (Fig. 2).

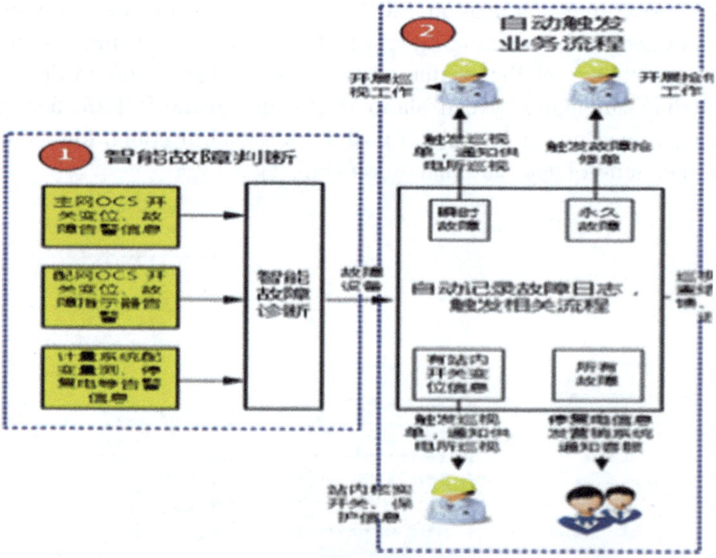

Fig. 2. Automatic alarm intelligent diagnosis chart

3.2 Distribution Transformer Terminal Failure Alarm Reverse Push Switch Trip

Nowadays, most of the distribution line switches in Kunming suburbs and rural areas are non-automatic switches. There is no automatic monitoring method for the fault tripping of the line switches. The tripping switches can only be determined by calling 95598 telephone and on-site inspection by the operation and maintenance team. This process usually takes a long time and breaks down. Inefficient investigation, seriously affecting the reliability of power supply, but also easy to cause customer complaints.

Based on the information of power failure alarm event, 15-min instantaneous data and terminal on-line status sent by metering automation monitoring terminal, and combined with the topology of power grid GIS, the "back-stepping fault point" is realized, and the switching tripping of distribution lines is detected and judged actively [12]. The visual fault diagnosis and information release is carried out by combining WebGIS. The realization of this requirement is expected to greatly improve the active detection ability of non-automatic switching tripping faults in medium-voltage distribution lines, shorten the time of switch tripping to a few minutes, thus greatly shortening the fault location time of distribution lines and improving the emergency repair of faults. Efficiency and enhance customer satisfaction (Fig. 3).

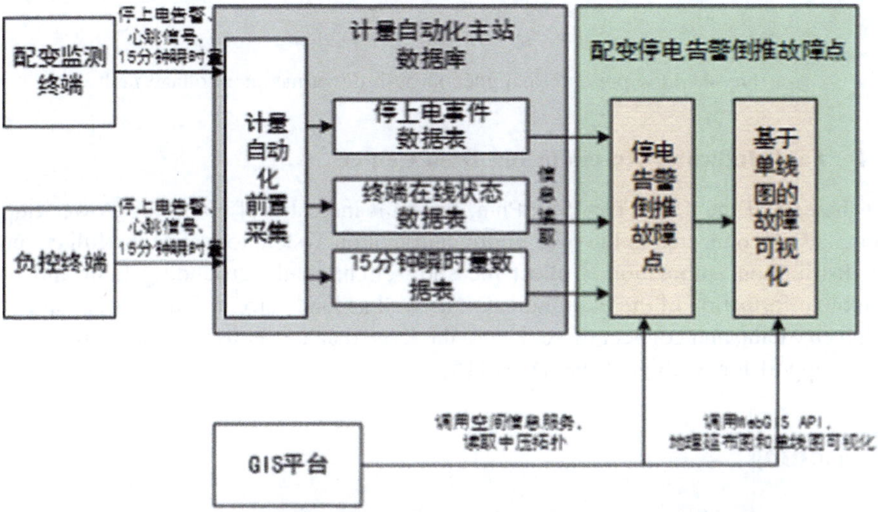

Fig. 3. Failure plan of distribution transformer alarm backward push

3.3 Low Voltage Obstacle Avoidance Medium Voltage Fault

According to the geographic location of multiple barrier work sheets, the spatial correlation judgment basis of the same residential area, and the electrical correlation of the same low-voltage station area and the same low-voltage switch outlet, the single-household fault, low-voltage switch tripping or distribution transformer blackout can be judged. According to the result of the fault diagnosis, according to the GIS topology, it can assist in judging the trip of the line switch [13, 14].

Display building address, residential district outline, distribution transformer power supply range and other information in low-voltage GIS, and graphical display of distribution transformer-low-voltage switch-low-voltage line-switch box-meter box-user power supply relationship by means of station extension map or single-line map, graphical display of unit location information of reporting obstacles, visual display of low-voltage reporting obstacles The reasoning logic and judgement result of the medium voltage fault are inverted (Fig. 4).

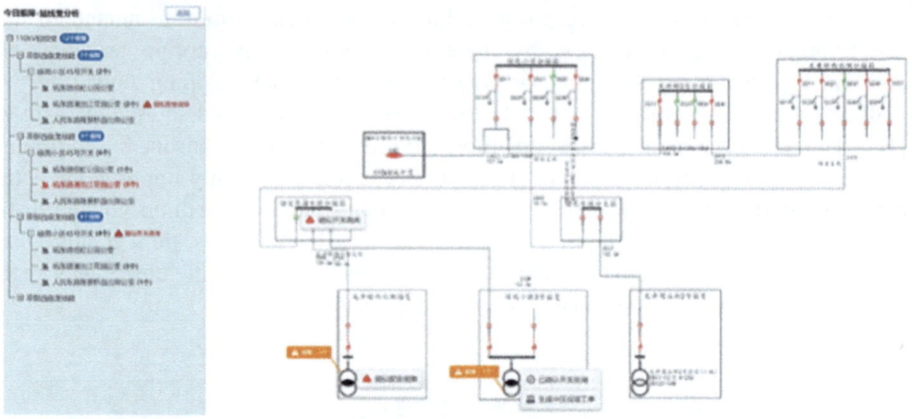

Fig. 4. Low pressure malfunction push down medium voltage fault

3.4 Fault Indicator Access to Big Data Center

At the end of the 13th Five-Year Plan, the fault indicator of Kunming Power Supply Bureau was connected to the distribution automation system to realize the full coverage of distribution automation. Collect the short-circuit fault, grounding fault and other remote information of the fault indicator, as well as load current, fault current and other telemetry data, and connect these data to the large data center to provide more powerful data support for intelligent diagnosis [15].

4 Ending

By constructing distribution automation, metering automation, 95598 customer service report work order and other large data centers, and connecting the fault indicators of uncovered distribution automation lines, the intelligent fault diagnosis and location of medium and low voltage distribution network can be realized, and the reliability of power supply can be improved.

References

1. Xin P et al (2011) Technical specification for distribution automation system of Kunming Power Suppl Bureau
2. Xu Z et al (2017) Implementation plan of Kunming Power Supply Bureau 2017 distribution network rush repair command center
3. Sheng R, Zheng H, Jing H (2010) Application of MMAS and rough set in fault diagnosis of bearing. Vibr Test Diagn 30(2):128–131
4. Yang J, Sun X, Che H et al (2009) Rolling force prediction of cold continuous rolling mill of neural network based on ant colony algorithm. Steel 44(3):52–55
5. Li P, Yan Y, Zheng W (2010) Short term load forecasting based on quantum neural network with evidence theory. Power Syst Prot Control 38(16):49–53

6. Li W, Zhang S (2010) Fault classification based on improved evidence theory and fusion of multiple neural networks. J Mech Eng 46(9):93–99
7. Yang J, Huang H (2008) Early fault diagnosis method for Aero Engine based on evidence theory. J Aerosp Power 23(12):2327–2331
8. Yang Z, Zhou J (2009) A turbine fault diagnosis method based on D-S evidence theory. Hydropower Energy Sci 27(2):152–154
9. Kang C, Xia Q, Liu M (2007) Power system load forecasting. China Electric Power Press, pp 196–199
10. Li Y, Chen D, Zhang Z et al (2001) Study on the improved time difference method for the identification of current transformer saturation. Protection 29(11):1–4
11. Jing S, Liu X (2004) Analysis of the error caused by the differential protection of the busbar differential protection caused by the saturation of the converter. Protection 32(2):70–71
12. Ding X, Zhao M, Pi X et al (2008) Measures to prevent the malfunction of busbar protection caused by AC series DC to DC bus. Power Syst Prot Control 36(22):97–99
13. Yuan J-X, Sheng H, Wu J (2004) Guide for application of current transformers for protection. China Electric Power Press, Beijing. (2000). Autom Electr Power Syst 24(6):54–56
14. Chen J-Y, Meng X, Zhang Z et al (2008) Analysis and Countermeasures of the influence of saturation of current transformer on relay protection. Protection 34(3):870–889
15. Li Y, Chen D-S, Zhang Z et al (2010) Study on improved time difference method for identification of TA saturation. Relay 29(11):1–5

Using Three-Frame Difference Algorithm to Detect Moving Objects

Zhigao Zhang[1(✉)], Hongmei Zhang[2], and Zhifeng Zhang[2]

[1] College of Math, Inner Mongolia University for Nationalities, Tongliao, China
zzgtongxin@163.com
[2] College of Computer Science and Technology,
Inner Mongolia University for Nationalities, Tongliao, China
Tongyu_007@163.com, zzfzyr@163.com

Abstract. Detection technology for moving targets is an important direction in computer vision research. This paper proposes a method to improve moving target detection, which is a three-frame difference algorithm combining edge information. This difference algorithm can detect moving objects with high accuracy. For the real-time image captured by the camera, the algorithm not only can reduce the processing time, but also judge the moving object with the fastest speed and the highest accuracy. In the process of the algorithm, Expansion and corrosion in mathematical morphology are used to remove noise from images. Due to the detection of moving targets, there will inevitably be some interference factors, and these factors will have a more serious impact on the detection sample. In order to eliminate the influence of noise on the processing results, the algorithm first divides the image into binary image, expansion and corrosion treatment of the image, and then according to the different pixel points between the three frame images, the shape of the object can be determined by the information of space and time, so as to identify the moving object, give an alarm and save the image to the local area.

Keywords: Three-frame difference · Expansion · Moving detection · Corrosion

1 Introduction

Moving object detection is the key point and difficult point in video image analysis. Currently, the inter-frame difference method should be mainly used in the still state of the camera head, where false targets are more likely to appear, and the reduplication of the two-frame object image will lead to detection failure. The calculation of optical flow method is complex and real-time monitoring can not be achieved. Regarding the issue above, the three-frame difference algorithm proposed here integrates edge information extraction and adaptive threshold calculation methods. The algorithm is simple to calculate and has high detection accuracy. When the dynamic image is captured, three images are continuously acquired, which are contiguous in the same video sequence, i.e., k frames, k − 1 frames and k + 1 frames. Subtract k − 1 frames

Z. Xu et al. (Eds.): CSIA 2019, AISC 928, pp. 923–928, 2020.
https://doi.org/10.1007/978-3-030-15235-2_123

from the k frames, subtract k frames from the k + 1 frames, obtain two frame difference images, and then perform "and" operations to obtain the binary image matrix [1].

The differential algorithm mentioned in this paper is based on the image frame difference algorithm. We know that the interframe difference algorithm can find the change area between two adjacent frames, which is derived from the theory of background image difference [2]. This changed area will contain information about the object before it was moved. Obviously, this region is larger than the actual contour of the moving object. Similarly, the difference image, between before and after frames, contains the same region. In this paper, the principle of the three-frame difference method is to obtain a difference image between two adjacent frames and then perform the "and" operation on the difference image. Since both images contain the region after the movement change, we "and" the two images, and take their intersection, so that we can get the similar outline of the object [3, 4].

2 The Basic Principle of Frame Difference Method

The principle of this differential algorithm is very simple. It is to obtain the approximate motion profile of the target by performing differential operations on double consecutive frame images in the sequence of video images [5]. When the abnormal target movement appeared in the surveillance scene, between two adjacent frames will appear obvious difference. In order to analyze the motion characteristics of the target object in the image sequence or video, two adjacent image frames can be subtracted. An absolute value of the pixel value difference can be obtained, which is from the same coordinate, is compared with a set threshold. Its mathematical formula is described as follows:

$$D(x, y) = \begin{cases} 1, if|(I(t) - I(t-1)| > T \\ 0, others \end{cases}$$

D (x, y), the differential one between the two pictures in a row; I(t) and I(t − 1) represent the pictures of two adjacent frames respectively; T is a selected threshold for the binarization of differential images, D(x, y) represents the foreground, when its value is 1, when it is 0, it means the background [6, 7].

3 Implementation of Three Frames Difference Algorithm

(1) Three continuous image frames are selected from the video sequence, the first frame image is $f_{k-1}(x, y)$, the second is $f_k(x, y)$, the third is $f_{k+1}(x, y)$. Decrease the amount of calculation and increase the speed of calculation, we first convert the color image to gray image, and then convert to binary image. The following formula can be used:

$$Y = 0.299 \times R + 0.587 \times G + 0.114 \times B$$

The corresponding grayscale image can be obtained by the above method.

(2) The basic frame difference algorithm is applied to the gray image to get the corresponding binarized image [8]. Calculate the difference between the $f_k(x, y)$ frame and the $f_{k-1}(x, y)$ frame $D_1(x, y)$, getting the absolute value of target changing, and then performing the frame difference processing to the image, we can obtain the two value image after the target change, and its mathematical expression is as follows:

$$\mathrm{D}_1(\mathrm{x}, \mathrm{y}) = \left\{ \begin{array}{ll} 255, & |f_k(x, y) - f_{k-1}(x, y)| \geq T \\ 0, & |f_k(x, y) - f_{k-1}(x, y)| \leq T \end{array} \right\}$$

(3) Calculated by a $f_{k+1}(x, y)$ image and the $f_k(x, y)$ image difference $D_2(x, y)$, get the target change, after the same frame difference operation, obtained by the difference of the $f_{k+1}(x, y)$ frame and the $f_k(x, y)$ of value images target formula is variation:

$$\mathrm{D}_2(\mathrm{x}, \mathrm{y}) = \left\{ \begin{array}{ll} 255, & |f_{k+1}(x, y) - f_k(x, y)| \geq T \\ 0, & |f_{k+1}(x, y) - f_k(x, y)| \leq T \end{array} \right\}$$

(4) Take the intersection of $D_1(x, y)$ and $D_2(x, y)$, Acquire a three-frame difference processed image $D(x, y)$, which is the moving region image of the object. $D(x, y)$ is expressed as a formula:

$$D(x, y) = \left\{ \begin{array}{ll} 255, & |D_1(x, y) \cap D_2(x, y)| \geq T \\ 0, & |D_1(x, y) \cap D_2(x, y)| \leq T \end{array} \right\}$$

In the formula, T represents an advance in the chosen threshold. In order to ensure that the background image difference comparison method, we also use the threshold extraction method used in background image difference, namely through the current gray image threshold value is obtained dynamically [9–11].

The moving target image is obtained by using the three-frame difference algorithm, which has been binarized, and many noise in the image is removed by mathematical morphology. This algorithm uses two basic mathematical morphological operations, expansion and corrosion, to obtain the target image. Because the three-frame difference algorithm has one more difference operation than the background image difference method, it has less noise than the background image difference method. However, when we get the intersection of two difference images, there are also some "glitch" phenomenon. Therefore, removing the noise in the image is a crucial step. From the theory of mathematical morphology, we can know that the corrosion operation has a reduction effect on the image. After etching the binary image obtained by frame difference algorithm, we can remove the excess part of the extracted target image, so as to make the target contour clearer [12].

The results of moving target detection using three-frame difference algorithm are shown in the following figure. These results are selected after many experiments and have representative results to analyze and compare.

Figure 1 shows the results of three effects: shadow, overlap between objects, and occlusion. Figure 1(d) is the difference image obtained by the three-frame difference algorithm. The algorithm is good for detecting moving targets from the detection result.

(a) 20th frames (b) 21th frames (c) 22th frames (d) Difference image

Fig. 1. Shadow and object overlap affect measurement results

Figure 2 is in the non static background; the extraction of the video continuous three images of the three-frame differencing operations, Fig. 2(d) is through the three-frame difference image obtained after operation, according to the experimental results can be drawn, the three-frame difference algorithm under dynamic background for moving target detection also showed better results.

(a) 79th frames (b) 80th frames (c) 81th frames (d) Difference image

Fig. 2. Non static background detection effect diagram

Figure 3 is the target detection result obtained by using the algorithm at high-speed motion of the object. Figure 3(d) is the three-frame difference image, the calculation results show that the three-frame difference operation in high-speed motion object, it can detect moving targets.

(a) 139th frames (b) 140th frames (c) 141th frames (d) Difference image

Fig. 3. Detection result of high speed moving object

With the background image difference processing method and denoising of the same value of the two images to the above algorithm, mathematical morphology is used to corrosion, and then expanded to deal with the noise, get the result shown in Fig. 4. The (a) in Fig. 4 is the (d) in the figure above, and (b) is the (d) in the figure above, Figure (c) is the (d) in the figure above.

(a) Corrosion Expansion

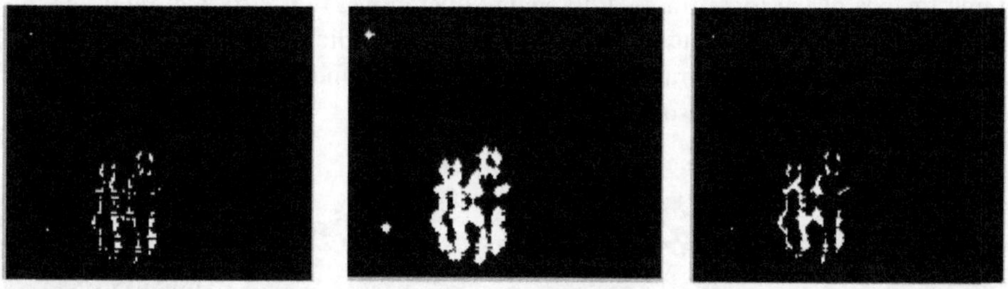

(b) Corrosion Expansion

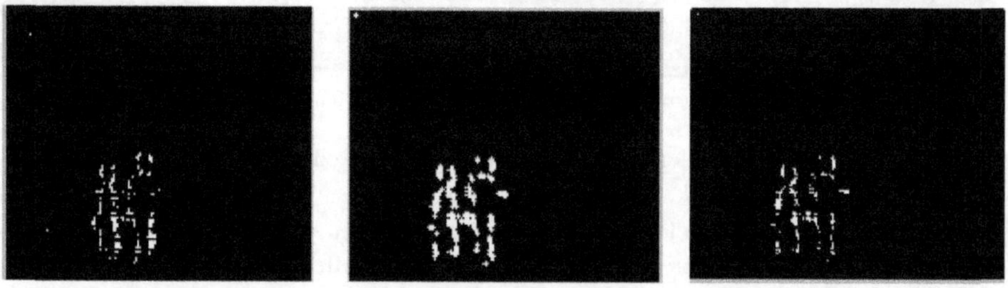

(c) Corrosion Expansion

Fig. 4. Morphological processing results of three-frame difference algorithm

4 Conclusion

According to the above results, the three-frame difference algorithm is outstanding in terms of a moving object detection, and the motion contours detected by the algorithm is clearer and more explicit.

From two experiments comparing the results we can see that the three-frame difference algorithm and the background image difference algorithm realize detection of moving objects, but the three-frame difference algorithm has higher accuracy and better detection effect.

Acknowledgement. This work is supported by the Scientific Research Foundation of Inner Mongolia University for Nationalities (NMDYB1757).

References

1. Qiu LK, Liu QL, Lei WL (2014) The motion detection based on background subtraction and three frame difference. J Hefei Univ Technol 5(37):572–577
2. Hua YL, Liu WJ (2014) Moving target detection algorithm based on improved mixed Gauss model. Comput Appl 34(2):580–584
3. Tong N, Duan X (2002) Research on detection algorithm for vehicle monitoring system. In: The first Chinese conference on intelligent surveillance, Beijing, pp 612–616
4. Fan W, Liu Y, Tang B (2016) Toward high efficiency for content-based multiattribute event matching via hybrid methods. Sci China (Inf Sci) 59(2):1–16
5. Morrison P, Zou JJ (2015) Inexact graph matching using a hierarchy of matching processes. Comput Vis Media 1(4):291–307
6. Zhao Y, Zhai Y, Dubois E, Wang S (2016) Image matching algorithm based on SIFT using color and exposure information. J Syst Eng Electron 27(3):691–699
7. Kim N-J, Lee H-J, Lee J-B (2008) Probabilistic global motion estimation based on Laplacian two-bit plane matching for fast digital image stabilization. EURASIP J Adv Signal Process 2008:180582
8. Ryu J-B, Lee C-G, Park H-H (2011) Formula for Harris corner detector. Electron Lett 47 (3):180–181
9. Nájera Juan J, Fochesatto Javier G, Last Deborah J, Percival Carl J, Horn Andrew B (2009) Infrared spectroscopic methods for the study of aerosol particles using white cell optics: development and characterization of a new aerosol flow tube. Rev Sci Instrum 79 (12):124102
10. Chai MC (2014) The complete extraction scheme of edge detection. Brand (9):169
11. Zheng JS (2008) The reach on extraction algorithm for vehicle edge based on adaptive threshold. J Shandong Jiaotong Univ 16(1):23–25
12. Tian P, Jin J, Li L et al (2007) A kind of biological characteristic recognition based on between-class variance and morphology. J Tsinghua Univ (Nat Sci) 47(z2):1747–1750

Research on Computer-Aided Ideological and Political Teaching Based on Constructivism

Yu Zhang(✉)

Marx Doctrine Teaching Department, Anhui Foreign Language University, Hefei 230001, Anhui, China
13499713@qq.com

Abstract. With the acceleration of the pace of reform and opening up in China and the promotion of quality education by the state, the current teaching of ideological and political courses in colleges and universities has achieved many achievements in the process of teaching and discussion. However, the teaching process of ideological and political courses is still the ideological and political course of colleges and universities. The weak link. In order to respond positively to the national call, it is of great significance to study the quality education of ideological and political education in colleges and universities. In the current curriculum and reform of ideological and political courses in colleges and universities, there is an urgent need to solve the theoretical and teaching requirements for strengthening teaching practice. The application of computer internet in the field of education and teaching has become increasingly widespread. Based on constructivism, this paper uses computer-aided ideological and political teaching services to broaden the channels for ideological and political teaching and to promote the sustainable and healthy development of ideological and political education.

Keywords: Computer-aided education · Internet · Constructivism · Ideological and political teaching

1 Introduction

The rapid development of computer technology in China has also greatly changed the way of education [1–5]. Facts have proved that the development of information technology in the new era has a great impact on education, which naturally includes ideological and political education in colleges and universities [6–8]. Modern college students have their own mobile phones, computers, etc. [9, 10]. It can be said that they are always in contact with the Internet, and it is easy to be invisibly affected by them. The development of the Internet has a major impact on the values and behaviors of college students [6, 11–13]. Combining the Internet with the university's ideological and political education, and innovating the teaching methods and contents, thus changing the way students learn. The Internet is a challenge and an opportunity for the ideological and political education of colleges and universities[12, 14]. It has brought about a major change in the educational mode and environment of the university's ideological and political education

Z. Xu et al. (Eds.): CSIA 2019, AISC 928, pp. 929–936, 2020.
https://doi.org/10.1007/978-3-030-15235-2_124

[15–18]. The ideological and political education of the university must grasp the favorable aspects and perfect the ideological and political education. This paper analyzes the innovation path of ideological and political education in colleges and universities in the era of computer technology development, and proposes relevant solutions based on constructivist ideological and political teaching design ideas.

2 The Development of Computer-Aided Education

2.1 The Development of Education Need Computer Help

We are in the information age. The information age is characterized by "information explosion". The update of knowledge is changing with each passing day. The information age puts forward higher requirements for education. How to solve the contradiction between the rapid update of knowledge and the limited learning time of students requires education and training. The number of people has surged and how to overcome the problem of lack of teaching staff. Solve the great development of education in the information age, meet people's growing educational needs and large-scale vocational training. This is the challenge facing education in the information age. The only solution to the challenge of solving the challenge of education is education informatization, that is, education requires computers to assist education. Computer-aided education can improve the teaching ability of teachers and promote the mode of education. Improve, promote management efficiency and improve the quality of teaching, meet the needs of lifelong learning, use computer-aided education to drive education modernization, and realize the leap-forward development of education.

2.2 The Change of Teaching Mode Requires the Support of Computer-Aided Teaching

Today, with the growth of information volume, people are more and more aware that it is difficult for the knowledge-accumulated talents cultivated in the past to cope with the fierce competition in the information society. The teaching activities of the information society should no longer be based on the development of human memory. The main goal should be to develop people's intelligence and creativity as the main goal. The education mode should be changed from "maintenance learning mode to "creative learning mode". The education field is undergoing a profound transformation. Computer-assisted instruction is needed support.

In the process of assisting teaching, the computer not only changes the traditional teaching mode, but also plays an active role in enriching subject knowledge, creating teaching scenarios, and optimizing classroom structure. The use of computer-aided teaching can enrich the subject knowledge and stimulate students' enthusiasm for exploring scientific knowledge. In the classroom activities, students can easily and quickly obtain a large number of subject-related information and enrich scientific knowledge through information technology. Creating a learning scenario allows students to experience a process of exploring knowledge and acquiring knowledge, cultivating students' practical ability and innovative spirit, and enriching and developing students' experience and experience. Optimizing the classroom structure and inspiring students to actively participate in the integration of information technology and activity classes can enable teachers to scientifically set the context of student activities, allowing students to be active and participate actively in learning.

Computer-supported classroom teaching strengthens and reforms traditional teaching methods, improves the quality of teaching and learning, and better plays the role of teachers in the classroom. Therefore, computer-supported classroom teaching is particularly imposing and necessary.

Reform requires the support of modern educational technology, and the main technology of educational technology is computer-aided education technology. Therefore, the requirements of the times and the need for education call for computer-aided education to exert its technological advantages.

3 The Reform Measures of Ideological and Political Courses for Different Majors in Colleges and Universities

3.1 Update Concepts and Clarify the Relationship Between Ideological and Political Courses and Professional Courses

Ideological and political courses do not exist in isolation in the curriculum system of colleges and universities, but are closely related to professional courses. Only by integrating the ideological and political curriculum into the curriculum system of colleges and universities, forming a closer relationship with the professional curriculum, and making different designs according to the different natural conditions of students, can produce better teaching effects. On the one hand, the ideological and political curriculum, like the professional curriculum, has a natural consistency in the teaching objectives. Both of them enable students to improve their ability to accept new things, while applying what they have learned to their future lives, creating more value for the country, society and themselves. The ideological and political course can promote the formation of better professional ethics and personality charm of college students. The professional courses can promote the formation of better professional operation skills for college students. On the other hand, the ideological and political courses and the professional courses are interdependent and mutually promoted relationship.

3.2 With the Goal of Talent Training as the Guiding Decision-Making Curriculum

The teaching of colleges and universities should be based on the students' own characteristics, which should enhance the social integration of students and make students diligent and knowledgeable. The use of teaching activities to strengthen students' communicative competence, hands-on ability and creative ability to promote students' all-round improvement in moral, intellectual, physical and aesthetic aspects. If you want to achieve the above goals, you need to have a certain difference in teaching activities depending on the training objectives. Taking Sizheng teaching as an example, we should aim at the actual needs of students, and aim at providing services for different professional students in colleges and universities, and stimulate the vividness of classroom teaching. For those content that are not the actual needs of students, we should make a bold abandonment, effectively highlight the pertinence of ideological and political education in colleges and universities, and reduce the pressure on students' curriculum. In this way, students' enthusiasm for knowledge can be fundamentally stimulated.

3.3 Promote the Integration of Ideological and Political Practice Activities with Professional Practice Activities

For colleges and universities, the focus of teaching is more theoretical. Therefore, we should promote the combination of Ideological and political practice and professional practice, so as to stimulate students' desire for knowledge and autonomy more effectively, so that students can better internalize knowledge into their own knowledge system. In teaching practice, we should make use of theoretical content to provide a solid foundation for teaching practice, and promote the internalization of knowledge through practical activities, so that students can smoothly go to society and work. After entering the society, students should not only apply their own theoretical knowledge to practice better, but also combine the corporate culture with themselves better, and constantly improve their professional skills, at the same time, they can also constantly enhance their professional ethics and personality value. Taking computer network specialty as an example, colleges and universities should organize students to go to network companies for a period of internship. Through practical activities, it can not only promote college students to transform theoretical knowledge into practical skills, but also enable students to more clearly define the needs of social employment in the process of work, and gradually fill in their theoretical gap. White and skill vacancies. The learning goal relationship is shown in Fig. 1.

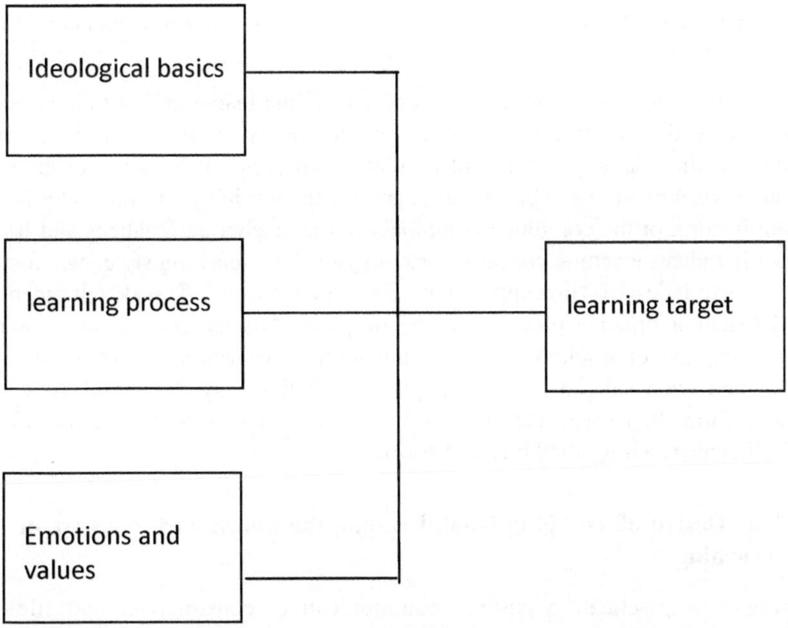

Fig. 1.

4 Based on Constructivism, Computer-Aided Ideological and Political Teaching Design Ideas

The related concepts and spiritual essence of the constructivist teaching theory are infiltrated into the teaching practice, which mainly includes two parts: teaching design and classroom teaching. Figure 2 design ideas.

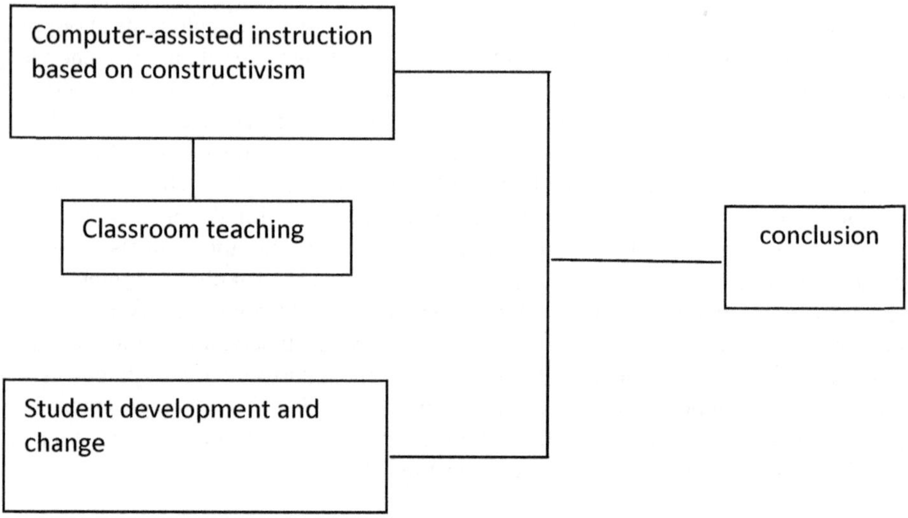

Fig. 2. The design idea of constructivist teaching theory in ideological and political teaching

Under the guidance of the teaching objectives, the teaching design is based on the system perspective, teaching concept and methodology, based on the inherent nature and laws of the teaching itself, and regulates and supports various resources in the teaching environment that support and guarantee the teaching activities. On the basis of the optimization of the combined combination, the teacher externalizes and formalizes the teaching ideas, teaching concepts, teaching wisdom, teaching style, etc., and has the dual characteristics of "presupposition" and "generation". The development of the special teaching practice process for the purpose. Any teaching is the result of the teacher's explicit or implicit teaching philosophy. In teaching, teachers always consciously and even subconsciously adopt the effective way they think to teach, and gradually form their own. Teaching style, in its own way to pursue an effective or called efficient teaching methods and forms.

4.1 The Design of Teaching Goal, Leading the Benchmark Classroom Teaching

Teaching is a practical, cognitive, communicative, constructive, and life-oriented practice that must be achieved through the bilateral interaction and cooperation of teachers and students, on the basis of the formation of synergy and emotional integration. In teaching, teachers can not be limited to "teaching" knowledge and skills, but also teachers to supervise and guide students to learn, create, create a harmonious teaching atmosphere and environment, stimulate students' interest in learning, build a deep friendship between students and so on… The behaviors and activities that teachers have made in teaching activities that promote positive development of students belong to the category of "teaching" of teachers in classroom teaching. It is necessary to judge the teacher's "teaching" with the value of teaching as the orientation, and to make the students learn more effectively, which is the "teaching" of value and efficacy. Teaching objectives enable teachers to reflect and supervise and regulate their own teaching behavior. The teaching goal is the rope of guiding and restraining the behavior of teachers and students. It is an important yardstick for classroom teaching evaluation, and an important reference for the generation and designation of teaching ideas and methods.

4.2 Learning Basic Analysis, Design the Starting Point of Student Learning

According to the relevant viewpoints of constructivist teaching theory, knowledge learning is based on the existing knowledge and experience of learners, and is obtained through meaning construction based on existing cognitive schemas. The basis and growth point of the occurrence and effective implementation of new learning is the "old knowledge" related to students. Without a growth point, or no growth point, students can't realize meaningful construction of knowledge even under a suitable learning environment. In the teaching design, helping (prompting) and guiding students to organize related old knowledge is the key link of learning. Focusing on different goals, analyzing the basic knowledge of students' learning needs, and then designing some problems (tasks) in specific teaching, so that students can self-test and organize the relevant knowledge.

4.3 Knowledge Combing, Design Core Knowledge Points and Key Knowledge Chains

The development of students in classroom teaching is mainly realized in the learning of knowledge, and adopts appropriate knowledge learning methods to enable students to achieve better development in the process of knowledge learning. Knowledge and skills are at the core of the classroom teaching of school education. It is better to learn basic knowledge, learn basic skills, and develop other aspects without becoming a sentence. On the basis of the intrinsic connection and consistency between the deep understanding of knowledge and knowledge, it is better to find a method suitable for guiding students to learn and choose the appropriate teaching media.

The construction of computer-aided ideological and political teaching methods based on constructivism has significantly enhanced the effect of ideological and political teaching. As shown in Fig. 3.

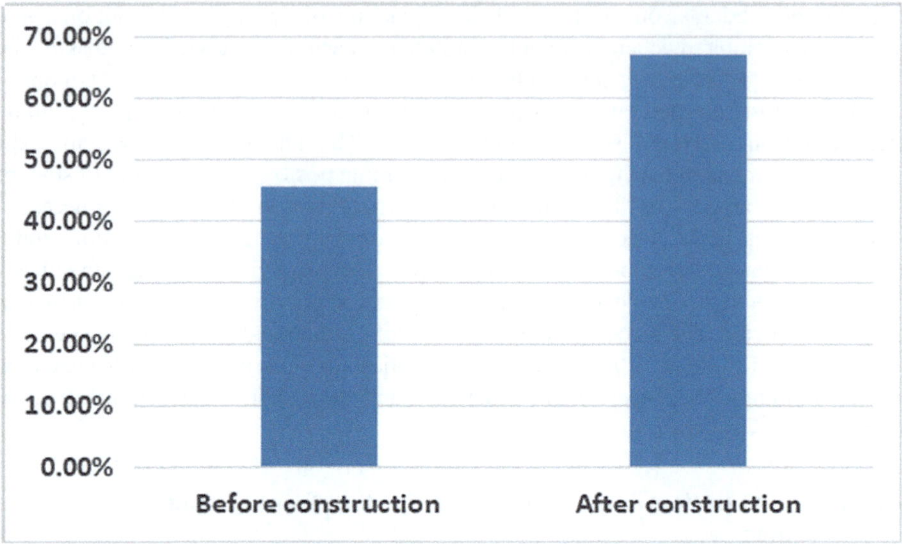

Fig. 3. Before and after construction

5 Conclusion

In short, the ideological and political education in Colleges and universities is of great significance to the development of our nation. In order to improve the educational effect, we must combine the convenience of the times and adopt diversified teaching methods. Today's college students have been accustomed to receiving information through the Internet, the ideological and political education of the university should also keep pace with the times, combined with the characteristics of College students, the computer-aided constructivism into the ideological and political education of colleges and universities, through the Internet, the ideological and political teaching of colleges and universities and reality are closely integrated, so that students can be more. For a deep understanding of ideology and politics. The Internet has changed the way contemporary college students receive information. Through computers, college students can learn more comprehensive and abundant knowledge and information, and can express their views in a timely manner. The ideological and political education in Colleges and Universities under the Internet era has been affected by its two sides, which is also the characteristics of the Internet. On the one hand, it can bring better technology to the ideological and political education in Colleges and universities, improve the quality and efficiency of education, on the other hand, it will also bring negative impact because of the free network environment. Therefore, universities should foster strengths and circumvent weaknesses so that the favorable side of the Internet can be applied to ideological and political education in Colleges and universities. To help students establish the right three concepts and cultivate more high-quality talents for the country.

Acknowledgements. Provincial Quality Engineering
Title: Reconstruction of Ideological and political education in universities in the "Internet+" era, Subject No: 2016jyxm0342.

References

1. Zhang CM (2010) Study on effectiveness improvement to ideological and political course teaching aided by famous historical and literary works. J Bohai Univ
2. Wang SQ (2014) Mold design and processing simulation software engineering based on creative industry pattern. Appl Mech Mater (608–609):124–128
3. Zhou YH (2016) The multimedia aided teaching system of ideological and political education based on Authorware. Electron Des Eng
4. Deek NF, Wei FC (2016) Computer-assisted surgery for segmental mandibular reconstruction with the osteoseptocutaneous fibula flap: can we instigate ideological and technological reforms? Plast Reconstr Surg 137(3):963
5. Chao X, Mantero M (2014) Church-based ESL adult programs: social mediators for empowering "Family Literacy Ecology of Communities". J Literacy Res 46(1):90–114
6. Hung HC, Young SC (2015) The effectiveness of adopting e-readers to facilitate EFL students' process-based academic writing. J Educ Technol Soc 18(1):250–263
7. Gould R (2015) Hijab as commodity form: veiling, unveiling, and misveiling in contemporary Iran. Feminist Theory 15(3):221–240
8. Carson JL, Sievert J (2015) Electoral reform and changes in legislative behavior: adoption of the secret ballot in congressional elections. Legislative Stud Q 40(1):83–110
9. Gray P (2014) The Coalition Government's policy on SEND: aspirations and challenges? J Res Spec Educ Needs 14(2):120
10. Rodrigues S (2014) Localising 'the rights of nature': a critical discourse analysis. Green Lett 18(2):170–184
11. Phemister A (2016) The grandest battle ever fought for the rights of human beings: radical republicanism and the universalization of the land war. Éire-Ireland 51(1–2):192–217
12. Sen D (2015) Anthropology of Work Review 36(1):37–41. From Modern Production to Imagined Primitive: The Social World of Coffee from Papua New Guinea by Paige West. Duke University Press, Durham, NC, 2012. Buying Into Fair Trade: Culture, Morality and Consumption by Keith R. Brown. NYU Press, New York, 2013
13. Mcguire RH (2014) Won with blood: archaeology and labor's struggle. Int J Hist Archaeol 18(2):259–271
14. Pratumsuwan P (2015) A conceptual framework and its application for project developing in mechatronics education. In: International conference on technology, informatics, management, engineering, and environment. IEEE, pp 222–227
15. Martone A, Sepe M, Immacolata Simeon M (2017) The process of urban regeneration in Budapest: approaching 2030. J Urban Regeneration Renewal 10(2):286–300
16. O'Kelly L (2017) Cold war on the airwaves: the radio propaganda war against East Germany. Am Journalism 33(3):350–351
17. Abedi A, Schneider S (2018) Big fish in small ponds: a comparison of dominant parties in the Canadian provinces and German Länder. J Mol Biol 34(3):643–654
18. Kuhn R (2018) Television and agenda-setting: the case of 'l'insécurité' and Le Pen in the 2002 French presidential election

Research and Implementation of Web Application System Vulnerability Location Technology

Lei Zheng(✉), Hui Yuan, Xiangli Peng, Guowei Zhu, Yue Guo, and Guoru Deng

Information and Communication Company of Hubei State Grid Corporation, No. 197 Xu Dong Street, Wuhan, Hubei, China
882148@qq.com

Abstract. In the era of rapid development of Internet technology, more and more Web application systems have emerged, and the security problems of Web applications have become more prominent. This paper analyzes the vulnerability detection methods of Web application systems and analyzes the scanners of black box testing. And the characteristics of the white box test tool, the scanner detects fast but can not locate the loophole, proposes a web application system vulnerability location method based on dynamic stain analysis technology, designs the system prototype and conducts experimental verification and testing.

Keywords: SQL injection · Dynamic stain analysis · Vulnerability location · Vulnerability detection

1 Introduction

There are various security issues in the Internet, most of which are caused by flaws in the software itself [1]. Software developers may not consider software security issues at the initial design stage, or may not pay enough attention to the security vulnerabilities that may exist in the system, or may inadvertently bring great risks to the security of the software [2]. Of course, It is impossible to rule out that someone intentionally implants malicious code in the system and leaves behind the door [3]. Attackers are exploiting these software security flaws to make security issues frequent [4–16]. This article analyzes the causes, classification, hazards, prevention, and detection methods of SQL injection vulnerabilities and XSS vulnerabilities. Inductive analysis of SQL injection and XSS cross-site scripting attack methods, design attack vector library. A vulnerability application method for Web application system based on dynamic stain analysis technology is proposed [17]. This method quickly obtains the injection points of SQL injection and XSS vulnerabilities in the fuzzy test phase [18]. The dynamic stain analysis stage traces the data of these injection points in the program, and obtains SQL injection and XSS vulnerabilities in the program from injection point to trap. The entire process of the point, complete the positioning of the vulnerability [19, 20].

Z. Xu et al. (Eds.): CSIA 2019, AISC 928, pp. 937–944, 2020.
https://doi.org/10.1007/978-3-030-15235-2_125

2 The Injection Vulnerability

The feature of the injection vulnerability is that the attacker forges special input data. Some of the information in the data is specific information written by the attacker to invade the system software. If the system software does not find the hidden intrusion in the data, it is still normal. If the process is executed, the information written by the intruder will be executed, so that the attack behavior will occur. The main solution is to discover the existence of these vulnerabilities, then filter the input information and not trust all the data input by the user.

2.1 SQL Injection

SQL injection is one of the most common injection class vulnerabilities in Web systems. The intruder passes into the background server by forging special input as a parameter, and most of the input data are basically statements conforming to the SQL query language. When the system executes these SQL statements, it will perform the operation that the attacker wants. The main reason is that the system does not filter the data input from the front end completely, which results in some illegal actions. Data is intruded into the system. SQL injection has many kinds of attacks, such as perpetual attack, joint query attack, Multi-Command statement attack, abnormal command attack, inference attack, encoding masquerade attack, stored procedure attack and so on. It is the most common and most dangerous security vulnerability.

2.2 Command Injection

Command injection is somewhat similar to SQL injection. This is also the intrusion behavior caused by unchecked data input by the user. SQL injection is mainly for database operations, and the intrusion behavior caused by the query language of the structured query language of the database is invoked. Most of the injection is for the system, the system shell script and other scripts or functions, the input information is forged and executed by the system, so that the attacker can obtain user rights or crash the system, etc. The main solution is also The input data information is filtered.

2.3 XPath Injection

XPath injection is a pointer to the attack technology of XML data information. XML (Extensible Markup Language) is a structured language used as a text mark. It is widely used in current web application systems, mainly used for data transmission and has a structure. Strong characteristics. XPath injection attacks use XPath · Parser's loose input and fault tolerance features to forge intrusive XPath query code in forms or other information to obtain certain permissions and modify the permissions file. XPath injection mainly attacks the server resources in the Internet. Its attack principle is very simple. Even if the attacker is not familiar with some relevant theoretical knowledge, it can complete the attack to steal the desired resources. Therefore, this attack method has a large Threatening. The XPath injection attack method also uses the construction attack parameters. These parameters are very common information, and do not violate the grammar requirements, but they have attack behavior in the actual sense. The system executes this information and the XPath attack behavior occurs. The solution is also to validate the parameters entered by the user, and to make some escaping of these parameters to defend against the attack.

3 The Vulnerability Detection Method

3.1 A Method Based on Symbolic Execution Techniques Vulnerability

The static symbol execution method is a technique for performing correlation analysis by using a symbol value to represent the value of a variable without executing a program, and performing the correlation analysis by simulating program execution. The advantage is that the program execution can be theoretically performed by collecting constraints generated during execution. All possible input values to somewhere, through the analog input to find loopholes in the execution of the program.

During the symbol execution process, when a conditional branch statement is encountered, a new state branch is generated, causing the total number of execution paths to grow exponentially, and there is a problem of path state space explosion. The dynamic symbol execution method uses a set of specific values to start the program, obtains the symbol constraint on the program input at the conditional statement branch in the target program execution process, generates a new path constraint condition according to the predefined test path traversal rule, and uses the constraint. The solver solves the new test input and causes the program to execute along the selectable program branch.

3.2 Flaw Detection Method Based on Analysis of the Stain

The core idea of stain analysis is to mark data from untrusted sources as tainted, to track the use of contaminated data and to track the use of contaminated data, and to monitor the use of pollution data to identify security vulnerabilities. This is an information flow analysis technology that provides an effective means of tracking the use of data. For example, stain analysis techniques mark external input data and new data generated by its operations as being contaminated, while ensuring that the data contaminated by these markers does not propagate outward to areas that may pose a security threat. Once the jump, call, and destination address of the data being moved are detected, these operations are considered illegal.

3.3 Vulnerability Detection Method Based on Software Testing Technology

After the location of the vulnerability injection point is found, the data from the injection point into the system can be observed and processed through relevant testing techniques to determine whether the vulnerability exists. The white box test can be used to track the flow and use of the data, and the feedback from the server is observed through the black box test to obtain the impact of the data on the system. At the same time, the test cases must fully reflect the means and input forms of the injection attack to determine the adequacy of the Web application defense mechanism and accurately locate the injection security vulnerability.

4 The Implementation of Vulnerability Localization Method Based on Dynamic Taint

4.1 Reptile Module Design

Crawler refers to a link from the address, recursive access to the corresponding page under the content and link address, until all the page content is obtained. For example, according to the URL of the Web site, the crawler module captures its content and all the URLs from the page under the URL, and then continues to capture the page content and URL corresponding to these URLs, so repeatedly, the termination condition is that all the page content under the URL is crawled. There are generally three crawling strategies: depth first, breadth first and best priority search strategy.

Crawler module is a very important part of WebPOS. The quality of the module design directly determines the acquisition of injection test points, and then affects the comprehensiveness and accuracy of SQL injection and XSS vulnerability security analysis of Web systems. According to the basic principle of network crawler, the breadth-first method is adopted to analyze the information of Web system and obtain the information of testable points through multithreading. The Crawler module is mainly composed of three parts: GETURL, GetHtmlCode and HTMLPaser, as shown in Fig. 1.

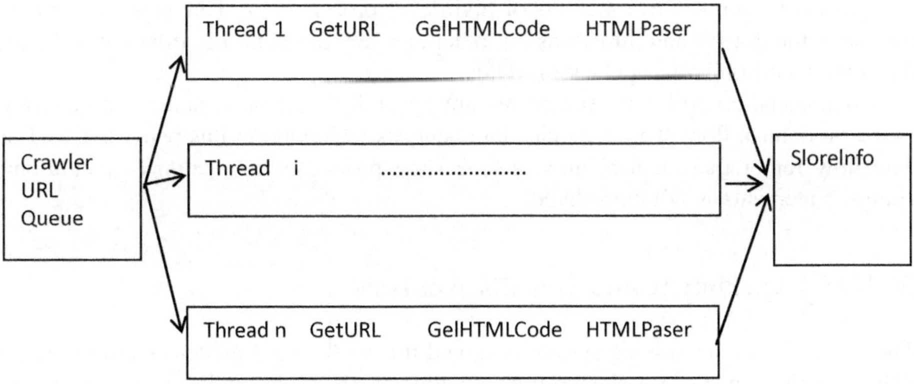

Fig. 1. Crawler module main structure.

4.2 The Stain Propagation Module

The taint mark module marks the untrusted data as smudge data. The smudge data undergoes a series of assignments, function calls, etc. during the running of the program, which causes the taint attribute of the taint data to be cleaned or propagated. In order to accurately track the spread of stain data, it is necessary to establish a rule for the spread of stains.

The stain propagation rules designed in this paper draw on the idea of traditional dynamic stain propagation rules. Compared with the traditional way, the difference is that the traditional dynamic stain propagation rules are classified according to the machine code instruction type of the application. The operation instructions are divided into two types: infectious operation instructions and non-infectious operation instructions. The instruction needs to smear or clear the source operand or the destination operand according to the stain propagation rule; the stain propagation rule designed in this paper classifies the various operations related to the data according to the characteristics of the high-level programming language, and analyzes each The class operates on the characteristics of smear propagation, and combines the specific forms of SQL injection and XSS cross-site scripting attacks to develop corresponding taint propagation rules. The dynamic smudge propagation rules based on assembly language classify machine instructions into four types of instruction types: data movement class instructions, arithmetic operation class instructions, memory operation class instructions, and non-propagation instructions. Different instruction types have different smear propagation rules. The following is a summary of the smudge propagation process of the above four types of instructions:

Arithmetic logic operation class statements include arithmetic operation class statements, relational operation statements, logical operation statements, and bit logic operation type statements.

The principle of stain propagation in assignment class statements is relatively simple. The stain state of the variable on the left side of the equation is affected by the state of the variable on the right side of the equation or the stain state of the expression.

The smudge propagation rules of function calls are relatively complicated, because the types and numbers of functions of high-level programming languages are numerous, and the forms and functions of functions are different for different software developers and different application fields.

Conditional control class statements are generally used in dynamic stain analysis based on control flow. The dynamic stain analysis technique in this paper is based on data flow rather than control flow, so the stain propagation function of conditional control statements is not considered.

5 The Experiment and Results Analysis

The vulnerability positioning system designed for verification can detect and locate the SQL injection and XSS vulnerabilities existing in the Web application system. The Eclipse integrated burst environment is used to implement Java programming for the WebPOS tool. The hardware platform uses the mainstream IBM- PC compatible machine, database management system is MySQL.

5.1 Time Complexity Analysis

Time complexity is the time it takes for each tool to test the application. According to the experimental data obtained from the above experimental process, it is analyzed whether WebPOS has an advantage in time complexity.

The time comparison of application vulnerability location is shown in Fig. 2.

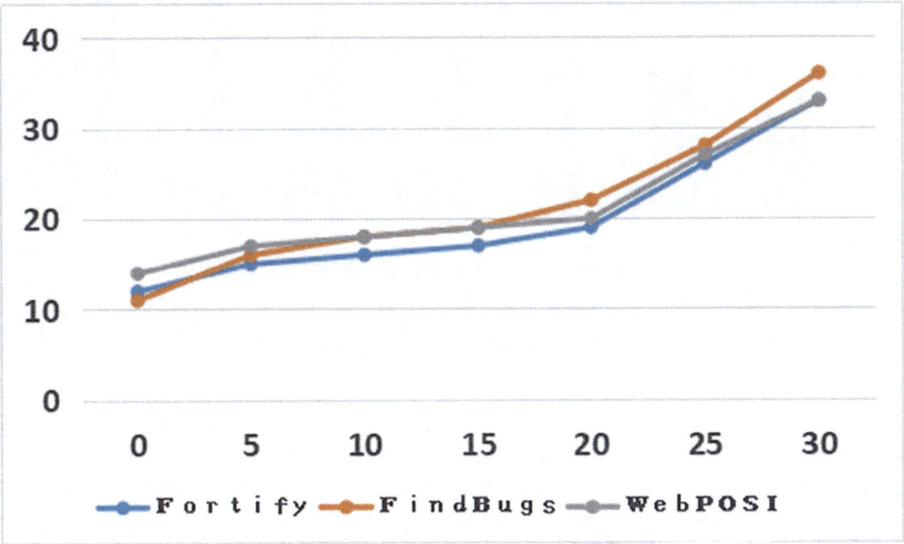

Fig. 2. Application time comparison chart positioned drain hole

Parsing Vulnerability positioning WebPOS due WebPOS need for the program to simulate the attack, Fuzzing testing phase there is a certain time-consuming, so for smaller applications that advantage is not obvious, but with the expansion of the scale of the program, Fuzzing test used The time consumption is smaller and smaller in the total positioning time, and in the dynamic stain analysis part, it only needs to mark the data of the injection point of the vulnerability that is obtained during the Fuzzing test phase, and the other two tools are analyzed. All injection point data, so the more source code lines, the more injection points there are, the more obvious the time advantage of WebPOS.

Experimental results show that WebPOS has an advantage in time complexity for large web applications.

5.2 False Positive Rate Analysis

False alarm rate (False · Positive), refers to procedures in place were not originally reported vulnerability probability of vulnerability. The bar chart is shown in Fig. 3

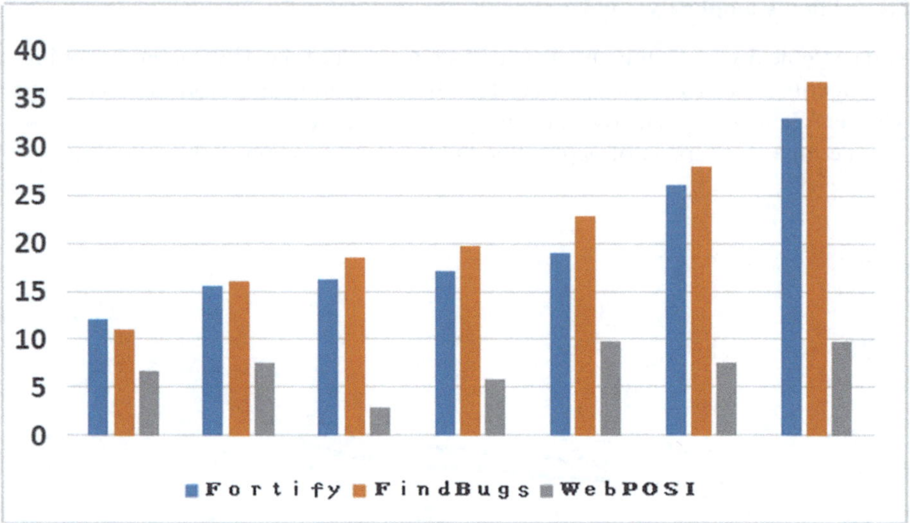

Fig. 3. Comparison of false positive rate.

As can be seen from Fig. 3, for the same application, the false alarm rate of WebPOS is much lower than that of Fortify and FindBugs. This paper analyzes the vulnerability location process of WebPOS. WebPOS obtains the possible vulnerabilities of SQL injection and XSS vulnerability injection point by simulating the program in the Fuzzing test phase, and dynamic stain analysis phase according to F. The results of fuzzing test phase track and analyze the input of the injection point, record the pollution propagation path, and check whether it reaches the sink point. This is both a positioning process and a verification process. The non-vulnerable injection points obtained in the fuzzy test phase will be excluded in the dynamic stain analysis phase, thus reducing the impact. The false positive rate of WebPOS.

6 Conclusion

The rapid development of information technology such as computer and network technology has accelerated and deepened the process of social informatization. Multi platform, networked and fully integrated Web application system has become the most popular processing mode. The security of Web application system has also become one of the important problems of network application. It is of great theoretical and practical significance to study the security testing of Web application system. This paper studies the vulnerability detection methods of Web application system, summarizes and analyzes the existing tools for detecting vulnerabilities of Web application system, and proposes a vulnerability location method of Web application system based on dynamic stain analysis technology. The injection points with SQL injection and XSS vulnerabilities can be quickly obtained. In the dynamic stain analysis stage, the whole process of SQL injection and XSS vulnerabilities in the program from the injection point to the trap point can be recorded by tracing the data transmission process of these injection points in the program.

References

1. Priya RL, Lifna CS, Jagli D, et al (2014) Rational unified treatment for web application vulnerability assessment. In: International conference on circuits, systems, communication and information technology applications. IEEE, pp 610–611
2. Wang YP, Cheng SY, Jiang F (2015) Web application vulnerabilities scan system. Comput Syst Appl
3. Salini P, Shenbagam J, Salini P, et al (2015) Prediction and classification of web application attacks using vulnerability ontology. In: IEEE international conference on computer & information technology workshops, pp 462–467
4. Madhusudhanan M, Saravanan M, Kumar DD (2015) Web security vulnerability assessment and recovery mechanism. Int J Eng Sci Res Technol 4(3)
5. Zscaler I (2017) Zero day threat detection based on fast flux detection and aggregation
6. Ying-Jie LI, Ren HM (2016) SQL injection vulnerability detection system based on Selenium. Modern Comput
7. Kumar P, Sheth RK (2016) A review on 0-day vulnerability testing in web application. In: International conference on information and communication technology for competitive strategies. ACM, pp 1–4
8. Chen CL, Zhang F, Han YU (2017) Design of vulnerability detection system for web application program. Comput Technol Dev
9. He H, Chen L, Guo W (2017) Research on web application vulnerability scanning system based on fingerprint feature. In: International conference on mechanical, electronic, control and automation engineering
10. Le VG, Nguyen HT, Lu DN et al (2016) A solution for automatically malicious web shell and web application vulnerability detection. International conference on computational collective intelligence. Springer, Heidelberg, pp 367–378
11. Oerton KJ (2016) Method of limiting use of a mobile wireless access point near a wireless local area network: US, US9241344[P]
12. Vmware I (2017) Methods and apparatus to identify priorities of compliance assessment results of a virtual computing environment
13. De Pauw W, Ammons G (2015) Visually analyzing, clustering, transforming and consolidating real and virtual machine images in a computing environment: US, US 8954859 B2[P]
14. Trumble B (2015) Using code inspection, code modification, and machine learning to prevent SQL injection. Dissertations & Theses - Gradworks
15. Rodríguez RJ, Merseguer J, Bernardi S (2016) Modelling security of critical infrastructures: a survivability assessment. Comput J 58(10):2313–2327
16. Gol D, Shah N (2016) Detection of web application vulnerability based on RUP model. In: Recent Advances in Electronics & Computer Engineering. IEEE, pp 96–100
17. Ramanujan RS, Trent BA, Sanders CM, et al (2015) Border gateway broker, network and method
18. Kumarshrestha A, Singh Maharjan P, Paudel S (2015) Identification and illustration of insecure direct object references and their countermeasures. Int J Comput Appl 39–44
19. Hassan MM, Sultana S, Akter M, et al (2018) Broken authentication and session management vulnerability: a case study of web application. Int J Simul Syst Sci Technol 19(2)

Analysis of Factors Affecting Construction Cost of Line Engineering and Cost Control Strategy

Chen Wu[1], Bing-Jie Li[1], Qian Ma[2], Yin Wu[1], Hong-Da Zhao[1], Dong-Xiao Niu[3], Hao Zhen[3(✉)], and Zhuoya Siqin[3]

[1] State Grid Jiangsu Electric Power Co., Ltd. Economic Research Institute, Nanjing 210008, China
cwusgcc@gmail.com, crazyjennylee@163.com, wuyinxf@163.com, 13912987815@yeah.net

[2] State Grid Jiangsu Electric Power Co., Ltd., Nanjing 210008, China
13770683400@139.com

[3] School of Economics and Management, North China Electric Power University, Beijing 102206, China
niudx@ncepu.edu.cn, mailofzhenhao@163.com, sqzhuoya@163.com

Abstract. The construction of power transmission and transformation project is a basic construction related to the national economy. The factors affecting the construction cost are intricate. In this paper, the fishbone analysis method is used to identify the influencing factors, with a total of 17 influencing factors being identified. The clustering analysis method is used to divide 17 factors into 5 categories. Then, through correlation analysis, 7 key factors are screened out; Gray comprehensive correlation is used to measure the impact of various key factors on investment. Based on the analysis of the influencing factors of cost, the whole process control strategy of overhead line engineering cost is proposed from the investment estimation stage, design stage, construction stage and completion settlement stage.

Keywords: Line engineering · Fishbone analysis method · Cluster analysis · Correlation analysis · Grey correlation · Cost control strategy

1 Introduction

The construction of power transmission and transformation projects is a basic construction related to the national economy and people's livelihood. The power transmission and transformation project not only has huge investment, long investment payback period, but also has many participants and complicated internal relations. Therefore, it requires a comprehensive identification of the factors affecting the cost of power transmission and transformation projects, judging the direction and degree of impact of various factors, and effective control, in order to better manage the cost of power transmission and transformation projects.

Z. Xu et al. (Eds.): CSIA 2019, AISC 928, pp. 945–954, 2020.
https://doi.org/10.1007/978-3-030-15235-2_126

In recent years, Yu et al. [1] gave a brief introduction to the identification, quantitative evaluation and correlation analysis of the factors affecting the cost of power transmission and transformation projects. Lei [2] analyzed the factors affecting the cost of each stage of the substation construction project, and determined the weight of the factors by the Delphi method and the expert scoring method. Yang [3] divided the factors affecting the cost of power transmission and transformation projects into four aspects: technical conditions, geological topography, construction land occupation and equipment price. Zhang [4] and Shen [5] began to study the influencing factors from various sub-items. Wang [6, 7] used qualitative analysis to eliminate the correlation between factors, and used SPSS to conduct independence test, linear test and sensitivity analysis. Some scholars [8–12] also used principal component analysis to deal with factors.

This paper expounds the basic theory of cost and control of overhead line engineering, and analyzes the influencing factors of transmission engineering cost by using fishbone analysis method. Finally, the paper puts forward the cost control strategy, which provides reference for cost management, comprehensively understanding the cost of power transmission and transformation projects and scientifically improving the cost control ability of power transmission and transformation projects.

2 Basic Theory

2.1 Basic Principles of Cluster Analysis

Cluster analysis is a practical data analysis technique. Based on the classification object, the cluster can be divided into sample clustering and variable clustering. Sample clustering is to classify the sample population according to the eigenvalues of each research object; variable clustering is to classify the variables describing the observed objects. In the analysis of the factors affecting the investment in power transmission and transformation projects, on the one hand, R-type clustering can be used to aggregate and classify the factors, so as to observe and explain the factor set; on the other hand, it can also determine the interdependence of these factors.

In the case of R-type clustering, the system clustering method is often used. The principle is: treat a certain number of variables as a class, and then combine the two classes with the highest degree of intimacy; then according to the degree of closeness between the merged class and other classes, combine the classes with a high degree of density. Repeat this process until all the variables are combined into one class [6].

2.2 Pearson Correlation Analysis Principle

A strong correlation between the factors, will result in duplication of information, increase the complexity of the research problem. Cluster analysis is based on the distance between factors, classifying factors with similar properties into one category.

Pearson correlation coefficient is often used to measure a given distance variable linear correlation and is the most widely used when calculating correlation coefficient. The calculation formula is:

$$\mathrm{r}_{jk} = \frac{\sum_{i=1}^{n}\left(X_J(i) - \overline{X_J}\right)\left(X_k(i) - \overline{X_k}\right)}{\sqrt{\sum_{i=1}^{n}\left(X_J(i) - \overline{X_J}\right)^2\left(X_k(i) - \overline{X_k}\right)^2}} = \frac{1}{n}\sum_{i=1}^{n}\left(\frac{\left(X_J(i) - \overline{X_J}\right)}{SX_J}\right)\left(\frac{X_k(i) - \overline{X_k}}{SX_k}\right) \quad (1)$$

Where n is the number of samples, $X_J(i)$ and $X_k(i)$ are the ith sample values of the J and k variables, respectively, and $\overline{X_J}$ and $\overline{X_k}$ are the sample mean of the J and k variables, respectively.

When the correlation analysis is performed on two variables, the joint distribution of the two variables is preset to a two-dimensional normal distribution. Propose the null hypothesis H_0: there is no significant linear correlation between the two variables, and construct the test statistic: $\mathrm{T} \sim \mathrm{t}(\mathrm{n} - 2)$.

$$\mathrm{T} = \frac{r\sqrt{n-2}}{\sqrt{1-r^3}} \quad (2)$$

Calculate the observations of the test statistic, check the table to obtain the significance of the corresponding observations and compare it with the significance level. If it is less than the significance level, the null hypothesis is rejected, that is, there is a significant linear correlation between the two variables [7].

2.3 Analysis of Grey Correlation

The grey correlation analysis is a multivariate statistical analysis method. It uses the gray correlation degree to describe the strength, size and order of the relationship between the variables based on the sample data of each variable. The basic idea is: taking the sample data of the variable as a sequence, the sequence will form a curve, and the closeness of a certain two variables is judged by the similarity of the two curves. The more similar the curves, the greater the degree of association between the corresponding sequences, and vice versa.

Grey relational analysis is often used to model and analyze the practical problems of various industries. The basic idea is to judge the degree of closeness between the different sequences by the similarity of geometric shapes in the same coordinate system. It is equally applicable when the sample values don't have obvious laws, and the calculation amount is not large, and the operation is very convenient, which largely compensates for the shortcomings of using statistical methods for system analysis. It is widely used in the correlation analysis between things and the comprehensive evaluation of engineering projects. Therefore, the degree of correlation can be used to measure the closeness of each influencing factor and investment in power transmission and transformation engineering, and provide a basis for managers to control engineering investment [8].

3 Analysis of Factors Affecting Investment in Overhead Line Engineering

Based on the investment sample data of 41 110 kV overhead line projects in a certain area, this paper uses cluster analysis method, correlation analysis and gray correlation analysis method to analyze from three aspects of factor identification, classification and measurement, and strives to be scientific and comprehensive. It analyzes the influencing factors of its engineering investment and provides reference for investment management and control.

3.1 Identification of Influencing Factors of Cost of Overhead Line Engineering Based on Fishbone Diagram Method

In this paper, the static investment final cost of the completed overhead line project is taken as the research object. The main engineering is composed of earthwork, foundation engineering, pole tower engineering and erecting engineering. Together with the other expenses, these five aspects are used to find out the possible Influencing factors, and draw a fishbone diagram (Fig. 1).

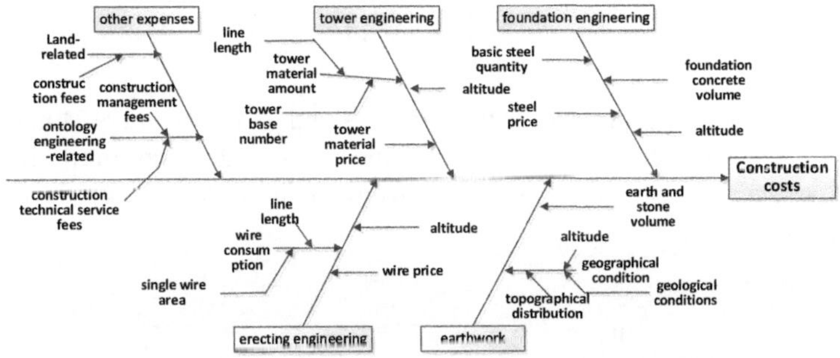

Fig. 1. Factors affecting the construction cost of 110 kV overhead line project

Finally, 17 influencing factors were identified, and the factors affecting the cost of overhead line engineering = {wire price, wire consumption, line length, single wire area, tower material price, tower material amount, tower base number, basic steel quantity, steel price, foundation concrete volume, earth and stone volume, altitude, topographical distribution, geological conditions, construction fees, construction management fees, construction technical service fees}.

3.2 Classification of Influencing Factors Based on Cluster Analysis

Based on the above seventeen influencing factors, this paper uses SPSS for system clustering. First, standardize the sample data, select the Pearson coefficient for the metric, then select the inter-group connection by the clustering method, finally run the clustering table of the influencing factors (Table 1).

Table 1. Influence factor clustering table

Order	Cluster		Coefficient	First appearance cluster		Next order
	Cluster1	Cluster2		Cluster1	Cluster2	
1	2	3	0.981	0	0	2
2	2	17	0.934	1	0	4
3	7	10	0.886	0	0	5
4	2	11	0.868	2	0	6
5	6	7	0.858	0	3	6
6	2	6	0.827	4	5	7
7	2	15	0.596	6	0	10
8	5	9	0.511	0	0	9
9	4	5	0.433	0	8	11
10	2	8	0.396	7	0	12
11	4	12	0.293	9	0	15
12	1	2	0.238	0	10	14
13	13	14	0.132	0	0	15
14	1	16	0.061	12	0	16
15	4	13	0.04	11	13	16
16	1	4	−0.067	14	15	0

It can be known from the cluster table that X_2 and X_3 can be merged into one class, then X_2, X_3 and X_{17} can be combined into one class, and so on, until all factors are grouped together. The clustering process of factors can be clearly seen through the tree graph (Fig. 2).

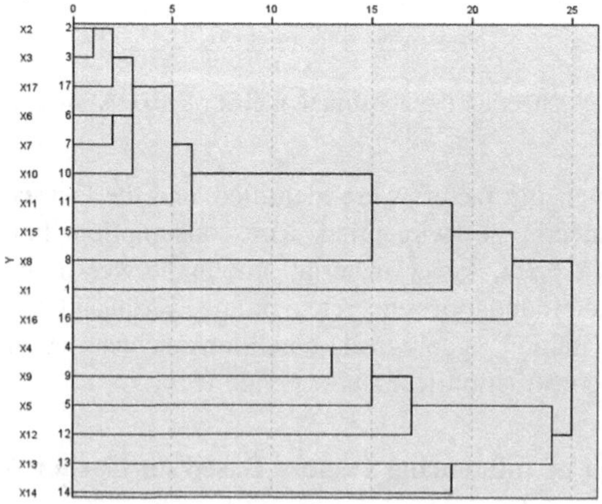

Fig. 2. Influencing factors clustering tree

At present, there is no unified understanding of the best systematic clustering time and the best factor classification number. A common method is to determine the time based on the jump degree of the tree and to classify according to the subjective judgment of the researcher. According to the cluster tree diagram of influencing factors, it can be recognized that factors jump significantly between 10 and 20, and it is appropriate to divide factors into 5 categories here. The classification results are as follows:

- First Type. Wire consumption, line length, construction technical service fees, earth and stone volume, tower base number, foundation concrete volume, tower material amount, construction fees, basic steel quantity, wire price.
- Second type. Construction management fees.
- Third type. Tower material price, steel price, single wire area, altitude.
- Fourth type. Topographical distribution.
- Fifth Type. Geological conditions.

The first type contain the largest number of factors, because the length of the line represents the scale of the entire project, and the scale of the project is closely related to the wire consumption, earth and stone volume, foundation concrete volume, tower material amount. These engineering factors are also closely related to the basic steel quantity, the number of tower bases, construction site expropriation and compensation fees. Therefore, these factors are classified into one category. The price factors of tower material price and steel price are classified into one category. The construction management fee mainly depends on the management level. The topographical distribution and geological conditions depend on the construction site selection.

3.3 Simplification of Investment Impact Factors Based on Correlation Analysis

Simplification of the First Type of Factors. The correlation coefficient between the first type of factors and the engineering investment and the correlation coefficient between the first type of factors are calculated separately (Table 2).

Table 2. Correlation coefficient between the first type of influencing factors and engineering investment

Correlation coefficient	r_j
Wire consumption	0.957**
Line length	0.985**
Construction technical service fees	0.903**
Earth and stone volume	0.867**
Tower base number	0.917**
Foundation concrete volume	0.859**
Tower material amount	0.946**
Construction fees	0.807**
Basic steel quantity	0.444**
Wire price	0.174

**Relevant at .01 level (both sides).
*Relevant at 0.05 level (both sides).

According to the correlation coefficient, the correlation between line length and engineering investment is the highest, and from Table 3, it can be found that the line length is related to the wire consumption, construction technical service fee, earth and stone volume, tower base number, foundation concrete volume and tower material amount. These coefficients are all greater than 0.8 and are highly correlated. Therefore, the length of the line can better represent these seven factors. The correlation coefficient between the construction fees, the amount of basic steel and the wire price is less than 0.3 and can be considered as independent. The first class is finally reduced to: line length, construction fee, base steel quantity and wire price.

Table 3. Correlation coefficient of the first type of influencing factors

r_{jk}	X_2	X_3	X_{17}	X_{11}	X_7	X_{10}	X_6	X_{15}	X_8	X_1
X_2	1	.981**	.931**	.897**	.865**	.834**	.860**	.565**	.428**	0.26
X_3	.981**	1	.936**	.897**	.907**	.851**	.871**	.615**	.448**	0.247
X_{17}	.931**	.936**	1	.810**	.855**	.808**	.824**	.560**	0.289	0.197
X_{11}	.897**	.897**	.810**	1	.774**	.730**	.747**	.497**	.386**	.306*
X_7	.865**	.907**	.855**	.774**	1	.886**	.885**	.684**	.453**	0.207
X_{10}	.834**	.851**	.808**	.730**	.886**	1	.831**	.677**	.417**	.375*
X_6	.860**	.871**	.824**	.747**	.885**	.831**	1	.572**	.519**	0.225
X_{15}	.565**	.615**	.560**	.497**	.684**	.677**	.572**	1	0.225	0.098
X_8	.428**	.448**	0.289	.386**	.453**	.417**	.519**	0.225	1	0.225
X_1	0.26	0.247	0.197	.306*	0.207	.375*	0.225	0.098	0.225	1

**Relevant at .01 level (both sides).

*Relevant at 0.05 level (both sides).

3.4 Simplification of Other Factors

According to other influencing factors and engineering investment correlation coefficient, the correlation coefficient between construction management fee, tower material price, single wire area, altitude and engineering investment is less than 0.1. It can be considered that the relationship between these four factors and engineering investment is very weak. Therefore, the four influencing factors are eliminated. The remaining steel prices, topographical distribution and geological conditions represent the third, fourth and fifth classes, respectively. At this time, there is only one factor left in each class, so there is no need to perform correlation analysis between factors. Finally, the 17 factors are reduced to seven key factors: line length, construction cost, basic steel quantity, wire price, steel price, topographic distribution, and geological conditions (Table 4).

Table 4. Table of other influencing factors and engineering investment correlation coefficient

Correlation coefficient	Construction management fees	Tower material price	Steel price	Single wire area	Altitude	Topographical distribution	Geological conditions
r_j	0.067	−0.066	−0.104	−0.221	0.079	−0.526	−0.171

Among them, the length of the line can represent the scale of the entire overhead line project, and also represents the engineering quantity of the line project and the tower project; the construction fee is other expenses related to the land, accounting for the largest proportion of all other expenses; the amount of basic steel can be Represents the engineering quantity of the basic project; the wire price and the steel price are price factors; the topographical distribution and geological conditions can indicate the geographical location of the process, and are closely related to the cost of the earthwork.

3.5 Analysis of Key Influencing Factors Based on Grey Correlation Analysis

When analyzing influencing factors, people tend to care about the impact of factors on investment. After the factor set is simplified, this section measures the degree of influence of the seven key influencing factors on the investment, calculates the gray comprehensive correlation degree between the key influencing factors and the engineering investment, and ranks the influence degree of the factors.

First, construct a behavior sequence, and record the line length, construction fee, basic steel quantity, wire price, steel price, topographical distribution, and geological conditions as $X_1, X_2, X_3, X_4, X_5, X_6, X_7$ and the project investment is recorded as X_0. i denotes the serial number of the sample project, $i = 1, 2, \cdots, 46$. The sample data uses an averaging transformation to eliminate the effects of different dimensions. The calculation is:

$$\varepsilon_{01} = 0.8818, \varepsilon_{02} = 0.8726, \varepsilon_{03} = 0.9575, \varepsilon_{04} = 0.5442$$

$$r_{01} = 0.6665, r_{02} = 0.3998, r_{03} = 0.3907, r_{04} = 0.5614$$

$$r_{05} = 0.5494, r_{06} = 0.6394, r_{07} = 0.3194$$

Taking $\theta = 0.5$, the gray comprehensive correlation degree can be obtained as shown in the following table (Table 5).

Table 5. Gray comprehensive correlation table

Correlation	X_1	X_2	X_3	X_4	X_5	X_6	X_7
ρ_{0j}	0.7741	0.6362	0.6741	0.5528	0.5915	0.7454	0.5847

Therefore, the impact of various key factors on engineering investment: line length > topographical distribution > basic steel quantity > construction fee > steel price > geological conditions > wire price.

According to the sorting results, the length of the line is the most important factor affecting the investment in overhead line engineering. This is also in line with the actual cognition. In practice, people often use unit length investment as an indicator of investment analysis. Topographical distribution is a secondary important factor affecting investment. Complex terrain will improve technical requirements and operational difficulty, reduce construction efficiency, and may cause inconvenience to transportation, resulting in further increase in engineering investment. The impact of basic steel volume and construction fees is third, and both directly and laterally reflect the engineering level of overhead line engineering. The construction fee accounts for about 10% of the static investment, and can directly affect the investment.

4 Research on Cost Control Strategy of Overhead Line Engineering

Cost management and control is a dynamic process, but also a technical, strong policy work. Based on the analysis of the influencing factors of cost, this chapter puts forward the cost control strategy in the investment decision stage, design stage, construction stage and completion settlement stage according to the actual situation of overhead line engineering cost and the whole process cost management theory of construction project.

In the investment decision-making stage, the construction unit conducts technical and economic research on the necessity and feasibility of the proposed project, analyzes the economic and social benefits of different programs, compares and selects the programs to achieve rational use of social resources.

In the design stage, it is necessary to design the overall plan of the overhead line project, prepare the project plan, construction drawing, and carry out the cost budget. Once the overall plan is determined, it is generally not allowed to change and modify at will.

In the construction phase, the construction unit will carry out the construction according to the plan and design drawings. Compared with other stages, the proportion of actual expenditure during the construction phase is the largest. Strengthening the construction cost control is an important means to obtain good economic benefits.

In order to reasonably control the final settlement price and safeguard the vital interests of the participating units, the following optimization measures can be taken: Carefully prepare the final accounts of the completion of the project, calculate the new fixed assets of the project; improve the overall quality of the staff; strictly review the authenticity, reliability and rationality of the final accounts.

5 Conclusion

In this paper, the fishbone analysis method is used to identify the influencing factors, and 17 influencing factors are identified. The clustering analysis method is used to classify 17 factors and divide the factors into 5 categories. Then, through correlation analysis, 7 key factors are selected. Then, the grey comprehensive correlation is then used to measure the impact of each key factor on the investment. Based on the analysis of the influencing factors of cost, this paper puts forward the whole process control strategy of overhead line engineering cost from the investment estimation stage, design stage, construction stage and completion settlement stage.

References

1. Yu X, Cai Z, Shang G, Yang Z, Liu J, Yan Y (2014) Research on influencing factors of power transmission and transformation cost based on whole process management. Sci Technol Ind (02):79–82
2. Lei Y (2015) Analysis of factors affecting construction cost of substation construction project and research on control strategy. North China Electric Power University
3. Yang R (2017) Analysis of factors affecting the cost of power transmission and transformation projects and countermeasures. China New Technol New Prod (01):106–107
4. Zhang Q (2011) Analysis of key influencing factors of construction cost based on 500 kV transmission lines. Sci Technol Commun (22):48–49
5. Shen Y, Fan Y (2009) Analysis of wind power cost sensitivity based on dynamic cost model. Power Demand Side Manag (02):15–17
6. Wang W (2012) Analysis of main influencing factors of 500 KV substation engineering cost. J Eng Manag (06):66–69
7. Wang W, Liu Y (2016) Research on new evaluation index system of substation engineering cost based on MLRA technology. Math Pract Theory (03):117–124
8. Zhao Z, Lv G, You W, Gao Y (2008) Evaluation model of construction cost evaluation for rural power grid 35 kV transmission lines. Power Syst Technol (14):96–100
9. Ji Y, Wu D, Peng W, Tan X (2014) Analysis of factors affecting the cost of substation engineering—based on SPSS software principal component analysis. Oper Manag (02): 125–130
10. Xiao J, Hao X, Tang X, Peng Y, Tan X (2014) Influencing factors of power engineering cost based on principal component analysis. Manag Manag (03):128–133
11. Hu J, Gao X (2016) Identification and data modeling analysis of influencing factors of power transmission and distribution engineering costs. J North China Electr Power Univ (Soc Sci Edn) (05):55–64
12. Yu C (2016) Analysis of factors affecting the cost of power grid project and evaluation model. North China Electric Power University, Beijing

Analysis and Application of Mapreduce Architecture and Working Principle

Hongsheng Xu[1,2(✉)], Ganglong Fan[1,2], and Ke Li[1,2]

[1] Luoyang Normal University, Luoyang 471934, China
85660190@qq.com
[2] Henan Key Laboratory for Big Data Processing & Analytics of Electronic Commerce, Luoyang 471934, China

Abstract. The core function of Mapreduce is to integrate the business logic code written by the user and the default components into a complete distributed operation program and run concurrently on a hadoop cluster. MapReduce is a set of software framework, which includes two stages: Map and Reduce. It can be used to partition the massive data, decompose the task and aggregate the results, so as to complete the parallel processing of the massive data. MapReduce's principle of work is actually the data - processing method. This article describes the analysis and application of MapReduce architecture and working principle in detail.

Keywords: MapReduce · Big data · Hadoop cluster · Parallel processing · Shuffle

1 Introduction

Big data is bound to rely on the cluster environment, and the cluster environment has three major challenges: parallelization, single point failure processing, resource sharing. Dynamic allocation of computing resources and other solutions to meet the challenges.

MapReduce is a programming model and an algorithm model for processing and generating large data sets [1]. The user first creates a Map function to process a set of data based on key/value pair, outputs the intermediate set of data based on key/value pair, and then creates a Reduce function to merge all the intermediate value values with the same intermediate key value. Therefore, many data processing problems can be transformed into the processing model of MapReduce.

Data partitioning and computing task scheduling, the system automatically divides big data, a job (Job) to be processed, into many data blocks. Each data block corresponds to a computing task (Task), and automatically schedules the computing node to process the corresponding data block. Job and task scheduling functions are mainly responsible for assigning and scheduling computing nodes (Map nodes or Reduce nodes), monitoring the execution status of these nodes, and taking charge of synchronization control of Map nodes.

Distributed parallel off-line computing framework is a programming framework of distributed computing program and the core framework of "data analysis and

Z. Xu et al. (Eds.): CSIA 2019, AISC 928, pp. 955–961, 2020.
https://doi.org/10.1007/978-3-030-15235-2_127

application based on hadoop" developed by users. The core function of Mapreduce is to integrate the business logic code written by the user and the default components into a complete distributed operation program and run concurrently on a hadoop cluster. Similar to the HDFS solution, large files are cut into small files and stored in each host of the cluster.

The MR framework is composed of a single JobTracker running on the primary node and a TaskTracker running on each cluster slave node. The master node is responsible for scheduling all tasks that constitute a job, and these tasks are distributed across different slave nodes. The master node monitors their execution and reexecutes previously failed tasks [2]. The slave node is responsible for only the tasks assigned by the primary node.

After mapper runs, we know that the output of mapper is such a key/value pair. In the end, the current key should be left to which reduce to do, it is necessary to decide now. MapReduce provides an Partitioner interface that determines which reduce task should ultimately handle the current pair of output data based on the number of key or value and reduce [3]. By default do hash to key and then to the number of reduce task model. The default mode is only for the average reduce processing power, if the user has a need for Partitioner, can be customized and set to the job.

Usually, the MapReduce framework and distributed file systems run on the same set of nodes, that is, computing nodes and storage nodes are usually together. This configuration allows the framework to efficiently schedule tasks on those nodes where the data is already stored, which makes the network bandwidth of the entire cluster very efficient.

2 Workflow and Mechanism Analysis of MapReduce

There are a large number of big data programming frameworks for cluster environment, first of all, Google's MapReduce, which shows us a simple general and automatic fault-tolerant batch computing model. But for other types of computing, such as interactive and streaming computing, MapReduce is not suitable. This has also led to the emergence of a large number of proprietary data processing models different from MapReduce, such as Storm, Impala and so on.

The Key-Value value pairs generated by the Map phase need to be transferred to the Reduce task for processing, but the MapReduce is used for distributed mass data processing, meaning that the data is not processed in memory on the same computer. It is necessary to carry out data transfer in each slaver [4]. Using HDFS as the medium for transmission. Map is used to write all the processed data into HDFS to pull the corresponding data from HDFS.

In order to reduce data communication, one of the basic principles is to localize data processing, that is, a computing node handles the data distributed on its local disk as much as possible, which realizes the migration of code to data. When this localized data processing is not possible, the Other available nodes are found and transmitted from the network to the node (data to code migration), but as far as possible, the available nodes are found from the local rack where the data is located, in order to reduce the communication delay.

Mapreduce divides a complex operation into several suboperations, and then gives them to each host in the cluster, which is run in parallel by each host [5]. With the introduction of mapreduce framework, developers can concentrate most of their work on the development of business logic, while the complexity of distributed computing can be handled by the framework (see Fig. 1).

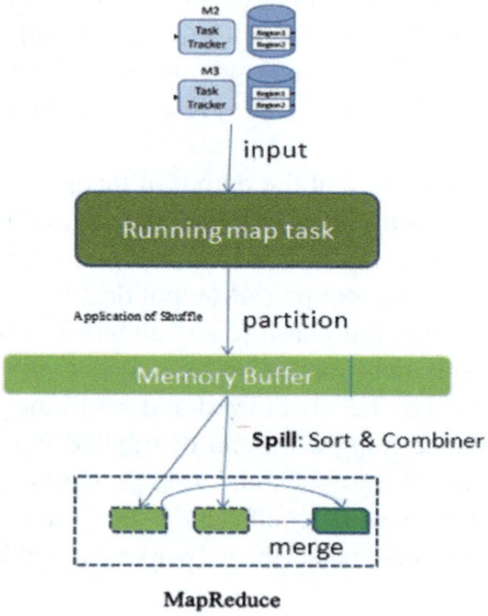

Fig. 1. Partial working principle in MapReduce.

When a Job is submitted, the JobTracker receives the submit job and configuration information, which is distributed to the slave node, Scheduling tasks and monitoring the execution of TaskTracker. JobTracker can be run on any computer in the cluster. TaskTracker is responsible for executing the task. It must run on DataNode and DataNode is a data storage node [6]. It is also the computing node. JobTracker distributes map tasks and reduce tasks to idle TaskTracker, tasks to run in parallel and monitors the running of tasks. If JobTracker fails, JobTracker will hand over the task to another idle TaskTracker to rerun.

After the JobTracker receives the job, it is placed in a job queue, waiting for the job scheduler to schedule it when the job scheduler schedules the job according to its own scheduling algorithm [7]. A map task is created for each partition based on the input partition information, and the map task is assigned to TaskTracker execution. For map and reduce tasks, TaskTracker has a fixed number of map slots and reduce slots based on the number of host cores and the size of memory. It is important to stress here that the: map task is not casually assigned to a TaskTracker, and it involves the above mentioned data localization (Data-Local).

In a Hadoop cluster, a TaskTracker normally communicates with JobTracker through a heartbeat mechanism. If a TaskTracker fails or runs slowly, it stops or rarely sends a heartbeat to the JobTracker. If a TaskTracker does not communicate with

JobTracker for a certain period of time (default is 1 min), then JobTracker removes the TaskTracker from the collection of TaskTracker waiting for task scheduling.

The application should at least specify the input/output location (path) and provide map and reduce functions by implementing appropriate interfaces or abstract classes. Plus the parameters of other jobs, this constitutes the job configuration (job configuration) [8]. Hadoop's job client submission jobs (jar packages/executables, etc.) and configuration information are then given to JobTracker, which is responsible for distributing these software and configuration information to slave, scheduling tasks and monitoring their execution, while providing status and diagnostics to job-client.

3 Research on the Important Application of Shuffle in MapReduce

In a cluster environment like Hadoop, most map task is performed on different nodes. Of course, in many cases, Reduce requires a cross - node to pull map task results on other nodes. If there are many jobs that the cluster is running, the normal execution of task will be severe for network resource consumption within the cluster. This network consumption is normal and we can't limit it to maximize the unnecessary consumption. Also within the node, the impact of disk IO on job completion time is significant compared to memory.

Map reads individual split for processing. If the file is large, it is automatically divided into multiple files and processed with multiple Map threads. Each Map thread generates the corresponding Key-Value output value and the partition value for which reduce to distribute. Here, there is a small episode, is about the memory buffer.

In order to reduce the overhead of data communication, the intermediate result data is merged before entering the Reduce node; the data processed by a Reduce node may come from more than one Map node. In order to avoid the intermediate result of data correlation-map node output in Reduce computing stage, we should use certain strategy to partition properly, and ensure that the correlation data is sent to the same Reduce node; in addition, the correlation data can be sent to the same Reduce node. The system also performs some performance optimization processes, such as multi-backup execution for the slowest computing tasks, and selection of the fastest finalists as the results.

After the maptask process is started, the data is processed according to the given range of data slicing [9]. The main process is to use the inputformat specified by the customer to get the RecordReader to read the data and form the input KV pair. The input KV (k is the line number of the file and v is the data of the file line) the map() method passed to the client is logically calculated, and the KV pair output from the map () method is collected to the cache. The KV pairs in the cache are sorted by K partition and are constantly overwritten to disk files.

Each map task has a memory buffer that stores the output of the map, and when the buffer is almost full, the buffer data needs to be stored on disk as a temporary file, When the entire map task is over, all the temporary files generated by this map task in the disk are merged to generate the final official output file, and then wait for the reduce task to pull the data.

HDFS and MR form the core of Hadoop distributed system architecture. HDFS implements distributed file system on cluster, and MR realizes distributed computing and task processing on cluster. HDFS provides support for file operation and storage during the process of MR tasks. MR realizes the task distribution, tracking, execution and other tasks on the basis of HDFS, and collects the results, which interact to accomplish the main tasks of distributed cluster.

Now that all work on the map end is complete, the resulting file is stored in a local directory within TaskTracker's reach. Each reduce task continuously retrieves information from the JobTracker through the RPC as to whether or not the map task has been completed, and if the reduce task is notified, it is known that the second half of the completion of the map task execution on a TaskTracker begins to start.

4 Analysis and Application of MapReduce Architecture and Working Principle

A large number of low-end servers are used in MapReduce cluster. Therefore, node hardware failures and software errors are the norm, so a well-designed parallel computing system with high fault tolerance can not affect the quality of computing service because of node failure. Any node failure should not lead to inconsistency or uncertainty of the result; when any node fails, the other nodes should be able to seamlessly take over the computing tasks of the failed node, and automatically join the cluster seamlessly when the failure node recovers. There is no need for the administrator to manually configure the system.

MRAppMaster monitors the completion of all maptask process tasks, starts the corresponding number of reducetask processes based on the parameters specified by the customer, and tells the reducetask process the data range (data partition) Reducetask process to handle when the Reducetask process starts, According to the location of the data to be processed by MRAppMaster, a number of maptask output files are obtained from several machines where maptask runs, and sorted locally, and then grouped according to the KV of the same key [10]. Call the customer-defined reduce() method for logical operation, collect the result of the operation output, KV, and then call the customer-specified outputformat to output the result data to the external storage mapreduce for how the data processed in the map phase is passed to the reduce phase. Is the most critical process in the mapreduce framework, called shuffle.

Parallel application development on Hadoop is based on MR programming framework. The principle of Mr programming model is that an input key-value pair set is used to generate an output key-value pair set. MR library implements this framework through two functions: Map and Reduce. The user-defined map function accepts an input key-value pair, and then produces a collection of intermediate key-value pairs. Mr combines all value with the same key value. Then pass a reduce function. Reduce function to accept the key and the associated value combined with the reduce function to merge these value values to form a smaller set of value. Usually we use an iterator to provide the intermediate value to the reduce function (the iterator's role is to collect these value values) so that we can handle a large collection of value values that cannot all be stored in memory.

In Hadoop Cluster, there is only one JobTracker, so that the JobTracker itself has a single point of failure. How to solve the single point problem of JobTracker? We can start one or more JobTracker standby nodes at the same time as we start the JobTracker master node. When the JobTracker master node has a problem, a primary node is re-selected from the standby JobTracker node by some election algorithm. Machine failure except the JobTracker error is the TaskTracker error. TaskTracker fault is relatively common. MapReduce usually resolves this fault by reexecuting the task.

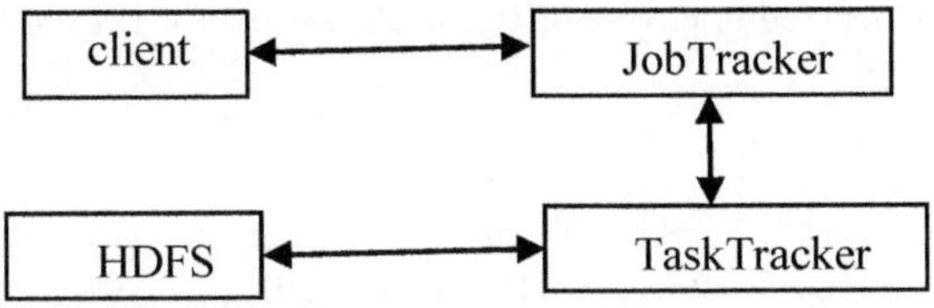

Fig. 2. Partial working principle in MapReduce.

MapReduce is custom-made for Apache Hadoop, as is shown by Fig. 2, it is very suitable for the use of Hadoop scenarios, that is, large-scale log processing system, batch data extraction and loading tools (ETL tools) and other similar operations. But as developers of Hadoop's sprawling turf discovered that MapReduce was not the best option in many scenarios, Hadoop began to put resource management into its own standalone component, YARN.

The Reduce process inherits the Reducer class in the org. apache.hadoop. mapreduce package and overrides the input parameter key of the reduce method reduce to a single word, while the values is a list of the count values of the corresponding words on each Mapper, so simply traverse the values and sum, The total number of occurrences of a word can be obtained.

The result values generated by Map are stored in memory first, but the memory buffer is size limited. The default is that 100 MB may burst memory when the output of map task is large. So you need to temporarily write the data in the buffer to disk under certain conditions, and then reuse the buffer. The process of writing data from memory to disk is called Spill.

MapReduce parallel computing software framework uses a variety of effective error detection and recovery mechanisms, such as node automatic reboot technology, which makes the cluster and computing framework robust against node failure, and can effectively handle the detection and recovery of failed nodes.

5 Summary

In MapReduce, the Job object is responsible for managing and running a computing task, and some methods of Job are used to set the parameters of the task. Here you set up the complete Map process using TokenizerMapper and the Combine and Reduce procedures using IntSumReduce. Also sets the output type of the Map procedure and the Reduce procedure: key of type Text, value is of type IntWritable. The input and output paths of the task are specified by command-line arguments and set by FileInputFormat and FileOutputFormat, respectively. The job.waitForCompletion() method can be called to execute the task when the parameters of the task are set.

Acknowledgements. This paper is supported by Henan key Laboratory for Big Data Processing & Analytics of Electronic Commerce, and also supported by the science and technology research major project of Henan province Education Department (17B520026), Key scientific research projects in Henan province universities (17A880020, 15A120012), and the Science and Technology Opening up Cooperation project of Henan Province (No. 172106000077).

References

1. Li W, Zhao H, Zhang Y, Wang Y (2013) Research on massive data mining based on MapReduce. Comput Eng Appl 20:100–110 (in Chinese)
2. Li B, Liu L (2012) Web log mining based on MapReduce. Comput Eng Appl (22):122–123 (in Chinese)
3. Li J, Cui J (2011) MapReduce parallel programming model. J Electron (11):520–526 (in Chinese)
4. Xin J, Cui Z (2011) Deep web data source discovery method based on MapReduce virtual machine. J Commun (07):320–330 (in Chinese)
5. Cheng M, Chen H (2011) Web log mining based on Hadoop. Comput Eng (11):108–111
6. Wang X, Wang Y, Zhu H (2012) Energy-efficient task scheduling model based on MapReduce for cloud computing using genetic algorithm. J Comput (12):522–526
7. Zhang G, Huang M, Ma L (2015) MapReduce simulator design for cloud computing environment. J Xinyang Normal Univ (Nat Sci Edn) 8(03):100–108 (in Chinese)
8. Xu H, Zhang R (2016) Novel approach of semantic annotation by fuzzy ontology based on variable precision rough set and concept lattice. Int J Hybrid Inf Technol 9(4):25–40
9. Jiang Y, Zhao Z (2015) Optimization of sorting algorithm based on MapReduce model. Comput Sci Explor (04):38–42 (in Chinese)
10. Jin X, Liu B (2016) Based on MapReduce location service optimization application. Inf Res 8(04):55–59

Design of Temperature Control System for BIW Phosphating Process

Weijie Gou[1(✉)], Lihong Wang[1], and Zhaokai An[2]

[1] Beijing Polytechnic, No. 9, Liangshuihe 1st Street, BDA, Beijing 100176, China
gvjie@126.com

[2] BBAC, No. 8, Boxing Road, BDA, Beijing 100176, China

Abstract. In automobile manufacturing, the phosphating process is required before the body painting is painted. This article introduces the phosphating liquid temperature of WinCC monitoring system. The main contents include the research and experiment of hardware, software design. The system consisted of WinCC monitor, Water-tank and PLC. The system has realized the measurement of PT100, temperature of solution of PID constant control, heating rod working duty cycle adjustment. This system not only greatly improves the automation level in the actual production line and realizes the remote control but also realizes the simulation teaching. This system has its own economy value, and it can save the teaching cost, it's a typical combination of practical application.

Keywords: Control system · PLC · Phosphating · Temperature

1 Introduction

Temperature is an important condition for many production processes. Cars need to obtain a durable, corrosion-resistant coating that is phosphated before painting. The phosphating treatment is to deposit an insoluble phosphating film on the surface of the degreased metal substrate by a dissociation reaction of phosphoric acid, and the function of the phosphating film is to improve the adhesion and corrosion resistance of the coating film coated thereon. The temperature of the phosphating solution is critical to the quality of the phosphating film formation. When the temperature is too high, a large amount of sediment is generated, and the phosphating solution loses the original concentration balance; when the temperature is too low, the filming ion concentration does not reach the concentration required for film formation, and the phosphate film is incomplete. Controlling the temperature control of the phosphating solution is an important process to ensure the quality of automotive paint. Remote control and visual management based on WinCC integration [1].

2 Working Principle of Temperature Control System

The phosphating solution temperature control system is a visual production process established by WinCC. The working principle of the system is shown in Fig. 1. A-PT100 b-mixer c-heater rod SY1-inlet valve SY2-drain valve. The system is mainly

Z. Xu et al. (Eds.): CSIA 2019, AISC 928, pp. 962–970, 2020.
https://doi.org/10.1007/978-3-030-15235-2_128

composed of WinCC monitoring interface, sink device and PLC. Set the water temperature setting value in the WinCC monitor screen, input the values of GAIN (proportional), TI (integral), TD (differential) and other parameters, select the working mode as "hardware environment", click the "start" button, these values will Feed to the corresponding address of the PLC. At this time, the current value of the water temperature is measured by the PT100, and then the resistance-voltage conversion is performed by the voltage transmitter, and then sent to the PIW100 of the PLC. The PLC internally obtains the heating parameters through the A/D conversion and the operations of the programs FB41, OB1, and FC100. The parameter value is output from the PQW100 of the PLC to the power adjustment module, and the power adjustment module controls the duty ratio of the heating rod after conversion, thereby achieving heating of the solution. The current value of the water temperature is sent to the PLC in cycles and compared with the set value of the water temperature, and the difference is PID-adjusted to form a closed-loop feedback system of temperature, thereby achieving constant control of the temperature of the phosphating solution.

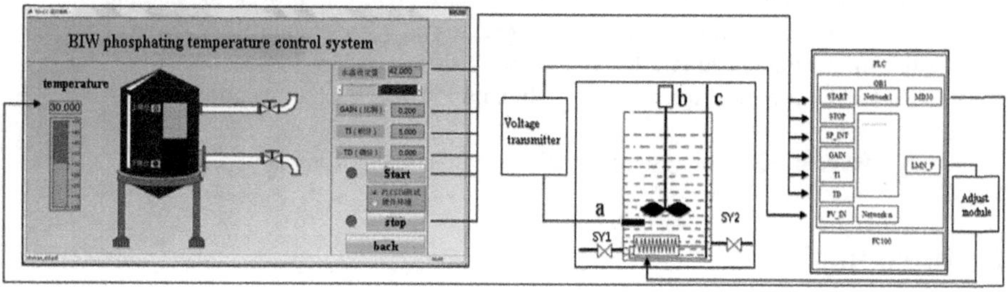

Fig. 1. Temperature control system

3 Temperature Control System Design

The monitoring part of the system uses WinCC V6.0, which offers flexible and powerful process visualization for field data display and control of the work process. The field data is collected and processed using the CPU314C2DP of Siemens S7-300. The controller is equipped with 5 channels of analog input and 2 channels of analog output. The input channel collects the current value of the water temperature measured by PT100, and the control channel outputs the control parameters of the heating bar. The program is written with the programming software STEP7 which is compatible with S7-300. The main application is FB41 to realize the temperature closed-loop feedback adjustment and control. The transfer of system variables is based on MPI communication and the network. The system can quickly and automatically realize real-time monitoring and control of the on-site production process.

3.1 Temperature Control System Monitoring Screen

The current value of the water temperature in the screen is the output field. The object outputs the value of the variable. The water temperature setting value, GAIN value, TI (integral) value and TD (differential value) are all input fields, and the input data will be input. Assigned to a variable; the bar graph below the current temperature of the water temperature is used to visually display the water temperature value; the PLCSIM test and the hardware environment are option groups. The system can open the PLCSIM for simulation test, or connect the experimental device for physical operation. Start and stop buttons to implement the call of related functions.

In the graphical editor of WinCC, click on the Standard palette to add objects. Double-click the object to open the Object Properties window and set the properties of the object. Attributes generally include parameters such as geometry, color, format, and font. The variables corresponding to the object are shown in Table 1. The variables in WinCC are imported from the PLC program, so each variable has a "S7$Program(2)/" section in front of it.

Table 1. Control object variable table

	Object	Connection variable	Control address
1	Current water temperature (bar graph)	S7$Program(2)wendu	MD30
2	Water temperature setting (slider)	S7$Program(2)wendu_shezhi	MD34
3	GAIN (proportion)	S7$Program(2)/PID_P	MD38
4	TI (integral)	S7$Program(2)/PID_I	MD42
5	TD (differential)	S7$Program(2)/PID_D	MD46
6	start up	S7$Program(2)/WinCC_qd	M10.0
7	PLCSIM test/hardware environment	S7$Program(2)/moshi_zj	MB13.0
8	stop	S7$Program(2)/WinCC_tzh	M10.1

3.2 Water Temperature Measurement

Since the resistance of the platinum resistance wire changes with temperature, it is often used as a temperature sensor. Platinum resistance temperature sensor is an ideal temperature measuring component widely used in industrial precision measurement and control systems because of its high stability, high precision, fast speed, and shock resistance. It is used as an international standard thermometer in the range of −100–600 °C. The system water temperature is measured by PT100. The meaning of Pt100 is that the nominal resistance value at 0 °C is 100 Ω [2–6].

3.2.1 Hardware Settings

Set the parameters related to Hardware in the SIMATIC Manager according to the actual device. Double-click the input and output item AI5/AO2 to open the analog input and output module setting dialog box, as shown in Fig. 2. In the Inputs item, the temperature unit is selected as Degrees Celsius, Input has 0–4 input channels, and the address is PIW100-PIW108, where 0–3 channels can receive voltage or current signals.

The system uses 0 channel to collect the current value of water temperature, the address is PIW100, and receives the voltage signal of 0–10 V. Thus, the measured value of the PT100 is sent from the channel to the PLC 300 after being converted by the voltage transmitter.

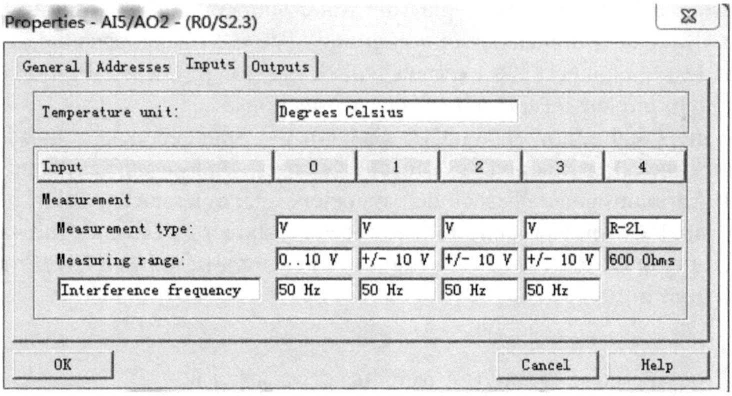

Fig. 2. Analog input and output module settings dialog box

3.2.2 Control Program

The temperature acquisition is realized by calling FC100 in the main program OB1. The FC100 mainly performs numerical transformation and calculation on the collected data. The collected temperature value is sent to FB41 for PID calculation.

FC100 is called in the OB1 program. The FC100 subroutine is called in the OB1 program. The interface input parameters of the subroutine are the temperature acquisition value of PIW100, the upper temperature limit set by #H_LIM, the lower temperature limit set by #L_LIM, and the output parameter of the interface is MD30. The current value of the water temperature is shown in Fig. 3.

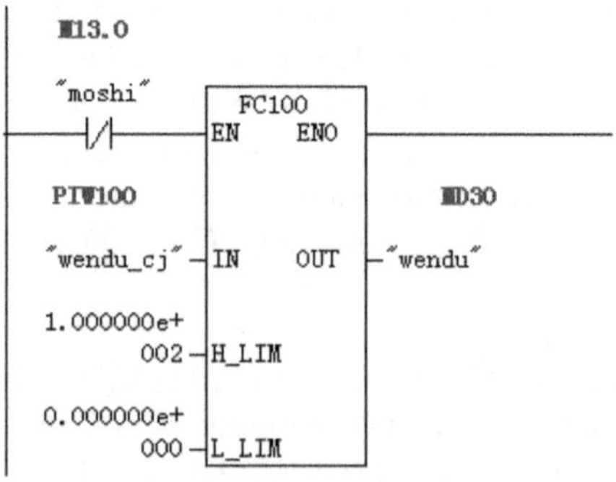

Fig. 3. Temperature display program

FC100 subroutine. Scale the acquired values. The field temperature value collected by the MOVE module is an integer 16-bit. In the FB41 module, PV_IN requires an input floating-point value of 32 bits. The data type and range cannot be matched and need to be converted. The acquired value is converted to a double integer by the I_DI module, and then converted to a floating point type by the DI_R module, as shown in Fig. 4.

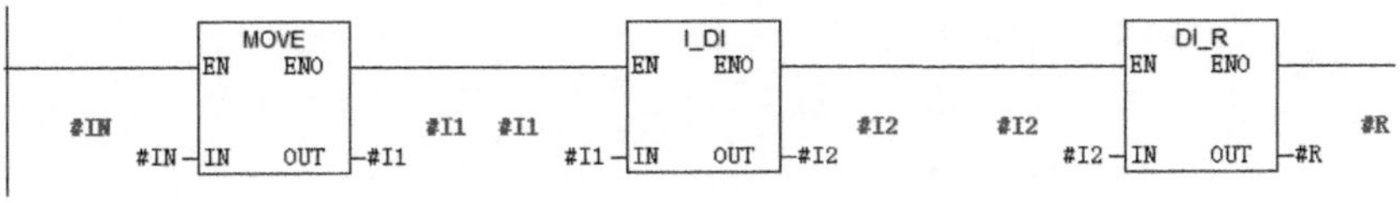

Fig. 4. Temperature value conversion program

The values collected by PIW100 range from 0–27648, and the temperature collected by PT100 is between 0–100 °C. The two are linearly related. The conversion method is shown in Eq. 1. The conversion formula calculates the value of the temperature effective range by the SUB_R module #rang=#H_LIM-#L_LIM, as shown in Fig. 5; the calculation process of Eq. 1 is implemented by the DIV-R, MUL-R and ADD-R modules, as shown in Fig. 6.

$$\#out = \frac{\#H\_LIM\text{-}\#L\_LIM}{27648}\#R + \#L\_LIM \tag{1}$$

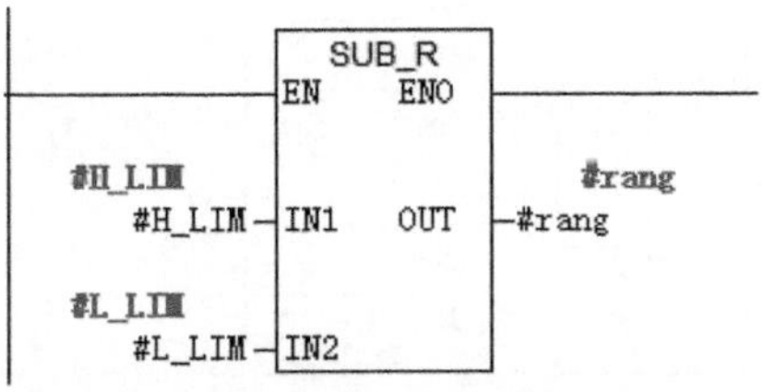

Fig. 5. A/D conversion sequence program

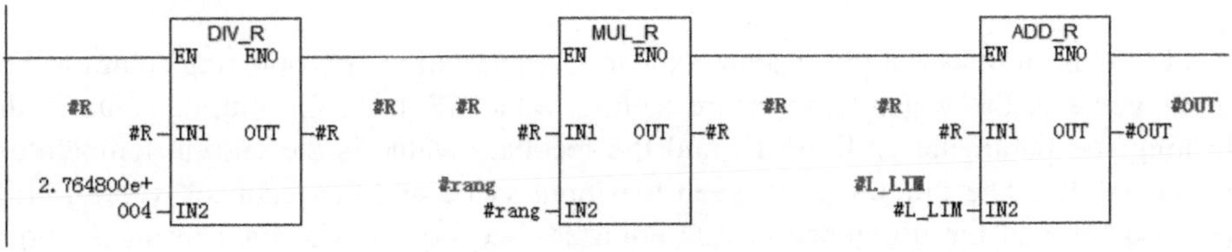

Fig. 6. A/D conversion calculation

The FB41 module of the OB1 program calls the current value of the water temperature, which is input from the PV-IN port, as shown in Fig. 7.

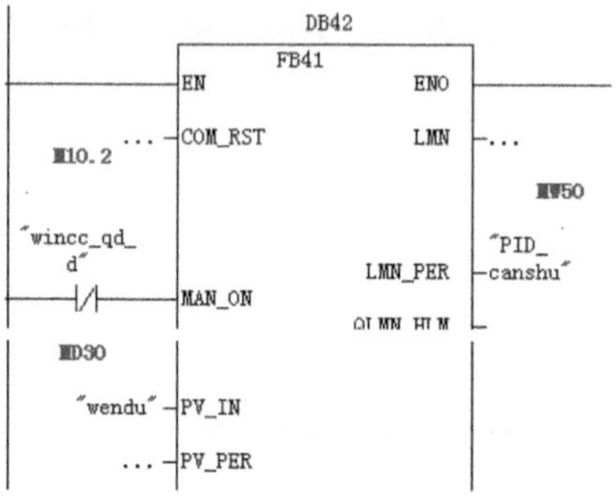

Fig. 7. Temperature acquisition program

3.3 Constant Temperature Control

FB4l is called "CONT_C" (continuous controller) and is a pure software PID controller [7–10] for system solid state. When calling this controller, you must specify the background data block and label. In this system, DB42 is specified as the instance data block of FB41. The working principle of FB41 is shown in Fig. 8.

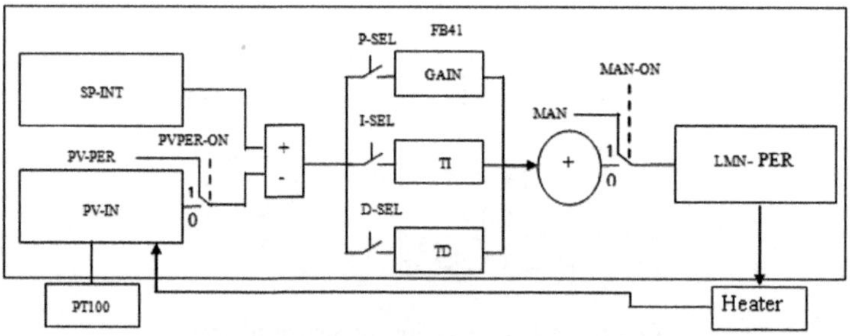

Fig. 8. Working principle of CONT_C

The control object of the system is the temperature of the phosphating solution. The input value is the water temperature setting value SP_INT, the output value is the heating rod parameter LMN-PER, and the feedback value is the current temperature value PV_IN. The difference between the input value and the feedback value is E(t) (see Eq. 2), and the difference is PID adjusted (see Eq. 3). The final result is output from the LMN-PER port to the heating rod. When PVPER-ON is 0, the PV_IN port is valid. When it is 1, the PV-PER port is valid. When MAN-ON is 0, the parameters of the system installation PID setting are automatically run. When it is 1, the parameters are manually input. P-SEL, I-SEL, and D-SEL control whether GAIN, TI, and TD are effective, respectively, so that the P, PI, and PID controllers can be flexibly implemented. The variables corresponding to each port are shown in Table 2.

$$E(t) = SP\_INT\text{-}PV\_IN \tag{2}$$

$$LMN\text{-}PER(t) = GAIN(E(t) + \int_{0}^{t} E(t)dt + \frac{dE(t)}{dt}) \tag{3}$$

It can be seen from Table 2. The integration time is TI and the derivative time is TD.

Table 2. Port corresponding variable.

	FB41 port	Input value	Address
1	MAN-ON	S7$Program(2)/WinCC_qd	M10.2
2	PVPER-ON	S7$Program(2)/WinCC_qd	M10.2
3	P-SEL	S7$Program(2)/WinCC_qd	M10.2
4	I-SEL	S7$Program(2)/WinCC_qd	M10.2
5	D-SEL	S7$Program(2)/WinCC_qd	M10.2
6	SP_INT	S7$Program(2)wendu_shezhi	MD34
7	PV_IN	S7$Program(2)wendu	MD30
8	GAIN	S7$Program(2)/PID_P	MD38
9	TI	MD42*1000	MD170
10	TD	MD46*1000	MD174
11	LMN-PER	S7$Program(2)/PID_canshu	MW50

3.4 Heating Temperature Control

There are two ways to control the temperature of the heating rod, voltage regulation control and power adjustment (duty cycle) control. This system uses a power adjustment module to perform numerical conversion between the PLC and the heating rod.

3.4.1 Parameter Setting

Set the parameters related to Hardware in the SIMATIC Manager according to the actual device. Double-click the input and output item AI5/AO2 to open the analog input and output module setting dialog box. Output has 0–1 output channels in the Output item, the address is PQW100-PQW102, which can output voltage or current signal. The system adopts the 0 channel output heating parameter jiare-csh, which will be sent to the power adjustment module to control the duty cycle of the heating rod after numerical conversion.

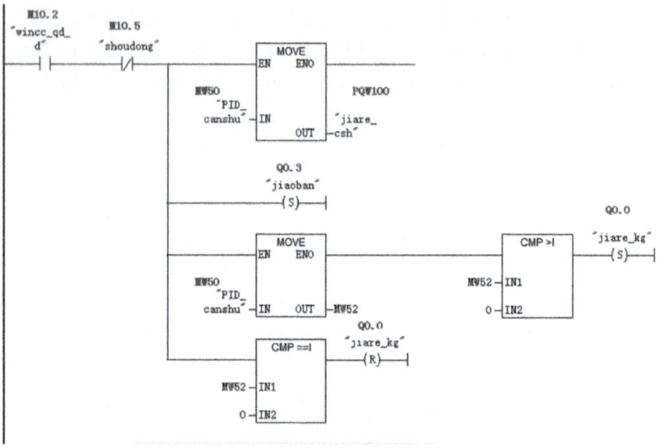

Fig. 9. Heating control program

3.4.2 Heating Control Program

In the OB1 main program, the parameters output by S7$Program(2)/PID_canshu are compared with 0. If it is greater than 0, the heating switch is started, and the parameter is output from the PQW100 channel to the variable jiare-csh, thereby controlling the working condition of the heating rod. If it is equal to 0, the heating rod is not activated, and if it is 1, the heating rod is activated. The program is shown in Fig. 9.

4 Temperature Control Test

The experimental platform is: the power of the heating rod is 1000 W, the volume of the solution is 3 L, the flow rate of the incoming and outgoing liquid is 1 L/min, the value of GAIN is 0.2, the value of TI is 5, and the value of TD is 0. After 5 min, the heating temperature is kept constant from 35° to 42°, and the overshoot of 2.3% is controlled within the allowable range. The experimental results are better. The experimental curve of the temperature control test results is shown in Fig. 10. The monitoring interface has good real-time response, sensitive control response, and stable and reliable system.

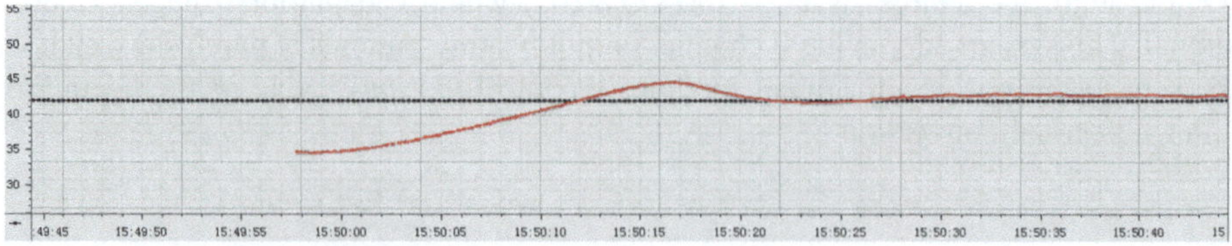

Fig. 10. Temperature control test results

5 Conclusion

Based on the WinCC phosphating solution temperature control system, the performance is stable and works well. The system better handles the data conversion and scale work between PT100, FB41 module and heating rod, and realizes the variable transfer between PLC and WinCC conveniently and quickly. The on-site control response is fast and the control is accurate. The system improves the efficiency of finding faults and solving faults, enhances the production capacity of automated production lines, reduces costs, and receives good economic benefits. The system realizes the combination of software integration control visualization and hardware execution functions, and is a project integrating enterprise practice functions and simulation.

Acknowledgments. Supported by Program for Research Team in Beijing Polytechnic.

References

1. Li J (2013) WinCC configuration skills and technical questions and answers. Mechanical Industry Press, Beijing
2. Zhang Y, Zhang S (2010) Design of high precision temperature detection system based on platinum resistance sensor. J Transduct Technol 03:311–314
3. Ren D, Zhou Q, Zhang X, Yu H (2010) A nonlinear correction method for platinum resistance temperature measurement circuit. Electron Dev 05:603–607
4. Zhang X, Hu X, Yan Y, Qin C, Zhang J (2010) Design and experimental research of high precision temperature acquisition system based on PT100. J Transduct Technol 06:812–815
5. Li A (1999) Scale transformation method of platinum resistance temperature measurement system. J. Xi'an Min Inst 01:74–77
6. Jiang S (2012) Robot controlled by PLC. Microcomputer 02:20–22
7. Yin H, Tian J (2011) Design of temperature control system for jacketed boiler based on FB41 and FB43. J Nanyang Inst Technol 06:58–62
8. Zheng B, Zeng Y (2012) Application of function block FB41 in CO_2 analysis and addition control system. Sci Technol Commun 11:133
9. Yuan W, Ai W, He X (2013) Simulation teaching system of power network-related accidents based on WinCC. Lab Res Explor 03:71–75
10. Gong Q (2012) Application of PLC PID controller in MPS automation control system. Hydraul Pneumatics 12:101–103

The Impact of Artificial Intelligence on the Accounting Industry

Yanling Shi(✉)

Finance Department, ShanDong University of Arts, Jinan, China
shiyanling@sdca.edu.cn

Abstract. With the development of artificial intelligence technology, artificial intelligence has entered the accounting field more and more deeply, which plays an important role in improving business efficiency, reducing work errors, preventing and controlling enterprise risks, improving enterprise competitiveness, and improving human resource efficiency. Artificial intelligence technology is like a double-edged sword. While promoting the development of accounting work, it will also cause accountants to face the crisis of unemployment in the workplace. Based on the concept of artificial intelligence technology and its application in the accounting industry, this paper discusses the impact of artificial intelligence on the accounting industry, and puts forward the challenges of the artificial intelligence technology accounting industry. It should take the lead in completing the skills upgrade; realize the transformation of the comprehensive management accounting role. Develop strategies such as designers and supervisors of artificial intelligence accounting systems.

Keywords: Artificial intelligence · Accounting industry · Influence · Countermeasure

1 Introduction

In recent years, China's artificial intelligence technology has developed rapidly and has surpassed the world's advanced level [1]. In the process of development, artificial intelligence brings great convenience to our production and life, but also brings a lot of problems [2]. The artificial intelligence robots invented by scientists have been similar in function to human beings [3]. Under such circumstances, the employees of basic accounting are seriously affected by their artificial intelligence, which has seriously threatened their professional quality [4–8]. In this regard, accountants must deeply understand the requirements of the development of the accounting industry, and actively respond to the opportunities and challenges that artificial intelligence technology brings to the accounting industry and its own development. In this regard, this paper explores the impact of artificial intelligence on the accounting industry from the concept of artificial intelligence technology and its application in the accounting industry, and puts forward the challenge of dealing with the artificial intelligence technology accounting industry. It should take the lead in completing the skills upgrade; [9–15] realize the comprehensive management accounting Role change; development strategies such as designers and supervisors of artificial intelligence accounting systems [16–20].

Z. Xu et al. (Eds.): CSIA 2019, AISC 928, pp. 971–978, 2020.
https://doi.org/10.1007/978-3-030-15235-2_129

2 Artificial Intelligence Overview

The term "artificial intelligence" first appeared in the 1956 Dartmouth Society. Since then, relevant scientific researchers have proposed many new related theories, and the concept of artificial intelligence has also developed. Artificial Intelligence, abbreviated as AI. It is a new technical science that researches and develops theories, methods, techniques, and applications that simulate, extend, and extend human intelligence. As a branch of computer science, artificial intelligence develops an intelligent machine product that reacts in a manner similar to human intelligence, based on the understanding of the essence of intelligence. Research in this area mainly covers image recognition, speech recognition, language processing, expert systems and robotics.

The definition of artificial intelligence can be divided into two parts, namely "artificial" and "intelligent". "Manual" is better understood and less controversial. Sometimes we have to think about what humans can do, or whether the level of intelligence of people is so high that they can create artificial intelligence, and so on. But in general, "artificial systems" are artificial systems in the usual sense.

There are a lot of questions about what is "intelligence". This involves other issues such as CONSCIOUSNESS, SELF, MIND (including unconscious thinking (UNCONSCIOUS_MIND)). The only intelligence that people understand is the intelligence of people themselves. This is a widely accepted view. But our understanding of our own intelligence is very limited, and we have limited understanding of the necessary elements that constitute human intelligence, so it is difficult to define what is "intelligence" of "manual" manufacturing. Therefore, the study of artificial intelligence often involves the study of human intelligence itself. Other intelligences about animals or other man-made systems are also generally considered to be research topics related to artificial intelligence.

With the deepening of research, artificial intelligence is combined with accounting information systems with its high-performance computing power and data storage capabilities. Next, big data, artificial intelligence, and blockchain technology will develop in the accounting industry in the next decade. Produce subversive changes. Accounting personnel engaged in a large number of repetitive, standardizable, process accounting, accounting, etc. will be completely replaced by more precise and rapid artificial intelligence. The emergence of "Deloitte Financial Robot" has further proved that artificial intelligence technology continues to extend to deep application. This will definitely create a huge panic for our current finance staff. First of all, we should clarify the impact of artificial intelligence on the accounting industry, so we will find our gaps and countermeasures.

3 Application Status and Prospects of Artificial Intelligence in Accounting Industry in China

3.1 Application Status of Artificial Intelligence in China for Accounting Industry

The two basic functions of accounting are accounting and supervisory functions. The accounting function includes accounting for various economic operations of the enterprise, such as filling in vouchers, finishing of journals, completion of financial statements, etc.; the supervisory function is mainly the separation of accounting incompatible positions, thus preventing the occurrence of fraud. At present, most companies use financial software to help companies complete some of their daily economic operations, such as the filling of accounting documents. Although accounting documents are used to complete the filling of documents, it is still necessary to manually input the data, then click on the review. The application of accounting software is only a substitute for some repetitive and complicated work of the enterprise. Most of the accounting work, such as statistics, analysis, and making appropriate accounting estimates, cannot be replaced by artificial intelligence. The accountant can spend more time doing other work.

3.2 Prospects of China's Artificial Intelligence to the Accounting Industry

Today, with the rapid economic development, the era of big data has arrived, and every industry is facing the challenge of dealing with massive data. On the one hand, in the face of massive data, complex calculations, it is unrealistic and infeasible to process these data by hand. At this time, with the aid of computer-aided systems, accounting software and computer ultra-fast computing capabilities play an increasingly important role in the financial work of collecting, calculating and analyzing large amounts of data. On the other hand, a complete accounting process is quite complicated and time consuming, especially for the acquisition and processing of accounting data. For most of the accounting staff, they all hope that this repetitive and unskilled accounting work can be done by computer. Although accounting software has replaced some financial work links, it is still far from enough, such as performance evaluation in management accounting, analysis of profit and loss, etc. These need to develop mechanisms and measurement principles that are suitable for the characteristics of the enterprise itself. However, we should believe that with the development of technology in the future, artificial intelligence will definitely be used more and more widely in the accounting industry.

4 The Impact of Artificial Intelligence on the Accounting Industry

4.1 Improve the Accuracy of Accounting

The significant performance of artificial intelligence in the accounting industry is the development and application of various accounting computerization systems and accounting software. After applying the accounting software, any one of the above three main bodies can handle the accounting of the day in a timely manner. Business and input information, and only need to log in to the accounting system, you can enter the corresponding business by inputting data and information. At the end of the month, the end of the quarter, and the end of the year, the software can automatically generate financial statements, saving the manual account statement. time. On the other hand, in the traditional accounting mode, most accounting and accounting records require manual calculation by the accountant, which is easy to increase the probability of error in the accounting business. However, in the accounting software, if there is a problem with the account entered by the accountant, the system Will automatically remind, to avoid further extension of the error, causing excessive impact on accounting, thereby improving the accuracy of accounting.

4.2 To Some Extent Reduce the Possibility of Financial Fraud

In the traditional accounting positions, incompatible positions do not achieve true separation, especially in small and medium-sized enterprises, financial personnel manage money and account, financial accounting accounts are chaotic, creating opportunities for financial fraud, give The criminals who seek personal gain can take advantage of it. The management is above the internal control, which damages the relevant interests of shareholders and is not conducive to the long-term development of the company. However, in the context of artificial intelligence, a large amount of accounting work has been handed over to the computer, and accounting personnel only need to review it. At the end of the period, the system automatically checks out the balance and makes a trial balance. In the accounting system, each financial staff has its own corresponding authority, and has different accounts and passwords. It can be said that the division of labor is clear, which reduces the possibility of financial fraud to a certain extent. However, the accounting system can not completely solve the problem of financial fraud from the root cause, because any system is ultimately controlled by people, and the setting of authority is completed by people, so the application of accounting system can not prevent management from overriding. Above the internal control.

4.3 Improve the Ability of Enterprises to Cope with Risks

The ability of enterprises to cope with risks needs to be supported by relevant information. The application of artificial intelligence has established a huge information base for the development of enterprises. Through the analysis of relevant information, the direction of future investment of enterprises is effectively predicted. The application of artificial intelligence quickly integrates data under high-speed computing capabilities, which promotes the establishment of enterprise risk prediction modules. Enterprises can use financial intelligence to predict financial crisis with the help of artificial intelligence, which can effectively identify financial risk issues, which is helpful for improving the competitiveness of enterprises in the market.

4.4 Threat to the Security of Accounting Information

The intelligent financial software stores the financial data of the accounting entity in each period in electronic form. It is undeniable that the electronic data storage form has the advantages of simple storage method, large capacity, convenient use and so on. However, on the one hand, if the system security protection measures are not comprehensive, the financial system is vulnerable to hackers, resulting in the disclosure of trade secrets. On the other hand, due to the low security of the network, when information is transmitted in the network, the financial information may be illegally intercepted, which seriously affects the security of the accounting information of the enterprise.

4.5 Improve the Pressure on Accountants

Artificial intelligence puts grassroots accountants at risk of losing their jobs. From the era of accounting computerization to the era of accounting intelligence, the number of financial jobs in China has become saturated, the incremental changes in posts are not significant, and the simple accounting work will be gradually replaced by intelligent financial software. It can be seen that with the continuous development of intelligent financial software, the basic work of the accounting industry will be completed by intelligent financial software, the demand for accounting talents in basic positions will be significantly reduced, and the grassroots accountants will face the pressure of unemployment. Artificial intelligence puts accountants under the pressure of skill transformation. Since basic and repetitive accounting work is done by intelligent financial software, accountants have more time and energy to invest in development strategies that focus on decision analysis and business management, which will greatly drive accounting staff to focus on their work. Emphasis on the transfer of accounting to focus on management, which puts the requirements for skill transformation for accountants, which is forced by the pressure of skills transformation from financial accounting to management accounting.

5 The Accounting Industry Personnel Training Strategy Under Artificial Intelligence

5.1 Improve the Ability to Use Professional Knowledge and Do Comprehensive Accounting Talents

In the current era, the accounting industry is a hot industry. The middle and low-end accounting talents are currently in a state of oversupply in the talent market, lacking core competitiveness and having strong substitutability. With the development of information technology, artificial intelligence is increasingly welcomed by all walks of life, then low-end accounting talents are easily replaced by artificial intelligence products. As the middle and low-end accountants, most of them should look to the future, be prepared for danger, and strive to have a place in the accounting industry. As an accountant, it is not enough to have a single accounting knowledge. It is necessary to improve its own capabilities, actively adapt to the changes in the functions of traditional accounting, and actively learn auditing, taxation, strategy, etc. while learning the constantly updated accounting knowledge. All aspects of knowledge, improve their ability to analyze and understand data, do work that artificial intelligence can't do, and become a comprehensive accounting talent. Consciously invest in the field of artificial intelligence, learn the principles and characteristics of artificial intelligence work, actively adapt to it, achieve the combination of labor and accounting software work, achieve greater efficiency, improve the ability to use professional knowledge, and become a comprehensive talent. As an accountant, if you stay in the traditional accounting treatment method in the intelligent era, it can only be eliminated by the times. This society is the survival of the fittest, new technical methods have been produced, you have not mastered the one that you are defeated. At least to keep up with the pace of the times. The state currently has requirements for accounting personnel to receive continuing education. Accounting personnel can use this platform to learn the current application of artificial intelligence in the field of accounting, and can also learn the related applications of accounting computerization.

5.2 Comprehensive Evaluation of Artificial Intelligence, Positive View of Artificial Intelligence

The use of artificial intelligence will not lead to the loss of accounting staff, but will promote the improvement of the overall quality of accountants, promote the transformation of traditional accounting, and adapt to the artificial environment. The use of artificial intelligence is to a large extent optimize the structure of accountants, and promote the transformation of low-end accountants to high-end accountants. Therefore, we must comprehensively evaluate artificial intelligence, positively treat artificial intelligence, and it is wrong to treat artificial intelligence with a negative attitude. This is not conducive to its own development, and is not conducive to the rapid development of the entire society. Artificial intelligence can't completely replace human intelligence and operational ability. Although artificial intelligence has great advantages in terms of computing power and responsiveness compared with accounting personnel, artificial intelligence is created by human beings, and there must be places where it is not as good as human beings. To this end, accountants need to correct their own attitudes, correctly view the relationship between traditional accounting models and artificial intelligence, and produce a clear understanding of the application of artificial intelligence in the accounting industry, avoiding the emergence of negative opinions and affecting accounting practitioners. Work confidence and enthusiasm.

5.3 Transformation to Management and High-End Accounting Talents

In the context of artificial intelligence, it is becoming more and more important to promote the rapid transformation of accountants. The reference of artificial intelligence is both a pressure and a driving force for the accounting profession and accounting personnel. In order to prevent themselves from being unemployed, this has forced accountants to shift to management and high-end accounting talent. The use of accounting software has largely replaced manual accounting, filling in vouchers, and preparation of financial statements, which has enabled a large number of accountants to be freed from these complicated accounting operations. Not only can they give them more time to learn more, but they also provide a good opportunity for their transformation. They are transformed from traditional accounting work to management, financial sharing, and business development.

5.4 Designing and Supervising the Artificial Intelligence Accounting System

The research and development of artificial intelligence accounting information system requires the cooperation of computer personnel who understand computer development and professional accounting personnel who understand accounting knowledge, and computer research and development personnel are the developers of basic program tools, and accounting personnel are practitioners of core accounting theory. Only by complementing each other, cooperating with each other, and complementing each other's strengths can we play a synergistic role in the research, development, maintenance and upgrade of artificial intelligence accounting systems, and promote the healthy development of artificial intelligence in the accounting industry. The completion of accounting work is impossible only by relying on accounting software based on programmatic and regularization. Some unexpected work that requires professional judgment still requires accountants to respond flexibly based on experience and knowledge. Moreover, the security of intelligent financial software is still a technical loophole. Accounting personnel should enhance their own risk prevention awareness, always supervise and prevent information leakage and other security issues, and act as the designer and supervisor of the accounting system in the era of artificial intelligence accounting.

6 Conclusion

The arrival of the era of artificial intelligence accounting is the inevitable result of the integration and development of Internet technology and artificial intelligence technology in the accounting industry. Artificial intelligence is an opportunity and a challenge for the development of the accounting industry. Every accounting worker should keep pace with the times, recognize the needs of his own skills improvement and functional transformation, actively change the resistance to artificial intelligence, tap his own advantages to make up for the shortcomings of intelligent accounting software, and seize the mentality of tolerance. Opportunities meet the challenges, making artificial intelligence technology a tool and partner for accounting work, exerting its own value in the transformation of the intelligent accounting era, and contributing to the development of the accounting industry.

References

1. Alhanshi M, Albraiki H (2015) Knowledge sharing and employee development in oil and gas companies in the United Arab Emirates. In: International conference on knowledge management in organizations. Springer, pp 190–208
2. Marwala T (2015) Impact of artificial intelligence on economic theory. Quant Financ
3. O'Keefe RM, O'Leary D, Rebne D et al (2015) The impact of expert systems in accounting: system characteristics, productivity and work unit effects. Intell Syst Acc Financ Manag 2(3):177–189

4. Broda M, Frank A (2015) Learning beyond the screen: assessing the impact of reflective artificial intelligence technology on the development of emergent literacy skills. Plant Physiol 151(2):681–690
5. Dirican C (2015) The impacts of robotics, artificial intelligence on business and economics. Procedia Soc Behav Sci 195:564–573
6. Makridakis S (2017) The forthcoming artificial intelligence (AI) revolution: its impact on society and firms. Futures 90:46–60
7. (2018) Response to technological innovation: the impact of stem graduates on employment opportunities in accounting services firms
8. Morikawa M (2017) Firms' expectations about the impact of ai and robotics: evidence from a survey. Econ Inq 55(2):1054–1063
9. Baldwin AA (2016) UOA, USA collected papers of the eleventh annual research workshop on: artificial intelligence and emerging technologies in accounting, auditing and tax
10. Galeshchuk S (2014) Neural-based method of measuring exchange-rate impact on international companies' revenue. In: 11th international conference distributed computing and artificial intelligence. Springer, pp 529–536
11. Vijayakumari AA, Thirunavukkarasu P, Lukose A, et al (2015) Exploration of the effect of demographic and clinical confounding variables on results of voxel-based morphometric analysis in schizophrenia. In: Artificial intelligence and evolutionary algorithms in engineering systems. Springer India, pp 139–149
12. Cockburn IM, Henderson R, Stern S (2018) The impact of artificial intelligence on innovation. NBER Chapters
13. Michaels A, Grüning M (2018) The impact of corporate identity on corporate social responsibility disclosure. Int J Corp Soc Responsib 3(1):3
14. Agwu OE, Akpabio JU, Alabi SB et al (2018) Artificial intelligence techniques and their applications in drilling fluid engineering: a review. J Petrol Sci Eng 167:300–315
15. Neo TK, Sabbaghan S (2014) The impact of the relationship between Gardner's multiple intelligence and Kolb's learning style. Knowl Discov Transfer Manag Inf Age 485(1–3):21–29
16. Sankararaman S, Teubert C (2015) Impact of uncertainty on the diagnostics and prognostics of a Current-Pressure transducer. In: Aerospace conference. IEEE, pp 1–10
17. Stejskal J, Hajek P (2015) Modelling knowledge spillover effects using moderated and mediation analysis – the case of Czech high-tech industries. LNBIP, vol 224, pp 329–341
18. Hsu YS, Lin SJ (2016) An emerging hybrid mechanism for information disclosure forecasting. Int J Mach Learn Cybernet 7(6):1–10
19. Dimiduk DM, Holm EA, Niezgoda SR (2018) Perspectives on the impact of machine learning, deep learning, and artificial intelligence on materials, processes, and structures engineering. Integr Mater Manuf Innov 7:157–172
20. Grosz BJ, Stone P (2018) A century long commitment to assessing artificial intelligence and its impact on society

Application and Realization of Genetic Algorithm Based on MATLAB Environment

Yan Li, Bo Yu(✉), Xiaodong Li, Shijun Luo, and Haibo Li

Mechanical and Electrical Engineering College,
Changchun Institute of Technology, Changchun, China
yubo745@163.com

Abstract. This paper introduces the principle and characteristics of genetic algorithm, and expounds the main functions and functions of the genetic algorithm toolbox used by the author. Through the simulation test of complex nonlinear and multi-peak function in MATLAB environment, the basic steps and calculation process of the genetic algorithm are explained in detail, and the efficiency and flexibility of the genetic algorithm in the global optimization problem are proved by examples.

Keywords: Genetic algorithm · MATLAB · Simulation test · Global optimization

1 Introduction

The Genetic Algorithm (GA) originated from the computers used in biological systems. In 1975, professor Holland from the university of Michigan put forward the theory of Adaptation in Natural and artificial Systems [1–5]. Genetic algorithm, as a practical, efficient, flexible and robust global optimization technology, has been highly concerned by domestic and foreign scholars and widely used [6–12].

2 Basic Principles and Features

Genetic algorithm (ga) is a random global search and optimization based on natural biological evolution mechanism Algorithm [2]. The basic principle is as follows: First of all, the solution of problems can be expressed as encoded string (biology called chromosomes, Chromosome), each encoded string representing a feasible solution, then a group of randomly generated string length must be encoded string (referred to as the initial Population, Population), and to adapt the encoded string into the corresponding value, then according to the corresponding target condition to adapt to the value selection, according to the encoding string of adaptive value of high and low, perform select (Reproduction), cross (Crossover, Mutation (Mutation) generates the next generation of group, through several generations of evolution, Finally, the condition optimal individual is obtained, that is, the optimal solution of the problem.

In view of the basic principles of the above genetic algorithm, the genetic algorithm has the following characteristics: the representation of feasible solutions is extensive. You have a group search feature. None of the auxiliary information is needed for the

Z. Xu et al. (Eds.): CSIA 2019, AISC 928, pp. 979–985, 2020.
https://doi.org/10.1007/978-3-030-15235-2_130

optimal solution. Triggered has inherent heuristic random search characteristics. Solver will not fall into local optimum. Rather, it can quickly and reliably solve complex and non-linear problems. Program has inherent parallelism and parallel computing power.

3 Main Functions and Functions of MATLAB Genetic Algorithm Toolbox

The function I use is a genetic algorithm toolbox function developed by the university of Sheffield in the UK. Genetic algorithm (ga) Toolbox is a genetic algorithm that realizes a wide range of applications through MATLAB matrix functions. The genetic algorithm tool is written as a command-line function in M files. No matter which programming method is adopted, the genetic algorithm toolbox needs to have practical functions such as population initialization, fitness, selection, crossover and variation, etc., which can be programmed according to the actual situation, and can be improved or extended.

3.1 Population Initialization Function

The first step of the genetic algorithm is to establish the initial population. Since the genetic algorithm cannot directly process the target variables, it must represent them as the string structure data of the genetic space through coding, and randomly generate N initial string structure data to form an initial population. Toolbox support: CRTBP (establish binary, integer population), CRTRP (establish real population) and other gene expression forms.

3.2 Fitness Function

Fitness function is called evaluation function, which is a standard determined according to the objective function to distinguish the good or bad of individuals in the group. It is the driving force of the algorithm evolution process and the only basis for natural selection. The fitness function is always non-negative, while the objective function can be positive or negative, that is, the maximum or minimum value. Therefore, it is often necessary to transform between the objective function and the fitness function. Toolbox support: Offsetting migration method (Goldberg), ranking (nonlinear evaluation), the ratio method and linear evaluation algorithm of shells.

3.3 Selection Function

Selection, also known as replication, is the process of selecting individuals with strong vitality in a group to generate new groups. The main purpose of selection operation is to avoid the loss of genetic information and to improve global convergence and computational efficiency. The selection function directly influences the calculation results of genetic algorithm. Toolkit support: RWS (roulette selection), SUS (random traversal sampling selection), etc.

3.4 Cross Function

Crossover, also known as recombination, is an important feature that distinguishes genetic algorithm from other evolutionary algorithms and plays a key role in genetic algorithm. Crossing, that is, choosing two individuals from the group with high probability, exchanging one or some bit information of two individuals, thus generating two new individuals with paternal characteristics. Toolkit support: xovsp (single point crossing), xovdp (two points crossing), xovsh (shuffle crossing), xovmp (multi-point crossing), etc.

3.5 Variation Function

Variation is the process of changing some or some bit value on the individual coding string with a small probability, such as "0" of binary coding becoming "1", "1" becoming "0", and then generating new individuals. Mutation operation is beneficial to maintain the diversity of the population and prevent premature convergence and local optimum. Toolkit support: mut (binary, integer variation), mutate (real value variation), etc.

4 Simulation Test

A typical nonlinear multimodal function is used to verify the efficiency of genetic algorithm in MATLAB environment. Local optimization characteristics. The Shubert function is:

$$\mathrm{Z} = \mathrm{F}(\mathrm{x},\mathrm{y}) = \sum_{i=1}^{5} i\cos[(i+1)\bullet x+i]\bullet\sum_{i=1}^{5} i\cos[(i+1)\bullet y+i] \quad \mathrm{x},\mathrm{y}\in[-10,10]$$

Find the maximum value of this function. The three-dimensional geometric characteristics of Shubert function are shown in Fig. 1. It can be seen from Fig. 1 that this function is a nonlinear, multi-peak function with numerous local maximum points, but this function only has one global maximum point. The following is the implementation code of genetic algorithm in MATLAB environment:

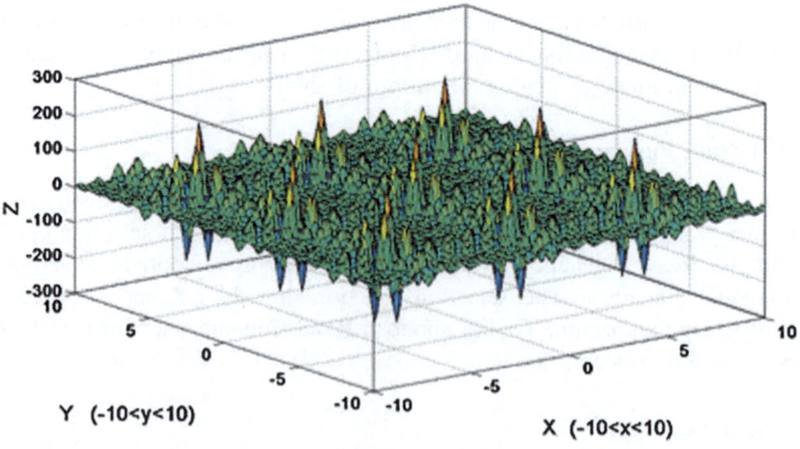

Fig. 1. Three-dimensional geometric characteristics of Shubert function

Population size N = 40, number of variables NVAR = 2, length of coding string of individual PRECI = 25, maximum genetic algebra MAXGEN = 50, generation gap GGAP = 0.9, crossover probability Px = 0.7, mutation probability PM = 0.7/(2 x PRECI) = 0.014.

The program code required to solve the target function is as follows:

```
Function Z = Shubert(x,y)
Z = zeros(2,5)
while(i<6)
Z1 • cos((i + 1) • x + i);
Z2 = i• cos((i + 1) • y + i);
Z(1;i) = Z1;     Z(2;i) = Z2;
i = i + 1;
end
Z1 = sum(1,:); Z2 = sum(2,:);
Z = Z1 • Z2;
```

Save it as a shubert.m file, which is used as a module for calling the main program.

The main program code is as follows:

```
NIND = 40;
MAXGEN = 100;
NVAR = 2;
PRECI = 25;
GGAP = 0.9;
FieldD = [rep([PRECI],[1,NVAR]);rep([-10;10],[1,NVAR]);rep([1;0;1;1],[1,NVAR])];
Chrom = crtbp(NIND,NVAR*PRECI);
gen = 0;
trace = zeros(MAXGEN,2);
x = bs2rv(Chrom,FieldD);
ObjV = Shubert(x(:,1),x(:,2));
while gen<MAXGEN
  FitnV = ranking(-ObjV);
  SelCh = select('sus',Chrom,FitnV,GGAP);
  SelCh = recombin('xovsp',SelCh,0.7);
  SelCh = mut(SelCh);
  x = bs2rv(SelCh,FieldD);
  ObjVSel = Shubert(x(:,1),x(:,2));
[Chrom ObjV] = reins(Chrom,SelCh,1,1,ObjV,ObjVSel);
  gen = gen+1;
  trace(gen,1) = max(ObjV);
  trace(gen,2) = sum(ObjV)/length(ObjV);
end
plot(trace(:,1),'r');
hold on;
plot(trace(:,2),'b');
grid on;
```

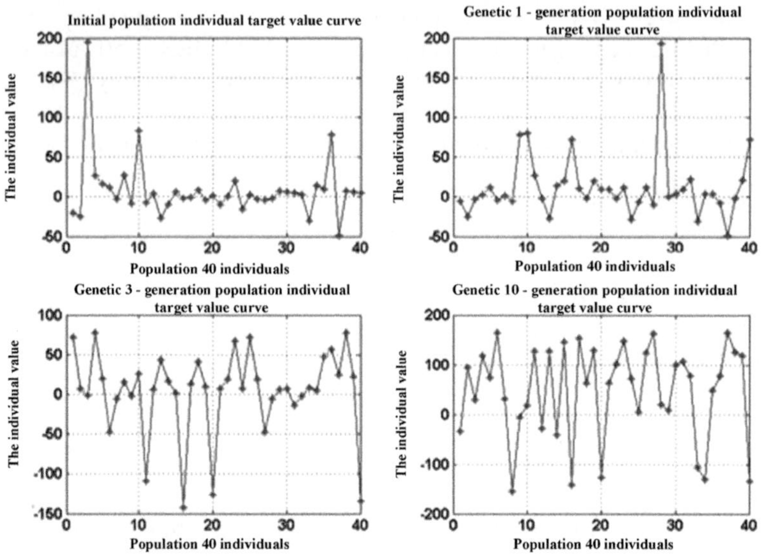

Fig. 2. Distribution of population target values

Figure 2 for different iterations of the population distribution of its individual values, Fig. 3 for the distribution of genetic population after 100 generations a target value, Fig. 4 for the optimization of genetic algorithm performance figure, from Figs. 2, 3 can clearly see the picture, along with the increase of iteration times, the in the target population is gradually towards the optimal evolution, after iterative 100 times, the target population has been largely for the optimal solution. Figure 4 shows the variation curve of population mean reconciliation during evolution. Figure 4 fully illustrates the efficient optimization performance of genetic algorithm.

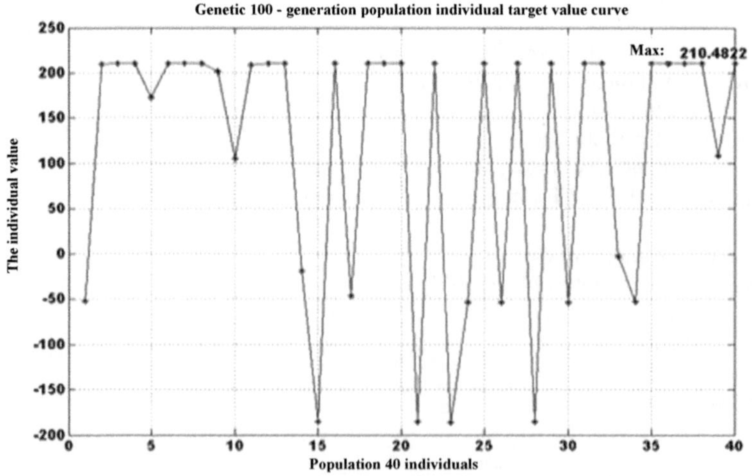

Fig. 3. Population target value distribution after 100 iterations

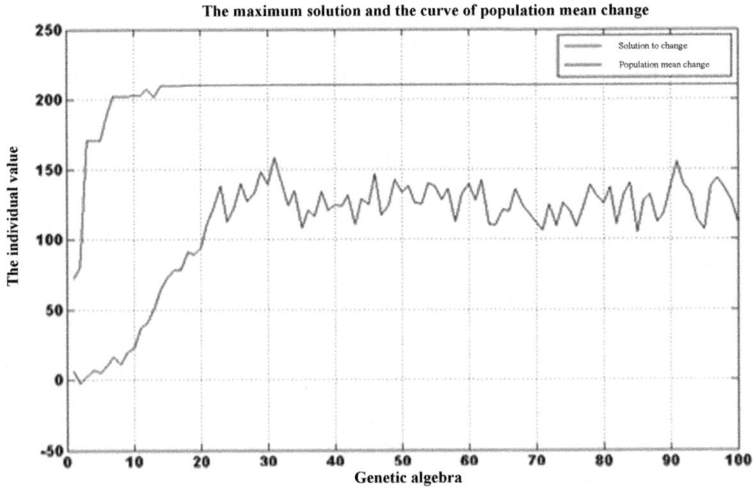

Fig. 4. Optimization performance of genetic algorithm

5 Conclusion

This paper verifies the high efficiency of genetic algorithm in the optimization problem through a typical example, and also illustrates that genetic algorithm is a global random search technology with directional guidance. With the gradual maturity of genetic algorithm, it is believed that genetic algorithm will have more application fields and wider development space.

References

1. Srinivas M, Patnaik L (2004) Adaptive probabilities of crossover and mutation in genetic algorithm. IEEE Trans Syst Man Cybern 24(4):656–666
2. Grefenstette JJ (2016) Optimization of control parameters for genetic algorithm. IEEE Trans Syst Man Cybern 16(1):122–128
3. Bauer RJ (1994) Genetic algorithms and investment strategies. Wiley, New York
4. Whitley LD, Vose MD (eds) (2005) Foundations of genetic algorithms, vol 3. Morgan Kaufmann, San Mateo
5. Mitchell M (1996) An introduction to genetic algorithms. The MIT Press, Cambridge
6. Schraudolph NN, Belew RK (2012) Dynamic parameter encoding for genetic algorithm. Mach. Learn. 9(1):9–21
7. De Jong KA (2001) Learning with genetic algorithm: an overview. Mach. Learn. 3:121–138
8. Lavine BK (2000) Pattern recognition analysis via genetic algorithm & multivariate statistical methods. CRC Press, Boca Raton
9. Ford LR, Fulkerson DR (2009) Maximal flow through a network. In: Classic papers in combinatorics. Birkhäuser, Boston, pp 243–248

10. Dinic EA (2007) An algorithm for the solution of the problem of maximal flow in a network with power estimation. Dokl Akad Nauk SSSR 754–757
11. Edmonds J, Karp RM (2001) Theoretical improvements in algorithmic efficiency for network flow problems. J Assoc Comput 19(2):248–264
12. Ahuja RK, Orlin JB (2001) Distance-directed augmenting path algorithms for maximum flow and parametric maximum flow problems. Naval Res Logistics 38(3):413–430

Research on the Integration and Innovation of Cloud Computing Technology and Enterprise Management by Internet Companies

Dian Jia(✉)

School of Business Administration, Qinghai Nationalities University, Xining 810007, Qinghai, People's Republic of China
jiatianabc@126.com

Abstract. With the rapid development of science and technology, the use and dependence of computers in all walks of life is increasing. Human beings have entered the era of "Internet +". In order to better meet the challenges brought by the current social development, enterprise management must recognize the importance of cloud data extraction technology in management, so as to continuously innovate the management model. This paper expounds the concept of cloud data extraction technology, the application and innovation of cloud data extraction technology by human resources management, the challenges faced by human resources management of enterprises in the era of cloud data extraction technology and the strategies of human resources management reform.

Keywords: Internet enterprise · Human resource management · Cloud data extraction technology · Innovation

1 Brief Introduction

With the deepening and development of knowledge economy, enterprises have increased the competition for talent resources, especially knowledge-based talents, which are the driving force of enterprise development. If enterprises want to develop continuously, they need to find and retain talents and stimulate their talents. At the same time, they need to establish an incentive system that suits their own enterprises and meets the needs of employees, so as to provide a good development platform for employees. As we all know, Internet enterprise is an enterprise with high knowledge literacy and knowledge reserve. It is an enterprise with fast replacement of employees. It is also a relatively centralized place for post-90s knowledge workers. The development of Internet enterprises depends on the development of knowledge-based talents [1]. Because of their growing environment, education and unique personality, post-90s knowledge workers are different from Post-70s and post-80s knowledge workers. Therefore, the traditional incentive methods can not play a very good incentive effect on post-90s knowledge workers. This paper expounds the concept of cloud data extraction technology, the application and innovation of cloud data extraction technology by human resources management, the challenges faced by human resources

Z. Xu et al. (Eds.): CSIA 2019, AISC 928, pp. 986–992, 2020.
https://doi.org/10.1007/978-3-030-15235-2_131

management of enterprises in the era of cloud data extraction technology and the strategies of human resources management reform [2, 3].

1, the characteristics of human resource management of Internet companies in cloud data extraction technology extraction technology.

In the 21st century, the post-90s employees as a new force enter the workplace, their unique personality and behavior once brought a lot of trouble to the development of enterprises. The post-90s knowledge-based employees once entered the enterprise from the campus, bringing the original campus life and the way of getting along with them into the work life, once they felt confused and confused about the work life. In view of the situation of post-90s knowledge workers, managers were at a loss for a time and did not know how to guide them. In people's impression, the post-90s generation is a more spoiled generation, with a unique personality, beliefs and values missing generation. Post-90s knowledge workers in enterprises show characteristics of disobedience to management, strong personality and great emotional fluctuation, which make many managers very dissatisfied with them [4, 5]. They only see that employees show bad aspects, and seldom examine whether their management style is suitable for post-90s knowledge workers. In the new era, how to make these post-90s employees with their unique personality adapt to the life of the workplace is a difficult problem that Internet business managers need to solve. Figure 1 is the distribution characteristics of human resources in Internet enterprises under the background of cloud data extraction technology.

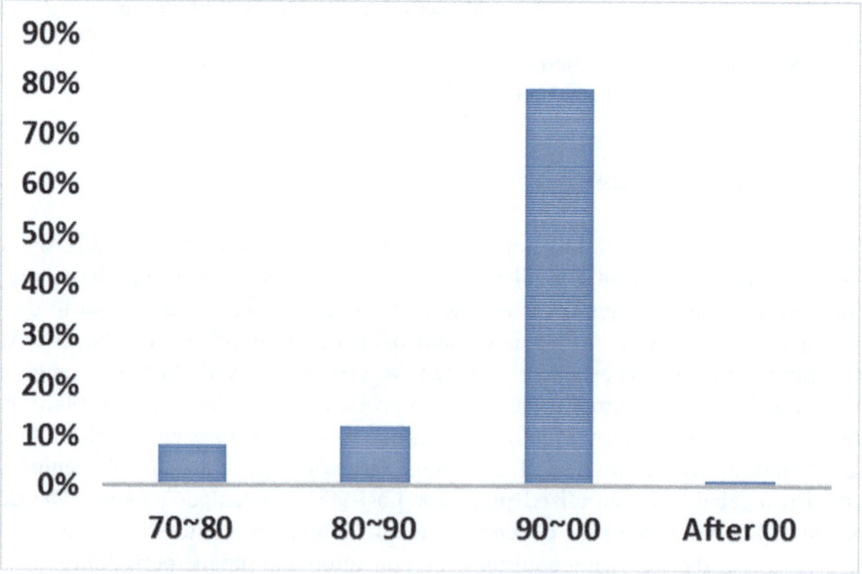

Fig. 1. Characteristics of talent distribution in Internet enterprises

The characteristics of human resource management are as follows.

1.1 The Structure of Human Resources Is Diverse

Talents are developing towards high level and specialization. Whether an enterprise can achieve long-term and stable development and maximize economic benefits largely depends on whether it has a large number of high-level professionals. High-level professionals have the characteristics of high education level, large knowledge reserve and diversified value orientation, but they often show their own characteristics in their work. New changes have taken place in workplace rules. The new generation of employees, represented by the post-80s and post-90s, are influenced by the new material and social environment, and their values and codes of conduct are more novel and diverse. Therefore, there are distinct differences between the "post-80s" and "post-90s" employees and the "older generation" in their ideas and behaviors. With the increasing number of such employees, the traditional human resources rules have changed.

1.2 The Scale and Flow of Human Resources Is Enhanced

In the past, the workers represented by peasant workers mainly migrated from underdeveloped areas to developed areas, while the stable and secure public and state-owned employees rarely migrated. However, with the continuous development and change of the times, the flow of talents is increasingly obvious and mobility is getting higher and higher. The social security welfare system has been gradually improved [6]. Under the background of the increasing level of social and economic development in China, the deepening reform of the market economic system has a certain impact on the change of government functions. The government pays more and more attention to social security and welfare [7]. By formulating and promulgating various laws, regulations and policies, it starts with salaries, benefits and other aspects. Gradually weakening the absolute advantages of the system, people's enthusiasm for the system gradually declined, but the free market is more popular at present.

1.3 The Potential of Human Resources Is the Core Capital

Innovation driven demand for experience is reduced. In the past growth mode, production factors occupy an incomparable important position. Affected by this, enterprises also require internal human resources to have good physical strength, solid and rich work experience and knowledge and skills [8]. Therefore, in the recruitment process, they tend to employ highly educated personnel with many skills certificates and professional counterparts, and for a long time regard them as valuable talents of enterprises. In the modern environment of gradual economic transformation, the above talent standards are no longer applicable, and innovation ability has become a key factor to measure the future development potential of talent.

2 Internet Enterprise Human Resources Management Mode Transformation Necessity Analysis

2.1 Accelerate the Transformation of Management Thinking

Internet information technology is not only a new way of information processing, but also a kind of modern ideological and cognitive concept. Under the background of Internet information technology, the communication mode between various departments and functional posts has undergone tremendous changes. The information processing mode of cloud data extraction technology connection has penetrated into the workflow of enterprise organization production, promotion and sales, R&D statistics [9, 10]. The Internet is not only a technology, but also a kind of thought and values. It is an innovation of business philosophy. The background of the Internet era helps enterprise employees maximize the transformation of operation mode from labor-oriented to intelligent. The reserve and application of innovative technicians has gradually become one of the components of enterprise human capital framework. As far as the current situation is concerned, part of the reason for the improvement of the production value of enterprises is that the value of human capital exceeds the actual reserves of the material capital and monetary capital of enterprises, and has become one of the main elements of the business activities of enterprises.

2.2 Accelerate the Transformation of Management Functions

Internet thinking is the thinking from “power center” to “service center”. Under the Internet thinking, the provision of any product or service needs to be based on the needs of users [11]. Human resources management should also be based on this concept. Following the principles of “user first” and “employee first”, we should change our management thinking, regard employees as market consumers, take consumer needs as the key to transformation, and build a service platform for information resource sharing. While providing adequate human resources support for the transformation, we should realize the humanized management of human resources reserve and professional talent reserve.

2.3 Accelerate the Transformation of Management Mode

Improvement and optimization of human resources management process: the large-scale development of the Internet era, so that the development concept of cross-regional management and operation of enterprises can be realized. Within the enterprise, the new organizational framework model built on the cross-regional sales management model has gradually entered the normal development process. The new cross-functional and cross-departmental management team has more prominent construction advantages in terms of both the setting of work content and the division of management authority. The optimization and integration among all functional teams can fully reflect the overall effectiveness of management [12, 13]. The original management mode of enterprises will lose its original application function and gradually enter a flat development state. On this basis, the traditional management mode is influenced by the differences of local cultural content. The development of talent management and reserve work has inherent drawbacks such as unclear rights and responsibilities and ambiguous performance indicators. Therefore, human resource managers should completely innovate the traditional management mode and optimize the existing management process. In the aspect of organization design and work design of human resources management, we should improve the frequency of information communication among staff in various departments. Promote the establishment of human resources management work, towards the direction of organization, convenience, transparency and simplification, rapid development, and ultimately achieve the strengthening of the core competitiveness of enterprises.

3 To Build an Incentive Mechanism for Enterprise Management Under the Cloud Data Extraction Technology

In the salary incentive model of post-90s knowledge workers in Internet enterprises, various strategies play a common role and constitute a relatively complete incentive model. Including salary and bonus incentive, salary and welfare incentive, career development incentive and work environment incentive, these four incentive strategies provide a reference for the motivation of post-90s knowledge workers in Internet enterprises from different angles, and ensure the effectiveness of the incentive strategies for post-90s knowledge workers.

3.1 Further Strengthen the Reform of Enterprise Staff Training

With the acceleration of information dissemination in the Internet era, enterprises put forward higher requirements for the working ability and professional quality of employees in the process of operation and development. In other words, enterprises' attention to the development of Internet technology will promote the reform of employee training, which can not only enhance the market value of employees, but also provide impetus for the sustainable development of enterprises. When reforming the training of employees, on the one hand, enterprises need to establish the relevant mechanism of training archives management, and create independent training archives with the help of Internet technology [13, 14]. On the other hand, enterprises should divide employees according to the results of performance appraisal and the development potential of different employees, and formulate different training programs, optimize the training process, and train employees scientifically and effectively.

3.2 Cloud Data Extraction Technology in the Application of Salary Management

The motivation of post-90s knowledge workers is the core of the management of Internet enterprises, and also runs through many links of the activities of Internet enterprises. Therefore, Internet enterprises should ensure the assistance and cooperation of other management mechanisms before running the motivation mechanism of post-90s knowledge workers. For example, the financial mechanism of Internet enterprises is the guarantee of incentive mechanism [15]. The operation of the incentive mechanism for post-90s knowledge-based employees needs the support of financial work. The financial mechanism not only provides capital support for the incentive mechanism for post-90s knowledge-based employees, but also ensures the effective implementation of incentive strategies [16, 17]. At the same time, it also forecasts and analyses the investment returns, ensure that investment is reasonable and effective. We should also improve the corresponding restraint mechanism, and at the same time have the cooperation of negative incentives while positive incentives [18, 19]. The setting of restraint mechanism is a powerful tool to ensure the effective and healthy role of the salary incentive mechanism for post-90s knowledge workers.

We should find and correct the wrong behavior in the process of implementing the incentive mechanism in time, and try our best to reduce the adverse effects of incorrect practices by following up and improving.

3.3 Cloud Data Extraction Technology Helps Career Design

Human resource managers can acquire data and information about employees' knowledge and skills, their behavior patterns, learning progress and learning effects by analyzing the relevant data of employees' training archives, so that the training is guided by employees' personal development. In addition, according to project training, daily evaluation and performance appraisal, record and analyze the employee's post competency, so as to formulate a personal career development plan for each employee.

4 Summary

In summary, with the advent of cloud data extraction technology era, human resources management is also facing new opportunities and challenges. Based on the application research of human resource management in cloud data extraction technology innovation, this paper analyses the obstacles of cloud data extraction technology in human resource management, and further explores the effective measures to realize the transformation of enterprise human resource management. At the same time, how to ensure the security of cloud data extraction technology application is worth the attention and solution of enterprise managers. Modern enterprises must keep up with the development trend of cloud data extraction technology era, adjust the traditional management mode and concept in time, learn to use cloud data extraction technology to make more accurate decisions, deal with various business problems, in order to establish a sound human resources management system.

References

1. Celesti A, Maria F, Romano A et al (2017) An OAIS-based hospital information system on the cloud: analysis of a NoSQL column-oriented approach. IEEE J Biomed Health Inf 22:912–918
2. Panarello A, Fazio M, Celesti A et al (2014) Cloud federation to elastically increase MapReduce processing resources. In: Euro-Par 2014: parallel processing workshops, pp 97–108

3. Celesti A, Fazio M, Giacobbe M et al (2016) Characterizing cloud federation in IoT. In: International conference on advanced information networking and applications workshops. IEEE, pp 93–98
4. Fazio M, Celesti A, Puliafito A et al (2015) Big data storage in the cloud for smart environment monitoring. Procedia Comput Sci 52:500–506
5. Mulfari D, Fazio M, Celesti A et al (2015) Design of an IoT cloud system for container virtualization on smart objects. In: European conference on service-oriented and cloud computing. Springer, pp 33–47
6. Carnevale L, Celesti A, Fazio M et al (2017) How to enable clinical workflows to integrate big healthcare data. In: Computers and communications. IEEE, pp 857–862
7. Pescosolido L, Berta R, Scalise L et al (2016) An IoT-inspired cloud-based web service architecture for e-Health applications. In: Smart cities conference. IEEE
8. Puliafito A (2014) SensorCloud: an integrated system for advanced multi-risk management. In: Network cloud computing and applications. IEEE, pp 1–8
9. Fazio M, Celesti A, Marquez FG et al (2016) Exploiting the FIWARE cloud platform to develop a remote patient monitoring system. In: Computers and communication. IEEE, pp 264–270
10. Celesti A, Fazio M, Romano A et al (2016) A hospital cloud-based archival information system for the efficient management of HL7 big data. In: International convention on information and communication technology, electronics and microelectronics. IEEE, pp 406–411
11. Galletta A, Ardo O, Celesti A et al (2017) C4E: cloud brokering platform for federated services aimed at European public administrations
12. Buzachis A, Galletta A, Celesti A et al (2018) An innovative MapReduce-based approach of Dijkstra's algorithm for SDN routing in hybrid cloud, edge and IoT scenarios. In: European conference on service-oriented and cloud computing. Springer, Cham, pp 185–198
13. Celesti F, Celesti A, Carnevale L et al (2017) Big data analytics in genomics: the point on deep learning solutions. In: Computers and communications. IEEE, pp 306–309
14. Fazio M, Celesti A, Puliafito A et al (2014) An integrated system for advanced multi-risk management based on cloud for IoT. In: Advances onto the internet of things, pp 253–269
15. Celesti A, Carnevale L, Galletta A et al (2017) A watchdog service making container-based micro-services reliable in IoT clouds. In: IEEE, international conference on future internet of things and cloud. IEEE, pp 372–378
16. Carnevale L, Celesti A, Galletta A et al (2018) From the cloud to edge and IoT: a smart orchestration architecture for enabling osmotic computing. In: International conference on advanced information networking and applications workshops. IEEE Computer Society, pp 419–424
17. Galletta A, Carnevale L, Celesti A et al (2017) BOSS: a multitenancy Ad-Hoc service orchestrator for federated openstack clouds. In: IEEE, international conference on future internet of things and cloud. IEEE, pp 351–357
18. Celesti A, Galletta A, Carnevale L et al (2017) An IoT cloud system for traffic monitoring and vehicular accidents prevention based on mobile sensor data processing. IEEE Sens. J. 18 (12):4795–4802
19. Galletta A, Carnevale L, Celesti A et al (2018) A cloud-based system for improving retention marketing loyalty programs in Industry 4.0: a study on big data storage implications. IEEE Access 6:5485–5492

Strategic Thinking on the Transformation and Development of Printing Industry Under the Background of Internet+

Guohua Song(✉) and Yongxin Liu

Media Academy, Jilin Engineering Normal University, Changchun, Jilin, China
1244534499@qq.com

Abstract. The printing and packaging industry is an important part of China's manufacturing industry. According to the "Made in China 2025" plan issued by the State Council, adhere to the basic principles of "innovation driven, quality first, green development, structural optimization, talent-based". In the wave of "industry 4.0", China's printing and packaging industry is facing an urgent need for transformation and upgrading. This paper analyses the advantages and problems of the printing industry as a basic and strategic part of the national economy, and tries to find the orientation of the printing industry as a characteristic industry according to the development trend of the printing industry. How to accurately grasp the direction of development in the new round of technological revolution, realize the transformation of development mode and structural adjustment, enhance the core competitiveness of the industry, and do a good job in characteristic industries?

Keywords: Packaging printing · Characteristic industry · Development strategy · Industrial transformation

1 Brief Introduction

Since 2008, affected by the international economic environment, the industrial environment at home and abroad has become increasingly severe, especially the rise of digital media, which makes China's printing and packaging industry face unprecedented difficulties and challenges [1, 2]. Moreover, due to the backwardness of traditional technology, low management efficiency and many other factors, sales revenue and profits of some enterprises in the industry show a more obvious decline [3–5]. The State Council issued the "Made in China 2025" plan, which put forward the basic principles of "innovation driven, quality first, green development, structural optimization and talent-oriented" [6–9]. Adhere to the basic principles of "market-oriented, government-led, current-oriented, long-term, overall promotion, key breakthroughs, independent development and open cooperation", and achieve the strategic goal of a manufacturing power through "three-step" approach. Printing industry, as an important part of traditional manufacturing industry, will also face the digital and intelligent industrial transformation in the tide of "Industry 4.0" [10–15].

Z. Xu et al. (Eds.): CSIA 2019, AISC 928, pp. 993–999, 2020.
https://doi.org/10.1007/978-3-030-15235-2_132

This paper takes printing enterprises as the research object. Combining with the existing conditions and resources inside and outside, how can enterprises make rational use of superior resources through strategic selection, seize opportunities at the critical moment of industrial transformation, and promote the transformation and development of traditional printing and packaging industry in Anhui and Jiangsu regions?

2 The Advantages of Packaging and Printing Industry

2.1 The Industrial Chain Is Complete

There are relatively perfect industrial systems of packaging, pre-press, printing, post-press, printing consumables equipment supply and reserve personnel transportation. Printing machinery, equipment manufacturers and agents, the world's major brands of printing equipment suppliers are equipped with multi-level agents [16–18]. On the supply of packaging and printing materials: there are various manufacturers and agents of packaging and printing materials, including paper, ink, gravure plate, aluminium plate, embossing plate, etc. They have printing and packaging of pre-press, printing, post-press and covering paper, plastic printing and packaging, metal printing and packaging, and printing and packaging of various anti-counterfeiting special materials. In packaging and printing education, many universities have set up printing technology, packaging technology and design specialties.

2.2 Advanced Equipment, Advanced Technology and Excellent Product Quality

The application level of packaging printing technology and equipment is in the leading position. It has CTP computer direct plate making system, commercial rotary press, single offset press with eight or more colors, single sheet offset press with four or more colors, gravure press, digital press and other advanced technical equipment, imported hardbound book automatic binding linkage production line, axle-less high-speed color newspaper printing machine production line, etc. For example, Dongguan's packaging and printing technology keeps pace with the global development, which can grasp the world's most advanced packaging and printing technology and technology at the first time, and quickly and effectively applied. Computer direct plate making, digital workflow, digital proofing, color management, printing standard certification, the application of these new technologies has promoted the vigorous development of packaging and printing industry.

2.3 Increase Communication with Customers

Printing and packaging enterprises can provide value-added services to customers through the process of obtaining products and services from customers, existing products and services themselves, products and services beyond the conventional ones, and customized products and services. From the perspective of business strategy selection, Kangqilai put forward seven transformation schemes: cross-industry transformation, production scale transformation, cooperative joint venture transformation, production technology transformation, production business transformation, production mode transformation, and production process transformation.

3 Problems Existing in Printing and Packaging Enterprises

In the course of enterprise operation, these enterprises have the following common problems:

3.1 The Business Model Is Backward

Small and medium-sized printing and packaging enterprises in the urban areas of Anhui River are generally under 50 employees. They are dominated by the traditional production-based (spindle) business model, that is, enterprises as suppliers in the middle and lower reaches of the industrial chain, and process products according to customers' orders. In the market, label other enterprises for sale. Therefore, these printing enterprises are only a part of the food industry, clothing industry or other consumer goods industry, and are not recognized by consumers in the market. Moreover, printing enterprises do not involve too much in the design and production of products. In the face of the industrial transformation under the new economic form, the operation mode of OEM exposes the problem of single profit model, which is not conducive to further structural optimization and strategic choice of enterprises.

3.2 There Is a Lack of Management Consciousness of Business Operators

Because these small and medium-sized printing enterprises are generally small in scale, with a small number of employees, and their comprehensive quality is basically not high, and they follow the traditional mode of OEM under the inertial thinking. When managers manage enterprises and communicate with customers, they still have a strong "small workshop" business philosophy and management consciousness. The concrete manifestations are: family management concept, extensive production management, disordered staff management, lack of overall planning of enterprise strategy, weak awareness of brand building, weak external public relations ability, etc. These drawbacks will seriously affect the transformation and upgrading of enterprises with the expansion of enterprise scale and the diversification of enterprise management objects.

3.3 Enterprises Lack High Level Technical and Business Talents

Because the barriers to entry of printing industry are relatively low compared with other manufacturing industries, printing and packaging enterprises are from owners to operators. Including enterprise technicians and company sales salesmen, there are many defects in the industry, such as low average education level, low technical level, weak management and communication ability, business ability is not prominent, and so on [19, 20]. Under the double challenges of the concept of green printing and the Internet+ era, such enterprises are an important part of the overall printing industry. If the owners, operators and technical operators are unable to see the changes of the times, understand the new needs of the consumer market, improve the level of business technology, fundamentally enhance the competitiveness of enterprises, seize the opportunity to integrate resources and optimize the structure, the so-called industrial transformation and upgrading will face enormous difficulties and obstacles.

3.4 Challenges of Emerging Media

From a macro point of view, in the 21st century, with the rapid rise of the Internet, electronic industry and new media based on digital technology, there is a fierce competition with traditional media. Consumers' reading habits have changed rapidly, and the advertising environment of traditional newspaper media has changed significantly. The rise of new media such as the Internet, mobile phones and e-books has broken the original mode of communication of traditional media, drastically reduced circulation and advertising costs, together with the sharp rise and fall of paper prices and the substantial increase of human costs, which has brought unprecedented hardship to the development of printing industry. The change of market and the progress of science and technology have impacted the living environment of packaging and printing industry. Traditional media can not compete with the emerging information industry. Traditional media has entered a historical recession.

4 Transformation and Upgrading of Printing Industry

4.1 Upgrading and Transferring Industries

Usually, the upgrading of printing industry can be divided into two stages. The first stage refers to the transformation and upgrading of printing industry as a labor-intensive industry in the process of transformation. The second stage is the printing industry, from labor-intensive industries to capital and technology intensive industries. The above two ways are two aspects for printing enterprises to upgrade and transfer their industries locally. In the process of development, the bottleneck facing the economy is the rising price of labor and land. Whether this problem can be solved completely depends on whether the printing industry can upgrade from the labor-intensive industry. At present, compared with other cities, the main characteristics and advantages of the printing industry are that it has been able to form a huge labor-intensive industrial cluster. Not only that but also for the printing industry, a relatively complete industrial chain has been formed, which makes the transformation path of the printing industry easier. Through long-term research and practice, the author believes that: It can realize partial transfer of printing industry, and achieve organic cooperation with other neighboring areas, and establish corresponding industrial transfer parks, so as to effectively avoid risks.

4.2 Change the Past Sales Channels

Previously, printing enterprises mostly realized outward sales, which has some problems. Under the economic crisis, printing enterprises have brought tremendous pressure. Therefore, we must realize the export of printing enterprises to domestic sales. Of course, this measure is a difficult thing for the printing enterprises at this stage. For a long time, the printing enterprises in our country have taken the foreign market as the main selling market. Transferring the market to the domestic market that the printing enterprises are not familiar with will result in the experience accumulated by the former printing enterprises and the expansion of sales channels not playing their due role, and even some printing enterprises have to start from scratch. The author believes that if printing enterprises want to open up the domestic market and survive in the fierce competition in the domestic market, they must create brand effect and realize brand competition. The author believes that the main reason why printing enterprises are reluctant to change from traditional OEM to sell their products is that they lack brand awareness and are difficult to establish a brand that meets their actual situation, which makes printing enterprises less competitive when competing with other industries.

4.3 Change the Past Packaging and Printing Path

First, the design aspects before printing. In the long-term development of traditional printing enterprises, the design of book shells, covers and books has gradually developed into a graphic design idea. However, in the process of transformation of printing industry, the author thinks that designers should reconsider the transformation of design style carriers. For example, when designing the cover of books and periodicals, they should pay attention to a kind of information conveyed by the picture of books and periodicals for readers, so as to realize all-round elaborate planning from book shells to writing and then to books. Printing design must be handled and constructed by specialists. The author believes that increasing the investment in pre-press design can bring huge returns to printing enterprises, and it can improve the core competitiveness of printing enterprises. Secondly, we must realize the color unification in packaging printing. The colours in trademark printing and packaging printing are not independent of each other. They should be organically combined to achieve the perfect unification of colours. For example, when quadrangle registration is used, many printing companies will encounter the problem that the pressure between the four corners and the middle of the trademark is different, resulting in the uneven ink color of the head and tail of the trademark. In this case, the printed products we designed are not up to the requirements. If it is not improved and put into the market, then the products we design will not be recognized by the vast number of consumers, and its competitiveness will naturally be difficult to improve. The solution of this approach can be achieved by using color management system. According to the different printing of books and periodicals and paper packaging, density design can be realized, so as to design products with brighter trademarks and give consumers visual impact. Thirdly, we should use advanced equipment after printing.

5 Develop Enterprise Competition Strategy Based on Digital Media

The digital media represented by the Internet, as the media channel with the widest radiation area and the fastest spreading speed, should be closely linked with the corporate strategy of printing enterprises. At present, small and medium-sized printing and packaging companies in Wanjiang City Belt only publish a small amount of enterprise information on some third-party platforms, some of which even lack contact information, which is extremely disadvantageous to tap potential customers in the market. At the same time, this kind of enterprise basically does not establish the company website, but publishes the enterprise information through the third party platform, exposes the company's backward management concept, which is not conducive to the enterprise market competition. Therefore, it is suggested that printing enterprises should innovate the market competition concept, and make efforts to broaden the business market through new media channels and communication with potential customers.

Summary

In a word, with the continuous development of market economy, if Dongguan printing industry wants to achieve sustainable development, it must take effective measures to realize industrial transformation. Only in this way can it survive in the fierce market competition, further improve the economic benefits of printing enterprises and serve the masses of the people. Of course, we should also realize that the transformation of Dongguan printing industry is not a one-off process. It is a long-term and systematic project, which requires our joint efforts to achieve.

References

1. Sun W, Kuang H, Yang Z (2015) 3D printing technology industry in hangzhou: its present situation and the development path. Modern City
2. Hu W (2014) On cultivation of printing high- quality talents under the background of industrial transformation and upgrading. J Shaoxing Univ
3. Tang L (2016) Development Strategy of anhui printing industry on the background of transformation and upgrading—based on swot analysis model. J Beijing Inst Graph Commun
4. Poblador KFK (2015) The transformation of property rights in the philippine timber and gold mining industries during the american colonial period
5. Zhang S, Wang F (2014) On the boost of cultural creative industries to the transformation of taiwan manufacturing industry. J Ocean Univ China
6. Zhu YF (2016) The research on the transformation and upgrading of traditional industries in Hebei Province. Value Eng
7. Ma Y (2016) Innovation and improve the system to guide the transformation and upgrading of cultural industries. J Comput Theor Nanosci 13:9303–9308
8. Huo P, Wei X (2017) Reflections on the transformation and upgrading of industries in China under the new industrial revolution. Acad J Zhongzhou

9. Wang JM (2017) A study on the system of promoting the transformation of resource based industries in western minority areas: from the perspective of incentives and constraints. Guizhou Ethn Stud
10. Yang YL (2015) Large data boost the transformation and upgrading of traditional industries. Heilongjiang Sci
11. Jia Y, Wang TS, Ling XU, et al (2016) Research on the mechanism of action of productive service industry in the transformation and upgrading of manufacturing industry. Technol Innov Manage
12. Weisen LI (2017) The geographic conditions monitoring promoting the transformation and upgrading of surveying, mapping and geoinformation industry. Geomat World
13. Cheng Q, Di WU (2015) Research on science and technology innovation drive the transformation and updating experience of traditional industries. Sci Manage Res
14. Chen XH (2015) Strategies on liuzhou to accelerate the transformation and upgrading of traditional industries and the advanced manufacturing industry development during the 13th five-year plan. J Liuzhou Vocat Techn Coll
15. Wen QQ (2017) Research on the transformation of minority nationality characteristic industries from the perspective of green development. Guizhou Ethn Stud
16. Guan N (2015) Creative design: to guide the transformation and upgrade of economic development: profound integration of industries in the new collective era. Hundred Schools Arts
17. Yang XF, Li XN (2018) The transformation and upgrading of coastal industries and innovative development of industries in nantong. J Yancheng Teach Univ
18. Zhu YY (2017) Study on the transformation of minority cultural industries to creative industries. Guizhou Ethn Stud
19. Song W (2016) "Internet+" to promote the transformation and upgrading of the industries in the central region. Acad J Zhongzhou
20. Xiong Z (2018) Can cultural and creative industries help to promote the transformation of economic development mode? Taking hunan province as an example. J Jishou Univ

Control Strategy of Unmanned Aerial Vehicle Based on Extended State Observer

Dan Wu(✉)

Department of Electronic Engineering, Sichuan Aerospace Vocational College, Chengdu, China
wjke654@163.com

Abstract. Due to the influence of engine vibration, the output noise of the sensor of the aircraft is large. However, in order to achieve the fast estimation of the disturbance, the observer gain is relatively large, but this will greatly increase the noise. This is a contradiction. In this paper, a linear state observer is used, because its stability and tracking performance have been well demonstrated and analyzed, and the parameter adjustment and circuit implementation are very simple. The filter equation is added to the ESO and the bandwidth is changed to realize the fast estimation of the internal and external interference, and the effect of the noise is greatly reduced. Besides, in the aspect of changing the bandwidth of the observer, this paper uses the desired trajectory and the state observer to output the error of the two to determine the size of the bandwidth, and the bandwidth is expressed as the hyperbolic tangent function of the error. The simulation analysis shows that the ability to track signal can be enhanced by improving the order of ESO.

Keywords: Unmanned aerial vehicle · Extended state observer · Noise · Dilatation state

1 Introduction

Generally speaking, UAV speed signals are used when designing control law [1, 2]. The speed signal can be obtained by differential location of GPS measurement, but the noise is large and the GPS signal frequency is low [3, 4]. It can also be obtained by the acceleration integral measured by the inertial measurement element. However, the noise and the zero drift in the acceleration signal will make a great drift in the error of the velocity measurement [5]. Usually, the measured values of GPS and IMU are multiplied by the weights less than 1 and then the final velocity measurement value is added, the choice of the weight value is to be used [6, 7]. A compromise between the measurement error and the noise suppression. The position measurement of GPS has a few meters of error, and the use of the differential global positioning system can greatly improve the measurement accuracy, but the signal in the room is not good. In this case, the position measurement method based on vision can be used in this case. Therefore, some literatures estimate the velocity value by designing observers and assume feedback control under the assumption that the position can be measured and the speed is unknown. In literature [8], it is difficult to realize the assumption that IMU can measure

Z. Xu et al. (Eds.): CSIA 2019, AISC 928, pp. 1000–1006, 2020.
https://doi.org/10.1007/978-3-030-15235-2_133

acceleration, angular velocity value and satisfy the PE condition by adding an adaptive observer to the measurement speed. Neural network on-line observer is used to estimate velocity, angular velocity and external wind disturbance. Without the speed measurement value, literature [9] skillfully introduces the intermediate variable to design the adaptive observer, and proves the global asymptotic stability of the system. The analysis and design process of these methods is rather complicated.

2 Extended State Observer

Give the system [10]

$$\begin{cases} x^{(n)} = f(x^{(n-1)}, x^{(n-2)}, \ldots, x, w, t) + bu \\ y = x \end{cases} \tag{1}$$

In formula (1), n is the order of the system, w is the external disturbance of the system, b is constant, and y is the output of the system. For this system, the idea of ESO is to represent the original system into the following system

$$\begin{cases} \dot{x}_1 = x_2 \\ \ldots \\ \dot{x}_{n-1} = x_n \\ \dot{x}_n = x_{n+1} + bu \\ \dot{x}_{n+1} = h(\cdot) \end{cases} \tag{2}$$

Use an extended state x_{n+1}, and let $x_{n+1} = f(x^{(n-1)}, x^{(n-2)}, \ldots, x, w, t)$, that is, an estimate of the external disturbance and the internal state of the state is an estimate of the internal and external disturbances, which realizes the decoupling of the internal and external disturbances regardless of its specific form. According to the above system, the observer structure is

$$\begin{cases} \dot{z}_1 = z_2 - \beta_1 fal(e_1, \alpha_1, \delta) \\ \ldots \\ \dot{z}_{n-1} = z_n - \beta_{n-1} fal(e_1, \alpha_{n-1}, \delta) \\ \dot{z}_n = z_{n+1} - \beta_n fal(e_1, \alpha_n, \delta) + bu \\ \dot{z}_{n+1} = -\beta_{n+1} fal(e_1, \alpha_{n+1}, \delta) \end{cases} \tag{3}$$

$[z_1, z_2, \ldots, z_{n+1}]^T \in R^{n+1}, e_1 = z_1 - x_1, \beta_i$ are state of observer, observation error and gain respectively. when the proper parameter values are selected, $z_i \rightarrow x_i(i \in \underline{n+1})$.

$$fal(e, \alpha, \delta) = \begin{cases} |e|^{\alpha}\mathrm{sgn}(e), |e| > \delta \\ e/\delta^{1-\alpha}, |e| < \delta \end{cases} 0 \le \alpha \le 1, \delta > 0 \tag{4}$$

This nonlinear observer lacks theoretical proof of stability, and the parameters of such observers are not well adjusted. When $\alpha = 0$ in function $fal(e, \alpha, \delta)$, formula (4) has the structure of the sliding mode observer. And when $\alpha = 1$, it becomes linear ESO.

$$\begin{cases} \dot{z}_1 = z_2 - \beta_1 e_1 \\ \cdots \\ \dot{z}_{n-1} = z_n - \beta_{n-1} e_1 \\ \dot{z}_n = z_{n+1} - \beta_n e_1 + bu \\ \dot{z}_{n+1} = -\beta_{n+1} e_1 \end{cases} \tag{5}$$

The parameter β_i in the observer can be designed to be

$$\beta_i = \frac{(n+1)!}{i!(n+1-i)!} \cdot w_o^i, i = 1, 2, \ldots, n+1 \tag{6}$$

The following formula can be obtained

$$s^{n+1} + \beta_1 s^n + \cdots + \beta_{n+1} = (s + w_o)^{n+1} \tag{7}$$

w_o is the bandwidth of the observer. This parameter is easier to design. If one parameter is selected, the observer must be stable.

The control law can be designed by decoupling the system with linear ESO. the gain of the controller is

$$u = [k_1(r_1 - z_1) + k_1(r_2 - z_2) + \cdots + k_n(r_n - z_n) - z_{n+1} + r_{n+1}]/b \tag{8}$$

Where r_i is the desired trajectory and the derivative values of the trajectory, which can be called the linear ADRC.

When the sensor is generally filtered, the noise is suppressed, but the real value is also lost in the amplitude and phase. Therefore, the filter equation is added to the state observer to form a new ESO structure. Assuming that the filtering equation is $\dot{y}_0 = f_f(y_0, y)$, y_0 is the filter output and y is the input signal of the filter, the new ESO structure is

$$\begin{cases} e_1 = z_0 - y_0 \\ \dot{z}_0 = f_f(z_0, z_1) - \beta_0 e_1 \\ \dot{z}_1 = z_2 - \beta_1 e_1 \\ \cdots \\ \dot{z}_{n-1} = z_n - \beta_{n-1} e_1 \\ \dot{z}_n = z_{n+1} - \beta_n e_1 + bu \\ \dot{z}_{n+1} = -\beta_{n+1} e_1 \end{cases} \tag{9}$$

The new ESO structure preserves the function of filtering and eliminates the effect of filters on real signals.

3 Simulation

The state observer is used to track two states. The filter Eq. (9) simply selects $\dot{y}_0 = -2y + 2y_0$, which requires a four order ESO. Figures 1 and 2 give state tracking cases with bandwidth of 5 dB and 10 dB respectively without noise at this time. The red dashed line is the actual system state trajectory, and the blue implementation is the estimated value. Obviously, the larger the bandwidth is, the better the tracking effect is.

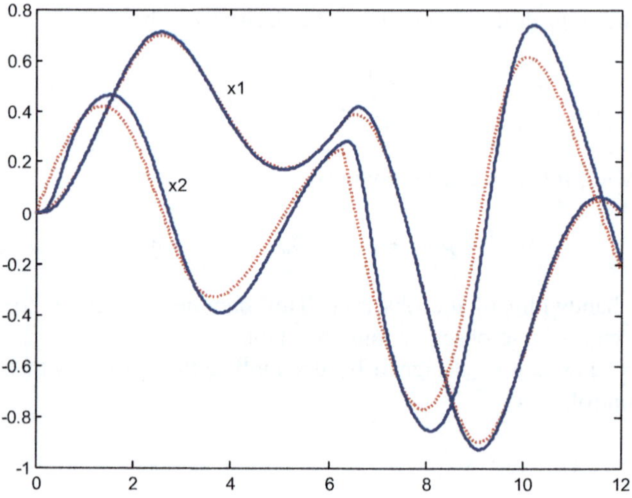

Fig. 1. The state tracking curve with a bandwidth of 5 dB without noise

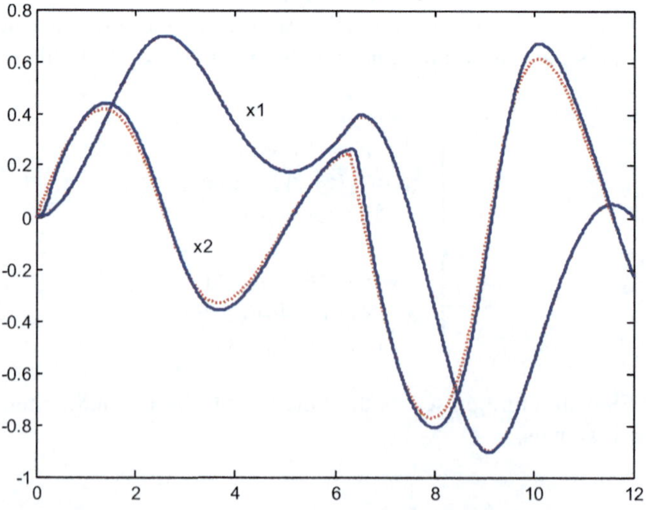

Fig. 2. The state tracking curve with a bandwidth of 10 dB without noise

When the random noise with zero mean variance is 0.01, the tracking curve is shown in Figs. 3 and 4.

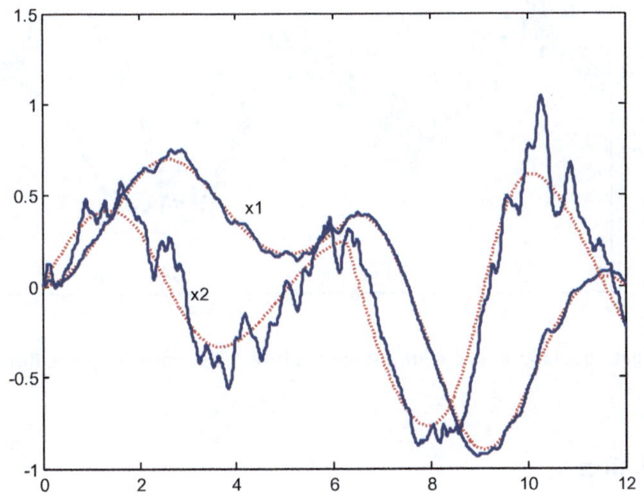

Fig. 3. The state tracking curve with a bandwidth of 5 dB with filter equation ESO and noise

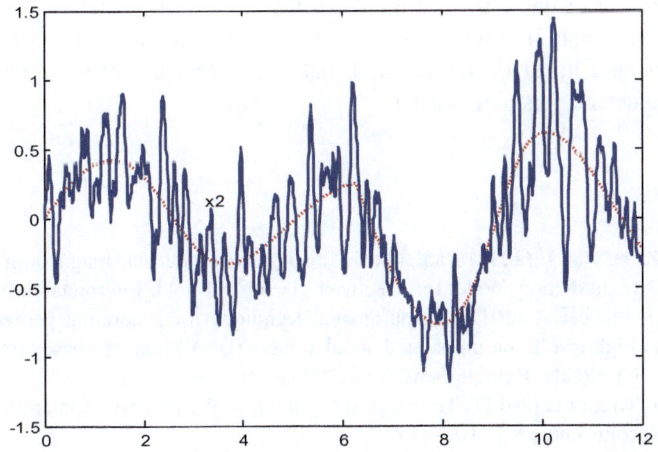

Fig. 4. The state tracking curve with a bandwidth of 10 dB with filter equation ESO and noise

Figure 4 shows only the tracking of x_2. Although the observer with a bandwidth of 10 dB can track the system signal very well, it can be seen that the filter can not completely filter noise, and the amplification effect of noise is very large. Figure 5 is a tracking curve with a bandwidth of 5 dB ESO without filtering equation. The noise is relatively large.

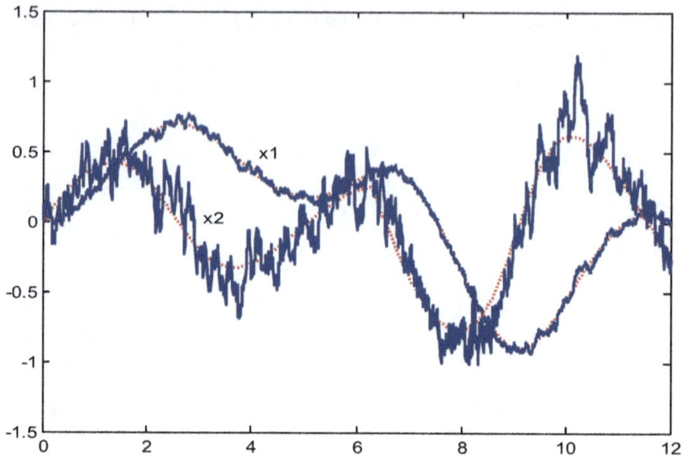

Fig. 5. The state tracking curve with a bandwidth of 5 dB under noise without filter equation ESO

4 Conclusion

The main research content of this paper is the design of control law based on six degree of freedom rigid body nonlinear model of unmanned aerial vehicle to control the tracking trajectory. The design of the control law takes into account the disturbance of wind, the change of the mass and inertia of the aircraft, the delay caused by the main rotor and the estimation of the velocity in the signal with the position of the noise, and the nonlinear and linear design method makes the structure of the controller simpler and the parameter adjustment easier.

References

1. Ahmad K, Hassan F (2016) Radial-basis-function-based nuclear magnetic resonance heavy oil viscosity prediction model for a Kuwait viscous oil field. Interpretation 4(2):81–92
2. Turner D, Lucieer A (2012) An automated technique for generating georectified mosaics from ultra-high resolution unmanned aerial vehicle (UAV) imagery based on structure from motion point clouds. Remote Sens 4(5):1392–1410
3. Baidyk T, Kussul E (2014) Flat image recognition in the process of microdevice assembly. Pattern Recogn Lett 25(1):107–117
4. Pantazis D, Joshi A (2010) Comparison of landmark-based and automatic methods for cortical surface registration. Neuro Image 49(3):2479–2493
5. Herwitz SR, Johnson LF (2014) Imaging from an unmanned aerial vehicle: agricultural surveillance and decision support. Comput Electron Agric 44(1):49–61
6. Courbon J, Mezouar Y (2010) Vision-based navigation of unmanned aerial vehicles. Control Eng Pract 18(7):789–799
7. Vachtsevanos G, Tang L (2015) From mission planning to flight control of unmanned aerial vehicles: strategies and implementation tools. Ann Rev Control 29(1):101–115

8. Yacef F, Bouhali O (2016) Observer-based adaptive fuzzy backstepping tracking control of quadrotor unmanned aerial vehicle powered by Li-ion battery. J. Intell. Robot. Syst. 84(4):1–19
9. Rizoug N (2014) Adaptive neural network control based on neural observer for quadrotor unmanned aerial vehicle. Adv Robot 28(17):1151–1164
10. Asl HJ, Yoon J (2016) Robust image-based control of the quadrotor unmanned aerial vehicle. Nonlinear Dyn 85(3):2035–2048

The Impact Factors of Neural Network Based Time Series Prediction: Taking Stock Price as an Example

Yue Hou[1(✉)], Heng Liu[1], Bin Xie[1], and Feng Ding[2]

[1] School of Electronic and Information Engineering, Lanzhou Jiaotong University, Lanzhou 730070, China
2016023148@qq.com

[2] Beijing Aerospace YILAI Electronic Technology Co., Ltd. China Aerospace Science and Industry Corp, Beijing 100074, China

Abstract. Compared with the traditional time series prediction model, neural network has obvious advantages for the analysis of nonlinear time series data. However, the topology structure and the training algorithm of neural network have a great influence on the prediction accuracy. Taking stock data as an instance, this paper analyzes the impacts factors of prediction ability of neural network such as topology structure, training algorithm and dataset. The experimental results show that the training algorithm and the size of dataset have significant influence on the performance of neural network.

Keywords: Neural network · Time series prediction · Impact factors

1 Introduction

Time series prediction is to predict the value of future data by observing historical time series data. Traditional time series forecasting model predicts future value by establishing a time series correlation identification model. [1–3] respectively proposed auto-regressive model, moving average model, auto-regressive and moving average model for time series prediction. However, the methods mentioned above are often based on conditions under certain assumptions and hence it is difficult to characterize the non-linear features of financial data. In the year of 1990, Wersino and Varfis first applied artificial neural network in economic field to model time series problems [4]. Afterwards, many scholars conducted in-depth research on it. [5–7] use neural network model to predict the future data. The previous work shows that higher prediction accuracy can be obtained by adopting neural network method which may help investors evaluate stock market risk and make better decision. Nevertheless, there is no mature methods to set the topology structure of neural network, and the best parameters can only be determined through multiple experiments.

In this paper, we analyzed the impact factors on the background of stock time series prediction in which three different neural network algorithms was used. The experimental results showed that the structure of network and the size of the dataset contributed a lot to the capability of the model. The more complex the constraints of the

Z. Xu et al. (Eds.): CSIA 2019, AISC 928, pp. 1007–1014, 2020.
https://doi.org/10.1007/978-3-030-15235-2_134

training algorithm, the stronger the generalization ability of the neural network, meanwhile the prediction error will decrease as the training dataset increases.

2 BP Neural Network Model

BP neural network is a multilayer back propagation algorithm. The common BP neural network consists of three layers: input layer, hidden layer and output layer (Given m input layer nodes, k hidden layer nodes and n output layer nodes, the topology of the network is depicted in Fig. 1). The purpose of this algorithm is to train neural network model with specific parameters, that is, we start from the input layer, pass our training data through the hidden layer and calculate the output of straightforwardly in the output layer. At this stage, we have the actual output of our model, and then calculate the loss between the expected output and the actual output. The loss is then propagated backward through the network from the output layer to the hidden layer, updating weights of the neural network until the loss reach the constraints. Finally, we will get the optimum parameters of our model after the training process is terminated.

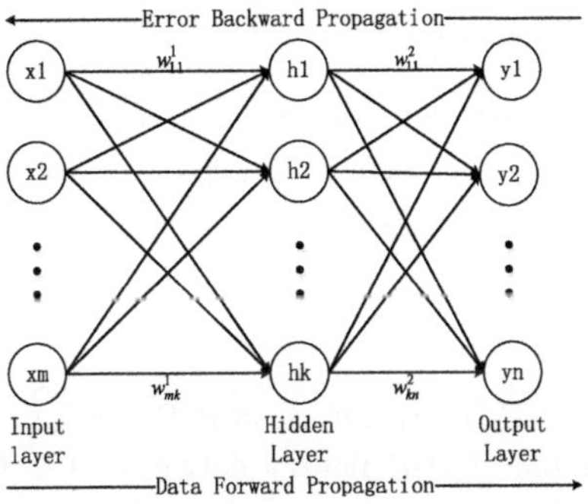

Fig. 1. Basic structure of BP neural network

2.1 LM-BP Algorithm

LM-BP algorithm uses Levenberg Marquardt method to optimize the BP neural network [8–10]. Having both the rapidity in local convergence of the Gauss-Newton method and the efficiency in global searching of gradient decent method, LM-BP algorithm can search in the optimal direction rather than stuck in the negative gradient direction during its iterations. The learning rule is defined as follows:

(1) Given a target precision ε, learning rate μ and proportional coefficient $\beta(0<\beta<1)$.
(2) Calculating the loss function $E(w^k)$ after k iterations:

$$E(w^k) = \frac{1}{2}\sum_{i=1}^{p} \|Y_i - Y_i'\|^2 = \frac{1}{2}\sum_{i=1}^{p} e_i^2(w^k) \tag{1}$$

The denotation Y_i is the expected output, Y_i' is the actual output, P is the number of samples, w is the weight vector, $e_i(w^k)$ is the MSE (Mean Square Error) after k iterations.

(3) If $E(w^k) < \varepsilon$, iterations will be terminated, and a predicted output can be computed. Conversely, step (4) will be executed.

(4) Calculating the Jacobian matrix $J(w^k)$:

$$J(w^k) = \begin{vmatrix} \frac{\partial e_1(w^k)}{\partial w_1} & \frac{\partial e_1(w^k)}{\partial w_2} & \cdots & \frac{\partial e_1(w^k)}{\partial w_n} \\ \frac{\partial e_2(w^k)}{\partial w_1} & \frac{\partial e_2(w^k)}{\partial w_2} & \cdots & \frac{\partial e_2(w^k)}{\partial w_n} \\ \vdots & \vdots & \ddots & \vdots \\ \frac{\partial e_N(w^k)}{\partial w_1} & \frac{\partial e_N(w^k)}{\partial w_2} & \cdots & \frac{\partial e_N(w^k)}{\partial w_n} \end{vmatrix} \tag{2}$$

(5) Calculating Δw:

$$\Delta w = \left[J^T(w)J(w) + \mu I\right]^{-1} J^T(w)e(w) \tag{3}$$

Where I is the identity matrix.

(6) Updating $w^{k+1} = w^k + \Delta w$ and compute a new $E(w^{k+1})$ by step (4). If $E(w^{k+1}) < E(w^k)$, set $k = k+1$, $\mu = \mu\beta$, and then turn to step (2), or if $E(w^{k+1}) < E(w^k)$, set $\mu = \mu/\beta$ and turn to step (5).

2.2 BR-BP Algorithm

BR (Bayesian Regulation)-BP algorithm uses the Bayesian regularization coefficient to improve the fitness function of BP neural network [11, 12]. It uses the uncertain information of historical data to conduct analytic reasoning and obtains the regularization term by determining the prior probability. Therefore, the loss function of the neural network will be optimized, the scale of the network can be effectively controlled, and the generalization ability can be improved.

The weight vector in the BR-BP neural network can be regarded as a multi-dimensional variable. Given the historical data D, the target is to train the network to get the best w (denoted by w^*) which can maximize the posterior probability $P(w|D)$, the formulation is as follows:

$$P(w|D) = \frac{p(D|w))p(w)}{\sum_{i=1}^{n} P(w/D_i)P(D_i)} \tag{4}$$

Where $P(w)$ is the priori probability of weight vector w, D_i is the subset of sample space D, $p(D|w) = \prod_{k=1}^{n} p(D_i|w)$ is the probability of the observation data D given the weight vector w. We now get w^*:

$$\begin{aligned} w^* &= \arg\max_w p(w|D) \\ &= \arg\max_w \frac{p(D|w) * p(w)}{p(D)} \\ &= \arg\max_w p(D|w)p(w) \end{aligned} \tag{5}$$

Taking the logarithm of the posterior likelihood to simplify our computation, we reach:

$$\begin{aligned} w_* &= \arg\max_w \sum_{k=0}^{n} \ln p(D|w) + \ln p(w) \\ &= \arg\min_w -\sum_{k=0}^{n} \ln p(D|w) - \ln p(w) \end{aligned} \tag{6}$$

Where w_* is the logarithmic result of w^*. When the prior probability satisfies a Gaussian distribution, that is:

$$\begin{aligned} p(w_i) &= N(w_i|\mu, \sigma^2) \\ &= \frac{1}{\sqrt{2\pi\sigma^2}} e^{-\frac{(w_i-\mu)^2}{2\sigma^2}} \end{aligned} \tag{7}$$

thus w_* can be formulated as:

$$\begin{aligned} w_* &= \arg\min_w -\ln \sum_{k=0}^{n} p(D_i|w) - \sum_{i=0}^{m} \ln p(w_i) \\ &= \arg\min_w -\ln \sum_{k=0}^{n} p(D_i|w) - \sum_{i=0}^{m} \frac{1}{\sigma^2}(w_i - \mu)^2 \\ &= \arg\min_w -\ln \sum_{k=0}^{n} p(D_i|w) + \lambda \sum_{i=0}^{m} (w_i)^2 \end{aligned} \tag{8}$$

$$\left(\mu = 0, \sigma = \sqrt{\frac{1}{\lambda}}\right)$$

With the above settings, the likelihood function portion corresponds to the fitness function in the target function of the neural network, and the prior probability portion corresponds to the regular term, from which the weight vector satisfying the target function of the neural network can be estimated.

3 Evaluation Protocol

To evaluate the performance of our model, we adopted RSME (Root mean squared error), PCD (Percentage of correct direction) and correlation coefficient C. Where RMSE is used to evaluate the precision of the model, C and PCD are used to examine the accuracy of stock fluctuations [13].

$$RMSE = \sqrt{\frac{1}{N}\sum_{n=1}^{N}(y(n) - \hat{y}(n))^2} \tag{9}$$

$$\begin{cases} PCD = \frac{1}{N}\sum_{n=1}^{N} Pcd_n \times 100\% \\ Pcd_n = \begin{cases} 1 & (y(n+1) - y(n))(y(n+1) - \hat{y}(n)) > 0 \\ 0 & \text{else} \end{cases} \end{cases} \tag{10}$$

Where $y(n)$ is the n th trading day's actual closing price, $\hat{y}(n)$ is the n th trading day's predicted closing price, N is the sample size.

4 Experiments

4.1 Preprocessing the Data

We experimented with the closing price of Baosteel (stock code: 600019) from October 10, 2005 to August 29, 2017 to establish our prediction model. We chose n consecutive trading days' closing price as a group of samples by adopting sliding window method [14], with n be the input size of sliding window, and split it into training set and test set by the portion 8:2 which means 80% of the original dataset is training set and the rest is test set. To accelerate the training process, the data were normalized to [0.2, 0.8] (Fig. 2).

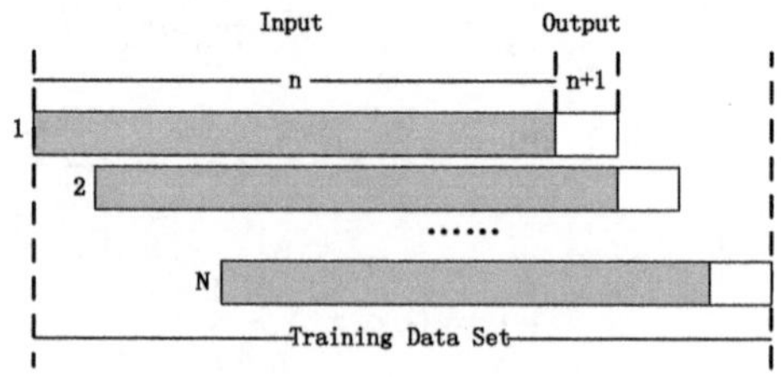

Fig. 2. Sliding window method with input size n

4.2 Training the Model with Different Network Structures

We built a three-layer neural network to conduct the experiment, intentionally set the input size n to 5, 10, 20 which represents the successive trading day of one week, half a month and one month. Each window with size n would be regarded as a sample of our input data, and the network was supposed to predict the stock price at time n + 1.

4.3 Performance Comparison

We separately trained the model with LM-BP algorithm and BR-BP algorithm to predict the closing price in twenty trading days and compared the results.

Figure 3 shows the prediction error of two algorithms with respect to the different datasets and network structures where the horizontal axis is the datasets and the vertical axis is the RMSE. The four different shaped curves represent the different net structures. (e.g., 5-2-1 mean 5 input nodes, 2 hidden nodes and 1 output node).

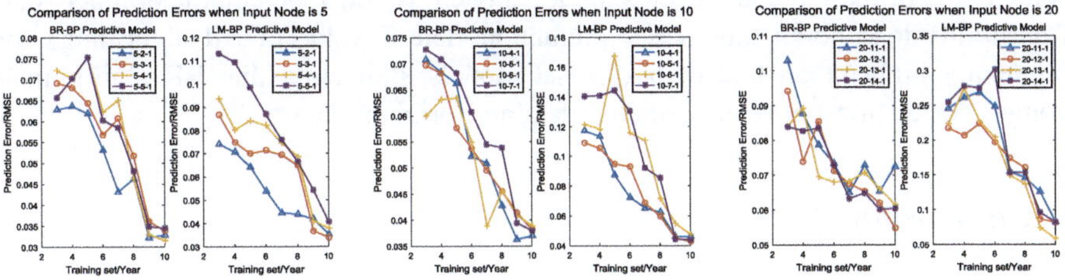

Fig. 3. The comparison between BR-BP and LM-BP with n = 5, 10, 20

5 Best Network Structure

Figure 3 shows that the prediction error under the structure 5-2-1 is significantly lower than that of other structures. Thus, we can assume that the best structure of neural network is 5-2-1. With the above settings, we then trained our model using GD algorithm, LM algorithm, and BR algorithm to find the optimum parameters, and got the closing price in twenty trading days. The result is shown in Fig. 4.

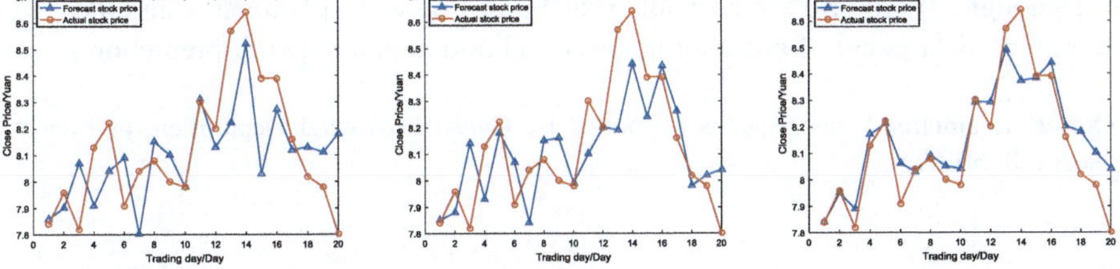

Fig. 4. The closing price in twenty trading days of three different algorithms

Table 1 demonstrates the comparison of three different algorithms.

Table 1. Comparison of three different algorithms

Algorithm	Error		
	RMSE	PCD	C
GD	0.1888	75%	0.6011
LM	0.1682	65%	0.6944
BR	0.1060	85%	0.9166

In terms of prediction accuracy, BR algorithm is superior to traditional GD algorithm and LM algorithm and has better generalization ability and prediction precision. The PCD of BR algorithm is also higher than the other two algorithms, means that BR algorithm also does well in forecasting the fluctuations. Besides, the correlation coefficient C of the three algorithms are all above 0.6, illustrates that neural network is of feasibility to conduct time series prediction. The C value of BR algorithm is predominantly higher than that of traditional models, indicating that BR algorithm has stronger correlation between predicted data and original data.

6 Conclusion

In this paper, we take time series stock price as an instance to discuss the impact factors of neural network prediction model. By setting different training algorithms, different volumes of dataset, and different topology structures of neural network, we build different models. The experimental result shows that the training algorithms and the size of dataset contribute to the prediction capability of the network. The BR algorithm which improves the constraints of the training algorithm can enhance the generalization ability of the network. The more complex the constraints of the network, the stronger the network prediction capability. Meanwhile, the prediction error will decrease as the training data set increases which indicates that the size of training data contributes a lot to the performance of the model. Moreover, the prediction accuracy of different topology structures under the same conditions is not large, and the network prediction errors of different topology structures tend to be stable when the historical data set is large enough. Therefore, a reasonable selection of network parameters and the size of the training dataset are of great significance to build neural network prediction models.

Acknowledgements. This paper is supported by Gansu Provincial Department of Education Project (2016B-027).

References

1. Akaike H (1969) Fitting autoregressive models for prediction. Ann Inst Stat Math 21 (1):243–247
2. Box GEP, Jenkins GM, Reinsel GC et al (2015) Time Series Analysis: Forecasting and Control. Wiley, Hoboken
3. Granger CWJ, Joyeux R (1980) An introduction to long-memory time series models and fractional differencing. J Time Ser Anal 1(1):15–29
4. Varfis A, Versino C (1990) Univariate economic time series forecasting by connectionist methods. In: Proceedings of INNC, vol 90, pp 342–345
5. Liu X (2016) Research on the mothed of forecasting stock price based on the BP neural network: taking military industry as an example. Beijing Jiaotong university, Beijing
6. Xiao Q (2017) The research and application of artificial neural networks in stock price forecasting. South China University of Technology, Guangzhou
7. Chen YY, Zhang ZX, Li WB (2014) Neural network based stock price prediction model. Comput Appl Softw 31(5):89–92
8. Han L (2016) Research on the stock prediction based on LM-BP neural networks. Northeast Agricultural University, Harbin
9. Liu XY (2018) Time series prediction and its application. Financ Theory Teach 1:010
10. Guo JF, Li Y, An D (2017) Prediction for short-term sock price based on LM-GA-BP neural network. Comput Technol Dev 27(01):152–155+15
11. Yang H, Ma JH (2017) Research on method of regularization parameter solution. Comput Measure Control 25(8):226–229
12. Jiao RQ (2017) Regularization parameters selection of Bayesian penalized regression. Southwest Jiaotong University, Chengdu
13. Wang L, Peng L, Xia D, Zeng Y (2015) BP neural network incorporating self-adaptive differential evolution algorithm for time series forecasting. Comput Eng Sci 37(12):2270–2275
14. Chou JS, Nguyen TK (2018) Forward forecast of stock price using sliding-window metaheuristic-optimized machine learning regression. IEEE Trans Ind Inf PP(99):1
15. Cai RH, Cui YX, Xue P (2017) Research on the methods of determining the number of hidden nodes in three layer BP neural network. Comput Inf Technol 25(5):29–33
16. Nielsen MA (2015) Neural Networks and Deep Learning. Determination press, USA

Laser Scanning Imaging System Research and Development Trend Analysis

Maoyun Zhang, Chen Tang(✉), Zhenglin Yu, and Fenglong Chen

College of Mechatronic Engineering,
Changchun University of Science and Technology, Changchun, China
563942951@qq.com

Abstract. Laser imaging technology has the advantages of good concealment and rich information of target image (such as distance, intensity and distance). It has broad application prospects in many fields such as military reconnaissance, topographic mapping and machine vision. It has become the focus and hot spot of research in many countries. This paper describes the basic principles of six kinds of laser scanning three-dimensional imaging radar systems and imaging technologies such as raster scanning, acousto-optic scanning, electro-optical scanning and galvanometer scanning, and traces and summarizes the research progress, and compares the advantages and disadvantages of various system technologies. The development trend is analyzed from the perspective of application. The conclusion is as follows: The method of realizing three-dimensional imaging by optical machine scanning is mature, with high resolution and large field of view.

Keywords: Laser scanning · Three-dimensional imaging · Development trend

1 Introduction

Lidar is widely used in aerospace, surveying, military, civil and other fields. Three-dimensional imaging laser radar technology has been proposed as a new type of imaging technology in the late 1990s, and is currently in a rapid development stage [1]. The three-dimensional imaging laser radar technology has the advantages of high imaging precision, long detection distance and fast acquisition of three-dimensional images. It is widely used in civil fields such as topographic mapping, urban modeling and highway detection; in weapon guidance, battlefield reconnaissance, underwater detection, etc. Military plays an important role; plays a key role in space rendezvous and docking, accurate landing of celestial surfaces, spacecraft orbital services and other aerospace fields [2].

Scanning imaging laser radar can use scanning imaging of unit detectors and non-scanning imaging of multi-element detectors, both of which have advantages and disadvantages. Scanning imaging is a method of performing point-by-point progressive scanning of a target using a transmission to achieve detection imaging. At present, the

Z. Xu et al. (Eds.): CSIA 2019, AISC 928, pp. 1015–1023, 2020.
https://doi.org/10.1007/978-3-030-15235-2_135

main methods of laser scanning include raster scanning, acousto-optic scanning, electro-optic scanning, galvanometer scanning, mirror scanning and wedge scanning. This paper sorts out the working principle of these six scanning laser 3D imaging radar technologies, traces and summarizes the research progress, analyzes the development trend from the application point of view, and clarifies its possible future development direction.

2 Scanning Laser Radar Working Mode

2.1 Raster Scanning

As shown in Fig. 1, the principle of raster scanning [3] is that the spatial frequency distribution is uneven for each part due to the different holograms. Therefore, when the laser beam is incident on the grating, different spatial frequencies at different positions cause different deflection angles of the diffracted light. Scanning is performed by different declinations of the diffracted light after passing through the converging lens. Raster scanning has great advantages in both scanning speed and scanning field of view. It is a typical high efficiency and small inertial scanning method. The disadvantage is that the mutual diffraction of the gratings causes the transmittance of the system to be too low, so that the imaging efficiency is low and the scanning effect is poor.

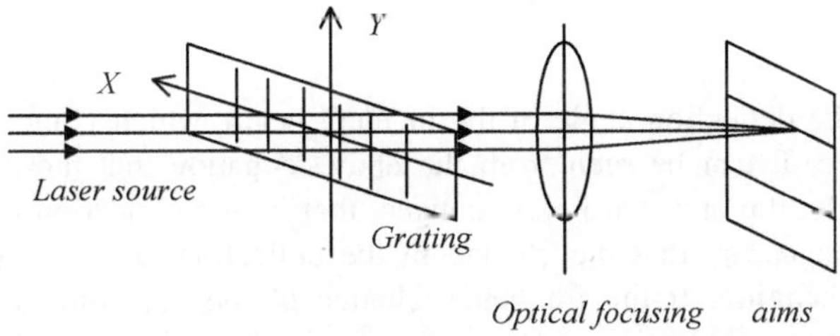

Fig. 1. Raster scanning structure principle

2.2 Sound and Light Scanning

Acousto-optic scanning [4] is a non-mechanical scanning technique. Its working principle is based on the acousto-optic effect. The beam of diffracted light is deflected by changing the frequency of the ultrasonic wave. Figure 2 is a schematic diagram of acousto-optic scanning.

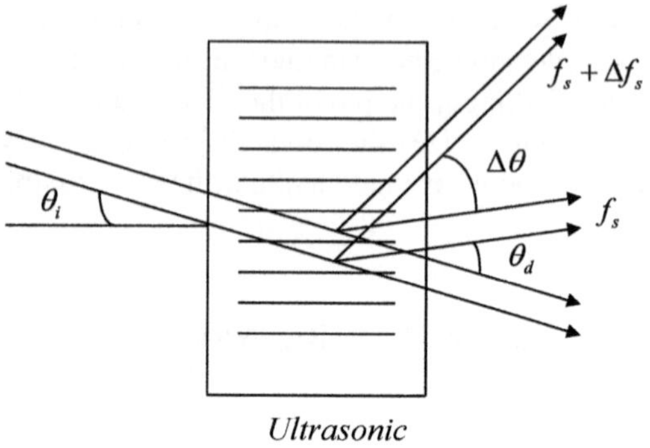

Fig. 2. Sound and light scanning structure principle

The two main parts of the acousto-optic scanner are the transmitting ultrasonic device and the acousto-optic crystal. With the injection of ultrasonic waves, the refractive index of the acousto-optic crystal will change gradually with the wave propagation direction. The incident light will undergo diffraction effect through the acousto-optic crystal. According to the Bragg diffraction theory and the incident angle, the diffraction limit is met. The Bragg condition that should be satisfied, and finally the relationship between the deflection angle of the beam and the ultrasonic frequency is given as Eq. 1:

$$\theta = \theta_i + \theta_d = 2\theta_B = \frac{\lambda}{nv_s} f_s \tag{1}$$

Where is the deflection angle of the incident beam, which is the frequency of the ultrasonic wave. It can be seen from the above equation that the proportional relationship between the and the direct changes, that is, the deflection angle of the laser beam also changes, so that the change in the deflection angle of the beam can be achieved by changing. If the frequency change of the ultrasonic wave is, then the change of the beam deflection angle can be obtained, as shown in the formula 2:

$$\Delta\theta = \frac{\lambda}{nv_s} \Delta f_s \tag{2}$$

Acousto-optic scanning is a non-mechanical scanning method, which is a non-inertial scanning, and the scanning speed is fast, but if the outgoing light intensity is sufficiently large, the diffraction must be maintained under Bragg diffraction conditions, and therefore, the viewing angle is small. When the acousto-optic scanning is not in the Bragg diffraction condition, the diffraction efficiency is very low.

2.3 Electro-Optic Scanning

Electro-optic scanning [5] is a scanner based on electro-optic effect. When the electro-optic crystal is subjected to an applied electric field, the refractive index in some directions of the crystal changes. As shown in Fig. 3, when the laser beam is incident on the electro-optic crystal in a specific direction, due to the poor refractive index, when the laser beam passes through the electro-optic crystal, a phase difference is generated, thereby deflecting the exit angle of the outgoing beam. Since the change in refractive index is related to the applied electric field, when only the applied electric field changes, the phase difference generated by the laser beam through the electro-optic crystal is only related to the applied voltage, and varies proportionally with the applied voltage. Therefore, when the laser beam is incident on the electro-optic crystal at a specific angle, changing the voltage of the applied electric field causes the laser beam exit angle to change accordingly, thereby forming a scan.

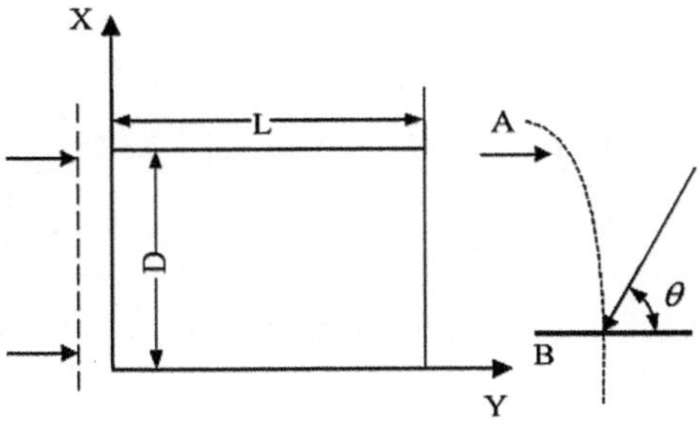

Fig. 3. Electro-optical scanning structure principle

Electro-optic scanning is a non-mechanical scan with a high scanning speed, but the scanning angle is relatively small. For example, for a KDP crystal, if the length, width, and height are both, the deflection angle is.

2.4 Galvanometer Scanning

The galvanometer scanning [6] schematic diagram of the two-dimensional scanning is shown in Fig. 4. Its principle is that the scanning motor drives the mirror to deflect rapidly, which deflects the angle of the incident laser. The two-dimensional galvanometer mainly consists of two scanning heads, X and Y, which constitute an optical deflector. The resonant scanning head X is used to realize fast scanning in the X direction, and the servo scanning head Y is used to realize frame scanning in the Y direction. After being expanded and collimated, the laser is first incident on the X-direction resonant scanning mirror, and the reflected laser light is collimated and then incident on the Y-direction scanning mirror, and is reflected by the Y-scan mirror to the target field. Galvanometer scanning is one of the most mature scanning methods. It has good line ability good repeatability and scanning efficiency high. However, due to the larger scanning angle of the galvanometer scanning, the scanning frequency is lower, so its scanning angle is Generally not large, about, and at this angle of view, the frequency of galvanometer scanning is generally low.

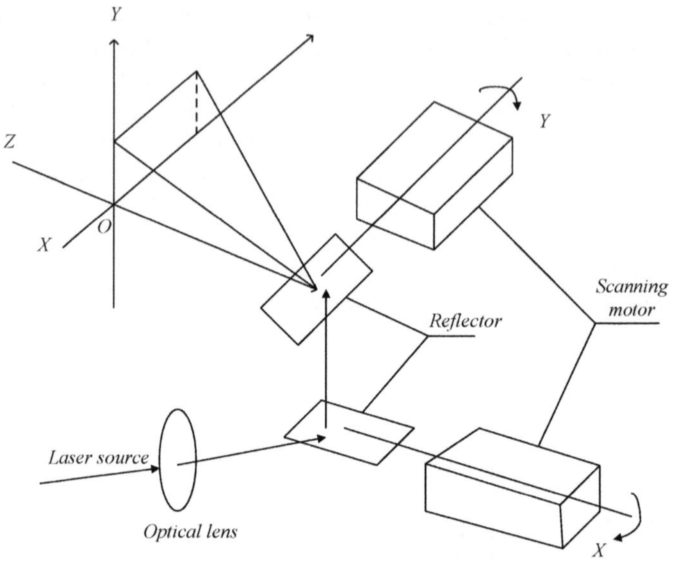

Fig. 4. Two-dimensional galvanometer scanning structure principle

2.5 Turn Scan

There are many types of mirror scanning [7, 8]. There are polygon mirrors and single-sided mirrors. There are trans missive and reflective types according to the function. The optical part and the mechanical part are combined. The schematic diagram of the scanning principle is shown in Figs. 5 and 6. The working principle is that the motor drives the polyhedral prism of the optical part to realize the rotation. When the incident light is incident at a certain angle, the rotation of the rotating mirror is the mirror. The rotation causes the reflected light to deflect, so that the mirror is continuously rotated by the mechanical motor to achieve scanning.

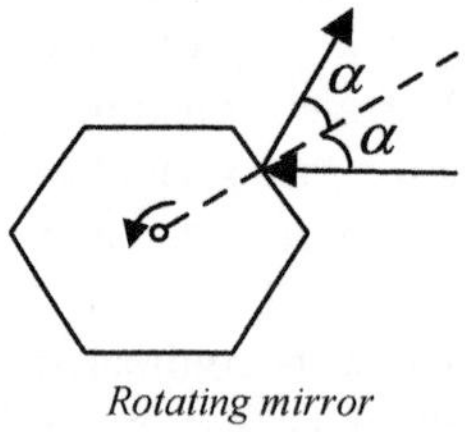

Fig. 5. Scanning mirror structure

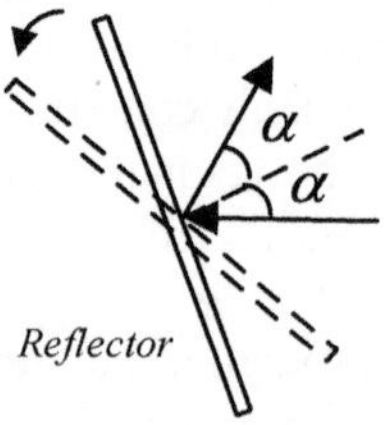

Fig. 6. Single mirror scanning structure

Since the motor speed can be very high, the scanning speed of the mirror is generally faster. And the scanning angle of the mirror is large, but the cost is also high and the stability is good. However, due to the large volume of the scanning mirror, the configuration of the scanning system is complicated, and the quality of the reflected beam is affected by the limitation of the processing technology of the rotating mirror.

2.6 Wedge Scanning

The wedge [9] is a prism with a small apex angle. According to the principle of light refraction, as shown in Fig. 7, when light passes through the prism, it is twice refracted, and the direction of the emitted light is deviated from the direction of the original incident ray.

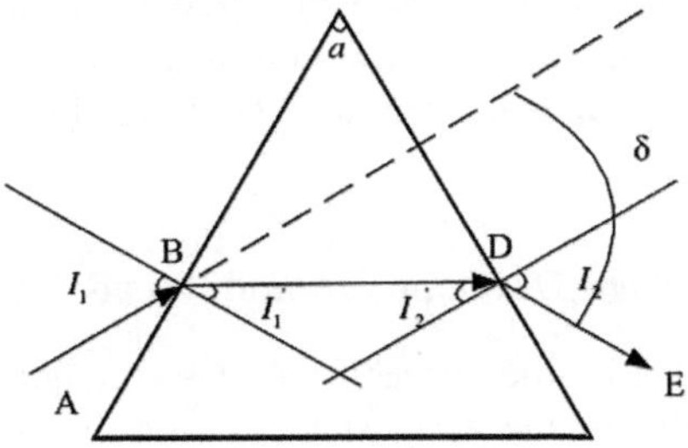

Fig. 7. Principle of wedge scanning structure

As shown in Fig. 8, when the two main wedge sections of the same wedge are placed in parallel, it can be known from the existing theory that the off-angle of the beam after passing through the two wedges is maximum, so that one wedge does not move and the other wedge edge When the optical axis rotates, the off-angle of the light beam passing through the two wedges becomes smaller and smaller. When the wedge is rotated, the off-angle is 0.

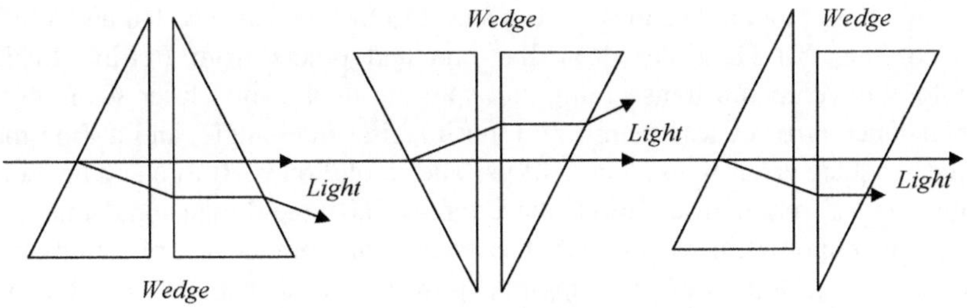

Fig. 8. Schematic diagram of wedge scanning principle

Wedge scanning is characterized by a large scanning angle and a fast scanning speed, but it cannot be applied to high-precision laser radar due to poor dispersion imaging quality due to light refraction.

3 Technical Comparison and Development Trend

3.1 Technical Comparison

Combining the various scanning techniques mentioned above, for the acousto-optic scanning technology without inertial scanning, there is a fast scanning speed, but only the scanning angle of the milli-arc metric can not achieve large-angle scanning, and at the same time, since the light beam passes through the crystal, it is transparent. The overshoot rate is not high, and the obtained beam quality is poor. Although the grating scanning has certain advantages in scanning speed and scanning field of view, the beam imaging quality is low due to the problem of diffraction efficiency; the optical scanning technology is relatively non-mechanical Compared with scanning technology, it has good performance in system stability, scanning angle and scanning speed, and beam imaging quality. Therefore, optical scanning technology has been widely used in laser radar technology.

3.2 Domestic and Foreign Development and Trend Analysis

Currently in China [10–13], the research on laser ranging and three-dimensional imaging lidar is generally in the early stage. Domestic units have followed up on various three-dimensional imaging schemes, and many institutions have conducted research on pulse flight time imaging systems. In 1999, Lu Zu-kang and Li Pei-yong of Zhejiang University developed a 5600-pixel laser vision system. In 2005, Hu Chun-sheng and Qin Shi-qiao of the National University of Defense Technology developed a laser with a fast-turning mirror as a scanning device and APD photoelectric receiving. 3D vision system, the distance measurement accuracy within 10 m can reach below 100 mm. In 2009, the Shanghai Institute of Physics of the Chinese Academy of Sciences successfully developed an on-board imaging system using a two-dimensional galvanometer scanning, and the imaging range was reached, but the corresponding large-angle scanning field of view resulted in a scanning frequency below 50 Hz. In 2010, Hua zhong University of Science and Technology proposed a new scheme to increase the scanning angle and scanning speed to Si-hua, Chen Si-hai and Wu Xin. In 2014, Yu Sen, Xu Da-xiong, Ren Jian-hua and others from Beijing Institute of Technology developed a transceiving and splitting dual-station laser scanning imager with a distance error of less than 0.2 m, an imaging field angle, and a time measurement mean square error of less than 340 ps. The resolution is 70 mm and the horizontal resolution is 1.5 mrad. In addition, the commercial three-dimensional imaging laser radar system imported in recent years has made many practical applications in digital object modeling, topographic mapping, power line detection, and forest cover detection.

Foreign research in the field of three-dimensional imaging laser radar started earlier, and the theory and practice are relatively mature. Many departments in the United States, Canada, Sweden, Australia and other countries have made due contributions to the development of laser radar. The system developed by the Hercules Defense Center in the United States uses raster scanning technology and a single InGaAs avalanche diode as a detector to achieve a maximum resolution of 0.25 m and a range of 2 km.

US Army Communications has developed a 3D laser radar system using Nd:YAG microchip lasers with a repetition rate of 3 kHz and a pulse width of 1.2 ns with a single pulse energy of 6 uJ. Using a dual galvanometer scan, full waveform acquisition can resolve four echo signals. The recognition of the camouflage on the target is achieved, and the total imaging pixels are 40–90 s per frame time and the detection distance is 50 m.

As the research progresses, increasing the imaging speed, that is, increasing the number of detection units is an effective method. The US Air Force White Lab began solid-state laser radar research in the late 1980s with the aim of attempting to use imaging laser radars with LD and detector arrays. The Lincoln Laboratory uses an array plus a two-dimensional laser radar. The Nd:YAG microchip laser is used to multiply the wavelength of 532 nm, the pulse width is 250 ps, and the single pulse energy is 3 uJ to achieve pixel and distance measurement accuracy of 3 cm. In the aircraft experimental system, the European Space Agency uses a linear array APD for dual-axis scanning. The Nd:YAG frequency doubled 532 nm laser has a pulse width of less than 10 ns, and its measuring range is 250 m. The ranging accuracy is up to 2 cm.

Based on the above summary, we found that the existing scanning methods only oscilloscope scanning and mirror scanning can be maturely applied in the laser imaging radar system, but it can not meet the requirements of today's large field of view and fast scanning. The scanning method generally has a problem that the transmittance of light is low or the angle of view is small. Therefore, laser three-dimensional imaging scanning is still developing toward a large field of view, high frame rate, and small volume.

4 Conclusion

The development of laser three-dimensional scanning imaging systems is mainly subject to the two core components of lasers and detectors. The laser is determined by the action distance. The narrow pulse width and high repetition frequency laser pulse realizes a far-reaching working distance with a small transmission power, exchanges energy with time, and uses the pulse emission intermittent to ensure the exposure time of the detector to ensure the accuracy of ranging. At the same time, high repetition rate laser pulses can also make breakthroughs in imaging resolution. The high-precision detection technology also determines the parameter performance of the laser three-dimensional scanning imaging system, and is also the focus of current optical machine technology development.

References

1. Li Z (2018) Research on laser 3D motion imaging technology. Laser J 39(10):119–123
2. Yang X, Ainiwai G, Wang Y, Hao, L (2018) Analysis and research of ultra-high resolution cluster pixel 3D imaging LIDAR. [J/OL] Laser J 1–4
3. Cheng Y, Huang X, Zhou J, Liu X (2010) Simulating raster scan-based high-resolution and long afterglow display of radar. Comput Appl Softw 27(12):226–229

4. Luo Y, He Y, Hu S, Zang H, Shang J, Wan Y, Chen W (2014) Three-dimensional video imaging lidar system based on acousto-optic laser scanning. Chin J Lasers 41(08):27–33
5. Wan L, Lu Z, Wang R (2011) Electro-optic laser scanner for arbitrary scanning in 8 rows. J. Appl Opt 2(02):323–328
6. Liu C (2018) Design and research of high speed scanning galvanometer control system. North University of China
7. Xie J (2011) Research on the key technologies of rotating mirror used on imaging ladar. National University of Defense Technology
8. Ji R, Zhao C, Chen G (2011) Analysis and calculation of scan trace of laser scanning rotation mirror. Chin J Lasers 38(04):204–208
9. Zhu J, Li F, Huang Q, Li M, Jiang Y, Liu R, Jiang C, Meng Z (2016) Design and realization of an airborne LiDAR dual—WEDGF scanning system. Infrared Laser Eng 45(05):9–14
10. Xing S, Chen S, Wu X, Zheng X, Xiao D (2010) Study and test on a novel fast laser scanner based on piezo-actuators. Chin J Lasers 37(02):408–413
11. Wang J, Hong G, Bu H, Xu W, Xiao G, He Z, Lin J, Shu R (2009) Study on airborne scanning ladar. Acta Optica Sinica 29(09):2584–2589
12. Hu C (2005) Investigation into the high-speed pulsed laser diode 3D-imaging ladar. National University of Defense Technology
13. Lu Z, Zang K, Li P, Hong Z, Wu B (1999) Study of 3D-imaging laser radar. J Zhejiang Univ Eng Sci (04):84–87

A Survey of Group Intelligence Optimization Algorithms

Chunguang Chang and Xi Wu(✉)

School of Management, Shenyang Jianzhu University, Shenyang 110168, China
wxy0102w@163.com

Abstract. The group intelligent optimization algorithm provides some new ideas for solving many practical problems. These algorithms have stronger robustness and stronger search ability, and are easy to implement in parallel. It is easy to combine with other algorithms to improve the performance of the algorithm and solve complex practical problems. The effect of the experiment is more obvious. In this paper, the improvement and application of particle swarm optimization algorithm, fireworks algorithm and artificial bee colony algorithm in intelligent algorithm are reviewed, and the advantages and disadvantages are analyzed. The future development of intelligent algorithm is prospected.

Keywords: Group intelligence algorithm · Particle swarm optimization · Fireworks algorithm · Artificial bee colony algorithm

1 Introduction

The method used to find the step of the optimization problem solution or the search process is called an optimization algorithm. The optimization algorithm can be generally divided into two categories: classic optimization algorithm and intelligent optimization algorithm. Because the classical optimization algorithm has the mathematical characteristics of over-reliance on the optimization problem, it has the disadvantages of high computational complexity and long solution time when solving a wide variety of complex problems with large problems. It is difficult to obtain the optimal solution of the actual optimization problem. In order to achieve a good balance between solution time and solution quality, the researchers have proposed a number of heuristic computational intelligence algorithms. The intelligent optimization algorithm has been widely concerned and applied by its rapid and effective salient features. Syntactic intelligence refers to the collective intelligence exhibited by a group of simple individuals in the present emerging reality. The swarm intelligence algorithm includes chaotic ant colony algorithm, ant colony optimization, bee colony algorithm, fish swarm algorithm, firefly algorithm, cuckoo algorithm, particle swarm optimization, bacterial foraging optimization algorithm and fireworks algorithm. The swarm intelligence algorithm is a method in which multiple individuals of the group cooperate with each other, using a probabilistic transfer method, combining certain heuristic rules, and performing parallel search on the solution space. The swarm intelligence algorithm is characterized by randomness, adaptability and parallelism. At present, the mathematical foundation of group intelligence is relatively scarce, and many researchers are

Z. Xu et al. (Eds.): CSIA 2019, AISC 928, pp. 1024–1033, 2020.
https://doi.org/10.1007/978-3-030-15235-2_136

advancing in constant exploration. The swarm intelligence algorithm has been continuously improved in terms of performance improvement and application range expansion. This paper mainly summarizes and analyzes the current situation of three kinds of intelligent algorithms, such as particle swarm optimization algorithm, fireworks algorithm and artificial bee colony algorithm, and looks forward to its future development trend.

2 Particle Swarm Optimization

Inspired by the bird's foraging behavior, Dr. Kennedy and Dr. Eberhart proposed a population-based optimization algorithm, Particle Swarm Optimization (PSO), in 1995. Compared with some other swarm intelligence algorithms, PSO is easy to implement and has better performance in solving some practical problems. The rise of artificial intelligence has promoted the development and progress of group intelligence algorithms. The particle swarm algorithm has been favored by many scholars and researchers by its own advantages, and has achieved good results in many applications. With the advancement of science and technology, the practical application has higher and higher requirements for accuracy, and the classification of specific problems is more comprehensive, which provides a theoretical basis and experimental environment for further application of solving problems in the future. The advantages of particle swarm optimization are as follows: simple concept, only basic mathematics knowledge, can be realized on the computer; low requirements for optimization problems, can be black box problem, no need for explicit expression; fast solution, the global search ability is strong, and in most cases, the local optimization of the optimization problem can be overcome. The shortcomings are as follows: lack of strict theoretical basis, can not ensure strict convergence; as a heuristic algorithm, can not ensure the feasibility and optimality of the solution, and can not even indicate the degree of approximation of the solution and the optimal solution; local search ability is weak. When dealing with multi-peak problems, it is still possible to fall into local optimum.

2.1 Improved Thinking

In PSO, each particle represents a potential solution to the optimization problem. The whole particle swarm is flying in the search space to find the optimal solution. The particle swarm algorithm continuously updates the particle's velocity and position toward the optimal objective function by continuously comparing the objective function values, individual extremum and group extremum searched by the particle. The algorithm search speed is fast, but it is easy to fall into local extremum due to the homogenization of particles, and the dependence on parameters is strong. If the parameters are set improperly, the quality of the solution will be reduced. The algorithm is easy to prematurely converge and is not suitable for high-dimensional multi-peak problems. To this end, many scholars have improved the particle swarm algorithm. After more than 20 years of development, these improved research work mainly has the following three aspects. (1) Make some adjustments based on the standard PSO, such as learning factor adjustment, inertia weight adjustment, speed simplification, etc. (2) Introduce the hybrid strategy to the basic particle swarm algorithm. (3) Fusion of standard particle swarm optimization algorithms with other intelligent optimization algorithms.

2.2 Research Status and Application

Guo [1] adjusted the fixed inertia weight dynamically. Zhang [2] used the inertia weight decrement to enhance the convergence efficiency of the algorithm and improved the robustness of the algorithm. Zhang [3] merged PSO with differential evolution algorithm; Zheng [4] applied improved genetic algorithm to particle swarm optimization algorithm to make particles have genetic variation ability. Wang [5] proposed a new hybrid algorithm combining the advantages of simulated annealing algorithm and PSO. Ren [6] and so on combined the artificial bee colony concept and particle swarm optimization algorithm to improve the search ability of the algorithm. Brabazon [7] proposed mixing the bacterial foraging algorithm with the particle swarm algorithm. Liu [8] and Liu [9] proposed the specific application of particle swarm optimization to neural network training. Zheng [10] and Yang [11] proposed the use of particle swarm optimization algorithm for PID control. Zhao [12] and Wang [13] proposed the particle swarm optimization algorithm for task scheduling under cloud computing. Jin [14] proposed the particle swarm optimization algorithm for image retrieval. Das [15] proposed the particle swarm optimization algorithm for non-stationary ECG signal denoising technology analysis. Cheng [16] and Wu [17] proposed the particle swarm optimization algorithm to solve the TSP problem.

3 Fireworks Algorithm

The Fireworks Algorithm (FWA) is a relatively new swarm intelligence algorithm proposed by Tan and Zhu in 2010 [18]. The design of the algorithm is inspired by the simulation of the beautiful scene generated by the night sky fireworks explosion. Like other optimization algorithms, fireworks algorithms are also based on iterative search. For each iteration, the four main operations of the explosion operator, mutation operator, mapping rule and selection strategy are used in sequence until the termination condition of the algorithm is satisfied. So far, fireworks algorithms have attracted the attention of more and more researchers. In view of the shortcomings of the fireworks algorithm, the researchers proposed many improved methods and hybrid algorithms. These efforts have greatly improved the performance of the fireworks algorithm, further enriching and promoting the research of fireworks algorithms. So far, fireworks algorithms have been successfully applied to many engineering fields.

3.1 Improved Thinking

The fireworks algorithm has received widely attention from researchers because of its ability to solve problems with good optimization problems. The optimization algorithm for fireworks algorithm has been proposed by various scholars in recent years. The optimization and improvement of different levels for different directions can be divided into two categories. One is the process of generating new spark particles in the process of the basic fireworks algorithm in its explosion process. The improvement is another type of optimization algorithm that is derived from the inspiration of other algorithms.

3.2 Research Status and Application

The Fireworks Algorithm (FWA) is a swarm intelligence algorithm inspired by the night sky fireworks explosion. In order to improve the performance of fireworks algorithms, researchers have proposed many improved versions. Zheng et al. [19] proposed two adaptive radius strategies, namely dynamic search fireworks algorithm (dynFWA) and adaptive fireworks algorithm (AFWA). In dynFWA, the particle blast radius is determined by spark fitness. Whether the value is improved or not, in AFWA, the explosion range of the spark particle is calculated from the distance between the individual with the best fitness value in the current population and a specific individual. These two algorithms for adaptive explosion range greatly improve the performance of the original algorithm. Liu [20] proposed the structural fireworks optimization algorithm (IFWA), which based on the original algorithm, modified the calculation of the explosion radius and the number of explosion sparks, using a new method, compared with the original fireworks algorithm. The algorithm has been improved in performance. Zheng et al. proposed an enhanced fireworks algorithm (EFWA) [21]. Compared to traditional FWA, FWA has five modifications. The experimental results show that the performance of EFWA on the displacement function is significantly better than the traditional FWA. Based on EFWA, Li et al. proposed an adaptive fireworks algorithm (AFWA) [22]. AFWA uses the sparks that have been generated to calculate the explosion amplitude of the core fireworks. Experimental results show that the new adaptive explosion amplitude can effectively improve the performance of the fireworks algorithm. Yu et al. proposed a dynamic search fireworks algorithm based on covariance variation, which used a simple and novel method to dynamically adjust the explosion amplitude [23]. Literature [24] and [25] proposed a method for integrating differential evolution operators into fireworks algorithms. The literature [26] proposed a cooperative framework for fireworks algorithms (CoFFWA). CoFFWA uses an independent selection method and crowd avoidance cooperation strategy to improve the performance of FWA. Literature [27] introduced a novel guiding spark in the fireworks algorithm. Through the spark of the explosion, the algorithm constructs a promising guide vector, which improves the search performance of the fireworks algorithm. Further, Li and Tan proposed a skeleton fireworks algorithm and a fireworks algorithm based on the knockout [28, 29]. Other aspects of the fireworks algorithm have also made great progress. The literature [30] used a fireworks algorithm to reconstruct the power system. Literature [31] used fireworks algorithms for network information retrieval. Literature [32] proposed a multi-task fireworks algorithm for cell tracking and contour estimation. The literature [33] proposed a multi-objective optimization algorithm and is used for multi-objective transportation network problems. The literature [34] used the fireworks algorithm to solve the TSP problem. Literature [27] made a comprehensive summary of the improvement research and application research results of fireworks algorithm.

The optimization performance of FWA is better as a new intelligent algorithm, which is applied to many fields of society, such as non-negative matrix factorization [35] and digital filter design [36]. The FWA is applied to the discrete optimization field and a reverse fireworks algorithm is solved to solve the multi-dimensional knapsack problem [37]. The maximum position method is used to map the continuous variables to the discrete space to solve the permutation flow shop problem [38]. The FWA is used to solve the problem of job shop scheduling with multiple constraints and multi-resource coordination [39]. The FWA is used to optimize the structural parameters of the fuzzy system model to improve the accuracy and interpretation of the model [40]. Using fireworks explosive immune algorithm to solve mobile body obstacle avoidance path planning problem [41]. The fuzzy system model is used to solve the fuzzy classification problem by combining the fireworks algorithm and the difference algorithm [42]. Using FWA to establish multi-objective scheduling model to solve the problem of user's service quality in cloud computing [43]. FWA is used to solve the multi-objective optimization model by association rules and mining algorithms [44, 45]. FWA is applied to the field of image segmentation and image feature extraction [46, 47]. Binary coding is adopted. FWA solves the optimal clustering problem [48]. Using FWA to establish discrete optimization problems and solve complex Web composition services [49]. Multi-objective nonlinear optimization model is established by adaptive fireworks algorithm to solve multi-UAV allocation problems and loading heavy-duty loading problems of large transport aircraft [50].

4 Artificial Bee Colony

Artificial Bee Colony (ABC) is a stochastic global search algorithm based on swarm intelligence that is developed by Karaboga to mimic the natural bee collecting process in nature. The algorithm contains three different functions of bees, namely: employment bee (representing a certain A specific food source), observation bees (observing the employment of bee feedback information to select food sources and reconnaissance bees (random search for new food sources), these bee colonies through the information sharing and communication to solve the problem. The ABC algorithm has simple structure, few parameters, high search precision and easy implementation. Compared with the classical optimization algorithm, the ABC algorithm also has the characteristics of low requirements on the objective function and constraints, and is basically in the process of finding the optimal solution. There is no need to use external information, only the fitness function is used as the basis for evolution. In addition, the ABC algorithm is clear and concise and has a strong global optimization ability, which is adopted by various fields to solve various complex optimization problems.

4.1 Improved Thinking

The ABC algorithm has the advantages of other swarm intelligence algorithms. It is self-organizing, adaptive, and robust. However, as such, it also has the disadvantage of being easily trapped in local optimum.

4.2 Research Status and Application

The ABC algorithm has developed rapidly. Since its introduction, it has achieved research results in many fields, such as neural network training, speech recognition, combinatorial optimization, and power system optimization. Experts and scholars at home and abroad have made important contributions to this. Literature [51] proposed a service-oriented S-ABC, which effectively applied the ABC algorithm to the solution of service computing optimization problems such as service selection and service resource scheduling. The literature [52] proposed an artificial bee colony algorithm for solving the link problem, which better solved the dependence and interaction between variables in the link problem. The literature [53] applied the ABC algorithm to adaptive The Adaptive Neural Fuzzy Inference System increases the two control parameters of the arithmetic crossover probability and the adaptive factor, effectively achieving the goal of fast convergence. Literature [54] improved the basic ABC algorithm based on bidirectional parallel search strategy and simulated annealing, and improved the algorithm to solve the problem of finding the optimal path for mobile robots. Literature [55] applied the artificial bee colony algorithm to the optimization of unmanned helicopter controllers, and significantly improved its tracking performance. Since then, more scholars have applied ABC algorithm to the slope safety factor solution [56], binary optimization problem solving [57] and cloud computing resource scheduling problem [58]. Nowadays, ABC algorithm has been successfully introduced into data mining, image analysis, speech recognition and many other application fields, and the results are remarkable. In the past few decades, ABC algorithm has been involved in many application fields. However, the research of artificial bee colony algorithm is still in the stage of continuous exploration and continuous improvement, and its NP-hard discrete domain optimization problem in multi-dimensional backpack and Bayesian network structure learning. And the engineering application has broad research prospects, the application will be more extensive, and the theory will be more and more mature and more perfect.

At this stage, the development of computational intelligence is also facing great challenges. The main problem is that computing intelligence lacks a solid mathematical foundation. Although neural networks have a relatively complete theoretical foundation, important intelligent technologies such as evolutionary computing have no perfect mathematical foundation. Numerical experiments and specific applications are important means to test the effectiveness and efficiency of intelligent algorithms. In this paper, the three-population intelligent optimization algorithm in domestic academic circles has been sorted out in recent years. It can be foreseen that various algorithms will be further integrated in the future to make up for their shortcomings.

5 Conclusion

(1) Many researchers have proposed a differential algorithm with adaptive control parameters. Applying these parameter adaptive strategies to improved algorithms should be a promising research direction. Many parameters of the algorithm itself do not adopt adaptive strategies. The adaptive strategy of mining the parameters of the

algorithm itself is a research direction. Since the function test set and optimization problems are more and more complicated, in order to make the algorithm have better performance on the optimization problem, it is indispensable to adopt an adaptive parameter strategy. (2) Because each algorithm has its own advantages and disadvantages, the hybrid algorithm can fuse different algorithm advantages, so it has always been a hot spot to study algorithm improvement. Mixing other strategies is also a valuable research direction. It is meaningful to study the role of relevant strategies in algorithms and their role in specific problems. It also makes sense to find a specific algorithm that is suitable for solving a particular problem. (3) Optimization is ubiquitous, and the application field of expanding group intelligence algorithms is a valuable direction. After all, the wide adoption of algorithms in the application field can show its strong vitality and value.

Acknowledgments. This research was supported by the National Natural Science Foundation of China (Project No. 51678375), Natural Science Foundation of Liaoning Province (Project No. 2015020603), and the basic scientific research project of Liaoning Higher Education (Project No. LJZ2017009).

References

1. Guo Y, Song Y, Song C, Liu L, Ren H (2017) A particle swarm target tracking algorithm with improved inertia weight. Foreign Electron Meas Technol 36(01):17–20 (in Chinese)
2. Zhang L, Tang Y, Hua C, Guan X (2015) A new particle swarm optimization algorithm with adaptive inertia weight based on Bayesian techniques. Appl Soft Comput 28:138–149
3. Zhang Q (2017) Study on particle swarm optimization algorithm and difference algorithm. Shandong University (in Chinese)
4. Zheng Y, Liu Y, Lu W et al (2016) A hybrid PSO-GA method for composing heterogeneous groups in collaborative learning In: International conference on computer science & education. IEEE
5. Wang Y, Cao J, Zhang F (2017) Improved chaotic particle swarm optimization algorithm based on simulated annealing. J Inner Mongolia Univ Technol (Nat Sci Ed) 6(03):173–177 (in Chinese)
6. Ren C, Ge H, Yang J, Yuan Y (2015) Artificial bee colony particle swarm optimization algorithm introducing mixed frog leap search strategy. Comput Eng Appl 51(22):38–41 (in Chinese)
7. Brabazon A, O'Neill M, McGarraghy S (2015) Bacterial foraging algorithms. Natural computing algorithms. Springer, Heidelberg, pp 187–199
8. Liu H, Shen X, Qu H, Wang P (2017) Study on temperature control of PID biogas dry fermentation based on particle swarm optimization. Comput Eng Des 38(03):784–788 (in Chinese)
9. Liu J, Mei Q, Yang D (2017) Neural network modeling of extreme speed learning machine based on blind moving particle swarm frequency decomposition. Inf Control 46(01):60–64 (in Chinese)
10. Zheng E, Jiang S (2017) Fractional order PID control based on improved particle swarm optimization algorithm. Control Eng 24(10):2082–2087 (in Chinese)
11. Yang Z, Chen Y (2016) Improved particle swarm optimization algorithm and its application in PID tuning. Control Eng 23(02):161–166 (in Chinese)

12. Zhao H, Li S (2016) Research on cloud computing resource scheduling method based on particle swarm optimization and RBF neural network. Comput Sci 43(03):113–117 (in Chinese)
13. Wang D, Liu X (2015) Resource scheduling of cloud computing platform based on improved particle swarm optimization algorithm. Appl Res Comput 32(11):3230–3234 (in Chinese)
14. Jin Y, Xue D, Zhang X, Li W (2018) Image retrieval research based on fusion-based scale-free particle swarm optimization algorithm. Microelectron Comput 35(01):36–40 (in Chinese)
15. Das AK, Biswas D, Halder S (2017) Analysis of de-noising techniques of non-stationary ECG signal based on wavelet and PSO optimized parameters for Savitzky golay filter. In: International conference on research in computational intelligence & communication networks, pp 39–44
16. Cheng B, Lu H, Huang Y, Xu K (2017) An adaptive excellent coefficient particle swarm optimization algorithm for solving TSP. J Comput Appl 37(03):750–754 (in Chinese)
17. Wu G (2016) Research on path planning problem based on particle swarm optimization algorithm. Yanshan University (in Chinese)
18. Tan Y, Zhu Y (2010) Fireworks algorithm for optimization. In: International conference in swarm intelligence. Springer, Heidelberg, pp 55–364
19. Zheng S, Janecek A, Li J et al (2014) Dynamic search in fireworks algorithm. In: IEEE evolutionary computation, pp 3222–3229
20. Liu J, Zheng S, Tan Y (2013) The improvement on controlling exploration and exploitation of firework algorithm 7928:11–23
21. Zheng S, Janecek A, Tan Y (2013) Enhanced fireworks algorithm. In: IEEE congress on evolutionary computation (CEC). IEEE, pp 2069–2077
22. Li J, Zheng S, Tan Y (2014) Adaptive fireworks algorith. In: 2014 IEEE congress on evolutionary computation (CEC). IEEE, pp 3214–3221
23. Yu C, Kelley LC, Tan Y (2015) Dynamic search fireworks algorithm with covariance mutation for solving the CEC 2015 learning based competition problems. In: 2015 IEEE congress on evolutionary computation (CEC). IEEE, pp 1106–1112
24. Zheng YJ, Xu XL, Ling HF et al (2015) A hybrid fireworks optimization method with differential evolution operators. Neurocomputing 148:75–82
25. Yu C, Kelley L, Zheng S et al (2014) Fireworks algorithm with differential mutation for solving the CEC 2014 competition problems. In: 2014 IEEE congress on evolutionary computation (CEC). IEEE, pp 3238–3245
26. Zheng S, Li J, Janecek A et al (2017) A cooperative framework for fireworks algorithm. IEEE/ACM Trans Comput Biol Bioinform 14(1):27–41
27. Li J, Zheng S, Tan Y (2017) The effect of information utilization: introducing a novel guiding spark in the fireworks algorithm. IEEE Trans Evol Comput 21(1):153–166
28. Li J, Tan Y (2018) The bare bones fireworks algorithm: a minimalist global optimizer. Appl Soft Comput 62:454–462
29. Li J, Tan Y (2017) Loser-out tournament based fireworks algorithm for multi-modal function optimization. IEEE Trans Evol Comput 22(5):679–691
30. Imran AM, Kowsalya M (2014) A new power system reconfiguration scheme for power loss minimization and voltage profile enhancement using Fireworks Algorithm. Int J Electr Power Energy Syst 62:312–322
31. Bouarara HA, Hamou RM, Amine A et al (2015) A fireworks algorithm for modern web information retrieval with visual results mining. Int J Swarm Intell Res (IJSIR) 6(3):1–23

32. Shi J, Xu B, Zhu P et al (2016) Multi-task firework algorithm for cell tracking and contour estimation. In: 2016 International conference on control, automation and information sciences (ICCAIS). IEEE, pp 27–31
33. Mnif M, Bouamama S (2017) Firework algorithm for multi-objective optimization of a multimodal transportation network problem. Procedia Comput Sci 112:1670–1682
34. Taidi Z, Benameur L, Chentoufi JA (2017) A fireworks algorithm for solving travelling salesman problem. Int J Comput Syst Eng 3(3):157–162
35. Janecek A, Tan Y (2011) Iterative improvement of the Multiplicative Update NMF algorithm using nature-inspired optimization. In: Seventh international conference on natural computation, Shanghai, China, pp 1668–1672
36. Gao HY, Diao M (2011) Clutural firework algorithm and its application for digital filters design. Int J Model Ident Control 14(4):324–331
37. Xue J, Wang W, Meng X et al (2017) Binary reverse learning fireworks algorithm for solving multi-dimensional Knapsack problem. Syst Eng Electron 39(2):451–458 (in Chinese)
38. Cao L, Ye C, Huang X (2016) Application of chaotic fireworks algorithm to solve the problem of replacement flow shop. Comput Appl Softw 33(11):188–192 (in Chinese)
39. Bao X, Ye C, Huang X (2017) Study on solving JSP problem by fireworks algorithm. Comput Eng Appl 53(3):247–252 (in Chinese)
40. Liu C (2016) Research on fuzzy modeling method based on fireworks algorithm. Zhengzhou University (in Chinese)
41. Ye Z, Yuan M, Cheng S et al (2013) A new firefly explosive new immune planning algorithm for mobile robots. Comput Simul 30(3):323–326 (in Chinese)
42. Zhu X, Liu C, Guo Y (2015) Design of fuzzy classification system based on fireworks algorithm and differential evolution algorithm. J Zhengzhou Univ (Eng Sci Ed) 36(6):47–51 (in Chinese)
43. Huang W, Guo F (2017) Cloud computing multi-objective task scheduling based on fireworks algorithm. Comput Appl Res 34(6):1718–1720 (in Chinese)
44. Wu Q (2016) Positive and negative quantitative association rule mining algorithm based on multi-target fireworks algorithm. Nanchang University (in Chinese)
45. Wu Q, Zeng Q (2017) Association rules mining based on multi-objective fireworks algorithm. Pattern Recogn Artif Intell 30(4):365–376 (in Chinese)
46. Chen H, Qi L, Ye Z (2018) Otsu multi-valued image segmentation method based on fireworks algorithm. J Hubei Univ Technol 33(1):55–58 (in Chinese)
47. Yan L (2017) Application of fireworks algorithm in image processing. Hubei University of Technology (in Chinese)
48. Li X, Cui Y (2016) Fireworks clustering algorithm based on binary code. Appl Technol 43 (1):36–39 (in Chinese)
49. Zhang Y, Wu J, Zhao M et al (2016) Web service composition optimization based on improved fireworks algorithm. Comput Integr Manuf Syst 22(2):422–432 (in Chinese)
50. Ma W, Zhao Y, Zhang W et al (2018) Multi-UAV task assignment based on adaptive fireworks algorithm. Electro-Opt Control 1:37–43 (in Chinese)
51. Xu X, Liu Z, Wang Z et al (2015) The artificial bee colony algorithm paradigm of S-ABC-oriented service domain. Chin J Comput 38(11):2301–2317 (in Chinese)
52. Hong PN, Ahn CW (2016) Linkage artificial bee colony for solving linkage problems. Expert Syst Appl 61:378–385
53. Karaboga D, Kaya E (2016) An adaptive and hybrid artificial bee colony algorithm(a ABC) for ANFIS training. Appl Soft Comput 49:423–436

54. Wen S, Xia J, Gao R et al (2016) Improved artificial bee colony algorithm based optimal navigation path for mobile robot. In: 2016 12th World congress on intelligent control and automation, Guilin, China, pp 2928–2933
55. Ma R, Wu H, Ding L (2016) Optimization design of LQG/LTR control law for unmanned helicopter based on artificial bee colony algorithm. Control Decis Making 31:1–7 (in Chinese)
56. Hu R, Cheng T, Xu W et al (2016) Seismic reliability analysis of slope based on artificial bee colony algorithm. J Wuhan Univ (Eng Sci) 49(5):796–800
57. Kiran MS (2015) The continuous artificial bee colony algorithm for binary optimization. Appl Soft Comput 33(4):15–23
58. Zhuo T, Zhan Y (2014) Cloud computing resource scheduling model based on artificial bee colony algorithm. Microelectron Comput 31(7):147–151 (in Chinese)

Design of Multi-layer Industrial Internet of Data Mine Network Model Based on Edge Computation

Haibo Peng(✉), Qiaoshun Wu, Jie Li, and Rong Zhou

Yunnan KISC Electronic Information Technology Co., Ltd., Kunming 650302, China
79517483@qq.com

Abstract. The main role of edge computing in industrial systems is the absorption and screening of data, storage analysis, which maximizes efficiency. In this paper, we implement the multi-layer industrial IoT data mining network model design based on edge computing. In this design, the functional model and the architecture model design are mainly composed of two parts. The functional model design senses the data through various processes such as data acquisition devices, and then the MES system can transmit the collected data that is barrier-free, highly reliable, and highly secure. The architecture model design integrates all key sites into a network platform, adopts software and hardware comprehensive modeling, and multi-language hybrid development to establish an open bus network. In addition, the data transmission mechanism between each site adopts synchronous and asynchronous combination to effectively ensure normal data transmission. This design can be applied to many types of steel enterprise production, testing data requirements and changeable testing and analysis tasks, effectively solving the real-time, convenient and efficient process of data transmission, reducing the intensity of manual operations, and helping to improve profit. And the security of edge computing is very high, which is one of the reasons why it has won the favor of many large enterprises.

Keywords: Edge computing · Industrial Internet of Things · Heterogeneous data exchange · SCADA · MES

1 Introduction

Steel and Iron Industry is a typical process production enterprise with many bases, wide area, long process and wide product coverage. The raw materials and auxiliary materials involved are complex. Also, there are many intermediate products and the production process has strong continuity. Increasing market competition requires companies to respond promptly and correctly to rapidly changing markets and production conditions that may change at any time. Simply relying on a planned ERP system or PCS field automation system can't cope with such a severe challenge. As a

Z. Xu et al. (Eds.): CSIA 2019, AISC 928, pp. 1034–1040, 2020.
https://doi.org/10.1007/978-3-030-15235-2_137

bridge between the ERP system and the PCS system, the MES (Manufacturing Execution System) realizes the data flow from the customer order and sales expectations to the personnel, materials and control equipment of the production and processing control layer, and also controls the layer. The production information such as personnel equipment and operation task status is fed back to the ERP system, which realizes the traceability of the product, improves the production efficiency of the enterprise, reduces the production cost, and improves the competitiveness of the enterprise.

How to adjust the procurement, production and sales plan according to the changes of the target market, organize the materials and design quality to produce and manufacture according to the customer's order, timely check the product quality, record the logistics supply and material consumption in the production and manufacturing in real time, and keep the data running According to the material entering the factory/product delivery, segmentation process, monomer production equipment unit. And this whole above process of production and manufacturing, refined control execution is the key to the MES to meet the design requirements. A real-time, controllable, trusted, scalable, deep-integrated computing, communication, and control capability enables real-time traceability and dynamic monitoring of production data in multi-base, large-scale complex and wide-area environments to meet a variety of differences. The data mining system of data exchange is the prerequisite for achieving the above objectives.

2 Idea and Method

The first step in building a SCADA system that meets the requirements of the above MES system is to accurately understand the technical requirements of product process specifications, manufacturing, etc. according to the characteristics and conditions of the production activities of the enterprise, determine the scope of the system, clearly define the system functions, and formulate a clearly designed, researched documentation. In the second step, the core is to understand the system's functional characteristics in a fundamental way according to modern management ideas, extract business elements and convert them into system specifications, effectively design business process models, and build a strong information system architecture. The third step is to combine and develop advanced information technologies, including distributed computer parallel processing technology, integrated automation network technology, heterogeneous system data interface switching technology, sensor fusion technology, data structure, and digging as well as database application technology.

3 Design of Functional Model

Data Acquisition Perception. The on-site collection and sensing of production data mainly utilizes data acquisition devices, IC, multimedia information collectors, QR identification codes, real-time positioning technologies and other events and data in the acquisition process, and multi-sensor data fusion with various types of test and measurement sensors and the collaborate on data. For example, design a multi-protocol data acquisition device for quality and measurement data for steel companies, including communication physical devices, communication processing, serial port management, data processing and application protocol management functions, which can automatically perform communication serial port parameter matching and data processing application protocol automatically. Matching is beneficial to improve interface reliability and reduce interface maintenance workload, save enterprise cost, improve quality, and measure data effectiveness.

Network Data Transmission. The MES system requires that the collected production and inspection data can be transmitted without barriers, high reliability, and high security. This requires the sensor network to be integrated with various communication technologies such as mobile communication technology and industrial bus network. Aiming at the various kinds of production, testing data requirements and changing test analysis tasks of iron and steel enterprises, it can meet the data transmission requirements of MES private network, and design an automatic matching method for multi-objective multi-task for data transmission of steel enterprises, based on XML [4] (Extensible Markup, Language) to deal with data packet problem, which effectively solves the real-time, convenient and reduced manual operation of data transmission, ensures the real-time and integrity of data transmission, and improves the quality and efficiency of measurement data.

Application of Network Data Service. It mainly includes the application support platform interface program and application service interface of the system. The application supporting platform interface program supports data collaboration, sharing, and interworking between departments, applications, and systems. The application service interface includes processes such as production, inspection, and metering, as well as calling standards and protocols for data exchange with systems such as ERP and MES. The data network points for steel enterprises are widely distributed, the physical distance between data points is far, and the working environment is harsh. The change of data processing is often centered on the database, and other data points are treated as clients. Put a large amount of data analysis and calculations that need to occupy bandwidth on the data side for multi-source data fusion processing, realize edge calculation [6], and only carry out necessary data packet delivery, providing the most direct, accurate and reliable for mining the information contained in the data packet and data support service.

4 Logic of System Operation

The system running process is shown as Fig. 1.

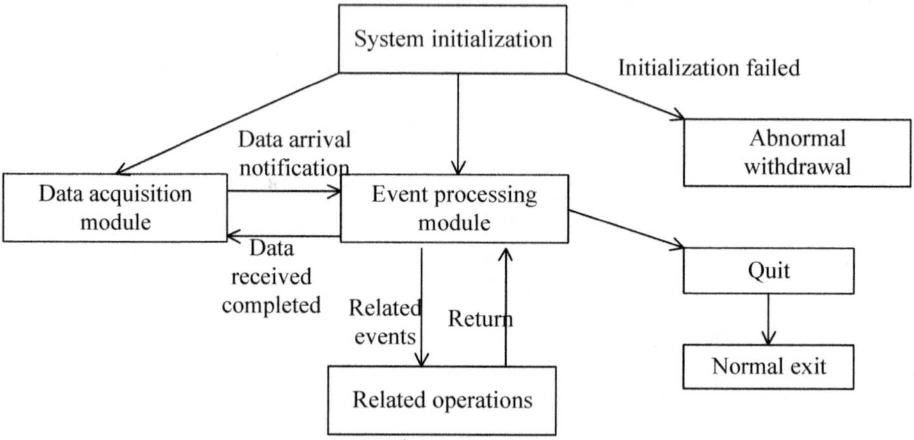

Fig. 1. Running system process

5 Architectural Model Design

Multi-layer industrial IoT [3, 9] data mining architecture model based on edge computing [7, 8] is based on enterprise information backbone network, industrial Ethernet backbone, industrial Internet of Things connected with production and testing equipment wireless sensor network, integrating all key sites into one network platform. The system forms a hierarchical and hierarchical network structure by the first, second and third level detection sites, and realizes various hardware device connections and interactive Internet of Things platforms of the enterprise base distribution units. On-site data collection and data management consists of a dedicated management computer station, operator station, engineering station and data collection station. The upper management level uses servers (including database server, WEB server, file server, etc.), personal computer terminals, and mobile terminals. The system private network uses industrial Ethernet as a technical standard, which is conducive to seamless connection and information sharing with the enterprise management network. Fieldbus and industrial Ethernet form a hybrid network. Various production and testing equipment, use the open fieldbus standard as the underlying communication interface. Industrial Ethernet is compatible with the largest number of hardware devices or subsystems to achieve flattening of production management. The wireless network segment and the wired network segment form a hybrid network, which overcomes the difficulty of field wiring and expands the application range of the distributed system. Using software and hardware integrated modeling, multi-language hybrid development, establishing a distributed open bus network structure, quantifying and extracting heterogeneous, spatio-temporal multi-dimensional information and measuring and verifying data device components; designing predictable data concentration and layering Storage technology, predictable real-time concurrency mechanism, customizable Web service technology, time/information-driven, publish/distribution mechanism; data acquisition and processing, data information is sent to the information layer via the network, and information layer components are targeted to the production process. Business and user requirements, configuration adjustments internal associations and applications.

In the overall structural design of the system, in order not to make the data server become the bottleneck of the system speed, the multi-region mode is adopted, which is divided into three levels. The overall structure of the system is shown as Fig. 2:

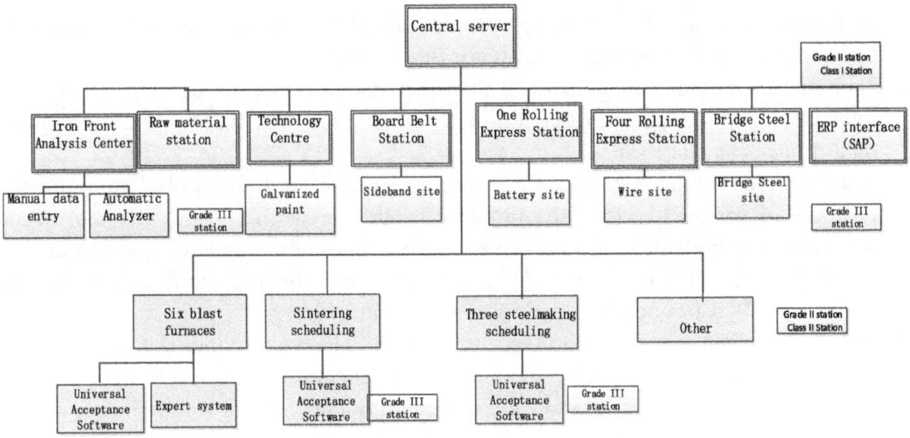

Fig. 2. Structural design of the system

The central site acts as the central data server for the central storage of all data, monitoring and data forwarding for each secondary site, and not directly communicating between the secondary stations, but through the central site for data exchange and sharing; Secondary-first site as a secondary data service site, the site receives data and messages sent from the input data uploaded by the third-level site and other secondary sites (including the secondary-first level site and the secondary-second level site), and simultaneously through the corresponding central site to other sites. The site sends data and messages manually or automatically; the secondary-second level site also serves as a secondary service site, and only receives data and messages sent from third-level site uploads and other secondary-first level sites for each quality. The management department provides comprehensive query and report service for quality data; the third-level site uploads various on-site data to the corresponding secondary site through the network, or queries analysis tasks and uploaded data information.

The way of data transmission between sites in the system is a combination of "push" and "pull". The so-called "push" means that once the underlying data generating site generates the latest data, or the station responsible for data forwarding receives the data information, it actively sends the data to the demanding data party; the so-called "pull" means the demand data unit, which can actively request data from the source data as needed. In addition, the inter-site data transmission mechanism adopts a combination of synchronous and asynchronous: since the data transmission result from the third level site to the second site has a direct impact on the next step of the third site, a synchronous transmission mechanism is adopted to ensure real-time data. Reliability of system and system operation; the central site and the secondary site do not have to be online at the same time during data transmission, and an asynchronous transmission mechanism can be adopted.

6 Key Technologies for Edge Computing

1. Develop a common data exchange protocol for data exchange and transmission for different systems or various links within the system.
2. To achieve unified management of data and standard data processing, to meet the interaction and management scheduling of production data, and to develop a unified data processing platform.
3. Multi-protocol data acquisition device. According to the serial communication protocol of various devices, the protocol header keyword and the protocol header keyword matching library are designed, the serial communication parameters and the data protocol are automatically matched, and the matching communication library is called to complete the communication process.
4. Data asynchronous transmission system. Aiming at asynchronous data transmission of remote unreliable circuits, hierarchical architecture of the designed data end (including the receiving end and the transmitting end), the processing end, and the data routing end. The data receiving end does not need to be always online, the transmitting end can send data at any time, the processing end performs data buffering, and the receiving end immediately transmits data when the receiving end is online; the receiving end sends a feedback signal to the transmitting end after receiving the data, and the transmitting end is certain The data is retransmitted when the feedback signal of the receiving end is not received within the time.
5. Automatic matching method for multi-target multi-task of data transmission. Mainly based on XML [10, 11], multi-objective data is packaged by matching the target information database, task data is packaged by matching the task information database, data packet is matched according to the type code of the number, and the data packet is transmitted through the network. Suitable for multi-site and multi-tasking needs.

7 Conclusion

The system design has the following advantages and effects: Today, the amount of data faced in the Internet of Things [1] application is extremely large, and the data transmission and interaction delay are very high. In order to be suitable for various data exchange and transmission, the system has developed a universal data exchange protocol. In order to achieve data unification and standards, a unified data processing platform was developed. It also uses a multi-protocol data acquisition device to transmit remote asynchronous data and receive data asynchronous transmission system, and data transmission automatic matching method. With the rapid development of the Internet of Things, edge computing [2] has become one of the most popular technologies, and his application has reduced the load on the cloud and greatly improved the efficiency. And it is safe and reliable, and there is no data loss problem when transmitting data remotely. The emergence of edge computing solves data latency and security issues. By controlling the device information flow and task status through the MES [5] system, it is possible to realize data transmission in a multi-base large-scale complex situation and a wide-area environment, which is beneficial to seamless connection and information sharing with the enterprise management network, and improves the production efficiency of the enterprise. This design is suitable for process production enterprises with wide coverage, variety and variety of materials, and a series of production processes with strong continuity. The design has a variety of heterogeneous data exchange data acquisition system, which collects application data and outputs structured data, with real-time, controllable, trusted, deep fusion computing, communication and control capabilities. The data collection and sensing application is beneficial to improve the interface and reduce the maintenance workload of the interface, save the enterprise cost, improve the effectiveness of quality and measurement data. Enterprises applying this design will increase the production efficiency of the enterprise, reduce the production cost, and improve the competitiveness of the enterprise.

References

1. Shi Y, Sun H, Cao J, Zhang Q, Liu W (2017) Edge computing: new computing model in the era of Internet of Everything. Comput Res Dev 5405:907–924
2. Guan X, Li W, Luo S (2018) Research on edge computing for Internet of Things. Inf Commun Technol Policy 07:53–56
3. Li S, Luo G (2014) Industrial IoT technology and application overview. Telecommun Netw Technol 03:26–31
4. Xie F, Ren W, Tang R (2004) XML-based heterogeneous data exchange integration technology and its implementation. Manufact Autom 04:1–4
5. Zhang Z (2004) Application and development of manufacturing execution system (MES) at home and abroad. Autom Expo 05:9–15+18
6. Song C (2017) Edge computing "No computing". Computer Word
7. Li D (2018) Edge computing architecture and key technologies. Autom Expo 3504:56–57
8. Wang L (2017) Application, architecture, capabilities and service challenges of edge computing. World Sci Technol Res Dev 3902:201
9. Wu Q, Kuang S, Peng H (2015) The design of quality and measurement control-execution system based on IOT bus. In: Proceedings of the 2015 Chinese intelligent automation conference, pp 531–540
10. Peng H, Wang X (2007) A method based on XML for creating EXCEL report in Java environment. MicroComputer Appl Technol 68:34–38
11. Wu Q, Peng H, Li J (2013) Design and application of custom dynamic report system. Mach Des Manuf Eng 42:80–82

Analysis and Research on Speech Enhancement Algorithms for Mobile Communication

Chunli Wang(✉) and Quanyu Wang

Department of Electronics and Information Engineering,
Lanzhou Jiaotong University, Lanzhou, Gansu Province, China
wcl@mail.lzjtu.cn

Abstract. In order to solve the problems of noise interference in mobile phone microphone array, the traditional algorithms and blind source separation algorithms are compared and analyzed to enhance the mobile speech. Under the conditions of unknown mobile communication environment, the blind source separation algorithm is adopted to solve the problem. The mixed matrix is derived from the observed signal and the needed source signal is obtained by the inverse matrix. The separation effect is good and the intelligibility of the separated speech is high.

Keywords: Microphone array · Blind source separation · Mixing matrix · Intelligibility

1 Introduction

Mobile communication environment is more complex, whether indoor or outdoor, in addition to the voice signal from the caller, there will be other people around the voice signal, the noise source is not a single, so the microphone array of mobile phone receives multiple signals aliasing. If we can separate the clear voice signal from this kind of aliasing signal, we can achieve the purpose of speech enhancement. The classical array speech enhancement algorithms include adaptive beamforming and blind source separation.

2 Adaptive Beamforming Algorithm

A microphone Array based speech Enhancement algorithm, also known as Linear constrained minimum Variance Beamforming (LCMV), proposed by Forst of the United States in the 1970s. This method keeps its gain unchanged in the direction of the desired signal and eliminates the noise by reducing the power of the output signal [1, 2]. On this basis, in 1980s, Grifiths and Jim put forward the concept of blocking matrix, and combined this matrix with Forst algorithm, the well-known generalized sidelobe canceller (GSC), was widely used because of its good noise suppression ability [3, 4].

Z. Xu et al. (Eds.): CSIA 2019, AISC 928, pp. 1041–1047, 2020.
https://doi.org/10.1007/978-3-030-15235-2_138

The GSC algorithm consists of three parts: one is a fixed beamformer, which is used to form a combined signal, the other is a blocking matrix, which is used to remove the desired speech signal and leave a noise signal. The third is the adaptive filter, through which the noise is removed further and the noise is eliminated [5, 6] (Fig. 1).

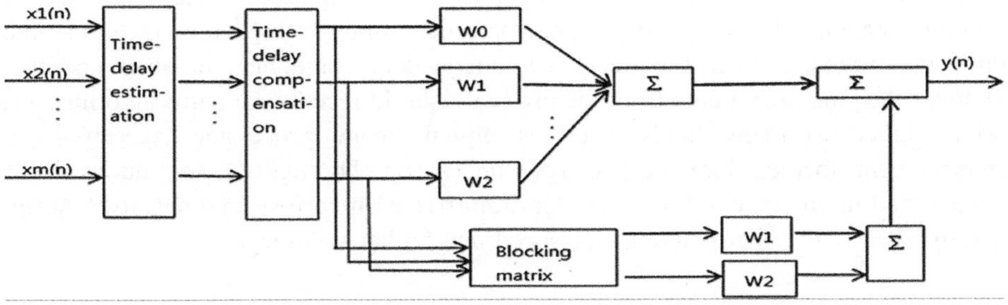

Fig. 1. Generalized sidelobe canceller structure

The implementation of the algorithm is as follows: first, the signal collected by the microphone array enters the fixed beamformer to form a composite signal. The other is the signal collected by the microphone array into the blocking matrix, the speech signal in the signal is blocked, and only the residual noise signal is left [7, 8]. The adaptive noise canceller estimates the noise components in the original signal according to the output of the blocking matrix. Finally, the enhanced speech signal can be obtained by subtracting the noise component from the synthetic signal. After the GSC algorithm, many improved algorithms are proposed, such as the TF-GSC algorithm based on acoustic transfer function [9, 10].

Although the performance of this algorithm is good, there are still some shortcomings. For example, when the number of noise sources is more than the number of microphone array elements, its ability to suppress noise will decrease. For mobile phone voice communication, the number of microphone array elements on mobile phone is usually not too many, but the noise source in the surrounding environment is obviously more than the number of array elements, so when GSC is applied to the speech enhancement of mobile phone microphone array, the effect is not very good.

3 Blind Source Separation Algorithm

In the speech enhancement method of microphone array, blind source separation is a rapid development in recent years. It can separate each signal (estimation of source signal) from the aliasing signal without any prior condition. The research of this algorithm started at the end of 1980s [11]. In the middle of 1990s, the independent component analysis (ICA) was proposed, which accelerated the development of this algorithm. Then the natural gradient algorithm proposed by Amari and others further improved the previous algorithm. Compared with the traditional speech enhancement algorithm, its advantage is that it is suitable for the environment with more unknown quantity, and can deduce the mixed matrix according to the observation signal, and calculate the needed signal according to its inverse matrix, and the separation effect is better.

The algorithm is divided into two steps, one is whitening and spheroidization, the other is orthogonal transformation. The separation methods are as follows: batch processing, processing directly according to the obtained speech data, adaptive processing, changing the processing parameters according to the different input data. Projection tracking process extracts the independent component in order and then removes the component data from the original data. In recent years, this algorithm has been applied to many fields, such as digital image processing, speech signal enhancement, medical biological analysis and so on. Through the continuous development and improvement, Fast ICA algorithm based on kurtosis and negative entropy has emerged with faster convergence speed and higher accuracy.

4 Simulation of Speech Enhancement Algorithm for Mobile Phone Based on Fast ICA

ICA's mathematical model is as following:

$$X(t) = AS_i(t) \qquad M \geq N \tag{1}$$

$$S_i(t) = [S_1(t), S_2(t), \ldots, S_N(t)]^T \tag{2}$$

$$X(t) = [X_1(t), X_2(t), \ldots X_M(t)]^T \tag{3}$$

$S_i(t)$ is the pure speech signal from each sound source without noise interference, t is the discrete time, A is the mixed matrix, $X(t)$ is the M observation signal. The goal of blind source separation is to estimate the original sound source signals at any t time, under the condition of an unknown, according to the existing observation signals.

If the noise is taken into account, if the ambient noise is $N_i(t)$, all kinds of noise constitute matrix $N(t)$, and let it be the noise matrix of K independent Gauss white noise, the observed signal is as follows:

$$X(t) = AS(t) + N(t) \qquad M \geq N \tag{4}$$

In the speech enhancement algorithm based on microphone array, the signal source can not be pure speech signal, and the noise can be expressed as:

$$S_i(t) = a_i(t) + n_i(t) \tag{5}$$

In the above formula, $a_i(t)$ is the first pure speech signal, $n_i(t)$ is the superposition noise signal. Finally, the best estimation. Fast ICA algorithm for noisy speech signal is obtained, as shown in Fig. 2:

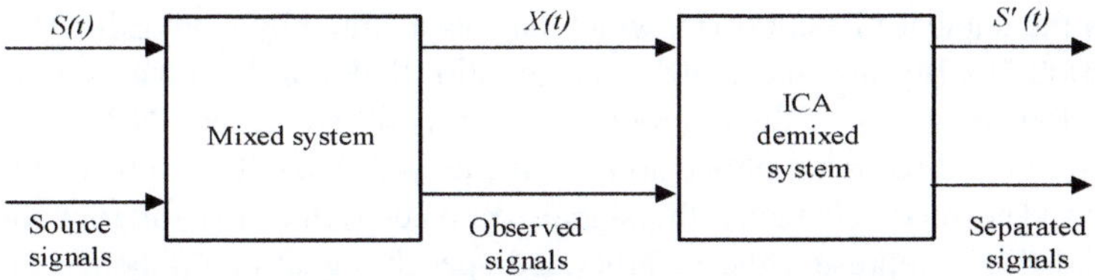

Fig. 2. Fast ICA algorithm schematic diagram

The flow of mobile phone speech enhancement algorithm based on microphone array is shown in Fig. 3.

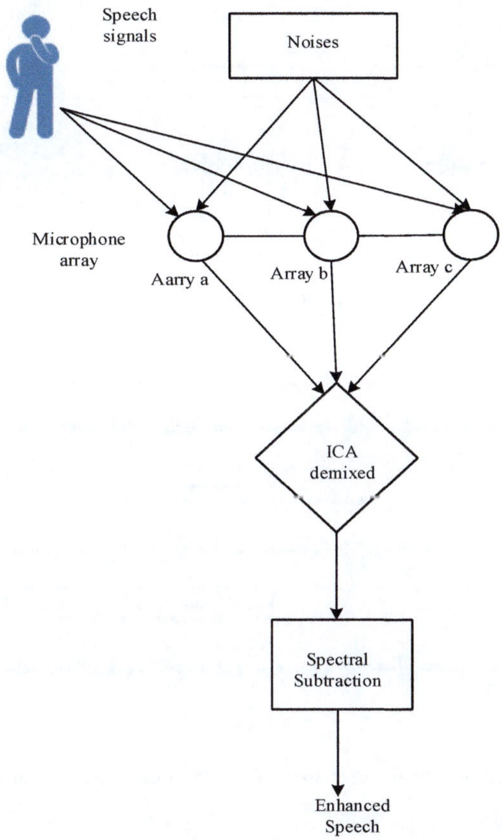

Fig. 3. Flow chart of speech enhancement algorithm based on microphone array

The speech signals used in this simulation experiment come from the Timit standard speech corpus. The sampling frequency is 16000 Hz. The selected noise is the noise signal from the noisex-92 standard noise database. The sampling rate of the noise signals in the database is 8,000 Hz, which has been edited by Cool Edit. The sampling rate is 16000 Hz. Because the signal to noise ratio (SNR) of the mixed signals received by the various elements of the microphone array is different, the SNR of the signal to noise ratio of the three microphone array elements is different by adjusting the signal to noise ratio. The mixi represents the signal received by the first microphone, and the noise-i and the xi represent the reverberated speech signal component and the noise component of the mixed signal received by the I microphone, respectively. The simulations are shown in Figs. 4 and 5.

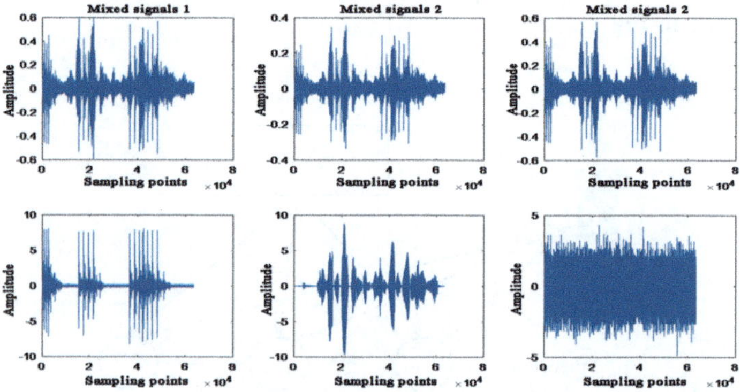

Fig. 4. ICA separation results

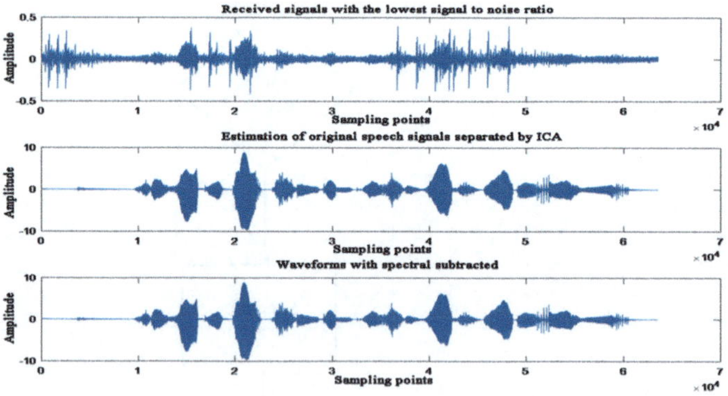

Fig. 5. Comparison of signals after spectral subtraction with separated signal waveforms

5 Comparison of Speech Enhancement Algorithms for Mobile Phones

The adaptive filtering method, especially the generalized sidelobe canceller, has complex structure and strong suppression ability to coherent noise. However, the algorithm requires a certain number of microphone elements, when the number of array elements is small, It will make the whole denoising effect worse, and when the incoherent noise is more, the applicability of the algorithm will become worse. The biggest advantage of blind source separation is that the noise signal can be separated from the speech signal without too much prior knowledge of the signal, and a better estimation of the original speech signal can be obtained. When the hardware performance can be satisfied, it is a better speech separation algorithm. The disadvantage is that the complexity of the algorithm is high (Table 1).

Table 1. Performance comparison of two algorithms

Algorithm	Advantages	Disadvantages
Adaptive beamforming algorithma	Good denoising performance	The number of microphones is related to the performance of the algorithm
Blind source separation algorithm	The separation ability is better and there is no need for too much priori condition	There is uncertainty in sorting separation signals

6 Conclusion

In the era of smart phone, the processing power of mobile phone chip has made a qualitative leap. The mobile phone has more and more functions and smaller size. It requires that the volume ratio of microphone array should not be too large, and generally it is appropriate to take 2 to 3 array elements. In the algorithm selection, we can choose some simple structure and moderate computation. For mobile phone speech communication, intelligibility is more important. Under the premise of ensuring intelligibility, it is the goal of mobile phone speech enhancement technology to maximize noise suppression, and many algorithms can suppress noise very well. However, the speech signal will be distorted and the intelligibility of the speech signal will be reduced. Therefore, through the analysis and comparison of various speech enhancement algorithms, the fast ICA algorithm based on blind source separation can be used as a speech enhancement algorithm for mobile phone microphone array.

References

1. Wan C (2017) Comparative study of typical near field beamforming methods for microphone arrays. Inner Mongolia University, Huhehaote (in Chinese)
2. Lei C (2016) Speech enhancement and realization of microphone array in noise background. Xiamen University, Xiamen (in Chinese)
3. Mao H (2005) Simulation and analysis of capon beamforming and spatial spectral algorithms based on Matlab 2(1):491–494 (in Chinese)
4. Zhang X (2016) Speech and audio coding, 2nd edn. Electronics Industry Press, Beijing (in Chinese)

5. Zhang X, Jia H (2011) Speech and audio coding. Xi'an University of Electronic Science and Technology Press, Xi'an (in Chinese)
6. Zhang Z (2011) Research and implementation of low-rate speech coding in single chip speech Cryptograph. Xi'an University of Electronic Science and Technology, Xi'an (in Chinese)
7. Cai Q, Liao Q, Jiang Z (2014) Research on signal processing of forming force based on wavelet transform and mean filter. Mach Tools Hydraulics 5:56–59 (in Chinese)
8. Zhong S (2014) Mathematical simulation experiment of double sliding window hysteresis algorithm for sinusoidal impulse signal. J Kunming Metall College 3:29–32 (in Chinese)
9. Huang H (2016) Detection of heart rate in motion state based on PPG signal. Southeast University, Nanjing (in Chinese)
10. Fu X (2015) Research on feedforward control of table active vibration isolation system based on LMS algorithm. University of Electronic Science and Technology, Chengdu (in Chinese)
11. Dong H (2016) Research on speech recognition based on spectral subtraction in noisy environment. Harbin Engineering University, Harbin (in Chinese)

Research on Three-Dimensional Localization Algorithm for WSN Based on RSSI

Yu Shi[1], Hua Liu[2(✉)], Weiyu Zhang[1], Yong Wei[1], and Jinfeng Dong[2]

[1] College of Engineering and Technology, Tianjin Agriculture University, Jinjing Ave., Tianjin 300384, China
[2] Student Center for Innovation and Entrepreneurship, Tianjin Agriculture University, Jinjing Ave., Tianjin 300384, China
syych83@tjau.edu.cn

Abstract. In recent years, with the wireless communication and electronic technology advances, making low-cost wireless sensor network WSN (Wireless Sensor Networks) technology has been greatly developed. It has a great impact on people's production and life, and is widely used in environmental, military, health care, agriculture, family, transportation and other business areas. Among them, the location information of the sensor nodes in the network has a very important role, for example, this location information can improve the routing efficiency and network topology self-configuration to provide support. Therefore, it is very important to study the sensor node localization technology in wireless sensor networks. In this paper, based on the RSSI value ranging algorithm, based on the study of weighted centroid localization algorithm, the algorithm is improved and the positioning accuracy is improved by adjusting the correction coefficient. The experiment is simulated on MTALAB R2014b, and the Gaussian filtering process is carried out. The influence of different correction coefficients on the positioning accuracy of the algorithm is discussed. The experimental results show that the improved algorithm achieves the purpose of improving the positioning accuracy of the nodes and has certain value in the application.

Keywords: Wireless sensor networks · RSSI · Weighted centroid localization · Algorithm improvement

1 Introduction

Wireless sensor network WSN (Wireless sensor network) is a large number of sensor nodes through the multi-hop, self-organized way. The sensors deployed internally can cooperate with each other to monitor the physical or environmental conditions such as temperature, sound, pressure, etc. throughout the area. With the development of electronic technology, Internet of things and cloud computing, WSN has been widely used in environmental and ecological monitoring, effective power monitoring, home automation and other civilian areas. In WSN technology, sensor node positioning technology plays a vital role. This location information can provide support for improved routing efficiency and self-provisioning of network topology. Therefore, if the location information of the target node can not be known, the related information to

Z. Xu et al. (Eds.): CSIA 2019, AISC 928, pp. 1048–1055, 2020.
https://doi.org/10.1007/978-3-030-15235-2_139

be monitored becomes meaningless. For all the sensor nodes such as China's Beidou, the United States' GPS and other receivers to obtain the specific location information of the sensor nodes, this approach is expensive to use, and not conducive to large-scale promotion and application.

It is realistic and important to locate the position information of the sensor nodes in three-dimensional space by means of research on three-dimensional positioning algorithm [1]. In view of one of the key technologies in WSN, so far, many methods have been proposed to solve the problem of node self-localization at home and abroad, such as the traditional APIT algorithm, DV-Hop algorithm and centroid algorithm proposed by foreign scholars [2]. Based on the traditional algorithm to improve the algorithm, many kinds of three-dimensional positioning algorithm are proposed. In the domestic research, Liu proposed to use the distance between the unknown node and the anchor node as the optimized weight factor, which can improve the convergence rate and adaptability of the algorithm [3]. The model proposed by Professor Li Peng's is superior to the traditional security location model in malicious node recognition and performance improvement [4]. How to improve the positioning accuracy and positioning efficiency effectively, become the key technical problems which the wireless sensor technology needs to solve. In this paper, by focusing on the centroid localization algorithm, use RSSI Ranging Technology to improve the algorithm based on the centroid localization algorithm. The improved algorithm can effectively improve the accuracy of positioning by data simulation.

2 Sensor Positioning Algorithm

Sensor node location is the main research direction of WSN. The principle is to rely on the anchor node location information in the network and wireless communication between nodes, to determine the location of unknown nodes in the network coordinates according to a positioning mechanism. For WSN node positioning technology research, national personnel have made a lot of results, put forward a number of different positioning algorithms. Among them, according to whether used the distance between the nodes in the positioning process, these positioning algorithms can generally be divided into two kinds. They are Range-Based positioning algorithm and Range-Free positioning algorithm [5, 6]. The Range-Based positioning algorithm needs to measure the distance or orientation between nodes using the actual distance to achieve positioning through a certain way. Range-Free localization algorithms include centroid algorithm and Approximate Point-in-triangulation Test (APIT) algorithm.

3 Analysis of Centroid Localization Algorithm Based on RSSI Value

In the WSN, the sensor nodes can communicate with each other. The anchor node will diffuse its own coordinates during the communication process. When the receiving node receives the signal, it will return the signal to the sending node, The transmitting node will get the RSSI value between it and the receiving node [7, 8].

RSSI ranging is based on the wireless signal propagation model, which can convert the power loss to the distance by comparing the transmit power and the received power. Its advantages are low power consumption, cost-effective; the disadvantage is vulnerable to external environmental impact. For many wireless signal propagation path loss models, we general use free space propagation model and log-normal distribution model [9, 10]. Due to the complexity of the actual environment, for any model, there is always an error in the RSSI value calculated by the model compared to the actual situation. The distance from the anchor node to the unknown node in the actual environment will always be greater than the true distance between the two nodes. As shown in Fig. 1, A, B, C is the three anchor nodes, D is an unknown node. According to the loss model $\mathrm{d_{AD}} = \mathrm{r_A}, \mathrm{d_{BD}} = \mathrm{r_B}, \mathrm{d_{CD}} = \mathrm{r_C}$. If the center of the hearts are A, B, C, use r_A, r_B, r_C as the radius for the circle. The resulting intersection area is ΔEFG. In this case, the basic idea of finding the position coordinates of the unknown node is to find the coordinates of the three points formed by the intersection of the three circles. These three points can form a triangle, we can see that the centroid of the triangle is the location of the unknown node coordinates. Here, the coordinates (x_e, y_e) of the intersection point E can be obtained by the following formula (1):

$$\begin{cases} \sqrt{(x_e - x_a)^2 + (y_e - y_a)^2} & \leq r_a \\ \sqrt{(x_e - x_b)^2 + (y_e - y_b)^2} & = r_b \\ \sqrt{(x_e - x_c)^2 + (y_e - y_c)^2} & = r_c \end{cases} \tag{1}$$

Similarly, find points $\mathrm{F}(\mathrm{x_f}, \mathrm{y_f})$, points $\mathrm{G}(\mathrm{x_g}, \mathrm{y_g})$. And the coordinates of the unknown point are obtained according to the centroid algorithm, which is $\left(\frac{x_a + x_b + x_c}{3}, \frac{y_a + y_b + y_c}{3}\right)$.

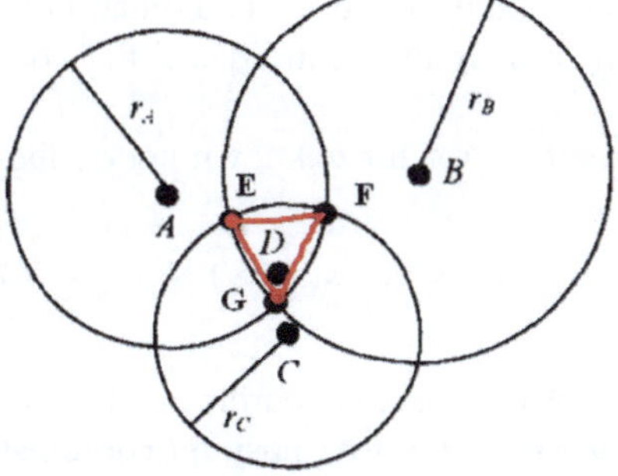

Fig. 1. The centroid algorithm in the actual environment

Centroid Location Algorithm Based on RSSI Value use RSSI technology to attenuate and convert the signal energy into the approximate distance between nodes in the network, so as to meet the ranging requirements of the algorithm without the need for additional network equipment. Combine with centroid localization algorithm to achieve positioning, which algorithm steps are as follows:

(1) The anchor node periodically transmits information containing the ID and its own position coordinates to the periphery. The node that received the message will take an average of the RSSI values from the same anchor node.
(2) Other nodes receive the information sent by some of the anchor nodes, after that, they will stop receiving information from other anchor nodes. The node then sorts the anchor nodes from large to small based on the received RSSI values. Get the following collection:

A collection of anchor nodes:

$$B\_set = \{a_1, a_2, \ldots, a_n\}$$

A collection of distances between unknown nodes and anchor nodes:

$$D\_set = \{d_1, d_2, \ldots, d_3\}, d_1 < d_2 < \cdots d_n$$

A collection of anchor nodes:

$$P\_set = \{(X_1, Y_1), (X_2, Y_2), \ldots, (X_n, Y_n)\}$$

(3) In order to improve the positioning accuracy, a large number of anchor nodes with large RSSI values must be selected from B_set to form a set. This collection is as follows:

$$T\_set = \{(a_1, a_2, a_3), \ldots (a_2, a_3, a_4), \ldots (a_3, a_4, a_5), \ldots\}$$

Then find the coordinates of each element in this set. We can get C_m^3 coordinates, among them, m is the number of selected anchor nodes, and $m < n$.
(4) Using the centroid algorithm to find the coordinates of the C_m^3 coordinates of the polygon, the coordinates of the centroid are the coordinates of the unknown nodes.
(5) Calculate the positioning error for unknown nodes, the formula is as follows:

$$error = \sqrt{(x_k - X)^2 + (y_k - Y)^2} \quad (2)$$

In the formula, (x_k, y_k) is the position coordinate of the unknown node obtained by the centroid algorithm, (X, Y) is the true position coordinates of the unknown node (Table 1).

The downside of this algorithm is that, after the anchor node is installed, there may be three anchor nodes, with which as the vertices of the interior of the triangle. There is a case where there is no unknown node. The farther the distance between the anchor node and the unknown node, the distance between the two is greater than the actual distance value according to the RSSI distance principle. The distance acquisition between the anchor node and the unknown node will produce a lot of error.

4 Improvement of Sublimation Algorithm Based on RSSI

4.1 Modified Weighted Centroid Localization Algorithm

The weighted centroid localization algorithm is modified by adjusting the weighting factor in order to change the dominant role of each anchor node to unknown nodes. If known, d_a, d_b, d_c is the distance between the anchor node and the unknown node, use $\frac{1}{d_a^{\beta}}, \frac{1}{d_b^{\beta}}, \frac{1}{d_c^{\beta}}$ as weighting factors. It can be seen that the anchor node, which is closer to the unknown node, has a greater effect. Such as the following formula:

$$x = \frac{x_a\left(\frac{1}{d_a^{\beta}} + \frac{1}{d_b^{\beta}}\right) + x_b\left(\frac{1}{d_b^{\beta}} + \frac{1}{d_c^{\beta}}\right) + x_c\left(\frac{1}{d_a^{\beta}} + \frac{1}{d_c^{\beta}}\right)}{2\left(\frac{1}{d_a^{\beta}} + \frac{1}{d_c^{\beta}} + \frac{1}{d_c^{\beta}}\right)} \tag{3}$$

$$y = \frac{y_a\left(\frac{1}{d_a^{\beta}} + \frac{1}{d_b^{\beta}}\right) + y_b\left(\frac{1}{d_b^{\beta}} + \frac{1}{d_c^{\beta}}\right) + y_c\left(\frac{1}{d_a^{\beta}} + \frac{1}{d_c^{\beta}}\right)}{2\left(\frac{1}{d_a^{\beta}} + \frac{1}{d_b^{\beta}} + \frac{1}{d_c^{\beta}}\right)} \tag{4}$$

Among them, β is a dynamic adjustment factor, when $\beta = 0$, the above formula is the basic centroid algorithm. Face different environment, reasonable arrange weight by adjusting β, in order to complete the estimation of the unknown node coordinates. This method can greatly improve the positioning accuracy.

4.2 Improved Algorithm Steps

(1) The anchor node periodically transmits information containing the ID and its own position coordinates to the surroundings. The unknown node that received the information will perform a Gaussian filtering process on the RSSI values from the same anchor node, which will take an average of the RSSI values from the same anchor node;

(2) The unknown node will take an average of these RSSI values after receiving some RSSI values from the same anchor node as the RSSI value received from this anchor node;

(3) The unknown node will stop receiving the information after receiving the information transmitted by some anchor nodes. Then the unknown node converts all the RSSI values it receives, according to the formula (5), into the distance value between the unknown node and the relevant anchor node. Finally, the reciprocal of the distance value is taken as the weighting factor;

$$PL(d) = \overline{PL}(d_0) + 10k\log_{10}\frac{d}{d_0} + X_\sigma \quad (5)$$

(4) Sort the distance values d from small to large, such as $d_1 < d_2 < \ldots < d_n$. We are most interested in is the three minimum distance value d_1, d_2, d_3. Suppose $A_1(X_1, Y_1)$, $A_2(X_2, Y_2)$, $A_3(X_3, Y_3)$ are the anchor node coordinates corresponding to the three minimum distance values, which can constitute ΔABC;
(5) The centroid of ΔABC is obtained by using the modified weighted centroid algorithm. The centroid is the position coordinates of the unknown node;
(6) Calculate the positioning error of the unknown node, the formula is as follows:

$$\text{error} = \sqrt{(x_k - X)^2 + (y_k - Y)^2} \quad (6)$$

Where (x_k, y_k) is the position coordinate of the unknown node obtained by the modified weighted centroid algorithm, (X, Y) is the true position coordinates of the unknown node.

Table 1. Related simulation data

Simulation platform	MATLAB R2014b
Simulation area	100 m × 100 m
Anchor node	100, Each communication radius is 20 m, distributed uniformly
Unknown node	50, distributed randomly

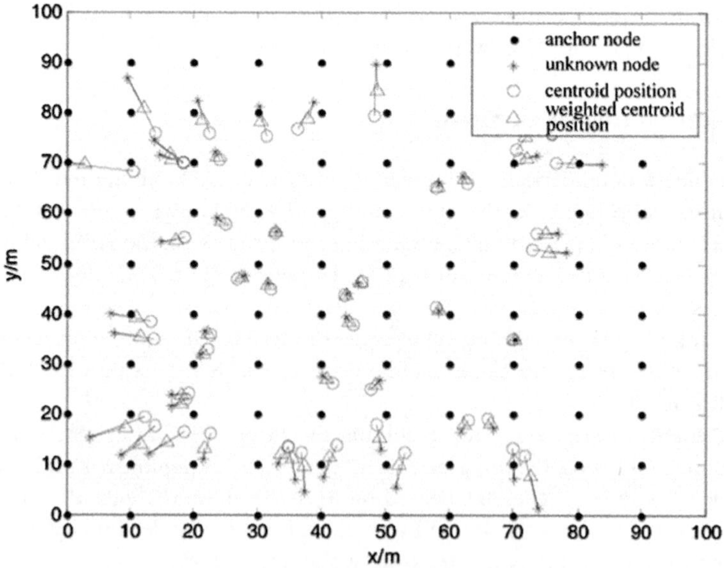

Fig. 2. Take the simulation results of $\beta = 1$

4.3 Simulation Results and Analysis

In order to replace the influence of obstacles, multipath and etc. in real environment, the Gauss noise with mean 0 and variance 6 is added in the simulation. The path loss index K takes value 2, according to the above algorithm step, the free space propagation model and the normal distribution model are simulated 100 times repeatedly, getting the average positioning error. The simulation result shows in Fig. 2.

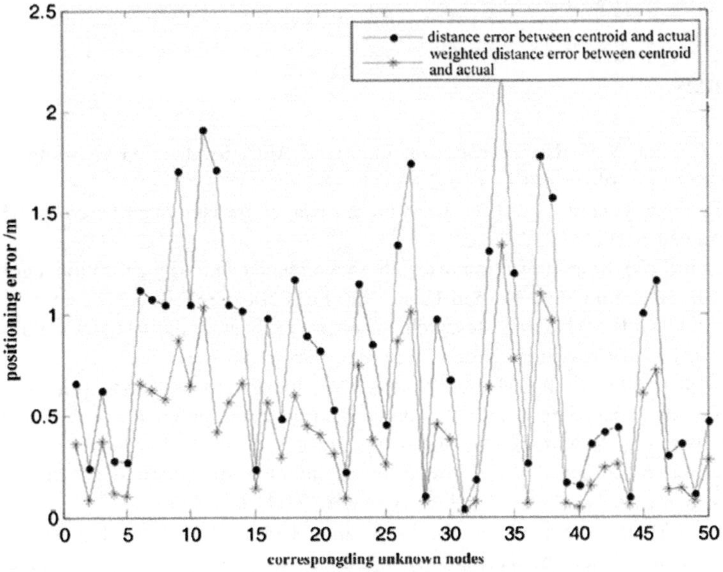

Fig. 3. Error curve of unknown node under condition $\beta = 1$

According to Fig. 3, it can be found that the location error of the traditional centroid algorithm is 0.8760 m, the average value of the location error of the revised algorithm is only 0.5848 m. Therefore, after adding the Gauss filtering model, the improved weighted centroid algorithm has higher localization accuracy than the traditional centroid localization algorithm.

5 Conclusion

Firstly, this paper briefly describes the structure knowledge, development status and practical application of wireless sensor networks (WSN), and then introduces some basic principles of localization algorithms. Among them, using the RSSI ranging technology, the centroid location algorithm is mainly analyzed; find that the selection of the weight has great effect on the positioning accuracy of the centroid localization algorithm. Finally, in order to further improve the positioning accuracy, the Gauss filter model is added to the weighted centroid localization algorithm during the simulation.

The simulation results show that this method can effectively improve the positioning accuracy. However, there is no location algorithm that can be applied to any environment. The algorithm in this paper is no exception, and the author's level is limited, and there are bound to be a lot of inadequacies, and I hope you can correct me.

Acknowledgments. This work was financially supported by Beijing-Tianjin-Hebei Science and Technology Achievements Transformation Project (17YFCZZC00330); Science and Technology Development Project of Wuqing District of Tianjin (WQKJ201715); Science and Technology Support Project of Tianjin (17YFZCNC00250).

References

1. Wang Z, Zhou X (2012) Research on improved AOA localization algorithm for wireless sensor network. Electron Des Eng 20(13):61–64
2. Zhen F, Zhan Z, Peng G (2007) Analysis of distance measurement based on RSSI. Chin J Sens Actuators 20(11):2526–2530
3. Liu Y, Liu J (2016) Optimization research on weighted centroid localization algorithm based on RSSI. J Central China Normal Univ (Nat. Sci.) 50(3):358–362
4. Li P, Yu X, Xu H et al (2017) Research on secure localization model based on trust valuation in wireless sensor networks. Secur Commun 1006–1015
5. T He, Huang CD, Blum BM (2003) Range-free localization schemes in large scale sensor networks. In: Proceeding of the 9th Annual International Conference on Mobile Computing and Networking, New York, NY, USA, pp 81–95
6. Liu XH, Li FM, Zheng P (2008) A distributed and range-free node localization algorithm in wireless sensor network. Chin J Sens Actuators 21(1):154–157
7. Zhang S (2010) A research on the localization technology of wireless sensor networks. University of Science and Technology of China
8. Zhang X Application and development of wireless sensor network [DB/OL]. 2014-08-01/2017-04-28
9. Arias J, Zuloaga A (2004) An RSSI Based Ad Hoc location algorithm. Microprocess. Microsyst. 28(5):403–405
10. Oka A, Lampe L (2010) Distributed target tracking using signal strength measurements by a wireless sensor network. IEEE J Sel Areas Commun 28(7):1006–1015

Intelligent Recognition System for High Precision Image Significant Features in Large Data Background

Kong Lu(✉)

Jiangxi Modern Polytechnic College, Nanchang 330095, Jiangxi Province, China
79364652@qq.com

Abstract. High precision image pattern recognition technology based on large data background is an important part of computer application technology. With the rapid development of digital image processing technology and pattern recognition technology, image pattern recognition technology has been applied more comprehensively in various fields. This paper briefly introduces image processing technology and its new development trend, focusing on image recognition technology and new development.

Keywords: Image features · Image intelligent recognition · Image processing

1 Introduction

With the development of social science and technology, the traditional image database retrieval technology can not meet the needs of people for image retrieval. The main reason is that the traditional method does not automatically and effectively describe image information, and the attribute annotation of image information needs a lot of manpower and material resources [1–3]. So the image retrieval technology, which combines image processing with computer vision technology and pattern recognition technology, content-based image retrieval technology, has become one of the hotspots of domestic and foreign research. Image processing technology is the technology of processing image information by computer [4–6]. It mainly includes image digitization, image enhancement and restoration, image data coding, image segmentation and image recognition [6–8]. One of the key technologies of content-based image retrieval is image feature extraction. At present, the extraction of image underlying features such as color, texture, shape, spatial relationship and so on is a more commonly used feature extraction method [9]. But the above methods of feature extraction have some limitations, so the research of feature extraction methods has become a hot spot [10–13]. Image is the main source for human to obtain and exchange information. Therefore, the application field of image processing inevitably involves all aspects of human life and work. Various algorithms of image recognition are constantly proposed and improved, which promotes the development of recognition system. [14–16]. Image segmentation is a key technology in image processing. At present, the research has a history of several decades, and people have always attached great importance to it. Up to now,

Z. Xu et al. (Eds.): CSIA 2019, AISC 928, pp. 1056–1062, 2020.
https://doi.org/10.1007/978-3-030-15235-2_140

thousands of segmentation algorithms have been proposed by virtue of various theories, and the research in this area is still active [17–19].

2 Significance of Intelligent Recognition of Image Features in Large Data

With the rapid development of multimedia technology and the World Wide Web, it is an urgent problem to retrieve the image information people need from the massive image data. Different from traditional text-based image retrieval methods, content-based image retrieval has become a new technology for efficient management and retrieval of large-scale multimedia databases. Content-based image retrieval is based on computer vision and image understanding and image analysis. It involves information retrieval, image processing, pattern recognition, computer graphics and database management. And many other aspects of technology. Content-based image retrieval is a hot research topic in the field of image information retrieval in recent years. With the rapid development of computer and network technology, people come into contact with more and more information. Especially since the development of multimedia technology, besides text information, people are facing more pictures, video and audio information. These massive non-text information is increasingly applied to all aspects of life. Compared with the text description information, people are more likely to get the information they want from pictures, videos and audio. Massive pictures and video information are absolutely dominant in the development of information technology. Effective organization, expression, storage, management and retrieval of these information become a key technology. The mathematical essence of image recognition problem belongs to the mapping problem from pattern space to category space.

3 Analysis of Intelligent Recognition of Image Characteristics

With the development of information technology, great progress has been made in image feature analysis, image fusion, image classification, image recognition and content-based image retrieval. These image processing technologies reflect human intelligence activities, and imitate, extend and expand human intelligence on the computer. They have intelligent processing functions, so they are called intelligent image processing technology. These intelligent technologies in image processing are developed on the basis of the traditional technology of image processing. Taking the traditional image processing technology as the pretreatment technology is the inevitable trend of the intelligent development of image processing. They can better meet the needs of human information processing.

3.1 Image Features

Image feature analysis and extraction is the basis of intelligent image processing. Commonly used image features include color, texture and shape. At present, the description of image content mainly uses the characteristics and combinations of images. High-precision image features include edges, angles, regions and ridges. Edge is the pixel that constitutes the boundary or edge between two image regions. Generally, the shape of an edge can be arbitrary and may include intersections. In practice, edges are generally defined as a subset of points with large gradients in an image. Some commonly used algorithms also link points with high gradients to form a better description of edges. These algorithms may also impose some limitations on edges; angle is a point-like feature of an image, and it has two-dimensional structure locally. Later, it is sometimes possible to find regions with the same angular characteristics where there are no corners in the image; regions differ from corners in that they describe a regional structure in an image, but regions may only consist of one pixel, so many region detection can also be used to detect corners. An area monitor detects an area in an image that is too smooth for an angle monitor. Region detection can be imagined as narrowing an image and then angular detection on the narrowed image; a long strip object is called a ridge. In practice, ridges can be regarded as one-dimensional curves representing symmetrical axes, in addition to having a ridge width locally for each ridge pixel. It is more difficult to extract ridges from gray gradient images than edges, corners and regions.

3.2 Image Fusion

Image fusion is the technology of spatial registration of the same object image data acquired by different types of sensors. Then a certain algorithm is used to combine the information advantages or complementarities contained in each image data to produce new image data. This new data has a better information representation to describe the object under study, and can be reduced or suppressed compared with a single information source. The information provided by various information sources can be utilized to the maximum extent for the ambiguity, incompleteness, uncertainty and errors that may exist in the interpretation of the perceived object or environment.

3.3 Image Recognition

Image recognition is the use of computers to identify objects in images and classify them as shown in Fig. 1. Machine intelligence is used instead of human intelligence. For example, the identification and classification of parts and components in mechanical processing; the identification of crops, forests, lakes and military facilities from remote sensing images; the accurate forecast of weather from meteorological observation data or meteorological satellite photos; the judgement of whether cancer occurs from X-ray photographs; the judgement of whether the examinee suffers from heart disease from the waveform of electrocardiogram; the realization of traffic control in traffic centers; and Identify vehicles and drivers who are driving in violation of regulations, etc.

3.4 Content-Based Image Retrieval

Content-based image retrieval is based on the semantic and perceptual features of the image. Specific implementation is to extract specific information clues or feature indicators from image data, and then search from a large number of images stored in the image database according to these clues to retrieve image data with similar features. Compared with the traditional keyword-based database retrieval methods, it has the characteristics of similarity retrieval, Approximate Retrieval and set restriction which requires the retrieval results to be given.

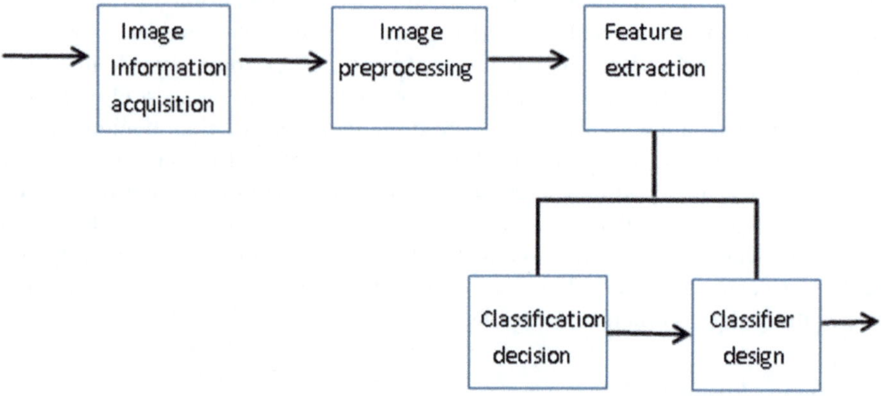

Fig. 1. Composition of image recognition system

4 Image Processing Technology

Image processing technology includes denoising, enhancement, segmentation, feature extraction, comparison and so on. The process of image recognition and retrieval completed in this paper is closely related to image segmentation. In a word, image processing technology is a technology that uses computer to process image information. It mainly includes image digitization, image enhancement and restoration, image data coding, image segmentation and image recognition.

4.1 Basic Concept of Image Segmentation

Image segmentation, generally the segmentation of exponential image, is the process of dividing the whole image into disjoint regions. The main idea is to cluster the image pixels according to the similarity criteria of some features or feature sets in the digital image target, divide the image into meaningful regions, reduce the amount of data contained in the image and retain the structural feature information of the image target, which is convenient for later image processing. The subsequent process includes the reduction of the amount of data of the target, and at the same time. Retain the feature information of the target structure.

4.2 Basic Theory of Image Segmentation

Image segmentation is to extract a specific object or part of the image that people are interested in. Image segmentation is one of the most basic steps in computer image processing. The quality of segmentation directly affects further image processing and analysis, and even further image recognition and understanding. Image segmentation is the process of dividing images into non-overlapping regions, and the definition of image segmentation. The segmented parts are all derived from the image and all parts are combined into one equal to the image. The segmented parts are independent and disjoint, and the segmented parts are all connected regions.

4.3 Common Methods of Image Segmentation

Image segmentation has always been attached great importance, and many segmentation methods have been proposed. Current segmentation methods include threshold segmentation, pixel segmentation, color segmentation, region-based growth method and so on. At present, there is no unified optimal segmentation algorithm for all fields. Each segmentation algorithm has its own scope of application. Different types of images need to adopt different segmentation algorithms. The most commonly used method of image segmentation is threshold segmentation, that is, by setting appropriate threshold, the object and background in the image are separated, through which the gray image is transformed into a binary black-and-white image. There are many methods to select the appropriate threshold.

5 Intelligent Recognition of High Precision Image Features

5.1 Intelligent Extraction of Image Features

Feature extraction is a concept in computer vision and image processing. It refers to the use of computers to extract image information and determine whether each image point belongs to an image feature. The result of feature extraction is to divide the points on the image into different subsets, which often belong to isolated points, continuous curves or continuous regions. A method of transforming a set of measurements of a mode to highlight the representative characteristics of the mode. The method of extracting the required features through image analysis and transformation.

5.2 Software Implementation of Image Recognition System

The software part of the image target recognition system is mainly divided into three modules: image processing module, recognition and classification module, stereo matching and positioning module. The image from the visual sensor enters the image processing module. Through image preprocessing and feature extraction, a joint feature vector about image features is obtained. After the joint feature vector enters the recognition and classification module, the recognition and classification are carried out. The recognition results are input into stereo matching and positioning module for stereo matching and positioning, and the three-dimensional coordinates of the target to be recognized are obtained.

5.3 Neural Network Intelligent Recognition System

The artificial neural network method based on neural network can deal with some problems such as complicated environmental information, unclear background knowledge and unclear reasoning rules. It allows samples to have larger defects and distortions. The disadvantage of the neural network method is that its model is constantly enriched and improved. At present, there are not enough pattern classes that can be recognized, and the neural network method allows samples to have more. It has large defect and distortion, fast running speed, good adaptive performance and high resolution. The image recognition system based on neural network is a kind of pattern recognition system based on neural network, and its principle is consistent. General neural network image recognition system consists of preprocessing, feature extraction and neural network classifier. Preprocessing is to delete, smooth, binarize and normalize the useless information in the original data. The feature extraction part of the neural network image recognition system does not necessarily exist, so it can be divided into two categories: the feature extraction part and the non-feature extraction part.

5.4 Image Intelligent Recognition Algorithms

The research of intelligent algorithm began in the early 1990s. Its basic idea is to draw lessons from and make use of the principle of survival of the fittest in natural phenomena, and to survive according to the adaptability of organisms to nature. The algorithm has parallelism. Intelligent algorithm is a random search algorithm based on biological intelligence. At present, typical intelligent algorithms include genetic algorithm, evolutionary algorithm, neural network, immune algorithm, ant colony algorithm, particle swarm optimization algorithm and its hybrid intelligent optimization algorithm. These intelligent algorithms simulate natural processes and have unique advantages in solving global optimal problems. Intelligent algorithms have broad application prospects, and there are many applications in image processing. Here we introduce two intelligent algorithms, genetic algorithm and artificial neural network.

6 Summary

Content-based image description, i.e. feature extraction, is a special focus and difficulty in the field of computer vision. At present, there are some related extraction methods, such as color feature, texture feature, shape and spatial relationship feature. The research on feature extraction has been a hot topic for many scholars. Intelligent optimization technology in image processing is particularly important. Image processing includes image denoising, enhancement, segmentation, edge extraction, feature extraction and recognition. The development of image processing has experienced a process from exploration to maturity. The amount of information to be processed in image processing is large, and there are many related technologies in image processing. It is very advantageous to introduce intelligent technology into image processing. Intelligent technology combines with traditional image processing technology and achieves good results that traditional image processing methods can not get. This new method attempts to broaden the new ideas of image processing methods. At present, more and more new technologies are applied to image processing, which should be paid attention to and studied deeply.

References

1. Jia X, Kuo BC, Crawford MM (2013) Feature mining for hyperspectral image classification. Proc IEEE 101(3):676–697
2. Dennis J, Tran HD, Chng ES (2013) Image feature representation of the subband power distribution for robust sound event classification. IEEE Trans Audio Speech Lang Process 21(2):367–377
3. Arashloo SR (2014) Class-specific kernel fusion of multiple descriptors for face verification using multiscale binarised statistical image features. IEEE Trans Inf Forensics Secur 9(12):2100–2109
4. Chen B, Ling C, Chen Y (2013) Efficient ant colony optimization for image feature selection. Sig Process 93(6):1566–1576
5. Kang X, Li S, Benediktsson JA (2014) Feature extraction of hyperspectral images with image fusion and recursive filtering. IEEE Trans Geosci Remote Sens 52(6):3742–3752
6. Grilo CM (2013) Why no cognitive body image feature such as overvaluation of shape/weight in the binge eating disorder diagnosis? Int J Eat Disord 46(3):208–211
7. Mckenna SJ (2014) Full body image feature representations for gender profiling
8. Yang Q, Li L, Zhang J et al (2014) A computerized global MR image feature analysis scheme to assist diagnosis of breast cancer: a preliminary assessment. Eur J Radiol 83 (7):1086–1091
9. Qin Z, Yan J, Ren K et al (2014) Towards efficient privacy-preserving image feature extraction in cloud computing. In: ACM International Conference on Multimedia
10. Jie J, Li X, Zhang G (2014) SIFT hardware implementation for real-time image feature extraction. IEEE Trans Circuits Syst Video Technol 24(7):1209–1220
11. Lategahn H, Beck J, Kitt B et al (2013) How to learn an illumination robust image feature for place recognition. In: Intelligent Vehicles Symposium
12. Hu Z (2013) Intelligent road sign inventory (IRSI) with image recognition and attribute computation from video log. Comput - Aided Civil Infrastruct Eng 28(2):130–145
13. Ali L, Hussain A, Li J et al (2014) Intelligent image processing techniques for cancer progression detection, recognition and prediction in the human liver. In: IEEE Symposium on Computational Intelligence in Healthcare & E-health
14. Jiang Z, Yang P, Liu S et al (2014) Study on intelligent image recognition for the tube welding defects in pressure vessels. Chin Weld 23(1):64–69
15. Lai H, Zhong J, Ying H (2014) Intelligent processing of computer image recognition application analysis. In: IEEE Workshop on Electronics, Computer & Applications
16. Wang X, Luo H (2013) Research on image recognition algorithm for a new type of intelligent ammeter system. In: International Conference on Digital Manufacturing & Automation
17. Milan S, Roger B, Vaclav H (2014) Image processing, analysis, and machine vision. J Electron Imaging xix(82):685–686
18. Ragan-Kelley J, Barnes C, Adams A et al (2013) Halide: a language and compiler for optimizing parallelism, locality, and recomputation in image processing pipelines. ACM Sigplan Not 48(6):519–530
19. Walt SVD, Schönberger JL, Nuneziglesias J et al (2014) scikit-image: image processing in Python. PeerJ 2(2):e453

Research and Guidance on the Use of New Media by Grassland Herdsmen in the Big Data Era

Yan Cui[1,2](✉)

[1] Faculty of Arts, Shaanxi Normal University, Xi'an, China
cuiyinhe66@sina.com
[2] Inner Mongolia University for Nationalities, Tongliao, China

Abstract. With the rapid development of economy and technology, new media has been widely promoted in urban and rural areas. The popularity of the Internet and smart phones especially increase the rate of communication among people. The combination of new media and communication technology brings mass communication into a new lane of development. For the northern prairie nomads whose economic development is slightly backward, it is necessary to make a intensive study on how the new media is used, what problems appear in the popularization process, and what impact it has on herdsmen's interpersonal communication, family life and national culture. So as to better understand the situation of the cultural transmission of farmers and herdsmen in grassland area. To formulate corresponding policies and promote the development of grassland national culture.

Keywords: Grassland pastoral area · New media · Internet

With the systematization and deepening of grassland culture research, on one hand, academic attention focuses more on the modern characteristics of grassland culture and the innovation of grassland culture, on the other hand, it turns to the inheritance and development of grassland culture. More and more scholars have realized that culture and communication are originally interactive and integrated relations. The formation and development of culture are inevitably affected by communication. It is communication that contributed to cultural integration, cultural proliferation, cultural accumulation, cultural stratification, cultural change and "homogenization" of culture [1]. This paper's research is based on the data of several herdsmen villages in Mongolian Autonomous County of Qian Gorlos. Mongolian Autonomous County of Qian Gorlos belongs to Songyuan City, Jilin Province, China. It is the only Mongolian Autonomous County in Jilin Province. From ancient times to modern times, this area belongs to the northern grassland corridor. Many villages under the jurisdiction of this county still maintain the traditional Mongolian herdsman culture. Some villages still use family animal husbandry as the main economic source. Therefore, the investigation on the former villages in this county is helpful to better understand the use of Internet and new media by the villagers. In this investigation, 20 complete questionnaires were collected by direct interviews and questionnaire survey. The contents of the questionnaire were input into SPSS software, and descriptive statistics were made by frequency statistics method. The data distribution can be observed intuitively. The gender distribution is as follows: (Fig. 1)

Z. Xu et al. (Eds.): CSIA 2019, AISC 928, pp. 1063–1069, 2020.
https://doi.org/10.1007/978-3-030-15235-2_141

Your gender

	Frequency	Percentage	Effective percentage	Cumulative percentage
Male	12	60.0	60.0	60.0
Famale	8	40.0	40.0	100.0
Total	20	100.0	100.0	

Fig. 1.

Among the 20 samples, 60% of them have a junior high school education or below, 20% of them have a senior high school education and their age are below 30 years old. All of the 20 samples are mainly engaged in animal husbandry or family animal husbandry.

1 Basic Situation of the Use of New Media by Grassland Herdsmen

Grassland herdsmen are limited by many factors in their specific area of life, such as remote geographical environment, backward technology, shortage of talents, and the current situation of industrialization in agricultural and forestry areas. Because the transportation is not very convenient in grassland area and herdsmen's cultural knowledge level is low, there are obvious differences between grassland area and developed area in people's acceptance and re-dissemination of information. For a long time, grassland herdsmen relied on interpersonal communication and organizational communication for information transmission. In recent years, the state has given policy, financial, material and information support to ethnic minorities. In the northern grassland area, the network signals have been fully covered. Herdsmen can use mobile phones to watch television and other video programs. Although 100% of the 20 herdsmen did not have broadband access in their homes, they could use touch-screen smartphones to access the Internet. The number of people with smartphones is 13, accounting for 65% of the total, and 75% of them spend less than 4 h a week surfing the Internet on average (Fig. 2).

How many hours do you spend online every week on average?

	Frequency	Percentage	Effective percentage	Cumulative percentage
4	9	42.9	75.0	75.0
6	2	9.5	16.7	91.7
8	1	4.8	8.3	100.0
Total	12	57.1	100.0	
Omission	9	42.9		
Total	21	100.0		

Fig. 2.

2 The Impact of New Media on Herdsmen's Life

2.1 The New Media Has Changed the Interpersonal Communication Among Grassland Herdsmen

Grassland culture is different from the Han culture, and it has diversity, which is fully reflected in the daily life of herdsmen. For example, Mongolian people usually toast each other in ceremonies, festival gatherings and normal interpersonal communication. If there are guests coming from afar, Hada will be presented as a representative of respect. Although these traditional interpersonal behaviors still exist in many areas, they have been greatly weakened. At present, only a few grassland minority areas with tourism as the main industry still retain such customs. Most herdsmen have gradually learned to use new media for interpersonal communication. The subjective judgments of the 20 herdsmen surveyed on the role of various media are as follows:

Which mode of communication has a greater impact on you?

	Frequency	Percentage	Effective percentage	Cumulative percentage
Television	5	25.0	25.0	25.0
Newspaper	1	5.0	5.0	30.0
Mobile phone	12	60.0	60.0	90.0
Internet	1	5.0	5.0	95.0
Broadcast	1	5.0	5.0	100.0
Total	20	100.0	100.0	

Fig. 3.

Figure 3 shows that 60% of herdsmen think that mobile phone have a greater impact on their lives, followed by television. As the most important means of communication, mobile phone plays a relatively important role in the daily life of herdsmen. After entering the information society, the ways of communication among people are becoming more and more diversified. The new media shorten the distance among people and break the restriction of interpersonal communication of grassland people originally because of their geographical relationship. Television is used to receive information, mobile phone is used to communicate with people. With the change of mobile terminals and the trend of digital media, herdsmen have more and more varied choices. New media's way of communication is special. It does not need paper, or any time limit for layout, printing and broadcasting. This efficient communication ensures that herdsmen can receive information in a timely manner. Its rapid development and abundant information forms contain a large number of pictures, texts, sounds and images. Various kinds of information not only expand the topic of people's communication, but also expand the scale of interpersonal communication. When young people use smartphones, dating software such as QQ and Wechat win their favor at the same time, which is also one of the important reasons why grassland people can not leave the new media.

2.2 While the New Media Refines the Audience, It also Increases the Misunderstanding of Communication

Figure 4 shows that the most trusted media for herdsmen is still television. Although the number of people who trust mobile media is not few, the credibility of new media is still worse than that of traditional media. While facilitating interpersonal communication, the new media also separates interpersonal communication into small social circles, clearly dividing the generation gap between the new generation and the old generation. This refined interpersonal communication makes the older generation unable to use new media such as Internet and mobile phone because of the influence of traditional culture and their limited knowledge level, but the younger generation can not do anything without mobile phone. The five herdsmen who trusted in mobile media were all under 30 years old, while the older generation of herdsmen preferred the television and believed that television was the most trustworthy media. In this case, the emotional changes between the young herdsmen and the old herdsmen can not be transformed through the new media, and their communication misunderstanding and information distortion become inevitable.

Which media do you trust the most?

	Frequency	Percentage	Effective percentage	Cumulative percentage
Television	8	40.0	40.0	40.0
Newspaper	3	15.0	15.0	55.0
Mobile phone	5	25.0	25.0	80.0
Internet	3	15.0	15.0	95.0
Broadcast	1	5.0	5.0	100.0
Total	20	100.0	100.0	

Fig. 4.

2.3 The Emergence of New Media Affects Herdsmen's Consumption Habits

By investigating the impact of the emergence of new media on herdsmen's lives, we get the statistical results as shown in Fig. 5. About half of the herdsmen believe that the emergence of new media such as the Internet and mobile phones has affected their lifestyle and consumption psychology, such as diet, consumption demand and popularization of scientific knowledge. 20.5% of herdsmen think that the new media can provide timely commodity information and play a guiding role in shopping and consumption. Other 25.6% of herdsmen think that the new media can only change their inherent habits occasionally. With the improvement of herdsmen's overall living standard, herdsmen's consumption also shows a rapid growth trend. According to relevant statistics, the per capita consumption of grassland herdsmen in Inner Mongolia Autonomous Region increased from 577.1 yuan in 1986 to 6164.4 yuan in 2018, which is an increase of 5587.3 yuan or an increase of 10.68 times [2]. With the emergence of new media, the way of life and consumption of herdsmen have gradually changed. The traditional market can no longer meet the needs of farmers and herdsmen. Some young herdsmen prefer to watch commodity advertisements through TV or other media, while a small number of herdsmen prefer to use Internet shopping to satisfy their consumption needs. The variety of commodities published by new media not only meets the herdsmen's choice, but also can fundamentally reduce the cost of commodities by means of new media shopping. Many elderly herdsmen say that even if they do not buy online, young people in their families have experienced online shopping. Influenced by the new consumption pattern, Mongolian herdsmen's consumption culture began to change. It is obvious that the traditional national consumption products have been replaced by modern popular products. Some hand-made food, clothing and other food and clothing cultures have no trace on the younger generation.

What kind of impact do you think network media and mobile media bring to your life? [a]

	Response		
	N	Percentage	Percentage of observed value
It can provide timely information about goods and play a guiding role in shopping and consumption.	8	20.5%	47.1%
It can affect my lifestyle and consumption psychology, such as diet, consumption and other needs, the popularization of scientific knowledge.	17	43.6%	100.0%
It can provide cultural and artistic appreciation.	4	10.3%	23.5%
It can change my inherent habits.	10	25.6%	58.8%
Total	39	100.0%	229.4%

a. Dichotomy Groups tabulated at Value 1.

Fig. 5.

3 Suggestions on the Development of New Media in Grassland Pastoral Area

3.1 New Media Should Be Used to Information Alleviate Poverty

As shown in Fig. 6, 45% of the 20 herdsmen surveyed use mobile phones to get news and 35% depend on watching TV to get all kinds of information. For a long time, grassland pastoral area has been in a disadvantaged position in the process of information dissemination because of the remote geographical environment and imperfect infrastructure. After the reform and open, the state has implemented various poverty alleviation plans and achieved remarkable results. However, with the acceleration of social modernization, the imbalance between information demand and supply in grassland area appears from time to time. Therefore, more attention should be paid to the effect of new media in information dissemination. If mobile phone usage is popularized, herdsmen can use mobile phones to access the Internet to understand all kinds

What media do you usually use to get all kinds of information?

	Frequency	Percentage	Effective percentage	Cumulative percentage
Television	7	35.0	35.0	35.0
Newspaper	2	10.0	10.0	45.0
Mobile phone	2	10.0	10.0	55.0
Internet	9	45.0	45.0	100.0
Broadcast	20	100.0	100.0	
Total	7	35.0	35.0	35.0

Fig. 6.

of information, which will greatly promote the transmission of all kinds of information among herdsmen. Nine out of 20 respondents regard mobile phones as an important channel to get information, accounting for nearly half of the total number. However, it can be seen from this data, there is still a large space for the development of new media.

3.2 We Should Adopt the Communication Mode Combined with Herdsmen's Life Style

In the past, the paper media played an important role in the communication activities in grassland pastoral area, which made the herdsmen develop a fixed reading habits and ways. With the emergence of new media, more and more new media information emerge. While people use the Internet and mobile phones to receive information, they not only broaden the herdsmen's vision, but also change their reading habits and interest. But this change is a long-term process. As far as herdsmen's cultural level and reading habits are concerned, mobile phones are still mainly used for answering calls, sending short messages and consulting mobile newspapers, which is obviously different from the new communication functions of mobile phones of urban residents (such as mobile radio, television, various client apps). In view of this difference, it is suggested that the use of new media should be combined with herdsmen's life to give full play to the advantages of new media. Text should be the main form of communication, supplemented by all kinds of pictures and audio. For ethnic minority areas, if we can seize the opportunity of rapid popularization of new media and combine with the reality of the region, develop mobile phone media with high practicability, strong timeliness, high popularization rate and outstanding characteristics. Then, it will play an obvious role in promoting the development of information dissemination industry, eliminating the phenomenon of information dissemination inequality, and promoting the economic and social development in minority areas [3]. It can also form the regional characteristics of national culture in the northern grassland corridor with independent identity marks. Some scholars pointed out that in the era of big data, if the use of new media in grassland herdsmen can be vigorously promoted, "In terms of economics, It can create good conditions for large-scale and long-distance nomadism. In terms of politics, it can create a political civilization adapted to the needs of animal husbandry economy characterized by nomadic production mode. In terms of culture, we can achieve groundbreaking achievements in life style, language, literature and art, sports and health, science and technology, mode of thinking, religious beliefs, ethical and moral concepts that are compatible with nomadic production" [4]. For grassland herdsmen, the emergence of new media is both an opportunity and a challenge. Nowadays, with the continuous development of economy, if we want to keep up with the trend of the times, we must integrate new media into their lives, especially grassland herdsmen. It is very important for the development of pastoral area to keep up with the pace of the times and popularize new media. In the process, we should combine the existing objective conditions of our nation, and let the new media play a role which is consistent with the needs of the local people in minority areas. At the same time, we should also pay attention to the negative impact of new media dissemination [5–10]. The local government should play an overall role, make full use of its strengths, avoid its weaknesses, and strive for the traditional media and new media together to play a role in the grassland nationalities, so that herdsmen can enjoy the convenient characteristics of media integration and information reception in the era of three-network integration, so as to contribute to economic development and social construction of pastoral area.

Acknowledgments. Research on the Excavation and Heritage Protection of Mongolian Endangered Cultural Heritage. Project Number: 18YJC850005.

References

1. Zhuang X (2002) Culture dissemination and disseminating culture. J Yunnan Arts Inst (1):76
2. Inner Mongolia Autonomous Region Statistics Bureau (2018) Inner mongolia statistical yearbook. China Statistics Press, Beijing, p 17
3. Jiang H (2009) How to use mobile media for effective information dissemination in ethnic areas: a case study of inner mongolia. Chin Minor Areas' Inf Commun Soc Dev Essay 213–223
4. He T (2007) Continuity and stage of grassland culture in ancient North China. Inner Mongolia Soc Sci (1) (Chinese version)
5. Song Y (2017) Research on the application of health big data from the perspective of artificial intelligence. China Dev
6. Zhai Q, Wei Z (2016) The practice of the "five relevance" audit ideas and methods of Henan provincial audit department in the context of big data. Auditing Res
7. O'Leary DE, O'Keefe RM (1997) The impact of artificial intelligence in accounting work: expert systems use in auditing and tax. AI Soc 11(1–2):36–47
8. Liu Z, Zhu Z (2015) Research prospects and application challenges of social stability: risk assessment in the context of big data. J East China Univ Sci Technol
9. Hemberg E, Rosen J, Warner G, et al (2015) Tax non-compliance detection using co-evolution of tax evasion risk and audit likelihood 79–88
10. Wang Q, Lu P (2018) Research on application of artificial intelligence in computer network technology. Int J Pattern Recognit Artif Intell (4)

Design and Implementation of Enterprise Network Security System Based on Firewall

Hui Yuan(✉), Lei Zheng, Shuang Qiu, Xiangli Peng, Yuan Liang, Yaodong Hu, and Guoru Deng

Information and Communication Company of Hubei State Grid Corporation, No. 197 Xu Dong Street, Wuhan, Hubei, China
882148@qq.com

Abstract. With the rapid development of the network, in recent years, the Internet has greatly improved people's lives, and the real-time, sharing and distance-removing characteristics of network information transmission have made the operation and management of enterprises more efficient and coordinated. The basis of refinement. At the same time, various network security incidents have followed, such as hacker attacks on computer network systems, and various types of viruses, Trojans and other active attacks emerge one after another. In this regard, this paper analyzes the enterprise network security system of firewall from the perspective of enterprise network security, briefly summarizes the background, advantages and disadvantages of firewall technology, and designs and implements a client software according to the actual needs of users. The network performs real-time intelligent security monitoring. After the system design is completed, the security is tested by building a simulation platform, including qualitative testing and quantitative testing, which are divided into security and performance to verify whether the system can achieve and guarantee performance.

Keywords: Firewall · Enterprise · Network security · Three-layer switch technology

1 Introduction

With the improvement of people's security awareness, enterprises or individuals know how to use a firewall to protect themselves when using the Internet, but the internal network has been invaded, and the phenomenon of server attacks is endless. This shows that network security is a systematic project, and it is not just relying on individual security technologies to solve the problem. At the same time, it is also dynamic. Today's security may seem unsafe in tomorrow. It is constantly moving forward in the contradiction between attack and defense. Therefore, how to develop a reasonable corporate network security strategy, better improve existing network security technologies, and provide maximum security for the network has become a very important thing. In this paper, the design and implementation of firewall-based

Z. Xu et al. (Eds.): CSIA 2019, AISC 928, pp. 1070–1078, 2020.
https://doi.org/10.1007/978-3-030-15235-2_142

enterprise network security are studied. The network security and firewall technology are summarized. In the design, in addition to the topology of the enterprise network overall module, for its sub-modules, the corresponding design is analyzed according to the requirements. And after the design is completed, the existing network equipment is used to build the simulation platform, and the implementation of the security policy is qualitatively and quantitatively tested. Its testing mainly includes two aspects of security and performance. By testing, verifying that the design and strategy are implemented and how they perform in real-world applications.

2 The Firewall Related Introduction

2.1 The Basic Principles of the Firewall

The firewall essentially implements the function of filtering the communication traffic between the networks by implementing an access control policy, and is a defense system for isolating the internal network and the external network. It is an analyzer that analyzes and checks data packets communicated between networks according to a preset security policy, and releases data flows that conform to policy rules. At the same time, the firewall itself needs to be able to successfully resist the penetration of external attacks. Therefore, the firewall can effectively monitor the activities between the networks and shield the internal network from the running status and specific structure, so that external unauthorized users cannot access and process the information of the internal network, thereby enhancing the internal network safety.

2.2 Firewall Function

Firewall is the first barrier to protect the internal network from external attacks. It has the following functions: (1) access control function. By configuring the corresponding security policy, the firewall can effectively control the network data flow. (2) firewall has the functions of security audit and exception monitoring. All access will be logged and formed a log, administrators can check the alarm log information to find firewall anomalies, and trace or make corresponding processing. (3) use the firewall to divide the internal network to ensure that the internal network information will not be leaked to the outside world. (4) firewall has the function of NAT address translation. The intranet host can be directly exposed to the external network. (5) flow control. Control and manage the traffic from IP address and user to ensure the stable connection between user and important interface.

2.3 Firewall Vulnerability Analysis

Vulnerability is also known as weakness or vulnerability. The vulnerability of the system can cause security threats and damage to it. As a combination of hardware and software, firewall itself must have vulnerabilities. This paper analyzes the potential vulnerability of firewalls from the following aspects: (1) The intrinsic vulnerability of firewalls is related to the corresponding types, and the exposure of firewall types means the exposure of their potential vulnerability. The identification of firewall system type is the first step to attack the firewall. At the same time, the attacker can download the corresponding version of firmware for detailed analysis, find the vulnerability of firmware and exploit it. (2) Filtering rules: rules set based on firewall bypass, such as Http Tunnel through firewall technology. Since the firewall allows data to access port 80 to pass through, you can use the Client end of Tunnel to direct data from any port to port 80 of the Tunnel Server, which listens on port 80 and then connects port 80 to the server. The data received is transferred to any service port of the machine. (3) Operating System: Each type of firewall depends on its own operating system support, attackers can use operating system vulnerabilities to achieve the use of firewall attacks. Therefore, the security of firewall depends to a large extent on the security of the operating system.

3 Enterprise Network Security Analysis

The object of network security design in this paper is L company. L Company is a subgroup of a large authoritative company in its field. After a long time of exploration, its information construction has been more comprehensive development trend, and its data systems are basically perfect, including office automation system, financial software system, personnel management, network, production operations, attendance. Backup and so on. The company has a network system involving personnel management, material management, production information, operation and sales and other departments. At present, the company has 500 computers, 13 servers, 1 router. The LAN covers the entire company system in an all-round way. The network is 1000 M. Through careful investigation and analysis of the company's network system structure, it is concluded that the basic structure of the enterprise network is star structure, so according to a long time of induction, the company's network topology is presented as shown in Fig. 1.

After several days of investigation, we found that the network chief command center on the first floor of the company's comprehensive office building is mainly responsible for managing the company's main network equipment, while the second-level three-level switch equipment is placed in each floor of the office building. The network system is stored in the box. There is a large amount of network information system devices in a company's memory, which requires special attention for its own security protection and daily maintenance, and the company has done a lot of work in this respect, which basically guarantees the service life and work of these network system devices effect. Here are a few aspects of the company's measures:

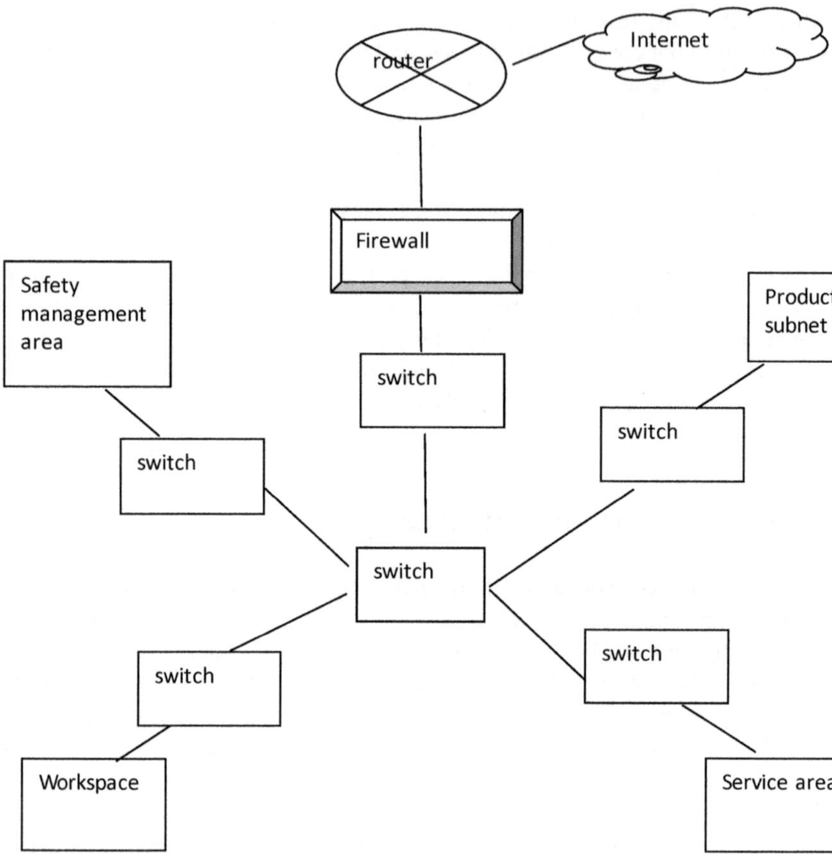

Fig. 1. L company's original network topology

1. The equipment of the network general command center with a large amount of memory on the negative layer will generate high heat every day without interruption, and the indoor ventilation is not smooth, which will affect the heat dissipation effect of the machine. Therefore, the company installed air-conditioning devices in the equipment room, which can adjust the temperature and humidity of the room in time to ensure that each machine can operate normally.
2. The network command center controls all the company's network systems. If the network is damaged, it will affect the normal operation of the entire company. Therefore, in order to ensure the safety of each device in the equipment room, the company sets outside the machine room. The facial recognition system, non-workers are not allowed to enter, and there is no dead angle monitoring facility installed in the machine room to ensure real-time observation of the dynamics in the machine room.

3. Since the power facilities are vulnerable to lightning strikes during thunderstorms, the company installed anti-lightning protection systems with relatively complete facilities to ensure that the company's network is not attacked by lightning, but the company also lacks its fire protection. The facilities are relatively simple and old, not enough to ensure normal use, and the coverage of fire-fighting facilities is too small to meet the relevant standards, which is not enough to protect against fires and other disasters.
4. The network command center contains the machine storage area and the staff office area. It is normal to stipulate that these two areas need to be isolated to avoid accidents, but the company is still not perfect enough in this respect to be further improved.

4 The Firewall-Based Enterprise Network Design and Implementation

4.1 Overall Design Requirements

According to the requirement analysis, on the basis of abiding by the general design principles, the overall design requirements are studied and formulated to meet the requirements of L enterprise network for reliability, confidentiality, manageability and scalability.

(1) rationally planning the network structure of enterprises to ensure physical safety;
(2) deploy the intrusion detection system IDS and the intrusion prevention system IPS to the key nodes.
(3) combining the firewall and waterproofing wall to protect the key sub network;
(4) install vulnerability scanner to scan the application layer and system layer regularly.
(5) configure VPN to provide a uniform external entry to isolate the intranet and external network.
(6) use the network system management software to manage the server and terminal system in a unified way.
(7) backup the key business in real time by using the hot standby disaster recovery method.
(8) formulate safety management related strategies.

4.2 DCFW18005 Multi-core Firewall Security Network Architecture

In this design topology, the firewall directly connects to the external network, which is the outlet of the entire enterprise network. At this point, the firewall is actually a masked host firewall, that is, generally speaking, the host on the Internet can connect to the system on the internal network (e.g., incoming e-mail). Even so, there are only certain types of connections that are allowed. Any external system attempting to access an internal system or service will have to be connected to the fortress host. Therefore, the fortress hosts need to have a high level of security.

In this design, policy configuration is the most important and key part of DCFW-1800 series firewalls to implement access control. Users can define the access control of various resources in the network where the firewall is located according to their needs. The resources used in these policies are all kinds of objects defined in the network configuration. For data flowing through the firewall, it checks the matching rules according to the policy rules defined by the user.

Each policy rule contains a uniquely identifiable sequence number of policy rules, attributes used by firewalls to match packets, access control attributes of firewalls to matching packets (e.g. pass, deny, authorization action and choice of local authentication mode), time control attributes, intrusion detection attributes, firewall's own behavior The property of the policy rule, the use property of the rule, that is, after the policy rule is defined, the rule can be disabled by forbidding the option. You can also customize the functions of IDS, anti-synflood, intrusion detection or fast path.

4.3 Network Basic Function Configuration

Network configuration includes configuring security domains, NIC interfaces, routing, DNS, address binding, and DHCP relay servers. The security domain is used to set up security domain-based access control. The interface settings are used to set the network address of each NIC installed in the firewall system, and whether to allow ping service, network port alias, and VLAN setting; the setting of the domain name server; the routing setting is used to tell the network topology around the firewall and the gateway configuration. The firewall proxy service needs to know the address of the domain name server in order to find the correspondence between the network address and the domain name address. The DHCP relay service still needs other DHCP servers on the network to assign IP addresses. The DCFW-1800s does not currently have the function of directly assigning IP addresses. In addition, in order to prevent IP address fraud, an IP address can be bound to its MAC address in the network configuration section.

5 System Testing and Analysis

The DCFW-18005 multi - core firewall and DCRS-55265 enterprise-level three-layer switch are used to build the main platform of enterprise network design, configure according to the strategy, and perform simulation test and comparison analysis according to the configuration system. In the analysis process, in order to verify the effect of the strategy, this design will perform another configuration horizontally in the comparison test: except for the basic network wanted, IP address allocation, no strategy, including VLAN division, anti- DOS Strategies and so on to verify the test results.

The experimental comparison compares the speed from the network speed from 201.5 KB/s to 231.2 KB/s. The contrast histogram is shown in Fig. 2.

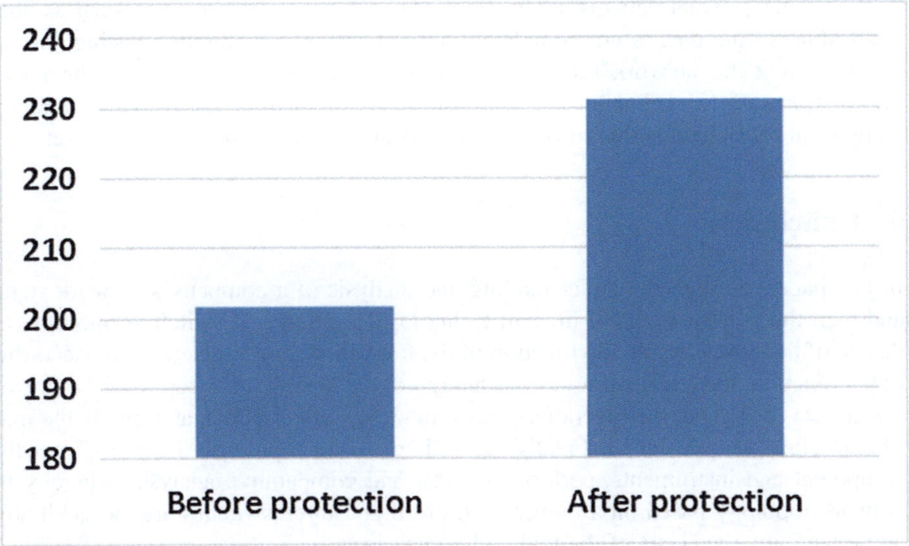

Fig. 2. Network speed comparison chart

We use the network stress test to compare the security, the overall effect of the LAN network external connection under the strategy, and the response time comparison chart using the WEB-CT repeated test is shown in Fig. 3.

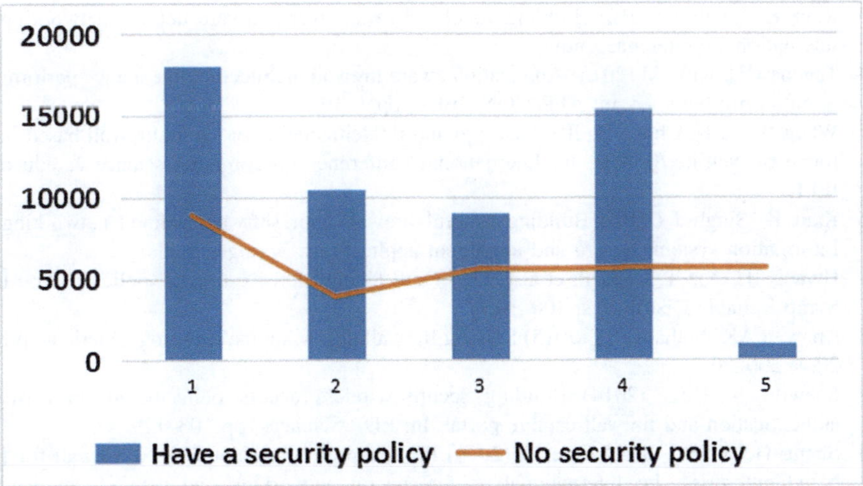

Fig. 3. Corresponding time comparison

Since the external network is dynamic, it is subject to uncertainties such as noise and traffic, so the data is not completely accurate. However, through testing, we can conclude that the network security policy configuration does not cause the packet information to be lost, but for the response. In terms of time, the response time will increase in milliseconds due to policy analysis and detection of the data packet.

6 Conclusion

In this paper, through the understanding and analysis of a company's network status, and then the current status of firewall technology and Layer 3 switch technology, the design of the host firewall, the function of the firewall system is determined. According to the function, the technical route was analyzed, the overall architecture of the firewall system was designed, the functions of each module were clarified, and finally the main file structure was designed. Finally, according to the topology, the use of existing equipment and instruments, performance test and comparative analysis, whereby the network topology based on a multicore firewall and three switches are the qualitative and quantitative analysis of the real and comparison.

References

1. Yin X, Xu J et al (2015) Research and application of multi-firewall technology in enterprise network security. Comput Appl Softw 9(5):153–162
2. Cheng Y, Wang W, Min G et al (2015) A new approach to designing firewall based on multidimensional matrix. Concurrency Comput Pract Exp 27(12):3075–3088
3. Kaur K, Singh J (2016) Building stateful firewall over software defined networking. In: International conference, India
4. Tegenaw H, Kifle M (2015) Application aware firewall architecture to enhance performance of enterprise network. In: AFRICON. IEEE, pp 1–10
5. Wang B, Lu K, Chang P (2016) Design and implementation of Linux firewall based on the frame of Netfilter/IPtable. In: International conference on computer science & education. IEEE
6. Kaur K, Singh J (2016) Building stateful firewall over software defined networking. In: Information systems design and intelligent applications. Springer, India
7. Hwang JH, Xie T, Chen F, et al (2015) Fault localization for firewall policies. Proc IEEE Symp Reliable Distrib Syst 100–106
8. Chawan AK, Mahajan SS (2015) Solving firewall policy anomalies using generic algorithm. 20(4):200–203
9. Soewito B, Hirzi (2014) Building secure wireless access point based on certificate authentication and firewall captive portal. In: EDP Sciences, pp 108–129
10. Sheng H, Wei L, Zhang C, et al (2016) Privacy-preserving cloud-based firewall for IaaS-based enterprise. In: International conference on networking and network applications. IEEE, pp 206–209
11. Majhi SK, Bera P (2015) Designing an adaptive firewall for enterprise cloud. In: International conference on parallel, distributed and grid computing. IEEE, pp 202–208
12. Zhang R (2017) Based on moves the firewall the enterprise wireless to search from the organization network initiative protection mechanism analyzes. Off Informatization

13. Cai F (2017) Research on the security method of enterprise network by using a linked model of firewall and intrusion detection system. Comput Knowl Technol
14. Wiegel B (2015) Securing enterprise email communication on both sides of the firewall
15. Tong M (2017) Research on development of firewall in cloud platform of enterprise. Wirel Internet Technol
16. Burchfield N (2015) Automatically recommending firewall rules during enterprise information technology transformation
17. Hwang J, Dotson CR, Peterson B, et al (2017) Automatically validating enterprise firewall rules and provisioning firewall rules in computer systems
18. Yang N (2018) Application of firewall in enterprise network. China Comput Commun
19. Han GL, Wang W, Sheng HL, et al (2018) Research on firewall strategy and its optimization methods. Electr Power Inf Commun Technol
20. Sujarwo A, Tan J (2018) Enterprise firewall virtualization design, p. 03004

Metadata Storage and Query of Hive Based on Hadoop Distributed Platform

Hongsheng Xu[1,2](✉), Lan Wang[1], and Ganglong Fan[1,2]

[1] Luoyang Normal University, Luoyang 471934, China
85660190@qq.com
[2] Henan Key Laboratory for Big Data Processing and Analytics of Electronic Commerce, Luoyang 471934, China

Abstract. Hive's data is stored in HDFS, and most of the queries are done by MapReduce, which is a large-scale data mechanism that can be stored, queried and analyzed in Hadoop. Hive can convert SQL statements into MapReduce tasks, which has the advantages of low learning cost and easy MapReduce statistics through SQL like statements. Most queries in Hive are executed through the MapReduce provided by Hadoop. This paper introduces the metadata storage and query of Hive based on Hadoop distributed platform.

Keywords: Metadata storage · Hive · Hadoop distributed platform · HiveQL · Hive on Spark

1 Introduction

Hive is an open source storage strategy based on Hadoop. Hive supports query expression of SQL like descriptive language-HiveQL, a query language that can be compiled into map-reduce jobs on Hadoop. Each table can have one or more partitions that determine the distribution of data in subdirectories under table directories. HiveQL supports multiple table inserts and users can execute multiple queries in the same input data by using a single HiveQL statement.

When starting the Client mode, you need to indicate the node where the Hive Server is located and start the Hive Server. at that node [1]. After all, there are more people who write SQL than JAVA, which gives a large number of operators direct access to huge amounts of data. In the construction of data warehouse, HIV E is flexible and easy to maintain, which is very suitable for statistical analysis of data warehouse.

Hive is the first step in an open source repository built on a scale map-reduce data processing system. Hive does not have a specific data format. Hive works well on top of Thrift, controls delimiters, and allows users to specify data formats. Because Hive uses SQL's query language HQL, it is easy to understand Hive as a database. In fact, there is no similarity in structure between Hive and database except that they have similar query language. Databases can be used in Online applications, but Hive is designed for data warehousing. Knowing this helps to understand the features of Hive from an application perspective.

Z. Xu et al. (Eds.): CSIA 2019, AISC 928, pp. 1079–1085, 2020.
https://doi.org/10.1007/978-3-030-15235-2_143

Hive stores metadata in RDBMS, and there are three ways to connect to a database: embedded mode: a Derby, that holds the metadata in an embedded database is generally used for unit testing, allowing only one session connection. Multiuser mode: install Mysql, locally to place metadata in Mysql, remote mode: metadata in remote Mysql database.

Hive's metastore component is the repository of hive metadata set. Metastore component consists of two parts: Metastore service and back-end data storage. Background data storage media is relational databases, such as hive default embedded disk database derby, and mysql database [2].

The core of Hive authorization is that the roles in the (Group), role (Role), Hive of the user (User), group are different from those in normal cognition. Hadoop is a popular open source map-reduce implementation that is being used based on general-purpose computers as an alternative to large data set storage and processing.

2 Architecture of Hive Operation Mechanism and Storage Mode

Because there is no need to convert from the user data format to the data format defined by Hive during data loading, the data itself is not modified during loading. Instead, copy or move the data content to the appropriate HDFS directory. In databases, different databases have different storage engines and define their own data formats. All data is stored in a structured way, so it takes time for the database to load the data.

The structured data file under Hadoop is mapped to a table in Zhang Cheng Hive, and provides sql like query function. Besides not supporting update, index and transaction SQL are all supported [3]. You can convert an sql statement to a MapReduce task to run as a sql-to-MapReduce mapper. Provide shell, JDBC/ODBC, Thrift, Web and other interfaces. As a data warehouse Hive data management can be used from metadata storage, data storage and data exchange according to the usage hierarchy.

Metadata Service component stores hive metadata the metadata stored in the relational database supports relational databases such as derby, mysql. The pure logical tables in Hive are the definitions of tables, that is, the metadata of tables. Using SQL to implement Hive is because SQL is familiar, conversion costs are low, and Pig with similar functions is not SQL, and decoupling hive services and metastore services.

HDFS is like a traditional hierarchical file system for external clients. You can create, delete, move, or rename files, and so on. But the architecture of HDFS. This is a disadvantage (single point failure) of HDFS because there is only one NameNode.

When Hive input is made up of many small files, because each small file starts a map task, if the file is so small that it takes longer to start and initialize the map task than the logical processing time, it can cause waste of resources, even OOM. Therefore, when we start a task and find that the input data is small but the number of tasks is large, as is shown by Fig. 1. We should pay attention to the input merging in the front end of Map [4].

By default, Hive uses MapReduce as the execution engine, or Hive on mr. In fact, Hive can also use Tez and Spark as its execution engines, Hive on Tez and Hive on

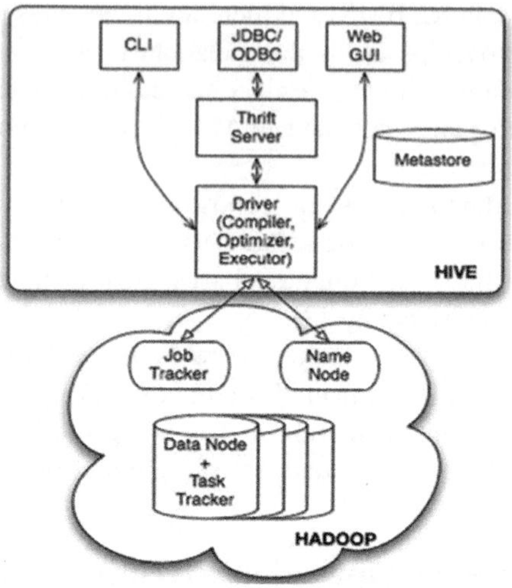

Fig. 1. Architecture of hive operation mechanism.

Spark, respectively. Because MapReduce intermediate computing needs to be written to disk, and Spark is in memory, Spark is generally much faster than MapReduce.

Hive data storage format common including TEXTFILE, SEQUENCEFILE, RCFILE and OCRFILE.TEXTFILE default format, data do not do compression, disk overhead, data parsing overhead large SequenceFile is a binary file support provided by Hadoop API, it is easy to use, can be divided, Compressible features. SequenceFile supports three compressed selections: no, RECORD, BLOCK. Record compression ratio is low, it is generally recommended to use BLOCK compression. TEXTFILE SEQUENC-EFILE is based on row storage.

Hive is built on Hadoop, and all Hive data is stored in HDFS. The database can save data in a block device or in a local file system [5]. There is no specific data format defined in the data format. Hive, the data format can be specified by the user, and the user-defined data format requires three attributes: column delimiters (usually spaces, "\ t", "\ x001", line delimiters ("\ n"), and methods for reading file data (there are three default file formats TextFile. in Hive).

3 Application of Hive on Spark in Hadoop Architecture

The metadata in Hive includes the name of the table, the column and partition of the table and its properties, the properties of the table (whether the table is an external table), the directory where the table data is located, and so on. It only needs to tell Hive column and row delimiters when creating tables, which can parse the data.

HiveQL supports generic map-reduce scripts that can embed queries. The language includes a system of this kind that supports the nesting of primitive data tables, array sets, and maps, and the same layers [6]. Roles in Hive can be understood as a collection of users or groups or roles with some of the same attributes. Here is the recursive concept that a character can be a collection of roles.

HBase is created for querying by organizing the memory of all machines in the node to provide a large memory Hash table, which needs to organize its own data structure, both on disk and in memory. Driver components: Complier, Optimizer and Executor, it parses, compiles, optimizes, and generates execution plans. The underlying MapReduce computing framework is then called.

NameNode decides whether to map files to replication blocks on DataNode. For the three most common replicating blocks, in Hive, a Partition in a table corresponds to a directory under the table, and all Partition data is stored in the corresponding directory.

So the hive on Spark will also be faster than the Hive on mr. To compare the speed of Hive on Spark and Hive on mr, you need to install the Spark cluster on a machine that already has a Hadoop cluster (the Spark cluster is built on top of the Hadoop cluster, that is, the Hadoop cluster is installed before the Spark cluster is installed). Because Spark uses Hadoop's HDFS, YARN etc.) and then sets the Hive execution engine to Spark.

RCFILE is a storage method that combines column and column storage. First, it divides the data into rows, ensuring that the same record is on one block and avoiding reading multiple block. To read a record Secondly, block data column storage is advantageous to data compression and fast column access.

Since Hive is designed for data warehouse applications, the content of data warehouse is read more than written [7]. Therefore, overwriting and adding data is not supported in Hive, all data is determined during loading. The data in the database usually needs to be modified frequently, so you can use INSERT INTO. VALUES adds data, using UPDATE. SET modifies data.

4 Metadata Storage and Query of Hive Based on Hadoop Distributed Platform

HiveQL is also very extensible. It supports user-defined column transformation (UDF) and aggregate (UDAF) functions implemented by Java. Users can associate tables with underlying data in serialized formats. Hive provides built-in serialization formats using compression and lazy deserialization [8]. Users can also add new data formats supported by SerDe methods, written in Java, called custom serialization and deserialization methods. The role definition in Hive is similar to that in relational databases. It is a mechanism that assigns certain permissions to all users who do not have the appropriate permissions.

Thrift is a software framework developed by facebook for the development of extensible and cross-language services. Interface. CLI: command line interface, command-line interface [9]. Thrift client that allows different programming languages to call hive: many of the client interfaces of the hive architecture are built on thrift clients, Including the JDBC and ODBC interface. WEBGUI: hive client provides a web access to the service provided by hive.

Hive is a distributed relational database. All queries, except "select * from table;", which are mainly used in hive, need to be executed through the way of Map\Reduce.

Because MapReduce, is a table with only one row and one column, it might take 8.9 s if it is not queried by select * from table;. But hive is better at handling large amounts of data. When there is a lot of data to be processed and the Hadoop cluster is large enough, its advantages can be demonstrated (see Fig. 1).

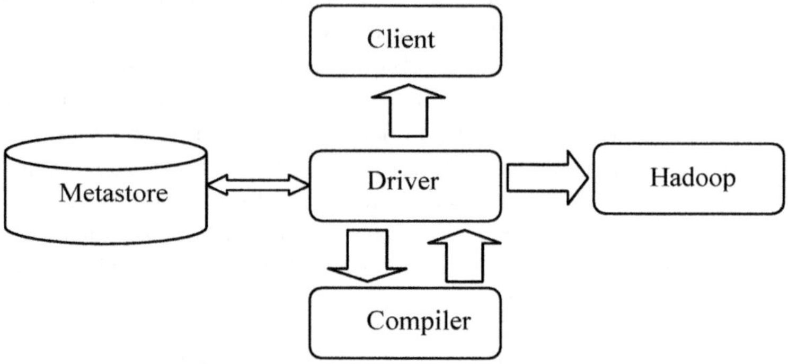

Fig. 2. Hive architecture & execution process.

To use the Spark version of Hive on Spark, you must not include Hive's related jar package "Note that you must have a version of Spark which does not include the Hive jars" on the website of on spark [10]. The compiled Spark downloaded on spark's website has integrated Hive, so you need to download the source code to compile it yourself, and you don't specify the Hive. at the time of compilation (Fig. 2).

By testing the time consuming of data import, row query and column query, and the storage space occupied by data table, the query efficiency and data compression ratio of different types of storage modes in hive are analyzed and compared. Test file path: HDFS/testr/container.txt, 4.8 GB, test storage type includes Textfile, Sequencefile, RCfile.

Hive does not process or even scan the data during data loading, and therefore does not index some of the Key in the data. Hive to access specific values in the data that meet the criteria, Violence is required to scan the entire data, so access latency is high. Because of the introduction of MapReduce, Hive can access data in parallel, so even if there is no index, the access to large amount of data can still reflect the advantage.

ExternalTable points to the data in the existing HDFS to create the Partition. Similar to Table in metadata organization structure, there is a big difference in the actual storage. After the application is submitted, the input and output directories included in the HDFS are provided. JobTracker uses block information (physical quantities and locations) to determine how to create additional TaskTracker dependencies. Column storage mode stores each column individually or several columns exist as column groups. Columns are stored to avoid reading unnecessary columns when executing queries.

Users can use a simple row-based stream interface to embed map-reduce custom scripts written in any language, that is, reading rows from standard input and writing out rows in standard output written in a language such as Java. The server can also support client. Thrift Hive clients in other languages to generate commonly used drivers in different languages.

Metastore service is a service component which is built on the background data storage medium and can interact with hive service. By default, the metastore service and hive service are installed together and run in the same process. I can also separate the metastore service from the hive service and install it independently in a cluster to remotely invoke the metastore service, so that we can put the metadata layer behind the firewall and the client can access the hive service. You can connect to the metadata layer, providing better management and security. The use of remote metastore services allows metastore services and hive services to run in different processes, which also ensures the stability of hive and improves the efficiency of hive services.

The intermediate results of the Map task are stored on the local disk as files after Combine and Partition are done. The location of the intermediate result file is notified to the master JobTracker. A hybrid storage mode is a structure that mixes row and column storage.

5 Summary

The driver controls the life cycle of a HiveQL statement during compilation, optimization, and execution, the column and partition of the table and its properties, the properties of the table (whether it is an external table, etc.), the directory where the data of the table is located, and so on. The organization of Partition in Hive is very different from that in databases. The MapReduce application is copied to each node where the input file block appears. Hive is a subproject under Apache. Client is the client of Hive, and the user connects to Hive Server.

Acknowledgements. This paper is supported by Henan key Laboratory for Big Data Processing & Analytics of Electronic Commerce, and also supported by the science and technology research major project of Henan province Education Department (17B520026), Key scientific research projects in Henan province universities (17A880020, 15A120012), and the Science and Technology Opening up Cooperation project of Henan Province (No. 172106000077).

References

1. Wang Y, Wang W, Meng D (2015) Hive data warehouse query optimization. Comput Res Dev (06):85–89 (in Chinese)
2. Zhang R (2017) Based on hive data warehouse of logistics big data platform research and design. Electron Des Eng 15(09):145–156 (in Chinese)
3. Yang R (2015) Big data environment dynamic data warehouse application research. Electron Technol Softw Eng 4(02):21–26 (in Chinese)
4. Li S (2014) About uses cloud computing technology to construct the large data warehouse platform the inquiry. Comput Opt Disk Softw Appl 8(16):258–262 (in Chinese)
5. Liu Y, Li J, Hu S (2016) Hive multidimensional index segmentation strategy selection algorithm based on cost estimation. Comput Res Dev 9(04):77–79

6. Xu H, Zhang R (2016) Novel approach of semantic annotation by fuzzy ontology based on variable precision rough set and concept lattice. Int J Hybrid Inf Technol 9(4):25–40
7. Jing H, Zheng J (2015) MapReduce and HBase based massive network data processing. Sci Technol Eng 34:800–807 (in Chinese)
8. Liao X, Ren C (2017) Research on heterogeneous data integration of logistics supply chain based on hive architecture. Logist Technol 4(03):389–396
9. Wang J, Li T (2017) Design and research of payment SDK log analysis system based on hive. Comput Appl Softw 12(07):445–469
10. Jiang H (2016) Research on log warehouse construction based on hive. Comput Age (11):100–120 (in Chinese)

Quality Evaluation of Tank Shooter Night Vision Image Fusion Based on Mark Watershed

Zhao Yao(✉)

Army Academy of Amored Forces, Changchun, China
3237610382@qq.com

Abstract. Aiming at the inconsistency between the evaluation results of traditional image fusion quality indicators and subjective perception results of human eyes, an image fusion quality evaluation method based on watershed algorithm is proposed. Structural similarity information graph between source images is obtained by using structural similarity theory, and information graph is segmented by watershed algorithm. In order to reduce over-segmentation, markers are used in watershed algorithm to divide the information of source images into common information and complementary information. Do not deal with common information and complementary information to complete the evaluation of fusion image quality. According to the requirements of video quality evaluation expert group Video Quality Expert Group (VQEG), the algorithm proposed in this paper is verified by experiments. The experimental results show that the algorithm is effective.

Keywords: Marker watershed · Image fusion · Quality evaluation · Tank shooter

1 Introduction

Image fusion plays an important role in the field of information fusion, and is widely used in the fields of hidden weapons inspection, night flight, important target surveillance, medical diagnosis, satellite remote sensing and so on [1]. The quality of fused image is an important aspect to measure the effect of image fusion. The research on the quality evaluation of fused image is of guiding significance to the development of fusion algorithm.

In the past, the quality of fused images was mainly measured by human subjective perception, but this evaluation method is time-consuming and laborious, and can not be integrated into the image fusion system, which is not conducive to the development of the system. Although this evaluation method has high accuracy, it is seldom used in practical production because of its poor practicability. With the development of machine vision, objective evaluation has gradually entered the field of vision. Mathematical statistics such as MSE [2], PSNR and sharpness are gradually used to evaluate the quality of image fusion, but these quantities are too simple to completely describe complex image information, so they can only be used in occasions where the

Z. Xu et al. (Eds.): CSIA 2019, AISC 928, pp. 1086–1093, 2020.
https://doi.org/10.1007/978-3-030-15235-2_144

evaluation accuracy is not high. With the emergence of SSIM [3], WMSSIM [4] and MWGS [5], the problem of high-precision fusion image quality assessment has become a reality. Piella and Heijmans introduced SSIM theory into the evaluation and put forward the method of image fusion quality evaluation based on SSIM [6]. Cvejic et al. put forward the method of image fusion quality evaluation based on local structure similarity by optimizing SSIM theory [7]. Zheng Yongan and others put forward the objective evaluation method of image fusion based on quality factor law [8–10]. However, no evaluation method includes measurement of common information and complementary information. Zheng Youzhi pointed out that common information and complementary information play an important role in the quality of fused images, and it is necessary to describe them accurately to achieve high-precision image fusion quality evaluation. In this paper, watershed algorithm is used to segment common information and complementary information, and a common information/complementary information response function is constructed to evaluate the quality of image fusion with high accuracy.

2 A Brief Introduction to the Theory SSIM

The SSIM theory was proposed by Zhou Wang in 2003. It assumes that the realization of the human eye's image function originates from the human eye's processing of image structure information. In view of this, by extracting and processing the structure of the image, we can achieve the evaluation effect of the human eye on the image. SSIM consists of 3 components: luminance comparison, contrast comparison and correlation comparison. Set $\mathrm{x} = \{\mathrm{xi} \mid \mathrm{i} = 1, 2, \ldots, \mathrm{N}\}$, $\mathrm{y} = \{\mathrm{yi} \mid \mathrm{i} = 1, 2, \ldots, \mathrm{N}\}$ as two structures to evaluate the image's signal, SSIM is defined as: $\mathrm{SSIM}(\mathrm{x}, \mathrm{y}) = \mathrm{l}(\mathrm{x}, \mathrm{y}) * \mathrm{c}(\mathrm{x}, \mathrm{y}) * \mathrm{s}(\mathrm{x}, \mathrm{y})$.

In the form:

$$\mathrm{l}(\mathrm{x}, \mathrm{y}) = \frac{2\mu_{\mathrm{x}}\mu_y + C_1}{\mu_x^2 + \mu_y^2 + C_1} \tag{1}$$

$$\mathrm{c}(\mathrm{x}, \mathrm{y}) = \frac{2\sigma_{\mathrm{x}}\sigma_y + C_2}{\sigma_x^2 + \sigma_y^2 + C_2} \tag{2}$$

$$\mathrm{s}(\mathrm{x}, \mathrm{y}) = \frac{\sigma_{xy} + C_3}{\sigma_x\sigma_y + C_3} \tag{3}$$

In the form:

$$\mu_x = \frac{1}{N}\sum_{i=1}^{N} x_i \tag{4}$$

$$\mu_y = \frac{1}{N}\sum_{i=1}^{N} y_i \tag{5}$$

$$\sigma_x^2 = \frac{1}{N-1}\sum_{i=1}^{N}(x_i - \mu_x) \tag{6}$$

$$\sigma_y^2 = \frac{1}{N-1}\sum_{i=1}^{N}(y_i - \mu_y)$$

$$\sigma_{xy} = \frac{1}{N-1}\sum_{i=1}^{N}(x_i - \mu_x)(y_i - \mu_y) \tag{7}$$

Among them, C_1, C_2 and C_3 are very small constants, which are used to keep the algorithm stable. The value of SSIM (x, y) is between 0 and 1. The smaller the value, the greater the similarity between X and y, and vice versa.

3 Segmentation of Common Information and Complementary Information

Image fusion synthesizes the information of multi-sensor images or images of the same sensor at different times, and synthesizes a composite image containing all the important information of the sensor, so as to achieve a better description of the target scene. Common information exists in multiple images, only one copy can be retained; complementary information exists in a separate image, and the information must be completely preserved in order to achieve a comprehensive description of the scene. In view of the different nature of common information and complementary information, their contribution to the quality of fused images is also different, so it is necessary to distinguish them in the quality evaluation.

Since what is meaningful to the human eye is the structural information of the image, the distinction between the complementarity and commonality of the structural information of the image is the distinction between the common information of the image. Considering the complexity of the image signal, the local similarity of each point of the image is $\mathrm{SSIM}(x, y \mid w)$ by sliding the window of size w from top to bottom and from left to right. The local structural similarity of the corresponding points of the two images forms a graph, which is called structural similarity information map SSIMMAP. The graph reflects the structural similarity of the corresponding regions between the two images.

Watershed algorithm is an important algorithm in image segmentation, which is widely used in the field of morphological image processing. Watershed algorithm regards the image as a 3 dimensional topographic map, and the pixel's gray value is its height. The high gray value corresponds to the peaks in the geography, and the low gray value corresponds to the basin in geography. A small hole is drilled at the bottom of each basin, and the water flows from the bottom to the basin and rises gradually. When the water in the basin is about to spill over the edge of the basin, a dam is constructed to prevent the water from spilling out of the basin. The dam is called a watershed. Watershed algorithm directly used in image segmentation can easily lead to over-segmentation, resulting in poor availability of segmentation results. In order to avoid this phenomenon, image segmentation algorithm based on marker watershed is adopted in this paper. The flow of algorithm is as follows:

(1) The horizontal Sobel operator and the vertical Sobel operator are used to filter the image respectively, and the horizontal gradient map FX and the vertical gradient map FY are obtained. The gradient image f of SSIMMAP is obtained by the mean square error of the horizontal gradient map and the vertical gradient map, as shown in Figs. 1 and 2.

$$f = \sqrt{f_x^2 + f_y^2} \tag{8}$$

1/8

1	0	-1
2	0	-2
1	0	-1

Fig. 1. Transverse Sobel operator

1/8

1	2	1
0	0	0
-1	-2	-1

Fig. 2. Longitudinal Sobel operator

(2) In order to reduce the effect of noise on the evaluation results, 3 * 3 linear smoothing filter is used to filter the image f; all local minimum points in the image are obtained; in order to improve the quality of local minimum points, the local minimum value of gray value less than 75 is set as the effective local minimum value, and it is marked as the internal marker. The watershed of the image with the effective local minimum is obtained by watershed segmentation, and the watershed under the action of the effective local minimum is marked as an external marker.
(3) divide the image into watershed and get different target regions including R1, R2,…RN, whose structure is similar as a whole, is called complementary information area, where complementary information is predominant. Background area RN + 1, which does not contain internal markers, is called common information area.

4 Construction of Information Processing Function

The purpose of image fusion is to synthesize the information from different channels, to synthesize a composite image containing all the important information of sensors, and to achieve a better description of the target scene. Therefore, we should preserve complementary information as far as possible in image fusion. All channels share the same information, and only keep one copy. In order to reduce the noise or distortion of the channel, the common information is retained as the average of the common information of each channel. Therefore, the construction of the information processing function is as follows:

$$Q(x,y,f) = \frac{1}{R_1 + R_2 + \ldots + R_N + R_{N+1}} \sum_{i=1}^{N+1} Q(x,y,f \mid R_i) * R_i \tag{9}$$

$$Q(x,y,f \mid R_i) = \frac{1}{2}[SSIM(x,f \mid R_i) + SSIM(y,f \mid R_i)] \quad \mathrm{i} = 1,2,\ldots\mathrm{N} \tag{10}$$

$$Q(x,y,f \mid R_{N+1}) = MAX(SSIM(x,f \mid R_{N+1}), SSIM(y,f \mid R_{N+1})) \tag{11}$$

In the formula, x, y are source images, f is fused images, R1, R2, ...RN, RN + 1 is the area corresponding to the target region and the fusion region, Q (x, y, f) is the quality of the fusion image, and Q(x, y, f | Ri) is the quality of the fusion image for each region.

5 Experimental Results and Analysis

In this paper, the IR and CCD images of seven different scenes, including Dune, Trees, UNcamp, faces, kayak, OCTEC, quad, are used as the source images in the standard fusion image database. Average, PCA and SIDWT fusion algorithms are used to fuse the images of seven scenes, and 21 fused images are obtained as the experimental data. Forty persons with normal vision, aged between 20 and 40, were selected as quality evaluation experts to evaluate the subjective quality of 21 fused images. The evaluation was carried out in an airtight darkroom with a brightness of about 0.6 lx. The display selected ViewSonic VG510 and the resolution was set to 1024 * 768 after checking for no color difference, bad points and distortion. The distance between the evaluation experts and the screen was about 0.5 m Room.

In order to verify the efficiency of this algorithm, the classical Piella algorithm and the new Zheng algorithm for image quality evaluation are selected as the comparison objects. The experimental data are shown in Table 1.

In this paper, the VQEG image quality evaluation algorithm quality evaluation criteria [validity test] proposed by VQEG, VQEG evaluation criteria include three aspects: (1) accuracy, subjective and objective evaluation data difference is large, this paper uses MSE for subjective and objective data difference calculation, MSE value is smaller means that the subjective and objective evaluation results of the difference is smaller. (2) monotonicity, objective evaluation data with the degree of monotonic changes in subjective evaluation data, this paper uses Spearman rank correlation coefficient measurement, the greater the Spearman value, means that the monotonicity of subjective and objective evaluation results is better; (3) consistency, objective evaluation data and subjective evaluation data consistency, this paper uses P Erson linear correlation measurement, the greater the Person value, the higher the consistency of subjective and objective evaluation results.

Table 1 shows that Zheng's algorithm is the best in terms of accuracy, followed by ISQP and Piella's worst in terms of monotonicity, Spearman's best, ISQP's second and Piella's worst in terms of consistency, Zheng's best, ISQP's second and Piella's worst.

Generally speaking, the ISQP and Zheng algorithms proposed in this paper have great improvement compared with Piella's classical algorithm, but their performance is not much different.

Table 1. Experimental data of subjective and objective evaluation under non interference conditions

Scene	Fusion algorithm	Subjective data	Piella	Zheng	ISQP
Dune	Ave	0.72	0.75	0.74	0.72
	PCA	0.85	0.80	0.86	0.89
	DWT	0.88	0.82	0.83	0.80
Trees	Ave	0.71	0.80	0.74	0.74
	PCA	0.84	0.82	0.86	0.82
	DWT	0.87	0.85	0.82	0.85
UNcamp	Ave	0.91	0.87	0.90	0.94
	PCA	0.88	0.92	0.87	0.86
	DWT	0.90	0.85	0.89	0.91
faces	Ave	0.69	0.64	0.71	0.65
	PCA	0.83	0.76	0.81	0.82
	DWT	0.86	0.78	0.84	0.84
kayak	Ave	0.77	0.69	0.75	0.75
	PCA	0.89	0.68	0.85	0.84
	DWT	0.89	0.88	0.90	0.86
OCTEC	Ave	0.69	0.72	0.67	0.66
	PCA	0.82	0.91	0.80	0.81
	DWT	0.86	0.86	0.88	0.85
quad	Ave	0.59	0.65	0.60	0.57
	PCA	0.75	0.79	0.81	0.77
	DWT	0.83	0.84	0.81	0.81

In order to adapt to the complex and changeable environment, 10% white noise is added to two fused images to verify the stability of the proposed algorithm (Table 2).

Table 2. Performance of objective evaluation algorithm without interference

	MSE	Spearman	Person
Piella	0.069	0.6130	0.6723
Zheng	0.027	0.9169	0.9496
ISQP	0.030	0.8935	0.9508

Table 3. Experimental data of subjective and objective evaluation under interference conditions

Scene	Fusion algorithm	Subjective data	Piella	Zheng	ISQP
Dune	Ave	0.62	0.68	0.67	0.61
	PCA	0.73	0.66	0.71	0.78
	DWT	0.74	0.83	0.78	0.71
Trees	Ave	0.65	0.72	0.69	0.65
	PCA	0.77	0.71	0.79	0.73
	DWT	0.72	0.69	0.73	0.72
UNcamp	Ave	0.83	0.76	0.80	0.93
	PCA	0.79	0.84	0.76	0.76
	DWT	0.82	0.73	0.76	0.84
faces	Ave	0.58	0.50	0.58	0.62
	PCA	0.74	0.66	0.65	0.73
	DWT	0.77	0.63	0.80	0.76
kayak	Ave	0.65	0.54	0.63	0.70
	PCA	0.76	0.64	0.61	0.74
	DWT	0.79	0.76	0.75	0.75
OCTEC	Ave	0.60	0.62	0.63	0.64
	PCA	0.71	0.80	0.79	0.69
	DWT	0.75	0.75	0.81	0.72
quad	Ave	0.52	0.56	0.63	0.49
	PCA	0.63	0.60	0.69	0.66
	DWT	0.72	0.83	0.75	0.77

After adding white noise, the experimental data are shown in Table 3. Under the condition of adding 10% Gauss white noise, the results are as follows: Table 4.

Table 4. Performance of objective evaluation algorithm under interference conditions

	MSE	Spearman	Person
Piella	0.077	0.5807	0.6466
Zheng	0.059	0.6660	0.7112
ISQP	0.037	0.8649	0.9042

As can be seen from Table 4, the performance of the three evaluation algorithms has a certain decline with the addition of noise, of which Zheng's algorithm has the most decline, ISQP's algorithm has the second place, Piella's algorithm has the least. It shows that the algorithm of Zheng is of low reliability under the condition of poor observation. Zhang used threshold segmentation to evaluate fused images, which resulted in meaningful image content segmentation and poor anti-jamming ability. The marker watershed algorithm used in this paper has a certain fault-tolerant ability and can be better applied to quality evaluation under interference conditions. Although

Piella has the strongest anti-jamming ability among the three algorithms, it is difficult to form high-quality evaluation criteria because of its performance cardinality.

6 Conclusion

In this paper, an image fusion quality evaluation method based on marker watershed algorithm is proposed through the research of image fusion algorithm. Experimental results show that the index is an effective evaluation index. In image quality evaluation, watershed-based image segmentation is more robust than threshold-based image segmentation. It can be predicted that with the further improvement of image segmentation algorithm, image fusion quality evaluation will achieve better results.

References

1. Hoffmann N, Weidner F, Urban P, Meyer T, Schnabel C, Radev Y, Schackert G, Petersohn U, Koch E, Gumhold S, Steiner G, Kirsch M (2017) Framework for 2D-3D image fusion of infrared thermography with preoperative MRI. Biomed Eng/Biomed Tech 62(6):85–92
2. Liu Z, Blasch E, John V (2017) Statistical comparison of image fusion algorithms: recommendations. Inf Fusion 3(6):112–131
3. Bavirisetti DP, Kollu V, Gang X, Dhuli R (2017) Fusion of MRI and CT images using guided image filter and image statistics. Int J Imaging Syst Technol 27(3):79–84
4. Yang T, Shah NM (2016) Molecular and neural control of sexually dimorphic social behaviors. Curr Opin Neurobiol 38(6):82–89
5. Lin M (2016) An improved threshold segmentation algorithm emphasizing trough information. Comput Syst Appl 25(8):162–165
6. Zhang J (2014) Infrared image threshold segmentation based on Otsu. Xiangtan University
7. Wang Q, Peng Z, Liu L (2003) An adaptive method of image segmentation. Trans Beijing Inst Technol 23(4):521–524
8. Wan Y, Bian F (2008) Design and implementation of inter active 2D&3D GIS architecture. Geomat World 6(2):48–52
9. Zhang G, Heng X, Ling Y, Lao S (2010) Interaction gesture analysis and design based on multi-touch surface. Appl Res Comput 27(5):1737–1739
10. Wang X, Chen G, Wang D, Wang C (2012) Research on multi-touch gesture analysis and recognition algorithm. Comput Sci 39(1):522–525

Research on Transformation and Innovation of Editing and Publishing Under the Background of Media Convergence

Hongyuan Li(✉) and Yanhua Yin

Media Academy, Jilin Engineering Normal University, Changchun, Jilin, China
592726666@qq.com

Abstract. In the era of media integration, the traditional publishing industry is experiencing unprecedented changes in content structure, communication means and business model, which puts forward new requirements for editors and publishers. How to innovate the training mode of editors and publishers to meet the development requirements of publishing industry in the era of media integration has become a subject that needs deep consideration in the industry. Starting from the characteristics of traditional paper periodicals in multimedia applications and the opportunities and challenges they face, this paper explores the media survival strategies of paper periodicals, and provides reference suggestions for paper media transformation under the integration of multimedia.

Keywords: Multimedia integration · Paper periodicals · Media

1 Introduction

With the emergence of audio books with pictures, texts and sounds, the audience is gradually turning from paper books to electronic books, which has brought a huge impact on the economic benefits of traditional paper media [1–4]. Therefore, the continuous development of traditional paper media is inseparable from the application of multimedia integration. In the future, journals will show three characteristics in the application of multimedia: first, content is king, the development of multimedia technology provides technical support for the digitization of paper journals, but technology can never replace content [5–8]. The key to the sustainable development of journals lies in the internal cause - excellent content quality. Only by enhancing the depth and breadth of content resources and adapting to the reading needs of the vast number of readers, can we have a stronger attraction. Secondly, the content presents richer forms [9–14]. With the development and application of multimedia, the contents and forms of periodicals are becoming richer and richer. At the same time, the interaction between authors and readers is becoming more and more close [15–18]. Periodicals can effectively interact with their audiences through questionnaires, articles, seminars and other forms. Finally, mobile Internet terminals are used to launch content publishing [19, 20].

In recent years, the development of mobile terminals based on smart phones has become the fifth media after newspapers, radio, television and network. In order to

Z. Xu et al. (Eds.): CSIA 2019, AISC 928, pp. 1094–1100, 2020.
https://doi.org/10.1007/978-3-030-15235-2_145

facilitate customers to read publications, various publications have developed APP based on mobile phones. The digital products of journals are gradually moving towards interaction, mobility and diversification of profit models. Mobile Internet terminals have brought the advantages of diversification and agglomeration of information to traditional paper journals.

2 The Concept and Characteristics of Media Convergence

The concept of media convergence was first proposed by Nicholas Negroponte, founder of the Media Laboratory at the Massachusetts Institute of Technology (MIT). In China, there is no general agreement on the concept of "media convergence", but intuitively speaking, media convergence refers to the use of digital technology and network technology as the basis of traditional media such as newspapers, television stations and radio stations in the face of the rapid development of information technology, derived from different forms of information products, and then transmitted to the audience through different platforms, to achieve complementary advantages and maximize dissemination benefits. This is an inevitable trend in the development of the media industry. It has the following characteristics:

2.1 Lightweight Reading Mode

In the new era with abundant information, once the audience could only accept the one-way information transmission mode of text-based from top to bottom mechanically and passively, each user no longer needed to subscribe to the content source in person, and could read it only by web browser, which saved the time and energy of users, and could also use the network data information. According to readers' different reading habits, we provide users with unique personalized content from multiple dimensions.

2.2 The Power of Communication Across Time and Space

Under the background of media convergence, the powerful transfer function of new media has changed the single linear transmission mode of traditional media in the past, realized cross-media and cross-platform communication, and broke through the weakness of lagging information transmission time. So far, publications are no longer independent research results, but through various social networks like snowballs gradually expand coverage, so that the target audience can easily and quickly get content, shorten the time cycle of content dissemination. At this time, the reader is not only passively and singly receiving information, but also the participant and promoter of information. They will reproduce and disseminate the content of information.

2.3 Convenient and Quick Search

In the new media age, besides the huge capacity, "easy search" is also an important feature. Every reader can not only store content at any time, but also get personalized information anytime, anywhere, conveniently and quickly. Moreover, network information can be reused by many people at the same time, without the limitation of time and space. Readers can read news information they need according to their interests and hobbies. For example, the current Internet knowledge platforms such as China HowNet, Weipu, Baidu Library, etc. Readers can search keywords through the knowledge platform, quickly and comprehensively find out the current research results of this research direction, timely grasp the latest research progress of this research direction, to meet readers' fragmented and differentiated reading needs.

3 Problems Existing in Editing and Publishing

3.1 The Release of Paper Magazines Is Blocked

With the continuous development of the Internet, these private circles, which are not originally belong to the media industry and cannot intervene in the media industry, but represent the fashion authority and taste, begin to be able to rely on the Internet platform to make their own voices, directly contact with the audience and reach the public. They want to publish their opinions and fashion-related information, and they don't have to follow suit and submit to traditional magazines as before. Therefore, under the background of media convergence, like other traditional paper media, magazines are also facing reform and thinking transformation. They need to cater to and interact with current audiences, and the traditional way of standing high and preaching is gone forever.

3.2 Multimedia Fusion Achieves the Two-Way Interaction of Journals

Multimedia technology aggregates various information expression methods such as text, image, animation and sound, and transforms the plane and one-way information transmission mode of traditional paper periodicals into three-dimensional and two-way communication. In addition, the network contribution platform promotes editorial department to better improve editing process and optimize service. On the one hand, the author can view the process and opinions of manuscripts in real time, and can communicate with editors and reviewers at any time. The new media represented by the Internet, with its prominent advantages of mass information, convenient retrieval, efficient interaction and low cost of subscription, have impacted the development of paper periodicals. Because the concept and content of multimedia and new media are overlapping, the development of paper periodicals is inseparable from the power of new media. In terms of journal solicitation and contributions compilation, the early way of sending and receiving manuscripts by mail has lagged behind the needs of the times. At present, most journals have adopted the form of website collecting and editing system or e-mail to collect manuscripts. In addition, in the process of editing and publishing, traditional paper media often take several days from reviewing, typesetting, printing to distribution. However, electronic publications can be published on the Internet in a few seconds. Obviously, in the face of digital publishing, the dissemination efficiency of traditional paper periodicals is relatively low.

3.3 Speed Up the Contents

The application of the network platform shortens the review cycle and processing speed of manuscripts, and facilitates the editorial department to analyze the information such as the situation of contributions and the source of authors. Multimedia integration transforms traditional publishing from one-way transmission to two-way interaction. With its personalized push, accurate link and search function, the display means of academic journal content become more three-dimensional and diversified, so as to provide readers with a more humane and high-quality experience. Secondly, multimedia fusion will change the channels and speed of periodicals dissemination. Influenced by the traditional publishing mode, the paper periodicals have a long publishing cycle and usually need more than one year to be officially published. This has a negative impact on the evaluation of academic periodicals, resulting in the blockage of dissemination and exchange of academic achievements, and is extremely harmful to the development of scientific research in the whole society. Multimedia integration technology provides a new opportunity for the dissemination of academic achievements. The use of periodical editing system can strengthen the management of a series of publishing activities, such as collecting, reviewing, compiling, editing and typesetting, and speed up the editing and typesetting of papers.

4 The Transformation of Editing and Publishing in the Context of Media Convergence

4.1 Improve Training System and Improve Comprehensive Quality

The internal training of publishing units should not only base on the basic skills of editing and publishing, but also rely on the strategic layout of "Internet+", and actively use new technologies and new media to build a diversified and open training system. To improve the comprehensive quality of editors and publishers in an all-round way, and to promote the transformation of the intellectual and omnipotent talent team. On the one hand, publishing units should strengthen vocational skills training for internal talents. The newly introduced talents in publishing units are basically theoretical and inexperienced. Publishing units should adopt internal training methods and innovate their own skills training modes in order to enhance the effectiveness of the training of publishing editors. For example, China Publishing Group has adopted the mentoring training mode to train talents, and has constructed a matching guarantee mechanism. On the other hand, publishing units should strengthen the training of rotation of internal talents. Through the training of editors and publishers in different positions in the business process, they can be fully familiar with the operation mechanism and post characteristics of the whole editing and publishing process, strengthen the sense of collaboration in transposition thinking, improve the ability of overall planning, and then promote the transformation of editors and publishers to compound editors and publishers.

4.2 Attach Importance to the Cultivation of Professional Values

Values have the characteristics of public goods in the field of informal institutions, and have economies of scale and externalities. The operation of every link in the publishing industry is not only a process of value realization, but also a process of value dissemination to meet the spiritual and cultural needs and disseminate the mainstream ideology. Whether from tradition to integration, or from single media to all media, the value orientation of the media industry will not change. Especially in the era of media convergence, the Internet has become the main battleground of public opinion struggle. On the basis of humanistic accomplishment, media accomplishment, marketing accomplishment and skill accomplishment, students also need to have political accomplishment, which depends on the cultivation and shaping of professional values in specialized education of colleges and universities.

4.3 Change the Way of Thinking and Strengthen the Role of Gatekeeper

At this stage, the integration of multimedia has changed the media's ecological environment, and a series of changes have taken place in the form of information presentation and dissemination. As an information processing and disseminator, periodical editors need to adjust and innovate the mode of communication. Paper periodicals should broaden their thinking, move towards the development path of multi-media integration, break the editorial concept and closed layout model that do not adapt to the development of the times, keep up with the current of the times and keep pace with the times. With the advent of the era of multimedia convergence, people's discourse expression tends to diversify, and different opinions can be more widely presented and confronted. The dissemination of information under the new media is fragmented and decentralized, and lacks the guidance of cultural orientation. In this context, the audience is presented with a large number of good and bad information, which has a negative impact on society. Editors of paper periodicals should strengthen their responsibility of cultural dissemination, strengthen the screening and checking of information, attach importance to the leading role of advanced culture, and give full play to the social guiding role of the mainstream discourse mode.

4.4 Humanized Development

As a complete ecosystem, the direction of evolution of media ecology is the result that various media factors constantly meet the new demands of audiences and develop together. The new media function is the inheritance and innovation of the old media function, and the media factors will be promoted with time, thus reflecting the inheritance side. Improving the quality of service and attracting more audience media convergence is literally a media-centered work, but in essence, it is based on winning users and serving users. Traditional periodicals are issued by post offices. Imagine that no one knows who the readers are and how to serve them well. Therefore, in the new media age, users must be the center to achieve their goals. But for a long time, the paper media and the audience can only communicate through simple questionnaire survey and mailbox interaction. The relationship is single and fragile, especially after the rise of social media on the Internet, this disadvantage is particularly prominent. In this case, the traditional media should create a "user-centered" service situation: first, editors should make use of powerful database platform to analyze the data of readers' educational level and professional characteristics, so as to grasp the personalized needs of users, and make good use of these data to understand the needs of readers. In order to narrow the distance from readers, we can create a three-dimensional media platform.

5 Summary

The development of multimedia convergence and the change of media environment are profoundly affecting the survival and development of traditional paper media. Under the application of multimedia technology, journals show the main characteristics of content-oriented, content-rich and content-publishing based on mobile Internet terminals. Multimedia fusion has brought opportunities for growth of traditional paper media, but it has also brought many impacts. The media survival strategies of paper media are: on the one hand, to enhance service awareness and let readers participate in production; on the other hand, to change the way of thinking and strengthen the role of "gatekeeper"; on the other hand, to base itself on paper-based communication and to spread on the Internet.

References

1. Song BA (2014) China's scientific and technological transformation and integration innovation and value on the development models and empirical analysis—research based on Yangzhou design rose valley straw technology transfer case. Technol Dev Enterp
2. Li W, Zhang X, Chen B (2016) The research on behavior pattern of transformation and upgrading driven by innovation of Hebei ceramic industry. Ceramics
3. Fan B (2016) Study on the policy of accelerating scientific and technological achievements transformation to promote innovation driven development. Innov Sci Technol
4. Jiao YB (2014) Research on SME model innovation under the transformation and upgrading background. Appl Mech Mater 687–691:4524–4527
5. Bouchard MJ, Trudelle C, Briand L et al (2015) A relational database to understand social innovation and its impact on social transformation. In: New frontiers in social innovation research. Palgrave Macmillan, Basingstoke
6. Huzair F, Sturdy S (2017) Biotechnology and the transformation of vaccine innovation: the case of the hepatitis B vaccines 1968–2000. Stud Hist Philos Biol Biomed Sci 64:11
7. Ponte D, Mierzejewska BI, Klein S (2017) The transformation of the academic publishing market: multiple perspectives on innovation. Electron Mark 27(2):1–4
8. Xia BH (2016) The research outline of social technological transformation theory and Chinese independent innovation. J Luoyang Norm Univ
9. Zhu B, Jiang H, Sha Q et al (2014) Research on experience of integration of cultural and technological innovation boosting urban transformation around major international metropolises. China Sci Technol Inf
10. Shaoya HE, Xiaonan BI (2017) The innovation and transformation of the traditional cultural resources in the grassroots social governance—a case study of Sidi Village in Wenxi County, Shanxi Province. Res Herit Preserv

11. Yuan Q, Dai B (2016) Research on transformation and innovation-driven development strategy for China's petrochemical industry. Pet Petrochem Today
12. He Q, Cheng Y, Zou J et al (2015) Research on the governance innovation of flexible employment relations under the internet economy. Hum Resour Dev China
13. Shi W, Cao CM, Feng JR (2017) The research on technological drive and publishing industry transformation in the late Qing Dynasty. Ed Friend
14. Chen M, Wei ZL et al (2017) The influence of service innovation on the transformation of economic growth pattern—a macro-level empirical investigation of China. J Shanxi Univ Finance Econ
15. Huang L, Guan Z et al (2017) Innovation and transformation of economic function of government management under the background of urbanization in China. Reform Strat
16. Zhuang ZB, Lin ZH et al (2014) The countermeasure research of transformation of China's manufacturing industry based on innovation-driven perspective. J Fujian Norm Univ
17. Liu XB (2017) On the creative transformation and innovative development of Chen Baisha's idealistic philosophy. J Wuyi Univ
18. Jin-Hua GU, Guo Y, Zhang GC et al (2015) Research on the practice and problems of Chinese veterinary medicine science and technology innovation and achievements transformation. Chin J Vet Drug
19. Gomber P, Kauffman RJ, Parker C et al (2018) On the fintech revolution: interpreting the forces of innovation, disruption and transformation in financial services. Soc Sci Electron Publ 35(1):220–265
20. Hinings B, Gegenhuber T, Greenwood R (2018) Digital innovation and transformation: an institutional perspective. Inf. Organ. 28:52–61

An Improved K-means Clustering Algorithm Based on Hadoop Platform

Xiangru Hou(✉)

Department of Information Engineering, Heilongjiang International University, Harbin 150025, China
3306530748@qq.com

Abstract. In order to solve the problem of poor clustering effect of K-means algorithm when dealing with massive high-dimensional data on Hadoop platform, and the existing improved algorithm is not conducive to parallelization. An improved K-means algorithm based on Hash is proposed on Hadoop platform. Firstly, the massive high-dimensional data is mapped to a compressed identification space, and then the clustering relationship is mined, and the initial clustering center is selected to avoid the sensitivity of the traditional K-means algorithm to randomly select the initial clustering center, and reduced the number of iterations of the K-means algorithm. Secondly, the overall parallelization of the algorithm is implemented in the framework of Map Reduce, and the degree of parallelization and execution efficiency is enhanced through the mechanisms of partition and combine. Finally, the experiments show that the algorithm not only improves the accuracy and stability of clustering, but also has a good processing speed.

Keywords: Big data · Hadoop · K-means · Clustering

1 Introduction

K-means algorithm is one of the classical clustering algorithms and has irreplaceable research value. Its advantages are simple thought, fast convergence speed and easy realization. The disadvantage is that it is sensitive to the initial clustering center, easy to form a local optimal solution with high operation complexity, especially in the big data environment [1, 2]. In order to solve the problems of poor clustering effect of K-means algorithm when processing massive high-dimensional data on Hadoop platform, and the existing improved algorithm's not conducive to parallelization, a parallelization scheme based on Hash improvement is proposed. Map massive high-dimensional data into a compressed identification space, then mine the clustering relationship and select the initial clustering center, which avoids the sensitivity of the traditional K-means algorithm to the randomly selecting initial clustering center and reduces the iteration times of the K-means algorithm [3]. Combining with Map Reduce framework, the algorithm is parallelized as a whole, and the parallelization degree and execution efficiency are enhanced by Partition, Combine and other mechanisms.

Z. Xu et al. (Eds.): CSIA 2019, AISC 928, pp. 1101–1109, 2020.
https://doi.org/10.1007/978-3-030-15235-2_146

The operation process of Map Reduce framework is executed in two stages: Map and Reduce. In MAP stage, each Map Task reads a block, calls Map function for processing, and then writes the results to the local disk. In Reduce stage, each Reduce Task reads data remotely from Map Task node, calls Reduce function for data processing, and then writes the results to HDFS. Obviously, both the results of Map and Reduce operations need to be written to disk. Although the performance of the operation is reduced, the reliability of the system is improved. Therefore, a large number of iterative calculations will greatly reduce the performance of the system.

Executing K-means algorithm on Hadoop platform can greatly reduce clustering time. Chu implemented many traditional data mining algorithms, such as Naïve Bayes, K-means, EM and so on based on Map Reduce distributed framework in cluster environment. [4] The parallel K-means algorithm based on Map Reduce distributed framework is implemented in multi-core environment. However, they did not consider the communication cost and calculation amount of execution, and the clustering accuracy and processing speed were not ideal. [5] A parallel clustering algorithm based on equivalent connection is proposed. Although the communication consumption caused by iteration is avoided to some extent, the clustering accuracy is greatly affected. [6] A clustering center optimization algorithm based on Hadoop platform is proposed. Although the clustering accuracy is improved, the algorithm is only parallelized in the clustering stage, and the center selection stage is also very resource - consuming, so the processing speed is not ideal. Although there have been many improvements in K-means algorithm, there are still few excellent algorithms transplanted to Hadoop platform, mainly for two reasons: First, the data coupling in the initial cluster center selection stage is strong and is not suitable for parallelization; Second, the initial cluster center selection still requires iterative calculation, and Map Reduce framework is very sensitive to iterative calculation [7].

Moreover, although most algorithms are parallelized, they do not make full use of Hadoop's various mechanisms. For example, most algorithms do not make good use of Partition mechanism and only use one Reducer to process when designing K-means algorithms to calculate new clustering centers, thus reducing the degree of parallelization. Many other algorithms do not use Combine mechanism to process data in shuffle stage, thus increasing the transmission burden of bandwidth and reducing the processing performance of the system [8, 9]. In addition, in practical applications, they often face massive and high-dimensional data, which is difficult to detect the overall distribution of such data in a distributed environment, which also increases the difficulty of selecting a reasonable initial clustering center. Therefore, this paper uses the principle of Hash algorithm to hash the attributes of each dimension of the data into a unified identification space, and then uses this reduced identification space to mine the clustering relationship of the data, so as to achieve the purpose of selecting the optimal initial clustering center.

2 Selection of Initial Clustering Center Based on Hash Algorithm

Hash algorithm transforms input of arbitrary length into output of fixed length through hash function, the output is a hash value. This transformation is a compression mapping. The hash space is usually smaller than the input space. Different inputs may be hashed into the same output.

The basic idea of the algorithm is to design a reasonable hash function to hash data with large similarity into the same address space and data with different similarity into different address spaces, and then select k initial cluster centers in k address spaces with the most synonyms, so that the selected initial cluster centers can satisfy the principle of minimum distance within clusters and maximum distance between clusters as much as possible. The basis of the algorithm can be summarized as follows:

(1) Mapping massive and high-dimensional data into a compressed address space by hash function is beneficial to controlling the data clustering relationship.
(2) After mapping, data with large similarity will "collide" and become synonyms. The centers of these densest data bands are closest to the clustering centers.
(3) By selecting different synonyms, the selected initial cluster centers are not in the same class as much as possible.
(4) Avoid selecting isolated points as initial clustering centers.

Definition 1: The step function is a linear combination of finite interval index functions, defining a step function $y = f(x)$. The domain is defined as $[a, b]$, the value range is $\{y_1, y_2 ... y_n\}$. Interval length is d, the step function can be expressed as:

$$f(x) = \begin{cases} y_1 \ [a, a+d] \\ y_2 \ [a+d, a+2d] \\ \cdots\cdots \\ y_k \ [b-d, b] \end{cases} \tag{1}$$

Definition 2: Design the hash function as:

$$H(key) = \varphi(key) \tag{2}$$

According to Definition 2, the hash function hashes the value of each one-dimensional attribute of the input data into k address spaces, each one-dimensional attribute of the data corresponds to a unique address space, and each address space is numbered, so each data can be represented by a row vector composed of m address space numbers, the data set can be represented by a matrix, the same row vectors are grouped together, and the numbers are counted to find the most k row vectors, and the k center points obtained by calculating each row vector correspond to the center points of all data are the selected initial cluster centers.

3 Improved K-means Algorithm Based on Hash

Algorithm Improved K-means algorithm based on Hash

Input: dataset (dataset); k (number of clusters).

Output: Clustering results.

Step1: Select k initial cluster centers:

1. Find the maximum and minimum values of each dimension of the data set;
2. Calculate the interval length d of each dimension attribute, construct an address space corresponding to each dimension attribute, and number it;
3. Hash all data to the corresponding address space;
4. Find the k most dense address spaces;
5. Calculate the center point of the data of each space in the k address spaces, these k center points are used as the initial clustering center of the K-means algorithm.

Step2: Perform K-means clustering algorithm:

1. Classify each sample point as the closest central point to it;
2. Reset the center point of each class;
3. Repeat steps (1) and (2) until convergence.

4 Implementation of Improve Algorithm on Map Reduce Framework

4.1 Implementation Strategy of Parallelization of Algorithms

The parallel strategy of this algorithm is to design three jobs to work in activity chain, each job runs independently, and the output of each job is used as the input of the next job until the end of the last job. For (1) and (2) in Step 1, since the operation of comparing each dimension attribute of each data is independent of each other and conforms to the parallel concept, and the calculation amount of the operation is huge, Map function is designed here. Reduce function is used to summarize the operation results of Map and construct address space. At this time, the calculation amount is already quite small, so only one Reducer is designed for processing. For (3), (4) and (5) of Step 1, since hashing each data into the corresponding address space is independent of each other and requires a large amount of computation, Map function is designed here. Reduce function summarizes the results of Map function operations and calculates the initial cluster center. At this time, the calculation amount is still large. Therefore, Partition mechanism is used to distribute data to each node for calculation according to the different number strings to maximize the performance of the cluster.

4.2 Implementation of Parallelization of Algorithms

Job 1's function is to construct hash tables, Map function finds out the extreme value of each dimension of data attribute, and Reduce function constructs corresponding address spaces for hash of each dimension of attribute. Job 2's function is to calculate the initial cluster center, Map function maps all data into the hash table so that each data has a unique address space number string. Combine's function is to combine data with the same number and count the number of these data to reduce the loss of bandwidth and the amount of Reducer calculation by data transmission. Partition's function is to partition the data so that the data can be transmitted to different Reducers to work, and Reduce function calculates the initial cluster center. Job 3 completes K-means clustering of all data.

Job1:

(1) Key formed after split is the byte offset of the current data relative to the starting position, and value is a string composed of attributes of each dimension of the current data.
(2) Mapper's operation is to analyze the value, compare the size of the dimension corresponding to the data, save the maximum and minimum values of each dimension attribute, output the number of each dimension attribute as a new key, and save the maximum and minimum values of the dimension.
(3) The operation performed by Reducer is to analyze the value, divide each dimension attribute into corresponding address space, and number each address space.
(4) The output result shows that key is the number of the address space and value is the value range of the address space.

Job2:

(1) Update the address space partitioned by Job1 to Job2.
(2) Key formed after split is the byte offset of the current data relative to the starting position, and value is a string composed of attributes of each dimension of the current data.
(3) Mapper's operation is to analyze the value, match the attributes of each dimension of the data with the corresponding address space, and record the number of the matching address space. Each dimension corresponds to a number, each data can be represented by a number string, and this number string is output as a new key.
(4) Partitioner performs the operation of partitioning the data so that the data with the same numbered string is in the same partition.
(5) Combiner performs the operation of merging data with the same number and counting the number of these data.
(6) Key formed after merge is the number string of the data, and value is a string array composed of all the dimensional attributes that own the number string data.
(7) The operation performed by Reducer is to resolve all the values on the first k arrays, calculate the center points of each array, and take the k center points as the initial clustering centers of the k-means algorithm.

Job3:

(1) Update the address space partitioned by Job2 to Job3.
(2) Mapper's operation is to analyze the value, compare the size of the dimension corresponding to the data, save the maximum and minimum values of each dimension attribute, output the number of each dimension attribute as a new key, and save the maximum and minimum values of the dimension.
(3) Mapper's operation is to analyze the value, calculating the distance from each point to the cluster center, and classifying the data into the nearest cluster center.
(4) The purpose of Partitioner execution is to partition the data according to the cluster center so that the data belonging to the same class are in the same partition.
(5) The operation performed by Combiner is to parse the value of value, and add the corresponding attributes of each data to each other. The new value contains the accumulated value of each dimension attribute and the total number of accumulated data.
(6) The key formed by the merged data is the value of the initial cluster center to which the current data belongs, and the value is an array of the value values of all the data belonging to the initial cluster center.
(7) The operation performed by the Reducer is to parse the values of all values on the array, calculate the new cluster center, and save.
(8) Determine the termination condition and whether to end the clustering.

5 Experimental Results and Analysis

5.1 Experimental Data and Environment

The experimental platform of this paper is built by 8 computers, one of which deploys Client node and is responsible for submitting Map Reduce and displaying the processing results, while another of which is taken as the master node to run Map Reduce and deploys name-node and job-tracker. The remaining 6 deploy data-node data nodes and task-tracker service nodes. The hardware configuration of the computer environment is as follows: 64-bit version of Ubuntu 13.10; Hadoop version 1.04; Jdk7.0 version. The experimental data come from UCI machine learning library, in which, iris, could and so on are commonly used numerical data sets to test clustering effect. The number, dimension and category of the data sets collected in this paper are listed in Table 1 respectively and are expanded by related tools.

Table 1. Experimental data set

Data set	Number of samples	Dimension	Number of categories	Attribute type
Synthetic control	700	70	8	Numerical
Could	1000	10	6	Numerical
Wine quality	4500	15	6	Numerical

5.2 Experimental Results

When testing the clustering accuracy, the author extended the above data to 1 GB. Compare the literature [4] algorithm (Algorithm 1), the literature [10] algorithm (Algorithm 2), the algorithm in this paper is algorithm 3, run 10 times, and use system sampling method to extract 10000 records for statistics. It is shown in Table 2.

Table 2. Algorithm accuracy ratio comparison

Dataset	Algorithm 1			Algorithm 2			Algorithm 3		
	Highest	Lowest	Average	Highest	Lowest	Average	Highest	Lowest	Average
Synthetic control	68.1	59.6	64.6	69.8	64.3	69.7	75.3	73.2	76.0
Could	64.2	55.6	60.3	68.3	65.3	63.5	74.5	72.6	75.3
Wine quality	61.3	53.1	55.6	65.3	30.2	60.3	69.3	64.2	68.0

Experiments show that the algorithm in this paper improves the accuracy by about 11% on the basis of the traditional parallel K-means algorithm. The traditional parallel K-means algorithm leads to unstable clustering results due to the random selection of the initial clustering center, and the difference between the highest and lowest is large. For example, the difference between the highest and lowest is 8.5% when dealing with Wine quality, and the accuracy of clustering is also poor. The accuracy of the algorithm in this paper is 7% higher than that of Algorithm 2, while the difference of algorithm 2 is about 5%, and the algorithm in this paper is basically maintained at 2%.

In order to test the processing speed of the algorithm in the big data environment, the author extended Synthetic control to five data sets of different sizes. They are 0.5 GB, 1 GB, 2 GB, 4 GB and 8 GB, respectively. Compared with the algorithms in Refs. [4] and [10], Table 3 records the iteration times of the above three algorithms when processing 8 GB, and Fig. 1 records the time taken by the three algorithms to process each data set.

Table 3. Iteration number comparison of algorithms

Number of times	1	2	3	4	5	6	7	8	9	10
Algorithm 1	42	27	24	16	50	33	28	34	21	18
Algorithm 2	28	24	15	22	18	16	26	20	25	22
Algorithm 3	6	9	9	5	9	7	8	8	9	9

Judging from iteration times, the algorithm in this paper is relatively stable and has a big gap with the comparison algorithm. It only takes about 8 times to reach the convergence condition. This is because the selected initial clustering center has approached the convergence state, greatly accelerating the convergence speed of K-means algorithm, while the traditional parallelized K-means algorithm has a slow and unstable convergence speed due to the randomness of the initial clustering center selection.

In terms of processing time, algorithm 1 is slightly better than algorithm 2 because algorithm 2 has one more center selection stage when the data set is small. With the expansion of the data set, algorithm 2 gradually embodies advantages because the initial clustering center selected by algorithm 2 reduces iteration times of K-means clustering. However, the algorithm in this paper is superior to the above two algorithms in terms of iteration times, adding Partition, Combine and other operations, and the whole process of the algorithm is fully parallelized. With the expansion of the data set, this advantage becomes more obvious, so the time performance is greatly superior to the above algorithms.

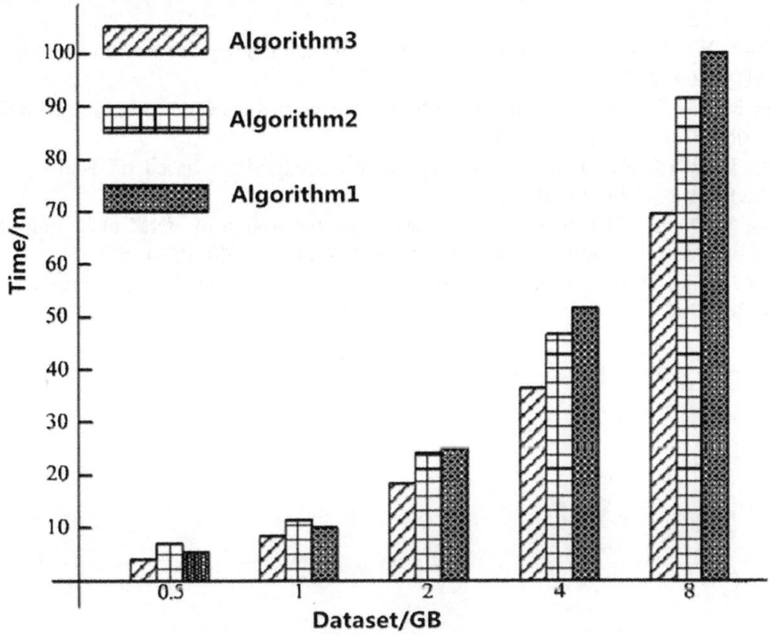

Fig. 1. Comparisons of algorithm processing time

6 Conclusion

In this paper, the optimization of K-means clustering algorithm on Hadoop platform is deeply analyzed and studied, and an initial clustering center selection scheme based on Hash algorithm principle is proposed, which hashes massive and high-dimensional data into a compressed space and then mines its clustering relationship, so that the selected initial clustering center approaches the convergence state as much as possible, which greatly reduces the iteration times of clustering and improves the clustering accuracy. At the same time, the algorithm is fully compatible with Map Reduce computing framework, and the parallelism is sufficient. Partition and Combine mechanisms improve the parallelism and processing speed of the algorithm. Finally, experiments on different UCI data sets show that the algorithm performs well in terms of accuracy, stability and processing speed.

References

1. Jinhai, Zhang J, Wu R (2018) A spectral clustering algorithm for large data based on improved sampling weighted kernel K-means. Surv Mapp Bull (11):78–82
2. Liu W, Zhang J (2018) An improved K-means clustering algorithm. Mod Bus Ind 39 (19):196–198
3. He M (2018) Research on power load data classification algorithm based on Hadoop platform. Xi'an University of Science and Technology
4. Zhao W, Ma H, He Q (2009) Parallel K-means clustering based on map reduce. In: CloudCom 2009. LNCS, vol 5931, pp 674–679
5. Miao Y, Zhang J et al (2014) New clustering algorithm based on Hadoop. Comput Sci 41 (4):269–272
6. Zhang S, Wu Z (2014) Clustering algorithm optimization research based on Hadoop. Comput Sci 41(4):269–272
7. Yang M, Ma C, Wang Y, Zhang Z (2019) An improved FCMM algorithm for K-means clustering. Comput Appl Res (07):1–6
8. Wang B (2018) Research on clustering K-means algorithm based on Hadoop platform. Comput Lett (04):18–20 (2018)
9. Zhang S, Dong Y, Chen X (2018) Research on the design of HKM clustering algorithm based on cloud computing platform Hadoop. J Appl Sci 36(03):524–534
10. Miu Y, Zhang J (2014) A new clustering algorithm based on Hadoop platform. Comput Sci 41(4):269–272

Research on Intelligent Detection System for Information Abnormal Defect Based on Personalized Recommendation of E-Book

Kong Lu(✉)

Jiangxi Modern Polytechnic College, Nanchang 330095, Jiangxi, China
79364652@qq.com

Abstract. With the accelerated pace of life, e-book reading has become a way for people to learn and play in their leisure time. When faced with a large number of e-books, the recommendation system and e-book rankings have become the entrance for readers to quickly find books of their own interest. Through the current situation of cash development of e-books, this paper analyzes the abnormality of information recommended by personalities, and discusses the problems of intelligent detection systems.

Keywords: E-book · Personalized recommendation · Intelligent detection

1 Introduction

The user's personalized recommendation accepts the influencing factor model, and according to the three stages of the e-book user's personalized recommendation technology, namely the knowledge stage, the decision stage and the acceptance stage, the measures and suggestions for the acceptance of the personalized recommendation technology of the e-book user are improved, and the Douban is added. The online and bibliographic recommendations provided by the China National Digital Library Network were analyzed [1–4]. In the process of user technology acceptance, users experience different stages and a series of activities, and finally make decisions to accept and use technology [5–7]. This paper uses the research results of the innovation diffusion theory as the main theoretical basis in the prior art to accept the research results of behavioral research, and deeply analyzes the different stages of the technology acceptance process. The electronic e-book user personalized recommendation technology accepts the intention. Based on the evolutionary law, a model of influencing factors for personalized recommendation acceptance of e-commerce users including knowledge, decision-making and acceptance is constructed [8–11]. Through analysis, this paper puts forward the influencing factors of user personalized recommendation technology at different stages: knowledge stage, user trust is the individual factor that influences the acceptance of personalized recommendation technology, user trust is influenced by personal trust tendency and system trust; decision stage, The technical characteristics of perceived usefulness and perceived ease of use are the technical factors that influence the acceptance of personalized recommendation technology; in the acceptance stage, subjective norms are the social factors that influence the

Z. Xu et al. (Eds.): CSIA 2019, AISC 928, pp. 1110–1117, 2020.
https://doi.org/10.1007/978-3-030-15235-2_147

acceptance of personalized recommendation technology [12–15]. All of these factors have an impact on the acceptance of technology acceptance behavior. The e-book user personalized recommendation technology was adopted to accept the influencing factor model, and relevant hypotheses were proposed. Most of the hypotheses were verified by using the structural equation model correlation method [16–19].

2 The Development and Current Status of E-Books

2.1 Basic Overview of E-Books

There are many definitions of e-books. At present, the community has initially identified e-books as different from traditional publications in the form of papers. Digitally, text, pictures, sounds, images and other information are recorded in light, electricity and magnetism. A digital publication that reads, copies, and transmits from a device in a medium. As a tool for reading e-books, readers are more widely available. These include personal computers, handheld digital devices and specialized e-book reading devices. Personal computers are subject to objective conditions such as size and weight. People spend less time sitting in front of a computer and use e-books with relatively little time and opportunity. Handheld digital devices, such as mobile phones, have high flexibility and take up little space. When people use smart electronic devices to read books, they can also obtain motion picture images for reading assistance. In the reader, the special e-book reader is similar to the traditional paper medium, the screen is moderate, the eye damage is small, and because of its functional specificity, it is more suitable for the reader to concentrate on reading for a long time.

2.2 E-Book Development History

After the launch of e-book readers in Amazon, it has become a global e-book reading boom, and e-book readers have become popular in Europe and the United States. A number of publishers have launched their own e-book readers. According to the e-reader industry market research report, the e-book reader market share is divided by North America, Europe, and China. Compared with computers, mobile phone color pictures or video image content multi-layer multimedia effects. Special e-book readers have room for improvement in meeting user reading requirements and improving user reading experience. The e-book reader industry chain consists of the design and production of the screen main control system. E-book publishers provide online services while providing reading content, and promote the subversion of traditional reading methods in the digital publishing and distribution industry. At present, the global e-reader sales momentum is very fast, the US e-book reader market has set off a wave of price cuts, Taiwan is fully promoting the pace of localization of e-book readers, the Japanese e-book reader industry has entered a rapid development track, and the UK e-book reader The market sales situation is getting better and the German e-book reader market has great potential for development.

2.3 E-Book Personalized Recommendation

In terms of the development of the e-book list, most of them are based on historical data statistics, so there is no predictive recommendation reflecting the development trend; in the personalized recommendation of e-books, the accuracy of the recommendation is made due to the lack of user-active feedback behavior data. affected. Therefore, in response to these problems, this paper has carried out research on individual e-book recommendation and group-oriented e-book list customization. Maximize the reading of books on the list by creating a list of popular books for group users. The development of an existing popular book list is only a matter of past statistics and does not reflect the future popularity of the book.

3 An Overview of the Basic Theory Based on User Personalized Recommendation Optimization Method

3.1 Personalized Recommendation Basic Theory

With the development of the Internet, more and more devices are able to access the Internet. While enjoying the vast amount of information on the Internet, they are also faced with the confusion of how to quickly find the information they need. Recommendations are an information screening technique designed to help users quickly access useful information. According to whether the user has put forward a clear recommendation keyword, the recommendation can be divided into explicit recommendation and implicit recommendation. The characteristic of explicit recommendation is that there are clear keywords, which can be recommended for users based on keywords. Implicit recommendation does not have clear keywords. It is necessary to predict the user's preferences based on the user's existing shopping records, evaluation records, browsing records and other historical information, so the implicit recommendation is more difficult. There are far more recommended application scenarios in the Internet than explicit recommendations. For example, most e-commerce companies need to give users implicit recommendations to attract users and increase sales. This chapter mainly introduces and analyzes the advantages and disadvantages of user personalized recommendation, context-aware recommendation, social network-based user recommendation, and collaborative filtering-based recommendation.

3.2 User Personalized Recommendation

Personalized recommendations give different recommendations for users with different backgrounds. The user's background includes information such as the user's income, education, social status, age, gender, and social relationships. The preferences of different users in the background are also largely different, and the expected results of the recommendations will be quite different. The fundamental purpose of personalized recommendations is to give accurate recommendations to users with different preferences. The personalized recommendation is based on the hidden information of the user to formulate a recommendation template or add an auxiliary query word based on the keyword given by the user, so as to achieve personalized recommendation for the user. In order to improve the quality of personalized recommendations, problems that need to be solved, for example, how to more comprehensively mine hidden information of users, better reflect the actual characteristics of users, and then give higher quality personalized recommendations; how to imply for multiple Information weighting value. Recommendation results based on different information are different in large probability. Accurately assigning reasonable weights to various information can improve the quality of personalized recommendations. Existing personalized recommendations increase the quality of personalized recommendations by incorporating recommendation filters into the user's preferences. The second screening is performed in all the recommendation results related to the user input keyword. By adding the user personalization factor, the user can be screened out for the personalized recommendation result. The method firstly discovers the seed closely related to the keyword. The webpage is further filtered by the algorithm to expand the link characteristics of the webpages associated with the keywords to improve the quality of the recommendation. One of the reasons for the impact of the recommendation is that the recommendation results include a certain amount of low-quality pages, so he believes that low-quality pages should be prioritized.

4 Research Status of Capable Detection Systems

4.1 Intelligent Detection System Overview

Intrusion detection is essentially an electronic data processing process. The collected security audit data is analyzed and processed according to a predetermined method, and the conclusion that the system is invaded is made based on the analysis result. The collected data is generally a system log or a network event log, a predetermined method, that is, an analysis technique used by the analysis engine. It is generally a pattern matching technique or a statistical analysis technique or a combination of the two. Key functions performed by IDS include: monitoring, analyzing user and system activity; identifying known attacks and responding; statistically analyzing abnormal behavior patterns; and assessing the integrity of critical systems and data files. Intrusion detection is generally divided into three steps, followed by information collection, data analysis, and response. Correspondingly, IDS generally consists of three functional modules: information collection, data analysis, and response, each of which undertakes the task of three steps.

4.2 Research on the Development of Intelligent Detection Systems

According to the analyzed data, the intrusion detection system can be divided into a host-based intrusion detection system and a network-based intrusion detection system. The host-based intrusion detection system usually uses audit data such as system logs and application logs as the detected data source, and then collects the information from the host for analysis; the network-based intrusion detection system uses the data packets transmitted on the network as the detection. data source. According to the technology used in the analysis, the intrusion detection system can be divided into an intrusion detection system based on misuse detection and an intrusion detection system based on anomaly detection. The method of misuse detection is quite similar to the method of anti-virus software. The attack method is expressed in a certain pattern or feature in advance, and the collected information is matched with known attack patterns or features to detect whether there is intrusion behavior. Anomaly detection is the pre-establishment of a description of the normal behavior of the network system. By analyzing the various collected information, it identifies those behaviors that deviate significantly from the normal behavior of the network system and treats them as intrusion attempts. According to different response strategies, intrusion detection systems can be divided into active response and passive response. It is a generic intrusion detection model, as shown in Fig. 1. The model is still widely used in intrusion detection systems. The generic intrusion detection system model consists of three main components: an event generator, an activity recorder, and a rule set. The event generator provides system activity information. The event comes from the system audit record, network communication or firewall, and the application subsystem such as the authentication server. The rule set is a reference engine that determines whether the intrusion occurs. It can be called a normal verification event. And state data checkers that use models, rules, patterns, and statistics to flag intrusion behavior; the activity logger holds the state of the system or network under surveillance. When an event occurs in the data source, the variables in the activity logger are changed, and the activity logger creates new variables based on the activity detected by the rule set. Feedback is an important part of the model. Some events may trigger rule learning and add new rules. Once the rule set detects a change in the threshold value in the active record set, the type, frequency, and other details of the event generated by the event generator are changed.

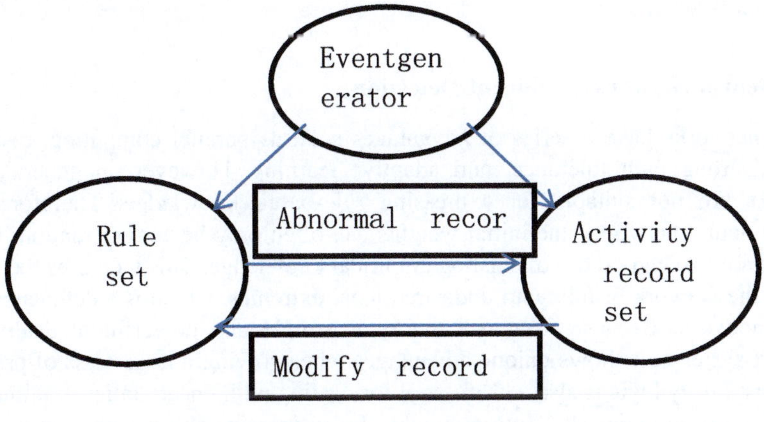

Fig. 1. Intrusion detection system model

4.3 Future Development Trend of Intelligent Detection System Based on Current Status

The Public Intrusion Detection Framework was developed by DARPA to allow ID components to interoperate and share information by developing a common IDS language, protocol, and application interface. The ultimate goal is to have different IDS systems share information and resources so they can use each other's ID parts. More and more organizations are joining the CIDF program, and it is expected that the IETF's Intrusion Detection Working Group will be established to develop intrusion detection specifications. The CIDF architecture model divides the intrusion detection system into four parts, describes and standardizes each part of the completed tasks, and exchanges and communicates between the parts through the general intrusion detection object format. Each GIDO encodes the facts that occur, which may be specific events that occur at a certain time, may be conclusions about a series of events, or may be instructions to perform an action. Each component in CIDF is a logical entity that can be generated or consumed. It can be a process on one computer or a collection of multiple processes on multiple computers. The event generator generates GIDOs, but does not consume them. Its task is to be sampled into a specific environment for sampling, and what happens is converted to GIDOs for use by other components; after the event analyzer receives the GIDOs, it analyzes it. Importance, draw conclusions and translate into another GIDOs; the event database stores events for retrieval purposes. The role of the event generator is to get events from a large computing environment outside of IDS and provide them to other parts of the system as GIDOs. The event analyzer is the core part of the IDS. It takes the GIDOs from other components, analyzes it, and then returns the new GIDOs, which is actually a summary or summary of the input events. The response unit consumes GIDOS. According to GIDOs, the response unit makes a decision to perform an action and performs the action. Such actions include ending the process, resetting the connection, changing file permissions, and so on.

4.4 Neural Network Intelligent Detection

Neural networks have a series of advantages such as parallel computing, distributed storage, strong fault tolerance, and adaptive learning. However, in general, neural networks are not suitable for expressing rule-based knowledge. Therefore, when training neural networks, the initial weights can often only be zero or random because they cannot make good use of existing empirical knowledge. This increases the training time of the network or falls into undesired local extremes, which is a deficiency of the neural network. Because fuzzy set theory is simple and powerful in dealing with complex systems, it shows unique advantages when solving a large class of prediction problems. Fuzzy logic is also a useful tool for dealing with uncertainties, nonlinearities, and other uncertainties. It is more suitable for expressing those vague or qualitative knowledge, and its way of reasoning is more similar to the way people think. However, although fuzzy logic has these significant advantages, its biggest drawback is the lack of self-learning and adaptive capabilities. The neural network and the fuzzy inference system have similar network structure forms in dealing with the nonlinear mapping relationship between input and output, but the processing is different. They can approximate a real continuous function with arbitrary precision under certain conditions. Fuzzy neural network control focuses on the characteristics of fuzzy control and neural network control. It tries to combine the two properly and absorb the strengths of the two to form a system with better performance than a single neural network or a separate fuzzy system. There are many forms of fuzzy neural networks, and fuzzy neural networks based on standard models are more common. In the design of the public intrusion detection framework of the big information platform, we noticed that the general architecture of IDS has striking similarities with the schematic of the fuzzy logic system. Using the fuzzy classification ability unique to fuzzy neural networks, the input events are reasonably summarized. The event analyzer constructed by the fuzzy neural network has higher reliability and flexibility.

5 Summary

People generally tend to trust familiar things. Therefore, e-book companies should focus on improving users' familiarity with personalized recommendation techniques. On the one hand, this familiarity is high in presentation rate, such as frequent advertising in the media, publicity, etc. On the other hand, familiarity also means that people know the laws governing the development of things. If the personalized recommendation system allows the user to know how the recommendation is generated by the input information, the user will trust the system more. The knowledge system indicates that the system should have a certain explanatory power.

References

1. Shen Y, Zhu X (2015) Intelligent particle filter and its application to fault detection of nonlinear system. IEEE Trans Industr Electron 62(6):3852–3861
2. Kum CH, Cho DC, Ra MS, et al (2014) Lane detection system with around view monitoring for intelligent vehicle. In: SoC design conference
3. Qian X, Feng H, Zhao G et al (2014) Personalized recommendation combining user interest and social circle. IEEE Trans Knowl Data Eng 26(7):1763–1777
4. West J, Bhattacharya M (2016) Intelligent financial fraud detection: a comprehensive review. Comput Secur 57:47–66
5. Liang T, Jiang Y, Lei L, et al (2014) Ensemble contextual bandits for personalized recommendation. In: ACM conference on recommender systems
6. Yin H, Cui B, Ling C et al (2015) Modeling location-based user rating profiles for personalized recommendation. ACM Trans Knowl Discov Data 9(3):1–41
7. Xie J, Knijnenburg BP, Jin H (2014) Location sharing privacy preference: analysis and personalized recommendation. In: International conference on intelligent user interfaces
8. Ghenname M, Abik M, Ajhoun R, et al (2014) Personalized recommendation based hashtags on e-learning systems. In: International symposium ISKO-Maghreb
9. Tang L, Jiang Y, Li L, et al (2015) Personalized recommendation via parameter-free contextual bandits. In: International ACM SIGIR conference on research and development in information retrieval

10. Xie Z (2014) Personalized recommendation algorithm based on preference features. Tsinghua Sci Technol 19(3):293–299
11. Amato A, Martino BD, Scialdone M, et al (2014) Personalized recommendation of semantically annotated media contents. In: International symposium on intelligent distributed computing
12. Yue H, Tan J (2015) Study on SINA micro-blog personalized recommendation based on semantic network. Expert Syst Appl 42(10):4797–4804
13. Shen Y, Jin H (2014) Privacy-preserving personalized recommendation: an instance-based approach via differential privacy. In: IEEE international conference on data mining
14. Zhang Y (2015) Incorporating phrase-level sentiment analysis on textual reviews for personalized recommendation
15. Zhu X, Tian H, Cai S (2014) Personalized recommendation with corrected similarity. J Stat Mech: Theory Exp 2014(7):P07004
16. Wang ZS, Qi L, Jing W, et al (2016) Real-time personalized recommendation based on implicit user feedback data stream. Chin J Comput
17. Xin L (2015) Modeling users' dynamic preference for personalized recommendation. In: International conference on artificial intelligence
18. Zhang Y (2015) Incorporating phrase-level sentiment analysis on textual reviews for personalized recommendation. In: Eighth ACM international conference on web search and data mining
19. Zhao G, Qian X, He F (2014) Personalized recommendation by exploring social users' behaviors. In: Anniversary international conference on multimedia modeling

Research on Distributed High Speed Network Intrusion Prevention System

Lei Zheng(✉), Hui Yuan, Xiangli Peng, Guowei Zhu, Yue Guo, Hao Xu, and Guoru Deng

Information and Communication Company of Hubei State Grid Corporation, No. 197 Xu Dong Street, Wuhan, Hubei, China
882148@qq.com

Abstract. The Internet is the darling of the information age. Its rapid development has brought a lot of wealth to the society, but it has also brought about increasingly serious security problems. In particular, the widespread application of e-commerce has made network security the most important part of the development of network technology. Network security technology is increasingly valued by computer researchers. Most of the existing security products are passive. The firewall can only be statically disabled. Although the Intrusion Detection System can dynamically detect the intrusion behavior, it cannot block the detected attack behavior. However, the impact of the intrusion prevention system on network performance and the high intrusion detection false alarm rate restrict the development and application of the IPS system. Especially on gigabit high-speed networks, performance has become the primary bottleneck of IPS systems. In view of the above problems, this paper proposes a distributed intrusion detection and blocking system that can run efficiently on high-speed networks. Such systems are also known as intrusion prevention systems IPS. Explain the structure of distributed high-speed network intrusion prevention system, and also introduce the related implementation technology and the realization of each part of distributed intrusion prevention system.

Keywords: Intrusion prevention system · High speed network · Distributed system · Host defense

1 Introduction

With the widespread use of the Internet, network security issues have become increasingly prominent [1]. The intrusion prevention system is a security defense system developed on the basis of the intrusion detection system [2]. It integrates the functions of firewall and intrusion detection, and can respond and intercept the detected intrusion behavior in real time, reducing the loss caused by network security incidents. To enhance network security, the intrusion prevention system has gradually gained people's attention and gradually applied to the network security defense system [3]. However, it is precisely because the intrusion prevention system will intercept the detected intrusion behavior in real time [4–8]. The intrusion prevention system itself also faces some challenges: how to identify the intrusion behavior efficiently and

Z. Xu et al. (Eds.): CSIA 2019, AISC 928, pp. 1118–1126, 2020.
https://doi.org/10.1007/978-3-030-15235-2_148

accurately; how to identify distributed and complex intrusion behaviors; How to intelligently respond to detected intrusions; how to provide good scalability and anti-aggression, and so on [9–14]. These challenges constrain the further widespread use of intrusion prevention systems. Aiming at the above problems, this paper introduces mobile agent technology into the intrusion prevention system, and proposes an anti-attack distributed intrusion prevention system [15] ARDIPS. The design goals, architecture, network deployment structure, module design, and cooperation mechanism of the ARDIPS system are Communication mechanisms and the like have been analyzed and described [12, 16–18].

2 Common Network Attack Methods

The network attack method can be classified according to different standards. But in general, at the highest level can be divided into active and passive attacks. Further classification Due to the complexity of cyber attacks, there is currently no uniform standard. This article will simply classify the attack according to the attack principle and the attack target.

2.1 Active and Passive Attacks

Active attack is an attacker who actively does something that is not conducive to the other system, including the intentional behavior of the attacker. For example, remotely log in to the specified machine's port 25 to find out the information of the mail server running by the company, or to forge an invalid IP address to connect to the server, so that the system receiving the wrong IP address wastes time connecting to the illegal address, etc. Attacks are all active attacks. Because of this, aggressive behavior is easier to detect.

Passive attacks mainly collect information rather than access it, and have no impact on the operation of the system itself. Therefore, it is relatively difficult to be noticed and detected, and managers are often not aware of such activities. Passive attacks include attack methods such as sniffing and information gathering.

2.2 According to the Principle of Attack Classification

According to the attack principle, most of the network attack methods can be divided into three categories:

(1) Using the system to implement the vulnerability
Such attacks exploit the operating system, application software, and even the implementation flaws of network devices and network architectures. The most common are buffer overflow attacks.
(2) Using network design flaws
Such attacks exploit the flaws of network protocol design to attack. Some attacks cause the software protocol stack to crash, while others provide false information to deceive users. Since the Internet is an open system, it is very resistant to

fundamentally modifying the protocol. Therefore, such attacks are generally difficult to completely block. Some solutions are based on maintaining compatibility with existing protocols and repairing the original protocols to some extent. In many cases, it cannot be completely avoided.

(3) Utilize a large number of normal requests
Such attacks are also called "violent" attacks. The idea is to send a large number of normal requests, causing the other server or network to be unavailable, or guessing the other party's network password. Generally, such attacks are DoS or DDoS attacks.

3 The Structure of Common Intrusion Prevention Systems

3.1 Online IDS (In-line IDS)

Most traditional NIDSs are equipped with network cards to capture network packets. By setting the network card to promiscuous mode, network packets can be collected into the system for intrusion detection. Then, a network card is set on such NIDS to allow packets to pass. Forwarded from another network card, the two network cards are connected to the internal and external networks. The whole structure is similar to a bridge. The IDS system with such a structure is called online IDS, and its structure is shown in Fig. 1.

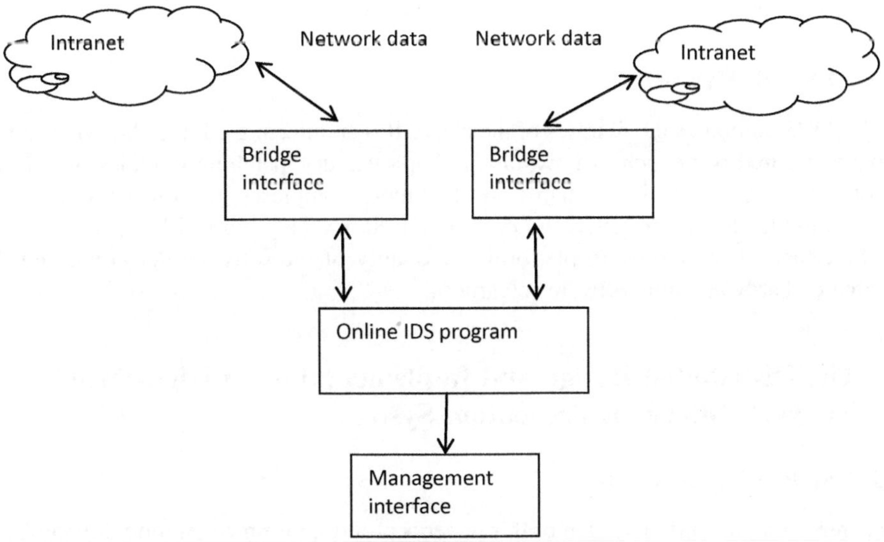

Fig. 1. Online IDS structure diagram

Online IDS is the simplest IPS system. Compared to traditional NIDS, the advancement of online IDS is to provide attack blocking capability. It has the characteristics of low cost and easy migration from existing IDS systems. Therefore, it is adopted by a large number of small security vendors. However, such a network card capture-based system can barely reach a load capacity of about 100 Mbps, and is completely unable to meet the needs of a high-speed network.

3.2 Seven-Layer Switch (Layer Seven Switches)

The traditional switch belongs to the Layer 2 network device. As the network speed increases, the routers originally implemented by software, and even some simple applications with higher performance requirements, gradually turn to hardware implementation. The result is a three-layer or seven-layer switch. Layer 3 switches can partially replace the functions of routers. The common use of Layer 7 switches is load balancing based on application protocols. To achieve adequate performance, switch vendors typically use specialized hardware to achieve high performance and easily handle gigabit-level network traffic in extreme situations. Many Layer 7 switch vendors have added a certain degree of additional features such as DoS attack prevention and DDoS functions to the application, which can perform application layer feature detection and linkage attack blocking.

3.3 Seven Layer Firewall (Layer Seven Firewall)

The seven-layer firewall is based on the traditional firewall, which adds an extension to the application layer check, and can also detect some known attacks with obvious features. Similar to the seven-layer switch, the seven-layer firewall is also relatively poorly scalable and can only be tested relatively easily.

3.4 Hybrid (Hybrid)

Hybrid IPS combines the features of the above IPS architectures: for high-performance, simple-featured parts such as firewalls or simple feature matching modules, which are implemented using dedicated hardware. For more complex detection functions, software is used. The performance and detection accuracy of a hybrid IPS depends on the performance of the hardware platform, the quality of the software detection, and the degree of hardware and software integration.

4 The Distributed Design and Implementation of High-Speed Network Intrusion Prevention System

4.1 System Design Goals

The intrusion prevention system of this paper is proposed for the common difficulties of the IPS system. In addition, the system has been extended in the concept of traditional IPS. The system design goals are as follows:

(1) The data throughput of the front-end firewall module reaches the gigabit level to meet the needs of high-speed networks without affecting network performance.
(2) The back-end data processing module reaches the quasi-Gigabit level.

(3) To solve the key problem of IPS with high false positive rate to some extent.
(4) It can block large-scale denial of service attacks that often exist on high-speed networks to a certain extent.
(5) With content filtering, it can filter harmful information on the network.

In the above objectives, the lack of processing performance and high false positive rate are the main difficulties in the current IPS system, and it is also the main problem that the system needs to solve.

4.2 Packet Collection and Distribution Module

The full-load traffic of the 1G duplex link can reach 2 Gbps, and all the data collected into the system memory will cause a large load on the forwarding system. Therefore, the message collection and distribution module should be implemented in hardware as much as possible, so that the network data is directly distributed to each network interface without going through the system bus. Some of the more complex distribution strategies (such as tracking distributions over TCP connections) are difficult to implement in hardware. In this case, only the scheme of collecting data into memory and distributing it by software can be adopted. At this time, the system processing capability is difficult to reach the peak of the Gigabit network, but it can meet the needs of the general situation.

Several distribution strategies that meet the requirements and their advantages and disadvantages are shown in Table 1.

Table 1. Several distribution strategies and comparison

Distribution strategy	Advantage	Disadvantage
The network data is processed separately according to the protocol: • Perform connection tracking on the TCP protocol and send the same connected data to the same data processor • Other non-connection-oriented protocols are distributed according to the combination of internal and external network addresses	The majority of the TCP data in the network data is distributed according to the connection, which can guarantee the finest granularity of negative Load balancing	It is not easy to implement in hardware. The software has a lot of work for connection tracking processing. In addition, attacks that involve multiple TCP connections, such as PortScan, may be distributed to different processors, increasing the difficulty of detection
Distributed according to the combination of internal and external network addresses	Simpler implementation	The equilibrium granularity is relatively rough
Distribute only by intranet address	Simple implementation	The balance granularity is rough. In the case of DDoS attacks, a large amount of load will be concentrated on the same processor and cannot be distributed

4.3 Intrusion Detection Module

The intrusion detection module is deployed on multiple systems using a distributed architecture. The detection capabilities of each system are identical, and they carry data from different network addresses.

The intrusion detection module is based on the traditional IDS. The distribution strategy of the distribution module tries to ensure that the data belonging to the same session is distributed to the same detection system. Therefore, the traditional IDS system can detect most of the intrusion behavior, and a few intrusion behaviors such as port scanning, DoS, DDoS, etc. involve multiple sessions and need to be processed separately for different behaviors. For example, for port scanning, packets containing the SYN flag can be recorded. The intrusion detection module submits the data that needs further processing and the detected message to the central processing module, and the central processing module comprehensively processes and makes an intrusion determination. The intrusion detection module itself does not determine the intrusion behavior.

A load monitoring agent is also installed on the intrusion detection system, and the load condition of the system is periodically submitted to the central processing module, and the central processing module dynamically adjusts the balance load of the distribution strategy in the previous stage according to the information.

4.4 System Data Processing and Performance Analysis

The session size of the intranet packet IP address is too coarse, and the data center IP network traffic distribution is rather uneven, resulting in poor traffic balancing. In the case of large traffic, it is easy to reach the upper limit of the traffic of a single NIC. Causes a lost message. In addition, 100M network cards usually do not interrupt the merge design, and it is also an important reason to use a large amount of system interrupt resources when sending messages. The solution is to use Gigabit network card or dedicated hardware to send messages. In order to test the upper limit of software packet processing capability, we use the message sending function of Wind Force 3.0,

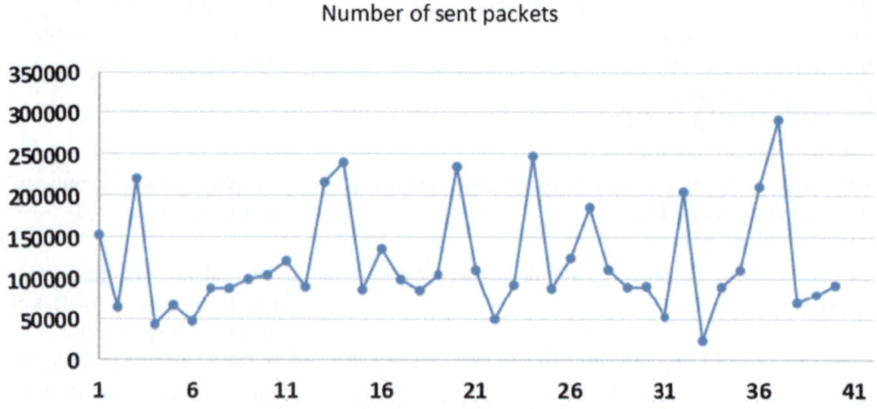

Fig. 2. Distribution module stress test

which is sent to the network card after the message is processed. Send the message through the send interface of Wind Force 3.0. The results of stress testing the forwarding module are shown in Figs. 2 and 3:

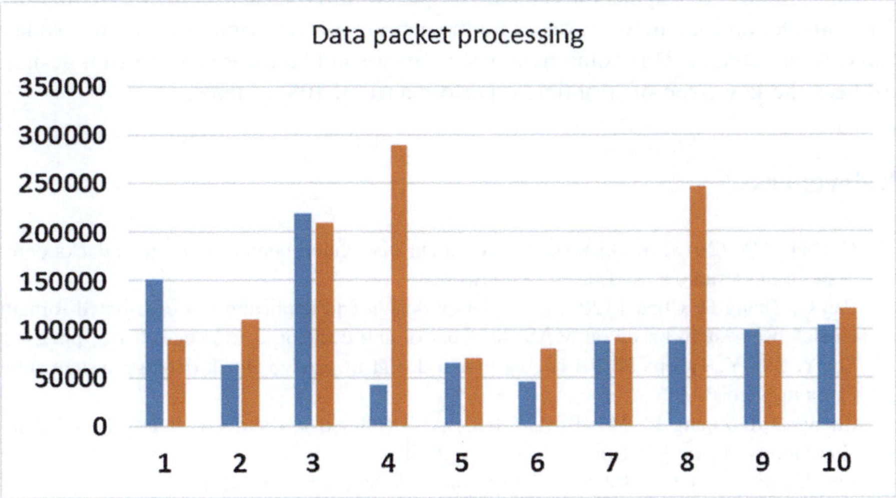

Fig. 3. Data packet processing

The data traffic of the data center is less than 1G. The test uses the software to process the collected data packets multiple times, and the data traffic is amplified by 30 times. The test duration is 1 min. The software sends 14133900 messages, totaling 7045248570 bytes. From the switch, the switch receives 14133677 messages, totaling 7045232207 bytes, the packet loss rate is 0.0016%, and the average report is sent every second. The number of texts is 235,565 and the average traffic is close to 940 Mbps. It can be seen that the processing and sending of messages through Wind Force 3 software can basically reach the Gigabit standard, considering that there is still room for further optimization of software and Wind Force hardware, such as distribution operations in Linux kernel mode. Therefore, it can be considered that the processing of the message by the optimized software and the distribution of the dedicated hardware can meet the needs of the gigabit message distribution.

5 Conclusion

The importance of network security has become increasingly prominent with the continuous development of the Internet. Static security products represented by firewalls can no longer meet the security needs. Dynamic security products represented by intrusion detection systems (IDS) have gradually become the mainstream of security products. However, many problems in the intrusion detection system affect its application, mainly in the absence of dynamic response mechanism, high false alarm rate, and can not adapt to the performance of high-speed network. In view of the difficulties in the implementation of IPS system, this paper proposes a model of distributed high-speed network intrusion prevention system. And given a pilot implementation. The distributed high-speed network intrusion prevention system uses a dedicated hardware expansion card as the packet filtering and collecting component. The software collects network data into the memory and distributes it to multiple back-end data processors. This combination of software and hardware can be well designed. Address the key issue of insufficient performance of IPS systems.

References

1. Hachem HY (2013) Sophisticated multi-agent distributed denial of service attacks defense system. Dissertations & Theses - Gradworks
2. Pan C, Zhang H, Chen J (2012) Simulation design and application of distributed formation air defense system based on MAS. In: Control and decision conference. IEEE, pp 23–26
3. Shi Y, Sun Y, Troops P (2014) Distributed denial of service attack defense system survey. Comput Secur
4. Zhang DM, Zhang K, Mei-Bo L (2014) A distributed sea surface IR attack and defense simulation system. Electron Opt Control (3):58–61
5. Liu B, Bi J (2015) DISCS: a DIStributed Collaboration System for inter-AS spoofing defense. In: International conference on parallel processing. IEEE, pp 160–169
6. Kwon YJ (2015) A survey on defense mechanism against distributed denial of service (DDoS) attacks in control system. KEPCO J Electric Power Energy 1(1):55–59
7. Lin Z, Li K, Hou H et al (2018) MDFS: a mimic defense theory based architecture for distributed file system. In: IEEE international conference on big data. IEEE, pp 2670–2675
8. Li Y, Zhou C, Huang M et al (2016) Lead tolerance mechanism in *Conyza canadensis*: subcellular distribution, ultrastructure, antioxidative defense system, and phytochelatins. J Plant Res 129(2):251–262
9. Li H, Hu J, Ma H et al (2017) The architecture of distributed storage system under mimic defense theory. In: IEEE international conference on big data. IEEE, pp 2658–2663
10. Falkner K, Chiprianov V, Falkner N et al (2013) Model-driven performance prediction of distributed real-time embedded defense systems. In: International conference on engineering of complex computer systems. IEEE Computer Society, pp 155–158
11. Shen D, Yu W, Blasch EP et al (2015) Towards an integrated defense system for cyber security situation awareness experiment. In: Sensors and systems for space applications VIII. SPIE, vol 9469, pp 946908–946908-8
12. Liu J, Lai Y, Zhang S (2017) FL-GUARD: a detection and defense system for DDoS attack in SDN. In: International conference, pp 107–111
13. Ni P, Liu JM, Liu YL et al (2014) Research on mission planning for distributed multi-sensors in anti-TBM combat based on multi-agent system. Sens Lett 12(2):325–331(7)
14. Wang C, Miu TTN, Luo X et al (2017) SkyShield: a sketch-based defense system against application layer DDoS attacks. IEEE Trans Inf Forensics Secur 13(3):559–573
15. Huang Z, Sheng Y, Chen M et al (2018) Liquiritigenin and liquiritin alleviated MCT-induced HSOS by activating Nrf2 antioxidative defense system. Toxicol Appl Pharmacol 355:18–27

16. Zegzhda DP, Stepanova TV (2012) Stochastic model of interaction between botnets and distributed computer defense systems. In: International conference on mathematical methods, MODELS and architectures for computer network security: computer network security. Springer, pp 218–225
17. Lai SF, Su HK, Hsiao WH et al (2016) Design and implementation of cloud security defense system with software defined networking technologies. In: International conference on information and communication technology convergence. IEEE, pp 292–297
18. Behal S, Kumar K, Sachdeva M (2018) D-FAC: a novel ϕ-divergence based distributed DDoS defense system. J King Saud Univ

Ecosystem Description of Hadoop Platform Based on HDFS, MapReduce and Data Warehouse Tool Hive

Hongsheng Xu[1,2](✉), Xiangkui Chen[1], and Ganglong Fan[1,2]

[1] Luoyang Normal University, Luoyang 471934, China
85660190@qq.com
[2] Henan Key Laboratory for Big Data Processing & Analytics of Electronic Commerce, Luoyang 471934, China

Abstract. This paper introduces the processing process of the distributed file system (HDFS, MapReduce) which is the core of the Hadoop distributed computing platform and introduces the data warehouse tool Hive and the distributed database Hbase. Spark is a big data distributed programming framework, which not only implements MapReduce operator map function and reduce function and calculation model, but also provides more abundant operators. This paper describes the ecosystem of Hadoop platform based on HDFS, MapReduce and data warehouse tool Hive.

Keywords: Hadoop · HDFS · MapReduce · Spark · Hive

1 Introduction

For Hadoop clusters, there are two broad categories of roles: Master and Salve. A HDFS cluster consists of a NameNode and several DataNode. NameNode, as the primary server, manages the namespace of the file system and the access operation of the client to the file system [1]. The DataNode in the cluster manages the stored data. The MapReduce framework is composed of a single JobTracker running on the primary node and a TaskTracker running on each cluster slave node.

Spark is a fast general-purpose computing engine designed for large-scale data processing. It is an iterative computation based on memory. Spark preserves the advantages of MapReduce and greatly improves its timeliness. Therefore, it provides a good support for the system which needs iterative calculation and high timeliness. Developers can use more than 80 advanced operators for data analysis in languages such as Java, Scala or Python.

MapReduce distributes the traditional query, decomposition and data analysis, and assigns processing tasks to different processing nodes, so it has stronger parallel processing capability. As a simplified parallel programming model, MapReduce also reduces the threshold for developing parallel applications.

Because Hive is built on Hadoop, the extensibility of Hive is consistent with that of Hadoop. Because of the strict restriction of ACID semantics, the extended rows are very limited. At present, the most advanced parallel database Oracle in the theory of

Z. Xu et al. (Eds.): CSIA 2019, AISC 928, pp. 1127–1133, 2020.
https://doi.org/10.1007/978-3-030-15235-2_149

expansion capacity is only about 100 Data size. Since Hive is built on a cluster and can be used for parallel computing using MapReduce, it can support very large scale data, whereas the database can support a smaller scale of data.

HDFS and MapReduce implementation are completely separate, not without HDFS cannot MapReduce operations. Hadoop and other cloud computing projects also have in common and goal: to achieve massive data computing. For mass computing, a stable, secure data container is needed before the Hadoop distributed file system. HDFS, Hadoop Distributed File System is available.

All data in Hive is stored in HDFS. The storage structure mainly includes database, file, table and view. Hive contains the following data models: Table internal table, External Table external table, Partition partition, Bucket bucket. Hive can load text file directly by default. Sequence file, RCFile is also supported.

Spark is a computing engine similar to MapReduce. Its memory mode solves the problem of slow read disk speed in MapReduce. In addition, it is based on the functional programming style of Scala and the efficiency of parallel computing in API.

2 Analysis of Interaction Between HDFS and MapReduce

HDFS uses a master-slave (Master/Slave) architecture model, and a HDFS cluster is made up of a single NameNode and several DataNode (multiple NameNode configurations have been implemented in the latest Hadoop2.2 version-which some large companies do by modifying the hadoop source code. In the latest version,). NameNode has been implemented as the primary server, managing file system namespaces and client access to files. DataNode manages stored data. HDFS supports data in the form of files.

Reduce receives data from different map tasks, and the data from each map is ordered. If the amount of data accepted by the reduce side is fairly small, it is stored directly in memory (the buffer size is controlled by the mapred.job.shuffle.input.buffer. percent property, Represents the percentage of heap space used for this purpose), and if the amount of data exceeds a certain percentage of the buffer size (determined by mapred.job.shuffle.merge.percent), the data is merged and spilled to disk.

MapReduce provides an Partitioner interface that determines which reduce task should ultimately handle the current pair of output data based on the number of key or value and reduce [2]. Default to the key hash and then to the number of reduce task modules. The default mode is only for the average reduce processing power, if the user has a need for Partitioner, can be customized and set to the job.

The core storage layer of Hadoop is called HDFS, full name is Hadoop file storage system, and with storage system, there is analysis system, so there is open source version of MapReduce, similar reference BigTable and Hbase. Once open source, the whole system will use more people, so everyone seems to want a variety of features.

In a large scale MapReduce computing cluster composed of low-end commercial servers, errors in node hardware (host, disk, memory, etc.) and software errors are the norm, so MapReduce needs to be able to detect and isolate error nodes. The new node takes over the computing task of the error node. At the same time, the system will maintain the reliability of the data storage, improve the reliability of the data storage by using the multi-backup redundant storage mechanism, and can detect and restore the wrong data in time.

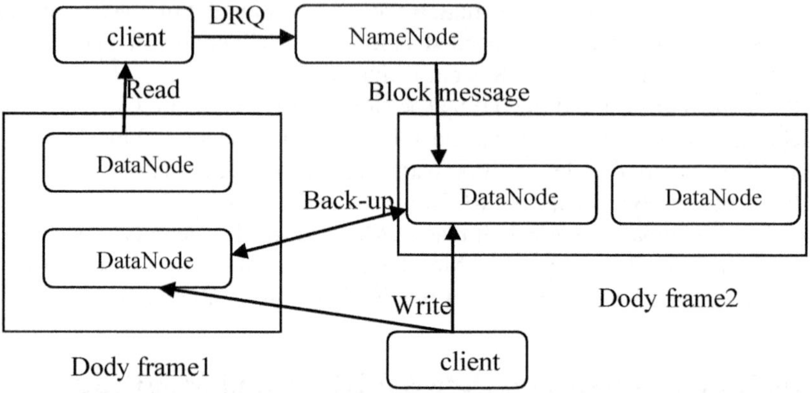

Fig. 1. HDFS architecture diagram.

Figure 1 involves three roles: NameNode, DataNode, Client.NameNode is the manager, DataNode is the file store, and Client is the application that needs to obtain a distributed file system [3]. MapReduce is suitable for data analysis, log analysis, business intelligence analysis, customer marketing, large-scale indexing and so on, and has very obvious effect. By combining MapReduce technology with real-time analysis, the credit calculation time of a household appliance company is shortened from 33 h to 8 s, while the time of gene analysis of MKI is shortened from several days to 20 min.

Internally, files are divided into blocks of data that are stored in a set of namespaces of the. NameNode execution file system on a set of DataNode, such as open, close, rename files or directories, etc. It is also responsible for mapping data blocks to specific DataNode [4]. DataNode is responsible for processing file reading and writing of file system clients, creating, deleting and copying databases under the unified scheduling of NameNode. NameNode is the manager of all HDFS metadata. User data never passes through NameNode.

HDFS and MapReduce together form the core of Hadoop distributed system architecture. HDFS implements distributed file system on cluster, MapReduce implements distributed computing and task processing on cluster. HDFS provides file operation in MapReduce task processing MapReduce implements task distribution on the basis of HDFS. The main tasks of Hadoop distributed cluster are accomplished by tracking, executing and collecting the results.

3 Processing Flow of Spark Based on RDD

Spark is a big data distributed programming framework, which not only implements MapReduce operator map function and reduce function and calculation model, but also provides more abundant operators. For example, filter, join, groupByKey, etc., Spark abstracts distributed data into elastic distributed data set (RDD), to implement application task scheduling, RPC, serialization and compression, and provides API. For upper layer components running on it [5]. The bottom layer is written in the functional language of Scala, and the API provides a programming interface similar to that of Scala, drawing on the Scala functional programming idea.

The goal of Spark ecosystem is to integrate batch processing, interactive processing and streaming processing into a software framework. Spark is an open source cluster computing system based on memory computing, which aims to make data analysis faster.

Shark is a data warehouse based on Spark and Hive. At present, Shark has completed its academic mission and terminated its development, but its architecture and principles are still useful for reference [6]. It provides a set of SQL interfaces capable of querying data stored in Hive, compatible with existing Hive QL syntax. In this way, users familiar with Hive QL or SQL can make quick SQL queries such as Ad-Hoc, Reporting based on Shark. Shark uses Hive parsers, optimizers, and metadata storage and serialization interfaces at the bottom of Shark. Shark compiles Hive QL into a set of Spark tasks. Perform distributed operations.

Spark is fully compatible with HDFS and can work in parallel with other Hadoop components including YARN and HBase. Spark can be used to handle a variety of job types such as real-time data analysis machine learning and graphics processing. It is widely used in recommendation and computing systems which can tolerate small delay.

Spark enables memory distributed datasets, which, in addition to providing interactive queries, also optimizes iterative workloads. Spark provides memory-based computing clusters that import data into memory when analyzing data for fast query. Spark was originally developed to handle iterative algorithms, such as machine learning, graph mining algorithms, and interactive data mining algorithms. In both scenarios, Spark can run hundreds of times faster than Hadoop.

From a communications point of view, if you use Hadoop's MapReduce computing framework, the communication and transfer of data between JobTracker and TaskTracker through heartbeat can lead to very slow execution. Spark has excellent and efficient Akka and Netty communication system, and the communication efficiency is very high [7].

Spark allows applications to save working sets in memory for efficient reuse. It supports a variety of data processing applications, while preserving the important features of MapReduce, such as high fault tolerance, data localization, large-scale data processing, and so on.

Spark Streaming implements large-scale stream data processing by accumulating stream data into RDD, according to specified time slice and batch processing each RDD. Its throughput can exceed the existing mainstream stream processing framework Storm, and provide rich API for stream data computing.

Spark's RDD concept can achieve the same performance as a proprietary system, and can also provide features that are lacking in proprietary systems, including fault-tolerant processing, delayed node processing, and so on [8]. Iterative algorithms: this is a very common application scenario for proprietary system implementations, such as iterative computing, which can be used for graph processing and machine learning. RDD can implement these models well, including Pregel, HaLoop and GraphLab.

Spark SQL provides SQL query functionality on big data, similar to the role of Shark in the entire ecosystem, which can be collectively called SQL on Spark. Previously, Shark's query compiler and optimizer relied on Hive, to force Shark to maintain a set of Hive branches, while Spark SQL used Catalyst for query parsing and optimizer, and used Spark as the underlying execution engine to implement SQL's Operator.

4 Ecosystem Description of Hadoop Platform Based on HDFS, MapReduce and Data Warehouse Tool Hive

At the bottom of the Hadoop is the HDFS, store files on all the storage nodes in the Hadoop cluster. The top layer of HDFS is the MapReduce engine, which consists of JobTrackers and TaskTrackers.

Hive provides a series of tools that can be used for data extraction, transformation, loading, (ETL), a mechanism for storing, querying, and analyzing large scale data stored in Hadoop [9]. Hive defines a simple SQL like query language. Called HQL, it allows users familiar with SQL to query data.

Hive, when querying data, needs to scan the entire table because there is no index, so the delay is high. Another factor that causes Hive to perform a delay is the MapReduce framework. Because MapReduce itself has a high latency, there will also be a higher delay when using MapReduce to execute the Hive query. Of course, this low is conditional, i.e., the data is smaller, and when the data size is large enough to exceed the processing capacity of the database, the parallel computing of the Archive clearly shows an advantage.

Files stored in the HDFS are divided into blocks, which are then copied to multiple computers in the (DataNode). This is very different from the traditional RAID architecture. The size of blocks (usually 64 MB) and the number of blocks copied are determined by the client when creating files. NameNode can control all file operations. All communication within HDFS is based on the standard TCP/IP protocol.

An important requirement for MapReduce is to run SQL queries, including long run, hours of batch jobs, and interactive queries. However, for MapReduce, comparing parallel databases for interactive queries has its inherent disadvantages, such as slow speed due to its fault-tolerant model. Using the RDD model, we can achieve good performance by implementing many common database engine features. MapReduce batch processing: the interface provided by RDD is the superset of MapReduce, so RDD can effectively run the application program implemented with MapReduce. In addition, RDD is also suitable for more abstract DAG-based applications. The simplified view of the Hadoop cluster is shown in Fig. 2.

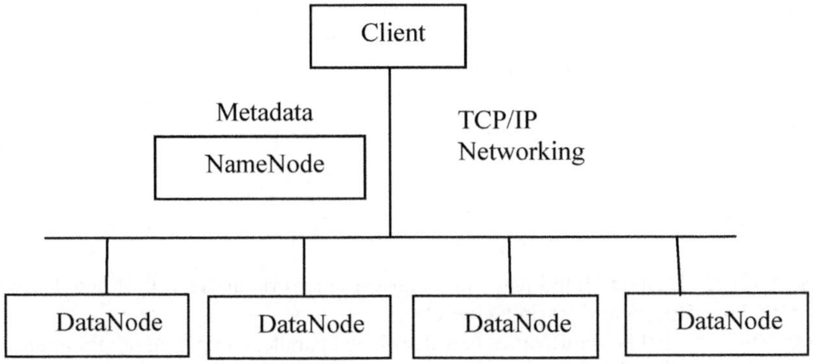

Fig. 2. Simplified views of Hadoop clusters.

DataNode is also a software that normally runs on a separate machine in an HDFS instance. DataNode is usually organized in the form of a rack. The rack connects all systems through a switch [10]. One of the assumptions of Hadoop is that the transmission speed between the internal nodes of the rack is faster than that between the nodes of the rack. The DataNode responds to the request from the HDFS client to read and write. They also respond to commands from NameNode to create, delete, and copy blocks.

Users can write SQL, directly on Spark, which is equivalent to extending a set of SQL operators for Spark, which undoubtedly enriches the operators and functions of Spark. Meanwhile, Spark SQL is compatible with different persistent storage (such as HDFS, Hive, etc.), which lays a wide space for its development.

Hadoop implements HDFS file system and MapRecue. As long as users inherit MapReduceBase, to provide two classes to implement Map and Reduce, and register Job, they can automatically run distributed. HDFS divides nodes into two classes: NameNode and DataNode.NameNode are the only nodes to communicate with, and then access files from DataNode. These operations are transparent and no different from normal file system API.

5 Summary

This paper introduces the HDFS, MapReduce processing process of the distributed file system (HDFS, MapReduce) which is the core of the Hadoop distributed computing platform and the introduction of the data warehouse tool Hive and the distributed database Hbase. It basically covers all the technical cores of the Hadoop distributed platform. From the point of view of internal mechanism, how HDFS, MapReduce, Hbase, Hive works and based on Hadoop. According to the warehouse construction and distributed database specific implementation.

Acknowledgements. This paper is supported by Henan key Laboratory for Big Data Processing & Analytics of Electronic Commerce, and also supported by the science and technology research major project of Henan province Education Department (17B520026), Key scientific research projects in Henan province universities (17A880020, 15A120012), and the Science and Technology Opening up Cooperation project of Henan Province (No. 172106000077).

References

1. Hao S (2012) Hadoop HDFS and MapReduce framework analysis. Post and Telecommun Des Technol 5(07):500–510 (in Chinese)
2. Li C, Zhang X (2011) MapReduce: new distributed parallel computing programming model. Comput Eng Sci 03:78–89
3. Chen J, Le J (2013) Hadoop ecosystem based big data solution overview. Comput Eng Sci 9 (10):125–136 (in Chinese)
4. Yang X (2016) The key technology of distributed storage of massive data based on Hadoop. Autom Instrum 10:387–390 (in Chinese)
5. Jiang Y, Zhao Z (2015) Optimization of sorting algorithm based on MapReduce model. Comput Sci Explor 12(04):38–42
6. Yuan X (2014) Small file distributed storage technology based on Hadoop. Electromech Eng Technol 12:102–109 (in Chinese)
7. Chang G (2016) Hadoop HDFS big data storage technology. Comput Program Skills Maint (06):31–39 (in Chinese)
8. Luo P, Gong X (2014) HDFS data storage strategy research and improvement. Comput Eng Des 5(04):856–860 (in Chinese)
9. Xu H, Zhang R (2016) Novel approach of semantic annotation by fuzzy ontology based on variable precision rough set and concept lattice. Int J Hybrid Inf Technol 9(4):25–40
10. Wan Y, Xiang G (2015) Research on distributed index cluster based on Hadoop and HBase. Inf Technol 01:90–101 (in Chinese)

Research on a Network Communication Data Privacy Protection System Based on OFDM Technology

Kong Lu(✉)

Jiangxi Modern Polytechnic College, Nanchang 330095, Jiangxi, China
79364652@qq.com

Abstract. At present, most data theft cases originate from the malicious intrusion of individual hackers to the production database. Therefore, more and more countries attach importance to the next generation of network communication, and a large amount of human and financial resources are invested in the research and development of data privacy protection of network communication. In order to perform real-time monitoring and intelligent control of network communication, the intelligent network communication control center needs to continuously collect the user's network communication data, and if the data leaks, it will expose the network communication rules and living habits of the individual users. In this paper, the actual system of high-speed data communication is realized by OFDM technology, and the problem of network communication data privacy protection is discussed and solved.

Keywords: OFDM technology · Network communication data · Privacy protection

1 Introduction

As a medium to achieve rapid interactive communication of information, in the process of information transmission, it faces direct outstanding information security problems. This is because the network can not only serve as a channel for information communication, but also become a hacker, a virus, a Trojan, and a criminal. It provides a place to steal information, so this makes the information data security problem faced by network communication also very prominent [1–3]. How to monitor regional network communication without revealing personal user network communication becomes a challenge [4]. The privacy data aggregation based on homomorphic encryption technology in public key cryptography successfully solved this problem [5–8]. The data aggregation technology can ensure that the control center can still calculate the sum of the user network communication data without leaking the personal network communication data at all, and at the same time, the communication overhead of the control center can be greatly reduced by aggregating the messages of a large number of users in advance. Among them, OFDM technology has a very broad development prospect [9–11]. At present, OFDM combines space-time coding, diversity, interference (including inter-symbol interference (ISD and adjacent channel interference (IC))

Z. Xu et al. (Eds.): CSIA 2019, AISC 928, pp. 1134–1141, 2020.
https://doi.org/10.1007/978-3-030-15235-2_150

suppression, and smart antenna technology to maximize the reliability of the physical layer; such as combining adaptive modulation, self Techniques such as adaptive coding and dynamic subcarrier allocation and dynamic bit allocation algorithms can further optimize their performance [12–15]. The development of network communication big data brings opportunities and challenges to personal life, enterprise management and even the country and society. Although big data has brought progress to society, it also needs to pay attention to the big data security problems it causes [14–19]. Based on this, it introduces the status quo and main problems of big data security, and analyzes the problems faced by big data. Many security threats further pointed out the causes of security problems, and on this basis, put forward effective data security and privacy protection measures to provide ideas for big data security construction [20, 21].

2 OFDM Technical Overview

2.1 OFDM Technological Development

OFDM was developed by Multi-Carrier Modulation (MCM). The military created the world's first MCM system in the 1950s and 1960s, and derived OFDM systems using large-scale subcarrier and frequency overlap techniques. In the 1980s, with the rapid development of VLSI and digital signal processing (DSP) technology, low-cost high-order FFT dedicated chips and DSP general-purpose chips appeared, making FFT operations convenient and efficient. Since then, OFDM has gradually entered the field of high-speed Modem digital mobile communications applications. In the 1990s, OFDM began to be widely used in broadband data communications for broadcast channels in Europe and Australia, such as digital audio broadcasting (DAB), high definition digital television (HDTV), and wireless local area network (WLAN) communications. At present, OFDM has become the core technology of 802.n, a wireless LAN standard developed by EIEE. In the power line communication, the core technology of the home power line network communication standard Homeplug1.0 developed by the Home Plug-in Alliance is a company's high-speed data transmission technology powerpacket, which uses OFDM modulation technology, and the transmission rate can reach 14 MbPs. At present, a transceiver chip dedicated to power line communication using OFDM technology has appeared.

2.2 Definition of OFDM

Orthogonal frequency division multiplexing is an orthogonal multi-carrier modulation method. In a conventional digital communication system, a symbol sequence is modulated onto a carrier for serial transmission, and the frequency of each symbol can occupy the entire available bandwidth of the channel. The OFDM modulation method divides the available spectrum into N sub-carriers with narrower and relatively low-rate transmission, and the amplitude-frequency responses of the sub-carriers overlap and orthogonal to each other. Each subcarrier can use different modulation methods in Sect. 3 OFDM technology or the same modulation method. BPSK, QPsK, QAM, etc. are commonly used. The serially transmitted symbol sequence is also divided into segments of length N, and the N symbols in each segment are modulated onto N subcarriers and transmitted together. That is to say, OFDM converts a set of high-speed serial data streams into low-speed parallel data streams, and then modulates the parallel data on mutually orthogonal subcarriers to realize parallel data transmission. Although the transmission rate of each subcarrier is not high, all the subchannels are added together to obtain a high transmission rate. In order to eliminate inter-symbol interference and sub-carrier interference, it is necessary to add a guard interval between OFDM symbols, so that the guard time is greater than the multipath delay of the channel. As a cyclic prefix, a sample with a tail length L of the OFDM symbol is usually copied to the front of the symbol. To separate the symbols.

2.3 Advantages of OFDM Technology Applied to Power Line Communication

The multi-path delay power line network is criss-crossed, and the low-voltage power line is an unbalanced and non-uniform transmission line. The connected load impedance is also constantly changing. Many power devices work in an impedance mismatch state, so the signal it will produce reflections, standing waves, and so on. When the same signal passes through different paths, the delay will be dispersed, causing interference before and after the received symbols, resulting in frequency selective fading and inter-code interference, which affect the communication quality. Inter-code interference is inseparable from the transmission rate. When the transmission rate is low, the period of the symbol is larger than the multipath delay spread on the power line, and multipath interference does not occur. OFDM allocates a high-speed data stream to N sub-channels, and the rate of symbols on each sub-channel becomes the original cow, and the period of the symbol is expanded by N times.

3 Data Security Issues in Network Communication

3.1 Authentication

Nowadays, the most common method for data information security in network communication is authentication, that is, information security verification is performed through network software and systems. This form of authentication mode is mainly for verifying account and password. Only if the verification is correct can you enter the system and obtain the permission. In the process of actual operation, in order to improve security, the password and the account may be stored separately, or divided into two different systems, and finally the information communication is carried out in the form of short message. With the continuous development of network technology, many of them are bio-encryption technologies, namely retina and fingerprint recognition.

3.2 Data Information Encryption Technology in Network Communication

Data information encryption is to encrypt and protect data information, so that hackers need to decipher the password before stealing the information, and set up obstacles for stealing information. This is also a very common form of security protection in network security communication at this stage. Data encryption has a significant effect on ensuring information security and is very flexible. Currently, the commonly used data information encryption technology is not unique. In specific applications, it can be selected. One or more encryption technologies are used in combination to maximize the security of data information. There are several types of commonly used data encryption technologies: network communication encryption. The so-called network communication encryption is based on the dynamic encryption in the network transmission process, and finally in the process of transmitting the communication data in the network in the process of online encryption; add encryption technology. Adding encryption technology is also the most common information security technology. It can combine node encryption and decryption encryption, and finally realize dynamic data dynamic encryption transmission; data end encryption. The final data-side encryption form is mainly to perform secondary encryption on the basis of encryption in the process of data information transmission, so that the secret code can be kept secret during the transmission process, and the encryption form belongs to the use of hardware. Decryption, can not be decrypted using ordinary software or a single encryption form.

3.3 Causes of Network Communication Security Risks

Causes of Data and Information Security Problems Caused by Network Communication. At present, the security of information data in network communication is not uncommon, and it has caused considerable economic losses and endangered social stability. For example, the network is open, and every user in the network can obtain data information in the network under certain permissions, which also greatly increases the efficiency of learning and work. However, it is precisely because of the open environment of the network that it also provides opportunities for lawless elements. They violate the rules, destroy the authority, and steal undisclosed data information, which seriously threatens network security. Nowadays, there are many networks. In order to quickly and easily control the user login port, the website will build a remote control system in the computer's settings management, but once this system mode is controlled by the network hacker, the hacker can invade the user through the remote control system. The computer system poses a huge threat to the security of the user's personal privacy information. At present, there are certain security problems in the network transmission protocol and network code. Although the network control system is constantly improving, according to the network hacking technology. The development situation, if the security method technology is not updated in real time, then sooner or later will be attacked by hackers. In order to effectively stop such things, international attempts to increase data security technology in network communication; in the end, many computer system personnel in the network system have insufficient attention to the security of network communication information and insufficient knowledge. It will also cause management loopholes in the network communication system. Even the computer responsible personnel use their own legal identity and authority to monitor and steal information from the stolen network system.

4 Network Communication Data Privacy Protection System

4.1 Privacy Protection in the Era of Big Data in Modern Society

The traditional method is used to protect the privacy of data in personalized retrieval, which resists the attack of illegal people to a certain extent, and protects the security of user privacy data, but leads to the reduced accuracy of personalized retrieval. Aiming at the above problems, this paper proposes a method to protect data privacy in personalized retrieval in big data environment. This method combines differential privacy with P-link technology to anonymize the user interest model in personalized retrieval to achieve data privacy protection. The differential privacy is used to generalize the user's identifier and add noise, and the initial anonymization of the privacy data is realized under the premise of ensuring the retrieval accuracy. The P-link technology is used to micro-aggregate the initial anonymized private data into a P-link equivalent group, and calculate the weight and centroid of the interest item to complete the secondary anonymization of the privacy data. It shows that compared with traditional distribution, the anti-theft rate and precision rate of this method are greatly improved, which resolves the contradiction between user privacy protection and retrieval performance in personalized retrieval technology.

4.2 Network Communication Security Protection

The network communication module is responsible for the processing of the initiation and response of all requests of the client. The network communication module includes a request policy processing and a network request module. The purpose of request policy processing is to classify and filter network requests, and customize the behavior of network requests according to the different needs of upper-level callers. The network request module consists of two parts: the underlying Http module encapsulates the network request module provided by the IOS SDK, and can globally configure the network request; the upper layer encryption and decryption module is a further secure processing of the transmitted data. The network request policy provides three types of network request configuration: one is to re-request data every time; the other is to use locally cached data first; the third is to use only locally cached data. The first configuration client will re-request the server-side data every time, which is generally applicable to requests that respond to frequent data changes. The second configuration client will first read the locally cached data. When the local cache does not exist or expires, the client the end will re-request the server-side data and update the local cache; the third configuration is a supplement to the second configuration, and returns data only if the local cache data exists and has not expired. The implementation of the HTTP request module includes three parts: a pair of upper layer modules open an interface of a configurable request type; rather, a configurable global internal parameter for the module, including a system version number, an API version, hardware device information, and a COOKIE; Externally, the HTTP request initiation, response, and data analysis are shown in Fig. 1.

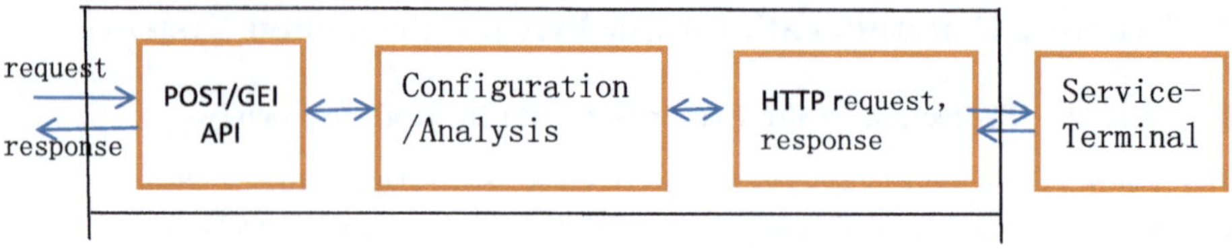

Fig. 1. HTTPRequest initiation and response process

4.3 Privacy Encryption Protection

In order to solve the problem of privacy leakage during the use of big data, a privacy protection method based on attribute-based proxy re-encryption is proposed. By using the attribute proxy re-encryption of different trust institutions in multiple domains, the encryption process of the attribute base is combined with the proxy re-encryption to improve the phase shift processing in the key generation process, and the calculation amount and the traffic amount of the algorithm are effectively reduced by the encrypted phase. Through the neighborhood allocation of multi-level attribute-based encryption, the domain is divided into big data, and the alienation technology is adopted to further reduce the complexity of key management. Simulation experiments further verify the effectiveness and superiority of the algorithm.

4.4 Information Privacy Protection

Information privacy system is a social platform based on protecting users' privacy, so it has two requirements: social and privacy protection. The social needs of the system are mainly account management, user information management, authentication management and data storage management. Privacy protection needs are mainly portrait privacy protection processing. That is, users can upload pictures to the platform to share information, express their mood and record their lives at will. At the same time, users can also protect the privacy of the portrait through the system, and display their own portrait information on the platform only to some authorized users, without exposing it to strangers.

5 Summary

With the comprehensive coverage of mobile networks, the popularity of social platforms and the intelligent development of mobile devices, the rapid upload and dissemination of pictures has become the main way of social platforms. Because of the multi-directional expansibility of information when it is transmitted on social platforms, user sensitive information will be exposed by other users, resulting in privacy leaks and unavoidable harm to users. Therefore, data security and fast performance are indispensable. With dynamic data shielding, organizations will be able to rapidly upgrade and expand to provide real-time protection for sensitive and privacy information without forcing some departments to make costly and time-consuming changes to applications and databases, thus avoiding affecting productivity and, more importantly, not interfering with employees' ability to perform their duties.

References

1. Thelwall M, Wilkinson D, Uppal S (2014) Data mining emotion in social network communication: Gender differences in MySpace. J Am Soc Inf Sci Technol 61(1):190–199
2. Goñi J, Mp VDH, Avenakoenigsberger A et al (2014) Resting-brain functional connectivity predicted by analytic measures of network communication. Proc Natl Acad Sci USA 111 (2):833
3. Voytek B, Knight RT (2015) Dynamic network communication as a unifying neural basis for cognition, development, aging, and disease. Biol Psychiatry 77(12):1089–1097
4. Ophir Y, Rosenberg H, Asterhan CSC et al (2016) In times of war, adolescents do not fall silent: teacher–student social network communication in wartime. J Adolesc 46:98–106
5. Joe MM, Ramakrishnan B (2015) Review of vehicular ad hoc network communication models including WVANET (Web VANET) model and WVANET future research directions. Wirel Netw 22(7):1–18
6. Ding T, Schotter A (2017) Matching and chatting: an experimental study of the impact of network communication on school-matching mechanisms ☆. Games Econ Behav S0899825616000294
7. Yang YI, Liu Y, Chen Y et al (2016) Research of network communication fault location technique in smart substation based on comprehensive information judgment. Power Syst Protect Control 44:135–140
8. Rios R, Cuellar J, Lopez J (2015) Probabilistic receiver-location privacy protection in wireless sensor networks. Inf Sci 321:205–223
9. Zuberi RS, Ahmad SN (2016) Secure mix-zones for privacy protection of road network location based services users
10. Memon I, Ling C, Arain QA et al (2018) Pseudonym changing strategy with multiple mix zones for trajectory privacy protection in road networks. Int J Commun Syst 31(1):e3437
11. Son J (2016) A new mobile online social network based location sharing with enhanced privacy protection. In: International conference on computer communication & networks
12. Wei J, Xiao L, Kang Z et al (2015) Design of WDM-RoF-PON based on improved OFDM mechanism and optical coherent technology. IEEE/OSA J Opt Commun Netw 7(2):74–82
13. Suganya M, Gandhiraj R (2016) Applicability of MIMO and OFDM technology to SATCOM. In: International conference on communication & signal processing
14. Moreolo MS, Fabrega JM, Nadal L et al (2014) Cost-effective data plane solutions based on OFDM technology for flexi-grid metro networks using sliceable bandwidth variable transponders. In: International conference on optical network design & modeling
15. Abdallah W, Boudriga N (2016) Enabling 5G wireless access using Li-Fi technology: an OFDM based approach. In: International conference on transparent optical networks
16. Luo RZ, Yang J, Rui LI, et al (2014) Research progress on synchronization technology for MIMO-OFDM system telecommunication engineering
17. Pandit A, Polina P, Kumar A (2014) CLOPRO: a framework for context cloaking privacy protection. In: Fourth international conference on communication systems & network technologies
18. Oliver I, Holtmanns S (2015) Aligning the conflicting needs of privacy, malware detection and network protection. In: TrustCom/BigDataSE/ISPA

19. Oliver I, Holtmanns S (2017) Providing for privacy in a network infrastructure protection context. In: Innovations in clouds, internet & networks
20. Gong C, Miao Z, Diao J (2014) Research of privacy protection mechanism for vehicles secure communication. In: International conference on information management
21. Feng DG, Zhang M, Hao LI (2014) Big data security and privacy protection. Chin J Comput 37(1):246–258

Research on College English Teaching System Based on Resource Library and Network Support Platform

Lu Wei[1(✉)] and Binquan Liu[2]

[1] Jingdezhen Ceramic Institute, Jingdezhen, China
weilu2700@haoxueshu.com
[2] Jingdezhen University, Jingdezhen, China

Abstract. These years, with the great development of electronic technology and the rise of the digital revolution, the advanced media of network multimedia, which integrates sound and picture animation, is being applied to college English teaching by more and more colleges and universities. Traditional education can meet the needs of information, digital and networked society anymore. A transformation that necessarily involves teaching content, teaching methods, teaching methods and teaching structure is taking place. Under the background of the limitations of thinking, material and technical conditions in China's current education system, the use of online multimedia English teaching will inevitably encounter many problems. For example, it is difficult for students to adapt and accept the method of learning English through network multimedia. The ability to fully utilize and accept multimedia networks is not available; unchanging courseware cannot adapt to different levels of students to learn independently according to their own abilities; formative assessment and summative assessment cannot be effectively combined; teaching management is arranged in class, The scores of records, credits, attendance registration, etc. are unchanged or there are no corresponding reasonable changes. In view of the problems existing in the current transition from college English to network multimedia mode, this paper analyzes the causes of these problems and puts forward the countermeasures to solve college English teaching problem under the condition of network multimedia.

Keywords: Network teaching support platform · English teaching system · Teaching form transformation · Strategy

1 Introduction

The network teaching management platform integrates online courses, teaching management, teaching evaluation and teaching and learning resources. The content is very rich, creating a relaxed and personalized and independent learning environment for students, and providing an interactive and convenient teaching for teachers. Management, resource sharing and information exchange platforms [1–5]. In long time, the college English teaching mode in our country is mainly based on teachers, mainly textbooks, and teaching. It ignores the students' initiative and the cultivation of

Z. Xu et al. (Eds.): CSIA 2019, AISC 928, pp. 1142–1149, 2020.
https://doi.org/10.1007/978-3-030-15235-2_151

learning interests, so that students are passively accepting learning and passive. Listening to the teacher's lectures without in-depth thinking, such teaching models and teaching methods are not conducive to students' accumulation of knowledge, but also not conducive to the students' initiative [6–8]. However, network information technology integration and college English curriculum has fundamentally changed the college English teaching essence. College English classroom teaching has changed from traditional classroom to college English classroom in the modern network environment [9–14]. The new network teaching support platform with computer multimedia technology and network technology as the core is gradually introduced into the field of English teaching. Under the guidance of the theory of second language acquisition and the theory of communicative teaching, it is to reform the traditional college English teaching [15–18]. Combine the advantages of traditional teaching with the advantages of online teaching in order to better improve the teaching effect [19, 20].

2 Network Teaching Support Platform and Teaching Ideas

Social development puts higher demands on the English level of English learners. In the basic stage of the university, college English can be said to be one of the courses that students spend more time, but the contradiction between the students' actual English level and the society's requirements for college students' comprehensive use of English is increasing. Many scholars even believe that there are problems such as time-consuming inefficiency, high scores and low energy, and "deaf-mute English" in college English teaching in China. Based on the above reasons, this paper is based on the theory of constructivism, the theory of autonomous learning, and the theory of social history development of Vygotsky. It builds a multi-interactive teaching model for college English, designs teaching procedures, implements experimental teaching, and comprehensively studies information technology. The relationship between the language learning activity of "interaction" and the effect of college English teaching in the environment. In the aspects of relevant theoretical exploration, research content, research methods, etc., this research has certain innovative significance and practical value.

2.1 Combining Theory with Practice, Enriching and Developing the Connotation of Teaching Mode

Based on a more in-depth analysis and reflection on the teaching meaning and interactive meaning of behaviorism, cognition and constructivism, this study draws on the essence of various modern teaching theories such as constructivism theory and proposes a unit-based model construction. The college English conceptual teaching model and the design of a multi-interaction teaching mode operation program map, guide the college English teachers in different types of teaching, different teaching stages of teaching design, flexible use of various interactive methods to achieve the best teaching results.

2.2 In Terms of Research Content, this Study Pays Attention to How Students Learn and How Teachers Teach

A key issue in the process of foreign language teaching is how teachers use appropriate methods to stimulate students' awareness of cognitive participation and to realize their learning potential. In order to study the teaching effect of the university English multi-individual interactive teaching mode under the information technology environment, this study takes the real or simulated "SLS task" as the starting point, and creates an English learning environment such as an extracurricular and online offline learning in the classroom to realize teachers and teachers. Students, students and students, students and teaching services (teaching activities) and experimental teaching. In addition, in order to ensure the reliability and validity of the university English teaching model research, the teaching beliefs of college English teachers are also investigated. The investigation of teacher's teaching beliefs makes us further realize that "personality" is the "bottle of the bottle" that restricts the implementation of the new teaching mode and whether the effectiveness of foreign language teaching can be greatly improved.

2.3 The Information Technology Development Calls for the Innovation of Traditional College English Teaching Mode and the Reconstruction of New Teaching Styles that the Times

China has a vast territory and unbalanced economic development. The foreign language education between regions varies greatly. Although our English education industry has developed rapidly and achieved many achievements in recent decades, it is undeniable that the overall effect of our English teaching is not high. We believe that college English teaching in the information technology environment is not only a simple knowledge inculcation, but a combination of knowledge dissemination, language use ability and learning ability; teachers are no longer the only source of knowledge; English teaching should not be a blind mountain teacher. Singing "one-man show", it should be a multi-dimensional and multi-form language and information interaction process based on "teacher-student interaction, life-time interaction and life-time interaction".

3 The Relationship Between Theory and English Teaching in a Network Environment

3.1 Constructivism and College English Teaching Under the Network Environment

The basic point of constructivism is to emphasize student-centeredness, requiring students to be transformed from external stimuli and indoctors of knowledge into subjects of information processing. Active constructors of knowledge meaning constructivist learning theory believes that meaning construction is learning The purpose is to rely on students to take the initiative to complete, the role of teachers and the external environment are to help and promote the meaning construction of students, but some researchers have some deviations from the theory to guide college English teaching under the network environment. Foreign language teaching includes four skills in listening, speaking, reading and writing. These contents mainly require memory rather than construction. For example, some grammar rules are conventional and there is no law to follow. Learners need to strengthen memory rather than logical reasoning. In the network environment, college English teaching uses multimedia display function to a certain extent, which is not conducive to students' memory. Once again, from the perspective of constructivist theory, students can only be self-constructed knowledge systems. This concept of objective transformation is not really a student's understanding. Constructivism emphasizes the construction of the learning environment. Foreign language learning requires constant imitation. It requires the use of the language knowledge to carry out the actual communication environment. However, in the context of multimedia network teaching, students are always faced with a cold computer machine. To a certain extent, it will affect the students' actual practice and their exercise emotions, and they will feel bored. Therefore, multimedia English network teaching is also a type of foreign language teaching. Considering the particularity of foreign languages, it is not appropriate to use constructivist theory to completely guide our foreign language teaching.

3.2 Humanistic Learning Theory and College English Teaching in Network Environment

Humanistic learning theory and constructivism are the two main theories that support college English teaching in the network environment. Humanistic psychology is a kind of psychological thought that emerged in the United States in the 1950s and 1960s. Humanistic learning The commentator believes that learning is the learner's acquisition of knowledge, skills and development of intelligence, exploring their own emotions, learning to communicate with teachers and class members, clarifying their values and attitudes, realizing their potential, and achieving the best realm. Humanistic theory emphasizes It is necessary to pay attention to learners and regard learners as the main body of learning activities; we must pay attention to the learners' wishes! Emotions! Needs and values, believe that normal learners can guide themselves and self-potentials. Under the network environment, college English teaching relies on the autonomy of students' learning, but many students have poor autonomy at this stage. According to a questionnaire survey on college students' online English teaching, data shows that 23% of students do not have online learning plans, and 50% of students lack management strategies. Lack of self-learning awareness and system theory knowledge, so go on, then the use of multimedia networks to teach is not conducive to the improvement of students' English performance. Humanism emphasizes that teachers are the promoters of learning. Rogers believes that the task of teachers is not to teach students knowledge, nor to teach students how to learn knowledge, but to teach Students improve the means of learning. However, because the concept of teaching has not completely changed, some teachers believe that self-study is to let students study independently in the online classroom, and then take care of their own work, which will be difficult for teachers to promote effect.

3.3 Input Hypothesis Theory and Multimedia Network English Teaching

The input hypothesis theory is the theoretical basis of Krashen's "input hypothesis model" for second language acquisition since the mid-20th century. Krashen believes that acquisition can only be produced when learners are exposed to understandable linguistic input and can focus on understanding the meaning or understanding of the information rather than the form. Although computers can provide supernormal language teaching information, students are not an automatic receiver. Even in advanced multimedia teaching environments, the input (input) of the computer to the learner cannot be freely converted into learner intake. As mentioned above, due to the particularity of English learning, language learning requires a lot of memory. If you only touch those languages and do not remember them, then it is not good for English learning. According to a survey, up to 70% the students admit that they rarely exchange English learning problems with teachers or classmates through the Internet. After using the multimedia network to teach English, it is found that the improvement of students' performance has no particularly significant effect. Such a situation has to be thought-provoking, perhaps in many cases. The difference between students is more likely to determine the effect of learning (Fig. 1).

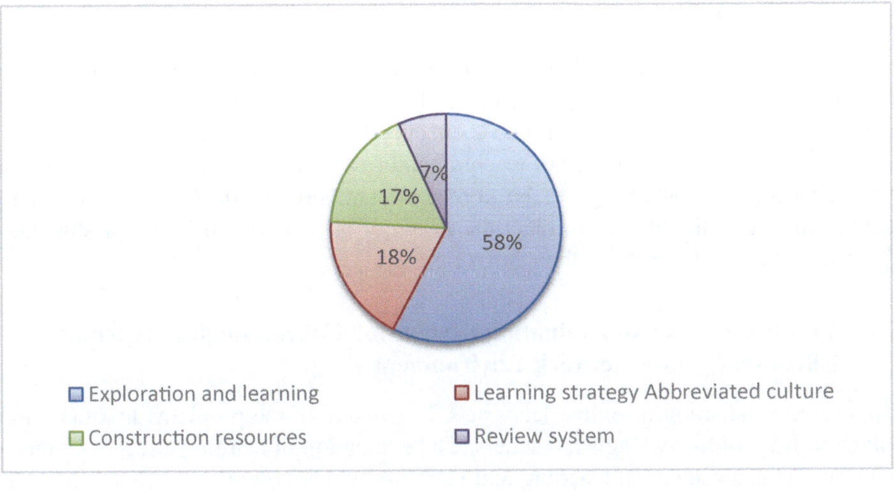

Fig. 1. Compare of different methods

4 Research on English Learning Methods Based on Resource Library and Network Construction

4.1 Strengthen the Exploration and Study of Theory

It is undeniable that constructivism, humanism and input hypothesis have profound guiding significance for English learning. However, the author believes that at this stage, some teachers have some misunderstandings about the guiding role of these theories in college English teaching under the network environment. These theories are all imported from abroad, and whether it is in line with China's current national conditions remains to be verified. The introduction of any theory cannot be at the expense of the original reasonable teaching philosophy. It should not go to extremes. It should be noted that it is in line with China's national conditions and the actual teaching, and it cannot be a good person. Therefore, it is indispensable to use the introduction theory to guide English teaching in the Chinese environment, to promote its longevity and avoid shortcomings.

4.2 Strengthen the Cultivation of Students' Learning Strategies and Stimulate the Intrinsic Motivation of Students' Learning

Students should gradually change from the passive recipient of knowledge to the initiative of learning, effectively establishing the student's self-learning subject status. In the course of teaching, teachers should consciously inspire students' self-learning ability, teach students learning strategies, stimulate interest in English learning and enhance motivation: self-control and attention.

4.3 Develop Flexible and Diverse ESP Elective Courses and Build a Rich Resource Library

ESP is an English course designed according to a specific major. It is different from ordinary English and is a unique teaching policy and teaching proposition. Universities can analyze their needs and combine their specific circumstances to form their own ESP courses. The characteristics of teaching and research enable university English and other professional knowledge to be combined and promoted. And establish a rich network resource library, try to meet the needs of all majors, all levels of students in English learning, and expand their horizons.

4.4 Create an Effective Evaluation System for College English Teaching Effectiveness in a Network Environment

The perfect evaluation of online learning effect is one of the problems that need to be solved in front of many English teachers. The evaluation of learning effect is connected with two related aspects of teaching and learning, which complement each other. "The author believes that the establishment of the evaluation system should be objective and comprehensive, pay attention to the process price, pay attention to the learning status, learning attitude, resilience and even emotion of the students in the activity, and find problems from it. Investigate and fill in the gaps in time to establish a reasonable teaching quality and teaching management evaluation system, or use the student evaluation system platform to provide students with convenient teaching evaluation.

5 Summary

The introduction of multimedia technology has brought tremendous opportunities for the reform of foreign language teaching in the 21st century, enriching the research scope of foreign language teaching. The network multimedia English teaching has the characteristics and advantages of openness, creativity, vividness, richness, practicability and interactivity. It is unparalleled in traditional English teaching and is a supplement and perfection to the lack of traditional teaching. The old concept of education, the lack of software and hardware resources, the lag of evaluation system reform and the lack of rationality of teaching management are the problems that need to be solved urgently in the transformation of college English teaching. It is also the bottleneck restricting the further deepening reform of network multimedia English teaching. In the process of solving the problem, this paper should emphasize the social, practical, active and influential of teachers as the leading, but also the autonomy, collaboration, development and creativity of students as the main body; The scientific, dynamic, standardized and structured construction, but also the construction of corresponding supporting mechanisms. It does not deny the great superiority brought about by college English teaching under the network environment, and is full of confidence.

Acknowledgement. This research originates from Social Science Research Projects of Jingdezhen Ceramic Institute in 2014, Analysis on the Deficiency of Chinese Culture in College English Teaching and Its Countermeasures.

References

1. Petcu D, Iancu B, Peculea A et al (2014) Integrating Cisco packet tracer with Moodle platform: support for teaching and automatic evaluation. In: Networking in education & research, RoEduNet international conference edition
2. Zhu T, Zhang L (2015) Flip classroom design and implementation of the literature retrieval course network teaching platform. In: International conference on computer science & education
3. Luan X (2017) Design and implementation of remote English teaching platform based on network technology. In: International conference on smart grid & electrical automation
4. Xiong MN (2014) Network architecture and functional development of the art teaching platform. Adv Mater Res 912–914:4
5. Yang J, Ming QI, Wen XU (2014) Construction and teaching of aviation maintenance practice platform based on network. Res Explor Lab
6. Liu Y (2014) The system design of the network teaching platform of learning based on the concept of development evaluation
7. Wang FP, Yi LI, Liu XN (2015) The design of "network virtual teaching training base" for turfgrass management major. Pratacult Sci 32(2):294–298
8. Bowers JS, Bowers PN (2017) Beyond phonics: the case for teaching children the logic of the English spelling system. Educ Psychol 2:124–141
9. Wang JF (2016) Design and implementation of online English multimedia teaching system based on B/S mode. In: Sixth international conference on intelligent systems design & engineering applications

10. Shen PP (2016) Research on the new modern English teaching mode in higher vocational colleges based on multimedia and interactive system. Int J Technol Manag 7:54–56
11. Bawazeer K (2015) A system for teaching English in Saudi Arabia. Teach Learn Saudi Arabia
12. Yao N (2018) Design and implementation of English teaching management system based on web. In: International conference on intelligent transportation
13. Wang B (2017) College English teaching assessment system in the era of big data. US-China Foreign Lang 4:227–231
14. Brown KM, Bright LM (2017) Teaching caring and competence: student transformation during an older adult focused service-learning course. Nurse Educ Pract 27:29–35
15. Senyshyn RM (2018) Teaching for transformation: converting the intercultural experience of preservice teachers into intercultural learning. Intercult Educ 29:1–22
16. Gitanjali B, Susan G (2016) Simply good teaching: supporting transformation and change through education for sustainability. Aust J Environ Educ 32(01):124–133
17. Gao S, Wang J (2014) Teaching transformation under centralized curriculum and teacher learning community: two Chinese chemistry teachers' experiences in developing inquiry-based instruction. Teach Teach Educ 44:1–11
18. Oxford RL, Rubin J, Chamot AU (2014) The learning strategy prism: perspectives of learning strategy experts. System 43(1):30–49
19. Tracey BD, Duraisamy K, Alonso JJ (2015) A machine learning strategy to assist turbulence model development. AIAA J
20. Mannodi-Kanakkithodi A, Pilania G, Huan TD et al (2016) Machine learning strategy for accelerated design of polymer dielectrics. Sci Rep 6:20952

Video Information Propagation Interruption Monitoring System Based on Electromagnetic Interference

Kong Lu(✉)

Jiangxi Modern Polytechnic College, Nanchang 330095, Jiangxi Province, China
79364652@qq.com

Abstract. With the rapid development of society, the rapid advancement of technology, more and more video spread in our lives, making us in a complex electromagnetic environment. This will cause wireless electromagnetic interference problems. In order to promote the good dissemination of video information, this paper has a deep understanding of the source of interference in the video information transmission monitoring system, and pays attention to the electromagnetic interference monitoring system. Through analysis and a series of discussions, a solution to the targeted suppression of electromagnetic interference.

Keywords: Electromagnetic interference · Video propagation monitoring · Interruption

1 Introduction

With the update of China's broadcast equipment and the improvement of technical indicators and stability, the failure rate and human error of equipment are decreasing, but it is still inevitable [1]. Electromagnetic wave radiation interference can cause adverse consequences such as interruption of wireless transmission or failure of computer operation facilities. According to the characteristics of radiated interference, we can reduce the damage caused by radiated interference to our production life by using less radiation interference source radiation, increasing the radiation interference propagation channel loss and reducing unwanted signals or noise received by the receiver [2–8]. All electronic circuits can be subject to electromagnetic interference. Although some of the electromagnetic interference is directly accepted by means of radio frequency radiation, most electromagnetic interference is accepted by transient conduction. In digital circuits, critical signals such as resets, interrupts, and control signals are most susceptible to electromagnetic interference [9, 10]. Control circuits, analog low-level amplifiers, and power conditioning circuits are also susceptible to noise. The video information monitoring service is not clearly defined [11–17]. The monitoring technology is not a purely single technology. It is an integrated application of several technologies used to accomplish a specific goal. As long as it helps the monitoring target to be achieved, it can be used to meet the cost performance. The latest

Z. Xu et al. (Eds.): CSIA 2019, AISC 928, pp. 1150–1157, 2020.
https://doi.org/10.1007/978-3-030-15235-2_152

achievements in various fields are absorbed as widely as possible, so the monitoring technology of different periods will always bear the brand of the times [17–19].

1.1 The Nature of Electromagnetic Waves

When the electromagnetic wave frequency is low, it can be transmitted mainly by a tangible electric conductor. The reason is that in the low-frequency electrical oscillation, the mutual change between magnetoelectricity is relatively slow, and almost all of its energy returns to the original circuit without energy radiation; when the electromagnetic wave frequency is high, it can be transmitted in free space, or it can be bound to the tangible Conducted in the body. The reason for the transmission in free space is that in the high-frequency electrical oscillation, the magnetoelectric interaction becomes very fast, and the energy cannot be returned to the original oscillating circuit. Therefore, the electric energy and the magnetic energy change to the space in the form of electromagnetic waves with the periodic changes of the electric field and the magnetic field. Spreading out, without the medium can also transfer energy outward, this is a kind of radiation. For example, the distance between the sun and the earth is very far away, but when outdoors, we can still feel the light and heat of the sun, which is like the principle that "electromagnetic radiation transfers energy through radiation." Propagation does not require media, electromagnetic waves of the same frequency, different speeds in different media. When electromagnetic waves of different frequencies propagate in the same medium, the higher the frequency, the larger the refractive index and the smaller the speed. And the electromagnetic wave can propagate along a straight line only in the same homogeneous medium. If the same medium is not uniform, the refractive index of the electromagnetic wave is different, and in such a medium, it propagates along the curve.

1.2 Principle of Electromagnetic Interference

Electromagnetic waves are a form of motion of an electromagnetic field. In the case of high-frequency electromagnetic oscillation, the general name of the electric wave and the magnetic wave formed by the partial propagation of energy from the space by radiation is called "electromagnetic wave". In the low-frequency electrical oscillation, the mutual change between the magnetisms is relatively slow, and almost all of the energy is reversed back to the original circuit without energy radiation. However, in high-frequency electrical oscillations, the magnetoelectric interaction becomes very fast. It is impossible for all the energy to return to the original oscillating circuit, so that the electric energy and the magnetic energy propagate to the space in the form of electromagnetic waves with the periodic changes of the electric field and the magnetic field. The electromagnetic wave is a transverse wave. The magnetic field, electric field and direction of travel of the electromagnetic wave are perpendicular to each other. The longer the wavelength of the electromagnetic wave, the easier it is to bypass the obstacle and continue to propagate. Air waves such as medium waves or short waves are transmitted by repeated reflections of the ionosphere and the earth surrounding the Earth. The amplitude is periodically alternating in the vertical direction of the propagation direction. The intensity is inversely proportional to the square of the distance.

The wave itself drives the energy. The energy of any position is proportional to the square of the amplitude. Its speed is equal to the speed of light. Light waves are electromagnetic waves. Radio waves also have the same characteristics as light waves, such as refraction, reflection, diffraction, scattering, and absorption when they pass through different media. The electromagnetic wave propagating in space is the same as the wavelength of the nearest electromagnetic field and the distance between the two points is the wavelength of the electromagnetic wave.

1.3 Electromagnetic Interference Type

Electromagnetic interference is divided into natural interference sources and human interference sources. The source of natural disturbances mainly comes from the sky-light noise in the atmosphere and the cosmic noise in the outer space of the earth. They are both an essential part of the Earth's electromagnetic environment and a source of interference that interferes with radio communications and space technology. Natural noise can interfere with the operation of satellites and spacecraft, and it can also interfere with the launch of ballistic missile launch vehicles. Human-induced interference sources are electromagnetic energy interference generated by electromechanical or other artificial devices, some of which are specifically used to emit electromagnetic energy. Devices such as radio, video, communications, radar, and navigation are known as intentional sources of interference. The other part is the launch of electromagnetic energy with the completion of its own functions, such as transportation vehicles, overhead transmission lines, lighting equipment, electric machinery, household appliances, industrial and medical RF equipment. This part has therefore become an unintentional source of interference.

2 The Need for Radio Frequency (RF) Monitoring Systems

2.1 Rapid Development of RF Information

Due to the rapid development of broadband networks in recent years around the world, high-quality audio and video compression technologies continue to evolve, higher compression ratios and wider bandwidth, making Internet users' desire to watch high-quality video programs on the Internet no longer fantasy. The network video market in the United States, Italy, France, Canada and other countries is becoming more and more mature. The small test knives in Harbin, Quanzhou and Shanghai in China have proved the network with stronger interaction as the selling point, based on Internet technology and P2P transmission technology. Video services have become a climate. Network video is a general term for so-called broadband video based on Internet technology. It can be user-generated, uploaded online or on-demand video programs, with autonomy and self-help. Various video websites and streaming media servers As people's demand for network video services grows rapidly, private network video companies are springing up. Network users use network video, becoming the third largest Internet application after music and instant messaging. This is the first time that online home entertainment applications have surpassed online business applications, namely traditional messaging applications such as mail, search engines and news. However, with the rapid growth of online video, various yellow, violent and reactionary spam messages are also mixed in the network video on the broadband network, which seriously affects people's normal work and life, as well as social spiritual civilization construction and the education of minors has brought huge hidden dangers.

2.2 Monitoring of RF Information

Due to the high-speed data packet transmission of broadband video networks, traditional information security monitoring devices are unable to do so in this respect. Therefore, we propose to apply key frame extraction technology to extract key frames in network video, thereby reducing the processing load and storage space. Reduce equipment costs and increase processing efficiency. The corresponding junk video key frame matching library is established, and the spam information is monitored from the high speed video stream through the video key frame matching algorithm and mode. Applying this video surveillance system and other network security devices, you can create a high-speed, clean online video environment for businesses, schools, and homes, making it easy for people to enjoy broadband video services.

3 RF Information Transmission Interruption Monitoring System

3.1 The Significance of RF Information Monitoring

In general, the main technologies related to monitoring technology include electronic technology, computer technology, network technology, microelectronic technology, and optoelectronic technology. Early monitoring is entirely manual monitoring and monitoring. The development of linear recording methods has led to the use of video recorders and recorders. Auxiliary recording and broadcasting programs became possible. In the late 1990s, the development of VLSI and software technology made the video and audio compression technology more and more mature. The development of nonlinear storage technology represented by computer storage made the hard disk video display gradually replace the video recorder and recorder. The trend of network technology has also made remote data transmission possible. The application of optoelectronic technology makes it possible to isolate and test the technical indicators of high-power high-voltage equipment. It is foreseeable that with the continuous development of new materials and new technologies in the future, monitoring technology. New changes will also take place in the form of expression.

3.2 Automated Monitoring System

From the perspective of automation, monitoring can be roughly divided into manual monitoring and automatic monitoring. At present, most monitoring institutions in China, including central, provincial and municipalities, mainly adopt the mode of manual and automatic coexistence, and the video information monitoring institutions at the municipal level. Most of them use a single method of manual monitoring, and some cities also use a combination of manual and automatic. The application of monitoring technology is closely combined with the characteristics of the video information technology process. For the city-level monitoring organization, the average failure rate of the small power link equipment such as studio and broadcast control is lower, and the fault occurs more frequently in the high-power launching process, especially In the case of low degree of solid state, the video information transmitting equipment with the tube amplifier as the core has poor stability. Therefore, the current practical monitoring system focuses on radio frequency (RF) signals, mainly implementing carrier frequency interruption and video signal interruption. Demodulation, audio signal amplitude, synchronization and other pointer monitoring, but for the video signal is not interrupted on the surface, the actual content has been interrupted, the phenomenon of black or other monochrome pad frame picture has not attracted attention, and this fault is It is not uncommon for studios and broadcast control. Especially in recent years, the insertion of criminals often leads to such failures in satellite receiving signals. Monitoring of this phenomenon is one of the important contents of this project.

3.3 RF Interrupt Impact

Regardless of wired or wireless TV, the RF signal works in the ultra-short band (48.SMHz–958MHz), and the modulation mode is vestigial sideband amplitude modulation (VSB-AM) to save bandwidth resources. The receiving device uses RF demodulated video. The signal establishes a synchronized reference for reception, controlling the line and field scanning of the display device. In the event of a radio frequency interruption, the built-in synchronization loses the reference source, and the thermal noise of the active device in the receiver will cause the image to appear "snowflake point". In recent years, the receiving device of the improved circuit outputs static in the case of synchronous loss of lock. The frame picture softens the response of the interrupt and provides an easy way to detect the interrupt. That is, by identifying the characteristic still frame picture after the RF interrupt of the specific receiving device, the occurrence of the RF interrupt can be effectively detected.

3.4 RF Interrupt Fault Detection Mode

The main equipment of the video transmitting station is a video transmitter, which is divided into two parts: a video exciter unit and a power amplifier unit. The video channel and the radio frequency channel are both in the exciter, and the attack and release is a single radio frequency channel. When the video channel in the exciter fails and the video is interrupted, the transmitter output is an equal amplitude wave that is not modulated by the video signal, and the video signal is not demodulated at the receiving end, and the receiver video channel input is a random clutter; When the RF channel and the power amplifier unit in the internal frequency modulation, intermediate frequency correction, frequency conversion, etc. are faulty, the RF signal is not interrupted, and the transmitter does not have the RF signal output. Naturally, the receiver cannot demodulate the video signal, and the receiver video channel input. The same is a random clutter. Obviously, the broadcast caused by the video and RF faults is the same at the receiving end, and the responsible departments of both faults are video transmitting stations. Therefore, by analyzing the clutter, the two faults are combined and detected. Completed in the video RF interrupt module.

4 Suppress Electromagnetic Interference from Radio Frequency Propagation

4.1 Using Switching Power Supply Suppression

Optimize circuit component layout to minimize parasitic and coupling capacitance. Delaying the turn-on and turn-off time of the switch, but this does not match the trend of high-frequency switching power supply. Apply a snubber circuit to slow down the rate of change of dvldt. The current in the converter is switched at high frequency, so that a high dvl towel is generated on the input and output filter capacitors, that is, the interference voltage is induced on the equivalent inductance or impedance of the filter capacitor. Normal mode interference will occur. Therefore, the use of high-quality filter capacitors (equivalent inductance or low impedance) can reduce the normal mode interference.

4.2 Common Mode Interference Suppression

It should be noted that the current phases of the different branches are not necessarily the same, which is especially important in the calculation of the magnetic field. The phase is different. First, there is a delay effect due to interference from the interference source to the measurement point. Second, the phase is different because of the characteristics of the components themselves. For example, the current phase in the inductor is lagging behind other components. The phase lag caused by the hysteresis effect is the result of the signal frequency, and the effect is only obvious when the frequency is high. For the power electronic device, the frequency is relatively low, so the hysteresis effect is not very large. Among the two types of interference generated by switching power supplies, conducted interference is transmitted through the power grid, causing serious interference to other electronic equipment, often causing more serious problems. Commonly used suppression methods include the buffer method, the reduced path method, and the parasitic element method. In recent years, with the stricter restrictions on electromagnetic interference of electronic equipment, some new suppression methods have emerged, mainly focusing on several aspects such as new control methods and design of new passive buffer circuits.

4.3 Use Shielding Technology to Reduce Electromagnetic Interference

In order to effectively suppress the radiation and conduction of electromagnetic waves and the noise current caused by higher harmonics, shielded cables must be used for elevator motor cables driven by inverters. The conductance of the shielding layer is at least 1/10 of that of the conductors of each phase conductor core. And the shielding layer should be reliably grounded. It is best to use shielded cables for control cables;

double-shielded twisted pairs should be used for analog signal transmission lines; different analog signal lines should be routed independently and have their own shielding layers. To reduce the coupling between the lines, do not put different analog signals in the same common return line; low-voltage digital signal lines are best to use double-shielded twisted pair or single-shielded twisted pair. Transmission cables for analog signals and digital signals should be shielded and routed separately for short use.

4.4 Use Filtering Technology to Reduce Electromagnetic Interference

Incoming reactors are used to reduce the harmonics generated by the frequency converter. They can also be used to increase the impedance of the power supply and help to absorb the surge voltage generated by nearby equipment and the peak voltage of the main power supply. The line reactor is connected in series between the power supply and the inverter power input. When the situation of the main power grid is unknown, it is best to add a line reactor. A low-pass filter (the same as FIR) can also be used in the above circuit. The FIR filter should be connected in series between the line reactor and the inverter. For elevator drives operating in noise-sensitive environments, FIR filters can be used to effectively reduce radiated interference from the transmission.

5 Summary

Due to the rich and colorful video information, snowflakes, black fields, etc. may be normal signals. In some videos, there may be long-term no-audio leopard phenomenon. The monitoring device itself may also have the possibility of malfunction. Therefore, it is possible to monitor the material after the event. Effectively identify system misjudgments and be able to present more accurate monitoring reports.

References

1. Liang J, Wang Y, Huang Y et al (2009) Electromagnetic interference shielding of graphene/epoxy composites. Carbon 47(3):922–925
2. Chung DDL (2001) Electromagnetic interference shielding effectiveness of carbon materials. Carbon 39(2):279–285
3. Al-Saleh MH, Sundararaj U (2009) Electromagnetic interference shielding mechanisms of CNT/polymer composites. Carbon 47(7):1738–1746
4. Middleton D (2007) Statistical-physical models of electromagnetic interference. IEEE Trans Electromagn Compat EMC-19(3):106–127
5. Li N, Huang Y, Du F et al (2006) Electromagnetic interference (EMI) shielding of single-walled carbon nanotube epoxy composites. Nano Lett 6(6):1141–1145
6. Zhang HB, Yan Q, Zheng WG et al (2011) Tough graphene-polymer microcellular foams for electromagnetic interference shielding. ACS Appl Mater Interfaces 3(3):918
7. Yang Y, Gupta MC, Dudley KL et al (2005) Novel carbon nanotube-polystyrene foam composites for electromagnetic interference shielding. Nano Lett 5(11):2131–2134

8. Liu Z, Gang B, Yi H et al (2007) Reflection and absorption contributions to the electromagnetic interference shielding of single-walled carbon nanotube/polyurethane composites. Carbon 45(4):821–827
9. Cao MS, Song W-L et al (2010) The effects of temperature and frequency on the dielectric properties, electromagnetic interference shielding and microwave-absorption of short carbon fiber/silica composites. Carbon 48(3):788–796
10. Witt T, Walter TR (2016) Video monitoring reveals pulsating vents and propagation path of fissure eruption during the March 2011 Pu'u 'Ō 'ō eruption, Kilauea volcano. J Volcanol Geoth Res 330:43–55
11. Sanchezlarsen A, Aznarlain G, Benito B et al (2017) Post-ictal atrial fibrillation detected during video-EEG monitoring: Case report, proposed physiopathologic mechanism and therapeutic considerations. Epilepsy Behav Case Rep 8:40–43
12. Anedda M, Murroni M, Muntean GM (2017) E-ARMANS: energy-aware device-oriented video delivery in heterogeneous wireless networks. In: IEEE international symposium on broadband multimedia systems & broadcasting
13. Qazi S, Siddiqui AS, Wagan AI (2016) UAV based real time video surveillance over 4G LTE. In: International conference on open source systems & technologies
14. Choi Y, Abbas SH, Lee JR (2018) Aircraft integrated structural health monitoring using lasers, piezoelectricity, and fiber optics. Measurement 125:294–302
15. Ghazi RM, Chen JG, Büyüköztürk O (2017) Pairwise graphical models for structural health monitoring with dense sensor arrays. Mech Syst Sig Process 93:578–592
16. Kijanka P, Packo P, Staszewski WJ et al (2013) Temperature effect modelling of piezoceramic transducers used for lamb wave propagation in damage detection applications. In: Health monitoring of structural & biological systems
17. Al-Majeed S, Fleury M (2014) Wireless handover with application to quadcopter video streaming over an IP network
18. Sujatha K, Pappa N, Nambi US et al (2013) Intelligent parallel networks for combustion quality monitoring in power station boilers. Adv Mater Res 699(699):7
19. Beniczky S, Polster T, Kjaer TW et al (2013) Detection of generalized tonic–clonic seizures by a wireless wrist accelerometer: a prospective, multicenter study. Epilepsia 54(4):e58–e61

Application Research of Intrusion Prevention System in Emergency Platform Network

GuoRu Deng(✉), Hui Yuan, Liang Dong, Shan Yang, Zheng Yu, Yan Zhuang, Haohua Meng, and Xuan Luo

Information and Communication Company of Hubei State Grid Corporation, No. 197 Xu Dong Street, Wuhan, Hubei, China
882148@qq.com

Abstract. With the in-depth construction of the national emergency platform project and the increasingly complex network environment, as well as the increasing diversification of intrusion methods, the defects of traditional firewall technology and intrusion detection system in network security protection are highlighted. The security of traditional network systems is mainly guaranteed by two pillar technologies: firewall and intrusion detection. However, network attack technologies are also constantly developing, and new technologies such as small fragmentation attacks, slow scanning, distributed denial of service attacks, and encryption attacks have emerged. Attack programs for network security software such as firewalls and intrusion detection systems have also emerged, all of which place new demands on the development of network security. This paper first analyzes various network intrusion behaviors, and elaborates the attack characteristics of different intrusion behaviors and the corresponding detection methods and anti-attack methods. Then it introduces the traditional network security defense technology, including password, identity authentication, firewall, intrusion detection, etc., and discusses these passive defense technologies in detail, pointing out their inherent shortcomings.

Keywords: Network security · Intrusion prevention system · Intrusion behavior · Emergency platform

1 Introduction

The continuous development of computer and network communication technology not only provides convenience for people's daily life, but also has a great impact on social progress [1]. At the same time, with the deepening of the national emergency platform system construction project, the security problems faced by the emergency network platform will become more and more complicated. Buzz overflow, worms, Trojans, rootkits and other malicious attacks seriously endanger the information [2]. Safety, in fact, according to the CSI/FBI security report, 86% of users used firewalls in network security incidents, 43% used intrusion detection, and 91% of intrusions bypassed the firewall [3–16]. It can be seen that the traditional firewall technology and intrusion detection system have obvious defects in network security protection. The human intrusion prevention system tends to provide proactive protection [17]. It is designed to

Z. Xu et al. (Eds.): CSIA 2019, AISC 928, pp. 1158–1166, 2020.
https://doi.org/10.1007/978-3-030-15235-2_153

intercept human intrusion activities and offensive network traffic in advance. To avoid causing losses, rather than simply issuing an alert when malicious traffic is transmitted or after transmission [18]. In order to deal with various types of attacks and viruses in the emergency platform network, this paper proposes an emergency platform network security solution based on the intrusion prevention system [19]. Not only need reliable, high-performance, flexible and rich equipment as a support, but also requires an easy-to-use management system, making the security protection and management of the entire network into a three-dimensional structure [20].

2 The Intrusion Prevention System

Intrusion Prevention System (IPS) is an emerging network security defense technology in the past two years. It has higher initiative and a certain degree of intelligence than firewall and IDS, and can protect the network from unknown types attack. It is deployed on the critical path of the network, and when an attack attempt is detected, it automatically drops the attack packet or blocks the attack source. IPS combines passive access control technology and proactive analysis and detection technology to integrate protection, detection and response in the entire network security protection system, so that network protection advances toward the goal of dynamic protection, deep protection and overall protection. The IPS system is more adaptive, proactive, intelligent and real-time, providing more reliable security for host and network security.

IPS has the following features: powerful intrusion detection capability, low false positive rate and false negative rate; real-time response, with certain firewall function, can dynamically configure BLOCK IP/CIDR; excellent processing power, In high-speed environments, there is no packet loss and normal intrusion detection. It uses multiple algorithms to block malicious behavior. It can immediately terminate the intrusion and block IP CIDR after the intrusion is discovered.

The principle behind IPS for real-time checking and blocking intrusions is that it has a large number of filters that prevent attacks. When a new attack is discovered, the IPS creates a new filter, and the IPS packet processing engine can deeply examine the contents of the packet. The traditional firewall packet filtering technology does not check every byte, and the IPS can check every byte, and all packets are classified according to the header information. Various filters are responsible for analyzing the corresponding data packets. Each filter has a corresponding filter rule, and these rules are broadly defined to ensure accuracy. When classifying the transmitted content, the filtering engine also needs to parse the data packet into a meaningful domain for context analysis to improve the filtering accuracy. The filter engine combines massively parallel processing hardware to perform thousands of packet filtering checks simultaneously. This hardware acceleration technology that does not increase system load is important for IPS.

Intrusion prevention technology is considered to be a promising security technology in the future. It can play the role of a level. All packets or network traffic destined for a critical network segment must pass the IPS check, so the attack data flow reaches the target. It was previously identified by the IPS, and the IPS was able to take immediate action to discard or block network packets for defense purposes. The IPS defense model is shown in Fig. 1.

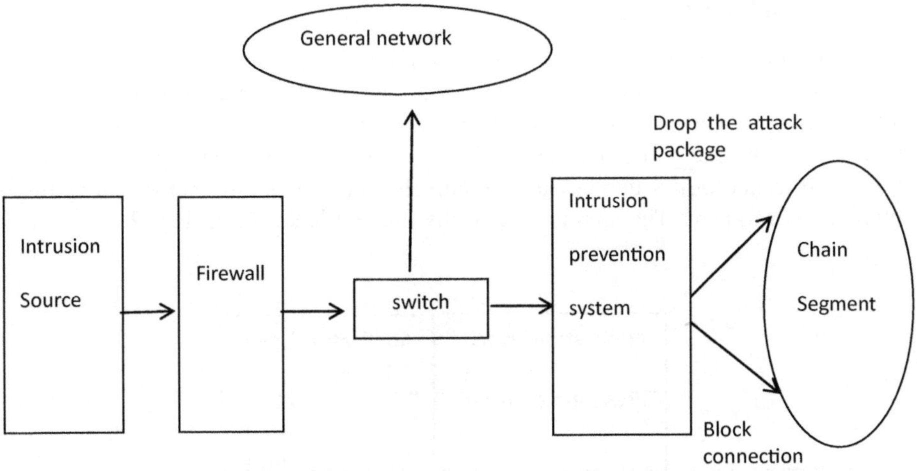

Fig. 1. IPS defense model

3 Common Network Security Defense Technology

3.1 Cryptography

To ensure the confidentiality of information in the process of communication, encryption algorithm is used to encrypt data or traffic. It can be used alone or in combination with other mechanisms. Encryption algorithm can be divided into two types: symmetric key system and asymmetric key system.

Symmetric cryptography is simple to operate, easy to implement, fast to encrypt, and takes up less resources at runtime, but it needs to exchange keys in a secure way before conducting secure communication. In the case of multi-user, the scale of key management is complex.

In asymmetric cryptography, the two sides of the communication do not need to exchange the key through the secret channel beforehand. The amount of key holdings is greatly reduced, but the large number of floating-point operations result in large amount of computation, and the slow speed of encryption and decryption requires more resources. This is particularly important for a large number of secure transactions in e-commerce.

3.2 Identity Recognition Technology

At present, there are mainly four kinds of technical methods for identity recognition, one is to use user identity, password, key and other technical measures for identity recognition, the other is to use user body features, fingerprints, signatures and other technical measures for identity recognition, the third is to use user-held certificates, such as optical cards, magnetic cards and other identification four is more. Interactive methods are used for identity recognition.

3.3 Firewall Technology

"Firewall" in the field of computer security refers to the device used to protect the internal network from illegal or unauthorized intrusion from the outside, it is located between two networks of the system. There are many kinds of firewalls, which can be divided into two categories: packet filtering type and proxy service type. The core idea of firewall technology is to construct a relatively safe subnet environment in an unsafe internet environment. The architecture of the firewall is shown in Fig. 2.

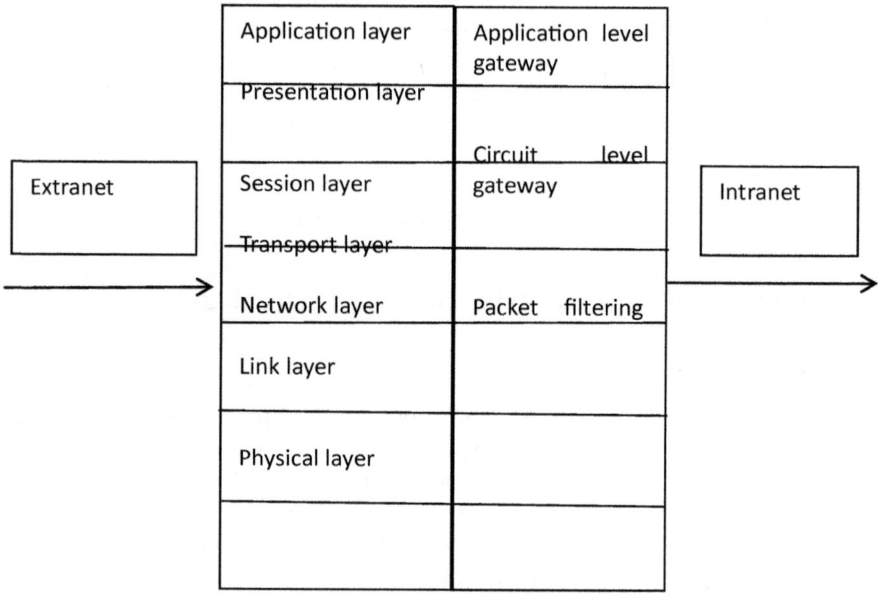

Fig. 2. Firewall architecture

3.4 Digital Signature Technology

Digital signature technology is a security technology to solve the problems of denial, forgery, impersonation and tampering in network communication. The sender attaches signature information encrypted by his private key to the message, and the receiver verifies the signature information with the signer's public key. It is a simulation of handwriting signature. It has the following properties:

(1) it can be verified as the author's signature and the date and time of signature.
(2) the content must be identified when signing.
(3) signatures must be confirmed by third parties in order to settle disputes.

4 The Comprehensive Linkage Program Design

At present, the more mature linkage system has been used commercially is to achieve intrusion prevention through the linkage of network intrusion detection system and firewall. When an attack is detected, the firewall will be notified to make dynamic changes to the relevant policies immediately, and block the source of the attack, such as blocking the source port, source and so on, so as to achieve the overall security control effect. The design of firewall and linkage fully embodies the idea of network security deep defense. The most important problem is that the interaction between firewalls and intrusion detection products does not have a commonly accepted standard. Most security vendors go their own way, which limits the development of technology and the range of products users choose.

Therefore, this paper proposes a comprehensive system linkage plan. In the comprehensive linkage plan, IPS is only a part of active protection, not all. Aiming at the characteristics of network topology of emergency platform, application-level firewall, security management center software, EAD (Endpoint Admission Defense) software, network version anti-virus software, network management software, SSL VPN access gateway and other hardware and software devices are added to the integrated linkage system. The comprehensive linkage plan of Hubei company is shown in Table 1.

Table 1. Configuration scheme of Hubei company's integrated linkage system

Serial number	Security system configuration	Implementation method and function
1	Firewall	A firewall is used to protect the trusted intranet for authorized access
2	Safety management center	Unified management of network products, security products and servers on the emergency platform, and visual monitoring and audit reports on network security status
3	EAD software	Through centralized deployment, the security status assessment and access rights of the user terminal are dynamically controlled, and the active defense capability of the network terminal in the emergency platform is strengthened to control the spread of viruses and worms
4	Network anti-virus software	The network virus server is deployed in the DMZ area, and the virus database of the access terminal and the server is upgraded in time to prevent virus intrusion
5	Network management software	Unified centralized management of network security devices
6	SSL VPN access gateway	Adopt SSL VPN technology to meet the needs of mobile office access
7	Intrusion prevention system	Intrusion prevention products are used to check the network or operating system to identify illegal intrusions and automatically respond and protect. Block DOS/DDOS attacks and virus intrusions from the Internet, protect intranet servers from vulnerabilities, and prevent web page tampering
8	Identity authentication system	Use digital certificates or dynamic passwords for authentication

The specific deployment strategies are as follows:

(1) the Internet outlet of the emergency platform network deploys firewalls and IPS. Firewall controls access from outside and protects against 2–4 layer network attacks from outside networks. IPS uses different rules to protect 2–7 layers of external network attacks and monitor internal traffic to restrict P2P, BT and other services to ensure the normal operation of the backbone service network of emergency platform, as shown in Figs. 3 and 4.

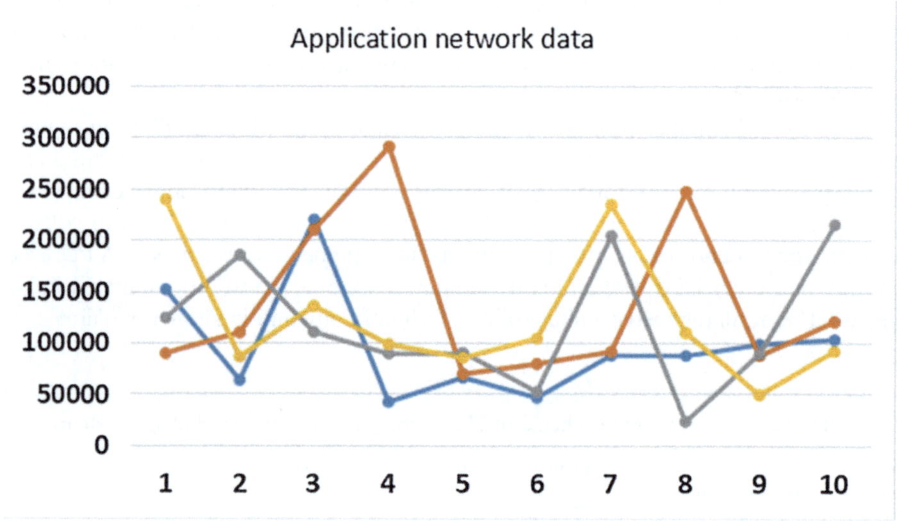

Fig. 3. Network attack simulation results of different methods

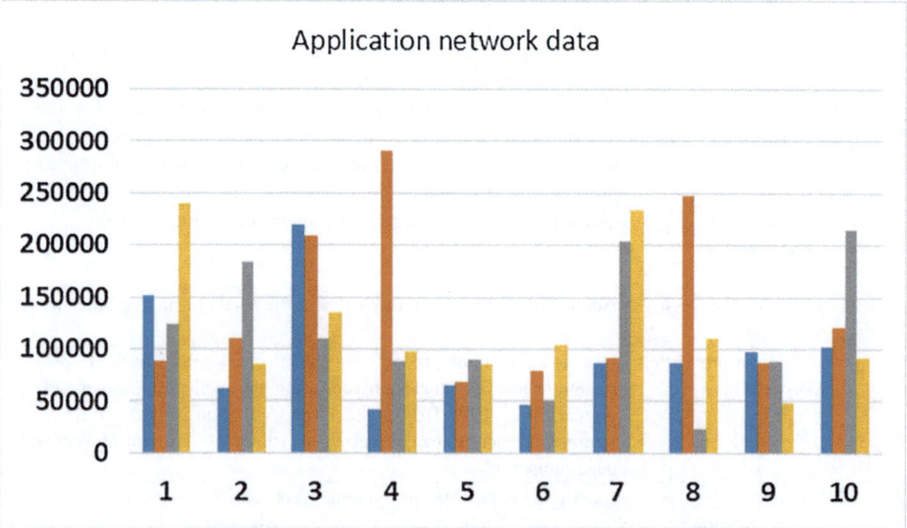

Fig. 4. Network simulation mean of different methods

(2) Two core switches bypass the deployment of SSL VPN equipment, and do a dual hot standby, in order to ensure the emergency platform network security, while meeting the needs of mobile office. At the same time, the mobile terminal accesses the emergency platform data by adding digital certificates to authenticate the identity, to ensure the security of mobile terminal access.
(3) important emergency platform server group front-end deploys IPS and firewall. It protects against attacks on operating system vulnerabilities and protects attacks from internal network 2–7 layer. The firewall virtualizes DMZ and internal trusted areas for the emergency platform server group, controls access to different units, and protects against attacks from 2 to 4 layers of the internal network.
(4) deploying network version of anti-virus software and EAD system in DMZ area. Network version of anti-virus server installed in the intranet office PC and server group, the software can update the virus library regularly and timely to protect the server group and Intranet office PC from virus attacks. Through centralized deployment, EAD can realize the security status evaluation of user terminals and dynamic control of access rights, thus strengthening the active defense capability of network terminals in emergency platform and controlling the spread of viruses and worms.
(5) the safety management software and the network management software centrally manage the emergency platform. Managers can manage and control network security and server equipment through network management software, update and modify the configuration of equipment, and reduce the difficulty and cost of management. The security events and logs of network, security and server are collected through the security management center software, such as attack event records and logs.

5 Conclusion

Firstly, this paper analyzes the network intrusion behavior, points out the common hacker attack behavior characteristics and protection technology, and studies the traditional anti-intrusion technology such as firewall and intrusion detection system, points out its shortcomings in security protection, and introduces a new network security. All-technology-intrusion prevention system. After analyzing and studying the working principle, characteristics and classification of Intrusion Prevention Technology in detail, the solution of intrusion prevention system in emergency platform network is designed, and the overall structure and main function structure of the system are given. According to the network environment of the emergency platform, the network security problem is solved from the overall situation, the whole and the equipment linkage. According to the unified security strategy and the security as the core, a complete set of integrated linkage security solution is proposed. According to the development of the times in the future, the advanced intrusion prevention system will synergize with other security products to form a synergistic network security protection system. Practice has proved that a single function product can not meet the security requirements. The integration, coordination and centralized management of security products are the important development direction of network security. Therefore, this study also complies with the future development trend of intrusion prevention system.

References

1. Jin H, Xiang G, Zou D et al (2013) A VMM-based intrusion prevention system in cloud computing environment. J Supercomput 66(3):1133–1151
2. Xing T, Huang D, Xu L et al (2013) SnortFlow: a OpenFlow-based intrusion prevention system in cloud environment. In: Second Geni research and educational experiment workshop. IEEE Computer Society, pp 89–92
3. Sun M, Zheng M, Lui JCS et al (2014) Design and implementation of an Android host-based intrusion prevention system. In: Computer security applications conference, pp 226–235
4. Xing T, Xiong Z, Huang D et al (2015) SDNIPS: enabling software-defined networking based intrusion prevention system in clouds. In: International conference on network and service management. IEEE, pp 308–311
5. Zhang L, Shou G, Hu Y et al (2014) Deployment of intrusion prevention system based on software defined networking. In: IEEE international conference on communication technology. IEEE, pp 26–31
6. Kenkre PS, Pai A, Colaco L (2015) Real time intrusion detection and prevention system. In: 2014 Proceedings of the 3rd international conference on frontiers of intelligent computing: theory and applications (FICTA). Springer International Publishing, Heidelberg, pp 25–41
7. Alqahtani SM, Balushi MA, John R (2014) An Intelligent intrusion prevention system for cloud computing (SIPSCC). In: International conference on computational science and computational intelligence. IEEE, pp 152–158
8. Lifliand V, Ryzhyk E, Sagiv Y et al (2016) Safe code for signature updates in an intrusion prevention system: US, US9389839
9. Huang NF, Wang C, Liao IJ et al (2015) An OpenFlow-based collaborative intrusion prevention system for cloud networking. In: IEEE international conference on communication software and networks. IEEE, pp 85–92
10. Chakraborty M, Chaki N, Cortesi A (2014) A new intrusion prevention system for protecting Smart Grids from ICMPv6 vulnerabilities. In: Computer science and information systems. IEEE, pp 1539–1547
11. Tomasek M, Cajkovsky M, Klimek I (2013) Cloud-centric application tracing and user monitoring intrusion prevention system. In: IEEE, international conference on intelligent engineering systems. IEEE, pp 339–343
12. Farhaoui Y (2016) How to secure web servers by the intrusion prevention system (IPS)? Int J Adv Res Comput Sci 6(23):65–71
13. Hock F, Kortiš P (2016) Commercial and open-source based intrusion detection system and intrusion prevention system (IDS/IPS) design for an IP networks. In: International conference on emerging Elearning technologies and applications. IEEE, pp 1–4
14. Shaghaghi A, Kaafar MA, Jha S (2017) WedgeTail: an intrusion prevention system for the data plane of software defined networks. In: Asia conference on computer and communications security
15. Shaghaghi A, Kaafar MA, Jha S (2017) WedgeTail: an intrusion prevention system for the data plane of software defined networks pp 849–861

16. Poongodi M, Bose S (2014) Design of intrusion detection and prevention system (IDPS) using DGSOTFC in collaborative protection networks. In: Fifth international conference on advanced computing. IEEE, pp 172–178
17. Liu W, Quan-Lin LI, Rui L et al (2015) A performance analysis method for intrusion prevention system. Netinfo Secur
18. Chen L, Li Y, Wang L (2017) Design and implementation of sybil intrusion prevention system based on internet of things. Comput Meas Control
19. Yerur SV, Natarajan P, Rangaswamy TR (2017) Proactive hybrid intrusion prevention system for mobile adhoc networks. Int J Intell Eng Syst 10(6):273–283
20. Swetha KV, Dara R (2018) Deployment of intrusion prevention system on multi-core processor based security hardware. Int J Comput Netw Commun 10(3):13–25

Research on Core Data Protection Based on Cloud Computing

Guoru Deng(✉), Shuai Hu, Hui Yuan, Liang Dong, Yan Zhuang, Shan Yang, Xuan Luo, and Yixi Wang

Information and Communication Company of Hubei State Grid Corporation, No. 197 Xu Dong Street, Wuhan, Hubei, China
882148@qq.com

Abstract. The rise of cloud computing has brought new challenges and opportunities to data protection technology. On the one hand, large-scale cloud storage systems contain huge amounts of data. Their system complexity and service characteristics make data reliability severely challenged, requiring stronger data protection technologies. At the same time, cloud host surfaces with important business data are stored. Against the intrusion threat of hackers around the world, the common data protection mechanism in the host can not resist the hacker's destruction behavior, and needs to adopt new data protection technology to deal with it. To this end, a cloud-based user core data protection model is designed to decompose user data into core data and general data. The core data will be stored in a user-controllable private cloud. The general data is filtered and stored in the public service provider. In the cloud, the protection and security of user core data is effectively solved. By utilizing the existing network security products and combining the designed data classification algorithms, the cloud-based enterprise core data protection system is constructed according to the model. The validity of the model is verified by the actual use, and the core data of the user in the cloud computing is used. Protection explores new ways.

Keywords: Cloud computing · Core data protection · Security model · Security threat

1 Introduction

With the popularity of cloud computing applications, many enterprises are preparing to migrate their business systems to cloud computing environments, so data security in cloud computing has become a concern of enterprise users [1]. Core data, sometimes referred to as internal data, contains important information such as user's key business process data, financial data, customer data, etc., and is the embodiment of the core competitiveness of user organizations. Therefore, users usually pay close attention to the security of such data [2]. Store this type of data within your own control, such as local storage [3–7]. According to the characteristics of user data storage in cloud computing environment, combined with the requirements of enterprise users' core data security protection, we propose a strategy of using hybrid cloud structure to protect user core data security, and fully analyze user's core data and general data. On the basis

Z. Xu et al. (Eds.): CSIA 2019, AISC 928, pp. 1167–1174, 2020.
https://doi.org/10.1007/978-3-030-15235-2_154

of different protection needs, the Hubei company used this model to establish a "cloud-based enterprise core data protection system", which was used to verify the practicability and effectiveness of the model. After the operation of Hubei Company, the system established by this model can better protect the user's core data [8–15]. The system basically meets the design requirements of the user in the protection of user core data, and protects the core data of users in the future cloud computing environment. The research has made a useful exploration [16, 17].

2 Cloud Computing

The so-called cloud computing refers to a new type of Internet-based network computing business service model, which integrates various IT resources including storage, computing, network, software and services, and provides on-demand application and dynamic scalability to customers through the network. Resource services that are paid for by usage - just like water and electricity. Cloud computing is characterized by scale, virtualization, generalization, platforming, on-demand customization, and high scalability. By using cloud computing resources, businesses and individuals no longer have to worry about the cumbersome IT infrastructure, infrastructure, infrastructure, and operational details, and can focus more on their own business, thereby reducing costs and accelerating industry innovation. From this perspective, cloud computing is an advanced production tool that boosts industry productivity.

As an extremely complex technology, industry, and commercial hybrid, cloud computing has several major advantages:

2.1 Low Cost

Cloud computing service providers have reduced the cost of construction by building large IT infrastructures on a large scale, and using the redundancy of multi-user services to improve the utilization of IT facilities, thereby effectively reducing the unit price of cloud services. Through the mode of actual usage payment, users can fully enjoy this low cost advantage.

2.2 Ease of Use

Through the mass procurement of hardware facilities and a unified virtualization platform, the cloud computing system can provide users with standardized virtual IT resources, so that users do not need to consider the operation and maintenance of the system too much, and the upper layer services do not need to face the complex heterogeneous hardware underlying. Fully reflects the ease of use of cloud computing.

2.3 High Reliability and High Availability

High reliability mainly means data is not lost, and high availability mainly means service is not interrupted. It can get higher data reliability and service availability than the IT facilities built by ordinary enterprises.

2.4 High Scalability

Benefiting from the cloud computing virtualization platform, users can flexibly use all kinds of cloud resources and cloud services: when the business scale increases, they will rent more resources and services; when new business needs appear, they will add new resources. And services; when resources and services are idle, they are scaled down.

3 The Data Security Threats Faced by Cloud Computing Facing Cloud Computing

Due to the huge scale of cloud computing systems, the application and privacy data of many users are concentrated. At the same time, cloud computing has unprecedented openness and complexity, and its security faces more severe challenges than traditional information systems. This article lists seven aspects of cloud computing security issues:

1. data loss and leakage. The security control of data in cloud computing is not high. The lack of security mechanisms and management deficiencies may cause data leakage. Whether it is private data or important national data, if it is lost or leaked, it will have bad consequences.
2. sharing technology vulnerabilities. Cloud computing is a large shared data center. The greater the degree of sharing, the more vulnerabilities and the more attacks.
3. vendor reliability is not easy to assess. To avoid the theft of sensitive information, a reliable service provider is needed, but how to conduct a credible assessment of the service provider remains to be studied.
4. weak authentication mechanism. Since a large amount of data, applications, and resources are concentrated in the cloud, if the authentication mechanism of the cloud computing is weak, the intruder can easily obtain the user account and log in to the user's virtual machine to perform various illegal operations.
5. unsafe application interface. The cloud computing application system is very complicated, and the security is more difficult to ensure. Some interfaces may be used by the attack program, which is prone to security problems.
6. without the right to run cloud computing. In terms of technology use, hackers may progress faster than technicians, use legal identity to fish in troubled waters, and illegally run cloud computing.
7. unknown risks. The transparency of the service allows the user to use only the web front-end interactive interface. It does not know which platform the vendor uses or which security mechanism to provide. In other words, the user cannot know whether the cloud service provider has fulfilled the service agreement as promised.

4 The Design of Core Data Protection Model Based on Cloud Computing

The design of this model depends on the deployment of cloud computing, so we must choose the most appropriate deployment scheme to play the role of this model. The deployment of cloud computing can be divided into four types: public cloud, private cloud, community cloud and hybrid cloud. These four deployment schemes have their own characteristics in data security transmission and storage.

This model is designed according to the safety requirements of enterprise users for core data. The structure is shown in Fig. 1:

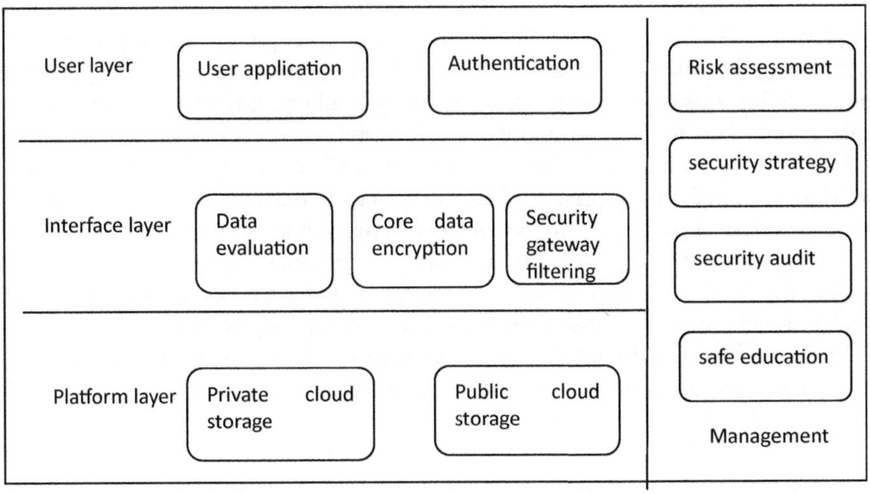

Fig. 1. User core data protection model based on cloud computing

The model is divided into four layers. The platform layer controls the basic data storage task. The interface layer is responsible for data classification and encryption. The user layer authenticates the user's identity and provides data. The management layer uses management methods and means to ensure the effective operation of all work. The specific functions of each layer are as follows:

User layer: including the user's application and login authentication, mainly using unified authentication and access control technology to achieve user identity authentication and management. Strict identity authentication can ensure the validity of identity and determine its access rights, thus effectively ensuring the security of cloud computing platform data. Complex authentication technologies can be deployed in cloud computing. One is the powerful processing power of cloud computing, which usually does not reduce its efficiency. The other is the openness of cloud computing, which makes the requirements of access control far higher than other web systems. Therefore, the authentication technology deployed by users in this layer should be designed for cloud computing with high-intensity authentication, otherwise it is difficult to ensure the effectiveness of access control.

Interface layer: data evaluation and classification, cloud computing gateway, data encryption technology and equipment. Data evaluation and classification technology is an algorithm designed to meet the needs of this model. The use of this algorithm will help users to control the core data, but also increase the strength of data security protection. Devices and programs in the interface layer are usually deployed at the entrance and exit of the private cloud, responsible for classifying, filtering, encrypting and other operations on user data. On the one hand, it ensures that users' core data will not easily flow out to the public cloud. On the other hand, if the core data needs to be stored in the public cloud, it must be encrypted to ensure its security. Interface layer devices and programs are the most important tasks in this model, and the quality of completion will directly affect the effect of core data protection. Therefore, in the practical application of this layer, we usually want users to choose advanced and mature products or technologies in the industry. Only in this way can we ensure the implementation of the core technology of this model.

Platform Layer: It includes both private and public cloud storage. Data classified as core data is stored in the private cloud in principle, but it can also be stored in the public cloud if it is encrypted intensively. This model is based on hybrid cloud architecture, and ordinary users do not have private cloud. System, so ordinary users can simplify the private cloud into a user intranet, as long as its Intranet has sufficient security protection, it can also meet the security requirements of this model.

Management: including safety risk assessment, safety strategy formulation, safety audit, safety education and other management tools. This layer is the support of the whole model implementation, and is also the guarantee for the whole model to run well. From the point of view of safety management, no matter how advanced technology, it also needs good management to support, otherwise its advanced technology is difficult to play its due role. Therefore, in order to protect the security of user's core data in cloud computing, users should formulate the corresponding security management strategy according to the relevant laws and regulations combined with their own enterprise's data security requirements, and strictly implement it in actual operation, in order to achieve the goal of core data protection required by this model.

5 The Example Verification of the Model

In the construction of protection system, the construction of interface layer is the most important part. There are not only subjective standards such as "data evaluation and classification" which need to be quantified, but also security gateway filtering which needs the corresponding functions of hardware products to support. So we spent a lot of time studying these aspects. After continuous experiments, we have created a "data importance evaluation" algorithm, which can solve the problem of data evaluation and classification.

Data importance evaluation algorithm evaluates the importance of data from two aspects: first, the value of data, that is, the importance of this kind of data to the enterprise, the criterion is how much loss this kind of data will cause to the enterprise; second, the strength of data needs to be protected, that is, the enterprise thinks that this kind of data. The intensity of confidentiality that should be achieved. To facilitate the implementation of the algorithm, the classification of user data in this system can be expressed by a simplified "Hubei Company Data Importance Classification Table" (see Table 1 and Experimental Results 1, 2).

Table 1. Hubei company data importance classification table

Value level	Protective strength			
	Advanced	Intermediate	Primary	Zero level
First level	–	General data	General data	General data
Second level	Core data	–	General data	General data
Third level	Core data	Core data	–	General data
Fourth level	Core data	Core data	Core data	–

The "value level" in the table is divided into four levels. The first level is the data with the importance score less than or equal to 10 points, the second level is the data with the importance score of 11 to 40 points, and the third level is the importance level score. Data from 41to 70 points, and the fourth level is data with an importance score greater than 70 points. The "protection strength" in the table is also divided into four levels. The confidential data is advanced strength protection, the confidential data is intermediate strength protection, the internal data is primary strength protection, and the open data is zero-level strength protection (Figs. 2 and 3).

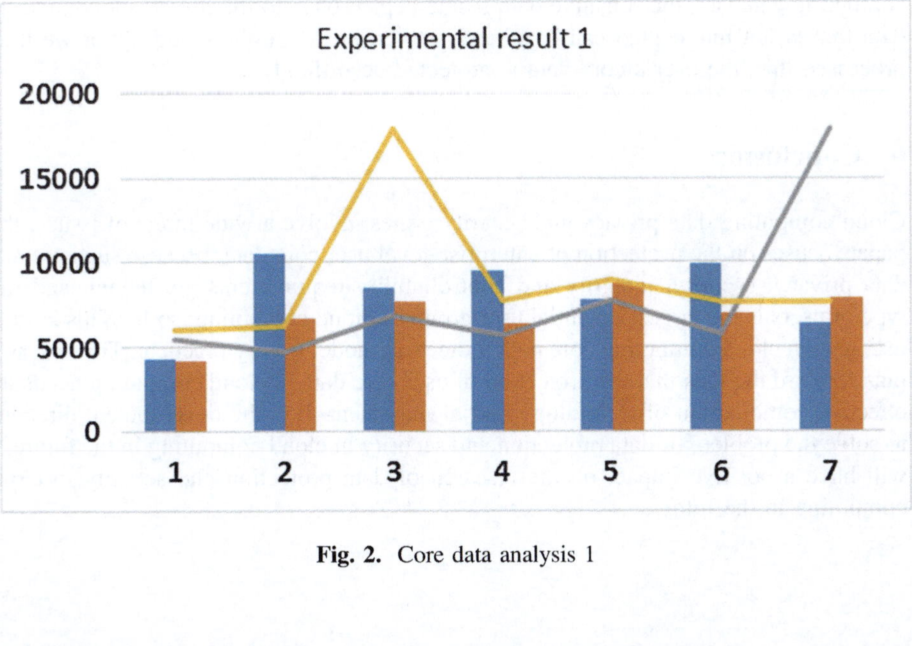

Fig. 2. Core data analysis 1

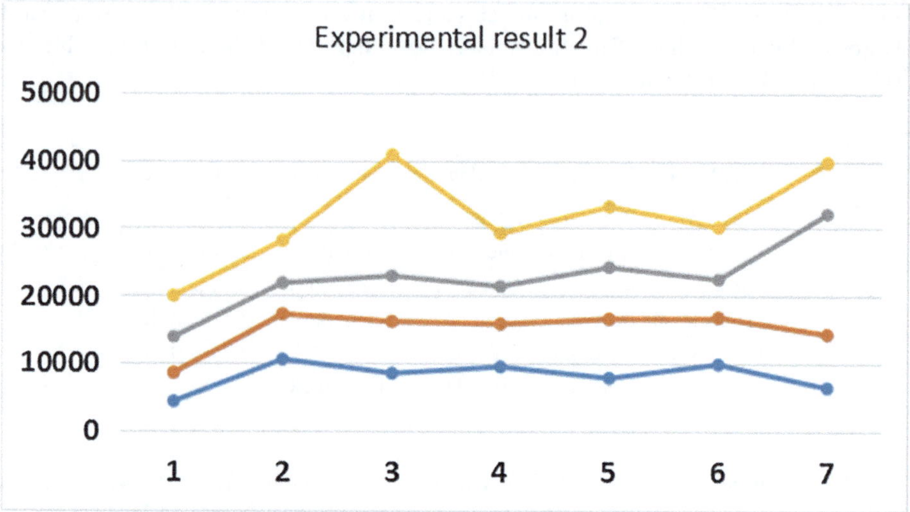

Fig. 3. Core data analysis 2

It can be known from Table 1 and Experimental Results 1 and 2 that the evaluated data does not appear on the diagonal of the table, so there is no need to distinguish whether it is core data. Data below the diagonal is evaluated as core data, which can only be stored in a private cloud. Of course, if it is encrypted, it can also be stored in the public cloud, and users need to protect the security and privacy of the data. The data above the diagonal is evaluated as general data. After filtering through the cloud computing gateway, the sensitive data is intercepted back to the private cloud, and the data that is not intercepted can be directly stored in the public cloud. After we have processed this, the user's core data is protected accordingly.

6 Conclusion

Cloud computing data privacy and security issues involve a wide range of issues, this paper focuses on the protection of enterprise-level user core data, because such users of data privacy, security, integrity and controllability requirements are higher, and this type of users is the largest potential user group of cloud computing, so for This kind of user design cloud computing core data protection model is very practical. This research puts forward the idea that the protection of user core data in cloud computing needs the effective combination of technology and management. It is the development direction to solve the problem of data protection and security in cloud computing in the future. It will have a positive impact on the research of data protection and security in cloud computing in the future.

References

1. King DA (2012) Notice of submission for OMB review; institute of education sciences; NPEFS 2011–2014: common core of data (CCD) national public education financial survey. Fed Reg
2. EDUCAUSE Connect Chicago, Solutions C C: Presentations and Seminars. A Crash Course in Object Storage: Massive Scalability, Cloud Stores, Self-Healing, and Data Protection, Chicago
3. Matthiä D, Meier MM, Reitz G (2014) Numerical calculation of the radiation exposure from galactic cosmic rays at aviation altitudes with the PANDOCA core model. Space Weather Int J Res Appl 12(3):161–171
4. Kosta E, Cuijpers C (2014) The draft data protection regulation and the development of data processing applications. In: IFIP PrimeLife international summer school on privacy and identity management for life, pp 12–32
5. Zhang X (2015) Research on the core database establishment for the "one map" of land and resources—taking Zengcheng as example. Urban Geotech Investig Surv
6. Zheng H, Guo S (2015) The design and research of petroleum resources database based on GIS vector data model. Comput Appl Pet
7. Zhu Y, Zhu Q, Feng Z et al (2015) Scientific big data sharing mechanisms research and suggestions for environmental information sharing. Chin J Environ Manag
8. Zhao H (2016) Research on the content and protection of individual privacy in the era of big data. Inf Stud Theory Appl
9. Danezis G, Domingoferrer J, Hansen M et al (2014) Privacy and data protection by design - from policy to engineering
10. Taylor MJ, Dove ES, Laurie G et al (2017) When can the child speak for herself? The limits of parental consent in data protection law for health research. Med Law Rev
11. Devries M, Fenchel M, Fogarty RE et al (2017) Name It! Store It! Protect It!: a systems approach to managing data in research core facilities. J Biomol Tech 28(4)
12. Zhang J, Zhang J, Huo X et al (2017) Research on the positioning of protection and utilization of historic districts under big data analysis. ISPRS – Int Arch Photogram Remote Sens Spat Inf Sci XLII-2/W5:731–735
13. Gibbs PEM, Tihomir M, Nicole LM et al (2016) Nanoparticle delivered human biliverdin reductase-based peptide increases glucose uptake by activating IRK/Akt/GSK3 axis: the peptide is effective in the cell and wild-type and diabetic Ob/Ob mice. J Diab Res 2016 (2):4712053
14. HTC Ltd (2017) System and method for wireless network access protection and security architecture
15. Singh U, Solanki NK, Varma MK et al (2017) A review on big data protection of Hadoop. In: International conference on communication and electronics systems, pp 943–950
16. Hui NC, Chang Y, Wong SF et al (2015) The implementation of the privacy protection policy for big data analytics: challenges faced in the malaysian telecommunications industry. In: European regional conference of the international telecommunications society
17. Kurtin JN (2016) Semiconductor structure having nanocrystalline core and nanocrystalline shell pairing with compositional transition layer

The Development Research of Gesture Recognition Based on Human Interaction

Jingliang Lai(✉)

Guangdong Industry Polytechnic, Guangzhou, Guangdong Province, China
laijingliang_gz@haoxueshu.com

Abstract. Firstly, the paper discusses the concept and common direction of virtual reality human-computer interaction. On this basis, it focuses on the foundation of function realization, and proposes to verify the multi-channel gestures through simulation to help improve the human-computer interaction process. The ability to simulate gestures. On this basis, the paper focuses on the tracking algorithm of multi-feature gesture recognition in virtual reality human-computer interaction environment, combined with the actual system design analysis, in order to be more clearly analyze the direction of human-computer interaction development.

Keywords: Gesture · Gesture recognition · Human interaction · Development

1 Introduction

With the rapid spread of computers and the Internet, human-computer interaction activities have gradually become an important part of people's daily lives. Studying the natural human-computer interaction method can reduce the difficulty of the operation itself, avoid the labor of a single part of the body, and reduce the chance of suffering from cervical spondylosis and lumbar disc herniation. Traditional human-computer interaction methods, such as keyboards, mice, remote controls, touch screens, etc., require people to adapt to the machine, and people need to operate according to preset specifications [1]. Nowadays, the development of technology has made the way of human-computer interaction more. Human-computer interaction based on gesture recognition is based on direct operation, which makes the human-computer interaction technology gradually shift from machine-centric to human-centered, in line with people's communication habits. Therefore, gesture recognition is gradually being developed and applied to engineering.

2 Gesture Recognition Overview

The gesture recognition device is a smart device for hand perception that has appeared in recent years. Its main principle is to use an advanced image fusion algorithm to identify and track the hand gesture and the fingertip trajectory, and then convert it into digital instructions.

The gesture recognition device gives the user a new way of interaction, enhances the user experience [1]. Which does not need to touch, and does not need to wear

Z. Xu et al. (Eds.): CSIA 2019, AISC 928, pp. 1175–1181, 2020.
https://doi.org/10.1007/978-3-030-15235-2_155

auxiliary equipment, so that the user can conveniently and intuitively manipulate electronic devices, such as computers through simple hand natural movements, so that users can enjoy. The joy brought by free manipulation has the functions of recognizing the overall shape of the hand, positioning the three-dimensional position of the fingertip, and capturing the sequence of hand movements [2].

From the perspective of sensory experience, the development of intelligent hardware has gone through three stages: from simple single sensory experience design to deep sensory interactive experience design to multi-sensory interactive experience design.

The gesture recognition based on the data glove requires the operator to wear the data glove, obtain the human hand information and the finger movement track and timing information through the sensor on the computer and the computer analyzes and recognizes the acquired data to achieve the effect of human-computer interaction [2]. Although this recognition method has high recognition accuracy, high speed, the device price is high, and the use comfort is poor, which is not a natural human-computer interaction mode. Vision-based gesture recognition is the acquisition of a sequence of images containing operator gestures by a camera, which is identified by image analysis. The equipment is cheap and easy to obtain, and easy to operate [3]. Today's cameras are no longer limited to just acquiring a 2D map of the scene, but also obtaining depth information for the scene. For example, Microsoft's somatosensory device Kinect can simultaneously acquire color images, depth images, human bone data, etc. of the scene, which is good for segmenting the target object, and its recognition process is not affected by light intensity, background, object color, texture, etc., and has good performance. Robustness [3]. Therefore, vision-based gesture recognition is receiving more and more attention from researchers.

3 Common Gesture Recognition Technology

Gesture recognition technology is currently divided into three main categories: based on template matching technology, based on probability and statistics technology and based on data classification technology. The template matching method first converts the image sequence into a set of static shape patterns, then compares it with the pre-stored behavior template in the recognition process, and finally selects the category of the known template with the closest similarity as the recognition result of the measured action. For example, Bobick transforms the motion information of the target into two two-dimensional templates of MEI (Motion Energy Image) and MHI (Motion History Image), and uses the Mahalanobis distance metric to test the similarity between the sample and the template [4]. The advantage of this method is that the computational complexity is low and the implementation is simple. The disadvantage is that the influence of the motion time cannot be solved. Template-based technologies mainly include template matching methods, dynamic time warping, and dynamic programming methods. The gesture recognition method based on probability and statistics is to apply the method of probability and statistics to the motion sequence, and define the action experienced in the middle as a state is arranged in a certain order, and the transition probability between state and state to represent [4]. The techniques based on probability statistics include hidden Markov models, dynamic Bayesian networks, and conditional random fields. Techniques based on data classification include neural networks, support vector machines, and the like.

Dynamic Time Warping Algorithm. Dynamic Time Warping Algorithm (DTW) is a nonlinear technique that combines time warping and distance measurement calculation. It is a classic template-matching algorithm. It is originally used in the speech recognition of isolated words, which can solve the sequence lengths. Template matching problem. The DTW algorithm involves two sequences, one is the template sequence and the other is the sequence to be tested. The main idea is to use the dynamic programming method to find a scientific time calibration-matching path, and the matching path is the mapping relationship between points and points on the sequence. For two sequences with different timelines, the DTW algorithm can eliminate the difference in the time axis and minimize the distortion between them. The method is to globally or locally expand, compress or deform the sequence, with another sequence [5].

Let the sequence of gestures to be tested be X = (x1, x2, ..., xn), the sequence of gesture templates is Y = (y1, y2, ..., ym), n and m represent the timing labels of the gesture frames, construct a matrix C, matrix Any element c(xi, yj) represents the distance between the feature vector of the first frame in the gesture sequence to be tested and the feature vector of the first frame in the template sequence. In general, the more similar xi and yj are, the smaller the value of c (xi, yj), that is, the shorter the distance between the two eigenvectors, we call the cost small. Conversely, the greater the distance between vectors, the greater the cost. This problem can be transformed into finding a path in the matrix that minimizes the distance between X and Y.

Hidden Markov Model. Compared with the DTW algorithm HMM has obvious advantages. It can model both spatiotemporal characteristics and its correlation, and has good performance time-varying data matching [6].

There are two random processes in the hidden Markov model: one is observable and the other is hidden. There is a certain relationship between the two processes, and the hidden process must be expressed through the observation sequence. An HMM can be represented by a 5-tuple {N, M, π, A, B}, where N is the number of hidden states, M is the number of observable states, π = {πi} is the initial state probability, A = {aij} is the transition matrix of the hidden state, and B = {bjk} represents the probability of a state observable at a certain time due to the hidden state.

Recognition Method of Finite Sequence State Machine for Posture Sequence. Lin Shuiqiang uses the finite state machine method to effectively recognize human motion. This method can also be used in gesture recognition [7]. The gesture motion is decomposed into the continuous motion trajectory of the corresponding joint point, and several discrete key points are selected in the motion trajectory. Different motion trajectories can be represented by different key point combinations, each key point represents a posture state, dynamic the process of identifying the state transition achieves the recognition of the gesture. According to this idea, the recognition method of the gesture sequence finite state machine is proposed to recognize a predefined gesture action [7, 8]. In addition, the gesture sequence represents a set of motion sequences in which a dynamic gesture is described by a plurality of static gestures on a time axis, and the gesture sequence finite state machine describes the finite state of each dynamic gesture and the transition process between states. Defining the pose sequence the finite state machine is A, which can be represented by a five-tuple:

$$A = (S, \sum, \delta, s0, F)$$

Where S denotes a state set {s0, s1, …, sn, f0, f1}, which describes each specific posture state of the dynamic gesture; $\sum$ denotes the input hand node feature vector and the restriction parameter alphabet {u, ┐p, ┐t}, where the symbol "┐" indicates logical negation; δ is the transfer function, defined as $S \times \sum \rightarrow S$, indicating that the posture sequence FSM transitions from the current state to the successor state; s0 represents the starting state; F = {F0, f1} is the final state set, which indicates the recognition success status and the identification invalid status.

In the alphabet, the variable u represents a set of all hand node feature vectors V corresponding to a certain dynamic gesture type, and the feature vector represents discrete point domain rules of the hand motion trajectory in the spatial grid, and the dynamics can be constructed by the dot domain rules. The trajectory of the gesture is a regular expression.

4 Implementation and Development of Human-Computer Interaction System Based on Gesture Recognition

The basic principle of the system is to use the camera acquisition method to obtain the user's gesture, and transfer the action to the computer for processing. The application in the computer divides, recognizes, processes according to the captured image, and finally drives the performance of the multimedia [9]. The system architecture is shown in Fig. 1.

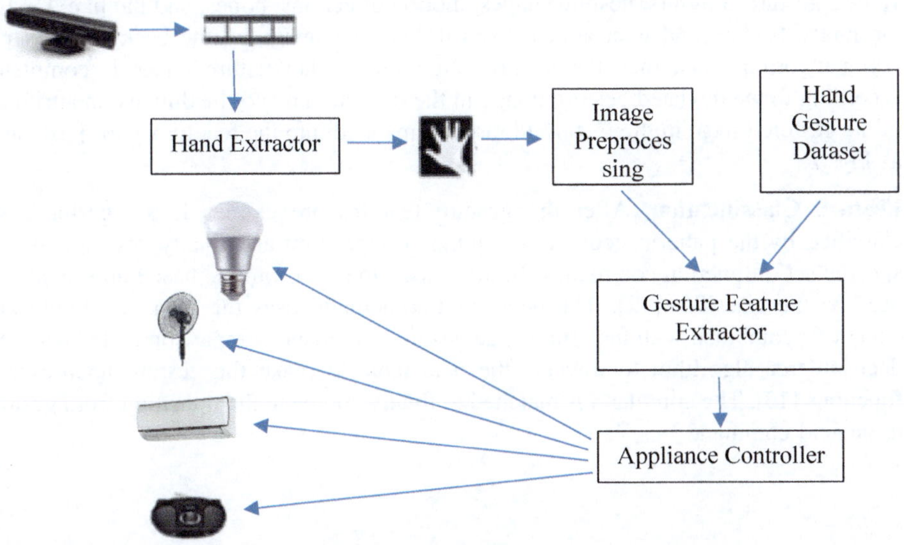

Fig. 1. System architecture

Gesture Input and Recognition. Using a high-definition camera as the acquisition unit ensures the detection and recognition of targets (gestures) within the appropriate field of view and depth of field. The detection process adopts a non-contact method, and the target (gesture) recognition detection rate is high. Then, the pattern recognition algorithm is used to analyze and process the input gesture image to detect the target (gesture) [10].

The high-definition camera obtains the video data stream, the data stream is segmented, identified, processed, the interactive gesture is stripped from the data stream, then the input gesture is registered with the gesture command library of the pre-mobile phone, and finally, the interaction of driving the related application is formed.

Noise Removal and Information Enhancement. From the input of video stream, to gesture recognition, to information conversion, various aspects such as electromagnetic interference of the device and limitations of the algorithm may affect every aspect of these processes. These interferences and effects will eventually form data noise and noise. Improper handling will distort the gesture image and affect the final interactive instructions [11].

Therefore, before the gesture image processing, this paper adds a noise filtering/sharpening noise filtering pre-processing, the purpose of which is to eliminate the noise to ensure the quality of the gesture image.

Gesture Segmentation and Feature Extraction. By implementing a gesture model database, the gestures in the data stream are segmented and feature extracted according to the database. In this paper, the serial boundary segmentation technique and parallel region segmentation technology are used to extract the feature parameters of the gesture model, and finally the final interactive command is formed according to the feature registration of the gesture model database [12]. In the gesture recognition process, the gesture feature vector may be established according to data such as image edge pixel values, gesture contours, gesture shapes, motion directions, bones, and the like. Firstly, the image background is separated from the gesture image by the background separation algorithm, and then the feature extraction of the gesture image is completed according to the deviated gesture image in the data stream and the dimension attributes in the gesture image in the feature library are mapped into the feature vector [13], such as Fig. 2.

Feature Classification. After the gesture features are extracted, the gestures are classified by the pattern recognition intelligent algorithm and finally correspond to a specific set of function commands. In this paper, the decision tree based on statistics is used as the classifier [12]. The decision tree actually uses the idea of "divide and conquer", combined with the established gesture-command comparison table, using the decision tree algorithm to traverse the data table to make the gesture features and functions [13]. The command is matched to finally complete the transition from gesture to antacid command.

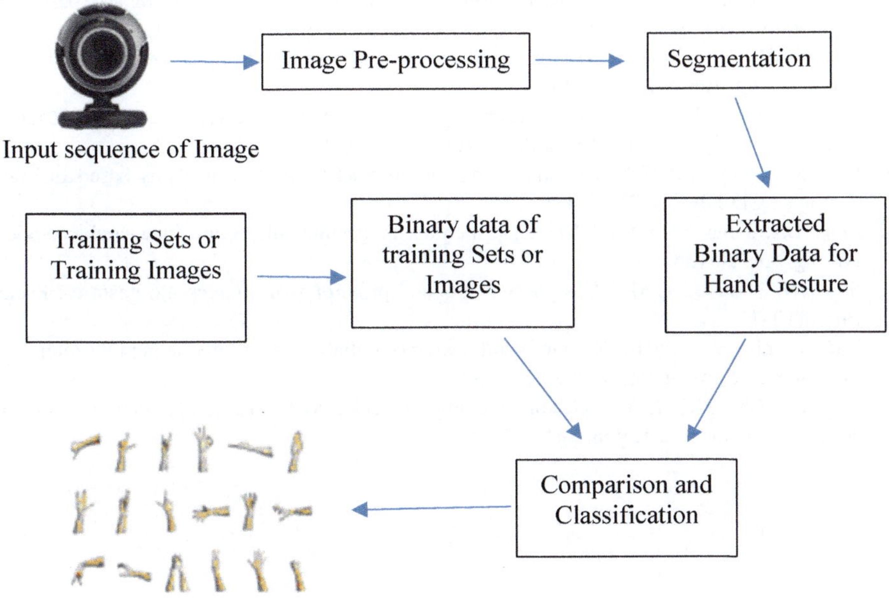

Fig. 2. Gesture recognition system

5 Summary

The human-computer interaction system based on virtual reality and gesture recognition computer understands people's gestures and responds accordingly through the camera, so that people can get rid of the constraints and drawbacks of traditional keyboard and mouse, in order to achieve more convenient and humanized interaction. The system can be used for home entertainment, conference presentations, merchandise displays, and campus displays. It has been widely used in many company product displays, but in the past many traditional display systems have been difficult to meet people's requirements. The system is more human, more beautiful and more intuitive.

References

1. Qi XF (2017) Virtual reality 3D scene modeling and human-computer interaction application technology research, art and design: theoretical edition, vol 4, pp 100–102
2. Lu JQ (2017) Software interface design and research based on virtual reality technology. J Chifeng Coll (Nat Ed) 1:6–8
3. Tan ZhY (2016) Research on 3D gesture design based on imagery. Packag Eng 4:61–65
4. Yan YZh, Xu DM (2001) Several key technologies of human-computer interaction. Comput Eng Appl 37(21):129–131
5. Wang ZhB, Ren LY (2012) Research on gesture interaction types and design principles in touchscreen mobile phones. Silicon Valley 9:108–109

6. Xu LSh, Cheng TG (2006) Classification of meningeal pen gestures and their experimental evaluation. J Softw 17:46–56
7. Zhang GH, Heng XG (2010) Interactive gesture analysis and design based on multi-touch. Comput Appl Res 5:1737–1739
8. Wu JX (2016) Research on the usability of 2D and 3D interactive gestures. Zhejiang University of Science and Technology, Hangzhou, pp 9–12
9. Li WSh, Deng ChJ (2011) Human-computer interaction gesture analysis based on touch display. LCD Display 2:194–199
10. Zeng LX, Jiang XT (2015) Design principles of gesture interaction in wearable devices. Packag Eng 20:135–138
11. Sun XH, Zhou BT (2015) Design elements and principles of intercepting gestures. Packag Eng 8:10–13
12. Liu YH, Zhu ZhM (2014) Research and design of collaborative human-computer interaction mechanism. Comput Eng Des 2:726–730
13. Li QSh, Fang ZhG (2002) Gesture recognition technology and its application in human-computer interaction. Ergonomics 32–34

Short Papers

Research on Computer Aided Design Software Innovation Based on VR Technology

Lei Zheng[1(✉)] and Ruibo Song[2]

[1] The Art Design School, Shandong Women's University, Jinan 250002, Shandong, China
yanbinwuhb@126.com

[2] The Design Art School, Shandong Youth University of Political Science, Jinan 250002, Shandong, China

Abstract. Focusing on the features of current computer-aided design software and the pain points faced by users in the use process, this paper analyzes the technical features of VR technology and discusses the path of computer-aided design software innovation. It clarifies the direction and content of the innovative development of computer-aided design software, which should be based on VR virtual reality technology's sensory expression system and virtual control system, create more realistic operating forms, strengthen man-machine interactive feedback, and improve users' immersive experience.

Keywords: VR virtual reality · Computer-aided design software · Innovate

1 Introduction

Computer-aided design software is based on computer technology to help designers better express ideas means. Since its inception, design has been mainly expressed by hand drawing, to achieve the idea in mind and to present to customers and audiences in a visual form [1]. With the emergence, development and continuous progress of computer technology, corresponding computer design software is constantly developed and applied, which greatly improves the efficiency of design, as well as the quality and expression effect of design.

2 Problems with Computer-Aided Design Software

However, with the continuous improvement of software functions, it is more difficult for designers to learn and operate the software. Generally, a designer should be proficient in at least two design software, including a graphic design software and a three-dimensional design software. Graphic design software includes Photoshop, AutoCAD, InDesign, Illustrator, CorelDRAW, PageMaker, etc.3d design software includes 3DMAX, Rhino, etc. Otherwise, it is difficult to express design ideas well. In addition, in order to better display the design works and processes, we also need to master the relevant video production software, such as After Effects, Premiere, Flash, etc.

Z. Xu et al. (Eds.): CSIA 2019, AISC 928, pp. 1185–1189, 2020.
https://doi.org/10.1007/978-3-030-15235-2_156

Before become an outstanding designer, need to spend a lot of time to study each command and functions of the software, even took the time to learn, but knowledge will soon be forgotten, because these functions and operations command requires a lot of practice to strengthen, in actual design process, many functions and commands are not commonly used or basic not to use [2–5]. At the same time, designers have to constantly adapt to the operating software keyboard, mouse, display and other hardware. To achieve efficient design expression, the human brain, hands and eyes must be highly coordinated. The brain is highly focused on the coordination and control of various organs of the body [6]. The lack of control space for creative conception and imagination has affected the overall expression of design.

Computer design software takes up a large amount of computer storage space because of its complex functions and many commands. It also needs a large temporary storage space in the process of software operation, which will seriously affect the normal operation of the computer. It often causes software crash, file loss or computer crash and other problems [7]. The original document of the finished design will also take up a lot of computer hard disk space.

The computer is a tool invented by human to improve work efficiency. It serves human beings. The goal is to adapt the computer to human beings. In this way, we can use our body language and sound language to participate in information processing and gain new experience of vision, hearing, touch and smell [8–10].

Computer-aided design software has the functions of material import, design expression, design output and development of new forms of design. Material import mainly aims at all kinds of graphic and image elements needed by design [11]. Design expression is to express design ideas more efficiently with the help of computer aided design software tools and commands. Design output is mainly for traditional media and new media. Traditional media is mainly planar and three-dimensional graphics and image content. New media focuses on dynamic, interactive, virtual graphics and images. Computer-aided design itself is a VR technology.

3 Introduction to VR Technology

VR is the full name of Virtual Reality, namely Virtual Reality. It uses computer technology to simulate the real environment and integrate all kinds of information to realize the simulation, multi-dimensional and interactive experience environment. VR technology involves the latest computer graphics technology, man-machine interface technology, network technology, multimedia technology and sensor technology in the field. There are many kinds of implementation software. Currently, it is in the continuous research and development stage in various fields, including VRP, Quest 3D, Patchwork3D and EON Reality, which are applied in education, industrial design, exhibition and art creation.

VR technology simulates the same virtual environment as the natural environment through corresponding technological means, and satisfies the perception of human vision, hearing, touch, smell, taste, force and movement, and realizes human behavioral movements, such as head rotation, eye rotation, limb movement, muscle twitch and other movements. The sensing device is used to feedback the content of the motion feelings to the human sensory organs and form a complete system. VR technology emphasizes the reality, reproduces the physical movement in the real environment, attaches importance to the multi-dimensional perception and interactive experience of human beings, and satisfies the sense of human existence in the virtual environment [3, 12].

Computer-aided design itself is a VR technology. It uses computer models to generate corresponding graphics and images, realizes the same two-dimensional and three-dimensional visual perception as reality, and adjusts and changes with the keyboard and mouse. However, in the real environment, the three-dimensional space has six degrees of freedom, and the movement mode of the mouse is plane motion, so it is difficult to realize the arbitrary motion of the three-dimensional space. In addition to graphics and images, sound is also an important part of realizing the real environment. The stereo effect formed by audio equipment can be used to simulate the real sound environment, but only limited to the fixed orientation perception of the left and right ears. When the head turns, the sound does not change significantly, which is inconsistent with the sound of the real world [13–15]. In terms of human perception feedback, computer-aided design is basically unable to realize the real environment. It can only achieve simple feedback through the keyboard keys, the spring device of the mouse or the way of touching the screen, and cannot achieve real sensory feedback with design content, graphics, images, etc. In the aspect of interaction, the lack of human-computer real-time interaction is limited to the difficulty and lack of technology of speech recognition, and computer-aided design of speech recognition has not been applied yet [16, 17].

The implementation of VR technology currently requires the support of relevant hardware equipment and software, including data gloves, digital helmet, head tracking, motion capture and position tracker. The data glove mainly realizes various motions of the hand, determines the position and direction of the fingers, palms and joints, connects with the palm in the virtual environment, and realizes movement and control of the virtual object [18–20]. Digital helmets mainly provide visual simulation, providing users with a strong sense of immersion. Secondly, there are motion capture devices for the human body, including HMD helmet display for head tracking, three-dimensional space sensor, MOCAP and position tracker for motion capture suite [15]. With these devices, users can move, rotate and move freely in virtual space, realizing six degrees of freedom. In the whole set of VR virtual reality technology, the most important contents are the integrated machine, the hand presentation in VR, and the head tracking with six degrees of freedom. At the Oculus Connect5 conference in 2018, Facebook, an internationally renowned company, announced that it has successfully developed Santa Quest, a VR all-in-one machine of 6DoF, which has achieved 3DoF head freedom and 6DoF body freedom (front and back, left and right, up and down), and has a wide range of tracking capability of over 4000 square meters, as well as a three-dimensional modeling capability. Modeling capability can realize the deep integration of real world and virtual world, and display objects in real world environment in virtual environment.

4 New Expression of Computer-Aided Design Software

Based on VR technology, computer-aided design software should be adjusted accordingly to solve a series of problems in learning and using computer-aided design software.

Using VR virtual reality technology in the motion capture technology, realize the virtual control, get rid of the restriction of the wiring harness, mixed reality environment, no longer bureau be confined to a desk, a computer, you can no longer subject to the influence of the monitor, keyboard, mouse, designers can take advantage of the head and eye movements, gestures and body movements, to control the design work, in order to reduce the operation difficulty, improve work efficiency.

The interactive feedback between human and computer-aided design software is strengthened. With the help of speech recognition technology, the voice control of each tool command is realized to input, adjust and input output specific parameters. Get rid of the mechanical interaction of keyboard input values and mouse position adjustment. And with the help of more advanced tactile technology, realize the feedback of color heating and cooling, the feedback of material texture, etc., which is helpful for the design results to be more realistic.

Designer's design expression process needs a lot of thinking movement, with the help of VR virtual reality technology intervention, so that designers have a good immersion experience, the design process is like a game, conducive to better innovation and creation.

The existing computer-aided design software is basically offline single operation, which cannot be effectively assisted and supported in use. By virtue of VR virtual reality technology, multiple ports can be accessed to realize the joint design and production of multiple people for complex internal structures such as buildings and mechanical products. With the great changes brought by 5G network technology, real-time communication, cooperation and design and production can be realized, as well as free cloud storage, download and sharing. The computer-aided design software PhotoshopCC2018 has added new functions and enhanced user experience in the cloud era, and design works can be freely obtained or Shared through software. Users no longer need to install the design software, produce temporary files to cause the computer-aided design software to crash, and do not need to occupy a large amount of computer storage space.

Computer-aided design software has been developed from scratch, and its functions have gradually become strong. It has solved a lot of problems for design activities and improved work efficiency and effectiveness. However, with the rapid development of VR technology and the gradual expansion of its application in various fields, computer-aided design software must be adjusted and changed accordingly, which may also be a qualitative change and will promote the innovation and development of the whole industry.

5 Conclusion

Computer-aided design software not only meets the needs of users and solves design problems, but also brings many new problems, which affect the efficiency of design expression and user experience. Through the application of VR technology, computer aided design software can be changed qualitatively, which promotes the innovation of the software industry and greatly improves the design.

References

1. Paar P (2006) Landscape visualizations: applications and requirements of 3D visualization software for environmental planning. Comput Environ Urban Syst 30(6):815–839
2. Burdea Grigore C, Coiffet P (1994) Virtual reality technology. Wiley-Interscience, London
3. Bao W, Zhou H, Wang L, Xie F (2016) The system of knowledge management using web based learning and education technology. Comput Syst Sci Eng 31(6):469–473
4. Schuemie MJ, Van Der Straaten P, Krijn M et al (2001) Research on presence in virtual reality: a survey. CyberPsychol Behav 4(2):183–201
5. Bailey C, Aguilera E, Espalin D et al (2018) Augmenting computer-aided design software with multi-functional capabilities to automate multi-process additive manufacturing. IEEE Access 6:1985–1994
6. Bao W, Zhou H, Xie F (2017) An optimal design of web based online English teaching by using struts framework. Bol Tecnico/Tech Bull 55(10):58–63
7. Tsur EE, Shamir A (2018) Computer-aided design of resistance micro-fluidic circuits for 3D printing. Comput-Aided Des 98:12–23
8. Chandrasegaran SK, Ramani K, Sriram RD et al (2013) The evolution, challenges, and future of knowledge representation in product design systems. Comput-aided Des 45 (2):204–228
9. Zhou Q, Luo J (2015) Artificial neural network based grid computing of E-government scheduling for emergency management. Comput Syst Sci Eng 30(5):335–343
10. Eves K, Salmon J, Olsen J et al (2018) A comparative analysis of computer-aided design team performance with collaboration software. Comput-Aided Des Appl 15(4):476–487
11. Berg LP, Vance JM (2017) Industry use of virtual reality in product design and manufacturing: a survey. Virtual Real 21(1):1–17
12. Hermann M, Pentek T, Otto B (2016) Design principles for industrie 4.0 scenarios. In: 2016 49th Hawaii international conference on system sciences (HICSS), pp 3928–3937. IEEE
13. Zhou Q (2016) Research on heterogeneous data integration model of group enterprise based on cluster computing. Clust Comput 19(3):1275–1282
14. Reddy SM, Chowdhury A, Charkrabarti D et al (2015) Role of colour and form in product choice and variation of preferences across product categories: a review. In: Research into design across boundaries, ICoRD 2015, vol 2. Springer, New Delhi, pp 631–640
15. Ye J, Campbell RI, Page T et al (2006) An investigation into the implementation of virtual reality technologies in support of conceptual design. Des Stud 27(1):77–97
16. Wang H, Rong YK, Li H et al (2010) Computer aided fixture design: Recent research and trends. Comput-Aided Des 42(12):1085–1094
17. Sampaio AZ, Ferreira MM, Rosário DP et al (2010) 3D and VR models in civil engineering education: construction, rehabilitation and maintenance. Autom Constr 19(7):819–828
18. Runhua T (2003) Progress of some problems in product design for innovation. Chin J Mech Eng 39(9):11–16
19. Bossak MA (1998) Simulation based design. J Mater Process Technol 76(1–3):8–11
20. Pappas M, Karabatsou V, Mavrikios D et al (2006) Development of a web-based collaboration platform for manufacturing product and process design evaluation using virtual reality techniques. Int J Comput Integr Manuf 19(8):805–814

Equipment and Application of Iris Recognition in Public Security

Cheng Cheng[1(✉)], Bo Zhao[1], Zheng Xu[2], and Xiao Wei[3]

[1] The Third Research Institute of the Ministry of Public Security, Key Lab of Information Network Security of Ministry of Public Security, 339 Bisheng Road, Shanghai, China
13916201644@139.com

[2] Guangxi Key Laboratory of Cryptography and Information Security, Guilin, China

[3] Shanghai University, Shanghai, China

Abstract. This paper briefly describes the concept and development history of iris recognition. Because of its high stability, high accuracy and uniqueness, iris recognition has been studied by many institutions and enterprises at home and abroad, and has been widely used. Especially in the field of social public safety, iris recognition as a precise biometric identification tool has a good application prospect in public security such as verification, pursuit, customs clearance, etc.

Keywords: Iris recognition · Biometric identification · Public security

1 Introduction

In the mid-1930s, people began to imagine using the iris to identify themselves, but it became a reality in the 1990s. In 1987, ophthalmologists Aran Safir and Leonard Flom first proposed the concept of automatic iris recognition using iris images. In 1991, Johnson of the Los Alamos National Laboratory in the United States implemented an automatic iris recognition system [1]. In 1993, John Daugman implemented a high-performance automatic iris recognition prototype system. Nowadays, most iris recognition systems still use the Daugman core algorithm. In 1996, Richard Wildes developed an iris-based identity card system. In recent years, iris recognition technology has developed rapidly [2]. The United States, China, South Korea, Japan, Israel and other countries have successively launched their own products, and applied them in airports, banks, prisons and other fields, forming a relatively complete industrial ecosystem.

The iris is part of the eyeball structure and belongs to the middle layer of the eyeball. It is located at the forefront of the vascular membrane. In front of the ciliary body, it is an annular region between the pupil and the sclera of the human eye. It is composed of many glandular fossa, folds and stains. The texture information automatically adjusts the pupil size to adjust the light entering the eye. Iris recognition technology is a multidisciplinary cross-tech that integrates physiology, optics, electronics, mathematics and computer science. The technology first uses the digital image

Z. Xu et al. (Eds.): CSIA 2019, AISC 928, pp. 1190–1194, 2020.
https://doi.org/10.1007/978-3-030-15235-2_157

acquisition device to acquire the iris image and convert it into digital coded information. When verifying, the collected iris coded information is compared with the pre-stored individual biological sample information to achieve accurate authentication of the individual biological identity.

2 Technical Advantages

Iris recognition technology has significant advantages:

1. Uniqueness. The formation of the iris is related to the local physical and chemical conditions of the tissue at the embryonic stage and has great randomness. Identical twins, the same person's left and right eye iris texture are not the same; that is, using cloning technology, cannot be copied.
2. High stability. The iris is formed in the fetal period and is shaped 6 to 12 months after birth. It disappears within a few hours after death and does not change with age.
3. High reliability. The iris contains a wealth of information. On the 11 mm diameter iris, the classic iris recognition algorithm uses 3 to 4 bytes of data to represent the iris information per square millimeter, and up to 266 independent quantized feature points can be obtained. 13 to 60 feature points higher than the general biometrics technology.
4. High accuracy. The possibility of two different irises producing the same iris code is 1:10^52, which is suitable for large-scale population iris library construction; and, in the case of one-thousandth of the rejection rate, one millionth of the misunderstanding can be achieved, and can achieve accurate identification of biological identity.
5. High detection speed. At present, the speed of iris recognition comparison is about 1.6 million images per second for single eye search by single-core processor, which can realize fast comparison recognition under large-scale database conditions.
6. High security. Under normal circumstances, wearing glasses and sunglasses does not affect the collection of iris; myopia, cataracts, etc. will not affect iris recognition, and even surgery is difficult to change the characteristics of the iris; at the same time, the iris is biologically active, using photos, videos, the iris of corpses instead of the living body can be tested.

3 Representative Iris Recognition Products

The In-Sight-Duo of Aoptix is a binocular long-distance iris recognition system. It is the world's first biometric identification system with synchronous iris and face capture in accordance with ISO standards. The collection space is large and the iris can be used. The image is extracted from the face image for recognition (Fig. 1).

Fig. 1. In-Sight-Duo

Iris ID's long-distance iris recognition product iCAM D1000 can collect face and iris information at the same time. It has the functions of fast speed, automatic zoom, auto focus, auto fill light, online coding and comparison, which can realize safe and convenient individual identification.

Carnegie Mellon University of the United States focuses on the research of ultra-distance iris recognition system. At present, the system can be used to collect and recognize the iris of the person in the rearview mirror of a distance of more than ten meters (Fig. 2).

Fig. 2. Ultra-distance iris recognition system of Carnegie Mellon University

The Institute of Automation of the Chinese Academy of Sciences is the first research base to start the research on iris recognition mechanism in China. Its self-developed iris recognition living body detection technology fills the gap in the international field. In addition, the iris image database of the State Key Laboratory of Pattern Recognition has become the largest iris shared library in the world, and has been applied for by more than 2,000 research institutions in 70 countries and regions. The high-definition iris collection instrument developed by the IrisKing, a company affiliated to the Institute of Automation, can be used for the collection and registration of iris images in large-scale populations, and also supports recognition functions. The instrument has the characteristics of fast recognition speed, high precision, and eye safety in accordance with IEC 62471 and IEC60825-1 standards.

The iris identification serialization product developed by the Second Academy of Aerospace Group is characterized by long-distance, fast and accurate identification, and is bound with ID card information. It has developed key personnel comprehensive identity information management and control, confidentiality key department access control, confidential system printing, and Employee attendance etc.

The Superred Technology's iris recognition products are mainly used in the fields of anti-terrorism combat and population precision management. The long-distance iris and face recognition device developed by the Irisian Optoelectronics can collect high-quality binocular iris images at a distance of 0.5–1 m, and can collect high-quality face images at a distance of 0.5–1.5 m; Support automatic lifting, rapid deployment, support for reading ID cards and other functions. In addition, the Iristar Technology, the EyeSmart technology, the EyeCool Technology, the YRDS, Hongshi Technology and other enterprises have representative products, each with its own characteristics.

4 Application of Iris Recognition Equipment

In some countries, iris recognition technology has developed earlier, but few large-scale applications have been carried out. In the United States, a few airports such as Kennedy, New Jersey, Albany, New York, and other irises have been installed for restricted access to staff; Frankfurt Airport in Berlin, Schiphol in the Netherlands, and Narita Airport in Japan have an iris entry and exit management system for Passengers self-service customs clearance; in India, the government is building a universal identification system that includes irises; in addition, the United Nations and the United States Federal Refugee Agency in Afghan Refugee Management, New Jersey Schools, German Hospital Management, and the Greek Olympics also have The application of iris recognition technology.

Domestic iris technology research has progressed rapidly in the past two decades, and related equipment and system applications are in the development stage. The Beijing-based iris research and development production base has been formed. The domestic iris recognition technology products are in banks, security, coal mines, Driving schools and other industries also have local applications for the precise identification of personnel in special occasions.

In the field of public safety, iris recognition technology has been initially applied in public security agencies in many places. Public security organs in Beijing and other places have also begun to collect key personnel irises for pre-production research. In the field of immigration management, the overall design of China's e-passport reissue has reserved relevant human biometric storage areas, providing technical support for the future use of iris immigration.

5 Applications in the Field of Public Security

Iris recognition technology is a method for human identity authentication using human biometrics. It is mainly used for individual one-to-one authentication and accurate identification of individual identities in large-scale populations. Through research on iris recognition technology products and applications at home and abroad, the author believes that in the field of public safety, iris recognition technology and equipment can be used for the following practical tasks:

1. In the field of criminal investigation. For high-throughput sites such as subways and station entrances and exits, it is used for insensitive collecting and accurately identifying fugitives. Based on the iris information recorded on the crime scene, and compared with the suspect information to identify the identity, it is used for the identity identification of criminal suspects. Other situations such as abduction, anti-spoofing, etc. require identity authentication.
2. In the field of law-and-order. For example, it is used for important venues, personnel control in key places, identification of the irises of participants, temporary confirmation of identity, and authorized activity areas. It is used for the management of potential criminals, used for identity registration and authentication, and behavior track management.
3. In the field Entry and exit control. For self-service customs clearance, on the basis of existing face and fingerprint self-service clearance, increase the iris verification channel or iris-assisted confirmation to improve the correct extraction rate and recognition rate of biometrics.
4. In the field of counter-terrorism. For example, it is used to pay attention to personnel control, identity authentication, trajectory association, etc. It is particularly effective in identifying terrorists who change their facial features.
5. In the other field. Such as the inspection of border personnel, the identification of illegal immigrants; the identification of regulatory sites; the verification of drug control personnel in high-risk sites.

Acknowledgement. This work is supported by National Key R&D Program of China (No. 2018YFC0809500), supported by Guangxi Key Laboratory of Cryptography and Information Security (No. GCIS201719), and supported by Key Lab of Information Network Security of Ministry of Public Security (The Third Research Institute of Ministry of Public Security) under grant no. C18607.

References

1. Cheng C, Zhao B (2018) Intelligent counter-terrorism equipment status and development. In: International conference on applications and techniques in cyber security and intelligence, ATCI 2018, pp 318–325. ISBN 978-3-319-98775-0
2. Cheng, C, Zhao B (2018) Prospect of application of hyperspectral imaging technology in public security. In: International conference on applications and techniques in cyber security and intelligence, ATCI 2018, pp 299–305. ISBN 978-3-319-98775-0

Study on the Risk and Analyze the Preventive Measures of We-Chat Pay

Yongxiang Ma(✉)

Economics and Management College, Longdong University,
Qingyang, Gansu, China
121408765@qq.com

Abstract. With the rapid development of Internet finance, various third-party electronic payment platforms are gradually known and dependent. We-Chat Pay, which has been widely used in recent years, is popular among merchants and consumers. However, while We-Chat Pay provides fast and efficient service, there are some risks, such as the lack of regulation, the security loophole of network technology, the lack of compensation clause, the weak security consciousness of users and so on. Accordingly, this paper puts forward corresponding countermeasures to these risks, and urges We-Chat Pay to better protect the rights and interests of financial consumers.

Keywords: We-Chat Pay · Payment risk · Countermeasures

1 Introduction

In 2011, Tencent launched We-Chat, a free messaging app for smart terminals, before launching We-Chat Pay in 2013 with Ten-pay, its third-party payment platform [1]. In the following months, We-Chat made a historic breakthrough, We-Chat users grew dramatically. According to the Ten-cent data of 2017 Q3, We-Chat and We-Chat have combined active accounts of 980 million per month. In an interview with reporters in early 2018, Huateng Ma, chairman and chief executive of Ten-cent, a deputy to National people's Congress, said that We-Chat monthly numbers of active users had exceeded the 1 billion mark during the 2018 Spring Festival, April 23, 2018 [2]. The world organization leading new economic industry data mining and analysis—iiMedia Research (Ai Media Consulting authoritative release of China 2017–2018 third party mobile payment market research report. The report said that in the first quarter of 2018, 34.4% of online consumers were more likely to use Ali-pay to pay, while 59.5% of respondents were using We-Chat Pay in offline consumption. The two giants, Ali-pay and Ten-pay, account for 90.6% of the market share of Chinese third party mobile payment transaction scale, of which Ali-pay accounts for 49.9%, Ten-pay 40.7 g, and the market concentration is high. The report also showed that 65.3% of respondents in small payments tended to use We-Chat Pay, while 59.5% of respondents preferred to use Ali-pay in large payments. Ai media consulting analysts believe that e-commerce advantage is obvious to Alibaba, Ali-pay more popular online consumption, but offline consumption scene, We-Chat advantage gradually appeared. However, while We-Chat Payment brings users the convenience of quick payment, there are also many risks.

Z. Xu et al. (Eds.): CSIA 2019, AISC 928, pp. 1195–1199, 2020.
https://doi.org/10.1007/978-3-030-15235-2_158

With the increase of users, these risks should be highly valued by We-Chat users, and the solutions should be implemented as soon as possible [3].

2 The Current Condition of We-Chat Pay

As one of the two largest third-party mobile payment giants in China, in terms of market share, We-Chat Pay is second only to Ali-pay, but the number of users is still increasing. We-Chat Pay originally based on We-Chat has a strong social nature, a large user base, and easy to use. After the user logs in to We-Chat, add the type of bank card to the bank card page, fill in the valid period, name, ID number and the mobile phone number of the bank card, and then set up the payment password after verifying the mobile phone number, then the We-Chat Pay can be opened. Later We-Chat Pay will be debited from the bound bank [4]. At present, We-Chat Pay has four basic capabilities: public number payment, Scroll payment, app payment and credit card payment. In addition, it has adopted a variety of marketing techniques, such as the cash red envelopes, vouchers, deductions and corporate payments. With the development of We-Chat platform, We-Chat Pay is more useful. Daily activities such as a shopping, taxi and movie tickets can be paid by We-Chat. Because We-Chat Pay is quick, wide range of application, avoid change and the existence of business activities and other advantages, more and more consumers choose We-Chat Pay. In addition to the popularity of buyers and sellers in the domestic market, We-Chat Pay has blossomed in Thailand, Malaysia, India and other Southeast Asian countries, for example, Thailand famous duty-free shop King Power can use We-Chat Pay to buy goods. And on June 7, 2017, Ten-cent teamed up with the Payment wall, a global online payment platform, to connect to We-Chat Pay in every online retail store. Businesses can also use We-Chat Pay to collect money without having to own entities in China, making it possible for We-Chat to collect money globally [5]. This cooperation helps We-Chat expand the global payment market and gain more overseas business opportunities.

3 The Risk of We-Chat Pay

Although We-Chat Pay allows consumers to hold a mobile phone in the world, We-Chat Pay faces many risks cannot be ignored. Only by facing these risks directly and putting forward preventive measures, we can better protect the rights and interests of financial consumers and maintain the national economic stability. At present, users recognize the main risks associated with We-Chat Pay are widely as follows.

3.1 The Relevant Laws and Regulations Are not Perfect

We-Chat Pay is a third-party payment, which ultimately belongs to the field of e-commerce. At present, the Electronic Commerce Law has not been issued in our country, and there are few laws and regulations on third-party payment, and the related laws and regulations are relatively low [6]. At the same time, the development of electronic commerce in China is still in the primary stage and involves a wide range. At present, the regulation of e-commerce also depends on other laws, such as contract Law, Electronic signature Law and so on. The existing third-party payment regulations and policies have a lot of room to move and the definition is not clear. The lack of relevant laws has led to a greater legal risk for third-party payment industries such as We-Chat Pay. Consumers encounter We-Chat financial fraud will face difficulties in filing evidence and litigation difficulties.

3.2 Network Technology Security Is Vulnerable

The increasing popularity of the network has brought about the problems of network attacks and information leaks [7]. Nowadays, network hackers are rampant, various viruses and fishing websites cannot be guarded against, and if they are not careful, they will be stolen by viruses, such as payment passwords, and other key information. The safety of the property of the user is greatly damaged. For example, criminals induce We-Chat Pay users to scan and install a Trojan QR code, and then automatically jump into fishing sites to defraud users of money. In addition, mobile payment relies on the public network, which imposes extremely high requirements for the security environment and stability of the network. If the network has a major failure, it will affect the operation and increase the risk.

3.3 The Compensation Clause Is Missing

According to the We-Chat Electronic Commerce Service Agreement, if a user has a dispute over the transaction of goods or services while using the service, the user irrevocably authorizes Ten-cent to issue instructions to Ten-pay Company according to the agreement and related service rules. Ask it to transfer all or all of the disputed money from the user Ten-pay account to a certain party, and users will consciously abide by and recognize Ten-cent ruling and exempt Ten-cent and Ten-pay from any liability [8]. This provision is clearly unfair. In addition, on the payment of We-Chat Pay users in the process of payment of funds stolen and other losses, Ten-pay did not specify in the terms of how to claim, to whom to claim. The lack of compensation clause and unfair dispute settlement both impair the user time claim [9].

3.4 The Security Consciousness of Users Is Weak

We-Chat and We-Chat Pay have become popular, and lawbreakers have come up with more ways to defraud users of their money, while less-conscious users will become criminal targets [10]. Common We-Chat fraud methods are number theft fraud, number exchange fraud, identity fraud, using QR code fraud and false public number fraud. Security-conscious users struggle to identify these tricks, they are insufficiently alert to strangers, and they do not heed and reject requests for property. In identity fraud, for example, the fraudsters pretend to be a rich-handsome or beauty, talk to single men and women, and borrow money by various means after gaining trust. If users raise their security awareness, they will not give criminals such a chance.

4 Measures to Prevent We-Chat Pay Risk

According to the above mentioned risks, there should be corresponding preventive measures, so that We-Chat Pay can better serve financial consumers, promote the development of Internet financing, and also make We-Chat Pay have a better development prospect.

4.1 Perfect Laws and Regulations

Speed up the establishment of a sound legal system and issue the Electronic Commerce Law as soon as possible. We should make practical and effective legal provisions for all aspects of electronic commerce, including operational and after-sales tracking services. Further standardize the operation flow of e-commerce. In addition, e-commerce depends on the network; we should further improve relevant laws related to network security, when users are damaged by network failures, so that they can claim compensation, and reduce the payment risk of electronic commerce by step up prevention of technological risks, make We-Chat Pay safer. We-Chat Pay platform should strengthen risk control and management to prevent risk and loss. For example, promote the payment card industry data security standard (PCIDSS) authentication, link the real name data of Tenpay with We-Chat account, carry on the strict security evaluation of security controls, data storage, and encryption authentication.

4.2 Fix the Holes Regularly

In addition, We-Chat should set up a database based on the registration information of We-Chat Pay users, operating habits and interpersonal networks, and monitor each account with the help of big data and machine learning. When a suspicious transaction occurs, it should be verified immediately. For example, if a user makes a large transfer immediately after adding another stranger as a friend, the operator will have to verify that the operator is himself or herself and make a risk prompt [11].

4.3 The Compensation Clause Favors Consumer Protection

Because the relevant laws and regulations are not perfect at present, the e-commerce is also in the initial stage of development, consumers know little about this, so they are at a disadvantage after losses when using We-Chat Pay. In order to protect consumers'rights, Tencent and Tenpay should put a proper emphasis on consumer protection in the relevant compensation clauses. For example, set up a risk compensation reserve; calculate according to a certain percentage of their business income. When the user has a loss, use the reserve to pay. In addition, cooperation with insurance institutions can be strengthened, and some specific clauses such as how to claim compensation from the insurance company and how to claim compensation from the insurance company can be set up in the user agreement, so that users can effectively make up for the losses suffered.

4.4 Users Raise Awareness of Risk Prevention

In this information society, false information flooding, network trading users should pay special attention to prevent property losses. We-Chat Pay users should raise their awareness of risk prevention and not scan dubious QR codes from unknown sources; be vigilant about the adding requests to stranger's friends, ascertain the identity each other, and refuse requests from strangers to transfer money. Report the case to police station if necessary; identify public numbers when shopping; in addition, do not install suspicious mobile phone software casually to avoid cell phone poisoning and information disclosure. The user raises the self-security consciousness to reduce the loss from the source, does not give the lawless element to take advantage of the opportunity.

References

1. Baidu baike. We-Chat[EB/OL]. https://baike.baidu.com/item/We-Chat/3905974?fr = aladdin
2. China Economic Weekly: Industrial Internet is promising[EB/OL]. http://www.ceweekly.cn/2018/0312/219994.shtml
3. iiMedia Research: China third Party Mobile payment Market report 2017–2018 [EB/OL]. http://www.iimedia.cn/61209.html
4. Baidu baike. We-Chat Pay[EB/OL]. https://baike.baidu.com/item/we-chatpay
5. Mina. We-chat pay, ali-pay bao in a fierce battle overseas. A survey of the reasons why Chinese entrepreneur chose We-Chat Pay. Mod Bus China 43–46
6. Gao Y, Wang W (2016) Risks and precautions in Mobile payments: a case study of We-Chat Pay. Spec Econ Zone (5):80–81
7. Yang B (2013) Study on effective supervision of third-party payment in China. Xiamen University Press, Xiamen, pp 210–215
8. WeChat e-commerce service[EB/OL], protocol. http://weixin.qq.com/cgi-bin/readtemplate?t=weixin_business_agreement&lang
9. Feng B (2016) Analysis of the risk situation of we-chat pay and study on the countermeasures to avoid it. J Anhui Vocat Tech Coll (4):36–38
10. Xu Z (2014) Influence of we-chat pay innovation on financial consumers. Zhejiang Jinrong (6):35–37
11. Zhou B, Huang W (2016) An investigation and analysis of the reasons for college students choice of We-Chat Pay. Mod Bus (26):190–191

Research on General Wearable Technology Based on Embedded Operating System

Ting Zhang(✉), Bingqian Li, Chenwang Xu, and Jiahao Wang

Xijing University, Xi'an 710123, Shaanxi, China
1046935520@qq.com

Abstract. Wearable device is a kind of portable device which is directly worn on the body or carried by the user as a jewelry. With the support of various software applications and data delivery, it can achieve more powerful functions. At present, there is a variety of wearable equipment on the market, whether in daily sports testing, medical health or livestock health monitoring system applications, which are favored, and is also growing. Most wearable devices have single functions and low data transmission requirements. However, the market expectation of wearable devices is not only a supplement to smart phones. With the development of miniaturization, networking and intelligence of various electronic products, it can be foreseen that more and more functions will be integrated to meet the needs of users in wearable devices.

Keywords: Embedded operation · General wearable · Sensor · LORA network

1 Introduction

According to statistics, global sales of smart wearable devices reached 116 million units in 2015, an increase of 53.6% over 2015, and sales revenue reached 18.167 billion US dollars, an increase of 84.7% over 2015. In the 2016–2020 year, the global smart wearable device market will continue to maintain healthy growth. In recent years, Apple, Google and Microsoft have each created different smart ecosystems. Tens of millions of developers have devoted their efforts to realizing the mysteries of smart devices, supported by sophisticated cloud services and big data technologies, relatively sound network environments, and rapidly advancing biometrics. Advances in mobile Internet technology have broadened the imagination of natives, and the dream of wearable devices seems to have come out. The Internet of Things (IOT) of the human body is a metaphor for wearable devices, which can detect the temperature, blood pressure, heart rate and other data of users through sensor. Wearable devices can be read by sensors. If users wear it for several years, the data are recorded and uploaded to the cloud, and a personal body database can be formed. If tens of thousands of people wear it, it will form a big data and return them back, which is very valuable [1–4].

Z. Xu et al. (Eds.): CSIA 2019, AISC 928, pp. 1200–1204, 2020.
https://doi.org/10.1007/978-3-030-15235-2_159

2 General Wearable Device Application Scenario

Using IMX6 UL of ARM Cortex-M4 kernel as hardware platform, embedded Linux as software platform, using modular structure, encapsulating various hardware interfaces, providing a common version of embedded software for different applications, and reserving a third-party interface, through the configuration of different parameters can be applied to different hardware and industry. In the coming wave of wearable devices, different devices will no longer fight individually, but form an organic whole. It can be applied in the following aspects [5–7].

(1) In livestock farming, it is mainly used for livestock. Through the built-in RFID tags and physiological indicators collected regularly, food safety traceability, through temperature, rumination times, steps and other data to warn livestock health status, collar shape, configuration of large-capacity batteries, full power can be used at least one year [8].
(2) In the army, through the comprehensive analysis of location information, body temperature, heart rate, steps, brain waves and other data, it is used for daily work training monitoring, task team physiological indicators monitoring, wrist shape, full power can be used for at least seven days, highlighting its portable performance.
(3) In prison management, through the comprehensive analysis of location information, body temperature, steps and other data, it is used for health monitoring and abnormal warning of prisoners, necklace or foot ring shape.

3 General Wearable Device Technology

3.1 Composition of General Wearable Devices

Universal wearable device terminal integrates low-power Internet of Things modules and various sensors, deploys LORA network, transmits collected health data back to the background, and builds a background cloud service system, including business platform and large data platform. The service platform has the function of viewing real-time data on the Internet and mobile Internet, and is healthy and healthy. The status diagnosis report generates query function and alerts the abnormal state of health. The big data platform uniformly stores health data, and carries out statistical analysis and real-time display. The driver program of wearable computer software system controls the normal operation of the equipment and guarantees the hardware realization of various functions. Software system provides users with interactive interface and firmware upgrade functions, and provides a unified programming interface and running environment for the upper application, which is related to the stability of the system [9, 10].

In order to improve the endurance of wearable devices, most of them do not even use wireless connection. Even if wireless connection is used, they also use Bluetooth and other low power connection to transmit data. The data transmission distance and quality are limited. For the camera equipment with high data transmission requirements, WIFI connection is mostly used, which has high transmission quality but high power consumption. At present, wearable devices on the market are often Bluetooth near-field communication, data back to the mobile phone, the application is very limited, in the terminal equipment encapsulated LORA, NBIOT and other narrow-band Internet of Things module data back, real-time monitoring can be carried out, for some high real-time requirements of the scene, such as unit patrol, prisoners monitoring and so on. Can play the most direct role. Secondly, the driver in the software system controls the normal operation of the device and guarantees the realization of its hardware functions. Software system provides users with interactive interface and firmware upgrade functions, and provides a unified programming interface and running environment for the upper application, which is related to the stability of the system. Therefore, the development of software system is very important for the development of equipment. The following aspects can be studied.

(1) Research the hardware equipment that needs to be encapsulated, including sensor equipment, network equipment and storage, power supply, etc.
(2) Multi-sensor cooperative processing, the core problem of multi-sensor system is to select the appropriate fusion algorithm, according to the different application, set different priority to the data collected by each sensor, filter invalid data, and sleep when not needed to specify sensors, improve the overall efficiency; choose a reasonable multi-sensor information fusion. Form of integration;
(3) Power control algorithms need to adopt different power control strategies according to different applications, so as to reduce the overall power consumption as much as possible and prolong the use time of equipment.
(4) Low-power embedded Linux platform, from the processor to the components need to use low-power devices, need to integrate more peripherals, using embedded Linux platform as a software platform, as far as possible to use the existing device driver and development platform.

3.2 Wearable Device for Detecting Livestock Life Signs

Wearable equipment for detecting signs of livestock life includes a collar body, which is provided with a sensor module, a processor module and a Lora terminal module. The signal output end of the sensor is connected to the signal input end of the processor, the signal output end of the processor is connected to the signal input end of the Lora terminal, and the Lora terminal signal output end is connected to the background cloud service through the Lora gateway [11–13].

Wearing the collar body around the neck of the livestock, the sensor module detects the temperature and pulse information of the livestock in real time. The processor compares the detected information with the reference value of the life signs of the healthy livestock stored in advance. If the deviation is greater than the set value, the livestock is judged to be in an unhealthy state and transmits the information to Lora. Terminals, otherwise, do not do any processing, Lora terminal will alarm information and intrinsic ID information through the LoRa gateway to the background cloud services, tracking and locating health problems of livestock, background cloud services in the health of abnormal livestock warning, and provide health status query function [14, 15]. Composition of wearable devices for detecting livestock life signs is shown in Fig. 1.

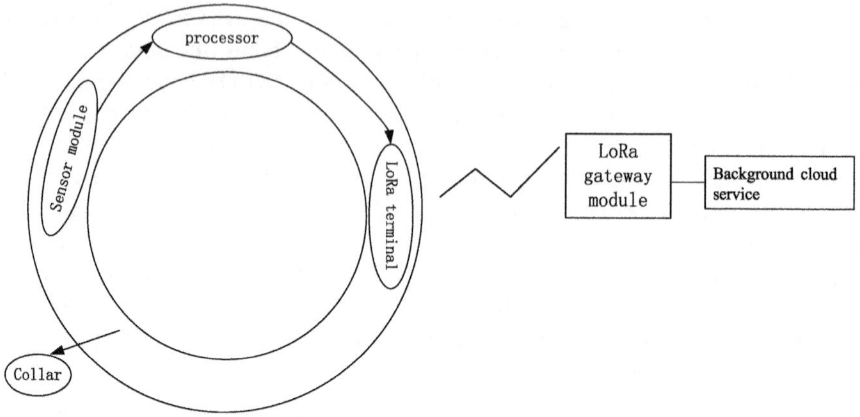

Fig. 1. The composition of wearable devices for detecting livestock life signs

By observing the health status of livestock closely, especially in the face of batches of livestock, farmers can avoid the occurrence of omissions or misjudgments. They can regularly perceive the life signs of livestock through a variety of sensor equipment, and compare with the stored reference data of the life signs of healthy livestock to give the health status of livestock and improve the management efficiency.

4 Conclusions

With the development of embedded software industry, embedded system is very mature both in software and hardware platform and development environment. Low power product is one of the directions. Especially in the combination with low power Internet of Things, it has a very broad market application space, and matching control software, especially power. The algorithm of rate control strategy will bring a brand-new professional direction in the face of complicated and different applications. The general wearable device based on embedded operating system adopts modular structure and encapsulates various hardware interfaces, including sensors, networks, displays, power supply and memory. It provides a general version of embedded software for different applications and reserves a third-party interface. Implementation can be applied to different hardware and industry functions by configuring different parameters.

Acknowledgements. This study was funded by Key Research and Development Plan Project of Shaanxi Provincial Science & Technology Department (Program No. 2018ZDXM-NY-014).

References

1. Hu C (2018) Low-power Bluetooth technology based on Android system [J/OL]. Electron Technol Softw Eng (16):45. http://kns.cnki.net/kcms/detail/10.1108.TP.20180824.1414.072.html. Accessed 04 Sept 2018
2. (2018) Nordic SoC powered low power bluetooth wearable device. Single Chip Microcomput Embed Syst Appl 18(07):94-95
3. Yang X, Guo Y (2018) Research on the development trend of sports wearable equipment. Fujian Sports Sci Technol 37(03):17–19+37
4. Ni L, Zhang Z, Jiao J, Yuan C, Wang M (2018) Classification of goat behavior based on wearable equipment. J Shandong Agric Univ (Nat Sci Edn) 49(02):235–239
5. Zhong J, Liu D, Luo Q, Huang Z, Qiu S, Cheng C, Yang L, Yi X, Zeng J (2018) Application of wearable equipment in the diagnosis of obstructive sleep apnea in children. J Otolaryngol Eye Shandong Univ 32(02):30–33
6. Liu H, Qiu L, Fan Q (2017) Application of sensor technology in wearable equipment. Wirel Interconn Technol (10):133–134
7. Liu Q, Li T, Yu Y, Cai Z, Zhou T (2018) Data security and privacy protection technologies for wearable devices. Comput Res Dev 55(01):14–29
8. Wang R, Lu R, Liang T (2018) Progress in the application of wearable equipment in disease management. Chin J Nurs 53(01):114–116
9. Zhang E, Zhao M, Liu C, Zhou L (2018) Design and implementation of wearable medical monitoring system application program. China Med Equip 33(01):53–56
10. Han G (2018) Wearable device product development design research. Design (01):84–85
11. Zhao J (2018) The application and development of wearable equipment in the field of human health monitoring. Electron World (01):67 + 69
12. Melody (2017) Design of elderly wearable devices based on negative emotions. Nanjing University of Science and Technology
13. Wang X, Xu K, Yang Z, Ge Z (2017) TinyLoc: an indoor localization algorithm for wearable equipment with limited energy consumption. J. Comput. Sci. 40(08):1813–1828
14. Cai Y, Huang W, Dong X (2017) Wearable flexible electronic strain sensor. Sci Bull 62 (07):635–649
15. Liang L (2017) Research and performance characterization of wearable ECG monitoring clothing. Tianjin University of Technology

Analysis of the Guiding Effect of Movie and TV Tourism Memes Based on Big Data

Yali Liu and Meiyun Zhang(✉)

Sanya University, Sanya, Hainan, China
570459549@qq.com

Abstract. The most influential information factors in movie and TV plays include tourism scenery, storyline, celebrity stars, folk culture and historical events. In the analysis of typical film and television works by using large data technology, it is found that in many film and television tourism memes, vivid storylines are the most important factors to impress the audience and the tourists. And the landscape meme is also very important, that is, "moving story + beautiful natural scenery" is the most influential factor. At the same time, we should avoid the negative effects caused by ecological damage.

Keywords: Big data · Tourism meme · Guiding effect

In recent years, with the development of social economy and the improvement of people's living standards, the tourism industry has developed rapidly. "Traveling with movies" has become a fashion. This phenomenon has not only caused a boom in the film and television circles, but also attracted the attention of experts from the tourism industry. With the rapid development of big data, we can fully discover and dig into the influence of tourism memes on tourism destinations and the supporting role of tourism destinations in maintaining the attention degree of film and television works.

1 Tourism Memes in Film and Television Plays

The word "meme" is translated from English "meme", and the interpretation of the Oxford English Dictionary for meme is that it is a basic cultural unit that is propagated through imitative and non-genetic ways [1, 2]. The interpretation of meme in Wechsler's dictionary is that: in the field of social culture, a kind of ideas, behavior habits, or style tastes spread among people through replication and imitation [3–6]. From the point of view of communication, "meme" refers to the unit of genetic and cultural imitation in the social and cultural field, and is a kind of information factor that exists in human thinking. Memes are transmitted by word of mouthand by books, computers, television and film [7].

The characters, plots, scenery and music, images, clothing and other information in movie and TV play can all be called memes [8]. These information factors are produced in the brain of the movie fan (meme host) and transmitted through the media to become a replication factor. Only the information factor in the process of replication and propagation is the real meme [9, 10]. Memes are not always duplicated

Z. Xu et al. (Eds.): CSIA 2019, AISC 928, pp. 1205–1210, 2020.
https://doi.org/10.1007/978-3-030-15235-2_160

independently. Like genes, memes and memes can be adapted to each other and combined to spread. As far as tourism information factor is concerned, it can be attributed to tourism memes. According to the research on the tourism memes of film and television works both at home and abroad, it is found that the factors which are strong in tourism influence include tourist scenery, story plot, celebrity star, folklore culture and historical event.

1.1 Scenery Memes

The natural scenery of the scene in the film and television works is an important factor in attracting filmmakers to shoot. These natural scenes not only bring a beautiful sense to the film, but also play a role without words. Bringing the connotation of scenery into film and television works, combining with themes, tourism memes are widely spread among movie fans and even the general public. After the movie "Lost in Thailand", the tropical scenery of Chiang Mai in Thailand, which is very impressed to Chinese tourists, is even more attractive.

1.2 Plot Memes

Story is an important part of film and television works, and also an important factor to attract audiences. In the film "If You Are the One 2", it not only spends about 50% of the time to show the charming natural scenery of Hainan, but also deduces the plot of "trial marriage" and "farewell party to life" and other stories. In the major tourism websites of Sanya, the "trial room" has become an important tourism destination.

1.3 Celebrity Memes

Many fans are willing to trace their directing or starring movies and TV plays because of their obsession with directors and stars. As a result, the memes of celebrities were gradually formed. In the film related to tourism, the typical "Shaolin Temple", starring Jet Li, as well as the first Oscar gold medal in Chinese film by Ang Lee, Zhou Runfa, Zhang Ziyi and other films, "Crouching Tiger, hidden dragon". After the films were released, there were more and more tourists to Shaolin Temple, Zhejiang, Huzhou.

1.4 Cultural Memes

In a broad sense, the core content of film and television communication is culture. However, this is mainly from the concrete representation of the film and television works, and based on the meme theory, especially the cultural information in the works. For example, the film "Raise the Red Lantern" and the television series "Courtyard of Family Qiao" shooting of the house of Qiao family, located in the beautiful and rich Jinzhong basin, is a collection of the historical features of the Jin merchants, reflecting the characteristics of the Ming and Qing Dynasties culture of the folk houses. The attraction of tourists is the flavor of national culture.

1.5 Historical Memes

Films drawn from historical themes and photographed at historical events will undoubtedly bring the satisfaction of historical reality to the audience. The opportunity to travel to the original place of historical events and the place of the film is the integration of the three images, and the historical memes formed from this will spread among the hosts. "Casablanca" drawn from World War II, tells the story of an unmoved and touching triangle in troubled times. The reproduction of historical memes also requires a story setting.

2 The Guiding Effect of Memesin Film and Television Tourism

The popularity of tourist attractions, including the increment of the number of tourists, is not directly proportional to the popularity of TV plays. Therefore, it is very necessary to make rational analysis of the guiding effect of movie and TV tourism memes by using big data technology, and make decisions after scientific judgment.

There is a certain meme playing a leading role in film and television works with tourism memes. Only in the process of shooting or propaganda, we can accurately grasp the dominant memes and combine the connotation of film and television memes with the characteristics of tourist attractions, so as to maximize the influence of the film and television tourism memes to the tourist attractions, and combine the two parties to promote their popularity and create greater value. The tourism models of 40 famous Chinese and foreign filmsare analyzed, such as "Mount Lu Love", "If You Are the One", "Lost in Hong Kong", "LostIn Thailand", "King of the Ring", "Transformers 4", "Sissi Princess", "007 series" and so on. The results are shown in Fig. 1.

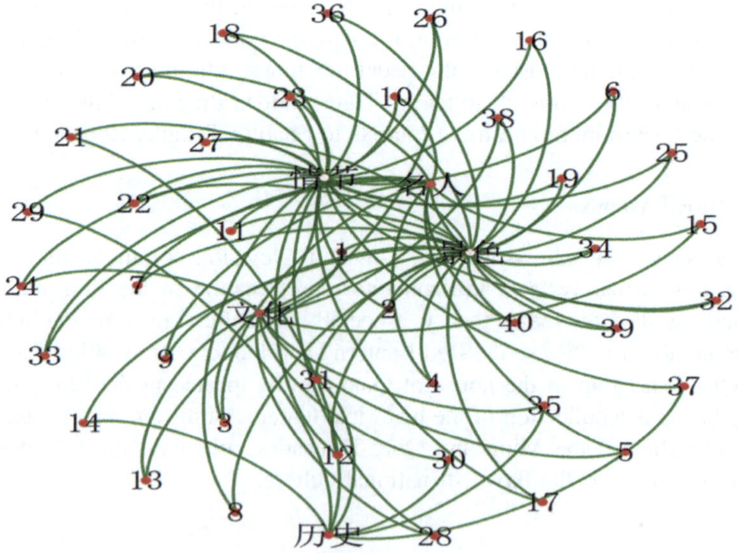

Fig. 1. Relationship between film and television works and tourism memes

From the results of the data analysis, we can see that the influence of scenery memes and plot memes in the 40 films is more prominent, the influence of celebrity memes and cultural memes is less, and the influence of historical memes is the least. In many movie and TV tourism meme, the vivid story plot is the most important factor to move the audience and the tourists. At the same time, the scenery meme is also indispensable, that is, "the moving story plot + the beautiful natural scenery", is the most influential factor.

3 The Negative Impact of Film and Television Shooting on Tourism

However, not all films and TV shows are mutually reinforcing. In the process of shooting, people will destroy the natural ecology of the scenic area. Some groups do not have the sense of ecological protection, they will build at will and destroy the environment. The most typical example is that the movie "The Promise" filmed badly damaged the azalea sea in Shangri-La, Diqing, Yunnan province. Two is the construction of the film city to maintain, although the city is not a natural landscape, but the city will generally choose beautiful scenery or cultural sites, the movie city will not only attract a large number of production groups due to the need, but also attract a large number of tourists to go, the management is not in place will cause certain damage to the surrounding environment. Three is the tourist after the film and TV play is released to a destination, which is bound to cause congestion. If the facilities are not in place, the unpleasant ending will be produced. Although the release of "Lost in Thailand" has brought huge income to Thailand's tourism industry, the influx of Chinese tourists has also made the Thais feel less satisfied, thinking that the quality of Chinese tourists needs to be improved. The movie "Star Wars 2: the Attack of the Clones", "Midnight Barcelona", which is known as the "Kingdom of tourism" in Spain, even broke out "anti-tourist" demonstrations.

4 Selection Strategy of the Meme of Film and Television Tourism

No matter what kind of tourism meme to show, first of all, it is necessary to fully demonstrate the possible negative effects and make a good plan, which is the prerequisite. On this basis, we can optimize the selection and design the plot, so as to achieve the mutual promotion with the tourist destination.

4.1 Optimizing the Scene

From the result of the analysis of the previous meme of tourism, we can see that the number of scenery meme is quite large, so it is very important to choose the best place to shoot for the film and TV play. The success of "The Lord of the Rings" is very much related to the selection of New Zealand's magical scenery. "If You Are the One 2" has finally identified Sanya in many candidate viewhouses. From the box office data and the comments of the netizens, this is a very wise choice. "007 Series" in many places in the world, the most classic scenery, such as Bond's hometown Scotland, gambling city Las Vegas, rich historical Istanbul and the modern international city Tokyo, Hongkong and so on, these places have made a lot of success in the film, and become one of the important "role".

4.2 Plot Design

Although the plot meme is less in number than the scene, but it's also very important. Audiences need not only to satisfy the pleasure of vision, but also to resonate with the soul. From the invention of films to the beginning of the twentieth Century, the film began to focus on long works. In the past more than 100 years, the film has always devoted itself to one thing: telling stories. From the beginning of the construction to the gradual conflict, until the solution is reached, whether the story can attract people will determine the success or failure of the movie. The success of "If You Are the One of 2" is crucial to the clever design of the plot. However, "The Love of the Blue Tone Sea" is also filmed in Sanya, Hainan, the audience's comments are quite different. There are 68 travel notes in the "Yalong Bay Tropical Paradise Forest Park" by Ctrip Community, and almost every one will mention "If You Are the One" and "The Love of the Blue Tone Sea" is rarely mentioned. This phenomenon is directly related to the attractiveness of the two films. In addition, the popularity of actors also has some influence, which is the result of multiple memes.

4.3 Mutual Promotion

The successful creation of scenic scenery, storyline, and so on, not only can contribute to the tourism industry, but also can get the "back feeding" of the tourism industry. People who like Wuzhen are likely to chase the TV series "The Years", and those who yearn for Zhangjiajie also want to see the beautiful and gorgeousLeah Road in "Afanda".

On the contrary, the film and television works produced by sacrificing the ecological environment of tourist attractions will make the audience and tourists unhappy. Therefore, the film and television works and the tourist attractions as filming sites are symbiotic and long, and this relationship needs mutual protection to promote each other.

Acknowledgement. HaiNan Philosophical and Social Sciences Planning Subject (2019 Key Research Project) Construction of a New Chinese Teaching Model Based on the Fourth Research Paradigm.

Foundation Project: National Social Science Foundation Project 2017 NO, 17XYY012.

References

1. Xu X (2015) On the two-way alignment between tourism industry and film culture–a case study of the film "Lost in Thailand". Movie Rev (18)
2. Ci X (2014) The modern paradox of exotic tourism films. Sichuan Drama (10)

3. Sun Y, Wu J (2015) On the cross-application of tourism destination image promotion and spread of micro-film. Contemp Cinema (01)
4. Gong Y (2014) The perception analysis of tourists on tourism microfilm. Business (05)
5. He Z (2016) Linguistic meme and its variant application. J Xinjiang Norm Univ (Philos Soc Sci) 37(02)
6. Cao J, Jin Y (2016) Theoretical interpretation on the communication power of internet strong language memes. Chin J J Commun 38(02)
7. Dong H (2015) An analysis on film tourism marketing based on the perspective of whole-process collaborations between film and tourism industries. Jiangsu Commer Forum (09)
8. Shan D, Wang Y, Yang X (2014) Theoretical model and empirical tests on film-induced tourism. Econ Geogr 34(08)
9. Qu Y (2018) A study of the transmission of internet catchphrases from the perspective of memetics. J Shenyang Norm Univ (Soc Sci Edn) 42(01)
10. He Z (2017) The forming process of linguistic memes and their spreading features: on Chinese memes and pragmatics in social ecology. Foreign Lang Literat Stud 34(03)

Research on Mutual Information Registration Method Based on Gradient Edge Information

Lianhuan Li(✉)

International Education School of Nanyang Medical College, Nanyang, Henan, China
computer20131222@163.com

Abstract. Aiming at the large difference of information of multi-source images, this paper proposes a registration method based on edge gradient information and normalized mutual information as the similarity criterion, and uses pyramid decomposition method to optimize the speed of the algorithm. The infrared image and the visible light image of the same scene are used as multi-source images, and the registration experiments are carried out. It is proved that the algorithm can achieve multi-source image registration.

Keywords: Multi-source image registration · Gradient edge information · Normalized mutual information · Pyramid decomposition

1 Introduction

The concept of image fusion has originated in the late 1970s. The multi-source image is an image acquired from different sensors [1–3]. Since the position of the sensor cannot be exactly the same when the image is acquired, the characteristics of each sensor and the spatial range of the acquisition are different, so the acquired source image is more or less present mismatched phenomenon [4–6]. Since image fusion requires all source images to be described as much as possible for the same target in the same scene, it is necessary to register the images before fusion to facilitate subsequent fusion processing.

2 Image Gradient Edge Extraction

The images acquired by different sensors may cause inconsistencies in the information characteristics of the images due to the difference in the representation method of the scene information [7, 8]. However, the edge of the image is the most basic feature of the image, so an effective algorithm must be used to detect the edge features of the image.

First define an extension structure Q:

$$Q = \begin{pmatrix} K_p * I_x^2 & K_p * I_x I_y \\ K_p * I_x I_y & K_p * I_y^2 \end{pmatrix} \tag{1}$$

Z. Xu et al. (Eds.): CSIA 2019, AISC 928, pp. 1211–1216, 2020.
https://doi.org/10.1007/978-3-030-15235-2_161

In the formula, the symbol "*" represents the convolution operation symbol, indicates K_p of a standard two-dimensional difference Nova, I_x and I_y respectively show component image gradient in the x and y direction, for each pixel in an image Q performs eigenvalue decomposition to obtain two eigenvectors w1 and w2, and two eigenvalues u1 and u2 (u1 > u2). If there is a large difference between two eigenvalues of one pixel pair, then This pixel is most likely located on the edge of the image. However, the difference between the eigenvalues corresponding to the points on the strong edge is much larger than that between the points on the weak edge and the corresponding eigenvalues.

In order to make the difference independent of the strength of the edge, for each pixel, define the parameter c as follows:

$$c = \begin{cases} 0 & else \\ (\mu_1 - \mu_2)/\mu_1 & if\ \mu_1 > \varepsilon \end{cases} \tag{2}$$

In the formula, c represents the confidence level of a pixel at the edge, in the range [0, 1]. The higher the value of c, the greater the probability that the pixel is located at the edge soil, c = 1 means that the pixel must be located on the edge, c = 0 means that the pixel is not on the edge, and the closer the value of c is to 1, the closer the pixel position is edge. Wherein, ε is the threshold, its role is to prevent the pixels in the homogeneous region of greater c. The value of ε is related to u1, and the proportion of pixels with non-zero c values to the total number of image pixels should be less than 50%. For each pixel, the corresponding image c is obtained to obtain the edge image c.

3 Normalized Mutual Information Registration

Assuming that the edge images obtained from the process in the first step are A and B, respectively, the entropy is $H(A)$ and $H(B)$, and the joint entropy is $H(A, B)$, then Its normalized mutual information is:

$$I_{NMI}(A, B) = \frac{H(A) + H(B)}{H(A, B)} \tag{3}$$

Among them:

$$H(A) = -\sum_a p_A(a) \log_2 p_A(a)\ a \in A \tag{4}$$

$$H(B) = -\sum_b p_B(b) \log_2 p_B(b)\ b \in B \tag{5}$$

$$H(A, B) = -\sum_{a,b} p_{AB}(a, b) \log_2 p_{AB}(a, b) \tag{6}$$

Among them, $p_A(a)$ and $p_B(b)$ are the edge probability distribution functions of A and B, and $p_{AB}(a, b)$ is the joint probability distribution function of A and B.

The specific implementation process is that the image A is used as a reference image, and the image B is spatially transformed as a floating image. The process of registering the edge images $A(m, n)$ and $B(m, n)$ is based on the definition of the similarity measure, and the process of finding the spatial transformation relationship that maximizes the similarity between the two images. The spatial transformation can be expressed as: $\mathrm{Ta} = \mathrm{a}(A(m, n), B(T(m, n)))$, wherein a is a similarity measure and T is a spatial transformation relationship. Therefore, the registration process can be expressed as follows:

$$a^* = \arg\max a(A(m, n), B(T(m, n))) \tag{7}$$

When edges A and B are optimally registered, the normalized mutual information of their corresponding image features should be maximized.

The further implementation process is: the first light calculates the mutual information of the multi-source image registration A and B according to the given initial point for the reference image A and the floating image B, and then uses the directional acceleration Powell algorithm to normalize the maximum mutual information. The process of "space geometric transformation - calculating mutual information value - optimal judgment" until the parameters satisfying the accuracy requirements are searched, and finally the registration parameters are output [9]. The multi-source image is registered with the obtained registration parameters to obtain the final registration result.

4 Pyramid Decomposition Optimization

The pyramid decomposition used in this paper is obtained by successive down-sampling of the original image by Gaussian pyramid. When using the Gaussian pyramid for down-sampling, to generate the i+1th layer from the i-th layer of the pyramid, we first convolve the i-th layer with a Gaussian kernel and then delete all even-numbered and even-numbered columns [10]. Of course, the newly obtained image area will become one quarter of the source image, and the entire pyramid can be obtained by performing a loop operation to set the number of stages.

The optimization process is implemented after the preprocessing of the source image, the processed source image is pyramid-decomposed, and then the normalized mutual information registration is started from the highest layer of the pyramid image, and the registration method is as described above until Obtain the best matching parameters of the layer, and then pass this parameter to the image registration process of the next layer as a registration guide to reduce the registration calculation of the next layer, and then obtain more accurate The registration parameters are cycled until the original edge image, which is the required matching parameter.

5 Overall Matching Process

Step (1): First determine the transformation model (generally projection transformation, including image translation, rotation, scaling).
Step (2): Preprocessing the visible light image and the infrared image to eliminate the noise of the infrared image and the visible image.
Step (3): Pyramid the processed image and select an appropriate decomposition series to obtain a pyramid image.
Step (4): Spatially transforming the i-th layer image of the infrared pyramid image to obtain a new i-layer image.
Step (5): The i-th layer image of the pyramid image (i is taken from the maximum start value) is processed according to the gradient edge acquisition method described above, and the edge image of the i-th layer image is acquired.
Step (6): Perform the registration of the normalized mutual information similarity measure on the acquired edge image to determine whether it is optimized. If the optimization is not achieved, return to step (4) until the layer image is optimized.
Step (7): Accept the registration result of the previous layer image. If it is not the pyramid level 0 layer, the result of obtaining the optimized registration parameter is used as a guide to reduce the registration calculation process, and repeat steps (4)–(6) until the final matching parameters are obtained.

6 Experiment and Result Analysis

In the experiment, visible image is used as reference image and infrared image as floating image. Taking the upper left corner of the visible light image as the origin, the right and the downward direction are the positive directions of x and y, and the clockwise direction is the positive direction of the rotation angle. The reference image and the image to be registered are decomposed into three layers by the pyramid decomposition method, and the edge detection is performed on each layer of the image to obtain the edge image.

Figure 1 shows the original image of the visible light image of the soldering iron (the reference image) and the image of each layer after the pyramid decomposition. Figure 2 shows the infrared image of the soldering iron (the image after the histogram equalization) and the images of the layers after the pyramid decomposition. Figure 3 shows the registration results. (a) is the unloaded source image overlay, and (b) is the effect of the registered source image. The registration parameters obtained are: displacement in the x direction, displacement in the y direction of 5, rotation in the range of $-1.4°$, and scaling of 1.02.

It can be seen from Fig. 3 that the method this paper proposed has good registration effect for visible and infrared images.

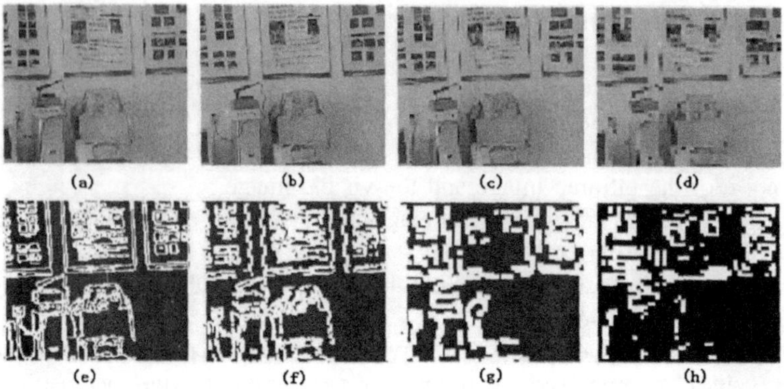

Fig. 1. The visible pyramid decomposition image of the soldering iron and the edge image of each layer

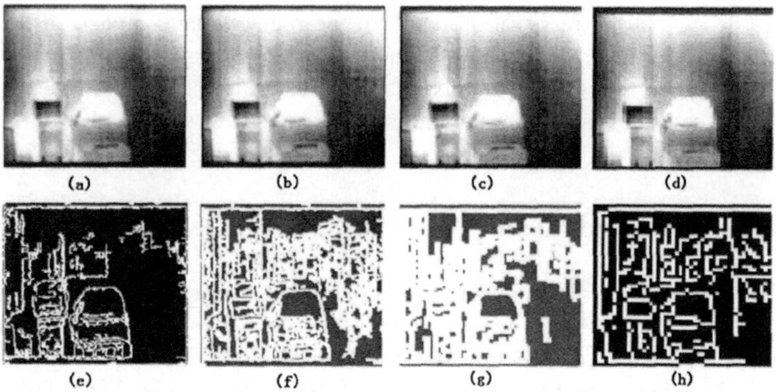

Fig. 2. The infrared image pyramid decomposition image of the soldering iron and edge images of each layer

Fig. 3. Registration effect of soldering iron

7 Conclusion

Aiming at the characteristics of infrared and visible images, an improved registration method of heterologous image based on normalized mutual information is proposed, and the algorithm is optimized by pyramid decomposition method. The registration of images as a verification experiment proves that the algorithm can achieve multi-source image registration better and lays a foundation for the fusion of multi-source image information.

References

1. Zheng Y, Tian X (2006) Development of medical image registration. Int J Biomed Eng 29 (2):88–92
2. Barnea DI, Silverman HF (1972) A class of algorithms for fast digital registration. IEEE Trans Comput C-21:179–186
3. Belongie S, Malik J, Puzicha J (2002) Shape matching and object recognition using shape contexts. Trans Pattern Anal Mach Intell 24(4):509–522
4. Wang C, Jiang M (2006) Review of image registration methods for medical images. CT Theor Appl 15(2):74–80
5. Zou B, Lin J (2008) Contour extraction research of image. Comput Eng Appl 44(25):161–165
6. Guo B, Zhang Q, Hou Y (2008) Region-based fusion of infrared and visible images using nonsubsampled contourlet transform. Chin Opt Lett 6(5):338–341
7. Piella G (2003) A general framework for multiresolution image fusion: from pixels to regions. Inf Fusion 4(4):259–280
8. Wang Z, Ziou D, Armenakis C et al (2005) A comparative analysis of image fusion methods. IEEE Trans Geosci Remote Sen 43(6):1391–1402
9. Shi W, Zhu C, Tian Y et al (2005) Wavelet-based image fusion and quality assessment. Int J Appl Earth Obs Geoinf 6(3):241–251
10. Moghaddam M, Dungan JL, Acker S (2002) Forest variable estimation from fusion of SAR and multispectral optical data. IEEE Trans Geosci Remote Sens 40(10):2176–2187

The Studied for the Positive and Negative Solutions of the 6-dof Motion Platform

Yiying Chen(✉)

Changchun Science and Technology University, Changchun, China
1206522865@qq.com

Abstract. With the rapid development of national economy, six degrees of freedom motion platform as its structure widely used in aircraft car simulator and dynamic movie large game consoles and other entertainment equipment. This article based on the six degrees of freedom parallel machine tool movement platform for the object to study the static position error and its simulation platform, for the research of high precision parallel machine tool simulator provides a basis for reference.

Keywords: 6-dof motion platform · Solution · Error analysis

1 Research Significance

This paper takes the 6-dof motion platform in the parallel machine tool as the research object, analyzes and establishes the mathematical model. The error source is determined and the static error kinematics model is analyzed by matrix method and the static pose error source of the platform is obtained. The main significance of this study is as follows:

Six degrees of freedom motion platform as a kind of parallel machine tool, the precision is difficult to compare with the traditional high precision machine tools, machine tool movement due to some factors on the manufacturing accuracy is not high, so accuracy is one of the problems in machine parameters must be considered, the error source and error analysis and simulation has the very vital significance.

Based on the single closed matrix vector analysis we can intuitively reflect the platform of static posture errors and affecting factors, and the simulation was carried out on the platform position error motion analysis, get the pose error of the trajectory of the platform, provides a theoretical basis for precision analysis and compensation.

2 Development Status at Domestic and Abroad

2.1 Foreign Development

Abroad, T.F.N. iaritsiry et al. studied various error sources and their influence degrees on the accuracy of parallel mechanism by using finite element analysis method, and found that temperature, manufacturing, installation errors and other factors affecting the motion accuracy of the mechanism were found [1]. Stephane et al. studied the change

Z. Xu et al. (Eds.): CSIA 2019, AISC 928, pp. 1217–1221, 2020.
https://doi.org/10.1007/978-3-030-15235-2_162

law of sensitivity of parallel machine tools, and analyzed the influence of dimensional tolerance change on posture accuracy of terminal platform based on kinematics method and differential vector method, as well as the influence of size and Angle change on posture accuracy of terminal platform [2–4]. Han et al. analyzed the problem of the error model matrix, studied the relationship between the error range of the fulcrum and the pose, and provided reference for the precision design of the parallel mechanism [5]. Masory Oren and Wang et al. found that the precision level of parallel platform and the series mechanism are on the same order of magnitude, and the boundary of the working space of mobile platform is the maximum area of error [6]. Wang et al. established the differential equation that can be directly input and output by using the coordinate transformation method, and analyzed the influence degree of various original errors on the pose of the moving platform from the sensitivity perspective. Philip et al. studied the influence of mechanism motion pair error on motion accuracy of parallel platform.

2.2 Domestic Development

In China, Li et al. took the 6-dof motion platform as the research object, deduced the transfer function equation of the mechanism from the input error to the output error, and analyzed the error transfer problem. Qiao et al. analyzed the spatial positioning error and rod length error of the hinge points of parallel mechanism by using mathematical statistics method. Based on the Stewart platform, Su et al. studied the large radio telescope, established its motion error model, and analyzed four factors that may lead to the reduction of the accuracy of the parallel platform mechanism [7, 8]. Lv et al. studied the process of analytical positive solution of the dynamic platform of parallel mechanism, and proposed an error analysis modeling method based on the positive solution of the pose of parallel mechanism. Yu et al. analyzed the original error of the motion simulator with parallel platform as the main structure and the posture deviation in the movement process, established the posture error model of the parallel platform mechanism, and provided reference for the precision design, error calibration and error compensation of the parallel platform. Wen-tao liu length is studied from the perspective of statistics such as the terminal pose the influence law of the moving platform respectively from two aspects of machining precision and working space of parallel machine tool research machine tool machining scope and main influence factors, draw a mechanism kinematic pair clearance, machine tool manufacturing and assembly errors of terminal influence on the posture error of moving platform, and analysis the result provides reference for the design of parallel machine tool.

Therefore, error and accuracy as one of the main performance indicators of machine tool directly affect the quality of work. The previous error and precision analysis mainly focuses on the error in the multi-factor manufacturing link. Based on this, this paper considers the error caused by separate factors and control to comprehensively and intuitively analyze the error of static posture. Therefore, the influence of the error of the research platform can provide theoretical basis for further calibration of pose compensation.

The control panel of the machine tool is used to directly control the movement or processing of the machine tool, including panel indicator light, operation mode indicator switch, multiplier switch, selection mode and other functions.

2.3 Handheld Unit

3 Kinematics and Error Analysis of 6-dof Motion Platform

3.1 Determination of Dof and Establishment of Platform Position Coordinate System

Generally speaking, the posture error of parallel machine tools can be divided into dynamic error and static error. Static error generally refers to the error does not change with time, in motion invariable error; In general, dynamic error refers to the error that changes with time and changes in motion. There are many reasons for static errors, such as errors in manufacturing and assembly, errors in temperature environment and errors in control system sensors. The dynamic error is caused by the action of the force on the mechanism in the motion of the machine, which leads to the vibration deformation and the posture error. This paper mainly considers the static posture error of the moving platform.

$$M = 6n - 6g - 6 + \sum_{i=1}^{m} fi$$

3.2 Program Contents

Where n is the number of active components (14), g is the number of moving components (18). Six cylinders have two degrees of freedom (1 translation, 1 rotation), so it's 6•2 = 12, tiger hinge has two degrees of freedom (2 rotation), so it's 12•2 = 24, M = 6, 14 − 6, 18 − 6 + 36 = 6.

The coordinate systems are set up on the upper and lower platforms, and o points are the geometric centers of two hexagons respectively. When the active platform stands, the two coordinate systems point to the same direction, as shown in the Fig. 1.

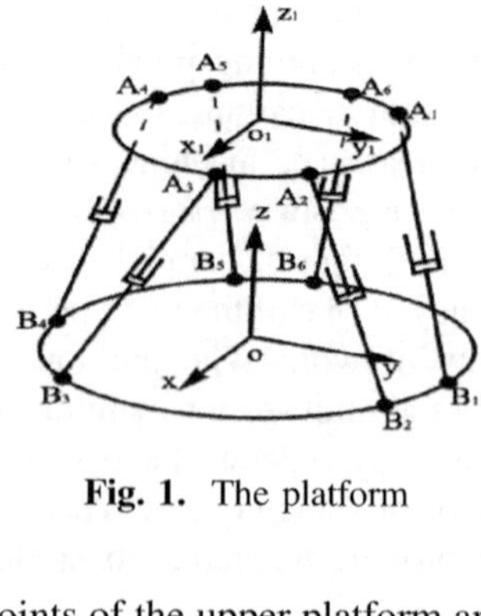

Fig. 1. The platform

A1 to A6 are the hinge points of the upper platform and the hydraulic cylinder, and B1 to B6 are the hinge points of the lower platform and the hydraulic cylinder. The transformation formula of the upper and lower platforms is:

Where the [T] is the rotation matrix, which rotates the case first around the z axis, and its transformation relation is as follows:

$X = x'\cos\gamma - y'\sin\gamma$

$Y = x'\sin\gamma + y'\cos\gamma$

$Z = z'$

In the same way, if we get the matrix [B], [A], then the rotation matrix [T] = [C]•[B]•[A].

3.3 Position Inverse and Positive Solutions

The inverse solution of position is to calculate the hydraulic cylinder expansion with known attitude parameters of the platform. The matrix [T] obtained by Sect. 3.1 can be substituted into the transformation formula to find the hydraulic cylinder length. The expression is as follows:

$Li^2 = (Xbi - Xai) + (Ybi - Yai) + (Zbi - Zai)$, the length of the hydraulic cylinder from L1 to L6 can be calculated.

The positive solution of position is the attitude parameter of platform with known hydraulic cylinder expansion. At present, there is no direct equation to find the positive solution, only the numerical iterative method can be used to approach the attitude parameters of the solution platform. The principle is to change the nonlinear equations into linear equations, find the approximate solution, and then further iterate on the basis of the approximate solution, and gradually approach the true solution.

After several iterations, the values of X, Y, Z, match and no can be obtained.

3.4 Pose Error and Error Model

The static error factors of the motion platform include manufacturing, installation and temperature control. For closed loop vector analysis the static error factor of platform is mainly composed of bar length and hinge.

Vector analysis of the single-chain closed loop of the platform can be expressed as: Bi is the hinge point of the lower platform; Libi is the actual length of the bar; P is the unit vector

The jacobian matrix is obtained by diff erentiating and differentiating the two sides. Pose error modeling is an important part of analyzing the impact of errors. First, vector analysis is carried out for a single dividing closed loop, then error model is established, and finally the impact of platform output parameters on pose is analyzed.

On the installation and control, there are also some factors that lead to the posture parameters of the movement platform, such as the influence of machine tool accuracy and the opening size of hydraulic valve electric valve. In the experiment, the error value is measured and compared with the real value.

3.5 Prototype Simulation Parameter Modeling and Simulation Analysis

The Solidworks is used for three-dimensional solid modeling of the mechanism and Adams virtual prototype is used for kinematics simulation analysis. Adams is a virtual prototype analysis software integrating modeling, solving and visualization. After modeling, the solution module (Adams/solver) is used to simulate the motion of the mechanism, and finally the simulation curve is drawn with the help of the processing module (Adams/postprocessor) [9, 10].

References

1. Allegedly H, Fellow GR (1997) The kinematic error estimation and transmission error bounding for stewart platform -based machine tools. Trans NAMRI/SME 11(1):245–265
2. Merlet JP (1990) On the infinitesimal motion of a parallel manipulators and Grassman geometry. Int J Robot Res 1(05):23–30
3. Shi X, Fenton RG (1994) A complete and general solution to the forward kinematics problem of platform type robotic manipulators. IEEE Preceding (28):105–114
4. Hunt KH (1978) Kinematic geometry of mechanisms, vol 23, no 2. Oxford Science Publications, Oxford, pp 45–65
5. Hunt KH (1983) Structural Kinematics of in-parallel actuated robot arms. ASME J Trans Autom Des 14(06):405–439
6. Fichter EF (1986) A stewart plan-based manipulator: general theory and practical construction. Int J Robot Res 02(02):49–57
7. Xu L, Fan S, Ma Y (2003) Precision modeling and error analysis of a new type of parallel machine tool. J Sichuan Univ (Eng Sci Ed) (04):15–19
8. Gao M, Li T, Zheng H, Wang J (2003) Compensation of manufacturing error of hinge of parallel machine tool. J Tsinghua Univ (Nat Sci Ed) (05):145–150
9. Ren F, Chen S, Gao S, Chang Y, Liu C (2012) Open pipe splicing special welding robot control system. J Welding (07)
10. Qin H, Xia Q, Fu Y (2009) PLC programming environment based on iec61131–3 standard. Comput Eng (23)

A Review of Context-Based Personalized Recommendation Research

Yi Ren(✉), Cuirong Chi, and Jintao Zhang

Shenyang Jianzhu University, Shenyang, Liaoning, China
1181134429@qq.com

Abstract. In recent years, the context-aware recommendation algorithm has become the main research direction in the field of recommendation systems. It becomes the main task of the context-aware recommendation system to use the context information to further improve the recommendation accuracy and user satisfaction. This paper studies and analyzes the context-aware recommendation system by context extraction and modeling. The key step is how to extract user preferences. At the same time, this article introduces the relevant context recommendation generation techniques. Finally, the full text is summarized and future work is proposed.

Keywords: Context-aware · Recommendation system · User preference

1 Introduction

With the advent and development of the era of intelligent Internet, the amount of information on the Internet has exploded, resulting in serious information overload, and information overload which has become a major obstacle for people to obtain information fast and effectively. The recommendation system is an important way to solve this problem.

In the 1990s, the concept of "personalized service" [1] was proposed to provide different needs for different users. Currently, the recommendation system is widely used in various fields, such as e-commerce, information retrieval, and mobile applications. With the development of these fields, the application of context information to improve user experience and system performance has become one of the hotspots of academic and industrial circles.

In the field of recommendation systems, researchers usually focus only on the binary relationship between "user-items" and rarely consider contextual factors. However, in many scenarios, relying solely on the "user-item" relationship does not produce recommendations well. For example, users may like to watch professional books on weekdays and enjoy reading novels during holidays. At this point, the time context has important determinants. When the user is with the child, choosing a cartoon movie and romance with the partner. At this time, the companion is an important contextual factor. Chen et al. [2] proposed a social-based context recommendation algorithm. The algorithm first uses the context extraction algorithm from the dataset to extract a variety of contextual information that may affect user preferences. Then, based

Z. Xu et al. (Eds.): CSIA 2019, AISC 928, pp. 1222–1227, 2020.
https://doi.org/10.1007/978-3-030-15235-2_163

on the context information, the random user tree is used to segment the existing user item scoring matrix. Based on the matrix decomposition model, the influence of user friends on user preferences in social networks is considered. He et al. [3] proposed a collaborative filtering recommendation based on context item scoring splitting. The algorithm first splits the item according to different splitting criteria under the condition of multi-dimensional context information. The split results are then clustered according to the context dimension. Finally, the collaborative filtering algorithm is merged to predict potential preferences. Liu et al. [4] proposed a contextual operation tensor (COT) model, using the context as a common semantic effect of the context manipulation tensor, and representing the context as a potential vector. The context manipulation matrix is generated from the context manipulation tensor and the context potential vector by simulating the semantic operations of the context combination. Karatzoglou et al. [5], Bell et al. [6] incorporated context information into a factorization model by treating the context as one or more dimensions with attributes of similar dimensions to the user and the item.

This paper reviews the context-aware recommendation algorithms. Section 2 mainly introduces related technologies for context recommendation. Section 3 analyzes extracting user preferences. Section 4 introduces context recommendation generation techniques. Section 5 summarizes the full text.

2 Related Technology Introduction

This section begins with an overview of the traditional recommendation system and introduces the formal definition of the context-aware recommendation system, then explains how to get context information and context modeling.

2.1 Traditional Recommendation Technique

The recommendation system involves multiple subjects such as information retrieval, management, and sociology. It was not until the 1990s that technologies about collaborative filtering appeared. The term "collaborative filtering" was first proposed by Goldberg et al. [7], and researched later as an independent disciplines. The recommendation system is based on a recommendation algorithm designed with user behavior data by establishing a binary relationship between the user and the item. From the perspective of information filtering, the recommendation system is mainly divided into the following categories:

(1) Content-based recommendation: According to the item that the user liked in the past, by explicit or implicit feedback to recommend the items similar to the those he liked in the past,the main idea is to calculate the similarity of the items. The content-based recommendation method relies on the users' preferences and the items' features, which is insensitive to the amount of data. Therefore, there is no data sparsity problem, but it is difficult to extract the item features

(2) Collaborative filtering recommendation: Collaborative filtering includes neighborhood-based recommendations and model-based recommendations. The former makes preference prediction by calculating similarities between users (or items). The latter primarily predicts a user's potential preference for a item by constructing a user preference model. Collaborative filtering only needs to use the user's historical rating data, so it is effective and the most successful recommendation method.

(3) Hybrid recommendation: According to different hybrid strategies (such as weighting, switching, mixed rendering, feature combination, concatenation, feature expansion, meta-level mixing, etc. [8]), different recommendation types or (algorithms) are combined until recommendations are generated.

2.2 Context-Aware Recommendation

The concept of the earliest context-aware recommender systems (CARS) was proposed by Adomavicius and Tuzhilin et al. [9]. The traditional "user-item" two-dimensional rating utility model: $u : Users \times Items \rightarrow R$ expand to a multidimensional scoring utility model with multiple contextual information $U : D_1 \times \ldots \times D_n \rightarrow R$ or $R : User \times Context \times Item \rightarrow Rating$. (If user A scores 5 for item B in the context of a, it can be expressed as: $A \times a \times B \rightarrow 5$).Then, the context-aware recommendation system is formalized as: Hypothesis: $D_{j1} \ldots D_{j1} (l < n)$ for the target dimension space to be predicted, $D_{i1} \ldots D_{ik} (k < n)$ is the dimension space for the recommendation result. And when $\{D_{j1}, \ldots D_{j1}\} \cap \{D_{i1}, \ldots D_{ik}\} = \emptyset$ is satisfied, utility function $u(\cdot)$ is used to calculate the user's preference for the item under multi-dimensional context conditions, then the context-aware recommendation system finds those tuples $d_{i1}, \ldots d_{ik}$ with the highest preference value for $d_{j1}, \ldots d_{jl}$. As is in formula (1) [10]:

$$\begin{aligned} &\forall (d_{j1}, \ldots d_{j1}) \in D_{j1} \times \ldots \times D_{j1}, \\ &(d_{i1}, \ldots d_{ik}) = \underset{\substack{d'_{i1}, \ldots, d'_{ik} \in D_{i1}, \ldots, D_{ik} \\ d'_{j1}, \ldots, d'_{jl} = (d_{j1}, \ldots, d_{jl})}}{\arg\max} u(d'_1, \ldots d'_n) d \end{aligned} \tag{1}$$

2.3 Context Extraction

In the context of context-aware research and application, the context extraction process is in the data collection phase of the system. The extraction methods mainly include:

(1) Explicit extraction: directly obtaining the context information associated with the user and the item through physical device sensing, UI interface inquiry, and user active setting. For example, user age, gender, etc.

(2) Implicit extraction: Indirectly obtaining some context information by using existing data or environmental factors. For example, using GPS positioning or base station positioning to obtain location context information such as latitude and longitude, region, etc.; using timestamps of user behavior data to obtain time context information of user behavior occurrence (such as time of day, week,

season); And time context information, obtaining information such as the weather of the user's area from a third-party server.

(3) Inferring extraction: It is necessary to use statistical methods or data mining techniques to obtain some context information. For example, the Bayesian classifier is used to obtain context information about whether the user is at home or at a company location.

Displaying the acquired context information is more accurate, and it is possible to clearly collect context information such as time, but it is difficult to obtain a large amount of display information. Implicit fetching does not require direct interaction with the user and is therefore more common, and most contexts are obtained by this method. Extracting valid context information from the context set plays an important role in the recommendation task. Considering all the context information not only increases the extraction and storage burden of the context data, but also greatly increases the computational complexity of the context-aware recommendation system, and may also reduce the recommendation accuracy rate. In practical applications, the application environment is considered to adopt specific extraction methods or combination methods to extract context information.

3 User Preference Extraction

Preference is a tendency in people's minds, with obvious individual differences. User preference extraction is a key step in context-aware recommendation. At present, context preference extraction techniques are mainly divided into two types: quantitative analysis and qualitative analysis.

3.1 Contextual User Preference Extraction Based on Quantitative Analysis

A contextual user preference extraction technique based on quantitative analysis refers to the use of numerical scores to represent contextual user preferences. At present, most of them use multidimensional matrix and hierarchical tree models for analysis. Contextual user preference extraction analysis is further divided into two categories:

(1) Heuristic-based methods: neighborhood-based algorithms, clustering, and similarity calculations.
(2) Model-based methods: naive Bayes classifiers, matrix decomposition, etc. Extract contextual preferences by modeling user preferences.

3.2 Contextual User Preference Extraction Based on Qualitative Analysis

The contextual user preference extraction technique based on qualitative analysis can ignore the user's quantitative value of the preference of the item and its attributes, and extract the user's partial order relationship of any two specific items or their attributes from the perspective of logical reasoning and partial order model. Table 1 compares two contextual user preference extraction techniques.

Table 1. Comparison of advantages and disadvantages of two contextual user preference extraction techniques

Contextual user preference extraction	Advantages	Disadvantages
Quantitative analysis	Conducive to quantitative representation and calculation	Forming a full-order representation between contextual user preferences, not allowing weak-order representations, and it is difficult to visually describe the relationship between two specific context user preferences
Qualitative analysis	Representing the relationship between any two contextual users' preference instances and be able to logically reason	Digital quantized representation and calculation cannot be performed

4 Context Recommendation Generation Technology

Adomavicius et al. [9] proposed three effective partitioning methods based on context information in the recommendation generation process: contextual pre-filtering, contextual post-filtering, and contextual modeling.

(1) Context pre-filtering: refers to the recommendation algorithm first filtering out data unrelated to user preferences after acquiring data, and then processing the filtered data by using traditional recommendation techniques such as collaborative filtering to predict the user. Adomavicius et al. [9] used context pre-filtering method to filter multi-dimensional context data out of invalid data, and used traditional two-dimensional collaborative filtering method to make different recommendations for users in various non-contextual instances.
(2) Post-context filtering: After inputting the original data to the recommendation algorithm to calculate the recommendation result, the item that satisfies the target user context to the user is recommended.
(3) Context Modeling: It is the most effective context recommendation generation technique by incorporating context information into user interest models (e.g., tensor decomposition, naive Bayes, etc.) as part of the recommendation algorithm.

5 Summary

With the increasing personalization needs of Internet users, the problem of "information overload" is heating up year by year, and the recommendation system plays an increasingly important role in various fields. In recent years, the context-aware recommendation system introduces context information into the recommendation system to further improve recommendation accuracy and user satisfaction, and promotes the research of cross-disciplinary integration. It has become one of the most active branches in the research of recommendation systems, and has been gradually applied to many industrial field. Based on the analysis of traditional recommendation algorithms, this paper analyzes the research status and progress of context-based recommendation system, and gives the future development direction.

References

1. Adomavivius G, Tuzhilin A (2005) Personalization technlogies: a process -oriented perspective. Commun ACM 48(10):83–90
2. Chen L, Li G et al (2015) Perceptual recommendation algorithm based on context extraction. Comput Sci 42(10):90–95
3. He M, Liu Y et al (2017) Collaborative filtering recommendation based on context item score splitting. Comput Sci 44(3):247–253. (in Chinese)
4. Liu Q, Wu S, Wang L (2015) COT: contextual operating tensor for context-aware recommender systems. Association for the Advancement of Articial Intelligence, pp 203–209 (2015). (in Chinese)
5. Karatzoglou A, Amatriain X, Baltrunas L et al (2010) Multiverse recommendation: n-dimensional tensor factorization for context-aware collaborative filtering. In: Proceedings of the fourth ACM conference on recommender systems, pp 79–86
6. Koren Y, Bell R (2011) Advances in collaborative filtering. In: Recommender Systems Handbook. Springer, pp 145–186
7. Goldberg D, Nichols D, Oki BM et al (1992) Using collaboration filtering to weave an information tapestry. Commun ACM 35(12):61–70
8. Burke R (2002) Hybrid recommender systems: survey and experiments. User Model User-Adap Inter 12(4):331–370
9. Adomavicius G, Sankaranarayanan R et al (2005) Incorporating contextual information in recommender systems using a multidimensional approach. ACM Trans Inf Syst (TOIS) 23 (1):103–145
10. Adomavicius G, Tuzhilin A (2005) Toward the next generation of recommender systems: a survey of the state-of-the-art and possible extensions. IEEE Trans Knowl Data Eng (TKDE) 17(6):734–749

Matching Technology of Internet of Things Based on Multiple Linear Regression Model in Urban Management

Peilu Feng[1(✉)] and Pingquan Wang[1,2]

[1] Hohhot Minzu College, Hohhot 010051, China
fpenglu@163.com
[2] School of Computer and Information Management, Inner Mongolia University of Finance and Economics, Hohhot 010070, China

Abstract. The acceleration of urbanization leads to higher standards and requirements for Internet of Things matching technology. Based on this, the matching technology of Internet of things based on multiple linear regression model in urban management is put forward. Data in the Internet of Things are processed accurately. Wireless sensors with optimal functions are selected, and mathematical models are established and solved. Through experimental demonstration, it is concluded that the Internet of Things matching technology based on multiple linear regression model greatly reduces the cost of urban management.

Keywords: City management · Multiple linear regression model · Internet of Things · Matching technology

1 Introduction

The city is a space-time convergence point of regional population concentration, social economic activity and resource concentration [1, 2]. It is also a mark of human social civilization and historical development. It is also the epitome of the combination of social productivity and production tools and the development of science and technology, and it is a whole undertaking a number of services in a region. Today, with the rapid development of society, the process of urbanization in China is also accelerating [3]. A large number of rural and urban collectives are pouring into the city. The people of society have a high standard of living conditions in the city, and their appreciation of the taste of the city and the continuous improvement of the quality of life in the city [4, 5]. Domestic cities have become trading and gathering centers for people to exchange commodities [6, 7]. However, in the face of unreasonable urban management means, backward large-scale infrastructure construction, and increasingly blocked urban traffic, urban emergency system which is difficult to play its practical role, and urban control system which is difficult to improve, we need to solve these problems urgently [8–10].

Z. Xu et al. (Eds.): CSIA 2019, AISC 928, pp. 1228–1233, 2020.
https://doi.org/10.1007/978-3-030-15235-2_164

2 Matching Technology of Internet of Things Based on Multiple Linear Regression Model

2.1 Implementation of Internet of Things Data Precision Processing

In wireless sensors, nets are usually set in outdoor environments, and sometimes their environments may be extremely harsh. Nodes themselves are relatively small, and very vulnerable to damage. Because environmental conditions sometimes directly or indirectly affect the network settings, it is very easy to cause damage and paralysis of wireless sensors, there is no way to timely and accurately guarantee the speed of data communication in the Internet of things. The lack or even omission of Internet of Things data in wireless sensor communication is a research topic which is often concerned by people. Lack of IOT data will lead to the lack of integrated data in the network, and even in some joint data, the lack of one data will lead to the loss of information accuracy of other related data. Lack of data and data omission will limit the wide use of wireless sensor settings within a large range. However, on the other hand, in some key data storage, such as economic, public affairs and other fields, the lack of data will cause immeasurable losses.

2.2 Best Choice of Wireless Sensor

As the main organization unit of the Internet of things, wireless sensor technology is developing rapidly. Sensors have even been widely used in people's social life and work. Sensors can collect data to the maximum extent and communicate by means of data transmission. The inductor can also be designed as a system operation with high concentration and low loss rate. Wireless sensor communication is formed by a large number of centralized network layout. Each node can collect data parameters within its own range and transmit them according to the communication protocols associated with wireless sensors. The purpose of data communication between nodes is achieved. Finally, the data can be transmitted to the host terminal by wireless nodes. As shown in Fig. 1.

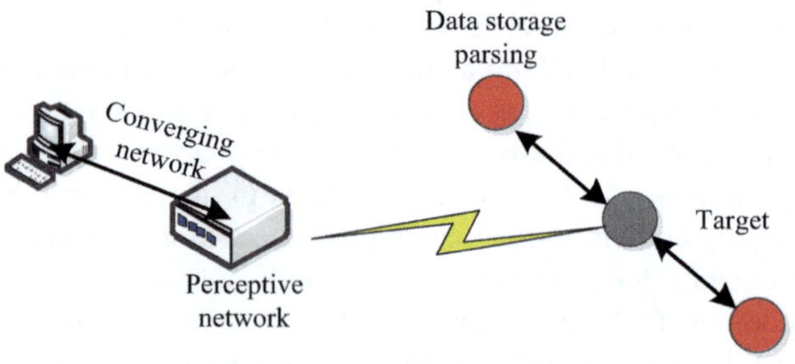

Fig. 1. Network composition diagram

Network settings are usually divided into collection points, router points and induction points. Sensor point is one of the most common settings, and its number range is very large. This is mainly achieved by collecting data and using router nodes for transmission. Router points are not necessarily set up, their existence is mainly determined by the actual environmental conditions around them. Router points also have some functions of induction points, and can transmit data to other nodes. The setup of wireless sensor nodes is shown in Fig. 2.

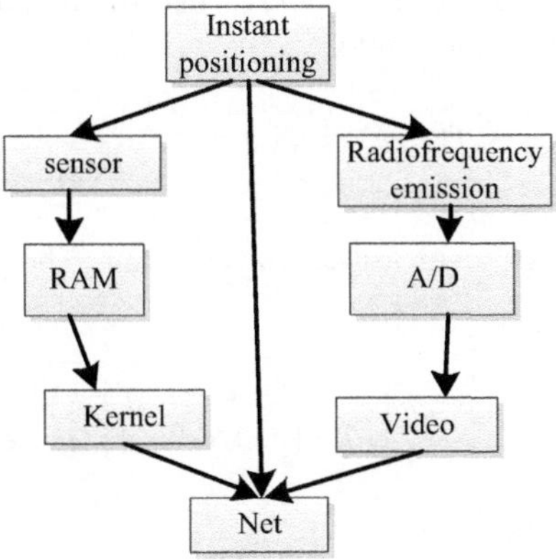

Fig. 2. Wireless sensor network settings

2.3 Establishment and Solution of Mathematical Model

SPSO is used to simulate the multivariate linear regression of common independent variables and dependent variables, and the results of the model are proved to be scientific and effective. In order to ensure the scientificity of the multiple linear regression model, the first step is to analyze the correlation of the information and data obtained, and the final result range is shown in Table 1.

Table 1. Area and scope of data coverage

System configuration	System operation	@sj@ design
Hsupa rate	kbpa	523
Downlink rate	kbps	1352
Communication channel	bd	Hsupa
Maximum path	km	139.10

Judging from the data obtained from previous analytical results, it is known that there is an obvious organic correlation among the original cost, transmission cost, packaging and loss cost, data and analytical cost and total micro-cost. Using the saliency test of horizontal communication a = 0.05, it is proved that the multivariate linear model is suitable for explaining the relationship between them. However, the obvious linear regression existed before the earliest independent variable and dependent variable, and the urban management prediction model in macro sense was obtained by SPSO method.

$$E(x/y) = 1^{'}p(y = 1/x) + 0 \bullet p(y = 0/x) = p(1/x) \tag{1}$$

E represents the corresponding weight, X represents the predicted value, Y represents the best measured value, and P represents the unknown quantity. In addition, the formula can also be translated into:

$$p(y = 1/x) = f(x, m) = \vee(x^{'}m) \equiv \frac{\longleftrightarrow}{1 + \exp(x^{'}m)} \exp(x^{'}m) \tag{2}$$

The m here represents the measurement constant. The formula also needs to be satisfied.

$$f(y/x, m) = \begin{cases} \triangleq (x, m),\ if\ y = 1 \\ \triangleq (1 - \vee(x^{'}, \mathrm{m})),\ if\ y = 0 \end{cases} \tag{3}$$

It can also be written as:

$$f(y/x, m) = \left\lfloor \vee(x^{'}m) \right\rfloor \overbrace{y = 1, 2, 3, 4 \cdots}^{x \neq 0, m \neq 0} \tag{4}$$

The final result is:

$$\begin{aligned} &f(y/x, m) = \left\lfloor \vee(x^{'}m) \right\rfloor^{y=1,2,3,4,\cdots} \\ &Inf(m/x, m) = yIn\lfloor \vee(x, m) \rfloor + (1 - y)In\left\lfloor 1 - \vee(x^{'}m) \right\rfloor \end{aligned} \tag{5}$$

3 Experimental Demonstration Analysis

In order to ensure the validity of the matching technology of the Internet of Things (IOT) based on the multiple linear regression model proposed in this paper, an experimental demonstration is carried out. In order to ensure the rigor of the experiment, the traditional matching technology of the Internet of Things is used as the experimental demonstration and comparison, and the urban cost is counted. The experimental results are shown in Fig. 3. According to the experimental data results, we can see that the matching technology course of the Internet of Things based on multiple linear regression model can minimize the effective cost of urban management and save national resources.

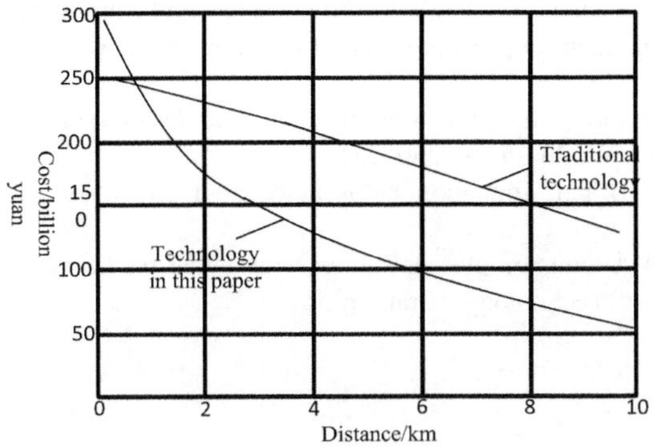

Fig. 3. Results of experiment

4 Conclusion

In this paper, the Internet of Things matching technology based on multiple linear regression model in urban management is preliminarily analyzed. Relying on the combination mechanism of Internet of Things matching in urban management, the matching technology of Internet of Things is optimized to realize the design of this paper according to the mathematical equation and data of multiple linear regression model. Experimental results show that the method designed in this paper is very effective. It is hoped that this study can provide a theoretical basis for the application of Internet of Things matching technology based on multiple linear regression model in urban management.

Acknowledgements. This research is funded by Scientific Studies Program of Higher Education of Inner Mongolia Municipality (NJZY18181).

References

1. Li-Jun F (2016) Energy consumption forecasting and energy saving analysis of urban buildings based on multiple linear regression model. Nat Sci J Xiangtan Univ
2. Man-Man H (2015) The evaluation of regional real estate investment based on a multiple linear regression model: the case of Wuhan urban agglomeration. Shanghai Land Res
3. Li L, Rong M, Zhang G (2015) An Internet of Things QoE evaluation method based on multiple linear regression analysis. In: International conference on computer science and education, IEEE
4. Chengwei T, He Z, Xiaomin Z, et al (2016) Analysis of logistics demand of shanghai based on multiple linear regression model. Logistics Technol
5. Sun Y (2018) Research and simulation of large data differentiation classification technology under the Internet of Things. In: International conference on intelligent transportation, IEEE Computer Society
6. Charpenay V, Nguyen H, Ibrahim M, et al (2018) Matching offerings and queries on an Internet of Things marketplace. In: European semantic web conference, Springer, Cham

7. Cheng Y, Tao F, Xu L, et al (2016) Advanced manufacturing systems: supply–demand matching of manufacturing resource based on complex networks and Internet of Things. Enterp Inf Syst 1–18
8. Rao J (2018) Exploring the innovation of urban road design under the background of smart city. Low Carbon World 150(9):250–251
9. Biyu W (2018) Urban simulation helps new smart city construction. Inf China Constr 21:14–15
10. Xiaoou D (2014) Urban complex design research under the background of smart city, MS., Harbin Institute of Technology, China, p 55

Optimization of Echo Parameter in Intelligent Instrument Under the Condition of Numerical Stability

Ke Song(✉)

Department of Electronic Engineering,
Sichuan Aerospace Vocational College, Chengdu, China
xucan264001@126.com

Abstract. The design of acquisition parameters is of great significance for intelligent instrument. In order to achieve better application of this method to formation fluid identification and reservoir evaluation, the observed echo amplitude and data kernel matrix are not affected by the diffusion coefficient and relaxation time. The FDTD method uses a set of finite difference equations to replace the Maxwell's rotation equation, that is, the solution of the differential equations is replaced by the solution of the difference equations. This substitution is meaningful only when the convergence and stability of the discrete differential equations are explained. Compared with the transmission of some broadband information, the use of a specific feature structure can increase the degree of freedom intelligent instrument, and give more detailed description of the echo parameter that can be used. By analyzing the basic principle of intelligent instrument, this paper uses the FDTD method to explain the signal of the instrument, and the simulation results are good.

Keywords: Echo parameter · Intelligent instrument · Numerical stability · FDTD method

1 Introduction

With the continuous development of science and technology, human society has entered the information age, which is more dependent on instruments. Modern instruments are characterized by digitalization, automation and intellectualization, and have developed rapidly [1, 2]. Because of the use of single-chip computer or micro-controller in intelligent instruments, many problems that were difficult to solve or simply impossible to solve by hardware logic can be solved by software very flexibly [3–5]. Because of the increasing memory capacity and working speed of the micro-computer, its data processing ability has been greatly improved. In this way, signal analysis technology can be introduced into intelligent instruments. The intelligent instruments can not only carry out the mentioned measurement, but also carry out complex data processing functions such as zero translation, average value, extremum calculation, statistical analysis and so on. It not only makes users from heavy workload.

Z. Xu et al. (Eds.): CSIA 2019, AISC 928, pp. 1234–1238, 2020.
https://doi.org/10.1007/978-3-030-15235-2_165

The data processing is liberated and the measuring accuracy of the instrument is effectively improved [6, 7].

Intelligent instrument has friendly man-machine conversation ability. Intelligent instruments use keyboards instead of switching switches in traditional instruments. Operators only need to input commands through keyboards to achieve certain measurement functions. At the same time, the intelligent instrument also tells the operator in time through the display screen about the convenient and intuitive operation. Intelligent instrument has self-test function and can provide more high quality information by reprocessing the measurement results [8]. The measurement process, software control and data processing functions of intelligent instruments make it easy to realize the multi-function of a single machine.

Geophysical technology is mainly based on quantum theory and classical theory [9]. It has been used to measure the magnetic moment [10]. Subsequently, intelligent instrument becomes an important means to study the geology structure between various substances. Geophysical technology combined with the FDTD method makes the use of pop more extensive, and has also led to the development of related technology.

2 Echo Parameter Optimization

Make $p(t)$ a specific implementation of $p(t; Z)$.

$$p(t) = \sum_{n=-\infty}^{\infty} P(n)e^{j\frac{2\pi}{T}nt}, t \in [0, T] \tag{1}$$

The integrator impact response is

$$h(t) = rect\left(\frac{2M}{T}t - 1\right) \tag{2}$$

The *rect* is the following rectangle window function

$$rect(x) = \begin{cases} 1, & for - 1 \leq x \leq 1, \\ 0, & otherwise. \end{cases} \tag{3}$$

The sampling interval T_S is $\frac{1}{N}$ times the initial time length in the low speed sampling step, and the sampling rate of the overall RD architecture is N/T HZ.

3 Numerical Stability Conditions

Stability refers to finding a condition that satisfies a discrete interval. Under this condition, the difference is bounded between the numerical solution of the difference equation and the strict solution of the original equation. The following discussion will give the stability time and the stability condition of the space step which limit the FDTD method.

The Courant stability condition must be satisfied for FDTD computation. The Courant stability condition of the three-dimensional FDTD problem under uniform mesh partition is

$$\upsilon \Delta t \leq \frac{\delta}{\sqrt{3}} \quad (4)$$

Among them, δ represents the mesh size of uniform mesh generation, and υ represents the phase velocity of wave field.

$$\upsilon = \frac{1}{\sqrt{\lambda \mu}} \quad (5)$$

The upper finished form can get the limitation of time step

$$\Delta t \leq \delta \sqrt{\frac{\lambda \mu}{3}} \quad (6)$$

Finishing the equation can get another form

$$\gamma \geq \frac{3}{\mu} (\frac{\Delta t}{\delta}) \quad (7)$$

The combination of three dimensional problems can be obtained

$$\Delta t \ll \delta \sqrt{\frac{\mu \sigma t}{6}} \quad (8)$$

4 Simulation

In order to better show the distribution of magnetic field and the outward diffusion of magnetic field at different times after the current is switched off. The contour map of vertical magnetic field intensity distribution was drawn at six moments after 1 s, 10 s, 100 s, 200 s, 400 s and 1000 s (Fig. 1).

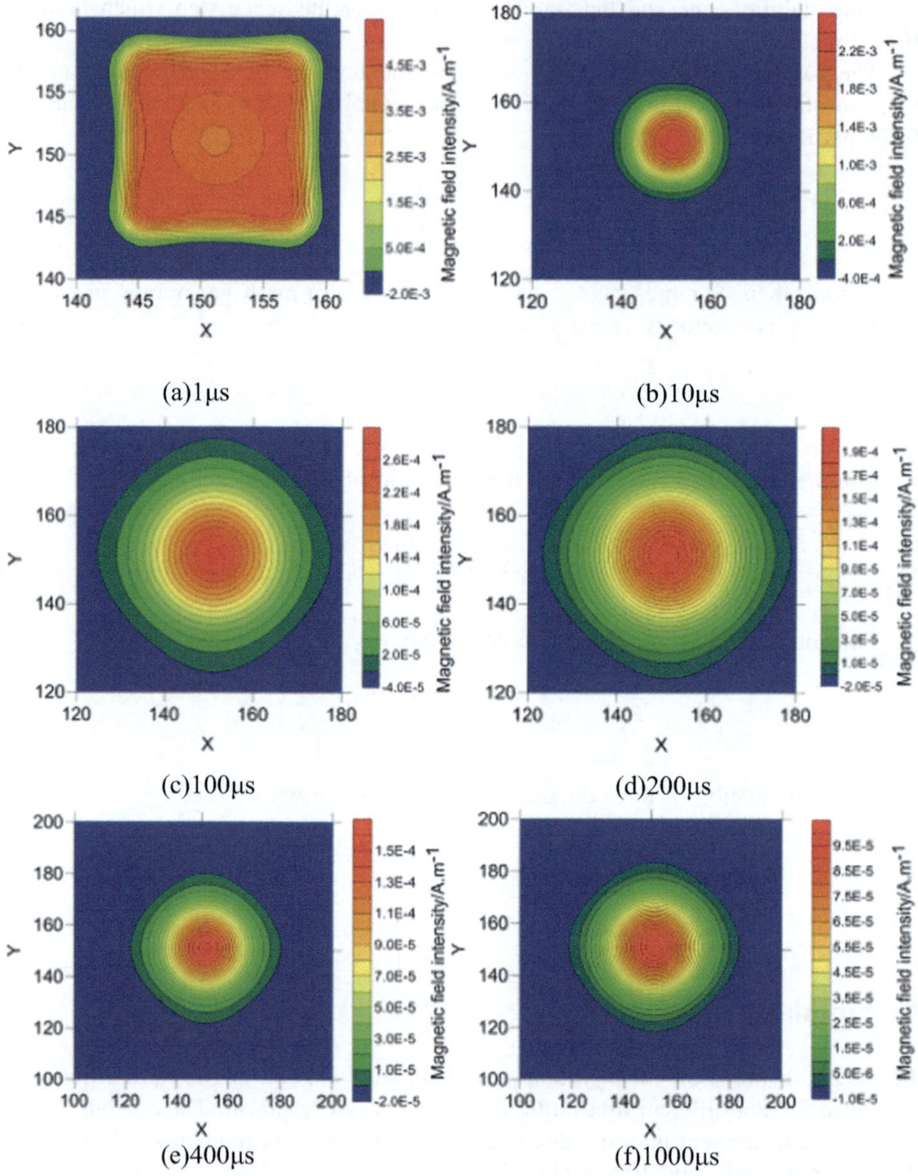

Fig. 1. The distribution of the vertical magnetic field of the ground at different times

5 Conclusion

With the introduction of the numerical stability theory and the pioneering application in the field of data acquisition, the optimization of echo parameter is applied to the field of broadband detection, which is a good solution to the defects of the ADC sampling frequency of the hardware. On the basis of numerical stability theory, the analysis of the collected signals is used to determine its structural characteristics. According to the detection mode of dynamic spectrum, the corresponding state of the related spectrum is evaluated without response to the initial signal, so that it satisfies the probability constraint conditions used in the detection of the spectrum state. Thus, a reliable solution for wide common detection is obtained by improving the scope of application of the spectrum monitoring belt.

References

1. Ahmad K, Hassan F (2016) Radial-basis-function-based nuclear magnetic resonance heavy oil viscosity prediction model for a Kuwait viscous oil field. Interpretation 4(2):81–92
2. Feng Q, He Z (2015) Development and application of CIFLog-CMR nuclear magnetic resonance data processing and interpretation software. Well Logging Technol 37(5):513–524 (in Chinese)
3. Baidyk T, Kussul E (2014) Flat image recognition in the process of microdevice assembly. Pattern Recogn Lett 25(1):107–117
4. Pantazis D, Joshi A (2017) Comparison of landmark-based and automatic methods for cortical surface registration. Neuro Image 49(3):2479–2493
5. Lindstr MA, Andersson CD (2015) Bone contrast optimization in magnetic resonance imaging using experimental design of ultra-short echo-time parameters. Chemometr Intell Lab Syst 125:33–39
6. Ongenae F, Looy SV (2016) Time series classification for the prediction of dialysis in critically ill patients using echo state networks. Eng Appl Artif Intell 26(3):984–996
7. Garcia-Piquer A, Ribas I (2014) Artificial intelligence for the EChO mission planning tool. Exp Astron 40(2):1–24
8. Coppe A, Haftka RT, Kim NH (2017) Optimization of distribution parameters for estimating probability of crack detection. J Aircr 46(6):2090–2097
9. Wu HT, Jiao CQ (2017) Transient electromagnetic disturbance induced on the ports of intelligent component of electronic instrument transformer due to switching operations in 500 kV GIS substations. IEEE Access 5(99):5104–5112 (in Chinese)
10. Chouikhi N, Ammar B (2017) PSO-based analysis of echo state network parameters for time series forecasting. Appl Soft Comput 55:211–225

Development of Position Detection Sensor Based on STM32

Jian Huang(✉) and Guangpeng Zhang

School of Mechanical and Precision Instrument Engineering,
Xi'an University of Technology, Xi'an 710048, China
565200245@qq.com

Abstract. To accurately detect the location of moving targets. Eight photoelectric sensors ST188 are arranged in a row. When an object passes directly above it, the output voltage of ST188 will change obviously. The voltage is connected to the A/D acquisition pin of STM32 to determine the position of the object according to the change of voltage. By adding a photosensitive detection circuit, the threshold of voltage detection can be adjusted in real time to achieve intelligent control. By introducing Bluetooth module, the communication between multiple detection modules can be realized, and a photoelectric sensor array can be formed to achieve a wider range of position detection. The test results show that the sensor module can detect the position of moving objects accurately and quickly, and has certain practical value.

Keywords: Position detection · Photoelectric sensor · Photosensitive · Bluetooth module

1 Introduction

In engineering practice and experiment, the location of moving objects is often detected. At present, there are two kinds of commonly used angle detection methods, the first is to rely on the geometry of the extract body to achieve, the second is to rely on the detection of the state of the object to achieve. In the first category, most of the algorithms used in pattern recognition and image correlation, such as pixel recursion and block matching, can estimate motion translation vectors or rotation angles between consecutive frames using affine transformation models. The second type is mainly realized by sensors, such as Hall sensor or photoelectric sensor [1–3], for the measurement of motor speed and position.

On the basis of previous studies, this paper proposes to use eight photoelectric sensors to form a row, which can detect the position of objects moving in a straight line. STM32F103RBT6 microprocessor is used as master control. Because ST188 is greatly affected by light and shade, a photosensitive detection circuit is introduced to detect the current brightness in real time and adjust the threshold of detection voltage of ST188 intelligently. All the above modules together form a position detection module. A sensor array is formed by combining multiple position detection modules. Bluetooth module is used to realize the communication and wireless interconnection between each detection module, which can detect the position of a moving object in a plane or in a larger range.

Z. Xu et al. (Eds.): CSIA 2019, AISC 928, pp. 1239–1244, 2020.
https://doi.org/10.1007/978-3-030-15235-2_166

2 System Design Block Diagram

The system design block diagram is shown in Fig. 1. The STM32F103RBT6 is the main control and the photoelectric sensor ST188 is used to detect the position of the object. The collected information is converted to A/D acquisition pin with voltage value connected to STM32F103RBT6. Photosensitivity is used to detect illumination in the current situation. When the illumination is different, the voltage value is different when no object passes through the ST188. Generally, a threshold value [4, 5] is adopted between the voltage value of an object directly above the object and the voltage value of an object directly above the object. Because of the addition of photosensitivity, the threshold will be a variable value. Intelligent control can be realized by adjusting the threshold intelligently according to the photosensitive acquisition value to ensure accurate, effective and real-time detection. By adding Bluetooth module, the interconnection of multiple detection modules can be realized to form a larger detection array.

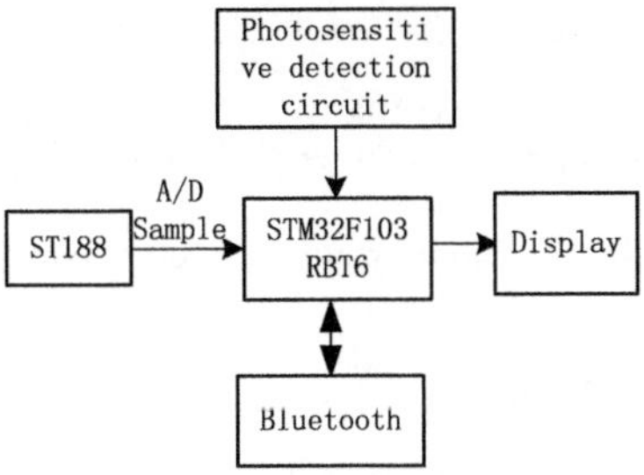

Fig. 1. System block diagram

3 Detailed Design

3.1 Design Circuit of Photoelectric Sensor ST188

The design circuit of the photoelectric sensor is shown in Fig. 2. Only one ST188 circuit diagram is drawn in the diagram, and the detection principle of the other methods is the same as that of the [6, 7]. The ST188 is composed of a light-emitting diode and a photosensitive triode. When illuminated, the transistor is close to conduction, and the AD0 outputs low level; when illuminated, the AD0 outputs high level. In practical application, ST188 receives and sends in one, so when there is object occlusion, there will be reflected light on the phototransistor. Because of different shielding materials, such as black paper or white paper, the amount of light reflected is different. So ST188 will not output an absolute high voltage or low level, it will only output a close value. So we often connect this pin to the A/D acquisition pin of STM32 to collect voltage, or to the comparator to get high and low levels.

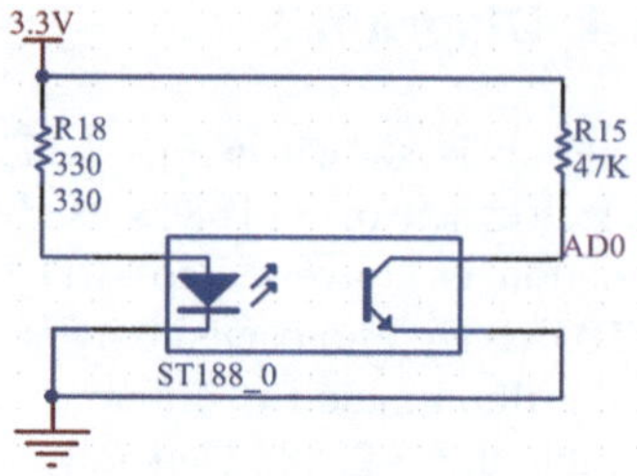

Fig. 2. ST188 circuit diagram of photoelectric sensor

3.2 Photosensitive Detection Circuit

The photosensitive detection circuit is shown in Fig. 3. Photoresistor R62 and resistor R61 are connected in series in the figure. The value of photoresistor varies with the brightness. Then the voltage value collected on AD8 will change. According to the different voltage value, the current brightness can be judged.

Fig. 3. Photosensitive detection circuit

3.3 Wireless Bluetooth Module

The wireless Bluetooth module is shown in Fig. 4. The Bluetooth module can receive and send data from RXD and TXD through serial port. The longest distance of wireless communication can reach 20 m.

Fig. 4. Wireless Bluetooth module

3.4 STM32F103RBT6

The main control adopts STM32F103RBT6, and is based on the Cortex-M3 kernel, which is a 32 bit microprocessor. The main frequency is 72 MHz, which contains 16 channels of A/D acquisition. The A/D of each channel is 12 bits, with 3 serial ports. In the circuit design, Bluetooth module is connected to serial port 3, eight ST188 voltage outputs are connected to AD0-AD7, and one photosensitive output terminal is connected to AD8. The PB port is connected to the TFT2.4 inch LCD, and its interface is compatible with 1602 and 12864 LCD interface [8].

4 Software

4.1 Software Design Flow Chart

The software design flow chart is shown in Fig. 5. First, the current illumination is read through the photosensitive detection circuit. The lower limit of the threshold is determined, and the read value is converted to the voltage value, which is increased by 0.5 V (empirical value, which can be adjusted appropriately according to the actual situation) as the threshold, so as to distinguish whether there is an object passing over ST188. If an object passes, the location of the moving object can be determined according to the location of the ST188 [9]. If the 8 photoelectric sensor ST188 is enough, no Bluetooth communication is needed. If the 8 ST188 is not enough, a group of 8 ST188 will be added to form 2 sets of ST188, a total of 16. It can realize 16 sensors in a straight line or 8 ST188 in two parallel lines. If not enough, it can be added. The combination and installation position of sensors can be determined according to actual needs. The communication between multiple sensors is realized by Bluetooth module.

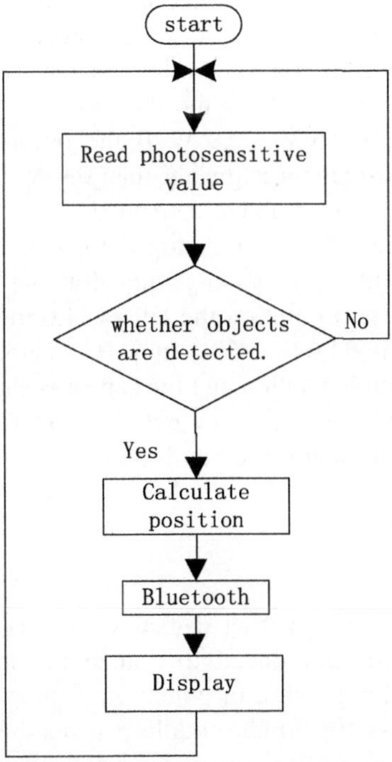

Fig. 5. Software design flow chart

If the moving object is not detected, the photosensitive value is re read and the threshold is adjusted in real time. Prepare for the next test.

5 Test Results

In the Altium Designer in the CPCB in the set in the Altium Designer, is can can can can can can can can can can can can can be be be the meta device and installed debugging, the the the view, in the the example, in the the example, the the the example, the the the the example, and the the example, and the the time, the example, the example, the the the example, the the the the example, the the the example.

Table 1. Output voltage value of photoelectric sensor in different environments

Environmental	Light on	Light off	Outdoor morning	Outdoor middle	Outdoor afternoon
Unshielded output voltage (V)	2.3	2.5	2.6	2.8	2.7
Shielded output voltage (V)	0.2	0.3	0.4	0.6	0.5

As can be seen from the table, the output voltage of the sensor is different in different environments with or without objects, and it is constantly changing with the change of the environment. Therefore, it is very necessary to adjust the threshold appropriately, so that intelligent control can be realized. Normally, the output voltage of the occlusion is added with 0.5 V as the threshold. For example, the threshold of outdoor morning is 0.4 V + 0.5 V = 0.9 V. If the output voltage measured by the software in the current environment is greater than 0.9 V, there is no object above the sensor; if less than, there is object above the sensor.

Assuming the location of ST188 on the top left is the origin O point, eight ST188s are arranged horizontally with equal spacing when drawing PCB. The distance between the second ST188 and the zero point on the left is 34.6 mm, and the third ST188 and the zero point on the left is 34.6*2 = 69.2 mm. By analogy, the corresponding relationship between the measured position and the sensor is shown in Table 1. The unit of distance in the table is mm. In order to get the voltage value of a certain point accurately, the mean filtering algorithm can be used.

6 Conclusion

In this paper, a linear array of position detection sensors is designed, and a photosensitive detection circuit is introduced to realize intelligent adjustment of object detection, avoiding manual regulation of potentiometers and realizing intelligent [10]. The introduction of wireless Bluetooth module realizes the combination and arrangement of larger arrays. Because of the use of wireless transmission, a large number of wired connections are avoided. It can be applied to the object detection of belt conveyor belt, motor rotor detection, intelligent anti-theft and so on. It has certain practical value.

References

1. Shi Z, Chen P et al (2004) High precision digital velocity measurement and dynamic position detection algorithm. J Tsinghua Univ (Nat Sci Ed) 44(8):1021–1024
2. Zhang Y, Liu J, Chen C (2003) Research on high precision position detection and location technology. J SE Univ (Nat Sci Ed) 33(4):495–497
3. Jin J, Liu Z, Lin Y (2012) Design of photoelectric sensor characteristic parameter testing system. J Sens Technol 25(12):1678–1683
4. Xu Z, Ge W et al (2009) Design of position detection system based on CMOS camera and FPGA. LCD Disp 24(5):746–750
5. Lu W, Wang W et al (2014) Design of wireless photoelectric sensor based on STM32. Sens Microsyst 33(9):74–80
6. Zhe Z, Yong X et al (2013) Measurement of wind speed based on photoelectric sensor. Meas Control Technol 32(7):38–40
7. Zhang S, Zhang C (2014) Maize disease identification method based on local discriminant mapping algorithm. J Agric Eng 30(11):167–172
8. Li Y, Yu Y (2010) Vision-based finger position detection technology. Comput Eng Des 31 (3):555–558
9. Jiang S, Cao Y et al (2013) Research on micro-high precision fiber Bragg grating earth pressure sensor. China Laser 40(4):1–6
10. Pan Q, Zhang L (2012) An object position detection system based on position sensitive elements. Comput Meas Control 20(7):1784–1786

Study on Intelligent Ventilator

Na Wang[1], Rui Wang[2], and Yuanyuan Wang[1(✉)]

[1] Department of Anesthesiology, The First Hospital of Jilin University, Changchun, China
lilyly12345@163.com
[2] Department of Computer Science, Jilin Business and Technology College, Changchun, China

Abstract. Mechanical ventilation plays an important role in life support for critically ill patients, but it has some complications. With the development of intelligent control and respiratory detection technology, intelligent ventilator has become possible, and it has solved many difficulties encountered in mechanical ventilation and brought comfort and convenience to patients.

Keywords: Intelligent ventilator · Intelligent control · Respiratory detection · Mechanical ventilation

1 Introduction

Using breathing machine for mechanical ventilation is to maintain basic breathing function of patients without spontaneous breath or with weak spontaneous breath, such as anesthetic state or critically ill state. It is the treatment of respiratory failure, but with long duration of mechanical ventilation, a series of complications might occur. It has been a problem of the goal of medical staff, how to obtain the advantages, avoid the disadvantages, reduce the occurrence of complications as far as possible. With the emergence and wide application of artificial intelligence, people try to combine artificial intelligence with ventilator to solve the problems.

2 Definition and History of Ventilator

Ventilator is a device that can replace, change or control respiration of an individual. By adjusting breathing parameters, including breathing frequency, tidal volume, airway pressure, etc., ventilator can improve respiratory function, provide oxygen, remove carbon dioxide, reduce respiratory function consumption and save heart reserve [1]. It not only plays an important role in various hospitals, as an essential respiratory support medical equipment in clinical medicine, but also enters the homes of patients with respiratory diseases.

In the mid-1600 s, Hooke inserted a tube into the dog's respiratory tract and vented it through a pair of bellows, finding that the dog could survive for more than an hour [2]. Tossach managed to resuscitate a patient with mouth-to-mouth breathing in 1774. In 1928, Drinker and Joh developed an artificial assisted breathing device called iron

Z. Xu et al. (Eds.): CSIA 2019, AISC 928, pp. 1245–1250, 2020.
https://doi.org/10.1007/978-3-030-15235-2_167

lung. It was followed by Bennett PR-IA and Bird mark VII as representative's first generation of breathing machine. [3] The breathing machine invented by Engstrom was the representative of the second generation of the breathing machine. It has been used from the end of the 20th century till the third generation of breathing machine appeared. Now the ventilator has upgraded to intelligent breathing machine. In this process, with the comprehensive understanding of respiratory physiology, as well as the improvement of scientific and technological level, the function of the ventilator is increasingly improved, and the range of its use is increasingly expanded. The ventilator developed from the endotracheal intubation ventilation to more powerful function. The adjustment of respiratory parameter was more detailed, the ventilation mode was more diversified, and the use method was more intelligent than old types.

3 Application of Intelligent Control Technology

Since the 20th century, with the progress of social science, control technology has developed vigorously and been introduced into mechanical ventilation, that is, electronic controlled volumetric ventilator, marking the ventilator from mechanical control into the precise electronic control. Then, in the clinical research and with experience accumulation, intelligent control was gradually developed and applied to the breathing machine. The performance of intelligent breathing machine was been improved to treat the patients with severe respiratory failure. At the same time, reducing the complications of mechanical ventilation was of special significance.

3.1 Respiratory Signal Detection Technology

Respiratory signal detection technology is an important part of mechanical ventilation technology. Clinical monitoring technology is an important indicator, because synchronization with breathing assisted ventilation only can be achieved by measuring respiratory signal, at the same time tide volume, respiratory frequency, airway pressure and other important physiological breathing indexes must be got, with the aid of disease diagnosis or therapy, etc. Many changes may occur in and out of the body as the body breathes, and these changes can be observed and applied to detecting respiratory signals. The methods of respiratory signal detection are various, and they are being innovated and optimized.

3.1.1 Respiratory Impedance Detection Technology

Impedance respiratory detection is the most commonly used method in current respiratory detection technology. The principle is that breathing movement is accompanied by relaxation of the chest wall muscle, the chest wall will be deformed alternately, and the electrical impedance of the chest will also produce corresponding changes. Respiratory impedance is directly proportional to lung volume. An alternating high-frequency electrical signal is added at both ends of the measuring electrode to detect its change and extract respiratory signal. Wang et al. designed a dual-frequency impedance respiratory detection system. They attached a pair of electrodes to the chest, respectively intervening the constant current carrier current of high frequency and relatively low frequency, and then introduced the modulated carrier voltage signal into the amplifying circuit through the external device, and finally processed the signal into the respiratory parameter display. Each heartbeat is generated by a wave front passing through different structures of the heart, and the activation/inactivation of these waves corresponds to different waves in the ECG. The ECG can be obtained by using multiple electrodes, providing a spatial perspective. However, the measured electrocardiogram does not completely reflect the heart's point activity, which is affected by respiration.

Studies have shown that respiration not only causes changes in the length of the heart cycle (physiological effect, through the main body), but also causes changes in the fluctuating shape caused by chest movement. The main reason is that the changes in lung volume during the respiratory cycle change the electrical impedance of the thorax, and the changes in cardiac vectors due to the changes in the displacement and orientation of the heart, as well as the changes in the autonomic nervous system caused by respiration. Therefore, changes in the peak value of electrocardiogram induced by changes in chest movement and heart position during the respiratory cycle can be observed by ECG. There are mainly three algorithms to get respiratory information from ECG: the algorithm based on principal component analysis, the algorithm based on r-r interval and QRS amplitude. Moody et al. obtained the frequency and waveform of respiratory signals from multi-channel ECG by studying the change of ECG vector and reference ECG vector due to respiration. Some studies have proposed the method of obtaining respiratory signal through adaptive filtering based on single lead ECG. This method can take the R wave amplitude time series and r-r interval time series extracted from ECG as the input of the filter, and estimate the parameters of respiratory movement through adaptive filtering. In recent years, Philip Langley et al. proposed PCA as a tool to analyze the change of electrocardiogram in accordance with the beat, and applied it to get respiratory information from ECG. PCA was used to describe the variability of ECG features, p wave, QRS complex and t wave caused by respiration.

3.1.2 Acquisition Through Breathing Sound

According to the European respiratory association, breath sounds include many sounds, such as the sound of breathing, and the sound of breathing muscles, but not the sound of breathing. Lung sounds are all breathing sounds that are heard or detected through the chest wall or inside the chest cavity, including breathing and other sounds detected at this location. The sound of the windpipe is the sound heard or detected in the outer part of the windpipe. During breathing, the airflow in the respiratory tract is correlated with the average voltage of sound. The sound of the trachea shows the dynamic characteristics of noise with broadband spectrum, and contains multiple resonant peaks. The sound of the trachea can show clear inhalation and exhalation phases, and its frequency content is higher than that of lung sounds. Therefore, the respiratory state can be determined by modeling the average value of airflow and sound voltage in the trachea.

3.1.3 Photoelectric Volume Pulse Wave

Photoelectric volume pulse wave recording (PPG) is a technique to detect microvascular volume changes in tissue using photoelectric technology. The researchers used a multichannel physiologic recorder collection at the same time by tem photoelectric pulse sensor and temperature sensor for human respiratory wave and PPG signals, wavelet transform the PPG signal decomposition, the decomposed of addition of approximate signal reconstruction for a breath, and then with the modified fast Fourier transform of frequency estimation method from the rate of respiration can be derived from the wave signals.

3.2 Intelligent Control of Breathing

Mechanical ventilation technology development, already has the original open-loop mode was upgraded to a closed loop mode, can through the feedback information of intelligent control, as shown in figure a simple breathing machine model for intelligence, most intelligent effects of breathing machine mainly include control device and device, patients breathe through various tests detect respiratory information feedback to the controller, the controller in real time adjustment and effector, effector is breathing machine parameters are adjusted to give patients (Fig. 1).

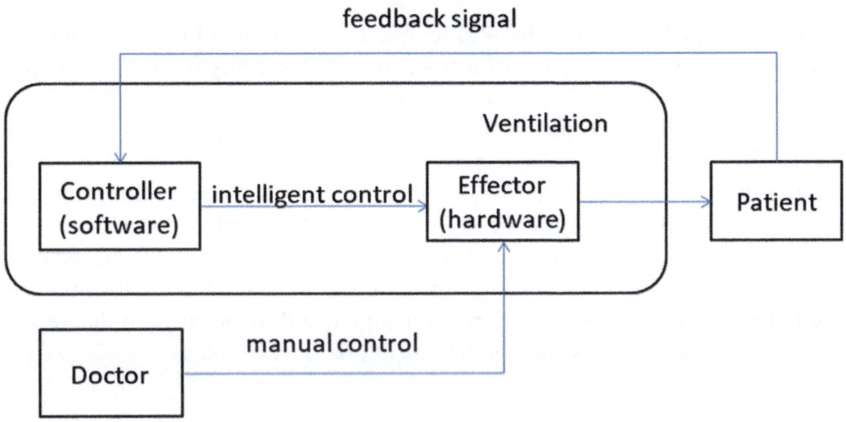

Fig. 1. VAV adjustment

Of course, there are various ventilator modes, and the adaptive support ventilation (ASV) adaptation is relatively extensive. Tehrani first described in 1991 that the design was designed to minimize the working rate of breathing, simulating natural breathing and stimulating spontaneous breathing. ASV is a type of servo-controlled ventilation mode, which USES the microcomputer in the ventilator to continuously monitor the respiratory status of patients, and automatically adjusts the ventilation parameters based on the respiratory mechanics and the degree of autonomous breathing to improve the degree of human-machine coordination. ASV simplifies the setting and adjustment of ventilation parameters as much as possible, avoiding operational differences. At the same time, it provides ventilation support of different degrees from complete control ventilation to complete autonomous respiration, because it can adapt to different conditions of patients. Patients are always in the state of minimum respiratory function until evacuation. In addition, ASV added some expert rules, such as limiting frequency and tidal volume, and reduced the risk of automatic pressure ventilation. In a sense, this model can be thought of as an intelligent target solution, or more properly a hybrid system (that is, using mathematical models and artificial intelligence). In the United States, the only commercial mechanical ventilation model to date is the installation of SmartCare/PS on the dragger ventilator, whose target program relies solely on expert-based systems. SmartCare/PS, as a special stress support mode, is designed for automatic offline use. The off-line controller USES preset acceptable ranges including spontaneous breathing rate, tidal volume and tidal end carbon dioxide tension, automatically adjusting the suction pressure to keep the patient in a "comfortable breathing zone". In addition, there are many other models, such as positive pressure ventilation and derivative model of dual-phase airway, dual-control ventilation, proportional assisted ventilation, etc. In recent years, modeling and simulation technology has also made great breakthroughs in the research of lung ventilation.

4 Summary and Outlook

Without breathing, there would be no life. Mechanical ventilation would flourish and continuously advance the progress of medical health, especially in the field of intensive critical care and anesthesia. Traditional mechanical ventilation in saving lives has some disadvantages, such as invasion, respiratory tract infection, diaphragm function decline, extubation difficulty, etc. In order to solve these problems, we must rely on the power of the high-tech to improve the level of intelligent control and optimization control scheme of existing ventilation technology. The synchronization performance of auxiliary ventilation and comfortable medical surgical development and rapid recovery are urgent to be improved. We have made great progress in the field of intelligent ventilator research, but it is still not perfect. Many of them are still in the stage of theoretical and clinical trials, which requires the continuous efforts of researchers.

References

1. Xie J, Zhang L (2014) The current situation and prospects of mechanical ventilator industry. China Med Device Inf 2:10–20
2. Liang X, Liang G (2008) The current situation and prospects of mechanical ventilation industry in China-a investigation report based on aeonmed. China Med Device Inf 14:30–36
3. Snider GL (1989) History perspective on mechanical ventilation: from simple life support system to ethical dilemma. Am Rev Respir Dis 140:52–57
4. Wang JB, Li T (2015) Design of dual frequency impedance type respiratory measurement system. Med Equip China 30:28–29
5. Sornmo L, Laguna P (2005) Bioelectrical signal processing in cardiac and neurological applications. Elsevier Academic Press, London
6. Noriega M, Martinez JP (2010) Respiration effect on single and multi lead ECG delineation strategies. In: Conference proceedings of IEEE engineering in medicine and biology society, pp 3575–3578
7. Hahn G, Sipinkov I, Baisch F, Hellige G (1995) Changes in the thoracic impedance distribution under different ventilatory conditions. Physiol Meas 16:161–173

8. Pallas-Areny R, Colominas-Balague J, Rosell FJ (1989) The effect of respiration-induced heart movements on the ECG. IEEE Trans Biomed Eng 36:585–590
9. Eckberg DL (2003) The human respiratory gate. J Physiol 548:339–352
10. Moody GB, Mark RG, Zoccola A (1985) Derivation of respiratory signals from multi-lead ECGs. Comput Cardiol 12:113–116
11. Varanini M, Emdin M, Allegri F et al (1990) Adaptive filtering of ECG signal for deriving respiratory activity. In: Computers in cardiology. IEEE Computer Society, Chicago, pp 621–624
12. Carro E, Laguna P, Wohlfart B (2000) Vectorcardiographic loop alignment and the measurement of morphologic beat-to-beat variability in noisy signal. IEEE Trans BME 47:497–506
13. Langley P, Bowers EJ, Murray A (2010) Principal component analysis as a tool for analyzing beat-to-beat changes in ECG features: application to ECG-derived respiration. IEEE Trans. Biomed. Eng. 57:821–829
14. Sovijarvi ARA, Dalmasso F, Vanderschoot J, Malmberg LP, Righini G, Stoneman SAT (2000) Definition of terms for applications of respiratory sounds. Eur Respir Rev 10:597–661
15. Beck R, Rosenhouse G, Mahagnah M, Chow RM, Cugell DW, Gavriely N (2005) Measurements and theory of normal tracheal breath sounds. Ann Biomed Eng 33:1344–1351
16. Pasterkamp H, Kraman SS, Wodicka GR (1997) Respiratory Sounds: Advances beyond the Stethoscope. Am J Respir Crit Care Med 156:974–987
17. Yap YL, Mussavi Z (2002) Accoustic airflow estimation from tracheal sound power. In: Electrical and computer engineering, IEEE CCECE, Canadian, vol 2, pp 1073–1076
18. Huang JP (2010) Human physiological parameters extraction research that based on the pulse signal. Harbin Institute of Technology, Harbin, pp 26–36
19. Zhao S-W, Gao F, Deng L (2016) Respiratory rate extracted from photoplethysmography signals by using wavelet transform and fast Fourier transform. Chin J Med Phys 33:39–43
20. Xiao M, Cai G (2008) A new method for the detection of the respiratory signal. J Biomed Eng Res 27:188–192
21. Tehrani FT (1991) Automatic control of an artificial respirator. In: Proceedings of IEEE EMBS Conference, vol 13, pp 1738–1739
22. Tehrani FT (2004) The origin of adaptive support ventilation. Int. J. Artif. Organs 27:709–716
23. Tassaux D, Dalmas E, Gratadour P et al (2002) Patient-ventilator interactions during partial ventilatory support: a preliminary study comparing the effects of adaptive support ventilation with synchronized intermittent mandatory ventilation plus inspiratory pressure support. Crit Care Med 30:801–807
24. Chatburn RL, Mireles-Cabodevila E (2011) Closed-loop control of mechanical ventilation: description and classification of targeting schemes. Respir Care 56:85–102
25. Rose L, Presneill JJ, Cade JF (2007) Update in computer-driven weaning from mechanical ventilation. Anesth Intensive Care 35:213–221

Analysis on the Importance of Price Support-Resistance Levels of Chinese Stock Market Based on the Proposed Information Granulation and FCM Clustering Algorithm

Xianchang Wang[1], Jiayu Wang[1], Xuhong Lin[1], Lin Xue[1], Meiying Zhu[1], Qianqian Song[1], and Xin Wang[2(✉)]

[1] School of Sciences, Dalian Ocean University, Dalian 116026, China
[2] College of Science, Dalian Maritime University, Dalian 116026, China
xenawang7811@hotmail.com

Abstract. With growing popularity of Big Data Analysis, Predicting the Support-Resistance Levels of stock prices is important problem, due to an investor in stock market ideally should get maximum returns on the investment made and for that should know how importance of Support-Resistance Levels. In this paper, we analysis the significance of price Support-Resistance Levels of Chinese Stock Market based on the proposed information granulation and FCM fuzzy clustering algorithm. The Proposed stock information granulation method considers the observed historical closing price of day K-line and 15-Minutes K-line. The research data set that has been used in this study is from Chinese Stock Market. Through analysis of experimental study, we found that the effectiveness of Support-Resistance Levels is nearly about Two-thirds.

Keywords: Fuzzy logic · Information granulation · Chinese Stock Market · Support-Resistance Levels · Stock data

1 Introduction

Fuzzy clustering based on fuzzy logic plays an important role in machine learning applications, such as text mining [1–3], graph clustering [4], web analysis [5–7], image segmentation [8–10], computational biology [11], stock data [12–15], and many others.

Predicting the Support-Resistance Levels of stock prices is important problem [16, 17], due to an investor in stock market ideally should get maximum returns on the investment made and for that should know how importance of Support-Resistance Levels. In this paper, we analysis the significance of price Support-Resistance Levels of Chinese Stock Market based on the proposed information granulation and FCM fuzzy clustering algorithm [18].

There are a lot of historical data of a stock usually, however, the most historical data is not valuable for predicting the Support-Resistance Levels. Thus, various information granulation methods [19–22] on stock data for reducing the number of data to be used. However, the traditional information granulation methods are not suitable for the reduction of stock data, Due to the traditional information granulation methods

Z. Xu et al. (Eds.): CSIA 2019, AISC 928, pp. 1251–1255, 2020.
https://doi.org/10.1007/978-3-030-15235-2_168

usually consider the observed historical closing price of day K-line. Thus, this paper proposed a new stock information granulation method considering the observed historical closing price of day K-line and 15-Minutes K-line.

2 The Proposed Stock Information Granulation Method

Let XD_t be the t-th observed historical closing price of day K-line, let XW_t be the t-th closing price of week K-line, let XM_t be the t-th closing price of month K-line, let XY_t be the t-th closing price of year K-line, let $X15$ be the t-th closing price of 15-Minutes K-line.

For the current time t, we defined the set $HD^* = \{XD_i\}$, for any one XD_i in HD^* satisfied that (1) $XD_i > \max(XD_{i-1}, \ldots, XD_{i-5})$; (2) $XD_i > \max(XD_{i+1}, \ldots, XD_{i+5})$. And we defined the set $LD^* = \{XD_i\}$, for any one XD_i in LD^* satisfied that (1) $XD_i < \min(XD_{i-1}, \ldots, XD_{i-5})$; (2) $XD_i < \min(XD_{i+1}, \ldots, XD_{i+5})$. Similarly, we defined the set $H15^* = \{X15_i\}$, for any one $X15_i$ in $H15^*$ satisfied that (1) $X15_i > \max(X15_{i-1}, \ldots, X15_{i-5})$; (2) $X15_i > \max(X15_{i+1}, \ldots, X15_{i+5})$. And we defined the set $L15^* = \{X15_i\}$, for any one $X15_i$ in $L15^*$ satisfied that (1) $X15_i < \min(X15_{i-1}, \ldots, X15_{i-5})$; (2) $X15_i < \min(X15_{i+1}, \ldots, X15_{i+5})$.

We defined the set HD be the two nearest elements in HD^*, LD be the two nearest elements of LD^*, $H15$ be the two nearest elements in $H15^*$, $L15$ be the two nearest elements of $L15^*$. There are only two elements HD_1 and HD_2 in HD, there are only two elements LD_1 and LD_2 in LD. There are only two elements $H15_1$ and $H15_2$ in $H15$, there are only two elements $L15_1$ and $L15_2$ in $L15$. See the examples in the Fig. 1. The Fig. 1 also shown the Support-Resistance Levels, let SD denote the line of Support Levels regarding to the day K-line, let RD denote the line of Resistance Levels regarding to the day K-line, let $S15$ denote the line of Support Levels regarding to the 15-Minutes K-line, let $R15$ denote the line of Resistance Levels regarding to the 15-Minutes K-line.

Fig. 1. The Support-Resistance Levels

Data granulation of the observed historical closing price for some stock is defined by the exemplar price vector $E = [LD_1, HD_1, LD_2, HD_2, L15_1, H15_1, L15_2, H15_2]^T$. The exemplar price vector E is a stock granular, it considers the observed historical closing price of day K-line and 15-Minutes K-line.

3 Experimental Study

The research data set that has been used in this study is from Chinese Stock Market. The series spans from 4th January 2016 to 28th September 2018, and we choose 683 different stocks at different times to analysis the importance of price Support Resistance Levels.

Firstly, we compute the exemplar price vector $E_i(i = 1,2,\ldots,683)$ for stock series data, and transform E_i the growth rate E_i^* was used to make sure the data are common, unity and complete. Then, we cluster these exemplar price vectors $E_i^*(i = 1,2,\ldots,683)$ into 20 different type of clusters by the well known FCM Clustering Algorithm. Last, the future closing price data were used to detect whether or not Support Resistance Levels worked effectively.

The results are shown in Fig. 2 for Support Levels, and the results are shown in Fig. 3 for Resistance Levels. In Fig. 2, these subfigures including A(60), C(56), D(55), E(49), F(46), G(42), H(42), M(26), N(25), O(20), Q(17) the Support Levels can work well, the curative rate was 64.1%. In Fig. 3, these subfigures including A(60), B(56), C (56), D(55), E(49), F(46), I(40), L(28), N(25), O(20), S(11) the Resistance Levels can work well, the curative rate was 65.3%. Through analysis of these results, the effectiveness of Support-Resistance Levels is nearly about Two-thirds.

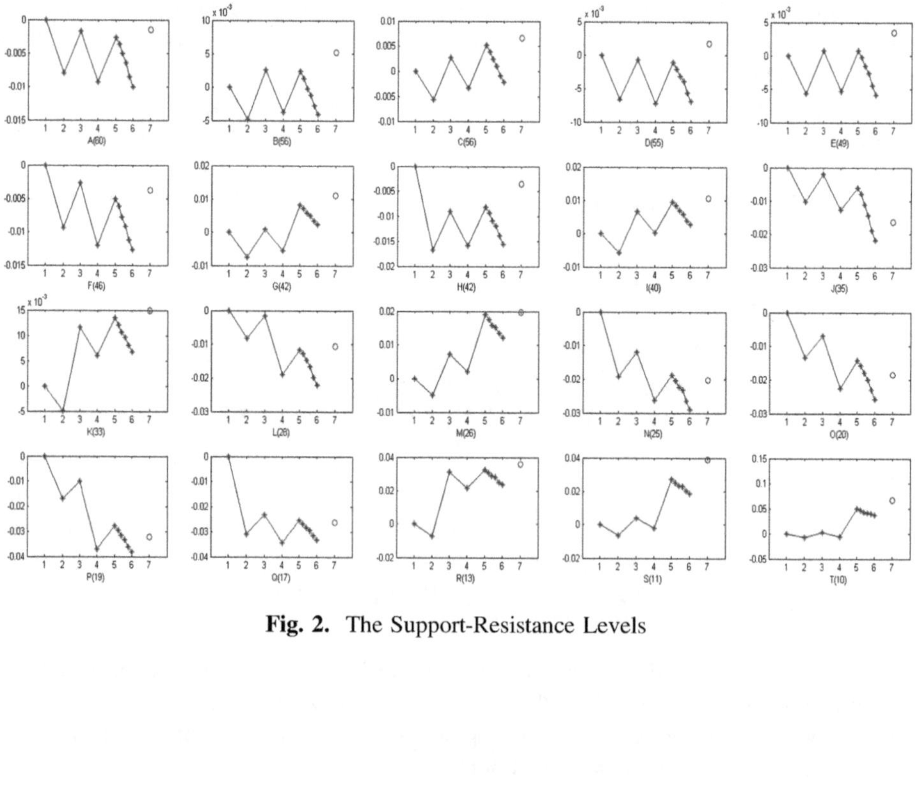

Fig. 2. The Support-Resistance Levels

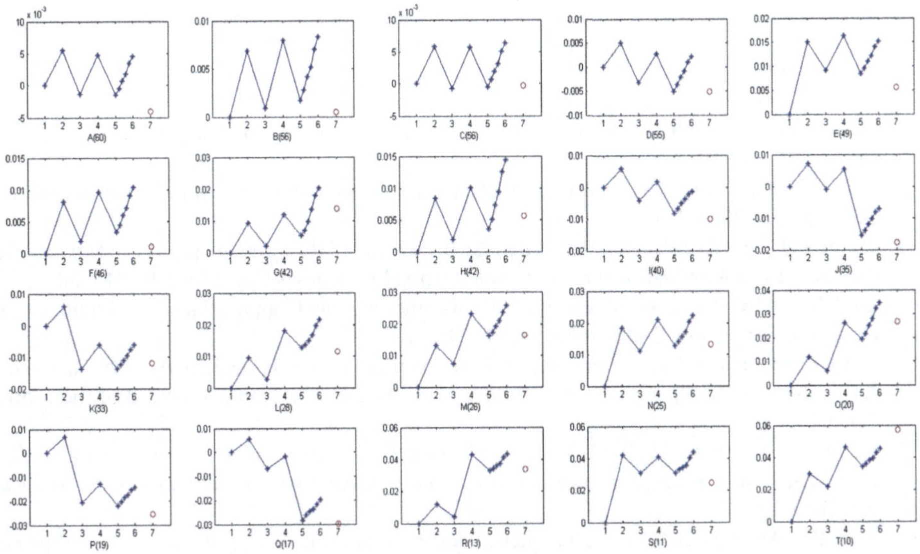

Fig. 3. The Support-Resistance Levels

4 Conclusion

In this paper, we proposed stock information granulation method considers the observed historical closing price of day K-line and 15-Minutes K-line, and analysis the significance of price Support-Resistance Levels of Chinese Stock Market based on the proposed information granulation and FCM fuzzy clustering algorithm. The research data set that has been used in this study is from Chinese Stock Market. Through analysis of experimental study, we found that the effectiveness of Support-Resistance Levels is nearly about Two thirds.

Acknowledgments. This work was supported in part by the Scientific Research Program for The Education Department of LiaoNing Province of China (Grant No. L201606, L201615) and Doctor Project (Grant No. 38/103816003). The National Natural Science Foundation of China under Grant 61803065.

References

1. Honda K, Sugiura N, Ichihashi H, Araki S (2001) Collaborative filtering using principal component analysis and fuzzy clustering. In: Web intelligence: research and development. Springer, Heidelberg (2001)
2. Deng J, Hu JL, Chi H, Wu J (2010) An improved fuzzy clustering method for text mining. In: International conference on networks security. IEEE Computer Society, vol 1, pp 65–69
3. Tjhi WC, Chen L (2009) Dual fuzzy-possibilistic coclustering for categorization of documents. IEEE Press (2009)
4. Lee YS, Cho SB (2012) Solving graph coloring problem by fuzzy clustering-based genetic algorithm simulated evolution and learning. Springer, Heidelberg, pp 351–360

5. Yang L, Geng X, Liao H (2016) A web sentiment analysis method on fuzzy clustering for mobile social media users. Eurasip J Wirel Commun Netw 1:1–13
6. Chen C (2013) Analysis of web log data mining based on improved fuzzy clustering algorithm. In: Advanced materials research, pp 760–762
7. Qi Y (2003) A web based computation software of fuzzy clustering analysis for webmetrics. Inf. Sci. 21(10):1065–1069
8. Thong PH, Le HS (2016) Picture fuzzy clustering: a new computational intelligence method. Soft Comput 20(9):1–14
9. Thong PH, Le HS (2016) A novel automatic picture fuzzy clustering method based on particle swarm optimization and picture composite cardinality. Knowl-Based Syst 109:48–60
10. Le HS (2016) Generalized picture distance measure and applications to picture fuzzy clustering. Appl Soft Comput 46(C):284–295
11. Ni Q, Pan Q, Du H, Cao C, Zhai Y (2017) A novel cluster head selection algorithm based on fuzzy clustering and particle swarm optimization. IEEE/ACM Trans Comput Biol Bioinform 14(1):76–84
12. Guo C, Jia H, Zhang N (2008) Time series clustering based on ICA for stock data analysis. In: International conference on wireless communications, networking and mobile computing. IEEE, pp 1–4
13. Tsay RS, Ando T (2012) Bayesian panel data analysis for exploring the impact of subprime financial crisis on the us stock market. Comput Stat Data Anal 56(11):3345–3365
14. George S, Changat M (2017) Network approach for stock market data mining and portfolio analysis. In: International conference on networks & advances in computational technologies. IEEE, pp 251–256
15. O'Shea, J (2014) Data analysis of stock exchanges
16. Angelis TD, Peskir G (2016) Optimal prediction of resistance and support levels. Appl Math Financ 23:465–483
17. IOSR Journal, Jain E (2014) Creating support-resistance levels using boll and predicting future market trend: a study of current scenario of Larsen & Toubro. Social Science Electronic Publishing
18. Dunn J (1973) A fuzzy relative of the ISODATA process and its use in detecting compact well-separated clusters. Taylor & Francis, New York
19. Lin T (1997) Granular computing: from rough sets and neighborhood systems to information granulation and computing in words. In: European congress on intelligent techniques and soft computing, pp 1602–1606
20. Pedrycz W (2013) Granular computing: analysis and design of intelligent systems. CRC Press, Boca Raton
21. Piotr H (2018) Recent granular computing frameworks for mining relational data. Artif Intell Rev (10):1–38
22. Sheng-Hua YU, Xiao YF (2011) Forecasting method of stock price based on information granulation and support vector machine. Theory Pract Finan Econ

Charging Analysis of Pipeline Robots Charged by Flow Power

Xiaomin Shan(✉) and Guangyu Liu

College of Mechanical Engineering, Inner Mongolia University for Nationalities, Tongliao, China
135351125@qq.com

Abstract. Refer to charging styles of pipeline robot, in this paper, the energy supply of the robot is satisfied by using the kinetic energy of the fluid. Verified issues of energy conversion for robot in cleaning oil and dirt in pipeline.

Keywords: Flow power · Energy conversion

1 Introduction

The energy which supported robot to work properly is provided by the power generation system. In this process, whether the power generated by the power generation system can meet the energy demand of the robot is related to the energy conversion of the power generation system [1, 2]. The pipeline robot converts the kinetic energy of the liquid in the oil pipeline into the working energy of the robot to complete the pipeline cleaning work.

1.1 Power Analyses for Energy Conversion Systems Charging by Flow Power

As cleaning work started, Robots walking slowly, At this time, the power generation system of the robot will convert the kinetic energy which fluid in the tube into electric energy and charges the lithium battery carried by the robot through the charging parts, so as to realize self-sufficiency of energy for the pipeline robot (the process of energy conversion device is shown in Fig. 1 as below).

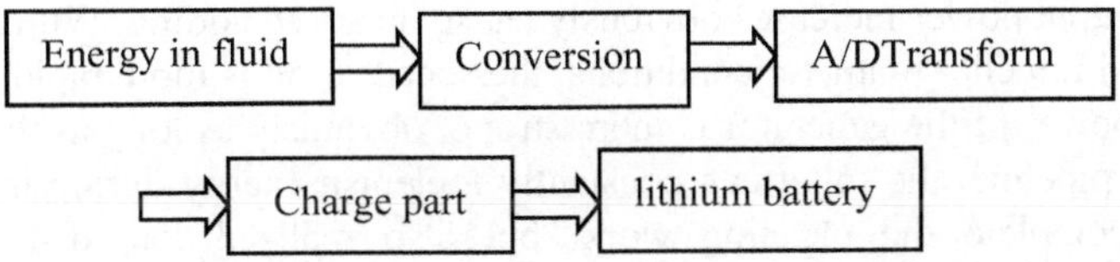

Fig. 1. Frame map for energy conversion process of power generation system

Z. Xu et al. (Eds.): CSIA 2019, AISC 928, pp. 1256–1261, 2020.
https://doi.org/10.1007/978-3-030-15235-2_169

Kinetic Energy Fluid in pipelines is:

$$E = \frac{1}{2}(\mathrm{m}v^2) \tag{1}$$

In it, m—Quality of Petroleum
v—Speed Rate of Petroleum
The power of the oil which flow to the energy conversion equipment in unit of time P_i is

$$P_i = \frac{1}{2}(\rho_1 \mathrm{A}v)v^2 = \frac{1}{2}(\rho_1 \mathrm{A}v^3) \tag{2}$$

In it, ρ_1—The density of Petroleum
A—Incident flow area for pipeline Robots
The output power of the energy conversion device P_0 is

$$P_0 = \eta \cdot P_i = \frac{1}{2} \cdot (\eta \rho_1 \mathrm{A}v^3) \tag{3}$$

In it, η—The efficiency of electromagnetic generator set is between 0.5 and 0.6.
As the fluid flows through the impeller [3, 4], the output power of the energy conversion device in the power generation system is:

$$P_0 = \eta \cdot P_i = \frac{1}{2} \cdot (\eta \rho_1 \mathrm{A}v^3) = \frac{1}{2}\pi\eta\rho_1\left(\frac{D}{2}\right)^2 v^3 \tag{4}$$

In it, A—The area which swept by the blade in impeller rotation
D—diameter of blade
ρ_1—the density of the fluid, which is 800 kg/m^3
For common small hydropower stations, the efficiency of the hydro generator units could attach above 0.6 [5] (the hydro generator part is 0.7–0.85, the generator part is 0.88–0.90, and the transmission part is 0.9–0.95). If depends $\eta = 50\%$, Data can be obtained in Fig. 2 as below: The output power of generator is related with fluid velocity and impeller diameter.

We can see in Fig. 2: due to the high density of oil, the energy which was gained in fluid from the power generation is enough. For pipelines with a diameter of 300 mm or more, the output power increases obviously cause oil speed adding. With a certain pipe diameter and impeller diameter conditions, the speed of oil is more rapidly, the greater the output power of the generator is more strong, obviously as long as there is enough fluid in the pipeline, the robot can constantly replenish energy during the movement. Not only complete the cleaning work, but also realized long-distance continue movement to complete the cleaning work of the entire pipeline.

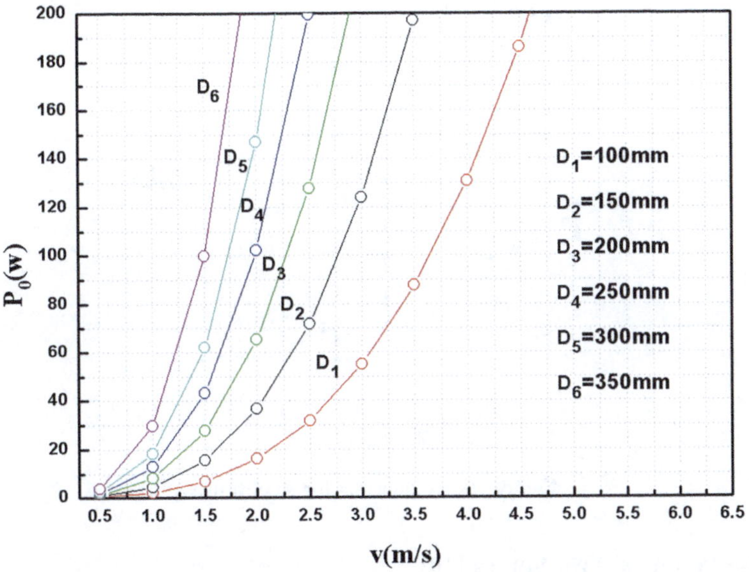

Fig. 2. Data of output power and oil speed are related to blade diameter

2 Provide Energy

The energy was product by the generator provide robot to clean up the system, namely the rotation of the steel brush. When the robot is working in the pipe for diameter = 300 mm and the speed of fluid is 1.5 m/s [6, 7], the power required by the steel brush for cleaning is calculated as follows:

2.1 Force Analysis for Steel Brush

Spring tensioning is F to The steel brush [8], and the friction between the pipe wall is f, the Angle formed by the axis is θ, At this time, the steel brush is subjected to the maximum tension in Fig. 3

and consist pull power

$$F = K_F \Delta l \tag{5}$$

In it, Δl—the stretching quantity of the spring, is 120 mm [9].

Friction with pipe wall

$$f = \mu N \tag{6}$$

In it, μ—friction factor between steel brush and pipe wall,

N—The force applied to the brush, i.e. the component of the tension force on the vertical axis $N = F \cdot \sin \theta$

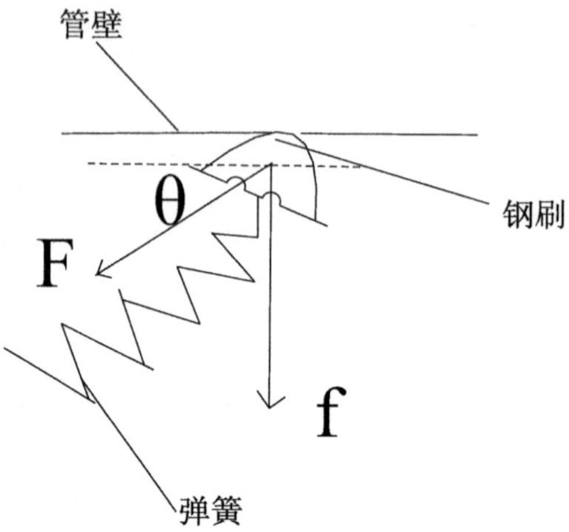

Fig. 3. Force analysis for steel brush

2.2 The Power of Two Forces [10]

(a) Elastic power P_1:

$$P_1 = F \cdot \cos\theta \cdot v \tag{7}$$

$$v = \omega r \tag{8}$$

$$\omega = 2\pi n \tag{9}$$

In it, v—Line speed of brush rotation
ω—The angular velocity of the brush rotation
n—Turing speed for DC motor
r—Pipe radius

Elastic power can be obtained from (5)– (9)

(b) Force of friction P_2:

$$P_2 = \mu F \cdot \sin\theta \cdot v \tag{10}$$

(c) The General power P:

$$P = P_1 + P_2 = F \cdot v(\mu\sin\theta + \cos\theta) \tag{11}$$

If $x = \mu \sin\theta + \cos\theta$, know as $x_{\max} = 1$, confirmed:

$$P_{\max} = F \cdot v = K_F \Delta l \cdot v = 11.3\,\mathrm{w}$$

General energy for 3 brushes

$$P_{总} = 3P_{\max} = 33.9\mathrm{w}$$

Result for calculation, the maximum power required by 3 steel brushes is 33.9 w. gain in Fig. 2, when the diameter of the pipe is 300 mm and the rate of fluid is 1.5 m/s, the output power of the generator P_0 is 60 w. The energy provided by the power generation system can meet the energy demand of robot in the whole working process. Therefore, this energy conversion device scheme is suitable for this pipeline robot. In view of the fact condition for robot which working in the oil pipeline, the above analysis shows that the robot designed in here can attach work requirements and will not resulted the robot was left in pipeline for insufficient power supply.

3 Conclusions

Analyzed energy conversion device entirely and confirmed the fluid kinetic energy could be transfer into electrical energy through energy conversion device, supply robot work energy for variously parts. From side of energy, by calculation, get the conclusions for fluid kinetic energy transformation, can satisfy demands of the robot, the robot can work uninterrupted for long time in pipeline. More faster the fluid moves, the more energy could be gain through conversion. As the fluid speeds become slowly, it could use charging battery carried by the robot to provide power.

References

1. Zhang Y, Yan G (2007) In-pipe inspection robot with active pipe-diameter adaptability and automatic tractive force adjusting. Mech Mach Theory 42:1618–1631
2. Lee D, Park J, Hyun D, Yook G, Yang H (2012) Novel mechanisms and simple locomotion strategies for an in-piperobot that can inspect various pipe types. Mech Mach Theory 56:52–68
3. Hansen P, Alismail H, Rander P, Browning B (2014) Visual mapping for natural gas pipe inspection. Int J Robot Res 34:532–558
4. Roh S, Choi HR (2005) Differential-drive in-pipe robot for moving inside urban gas pipelines. IEEE Trans Robot 21(1):1
5. Xu H, Lin P, Wang Y (2015) Design of a new peristaltic pipeline robot. J Jiangsu Univ (Nat Sci Ed) 36:561–565
6. Yu Q, Yu J, Wang J, Liu J (2013) The spiral driven and control method research of the pipe cleaning robot. Int J Adv Inf Sci Serv Sci 5(1):484–490
7. Hu Z, Appleton E (2005) Dynamic characteristics of a novel self-drive pipeline pig. IEEE Trans Robot 21:781–789
8. Choi C (2012) Robot design for leak detection in water-pipe systems. MS thesis. MIT

9. Choi C, Kamal Y-T (2013) Robot design for high flow liquid pipe networks. In: IEEE/RSJ international conference on intelligent robots, pp 246–251
10. Chatzigeorgiou D, Youcef-Toumi K, Khalifa A, Ben-Mansour R (2011) Analysis and design of an in-pipe system for water leak detection. In: ASME international design engineering technical conferences & design automation conference

Reflections on the Application of AI in Auditing Practice in the Context of Big Data

Xiaohong Wang(✉)

Auditing Department, Shandong University of Arts, Jinan, China
962238629@qq.com

Abstract. In recent years, big data and cloud computing technology have been widely used, which has led to profound changes in work and life. In the field of finance, "Internet + accounting" and big data auditing have also become hot topics in the industry. The Ministry of Finance and the Audit Office have also issued relevant documents in succession, proposing to strengthen the construction of information technology and increase the use of large data. With the emergence of cloud accounting and financial sharing centers, the trend of computerization of accounting data is further strengthened, which makes it possible to obtain direct activity information of enterprises through computers. On the other hand, the abundant data resources make the quantification process begin in various fields, and when big data is applied more and more widely, the acquisition of industry data and industry data will become more and more convenient. After introducing the research background and significance, this paper analyses the characteristics of audit analysis procedures in different stages of development, points out the limitations of traditional audit analysis procedures, and then leads to the significance of applying big data analysis to audit work. Next, we discuss the application of big data in audit analysis procedure.

Keywords: AI · Audit · Big data

1 Brief Introduction

Since twenty-first Century, the concepts of "AI", "big data" and "cloud computing" have begun to enter the public view [1]. At present, big data analysis has achieved good application results in e-commerce, statistical prediction, scientific research, business decision-making and other aspects, and the related technologies are becoming more and more mature [2–6]. The wide application of these technologies has improved the degree and depth of accounting and auditing informatization. "Internet + accounting", "Internet + audit" and big data audit have become the current research hotspots [3, 7–12]. The National Audit Office has also issued relevant documents to clarify the importance of information construction, aiming at improving the efficiency and effectiveness of audit. At the same time, vigorously promote "cloud computing" and data mining and other emerging technologies, more efficient analysis of data, improve audit efficiency [3]. At present, big data, cloud computing and other emerging technologies are booming, and are in the ascendant. At the same time, the scale of enterprises is bigger and bigger, and the degree of accounting informationization is getting

Z. Xu et al. (Eds.): CSIA 2019, AISC 928, pp. 1262–1267, 2020.
https://doi.org/10.1007/978-3-030-15235-2_170

higher and higher [4]. For auditors, informatization is not simply to improve the efficiency of audit manuscript compilation through audit software. More importantly, how to make full use of information technology and improve the current audit mode, methods and concepts through big data and advanced industry experience [7].

After introducing the research background and significance, this paper analyses the characteristics of audit analysis procedures in different stages of development, points out the limitations of traditional audit analysis procedures, and then leads to the significance of applying big data analysis to audit work. Next, we discuss the application of big data in audit analysis procedure [13, 14].

2 Artificial Intelligence

Artificial intelligence is popular in that it enables machines to have the same intelligence and ability as human beings through artificial methods. At present, the scientific community has not yet made an accurate definition of AI. The main reason is that scientists do not understand why AI is. At present, as the only highly intelligent creature on earth, human intelligence comes from human brain. But there are still many mysteries about how the brain works, so it is still impossible to make a scientific and rational exposition of intelligence. As we mentioned earlier, the concept of AI was first put forward by Turing, the father of computer science, but the development of AI is the result of the mutual efforts of generations of scientists, and its development process is also abnormal twists and turns. The term "artificial intelligence" was formally used as a technical term in the summer of 1956, when McCarthy, the father of artificial intelligence, mentioned it in a speech. Artificial intelligence (AI) was heated by the media at that time. Various countries also launched investment and Research on AI. Especially western capitalist countries invested a lot of manpower, material resources and financial resources. However, due to the maturity of theory and technology, coupled with the lack of effectiveness, western capitalist countries have reduced research funding, resulting in artificial intelligence in 1971 to 1980 in a stagnant period, people have gradually reduced the attention and enthusiasm for artificial intelligence. However, with the maturity of theory and technology, new theory and technology have solved the problems that have plagued scientists in AI for many years, and AI has entered the era of rapid development. Until today, more and more products related to AI have entered the lives of ordinary people, bringing endless convenience and fun to people's lives.

We can imagine the following scenarios: in the future, when you get off work, the car will automatically come out of the parking lot and wait for you downstairs. When you get on the bus, a soothing piece of music will make you relax from a heavy day's work. And you don't need to drive yourself, it will take you home automatically… This scenario that used to only appear in science fiction will be realized in the near future, depending on the development of artificial intelligence. With the advent of 5G era, all kinds of intelligent devices will achieve seamless docking, even on the fast-moving high-speed railway, you can enjoy the pleasure of watching video smoothly. Artificial intelligence is being applied in more and more fields. With the maturity of theory and technology, more and more products related to artificial intelligence will be integrated into our life.

3 The Advantages of Introducing Artificial Intelligence into Auditing Under the Background of Big Data

3.1 Get More Comprehensive Data and Create a Good Foundation for Auditing

In the era of big data, the amount of information is so large that we need to make full use of data analysis tools to analyze comprehensive data. For example, if the relevant financial information and non-financial information of the enterprise are input into the audit software, the relevant information can be collected in the background. Auditors must judge the audit opinions provided by audit software professionally according to the professional knowledge of audit, so as to make reasonable choices. In addition, auditors can also obtain financial information and operation status of other companies in the same industry through data sharing platform, so that they can have a good understanding of the development of the industry and the situation of competitors. In the process of auditing enterprises, auditors are faced with not only the financial data of enterprises, but also the data related to the operation of enterprises and the analysis and comparison of different data of enterprises.

3.2 Identify Risk Points Through Model Validation Analysis

Analytical procedures can be used to understand the auditees and assess their total risk of material misstatement, to help auditors find abnormal data in financial information and identify areas where there is significant risk of material misstatement. Sometimes appropriate analysis is more likely to identify problems than detailed tests. At present, large data analysis is more and more widely used, such as predictive analysis. By establishing scientific models and bringing in data, future data can be predicted and validated. In the past practice, the trend analysis of audited units is the main focus of financial statement analysis. Today, in the form of large data and computer data widely used, auditors can fully obtain the historical data of the auditees, at the same time, they can collect a large number of external data, and use appropriate statistical methods to process and extract data.

3.3 Improve Audit Efficiency and Reduce Sampling Risk

In the past, due to the low level of data recording and storage informationization, only a small number of samples can be extracted for verification. However, the application of big data technology to audit sampling has greatly increased the amount of data processed, although the scale of data that can be processed is still limited. In the case of high degree of enterprise informationization, more and more paper documents have been replaced by electronic documents in the past. For example, to go to the bank for business, it used to be necessary to sign paper documents. Nowadays, many documents only need to be signed on the electronic screen at the counter. This kind of documents also omit the link of staff scanning and filing.

4 The Application of Artificial Intelligence in Auditing Practice

4.1 Impact on Audit Practice

At present, AI is still relatively shallow in the audit work. With its intelligent characteristics, AI has great advantages in solving the specific work of audit practice, but its ability to solve problems is limited and there are some deficiencies that cannot be ignored. The advantages lie in the following aspects: Firstly, the current financial artificial intelligence technology can help financial personnel to carry out basic manual repetitive operations, such as input data change information. Secondly, AI can also process data with high quality and efficiency, and provide data needed by management with high quality and efficiency, save a lot of working time of financial personnel, reduce work pressure, improve professional well-being, reduce the opportunity cost of human resources, and create greater value.

There are still many deficiencies in the application of artificial intelligence in auditing. First of all, AI cannot completely replace labor. The problems encountered in audit practice are ever-changing, most of the time rely on the professional judgment of auditors. The final decision-making and reasonable questioning of audit work need to be carried out manually, which cannot be replaced by artificial intelligence for the time being. Secondly, because AI technology is still in the exploratory stage, the efficiency of solving practical problems is not high. Auditors also need to take time to learn how to use AI in practice, which will inevitably increase the workload and reduce the work efficiency. Of course, the introduction of AI will bring great changes to auditing practice. The financial robot can monitor every business of the enterprise in a comprehensive way. At the same time, AI can track the whole accounting process of the company, standardize the financial work of the enterprise, and reduce financial violations.

4.2 Impact on Auditors

With the advent of artificial intelligence, auditors need to have comprehensive information technology innovation ability and rich business knowledge. The value of the financial robots introduced by the four major accounting firms lies in high accuracy, long-term uninterrupted work, process automation, optimization of financial processes and standards, monitoring and recording audit evidence, short payback period of investment in process automation technology, low-cost integration, etc.

Artificial intelligence lacks audit judgment. The way of thinking that auditors form professional judgment cannot be achieved by artificial intelligence nowadays, so artificial intelligence cannot replace auditors to make professional judgment for the time being. Therefore, auditors should pay attention to the understanding and communication of emerging issues, the construction of business cooperation and relationship, and the evaluation and analysis of senior investment in communication. In terms of thinking judgment, we should use strategic thinking to evaluate the audited units comprehensively and correctly, find the key points from the huge data information and make accurate judgments. We should have a deep understanding of the whole business economic environment and data analysis, and use the advantages of artificial intelligence to better assist our own soft skills and professional judgment.

4.3 Internal and External Support for the Use of AI

Although AI reduces audit risk, improves audit efficiency and brings many opportunities, there are still some problems in the application of AI to audit practice. Firstly, AI can't guarantee information security, such as machine internal error programs, malicious attacks from external personnel of enterprises, etc. These reasons will lead to system operation errors, leading to internal out of control of enterprises.

Secondly, the cost of troubleshooting and behavior supervision has been greatly improved. Because of the complexity of AI itself and the dramatic increase of AI system risk, the cost of troubleshooting will also be greatly increased. At the same time, the existing legal and regulatory system for artificial intelligence failure or behavior caused by social problems, such as responsibility definition, behavior supervision judgment is more difficult. When the behavior cannot be traced back, it is difficult to define the subject of responsibility, and the cost of dealing with the chain consequences caused by minor mistakes will increase greatly. To popularize AI in auditing practice, first of all, the improvement of technology is required to make AI change from traditional linear thinking, to simulate human brain for thinking and decision-making, to further obtain the results of financial decision-making, and to flexibly respond to changes in financial environment. Secondly, aiming at the difficult problem of regulation and regulation in the industry, the state should escort AI with strong development momentum. Relevant departments should promulgate relevant laws and regulations, solve the gray area of legal norms such as responsibility definition, clarify the relationship subject, and avoid financial and security risks.

5 Summary

Accounting experience from the era of manual accounting to computerized accounting, is now in the transition to the era of intelligent accounting, audit work has also entered the transition stage. Accounting professionals have always been very sensitive to the application potential of emerging technologies, so that they can better play their business capabilities through emerging technologies, and promote the development of the accounting industry to today's level. Auditors should seize the opportunity of the era of artificial intelligence, make use of the characteristics of artificial intelligence, improve business ability, actively adapt to the transformation, and enter a new era with the audit work.

References

1. Omoteso K (2012) The application of artificial intelligence in auditing: looking back to the future. Expert Syst Appl 39(9):8490–8495
2. Han FY (2017) The research on auditing fundamental course teaching based on rational integration and its practice—Taking Chongqing business vocational college as an example. J Chongqing Ind Trade Polytech

3. Zhai Q, Wei Z (2016) The practice of the "five relevance" audit ideas and methods of Henan provincial audit department in the context of big data. Audit Res
4. O'Leary DE, O'Keefe RM (1997) The impact of artificial intelligence in accounting work: expert systems use in auditing and tax. AI Soc 11(1–2):36–47
5. Hughes G, Dobbins C (2015) The utilization of data analysis techniques in predicting student performance in massive open online courses (MOOCs). Res Pract Technol Enhanc Learn 10(1):10
6. Usa UOA (2016) Collected Papers of the eleventh annual research workshop on: artificial intelligence and emerging technologies in accounting, auditing and tax. Amelia A Baldwin
7. Liu Z, Zhu Z (2015) Research prospects and application challenges of social stability: risk assessment in the context of big data. J East China Univ Sci Technol
8. Peng D, University UV (2016) Exploration on cloud classroom learning in the context of big data. Wirel Internet Technol
9. Wang XZ, Song YF (2016) Research on the big data application for practice of quality education in colleges and universities. Teach Educ Forum
10. Abidoye RB, Chan APC (2017) Valuers' receptiveness to the application of artificial intelligence in property valuation. Pac Rim Prop Res J 23(2):1–19
11. Bukhsh FA, Weigand H (2011) Evaluating the application of service-oriented auditing in the B2G domain: a case study. In: Perspectives in business informatics research - international conference, Bir 2011, Riga, Latvia, 6–8 October 2011, Proceedings, pp 281–295
12. Song Y (2017) Research on the application of health big data from the perspective of artificial intelligence. China Dev
13. Hemberg E, Rosen J, Warner G et al (2015) Tax non-compliance detection using co-evolution of tax evasion risk and audit likelihood, pp 79–88
14. Wang, Q, Lu P (2014) Research on application of artificial intelligence in computer network technology. Int J Pattern Recognit Artif Intell (4)

Research on Safety Cost Optimization Model of Prefabricated Building

Chunguang Chang and Xi Wu(✉)

School of Management, Shenyang Jianzhu University, Shenyang 110168, China
wxy0102w@163.com

Abstract. Aiming at the nonlinear characteristics of the safety cost of prefabricated building, the nonlinear optimization theory is used to optimize the loss-reduction effect of the total cost of the system, and the safety cost optimization control model is established. The matlab optimization tool is combined with the example for empirical analysis and simulation. The results show that the cost of the optimized security risk control is lower than the average, which verifies the validity of the model.

Keywords: Prefabricated building · Safety cost · Nonlinear model · Cost loss reduction effect

1 Introduction

Since the 1970s, fabricated building technology has evolved [1–3]. In the past three decades, these technologies have been further developed and improved, but China's prefabricated buildings are still in their infancy, and their on-site construction safety production management is imperfect. Therefore, strengthening the on-site construction safety management of the prefabricated building is not only conducive to the further development of the prefabricated building, but also an important prerequisite for the healthy and sustained development of the construction industry [4–6]. At present, the research on fabricated buildings at home and abroad involves BIM technology [7], earthquake resistance [8], etc. There are few researches on the safety cost of fabricated buildings. Due to the existence of many dangerous sources in the prefabricated building, comprehensive prevention and control, the risk of risk management and control is relatively large, and how to control the risk cost within a reasonable range has become an important issue in the research of assembly-type construction risk management. In the existing literature, domestic and foreign scholars have divided security costs into guaranteed security costs and loss security costs [9]. According to the ergonomic research method, the guaranteed safety cost of prefabricated building construction can be divided into four directions: human, machine, management and environment [10]. When optimizing the system security cost, it is necessary to study the relationship between the four and the loss safety cost, so that the guaranteed safety cost can reach the optimal ratio, thus ensuring the safe, efficient and reasonable operation of the system.

Z. Xu et al. (Eds.): CSIA 2019, AISC 928, pp. 1268–1273, 2020.
https://doi.org/10.1007/978-3-030-15235-2_171

2 Model Building

Guaranteed safety input costs are expenses incurred to ensure a reasonable level of safety, including safety training inputs, safety protection fees, safety construction fees, and safety management fees. Loss-safe cost refers to the cost of dealing with accidents after an accident occurs, including accident handling fees, occupational disease treatment and rehabilitation costs. The safety status of the prefabricated construction project system can be determined by the casualty rate and safety as an indicator of the degree of safety assurance. The relationship between safety costs, guaranteed safety input costs, and lossy safety costs and system safety conditions is the key to safety cost optimization.

2.1 System Total Loss Reduction Effect Model

Establish a system safety cost control model. The relationship is as follows:

$$T(x_1, \ldots, x_n) = L - G \tag{1}$$

T is the total loss reduction effect of the system, L is the loss reduction effect brought by safety investment, $G = \sum_{t=1}^{n} x_i$ is the total cost of each guaranteed safety input, and $(x_1, x_2, \ldots, x_n)$ is the guaranteed safety input cost of each item.

2.2 Loss-Safe Cost-Guarantee Safety Input Cost Reduction Effect Model

Analyzing the relationship between the loss-reducing cost reduction effect and the various guaranteed safety input costs. The inherent law between the guarantee safety sub-input and the accident economic loss reduction effect can be approximated by Cobb-Douglas. The input-output relationship of the function indicates that the loss-reducing cost reduction effect and the guaranteed safety input cost model are as follows:

$$L = f(x_1, x_2, \ldots, x_n, t) = Ax_1^{\beta_1} x_2^{\beta_2} \ldots x_n^{\beta n} \lambda^t \tag{2}$$

L is the loss safety cost reduction effect, $(\beta_1, \beta_2, \ldots, \beta_n)$ is the elastic coefficient of the guaranteed safety input cost of each item, A is a constant, and λ is the technological progress coefficients as a function of time t.

According to the relationship between loss safety cost and guaranteed safety input cost, function (2) should meet the following conditions: (1) The loss safety cost cannot exceed the specified upper limit (i.e. $\sum_{t=1}^{n} x_i \leq G_0$), and (2) Under the premise that the guarantee safety inputs of other sub-items remain unchanged, the safety investment for a certain sub-item will increase, and the effect of reducing the loss-safe cost will increase (i.e. $\frac{\partial \ln(f)}{\partial x_i} = \frac{\beta_i}{x_i} > 0, \beta_i > 0$).

2.3 System Security Cost-Guarantee Safety Input Cost Reduction Effect Optimization Model

The system safety cost reduction effect is the maximum objective function. According to (1) and formula (2) can establish the safety input cost is not greater than G_0, and the sub-item safety input cost is not greater than k. Nonlinear programming model is as follows:

$$\begin{cases} \max T(x_1, x_2, \ldots, x_n, t) = Ax_1^{\beta_1} x_2^{\beta_2} \ldots x_n^{\beta_n} \lambda^t - \sum_{i=1}^{m} x_i \\ T(x_1, x_2, \ldots, x_n, t) \geq 0 \\ \sum_{t=1}^{n} x_i \leq G_0, i = 1, 2, \ldots, n \\ 0 < x_i < k, i = 1, 2, \ldots, n \end{cases} \quad (3)$$

By solving it by Matlab, the optimal safety input cost of the system sub-item safety measures and the optimal system safety input cost of the system can be obtained.

3 Empirical Analysis

3.1 This Paper Takes a PH Prefabricated Construction Enterprise in D City as an Example to Analyze the Project Safety Cost Index Data Analysis

Data of 2013–2018. The guaranteed safety input cost can be divided into four aspects (including personnel safety investment, equipment safety investment, Manage safety investment and environmental safety investment). As shown in the data in Table 1, the average value of the guaranteed safety input cost of the enterprise is 10.07 million yuan, and the average effect of the loss safety cost reduction effect is 18.36 million yuan. The other sub-items are shown in Table 1. The casualty rate of enterprises has been declining year by year, the safety has increased steadily, and the overall security form of enterprises is better.

Table 1. System safety cost and safety status level information (million yuan)

Years	x_1	x_2	x_3	x_4	G	L	T	Thousand casualties	Safety
2013	3.42	3.54	2.03	0.59	9.57	0.22	9.79	0.826	0.780 9
2014	3.28	3.47	2.03	0.78	9.56	0.21	9.77	0.569	0.821 9
2015	3.15	3.58	2.08	0.65	9.45	0.21	9.67	0.604	0.815 3
2016	3.50	3.53	2.04	0.76	9.82	0.21	10.04	0.493	0.837 7
2017	4.58	3.67	2.05	0.92	11.22	0.21	11.42	0.373	0.868 3
2018	3.59	3.62	2.54	0.99	10.75	0.21	10.95	0.373	0.868 3
Mean	3.59	3.57	2.13	0.78	10.06	0.21	10.27		

3.2 Instance Verification

Taking the natural logarithm of the actual data of the survey, and combine the formula (2) to perform multiple linear regression on these natural logarithms, the mathematical expression of the result is as follows:

$$\ln L = \ln A + \beta_1 \ln x_1 + \beta_2 \ln x_2 + \beta_3 \ln x_4 + t \ln \lambda \tag{4}$$

Since the regression test of the technological progress coefficient and the time variable t is not significant, the re-fitting after t is deleted to obtain the following expression.

$$\ln L = 2.342 + 0.017 \ln x_1 + 0.422 \ln x_2 + 0.040 \ln x_3 + 0.083 \ln x_4 \tag{5}$$

Therefore, the loss safety cost-guaranteed safety input cost model of the project is obtained as follows:

$$L = f(x_1, x_2, \ldots, x_n, t) = 14.409 x_1^{0.017} x_2^{0.422} x_3^{0.04} x_4^{0.083} \tag{6}$$

According to the formulas (1), (3), (6), combined with the safety status of the project, the safety cost optimization model of the project is established as follows:

$$\begin{cases} \max T(x_1, x_2, \ldots, x_n, t) = 14.409 x_1^{0.017} x_2^{0.422} x_3^{0.04} x_4^{0.083} - \sum_{i=1}^{n} x_i \\ T(x_1, x_2, \ldots, x_n, t) \geq 0 \\ G = \sum_{1}^{n} x_i \leq G_0, i = 1, 2, 3, 4 \\ 0 < x_i < k, i = 1, 2, 3, 4 \end{cases} \tag{7}$$

3.3 Optimization Model Solution

According to the safety situation and safety cost data analysis in recent years, the overall safety situation of the project is good, the casualty rate is low, and the safety situation is stable. The general level of safety of the project is optimized (Table 1), ensuring safety. The upper limit of input cost G is the highest value of 11.22 million yuan, and the lower limit of the safety input cost of each sub-item is 0, and the upper limit is the highest value of the previous year. Based on this, the constraints can be determined: $G < 11.22$, $k_1 = 4.58$, $k_2 = 3.67$, $k_3 = 2.54$, $k_3 = 0.99$.

Using Matlab programming to deal with the constrained nonlinear multivariate function optimization method, the project's guaranteed safety input cost is up to 9.94 million yuan, and the optimal safety total cost reduction effect is 8.16 million yuan. Among them, the personnel safety input cost is 3.49 million yuan, the equipment safety input cost is 2.28 million yuan, the management safety input cost is 1.68 million yuan, and the environmental safety input cost is 1.37 million yuan. The total cost of safety of the project decreased by 0.13 million yuan compared with the annual average, and the guaranteed safety input cost decreased by 0.13 million yuan compared with the annual average.

As shown in Table 2, the allocation plan for the proportion of safety investment in each project and the optimized ratio of guaranteed safety input costs are: 0.3553:0.3557:0.2118:0.0772, and the optimal allocation plan after optimization is: 0.4276:0.2790:0.2062:0.1678. The proportion of investment in equipment safety is generally high, and the proportion of personnel safety investment and environmental safety investment is obviously insufficient. In order to ensure the efficient and economic operation of the safety situation of the project, the safety investment in equipment safety should be appropriately reduced, and the personnel and environmental safety inputs should be appropriately increased, and the proportions should be controlled at 0.4276 and 0.1678 respectively.

Table 2. Distribution plan of safety investment proportion of PH enterprises in each year

Years	x_1	x_3	x_3	x_4
2013	0.357 0	0.369 5	0.211 9	0.061 6
2014	0.343 1	0.363 0	0.212 3	0.081 6
2015	0.333 0	0.378 4	0.219 9	0.068 7
2016	0.356 1	0.359 1	0.207 5	0.077 3
2017	0.408 2	0.327 1	0.182 7	0.082 0
2018	0.334 3	0.337 1	0.236 5	0.092 2
Average ratio	0.355 3	0.355 7	0.211 8	0.077 2
Optimized ratio	0.427 6	0.279 0	0.206 2	0.167 8

4 Conclusion

Studying the prefabricated building safety cost optimization control model can provide a scientific and systematic basis for enterprises to make safety investment decisions, and has strong practicability, but the safety cost in this model is related to the guaranteed safety input cost and the loss safety cost. In addition, factors such as the scale of production and the number of personnel of the project should also be considered. This is the next research direction.

Acknowledgments. This research was supported by the National Natural Science Foundation of China (Project No. 51678375), Natural Science Foundation of Liaoning Province (Project No. 2015020603), and the basic scientific research project of Liaoning Higher Education (Project No. LJZ2017009).

References

1. Khalili A, Chua DKH (2013) IFC-Based framework to move beyond individual building elements toward configuring a higher level of prefabrication. J Comput Civil Eng 27(3):243–253
2. Tumminia G, Guarino F, Longo S, Ferraro M, Cellura M, Antonucci V (2018) Life cycle energy performances and environmental impacts of a prefabricated building module. Renew Sustain Energy Rev 92:272–283

3. Said HM, Kandimalla P (2018) Performance measurement of building sheet-metal ductwork prefabrication under batch production settings. J Constr Eng Manag 144(2):04017107
4. Hong JK, Shen GQP, Li ZD, Zhang BY, Zhang WQ (2018) Barriers to promoting prefabricated construction in China: a cost–benefit analysis. J Cleaner Prod 172:649–660
5. Yuan ZM, Sun CS, Wang YW (2018) Design for manufacture and assembly-oriented parametric design of prefabricated buildings. Autom Constr 88:13–22
6. Yoders J (2017) Manufacturing's quest for process efficiency: clients desire prefabrication and even design management. ENR: Eng News-Rec 31:76–77
7. Zhang LM, Wu XG, Ding LY, Skibniewski MJ, Lu YJ (2016) Bim-Based risk identification system in tunnel construction. J Civil Eng Manag 22(4):529–539
8. Ercolino M, Magliulo G, Manfredi G (2016) Failure of a precast RC building due to Emilia-Romagna earthquakes. Eng Struct 118:262–273
9. Yun L (2004) Security economics. Industrial Press, Beijing, pp 64–69. (in Chinese)
10. He X (2000) Safety engineering. China University of Mining and Technology Press, Xuzhou (in Chinese)

Study on Distortion Characteristics of Analog Circuit by Nonlinear Degree of Integrated Circuit Amplifier

Wang Tao[1(✉)] and Sun Wen[2]

[1] Xianning Vocational Technical College, Xianning, China
zhaoleies@163.com
[2] Tellhow Polytron Technologies Inc., Shanghai, China

Abstract. The application of large scale system integrated circuit can not be solved by digital circuit. Many signal acquisition and digital-analog conversion in nature require the participation of analog circuits. Linear integrated circuit amplifiers amplify analog circuit signals to transmit signals and maintain the accuracy of the signals. The linearity of the circuit amplifier is directly related to the distortion characteristics of the analog circuit. The distortion characteristics of single-stage circuits are studied in this paper. The efficiency and accuracy of calculation are improved by deducing the expression of distortion factor of single-stage circuits. Finally, the distortion factor of single stage circuit is calculated by simulation, and the theoretical results are verified.

Keywords: Artificial circuit · Nonlinear degree · Distortion characteristic · Single-stage circuit

1 Introduction

It is an important research direction to accurately analyze the distortion characteristics of analog circuits. The key component of IC amplifier is also the key to study the distortion characteristics of analog circuits. The analog circuit increases the amplitude of the electric signal through the circuit amplifier, so that the information can be transmitted. The accuracy of the amplifier linearity is directly related to whether the electrical signal is accurate to achieve amplitude enhancement characteristics, to ensure the authenticity of the analog circuit, and to prevent the analog circuit from distortion. At present, many methods have been used in the research at home and abroad. It is difficult to analyze the distortion characteristics of analog circuits. Nonlinear Analysis of degenerate Impedance by Volterra Series method by Liu et al. [1]. Darliri et al. studied the distortion characteristics of boot belt switch by mathematical modeling [2].

This paper focuses on the influence of the nonlinearity of the integrated circuit amplifier on the distortion characteristics of the analog circuit. Through simulation analysis, the law of amplifier nonlinearity distortion to analog circuit is obtained.

Z. Xu et al. (Eds.): CSIA 2019, AISC 928, pp. 1274–1279, 2020.
https://doi.org/10.1007/978-3-030-15235-2_172

2 Theoretical Basis of Analog Circuit Distortion Analysis

At present, there have been a lot of research results about the distortion characteristics of analog circuits. This chapter focuses on the theoretical basis of the popular Volterra series method and vector method, and makes relevant derivation and analysis [3, 4].

2.1 Single Frequency Signal Excitation

The input excitation of the analog circuit is assumed to be a sinusoidal signal with a frequency of 1. When the input signal amplitude is small enough, the output spectrum contains only the first order component, which is the linear response of the circuit. After the input signal passes through the circuit, the output signal has the same frequency as the input signal, and the output fundamental wave component is proportional to the amplitude of the input signal [5–7].

When the amplitude of the input signal increases, the output spectrum consists of second-order and third-order components, and the circuit contains both linear and nonlinear responses [8–10]. If the input signal continues to increase, the degree of nonlinearity will gradually increase. In general, the analog circuit design needs the linear response to transfer signal, the nonlinear part is the superfluous component. Therefore, these nonlinear components are defined as distortion. The ratio of the nonlinear harmonic component to the reference component can be used to judge the distortion. Considering the positive and negative characteristics of the output signal and the sensitivity of the distortion factor, the square of distortion is taken as the index to evaluate the distortion factor. The second and third order distortion factors are defined as follows.

$$\mu_2 = \left(\frac{Y_{O,2\omega 1}}{Y_{O,1\omega 1}}\right)^2 \tag{1}$$

$$\mu_3 = \left(\frac{Y_{O,3\omega 1}}{Y_{O,1\omega 1}}\right)^2 \tag{2}$$

Type center:

$Y_{O,3\omega 1}$—Representation of third-order output components;
$Y_{O,2\omega 1}$—Representation of second-order output components;
$Y_{O,1\omega 1}$—Representation reference component;

The above distortion factor can be used to draw dimensionless curves of input signals. These figures can be used to determine the nonlinear behavior of analog circuits with high sensitivity and simple calculation process.

Suppose the input signal of the circuit is R(t). The output signal is C(t). Then the relationship between the input signal and the output signal is as follows.

$$C(t) = c_1 R(t) + c_2[R(t)]^2 + c_3[R(t)]^3 + \ldots \tag{3}$$

c_1 can be defined as a linear factor, c_2 and c_3 are second order and third order nonlinear factors, respectively.

The second order distortion factor is determined by Taylor series method.

$$\mu_2 = (c_2)^2 = (\frac{1}{2}\frac{d^2 f}{d^2 r})^2 \tag{4}$$

2.2 Vector Method

Assuming that the current circuit is stable, the voltage and current are sinusoidal. Change the amplitude and phase of the input signal to get the output signal. Let the adjustable transfer function be $K(j\omega)$, Phase is $\Psi(\omega)$, The range is A. The output signal can be represented as follows.

$$C(t) = |K(j\omega)| A \cos(\omega t + \Psi(\omega)) \tag{5}$$

When the circuit is in a stable state, the nonlinear components can also be expressed by vector derivation, and the excitation of the system becomes the nonlinear coefficient embedded in the system.

Vector method is more convenient and faster than Volterra series method. The vector method directly calculates the required core function and omits the hyperactive part of the series.

3 Analysis of Distortion Characteristics of Single Stage Amplifier

This section uses the commonly used vector method to investigate the distortion characteristics of feedback single stage amplifiers.

After the linear signal function is obtained, the multi-order nonlinear response signal is obtained by polynomial combination function. In this section, the accuracy of the inverter is verified by simulation analysis. The model is shown in Fig. 1 below.

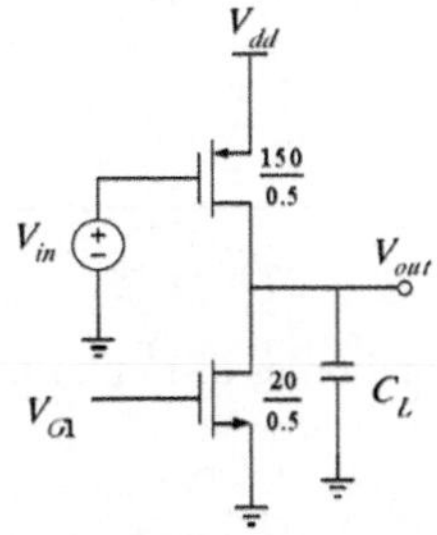

Fig. 1. Inverter with current leakage as load.

4 Simulation of Distortion Characteristics of Single Stage Amplifier

The accuracy of the above model is verified by comparing the theoretical analysis and simulation results. A single stage inverter with current leakage as load is used to verify the applicability of this method. A 0.35 μm CMOS process is used, and the single stage amplifier is configured in closed loop with reverse end input. The feedback amplifiers are fed into 100 MV sinusoidal signals and simulated in spectre (Table 1).

Table 1. Parameters of current amplifier.

Amplifier parameter			
Parameter	Name	Figure	Unit
A0	Open-loop DC gain	30	dB
FGgw	Unity gain band width	9.0	MHz
CL	Load capacitor	5	pF
f	Feedback factor	1/3	V/V
A0	Open-loop DC gain	30	dB

The distortion factor of the closed-loop amplifier can be obtained by Fourier analysis of the simulated output signal. The second and third order distortion factors obtained by the simulation of the inverter model with current leakage as load are shown in Figs. 2 and 3 below.

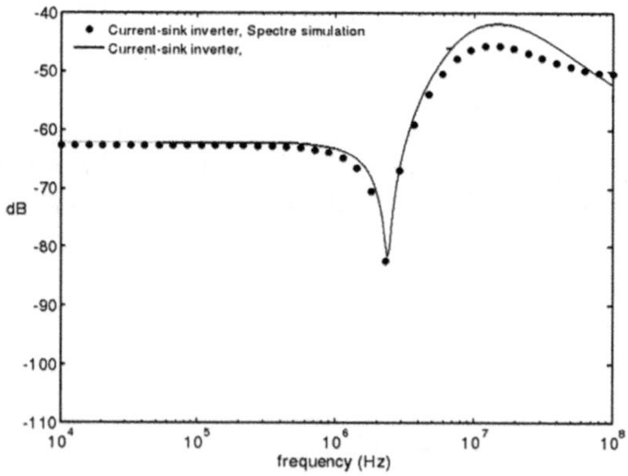

Fig. 2. Second-order distortion factor graph.

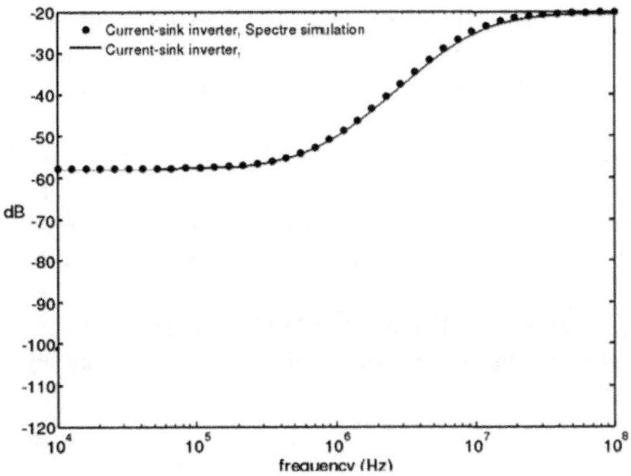

Fig. 3. Third-order distortion factor graph.

It can be seen from Figs. 2 and 3 that the simulation results of second and third order distortion factors are in good agreement. The distortion characteristics of the circuit can be calculated with high accuracy.

5 Summary

In this paper, the vector method is used to model and simulate the distortion characteristics of inverter with current leakage as load, and the expression of nonlinear distortion factor is derived. Improving the sensitivity of distortion factor is helpful to better reflect the distortion characteristics of the circuit. It is helpful to better understand the nonlinear problems of amplifiers and the analysis of circuit distortion characteristics, and provide guidance for the simulation analysis of circuit distortion characteristics.

References

1. Liu L, Wang ZH, Li GL (2005) Calculation of intermodulation distortion in CMOS transconductance stage. In: Proceedings of international symposium on circuits system, pp 3700–3703
2. Daliri M, Maymandi-Nejad M, Mafinezhad K (2009) Distortion analysis of bootstrap switch using volterra series. IET Circ Devices Syst 3(6):359–364
3. Yuan F, Opal A (2001) Distortion analysis of periodically switched nonlinear circuits using time-varying Volterra series. IEEE Trans Circuits Syst I Fund Theor Appl 48(6):726–738
4. Wambacq P, Vanthienen J, Gielen G, et al (1991) A design tool for weakly nonlinear analog integrated circuits with multiple inputs (mixers, multipliers). In: Proceedings of IEEE custom integrated circuit conference, pp 5.1/1–5.1/4
5. Eynde FO, Wambacq P, Sansen W (1989) On the relationship between the CMRR or PSRR and the second harmonic distortion in differential amplifiers. IEEE J Solid-State Circ 24 (6):1740–1744

6. Wambacq P, Gielen GGE, Kinget PR et al (1999) High-frequency distortion analysis of analog integrated circuits. IEEE Trans Circ Syst II 46(3):335–345
7. Hernes B, Sather T (2003) Design criteria for low distortion in feedback opamp circuits. Kluwer, Norwell
8. Palumbo G, Pennisi M, Pennisi S (2006) Analysis of harmonic dis-tortion in the Colpitts oscillator. In: IEEE international conference on electronics, circuits and systems, pp 196–199
9. Giustolisi G, Palumbo G, Pennisi S (2002) Harmonic distortion in single-stage amplifiers. In: Proceedings of international symposium on circuits and system (ISCAS 2002), vol 2, pp II-33–II-36
10. Cannizzaro SO, Palumbo G, Pennisi S (2008) An approach to model high-frequency distortion in negative-feedback amplifiers. Int J Circ Theor Appl 36(1):3–18

Gronwall Extension and Application to First Order Delay Differential Equations

Zhongqian Wang and Zhibin Yan(✉)

School of Mathematics, Harbin Institute of Technology, Shenzhen, Guangdong, China
1030232555@qq.com

Abstract. In this paper, a wider range of nonlinear delay integral inequalities is studied. The right side of the inequality includes two nonlinear factors with different unknown coefficients. By establishing a new Gronwall-Bellman delay integral inequality and basic inequality, some simple results are obtained. Finally, the results of inequality study are used to simplify the equation.

Keywords: Nonlinear integral inequalities · Delay Gronwall-Bellman inequalities

1 Introduction

In all kinds of solutions of differential equations and integral equations, it is important to study existence, stability and other qualitate properties. Gronwall inequality can help us to get some results on its generalization. There are some examples in [1–8]. What we want to study is Bihari's [9] for the nonlinear inequality

$$u(x) \leq a + \int_0^x \lambda(y)\omega(u(y))dy, x \geq 0, \tag{1.1}$$

Where $a > 0$ is a constant. Replacing x by a function b(y) in (1.1), Lipovan [10] investigates the retarded inequalities

$$u(x) \leq a + \int_{b(x_0)}^{b(x)} f(y)w(u(y))dy, x_0 \leq x < x_1, \tag{1.2}$$

And

$$u(x) \leq a + \int_{x_0}^{x} f(y)w(u(y))dy + \int_{b(x_0)}^{b(x)} g(y)w(u(y))dy, x_0 \leq x < x_1 \tag{1.3}$$

In this paper we consider such an inequality

Z. Xu et al. (Eds.): CSIA 2019, AISC 928, pp. 1280–1286, 2020.
https://doi.org/10.1007/978-3-030-15235-2_173

$$u(x) \le k + \int_0^x f(y)(\tau(y)) + g(y)u^a(\tau(y)) + h(y)u^\beta(\tau(y))dy, 0<x<x_1, \qquad (1.4)$$

in a general form. Some of our results can be deduced from [8, 9].

As an application of this formula, we show that the global existence lies in the neutralization of solutions of delay differential equations for functional differential equations.

2 Problem Formation and Preliminaries

Consider inequality (1.4) and suppose that

$(H_1)\omega_1(y) = u(y), \omega_2(y) = u^\alpha(y), \omega_3(y) = u^\beta(y)$ are continuous and are nondecreasing functions on $[0, +\infty)$ that $\omega_1 \propto \omega_2 \propto \omega_3$;

$(H_2)\alpha, \beta \epsilon (1, +\infty)$ and $\beta > \alpha$;

$(H_3) f(y), g(y), h(y)$ are continuous and nonnegative functions on $[x_0, x_1)$.

Take the notation $W_I(u, u_i) := \int_{u_i}^u \frac{d_z}{\omega_{i(z)}}$ for u > 0, where $u_i > 0$ is a given constant. $W_i(u)$ is simply denoted while it is not confusion. Syllabify, W_i is increasing, therefore, its inverse W_i^{-1} is great defined. It is growing in its corresponding fields.

Lemma 2.1. Let $z(x)$,$f(x)$ and $g(x)$ be nonnegative functions satisfying the inequality

$$z(x) \le k + \int_a^x [f(y)z(y) + g(y)z^n(y)]dy, \text{ for } t \in I = [a, b], \qquad (2.1)$$

where k $\ge$ 0 and n $\ge$ 1 are constants. If the following inequality:

$$k^{1-n} - (n-1)\int_a^x g(y)e^{\int_a^s (n-1)f(\tau)d\tau}dy > 0 \qquad (2.2)$$

Holds, then, for t $\in$ I,

$$z(x) \le \frac{e^{\int_a^x f(y)dy}}{\left(k^{1-n} - (n-1)\int_a^t g(y)e^{\int_a^x (n-1)f(\tau)d\tau}dy\right)^{\frac{1}{n-1}}}. \qquad (2.3)$$

Lemma 2.2. Assume that k $\ge$ 0, and $u(x)$ conditions that satisfy the delay integral inequalities listed below

$$u(x) \le k + \int_0^x f(y)(\tau(y)) + g(y)u^a(\tau(y)) + h(y)u^\beta(\tau(t))dy, 0<x<x_1, \qquad (2.4)$$

with initial condition u(t) = ∅(t)t ∈ $[t_1, 0]$, Then we get

$$u(x) \le e^{\int_0^x f(y)dy} + \left[(1-\alpha)\int_0^x g(y)e^{\alpha-1}dy\right]^{\frac{1}{1-\alpha}} + \left[(1-\beta)\int_0^x h(y)e^{\beta-1}dy\right]^{\frac{1}{1-\beta}}, \quad (2.5)$$

where

$$\begin{gathered}(1-\alpha)\int_0^x g(y)e^{\alpha-1}dy > 0, (1-\beta)\int_0^x h(y)e^{\beta-1}dy > 0.\\ K = k + \|\phi\|\int_0^{x^*} f(y)dy + \|\phi\|^\alpha \int_0^{x^*} g(y)dy + \|\phi\|^\beta \int_0^{x^*} h(y)dy,\\ x^* = \sup\{x : \tau(x) \le 0\}.\end{gathered} \quad (2.6)$$

Proof. Define a function v(t) by

$$v(x) = k + \int_0^x f(y)u(\tau(y)) + g(y)u^\alpha(\tau(y)) + h(y)u^\beta(\tau(y))dy. \quad (2.7)$$

Then, v(0) = k, v(x) is nondecreasing, and $u(x) \le v(x), x \ge 0$. It follows from (2.5) and (2.6) that

$$\begin{aligned} v(x) &= k + \int_0^{x^*} f(y)u(\tau(y))dy + \int_0^{x^*} g(y)u^\alpha(\tau(y))dy + \int_0^{x^*} h(y)u^\beta(\tau(y))dy\\ &+ \int_{x^*}^x f(y)u(\tau(y))dy + \int_{x^*}^x g(y)u^\alpha(\tau(y))dy + \int_{x^*}^x h(y)u^\beta(\tau(y))dy\\ &\le K + \int_{x^*}^x \left[f(y)u(\tau(y)) + g(y)u^\alpha(\tau(y)) + h(y)u^\beta(\tau(y))\right]dy \end{aligned} \quad (2.8)$$

where x^* is defined as in (2.5). Since $x^* \le y \le x$, we have

$$u(t) \le K + \int_0^x \left[f(y)u(y) + g(y)u^\alpha(y) + h(y)u^\beta(y)\right]dy, 0 \le x \le T, T \in [x_0, T_1].$$

3 Proof of Theorem

Theorem 3.1. Suppose $(H_1) - (H_3)$ hold.

$$\begin{aligned} v(x) &\le k + \int_0^x \left[f(y)u(\tau(y)) + g(y)u^\alpha(\tau(y)) + h(y)u^\beta(\tau(y))\right]\\ &\le \ln\frac{v}{v_1} + \frac{1}{1-\alpha}\left(v^{1-\alpha} - v_2^{1-\alpha}\right) + \frac{1}{1-\beta}\left(v^{1-\beta} - v_3^{1-\beta}\right) \end{aligned} \quad (3.1)$$

Proof. Having (3.1) we claim

$$u(x) \leq W_1^{-1}\left[W_1(k) + \int_0^x f(y)dy\right], 0 \leq x \leq T \leq T_2, \tag{3.2}$$

where

$$T_2 < x, W_1(k) + \int_0^{T_2} f(y)dy \leq \int_{v_1}^{\infty} \frac{du}{u} \leq \ln \frac{x}{v_1} \tag{3.3}$$

The following equation equals

$$u(x) \leq k + z(x), x \in [0, T], \tag{3.4}$$

where $z(x) := \int_0^x f(y)u(y)dy$ is differentiable, nonnegative and nondecreasing on $[0.y]$.

We have $\frac{z'(x)+k}{w_1(k+z(x))} \leq \frac{f_1(x)u(x)}{w_1(z(x)+k)} \leq \frac{f_1(x)u(z(x)+k)}{w_1(z(x)+k)} \leq f(x)$,
by differentiating inequalities on both sides from 0 to t, we get

$$W_1(z(x)+k) \leq W_1(k) + \int_0^x f(y)dy, 0 \leq x \leq T \tag{3.5}$$

Thus we conclude W_1^{-1} is nondecreasing,

$$u(x) \leq k + z(x) \leq W_1^{-1}\left[W_1(k) + \int_0^x f(y)dy\right], 0 \leq x \leq T \leq T_2 \tag{3.6}$$

Here we have

$$\begin{aligned} u(x) &\leq k + \int_0^x f(y)u(y)dy \leq k + z(x) \\ &\leq \omega_1^{-1}\left[W_1(k) + \int_0^x f(y)dy\right] \leq \ln \frac{x}{v_1}, 0 \leq x \leq T \leq T_2 \end{aligned} \tag{3.7}$$

Then we consider

$$u(x) \leq k + \int_0^x f(y)u(y) + g(y)u^{\alpha}(y)dy \tag{3.8}$$

Let $z(x) = k + \int_0^x f(y)u(y) + g(y)u^a(y)dy$, it is obviously that z(y) is differentiable, nonnegative and nondecreasing on $[0, x]$.

Thus we have

$$\begin{aligned}\frac{z'(x)+k}{w_1(k+z(x))} &\le \frac{f_1(x)u(x)+g(x)u(x)}{w_1(z(x)+k)}\\ &\le \frac{f_1(x)u(z(x)+k)}{w_1(z(x)+k)}+\frac{g(x)u^{\alpha}(z(x)+k)}{w_1(z(x)+k)}.\\ &\le f(x)+g(x)\phi_2(z(x)+k)\end{aligned} \tag{3.9}$$

where $\phi_2(m)=u^{\alpha-1}(m)$.

Then we get $\omega_1(z(x)+k)\le\omega_1(k)+\int_0^x f(y)dy+\int_0^x g(y)\phi_2[z(y)+k]dy, 0\le x\le T,$

$$c_1(t)=w_1(k)+\int_0^x f(y)dy, 0\le x\le T. \tag{3.10}$$

Let

$$\begin{aligned}&\xi(x)\le c_1(x)+\textstyle\int_0^x g(y)\phi_2[z(y)+k]dy\\ &\le\phi_2^{-1}\left[\phi_2 c_1(x)+\textstyle\int_0^x g(y)dy\right], x_0\le x\le\min\{T,T_3\}.'\end{aligned} \tag{3.11}$$

Where

$$\begin{aligned}&\phi_2(u)=\textstyle\int_{\overline{u_2}}^{u}\frac{dz}{\phi_2\left(\omega_1^{-1}(z)\right)}, u>0, \overline{u^{\alpha}}=\omega_1(u^{\alpha}).\\ &c_2(t)=\phi_2^{-1}\left[\phi_2 c_1(x)+\textstyle\int_0^x g(y)dy\right],\\ &\phi_2(c_1(T_3))+\textstyle\int_0^x g(y)dy\le\int_{\overline{u_2}}^{W_1(\infty)}\frac{dz}{\phi_2\left(\omega_1^{-1}(z)\right)}.\end{aligned}$$

$$\begin{aligned}\phi_2(u)&=\int_{\overline{u_2}}^{u}\frac{dz}{\phi_2\left(\omega_1^{-1}(z)\right)}=\int_{w_1(u^{\alpha})}^{u}\frac{u\left(w_1^{-1}(z)\right)dz}{u^{\alpha}\left(\omega_1^{-1}(z)\right)}\\ &=\int_{u_2}^{w_1^{-1}(u)}\frac{dz}{u^{\alpha}(z)}=w_2\left(w_1^{-1}(u)\right).\end{aligned} \tag{3.12}$$

Then we get

$$\begin{aligned}&u(x)\le k+\tau(t)=\omega_1^{-1}(\zeta(x))\\ &\le\omega_2^{-1}\left[\omega_2(\omega_1^{-1}(c_1(x)))+\int_0^x g(y)dy\right]'\end{aligned} \tag{3.13}$$

Let $\overline{c_2(x)}=W_1^{-1}(c_1(x))$,

$$\overline{c_1(x)}=W_1^{-1}(c_1(x))=W_1^{-1}\left(W_1(k)+\int_0^x f(y)dy\right)=\overline{r_3(x)}.$$

$$\begin{aligned}\overline{c_2(x)} &= \omega_1^{-1}\left\{\phi_2^{-1}\left[\phi_2(c_1(x)) + \int_0^x g(y)dy\right]\right\}\\ &= \omega_2^{-1}\left\{\omega_2\left[\omega_1^{-1}(c_1(x)) + \int_0^x g(y)dy\right]\right\}\\ &= \omega_2^{-1}\left\{\omega_2\left[\overline{c_1(x)} + \int_0^x g(y)dy\right]\right\}\\ &= W_{21}^{-1}\left(W_2\left(\overline{r_2(x)}\right) + \int_0^x g(y)dy\right) = \overline{r_3(x)}\end{aligned} \tag{3.14}$$

It is easily to get $\overline{c_2(x)} = \overline{r_4(x)}$.
Then we can get

$$\begin{aligned} W_2\left(\overline{r_2(x)}\right) + \int_0^x g(y)dy &\leq \int_{\overline{u^\alpha}}^{u(\infty)} \frac{dz}{\phi_2\left(W_1^{-1}(z)\right)} = \int_u^\infty \frac{dz}{u^\alpha(z)}\\ u(x) \leq W_2^{-1}\left[W_2\left(W_1^{-1}(c_1(x))\right) + \int_0^x g(y)dy\right] &\leq \int_u^\infty \frac{dz}{u^\alpha(z)} = \ln\frac{v}{v_1} + \frac{1}{1-\alpha}\left(v^{1-\alpha} - v_2^{1-\alpha}\right).\end{aligned} \tag{3.15}$$

Repeat the above algorithm, we can get

$$\begin{aligned} v(x) &\leq k + \int_0^x \left[f(y)u(\tau(y)) + g(y)u^\alpha(\tau(y)) + h(y)u^\beta(\tau(y))\right]\\ &\leq \ln\frac{v}{v_1} + \frac{1}{1-\alpha}\left(v^{1-\alpha} - v_2^{1-\alpha}\right) + \frac{1}{1-\beta}\left(v^{1-\beta} - v_3^{1-\beta}\right).\end{aligned} \tag{3.16}$$

Example 4.1. The exequality

$$u(x) \leq 1 + 2\int_0^x (y+1)\sqrt{u(y)}dy + 2\int_0^{\sqrt{x}} yu(y)dy, 0 \leq x \leq x_1 \tag{4.1}$$

implies

$$u(x) \leq 1 + 2\int_0^x (y+1)\sqrt{u(y)}dy + 2\int_0^x yu(y)dy, 0 \leq x \leq x_1 \tag{4.2}$$

By enlarging $\sqrt{x}$ to x. Apply our Theorem 3.1 we obtain

$$u(x) \leq \frac{1 + (1+x)^2}{2} e^x, 0 \leq x \leq x_1, \tag{4.3}$$

where $T_1 = t_1$ because $\int_{u_1}^\infty \frac{dz}{\sqrt{z}} = \infty$ and $\int_{u_2}^\infty \frac{dz}{z} = \infty$. On the other hand, Theorem 1 of [10] gives that

$$u(x) \leq \frac{1 + (1+x_1)^2}{2} e^{x^2}, 0 \leq x \leq x_1. \tag{4.4}$$

Clearly, (4.3) is sharper than (4.4) or large x.

References

1. Podlubny I (1999) Fractional differential equations, mathematics in science and engineering. Academic Press, New York
2. Kilbas A, Srivastava KM, Trujillo JJ (2006) Theory and applications of fractional differential equations. Elsevier, Amsterdam
3. Xu L, Hu H, Qin F (2016) Ultimate boundedness of impulsive fractional differential equations. Appl Math Lett 62:110–117
4. Liu Z, Li X (2013) Existence and uniqueness of solutions for the nonlinear impulsive fractional differential equations. Commun Nonlinear Sci Numer Simul 18:1362–1373
5. Khalil R, Horani M et al (2014) A new definition of fractional derivative. J Comput Appl Math 264:65–70
6. Abdeljawad T (2015) On conformable fractional calculus. J Comput Appl Math 279:57–66
7. Batarfi H et al (2015) Three-point boundary value problems for conformable fractional differential equations. J Funct Spaces 15:1–6
8. Hammad M, Khalil R (2014) Ablel's formula and wronskian for conformable fractional differential equations. Int J Differ Equ Appl 13(3):177–183
9. Gokdodgan A, Unal E (2015) Existence and uniqueness theorems for sequential linear conformable fractional differential equations. Mathematics 1–162
10. Khalil R, Abu-Shcab H (2015) Solution of some conformable fractional differential equations. Int J Pure Appl Math 103(4):667–673

Research on Improvement of Particle Swarm Optimization

Chunguang Chang and Xi Wu(✉)

School of Management, Shenyang Jianzhu University, Shenyang 110168, China
wxy0102w@163.com

Abstract. Although the particle swarm optimization algorithm has simple principle, few parameters and easy implementation, the particle swarm optimization algorithm is easy to fall into local optimum on multi-mode function and the local search ability is relatively weak. In this paper, the improvement of these two defects is carried out. The particle motion formula with learning model is added, and the generation strategy of a guided vector is added to improve the particle swarm optimization algorithm. The improved algorithm has a two-layer structure, and finally the research direction is prospected.

Keywords: Particle swarm algorithm · Two-layer structure · Improvement

1 Introduction

In 1987, Reynolds proposed a Boid (Bird-oid) model that simulates the collective flight behavior of birds. In this model, a Boid represents a flying bird with its own flight position and speed. Each bird can obtain information about the flight status of other birds in the population while flying, and it can adjust its current flight speed and direction based on this information to reach the desired destination. The model completely represents the group behavior of birds in flight in nature, but it is also limited to the flight process itself, and does not consider the purpose and result of the flight. The model shows that birds rely on group information and individual information to make decisions about their behavior during flight. The flight behavior of birds is obviously purposeful, so the model has perfect space. In 1990, Heppner combined this idea with the Boid model and proposed a new bird model. In 1995, American scholars James Kennedy and Russell Eberhart were inspired by the model to propose a particle swarm algorithm. The particle swarm algorithm has a simple principle and good performance. Therefore, it has been loved by many scholars and researchers at home and abroad, and has conducted in-depth research. Particle swarm optimization also has defects such as easy to fall into local minimum points, large dependence on search performance on parameters, and insufficient theory. In response to these shortcomings, many improvements have been made at home and abroad to improve its ability to solve complex function problems. At present, the research on particle swarm optimization at home and abroad is mainly divided into three aspects: optimization of particle swarm theory analysis, strategy improvement of particle swarm optimization algorithm and practical application of particle swarm optimization algorithm in practical problems.

Z. Xu et al. (Eds.): CSIA 2019, AISC 928, pp. 1287–1292, 2020.
https://doi.org/10.1007/978-3-030-15235-2_174

2 Research on Improvement of Particle Swarm Optimization Algorithm Parameters

2.1 PSO Algorithm

In PSO, each particle represents a latent solution to the optimization problem, and the entire particle swarm is flying in the search space to find the optimal solution. In the D-dimensional search space, let the particle velocity vector be $V_i = (V_{i1}, V_{i2}, \ldots, V_{iD})$ and the position vector be $X_i = (x_{i1}, x_{i2}, \ldots, x_{iD})$. According to the search space, the velocity vector and the position vector are randomly initialized for each particle. The update formula of particle and velocity is as follows:

$$v_{id}^{t+1} = wv_{id}^{t} + c_1 r_{1d}\left(p_{id}^{t} - x_{id}^{t}\right) + c_2 r_{2d}\left(p_{gd}^{t} - x_{id}^{t}\right) \tag{1}$$

$$x_{id}^{t+1} = x_{id}^{t} + v_{id}^{t+1} \tag{2}$$

w represents the inertia weight, c_1 and c_2 represent the acceleration factor, and r_1 and r_2 represent the random number uniformly distributed between [0, 1]. The variable d represents a certain dimension of a particle ($d \in [1, D]$), p_g represents the historical optimal position of the entire particle swarm discovery, p_i represents the historical optimal position found by particle i, and the variable t represents the current number of iterations.

2.2 Improvement Ideas

From the formula of the basic particle swarm algorithm, it can be seen that the particle swarm algorithm is affected by the parameters in the running process. Therefore, the improvement and optimization of the particle swarm parameters has been a hot topic for many scholars. Among them, the most important one is the improvement around the inertia weight and learning factor. However, the improved optimization of these simple parameters is not ideal. Therefore, some scholars consider starting from the fundamental principle of particle swarm optimization to improve the optimization effect. Literature [1] introduced the concepts of scalar operators and learning operators on the basis of standard particle swarms, and proposed a new vector cooperative particle swarm optimization algorithm. In [2], an adaptive particle swarm optimization algorithm based on gradient search algorithm was proposed. The particle position is updated with a linearly increasing probability to update the negative gradient direction, which can effectively avoid the particles falling into the local optimal position. In [3], a particle swarm optimization algorithm based on neighborhood search was proposed. Through the neighborhood search strategy, neighboring particles learn from each other and balance the ability of particle exploration and development. The convergence accuracy of the algorithm is greatly improved. Literature [4] proposed a particle swarm optimization algorithm based on lens imaging reverse learning strategy. The algorithm also introduces the search and development performance of scaling factor and search radius balance algorithm, which improves population diversity and convergence accuracy. Literature

[5] introduces two mechanisms: competitive group optimizer and reverse learning. According to the fitness value, different learning mechanisms are selected, and an opposite learning competition particle swarm optimization algorithm is proposed. In [6], an adaptive particle swarm optimization algorithm is proposed. In the process of particle running, according to the changes of the evolutionary environment, it is dynamically adapted to the operating environment and improves the performance of the algorithm.

Since many particle swarm versions use only global optimization and historical optimization, the optimization performance of the algorithm in complex environments is limited. The DE algorithm can help improve the performance of the PSO algorithm. The PSO algorithm updates the flight speed and the position of the child through the individual history optimization and the population optimization. The DE algorithm updates the children by combining the parent difference vector with the target individual and competing with the parent. So far, many hybrid algorithms for DE and PSO have been proposed. Literature [7] proposed a particle swarm optimization algorithm (DEPSO) with mixed differential variation. In DEPSO, a global version of PSO and bell-shaped variants are used. The hybrid algorithm (DEPSO-MV) was proposed in [8]. The EPSO-MV uses the DE/rand/2 variant and the particle swarm algorithm with ring topology. The literature [9] proposes a hybrid framework that uses different DE variants to evolve individual historical optimal particles of different PSO versions. The literature [10] proposed a chaotic-based co-evolution algorithm (CCDEPSO). However, many hybrid algorithm versions still have difficulty avoiding local optimization. In the past two decades, researchers have proposed many differential variability schemes. The results show that some differential variants have better global search ability, and some differential variants have better local search capabilities. In recent years, speed update formulas with learning models have been widely used in the research of particle swarm optimization. Based on these observations, this paper adopts the particle motion formula with learning model, and adds a guiding vector generation strategy to improve the particle swarm optimization algorithm. The improved algorithm has a two-tier structure: top and bottom. The top layer consists of all Pis and the bottom layer consists of all Xis. According to the division of the global search and the local search function, the top-level particles are divided into two sub-groups, which are represented by swarm1 and swarm2, respectively.

The particle speed update formula is as follows:

$$v_{id} = wv_{id} + cr_d(GV_{id} - x_{id}) \tag{3}$$

c is the acceleration constant, r_d is a uniformly distributed random number between 0 and 1, and GV_{id} is the steering vector.

In this paper, a differential evolution algorithm is used to generate the steering vector. DE has a good global search capability. Therefore, the differential mutation operation can generate a variety of guidance vectors, which can make the improved algorithm avoid premature convergence and enhance local search ability.

In the DE algorithm, each individual is a potential solution to the problem $X = (x_{i1}, x_{i2}, \cdots, x_{iD})$, where X represents the i-th individual. When DE is initialized, the algorithm randomly generates N individuals to form the initial population. For each iteration, according to the corresponding mutation strategy, a variation vector

$V_{im} = (v_{i1}, v_{i2}, \cdots, v_{iD})$ is generated for the individual i. The usual mutation operations are as follows:

$$\text{DE/rand/1} \quad V_{im,d} = X_{r1,d} + F \cdot (X_{r2,d} - X_{r3,d}) \tag{4}$$

$$\text{DE/current-to-best/1} \quad V_{im,d} = X_{i,d} + F \cdot (X_{best,d} - X_{i,d}) + F \cdot (X_{r1,d} - X_{r2,d}) \tag{5}$$

$$\text{DE/rand/1} \quad V_{im,d} = X_{best,d} + F \cdot (X_{r1,d} - X_{r2,d}) \tag{6}$$

$$\text{DE/rand/2} \quad V_{im,d} = X_{best,d} + F \cdot (X_{r1,d} - X_{r2,d}) + F \cdot (X_{r3,d} - X_{r4,d}) \tag{7}$$

$$\text{DE/rand/2} \quad V_{im,d} = X_{r1,d} + F \cdot (X_{r2,d} - X_{r3,d}) + F \cdot (X_{r4,d} - X_{r5,d}) \tag{8}$$

Where $r_1, r_2, r_3, r_4, r_5 \in \{1, 2, \ldots, N\}$ are mutually unequal integers not equal to i, and F is a scaling factor between values (0, 1). X_{best} represents the best individual in the current population.

After the mutation, a binomial crossover operator is performed on X_i and V_{im} to generate a new test vector U_i.

The specific implementation of the cross operation is as follows:

$$U_{i,d} = \begin{cases} Vim, d, \text{if } \mathrm{r}_3 \leq CR \quad or \quad j = j_{rand} \\ X_{i,d}, \ otherwise \end{cases} \tag{9}$$

Among them, the crossover probability CR is a predetermined constant, and the value range is [0.1]. j_{rand} is an evenly distributed integer between [1, D].

After the crossover operation is the selection operation. The main purpose of the selection operation is to select individuals with better fitness to enter the next generation. The specific implementation of the selection operation is as follows:

$$X_i = \begin{cases} U_i, \text{if } f(U_i) \leq f(X_i) \\ X_{i,d}, \ otherwise \end{cases} \tag{10}$$

Where $f(X_i)$ is the fitness value of the individual X_i. Through the selection operation, it is ensured that the one-to-one individuals proceed in a direction of good fitness, thereby improving the average fitness of the entire group. After the formation of a new generation of groups, the differential algorithm continuously evolves the group through mutation, intersection, and selection operations until the corresponding exit conditions are met.

The steps for generating the boot vector are as follows: (1) Cross variation: In order to ensure the simplicity and functional requirements of the algorithm, two differential variations of DE/rand/1 and DE/current-to-best/1 are used in this paper. (2) Crossover: Binomial crossover using the DE algorithm, refer to Eq. (9). Since the improved algorithm uses two differential variations, two different cross-parameter values are required. (3) Selection: The selection operation of DE refers to Eq. (10). The selection operation ensures that the top-level particles evolve in a good direction for each generation.

2.3 Main Steps to Improve the Algorithm

The main steps are described as follows: (1) Randomly initialize the speed and position of N particles and set some necessary parameter values. (2) Evaluate the fitness values of all particles and set Pi, Pg and t = 0. (3) While t < Maxiter do. (4) Use the formula (4) variation. (5) According to the subgroup where the particles are located, select different cross values and use the formula (9) for cross operation. (6) The selection operation is performed using the formula (10), and the guidance vector is updated. (7) Calculate the velocity and position of each particle using Eqs. (3) and (2). (8) Evaluate the fitness value of each particle and update Pi and Pg. (9) t = t + 1. (10) end while.

3 Conclusion

In this paper, two different differential variants are introduced into the PSO. Based on two differential mutation operations, the improved algorithm adopts a two-layer and two-group structure. One subgroup has better global search capabilities, while another subgroup has better local search capabilities. So far, some effective adaptive strategies for DE parameters have been proposed. Obviously, these adaptive strategies can be used to improve the PSO based on this. Trying to integrate into other hybrid technologies and parametric adaptive strategies is a potential research direction.

Acknowledgments. This research was supported by the National Natural Science Foundation of China (Project No. 51678375), Natural Science Foundation of Liaoning Province (Project No. 2015020603), and the basic scientific research project of Liaoning Higher Education (Project No. LJZ2017009).

References

1. Zhang Q, Liu W, Meng X, et al (2017) Vector coevolving particle swarm optimization algorithm. Inf Sci 394(C):273–298
2. Li R, Shen Y, Liu J (2015) Improved adaptive particle swarm optimization algorithm. Comput Eng Appl 51(13):31–36. (in Chinese)
3. Wang H, Sun H, Li C et al (2013) Diversity enhanced particle swarm optimization with neighborhood search. Inf Sci Int J 223(2):119–135
4. Fei Yu, Yuanxiang L, Bo W et al (2014) Application of lens imaging inverse learning strategy in particle swarm optimization algorithm. Chin J Electron 42(2):230–235
5. Zhou J, Fang W, Wu X, et al (2016) An opposition-based learning competitive particle swarm optimizer. In: Evolutionary computation. IEEE
6. Wang Y, Li B, Weise T et al (2010) Self-adaptive learning based particle swarm optimization. Inf Sci 81(20):4515–4538
7. Zhang WJ, Xie XF (2003) DEPSO: hybrid particle swarm with differential evolution operator. In: 2003 IEEE international conference on systems, man and cybernetics, vol 4. IEEE, pp 3816–3821
8. Moore PW, Venayagamoorthy GK (2006) Evolving digital circuits using hybrid particle swarm optimization and differential evolution. Int J Neural Syst 16(03):163–177

9. Epitropakis MG, Plagianakos VP, Vrahatis MN (2012) Evolving cognitive and social experience in particle swarm optimization through differential evolution: a hybrid approach. Inf Sci 216:50–92
10. Zhang M, Zhang W, Sun Y (2009) Chaotic co-evolutionary algorithm based on differential evolution and particle swarm optimization. In: 2009 IEEE international conference on automation and logistics, ICAL 2009. IEEE, pp 885–889

The Rolling Process Analysis and Groove Optimization of 16# I-Beam Based on FEM

Rui Tang[1(✉)] and Qi Zhang[2]

[1] Aviation Engineering Institute, Civil Aviation Flight University of China, Guanghan, Sichuan, China
904200315@qq.com

[2] School of Intelligent Manufacturing, Panzhihua University, Panzhihua, Sichuan, China

Abstract. This paper points out that using the finite element software of a production enterprise of conjugate pass system has carried on the simulation of rolling process, in view of the rolled piece in the process of rolling bending, torsion and other issues, through the way of quantitative analysis and deformation analysis to find out the causes of these problems, the roller in rolling process based on sharing under the premise of groove parameters optimization design, and the groove of the optimized finite element simulation, the results showed that after the adjustment groove is better than the original value of the parameters, can satisfy the requirement of the actual production technical innovation.

Keywords: I beam · FEM simulation · Bend · Twist · Pass optimization

1 Introduction

An enterprise now USES 150 mm × 150 mm square billet to roll no. 16 i-beam, which is required to roll without changing the original equipment of the enterprise [1] (two three-high rolling mills and one two-high rolling mill). According to the characteristic of rolling mill, the engineer designs a set of conjugate pass system [2].

Reasonable pass design should guarantee the quality of products, improve the output of rolling mills, reduce the cost of products, and adapt to the equipment in the workshop [3]. The finite element numerical simulation technology can be used to assist the optimization design of the pass, and at the same time, it can avoid the use of the actual test cost of manpower, funds and time [4, 5]. In this paper using by MSC, to simulate the process of rolling, found the pass system of poor stability in the process of rolling groove, and the groove is bend torsion and deformation analysis, find out the cause of the defects, and put forward the optimization scheme of pass, design a set of the pass system is more reasonable.

2 Finite Element Simulation of Rolling Process

Hot rolled 16 beams belongs to the large deformation of metal plastic deformation process, and the rolled piece can ignore the elastic deformation and by using the rigid-plastic material model, the coupled thermo-mechanical analysis process [6], workpiece

Z. Xu et al. (Eds.): CSIA 2019, AISC 928, pp. 1293–1298, 2020.
https://doi.org/10.1007/978-3-030-15235-2_175

material is Q235, material stress-strain curve obtained by GLEE experiments, and the young's modulus, specific heat, coefficient of thermal conductivity, convective heat transfer coefficient as are required to consider the influence of the temperature. The material density was, poisson's ratio was 0.3, thermal expansion coefficient was 0.9, thermal radiation coefficient was 0.9, and contact heat transfer coefficient was taken.

The roller is set as rigid body, and the roller temperature is. Since the groove is the skew rolling process, only the whole modeling can be adopted for modeling. The model of each pass rolling piece is constructed by extracting the peripheral node information of the section of the last stable rolling section, taking the length of 900 mm and adopting the 8-node hexahedral element, with the initial temperature of [7]. Shear friction is applied between the rolls and the friction coefficient is 0.3. In the rolling process, with the rolling speed of 5 m/s, a push plate shall be established to push the rolled piece smoothly into the rolling process at the initial stage of rolling and return it after the rolled piece enters stable rolling.

3 The Simulation Results and Analysis

3.1 Quantitative Analysis

Check the whole rolling process simulation results show that K4 passes the larger bending and torsion, as shown in Fig. 1, serious bend torsion will adverse effects on the next time the rolling, need through the quantitative analysis for the actual production to assess [8].

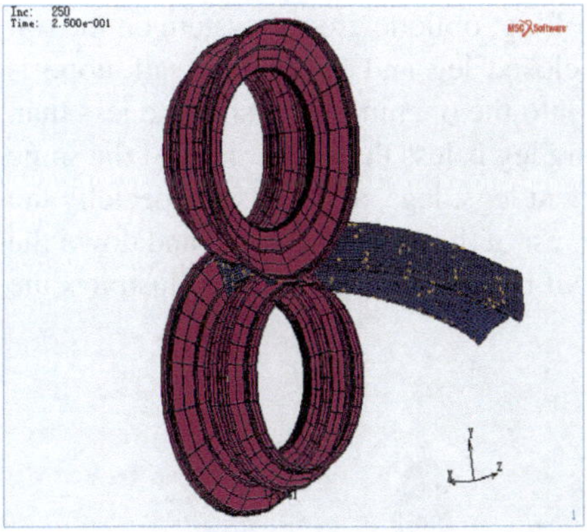

Fig. 1. Simulation result of K4

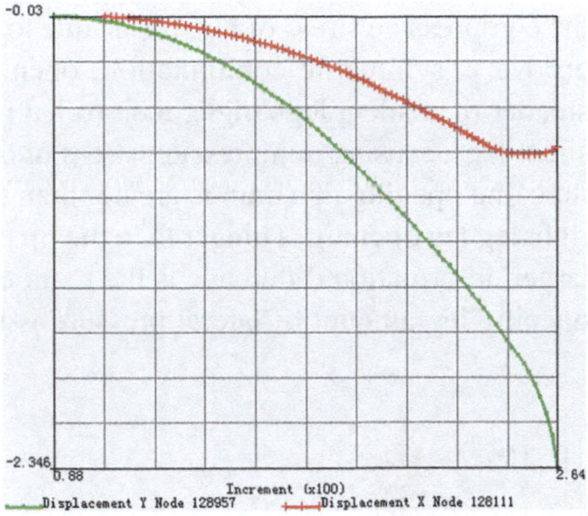

Fig. 2. X and Y direction displacements of node 128111

Within 150 mm cross section of the rolled piece face took on a node, 128111, through dynamic demo to find out the cross section is located in the export of rolling incremental step 88, extract the node from the 88th incremental step to complete the process of rolling in the X direction of rotation (roll) displacement, as shown in Fig. 2. Results show rolled piece 600 mm length upper curved quantity is 68.37 mm, can estimate the amount of lateral rolling 12 m beams is 1367.4 mm.

Extract the node from the 88th incremental step to Y in the complete process of rolling direction (vertical direction) of the displacement, as shown in Fig. 2. Results show rolled piece 600 mm length and amount of bend is 231.6 mm, can estimate the amount of rolling 12 m beams under bending is 4632 mm.

Within 150 mm cross section of the rolled piece face again take a node on the 123504, and extract the two nodes in the incremental step 88 and finish rolling (264) incremental step coordinate information, as shown in Table 1. Results show rolled piece on the 600 mm length for torsional Angle, can estimate the rolling 12 m beams for torsion Angle [9].

Table 1. Coordinates of nodes

Node	X(88 step)	Y(88 step)	X(264 step)	Y(264 step)
123504	94.5480	16.9473	20.4329	−220.7761
128111	−88.7697	−7.9527	−155.1439	−236.3581

3.2 Deformation Analysis

As shown in Figs. 3 and 4 for K4 rolling rolling piece for export of equivalent stress and strain diagram, you can see the whole cross section, uneven distribution of stress, strain and rolled piece middle metal waist by roll, under the pressure of the metal to flow on both sides of the free end, and the middle position furthest from the free end, and metal flow is difficult, by large compressive stress, and direct contact with roll waist under the surface of the maximum compressive stress [10]. Leg is the stress distribution is layered, from external to internal can decrease step by step. Open leg slightly less than silent by the compressive stress of leg, this is due to the rolling, oblique groove system on the roll groove is symmetric configuration, open and closed leg and leg inside wall slope is smaller than silent leg Angle, then rolled piece into the opening leg resistance less than silent legs, causing compression stress of opening leg is less than silent leg. At the same time, the opening tip strain is greater than the silent legs, legs, at the base, especially the right leg leg opening is bigger than the tip of the rest of the leg, right leg up and down the larger deformation difference is the main cause of rolled piece to reverse, illustrates the opening leg amount of lateral pressure is big.

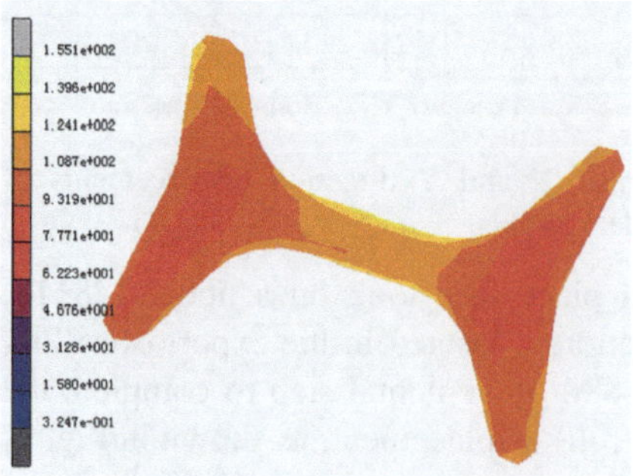

Fig. 3. Stress contour of K4

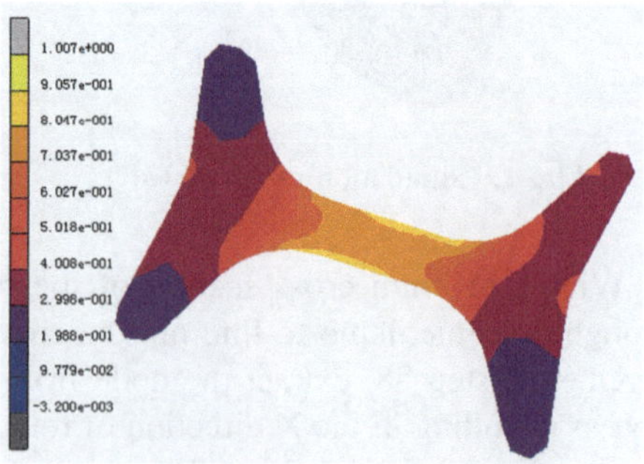

Fig. 4. Strain contour of K4

3.3 Extension Analysis

As shown in Table 2, K4 hole upper elongation is greater than the lower elongation, and rolling workpiece under bending phenomenon, and the main reason is because there are many differences between the waist and elongation. You can also see K4 silent leg extension rate is greater than the opening on the right side leg, caused in the process of rolling torsion of the rolled piece.

Table 2. Ductility of parts of K4 hole pattern

	Upper	Lower	Upper waist	Lower waist	Upper leg
Elongation	1.4082	1.3111	2.1710	1.5857	1.0991
	Lower leg	Right side of the open mouth leg	Left side of the open mouth leg		
Elongation	1.0912	1.1264	1.0951		

4 Pass to Optimize

To improve rolling, can take the main reduce the opening on the right side leg legs tip and root amount of lateral pressure, appropriately increasing the silent root lateral pressure leg leg and right leg leg held pointed the amount of lateral pressure method to improve the lateral bending and torsion; By reducing the waist upper reduction to improve under bending. At the same time, because of the particularity of the pass system, namely the three roll mill roll in up and down two times sharing, K3, K4 with roller is shown in Fig. 5, for K4, on the right side of the legs pass changes should consider its impact on the pass of the K3. Rolled piece in K3 passes slightly upward in the process of rolling, rolling export Fig. 6 for K3 passes slice equivalent strain figure, it can be seen on the right side silent leg strain is less than the opening leg, enlargement of K3, K4) on the right side silent leg deformation, can at the same time become warped on improvement of K3, K4 tao time and bending [11].

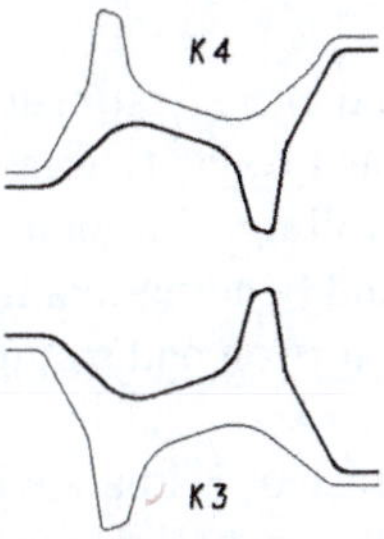

Fig. 5. Roll-arranging diagram of K3, K4

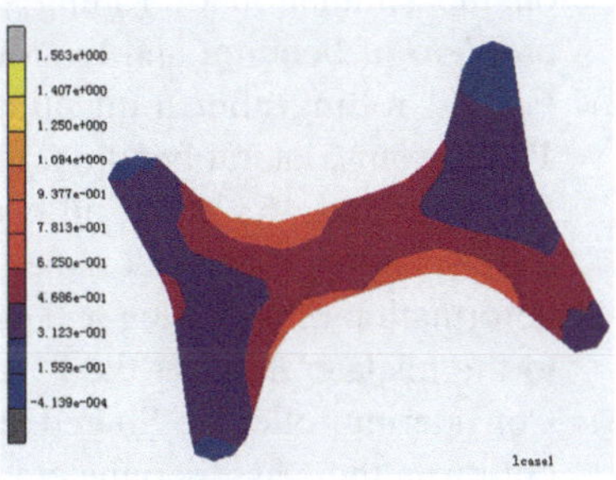

Fig. 6. Strain contour of K3

Based on the deformation characteristics and the process conditions of K4 groove is optimized, as shown in Fig. 6, increase the width between the tips of the right leg leg opening (increased by 14 mm for 17 mm) and the width of the leg root (increased by 32 mm is 34 mm), silent root width reduced 1 mm leg leg, right leg leg held pointed reduced 1 mm width, in order to ensure the workpiece deformation is relatively consistent, avoid rolled piece side bending and torsion; The waist upper reduced reduction (waist increased by 2.5 mm thick), decreased the upper waist elongation to control the bending of the rolled piece (Fig. 7).

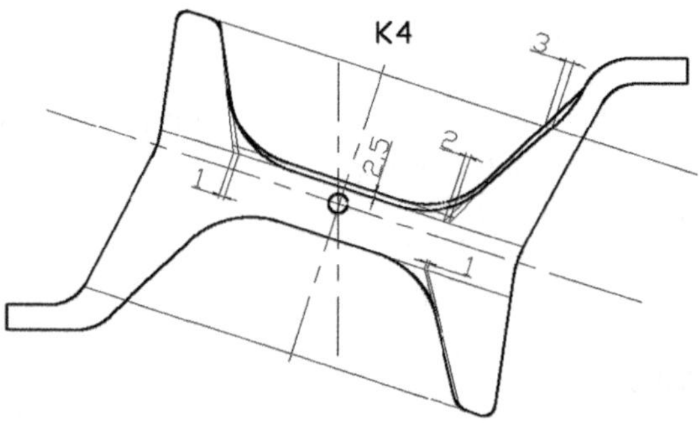

Fig. 7. Hole pattern optimization of K4

By using the optimized roller to roll model is established, and the same conditions in finite element simulation of rolling process. View the results in the groove after the optimization, 600 mm in length of rolled piece to the displacement of the 9.55 mm X, Y to the displacement of the 11.85 mm, for the torsional Angle, both can satisfy the requirement of rolling.

5 Conclusion

(1) Using finite element method (fem) to 16 beams conjugate pass system has carried on the simulation of rolling process, found the K4 including a more serious problem of bending and torsion.

(2) For K4 rolling after a quantitative analysis of rolled piece, estimate the rolling 12 m beams, lateral bending, the bending and torsional capacity were 1367.4 and 53.2 mm and 4632 mm, all can affect a time after rolling. Through deformation analysis pointed out that under the lateral bending and bending mainly due to the deformation of upper leg and elongation than vol. 6, torsion and strain mainly due to the ipsilateral leg at the base.

(3) Considering roller are Shared, change under the premise of K4 pass will affect K3, optimize the pass parameters, increase the K4 pass right leg opening width, reduced the silent leg width on the right side, reduced the silent leg root on both sides with the size of the waist joint rounded corners. Through the finite element verification, optimization scheme is feasible.

(4) Based on the finite element analysis, found the deficiencies in the design of pass system, provides a way for similar rolling process research, has higher reference value for practical production applications.

References

1. Songyun Z, Wenlin T (2005) Pass design of section steel. Metallurgical Industry Press, Beijing
2. Tao C (2014) Section rolling. Metallurgical Industry Press, Beijing
3. Wang Y et al (2014) Modern steel rolling. Metallurgical Industry Press, Beijing
4. Wang Y, Qi K (2012) Metal and plastic processing: rolling theory and process. Metallurgical Industry Press, Beijing
5. Zhang Y, Chen H et al (2012) FEM simulation and pass system adjustment of hot rolling of 150 mm × 168 mm billet. Hot Working Technol 41(32)
6. Zhang S, Liu J et al (2015) Advanced materials processing technology and realization of MSC.Marc. National defense industry press, Beijing
7. Liu H, Zhao X, Wu D (2006) Profiled billet deformation simulation of H beam slab by FEM. J Plast Eng 13(5)
8. Tao G, Cheng C, Feng W (2010) Finite element analysis of twist of 60D40 switch rail during rolling. Steel Rolling 27(1)
9. Lee Y (2012) An analytical study of mean roll radius in rod rolling. ISIJ Int 41(11):1414–1416
10. Yan G, Yong Z (2006) Finite element simulation of section deflection during H-beam roller straightening. J Univ Sci Technol Beijing 28(12):1157
11. Galantucci LM, Tricarico L (1999) Thermo-mechanical simulation of a rolling process with an FEM approach. J Mater Proc Technol 92:494–501

Study on the Management Mode of Asphalt Pavement Cracks in Different Climatic Zones

Xin Lan[1(✉)] and Xiangguo Chang[2]

[1] Department of Geological Engineering, Chang'an University, Xi'an, Shaanxi, China
598274383@qq.com

[2] Key Laboratory for Special Area Highway Engineering of Ministry of Education, Chang'an University, Xi'an, Shaanxi, China

Abstract. According to the difference and uncertainty of the destructional forms of asphalt pavement cracks in different regions of China, through investigation and analysis, referring to climatic zoning for highway, the different destructional forms of cracks in Northern permafrost regions, Southern hot and humid regions, Northwest arid regions and Qinghai Tibet Plateau permafrost region were introduced, then combined with different climatic conditions and traffic conditions in different regions, the paper puts forward the management mode of asphalt pavement in different climate areas, provided a reference for the prevention, detection and effective repair of asphalt pavement cracks in different climatic regions in China.

Keywords: Asphalt pavement cracks · Climatic zones · Destructional forms · Management mode · Prevention · Detection · Repair

1 Introduction

Asphalt pavement is widely used in urban roads and highways because of its excellent road performance, and it has become the main pavement structure form of high-grade highway in China. According to the relevant survey data, the proportion of asphalt pavement is over 90% in the high grade highways that have been built [1]. Although asphalt pavement with advantages of good comfort, smooth running and low noise, under the combined action of environmental conditions, traffic load and other factors, the asphalt pavement is prone to various kinds of diseases such as cracks, pits, tracks and so on, this situation directly affects the service performance and service life of the highway. Crack is the most common type of damage in the asphalt pavement, It not only damages the integrity of pavement structure, but also reduces the overall service performance of the road.

China's climate is also complex and diverse. In different climatic zones, there are great differences in water temperature, geological conditions and traffic load distribution, so the inducing factors, manifestations and development trends of asphalt pavement cracks are different. This paper is aimed at the difference of crack failure modes of asphalt pavement under different climatic conditions in China. According to the natural division of highways, this paper comprehensively summarizes and classifies the

Z. Xu et al. (Eds.): CSIA 2019, AISC 928, pp. 1299–1304, 2020.
https://doi.org/10.1007/978-3-030-15235-2_176

formation mechanism, manifestation and influencing factors of cracks in different climate zones, and discuss the management mode of asphalt in different areas. This further enriches the classification form of asphalt pavement cracks and provides theoretical reference for the prevention and maintenance of asphalt pavement cracks in various regions.

2 The Northern Permafrost Region

The northern permafrost region belongs to the high latitude and low altitude permafrost region, mainly located in northern Heilongjiang, northern Inner Mongolia and parts of Xinjiang.

The surface cracks in the northern permafrost region can be divided into two types: temperature contraction cracks and base reflective cracks.

①Temperature contraction cracks: This kind of cracks is mainly caused by insufficient bonding strength of base asphalt and aggregate or poor temperature stability of asphalt materials. At the beginning, the cracks only occur in the surface layer and the depth is shallow, it can heal automatically at high temperatures in summer. But if the cracks are not repaired in time, the stress relaxation ability of the materials will deteriorate, the width and depth of cracks will develop rapidly under the effect of long-term vehicle load and frequent freeze-thaw cycles, which provides a channel for water to enter the substrate.

②Reflective cracking of the base: When the temperature changes, the frost heave phenomenon occurs on the interlayer water in the semi-rigid base layer of the road surface, The stress generated by the volume expansion of the base material causes cracking of the base layer, when the tensile stress increases to more than the ultimate tensile stress of the asphalt mixture, the crack spreads from the bottom to the surface layer, eventually leading to cracks on the road surface. The reflective cracking of the base mainly manifest as longitudinal crack, and most of them appear on the south faced slope of the high embankment road, generally close to the shoulder [2]. If it is not repaired in time, the cracks will develop rapidly under the repeated action of rain, snow and load, which will affect the driving comfort and even threaten the driving safety.

3 The Southern Wet-Heat Region

In the southern wet-heat region, investigation shows that water is the leading factor in the occurrence of disease.

The surface cracks in the southern wet-heat region can be divided into three types: water-damage cracks, loading type cracks and temperature fatigue cracks.

①Water-damage cracks: The southern humid hot zone has large rainfall and concentrated time, resulting in a high groundwater level. Such cracks often occur in the form of longitudinal cracks. If they are not repaired, the water will cause further damage to the base layer and seriously affect the road service performance. Through engineering practice, it is found that if the soil foundation adopts effective waterproof measures and the roadbed is layered and filled, the degree of compaction meets the standard, which can greatly reduce the number of longitudinal cracks and delay the occurrence of time [1]. Therefore, in such areas where cracks occur frequently, road management should focus on the above aspects.

②Loading type cracks: Under the double action of high continuous load and environmental factors, local stress concentration occurs in asphalt pavement, and the appearance of micro-cracks leads to the decrease of bearing pressure area and the increase of effective stress. Under the driving pressure of the vehicle, high shear stress occurs repeatedly on the road surface in the longitudinal direction of the wheel edge, and divergent longitudinal cracks and mesh cracks are generated on the asphalt pavement surface [3]. At the same time, due to heavy precipitation and frequent rainfall in the southeast region, it is easy for rain water to penetrate deep into the pavement structure from road surface cracks. The dynamic water pressure and suction force caused by the driving force continuously impact the road surface, making the asphalt film and aggregate fall off and the overall structural strength of the surface layer gradually lose. If the crack is not treated in time, it will develop rapidly, and then there will be loose, pit and other diseases.

③Temperature fatigue cracks: Such cracks often occur in areas with high temperature and frequent temperature changes in southern China. Under the effect of temperature stress caused by the temperature cycle of daytime high temperature and night low temperature, sunny high temperature and short rainstorm low temperature, the ultimate tensile strain and stiffness modulus of asphalt concrete become smaller, and the stress relaxation ability decreases, and some of the deformation generated cannot be recovered again. After a period of time, the pavement cracked at a temperature that was not too low [4].

4 The Northwest Arid Region

The northwestern arid region is mainly distributed in most parts of Xinjiang, northern part of Ningxia, Shaanxi and Gansu, and most parts of Inner Mongolia.

The surface cracks in the northwest arid region can be divided into two types: temperature cracks and reflection cracks on asphalt pavement base.

①Temperature cracks: Temperature cracks in the northwest arid region mainly include temperature fatigue cracks and low- temperature shrink cracks. In the northwest arid region, the temperature changes dramatically and the ultraviolet light is strong, which leads to the severe aging of asphalt. The temperature stress generated by the huge temperature changes in a short time also stretches and compresses the asphalt concrete, resulting in the reduced ultimate tensile strength of asphalt concrete. Therefore, asphalt pavement will produce temperature fatigue cracks earlier [5]. The low-temperature shrink cracks are mainly caused by the extreme low temperature in winter. These two kinds of cracks appear very frequently, and there is a crack in the road every certain distance. The fracture occurs in the surface layer and then spreads down over time.

②Reflection cracks on asphalt pavement base: There are two situations for the occurrence of such cracks. One is that due to the high latitude, the onset of winter is earlier and the crack is located in the inland hinterland. In places with high underground water level, the freezing depth of subgrade in winter is very great. In the spring of the next year, when the temperature warmed up, the ice in the subgrade began to melt, and the water moved and could not be removed in time, resulting in the unstable state of the subgrade soil. The consolidation subsidence formed by the melting of permafrost weakened the load-bearing effect of the subgrade and the base layer, resulting in subsidence [6]. The second situation occurs in dry climate, low underground water level, but soil desertification serious areas. In this region, if the treatment is not perfect in the construction process, under the action of high strength driving load, the soil foundation and the base layer have insufficient bearing capacity, which leads to subsidence and fracture. The difference in vertical displacement between plates leads to huge shear force in the surface layer, and cracks will be transferred from the base layer to the surface layer, and then develop into faults, subsidence and other diseases.

5 The Qinghai-Tibet Alpine-Cold and Frozen Soil Region

The Qinghai-Tibet alpine-cold area is mainly distributed in Tibet, Qinghai province, western Sichuan province and other regions, with the following characteristics: low annual average temperature, small annual temperature difference and large daily temperature difference, less precipitation and uneven seasonal distribution, high elevation and strong solar radiation and long hours of sunshine. The Qinghai-Tibet alpine-cold area is the largest permafrost region in China. Soil is a kind of negative ice temperature geological body which is very sensitive to temperature and external factors. The permafrost is the soil that has been frozen for more than two years. It is the product of interaction of earth atmosphere system and geological history [7]. Its typical characteristics are heat sensitivity and thermal instability, coupled with the harsh natural environment, road surface cracking easily.

The surface cracks in the Qinghai-Tibet alpine-cold area can be divided into two types: temperature cracks in surface layer and reflection cracks.

①Temperature cracks in surface layer: It can be divided into two types: temperature fatigue cracks and low- temperature shrink cracks.

(1) Temperature fatigue cracks: The sunshine in the Qinghai-Tibet alpine-cold area intense and long-lasting, and the amount of radiation is significantly higher than that in the plain area [7]. Temperature fatigue cracks first appear on the surface of asphalt road, under the action of vehicle dynamic load and temperature cycle, the uneven deformation of base and soil foundation will occur, which in turn accelerates the crack of pavement. The occurrence frequency of such cracks is very high, but the general damage degree is relatively light. The primary form of the cracks in the early stage is fine transverse cracks and reticular cracks, which should be timely sealed and filled after cracking to avoid further invasion of rain and snow.
(2) Low- temperature shrink cracks: In rapid cooling and continuous low temperature phase, the sudden decrease of pavement temperature, improve its stiffness, deformation capacity along with the increase of stiffness and reduce, but in the process of cooling, along the road produce low high temperature gradient in the direction of depth, due to the layer below the restraint of grassroots and cannot free shrinkage,

therefore in the tensile stress is generated in the surface layer and the compressive stress at the grassroots [8]. Generally, this kind of crack is transverse cracking at intervals along the width direction of the road. If not treated in time, the crack will continue to develop and form such diseases as net cracking and pit groove.

②Reflection cracks: Reflection fracture is a common disease in the Qinghai-Tibet alpine-cold area, such cracks appears mainly for the following reasons:

(1) In the high altitude area, the soil subgrade has a long freezing time and the temperature during the seasonal freezing period is extremely low. When the subgrade is lower than the critical height, the groundwater in the subgrade rises and freezes repeatedly, which makes the subgrade swell. At the same time, the ultraviolet radiation in the high-cold frozen soil area is intense, the aging rate of asphalt is accelerated, the tensile property is seriously reduced, and the frost expansion and cracking of roadbed will lead to the crack of asphalt surface.
(2) In order to minimize the influence of seasonal frozen soil and groundwater on the stability of subgrade, it is generally chosen to increase the subgrade height in engineering. However, with the increase of subgrade height, the area of the slope increases significantly, resulting in uneven absorption of solar radiation by the slope on both sides of the subgrade. It leads to a large temperature difference in the frozen soil layer under the two sides of the slope, which destroys the temperature balance on both sides of the subgrade, resulting in different settlement amounts of the two sides of the slope, and thus the longitudinal cracks of the road surface are generated. In addition, the improvement of subgrade puts forward higher requirements for the bearing capacity and shear strength of the original ground at the foot of slope. When the bearing capacity and shear strength of the slope are less than the sliding force increased by the improvement of the subgrade, the instability of the subgrade will also lead to longitudinal cracks in the pavement [9].
(3) In Qinghai-Tibet area, roadbed construction is limited to natural conditions, and roadbed filling is often excavated from both sides of the roadbed. As a result, the natural vegetation on the surface was destroyed and the thermal characteristics of the surface were changed. The thermal effect caused by seepage of water makes permafrost gradually melt, and the soil layer that melts will be drained and consolidated under the action of load, resulting in compression deformation and settlement deformation of roadbed. It makes the pavement bear the shear stress in the vertical direction, and when the shear stress exceeds the shear strength of the pavement, cracking failure occurs. If the water permeability of the active layer is poor, the melted ice water cannot be removed quickly, and more serious longitudinal cracks will be caused [10].

6 Conclusion

During the 13th five-year plan period, with the gradual construction and improvement of China's highway network, the highway industry has been transformed from the construction stage to the construction and maintenance with equal emphasis, and the maintenance is the main. Under this new industry background, highway management, highway service performance maintenance and improvement have become the key problems that must be faced with and solved. As the most common diseases in asphalt pavement, this article through to in different climate area crack of asphalt pavement comprehensive summary analysis, has enriched the classification of the asphalt pavement crack forms. Not only helps managers adopt the right way to manage, also help to maintenance personnel based on the destruction mechanism of the crack under different climatic conditions and destruction form of targeted prevention and repair, improving the service performance of asphalt pavement.

References

1. Sha A (2011) Subgrade and pavement engineering. Higher Education Press, Beijing (in Chinese)
2. Xu Y (2017) Discussion on road diseases and countermeasures in permafrost region. Northern Commun (07):99–102+105. (in Chinese)
3. Pang Q (2013) Research on crack repair technology of asphalt concrete pavement. Central South University, Changsha. (in Chinese)
4. Sheng J, Li F, Chen J (2004) Analysis and preventive techniques of premature damage of asphalt pavement in expressway. China Communications Press, Beijing (in Chinese)
5. Zhu H, Yang S, Li Y (2017) Analysis on the influence of oasis and desert climate on asphalt pavement crack in Xinjiang. J Chin Foreign Highw 37(01):46–48 (in Chinese)
6. Liu B (2013) Analysis on the causes of diseases in semi-rigid base asphalt pavement in Xinjiang. Chang'an University, Xi'an. (in Chinese)
7. Gao G (2012) Study on climatic zoning of asphalt pavement and adaptability of modified asphalt in Tibet. Chang'an University, Xi'an. (in Chinese)
8. Wu C (2016) Study on crack diseases and treatment measures of asphalt pavement in Tibet. Chang'an University, Xi'an. (in Chinese)
9. Wu Q, Liu Y, Tong C, Zhang J, Shen Z (2000) Highway engineering geology research in plateau permafrost region. Highway (02):1–4. (in Chinese)
10. Le T (2012) Exploration and practice of new treatment technology for roadbed diseases in permafrost region. Chang'an University, Xi'an. (in Chinese)

Research on Target Recognition Method Based on Laser Point Cloud Data

Fan Yu(✉), Yanxi Wei, and Haige Yu

School of Computer Science and Engineering, Xi'an Technological University, Xi'an 710021, Shaanxi, China
407171251@qq.com

Abstract. High resolution 3d point cloud data obtained by 3d laser scanning system has become a research hotspot and difficulty in recent years due to its large data volume, irregular data and high scene complexity. Target detection is the basis of scene analysis and understanding, which provides the underlying object and analysis basis for high-level scene understanding. Based on high resolution three-dimensional point cloud data of target recognition and tracking problem both in theory and application is facing great challenge, is a new research topic in this paper, according to the laser point cloud data processing as the research object, analyses the characteristics of lidar point cloud data and data processing of train of thought, analysis of lidar point cloud data storage and retrieval strategy, on the basis of the target recognition based on the laser point cloud data. The lidar data are distributed discretely in form. The discretization here refers to the irregular distribution of the positions and intervals of exponential data points in the three-dimensional space, namely the irregular distribution of data. In recent years, with the rise of deep learning and the large-scale application of deep learning in image detection, speech recognition, text processing and other related fields, it has become one of the current important research topics to use the method of deep learning for target recognition of three-dimensional point cloud data. Its main idea is to learn hierarchical feature expression through supervised way and describe the object from the bottom to the top. This method can effectively improve the ability of object feature representation and the performance of object recognition. Deep learning is also widely used in object recognition, object detection, scene segmentation and other image processing. Therefore, this paper adopts the method of deep learning to classify and identify 3d objects.

Keywords: Point cloud · Convolution Neural Network · Lidar · Target recognition

1 Introduction

In the past few decades, with the development and progress of science and technology and the improvement of computer computing power, image recognition technology has developed rapidly and been widely used in various fields [1]. The real environment is very complex and changeable, and it is difficult to make reliable inference in the real world only by using two-dimensional images, which requires us

Z. Xu et al. (Eds.): CSIA 2019, AISC 928, pp. 1305–1310, 2020.
https://doi.org/10.1007/978-3-030-15235-2_177

to use three-dimensional objects for automatic recognition and retrieval. Three-dimensional point cloud has all the spatial information of the target and can overcome the difficulties faced by two-dimensional images [2].

1.1 Research Background and Significance

With the continuous development of laser scanning technology, in recent decades, the means of human perception of the world have developed from 2D perception means mainly based on optical imaging to 3D perception means mainly based on laser scanning technology. Three-dimensional laser scanning system has become an important remote sensing sensor after visible light, infrared, microwave, multispectral and hyperspectral. With the popularity of computer hardware and the rapid development of computer theory, the production cost of 3D scanning devices has been gradually reduced, such as Microsoft Kinect and PrimeSense Carmine, RGB-D cameras and lidar, distance sensors. Therefore, the traditional two-dimensional image form is gradually replaced by the three-dimensional method [3]. At the same time, the rapid increase of 3D model database and scene database also provides researchers with enough reliable data for training and testing object recognition. More and more companies are using three-dimensional images instead of simple two-dimensional images to show users.

1.2 Research Status of Convolution Neural Network

Accurate target recognition is the main challenge and difficulty for computers to understand scenes, and it is also a key skill for intelligent robots to behave as freely as human beings in the real world. Deep learning is also widely used in object recognition, object detection, scene segmentation and other image processing. Convolution Neural Network (Convolution Neural Network, CNN) is a kind of deep learning framework, it to process the data, by means of multi-layer matrix than the traditional method in many practical applications, mainly because it is easy to train and has good generalization ability, and this makes the convolutional Neural Network is widely used in object recognition, object detection, scene segmentation, such as image processing, it has become the standard deals with the problem of target identification method. Convolutional neural network (CNN) has been applied in many visual pattern recognition systems because of its good effect in the field of visual recognition. However, only a small part of convolutional neural networks can process 3D data, so there is still a lot of room for further development and exploration of convolutional neural networks based on 3D data processing. At present, the input data formats of most 3D convolutional neural networks are regular 3D pixel grids or picture sets [4]. When encountering irregular data forms such as point clouds, most researchers will convert them into the form of physique, which will lead to the loss of some data.

1.3 Grid-Based 3D Target Recognition Method

This 3D target recognition technology no longer relies on 2D images, more and more experts are paying attention to 3D target recognition methods based on 3D point cloud and 3D mesh. Such as VoxNet proposed by Daniel Maturana et al. VoxNet is mainly divided into two major modules, one is to estimate the three-dimensional grid according to the space occupancy rate, and the other is to be able to directly predict the three-dimensional convolutional neural network based on the target category of the grid. They conducted experimental studies on the Binary occupancy grid, the Density grid, and the Hit grid, all of which achieved good results. In this paper, based on the ModelNet dataset, the data is preprocessed and convolutional neural networks are used for classification and recognition (Fig. 1).

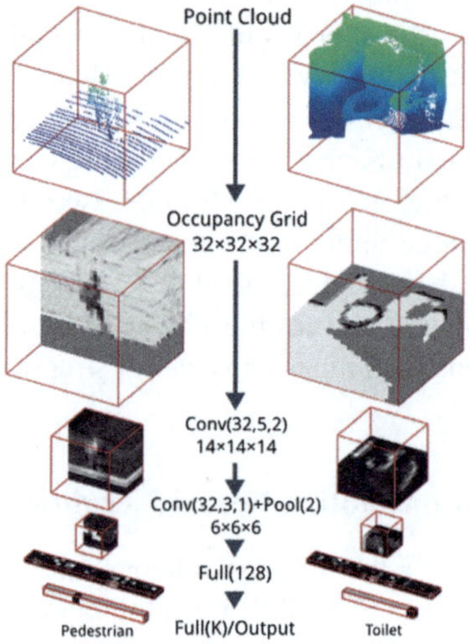

Fig. 1. The left side is the Lidar point cloud image classification, and the right side is the RGBD point cloud image classification.

2 Convolutional Neural Network

Traditional neural networks are composed of simple artificial neurons connected to each other. According to the connection between neurons, the flow of information is different, which constitutes a variety of neural network models. As the network layer data gradually increases, a deep neural network is formed. This paper first introduces the structure of artificial neurons and artificial neural networks, and then studies deep neural networks [6]. Based on this, the model structure of classical convolutional neural networks is studied, and the local connections and weights of convolutional neural network models are studied. In-depth study of structural features such as sharing. The network training algorithm uses the BP algorithm, which performs the back-propagation of the residuals of the network to complete the adjustment of the network parameters.

The convolutional neural network is inspired by the neural mechanism of the visual system and is based on its structural principle combined with artificial neural network. It is an artificial neural network system with deep learning ability. A convolutional neural network usually consists of an input layer, a convolutional layer, an activation function, a pooling layer, a fully connected layer, and an output layer. In convolutional neural networks, the input layer is usually a matrix for receiving the original image; the convolution layer is used for image feature extraction; the convolution layer shares local weights, which makes CNN have unique advantages in the field of image processing [7]. In this project, a target recognition and tracking method based on laser point cloud data is studied. Firstly, the original point cloud data is preprocessed, and the features are extracted from the obtained point cloud data using the convolutional neural network. Then, the classification and recognition of the model are completed.

3 Improved Convolutional Neural Network for Recognition of Point Clouds

The above methods have made significant progress in 3D target classification, matching and retrieval, but there are still deficiencies in feature extraction. It is far from enough to understand 3D models from a single mode. In recent years, target recognition and tracking algorithms based on laser data are booming. The laser point cloud data fast classification and target extraction, it will point cloud data projection to planned plane grid, through the analysis of the spatial distribution of point cloud data network characteristics of the image, and using image processing algorithms such as threshold segmentation, contour extraction for building the boundary of the target information, classification of the target object.

As is Fig. 2 is a network data flow diagram of VoxNet, the input layer accepts data in the form. There are two convolutional layers in total, and the number of feature maps is 32 × 32 × 32, respectively using the convolution kernel of the sum. The dropout rate of the Dropout layer is 0.1 and 0.2, respectively, which prevents overfitting and reduces the amount of calculation. The largest pooling layer, the filter used.

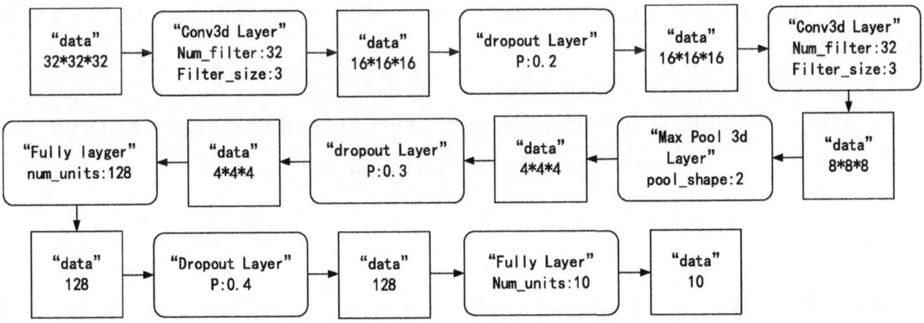

Fig. 2. VoxNet network data flow diagram

4 Application of Improved Convolutional Neural Network in Point Cloud Recognition

There are two main directions for classification and identification of point clouds using neural networks [8]. One is the three-dimensional target recognition algorithm for point cloud cell images and the other is grid-based three-dimensional target recognition algorithm. The algorithm has the highest recognition rate. It is a VoxNet network. In this chapter we will use the same data set to compare the recognition rates of point cloud and point cloud cells.

The environment used in this experiment is TensorFlow-gpu0.12.1 open source software library, Windows7 operating system, and NVIDIA GTX950 graphics card. Use Qt to write a point cloud data generator, use Eigen3 for matrix operations, and Python 3 to process the data in use. In this experiment, the data set is divided into three parts, namely training set, verification set and test set, wherein the training set accounts for 50%, while the verification set and the test set each account for 25%. Train the network using the training set and use the validation set data for testing. The verification set can prevent the model from overfitting. If there is no verification set, the model parameters are adjusted according to the test set, and the generalization ability of the model to the new sample data cannot be guaranteed.

The main principle of designing convolutional neural network and the selection of convolution template, developed from AlexNet model in 2012 to Deep Residual Learning model at the end of 2015, the convolution size was basically selected at 3×3, due to its effectiveness and simplicity in design. In this project, replacing the convolution kernel of 3×3 with the convolution kernel of 1×1 can reduce the parameter by 9X. But in order not to affect the accuracy of identification, not all substitution, but part with 3×3, part with 1×1. And then reduce the number of input feature graphs convolved with 3×3, if the convolution layer is directly connected, then in fact there is no way to reduce the number of input feature graphs in the next layer. In addition, pooling should be reduced so that the convolutional neural network is more lightweight and can be identified quickly. The experimental results are shown in Table 1.

Table 1. Comparison of accuracy between point cloud cell image and recognition

Network type	VoxNet	Point cloud cell image
accuracy	0.885	0.933

5 Conclusion

For the application of convolutional neural networks in image classification, the principle of extracting features and the methods and techniques used in building networks are analyzed. This paper introduces the method of enhancing network generalization ability and preventing over-fitting. At the same time, the network design of the point cloud cell is carried out. The effects of parameters such as batch value, local response normalization and momental momentum value on the network are analyzed. Experiments are carried out to verify the influence of each parameter on the network.

Finally, using tensorflow to build a network of point cloud cell images and a VoxNet network, respectively, using the dataset transformed by ModelNet into point cloud cells and grids. The classification results based on the point cloud cell and the experimental results of the VoxNet method were compared. It can be seen from experiments that the recognition rate of the network based on the point cloud cell image is higher than that of the VoxNet network.

References

1. Shao T, Xu W, Yin K, Wang J, Zhou K, Guo B (2011) Discriminative sketch-based 3D model retrieval via robust shape matching. In: Computer graphics forum, vol 30. Wiley Online Library
2. Simonyan K, Parkhi OM, Vedaldi A, Zisserman A (2013) Fisher vector faces in the wild. In: Proceedings of BMVC
3. Xu X, Corrigan D, Dehghani A, Caulfield S, Moloney D (2016) 3D object recognition based on volumetric representation using convolutional neural networks. In: International conference on articulated motion and deformable objects, pp 147–156
4. Li Y, Pirk S, Su H, Qi CR, Guibas LJ (2016) FPNN: field probing neural networks for 3D data. In: NIPS, pp 307–315
5. Qi CR, Su H, Niessner M, Dai A, Yan M, Guibas LJ (2016) Volumetric and multi-view CNNs for object classification on 3D data. arXiv
6. Gupta S, Girshick R, Arbelaez P, Malik J (2014) Learning rich features from RGB-D images for object detection and segmentation. In: ECCV
7. Hinton GE, Osindero S, Teh Y-W (2006) A fast learning algorithm for deep belief nets. Neural Comput
8. Jia Z, Chang Y-J, Chen T (2009) Active view selection for object and pose recognition. In: ICCV workshops
9. Qi CR, Su H, Mo K, Guibas LJ (2016) PointNet: deep learning on point sets for 3D classification and segmentation. arXiv preprint arXiv:1612.00593
10. Su H, Maji S, Kalogerakis E, Learned-Miller EG (2015) Multi-view convolutional neural networks for 3d shape recognition. In: Proceedings of ICCV. To appear
11. Vinyals O, Bengio S, Kudlur M (2015) Order matters: sequence to sequence for sets. arXiv preprint arXiv:1511.06391
12. Macrini D, Shokoufandeh A, Dickinson S., Siddiqi K, Zucker S (2002) View-based 3-D object recognition using shock graphs. In: Proceedings of ICPR, vol 3
13. Su H, Maji S, Kalogerakis E, Learned-Miller E (2015) Multi-view convolutional neural networks for 3D shape recognition. In: ICCV
14. Shi B, Bai S, Zhou Z, Bai X (2015) DeepPano: deep panoramic representation for 3-D shape recognition. IEEE Sign Process Lett 22:2339–2343
15. Sinha A, Bai J, Ramani K (2016) Deep learning 3D shape surfaces using geometry images. In: ECCV, pp 223–240

Summary of Research on Computing and Cloud Computing

Xin Sui[1] and Yi Sui[2(✉)]

[1] College of Humanities and Sciences of Northeast Normal University, Changchun 130117, People's Republic of China
Suixin1997@126.com
[2] China Telecom, Beijing Branch, Beijing 100124, People's Republic of China
ericsuiyi@qq.com

Abstract. Computing is one of the oldest achievements of human civilization. From ancient finger counting and not counting to ancient Chinese calculation and abacus calculation, to modern western Nepal domino calculation and Pascal calculator, to modern computer calculation, the infinite development and tremendous role of calculating methods and calculating tools, computing innovation occupies a very important position in human history. We are now in the "cloud computing" era, where users use the "cloud" to store and calculate. "Cloud" includes hundreds of thousands or even millions of computers one by one.

Keywords: Computing · Calculator · Calculating methods · Cloud computing

1 Development of Computing in China

Around the Spring and Autumn Period, the Chinese invented the use of calculation as a calculating tool, which was arranged in vertical and horizontal forms. According to the principle of intersection of vertical and horizontal, natural numbers can be expressed, and can be added, subtracted, multiplied, divided, square and other algebraic operations [1]. In order to facilitate the calculation of negative numbers, the calculation strategy evolves into red and black, red chips represent positive numbers and black chips represent negative numbers. As the oldest calculating tool in the world, planning played an important role in the development of ancient Chinese society. Zu Chongzhi an ancient Chinese mathematician calculated the value of circumference by means of calculation. With the advent of computational planning, the decimal system of counting was also one of the important inventions in the field of computational theory in ancient China.

The idea of mathematical mechanization also comes from ancient Chinese arithmetic. In the process of development of traditional mathematics in China, which is based on solving practical problems and starting from problems, an algorithm system featuring structure and mechanization has been formed, which is far from the axiomatic deduction system represented by Euclid's Geometric Origin [2].

Chinese traditional mathematics takes solving practical problems as its ultimate goal, which is more practical. This practical idea of mathematics is directly related to the traditional Chinese mathematical mechanization and numerical calculation

Z. Xu et al. (Eds.): CSIA 2019, AISC 928, pp. 1311–1314, 2020.
https://doi.org/10.1007/978-3-030-15235-2_178

thinking. The wide use and continuous development of computing tools such as calculation, abacus and mathematical mechanization algorithms have formed the idea of nominalization [3]. Ancient Chinese people used to digitalize the problems, turning some complex theoretical or applied problems into computable ones, and then solving them through specific numerical calculations. The abacus relies on the arithmetic formula, which generalizes a variety of calculation programs into a formula, which is similar to the process of modern computer using pre-programmed programs to carry out operations. Therefore, Mr. Wu Wenjun, a famous mathematician in China, calls the abacus "a simple computer without storage devices". The ancient Chinese computational thinking not only made the ancient Chinese mathematics achieve glorious achievements with world historical significance, but also put forward an idea and ability to solve problems by using computational methods [4].

In the long history, not only ancient China used the idea of Computational Thinking to solve problems, but also many people abroad have indelible contributions to the evolution and development of computational thinking [5].

2 Computing and Cloud Computing

In 1936, British mathematician Alan Machines Turing proposed an abstract computing model, which abstracted the process of using paper and pencil to perform mathematical operations, and replaced people with a virtual machine to perform mathematical operations. This is the famous Turing computer [6].

The so-called Turing Machine is an abstract machine. It has an infinite length of paper tape, which is divided into small squares, each with different colors. There is a machine head moving up and down on the tape [7]. The machine head has a set of internal states and some fixed procedures. At each moment, the machine head reads grid information from the current tape, then combines its internal state to find the program table, outputs information to the tape grid according to the program, and changes its internal state, and then moves.

Turing machine realizes the process of simulating human mathematical operation with paper and pen, and also realizes the leap-forward development from manual calculation to automatic mechanical calculation [8]. In ancient China, the calculation and abacus were stored in the human brain and expressed in the form of a formula. The whole calculation process was completed in the brain. Turing machine is to load the arithmetic program into the memory of the controller, and then the controller controls the execution of the program to complete the whole calculation process. Although they have different forms of calculation, they have the same computing power, that is, all computable problems can be calculated by Turing machine or abacus [9]. The common characteristics of the two methods are: when solving complex application problems, we must first digitalize the problems into computable problems, then find the algorithms and programs to solve the problems, control the calculation process through the algorithms and programs, and finally get the results.

In the 1980s, on the basis of summing up his predecessors, classified the science of thinking as one of 11 categories of science and technology, juxtaposed with natural science, social science, mathematics science, system science, human body science, behavioral science, military science, geographic science, architectural science, literature and art. Practice has proved that under the advocacy and influence of his thinking science, various disciplines of thinking gradually began to form and develop, such as mathematical thinking, physical thinking and so on.

Since Mr. Qian put forward the science of thinking, various disciplines have gradually developed under the guidance of the science of thinking, and computational disciplines are no exception. In 1992, Huang Chong-fu gave the definition of computational thinking: "Computational thinking is the computational simulation methodology of thinking process or function. The purpose of his research is to provide appropriate methods so that people can gradually achieve the higher goal of artificial intelligence with the help of modern and future computers".

In 2002, Dong Rongsheng put forward and constructed the methodology of computer science and technology. In the study of Computational Thinking and computer methodology, he pointed out that although Computational Thinking and computer methodology have their own research contents and characteristics, they complement each other very well and can promote each other. Computer methodology can be used for computational thinking. Re-study and assimilation of the research results will enrich the content of computer methodology. Conversely, the cultivation of computational thinking ability can also be greatly improved through the study of computer methodology. The relationship between them is very similar to that between modern mathematical thinking and mathematical methodology.

Cloud computing carries tens of thousands of types of services, and the same types of services have different requirements for security [10]. Different types of services have different security requirements.

Computer scientist John McCarthy proposed as early as the 1960s that "calculation will one day become a public service, like water, electricity, coal, etc., become a public infrastructure, easy to access, and cheap".

Cloud computing has a number of column features, such as scalability, elasticity, on-demand charges, etc. It will store resources, network resources, and computing resources to be submitted via the network in a virtualized manner. Companies pay as much as they use hydropower resources to get all the resources without spending large sums of money on servers, software, hard drives, etc. [11]. The use of cloud computing has brought huge advantages to enterprises. Enterprises can cope with changes in demand, reduce the cost of informatization, and be able to carry out more business. It is more conducive to enhancing the competitiveness of enterprises and creating more value.

3 Threats of Cloud Security and Cloud Computing Security

Cloud service providers inadvertently cause data loss, hackers delete data resources on cloud platforms, and other reasons lead to lost data [12]. There is also malicious internal data loss caused by people with access to the system.

Communicators carry disease software; crack the secrets of cloud services and other abuse services. Cloud service providers provide better infrastructure, applications, platforms, and shared use. Services also bring shared security vulnerabilities.

The security threats faced by each layer of cloud computing are not the same. The main security threats in the physical layer include hardware damage, natural disasters, and cyber-attacks. The main security threats of the virtual layer include programming loopholes, software detection, and data integrity destruction; the security threats of the application layer mainly include: tampering with data, destroying data, stealing data, and hacking sessions.

4 Conclusion

From the analysis of the attack source, the attack is not only from the external network, but also from the attack between the internal networks. Cloud computing security has become an important issue for cloud security. It not only distorts data, causes data loss, etc., but even leads to the collapse of the entire cloud computing platform and poses a fatal threat to cloud computing. Cloud computing is the top priority of cyber security.

Acknowledgements. 2018 Jilin Province Education Department "Thirteen-Five" Science and Technology Project "Enterprise Private Cloud Construction Design and Research ", Project No.: JJKH20181306KJ.

References

1. Cao Y (2018) The role of cloud computing in promoting the establishment of the status of trial center. J Henan Univ Technol (Soc Sci Ed) (06):27–33+41. https://doi.org/10.16433/j.cnki.cn41-1379.2018.06.004
2. Li Z (2018) Research on domain-oriented data mining service platform in cloud computing environment. Mod Inf Technol (12):79–80+83
3. Wen X (2018) Brief analysis of mobile internet security under cloud computing application mode. Netw Secur Technol Appl (12): 80
4. Sun P (2018) Strengthen the innovation of intelligent computing system and promote the development of artificial intelligence. China Natl People's Congr (21): 49
5. Li Y (2018) From sentence compilation to algorithmic design-the development path of computational thinking. Sci Wkly (30):179–180. https://doi.org/10.16657/j.cnki.issn1673-9132.2018.30.112
6. Zeng Y (2018) Development of text similarity computing method. Digit Commun World (10):218
7. Jazin (2018) Cloud-based database technology. Electron Technol Softw Eng (22):156
8. Wen C, Qin W (2018) Security prevention and control strategy of cloud computing technology. Electron Technol Softw Eng (22):187
9. Liu J (2018) Selection of cloud computing service providers based on hesitant fuzzy group decision model. Comput Eng Appl 54(23):109–114+119
10. Li S (2018) Application of cloud computing technology in computer data processing. Style Sci Technol (34):99
11. Hao L, Liu X, Zhu Y (2018) Application analysis of cloud computing technology in basic computer teaching in colleges and universities. South Agric Mach 49(21):166–167
12. Jin X (2018) Design and development of computer network security storage system based on cloud computing technology. Inf Comput (Theor Version) (21):209–211

Prediction Model of Milling Surface Roughness Based on Genetic Algorithms

Ying Chen(✉), Yanhong Sun, Han Lin, and Bing Zhang

Jilin Teachers Institute of Engineering and Technology,
Changchun 130000, China
823068684@qq.com

Abstract. According to the orthogonal test results, the surface roughness prediction model based on BP artificial neural network algorithm combined with genetic algorithm and considering material removal rate, a multi-objective optimization mathematical model for high-speed milling process parameters optimization was established, and the optimal combination of parameters satisfying the requirements was found within the given parameters range. The method is validated by comparing the surface roughness and processing efficiency with the optimization parameters determined by range analysis method.

Keywords: Surface roughness · High speed milling · Genetic algorithm · Prediction model

1 Introduction

In NC machining, surface roughness is one of the important indexes to design parts and measure the machined surface quality [1]. In order to find the optimal cutting parameters to predict and control the surface roughness, reduce the test report time and cost of cutting, and get the best processing plan before actual processing, domestic and foreign scholars have carried out extensive research on it [2–10].

Because the mechanism of surface roughness formation in high speed cutting is not yet mature, it is still mostly based on the experimental data analysis method. At present, the commonly used methods are range analysis [11] method and regression analysis [12, 13] method. However, range analysis can only roughly determine a combination of parameters at the level of known parameters, and orthogonal regression analysis can only predict surface roughness. Therefore, this paper establishes surface roughness prediction model based on BP algorithm and genetic algorithm, which provides a reliable basis for reasonable selection of milling parameters.

2 Orthogonal Test and Data Analysis

2.1 Test Conditions

Test equipment: DMU125P five axis milling machine
Cutter: toroidal cutter with a diameter of 25

Z. Xu et al. (Eds.): CSIA 2019, AISC 928, pp. 1315–1320, 2020.
https://doi.org/10.1007/978-3-030-15235-2_179

Workpiece material: P1.2738 plastic mould steel
Cooling method: oil mist
Measuring instrument: measuring instrument of surface roughness, each parameter test result is measured 10 times, taking mean value

2.2 Test Method

Orthogonal experimental design is an efficient, fast and economical experimental design method for studying multi-factors and multi-levels. It is an effective method to explore the relationship among the factors in high speed milling process by using orthogonal table to select the test conditions and to analyze the data using the characteristics of orthogonal table. The main cutting parameters in this experiment are cutting speed (spindle speed), feed speed, cutting depth and radial feed. The table is based on four factors and four levels standard orthogonal table. The table of four factors and four levels is shown in Table 1. The table head design and test results of four factors and four levels orthogonal test are listed in Table 2.

Table 1. Level of four factor and four level test factor

Level	Test factor			
	Milling depth $a_p[mm]$	Spindle speed $n[r/\min]$	Feed per tooth $f_z[mm/r]$	Milling spacing $a_e[mm]$
1	0.05	6000	0.05	2
2	0.10	6500	0.10	4
3	0.15	7000	0.15	6
4	0.20	7500	0.20	8

3 Establishment of Surface Roughness Prediction Model

The prediction accuracy of the model based on BP algorithm is higher than that of the orthogonal regression analysis model. In this paper, the surface roughness prediction model based on BP algorithm and genetic algorithm [14, 15] are selected to find the optimal combination of parameters within the given parameters.

3.1 Mathematical Model for Optimizing High Speed Milling Parameters

In multi-objective optimization problems, because each objective is incompatible with each other, it is necessary to determine the relative importance of each objective to obtain a relatively satisfactory solution according to the actual situation. In the process of multi-objective optimization, a mathematical model composed of parameters to be optimized, objective functions and constraints must be established first.

Table 2. Four factors and four levels orthogonal table head and test results

No.	Factor (level)				Roughness $Ra(um)$
	Milling depth	Spindle speed	Feed per tooth	Milling spacing	
1	1	1	1	1	0.434
2	1	2	2	2	0.536
3	1	3	3	3	0.599
4	1	4	4	4	0.682
5	2	2	3	4	0.664
6	2	1	4	3	0.743
7	2	4	1	2	0.389
8	2	3	2	1	0.378
9	3	3	4	2	0.654
10	3	4	3	1	0.610
11	3	1	2	4	0.631
12	3	2	1	3	0.434
13	4	4	2	3	0.723
14	4	3	1	4	0.535
15	4	2	4	1	0.555
16	4	1	3	2	0.667

(1) Optimization parameters

Surface roughness prediction model based on BP algorithm optimizes milling parameters under other conditions: milling depth $a_p(mm)$, spindle speed $n(r/\text{min})$, feed per tooth $f_z(mm/z)$, milling row spacing $a_e(mm)$.

(2) objective function

Surface roughness $Ra, Min f_1(x) = f(a_p, n, f_z, a_e)$, is a surface roughness prediction model based on BP algorithm.

Material removal rate, $Ra, Min f_1(x) = f(a_p, n, f_z, a_e)$,

(3) Parameter range

$0.05 \leq a_p \leq 0.20$ (mm), $6000 \leq n \leq 7500$ (r/min), $0.05 \leq f_z \leq 0.20$, $2 \leq a_e \leq 8$ (mm)

(4) Fitness function

In order to avoid conflicts among optimization objectives in multi-objective optimization problems, multi-objective optimization problems need to be transformed into single-objective optimization problems. In this paper, the weight coefficient method is used to determine the objective fitness function as follows.

$$G(x) = 1/(K_1 + w_1 f_1(x) - w_2 f_2(x))$$

In the formula, K_1 is a constant, w_1 and w_2 is the weight coefficient of the objective function $f_1(x)$, $f_2(x)$. In order to calculate the fitness value of genetic algorithm and eliminate the difference in unit and order of magnitude between the objective functions, it is necessary to process the data of each objective function value.

3.2 Data Optimization Based on Genetic Algorithm

The initialization parameters of the genetic algorithm for the experimental data in this paper are shown in Table 3 below.

Table 3. Initialization parameters of genetic algorithm

Evolution algebra	Population number	Overlapping probability	Variation probability	Character length
70	40	0.9	0.03	80
Variable digit	K_1	w_1	w_2	
20	1	0.5	0.5	

The parameters of high-speed milling die were optimized, The variation of surface roughness, material removal rate and fitness with the growth of evolutionary algebra is shown in Fig. 1(a) (b) (c), respectively. The results show that the surface roughness decreases with the increase of evolutionary algebra, while the material removal rate and fitness value increase. When the evolutionary algebra increases to 100, the fitness value is 0.0493, and the optimization results are as follows:

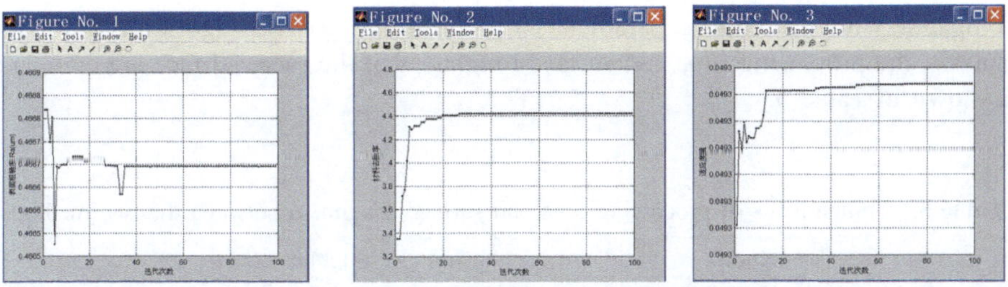

(a) (b) (c)

(a) The relationship between surface roughness and evolutionary algebra
(b) The relationship between material removal rate and evolutionary algebra
(c) The relationship between fitness and evolutionary algebra

Fig. 1. Multi-objective optimization results of genetic algorithm

Milling depth 0.1 mm, spindle speed 7332.3 r/min, feed per tooth 0.1 mm/z, milling row spacing 7.9 mm, corresponding surface roughness 0.4666 um, material removal rate 4.4220 cm^3/min.

The optimum combination of parameters obtained by range analysis and genetic algorithm and the value of surface roughness predicted by orthogonal regression are listed in Table 4.

From the cutting parameters predicted by the two methods, the value of milling depth is the same; the speed is slightly changed, but basically close to the upper limit of the parameter range. The two cases of genetic algorithm are larger than the range analysis method, slightly increased, the cutting speed greatly helps to improve efficiency and reduce surface roughness; the radial cutting is 2 mm in range analysis method, and the diameter in genetic algorithm is 7.9 mm. The tangential depth is close to the limit of the parameter range. According to the material removal rate formula, this is mainly related to the improvement of material removal rate and processing efficiency.

Table 4. Optimizing parameters and predicting surface roughness

Method	Milling parameters				Surface roughness (um)	
	Milling depth $a_p(mm)$	Spindle speed $n(r/\min)$	Feed per tooth $f_z(mm/z)$	Milling row spacing $a_e(mm)$	Inheritance forecast	Orthogonal forecast
Range analysis	0.1	7000	0.05	2		0.3760
Genetic algorithm	0.1	7332.3	0.1	7.9	0.4666	0.4933

4 Test Verification

Compared with the cutting parameters optimized by genetic algorithm and range analysis, the processing time and surface roughness of the same surface are compared as shown in Table 5.

Table 5. Comparisons of processing time and surface roughness between the two methods

Method	Processing time	Roughness (um)
Range analysis	70 min and 43 s	0.4156
Genetic algorithm	40 min and 28 s	0.4985

It can be seen from the table that the processing time of range analysis method is nearly twice as long as that of this algorithm, and the surface roughness is changed from 0.4156 um to 0.4985 um. The difference between them is not significant. Therefore, the optimal combination of parameters obtained by this method can effectively improve the processing efficiency on the premise of ensuring the accuracy.

References

1. Wang S, Ai X, Zhao J (2006) Modeling and prediction of surface roughness in high speed milling. Manuf Technol Mach Tools 8:65–68 (in Chinese)
2. Yang J, Guo H, Li H (2011) Experimental study on surface roughness of aeronautical aluminum 7050 high speed milling. Mech Manuf Res 40(3):34–35 (in Chinese)
3. Tian X, Yu A (2008) Establishment of milling surface roughness prediction model based on regression analysis. Manuf Technol Mach Tools 11:101–104 (in Chinese)
4. Li S, Sun L, Guo L (2000) Roughness prediction of surface machining in NC milling. Mech Des Manuf Eng 29(4):35–37 (in Chinese)
5. Liu M, Yang M, Huo Y (2005) Key technologies for surface roughness prediction in five-axis NC milling of complex surfaces. Mach Manuf 43(495):11, 12–14 (in Chinese)
6. Wang W, Tang S, Zhang Y (2010) Prediction of surface roughness in high speed milling based on neural network. Mech Des Manuf 3:216–217 (in Chinese)
7. Tian M, Li Z, Yan B (2004) Research on roughness prediction of high speed milling of hard-to-machine materials based on RBF neural network. Tool Technol 42(3):35–37 (in Chinese)
8. Xiao J (2010) Establishment of surface roughness model for aluminium alloy milling based on processing residual height. Modul Mach Tools Autom Process Technol 3:76–78 (in Chinese)
9. Baskar N, Asokan P, Saravanan R, Prabhaharan G (2005) Selection of optimum tool geometry and cutting conditions using a surface roughness prediction model for end milling. Int J Adv Manuf Technol 26:1202–1210
10. Feng D (2005) Countermeasure of reducing surface roughness in nc milling of aluminum alloy parts. Mech Eng 12:78–79 (in Chinese)
11. Wang S, Zhu X (2009) Orthogonal optimization of milling parameters for TC4 titanium alloy. Mech Electr 12:39 (in Chinese)
12. Guo X, Chen X (2011) Experimental study on surface roughness of aluminium alloy 6061 based on high speed milling. Mach Tools Hydraul Press 39(6):38–3913(2011) (in Chinese)
13. Hu Z, Meng G, Xia H (2011) Study on surface roughness of GH169 high speed milling based on orthogonal test method. Manuf Technol Mach Tools 1:44–46 (in Chinese)
14. Fang Y, Li F (2006) Prediction model of surface roughness for high speed machining based on artificial neural network. Tool Technol 40(11):78–80 (in Chinese)
15. Lei Y, Zhang S, Li X (2005) MATLAB genetic algorithm toolbox and its application. Bureau of Electronic Commerce University Press, Xi'an (in Chinese)

The Research on Network Security Situation Awareness Technology

Yongmei Zhang(✉), Yanmei Jia, and Jinxiang Zhong

China West Normal University Sichuan, Nanchong 637009, China
zymface@163.com

Abstract. With the continuous development of information technology, the scope of network application is constantly expanding, and a variety of virus, hacker and other attack methods emerge in endlessly. In the face of such a serious security threat, we know little or nothing about the attacker, the way of attack, the purpose of attack or the means of attack. In order to change the asymmetry of attack and defense, decrease the cost of attack and reduce the security threat to the actual system, the attacker's attack tools and methods are studied, and the source of attack is tracked in this research. Situation awareness technology emerges as the times require.

Keywords: Network security · Situation awareness · Situation prediction

1 Introduction

Dynamic perception technology integrates various security measures, realizes the evaluation of the current network situation, and predicts the trend of future network changes [1]. It can realize the optimal management of the network and effective protection of network security [2–4]. Network security situation awareness is an important technology in information security management [5]. It is the combination and enhancement of many security technologies. It emphasizes the real-time capture of changes in network security situation and evaluates the network security situation accordingly [6]. Network security situation awareness technology can synthesize various security factors, and reflect the network security situation dynamically on the whole [7]. Analyze and evaluate it with timely inform early warning so as to enhance the ability of network security monitoring, along with early warning and protection in China [8–10].

2 The Origin of Network Security Situation Awareness

Network security situation awareness technology originated in the 1980s and was proposed by the US Air Force. It covers three aspects: perception, understanding and prediction. Network security situation awareness is to use various network security technologies in data mining, research, analysis and processing, and then provide a current network security schematic map, so that network security administrators can clearly understand the current network security situation. Through the analysis of the situation,

Z. Xu et al. (Eds.): CSIA 2019, AISC 928, pp. 1321–1326, 2020.
https://doi.org/10.1007/978-3-030-15235-2_180

corresponding protection methods are taken, in order to achieve the role of protecting network security. Figure 1 shows the three-level model of situation awareness.

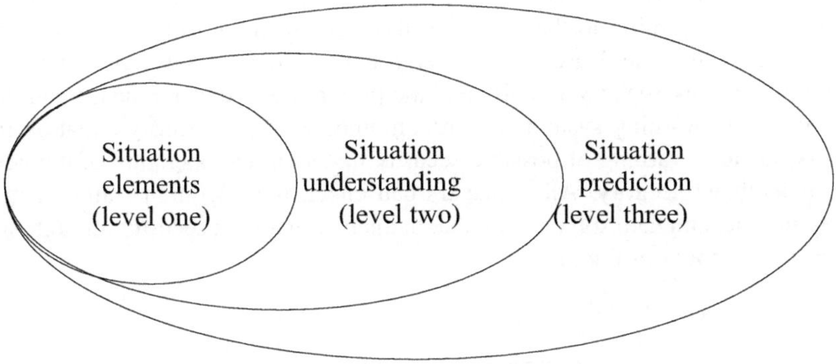

Fig. 1. Three level model

Data mining technology, data fusion technology, intelligent analysis and visualization technology can help network security situation awareness to achieve better network protection. Network security administrators use security situation awareness technology to understand the network situation in real time, and take effective measures to protect network security according to the information they know.

3 Network Security Situation Awareness Architecture

3.1 Main Technologies of the System

Network security situation awareness has a good effect on the management of network security information. Its effect is achieved by combining a variety of network information security technologies, such as firewall, anti-virus software, intrusion detection system and so on. Its role is mainly reflected in real-time detection and rapid early warning of network security. Through real-time detection, network security situation awareness can evaluate the security situation of the running network, and predict the trend of the network in a certain period of time.

3.2 System Components

Network security situation awareness system can be divided into four parts. The first part is feature extraction. The main function of this layer is to sort out and delete a large number of data information in network system through firewall, intrusion detection system, anti-virus, flow control, log audit and other systems, and then extract the network security situation information needed by the system. The second part is security assessment, which belongs to the core part of network security situation awareness system. The function of this part is to analyze the information presented in the first part and to evaluate the operation status of network information security with other network security technologies (firewalls, intrusion detection systems, etc.) in the system, and to give the evaluation model, vulnerability scanning and threat assessment. The third part is situation awareness. The role of this part is to identify the information and information sources of network security assessment, and then clarify the double. At the same time, according to the results of the assessment, a security situation map is formed to determine the degree of network security threat, and to reflect the real-time situation of network security visually and the possibility of development trend; the last part is the early warning system, which combines with the security situation map to give a rapid early warning of possible security threats in the operation of the network, so as to facilitate security. All managers can check the operation status of network security in time, and then solve the hidden dangers of network security through targeted measures. As shown in Fig. 2.

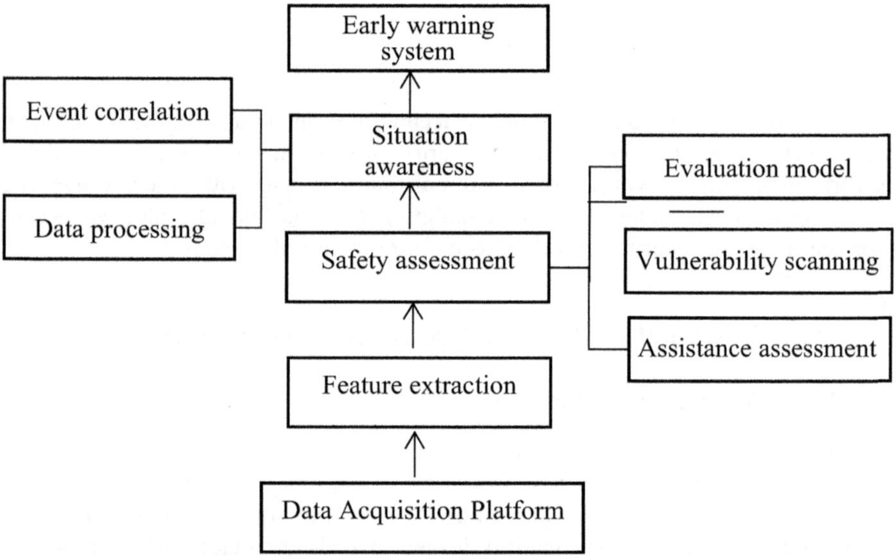

Fig. 2. Network perception architecture diagram

4 Key Technologies of Network Security Situation Awareness

4.1 Data Fusion Technology

The concept of data fusion technology originated in the 1970s, and it did not get people's attention until the 1990s. At present, data fusion technology has been widely used in target recognition, tracking and situation awareness in network security. Data fusion is the processing of data information from various sources. It has the function of combining data from various data sources for formal description. The amount of data obtained from multiple sources is significantly better than that from a single source. Data fusion technology is a multi-level and multi-category data processing method. Its function is to supplement and integrate information from various sources of similar or different feature modes in the network. The data will be detected and analyzed to clarify the correlation between data, correlation and so on, making the data results more accurate and reliable.

Data fusion technology includes feature level fusion, data level fusion and decision level fusion. Feature level fusion is to extract features from sensor information, and then integrate, analyze and process them. Data layer fusion is to fuse data directly in the data layer, and integrate and analyze information without pretreatment in the initial test. Decision-level fusion is to localize different types of sensors, including preprocessing, feature extraction, recognition or judgment, and to establish preliminary conclusions about the observed objects. Then the decision level fusion is made through the association process, and the joint inference results are finally obtained.

4.2 Data Mining Technology

Data mining technology discovers the law between data and the implied meaning of data from a large number of incomplete, noisy, fuzzy and random practical applications. Nowadays, the existing technologies of data mining technology in the field of network security situation awareness are clustering analysis and association analysis. Clustering analysis is to divide data into different clusters according to different characteristics and properties of data. No cluster has certain similarities in the characteristics of data. So is the correlation analysis. By analyzing massive and complex data, we can find the dependence and correlation degree between the data and find the correlation information of the data.

4.3 Situation Assessment Technology

Network security situation assessment is a mapping from real-time network information to evaluation indicators. The definition of risk assessment in "Rules for the Implementation of Information Security Management" is: to evaluate information security, identify potential threats, and predict and warn the occurrence of threats.

4.4 Information Visualization Technology

Information visualization technology is the use of computer image processing technology and data information into image information, so that it can be displayed on the screen graphically and graphically, while using interactive technology to achieve network information processing. By using information visualization technology, the rules hidden in data information can be effectively known, and the reliable basis for network information processing can be obtained. Nowadays, network security devices can only display the results of analysis by short ones.

Text descriptions or graphs, however, are difficult to extract important information from them. The main function of network security situation awareness system is to integrate and classify multi-source data, so that network security managers can make clear entry points when making decisions or adopting measures. At this time, the importance of information visualization technology is realized. The results of multi-source information data fusion and analysis are extracted and displayed in the computer system through visualization, so as to ensure that the network security status can be effectively predicted and monitored.

4.5 Hierarchical Perception Technology

Hierarchical network security perception technology uses IDS alarm information and network performance indicators to evaluate network security quantitatively, and constructs a hierarchical quantitative evaluation model from three aspects: system, host and service. From top to bottom, the model is divided into four levels: network system, host, service, and attack/vulnerability. According to the alarm and vulnerability information provided by IDS and the consumption of network resources, we can find out the threats faced by the services provided by the hosts, and analyze the severity of the attacks, the number of attacks and the occupancy rate of network bandwidth. According to these indicators, we can evaluate the security status of the services. On this basis, we can evaluate the security status of the hosts in the network system comprehensively.

5 Concluding Remarks

This paper introduces the research framework of network security situation awareness. From the aspects of data acquisition, preprocessing, situation assessment, situation prediction and situation visualization, it expounds the current system structure, main research ideas and key technical methods of network security situation awareness. The research of network security situation awareness is of great significance in the field of information security. With the development of network security situation awareness technology, many methods and algorithms are relatively mature, but there are still many problems to be improved: situation awareness-related Internet of Things technology and cloud computing technology are still in the stage of theoretical research; massive data acquisition and high-speed processing technology need to be further improved.

References

1. Wang H, Lai J, Hu M (2008) Research on key implementation technologies of network security situation awareness. J Wuhan Univ Inf Sci Ed 33(10):995–998 (in Chinese)
2. Wang J, Shen L, Wang K (2010) Network security situation prediction and its application in intelligent protection. Comput Appl 30(6):1480–1488 (in Chinese)
3. Huang S (2016) Solution to network security problem. Netw Secur Technol Appl (in Chinese)
4. Chen N (2015) Research on network security situational awareness system and key technologies. Autom Instrum Tables (01):47–49 (in Chinese)
5. Cao R (2014) Research on network security situational awareness in big data environment. Digit Libr Forum (02):11–15 (in Chinese)

6. Zhao P, Liu F, Zhang H, Wang S (2008) Large-scale network security situation assessment system. Comput Eng Appl (33):122–124+127 (in Chinese)
7. Feng J, Chen S (2010) Research on network security situation prediction method based on GEP. Fujian Comput (10):4–7 (in Chinese)
8. Zhu L, Wang H, Zheng L. Review on visualization of network security situation. http://www.paper.edu.cn
9. Wang H, Lai J, Zhu L et al (2006) A review of network situational awareness system research. Comput Sci 2006 (in Chinese)
10. Ye P (2010) Application of network security situational awareness in security management platform. Inf Netw Secur (in Chinese)

The Research on Street Landscape Design in Smart City Based on Big Data

Wenjun Wang(✉)

City College of WUST, Wuhan, China
15827425957@163.com

Abstract. The traditional urban planning and management model can no longer meet the needs of the contemporary people. More and more cities are moving towards smarter. Wisdom is an important part of urban planning and a technical basis for urban development. In the process of development, a lot of financial and material resources are invested to build a smart city street landscape. The continuous development of street landscape construction has played a positive role in promoting the development of smart cities. The emergence of smart cities is not only an effective means of urban planning, but also an urban development. premise. The article first introduces the background and significance of the research, analyzes the current situation of the application of street landscape design in smart city planning, and combines the current practical characteristics to give a plan for smart city street landscape planning.

Keywords: Smart city · Big data · Street landscape · Design

1 Background Overview

The traditional urban planning and management model can no longer meet the needs of contemporary people [1]. Therefore, the introduction of intelligent information into the urban planning process is an inevitable trend of social development and an indispensable part of China's information construction process [2]. In the process of smart city planning, the intelligent of street landscape design is a process of the development of smart cities, and it is also a stage that must be experienced, which is in line with the development of the times [3–5].

Urban intelligence is an important part of urban planning and a technical basis for urban development [6]. Under the traditional urban development model, the management efficiency of various resources in the city is low, the management process is disorderly, and there are many human factors in the management process [7–9]. Therefore, in view of the problems existing in the development of traditional urban road landscape planning under the traditional mode, the road landscape will be The design is introduced into the smart city planning, which makes up for the shortcomings in the traditional urban road landscape design process and effectively avoids the problems existing in the traditional road landscape planning process [10].

The urban landscape design process can't be limited to the beautiful visual experience created by flowers and trees, but also the landscape design and urban ecological construction. It can be seen that urban landscape construction not only needs to meet

Z. Xu et al. (Eds.): CSIA 2019, AISC 928, pp. 1327–1331, 2020.
https://doi.org/10.1007/978-3-030-15235-2_181

people's viewing needs, but also should build a good ecological environment. It can be said that urban landscape design has positive significance for urban construction, improving the artistic quality of residents' living environment and ensuring the environment. Cleanliness plays an important role.

The construction of urban street landscapes highlights the dependence of cities and natural scenery, and handles the relationship between historical ancient capitals and modern metropolises. According to the regional function and historical and cultural protection requirements, the street landscape is designed separately. With the goal of high and low fluctuations and scattered, we will strengthen the control of urban contours, and protect and promote the urban landscape in harmony with natural landscapes and historical humanities. Urban street buildings should be combined with landscape green space landscape, combined with water landscape, compact layout, saving land and controlling street landscape density. Promote the diversity of street landscape design styles and maintain the overall coordination of street rules.

2 The Role of Street Landscape in the Construction of Smart Cities

Street landscapes play a vital role in the construction of smart cities. Combined with the actual characteristics of smart cities, full consideration of street landscape design planning is conducive to the construction of smart cities, and has a profound impact on urban residents' living and outdoor activities.

The traditional urban street landscape design pattern can no longer meet the needs of contemporary people. Therefore, applying scientific and rational street landscape design to the process of smart city construction is an important part of China's urban development and construction process. Street landscape is an important part of smart city planning and the technical foundation of green city. With the global awareness of environmental protection, the city is developing in an important direction of green, low-carbon and sustainable development. It is urgent to build a city into a green city, and the focus of building a green city is on the street landscape. Reasonable configuration.

The whole street landscape design process can ultimately be attributed to the configuration of plant materials. The rationality of plant configuration will directly affect the later use of street landscapes and the sustainable development of human ecological environment. In the process of plant configuration, different plant configuration schemes should be designed for different street landscapes in order to ensure that the completed street landscape has a good application effect, and has its own unique style, which can reflect the diversity of plants in nature. Fully reflected. The plant configuration should be as rich as possible, and at the same time ensure the rules of the tree species, do not be chaotic, the rationality of the plant configuration in the street landscape, whether the street landscape can become a clear landmark of the city.

3 Planning of Street Landscapes in Smart Cities

The design of street landscapes in smart cities must follow the scientific nature, and must be scientific. It is the unity of art and science. According to the scientific principles of plant configuration, the characteristics of plants, colors, contours and lines in smart cities can be configured. The height is perfectly unified to achieve a better natural beauty effect. The scientific nature of street landscape design in smart cities is mainly reflected in the following aspects:

3.1 Embody the Plant Plasticity of Street Landscape Design in Smart Cities

The so-called plant plasticity of the street landscape refers to the germination of plants and the degree of toughness of branches and stems. Different plants have different germination characteristics. Many plants can grow new shoots quickly after pruning, while some plants can't grow new shoots in a short time. Some plants have branches and stems with high toughness, while some plants do not have better toughness. In order to be able to rationally allocate the shrinkage of plants, the smart city is mainly based on Mexican cedar, supplemented by ginkgo and citron, and planted a variety of aquatic plants in water-rich areas.

3.2 Reflect the Adaptability of Plants to the Environment in Smart Cities

In the construction of street landscapes, it is necessary to fully consider the interaction between each plant and the natural environment, plant different plants in different places, ensure that the plants planted can adapt to the environment, and the main factors affecting the plant growth environment include water, sunshine, air, temperature, humidity and other factors, the street landscape in the smart city needs to choose the species suitable for the urban street landscape design, planting large-scale ginkgo and camphor along the landscape axis.

At the same time, studies have shown significant differences in the dust retention and purification effects of different green belts with the same width. Set H-1, H-2, H-3 and H-4 road landscape green belts with the same width, but the plant configuration is different. Check the dust retention effect after 3d and 10d, compare the dust holding capacity of the above green belt. The difference is shown in Table 1.

Table 1. The same width green belt dust amount of data

Road landscape green belt	Dust on the third day (kg/hm^2)	Dust on the tenth day (kg/hm^2)
H-1	95.5	190.1
H-2	150.5	210.2
H-3	76.1	120.8
H-4	86.4	160.7

It can be seen from the above table that the four vertical green belts have slightly different effects on the roads, and the highest total dust retention is the H-2 green belt, and the least total dust retention is the H-3 green belt. The reason is that the dust-removing plants selected by the H-3 green belt are inferior.

3.3 Reflect the Diversity of Street Landscapes in Smart Cities

When planning smart cities and selecting plants, following the principle of plant diversity, we also fully consider the group, shape, ecological relationship of the plants, and the aesthetics of the public to ensure that the selected plants present a beautiful shape.

In the process of building a street landscape of a smart city, the design is based on the "Spring Blossom Autumn Scenery" as the main line of greening construction, and the autumn leaf tree species runs through the city, following the following configuration principles.

The principle of diversity and unity is also understood as the principle of unity and variability, which is the basic principle for designing a smart city. The principle of street landscape in a smart city must follow the principle of "pursuing change in unified configuration and striving for unity in the process of change". The principles of diversity and unity of smart cities mainly include three aspects, namely, the variability and unity of plant forms, the variability and unity of line shapes, and the variability and unity of parts and wholes. The variability and unity of the shape means that the single shape of the plant is combined with various forms to create a more perfect shape. The variability and unity of the shape means that the branch shape of the plant needs to adhere to the principle of variability. It is also necessary to abide by the variability and unity of the principle of unity and unity. It means that the street landscape design must be coordinated with the whole city.

Balance and stability. This principle is the basic principle of smart city street landscape planning. The principle of street landscape design in a smart city must follow the principle of "balance and stability". The principle of balance mainly refers to the equilibrium relationship between plants on the three-dimensional plane and the balance surface. The principle of stability is mainly reflected in the sense of weight of the plant moving down on the three-dimensional level. The principles of balance and stability in plant configuration are mutually unified, and they are inseparable.

Contrast and reconcile. This principle is the basic principle of streetscape design in smart cities. The principle of plant allocation in a smart city must follow the principle of "contrast and reconciliation". The so-called contrast principle refers to the combination of many aspects such as the shape of the plant, the volume of the plant, the color of the plant, the brightness of the plant, the line of the plant, etc., and the visual effect is strong, and the contrast is relatively large. When using the principle of contrast, we need to pay attention to the principle of coordination at all times. The contrast is reflected in the local part. The contrast is reflected in the overall aspect. The principle of contrast and coordination is mainly reflected in the contrast and reconciliation of color, the contrast and reconciliation of images, and the contrast and reconciliation between the virtual and the real.

4 Summary

The smart city is accompanied by the development of garden technology. In the process of construction, the design of street landscape is comprehensively applied with botany, gardening and spatial geographic information technology. This paper aims at the current situation of urban development in China, combined with the design of street landscape in the development of smart city. In reality, the application of street landscape design to the smart city planning process has played a positive role in promoting the development of the city. In the urban planning process, the street landscape is not only an effective means to improve the planning of smart green cities, but also a prerequisite for the city to develop towards green. In this paper, the problems existing in the planning process of the smart city street landscape in the traditional mode are introduced into the smart city planning, which makes up for the shortcomings of the traditional city in the planning process and effectively avoids the existence of the traditional urban planning process. The problem has raised the people's living standards and made every citizen of urban life feel the environment constantly improving.

Acknowledgement. The research topic of City College of WUST 2018, Exploration and Research on the Teaching Mode of Landscape Design Under the Background of Smart City. Item number: 2018CYYBJY013.

References

1. Yihong G, Xu J, Yongli W (2018) Reflecting the needs of smart city construction in the urban planning system. Shanghai Informatiz (12):24–27
2. Lu Z (2016) Evaluation of urban road landscape in Ningbo. MS, Nanjing Forestry University, China, p 86
3. Zhao Y, Hongmei W (2018) Research on the construction of smart city based on big data. Value Eng 48(2):143–144
4. Tingting L (2018) Urban shared transportation space landscape planning and design. MS, Qingdao University of Technology, China, p 82
5. Li C (2017) Teaching reform practice of environmental art design drawing and mapping. Archit Cult 117–119 (2017)
6. Xuehen S (2012) Planning and design of plant landscape. China Forestry Publishing House, Beijing
7. Kaijun Y, Lin L (2016) The role and value of garden landscape in smart cities. J Liaoning Univ Technol (Soc Sci Ed) 24(1):80–82
8. Chen Y (2017) Research on urban waterfront landscape space design based on low impact development–taking Nanjing Hexi riverside scenery belt as an example. MS, Nanjing Forestry University, China, p 12
9. Rao J (2018) Exploring the innovation of urban road design under the background of "smart city". Low Carbon World 150(9):250–251
10. Biyu W (2018) Urban simulation helps new smart city construction. Informatiz China Constr 21:14–15
11. Xiaoou D (2014) Urban complex design research under the background of smart city. MS, Harbin Institute of Technology, China, p 55

Adaptive Scheduling Algorithm for Hadoop Node Capability in Heterogeneous Resource Environment

Ming Zheng and Mugui Zhuo(✉)

Guangxi Colleges and Universities Key Laboratory
of Professional Software Technology, Wuzhou University, Wuzhou, China
370505375@qq.com

Abstract. In order to overcome the shortcomings of the existing scheduling allocation methods for Hadoop clusters in heterogeneous resource environments, an adaptive scheduling algorithm NCAS (node capacity adaptive scheduling) based on node capability is proposed. Firstly, NCAS algorithm calculates the scheduling factor according to the node performance and task characteristics; then, the scheduling factor determines the amount of data and task slots that each node should share; finally, the data and tasks are distributed more to fast nodes and less to slow nodes. The experimental results show that compared with the traditional scheduling algorithm, NCAS algorithm greatly reduces the number of backup tasks to start, significantly reduces job completion time, and improves the efficiency of task execution.

Keywords: Adaptive · Node capability · Hadoop · Heterogeneous resource

1 Introduction

As an open source solution for cloud storage and cloud computing, Hadoop [1] has been widely used in academia and industry. Job scheduling algorithm and task scheduling algorithm play an important role in the performance of Hadoop. At present, several common job scheduling algorithms in Hadoop are first in first out [2], fair scheduler [3], capacity scheduler [4] and so on. These Hadoop job scheduling algorithms are designed for homogeneous cluster resources, which are inefficient in heterogeneous resource environments. In order to overcome the shortcomings of Hadoop's default speculative task [5] scheduling algorithm Speculative Task in heterogeneous environments, Zaharia et al. proposed a LATE scheduler, which improves Hadoop's task execution efficiency by starting backup tasks for tasks with the longest remaining completion time, but estimates the remaining completion time of tasks need to be improved. Tao et al. proposed an adaptive MapReduce scheduler [6]. This algorithm solves the problem of uneven load distribution of Hadoop in heterogeneous resource environment to some extent, but it is difficult to determine the expected completion time of tasks. Zheng et al. proposed a task adaptive scheduling method based on node capability, which fully considers the heterogeneity of node resources in the cluster, but it is easy to cause

Z. Xu et al. (Eds.): CSIA 2019, AISC 928, pp. 1332–1336, 2020.
https://doi.org/10.1007/978-3-030-15235-2_182

frequent data transmission between nodes, occupy network bandwidth, and reduce network bandwidth. Low system performance.

In order to solve the problem of inefficiency of Hadoop scheduling algorithm in heterogeneous environment, an adaptive node capacity scheduling algorithm NCAS is proposed. The algorithm calculates the value of the scheduling factor which represents the computing power of each node. According to the scheduling factor, the number of task slots and the amount of data are allocated to the fast or slow nodes, so as to improve the overall efficiency of the system.

2 Method

NCAS algorithm first partitions the user's files after receiving them, then distributes the data blocks to HDFS to save them in turn, and then carries out Map task scheduling and Reduce task scheduling. In order to explain clearly, two related concepts are introduced at first, and then an adaptive data distribution algorithm and an adaptive task scheduling algorithm are proposed to constitute NCAS algorithm.

The core of Hadoop consists of two parts: Hadoop Distributed File System (HDFS) [7] and MapReduce implementation system. The system architecture of Hadoop cluster consists of a master node and a group of slave nodes. In HDFS, a NameNode and DataNode processes are run on the master and slave nodes respectively. NameNode stores metadata in HDFS and responds to user's access to HDFS file system; DataNode stores data, executes NameNode's commands, creates, replicates and deletes data blocks, and the client can directly read and write to DataNode. HDFS receives the file and divides it into equal-sized data blocks, which are copied three times and stored in different nodes.

For MapReduce system, user-submitted jobs are divided into several map tasks and reduce tasks [8]. Each map task processes a data block and outputs corresponding key-value pairs. Reduce tasks process these key-value pairs to get the final output results. Each slave node has a certain number of map task slots and reduce task slots, one slot performs a corresponding type of task, slot configuration plays a vital role in the performance of Hadoop. A Job Tracker and a Task Tracker process are run on the master and slave nodes respectively. Job Tracker is responsible for dispatching Map tasks and Reduce tasks to the corresponding Task Tracker, and for task execution monitoring and fault-tolerant management; Task Tracker is responsible for performing assigned Map tasks and Reduce tasks, collecting and storing the results, and reporting the current status and resource utilization of nodes to Job Tracker through periodic heartbeat. The system starts backup tasks for backward tasks and reschedules tasks that fail to run.

Scheduling factor is related to node performance and task characteristics, which represents the strength of node computing power. The performance of the node can be determined by the hardware parameters of the node. The larger the hardware parameters, the better the performance of the node. In heterogeneous environments, the same slot shows different operation speeds when handling different jobs. Task characteristics are defined to represent the different performance of the same node when performing different tasks. There are three main types of jobs handled by Hadoop cluster: CPU-bound,

I/O-bound and class sway [9]. In this paper, CPU-bound and I/O-bound tasks are selected, and the value of task characteristics is calculated by taking the time spent by different types of tasks as parameters. With the continuous execution of tasks, task feature parameters may change, and a certain period of update is set to calculate task feature parameters. This paper reads and calculates various node information values through scripts, and saves the results in files.

From the local user log, we can find the historical time record of the node completing tasks. The average completion time of CPU-Bound type and I/O-Bound type is tt_{cmj} and tt_{iomj}, the average completion time of CPU-Bound type and I/O-Bound type is tt_{crj} and tt_{iorj}, and the average completion time of CPU-Bound type and I/O-Bound type is avg_{cm}. With avg_{iom}, the average completion time of running Reduce tasks CPU-Bound and I/O-Bound is avg_{cr} and avg_{ior}. Task feature tt_j is represented as

$$N_{rj} = w_1 \times \frac{tt_{cj}}{avg_c} + w_2 \times \frac{tt_{mj}}{avg_m} + w_3 \times \frac{tt_{nj}}{avg_n} w_i \times \frac{tt_{dj}}{avg_d} \quad (1)$$

In heterogeneous resource environment, the computing power of each node varies greatly. Each node has the same amount of data. The fast node that processes the data of the node quickly needs to process the data of the slow node, and the transmission of large amounts of data between the long-distance fast and slow nodes requires a huge cost. In order to avoid this situation as far as possible, the amount of data stored by each node will be directly proportional to its computing power, and the amount of data that needs to be transmitted remotely will be greatly reduced. The adaptive data distribution algorithm allocates a large amount of data to fast nodes according to scheduling factors, and a small amount of data to slow nodes to avoid remote transmission of large amounts of data [10]. Current scheduling methods face the problem of uneven load distribution in heterogeneous clusters. In order to balance the load as much as possible, an adaptive task scheduling algorithm is proposed. According to the scheduling factor operation, the number of task slots matching the computing power of each node is allocated.

3 Experiment

To verify the algorithm, a cluster consisting of three racks is built. Each rack consists of a set of computer nodes with different configurations, and the internal rack and the rack are connected by switches.

Figure 1 shows a comparison of the number of backup tasks initiated by the default push task scheduling algorithm and NCAS algorithm in Hadoop when the amount of start job data is 2 GB, 4 GB and 8 GB, respectively. The graph shows that the number of backup tasks enabled by NCAS algorithm decreases by 70.0% on average compared with the speculative task scheduling algorithm. The reasons for the analysis are as follows: the resources in the default Hadoop cluster are isomorphic, each node divides tasks into slots and data, and many tasks on the slow node run backward, which makes the system start many backup tasks; while NCAS algorithm determines the number of slots and data for each node according to the scheduling factor, which makes the progress of each node in the running process of the cluster large. The small relative balance reduces the number of backup tasks and optimizes the performance of the cluster.

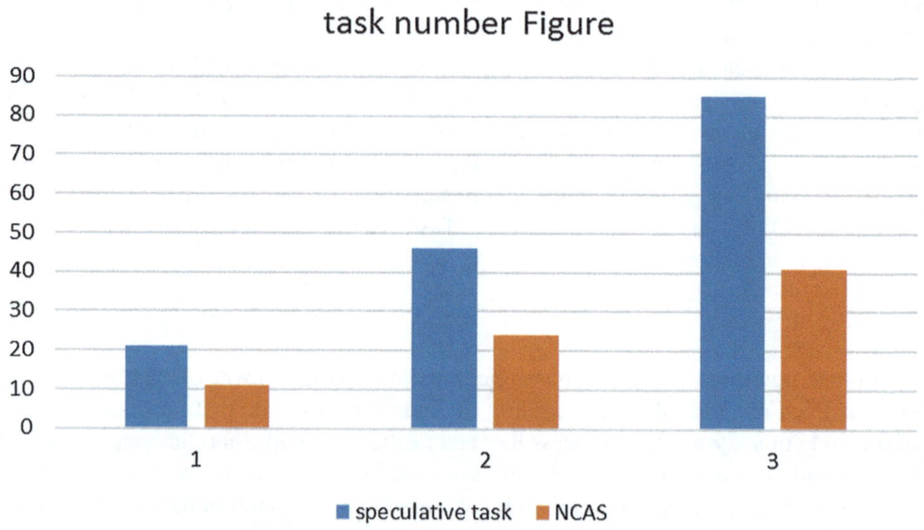

Fig. 1. Comparison of running backup tasks

The data volume of the experimental program is set to 4 GB, and the Hadoop cluster is run under the Hadoop scheduler, the speculative task scheduling algorithm, the LATE algorithm and the NCAS algorithm of the non-startup speculative task scheduling algorithm, respectively. The programs of each task type are executed three times under the four algorithms to get the mean value.

4 Conclusion

This paper studies the main architecture and operation principle of Hadoop, and proposes an adaptive scheduling algorithm NCAS for node capability in heterogeneous resource environment. The scheduling factor is obtained by calculating the correlative quantity of the computing power of the nodes. The proportion of the scheduling factor to the total of the cluster scheduling factors determines the amount of data and the number of task slots that the nodes should share. The fast nodes have more nodes and the slow nodes have fewer points, so that the load of the cluster is always in a relatively balanced state. The experimental results show that NCAS algorithm improves the resource utilization of Hadoop in heterogeneous resource environment, and improves the system performance of Hadoop.

Acknowledgements. This work was supported by grants from The National Natural Science Foundation of China (No. 61862056), the Guangxi Natural Science Foundation (No. 2017GXNSFAA198148) foundation of Wuzhou University (No. 2017B001) and Guangxi Colleges and Universities Key Laboratory of Professional Software Technology, Wuzhou University.

References

1. Glushkova D, Jovanovic P, Abello A (2019) Mapreduce performance model for Hadoop 2.x. Inf Syst 79:32–43
2. Qin P, Dai B, Huang BX et al (2017) Bandwidth-aware scheduling with SDN in Hadoop: a new trend for big data. IEEE Syst J 11(4):2337–2344
3. Pastorelli M, Carra D, Dell'Amico M et al (2017) HFSP: bringing size-based scheduling to Hadoop. IEEE Trans Cloud Comput 5(1):43–56
4. Quresh NMF, Shin DR, Siddiqui IF et al (2017) Storage-tag-aware scheduler for Hadoop cluster. IEEE Access 5:13742–13755
5. Guo YF, Rao J, Jiang CJ et al (2017) Moving Hadoop into the cloud with flexible slot management and speculative execution. IEEE Trans Parallel Distrib Syst 28(3):798–812
6. Ferrucci F, Salza P, Sarro F (2018) Using Hadoop MapReduce for parallel genetic algorithms: a comparison of the global, grid and island models. Evol Comput 26(4):535–567
7. Lin CY, Lin YC (2017) An overall approach to achieve load balancing for Hadoop distributed file system. Int J Web Grid Serv 13(4):448–466
8. Alarabi L, Mokbel MF, Musleh M (2018) ST-Hadoop: a MapReduce framework for spatio-temporal data. Geoinformatica 22(4):785–813
9. Lu XZ, Phang K (2018) An enhanced Hadoop heartbeat mechanism for MapReduce task scheduler using dynamic calibration. China Commun 15(11):93–110
10. Oo MN, Parvin S, Thein T (2018) Forensic investigation through data remnants on Hadoop big data storage system. Comput Syst Sci Eng 33(3):203–217

Application and Practice of Deep Learning Platform in Automobile Field

Yingzi Wang(✉), Xiangyi Fang, and Jue Hou

China Automotive Technology and Research Center Co., Ltd., Tianjin 300300, China
yingzimizhan@sina.com

Abstract. Starting from the development trend of the automotive field, this paper describes the development of the automotive field at home and abroad, and mainly studies the application examples of the deep learning platform in the automotive field, and explores the convenience and advantages brought by the deep learning platform for the automotive field, which lays a good theoretical and practical foundation for our country's driverless technology.

Keywords: Deep learning · Automotive field · Application value · Driverless

With the continuous development of various fields, the machine has brought countless conveniences to people, which not only enriches people's lives, but also replaces manpower in many fields, reducing people's work intensity. Therefore, there is no exception in the automotive field, and people's expectations for the automotive field are also increasing, among which people are very interested in driverless technology. Driverless can reduce the restrictions on driving, increase the safety of traffic, and reduce accidents caused by human causes, which greatly improves people's work efficiency, and brings people physical and mental benefits. The basic technology of driverless technology is its learning ability [1]. Therefore, the deep learning platform plays an important role in the development of the automotive field. After collecting a large amount of data artificially, the number is analyzed, so that the vehicle can automatically process the feedback information of the surrounding environment, and continuously improve and perfect the driverless technology through the algorithm of the deep learning platform. This paper will focus on the application and practice of deep learning platform in driverless technology, and explore the significance of deep learning [2–6].

1 Principle of Technology of Driverless Car

The driverless system is made up of ranging, camera, radar, database and processor. A laser range finder is installed on the top of the car. The distribution of obstacles around the car can be calculated by receiving the laser [6]. Radar device can identify the fixed obstacles in a long distance. When the signal is captured by the automobile processing system, it can be processed in advance to avoid the roadblock. When a car

Z. Xu et al. (Eds.): CSIA 2019, AISC 928, pp. 1337–1341, 2020.
https://doi.org/10.1007/978-3-030-15235-2_183

changes lanes, the radar in the rear of the car can judge whether there is a vehicle in the left and right rear of the car. At the same time, the laser ranging system is used to measure the distance between vehicles to avoid side impact [7]. The radar in front of the vehicle can identify the intersection in front of the vehicle and send the data to the computer processing system for processing and analysis. If there is a vehicle in front of the vehicle, the car will brake. When car is reversing, the rear radar can accurately know the position and distance of the rear obstacle, and then judge the mode and distance of reversing. If there is a vehicle in the rear measured by a laser range finder during driving, the computer will analyze the distance and retrieve the data from the database to keep the distance within the safe range [8, 9].

In addition, parameters such as acceleration and angular velocity can be monitored at the bottom of the vehicle, and processed and analyzed by the processor with the GPS data. The state of the vehicle can be monitored in real time by combining the feedback information of the micro-sensor, and the normal driving of the vehicle can be ensured.

2 Basic Situation of Deep Learning Platform

The deep learning platform is inspired by artificial neural networks and is an emerging platform for machine learning research. In the deep learning platform, people can collect a large amount of data through pre-investigation and research to build a database, and then simulate the neural network in the human brain, giving the machine the ability to "think". An abstract and complex attribute category and feature can be constructed through one simple combination feature after another. For example, in the deep learning platform, a single image, sound and text information can be synthesized like human brain processing and analyzing data to construct a multi-dimensional object. The deep machine learning method, like the ordinary machine learning method, can be roughly divided into two major sections, namely, supervised learning and unsupervised learning. The difference in learning patterns is determined by different learning frameworks. For example, the machine's convolutional neural network learning model belongs to the supervised learning model in deep learning, while the deep belief network is the unsupervised learning model in machine deep learning.

Deep learning is not a simple data processing, but a comprehensive calculation of many data. Therefore, it can be defined as a family of functions in all nodes and possible graphic structures. There is no child at the input node and no father at the output node.

3 Principle of Deep Learning Platform and Its Application in the Automotive Field

3.1 The Calculation Principle of the Deep Learning Platform

The deep learning platform is not the same as the ordinary data processing or learning platform. It not only needs to process simple data but also integrates the obtained data and implements the data into the automotive field. In the automotive field, deep learning is mainly reflected in the aspect of driverless technology, and several modules need to be worked if the deep learning platform is served with the driverless technology. Firstly, the in-depth learning platform needs to collect a large amount of data in the preparation stage, and preprocess these data. Through preprocessing, the appropriate data structure is screened out and stored, and then the training data and test tuples are constructed. Next, a large amount of data is input into the training data and the test tuple to perform unsupervised learning of the first layer, and the data is clustered according to the result, and the approximated data is grouped into one class for random discrimination. The supervised learning mode is used to adjust the thresholds of the nodes in the second layer to increase the accuracy of the input data of the second layer.

Then learn unsupervisedly each layer of data on the deep learning platform, and each unsupervised learning only exercises the same layer of data, and outputs the results of the exercise to the higher level of data. Finally, in the supervised learning mode, the data of each layer should be adjusted.

3.2 Application of Deep Learning Platform in the Automotive Field

When the car receives data fed back by a measuring instrument such as a radar or a laser range finder, the obtained raw data needs to be preprocessed and converted into corresponding spatial information. When calculating the average value, it is necessary to perform principal component analysis on the original data, and blank the data using PCA and ZCA processing, and standardize the calculated average value. For example, when the laser sensor receives the laser feedback signal, the walking time of the laser should be converted into the displacement between the automobile and the object according to the formula; when the vehicle camera captures the image information around the automobile, the image information is fed back to the processor. The system allows the processor to determine the location of the obstacle, and can also process traffic lights and pedestrians, plan the direction of the car, and convert the data detected by the radar system into spatial information. Next, the application of deep learning in the acceleration and deceleration of automobiles will be focused on.

The brake of a car is related to the presence of pedestrians in front of the car and the distance between pedestrians. By accumulating a large amount of input data, the learning platform will divide the distance between the car and pedestrians into one kind, and supervise and learn different distances. When the distance between the car and pedestrians is within a certain range, it will adjust the state of the car, perform braking and whistling. At the same time, it will continue to drive at a certain speed to enhance the connection and the validity and correctness of classification of the second level. For example, in this case, there are “n” cases, each case corresponds to a data, and the threshold of braking whistle and moving forward is “m”. “m” is used as the node to judge whether to perform braking whistle operation, and to divide “n” data into several categories, so that the same kind of data can perform the same operation. If the result of execution is not consistent with the actual situation, the threshold value of low brake whistle should be adjusted appropriately. If the execution results of the same kind of data are not only wrong whistling and braking, but also moving at the wrong speed, these similar errors are classified into the same type.

The number of surrounding vehicles is collected by the detection system, and the vehicle with the shortest distance is used as the input data of the distance and the traveling speed. By analyzing and learning a large amount of input data, the second layer network then classifies the number of reserves in a certain range into one category, supervising and learning different types of situations. When the number of surrounding vehicles is in a certain range, the corresponding speed is obtained to drive, and judge whether to accelerate, decelerate or travel at a constant speed according to the distance between the vehicles. Assume that there are x cases. When the threshold is y, the vehicle speed is changed, the distance and speed are kept at the preset nodes, and the situation in "x" is summarized into several execution results, and the same kind of situation is ensured with the same processing. When the speed is constant and the speed is decelerated, the threshold is appropriately lowered, and the threshold is increased when the car accelerates.

4 Deep Learning Platform in the Automotive Field Development Prospects

With the continuous development of intelligent technology and automobile active safety technology, people gradually pay attention to the development of this area. Therefore, many enterprises are constantly investing in the field of automobile driverless technology. At the same time, the sensor technology involved in the driverless technology is constantly innovating, which greatly reduces the cost of technology research and development, and has a bright future. The in-depth learning platform has better image recognition and processing technology, which has injected strong impetus into the development of unmanned driving technology. GUP technology can capture images in real time, and use the processing and analysis system to make timely and correct processing, which makes up for the shortcomings of human drivers and greatly improves the safety of driving. In the field of deep learning in the automotive field, considerable research results have been achieved at home and abroad, but there are still many problems in the experiment, which need continuous improvement by researchers.

In addition, that the development open source platforms for automatic containers such as Docker and k8s provides technology platform for driverless. Among them, Openshift is an application obtained by organically combining Docker and k8s. The developers of the cloud computing platform can create, test and run activities on the platform, and deploy the running results to the cloud computing. In Openshift, the role of the k8s cluster is mainly to provide computing power, while the persistence of data requires the cooperation of other cloud services. Web Honeycomb is also a container service based on Docker and k8s, and it has been put into operation in practice, serving many domestic enterprises, bringing stable, safe and convenient efficient cloud computing services to these enterprises. On the other hand, with the development and reform of cloud computing containers, the resource management of servers has also made great progress in the continuous process of time, and has been applied to hospitals, schools, transportation and other industries. A cluster that can solve most problems can be built through a small number of high-performance servers, which reduces the occurrence of adverse events such as business interruption caused by server hardware damage. In the automotive field, efficient resource management can improve the practicality and safety of autonomous vehicles, which is of great significance. Server resource management can collect a large amount of data, which lays a good foundation for the goal of automotive automation driving and greatly reduces labor costs and improves the level of resource management and integration.

In short, the deep learning platform mainly involves driverless technology in the automotive field, and the purpose of the driverless technology is to realize the driverless driving of the vehicle through the network and information technology. Therefore, researchers can continuously improve the driverless technology of the car on the platform of deep learning, and continue to promote to other aspects of the automotive field. It can not only promote the development of the automotive field, but also improve the level of social labor productivity, optimize the way people travel, and give people bring more security and convenience.

References

1. Cheng X, Hu H, Ji G, Sun L (2018) Research on multiscale target detection algorithm based on deep learning monitoring scene. J Nanjing Normal Univ (Eng Technol) 18(03):33–38
2. Wang N, Yang M (2018) Image-based paper-cutting platform based on deep learning and image processing algorithms. Comput Knowl Technol 14(25):61–63+70
3. Gao Y, Zhang L, Fu Y (2018) Deep learning and its significance. Sci Pop (Sci Educ) (09):139
4. Wang W, Zhang Z, Gao N, Zhao Y Progress of research on big data analysis methods based on artificial intelligence technology. Comput Integr Manuf Syst 1–33
5. Liu M, Zhan Q (2014) Practical application of curriculum system in higher vocational automobile majors. J Mudanjiang Coll Educ (11):87–88
6. Lu H, Liu D, Sun J (2010) From the driverless car to the World Expo to see the future car. Mech Electr Prod Dev Innov
7. Li C, Peng X (2011) Driverless car: feasible or not feasible? Today Sci Court
8. Cui Y (2002) Discussion on compatibility of control management software in security field. China Secur Prod Inf
9. Tang Z, Li W, Shen D (2010) Application and development of intelligent high-definition video surveillance in security field. China Secur

Exploration and Practice of Market-Oriented Photoshop Image Processing Course

Xiao Wang(✉)

Xi'an Fanyi University, Xi'an, Shaanxi, China
wxzw_1021@163.com

Abstract. With the development of science and technology, the demand of society is also changing constantly. To some extent, the change of demand leads to the different kinds of curriculums offered by colleges and universities. As for private colleges and universities that focus on train practical and high-skilled talents, fostering graduates who can handle many skills have become teaching important point. Photoshop image processing course can better integrate students into society, while traditional teaching methods can not well link up education and market. Therefore, in order to improve the teaching effect, this essay proposes to introduce enterprise or industry working mode. Aimed at project procedure as project teaching, students can meet the integration of universities and enterprises.

Keywords: Collaborative education · Enterprise project · Evaluation system · Work-study alternation

1 Introduction

With the rapid development of science and technology, Photoshop, as a powerful image processing software, has been applied to various industries, such as web page design, packaging advertising design, album design and so on [1]. Therefore, according to the needs of the society, colleges and universities open up Photoshop. In order to enable students to master one skill, they also train a group of graphic design talents for the society [2]. The main purpose of this course is to enable students to master the relevant knowledge of image production, to analyze and process pictures independently according to user needs, and to achieve image filtering, synthesis and other effects [3]. With the arrival of market economy, the demand standard for professional talents is constantly improving and greatly made the competition of talent market more fierce than before [4]. The training objectives of all universities are towards the direction of compound applied technical talents [5]. While stressing practical teaching, the training of students' practical ability and cognitive ability should be strengthened so that students can adapt to the needs of their jobs as soon as they graduate.

Z. Xu et al. (Eds.): CSIA 2019, AISC 928, pp. 1342–1347, 2020.
https://doi.org/10.1007/978-3-030-15235-2_184

2 Teaching Model of Integration of Theory and Practice

Photoshop image processing is a highly artistic, practical, innovative and abstract course. Students should not only master professional operation skills, but also have certain expressive and independent aesthetic abilities in the process of learning. The teaching mode of separating theory from practice is not conducive to students to master basic knowledge, but also to better cultivate students' innovative ability and interest in learning [6]. Therefore, it's better to build a mode of integrating theory with practice and combining students' practice with multimedia technology can effectively achieve the teaching objectives. Students can consolidate the basic knowledge learned in the classroom through the operation of teaching cases or teaching projects. After that, it will not only fully reflect the curriculum characteristics of Photoshop, but raise the students' interest in learning and improve their learning ability [7].

However, through the tracking of graduates and a large number of surveys, the results show that although most students can master the use of software design skills through practical courses in colleges and even better on this basis to deal with daily graphics, but it is difficult to meet the requirements of enterprise front-line design. The reason is that although the school has always emphasized the integration of theory and practice as well as project-teaching way in the teaching process, due to the lack of support from practical projects, the integration of theory and practice teaching can only be simply implemented as the combination of theory and practical training exercises. Practice can only come from textbooks, examinations or reference books. The practice teaching completed in this way is still out of line with the actual needs of the market. The limitation of this teaching mode is not only reflected in the unreasonable practice projects, but also in the incomplete evaluation system of the practice projects [8]. The students' projects are basically completed by the teaching teachers, and they do not accept test from the market. Therefore, it is inevitable to have deviation from market demand. In order to change this phenomenon, the most effective way is to realize the collaborative education between universities and enterprises, to introduce projects from enterprises into universities, to bring students into enterprises, to adjust the traditional teaching content, teaching emphasis and teaching difficulties, to be jointly participated by front-line personnel of enterprises and teachers of this course through the analysis of enterprise projects [9]. We can integrate tasks into classroom teaching, and improve curriculum resources, including handouts or textbooks, cases and materials, so as to improve the quality of teaching with the joint efforts of both sides.

3 Project Teaching Method Under College-Enterprise Cooperation

3.1 Developing Enterprise Project Plan Based on Teaching Materials

In the course of Photoshop Image processing, we should emphasize practicality and interest in learning. Therefore, when choosing textbooks, we should follow the principles of "explaining profound theories in simple language", "rich colors" and "clear and fashionable typesetting", so that students can establish a good interest-oriented curriculum.

Teaching based on textbooks can't be confined to textbooks only in content. If the content of knowledge and practice is derived from textbooks, students will lose interest and creativity in the curriculum very soon. Students trained in this way can't express their aesthetic ability and artistic accomplishment perfectly, and at the same time, they can't compare their skills with enterprises. Combination. In order to solve this problem, teachers should combine students' interests or professional orientation, select relevant resources from other material for class exercises, and stimulate students' learning initiative. When universities and enterprises achieve collaborative education, the selection of practical projects can be obtained from enterprises. The market of enterprises is large and there are many projects. Teachers choose projects which are suitable for students to implement from enterprise projects and deliver them to students. Enterprise personnel clarify project objectives and project tasks, while reserving certain creative space for students, so that students can have more clear objectives in the teaching process. We will actually bring the content of project teaching into line with the market, stimulate students' enthusiasm for learning, improve practical operation ability, accumulate technical experience in the process of project implementation, and improve the sense of collaboration and comprehensive application ability. At the same time, through the implementation of enterprise projects, students can not only grasp the production norms of projects, but understand the production technology and process of related industries.

3.2 Developing Project Tasks by Combining Enterprise Tutors with Professional Teachers

After introducing enterprise project into teaching, in the following teaching process, teachers need to decompose the project according to the content of specific project. For example, before making a website, they will do the effect map of the web page to show customers. Teachers will guide students to decompose the task of making the effect map of the web page into a serious small projects, such as Logo design, Banner design, navigation bar design, web background design and page layout design. The knowledge points involved in the course are: basic image editing, selection tools, image adjustment commands; pen tools and vector graphics; text input and editing; layers, channels and masks; color composition, etc. When students decompose the project, the enterprise tutor needs to identify and adjust the decomposition of the project, and make clear the goals to be achieved for each sub-project, so as to facilitate follow-up in the implementation process. In the following practical links, teachers should take into account the principle of complementary advantages of students, assist students in grouping and identifying projects, cultivate the sense of teamwork and spirit of resource sharing, and mobilize their sense of competition among groups to promote mutual learning. Each group appoints project leaders, who are responsible for clarifying the division of labor and problems arising from consultation. Detailed progress plans should be made to monitor the efficiency of team members. Teachers and business mentors should formulate overall creative requirements for the project and require students not to change at will in the process of production. After the project is set up, the teacher will issue the project task book to each group, at the same time, briefly explain the main knowledge points involved in the project, and give help and guidance to the students in the process of completing the project. Through the development of group teaching, we can cultivate the team spirit of cooperation among students, problems in the process of group teaching, or corresponding solutions are obtained through discussion and consultation among the members of the group. This can also train interpersonal communication ability, organizational ability and independent thinking ability.

3.3 Improving the Evaluation System

Teachers should specify the criteria for project evaluation in the project task book. The evaluation of the project is divided into three stages: student self-evaluation stage, tutor evaluation stage and market evaluation stage.

In the self-evaluation stage, the students summarize the completion of the project. They can express the background, highlights and technical difficulties of the project, and cultivate the habit of self-summary and reflection. At the same time, it accepts the mutual evaluation among various project groups, finds out the shortcomings, and forms a relatively complete evaluation system [10]. According to the evaluation, the students revise and improve again until the project is completed.

According to the actual situation of the project, the teacher evaluation in the tutor evaluation stage mainly carries on the objective and fair evaluation from the technical aspects, summarizes the advantages and disadvantages of each group of projects, and puts forward pertinent suggestions to make the students' works more complete. Enterprise mentors mainly analyze the feasibility of the project, and evaluate the results from the aspects of economic and social effects.

In the stage of market evaluation, after passing the first two evaluations smoothly, projects can also be directly tested by the market and tested by market feedback. The feedback from the market objectively and effectively evaluates the results of the project. Through the feedback from the market, we can find out the pertinent solutions to the problems. Under such a mode, we should guide students' research, constantly develop their attitudes, and the trained talents will be more in line with the market demand.

4 Promoting the Mode of "Work-Study Alternation" to Achieve Win-Win Situation

Practice teaching is the characteristic of Photoshop Image Processing course. In order to make practice teaching play its important role, it is necessary to adjust the existing teaching mode. Combining the practical working mode of enterprise front line with universities, students can get a comprehensive understanding of the theoretical knowledge in the textbook and the specific operation in class practice. In this way, students can correct the mistakes in the learning process in time, promote their interest in learning, and use the skills flexibly. In order to realize the teaching mode of "work-study alternation", it is better to step by step and gradually deepen the teaching mode [11]. For example, during the course, students can be brought into the enterprise to visit and learn according to the time node of the project, to understand how a project in the enterprise is from market research to the formulation of the project implementation plan, to define the project objectives, to complete the project plan, and finally to pass the project acceptance. Through learning the specific work content of enterprise personnel in different nodes, so students cam make the project clear. When students return to school, they can arrange tasks for their own projects to make their practice more purposeful. In this way, students can learn in practice, fully integrate theory with practice, constantly improve and complement each other, and promote their own comprehensive quality and ability.

Under the guidance of enterprises and markets, teaching method based on upgrading program has achieved a win-win situation for students, teachers and enterprises. Through the application of real enterprise projects in school, students understand the needs of specific jobs, which is conducive to transformation from knowledge to ability, information literacy has been greatly improved, and lay a solid foundation for graduation into society in the future. Teachers, in the university-enterprise cooperation mode, also provide more practical resources, cases and materials for teaching. The diversity of enterprise projects puts forward higher requirements for teachers' teaching and teaching, and promotes continuous learning and upgrading of professional fields in the process of guiding students. In this process, enterprises have realized resource optimization. The most important thing is that students trained through project teaching are more in line with the needs of enterprises and the market. After graduation, students can start their work quickly without spending time on pre-job training. Such a win-win situation provides learning opportunities for more courses to carry out project teaching of university-enterprise cooperation.

5 Conclusion

To sum up, in today's rapid development of science and technology, training innovative and applied talents is far more meaningful than excellent students. Only when students learn to use the knowledge flexibly, can they realize the seamless connection between colleges and the market, and meet the needs of high-skilled talents in social posts. The teaching method driven by enterprise project can make students' learning objectives clearer and more effectively promote students' learning enthusiasm and initiative. It also plays a positive role in the daily management of students. Therefore, the market-oriented curriculum reform of Photoshop Image Processing provides a good platform for students, teachers, and schools, so that all roles can perform brilliantly and smoothly. I hope this method can provide a reference for professionals in the field of education.

Acknowledgments. This research was supported by Scientific Research team in Xi'an Fanyi University (XFU17KYTDB02).

References

1. Lin J (2017) Photoshop image processing course teaching exploration. Art Educ Res (10) (2017) (in Chinese)
2. Bao F (2017) Method application of project teaching method in photoshop image processing course. Mod Educ (32):231–232 (in Chinese)

3. Tao S (2007) Experiences and suggestions in the application of project teaching method. China Prof Tech Educ (28) (in Chinese)
4. Neo Y, Liu Q (2007) Application of task-driven teaching method in computer teaching. Sci Technol Inf (36) (in Chinese)
5. Wang B (2015) Taking photoshop of image processing as an example—the project teaching under the background of school-enterprise cooperation. Asia-Pacific Educ (09) (in Chinese)
6. Wang Z (2014) Exploration of photoshop course teaching. J Harbin Vocat Tech Coll (3):112–113 (in Chinese)
7. Kan Q, Fei X (2009) Discussion on the modularization and case-based teaching method of PS course. Comput Age (1):63–65 (in Chinese)
8. Zhang J (2010) Discussions on cooperative education between industries, universities and research in applied shell universities. J Huainan Normal Univ (3) (in Chinese)
9. Lu X (2018) Exploration and practice of innovation and entrepreneurship education for college students driven by project. Res Pract Innov Entrep Theory (01) (in Chinese)
10. Xiang D (2008) A discussion on the operation of efficient school-enterprise cooperation mode under the new situation. J Xiangtan Normal Univ (Nat Sci Ed) (04) (in Chinese)
11. Zhang H (2016) Research on the importance of school-enterprise cooperation in photoshop image production teaching. Curric Educ Res (32) (in Chinese)

Advertising Icon Design and Communication Conception Under the Condition of EEG and Eye Movement Experiments—Taking the Lingmei Omnimedia E-Commerce Platform Mobile APP as an Example

Yan Cui[1,2](✉)

[1] Faculty of Arts, Shaanxi Normal University, Xi'an, China
cuiyinhe66@sina.com
[2] Inner Mongolia University for Nationalities, Tongliao, China

Abstract. "With the development of social productivity, the advancement of science and technology, the way of mass communication has also been constantly changing, the scope of communication has become more wider, and the effect of communication has become more stronger; Due to media update, the media has more impact on the people, people's spiritual and cultural life has become more colorful, and the spiritual and cultural needs of the public have been greatly satisfied". Indeed, in recent years, With the rapid development of information technology and Internet technology, the content and application of mobile intelligent communication device are continuously enriched, the hardware capabilities are continuously improved, which promotes the innovation and progress of mobile intelligent communication device continuously; the growing spiritual and cultural needs of the public are greatly satisfied. Taking the smart phone as an example, the China Internet Network Information Center (CNNIC) released the "Statistical Report on China's Internet Development Status": "As of June 2018, the number of netizen in China was 8.02 billion, The number added in the first half of the year was 29.68 million and the Internet penetration rate reached 57.7%. As of June 2018, the number of mobile netizen in China reached 7.88 billion. The number added in the first half of the year was 35.09 million. Compared with the end of 2017, it has increased by 4.7%, and 98.3% of netizen use mobile phones to access the Internet".

Keywords: Advertising icon · Movement Experiments · EEG

1 Introduction

On the basis of high base, the proportion of mobile netizen has further increased. Advertising As a important chart component of mobile smart device user-interface, advertisement is "a language that are understandable to the interface designer and users of specific applications", advertisement is also an important way for advertisers for information dissemination and user acceptance of information through a variety of systems. In the deeper, User awareness of icons is part of system awareness [1–3]. In

Z. Xu et al. (Eds.): CSIA 2019, AISC 928, pp. 1348–1353, 2020.
https://doi.org/10.1007/978-3-030-15235-2_185

this case, advertising icon design should be simple, natural, friendly, convenient, consistent and reflect the "people-oriented" design philosophy, it can quickly be identified and remembered, and eliminating communication barriers between users and the computer, allowing users prefer to read Figure [4, 5]. On the other hand, the ideal state of simplicity, intuition, and metaphor of icon design is that you not need words to tell people what they can see the information spread by the figure. In order to achieve this ideal state, people's requirements for icon design are constantly improving, and the standard is more and more strict. Because improperly designed icons can not improve cognitive efficiency, it will affect the user's operation process and even cause wrong operation. In response to this situation, some scholars pointed out: "The core of icon design is to 'communicate', to transmit information to the audience through the visual symbol, not only to 'pass', but also to 'reach' … Therefore, how to communicate and how effective, is the primary problem for icon design" [6–10].

On the other hand, with the rapid development of computer technology, big data and cloud computing have become an important supporting foundation for modern scientific research. Under this favorable situation, it is a valuable research topic that study "Advertising icon design and Communication under the Condition of EEG and Eye Movement Experiments" by computer technology. Armed with this research idea, this article takes the "Lingmei omnimedia e-commerce platform" mobile APP as an example to carry out the test. The specific design concept has the following aspects:

(1) Establish an icon recognition model of "Lingmei omnimedia e-commerce platform" mobile APP users. The design philosophy is the case that the main body that interacts with the icon is the user, not the designer. In the design process, designers can't replace user thinking subjectively, and can't substitute user evaluation for self-reference design. The user model can be established by using eye movement and EEG technology to deeply analyze the user's cognitive rules and mental activity mechanism. This model helps designers distinguish user groups and form a user-centered design and evaluation mechanism.
(2) Establish an icon interpretation rules. The expression and interpretation of rules contribute to operable and controllable design, but also guide users to enhance their understanding of icons. Use eye movement and EEG technology to explore "Lingmei omnimedia e-commerce platform" Mobile APP icon design model and cognitive rules, will be able to establish systematic rules of icon-interpretation, will greatly enhance the scientific of icon design and evaluation.
(3) Using big data, cloud computing and eye movement and EEG technology to study the psychological phenomena and their interrelationships in the field of mobile APP icon design of "Lingmei omnimedia e-commerce platform", and the related factors and laws of these psychological phenomena. This idea is not only a strong complement to the modern theory of design, but also further promotes the development of cross-disciplinary.
(4) Based on user cognition, constructing the systematic model and method of icon design and cognitive theory, it will help to design icons that are close to the user's mental model, and achieve more intuitive, humanized and emotional advertising experience of "Lingmei omnimedia e-commerce platform" mobile APP.

(5) Provide the theoretical basis for icon design and evaluation, which helps designers to design or choose to use icons that convey information greatly, achieve online and offline multidimensional image information communication.
(6) It helps to overcome cognitive limitations due to the cultural level, aging cognitive and cultural difference, enhance the penetration rate of mobile smart devices.

Specific research can be carried out from the following aspects:

2 The Analysis Factors that Affect Icon Cognition and Design and Quantitative Assessment Study

First, fully analyze, summarize and summarize the factors that affect icon design and cognitive, such as user factors (user cognitive habits, cultural level, experience, etc.), environmental factors (device screen size, environmental brightness, etc.) and icons factors (the physical properties as a component for a single icon such as color, size, shape, etc., the spatial attributes as a set, such as pitch, group, arrangement, etc., the cognitive attribute that convey meaning, such as familiarity, particularly, semantic relations, the visual complexity, etc.). Secondly, through the relevant literature, mobile smart device and Internet, we collect icon and establish icon library. Through questionnaire, we quantitative assess cognitive attributes of each icon of the "Lingmei omnimedia e-commerce platform" mobile APP. According to evaluation of results, we use SPSS to make correlation analysis to study what cognitive attributes affect the understanding of the icon and the correlation between each cognitive attributes, provide research materials and data for the follow-up study eye movement and EEG studies Research materials and data.

1. The eye movement of icon visual search study

With the explosive growth of smart mobile devices in a variety of applications, designers and researchers first should pay attention to how the user can search useful icons quickly and efficiently in the interactive process. As a complex cognitive process, visual search means acquire the external stimulus information through a series of gazing and eye hoping process, thereby completing the processing of information; Generally, it require individuals to find a particular stimulus in a certain context, it has a more strong purpose. Eye movement research collects task-related information from visual scenes. Research shows that various modes of eye movement have been associated with human psychological changes. Among them, eye movement research on visual search is widely regarded as the most effective means in the research of visual information processing. This topic is based on the "Lingmei omnimedia e-commerce platform" advertising communication under the "Yi YOUYA" company, using SPSS to analyze user behavior data, and using eye tracker to record and analyze the eye movement process and data of the audience (gaze time, number of gaze, squint, etc.), Analysis of the factors affecting the design and cognition of advertising icons is how to obtain information such as the user's attention distribution and cognitive load, and deeply explore the user's visual search characteristics, understand their visual attention distribution rules and visual information processing. Analyze how users perform visual search, what methods are used, what kind of visual search model is formed, and provide designers with scientific and effective icon evaluation indicators.

3 EEG Research on Icon Understanding

The use of icons to represent objects, concepts, or functions depends on the ability of people to learn the meaning of icons by using prior knowledge. When design the series icon for the specific application, the meaning of each icon needs to be particularly clear, its meaning if it is not obvious, it must be able to learn quickly, and can not confuse with other icons in this icon. It is a big challenge for designers and researchers to have a consistent interpretation of icons for audiences of different ages, cultures, and knowledge backgrounds. The event-related potential (ERP) is a special brain evoked potential that reflects the physiological changes in the brain's nerve points during cognitive process by intentionally giving stimulation a special psychological meaning and using brain potentials caused by multiple or multiple stimuli, this method is called cognitive potential. This research is based on "Lingmei omnimedia e-commerce platform" Mobile APP icon library and quantitative assessment of the Icon cognitive attributes, research the cognitive attributes (such as familiarity, concreteness, semantic relations, visual complexity, etc.) the response characteristics of each brain region corresponding to the early stages of icon understanding that affects processing. Taking EEG components such as P300, N400 and RP in event-related potentials as the main analytical indicators, design EEG experiments and record user behavior data and EEG data. SPSS software was used to analyze user behavior data and EEG data. The brain topographic map provides an in-depth analysis of the brain's response characteristics in different brain regions and cerebral hemispheres during the process of icon comprehension processing and the corresponding brain processing mechanism, providing scientific and effective evaluation indicators and basis for establishing icon interpretation rules.

4 The Theoretical Example Verification Study

Taking the YIYOUYA's "Lingmei omnimedia e-commerce platform" Mobile APP icon interface design as an example, to verify the effect of the application of theory, to evaluate the optimization of icon design and cognition, enhance user interaction efficiency with smart phones, enhance user experience, feedback correction deepening theory.

5 Research Purposes

① Through the quantitative evaluation of the cognitive attributes of icons, the influence of various cognitive attributes on icon comprehension and the correlation between various cognitive attributes can be found.

② Deeply analysis of how various factors of the design icon and cognitive influence access to customers' attention distribution and cognitive load distribution, to explore the customer's visual search features and strategies, understand the situation about s visual attention distribution rules and visual information processing, form a visual search model related to icon design and cognitive influence factors; provide an academic basis for evaluation of advertising effectiveness.
③ Using behavioral data and EEG data, combined with brain topographic maps to deeply analyze the brain's response characteristics in different brain regions and cerebral hemispheres during the process of icon comprehension processing and corresponding brain processing mechanisms, and establish icon interpretation rules.

6 Possible Difficulties Encountered in the Study

The construction of the icon library is one of the research difficulties. The construction of the icon library not only provides basic data for subsequent research, but also provides data for relevant subsequent research to facilitate comparison of relevant research results. Therefore, the icon library construction must have a sufficient number of icons, the icon in library is representative.

(1) The cognitive attributes of icon are related, during the EEG experiment, when study the impact of a attribute on the icon understanding how to control other attributes is the another difficulty.

Faced with the above difficulties, eye movement technology and EEG technology will be adopted. The icon design and cognitive research will be carried out mainly on the two levels of icon visual search and understanding. The icon library will be constructed to quantify the cognitive attributes of icons and lay the foundation for subsequent research. Foundation; Specific strategies are as follows:

(1) Eye movement and EEG experimental research. In the "Lingmei omnimedia e-commerce platform" Mobile APP experiment, use the eye tracker to record data, and analysis user's eye movement index during the icon visual search processing (such as the fixation point, gaze count, eye hoping distance, Gaze time, scan path, heat map, etc.). Through the analysis, study the eye movement rules, attention distribution and search strategies when people complete visual tasks. It comes down to the theoretical results and constructs the theoretical model and interpretation rules of icon design and cognition.
(2) Adopt P300, N400 in ERP and RP as the main index, to study cognitive property affects the Brain processing mechanism of the icon understanding. Through the "Lingmei omnimedia e-commerce platform" the mobile APP example verification, evaluate and feedback, cycle optimization theory system.

This topic will fully draw on relevant research results, use the eye movement technology and EEG technology, systematic study the icon design and cognitive of the "Lingmei omnimedia e-commerce platform" smart phone APP interface, by analyzing the user's cognitive rules and mental activity mechanism, establish a user model of icon cognition, form a user-centered design and evaluation mechanism, and evaluate the effect of advertising communication more scientifically and effectively. At the same time, establish the systematic icon interpretation rules to improve the scientific of icon design and dissemination; realize the organic combination of information dissemination and social culture. As scholars have pointed out: "Designers must assume responsibility for the present and the future in society and culture, design must reduce production and operating costs, ensure that the environment can withstand, guide the correct behavior of consumption".

References

1. Cui Y (2015) Mass Media and Culture: People's Publishing House, p 56
2. Forty-second China Internet Development Statistics Report. China Internet Network Information Center
3. He Y, Cui Y (2015) Research on creative thinking of visual communication design. Inner Mongolia University Press, p 3
4. Li Y (2006) Foreign Design Classic Art Works Readings. Tsinghua University Press, pp 59–60
5. Lazard A, Mackert M (2014) User evaluations of design complexity: the impact of visual perceptions for effective online health communication. Int J Med Inform 83(10):726–735
6. Mcnely BJ (2014) Visual research methods and communication design. Inf Sci 289 (289):190–205
7. Mitton M (2014) Interior design visual presentation: a guide to graphics, models and presentation techniques, 4th edn. Ann Emerg Med 51(1):66–69
8. Roxburgh M (2001) Design and the aesthetics of research: visual communication journal. Curr Opin Microbiol 4(5):526–534
9. Vanhees H (2012) The influence of the design directive and the regulation on community designs on the benelux design law. Plant Physiol 159(1):131–143
10. Zamzow JP, Losey GS (2002) Ultraviolet radiation absorbance by coral reef fish mucus: photo-protection and visual communication. Environ Biol Fishes 63(1):41–47

Research on the Influencing Factors of Residents' Travel Based on Bayesian Network

Fengying Wang(✉), Liming Du, Gui Li, and Jie Dong

Shenyang Jianzhu University, No. 9, Hunnan East Road, Hunnan District, Shenyang, Liaoning, People's Republic of China
wangfy678@163.com

Abstract. Traffic has become an important factor affecting the development of a city and the choice of mode of transport is an important and indispensable component of traffic planning and policy development. In this paper, the urban residents of Shenyang City as the object of study, the application of Bayesian network method, the use of Shenyang city residents travel mode survey data to calculate the influencing factors of the relevant factors and behavioral economics theory of urban residents Travel mode selection to do a whole analysis and research. On the basis of reading a lot of literature, this paper briefly introduces the influencing factors of urban residents 'travel mode, and makes a detailed analysis of residents' travel behavior by using the results of previous literature research. The contents of the analysis mainly include the relative deterministic factors and the relative uncertainty factors that affect the residents' travel mode. Then, the related knowledge and learning methods and parameter estimation of the Bayesian network are introduced. The Bayesian network method and the economic theory Combined to further analyze and study the influencing factors of residents' travel mode. Draw conclusions and provide some suggestions and reference for the improvement of traffic policy.

Keywords: Influencing factors · Bayesian network · K2 algorithm

1 Introduction

In recent years, urban economic development is becoming more and more developed, people's life becomes more and more rich and comfortable, with the rapid development of private cars, the urban road traffic congestion, lead to more and more urban residents travel problems, more and more obvious, different individuals choose different way to travel, the formation of the urban traffic layout. The choice of transportation mode is an important and indispensable part in the transportation planning and policy making, and transportation has become an important factor influencing the development of a city. Therefore, it is necessary to analyze the influencing factors of urban residents' travel modes.

The direct hazard of traffic problems is to increase traffic delays, reduce driving speed, and bring time loss. Low-speed driving also leads to increased fuel consumption and increased travel costs. By studying 39 major cities in the United States, the Texas

Z. Xu et al. (Eds.): CSIA 2019, AISC 928, pp. 1354–1359, 2020.
https://doi.org/10.1007/978-3-030-15235-2_186

Transportation Research Institute estimates that the annual economic loss caused by traffic congestion in the United States is approximately $41 billion [1, 2]. The annual loss of the 12 largest cities exceeds $1 billion. In the Tokyo metropolitan area of Japan, there are 219 heavily crowded locations. On the heavily congested sections of the Capital Expressway, the congestion lasts for 17 h and the length of the crowd is 9.87 km. The traffic loss of traffic participants is quite equal in Tokyo every year due to traffic congestion. At 12.3 billion yen. The annual economic losses caused by traffic accidents, traffic congestion and environmental pollution in Europe are 50 billion euros, 500 billion euros and 5 billion to 50 billion euros respectively.

Since the 1970s, the interdependence among population structure, urban form and travel has developed into the field of space science and transportation science [4–6]. It is based on the understanding that travel can be explained in urban form to a considerable extent. With the comprehensive development of space and traffic planning, this insight gradually developed into the science of traditional no-space traffic planning. The aim is to achieve more sustainable transport needs by implementing land use and urban morphology concepts [7, 8]. However, some of the disappointments of the 1990s were the increasing frequency of studies of transport in urban form [9–12]. It is increasingly clear that demographic differences in different fields are becoming more and more evident, that simple spatial comparisons of travel behavior may lead to wrong conclusions, and that there are entirely different mechanisms behind the presumed spatial causes of distance behavior and pattern use.

2 Assumptions (Prerequisites)

In this paper, the factors influencing the choice of travel mode of urban residents are analyzed and studied by using the bayesian network model.

In addition, each participant must be completely rational, with the goal of maximizing personal interests. This is in line with some personal experiences, while ignoring others, such as the influence of emotional factors, the altruistic moral inclination in nature (which stems from the instinct to reproduce a race in any species), the rational man (economic man) assumption that human thinking is rational; And the impact of emergency factors such as temporary changes of transportation policy on residents' choice of travel mode is not considered. That is to say, people act rationally. The idea of rational behavior is used to describe the decision-making process. Generally speaking, rational behavior refers to the process of considering and calculating before making a decision. In this process, the decision makers will choose according to their own purposes. Rational behavior is opposite to conscious impulse.

3 Improvement of K2 Algorithm Based on Influencing Factors

Cooper et al. proposed a K2 scoring function combining prior information []. Given the prior information of node order, K2 scoring function can be used as a standard to evaluate the fitting degree of network structure and observation data. However, before learning bayesian network structure, the node order is not clear in most cases. Although the calculation efficiency of K2 scoring function is much higher than that of BIC, it has certain limitations in practical application. As K2 score function improvement, Heckerman et al. in 1995 proposed the BDe (Bayesian Dirichlet equivalent) score, this method, the prior distribution of the bayesian network parameters are assumed to be the Dirichlet distribution, in the process of computing nodes do not need to obtain order, expanded the application field of scoring function. Bouchaala et al. proposed a scoring function named IS (implicitscore), which used the implicit estimation method to estimate the bayes network parameters, avoiding the situation of first determining the distribution of node variables, reducing the error caused by the distribution of node variables, and improving the accuracy of the scoring function. Recently, Campos et al. proposed MIT (mutual information tests), a rating function based on conditional independence testing. The function evaluated the network structure by measuring the KL distance between the network structure and the observed data. This method USES the principle of information theory to reduce the computational complexity.

The basic idea is: start from an empty network, select the node with the highest probability of posterior structure as the parent node of the node according to the predetermined node order (prior knowledge, expert experience), traverse all nodes in turn, and tablecloth adds the optimal parent node for each variable.

As K2 algorithm determines the topology based on expert opinions or experience, it is often affected by subjective intention. Therefore, K2 algorithm combined with correlation analysis is adopted in this paper for analysis. The specific process is as follows: firstly, the correlation coefficient is used to determine the variables with strong correlation and provide the basis for orientation. K2 algorithm is used to study the network structure, and the order of variables is adjusted constantly, and finally the reasonable topology is determined.

4 Data Collection

The research data provided in this paper is from the survey results of urban residents in Shenyang. On weekdays and weekends respectively according to different populations were investigated in Shenyang, select the address of a questionnaire for parking lots in urban and suburban, peripheral part of the park, public transportation station, large shopping entertainment venues, colleges and universities around, and the questionnaire is the combination of paper and electronic questionnaire of questionnaire form, eventually to collect all the survey data. The survey method is a combination of questionnaire survey and face-to-face interview and inquiry.

The survey mainly includes the choice of travel mode (means of transport). Characteristics of traveler: gender, age, occupation and income; Family property: whether and the type of transport; Traffic property: travel purpose, travel distance, travel cost, travel time, etc. In addition, the weather conditions on the day the questionnaire was issued were recorded in detail, and the electronic version of the questionnaire paid attention to the completion status in real time, and the weather conditions were recorded. A total of 236 questionnaires were issued and 236 questionnaires were recovered, with a 100% recovery rate. A total of 100 interviewees were interviewed.

Among them, 236 valid samples were obtained from questionnaires and 100 valid samples were obtained from interview asking samples. The specific content of the questionnaire is shown in Appendix iii and the interview content in Appendix iv.

In order to make more objective analysis, the variable of attribute is coded as a dummy variable, and the continuous variable is coded as a discrete variable. In combination with relevant standards and modeling experience, the variables of the factor analysis of travel mode selection are listed as follows (Table 1):

Table 1. Travel behavior analysis bayesian network model node variable definition and value

	Variable name	Symbol	Variable value
Traveler attribute	Gender	Sex	S1. Male S2. Female
	Age	Age	A1. under-18; A2. 19–29; A3. 30–39; A4. 40–49 years old; A5. 50 years old and above
	Professional	Job	J1. student; J2. farmer/worker; J3. public institution and enterprise employee; J4. retiree; J5. others
	Income	Inc	I1. No income; I2. below 2000 Yuan; I3. 2001–5000 Yuan; I4. 5000 Yuan above
Family attribute	Possess vehicle	Tra	T1. Private car T2. Bicycle/electric car/motorcycle T3 T4. Other
Traffic attribute	Travel purpose	Goa	G1. Business; G2. Entertainment shopping; G3. Social (visit relatives and friends); G4. Other
	Travel distance	Dis	D1. 2 km below; D2. 2 to 5 km; D3. 5–10 km between; D4. 10 km above
	Travel cost	Cos	C1. 0–3 yuan; C2. 4–8 Yuan; C3. 9–15 Yuan C4. 15–30 Yuan; C5. 30 Yuan and above
	Travel time	Tim	Ti1. 5:00 before Ti2. 5:00–9:00 (morning peak) Ti3. 9:00–16:00 (usual time) Ti4. 16:00–19:00 (evening peak) Ti5. 19:00 later
Residence attribute	Traffic lights	Qua	Q1. 0–3; Q2. 3–6; Q3. 6 or more
	Road conditions	Roa	R1. Unblocked; R2. Relatively congested; R3. Very congested
Travel way	Travel vehicle	Cho	Ch1. Walking; Ch2. Bicycle/electric ar/motorcycle; Ch3. Bus/subway; Ch4. Taxi Ch5. Private car

5 Correlation Analysis of Influencing Factors

In this study, the correlation analysis is first carried out to investigate the correlation degree between two things (called variables in the data), so as to confirm the correlation between various influencing factors. See Table 2 for the correlation analysis.

$$\rho_{xy} = \frac{Cov(X,Y)}{\sqrt{DX}\sqrt{DY}} = \frac{E[XY] - E[X]E[Y]}{\sqrt{DX}\sqrt{DY}} \quad (1)$$

Table 2. Correlation analysis of influencing factors

Variable	Correlation coefficient	Significant degree
Income and travel distance	0.85290022	√
Income and ownership of transportation	0.60876487	√
Income and travel purpose	−0.463053416	
Travel distance and travel purpose	−0.559112277	
Number of traffic lights and traffic congestion	−0.323924259	
Travel distance and own vehicle	0.770841617	√
Own vehicle and travel purpose	0.78264603	√
Age and travel cost	0.677756096	√
Professional and travel cost	−0.60749012	
Professional and travel way	0.290300048	√
Professional and travel time	0.973241494	√
Age and travel way	0.234705617	√

6 Conclusion

From the correlation analysis, it can be seen that the traveler attribute has certain influence on the uncertainty factors such as single trip. Residential property has a significant impact on traffic property factors.

References

1. Abdel-Aty MA, Kitamura R, Jovanis PP (1996) Investigating effect of travel time reliability on route choice using repeated measurement stated preference data. Transportation Research Record 1493, Washington DC, TRB, pp 39–45
2. Berdica K (2002) An introduction to road vulnerability: what has been done, is done and should be done. Transp Policy 9:117–127
3. Ma H (2014) A study on the influencing factors of the choice of residents' travel mode based on non-lump-sum model [master's thesis]. Nanjing university of finance and economics, Nanjing (in Chinese)
4. Nicholson A, Du Z (1997) Degradable transportation systems: an integrated equilibrium model. Transp Res B 31(3):209–223
5. Scheiner J, Holz-Rau C (2007) Travel mode choice: affected by objective or subjective determinants? Transportation 34:487–511
6. Chen Y, Gao A (2002) A study of the international unblocked reliability based on the artificial neural network. In: International conference of ICMLC 2002, Beijing, pp 1306–1309

7. Zhang C, Chen X, Sumalee A (2011) Robust Wardrop's user equilibrium assignment under stochastic demand and supply: expected residual minimization approach. Transp Res Part B Methodol 45(3):534–552
8. Hate M, Hashemi SM (2009) Traffic assignment model with fuzzy level of travel demand: an efficient algorithm based on quasi-Logit formulas. Eur J Oper Res 194(2):432–451
9. Lee BD (2005) Motives, behaviors, and attachments: a comparative study between older travelers and younger travelers in national science area. The Pennsylvania State University, United States
10. Katsiko Poulos KV, Fisher DL, Duse-Anthony Y et al (2002) Risk attitude reversal sin drivers, route choice when range of travel time is provided. Hum Factors 44(3):466–473
11. Fan ZP, Zhang X, Chen FD et al (2013) Multiple attribute decision making considering aspiration-levels: a method based on prospect theory. Comput Ind Eng 65(2):341–350
12. Li ZB, Wang W, Liu P, Ragland DR (2012) Physical environments influencing bicyclists' perception of comfort on separated and on-street bicycle facilities. Transp Res Part D: Transp Environ 17(3):256–261

Research on the Development of Western Coal Industry Under the Background of Big Data

Xing Li(✉), Yadi Nan, and Ting Li

College of Economy and Management, Longdong University, Qingyang 745000, Gansu, China
leebj@189.cn

Abstract. This paper Research on the method of big data, During the 40 years of reform and opening up, Analysis of coal industry in the western region from 1979–2018. Found in recent years, impact of imported coal, environmental protection, energy conservation and consumption reduction, the northwest coal industry has turned into a period of deep adjustment of production capacity structure. This article will combine the new normal of coal industry, revolve around the northwest coal industry economic transformation and upgrade, from the northwest coal industry economic development pressure effective transformation power, explore to adapt to the northwest coal industry development fast and good new development ideas.

Keywords: Big data · Coal industry economy · Transformation and upgrading

1 Introduction

Coal mining industry is an earlier form of mining [1]. Many old industrial areas in Europe and America have taken the coal mining industry as a priority industry in the early stage of development [2–5]. As far as China is concerned, coal occupies 2/3 of the primary energy production and consumption [6–8]. China's reserves and utilization of resources show that coal will remain the dominant primary energy for a long time [9]. The following will be combined with the northwest of the significance of economic transformation and upgrading of coal industry and constraints to proceed, on this basis, put forward the corresponding countermeasures and suggestions [10–15].

2 Literature Review

2.1 Significance of Transformation and Upgrading of Coal Industry in Northwest China

The economic development in Northwest China is relatively backward. GDP accounted for 6.1% of the country, investment in fixed assets accounted for 7.3% of the whole society, local public revenue accounted for 5.7%, total retail sales of consumer goods accounted for 4.4%, import and export volume accounted for 1.4%, and industrial revenue accounted for 3.9%. Northwest China is dominated by resource industries and

Z. Xu et al. (Eds.): CSIA 2019, AISC 928, pp. 1360–1365, 2020.
https://doi.org/10.1007/978-3-030-15235-2_187

heavy chemical industries, including oil, natural gas, coal and other mining industries, as well as chemical, metallurgical, electric power, food, machinery and other industries. The economic slowdown in the country has reduced energy demand in the northwest and overcapacity in some sectors. Accelerating the adjustment of industrial structure and eliminating backward production capacity, the growth rate of traditional heavy and chemical industry in Northwest China has slowed down significantly.

Affected by comprehensive factors such as excessive structural capacity, declining consumption of major energy-consuming industries, outstanding release of coal capacity and stocks ahead of schedule, impact of imported coal, environmental protection, energy saving and consumption reduction, after years of rapid development, China's coal industry has ended the "golden decade" and entered the period of deep adjustment of capacity structure. Since the first quarter of 2013, many coal enterprises in Northwest China have experienced a slow market demand, a sharp drop in sales, a drop in coal prices, and a sustained decline in efficiency to the prosperity of the northwest coal market in 2017, resulting in increased operational difficulties for enterprises. It is urgent to explore the transformation and upgrading of the northwest coal industry.

3 Analysis Factors Restricting Economic Transformation and Development of Coal Industry in Northwest China

3.1 Analysis of the Industrial Mode Restricting the Economic Transformation and Development of the Coal Industry in Northwest China

The scale of coal enterprises is small, the product structure is single, the coal industry chain is short, and the utilization efficiency of resources is low. We know that the larger scale of coal enterprises, the diversified product structure and the longer coal industry chain are the important backing for the development of circular economy in the northwest coal industry. It can make the enterprises in the industry promote each other, optimize each other, make full use of resources, eliminate environmental damage, and coordinate nature, society and economy. The sustained development of the economy; on the contrary, the enterprises in the industry compete viciously with each other, resulting in waste of resources and environmental damage.

However, the Northwest Coal Enterprises have long taken the extensive and extended road of operation and development. The coal enterprises are small in scale, the product structure is single, and the coal industry chain is short. On the one hand, in the process of socialist market economy development and reform and opening up, the northwest coal enterprises are facing a huge test, on the one hand, the benefits and profits of enterprises, on the other hand, environmental pollution, energy conservation and emission reduction, but in these two aspects, some business managers will not hesitate to choose the former, because they are short-sighted, rat. We only see the driving force of immediate interests, but not for the next generation and the next generation. There is only one earth, to protect the environment, to let future generations have clean water to drink, and fresh air to enjoy. We should actively carry out the construction of new energy and maintain the sustainable development of the coal industry in the northwest. Long-term single development of coal production, low level of comprehensive utilization of resources, single product structure, poor economic benefits, serious destruction and waste of resources.

3.2 Analysis of the Driving Mechanism Restricting the Economic Transformation and Development of the Coal Industry in Northwest China

As the northwest coal enterprise's circular economy needs to carry on from the market and the government two stratification planes, on the one hand the coal enterprise's circular economy function in the market cannot be neglected, because the northwest region traditional industry pattern development, causes some systems to be difficult to change suddenly, needs from each stratification plane to carry on the control and the treaty Under the stimulation of great interests, we should actively explore new energy resources and new industrial development, and not exist in a single economic development model, so that one day we will lose the source of competitive power. On the other hand, in the process of market allocation, the local government in Northwest China also plays a very important leading role. Although the separation of government and enterprise is conducive to the development of enterprises themselves, the mediation role of the government is indispensable. Although the market system can automatically restrain coal enterprises from polluting the environment, there is no government. With the control and adjustment of the government, the development of the coal industry will go into a dead end and there is no way out. If excessive mining, will cause geological changes, environmental changes, all these consequences will appear in a period of time or in the next generation, for the sake of the entire human survival environment, the transformation of coal enterprise economic development mode is imperative.

4 Transformation and Upgrading of Coal Industry in Northwest China and Sustainable Development

4.1 Co-ordinate the Development Plan of Coal Resources, and Strengthen the Regulation of the Coal Industry

At present, the state on the development of coal industry, from the macro view of the coal industry as an industry with excess capacity, in the construction scale and output has increased the intensity of regulation and control. Under such favorable conditions, we must increase the planning and control of the coal industry in the northwest. The first is to strengthen the planning and guidance of coal mining. Strengthen the exploration of coal resources, with a good overall plan for the development of coal industry in Northwest reserve energy; improve the safety of existing production mines, strictly according to the approved capacity to organize production, do a good job in the old mining area (mine) production continuity, strive to stabilize coal production in a long period of time; Running a coal mine must be in line with the reserves of mineral resources and the construction plan of a large coal mine base in the province. It is strictly forbidden to declare new coal mine projects that do not meet the requirements of the state. Two, we should continue to eliminate small coal mines which do not meet safety standards, do not conform to environmental protection requirements and waste resources. At the same time, we should change the incentive mechanism of talents, from providing relatively favorable living conditions to providing development opportunities on the premise of equal competition, and adopt various forms to introduce outstanding talents to work in the coal industry.

4.2 Formulate Incentive Policies to Guide Market Behavior Towards the Goal of Circular Economy

Resources and environment have the nature of public goods. The technically feasible "cycle" will not necessarily become "economic" behavior in practice. To develop circular economy, the government's macro-control means must be considered. The role of the government is mainly manifested in two aspects: regulation and motivation. On the one hand, the government can restrict and regulate the behavior of economic participants through institutional arrangements. This system includes both formal systems, such as formal regulations and policies, and informal systems, such as industry norms, ethical standards, etc. On the other hand, the government can guide by formulating incentive policies. Market behavior is developing towards the goal of circular economy. Norms make the interests of economic subjects clear and their behaviors rules can be followed, while i.

4.3 Improve the Utilization Ratio of Resources and Support the Development of Coal Continuous Industries

In the long run, great efforts should be made to foster the development of non-coal industry and protect the development of coal resources, so as to make full and rational use of precious coal resources, and lay a solid foundation for the long-term development of Northwest coal industry in the future. One is to improve the utilization rate of resources, especially to study the matching mining technology of thin and thick coal seams, increase the matching mining intensity, improve the recovery rate of resources, make an article on saving and reducing costs, so as to achieve stable and efficient production. Two, we should intensify structural readjustment and speed up the development of coal alternative industries. Adhere to the principle of giving priority to coal and co-development of coal and non-coal, highlight the development of coal power, coal chemical industry, coal building materials and other advanced industries in deep processing of coal, steadily implement coal liquefaction and gasification projects, speed up the construction of demonstration projects such as underground gasification of low-grade and difficult-to-mine coal, and promote new energy and chemical industries based on coal Development.

5 Conclusion

Along with the release of infrastructure construction demand in Central Asia, South Asia and Southeast Asia and the increase of investment in the government of this area, some parts of the countries along the belt and road are rich in resources, and have the necessary raw materials for developing iron and steel, energy, manufacturing and other industries, thus becoming a new growth point of global capacity cooperation and driving our state-owned enterprises. Industry "go out". The economic transformation and upgrading of Northwest coal industry also need to adjust the development strategy in foreign cooperation, and the coal enterprises need to "go out" as an important direction of strategic transformation. It is necessary to provide relevant information, policies, assistance and other support for the northwest coal enterprises to go out, formulate incentive measures and implement the mechanism of "replacing compensation with awards". The research institutions, financial institutions, industry associations and so on will be brought together to form an industrial alliance and realize the strategy of "going out integration".

Acknowledgements. Supported by a project grant from Longdong University doctoral research (Grand No. XYBE1605). Qingyang youth social science research project (No. QYB201712C1).

References

1. Xinglei (2018) Research on the conversion of new and old kinetic energy in coal enterprises. Coal Econ Res (08):6–12
2. Li A, Zhu D, Xue Z (2014) Study on service model of collaborative manufacturing industry cluster innovation platform. In: Proceedings of the tenth annual conference on science and technology policy and management in China, Jilin, Changchun
3. Li X, Qu T, He JM, Hou BJ (2016) Seek excellence on the hospital quality management competition. In: Basic & clinical pharmacology & toxicology, December, vol 119, no S4, HHME16-H24
4. Wahlster W (2012) Industry 4: From the internet of things to smart factories, 3rd European Summit on Future Internet
5. Li X, Qiu W, Zhang P (2017) Discussion on service innovation of cultural and creative park: cultural value perspective. Macroecon Manag (S1):34–36
6. Zhou X, Guo S, Zhang C, Guo P (2017) Research on the relationship between technological innovation ability and efficiency of China's coal industry. Econ Issues (12):92–99
7. Wang X, Li Y (2018) Analysis of the development path of coal industry in shandong province under the background of new and old kinetic energy conversion. Coal Econ Res (08):13–17
8. Sun Y (2018) China coal industry prosperity measurement and its operational characteristics analysis. Stat Decis-Making 34(17):116–120
9. High Spring Rain, Soviet Union and Germany (2018) The impact of coal production and development layout westward on the environment of Shanxi-inner mongolia new area and suggestions. Shandong Coal Sci Technol (08):204–205+208
10. Ma G, Li N (2018) Research on optimization of profit model of coal listed companies under the background of supply-side reform. China Coal 44(08):23–28

11. Li P (2018) Current situation and sustainable development of coal industry in China. Decis Making Explor (08):16–17
12. Sun Z, Jiang Y (2018) How can coal enterprises better participate in the precise poverty alleviation - take inner mongolia autonomous region as an example. Inner Mongolia Coal Econ (15):16+54
13. Li Z, Zhang Y, Chen H (2018) Research on the development of coal industry in Hebei Province under the background of "de-productivity". China Coal 44(02):26–28
14. Jiao R, Zhao G, Zhang B (2018) Strategies for sustainable development of China's coal industry - based on system basis model. Econ Issues (03):79–84
15. Xu J (2018) Research on green development path of coal resource-based cities. Anhui University

Research and Application of Substation Safety Control Technology Based on Internet of Things Technology

Tianzheng Wang[1(✉)], Zhumao Lu[1], Shaohui Feng[2], Hua Yu[1], and Yongxin Liu[1]

[1] State Grid Shanxi Electric Power Research Institute, Taiyuan 030001, Shanxi, People's Republic of China
Wtz2000@163.com

[2] State Grid Taiyuan Power Supply Company, Taiyuan 030012, Shanxi, People's Republic of China

Abstract. The Internet of Things (IOT) technology is a new type of technology. It is applied to the safety management and control of substations. And it is perfected according to the relevant conditions of substations to form a safe management and control technology suitable for substations. The application of this technology can not only monitor the staff of substation maintenance operation on-line, but also carry out safety positioning. At the same time, the substation safety management and control technology based on IOT is mainly operated on the computer, and has three-dimensional display technology of GIS. It is a modern technology of safety inspection and management technology, and can realize the role of real-time inspection. In addition, during the operation, the safety management technology based on IOT can be used to understand the work situation of the on-site maintenance staff and standardize their maintenance work. Moreover, under the 3D technology, the scene scene ARCGIS is further realized, and its visual centralized control is carried out.

Keywords: Internet of Things technology · Substation · Safety control technology

With the rapid development of living standards and economy in China, people pay more and more attention to power plants and power grids, and the construction of basic equipment is also in constant improvement and transformation. In the process of its safe operation, there is a higher requirement. Therefore, power plants, power companies and other companies attach importance to the power lines, electrical equipment and other related settings [1–4]. The inspection and maintenance of electronic facilities are highly valued and a lot of manpower and material resources are invested. However, the past safety control technology has some shortcomings, such as low efficiency of patrol inspection, inconvenient management and so on, and the form of manual record has great limitations. On the other hand, the on-site safety management and control technology based on IOT in substations can make up for the shortcomings of the previous management methods, which integrates the advanced technologies such as network technology, communication technology and computer technology [5–7]. It has

Z. Xu et al. (Eds.): CSIA 2019, AISC 928, pp. 1366–1370, 2020.
https://doi.org/10.1007/978-3-030-15235-2_188

the characteristics of fast running speed and high precision, and it is also possible to understand the on-site maintenance and inspection circuit online, making high-level-on-site-safety control more efficient, more convenient, and improving safety [8–10].

1 Brief Introduction of the Internet of Things Technology

Electric power resources are still important resources for our society, life and work, and substation is an important unit for its normal operation in the power system. The equipment of substation is generally high voltage live, which brings certain risks to the work of maintenance staff. It is necessary to pay special attention to the safety control of maintenance staff and provide security guarantee for maintenance staff. Therefore, it is one of the necessary work for maintenance personnel to inspect and repair the equipment. Under the condition of Internet of Things technology, there are five advantages in the safety management and control of the maintenance staff of substations. (1) Online recording by the handled patrol. Tour the situation and get real-time information about the device. After the inspection, the patrol personnel can also learn about the work of the patrol personnel through the recording of the patrol, which is more efficient and faster. (2) After recording the situation of the inspection equipment online, you can use the Internet of Things technology to statistically analyze the inspection situation, and accurately understand the time and path of the inspection. At the same time, the data can be sent to the day after tomorrow after reading the data. (3) Real-time connection of maintenance personnel's access time and maintenance. (4) Special barriers are provided in sensitive and dangerous areas. When the maintenance personnel enters the area, they can remind the maintenance personnel to enhance their safety awareness. In the event of an illegal cross-border situation, an alert is sent and sent to the background. (5) Through the camera and other equipment to achieve remote monitoring and maintenance.

2 Composition of the System Structure

The safety management and control technology based on the Internet of Things also uses many kinds of technologies at the same time, and combines them with each other to form a new system suitable for substation application. Some of the technologies are used, such as infinite transmission technology, electronic safety fence technology of leaky cable, scanning and positioning technology, etc., and are supported by 3D technology and ARCGIS technology. We have built a real scene defense platform for substation. The location of RFID identification card and electronic security fence is determined according to the situation of the field equipment and the past experience, which can realize the patrol work of the field workers and correct the irregular behavior in real time. The structure of the whole system is simplified as follows: RFID tags (high-definition surveillance cameras) on the required patrol equipment and its equipment - Handheld patrol recognition - 3D GIS management and control platform.

2.1 Equipment Patrol System

In the past, the form of the paper file was used to record the inspection situation, but the recording method is prone to missed inspection and misdetection, and the restriction is large, and it is difficult to record the maintenance condition normally due to the weather and climate. The use of RFID radio frequency identification technology can save the manual paper quality record, save time and reduce the impact of weather and climate. At the same time, the patrol route can be set in advance, and when there is a missed inspection, a reminder will be issued. If the maintenance personnel carry out the inspection route for the safety specification, a reminder will be issued to enhance the standardization and safety of the maintenance. The maintenance and recording of the inspection information by the handheld patrol device is transmitted to the background computer for saving, saving time and space.

2.2 Maintenance Area Safety Positioning System

In the equipment that needs to be inspected and overhauled, the high-risk position is specially divided by the isolation device, and the maintenance personnel need to wear the safety positioning identifier when carrying out the inspection work. The maintenance personnel should work at the designated position. If they go to the isolation area at will, the alarm will be issued to prompt the maintenance personnel to return to the safe working area, and the system can record the time and duration of the maintenance personnel, and upload and back up the information to the background, which is convenient for the management and supervision of the maintenance personnel.

3 Introduction of 3D GIS System Function

Using database technology and monitoring technology to transform the real scene into online virtual scene, and to create three-dimensional virtual scene. It is not only conducive to the real equipment for current affairs query, and management, but also can accurately locate the location of maintenance personnel, and will look at the inspection route of maintenance personnel, inspection inspection inspection inspection inspection inspection inspection inspection time. With virtual scene simulation operation and adjustment, it can also be synchronized with the actual scene. For example, in a virtual three-dimensional scene to manipulate graphical wounds to display information, or through navigation operations, bird's eye view of the work of the scene, or roaming patrol. It can also analyze the installation, spacing, height and operation of the equipment, and comprehensively understand the equipment, working range and work content through observation. When the 3D GIS system locates the maintenance personnel, it also determines the work area of the maintenance personnel to prevent the maintenance personnel from entering the sensitive and dangerous areas, thereby enhancing the safety of the maintenance personnel and facilitating the safety of the maintenance personnel. Management, and when the accident is discovered, the location can be determined in time, and the matter can be understood, so that scientific and reasonable solutions can be taken in time.

4 Characteristics of the System

The substation safety management and control technology studied in this paper is based on the Internet of Things technology, which transforms the industry into the need of automation development process. The technology integrates the substation safety management, monitoring, early warning, protection and other aspects, greatly saving production time and manpower, and improving the efficiency and safety of production. Through the technology of computer and camera, real working scene is transformed into virtual scene, and automatic production management is carried out. It conforms to the trend of the times, enters the field of automatic production, reduces production cost, achieves the effect of both on-site control and remote control, and realizes the operation of maintenance personnel. The whole process of on-site supervision can stop the irregular behavior and operation of the maintenance personnel in time and carry out the maintenance work efficiently.

5 Conclusion

In modern society, all walks of life keep up with the pace of the times, introducing advanced plans, improving work efficiency and quality, and maintaining safety management. Automation is the trend of the industry, which has the advantages of saving manpower, material and financial resources. Substation automation and its management have also been applied and promoted, but the work needs to maintain a certain degree of security. On this basis, the substation according to its actual situation will be the Internet of Things technology into the safety management, the formation of a unique substation safety management and control technology, improve work efficiency, but also improve the safety of operation. However, the safety of on-site operation in substation is still a key link in the work, so the application of management and control technology at the same time, we need to focus on the application of on-site operation. The substation safety management and control technology based on the Internet of Things technology has been tried in reality, and found that its application effect is remarkable in practice, and achieved the desired results.

References

1. Yang Y, Lu Y (2018) Safety and process control of installation and construction of electrical primary equipment in substation. Sci Technol Wind (25):101
2. Li Z, Wang X, Zhang L, Xue W (2018) Research on intelligent monitoring system of substation operation safety based on area identification. Electric Power Inf Commun Technol 16(07):28–33
3. Wang S (2018) Analysis on integrated management mode of substation operation and maintenance. Commun World (05):143–144
4. Qi H, Wang Y, Zhou Z, Qian J, Zheng Z (2018) Design of high precision location safety operation control platform in substation. China Hi-tech Zone (08):123

5. Zhang X, Ma Q (2017) The "May 4th 3rd" management and control mode of substation in power supply enterprises under the guidance of integratio. Enterprise Manag (S2):232–233
6. Yu L (2017) Safety risk management and control strategy for relay protection maintenance operation of intelligent substation. Res Urban Constr Theory (Electron Version) (34):71
7. Zhang G (2017) Research and application of intelligent substation safety inspection technology. North China Electric Power University (Beijing)
8. Lin F, Xu X, An Y, Gu H, Yang W (2015) Visual identification of human body inspection in substation safety monitoring. Electrical Technol (10):23–25
9. Xiao B, He Q, Mao Y (2015) Practice of substation operation safety management and control system. Qinghai Electric Power 34(01):71–72
10. Wang Q, Lu P (2018) Research on application of artificial intelligence in computer network technology. Int J Pattern Recogn Artif Intell (4)

Research on Multi-source Image Fusion Method Based on FCM and Wavelet Transform

Lianhuan Li(✉)

International Education School of Nanyang Medical College, Nanyang, Henan, China
computer20131222@163.com

Abstract. Based on the information complementarity relationship of heterogeneous images, this paper proposes a wavelet transform fusion method based on target feature regions. Firstly, the method based on fuzzy C-means clustering is used to extract the target feature region of the infrared image, which is used for local information fusion of the target region of the heterogeneous image to achieve the effect of adding infrared target information in the visible image. Secondly, the original visible image is replaced by the image merged in the first step, and the fusion with the infrared image is realized by wavelet transform to obtain the final fused image. The experimental results of the proposed algorithm and other fusion algorithms are analyzed and compared using subjective and objective evaluation criteria.

Keywords: Multi-source image fusion · Fuzzy C-means clustering · Wavelet transform

1 Introduction

Infrared image is the thermal radiation information of the acquired scene, so its characteristics are generally gray level is small, the image is easy to be directly understood by people, but the thermal target in the scene contained in the information is generally very obvious; the visible image is due to its The imaging mechanism is different from the infrared image [1–3]. It is not very sensitive to the thermal target in the scene, but it can record the visible light information in the scene very well, because its image has rich gray level and is more easily understood by people [4–6]. The main purpose of merging the visible light image and the infrared image is to reflect the hot target information in the infrared scene while keeping the rich information in the visible light image as much as possible, so that people can directly view all the information of the image.

Z. Xu et al. (Eds.): CSIA 2019, AISC 928, pp. 1371–1376, 2020.
https://doi.org/10.1007/978-3-030-15235-2_189

2 Local Fusion of Feature Regions Based on FCM

FCM was proposed by Ruspini and Bezdek in 1981. It is a very effective fuzzy clustering algorithm, using the membership degree of each sample belonging to a certain cluster, even for variables that are difficult to classify, FCM can get more satisfactory clustering effect [7].

When the FCM is used to extract the target region in the infrared image, the feature vector is first established for each pixel in the image, that is, the pixel point of the image is regarded as the sample point of the data set, and the feature of the pixel point is regarded as the feature of the sample point [8]. Using these feature vector FCM algorithms will establish a fuzzy membership partition that gives each pixel a fuzzy membership value for each class.

In the process of using the FCM method to perform the infrared target feature region, the selection of the number of cluster categories is very important, which directly affects the accuracy of the target region extraction. Generally, the number of clusters needs to be manually input, and it is difficult to determine. For this problem, this paper starts from the characteristic analysis of infrared images, and uses the method based on image gray histogram information to automatically determine the number of clusters. The distribution of gray information in infrared images is concentrated, and there are generally multiple peaks. These peaks represent the aggregation of image gray information to some extent. Therefore, the clustering categories can be obtained directly by calculating these peaks. The number is the number of these peaks plus one.

The FCM method is simply to segment the image. Although the target area in the infrared image can be well segmented, it is not possible for the computer to directly determine which area is the target feature area of the infrared image. Aiming at this problem, this paper proposes a method for automatically determining the target region based on the high gray value of the target region in the infrared image. That is, the mean value of each region of the image after clustering is determined, and the region with the largest mean value of all the pixels in each region is taken as the target region, which is expressed by the formula:

$$c = \max\left\{ M_i = \frac{\sum_{j=1}^{n} P_j}{n} \right\}, i = 1, 2, \cdots, c \tag{1}$$

Where n is the number of pixels in each region and p is the gray value of each pixel.

3 Global Fusion Based on Wavelet Transform

Wavelet theory is a new signal processing tool developed in the late 1980s [9]. Because of its very good time-frequency localization characteristics, scale variation characteristics and directional characteristics, it has been widely used in image processing, pattern recognition, computer vision, fractal analysis and other research fields [10].

The image fusion method based on wavelet transform can be said to be based on the direct expansion of the traditional multi-resolution pyramid image fusion method, and is also a multi-resolution and multi-scale decomposition of images. The basic steps of image fusion based on wavelet decomposition are as follows:

(1) Each of a source image after registration decomposition using wavelet transform, the wavelet pyramid image is formed;
(2) The respective decomposition layers are separately processed, and the wavelet coefficients of each decomposition layer can be merged by different fusion operators according to the characteristics of different frequency components to form a merged wavelet decomposition pyramid image;
(3) Perform wavelet inverse transform on the fused wavelet pyramid image, and the reconstructed image obtained is a fused image.

4 Algorithm Implementation Process and Steps

In summary, the specific steps of the wavelet transform fusion method based on the target feature proposed in this paper are as follows:

(1) Using the target extraction algorithm based on the FCM method for the infrared image that has been registered, the target region is extracted. In the extraction, according to the peak information of the gray histogram of the infrared image, the number of categories that need to be clustered is automatically determined, and then the target area to be extracted is determined based on the principle of the mean value of each divided area, and the area is output.
(2) Based on the target region extracted in the first step, the first partial fusion of the visible light image and the corresponding region of the infrared light image is performed. In this fusion process, only the previously extracted target region is used, and other regions are directly using information from visible images. In the local fusion of the target region, a pixel-weighted fusion criterion is employed. The image merged in the first step enhances the target information in the infrared image on the basis of most of the information including the visible light image.
(3) On the basis of completing the first step of fusion, carry out the second step of fusion. The fusion of the step is to replace the original visible image with the new fused image obtained in the first step of fusion, and directly merge with the infrared source image. The fusion method at the place adopts fusion based on wavelet transform, and each image in the wavelet pyramid image the fusion of layers uses a wavelet coefficient to take a large fusion operator, and the number of decomposition layers is two. The final fused image can be obtained by this step fusion.

5 Experiment and Result Analysis

In this paper, an experiment of infrared image and visible image fusion is used to verify the effect of the above method. The methods used as comparative experiments are a weighted fusion method, an average fusion method, a pixel-large fusion method, and a pixel-based fusion method. The evaluation of the experimental results uses a combination of subjective and objective evaluation criteria. The experimental results and evaluation are as follows:

Figure 1 shows the experimental results, in which (a) is the fusion result of the fusion method of the infrared and visible images of the laboratory soldering iron, and (b) is the fusion result of the fusion method based on the pixel is small, (c) is The graph is the fusion result based on the weighted fusion method, (d) is the fusion result based on the average fusion method, (e) is the result of the first fusion of the method, and (f) is the final fusion result of the project method.

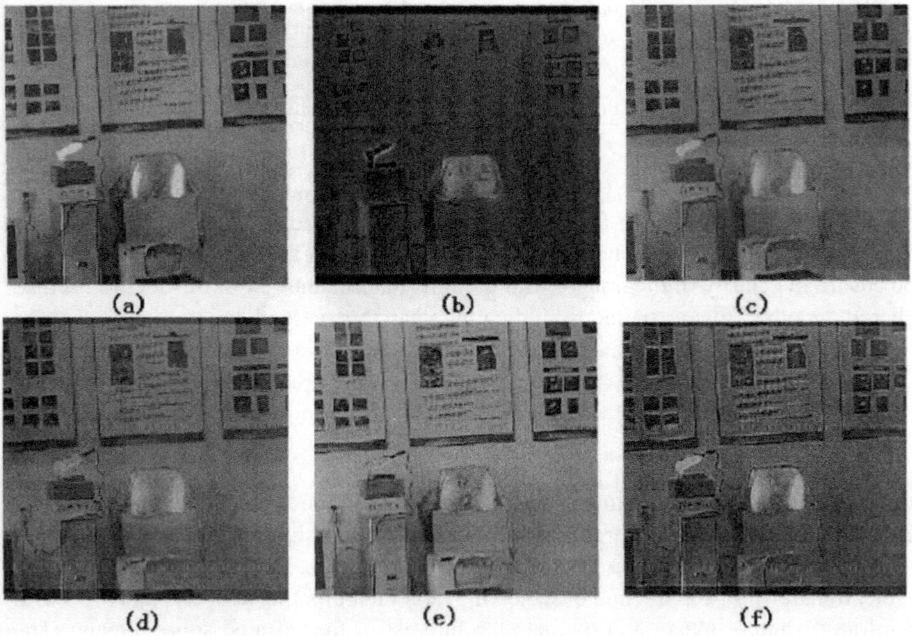

Fig. 1. Fusion experiment results

The subjective scores of the experiments based on subjective evaluation scales are as Table 1:

Table 1. Experimental subjective evaluation scale score sheet.

Evaluation scale	1(a)	1(b)	1(c)	1(d)	1(e)	1(f)
Quality scale	4	1	3	3	3	4
Obstruction scale	5	2	4	4	4	5

For the objective evaluation of the experimental results, the standard deviation, the average gradient and the information entropy of the image were selected as the evaluation criteria. The parameters of each image are calculated as follows:

Table 2. Convergence experiment results objective evaluation parameter comparison table

Image	Standard deviation	Average gradient	Information entropy
Visible light image	24.6717	5.9551	6.4175
Infrared source image	18.8310	1.9423	5.3317
Large pixel fusion	24.8969	5.4148	6.3742
Small pixel fusion	10.6574	2.1610	5.0049
Weighted fusion	18.0865	4.0122	5.9540
Average fusion	14.3984	3.1812	5.6624
First step fusion	24.8377	5.9556	6.1641
Final fusion	20.0609	6.2031	6.4407

It can be seen from the Table 2 that the average gradient of the image fusion method is higher than other fusion methods, which indicates that the method can preserve and enhance the detail and texture information in the image, and at the same time ensure the clarity of the image. And the information entropy of this method is also higher than other fusion methods, indicating that the merged image contains more information. This shows the fusion effect of the method.

6 Conclusion

The purpose of multi-source image fusion is to include the fused image with complementary information of the source image. In order to better highlight the enhancement of this kind of complementary information in the fused image, this paper proposes a new wavelet transform fusion method based on the target feature, first analyzes and processes the infrared source image, and extracts the interest in the infrared source image. The target area, and based on the target area, performs the first partial fusion on the registered visible light image to obtain a new fused image to enhance the information of the infrared target in the fused image. Then, the fused image is used as a new image source, and the infrared source image is subjected to quadratic global fusion based on wavelet transform, which greatly enhances the information of the feature target in the infrared image. Finally, through contrast experiments, the method and other methods are compared and analyzed to verify the effect of the method.

References

1. Zheng Y, Tian X (2006) Development of medical image registration. Int J Biomed Eng 29 (2):88–92
2. Wang C, Jiang M (2006) Review of image registration methods for medical images. CT Theory Appl 15(2):74–80

3. Zou B, Lin J (2008) Contour extraction research of image. Comput Eng Appl 44(25):161–165
4. Lowe D (2004) Distinctive image features from scale-invariant key points. Int J Comput Vis 2(60):91–110
5. Qu G, Zhang D, Yan P (2002) Information measure for performance of image fusion. Electron Lett 38(7):313–315
6. Mounce SR (2003) Sensor-fusion of hydraulic data for burst detection and location in treated distribution system. Inf Fusion 3:217–229
7. Dou W, Chen Y, Li X, Sui DZ (2007) A general framework for component substitution image fusion: an implementation using the fast image fusion method. Comput Geosci 33 (2):219–228
8. Wang ZJ, Djemel Z, Armenakis C et al (2005) A comparative analysis of image fusion methods. IEEE Trans Geosci Remote Sens 43(6):1391–1402
9. Barnea DI, Silverman HF (1972) A class of algorithms for fast digital registration. Trans Comput 100:179–186
10. Belongie S, Malik J, Puzicha J (2002) Shape matching and object recognition using shape contexts. Trans Pattern Anal Mach Intell 24(4):509–522

The Analysis and Research of Lifting Scheme Based on Wavelet Transform

Li Ding[1(✉)] and Weiqing Chen[2]

[1] Xi'an Medical University, Xi'an 710021, China
370486946@qq.com
[2] Xi'an Yuetai Science and Technology Co., Ltd., Xi'an 710075, China

Abstract. Wavelet transform has the good characteristic of time domain and frequency domain, have been widely used in areas such as signal processing. With the development of science and technology there is a new wavelet transform method has appeared, and used as the core transforming technology in JPEG2000, a newest image compression standard. Based on the principle of lifting wavelet algorithm, this paper analyzes its characteristics. Analysis of the JPEG2000 algorithm used in Le Gall 5/3 and Daubechies 9/7 two wavelet transform.

Keywords: JPEG2000 · Wavelet transform · Lifting scheme · Structure

1 Introduction

Among the modern algorithms for two-dimensional discrete wavelet, Mallat algorithm is the most commonly used one, which is a discrete wavelet transform algorithm based on convolution. The Mallat algorithm uses a low-pass filter and a high-pass filter to perform uninterrupted alternating in both horizontal and vertical directions, thereby implementing wavelet transform. However, the disadvantages of this algorithm lie in its large computation amount, high complexity, high requirements for storage space and relatively difficult hardware implementation. In this paper, the lifting wavelet algorithm is adopted to effectively solve the above problems [1]. Lifting algorithm is a kind of wavelet construction method based on spatial domain, and it is a faster and more effective wavelet implementation method. It not only has simple structure, low computational cost, in situ operation, but also saves storage space. When carrying out inverse transformation, it can be directly reversed to achieve, which is called the second generation of wavelet transform.

2 Principle of Lifting Wavelet Transform

Steps

Wavelet lifting algorithm adopts modular method to solve the problem. The existing wavelet filter is divided into several construction modules to complete the wavelet transformation step by step, and the process is divided into three steps: splitting, prediction and update [2]. The specific implementation steps are as follows:

Z. Xu et al. (Eds.): CSIA 2019, AISC 928, pp. 1377–1382, 2020.
https://doi.org/10.1007/978-3-030-15235-2_190

(1) **Split**

Split is to divide the original signal $s_j = \{s_{j,k}\}$ into two subsets and, the two subsets do not intersect each other, and their lengths are half of the atomic set. Generally, an array is divided into even sequence e_{j-1} and odd sequence o_{j-1} [3], as shown in Eq. (1):

$$Split(s_j) = (e_{j-1}, o_{j-1}) \tag{1}$$

There into, $e_{j-1} = \{e_{j-1,k} = s_{j,2k}\}$, $o_{j-1} = \{o_{j-1,k} = s_{j,2k+1}\}$.

(2) **Predict**

Predict refers to the application of the correlation between odd-even sequences. If you need to predict an odd sequence (o_{j-1}), you need to do it with another even sequence (e_{j-1}). The difference between the actual and predicted values reflects the degree of similarity between the two. In the calculation process, the detail coefficient or wavelet coefficient of the high frequency part of s_j. is generally used to express the similarity. In general, Data correlation directly affect the value of the wavelet coefficients of both the stronger the correlation, the smaller the replication, whereas correlation low-rising value is more and more small. If the prediction is reasonable, d_{j-1} will have more relevant information, which is conducive to the processing of subsequent problems. The prediction process is shown in (2) [4]

$$d_{j-1} = \overline{o}_{j-1} - P(e_{j-1}) \tag{2}$$

The prediction operator is called P. It can be represented by the prediction function P_k, Function P_k can be the corresponding data in function e_{j-1}, as shown in Eq. (3):

$$P_k(e_{j-1,k}) = e_{j-1,k} = s_{j,2k} \tag{3}$$

Otherwise, the average value of adjacent data of corresponding data in e_{j-1}, as shown in formula (4):

$$P_k(e_{j-1}) = (e_{j-1,k} + e_{j-1,k+1})/2 = (s_{j,2k} + s_{j,2k+1})/2 \tag{4}$$

Perhaps some other more complicated function

(3) **Update**

Some of the overall characteristics (such as averages) of the subsets that are different from the original data are generated after the splitting step. In order to ensure the overall characteristics of the data, update process is adopted in the re-operation process. The update process is represented by U, This process is shown in the following Formula (5)

$$U_k(d_{j-1}) = d_{j-1,k}/2 \tag{5}$$

Where, The low frequency part of s_j is s_{j-1}; Different functions are applied to the update operator, so that the prediction function is shown in Formula (6):

Or as shown in Formula (7) :

$$U_k(d_{j-1}) = (d_{j-1,k-1} + d_{j-1k})/4 + 1/2 \tag{7}$$

Taking different functions of *P* and *U*, different wavelet transforms can be constructed.

Decomposition and Reconstruction

After lifting the wavelet, the original signal s_j is decomposed into two parts, namely, the low-frequency part s_{j-1} and the high-frequency part d_{j-1}. Then split, predict and update s_{j-1} again for the subset of low-frequency data. s_{j-1} is further decomposed into d_{j-2} and s_{j-2}. In this way, after n times of factorization, the wavelet of the data is decomposed into $\{s_{j-n}, d_{j-n}, d_{j-n+1}, \ldots, d_{j-1}\}$. The low frequency part of the signal is representation by s_{j-n}, and the high frequency series is part of the signal from low frequency to high frequency, namely $\{d_{j-n}, d_{j-n+1}, \ldots, d_{j-1}\}$. Each decomposition corresponds to three steps of ascension – splitting, prediction and update [5], as shown in Formula (8):

$$\begin{cases} Split(s_j) = (e_{j-1}, o_{j-1}) \\ d_{j-1} = o_{j-1} - P(e_{j-1}) \\ s_{j-1} = e_{j-1} + U(d_{j-1}) \end{cases} \tag{8}$$

Wavelet lifting is a completely reversible process, and the steps of its inverse transformation are as follows:

$$\begin{cases} e_{j-1} = s_{j-1} - U(d_{j-1}) \\ o_{j-1} = d_{j-1} + P(e_{j-1}) \\ s_j = Merge(e_{j-1}, o_{j-1}) \end{cases} \tag{9}$$

The decomposition and reconstruction principle of the promotion method is shown in Fig. 1:

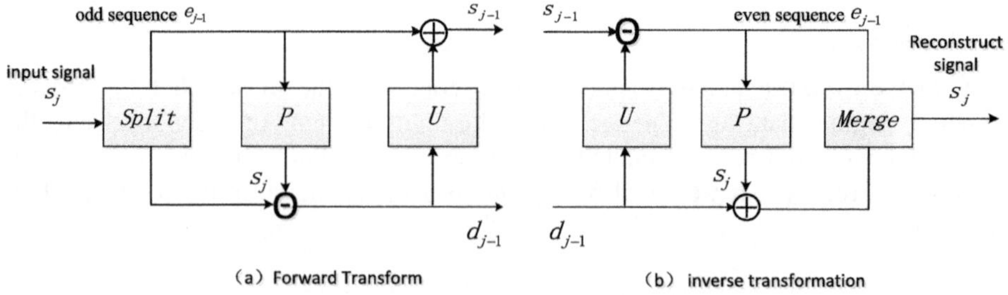

Fig. 1. Decomposition and refactoring of promotion methods

3 Wavelet Transform of JPEG2000

Wavelet Transform Le Gall 5/3

In JPEG2000 core coding, Le Gall 5/3 filter promotion algorithm is used for integer to integer transformation, which is reversible discrete wavelet transform [6]. The low-pass filter at the decomposition end has five coefficients, and the low-pass filter at the merge end has three coefficients, which are used for loss compression or lossy or lossless compression of picture. The implementation formula of the specific algorithm is shown in (10) and (11):

(1) Inverse Le Gall 5/3 forward wavelet transform:

$$\begin{aligned} Y[2n+1] &= X[2n+1] - \left\lfloor \frac{X[2n]+X[2n+2]}{2} \right\rfloor \\ Y[2n] &= X[2n] + \left\lfloor \frac{Y[2n-1]+y[2n+1]+2}{4} \right\rfloor \end{aligned} \tag{10}$$

(2) Invertible Le Gall 5/3 inverse wavelet transform:

$$\begin{aligned} X[2n] &= Y[2n] - \left\lfloor \frac{Y[2n-1]+Y[2n+1]+2}{4} \right\rfloor \\ X[2n+1] &= Y[2n+1] + \left\lfloor \frac{X[2n]+X[2n+2]}{2} \right\rfloor \end{aligned} \tag{11}$$

4 Wavelet Transform Daubechies 9/7

Daubechies 9/7 filter improvement algorithm for real to real number conversion that is irreversible Discrete Wavelet Transformation [7]. Among them, 9 coefficients are used at the decomposition end of the low-pass filter and 7 coefficients are used at the combination end of the high-pass filter, which is used in the case of lossy image compression [8]. The implementation formula of the specific algorithm is shown in (12) and (13):

(1) Irreversible Daubechies 9/7 forward wavelet transform need to execute six steps: two-step resize and four-step lifting
Resize:

$$\begin{aligned} Y[2n+1] &= X[2n+1] + \alpha \times (X[2n] + X[2n+2]) \\ Y[2n] &= X[2n] + \beta \times (Y[2n-1] + Y[2n+1]) \\ Y[2n+1] &= Y[2n+1] + \gamma \times (Y[2n] + Y[2n+2]) \\ Y[2n] &= Y[2n] + \delta \times (Y[2n-1] + Y[2n+1]) \end{aligned}$$

Lifting:

$$\begin{aligned} Y[2n+1] &= -K \times Y[2n+1] \\ Y[2n] &= \tfrac{1}{K} \times Y[2n] \end{aligned} \tag{12}$$

(2) Irreversible Daubechies 9/7 invert wavelet transform need to execute six steps: two-step resize and four-step lifting
Resize:

$$\begin{aligned} X[2n] &= K \times Y[2n] \\ X[2n+1] &= -\tfrac{1}{K} \times Y[2n+1] \end{aligned}$$

Lifting:

$$\begin{aligned} X[2n] &= X[2n] - \delta \times (X[2n-1] + X[2n+1]) \\ X[2n+1] &= X[2n+1] - \gamma \times (X[2n] + X[2n+2]) \\ X[2n] &= X[2n] - \beta \times (X[2n-1] + X[2n+1]) \\ X[2n+1] &= X[2n+1] - \alpha \times (X[2n] + X[2n+2]) \end{aligned} \tag{13}$$

The value of the parameter is $\alpha = 1.586134342$, $\beta = 0.052980118$, $\gamma = 0.882911075$, $\delta = 0.443506852$, $K = 1.230174105$.

5 The Experimental Results

In JPEG2000 standard, Mallat algorithm and wavelet lifting algorithm are used to transform two pixels respectively. Through experiments, it is found that the multiplication and addition times of the two algorithms are different. The wavelet lifting algorithm is less than mallat algorithm in terms of the number of operations, which is about 1/2–2/3. Experimental results prove the improved wavelet algorithm in this paper can reduce computational complexity and compress the operation time [9, 10].

6 Conclusion

The wavelet lifting algorithm not only have multi-resolution property of the first generation wavelet, but also does not depend on Fourier transform, The wavelet transform can be completed directly in the running process. With the advantages of simple algorithm, fast operation speed and small memory demand, wavelet transform of arbitrary image size can be realized, which has been widely used in JPEG2000.

References

1. Zhang Z, Ma S, Tan K (2010) Gauss noise image recovering method based on directional wavelet transform. J Jilin Univ (Sci Ed) 48(06):987–994
2. Hu H (2010) Based on integer wavelet transform image processing algorithm. J Hunan Univ Arts Sci (Sci Technol) (01):58–60
3. Liu B, Fu Z (2018) Multi-focus image fusion based on four-channel non-separable lifting wavelet. Syst Eng Electron 40(2)
4. Liu H, Wei Z (2009) Image denoising based on maxima child node dependence coefficients in wavelet domain. Comput Eng (13):214–215

5. He W (2013) Application of lifting wavelet transform in image edge detection. Comput Knowl Technol (25):5703–5704
6. Kang Y, Xu H, Wang Y (2007) Application and realization of the lifting wavelet algorithm in reversible transforms of JPEG2000. Ship Electron Eng (6):137–139
7. Sun Y (2005) Wavelet analysis and application, vol 3. China Machine Press, pp 36–37, 52–54
8. Wang C, Gao X (2018) Despeckling algorithm for ultrasound images based on variational filter in wavelet domain. J Southwest China Normal Univ (Nat Sci Ed) 43(7)
9. Luo Le, Chen Q, Dai H, Gu G, He W (2018) Adaptive compression sampling with compressive sensing and extended wavelet tree. Chin J Lumin 39(10)
10. Huang Y, Tian X (2018) Design and implementation of fuzzy image processing system based on wavelet transform. Modern Electron Tech 41(19)

A Survey of Personalized Recommendation Algorithm Selection Based on Meta-learning

Yi Ren(✉), Cuirong Chi, and Zhang Jintao

Shenyang Jianzhu University, Shenyang, Liaoning, China
1181134429@qq.com

Abstract. The purpose of algorithm selection is to automatically select the most suitable one for the current problem from among the many available optimization algorithms. For this problem, this paper describes the recommendation algorithm selection of meta-learning. Firstly, the related techniques based on meta-learning are analyzed. Then the algorithm selection framework and the extraction of meta-features are constructed. Finally, the problems of algorithm selection based on meta-learning ideas are proposed, and the future development direction is pointed out.

Keywords: Algorithm selection · Meta-learning · Meta-feature

1 Introduction

The diversification of recommended data leads to a single recommendation algorithm that is difficult to obtain optimal recommendation performance in all recommended prediction processes, based on the No-Free Lunch (NFL) theorem [1]: there is no specific application unrelated, universally applicable "general algorithms" can solve all optimization problems once and for all. The deeper meaning is that the most suitable recommendation algorithms on different data sets are not the same.

In this case, the establishment of a recommendation model based on meta-learning is particularly important. Meta-learning was first applied in the discipline of psychology, and John Biggs, one of the researchers in this field, described meta-learning as realizing and grasping his own learning [2]. Therefore, meta-learning is seen as an understanding and adaptation of the learning itself, not just the acquisition of subject knowledge. Afterwards, it is widely used in various fields such as computer science, artificial intelligence, operations research, statistics and so on. Some researchers have used meta-learning techniques to have some research in the area of personalized recommendation [3], which aggregated information in a dataset by defining meta-features, and supervised machine learning is used to learn the relationship between the meta-features and the performance of the recommendation algorithm. At last, measuring the optimal algorithm for the data set with standard metric. Wolpert [4] used predictive combination techniques to construct models that forecast the performance of basic classifiers, including the predictive classifier and the characteristics of the input data.

This paper mainly introduces the selection of personalized recommendation algorithms based on meta-learning. Section 2 focuses on the concepts related to

Z. Xu et al. (Eds.): CSIA 2019, AISC 928, pp. 1383–1388, 2020.
https://doi.org/10.1007/978-3-030-15235-2_191

meta-learning. Section 3 analyzes the meta-learning algorithm selection framework and related meta-feature extraction techniques. Section 4 describes several common algorithm performance metrics. Section 5 summarizes the full text.

2 Related Concept

In the past 20 years, machine learning has involved a number of optimization algorithms, including parameterization, pre-processing and post-processing, as well as a wide range of applications due to increased calculating ability. Meta-learning can be a great help for further understanding of machine learning itself, selecting better algorithm and appropriate parameterization.

2.1 Meta-learning Definition

There are many definitions of meta-learning. In simple terms, meta-learning is learning to learn. It is achieved by learning the relationship between data characteristics and the performance of the data algorithm. Meta-learning concept was first proposed by Rendell [5] to describe the characteristics of classification problems and verify the influence of features on algorithm behavior. In 2002, Vilalta and Drissi [6] proposed meta-learning to study learning systems how to improve efficiency through experience; the goal is to understand how learning itself becomes flexible based on the field or task being studied. In 2009, Brazdil et al. [7] showed that meta-learning is a principle method for studying the use of meta-knowledge to obtain effective models and solutions by adjusting machine learning and data mining processes. In 2010, Vanschoren [8] proposed meta-learning to monitor the auto-learning process itself in the context of the learning problems it encountered and to try to adjust its behavior to make better use of it. In 2014, Giraud-Carrier [9] pointed out that the main goal of meta-learning is to understand the interaction between the learning mechanism and the specific context in which the mechanism applies.

2.2 Meta-learning Goal

From a practical perspective, the purpose of meta-learning is twofold. On the one hand, in order to overcome some of the challenges faced by users using current data analysis tools and help users choose the appropriate predictive model (or combination of models) while considering the application domain. On the other hand, it is desirable to address the common problems in the practical use of data analysis tools, namely how to benefit from reusing predictive models rather than similar tasks. The successful application of models in real-world scenarios requires constant adaptation to new demands and relearn through the learning mechanism itself, rather than restarting new tasks.

3 Related Technology

Some key technologies to be studied in the selection of recommendation algorithms based on meta-learning are as follows: the construction of algorithm selection framework, the extraction of meta-features and the selection of algorithm performance indicators. Next, these aspects are elaborated.

3.1 Recommendation Algorithm Selection Framework Based on Meta-learning

Meta-learning refers to the application of machine learning (meta-algorithm) to find the mapping between the feature (meta-feature) of the problem and the relative performance measure of the algorithm, thus forming the learning process of meta-knowledge [7]. Through the existing research on algorithm selection and meta-learning, a unified selection framework for recommendation algorithm based on meta-learning can be proposed as shown in Fig. 1 [10]:

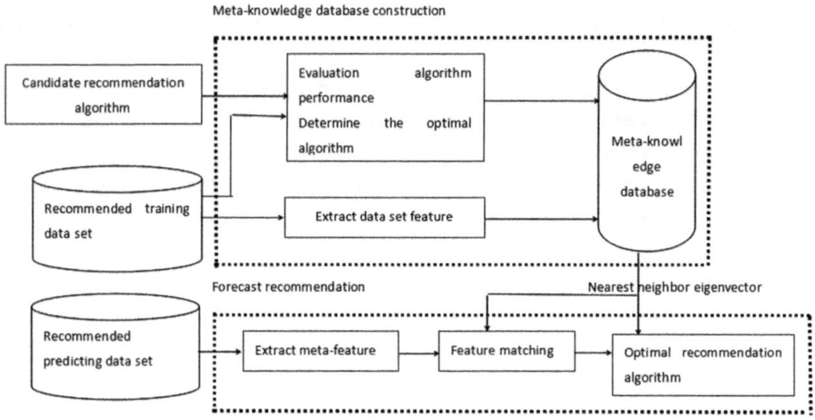

Fig. 1. Recommendation algorithm selection framework based on meta-learning

The meta-learning model is mainly composed of two parts: the meta-knowledge database and the prediction algorithm. First, extracting the metrics describing the characteristics of the data set in each recommendation data set, generating corresponding feature vectors, and evaluating the performance of all candidate recommendation prediction algorithms on each data set, then select the optimal prediction algorithm, finally, setting the data sets. The feature vector is in one-to-one correspondence with the optimal recommendation prediction algorithm, and a meta-knowledge database of “data set feature-optimal recommendation prediction algorithm” is established. When the predicted data set to be predicted arrives, the feature vectors of the data set are extracted; then, the collected data set feature is extracted from the meta-knowledge database for feature matching, and the first k algorithms are selected for voting. The optimal recommendation prediction algorithm of the dataset will be selected.

3.2 Extraction of Meta-features

It can be seen from Fig. 1 that the key to the recommendation algorithm selection based on meta-learning is to extract meta-features. The extracted meta-features must be able to provide a reasonable explanation for the difference in algorithm performance. Representative meta-features can be divided into three categories: statistics and information theory; landmarking and models.

Meta-feature Based on Statistics and Information Theory. The meta-characteristics based on statistics and information theory mainly include the simple features of the data set (data set size, number of attributes, etc.); the statistical characteristics of the data set (geometric average, harmonic mean, variance, offset, etc.) mainly reflect the central trend of the data. And the degree of dispersion of attribute points; the information characteristics of the data set (information entropy of the attribute variable, noise rate, etc.) reflect the degree of association between different attributes. As shown in Table 1.

Table 1. Meta-feature based on statistics and information theory

Simple feature	Statistics feature	Information feature
Sample size	Median	Class entropy
Number of attributes	Mode	Average entropy of attributes
Number of classes	Variance	Mutual entropy between classes and attributes
Positive percentage	Arithmetic average	Valid attribute
Negative percentage	Maximum and minimum eigenvalues	Noise rate
Missing value percentage	Harmonic average	
Percentage of majority and minority	Geometric mean	

Meta-feature Based on Landmarking. The main idea of the Landmarking method [11] is: Given two simple classifiers A and B, as a benchmark classifier, if classifier A performs better than B in a given learning task, then When performing a similar mining task, selecting a classifier that has the same inductive bias as A. This metric not only can distinguish different types of classification problems, but also highlight the scope of application of classification algorithms.

Model-feature Based on Model. Meta-feature based on model refer to training a model through a data set, and then taking some structural characteristics of the model as feature measures of the data set. Bensusan et al. [12] proposed to obtain information from the obtained decision tree model to characterize the learning complexity. Based on the decision tree, 10 feature measures were listed, such as the ratio of the number of decision tree nodes to the number of attributes, the number of nodes and training examples ratio and so on. Detailed model-based meta-features are shown in Table 2.

4 Algorithm Evaluation Index Selection

There are several measures to evaluate the performance of the algorithm in the field of machine learning. The more common performance measures have accuracy, true case ratio, true negative case ratio, precision ratio, F-measurement, ROC curve area, mean absolute error, training time, and testing time, interpretability and so on. The algorithm performance measures that most researchers consider when using meta-learning methods for algorithm selection are more focused on accuracy and training time, while ignoring other performance measures. The algorithm performance measure has the accuracy and training time of the algorithm, and combines the two by ARR measure. The evaluation of the project recommendation task is based on the prediction ranking using predictive ranking indicators such as Mean Forecast (MAP) and Standardized Discount Cumulative Income (NDCG).

Table 2. Meta-feature based on model

Meta-feature of the model		
Tree breadth	Average number of nodes	Branch length standard deviation
Depth of the tree	Standard deviation of the number of nodes	Maximum attribute
Number of nodes	Length of the longest branch	Minimum attribute
Number of leaf nodes	Minimum branch length	Average attribute
Maximum number of nodes	Average branch length	Standard deviation of attributes

5 Summary

Algorithm selection based on meta-learning has been widely used in various subject areas. The meta-learning model can effectively mine meta-knowledge and help users choose appropriate algorithms. The extraction of data element features is a key technique when building meta-models. There are still deficiencies in algorithm selection based on meta-learning ideas. Each type of algorithm has its corresponding scope and limitations. On the other hand, the algorithm selection methods based on meta-learning are mostly in the form of black boxes, and the acquired meta-knowledge lacks interpretability.

This paper first summarizes the knowledge related to meta-learning, then proposes a model framework based on meta-learning ideas. Finally, it analyzes the extraction of key technical meta-features of meta-learning and points out the shortcomings of current research, and provides a theory for improving the problem of algorithm selection and technical references.

References

1. Wolpert DH, Macready WG (1997) No free lunch theorems for optimization. IEEE Trans Evol Comput 1(1):67–82
2. Biggs JB (1985) The role of meta-learning in study process. Br J Educ Psychol 55:185–212
3. Hutter F, Hoos H, Stutzle T (2007) Automatic algorithm configuration based on local search. In: Proceedings of the 22nd national conference on artificial intelligence, AAAI 2007, pp 1152–1157
4. Wolpert DH (1992) Stacked generalization. Neural Netw 5:241–259
5. Rendell L, Cho H (1990) Empirical learning as a function of concept character. Mach Learn 5(3):267–298
6. Vilalta R, Drissi Y (2002) A perspective view and survey of meta-learning. Artif Intell Rev 18:77–95
7. Brazdil P, Giraud-Carrier C et al (2009) Metalearning: applications to data mining. Springer, Heidelberg, pp 31–60
8. Vanschoren J, Blockeel H (2010) Towards understanding learning behavior. In: Proceedings of the annual machine learning conference of Belgium and the Netherlands, pp 89–96
9. Giraud-Carrier C (2014) Metalearning a tutorial. In: Tutorial at the 7th international conference on machine learning and applications (ICMLA), pp 233–317
10. Cheng J, Zhang X et al (2015) Software defect prediction recommendation method based on meta-learning. J China Acad Electron Sci 10(6):620–627 (in Chinese)
11. Pfahringer B, Bensusan H et al (2000) Meta-learning by landmarking various learning algorithms. In: Proceedings of the 17th international conference on machine learning, pp 743–750
12. Bensusan H, Giraud C, Kennedy C (2000) Higher-order approachto meta-learning. In: The ECML 2000 workshop on meta-learning: building automatic advice strategies for model selection and method combination. Springer, Heidelberg, pp 109–117

Study of Signal Remote Monitoring System Based on Template Technology in Timing System

Wei Wu(✉) and Haidong Zou

China Satellite Maritime Tracking and Control Department, Jiangyin, Jiangsu, China
605571975@qq.com

Abstract. This paper proposes a design of remote monitoring system for timing system based on template technology. The monitoring signal of oscillograph is collected by the extension module TDS2CM, which is processed by micro controller unit and network module, and is transmitted to IP network to realize remote monitoring. At the time, all the indicators of the system exceeded the set value will trigger the sound alarm. This will help to remind of carrying out the corresponding operation, preventing the timing system of exceeding the specified range of technical indicators. The result shows that this system does well in achieving the purpose of fault warning in timing system.

Keywords: Timing system · Remote monitoring · Template technology

1 Introduction

The timing system is responsible for providing standard time and frequency signals to realize the time synchronization for the measurement and communication system. In the course of the experiment, the time series should be tested regularly, including 1PPs, B(DC) code, and 10 MHz frequency signal. The amplitude, front and synchronization error of each signal should be monitored especially. Taking the time synchronization 1PPs synchronous test as an example, time synchronization equipment needs "timing" and "punctuality" operation. The so-called "time to time" uses the GPS second signal [1, 2], the rubidium clock or other external second signal as the time standard. So that the second frontier of the local second signal and external second signal are homogeneous. The so-called "punctuality" is that when the time to time procedure is complete, the timing equipment will works according to its own frequency and transmits the timing signal to users [3, 4].

Due to lack of effective fault monitoring and warning means for the timing system equipments, failures in the equipment can't be found in time. When using the oscilloscope to monitor all the indicators, the operators need to watch the state of the oscilloscope closely for a long time. Therefore, it is necessary to design a remote monitoring system of time series signal based on template technology. When the values of the timing system exceed a set range, it triggers sound alarm, and reminds of operation and preventing the timing system from exceeding the prescribed range of technical indicators.

Z. Xu et al. (Eds.): CSIA 2019, AISC 928, pp. 1389–1394, 2020.
https://doi.org/10.1007/978-3-030-15235-2_192

2 Signal Template Technology

The signal template technology is to establish one or more dimensions of the template signal based on the detailed characteristics of the existing signal [5]. Then make a comparison of the signal to be detected with the template signal, and draw conclusions according to the results [6]. This process of signal processing is referred to template matching.

The 1PPs second signal in the timing system is taken as an example. The indexes reflecting the detailed characteristics of the signal mainly include the amplitude, the second edge, the width of the second pulse, and the synchronization deviation of the local second signal relative to the external second signal. The key points of the waveform are 1PPs second signal amplitude and second synchronization accuracy. The actual monitoring waveform is shown as Fig. 1.

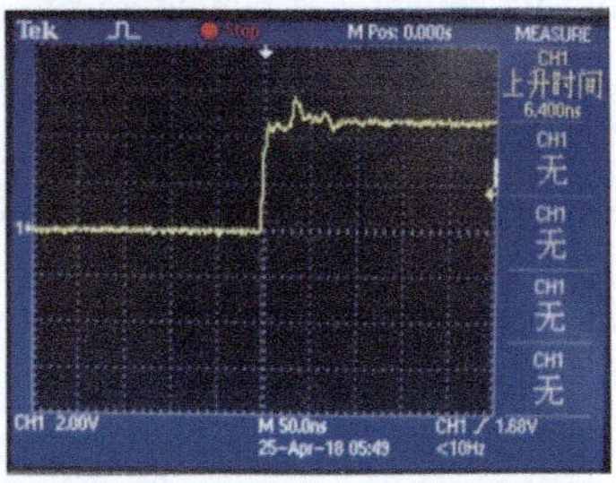

Fig. 1. Front edge of 1PPs second signal.

The similarity between data vectors $\vec{x} = (x_1, x_2, \ldots, x_n)^T$ and data samples $\vec{y} = (x_1, x_2, \ldots, x_n)^T$ is defined as:

$$S(\vec{x}, \vec{y}) = \frac{\vec{x} \cdot \vec{y}}{|\vec{x}||\vec{y}|} \tag{1}$$

In the formula, the modules of vectors $\vec{x}$ and $\vec{y}$ can be obtained, and $-1 \leq s(\vec{x}, \vec{y}) \leq 1$ can be deduced. The greater the value of $s(\vec{x}, \vec{y})$, the higher similarity between the vectors [7]. This index can be used as an important reference for judging the quality of the measured signal.

Taking the amplitude waveform of 1PPs second signal as an example, it is required that the amplitude area is [2.4, 5.0] V. Take the value of 3.7 V, define its template vector as $\overline{Amp}$, then use $\overline{A_{max}} = \overline{Amp} + 1.3V$ and $\overline{A_{min}} = \overline{Amp} - 1.3V$ as the boundary of the safety value. For the measured sample vector, the calculated range is within the interval [−1.3, 1.3] V as a criteria. If then, the sample data can meet the requirements of the index. Otherwise, the decision signal does not meet the requirements of the target.

3 System Hardware Design

The system hardware structure is shown in Fig. 2.

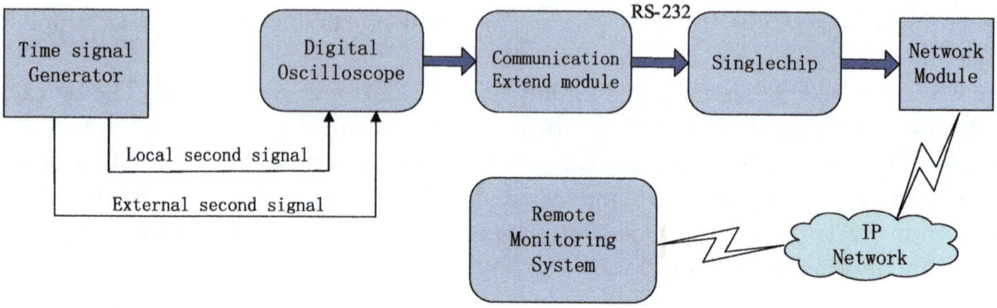

Fig. 2. Hardware structure of remote monitoring system.

The TDS2CM communication expansion module is adopted in the system from Fig. 2, and its function is to collect signals from digital oscilloscope. When processing a high frequency signal (for example, up to 100 MHz), an ultra high speed hardware acquisition circuit is usually designed, including magnification, filtering, A/D and D/A conversion. This circuit has very high requirements, which requires the acquisition edge storage, the high speed of the circuit, and the consideration of various radiation interference. And according to the sampling theorem, the sampling frequency F should be greater than or equal to 2 times the maximum frequency f of the sampled signal. That is, F is no less than 2f. The low pass filter, considering the actual recovery waveform, can not have completely ideal characteristics. In order to restore the signal correctly, it usually takes F = (2.5–5) * f or higher [8]. When the sampling signal reaches as high as 100 MHz, the sampling rate of 500 MHz should be achieved. The synchronization precision of the time and second signal in this machine usually needs to reach dozens of nanoseconds to meet the technical requirements. Therefore, to sample the time-series signal, the signal acquisition equipment needs to reach the sampling rate of about 1 Gs/s.

The TDS200 series digital oscilloscope of Tektronix has been widely used all over the world, and its supporting extension module TDS2CM. It has the function of two-way communication with the external equipment. It can connect directly with the printer and computer, and make the work of storage and printing of the waveform very square. The TDS220 digital oscilloscope has 100 MHz bandwidth and achieves 1 Gs/s sampling rate by 10 times scanning mode. The data and waveform of the oscilloscope can be read and processed directly by using the corresponding software (such as Matlab) when the RS232 cable is connected with the computer by serial communication with the serial port of the TDS2CM module [9]. Therefore, after considering the timing synchronization fault remote early warning system, the TDS2CM extension module is used as signal acquisition device.

TDS2CM is the communication extension module. It can be directly inserted into the rear panel of any TDS200 series oscilloscope, and can collect and process the signal of the oscilloscope [10]. The module has two interfaces, GPIB and RS232, and is equipped with a centronics hard copy print port.

In this system, the local second signal and external second signal output by the time code device are input to the TDS220 digital oscilloscope through the oscilloscope probe, and be transmitted to the MCU through the RS232 interface with the TDS2CM communication expansion module is collected. The processed signal is sent to the network module and transmitted to the remote monitoring terminal through the IP network to realize the remote monitoring of the time synchronization system.

4 System Software Design

The software design of the system mainly involves two parts: the single chip micro-computer system and the network module are used to analyze and repackage the serial data collected from the TDS2CM communication extension module to facilitate the transmission of the network. Storage, query and real-time warning of the acquired data are needed of the remote monitoring terminal.

4.1 Single Chip Microcomputer System Software Processing

The software of the MCU part mainly completes the protocol conversion and remote transmission of the field monitoring data, which is to convert the serial data of RS232 into a custom data packet for network transmission, and then realize the remote transmission of the network through the network module. It is mainly divided into three parts: integrity checking of serial packets, data precomputation and early warning, data re encapsulation and network transmission. The basic implementation process is shown in Fig. 3.

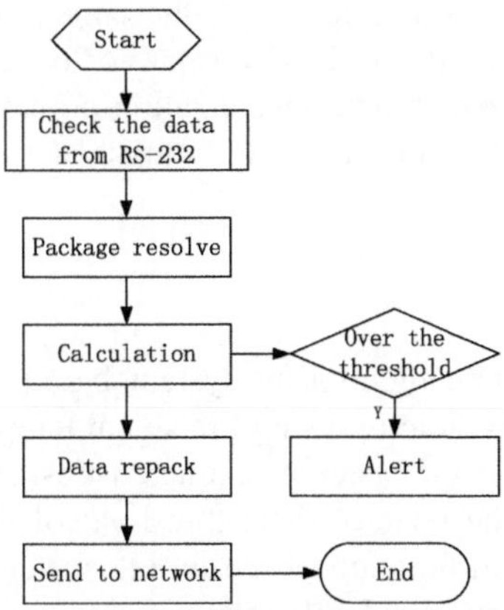

Fig. 3. Diagram of the MCU software processing flow.

4.2 Remote Monitoring Terminal Software Processing

The remote monitoring terminal mainly completes the storage, response query, real-time fault warning and so on. In order to provide data support for the overall decision analysis of communication accurately, a storage database system for the data collected by the system is needed. Remote monitoring system can use JSP programming to realize its basic software processing flow as shown in Fig. 4.

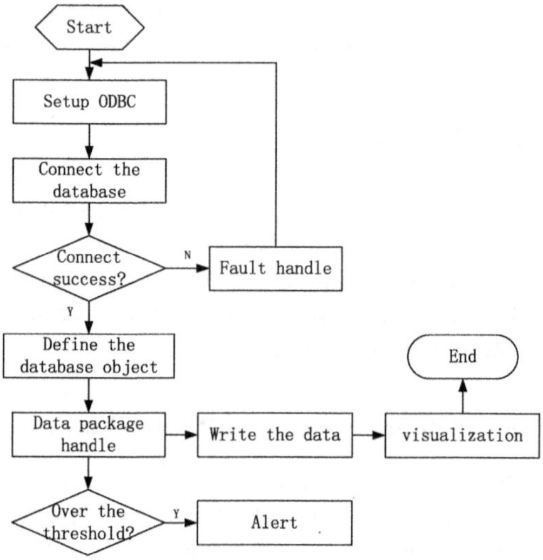

Fig. 4. Diagram of the MCU software processing flow.

After the operation of the remote monitoring system, the connection with the local database is established. After the connection is successful, the system receives a remote transmission packet on a fixed port. After parsing the packet, the system can judge whether it exceeds the predetermined threshold. If the result is true, then the remote alarm and manual processing is carried out. At the same time, the parsed data is written to the local database in a predetermined format. After that, a visual display of the collected data is realized through data visualization processing. Thus a complete process of data acquisition and remote warning is finished.

5 Conclusions

This paper proposes a remote monitoring system based on digital oscilloscope and communication extension module by using the signal template technology. The signal template, which is based on the specific characteristics of the existing measurement signals, can easily define the characteristic threshold of the signal. In hardware, the remote monitoring and alarm function of the timing system can be realized by adding the communication extension template to the existing oscillograph, and the software programming can effectively improve the efficiency of the system.

References

1. Lin X, Zhang R (2016) 2G-ALE signal recognition technology based on template matching. Radio Commun Technol 42(3):46–48
2. Wu L, Zheng Z, Xu Q (2016) Sample extraction technology of periodic signal based on full pulse. Aerosp Electron Countermeas 32(4):41–43
3. Tong B (2003) Time unification system. National Defense Industry Press
4. Liu K (2010) Time unification technology research and application. Xi'an Electronic and Science University
5. Fan Y, Yu Y, Li Y et al (2016) Remote monitoring system based on ZigBee wireless sensor network. Lab Res Explor 35(239) (1):80–84
6. Zhu Y, Li W (2016) Applied research of remote monitoring system based on computer network technology. Digit Technol Appl (7):83
7. Zhu W, Lv C (2016) Design of remote monitoring system based on GPRS. Inf Syst Eng (2):21–22
8. Peng K, Feng J, Zheng H et al (2016) Design and development of remote monitoring platform for urban LED lighting system. Comput Meas Control 24(9):103–106
9. Chen H (2015) Design of time synchronization module based on PCI9052. Electron Technol Softw Eng (12)
10. Sun Z (2016) Testing system for time sync equipment based on MCU and FPGA. Ind Control Comput (04)

Research on E-learning Teaching Assistant System Based on Improved Particle Swarm Optimization Algorithm

Yue Liu, Jiamei Xue(✉), and Meishan Li

College of Information Science and Electronic Technique, Jiamusi University, Jiamusi 154007, China
xuejiameixzy@sina.com

Abstract. With the development of information technology, e-learning has become an important way of learning. Compared to the traditional way of learning, E-learning is not limited by time and space and can meet student' learning needs at any time. In order to improve students' autonomous learning efficiency of E-learning and teachers' efficiency in managing students' study, this paper puts forward that we shall apply the particle swarm optimization algorithm to the digital learning platform. Aiming at the problem of slow recommendation speed in recommendation methods of E-learning resources, should use particle swarm optimization (PSO) to seek the optimal teaching objective. Therefore, this paper designs the E-learning teaching assistants system based on the improved PSO. Experiments show that the improved PSO is more effective in solving optimization problems of group learning features in colleges and universities and the optimization results are ideal, which can improve the learning effect of college students.

Keywords: E-learning · Particle swarm optimization · Autonomous learning

1 Introduction

E-learning (Electronic Learning) is also called as "digital learning". It refers to a new student-centered learning mode in which students use digital learning resources on the online learning platform for independent learning. At present, more and more colleges and universities begin to use E-learning platform as an auxiliary system of traditional classroom teaching so as to form a hybrid learning integrating offline learning and online learning into one. This paper uses data mining technology to analyze learning process of online groups so as to improve the efficiency of online learning. At present, the optimization design of group learning behaviors has become a hot topic in education field [1].

In order to solve at the problem of slow recommendation speed of online learning resource recommendation methods [2], this paper proposes a personalized online learning resource recommendation method based on improved particle swarm optimization algorithm by referring to research results of many scholars. Particle swarm optimization algorithm is simple and easy to implement. The algorithm can be

Z. Xu et al. (Eds.): CSIA 2019, AISC 928, pp. 1395–1400, 2020.
https://doi.org/10.1007/978-3-030-15235-2_193

continuously optimized through system simulation, which can improve the learning efficiency and learning effect of students and achieve better learning effect with less learning time and energy [3].

2 Particle Swarm Optimization Algorithm

Particle swarm optimization (PSO) algorithm is an evolutionary computing technology based on swarm intelligence. It is proposed under the inspiration of behavior rules of birds, fish and human society. Particle swarm optimization algorithm guides the optimization search through the swarm intelligence generated by the cooperation and competition among particles in the group [4]. Imagine a situation where there is only one piece of food in an area, but a group of birds are randomly searching for food in that area. All birds don't know where the food is, but they know how far away it is from the food. So what's the best strategy for finding food? The simplest and most effective method is to search the area around the bird which is nearest to the food at present. They can find global optimal values by following the optimal value currently searched [6]. In the PSO system, particles refer to birds. Each particle has its own position vector, velocity vector and an adaptive value used to evaluate the position of particles. Position vector represents a point in the solution space of the problem, that is, a valid solution [5]. The velocity vector determines the distance and direction the particle flies in the next iteration. It is affected by the historical optimal position Pbest of the particle itself and the historical optimal position Gbest of the entire particle swarm so that particles can dynamically adjust their position under the individual-optimal and global-optimal guidance so that the whole group can converge to the global-optimal position. Each particle is a random effective solution in the solution space; fitness (x_i) is the fitness value to calculate the particle position. The larger the value is, the closer x_i is to the theoretical optimal solution. The historical optimal position of particle individuals and the optimal position of the group are updated by the following formula.

$$v_{i,d}^{k+1} = wv_{i,d}^{k}(t) + c_1 rand()\left(Pbest_{i,d}^{k} - x_{i,d}^{k}\right) + c_2 rand()\left(Gbest_{i,d}^{k} - x_{i,d}^{k}\right) \tag{1}$$

$$x_{i,d}^{k+1} = x_{i,d}^{k} + v_{i,d}^{k+1} \tag{2}$$

In the formula, c1 and c2 refer to the accelerated factor; rand () means the random number between [0, 1]; $v_{i,d}^{k+1}, x_{i,d}^{k+1}$ refer to the d component of speed v_i and x_i in the k + 1 iteration. The position range of the $d(1 \leqslant d \leqslant D)$ dimension is $[-XMAX_d, XMAX_d]$. The speed variation scope is $[-VMAX_d, VMAX_d]$, which means that if $x_{i,d}$ and $v_{i,d}$ in the iteration exceed the boundary value, they will be set as the boundary value. ω is called as the inertia factor and it is put forward by Shi and Eberhart and other experts. ω means the effect of the velocity of a particle in the previous iteration on its current velocity. Search interval and search accuracy of balance particle enables the algorithm a strong search capability in the early search stage and more accurate results in the later stage.

The optimization algorithm of basic particle swarms is as follows:

(1) Randomly initialize the swarm. The fitness value was calculated according to the fitness function, and the individual optimal solution Pbest and the group optimal solution Gbest were determined according to the fitness value.
(2) Update particle velocity and position according to Eqs. (1) and (2)
(3) Calculate the fitness value of particles and update the individual optimal solution Pbest and the group optimal solution Gbest according to the fitness value.
(4) Determines whether the loop ends; if not, return to Step 2.

3 Improved Particle Swarm Optimization Algorithm

In order to solve the situation that PSO algorithm is prone to produce premature convergence and has poor local optimization ability [7], this paper puts forward an improved particle swarm optimization algorithm based on selection and crossover in genetic strategy so as to enhance the searching ability. In addition, the inertial weight ω is dynamically adjusted in the improved algorithm to further improve the development ability of particle swarm optimization in the later flight stage. Here, the formula combining inertia weight and contraction factor is adopted to calculate the velocity, as shown in formula (3).

$$v_{i,d}^{k+1} = \mathrm{k}\left(wv_{i,d}^{k}(t) + c_1 rand()\left(Pbest_{i,d}^{k} - x_{i,d}^{k}\right) + c_2 rand()\left(Gbest_{i,d}^{k} - x_{i,d}^{k}\right)\right) \quad (3)$$

k is the contraction factor and the function of c1 and c2.

$$\mathrm{k} = \frac{2}{\left|2 - (c_1 + c_2) - \sqrt{(c_1 + c_2)^2 - 4(c_1 + c_2)}\right|}, c_1 + c_2 > 4 \quad (4)$$

Generally speaking, particle swarm optimization is expected to have a good exploration ability at the beginning of flight, and with the increase of iteration times, it is expected to have a good development ability at the later stage of flight [8]. This can be realized by dynamically adjusting the inertia weight in formula (4). This project uses the way of time-varying weight to dynamically adjust the inertia weight ω. Suppose that the value range of inertia weight is $[\omega_{min}, \omega_{max}]$ and the maximum number of iterations is D_max, the inertia weight during the i iteration shall be

$$\omega_i = \omega_{max} - \frac{\omega_{max} - \omega_{min}}{D\_max} \times i \quad (5)$$

The interleaved mode is shown as follows: at each iteration, a certain number of particles are selected from the particle swarm according to a certain probability and put into a pool. The particles in the pool are randomly cross-bred to produce a corresponding number of offspring particles. In order to keep the population size unchanged, the offspring particles are used to replace the parent particles.

The positions of the offspring particles in each dimension are obtained by the arithmetic cross calculation of the corresponding positions of the parent generation.

$$child_1(x_i) = p_i \times parnet_1(x_i) + (1 - p_i) \times parent_2(x_i) \tag{6}$$

$$child_2(x_i) = p_i \times parnet_2(x_i) + (1 - p_i) \times parent_1(x_i) \tag{7}$$

p_i means the pseudo-random numbers evenly distributed between 0 and 1.

Velocity vector of offspring particles is obtained by normalization of the sum of parent velocity vector.

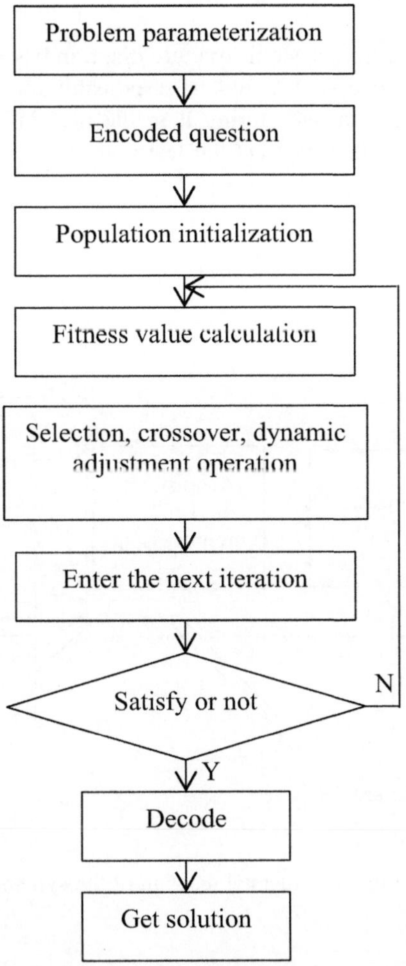

Fig. 1. Flow chart of improved PSO algorithm

$$child_1(v) = \frac{parent_1(v) + parent_2(v)}{|parent_1(v) + parent_2(v)|}|parent_1(v)| \quad (8)$$

$$child_2(v) = \frac{parent_1(v) + parent_2(v)}{|parent_1(v) + parent_2(v)|}|parent_2(v)| \quad (9)$$

The introduction of selection operation can improve the local optimization ability of PSO algorithm, cross on the basis of selection, increase the diversity of particles, make the particles benefit from both parents, easy to jump out of the local optimal solution, enhance the search ability, and also improve the convergence speed of the algorithm [9, 10]. Figure 1 show the improved particle swarm optimization process.

4 System Architecture Design

Figure 2 shows the E-Learning system structure diagram based on improved PSO. The data acquisition and preprocessing module is responsible for collecting and processing students' online learning data and storing it in the user information base. The optimization analysis module then extracts the learning feature data from the library for optimization analysis.

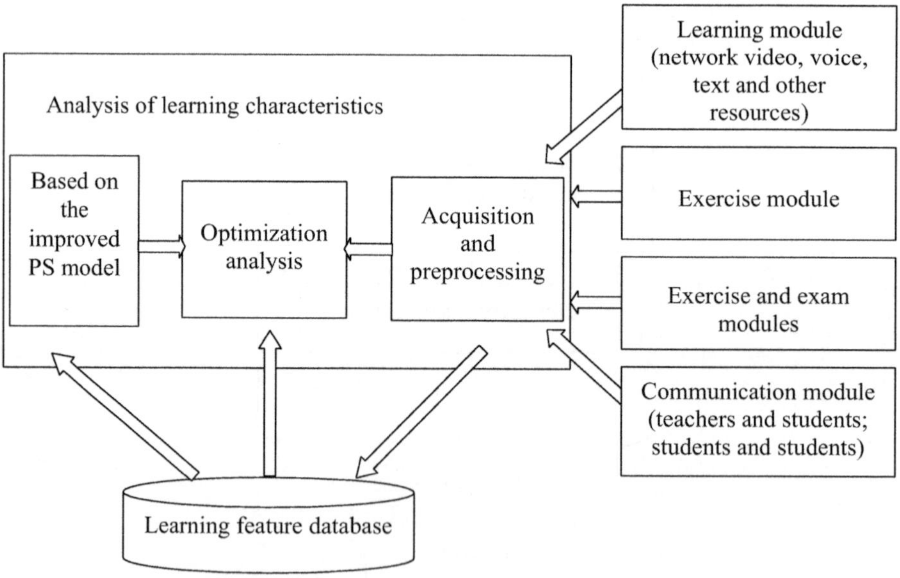

Fig. 2. Structural diagram of the system

5 Conclusion

The in-depth development of E-learning lowers the learning threshold and breaks the learning time and space restriction. However, learners need to spend time selecting suitable learning resources, which will cause learning loads. The improved PSO algorithm dynamically adjusts inertia weight to improve the convergence of the algorithm through the way of linear time-varying weights. It can reduce the search process and it is of great significance to improve students' learning efficiency, learning effect and teaching quality.

Acknowledgments. This paper was supported by teaching research project of Jiamusi university (Grant No. 2017LGL-018), teaching research project of Jiamusi university (Grant No. 2018JYXB-042), teaching research project of Jiamusi university (Grant No. 2018JYXB-041) and planning project on Educational Science of Heilongjiang Province (Grant No. GBD1317136).

References

1. Xie X, Li X, Cao F, Sun L (2018) Research and implementation of e-learning teaching assistant system based on improving C4.5. J Jiamusi Univ (Nat Sci Ed) 64–67
2. Li H, Liu Z, Li S, Wang W (2017) A personalized e-learning resource recommendation method based on an improved binary particle swam optimization algorithm. J Syst Sci Math Sci 1770–1779 (2017)
3. Lin D, Li J (2010) Research on particle swarm optimization applied in group learning behavior design. J Hunan Univ Sci Technol (Nat Sci Ed) 91–93
4. Duan XD, Wang CR, Liu XD (2007) Particle Swarm Optimization and Its Application. Liaoning University Press, Shenyang
5. Kennedy J, Eberhart RC (1995) Particle swarm optimization. In: Proceedings of IEEE international conference oil neural networks. IEEE Press, Proceedings of IEEE international conference oil neural networks, Piscaltaway, NJ, pp 1942–1948
6. Zhang S (2011) Research on multi-object intelligent test paper generation based on improved PSO algorithm. J Fujian Univ Technol 86–91 (2011)
7. Gong Y (2007) The study of PSO with GA. J Jining Univ
8. Yang X, Jiang Z, Zhang W (2010) A particle swarm optimization algorithm-based solid launch vehicle ascent trajectory optimum design. J Astronaut 1304–1309
9. Bai L, Xu S (2016) Computer experiment teaching based on improved PSO algorithm. Fujian Comput 119–120
10. Liu Z (2017) Personalized e-learning resource recommendation method based on multi-objective particle swarm optimization algorithm with neighborhood learning strategy. Zhejiang University of Technology

Design of Tracing Car Based on Photoelectric Sensor

Huang Jian(✉)

XiJing University, Xi'an 710123, China
565200245@qq.com

Abstract. In order to identify black and white lines accurately, ST188 is used as photoelectric sensor to detect the black line runway. The reflection ability of the black line to light is weaker, and the white line has stronger ability to reflect light. According to the strong and weak reflection light, we can judge the black and white line. Usually, 2 sensors are used to place the runway at the center of the sensor so that it can be easily detected. The experimental results show that this method can detect the black line track accurately and achieve automatic tracing.

Keywords: Black and white line · Photoelectric sensor · Automatic tracing

1 Introduction

In the control of smart cars, runway is often detected by photoelectric sensors, while ST188 is a reflective photoelectric sensor, transmitting and receiving are integrated. When illumination reaches the black line, the reflection of light is weak; when illumination reaches the white line, the reflection of light is strong. Accordingly, we can judge the black and white line [1–3].

2 System Design Block Diagram

The system design block diagram is shown in Fig. 1. The picture is dominated by STM32F103RBT6. The photoelectric sensor ST188 detects the different illumination of black and white light, and the voltage value when no object passes over ST188 is different. Generally, the threshold value is a value between the voltage value of an object directly above the object and the voltage value of an object directly above the object [4–6]. According to whether it is larger than the threshold or less than the threshold, we can judge whether it is a black line or a white line.

Z. Xu et al. (Eds.): CSIA 2019, AISC 928, pp. 1401–1405, 2020.
https://doi.org/10.1007/978-3-030-15235-2_194

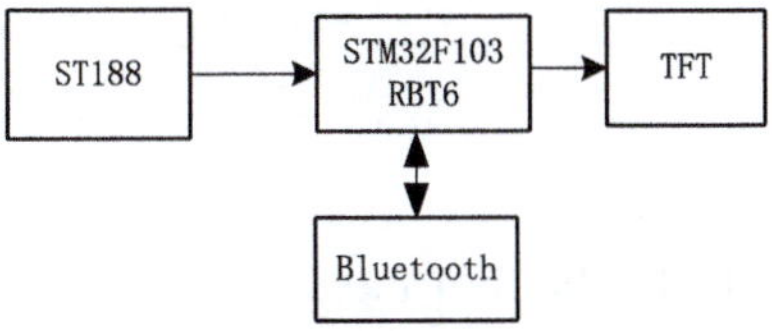

Fig. 1. System block diagram

3 Detailed Design

3.1 ST188 Circuit

The design circuit of the photoelectric sensor is shown in Fig. 2. Only one circuit diagram of ST188 is drawn. The ST188 is composed of a light emitting diode and a phototransistor. When illuminated, the transistor is close to conduction, and the AD0 outputs low level; when illuminated, the AD0 outputs high level. So we often connect this pin to the A/D acquisition pin of STM32 to collect voltage, or to the comparator to get high and low levels.

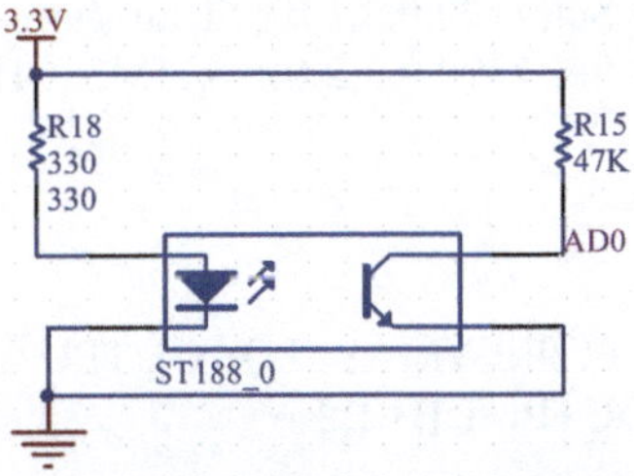

Fig. 2. ST188 circuit diagram of photoelectric sensor

3.2 STM32F103RBT6

The main control adopts STM32F103RBT6, and is based on the Cortex-M3 kernel, which is a 32 bit microprocessor. The main frequency is 72 MHz, which contains 16 channels of A/D acquisition. The A/D of each channel is 12 bits, with 3 serial ports. Any IO interface can connect to ST188 [7, 8].

4 Software Design

```
void motor_init(void)
{
        GPIO_InitTypeDef GPIO_InitStructure;
RCC_APB2PeriphClockCmd(RCC_APB2Periph_GPIOF|RCC_APB2Periph_GPIOG
, ENABLE);
            GPIO_InitStructure.GPIO_Pin                                        =
GPIO_Pin_13|GPIO_Pin_14|GPIO_Pin_15;
            GPIO_InitStructure.GPIO_Mode = GPIO_Mode_Out_PP;
            GPIO_InitStructure.GPIO_Speed = GPIO_Speed_50MHz;
            GPIO_Init(GPIOF, &GPIO_InitStructure);
            GPIO_ResetBits(GPIOF,GPIO_Pin_13|GPIO_Pin_14|GPIO_Pin_15);

            GPIO_InitStructure.GPIO_Pin = GPIO_Pin_0;
            GPIO_InitStructure.GPIO_Mode = GPIO_Mode_Out_PP;
            GPIO_InitStructure.GPIO_Speed = GPIO_Speed_50MHz;
            GPIO_Init(GPIOG, &GPIO_InitStructure);
            GPIO_ResetBits(GPIOG,GPIO_Pin_0);

                TIM3_PWM_Set(7199,0,3,1,0);//Tout=(arr+(psc+1))/Tclk PC6
                TIM3_PWM_Set(7199,0,3,2,0); //TIM3 CH1-CH4 OUTPUT PWM
PC6 PC7 PC8 PC9 1K PC7

}

//PE9(AIN2) PE8((AIN1)) PC9(PWMA) TO OUTPUT A1 A2; PC8(PWMB)
PG1(BIN2) PE7(BIN1) TO OUTPUT B1 B2

void motor2_init(void)
{
        GPIO_InitTypeDef GPIO_InitStructure;

RCC_APB2PeriphClockCmd(RCC_APB2Periph_GPIOE|RCC_APB2Periph_GPIOG
|RCC_APB2Periph_GPIOD, ENABLE);
            GPIO_InitStructure.GPIO_Pin = GPIO_Pin_7|GPIO_Pin_9;
            GPIO_InitStructure.GPIO_Mode = GPIO_Mode_Out_PP;
            GPIO_InitStructure.GPIO_Speed = GPIO_Speed_50MHz;
            GPIO_Init(GPIOE, &GPIO_InitStructure);
            GPIO_ResetBits(GPIOE,GPIO_Pin_7|GPIO_Pin_9);

            GPIO_InitStructure.GPIO_Pin = GPIO_Pin_1;
            GPIO_InitStructure.GPIO_Mode = GPIO_Mode_Out_PP;
            GPIO_InitStructure.GPIO_Speed = GPIO_Speed_50MHz;
            GPIO_Init(GPIOG, &GPIO_InitStructure);
            GPIO_ResetBits(GPIOG,GPIO_Pin_1); //clear

        GPIO_InitStructure.GPIO_Pin = GPIO_Pin_8;
            GPIO_InitStructure.GPIO_Mode = GPIO_Mode_Out_PP;
```

```
        GPIO_InitStructure.GPIO_Speed = GPIO_Speed_50MHz;
        GPIO_Init(GPIOE, &GPIO_InitStructure);
        GPIO_ResetBits(GPIOE,GPIO_Pin_8); //clear

            TIM3_PWM_Set(7199,0,3,3,0);//Tout=(arr+(psc+1))/Tclk PC8
            TIM3_PWM_Set(7199,0,3,4,0); //TIM3 CH1-CH4 OUTPUT PWM
PC6 PC7 PC8 PC9 1K PC9
}
void motor_go(int pwm1,int pwm2)//初始化 CLOSE ALL LED
{
    PWMA=pwm1;
    PWMB=pwm2;
    AIN1=1;
    AIN2=0;
    BIN1=1;
    BIN2=0;
    }
void motor_back(int pwm1,int pwm2)//初始化 CLOSE ALL LED
{
    PWMA=pwm1;
    PWMB=pwm2;
    AIN1=0;
    AIN2=1;
    BIN1=0;
    BIN2=1;
    }
void motor_stop(int pwm1,int pwm2)
    {
        PWMA=pwm1;
        PWMB=pwm2;
        AIN1=0;
        AIN2=0;
        BIN1=0;
        BIN2=0;
    }
    void motor_turn_right(int pwm1,int pwm2)
    {
        PWMA=pwm1;
        PWMB=pwm2;
        AIN1=0;
        AIN2=0;
        BIN1=1;
        BIN2=0;
}
void motor_turn_left(int pwm1,int pwm2)//初始化 CLOSE ALL LED
{
```

```
    PWMA=pwm1;
    PWMB=pwm2;
    AIN1=0;
    AIN2=1;
    BIN1=0;
    BIN2=0;
}
```

5 Conclusion

This paper designs an automatic tracing intelligent car, uses photoelectric sensor to detect black and white lines, designs hardware circuit, and compiles a program to realize the automatic tracing function [9, 10]. It has certain practical value.

References

1. Shi Z, Chen P et al (2004) High precision digital velocity measurement and dynamic position detection algorithm. J Tsinghua Univ (Nat Sci Ed) 44(8):1021–1024
2. Zhang Y, Liu J, Chen C (2003) Research on high precision position detection and location technology. J Southeast Univ (Nat Sci Ed) 33(4):495–497
3. Jin J, Liu Z, Lin Y (2012) Design of photoelectric sensor characteristic parameter testing system. J Sens Technol 25(12):1678–1683
4. Xu Z, Ge W et al (2009) Design of position detection system based on CMOS camera and FPGA. LCD Disp 24(5):746–750
5. Lu W, Wang W et al (2014) Design of wireless photoelectric sensor based on STM32. Sens Microsyst 33(9):74–80
6. Duan Q, Yuan H, Jin X (2013) Simulation study on speed sensorless balance control of two-wheeled self-balancing vehicle. Control Eng 20(4):618–622
7. Wen J, Ma C (2016) Design of fuzzy PI control system for brushless DC motor. J Motor Control 20(3):102–108
8. Guo W, Chen Y, Zhou L, Ni J (2013) Research on fractional PI predictive function control of brushless DC motor. J Wuhan Univ Technol 35(3):130–135
9. Jiang W, Wu J (2012) DC motor double closed loop PI control technology research. Mach Tool Hydraul 40(11):21–24
10. Wang X, Zhu J (2014) BLDC motor speed control system based on fuzzy PI control. Electric Drive 44(1):63–67

An Improved Particle Swarm Optimization Algorithm

Chunguang Chang and Xi Wu(✉)

School of Management, Shenyang Jianzhu University, Shenyang 110168, China
wxy0102w@163.com

Abstract. Based on a brief introduction to the principle of particle swarm optimization (PSO) and different improved methods of PSO at home and abroad, the particle swarm optimization algorithm is improved for the shortcomings of particle swarm optimization. This paper selects the particle velocity formula with a learning model, which has good exploration ability and can effectively avoid the algorithm falling into local optimum, and recon figure some parameters of the algorithm. A PSO with two crossover operations (PSOCO) is put forward, and the next research direction of PSOCO algorithm is given.

Keywords: PSO · Crossover operator · PSOCO

1 Introduction

As a branch of computer science, artificial intelligence aims to produce intelligent machines that respond in a manner similar to human intelligence. At present, artificial intelligence has affected all aspects of human economic interests, cultural life, thinking and concepts. PSO is one of the most popular and effective swarm intelligence algorithms. It is a population-based meta heuristic algorithm. The main idea of PSO is to simulate the collective collaborative behavior of the bird population. PSO is a population-based iterative algorithm and it uses a principle that mimics the behavior of flocks of birds to guide these particles to search for global optimal solutions. Due to the simple implementation steps of PSO, PSO has been successfully applied to solve many real-world problems. Particle swarm optimization algorithms have two major drawbacks: relatively weak mining capabilities and premature convergence on complex multimodal problems. Therefore, the improvement of the particle swarm algorithm is very challenging and meaningful. Particle swarm optimization has attracted the attention of many researchers in related fields. Many researchers at home and abroad have made effective improvement work from different angles and methods. After more than 20 years of development, these improved research work mainly has the following two aspects, (1) adjusting the parameters, topology and running formula of the algorithm, and (2) mixing other mechanisms, strategies and algorithms.

Crossover operators have long been considered to be one of the main search operators of genetic algorithms. So far, a large number of crossover operators have been proposed. Crossover operators can effectively use the information of previous samples, which in turn affects future searches. Cross-over operations can combine parts

Z. Xu et al. (Eds.): CSIA 2019, AISC 928, pp. 1406–1410, 2020.
https://doi.org/10.1007/978-3-030-15235-2_195

of an excellent solution to form a potential good solution. Due to these advantages of cross-operation, cross-operation can improve the performance of the particle swarm algorithm.

In the past decade, the combination of cross-operation and particle swarm optimization has yielded some research results. Literature [1] proposed a dynamic particle swarm optimization algorithm based on arithmetic crossover. In literature [2] two different crossover operations were used to propagate promising samples. By intersecting the best positions of each particle's personal history, build effective guidance paradigms and maintain good diversity. A scheme for generating better candidate solutions using Laplace crossover operators is proposed in [3]. Literature [4] the particle swarm optimization algorithm was combined with the genetic arithmetic crossover operator to solve the global optimization problem to avoid the problem of group stagnation and premature convergence. Literature [5] proposed a method of acting on historically optimal particles by crossover. Literature [6] proposed a new PSO algorithm with a mufti-parent crossover operator. According to the multi-parent crossover operator, the descendants still stay in a linear space composed of four different parent individuals. In [7], a hybrid particle swarm optimization algorithm with crossover operator (represented as C-PSO) was proposed, which uses the idea of linear combination of two vectors to implement crossover operators, one of which comes from particles. Another vector is randomly selected from the elite collection. A review of a class of PSO algorithms using crossover operations was given in [1]. Most of these research results use a crossover operation, and combined with the basic motion formula of the particle swarm algorithm, there are few studies using two cross operations. Based on these observations, this paper selects the particle velocity formula with a learning model, which has good exploration ability and can effectively avoid the algorithm falling into local optimum, and improve some parameter configuration of the algorithm. Cross-operative particle swarm optimization algorithm (PSOCO).

2 PSO Algorithm and PSOCO Algorithm

2.1 PSO Algorithm

In PSO, each particle represents a latent solution to the optimization problem, and the entire particle swarm is flying in the search space to find the optimal solution. In the D-dimensional search space, let the particle velocity vector be $V_i = (V_{i1}, V_{i2}, \ldots, V_{iD})$ and the position vector be $X_i = (x_{i1}, x_{i2}, \ldots, x_{iD})$. According to the search space, the position vector and the velocity vector are randomly initialized for each particle. The update formula of particle and velocity is as follows:

$$v_{id}^{t+1} = wv_{id}^{t} + c_1 r_{1d}(p_{id}^{t} - x_{id}^{t}) + c_2 r_{2d}(p_{gd}^{t} - x_{id}^{t}) \quad (1)$$

$$x_{id}^{t+1} = x_{id}^{t} + v_{id}^{t+1} \quad (2)$$

w represents the inertia weight, c_1 and c_2 represent the acceleration factor, and r_1 and r_2 represent the random number uniformly distributed between [0, 1]. The variable d

represents a certain dimension of a particle ($d \in [1, D]$), p_g represents the historical optimal position of the entire particle swarm discovery, p_i represents the historical optimal position found by particle i, and the variable t represents the current number of iterations.

2.2 PSOCO Algorithm

In the PSO algorithm, according to the motion formula (1), it can be seen that the individual historical optimal particles and the group history optimal particles determine the search behavior and direction of the particles. The results of the literature [8] show that the PSO motion formula is flawed, which limits the ability of particles to explore. That is, the motion formula of the particle tends to fall into the local optimum in some cases, so that the algorithm falls into premature convergence. Therefore, a particle motion formula with a learning model is used [8, 9].

The formula for updating the velocity of a particle is as follows:

$$v_{id} = wv_{id} + cr_d(GV_{id} - x_{id}) \tag{3}$$

c is the acceleration constant, r_d is a uniformly distributed random number between 0 and 1, and GV_{id} is the steering vector. In this paper, a crossover operation is used to generate the steering vector.

2.2.1 Cross-Operation Generates a Boot Vector GV_{id}

(1) Arithmetic intersection: For each particle i, the cross operation acts on P_i and P_j to generate a new individual $V_{ic} = [V_{ic,1}, V_{ic,2}, \ldots, V_{ic,D}]$.

The operation expression is as follows:

$$V_{ic,d} = r_{1,d}P_{i,d} + (1 - r_{1,d})P_{j,d} \tag{4}$$

$r_{1,d}$ is a random number uniformly distributed between 0 and 1.

(2) Differential evolutionary crossover: Randomly permuting the historical optimal position $(P_1, P_2, \ldots, P_N)$ of all particles before the crossover operation.

The mathematical expression is as follows:

$$\begin{bmatrix} P_{j1}, P_{j2}, \ldots, P_{jN} \\ P_1, P_2, \ldots, P_N \end{bmatrix} \tag{5}$$

In the formula, the upper layer $P_{j1}, P_{j2}, \ldots, P_{jN}$ is a random permutation arrangement of the lower layer $P_1, P_2, \ldots, P_N$. Cross-operations use elements of the upper and lower layers, which can produce diverse descendants. However, as the number of iterations increases, in order to avoid the algorithm falling into local optimum, more local search should be done near the group history optimal particle p_g. Therefore, the crossover probability of algorithms p_i and p_g should be increased. This paper defines an alternative pressure variable R, which represents the number of p_g instead of p_i in the permutation group $(P_{j1}, P_{j2}, \ldots, P_{jN})$. The expression of R is as follows:

$$R = \lfloor (t/Maxiter) \times N \rfloor \tag{6}$$

The differential evolution cross energy exchange vector V_i and the target vector P_i form a new vector U_i.

The expression of U_i is as follows:

$$U_i = \begin{cases} V_{ic,d}, & \text{if } r \leq CR \quad or \quad j = j_{rand} \\ P_{j,d}, & otherwise \end{cases} \tag{7}$$

(3) Select operation: Through the above two cross operations, generate descendant U_i, perform selection operation on U_i and P_j, and the boot vector expression is as follows:

$$GV_i = \begin{cases} U_i, & if\ (U_i \leq f(P_i) \\ P_i, & otherwise \end{cases} \tag{8}$$

2.2.2 Implementation Steps of the Improved Algorithm

PSOCO uses the cross-operation to generate the guidance vector based on the standard PSO algorithm. The specific steps are as follows: (1) Randomly initialize the velocity and position of the particle and set the relevant parameters. (2) Estimating the fitness values of all particles, settings p_i, p_g and $t = 0$. (3) While $t < Maxiter$ do. (4) Generating a steering vector according to Eqs. (4), (7), and (8). (5) Calculate the velocity of each particle using Eq. (3), and calculating the position of each particle using Eq. (2). (6) Evaluating the fitness value of each particle and updating p_i and p_g. (7) $t = t + 1$. (8) End while.

3 Conclusion

Two different crossover operations are introduced into the PSOCO algorithm. One is an arithmetic crossover operation and the other is a differential evolution crossover operation. These two cross operations enable the generation of diverse and high quality boot vectors. These vectors are better able to guide particles' flight. Introducing different cross operations into PSOCO is the next step in research.

Acknowledgments. This research was supported by the National Natural Science Foundation of China (Project No. 51678375), Natural Science Foundation of Liaoning Province (Project No. 2015020603), and the Basic Scientific Research Project of Liaoning Higher Education (Project No. LJZ2017009).

References

1. Engelbrecht AP (2016) Particle swarm optimization with crossover: a review and empirical analysis. Artif Intell Rev 45(2):131–165
2. Chen YG, Li LX, Xiao JH, Yang YX, Liang J, Li T (2018) Particle swarm optimizer with crossover operation. Eng Appl Artif Intell 70:59–169
3. Xie J, Yang J (2010) A novel crossover operator for particle swarm algorithm. In: 2010 International Conference on Machine Vision and Human-Machine Interface (MVHI). IEEE, pp 161–164
4. Mohamed A, Tawhid AF (2016) Simplex particle swarm optimization with arithmetical crossover for solving global optimization problems. Opsearch 53(4):705–740
5. Chen S (2012) Particle optimization with pbest crossover. In: 2012 IEEE Congress on Evolutionary Computation (CEC). IEEE, pp 1–6
6. Wang H, Wu Z, Liu Y et al (2008) Particle swarm optimization with a novel mufti-parent crossover operator. In: Fourth International Conference on Natural Computation, ICNC 2008, vol 7. IEEE, pp 664–668
7. Zhang T, Hu TS, Guo XN, Chen Z, Zheng Y (2013) Solving high dimensional bilevel multiobjective programming problem using a hybrid particle swarm optimization algorithm with crossover operator. Knowl-Based Syst 53:13–19
8. Liang JJ, Qin AK, Suganthan PN et al (2006) Comprehensive learning particle swarm optimizer for global optimization of multimodal functions. IEEE Trans Evol Comput 10 (3):281–295
9. Chen Y (2018) Research on some improvement of swarm intelligence algorithm. Beijing University of Posts and Telecommunications (in Chinese)

A Statistical Process Control Approach to Global Optimization of System Integration

Hequn Wu(✉)

Network Management Center, Hohhot Vocational College, Hohhot, China
wuhequn53@163.com

Abstract. Although the traditional control algorithm produces many successful results on system integration applications, there still exist insufficiencies need to be improved. For traditional control approach, it is well known that the search equation is superior at local range but constrained at global range for system integration, which will transform the optimal performance of the algorithm. Therefore, the search ability is the most important goal in algorithm modification on system integration. To solve the faults in traditional control algorithm and achieve the goal of improvement, a new statistical process control approach is proposed to global optimization of system integration. In order to balance the search ability, search algorithms are made better by search strategies that search probability and random variable is related with a certain degree of correlation. In addition, to deepen the convergence degree, the local search operator is also utilized. The simulation results tested show that the proposed process control approach can outperform control approach in most of the experiments.

Keywords: Statistical process control · Global optimization · System integration · Search ability

1 Introduction

Statistical process control approach is used to monitor all stages of the process so as to ensure product quality [1]. Statistical process control approach ensures that the process is stable and predictable [2], improves product quality [3], production capacity and reduces costs [4], and provides a basis for process analysis [5]. Differentiate between the special and common causes of variation as a guide for taking local or systematic measures. Statistical process control is a system-wide, whole-process, using scientific methods to ensure the whole process of prevention [6]. Statistical process control is a technology that uses statistical technology to evaluate and monitor the various stages of the process [7], to establish and maintain an acceptable and stable level of the process, so as to ensure that products and services meet the required requirements [8]. The control chart can be used to analyze the stability of the process and to warn the abnormal factors in the process [9]. The process capability index can be calculated to analyze the degree to which the stable process capability meets the technical requirements and to evaluate the process quality.

Z. Xu et al. (Eds.): CSIA 2019, AISC 928, pp. 1411–1415, 2020.
https://doi.org/10.1007/978-3-030-15235-2_196

2 A Process Control Approach with Global Optimization

The search ability is crucial for the search equations to find the optima in searching space [10]. So some new solution searching equations are proposed. In differential evolution, the general steps of evolutionary algorithms and three operations will be executed, including mutation, crossover and selection. The mutation can form different DE algorithm. In all mutation operators, v_{ij} has the great search ability

$$v_{i,j} = x_{best,j} + \varphi_{i,j}(x_{best,j} - x_{i,j}) \tag{1}$$

where $i \in \{1, 2, \cdots, SN\}$; $x_{best,j}$ is the global best solution; $j \in \{1, 2, \cdots, D\}$ is a randomly selected index and $\varphi_{ij} \in [-1, 1]$ is uniformly distributed random number. In addition, the search equation can enhance the search ability to improve the convergence performance of the algorithm.

The optimized algorithm is proposed to improve the search ability by taking the advantages of the search equation. In this paper, the modified search equation is described as follows

$$v_{ij} = x_{ij} + \phi_{ij}(x_{ij} - x_{kj}) + \varphi_{ij}(x_{best,j} - x_{lj}) \tag{2}$$

where $k, l \in \{1, 2, \ldots, SN\}$ is a random selected index which is different from i, $\phi_{ij} \in [-1, 1]$ and $\varphi_{ij} \in [0, 1.5]$ are both uniformly distributed random numbers.

To further improve the search ability, the local search is executed after employed bee and onlooker bee search. Because of the randomness, ergodicity and irregularity of chaotic maps, chaotic local search is employed to search around the best food source. In this chaotic local search method, a contraction strategy is designed, which makes the search area larger at beginning and smaller at the end. The algorithm for chaotic local search is given as follows.

Step 1: Choose the best solution x_{best} achieved so far from food source.
Step 2: Generate the logistic variable x_i.
Step 3: Map the chaos variable x_i into chaos vector X_i.
Step 4: Generate the new food source V_i by the following equation

$$X_i = (1 - \lambda) \times x_{best} + \lambda \times x_i; \quad i = 1, \cdots n \tag{3}$$

where λ is the contract factor, defined as

$$\lambda = \frac{Maxcycle - cycle + 1}{Maxcycle} \tag{4}$$

Here, *Maxcycle* represents the largest iteration number and *cycle* is the current iteration number.

Step 5: If the above steps are not valid, it will jump into Step 2.

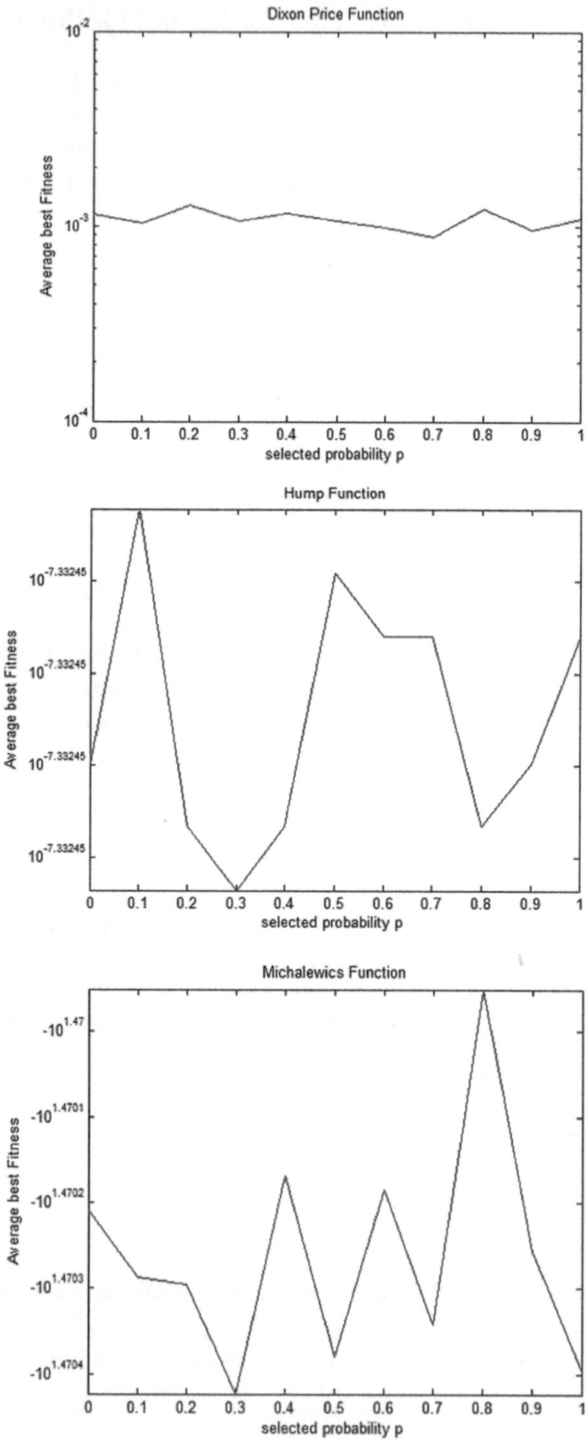

Fig. 1. Results on four test functions with different selective probability *p*.

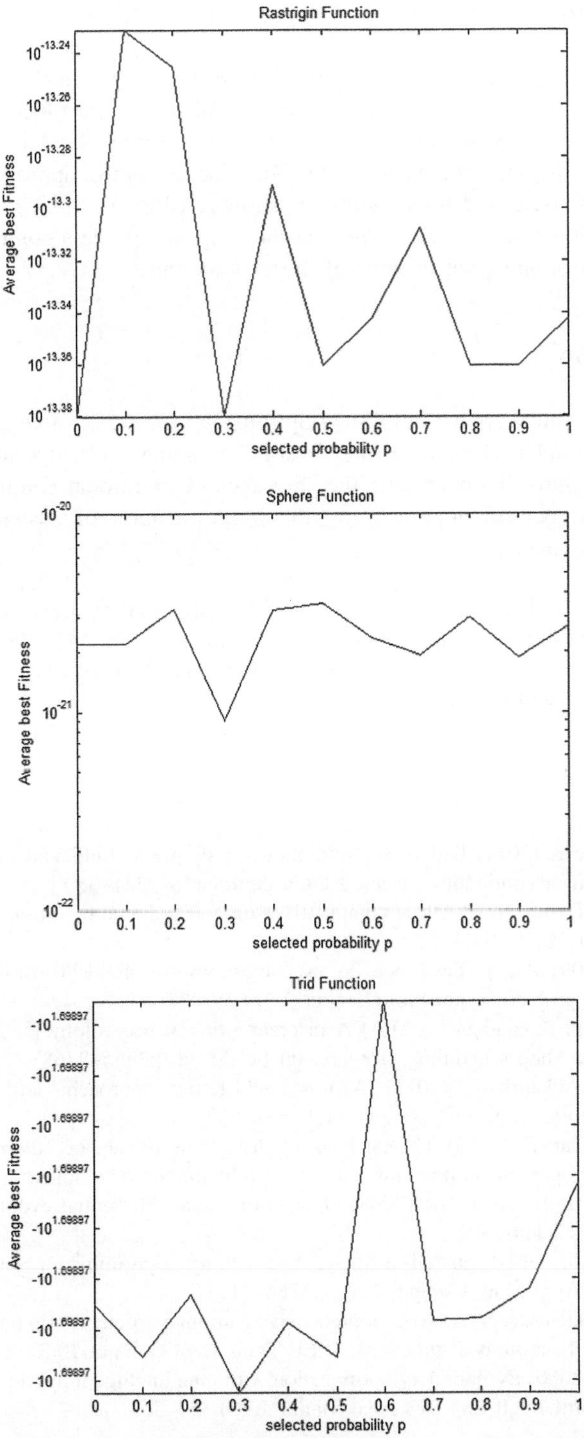

Fig. 1. (*continued*)

3 Simulation

In process control approach, there is a selective probability p, which controls the usage of searching Eqs. (5) and (6). To test the impact of p, six test functions are tested as p vary from 0 to 1. These test functions are Dixon-Price, Six Hump Camel Back, Michalewicz, Rastrigin, Sphere and Trid6. The process control approach runs 10 times on each test functions, and final results are shown in Fig. 1.

The simulation results tested show that the proposed process control approach can outperform control approach in most of the experiments.

4 Conclusion

The traditional control approach to local optimization of system integration shows the competitive optimal performance, and it still has some problems suffered by other stochastic algorithms. To overcome the shortages of traditional control algorithm, an effective process control approach to global optimization of system integration is proposed in this paper.

Acknowledgments. This research was supported by the Key Projects of Natural Science Research in Inner Mongolia Higher Education Institutions (Grant No. NJZZ17647), and the Project of Humanities and Social Sciences Research in Inner Mongolia higher Education Institutions (Grant No. NJSY17149).

References

1. Storn R, Price K (2011) Differential evolution - a simple and efficient heuristic for global optimization over continuous spaces. J Glob Optim 11(4):341–359
2. Karaboga D, Basturk B (2009) A comparative study of artificial bee colony algorithm. Appl Math Comput 214(1):108–132
3. Singh A (2009) An artificial bee colony algorithm for the leaf constrained minimum spanning tree problem. Appl Soft Comput 9(2):625–631
4. Tasgetiren MF, Suganthan P (2011) A discrete artificial bee colony algorithm for the lot-streaming flow shop scheduling problem. Inf Sci 181(12):2455–2468
5. Karaboga D, Ozturk C (2011) A novel clustering approach: artificial bee colony (ABC) algorithm. Appl Soft Comput 11(1):652–657
6. Kıran MS, İşcan H (2013) The analysis of discrete artificial bee colony algorithm with neighborhood operator on traveling salesman problem. Neural Comput Appl 23(1):9–21
7. Rahnamayan S, Tizhoosh HR (2008) Opposition-based differential evolution. IEEE Trans Evol Comput 12(1):64–79
8. Sam K (2010) Gbest guided artificial bee colony algorithm for numerical function optimization. Appl Math Comput 217(7):3166–3173
9. Suganthan PN, Baskar S (2006) Comprehensive learning particle swarm optimizer for global optimization of multimodal functions. IEEE Trans Evol Comput 10(3):281–295
10. Wakelam M (2000) Evolutionary optimization within an intelligent hybrid system for design integration. Artif Intell Eng Des Anal Manuf 13(5):351–363

Research on 3-D Laser Point Cloud Recognition Based on Depth Neural Network

Fan Yu(✉), Yanxi Wei, and Haige Yu

School of Computer Science and Engineering, Xi'an Techonolgical University, Xi'an 710021, Shananxi, China
407171251@qq.com

Abstract. Typical convolution architectures require fairly conventional input data formats, such as image grids or three-dimensional pixels, to show shared weights and other kernel optimizations. Because point clouds and grids are not typical formats, most researchers usually convert these data into conventional three-dimensional pixel grids or picture sets before providing them to deep-net architectures. However, this data representation transformation presents unnecessary result data and introduces the natural invariance of quantified workpiece fuzzy data. For this reason, we focus on using a different simple point cloud input representation for three-dimensional geometry, and named our deep network as point network. Point cloud is a simple and unified structure, which avoids the combination of irregularity and complex grids, so it is easier to learn. This topic takes point cloud as input directly, and outputs the whole input classification label or every part label of each point input. In the basic settings, each point is represented by three coordinates (x, y, z), and additional dimensions can be added by calculating normals and other local or global characteristics.

Keywords: Point cloud · Convolution neural network · Lidar · Depth network

1 Introduction

With the continuous development of laser scanning technology, in recent decades, the means of human perception of the world has evolved from two-dimensional perception based on optical imaging to three-dimensional perception based on laser scanning technology [1]. Three-dimensional laser scanning system has become an important remote sensing sensor after visible light, infrared, microwave, multispectral and hyperspectral. The high resolution point cloud data obtained by three-dimensional laser scanning system has become a research hotspot and difficulty in recent years because of its large amount of data, irregular data and high complexity of scene. Target detection is the basis of scenario analysis and understanding, which provides the underlying objects and analysis basis for high-level scenario understanding. Target detection based on high-resolution three-dimensional point cloud data is a new research topic, which faces great challenges in theory and application. In recent years, with the rise of in-depth learning and the large-scale application of in-depth learning in image detection, speech recognition and text processing, target recognition using in-depth learning method for three-dimensional point cloud data has become one of the important research topics [2].

Z. Xu et al. (Eds.): CSIA 2019, AISC 928, pp. 1416–1420, 2020.
https://doi.org/10.1007/978-3-030-15235-2_197

1.1 Research Background and Significance

Human beings live in a three-dimensional world. It is an obvious and indispensable fact that the best visual system, that is, the human visual system possessed by human beings and beyond which machines can not surpass, is oriented to the three-dimensional world. Psychological research also shows that human visual system uses a lot of depth information based on vision when understanding and recognizing scenes, which gives computer vision researchers an important inspiration: we can study depth image-based visual system directly from depth information. Therefore, the analysis and research of depth image has an important role in promoting the development of computer vision.

In the past decades, ordinary two-dimensional optical image is the most widely used image data. The imaging process of two-dimensional image is a mapping from three-dimensional space to two-dimensional space, which leads to the serious loss of information [3]. However, with the widespread application of computer vision and the improvement of automation, people have higher and higher requirements for computer vision systems. In the fields of computer vision applications requiring three-dimensional scene analysis, such as robot navigation, aircraft navigation, industrial parts detection and capture, and assembly line, three-dimensional depth information is essential for the task completion and performance of the system. Achievement is essential [4].

1.2 Research Status of Convolution Neural Network

In recent years, with the rapid development of laser sensor technology, the acquisition of depth image data containing depth information has become possible, and computer vision system based on distance information has also attracted people's attention. The depth imaging sensor is used to measure the three-dimensional coordinate data of the scene surface. Its output is called depth data, and these depth data are represented as depth images.

With the rapid development of three-dimensional imaging technology, a large number of low-cost miniaturized three-dimensional sensors have emerged in recent years and gradually equipped in mobile devices, such as Kinect, Realsense and Google Tango [5]. The three-dimensional sensor can capture the three-dimensional information of the scene well, and make the intelligent device better perceive and understand the surrounding environment. It has broad application prospects in robots, AR/VR, human-computer interaction, remote sensing mapping and other fields.

2 3-D Object Recognition from Point Cloud Cell Image

In the whole process of image recognition, feature extraction plays an important role, which largely determines the recognition performance. For the target to be classified and recognized, if the extracted features have strong descriptive ability and distinguishing ability, then a simple linear classifier can be used to get a good recognition rate. On the contrary, if the quality of extracted features is not good, the recognition effect will be poor. The features commonly used in image recognition include boundary feature, shape feature, color feature, scale-invariant feature transform (SIFT), direction gradient histogram feature (HOG) and combination feature. In recognition of different targets, a lot of experiments are needed to select artificial features. Although traditional image recognition methods have made some achievements, there are many subjective factors in extracting features by artificial design. Moreover, HOG, SIFT and other features are mostly local shallow features, which can not adequately represent the essential attributes of the target. Therefore, in the face of massive data or complex environment, traditional image recognition methods are powerless [6].

With the advent of the era of big data and the rapid improvement of computer computing ability, image recognition technology based on deep learning has gradually been realized, and has become the focus and hot spot of research in the field of artificial intelligence [7]. Deep neural network has more layers than shallow network, so it has more powerful generalization ability. Deep neural network simulates human nervous system to analyze samples. It can learn deeper feature representation of samples, and deep neural network can express complex functions in a simpler way. Compared with traditional image recognition methods, image recognition methods based on depth learning do not need to design features manually. It can automatically learn and summarize Abstract features. These abstract features are difficult for human beings to understand, but the use of these abstract features can achieve high recognition accuracy. At present, image recognition system based on depth learning has reached or even surpassed the recognition ability of human beings in terms of accuracy. It is believed that in the near future, computers will help people deal with the work related to image recognition. The data set is scanned by the hdl-64e VELODYNE lidar in Sydney and Australia. It contains a variety of common urban roads, vehicles, pedestrians, signs and trees. There are 631 objects in total, divided into 26 categories as shown in Fig. 1.

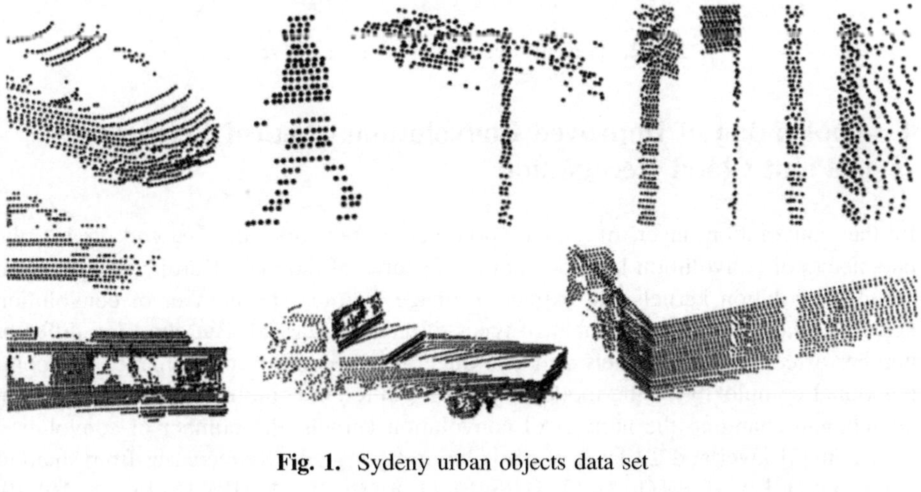

Fig. 1. Sydeny urban objects data set

3 Convolutional Neural Network for Recognition of Point Clouds

When the design of neural network model is complex and the number of samples is relatively small, the network will appear over-fitting phenomenon. Overfitting means that with the increase of training times, the recognition rate of the network on the training set increases, even up to 100%, but the recognition rate on the test set is very low [8]. The main reason for this phenomenon is that the existing data sets can not meet the requirements of network training, which leads to the over-fitting of training set, but the data of test set can not be well fitted. As shown in Fig. 2.

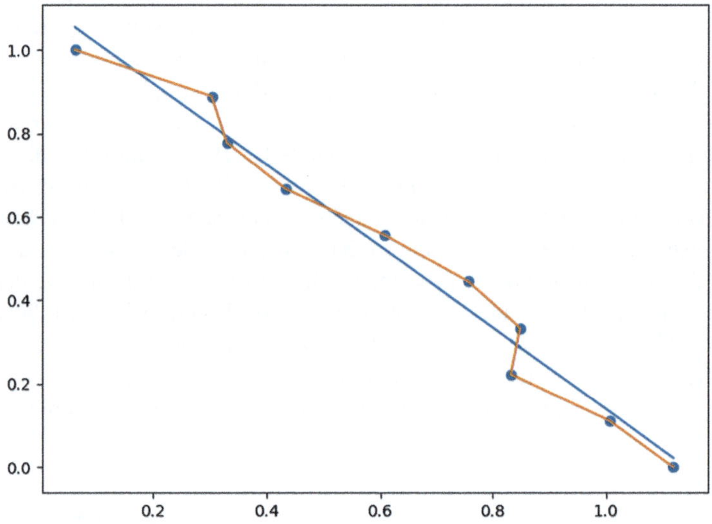

Fig. 2. Prevents over-fitting after regularization

4 Application of Improved Convolutional Neural Network in Point Cloud Recognition

In the convolution layer of convolution neural network, the network trains the parameters of convolution kernels from the features of the main learning image. Each set of convolution kernels can extract an image feature. The number of convolution kernels is the same as the number of types of features learned. But choosing different number of convolution kernels will also affect the recognition performance and computational complexity of the model. By setting different combinations of convolution kernels and changing the number of convolution kernels, the number of convolution kernels in C1 layer and C3 layer of convolution layer gradually increases from small to large, and {C1, C3} = {(1, 2), (2, 4), (3, 6), (4, 8), (5, 10), (6, 12), (7, 14), (8, 16), (9, 18), (10, 20)}, a total of 10 groups of models are obtained, and the recognition results are shown in Table 1.

Table 1. Contrastive experiments on the number of convolution kernels

(C1, C3)	Accuracy rate (%)	(C1, C3)	Accuracy rate (%)
(1, 2)	60.47	(6, 12)	81.5
(2, 4)	60.35	(7, 14)	81.75
(3, 6)	70.53	(8, 16)	82.5
(4, 8)	77.76	(9, 18)	82.4
(5, 10)	78.89	(10, 20)	81

5 Conclusion

The generation of point cloud data is introduced, and the network model of point cloud cell image and the network model of point cloud grid image are built. In this chapter, tensorflow is used to build these two networks, and the effect of these parameters on accuracy is observed by changing the parameters of the network. Finally, by comparing the recognition rates of the two networks, it is concluded that the convolution neural network proposed in this paper has a higher accuracy in the recognition of point cloud cells.

References

1. Qi CR, Su H, Niessner M, Dai A, Yan M, Guibas LJ (2016) Volumetric and multi-view CNNs for object classification on 3D data, arXiv
2. Gupta S, Girshick R, Arbelaez P, Malik J (2014) Learning rich features from RGB-D images for object detection and segmentation. In: ECCV
3. Hinton GE, Osindero S, Teh Y-W (2006) A fast learning algorithm for deep belief nets. Neural Comput 18(7):1527–1554
4. Jia Z, Chang Y-J, Chen T (2009) Active view selection for object and pose recognition. In: ICCV workshops
5. Qi CR, Su H, Mo K, Guibas LJ (2016) PointNet: deep learning on point sets for 3D classification and segmentation. arXiv preprint arXiv:1612.00593
6. Su H, Maji S, Kalogerakis E, Learned-Miller EG (2015) Multi-view convolutional neural networks for 3D shape recognition. In: Proceedings ICCV (to appear)
7. Vinyals O, Bengio S, Kudlur M (2015) Order matters: sequence to sequence for sets. arXiv preprint arXiv:1511.06391
8. Macrini D, Shokoufandeh A, Dickinson S, Siddiqi K, Zucker S (2002) View-based 3-D object recognition using shock graphs. In: Proceedings of ICPR, vol 3
9. Shi B, Bai S, Zhou Z, Bai X (2015) DeepPano: deep panoramic representation for 3-D shape recognition. IEEE Sig Process Lett 22:2339–2343
10. Sinha A, Bai J, Ramani K (2016) Deep learning 3D shape surfaces using geometry images. In: ECCV, pp 223–240

Information Management System and Supply Chain Management (SCM)

Yefu Tang(✉) and Yanju Liu

Guangdong University of Science and Technology,
Dongguan 523083, Guangdong, China
76092313@qq.com

Abstract. This paper expounds the concepts of information management system, supply chain and supply chain management (SCM), analyses the information problems in SCM and the relationship between SCM and information management system, puts forward the logical structure model of information management system in SCM for data and information processing, and clarifies that it has certain positive significance for enterprises to build a scientific and efficient supply chain management information system.

Keywords: Supply chain management (SCM) · Information management system · Decision support system · Information flow

1 Introduction

Modern information technology has laid the foundation of the information age, promoted the arrival of the information age, and the information age has promoted the development and innovation of supply chain management. Enterprises can use modern information technology (IT) to improve the weak links in the supply chain, improve its operational efficiency, reduce operating costs, and establish rapid response strategies, so as to better face the diversity of consumers. Individualized demand, as well as unpredictable and competitive market environment, enables enterprises to maintain competitiveness for a long time. In order to gain a dominant position in such a competitive environment, enterprises must change the traditional information system, adopt modern advanced information technology, optimize and reorganize the supply chain, so that information can be transmitted and shared quickly and accurately among all nodes of the supply chain, so as to respond to customer needs more quickly and serve customers better. Therefore, effective supply chain management can not be separated from the reliable support of information management system. This paper will study and explore supply chain management from the perspective of information system.

2 Concepts of Information Management System, Supply Chain and Supply Chain Management

Information management system is a pure software business management system based on data acquisition and transmission technology [1], computer network technology, database construction, multimedia technology, business needs and so on. It realizes

Z. Xu et al. (Eds.): CSIA 2019, AISC 928, pp. 1421–1426, 2020.
https://doi.org/10.1007/978-3-030-15235-2_198

data and information sharing among business systems, and builds query and adjustment on this basis. Degree or assistant decision-making system.

So far, there is no uniform definition of supply chain and supply chain management in the world. China's current national standard "Logistics Terminology" defines supply chain as "supply chain, that is, the network chain structure formed by the upstream and downstream enterprises involved in providing products or services to end-user activities in the process of production and circulation". Supply chain emphasizes an integrated management idea and method. It pays attention to the cooperation between enterprises with supply-demand relationship, organically combines all links of supply chain, and achieves the highest overall efficiency of supply chain. In Logistics Terminology, supply chain management is defined as "supply chain management, that is, to plan, organize, coordinate and control the business flow, logistics, information flow and capital flow in the supply chain by using computer network technology".

3 Information Problems in SCM

Information is one of the main factors to strengthen the competitiveness of supply chain [2]. The benefits of supply chain management are based on coordination among members, and the basis of coordination depends on information sharing. Due to the insufficient information sharing and the backward application of information technology, it is difficult to coordinate or even divorce the business activities between the upstream and downstream enterprises in the supply chain, which makes the business activities become a blurred black hole, resulting in high cost and poor controllability, which seriously restricts the development of enterprises in China. At present, there are three problems in supply chain management:

First, members of the supply chain are reluctant to share their business information with others.

Secondly, information processing methods are still mainly manual and semi-automated. Information systems divided according to their functions act as isolated islands, such as customer service system, accounting and settlement system, manufacturer and distribution system. Through their independent systems, they only pay attention to some operation activities of their own functional departments, thus affecting the sharing of information. As a result, the members of the supply chain can't get the information in time and accurately, which increases the uncertainty of the enterprise plan. Therefore, the members of each link have to adopt the way of buffer inventory or safe inventory to adapt to this uncertainty, which reduces the operation efficiency and increases the inventory cost.

Thirdly, because the availability and timeliness of information are affected, enterprises are slow to respond to market demand. The change of client demand in supply chain moves up the supply chain step by step. At the same time, it can not communicate with potential customer demand in time. It often takes a long time to feed back to manufacturer and upstream supplier, so it is impossible to supply products to the market faster.

Therefore, we must speed up the pace of enterprise information construction, provide a good information management system platform for Chinese enterprises to implement supply chain management, make the enterprise competitive strategy innovate constantly, and improve the competitiveness of enterprises.

4 The Relationship Between Supply Chain Management and Information Management

4.1 Processing Flow of Information Management System in Supply Chain Management (Fig. 1)

At present, information management system includes five kinds of information systems, including artificial intelligence system (AIS), management information system (MIS), decision support system (DSS), knowledge management system (KBS), office automation system (OA). Among them, MIS is used in specific functional departments and functional information system (FIS) is produced. It also includes manager information system, marketing information system and sales information system. Financial information system, human resources information system, information resources system, manufacturing information system, etc. Manager information system is a tool for managers to carry out daily management, it is the management of other functional information systems [3].

Management Information System (MIS) is a comprehensive system consisting of computer technology, network communication technology, information processing technology, management science, economics, etc. It supports the operation and management of enterprises [4]. Among them, it supports the focus of supply chain management, because the object of supply chain management - people, finance, goods and the process of supply chain management - production, supply and marketing, all involve various departments inside and outside the enterprise, such as raw material warehouse, production workshop, finished product warehouse, transportation department, sales department, finance department and so on, and outside the enterprise, including raw material suppliers, distributors and associations. Partners, customers, etc. It can be imagined that if the enterprise supply chain does not have the support of information system, then the supply chain management can not be carried out. Information system not only manages the internal enterprise, but also manages the inter-enterprise. It realizes the management of the supply chain through the management of "information flow" inside and outside the enterprise.

In supply chain management, including supply chain process operation, supply chain relationship, supply chain logistics management and so on, and decision support system (DSS) plays an important role in it. It obtains various reports and mathematical models from MIS, generates decision information, and transmits these information to solve the special problems and semi-structural problems of enterprises. Supply chain management system is a dynamic and complex system. To solve the problem of non-linearity in supply chain, we ultimately have to rely on knowledge-based system (KBS). At present, people are continually carrying out research in this area. It is expected that people will combine information technology with biological science, which will inject new vitality into future enterprise management and enable people to use intelligent means to solve it. Complex business problems are possible.

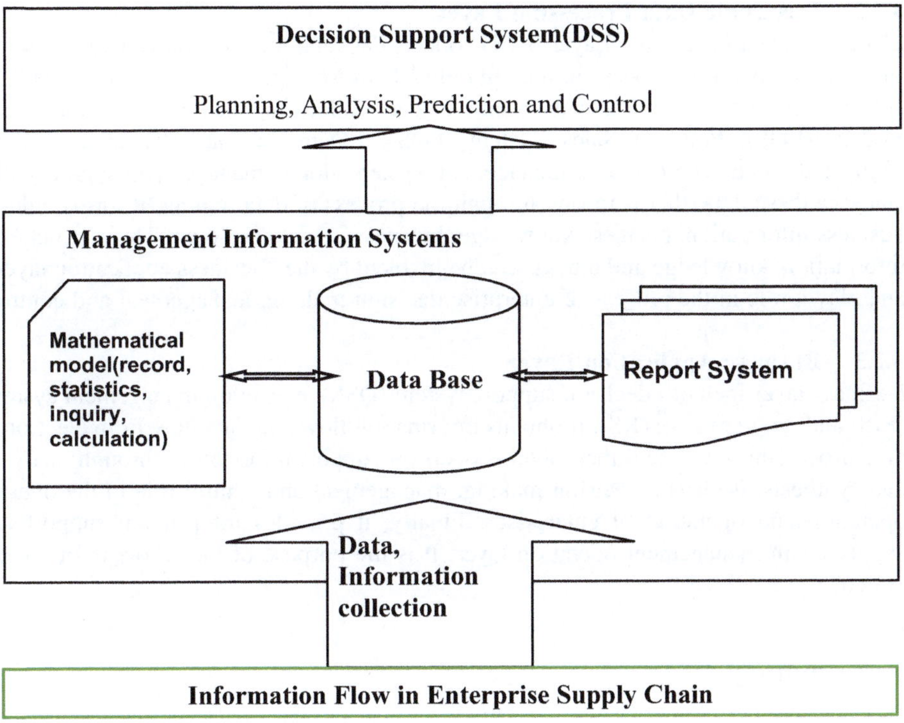

Fig. 1. Processing flow of information management system in supply chain management

4.2 Analysis of Logical Structure Model of MIS for Data and Information Processing in SCM

The logical structure model of data and information processing in enterprise supply chain management information system that it is composed of supply chain management operation layer, electronic data processing layer and business application layer. It is only a logical conceptual hierarchical division and does not exist entity. It only serves as a reference model in the process of building enterprise supply chain management information system.

4.2.1 Supply Chain Management Operational Level

At this level, supply chain management carries out substantive operations, including physical management, warehousing management, transportation management, order management, distribution management, manufacturing management, financial management, electronic procurement management, relationship management and so on. These specific operations are based on the "business decision-making, management, control" information in the "business application layer".

4.2.2 Electronic Data Processing Layer

Electronic Data Processing Layer (EDI) collects data and information generated by the substantive operation process in the "Supply Chain Management Operating Layer". It collects data through various subsystems of data collection, such as Electronic Order System (EOS), Point of Sales System (POS), Electronic Data Exchange System (EDI) and so on. The database management system stores, manages and synthetically analyses these data, that is to say, through the process of data mining, it forms unique business information, business knowledge, business model and so on. These structured information, knowledge and models can be invoked by the "business application layer" and play a role in the process of enterprise decision-making, management and control.

4.2.3 Business Application Layer

Business layer includes decision support system (DSS), execution management system (EIS) and report system (RS). It obtains information flow and data flow from electronic data processing layer, and then obtains decision support information through analysis and synthesis. It plays a decision-making, management and control role in the overall operation and operation of enterprises. Finally, it provides information support for supply chain management operation layer. It is the purpose of the whole information system.

5 Summary

The extensive application of modern information technology can effectively reduce the management costs of enterprises, help to coordinate and control the supply chain nodes among enterprises. Enterprises integrate the construction of information management system with supply chain management, and build a scientific and efficient enterprise supply chain management information system, so as to improve the efficiency of supply chain management activities and enhance the operational decision-making ability of the whole supply chain. The processing flow of information management system in supply chain management and the logical model structure of data and information processing proposed in this paper have a certain guiding role for enterprises to build a scientific and efficient supply chain management information system, and have a certain positive significance for Chinese enterprises to carry out effective supply chain management in the environment of economic globalization and improve their competitiveness.

References

1. Ma S, Lin Y (2006) Supply Chain Management, 2nd edn. Higher Education Press, Beijing
2. Shi X, Li Y (2006) Principle and Application of Supply Chain Management. Tsinghua University Press, Beijing
3. Zhang Y (2002) Application of information technology in supply chain management. Enterp Informatiz (4):4–5
4. Mou X, Xiong Z (2006) Discussion on the information transmission and management mode in the supply chain of real-time response. Sci Technol Progress Countermeas (7):173–175

5. Xiong B, Miu J, Xing F Effective Supply Chain Management Information System. http://www.chinachunyun.com
6. Mashuahua, Ming G (2009) Supply chain cooperative technology and management principle and application based on supply driven. Huazhong University of Science and Technology, Wuhan. Publishing House, pp 32–46
7. Teng R (2009) Research on information sharing and coordination based on supply Chain. China Collect Econ (7):64–65
8. Tian Z (2006) Information sharing and strategy in supply chain management. Contemp Manag (5):157–158
9. Victor M-S (2013) Big Data Age. Zhejiang People's Publishing House
10. Wang Y, Huawei (2012) Integrated supply chain change. Petrol Petrochem Mater Purchase (8):31–34

Development of Hadoop Massive Data Migration System

Ming Zheng(✉) and Mugui Zhuo

Guangxi Colleges and Universities Key Laboratory of Professional Software Technology, Wuzhou University, Wuzhou, China
370505375@qq.com

Abstract. At present, the amount of data generated by high-energy physics experiments is increasing. When Hadoop, a large data processing platform, is used to process high-energy physics data, it is faced with the actual needs of data migration. However, the existing migration tools do not support data transmission between HDFS and other file systems, and their performance has obvious defects. Starting from the requirements of synchronization and archiving of high energy physical data, this paper designs and implements a universal mass data migration system. By extending the access mode of HDFS data, MapReduce is used to migrate data directly between HDFS data nodes and other storage systems/media. In addition, the system designs and implements the dynamic priority scheduling model, and evaluates and chooses the dynamic priority of multi-task. The system has been applied to data migration in large high altitude air shower Observatory (LHAASO) cosmic ray and other physical experiments. The actual operation results show that the system has good performance and can meet the data migration requirements of various experiments.

Keywords: Data migration · GridFTP · Dynamic priority scheduling · Multi-attribute decision making · Hadoop

1 Introduction

In the field of high energy physics, the storage and processing of massive experimental data, global sharing and long-term preservation need the support of advanced computing environment. The traditional distributed computing mode of storage and calculation separation can not meet the needs of fast data processing and analysis [1]. In order to solve this problem, researchers propose a technical scheme for data processing and analysis of high-energy physics based on large data processing framework, which changes from traditional computing cluster to data-centric Hadoop [2] computing cluster.

Data generated by high energy physics experiments are transmitted to distributed file systems and tape libraries through an online acquisition system. When turning to Hadoop for mass data processing, Hadoop's data localization requires that data be transferred to Hadoop Distributed File System (HDFS) [3] online, while data archiving and backup also need to migrate data out of HDFS. So data migration is of great significance to improve Hadoop ecosystem. At present, there is no special tool for data migration between HDFS and other storage systems/media, so this paper designs and

Z. Xu et al. (Eds.): CSIA 2019, AISC 928, pp. 1427–1431, 2020.
https://doi.org/10.1007/978-3-030-15235-2_199

implements a massive data migration system in order to achieve efficient and parallel data migration between HDFS and different storage systems/media. A scheduling model based on dynamic priority index is proposed. Tasks with the highest priority index are selected and submitted to Hadoop cluster. The original data access mode of HDFS is extended. Data migration between the local file system of HDFS data node and other file systems is realized by parallel tasks of MapReduce [4]. Finally, the migration performance of the massive data migration system is analyzed through the actual test task of the system.

In terms of Hadoop data migration, Hadoop itself provides two data migration tools, DistCP and Sqoop [5], for specific scenarios. GridFTP [6] is an efficient, secure and robust communication protocol provided by Globus project [7], which is improved on the basis of FTP protocol to adapt to large data transmission. GridFTP protocol supports different levels of security authentication and integrity checking, supports data transmission controlled by third parties, and facilitates the control of large data transmission process in distributed systems. In data transmission, the GridFTP protocol supports parallel transmission and strip transmission, effectively improves the speed and bandwidth of data transmission, allows automatic negotiation of buffer size, and makes data transmission fast and efficient. GridFTP also supports data retransmitting and partial transmission, and the transmission process is stable and reliable. The superior transmission performance of GridFTP protocol has been widely recognized in the field of high energy physics. It has been widely used in large Hadron Collider and other scientific projects. It is closely integrated with the application scenarios of Hadoop Massive Data Migration System [8] in this paper.

2 Method

Based on the above analysis, in order to improve the application of Hadoop in the field of high-energy physics, this paper designs and implements Hadoop massive data migration system based on the research of existing high-energy physics data processing methods, which is used for data migration between HDFS and other storage systems/media. As the support layer of Hadoop computing cluster in the field of high energy physics, this system effectively manages the data interaction inside and outside Hadoop ecology. Its core design ideas are: (1) After pre-processing the migration tasks submitted by users, the migration tasks are measured by dynamic priority scheduling model based on multi-attribute decision-making from multiple perspectives, and the tasks with the highest priority index are selected from the queue and submitted to the service layer (2) The service layer determines the migration mode of data according to the pre-processing results of the migration tasks, and completes the migration service workers accordingly. (3) Using GridFTP protocol, the migration layer can migrate data efficiently and concurrently between HDFS data nodes and target system.

Data migration can be divided into two migration modes [9]: import and export, which correspond to the migration direction of data. The front-end of the system provides two kinds of services: Periodic Migration and instant migration of data to meet the needs of users in terms of Periodic Migration of specific data sets, sudden batch data migration, data synchronization, archiving and backup. Task management preprocesses many parameters of migration task, constructs evaluation index of migration task, and determines the task with the highest priority index and corresponding migration mode by scheduling strategy within migration system. The service layer serves the target task and completes the migration preparation. The migration layer calls the GridFTP protocol in the migration sub-task to migrate data between HDFS data nodes and other systems. The task monitoring layer monitors the migration process in real time and provides feedback to users.

In this paper, a dynamic priority task scheduling model is proposed to evaluate and select the dynamic priority of multiple tasks according to some decision-making principles. For priority ranking of migrating tasks, the urgency P, waiting time WT and attractiveness JA of migrating tasks are selected as evaluation indicators of task priority. Among them, task urgency P represents the migration urgency of migration tasks, reflecting the urgency and importance of migration tasks; waiting time WT is to avoid the situation that migration tasks with advanced entry into the queue are not executed for a long time, setting waiting time for each task, and taking the order of tasks entering the queue as a reference to assess the priority of migration tasks; migration task attractiveness JA Referring to the strategy of the Shortest Job Priority Scheduling algorithm [10], it shows that the tasks expected to be completed earliest have the weakest and the strongest attraction to resources.

Set the task set in the task queue as $T = \{T_1, T_2, \ldots, T_n\}$. The goal of dynamic priority scheduling is to select the task with the highest priority index in T to execute. The evaluation index set $A = \{a_1, a_2, a_3\}$ corresponds to the urgency, attractiveness and waiting time of migration tasks respectively. For any task T_i, there are three evaluation indicators from different angles, namely T_i evaluation indicators (a_{i1}, a_{i2}, a_{i3}). According to the evaluation index set A, the evaluation indexes of each task in the migration task set T are collected, and the following initial decision matrix is formed:

$$A = \begin{pmatrix} a_{11} & \cdots & a_{1n} \\ \vdots & \ddots & \vdots \\ a_{m1} & \cdots & a_{mn} \end{pmatrix} \quad (1)$$

The function of migration service layer is to migrate service in MapReduce sub-task program according to different migration modes before actual migration of data. The work includes batch data set splitting, data logical location mapping and HDFS actual storage location mapping. In order to provide more high-performance transmission services, the migration service layer extends the original data access mode of HDFS, so that the data migration process can be carried out directly between the local file system of the HDFS data node and other file systems.

3 Experiment

In order to verify the data migration performance of the system, the experimental data from the high-energy physical storage cluster are selected and tested in the actual Hadoop data processing environment of high-energy physics. The test contents include the system data migration performance and the performance of dynamic priority scheduling model under multi-migration tasks.

In order to test the migration performance of Hadoop mass data migration system, firstly, the migration performance of DistCP is used as a comparison group, and different size data sets are used to test. Hadoop is selected to test the utilization rate of cluster network resources as an evaluation index. The comparison results are shown in Fig. 1.

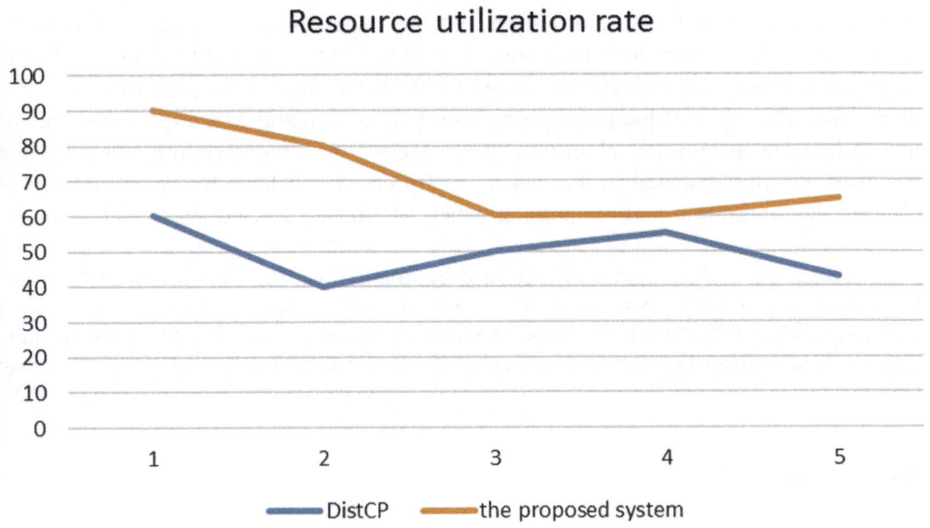

Fig. 1. Comparison of network resource utilization rate

Performance comparison test compares dynamic priority task scheduling model with first-in-first-out scheduling algorithm and short-job priority scheduling algorithm. When testing the scheduling performance of each algorithm model, each algorithm has 20 rounds of testing, each round submitting 40 migration tasks to the migration system, each task submitting time interval is 20 s, the total size of migration files is 2.1T. When testing the dynamic priority scheduling model, according to the above 2.1.1 task scheduling model based on dynamic priority, assuming that the importance ranking of migration task evaluation indicators is: urgency > attractiveness > waiting time, the proportion scaling method is selected to construct the judgment matrix and determine the importance weights of the three indicators: urgency, attractiveness and waiting time. Using the dynamic priority scheduling model proposed in this paper, under the condition of limited system resources, better system performance can be achieved by considering the attributes of migrating tasks and arranging the execution order of tasks reasonably.

4 Conclusion

Aiming at the data migration problem of Hadoop in high energy physics applications, this paper designs and implements a massive data migration system based on the actual needs. By using MapReduce parallel tasks and GridFTP protocol, data can be migrated directly between HDFS data nodes and other storage systems/media to further improve the application ecology of Hadoop in the field of high energy physics data processing. From the test and actual operation results of high-energy physical data migration, the massive data migration system in this paper performs well in data migration. The dynamic priority scheduling model proposed in this paper introduces multi-attribute decision-making theory, uses multi-index and multi-angle to evaluate the dynamic priority of migration tasks, and screens out the most priority migration tasks to be submitted to the system for processing. The algorithm is in multi-migration. In the application scenario of task-shifting, it shows great advantages. Its performance is 7% higher than that of short job priority scheduling algorithm and 11% higher than that of first-in-first-out scheduling algorithm. The Hadoop massive data migration system designed and implemented in this paper is of great significance to the application of Hadoop data migration and the popularization of Hadoop computing model.

Acknowledgments. This work was supported by grants from The National Natural Science Foundation of China (No. 61862056), the Guangxi Natural Science Foundation (No. 2017GXNSFAA198148) foundation of Wuzhou University (No. 2017B001) and Guangxi Colleges and Universities Key Laboratory of Professional Software Technology, Wuzhou University.

References

1. Sahadat MN, Alreja A, Mikail N et al (2018) Comparing the use of single versus multiple combined abilities in conducting complex computer tasks hands-free. IEEE Trans Neural Syst Rehabil Eng 26(9):1868–1877
2. Glushkova D, Jovanovic P, Abello A (2019) Mapreduce performance model for Hadoop 2.x. Inf Syst 79:32–43
3. Lin CY, Lin YC (2017) An overall approach to achieve load balancing for hadoop distributed file system. Int J Web Grid Serv 13(4):448–466
4. Khalil Y, Alshayeji M, Ahmad I (2019) Distributed whale optimization algorithm based on MapReduce. Concur Comput-Pract Exp 31(1):e4872
5. Zhang H, Huang T, Lv ZH et al (2018) MCRS: a course recommendation system for MOOCs. Multimedia Tools Appl 77(6):7051–7069
6. Rashti MJ, Sabin G, Kettimuthu R (2016) Long-haul secure data transfer using hardware-assisted GridFTP. Future Gener Comput Syst-Int J Escience 56:265–276
7. Suryanarayana SM, Kotaleski JH, Grillner S et al (2019) Roles for globus pallidus externa revealed in a computational model of action selection in the basal ganglia. Neural Netw 109:113–136
8. Nunez-Gaona MA, Marcelin-Jimenez R, Gutierrez-Martinez J et al (2018) A dependable massive storage service for medical imaging. J Digit Imaging 31(5):628–639
9. Cao Z, Zheng XY, Liu YS et al (2018) Exploring the changing patterns of China's migration and its determinants using census data of 2000 and 2010. Habitat Int 82:72–82
10. Komarasamy D, Muthuswamy V (2018) Priority scheduling with consolidation based backfilling algorithm in cloud. World Wide Web-Internet Web Inf Syst 21(6):1453–1471

Talent-Training Mode Exploration in Software Major Between Universities and Enterprises Based on the Perspective of Big Data

Xiaoming Yang(✉)

College of Engineering and Technology, Xi'an Fanyi University, Xi'an 710105, China
26254588@qq.com

Abstract. This paper puts forward the existing problems and correction proposal for software major in the big data era, and gives the feasible reform program for talent cultivation of between universities and enterprises.

Keywords: Big data · Construction between universities and enterprises · Talent-training

1 Introduction

Big data has penetrated into every industry and business area. In the outline of the 13th Five-Year Plan of the State, it is clearly stated that "the implementation of the national big data strategy and the promotion of openly sharing of data resources" should be carried out. In June 2015, the State Council promulgated "Several Opinions on Strengthening the Service and Supervision of Market Subjects by Using Big Data". On August 19, the Executive Meeting of the State Council reviewed and approved the "Platform for Action on Promoting Big Data Development". On September 5, the State Council formally issued the "Platform for Action on Promoting Big Data Development". At the same time, the General Office of the State Council issued No. 36 National file named "Opinions on Deepening the Reform of Innovation and Entrepreneurship Education in Colleges and Universities." These all mean that big data has formally become the national strategy. Deepening the integration of industry and education, enterprises-university cooperation, collaborative education, pooling enterprise resources to support comprehensive reform and innovation and entrepreneurship education in Colleges and universities has become a new mode for enterprises and colleges to jointly cultivate talents [9, 10].

Software industry, as the fastest and most active industry in IT field, promotes the demand for a large number of software talents with its rapid development. Software development talents have been in short supply. At present, there are software majors in colleges and universities. Every year, plenty of computer software talents can feed the society. However, nowadays, the traditional training mode and courses of software majors can not meet the needs of society and enterprises. Combining with the characteristics of big data era, building curriculum system with enterprises, assisting universities in curriculum construction and improving teaching quality, and according to

Z. Xu et al. (Eds.): CSIA 2019, AISC 928, pp. 1432–1436, 2020.
https://doi.org/10.1007/978-3-030-15235-2_200

the development trend of computer software industry, formulating curriculum content that meets the needs of professionals, as well as exploring new talent training mode and reforming curriculum settings are of great significance for promoting the sustainable development of software major [1, 3].

2 The Impact of Universities-Enterprise Cooperation on Software Professional Talents Training in the Big Data Era

Under the big data era, computer software major is facing severe opportunities and challenges. With the soaring growth of data volume, the increasing types and quantities of processing data structures, the application of distributed storage and computing, and the enhancement of capability of mobile terminals, the demand for storage technology talents, data processing and analysis mining talents, data development and Application talents should be raised attention to. Therefore, the training of software professionals should be closely integrated with the current market demand, so as to avoid the problem of the disconnection between the training talents and the market needs.

Nowadays, the personnel training mode and curriculum of software technology major have made some adjustments to the practice of emphasizing theory rather than practice, and strengthened the practice. But generally speaking, the pertinence of the curriculum is poor. The technology updating in the frontier of the industry is slow. Most of teachers have no experience in enterprise development. This situation can not adapt to the current development of big data industry for software major. The principles and policies of university-enterprise cooperation of the state have brought excellent opportunities for the training of software professionals. By utilizing the advantages of university-enterprise cooperation, we can find a suitable point between students' employment and social needs. Focusing on the purpose of cultivating applied talents, we should coordinate the relationship between universities and enterprises, and seize the connection between major settings, local industrial sectors, social needs, the goal of talent cultivation and the needs of enterprises. To achieve personnel training specifications and post requirements, deepen curriculum construction and practical teaching construction, highlight the cultivation of students' practice and innovative abilities, it will truly realize "learning for application" and provide software professionals with actual needs for the development of large data industry [7].

3 Training Target of Software Talents from the Perspective of Big Data

Talents training must be student-oriented and aim at adapting to social needs. It is necessary not only to cultivate students' ability to learn knowledge, practice and adapt to society, but also to tap the potential of each student, give full space for students' characteristics, so that each student's ability can be maximized.

3.1 The Goal of Comprehensive Quality

To cultivate all-round development in morality, intelligence, physique and aesthetics, to meet the needs of regional economic and social development, to have good professional ethics, humanistic accomplishment, strong innovative spirit and practical ability, to have a sense of teamwork, to have a strong ability of communication and expression, analysis and understanding, to write professional documents, innovative ability, project management awareness and other comprehensive qualities [4].

3.2 Professional Skill Objectives

To cultivate high-quality technical talents with good basic and programming thinking ability, basic theoretical knowledge of software technology specialty, ability of programming, software testing and application development of mobile Internet and mobile terminal, engaged in software development, software testing and maintenance, mobile Internet and mobile terminal application development in IT industry, enterprises and other related posts [5].

4 Thinking and Countermeasure of Software Professional Training in Xi'an Fanyi University

At present, the compulsory courses offered by software major include program design foundation, data structure and algorithm, software comprehensive training, software testing, software engineering, JAVA programming, database application technology, HTML5 technology, XML language, JAVA EE, UI design and implementation of mobile terminals, Android foundation, etc., We also set up professional practice links. At present, our curriculum is reasonable. However, with the rapid development of big data, we also need to improve and adjust the curriculum. At the same time, we need to break the original curriculum system, optimize and arrange the curriculum content according to the professional and technical abilities required by applied talents, emphasizing on optimizing the curriculum content and setting up practical projects based on the professional abilities required by industry enterprises, and alternating theoretical curriculum learning with enterprise practical training. We should pay attention to the pertinence and practicality of the curriculum system, highlight practical teaching, and the proportion of professional practice is relatively large. We should attach importance to the practical training of students in industrial enterprises, and pay attention to the cultivation of students' innovative spirit and entrepreneurial abilities and practical abilities [8].

5 The Mode of Software Talents Co-constructed Between Universities and Enterprises from the Perspective of Big Data

5.1 Co-construction of Curriculum Resources Between Universities and Enterprises

Combining with the related courses or experimental needs in the colleges and the teaching resources and software & hardware platform provided by Daniel Times Science and Technology Group Co., Ltd., We can develop courseware, experimental projects and real case base for enterprises in order to provide effective teaching resources for computer related professional program design and data structure course teaching.

5.2 One Lesson, Two Ways

The unified teaching plan for the core courses of software major enables students to complete a single task of experimental content to solve the sublimation of medium-sized and complete practical cases, process the teaching content with different methods, and form a complete curriculum system according to the needs of enterprises and industries. The theory class can be put in classroom and practice class in laboratories or enterprises. The theory class is mainly about understanding, and the practice class is mainly about application, which brings students multi-angle cognition and deeper understanding, and achieves in-depth understanding and skill growth of the theory in the application, so as to achieve "understanding first, come into being as the times require" [6].

5.3 Practical Teaching Base Between Universities and Enterprises

Construct a mutually beneficial and win-win benefit-driven mechanism, accurately grasp the common interests of both sides, continue to build and improve the school-enterprise cooperation management platform and institutional mechanism, further carry out the implementation of the "project introduction + practical training" cooperation mode, establish training bases inside and outside schools, solve the problems of inadequate conditions for practical training in schools and students' employment difficulties.

5.4 Fostering Students' Practical and Innovative Abilities Guided by the Needs of Enterprises

Utilizing the advantages of school-enterprise cooperation, we should find a suitable point between students' employment and social needs, coordinate the relationship between universities and enterprises around the purpose of training applied talents, grasp the connection between major setting based on local industry and social needs, talent training objectives and enterprise needs, talent training specifications and post requirements. We need to deepen curriculum construction and practical teaching construction, highlight the cultivation of students' practical and innovative abilities so as to truly realize "learning for application".

6 Conclusion

The arrival of the era of big data has brought profound and tremendous impact on people's way of thinking, and put forward new requirements for the training of software professionals. To cope with these new situations well, we must reform the curriculum, teaching methods, training objectives, training modes and so on, so as to develop practical new talents for society and enterprises.

Acknowledgments. This research was supported by Scientific research team in Xi'an Fanyi University (XFU17KYTDB02).

References

1. Luo L (2017) Comprehensive reform of computer science and technology in the age of big data. Digit Place (in Chinese)
2. Chen X, Zhou L, Cao Y (2017) Exploring the construction of talent training program for applied undergraduate data science and big data technology. Mod Ind Econ Inf Technol (in Chinese)
3. Hao S, Guo Y (2016) Exploration and research on the training model of personnel majoring in information and accounting from the perspective of big data. J Jiangsu Normal Univ (in Chinese)
4. Sun L, Zhao E et al (2016) Research on the reform of mathematics classroom teaching in engineering universities based on the training of applied talents. In: Thirteenth annual conference of Shenyang science (in Chinese)
5. Chen Z, Zhang H, Wang C et al (2015) Research and practice on the training mode of applied talents in computer specialty with the ability of programming and software development as the main part. Comput Educ (in Chinese)
6. Gu X (2016) One lesson, two lessons, three analyses. School-based teaching and research model inquiry. Main line of teaching and research (in Chinese)
7. Li D (2018) Exploring the training model of applied talents in private independent colleges based on school-enterprise cooperation. New Curric Res (in Chinese)
8. Li D (2017) Training mode of software technology professionals in the "Internet+" environment. Economic outlook for Bohai rim (in Chinese)
9. Zou H (2017) The innovative direction of computer science and technological teaching in the era of exploring big data. Wind Sci Technol (in Chinese)
10. Historical opportunities in the era of big data: Industrial revolution and date science. Tsinghua University Press, Beijing (in Chinese)

Analysis of Factors Affecting Power Grid Investment Based on Johansen Cointegration Analysis Theory

Wang Zhang[1], Kaihui Nan[1], Qinggang Yang[1], Jianfeng Zhang[1], Hong Chen[1], and Xinyan Zhang[2](✉)

[1] State Grid Jiangsu Electric Power Co., Ltd. Economic Research Institute, Nanjing 210008, Jiangsu, China
13913926178@163.com, 13809022300@139.com, YGQLYG@163.com, 648594915@qq.com, victory0326@126.com

[2] School of Economics and Management, North China Electric Power University, Beijing 102206, China
1070344204@qq.com

Abstract. The power grid is one of the foundations of national economic construction. Considering the future development trend of power grid and power market, and the important challenges of grid investment decision, this paper mainly studies various factors affecting grid investment from two aspects: internal and external. Therefore, the grid enterprises can accurately grasp the investment ability, make reasonable investment decisions, increase the profit margin, and adapt to the new situation of power development. The ARMA model and Johansen cointegration analysis theory of grid investment are used to analyze the relationship between power grid and various influencing factors, and the relationship between influencing factors and grid investment is obtained. The validity of this relationship is demonstrated by using data from the State Grid Corporation of 2005–2015. It is of great practical significance for grid companies to further understand the factors affecting investment and how to find effective ways to make investment decisions.

Keywords: Investment · Power grid enterprise · Cointegration analysis

1 Introduction

In recent years, China's economy is in a long-term "new normal", industrial electricity consumption is growing less, and the industrial structure has undergone tremendous changes. The secondary industry accounts for less and less GDP, and the tertiary industry is growing. Need to conduct a more in-depth analysis of the factors affecting grid investment [1]. Since the reform and opening up, China's economic construction has made great achievements, and the living conditions of the residents have also been greatly improved. At the same time, the electricity consumption of the whole society is also increasing. The power industry has maintained rapid growth in investment over the past two decades, with an average annual growth rate of 20.4%, of which the power

Z. Xu et al. (Eds.): CSIA 2019, AISC 928, pp. 1437–1442, 2020.
https://doi.org/10.1007/978-3-030-15235-2_201

grid accounts for 45% to 50% of the total investment. The importance of power grid investment is increasingly evident [2].

The power grid is one of the foundations of national economic construction. It is of great significance in supporting industrial production, ensuring the lives of residents and maintaining stable social development. In the process of infrastructure construction, maintenance and maintenance, power grid enterprises will inevitably involve the operation of a large amount of funds. The investment in power grid construction is huge, and the long-term cost recovery and profit cycle will bring greater uncertainty and risk. Therefore, under the conditions of limited market financing, investment efficiency and cost recovery cycle, it is necessary to study and analyze the factors affecting grid investment. Therefore, to improve the economics of power grid construction and operation, to reasonably control costs and expenses, and to achieve sustainable development of enterprises has become one of the important goals of modern power companies.

At present, there are few research literatures on grid investment at home and abroad, mainly focusing on the factors affecting power consumption, factors affecting power demand, and the coordination relationship between power consumption and economic development [3]. Due to the non-stationary nature of economic time series, cointegration theory has become the main method to study the relationship between economy and power [4]. The research on the factors affecting the grid investment is mainly from the financial point of view, studying the impact of a few financial indicators on investment ability, and failing to fully consider the impact of external constraints on the investment capacity of the company's internal management requirements and policies. The analysis of the factors affecting investment is one-sided. At the same time, the operation status of the enterprise itself has not been well considered, and the investment risk of the power grid enterprises has been increased. Therefore, the research on the factors affecting investment ability needs further research.

As the scale of power grid investment continues to expand and the pace of construction continues to accelerate, grasping the law of grid investment and analyzing the influencing factors affecting grid investment construction has become an important issue to be considered in the management of power grid enterprises. At present, during the 13th Five-Year Plan period, China's power grid investment is in the third stage of development (2016–2020), and it is of great practical significance to analyze the influencing factors of power grid investment. This paper will comprehensively analyze various factors affecting grid investment from internal and external aspects, and analyze the relationship between power grid and various influencing factors by using ARMA model of grid investment and Johansen cointegration analysis theory [5]. To grasp the law of investment in power grid development, and to realize the scientific and sustainable development of power grid enterprises on the basis of ensuring the safe and reliable technical conditions of power grids and the grid investment to meet the maximum social benefits.

2 Analysis of Influencing Factors

2.1 Internal Factors

Grid investment belongs to the category of fixed assets investment and has the characteristics of general fixed assets. Fixed asset investment is affected by many factors, including macroeconomic factors such as gross domestic product, inflation, and interest rates [6]. However, due to the inability to store electrical energy, the grid has real-time performance, power usage and transmission are networked, and grid enterprises have the characteristics of natural monopoly and public service. The grid investment has some characteristics that are not available in fixed assets investment in other industries. This paper will analyze the factors affecting grid investment from two aspects: internal factors and external factors. Internal factors are affected by the company's own situation, mainly including operating conditions and management levels. The business status of an enterprise refers to the development status of the sales and service of the products of the enterprise in the commodity market, which can be reflected by financial indicators. The management level is the soft power of the enterprise. The fund raising, use, investment decision making, investment cycle arrangement, personnel distribution and scheduling are all closely related to management. The management level has a positive impact on the investment ability of the enterprise.

2.2 External Factors

External factors mainly include macroeconomic factors, electricity market factors and policy environmental factors. Macroeconomic factors involve a wide range of factors. Generally, two indicators, gross domestic product (GDP) and inflation index (GDP deflator), are selected as factors to measure grid investment. Gross domestic product refers to the value of all the final results of a country's production activities within a certain period of time, and is an important indicator of the comprehensive financial resources of a country or region [7]. The inflation index refers to the currency depreciation caused by the currency in the market exceeding the actual demand under the credit monetary system, accompanied by a comprehensive and sustained rise in the price level.

Electricity market factors are external factors that can have an impact on the production and sales of a product and are closely related to grid marketing activities. The grid can analyze market demand based on these factors, so as to conduct sales analysis and revenue analysis. The changes in the market environment have two sides. It can not only promote the development of enterprises, but also the ribs of enterprises [8]. Therefore, conducting a comprehensive market environment analysis plays an important role in measuring the investment capacity of the power grid.

The policy environmental factors refer to the factors that may affect the investment in power grid enterprises due to the social system, institutional conditions and political culture, relevant industrial policies, legal provisions and national guidance documents [9]. Government behavior affects investment, and corporate investment will be affected by the policies introduced. If the state is strongly supported, enterprises will enjoy certain preferential treatment when investing. If the investment process violates or violates relevant regulations, it may increase the enterprise's Additional investment costs even hinder the normal conduct of investment activities [10].

3 Grid Investment Model

In order to study the relationship between grid investment and various influencing factors, and based on literature comparison research, select gross domestic product (GDP), electricity consumption (ydl), industrial structure (cyjg), line loss rate (xs), reliable power supply. Sex (gdkkx) and profit rate (lrl) as independent variables, corresponding grid investment as dependent variable. Establish the grid investment function equation as follows:

$$Q = f(GDP, ydl, cyjg, xs, gdkkl, lrl) \tag{1}$$

The moments of a certain economic time series, such as its mean, variance and other statistics, generally do not change with time, appearing non-stationary features, but the linear combination of these non-stationary time series can remain stable, that is, there is no certainty Sexual trends or random trends. "Co-integration" has become the main method of analyzing and studying economic law in econometrics. Among them, Johansen cointegration analysis is based on the vector autoregressive (VAR) model to test the regression coefficient for multivariate cointegration analysis. Now Johansen cointegration analysis has been widely used in multivariate cointegration test. Take the micro data of State Grid Corporation from 2005 to 2015 as an example, based on the ARMA model of grid investment:

$$Lndw_t = 7.67 + 1.72(Lndw_{t-1} - 7.67) - 0.78(Lndw_{t-2} - 7.678) \tag{2}$$

Using the Johansen cointegration test, it is assumed in the test form that the cointegration contains trend and Intercept terms, as shown in the following table.

Table 1. Johansen test - maximum eigenvalue.

Characteristic root	Trace statistics	5% confidence interval	P value	Null hypothesis
0.94	55.18	47.21	0.94	None
0.90	26.81	26.62	0.27	At most 1
0.39	4.88	15.44	0.23	At most 2
0.0003	0.003	3.75	0.28	At most 3

It is known from Table 1 that the maximum eigenvalue test indicates that the model has a cointegration vector at the % confidence level. According to the cointegration analysis, the cointegration equations after the normalization coefficients are extracted are shown in Table 2:

Table 2. Standardization cointegration coefficient.

Lndw	GDP	Lnydl	Lncyjg	C
1.00	−8.00	11.75	2.92	−28.98

The equation for long-term cointegration can be obtained from Table 2 as:

$$Lndw = 28.98 + 8.00LnGDP - 11.75Lnydl - 2.92Lncyjg \tag{3}$$

The above co-integration results show that there is a long-term equilibrium relationship between grid investment and electricity consumption, GDP, and industrial structure between 2005 and 2015. The elasticity of power grid investment for electricity consumption, gross domestic product, and industrial structure was 11.75, 8.00, and 2.92, respectively. Explain that under the premise of other influencing factors, when GDP increases (decreases) by 1%, grid investment increases (decreases) by 8.00%; when electricity consumption increases (decreases) by 1%, grid investment increases (decreases) by 11.75. When the industrial structure increases (decreases) by 1%, grid investment increases (decreases) by 2.92%. The sum of the electricity consumption, GDP and industrial structure is 6.6. When all three increase, 1%, and grid investment increases by 6.6%.

Based on the above cointegration relationship, the raw data of the explanatory variables are brought in, and the predicted value of the grid investment is obtained, as shown in Fig. 1. It can be seen that the error between the predicted value and the actual value fluctuates within ±5%, and the fitting effect is better.

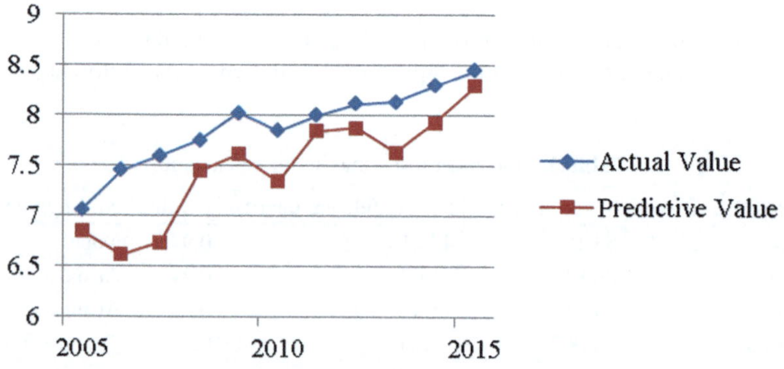

Fig. 1. The comparison chart of actual values and predicted values

4 Conclusion

This paper introduces the background of factors affecting grid investment, the status quo of research at home and abroad, and the factors affecting grid investment. The ARMA model of grid investment and Johansen cointegration analysis theory are used to analyze the relationship between China's power grid investment and its influencing factors. The grid investment relationship equation of gross domestic product (GDP), electricity consumption (ydl), industrial structure (cyjg), line loss rate (xs), power supply reliability (gdkkx) and profit rate (lrl) as independent variables. The data test proves that the relationship fits well.

Acknowledgments. This research was one of the results of the science and technology project of State Grid Jiangsu Electric Power Co. ltd. Economic Research Institute called "Evaluation and Analysis of Differential Sensitive Factors in the Whole Process of Power Grid Project Investment".

References

1. Deng G (2015) Research on long-term and dynamic relationship of factors affecting grid investment based on time series analysis. Zhejiang University (in Chinese)
2. Xu X (2017) Research on investment decision-making of complex grid optimization based on power demand and investment capacity. North China Electric Power University, Beijing (in Chinese)
3. Ji L, Yang L, Fei G (2016) Analysis and forecast of factors affecting power grid engineering investment. China Power Enterp Manag (in Chinese)
4. Cheng Y, Zhang Z (2006) Co-integration modeling analysis of sales price and electricity demand. In: Proceedings of the CSEE (in Chinese)
5. Zhao H, Yang W, Li C (2011) Predictive research on grid investment demand based on cointegration theory and error correction model. Electric Netw Technol (in Chinese)
6. Cui H, Wang W (2010) Research on China's energy-economy-environment (3E) system based on VAR model. J Beijing Inst Technol (in Chinese)
7. Yuan J, Ding W, Hu Z (2006) Cointegration and volatility analysis of power consumption and China's economic development. Power Syst Technol (in Chinese)
8. Zhang X, Niu Y, Zhao X (2008) Model of coordination relationship in China's power consumption. In: Proceedings of the CSEE (in Chinese)
9. Wang C, Liu C, Zhou J (2012) Analysis of the impact of power grid investment on the operating efficiency of power grid enterprises. China High-tech Enterp (in Chinese)
10. Wang S, Hu J (2009) Trend cycle decomposition of China's GDP and the persistence effect of random impact. Econ Res (in Chinese)

Direct Torque Control System of Electric Vehicle Based on Torque Hysteresis Adjustment

Taihua Jia(✉)

Department of Mechanical and Electrical Engineering,
Guangdong University of Science and Technology, Dongguan 523083, China
jipbqd@yeah.net

Abstract. By analyzing and comparing the advantages and disadvantages of all kinds of motor drive control strategy, and considering the special requirements of electric motor drive system of electric vehicle, direct torque control method is chosen as the control strategy of motor driven in this paper. Based on the modeling, the principle of direct torque control strategy is explained, and a torque hysteresis regulator is designed. The simulation results show that when the motor speed is very low, the calculation error is large, causing the magnetic chain track to become more serious. With the increase of speed, the distortion of flux linkage will decrease gradually.

Keywords: Electric motor · Direct torque control · Electric vehicle · Torque hysteresis regulation

1 Introduction

With the rapid development of economy, more and more fuel vehicles have entered people's daily life. At present, the two major problems facing the world are environmental pollution and energy depletion [1, 2]. At the same time, because of the rapid development of motor drive control technology, modern industry is more easy to develop electric vehicles with no pollution, simple structure and low operating cost [3].

An electric vehicle is a vehicle driven by a vehicle powered by an electric vehicle, driven by the driving motor of an electric vehicle, and in accordance with the requirements of the traffic regulations [4, 5]. The scientific research institutions of many developed countries, electric power companies and vehicle companies have introduced the concept cars of electric vehicles very early, and some of the more advanced electric vehicle enterprises have entered the production stage [6]. The vigorous development of electric vehicles can not only achieve low emission but also reduce the environmental pollution, and alleviate the exhaustion of oil resources. Therefore, the research of electric vehicles has become the top priority in the field of automotive research.

Z. Xu et al. (Eds.): CSIA 2019, AISC 928, pp. 1443–1448, 2020.
https://doi.org/10.1007/978-3-030-15235-2_202

2 Electric Motor Direct Torque Control System of Electric Vehicle

The electric vehicle is composed of three subsystems, namely the energy subsystem, the motor drive subsystem and the auxiliary control system [7]. The electrical energy required by the motor drive system of an electric vehicle is provided by the vehicle battery, and the electric energy output from the vehicle battery is converted to the mechanical energy required by the electric vehicle [8]. The output shaft of the driving motor is connected to the drive system of the electric vehicle. The transmission device is produced by the transmission device which is driven by the basic structure of the drive system. The driving force drives the electric vehicle to run normally.

Direct torque control (DTC) is used to calculate and control the torque of AC motor in the stator coordinate system by analyzing the space voltage vector and using the stator magnetic field orientation analysis method [9]. The pulse width modulation signal is generated by the discrete two point regulator, and the switching condition of the inverter is directly controlled to obtain high motion, which solves the problems in vector control to a certain extent.

The mathematical model of three-phase asynchronous motor consists of four equations, namely voltage equation, flux linkage equation, torque equation and motion equation.

Voltage equation is

$$\begin{bmatrix} u_A \\ u_B \\ u_C \\ u_a \\ u_b \\ u_c \end{bmatrix} = \begin{bmatrix} R_s & 0 & 0 & 0 & 0 & 0 \\ 0 & R_s & 0 & 0 & 0 & 0 \\ 0 & 0 & R_s & 0 & 0 & 0 \\ 0 & 0 & 0 & R_s & 0 & 0 \\ 0 & 0 & 0 & 0 & R_s & 0 \\ 0 & 0 & 0 & 0 & 0 & R_s \end{bmatrix} \begin{bmatrix} i_A \\ i_B \\ i_C \\ i_a \\ i_b \\ i_c \end{bmatrix} + p \begin{bmatrix} \psi_A \\ \psi_B \\ \psi_C \\ \psi_a \\ \psi_b \\ \psi_c \end{bmatrix} \tag{1}$$

where u_A, u_B, u_C, u_a, u_b, u_c are the instantaneous value of phase voltage between the stator of a rotor, i_A, i_B, i_C, i_a, i_b, i_c are the instantaneous value of phase current between the stator of a rotor, ψ_A, ψ_B, ψ_C, ψ_a, ψ_b, ψ_c are full magnetic chain of rotor stator winding.

Magnetic chain equation is

$$\begin{bmatrix} \psi_A \\ \psi_B \\ \psi_C \\ \psi_a \\ \psi_b \\ \psi_c \end{bmatrix} = \begin{bmatrix} \mathrm{L_A} & \mathrm{M_{AB}} & \mathrm{M_{AC}} & \mathrm{M_{Aa}} & \mathrm{M_{Ab}} & \mathrm{M_{Ac}} \\ \mathrm{M_{BA}} & \mathrm{L_B} & \mathrm{M_{BC}} & \mathrm{M_{Ba}} & \mathrm{M_{Bb}} & \mathrm{M_{Bc}} \\ \mathrm{M_{CA}} & \mathrm{M_{CB}} & \mathrm{L_c} & \mathrm{M_{Ca}} & \mathrm{M_{cb}} & \mathrm{M_{Cc}} \\ \mathrm{M_{aA}} & \mathrm{M_{aB}} & \mathrm{M_{ac}} & \mathrm{L_a} & \mathrm{M_{ab}} & \mathrm{M_{ac}} \\ \mathrm{M_{bA}} & \mathrm{M_{bB}} & \mathrm{M_{bC}} & \mathrm{M_{ba}} & \mathrm{L_b} & \mathrm{M_{bc}} \\ \mathrm{M_{cA}} & \mathrm{M_{cB}} & \mathrm{M_{cC}} & \mathrm{M_{ca}} & \mathrm{M_{cb}} & \mathrm{L_c} \end{bmatrix} \begin{bmatrix} \mathrm{i_A} \\ \mathrm{i_B} \\ \mathrm{i_C} \\ \mathrm{i_a} \\ \mathrm{i_b} \\ \mathrm{i_c} \end{bmatrix} \tag{2}$$

where L_A, L_B, L_C, L_a, L_b are self inductance between the stator and rotor, and other elements represent mutual inductance.

Electromagnetic torque can be derived from the law of conservation of energy. According to the basic principle of energy conversion, when the motor is a plurality of winding motors, the energy storage of the magnetic field is

$$W_m = \frac{1}{2} i^T \psi \tag{3}$$

According to the principle of energy conservation, when the asynchronous motor runs, the electromagnetic torque T_e of the asynchronous motor is equal to the deviation of the angular displacement θ_m of the magnetic field energy storage energy when the current is constant. That is,

$$T_e \frac{\partial W_m}{\partial \theta_m}|_{i=c} = p_n \frac{\partial W_m}{\partial \theta_r}|_{i=c} \tag{4}$$

$$\theta_r = p_n \theta_m \tag{5}$$

In this formula, p_n is the number of pole pairs, θ_r is angular displacement.

$$\begin{aligned} T_e &= \frac{1}{2} p_n \left[i_r^T \frac{\partial M_{rs}}{\partial \theta_r} i_s + i_s^T \frac{\partial M_{sr}}{\partial \theta_r} i_r \right] \\ &= -p_n M_{sr} + [(i_A i_a + i_B i_b + i_C i_c) \sin \theta_r \\ &+ (i_A i_b + i_B i_c + i_C i_a) \sin(\theta_r + 120^{\circ}) \\ &+ (i_A i_c + i_B i_a + i_C i_b) \sin(\theta_r - 120^{\circ}) \end{aligned} \tag{6}$$

where M_{sr} is mutual inductance between the stator and the rotor.

Motion equation is

$$\begin{aligned} T_e &= T_L + \frac{J}{p_n} \frac{d^2 \theta_r}{dt^2} + \frac{D}{p_n} \frac{d\theta_r}{dt} \\ &= T_L + \frac{J}{p_n} \frac{d^2 \omega_r}{dt} + \frac{D}{p_n} \omega_r \end{aligned} \tag{7}$$

In this formula, T_L is resistance torque of load, J is moment of inertia of a unit, D is torque damping coefficient.

3 Torque Hysteresis Regulation

For the direct torque control system, if the higher dynamic performance is required, the electromagnetic torque of the motor must be directly controlled [10]. To achieve torque regulation and control, the torque regulator can be used. The input signal of the torque regulator is the signal difference of the given torque T_g and the feedback value T_f, and the switch signal TQ is the output signal corresponding to the torque regulator. The tolerance of the torque two point regulator is $\pm\varepsilon_m$, and the torque fluctuation can be restricted to the tolerance range given the value by using the discrete two point regulation method. When the torque ripple is within the tolerance range of the given value, the switch signal $TQ = 1$ will output the corresponding space voltage vector, which can make the stator flux spin and the torque will rise. When the difference between the output torque and the given torque is greater than the allowable deviation, the switch signal $TQ = 0$, at this time the output space voltage vector is zero, and the stator flux will not operate normally, but the torque is reduced at this time.

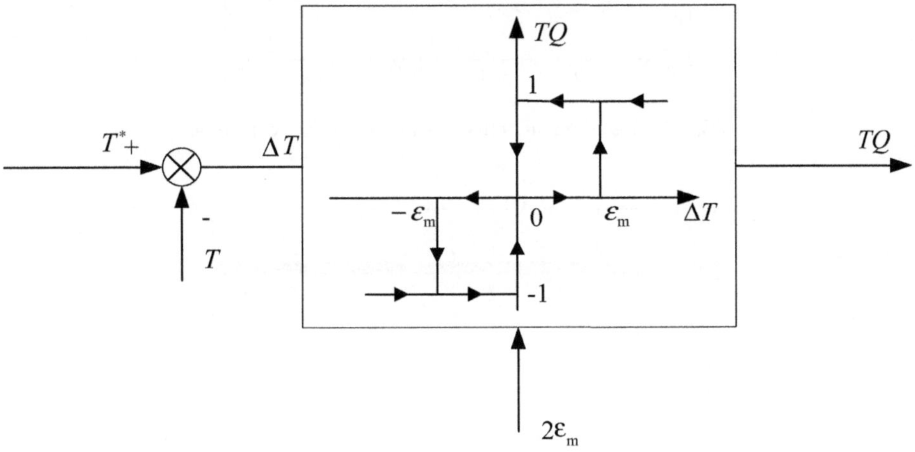

Fig. 1. The torque hysteresis regulator

The torque hysteresis regulator uses a double hysteresis regulator. The input value of the double hysteresis regulator is ΔT, and the output value is the TQ in the diagram. The operating principle of the torque hysteresis regulator sets the hysteresis width ε_m, as shown in Fig. 1, and TQ is judged by ΔT.

If $\Delta T < -\varepsilon_m$, $TQ = -1$.
If $\Delta T > -\varepsilon_m$, $TQ = 1$.
If $\Delta T = 0$, $TQ = 0$.

4 Simulation of Direct Torque Control

When the motor type is the squirrel cage asynchronous motor, the rated power parameter is set to 7.5 kW, the rated speed parameter is set to 1440r/min, the rated frequency parameter is set to 50 Hz, the inverter DC power source takes 100 V, the torque tolerance is set to 0.5N · M, the torque is set to 10N · M, and the simulation time is set to 0.25 s. The simulation results are as follows (Figs. 2, 3 and 4).

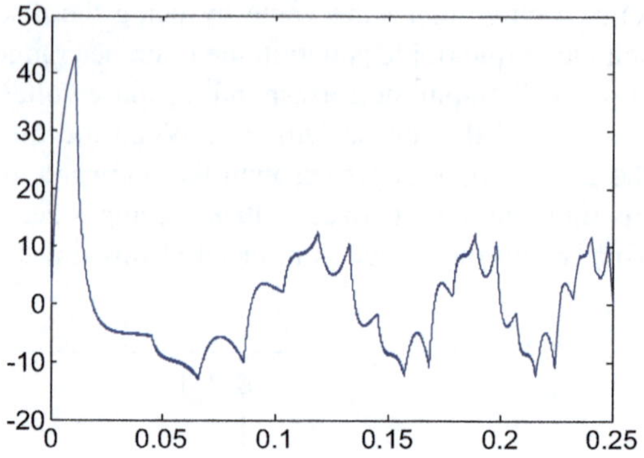

Fig. 2. The dynamic curve of phase current with time

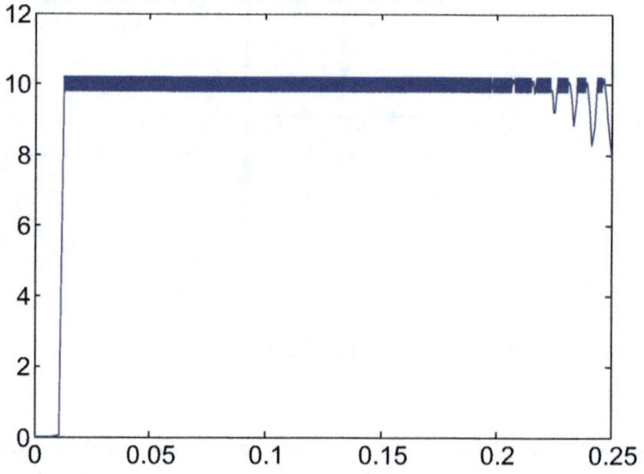

Fig. 3. The dynamic curve of electromagnetic torque with time

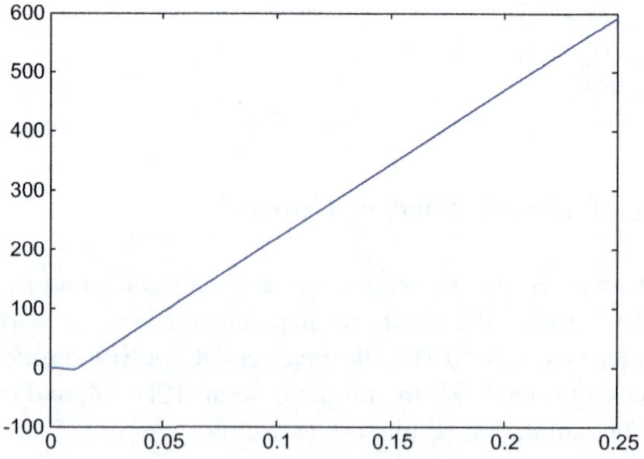

Fig. 4. The dynamic curve of motor speed with time

It can be seen that when the motor speed is very low, the calculation error is large, causing the magnetic chain track to become more serious. With the increase of speed, the distortion of flux linkage will decrease gradually. The a phase current of the motor stator is larger when starting. As the speed increases, the current gradually approaches the sine. When the electromagnetic torque is at 0.01 s, it reaches the specified torque 10N · M, and realizes the fast response of the torque.

5 Conclusion

Electric vehicle is very popular with the modern people from the whole international market. The motor drive part is the main research content of the electric vehicle. As described in this paper, the asynchronous motor is selected as the driving motor of this paper by comparing the four kinds of motor, and the direct torque control is chosen as the electric vehicle. The motor drive control strategy is explained carefully, and the corresponding modeling is carried out under the MATLAB/Simulink platform. At the same time, the results of simulation experiments are analyzed.

References

1. Roy JV, Leemput N (2017) Electric vehicle charging in an office building microgrid with distributed energy resources. IEEE Trans Sustain Energ 5(4):1389–1396
2. Martinez CM (2017) Energy management in plug-in hybrid electric vehicles: recent progress and a connected vehicles perspective. IEEE Trans Veh Technol 66(6):4534–4549
3. Martinez CM (2017) Charging, power management, and battery degradation mitigation in plug-in hybrid electric vehicles: a unified cost-optimal approach. Mech Syst Signal Process 87(12):4–16
4. Pantazis D, Joshi A (2010) Comparison of landmark-based and automatic methods for cortical surface registration. Neuro Image 49(3):2479–2493
5. Xiong R, Yu Q (2017) A novel method to obtain the open circuit voltage for the state of charge of lithium ion batteries in electric vehicles by using H infinity filter. Appl Energy 207 (45):134–145
6. Lv C, Liu Y (2017) Simultaneous observation of hybrid states for cyber-physical systems: a case study of electric vehicle powertrain. IEEE Trans Cybern 48(8):2357–2367
7. Jidin A, Idris NRN (2014) An optimized switching strategy for quick dynamic torque control in DTC-hysteresis-based induction machines. IEEE Trans Industr Electron 58(8):3391–3400
8. Sutikno T, Idris NRN (2014) A review of direct torque control of induction motors for sustainable reliability and energy efficient drives. Renew Sustain Energy Rev 32(2):548–558
9. Inoue Y, Morimoto S (2012) Investigation and improvement of torque response of control system based on direct torque control in interior permanent magnet synchronous motors. Electr Eng Jpn 181(2):55–65
10. Sahoo SK, Dasgupta S (2012) A lyapunov function-based robust direct torque controller for a switched reluctance motor drive system. IEEE Trans Power Electron 27(2):555–564

Author Index

Z. Xu et al. (Eds.): CSIA 2019, AISC 928, pp. 1449–1453, 2020.
https://doi.org/10.1007/978-3-030-15235-2

GPSR Compliance

The European Union's (EU) General Product Safety Regulation (GPSR) is a set of rules that requires consumer products to be safe and our obligations to ensure this.

If you have any concerns about our products, you can contact us on ProductSafety@springernature.com

In case Publisher is established outside the EU, the EU authorized representative is:

Springer Nature Customer Service Center GmbH
Europaplatz 3
69115 Heidelberg, Germany

Batch number: 10844661

Printed by Printforce, the Netherlands

Springer Texts in Business and Economics

Pasquale De Luca
Faculty of Economics
University of Rome Sapienza
Rome, Italy

ISSN 2192-4333 ISSN 2192-4341 (electronic)
Springer Texts in Business and Economics
ISBN 978-3-031-18299-0 ISBN 978-3-031-18300-3 (eBook)
https://doi.org/10.1007/978-3-031-18300-3

This Springer imprint is published by the registered company Springer Nature Switzerland AG
The registered company address is: Gewerbestrasse 11, 6330 Cham, Switzerland

Springer Texts in Business and Economics (STBE) delivers high-quality instructional content for undergraduates and graduates in all areas of Business/Management Science and Economics. The series is comprised of self-contained books with a broad and comprehensive coverage that are suitable for class as well as for individual self-study. All texts are authored by established experts in their fields and offer a solid methodological background, often accompanied by problems and exercises.

Pasquale De Luca

Corporate Finance

Fundamentals of Value and Price

Springer

A Livia, amatissima figlia.
Abbi sempre il Coraggio della tua Unicità,
e divieni esattamente ciò che Sei.

Introduction

This book of Corporate Finance tries to systemically integrate firms' approach on the market, on which the fundamentals of value depend, with that of investors in the financial markets on which prices depend.

The book of Corporate Finance is built on the basis of four strong beliefs.

First, the main aim of the firm is to maximize the equity value over time, and then for current and future shareholders. Then this aim must always be considered in the long run where pursuing the shareholders' value creation implies and requires satisfying of other stakeholders as well. It is in a perspective of short run that we may have distortions of the shareholder value theory able to attribute to it the blame for the incorrect behaviour of managers. Indeed, the maximization of the equity value in the long run is different and, most relevant, commonly in contrast with the maximization of the equity value in the short run. Therefore, the problem is not the shareholder-oriented capitalism but the distortion due to the short-termism of some managers.

Second, finance has a fundamental role in the structured growth process of the firm. Corporate finance goes far beyond the narrow boundaries as defined in the past by influencing directly and in relevant way the most important strategic and operating choices of the firm. Today for the firm is not possible to image to make well business without to make well finance as well. Since the aim of the firm is to maximize the equity value in order to grow in a structured way, a good financial manager must always think in terms of value creation. It requires a deep knowledge of the firm's business and the behaviour of all its actors (customers, suppliers, employees, competitors, etc.), to invest capital with profit, as well as a deep knowledge of financial markets and investors' behaviour about risk and expected return, to raise capital to be invested in the business.

Third, fundamental analysis of the firm is a relevant part of the corporate finance and it is the starting point for financial managers, financial analysts, investors, financial advisors, and bankers, to well-understand the current state of the firm's health, where it comes from and where it is going.

In this contest, the fundamental analysis of the firm is based on the *Economic and Financial Dynamic Analysis (EFDA)* of the firm. It is more than the simple financial analysis commonly based on the financial statements and then focused on the past performance of the firm. The EFDA is not an accounting analysis and it must be

never confused with the analysis of the accuracy of numbers on the basis of the accounting principles.

The EFDA is based on economic and financial aggregates (operating and net income, invested capital and capital structure, free cash-flows to the firm and to equity) able to show clearly, simple and intuitively the effective economic and financial dynamic of the firm over time by considering both the past and the future connected in a single and unique evolution path. In this dynamic perspective, the focus is on evolution over time of the economic and financial items rather than on their static analysis with regard to a specific moment. Indeed each single number must be analysed in a systemic way with regard all other numbers on the basis of their dynamic evolution over time.

Indeed, the main aim of the EFDA is to support the decision-making process by evaluating the firm's ability to create and to maximize the equity value over time through the systemic, constant, and continuous measurement of the effects of the strategic and operating decisions of CEO and managers on the economic and financial dynamic of the firm with regard to the past and the future. Specifically, the EFDA supports the decision-making process by measuring and evaluating *i) ex ante*, the expected effects of the strategic and operational decisions on the expected economic and financial dynamic of the firm and then on its ability to create and to maximize value, and *ii) ex post*, the real effects of the strategic and operational decisions made on the actual economic and financial dynamic of the firm and then on the effective value created.

Since the main aim of the firm is to create value, the future time is more relevant to the past time. Therefore, the EFDA is based more on the expected future dynamic rather than the past. The past analysis is relevant to well-understand the performance effectively realized by the firm in order mainly to evaluate the accuracy and reliability of the assumptions on which the expected value of economic and financial items is made in the expected dynamic.

Fourth, the firm's ability to create and to maximize the equity value must be measured by considering jointly the fundamental analysis of the firm, based on the Economic and Financial Dynamic Analysis (EFDA), with the dynamic of financial markets. Indeed, the firm valuation is one of the most relevant fields in which the fundamentals of value based on the firm's analysis meet the fundamental of asset pricing based on financial market analysis about risk and expected return. In this sense, the baseline equation of value creation states that the firm creates value if and only if the return on capital invested in the business exceeds the cost of capital raised in the financial market. Consequently, the maximization of the firm's equity value is based on two variables: 1) *return on invested capital*, where its maximization requires a deep knowledge of real markets and the business model of the firm and 2) *cost of capital*, where its minimization requires a deep knowledge of the financial markets and the behaviour of investors with regard to the risk and expected return.

I believe that in the field of Corporate Finance theory and practice must be considered jointly. Then the book is defined by thinking of master's degree and

doctoral students as well as financial managers, financial analysts and advisors, investors and bankers.

The approach used in the book is based on a rigorous quantitative analysis. All equations used, although they can be frightening at first reading, they always have a direct application and their main aim is to help the decision-making process both at strategic and operating level in order to maximize the firm's equity value.

To avoid weighing down the text no citations have been inserted except as deemed necessary (and if any of these are missing, I apologize in advance). All the texts and papers from which I drew are indicated in the bibliography at the end of the book and also in this case I hope I have not forgotten anyone.

The book is organized into seven parts.

Part I named "*Economic and Financial Analysis of the Firm*" is focused on the Economic and Financial variables of the firm analysed in the perspective of the maximization of the equity value creation.

Chapters 1–3 investigate the firm's ability to create profit over time on the basis of the analysis of revenues, cost, and margin structures. The aim is to investigate the firm's ability to produce profit margin over time in a stable and structural way at level of product, business unit, and corporate. Therefore, they analyse the main economic variables and their functions in order to maximize the profit and to minimize the cost structure.

Chapters 4–6 are focused on the Economic and Financial Dynamic Analysis (EFDA). The analysis refers to the operating and net income, the invested capital and capital structure, and the free cash-flows to the firm and to equity. The main aim is to investigate the structural ability of the firm to create profit in its business, the sustainability of the invested capital and capital structure, and the firm's ability to generate free cash-flows to equity that are structural, stable and in line with investors' expectations.

Chapters 7–8 complete the economic and financial analysis by focusing on the analysis of the main financial ratios used in financial community and the basic tool that firm commonly use to evaluate its investment projects.

Part II named "*Risk and Return in Capital Markets*" is focused on the analysis of investors' behaviour about risk and expected return.

Chapters 9–12 are focused on the investor's choice about risk and expected return. Three steps are followed: first, we introduce the measurement of portfolio's expected return and risk, second, we determine the efficient frontier for all investors on the market, third we introduce the expected utility for the definition of the optimum portfolio for each investor. The analysis is completed by the introduction of the Single Index Model that is one of the most common models used to simplify the portfolio theory.

Chapters 13–14 are focused on the analysis of the Capital Asset Pricing Model (CAPM) that is the most common and used general equilibrium model in the capital markets. The CAPM is analysed in its standard form and in its most common non-standard form.

Part III named "*Money, Interest Rates and Bond Markets*" is focused on the analysis of interest rates behaviour and the bond price.

Chapters 15–16 are focused on the analysis of definition of the equilibrium interest rate on the basis of the demand and supply of bond and the behaviour interest rate with regard to the effects of shifts in demand and supply curves.

Chapter 17 introduces the analysis of the risk and term structure of interest rate.

Part IV named "*Financial Policies and Capital Structure Choices*" is focused on the analysis of the firm's financial policies and its capital structure choices.

Chapters 18–19 analyse the two main source of financing equity and debt and the optimum capital structure choices on the basis of the theories about the relationship between these choices and the firm's value.

Chapter 20 analyses the dividend policy of the firm and its connection with the firm's value creation.

Chapter 21 analyses the cost of capital on the basis of the firm's choices about capital structure and the dynamic of financial markets on the basis of the asset pricing.

Part V named "*Valuation*" is focused on the models for firm's valuation.

Chapters 22–24 introduce the general equation of valuation and its application in the perspective of equity side, by analysing the equity valuation models, and asset side by analysing the firm's valuation models.

Chapter 25 introduces the firm's valuation on the basis of multiples approach by analysing the most common multiples used.

Part VI named "*Options*" is focused on the analysis and valuation of financial options.

Chapter 26 is focused on the analysis of the main characteristics of financial options while *Chapter* 27 introduces the main models to pricing financial options.

Part VII named "*Special Topics*" is focused on the main financial extraordinary operations.

Chapter 28 analyses the Mergers & Acquisitions in the perspective of buy-side and sell-side.

Chapter 29 analyses the investment in the firm in the perspective of Private Equity, Venture Capital, and Head Fund.

Chapter 30 analyses the main aspect concerning the Initial Public Offering of the firm.

I hope you enjoy this book as much as I enjoyed writing it.

Rome, Italy
August 2022

Pasquale De Luca

Contents

Part V Valuation

Part VII Special Topics

Part I

Economic and Financial Analysis of the Firm

Production Functions, Cost Minimization, and Profit Maximization

1

1.1 Production Functions

The production function of the firm must always be defined on the basis of the technological constraints: they limit the firm's ability to produce the output as well as a defined level of it. Therefore, the technology analysis refers to the right definition of technological constraints and their impact on the production system.

The analysis of the production function of the firm requires the right definition of the combination of inputs–outputs that are effectively feasible first in a technical way, and second in an economic way.

In this context, we limit the discussion around few main elements of the analysis of the production function.

1.1.1 Baseline Concepts

Preliminarily, we need to introduce some essential baseline concepts (Varian, 1992).

Net Output

Assume that the firm can use n goods as output (production products) and input (factors of production). The Net Output of the jth asset (y_j) is equal to the difference between the units of output of jth asset $\left(y_j^0\right)$ and the units of the input of jth asset $\left(y_j^i\right)$ as follows:

$$y_j = y_j^0 - y_j^i$$

Therefore, if:

P. De Luca, *Corporate Finance*, Springer Texts in Business and Economics,
https://doi.org/10.1007/978-3-031-18300-3_1

(a) $y_j > 0 \rightarrow y_j^0 > y_j^i$: Net Output is positive, and then the firm produces units of output of the asset j $\left(y_j^0\right)$ greater than the units of input of asset j $\left(y_j^i\right)$ used;

(b) $y_j < 0 \rightarrow y_j^0 < y_j^i$: Net Output is negative, and the firm produces units of output of the asset j $\left(y_j^0\right)$ lower than the units of input of asset j $\left(y_j^i\right)$ used.

Production Plan

It is the list of Net Output effectively available for the firm. It can be defined as a vector y in R_n whose component y_j is negative if the j-asset is an input and positive if the j-asset is an output.

Production Possibilities Set

It is the set of Production Plans technically feasible for the firm. Then, it is the set of all combinations of inputs and outputs that comprise a technologically feasible way to produce. It can be represented by Y that is a subset of R_n. Consequently, the set Y represents all combinations of input and output that are technically feasible of the firm and then it gives a clear definition of the technology of the firm.

Assume that: (i) the firm produces only one output by using only two factors (inputs); (ii) the firm produces y units of output by using x_1 units of factor 1 and x_2 units of factors 2.

We can define the *Production Set* ($Y(x_1, x_2)$) as follows:

$$Y(x_1, x_2) = \{(y, \ -x_1, \ -x_2) \text{ in } Y\}$$

It is possible that the production set feasible in the short run is different in the long run. Then, we can define the ***Short-run Production Possible Set*** the set of all combinations of inputs and outputs that are technically feasible only in the short run. It is a vector z in R_n and denoted by $Y(z)$ that is a subset of Y. We can interpret the vector z as the maximum amount of input that is possible to use in the short run or the maximum amount of output that is possible to produce in the short run.

Consider the previous case and assume that in the short run we can use the factor 2 at a fixed level $\overline{x_2}$. The Short-run Production Possible Set ($Y(\overline{x_2})$) is defined as follows:

$$Y(\overline{x_2}) = \{(y, \ -x_1, \ -x_2) \text{ in } Y : x_2 = \overline{x_2}\}$$

Inputs Requirement Set

It is the set of all input bundles that produce at least y units of output. Assume that firm produces only one output. We can write the Net Output bundle as $(y, -\boldsymbol{x})$ where $\boldsymbol{x}$ is the vector of inputs necessary to produce y units of output. The Inputs Requirement Set can be denoted with $V(y)$ and it is defined as follows:

$$V(y) = \{x \text{ in } R^n_+ : (y, \quad -x) \text{ is in } Y\}$$

Note that inputs are represented as a positive number because we use the sign minus in the vector of net output $(y, -x)$.

Isoquant

It groups all combinations of inputs (x) able to produce y units of output exactly (no more (y') and no less (y'')). Therefore, considering Inputs Requirement Set need for production $V(y)$, the *Isoquant* $Q(y)$ can be defined as follows:

$$Q(y) = \{x \text{ in } R^n_+ : x \text{ is in } V(y)\}$$

where x is not in $V(y')$ for $y' > y$ and in $V(y'')$ for $y'' < y$

We can represent isoquant as in Fig. 1.1.

In the case of two inputs, the isoquant is the set of all possible combinations of inputs 1 (x_1) and 2 (x_2) that are needed exactly to produce a given amount of output y.

Note that even if isoquant is similar to the Indifference Curve (that defines the different consumption bundles that are just sufficient to produce a certain level of utility), however there is a fundamental difference: Isoquant is based on the amount of output able to produce and not on the utility level. It implies that isoquant is fixed by the technology and it does not have the kind of arbitrary nature that the utility on the contrary has.

If we assume that there are many slightly different ways to produce a given level of output, then technology can be represented by ***Parametric Function*** involving a few unknown parameters. Therefore, we could to fit the curve on the basis of the possible production points by having a smooth approximation of an isoquant as shown in Fig. 1.2.

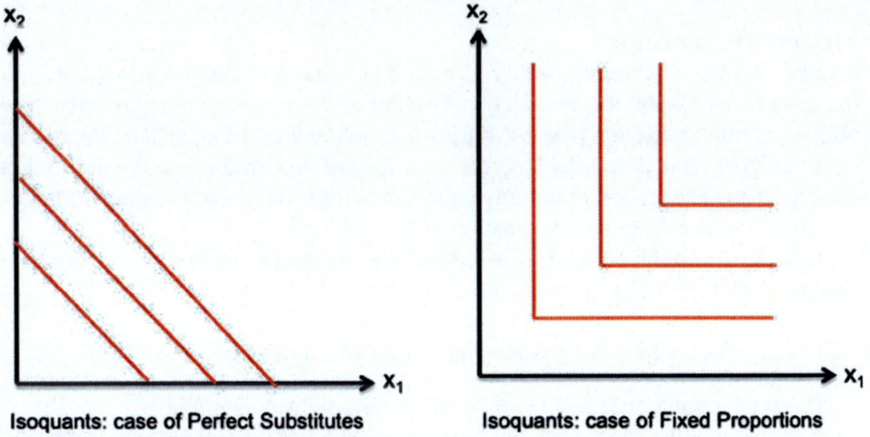

Fig. 1.1 Isoquants

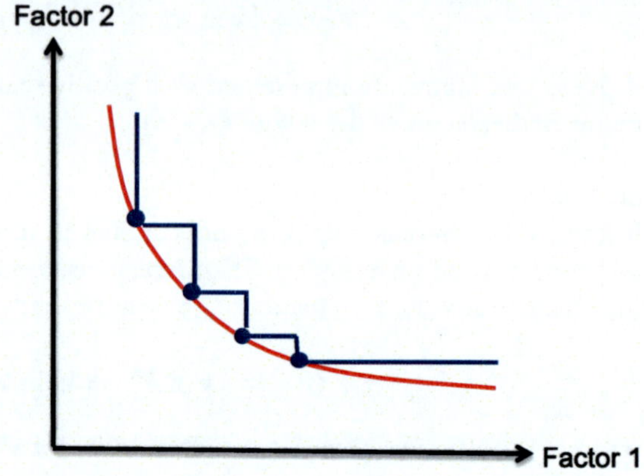

Fig. 1.2 Smooth approximation of an isoquant

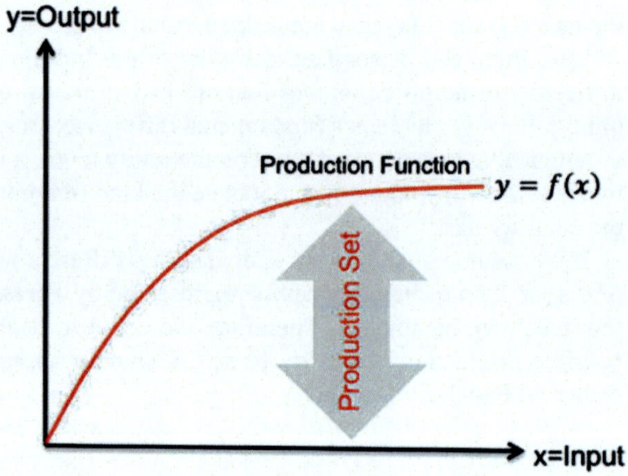

Fig. 1.3 Production function

Production Function

It represents the maximum quantity of output in units. Because inputs are costly, in the analysis of all possible Production Possibility Set we must consider only those able to give the maximum possible output for a given level of input. The Production Function is the function describing the boundary of this Production Possibility Set. Therefore, the Production Function measures the maximum possible output that it is possible to obtain from a given amount of input.

Assume firm produces only one output. We can define the Production Function ($f(x)$) as follows:

$$f(\boldsymbol{x}) = \{y \text{ in } R : y \text{ is the max units of output for} - \boldsymbol{x} \text{ in } Y\}$$

The Production Function ($y = f(x)$) can be represented as in Fig. 1.3.

If we assume that firm uses only two inputs, the Production Function ($f(x_1, x_2)$) measures the maximum amount of output y, so that:

$$y=f(x_1, x_2)$$

where x_1 and x_2 are the units of Factor 1 and Factor 2, respectively.

Note that it is reasonable to assume to describe the efficient (in a technological way) Production Plan by a *Transformation Function*.

If the Production Plan (vector $\boldsymbol{y}$) in Y is efficient, there is not possible to find another Production Plan (vector $\boldsymbol{y}'$) in Y so that $\boldsymbol{y}' \neq \boldsymbol{y}$ and $\boldsymbol{y}' \geq \boldsymbol{y}$. It means that it is not possible to produce more unit of output by using the same level of inputs, or similarly, it is not possible to produce the same unit of output by using less level of inputs.

By using a Transformation Function (T), the efficient Production Plan (vector $\boldsymbol{y}$) can be defined as follows:

$$T : R_n \rightarrow R \text{ where } T(\boldsymbol{y}) = 0 \text{ only if } \boldsymbol{y} \text{ is efficient}$$

If the Production Function represents the maximum *scalar* quantity of output units as the function of the output, the Transformation Function represents the optimal combination of the vectors of Net Output.

1.1.2 Assumptions

There are two main assumptions regarding the properties of technology: monotonicity and convexity.

Assumption 1: Monotonicity

The assumption that technology is monotonic implies that if we increase the amount of at least one of the inputs, it is always possible to produce at least as much output as before.

Assume a condition of *free disposal* of inputs: the firm can dispose of any inputs costless.

Assume two vectors of input, $\boldsymbol{x}$ and $\boldsymbol{x}'$. Assume they are able to produce y units of output where each component in the vector of input $\boldsymbol{x}'$ is equal or greater than the correspond in the vector of input $\boldsymbol{x}$.

We can formalize the assumption of monotonicity on the basis of:

(a) The Inputs Requirement Set $V(y)$: *if* $\boldsymbol{x} \in V(y)$ and $\boldsymbol{x}' \geq \boldsymbol{x}$ then $\boldsymbol{x}' \in V(y)$.
(b) The Production Possibilities Set (Y): *if* $\boldsymbol{y} \in Y$ and $\boldsymbol{y}' \leq \boldsymbol{y}$ then $\boldsymbol{y}' \in Y$.

Note that in case of Production Possibilities Set (Y) we say $\boldsymbol{y}' \leq \boldsymbol{y}$ while $\boldsymbol{x}' \geq \boldsymbol{x}$ in Inputs Requirement Set $V(y)$. It implies that each component of the vector $\boldsymbol{y}'$ must be equal or lower than the corresponding component in the vector $\boldsymbol{y}$. Then, the vector $\boldsymbol{y}'$ is able to produce y units of output equal or lower than the vector $\boldsymbol{y}$ by using an amount of inputs at least equal. Consequently, it is reasonable to assume that if $\boldsymbol{y}$ is feasible, $\boldsymbol{y}'$ is feasible too.

Assumption 2: Convexity

The assumption that *technology is convex* implies that if we have two production techniques able to produce y units of output, then their weighted average will produce at least y units of output. Therefore, if we choose the level at which we can use the two production techniques, it is always possible to produce a given amount of output y by combining in a variety of different ways the two production techniques.

Assume two vectors of input $\boldsymbol{x}$ and $\boldsymbol{x}'$ to produce the y units of output. The assumption of convexity can be formalized on the basis of:

(a) The Inputs Requirement Set $V(y)$: *if* $\boldsymbol{x}$ and $\boldsymbol{x}' \in V(y)$ then $t\boldsymbol{x} + (1-t)\boldsymbol{x}' \in V(y)$ for $0 \leq t \leq 1$.
(b) The Production Possibilities Set (Y): *if* $\boldsymbol{y}$ and $\boldsymbol{y}' \in Y$ then $t\boldsymbol{y} + (1-t)\boldsymbol{y}' \in Y$ for $0 \leq t \leq 1$.

Note that:

1. The convexity of the *Inputs Requirement Set* $V(y)$ implies the scalar of technology. If we want to produce an increasing amount of y units by reproducing the production process, the technology must be convex.
2. The convexity of the *Production Possibilities Set* (Y) implies the convexity of the *Inputs Requirement Set* $V(y)$. If Y is convex, then for each vector $\boldsymbol{x}$ and $\boldsymbol{x}'$ it gets:

$$(y, -\boldsymbol{x}) \text{ and } (y, -\boldsymbol{x}') \in Y, \text{then } (ty + (1-t)y, -t\boldsymbol{x} - (1-t)\boldsymbol{x}') \in Y$$

it implies that:

$$(y, -(t\boldsymbol{x} + (1-t)\boldsymbol{x}')) \in Y$$

and by considering that:

$$\boldsymbol{x} \text{ and } \boldsymbol{x}' \in V(y)$$

then:

$$t\boldsymbol{x} + (1-t)\boldsymbol{x}' \in V(y)$$

Consequently, $V(y)$ is convex as Y.

1.1.3 Marginal Product of Factor (MP)

The Marginal Product of Factor (MP) measures the increase in output (Δy) due to "one" more unit of one factor by keeping at the same level the other factor.

Assume the firm produces y units of output by using a production function derivable and two factors: Factor 1 at level of unit of input x_1 and Factor 2 at level of unit of input x_2.

Therefore, by using the Production Function (f) based on the amount of the two factors (x_1, x_2), so that the $f(x_1, x_2)$, the y units of output is equal to:

$$y = f(x_1, x_2) \quad \leftrightarrow \quad y = f(\boldsymbol{x}) \quad \text{where } \boldsymbol{x} = \{x_1, x_2\}$$

Assume to increase the Factor 1 of amount Δx_1 so that its level shifts from x_1 to $x_1 + \Delta x_1$, and to keep fixed the Factor 2 at the level $\overline{x_2}$.

The ***Marginal Product of Factor 1*** ($\text{MP}_1(x_1, \overline{x_2})$) measures the increase in output (Δy) per unit change in Factor 1 (Δx_1), and it is equal to:

$$\text{MP}_1(x_1, \overline{x_2}) = \frac{\Delta y}{\Delta x_1} = \frac{f(x_1 + \Delta x_1, x_2) - f(x_1, x_2)}{\Delta x_1} \tag{1.1}$$

Similarly, assume to increase the Factor 2 of amount Δx_2 so that its level shifts from x_2 to $x_2 + \Delta x_2$, and to keep fixed the Factor 1 at the level $\overline{x_1}$.

The ***Marginal Product of Factor 2*** ($\text{MP}_2(\overline{x_1}, x_2)$) measures the increase in output (Δy) per unit change in Factor 2 (Δx_2), and it is equal to:

$$\text{MP}_2(\overline{x_1}, x_2) = \frac{\Delta y}{\Delta x_2} = \frac{f(x_1, x_2 + \Delta x_2) - f(x_1, x_2)}{\Delta x_2} \tag{1.2}$$

Because Δy, Δx_1, and Δx_2 are relative to an amount, the Marginal Product of Factor (MP_f) is a rate: it is the extra amount of output per unit of extra input ($\Delta y/\Delta x_1$ if we consider the Factor 1 and $\Delta y/\Delta x_2$ if we consider the Factor 2).

One of the most relevant concepts is the ***Law of Diminishing Marginal Product***: *the MP will diminish as we get more and more of that factor.*

Note that the law of diminishing marginal product can be applied only when one factor changes while the other is being held fixed: it shows how the marginal product changes to the increase in the amount of one factor, holding the other factor fixed.

The law of diminishing marginal product is strictly related to the assumption of monotonicity of the technology.

Therefore, considering them both, the *total output level will increase to the increase in the amount of a factor but a decreasing rate.*

1.1.4 Technical Rate of Substitution of Factor (TRS)

The Technical Rate of Substitution of Factor (TRS) measures the rate at which the firm can substitute one input for another in order to keep output level constant: it shows *the ratio of the marginal product changes as we increase the amount of one factor and reduce the amount of the other factor so as to stay on the same isoquant.* Consequently, TRS measures the *slope* of isoquant.

If we consider only two factors, the TRS measures the slope of isoquant and then the change of one factor when we change the other factor in order to realize the same level of output. If we consider n factors, the TRS measures the slope of an isoquant surface measured in a particular direction.

Assume to produce y units of output by using a production function derivable and two factors: Factor 1 at level of unit of input x_1 and Factor 2 at level of unit of input x_2.

Therefore, by using the production function (f) based on the amount of the two factors (x_1, x_2), so that the $f(x_1, x_2)$, the y units of output is equal to:

$$y = f(x_1, x_2) \quad \leftrightarrow \quad y = f(\boldsymbol{x}) \ \text{ where } \boldsymbol{x} = \{x_1, x_2\}$$

Assume to increase a little bit of Factor 1 and using less of Factor 2 to produce the same amount of output y.

The problem is to compute the amount of reduction of the Factor 2 able to compensate the increase of Factor 1 in order to produce the same amount of output y.

We can derive the formula of the TRS by using the marginal product. Consider the Marginal Product of Factor 1 ($\mathrm{MP}_1(x_1, x_2)$) and Factor 2 ($\mathrm{MP}_2(x_1, x_2)$):

$$\mathrm{MP}_1(x_1, x_2) = \frac{\Delta y}{\Delta x_1} \quad \rightarrow \quad \Delta y = \mathrm{MP}_1(x_1, x_2) \cdot \Delta x_1$$

$$\mathrm{MP}_2(x_1, x_2) = \frac{\Delta y}{\Delta x_2} \quad \rightarrow \quad \Delta y = \mathrm{MP}_2(x_1, x_2) \cdot \Delta x_2$$

By considering both, it gets:

$$\Delta y = \mathrm{MP}_1(x_1, x_2) \cdot \Delta x_1 + \mathrm{MP}_2(x_1, x_2) \cdot \Delta x_2$$

Since the amount of output remains constant ($\Delta y = 0$), it gets:

$$\Delta y = 0 \quad \rightarrow \quad \mathrm{MP}_1(x_1, x_2) \cdot \Delta x_1 + \mathrm{MP}_2(x_1, x_2) \cdot \Delta x_2 = 0$$

and then:

$$\mathrm{MP}_2(x_1, x_2) \cdot \Delta x_2 = -\mathrm{MP}_1(x_1, x_2) \cdot \Delta x_1$$

$$\mathrm{TRS}(x_1, x_2) = \frac{\Delta x_2}{\Delta x_1} = -\frac{\mathrm{MP}_1(x_1, x_2)}{\mathrm{MP}_2(x_1, x_2)} \tag{1.3}$$

Note that also in this case the one of the most relevant concepts is the ***Law of Diminishing Technical Rate of Substitution of Factor*** (TRS): *the TRS will diminish as we get more and more of that factor.*

The Law of Diminishing Technical Rate of Substitution of Factor is strictly related to the assumption of Convexity of the Technology. It implies that the slope of an isoquant decreases in absolute value as we move along the isoquant in the direction of increasing one factor, as well as it increases in absolute value as we move in the direction of increasing of the other factor.

1.1.5 Elasticity of Substitution (ES)

The Elasticity of Substitution (ES) measures the curvature of isoquant: it shows how the ratio of factor inputs changes as the slope of the isoquant changes.

Therefore, while the Technical Rate of Substitution (TRS) measures the slope of isoquant, the Elasticity of Substitution (ES) measures the curvature of isoquant.

Formally, the Elasticity of Substitution (ES) is equal to the ratio between the change in the factor ratio ($\Delta(x_2/x_1)$) and the change in the Technical Rate of Substitution (ΔTRS), as follows:

$$\mathrm{ES} = \frac{\frac{\Delta(x_2/x_1)}{x_2/x_1}}{\frac{\Delta \mathrm{TRS}}{\mathrm{TRS}}} \tag{1.4}$$

Therefore, the ES measures the percentage change in the factor ratio divided by the percentage change in the TRS, by remaining fixed the level y of output.

Consequently, if a small change in slope generates a large change in the factor input ratio, the isoquant is relatively flat and then the elasticity of substitution is large.

The Elasticity of Substitution (ES) is commonly derived by suing the logarithmic derivate method. Consider a general function $y = g(x)$. The elasticity (ϵ) of y with respect to x measures the percentage change in y due to a small percentage change in x. It is equal to:

$$\epsilon = \frac{\frac{dy}{y}}{\frac{dx}{x}} = \frac{dy}{dx} \cdot \frac{x}{y}$$

By considering that $\frac{d}{dx}[\ln x] = \frac{1}{x}$ as well as $\frac{d}{dy}[\ln y] = \frac{1}{y}$, if x and y are positive, we can rewrite the elasticity (ϵ) as follows:

$$\epsilon = \frac{d \ln y}{d \ln x}$$

By using the role of the derivation of the compost function, it gets:

$$\frac{d \ln y}{d \ln x} \cdot \frac{d \ln x}{dx} = \frac{d \ln y}{dx}$$

By considering the derivate of left-hand and the right-hand side of the equation, it gets:

Fig. 1.4 Technical Rate of Substitution (TRS) and the Elasticity of Substitution (ES)

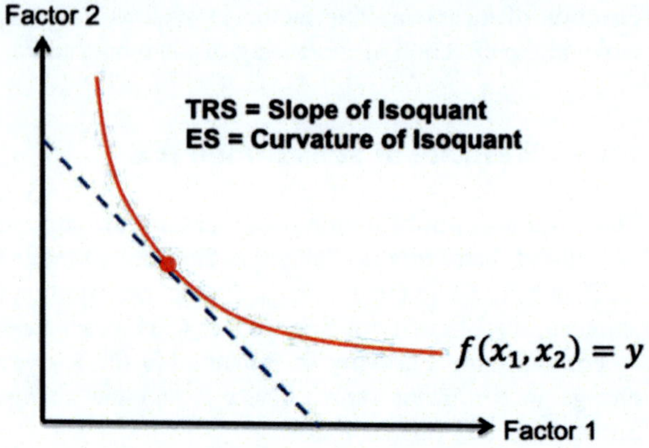

$$\frac{d\ln y}{d\ln x}\cdot\frac{1}{x} = \frac{1}{y}\frac{dy}{dx}$$

$$\frac{d\ln y}{d\ln x} = \frac{x}{y}\frac{dy}{dx}$$

Therefore, the ***Elasticity of Substitution*** (**ES**) can be defined as follows:

$$\mathrm{ES} = \frac{d\ln(x_2/x_1)}{d\ln|\mathrm{TRS}|} \tag{1.5}$$

Note that the absolute value in the denominator is necessary to convert the TRS to a positive number in order to calculate the logarithm.

We can represent the Technical Rate of Substitution (TRS), that it measures the *slope* of isoquant, and the Elasticity of Substitution (ES), that it measures the *curvature* of isoquant, as in Fig. 1.4.

1.1.6 Returns to Scale

Returns to Scale describes what happens to output level (y) when we increase all inputs ($\boldsymbol{x}$).

Assume to use a vector of input ($\boldsymbol{x}$) to produce a certain level of output y. Assume to increase or decrease the amount of all inputs of production function. The problem is to define the effects on the level of output y. We can have three main cases:

1. *Constant Returns to Scale*. If we scale up all of the inputs by some amount t, we obtain t times as much output: $tf(\boldsymbol{x}) = f(t\boldsymbol{x})$ *for all* $t \geq 0$.
   The firm can replicate what it was doing before in the exactly way. Then, if we use twice as much of each input, we will get twice of much output. In terms of the production function, it means that two times as much of each input gives two

times as much output. Note that by considering that a first-degree homogeneous function is one for which $f(tx) = tf(x)$ (while a zero-degree homogeneous function is one for which $f(tx) = f(x)$), we can have constant returns to scale if and only if the production function is homogeneous of degree 1.

2. *Increasing Returns to Scale*. If we scale up all of the inputs by some amount t, we obtain more than t times as much output: $tf(x) < f(tx)$ for all $t > 1$.
3. *Decreasing Returns to Scale*. If we scale up all of the inputs by some amount t, we obtain less than t times as much output: $tf(x) > f(tx)$ for all $t > 1$.

These three cases describe a general form. However, it is always possible that a technology is characterized by a Constant Returns to Scale for certain input and a Decreasing or Increasing Returns to Scale for other certain input in the vector $\boldsymbol{x}$.

We can calculate the local measure of returns to scale by using the ***Elasticity of Scale (ESC)***: it measures the percentage increase in the level of output y due to one percentage increase in all inputs.

Assume a production function equal to $y = f(x)$ and a positive scalar t ($t > 0$) so that $y(t) = f(tx)$. Consequently, if:

(a) $t = 1$, we have the current scale of operations
(b) $t > 1$, we are scaling all inputs up by t
(c) $t < 1$, we are scaling all inputs down by t

The Elasticity of Scale (ESC) can be defined as follows:

$$\mathrm{ESC} = \frac{\frac{dy(t)}{y(t)}}{\frac{dt}{t}}$$

The Elasticity of Scale (ESC) must be evaluated at $t = 1$, so that:

$$\mathrm{ESC} = \frac{dy(t)}{dt}\frac{t}{y(t)}\bigg|_{t=1} = \frac{df(tx)}{dt}\frac{t}{f(tx)}\bigg|_{t=1}$$

And consequently, the technology presents:

(a) ESC > 1: a locally increasing returns to scale
(b) ESC $= 1$: a locally constant returns to scale
(c) If ESC < 1: a locally decreasing returns to scale

1.2 Cost Minimization

The problem of cost minimization can be formalized as follows (Varian, 1992):

$$\begin{cases} \min_{x} \boldsymbol{wx} \\ f(\boldsymbol{x}) = y \end{cases} \tag{1.6}$$

where:

- $\boldsymbol{x}$: is the vector of inputs, so that $\boldsymbol{x} = (x_1, x_2, \ldots, x_n)$
- $\boldsymbol{w}$: is the vector of inputs price, so that $\boldsymbol{w} = (w_1, w_2, \ldots, w_n)$
- y: is the level of output
- $f(\boldsymbol{x})$: is the production function.

The problem of cost minimization can be formalized as a constrained minimum problem where the first is the function objective and the second the constraint.

To solve this constrained minimum problem, we can use the method of Lagrange multipliers. The Lagrangian is equal to:

$$\mathcal{L}(\lambda, \boldsymbol{x}) = \boldsymbol{wx} - \lambda(f(\boldsymbol{x}) - y)$$

By differentiating it with respect to each of the choice variables (x_i) and the Lagrange Multiplier (λ), the first-order conditions characterizing an interior solution $\boldsymbol{x}^*$ are the following:

$$\frac{\partial \mathcal{L}(\lambda, \boldsymbol{x})}{\partial x_i} = w_i - \lambda \frac{\partial f(\boldsymbol{x}^*)}{\partial x_i}$$
$$\frac{\partial \mathcal{L}(\lambda, \boldsymbol{x})}{\partial \lambda} = f(\boldsymbol{x}^*) - y$$

and pointing the first-order conditions equal to zero, it gets:

$$\begin{cases} w_i - \lambda \frac{\partial f(\boldsymbol{x}^*)}{\partial x_i} = 0 \\ f(\boldsymbol{x}^*) - y = 0 \end{cases} \rightarrow \begin{cases} w_i = \lambda \frac{\partial f(\boldsymbol{x}^*)}{\partial x_i} & \textit{for } i = 1, 2, \ldots, n \\ f(\boldsymbol{x}^*) = y \end{cases}$$

If we use the vector notion, by denoting with $\boldsymbol{D}f(\boldsymbol{x})$ the gradient vector, the vector of partial derivatives of $f(\boldsymbol{x})$, we can rewrite these conditions of the first-order as follows:

$$\boldsymbol{w} - \lambda \boldsymbol{D}f(\boldsymbol{x}^*) = 0 \rightarrow \boldsymbol{w} = \lambda \boldsymbol{D}f(\boldsymbol{x}^*)$$

where:

$$\boldsymbol{D}f(\boldsymbol{x}^*) = \left(\frac{\partial f(\boldsymbol{x}^*)}{\partial x_1}, \frac{\partial f(\boldsymbol{x}^*)}{\partial x_2}, \ldots, \frac{\partial f(\boldsymbol{x}^*)}{\partial x_n} \right)$$

In order to interpret the first-order conditions, consider the *i*th factor and the *j*th factor as follows:

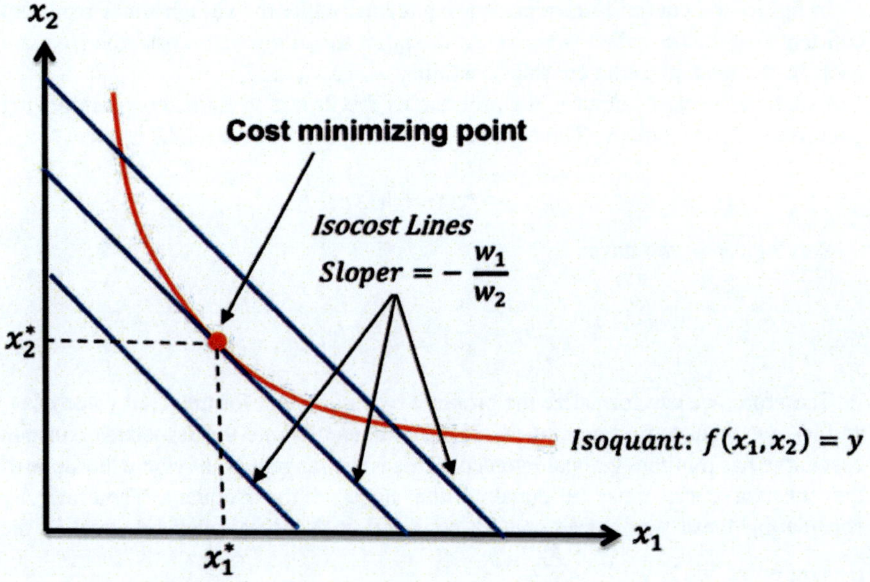

Fig. 1.5 Cost minimization

$$w_i = \lambda \frac{\partial f(x^*)}{\partial x_i}; \quad w_j = \lambda \frac{\partial f(x^*)}{\partial x_j} \quad \textit{for } i \text{ and } j = 1,2,\ldots,n$$

By dividing w_i by the w_j, it gets:

$$\frac{w_i}{w_j} = \frac{\frac{\partial f(x^*)}{\partial x_i}}{\frac{\partial f(x^*)}{\partial x_j}} \quad \textit{for } i \text{ and } j = 1,2,\ldots,n \tag{1.7}$$

where:

- the right-hand side: is the Technical Rate of Substitution of Factor (TRS) and it measures the rate at which factor j can be substituted for factor i by maintaining a constant level of output.
- the left-hand side: is the Economic Rate of Substitution of Factor (ERS) and it measures at what rate factor j can be substituted for factor i while maintaining a constant cost.

Therefore, the first-order condition requires that the Technical Rate of Substitution for Factor (TRS) must be equal to the Economic Rate of Substitution of Factor (ERS). If it is not, there would be some kind of adjustment that would result in a lower cost way of producing the same output. We can represent the first-order condition as in Fig. 1.5.

In figure, the curved lines represent isoquants, while the straight-lines represent constant cost curves called *isocosts*. At the point that minimizes costs, the isoquant must be the tangent to the constant cost line.

Fixed the level of output y, the problem of the firm is to find a cost-minimizing point on a given isoquant. The equation of a *constant cost curve* (C) is equal to:

$$C = w_1 x_1 + w_2 x_2$$

Solving for x_2, we have:

$$x_2 = \frac{C}{w_2} - \left(\frac{w_1}{w_2}\right) x_1$$

Therefore, we can formalize the problem by saying that for the fixed value of w_1 and w_2, we want to find a point on a given isoquant where the associated constant cost curve has minimal vertical intercept. This is the tangent point where the slope of the constant curve must be equal to the slope of the isoquant. Therefore, by considering these two slopes and by considering that they must be equal in the tangent point, we have: $\frac{w_i}{w_j} = \frac{\frac{\partial f(x^*)}{\partial x_i}}{\frac{\partial f(x^*)}{\partial x_j}}$.

Note that there is a second-order condition that must be satisfied at a cost-minimizing choice: the isoquant must lie above the isocost line.

1.2.1 Weak Axiom of Cost Minimization (WACM)

If we assume that the firm chooses factors to minimize the cost of output λ, the main implication is that the factors change as prices change.

Assume that the output level is y^t, the vector of factor prices is $\boldsymbol{w}^t$, the vector of factor levels is $\boldsymbol{x}^t$, for $t = 1, 2, \ldots, T$.

The cost minimization implies that the observed choice of inputs ($\boldsymbol{w}^t\boldsymbol{x}^t$) is no greater than the cost of any other level of inputs ($\boldsymbol{w}^s\boldsymbol{x}^s$) able to produce at least as much output y. Formally:

$$\boldsymbol{w}^t\boldsymbol{x}^t \leq \boldsymbol{w}^s\boldsymbol{x}^s \quad \text{for all } s \text{ and } t \text{ such that } y^t \leq y^s \tag{1.8}$$

This condition is called ***Weak Axiom of Cost Minimization (WACM)***.

Assume two choices of output $\boldsymbol{w}^t\boldsymbol{x}^t$ and $\boldsymbol{w}^s\boldsymbol{x}^s$ with the same level of output y. The cost minimization implies that (Varian, 1992):

$$1.\boldsymbol{w}^t\boldsymbol{x}^t \leq \boldsymbol{w}^t\boldsymbol{x}^s \quad \rightarrow \quad \overline{\boldsymbol{w}^t} \text{ and } \boldsymbol{x}^t \leq \boldsymbol{x}^s$$
$$2.\boldsymbol{w}^s\boldsymbol{x}^s \leq \boldsymbol{w}^s\boldsymbol{x}^t \quad \rightarrow \quad \overline{\boldsymbol{w}^s} \text{ and } \boldsymbol{x}^s \leq \boldsymbol{x}^t$$

where:

1. the first inequality states that by considering the tth observation, the cost minimization is realized at tth prices.

2. the second inequality states that by considering the *s*th observation, the cost minimization is realized at *s*th prices.

Consider the second inequality and change the sign by passing from positive to negative:

$$\mathbf{w}^s\mathbf{x}^s \leq \mathbf{w}^s\mathbf{x}^t \quad \leftrightarrow \quad -\mathbf{w}^s\mathbf{x}^t \leq -\mathbf{w}^s\mathbf{x}^s$$

Add to the second inequality the first inequality:

$$\mathbf{w}^t\mathbf{x}^t - \mathbf{w}^s\mathbf{x}^t \leq \mathbf{w}^t\mathbf{x}^s - \mathbf{w}^s\mathbf{x}^s$$

and rearranging we have:

$$\mathbf{w}^t\mathbf{x}^t - \mathbf{w}^s\mathbf{x}^t - \mathbf{w}^t\mathbf{x}^s + \mathbf{w}^s\mathbf{x}^s \leq 0$$

$$\mathbf{x}^t(\mathbf{w}^t - \mathbf{w}^s) - \mathbf{x}^s(\mathbf{w}^t - \mathbf{w}^s) \leq 0$$

$$(\mathbf{w}^t - \mathbf{w}^s)(\mathbf{x}^t - \mathbf{x}^s) \leq 0$$

and then:

$$\Delta\mathbf{w}\Delta\mathbf{x} \leq 0 \tag{1.9}$$

where Δx is the change in factor levels and Δw is the change in factor prices.

It implies that the vector of factor levels must move opposite to the vector of factor prices. Therefore, based on the cost minimization aim of the firm, the equation states how the firm's choice about factor levels must change if the input prices change and the output remains constant to minimize the costs.

To well-understand assume the case of two factors. In this case, we have two set of prices (w_1^t, w_2^t) and (w_1^s, w_2^s) and two set of factor levels (x_1^t, x_2^t) and (x_1^s, x_2^s). Assume that each of these choices produces the same output level *y* (Varian, 1992).

If each of these choices is cost minimizing, we have:

$$1. w_1^t x_1^t + w_2^t x_2^t \leq w_1^t x_1^s + w_2^t x_2^s \quad \rightarrow \quad \overline{w_1^t}; \overline{w_2^t} \text{ and } x_1^t + x_2^t \leq x_1^s + x_2^s$$

$$2. w_1^s x_1^s + w_2^s x_2^s \leq w_1^s x_1^t + w_2^s x_2^t \quad \rightarrow \quad \overline{w_1^S}; \overline{w_2^S} \text{ and } x_1^s + x_2^s \leq x_1^t + x_2^t$$

Based on WACM if the firm chooses the cost minimization to produce *y* units of output, then the firm's choices at time *t* and *s* must satisfy these inequalities.

Rewrite the second inequality by changing the sign passing from positive to negative as follows:

$$w_1^s x_1^s + w_2^s x_2^s \leq w_1^s x_1^t + w_2^s x_2^t \quad \leftrightarrow \quad -w_1^s x_1^t - w_2^s x_2^t \leq -w_1^s x_1^s - w_2^s x_2^s$$

Add the first inequality to the second as follows:

$$w_1^t x_1^t + w_2^t x_2^t - w_1^s x_1^t - w_2^s x_2^t \leq w_1^t x_1^s + w_2^t x_2^s - w_1^s x_1^s - w_2^s x_2^s$$

And rearranging, we have:

$$w_1^t x_1^t + w_2^t x_2^t - w_1^s x_1^t - w_2^s x_2^t - w_1^t x_1^s - w_2^t x_2^s + w_1^s x_1^s + w_2^s x_2^s \leq 0$$

$$(w_1^t - w_1^s) x_1^t + (w_2^t - w_2^s) x_2^t - (w_1^t - w_1^s) x_1^s - (w_2^t - w_2^s) x_2^s \leq 0$$

$$(w_1^t - w_1^s)(x_1^t - x_1^s) + (w_2^t - w_2^s)(x_2^t - x_2^s) \leq 0$$

And then:

$$\Delta w_1 \Delta x_1 + \Delta w_2 \Delta x_2 \leq 0$$

where Δx is the changes in factor levels and Δw is the change in factor prices.

Therefore, if we assume that the price of the first factor increases ($\Delta w_1 \neq 0$) and the price of second factor remains constant ($\Delta w_2 = 0$), the inequality becomes:

$$\Delta w_1 \Delta x_1 \leq 0$$

Therefore, if the price of factor 1 increases, the level of factor 1 must decrease. Therefore, the inequality states in which way the firm's choice about factor levels must change if the input prices change and the output remains constant to minimize the costs.

Note that the right application of this calculus requires that the production function is well defined and derivable. Therefore, there are many cases in which it is not possible.

1.3 Profit Maximization

The ***Profit of the firm*** (π_F) can be defined easy as the positive difference between total revenues (R_T) and total costs (C_T) as follows:

$$\pi = R_T - C_T$$

Both revenues and costs are strictly related to the firm's activities. If we denote with $\boldsymbol{a}$ the vector of all activities of the firm, so that $\boldsymbol{a} = (a_1, a_2, \ldots, a_n)$, the firm's profit ($\pi_F$) is equal to:

$$\pi = R(a_1, a_2, \ldots, a_n) - C(a_1, a_2, \ldots, a_n)$$

The firm can maximize the profit by choosing those activities $(a_1, a_2, \ldots, a_n)$ able to maximize the difference between revenues and costs, as follows:

$$\max_{a_1,a_2,\ldots,a_n} \pi = \max_{a_1,a_2,\ldots,a_n} R(a_1, a_2, \ldots, a_n) - C(a_1, a_2, \ldots, a_n) \tag{1.10}$$

The vector of activities able to maximize the firm's profit $\boldsymbol{a}^* = \left(a_1^*, a_2^*, \ldots, a_n^*\right)$ is characterized by the following condition:

$$\frac{\partial R(\boldsymbol{a}^*)}{\partial a_i} = \frac{\partial C(\boldsymbol{a}^*)}{\partial a_i} \quad \leftrightarrow \quad \frac{\partial R(\boldsymbol{a}^*)}{\partial a_i} - \frac{\partial C(\boldsymbol{a}^*)}{\partial a_i} = 0 \quad for\ i = 1,2,\ldots,n \tag{1.11}$$

or in simpler form:

$$R_i' = C_i' \quad \leftrightarrow \quad R_i' - C_i' = 0 \quad for\ i = 1,2,\ldots,n$$

where R_i' is the *Marginal Revenue* of the *i*th activity, so that $R_i' = \frac{\partial R(\boldsymbol{a}^*)}{\partial a_i}$, and with C_i' is the *Marginal Cost* of the *i*th activity, so that $C_i' = \frac{\partial C(\boldsymbol{a}^*)}{\partial a_i}$.

This equality states the *Optimization Rule*: the firm increases the level of its activity until the marginal revenue of *i*th activity $(\partial R(\boldsymbol{a}^*)/\partial a_i)$ is equal to its marginal cost $(\partial C(\boldsymbol{a}^*)/\partial a_i)$.

Therefore, the equality between marginal revenue and marginal cost of the *i*th activity $\left(R_i' = C_i'\right)$ states the fundamental condition of the profit maximization so that it is not convenient to increase or decrease the level of the activity. Indeed, if:

(a) The marginal revenue is greater than marginal cost $\left(R_i' > C_i'\right)$, we will increase the level of the activities.
(b) The marginal revenue is lower than marginal cost $\left(R_i' < C_i'\right)$, we will decrease the level of the activity.

The optimization rule has two relevant and concrete implication in the firm's decision-making process. Indeed, it is fundamental to:

1. *Define the level of a specific input*: the firm maximize the profit if it uses a level (in units) of a input so that the use of *one more unit of input* produces a marginal revenue equal to the marginal cost of its use.
2. *Define the level of output*: the firm maximize the profit if it defines a level (in units) of output so that the production of *one more unit of output* produces a marginal revenue equal to its marginal cost of production.

Assume that the firm:

- produces *n* output goods: y_i for $i = 1, 2, \ldots, n$
- uses all *n* factor inputs: x_i for $i = 1, 2, \ldots, n$
- the prices of *n* output goods: p_i for $i = 1, 2, \ldots, n$
- the prices *n* factor inputs w_i: for $i = 1, 2, \ldots, n$

It gets that:

$$\begin{aligned} R_T &= \sum_{i=1}^{n} p_i y_i \\ C_T &= \sum_{i=1}^{m} w_i x_i \end{aligned} \quad \rightarrow \quad \pi = \sum_{i=1}^{n} p_i y_i - \sum_{i=1}^{m} w_i x_i$$

Therefore, the firm's profit is the function of four variables:

- the price of each input (w_i) the price of each output ($p_{i,}$)
- the level (in units) of each input (x_i) and of each output (y_i)

All variables considered must be defined by the firm taking into account the constraints that exist with regard three main aspects: technology, business, capital markets.

Consider a competitive market in which the firm is a price-taking for both inputs and outputs. Therefore, firm faces fixed prices for inputs (w_i) and output (p_i), and it defines the level (in units) of input and output able to maximize the profit. If we denote with $\boldsymbol{p}$ the vector of fixed prices of inputs and outputs and $\boldsymbol{y}$ the vector of inputs (with negative sign) and outputs (with positive sign) so that $\boldsymbol{y} \epsilon Ym$, the profit maximization problem of the firm can be formalized as follows (Varian, 1992):

$$\pi(\boldsymbol{p}) = \max \boldsymbol{yp} \tag{1.12}$$

where $\pi(\boldsymbol{p})$ is the profit function that gives the maximum profits as a function of the prices.

Assume that the firm produces only one product (one output) whose price is fixed, so that p is the scalar price of output. By considering the vector $\boldsymbol{x}$ (nonnegative) of inputs (nonnegative vector $\boldsymbol{x} = (x_1, x_2, \ldots, x_n)$) and the vector $\boldsymbol{w}$ of the price of the inputs (so that $\boldsymbol{w} = (w_1, w_2, \ldots, w_n)$, the *profit function* is equal to:

$$\pi(p, \boldsymbol{w}) = \max pf(\boldsymbol{x}) - \boldsymbol{wx}$$

where:

- $pf(\boldsymbol{x})$: is the total revenue based on the price of output (p) and the production function $f(\boldsymbol{x})$ on the basis of input ($\boldsymbol{x}$)
- $\boldsymbol{wx}$: is the total cost based on the price of input ($\boldsymbol{w}$) and the input used ($\boldsymbol{x}$).

The profit maximization can be analysed on the basis of the ***first-order condition***.

Consider the case of one product (one output). The first-order conditions for the single output profit maximization problem is equal to:

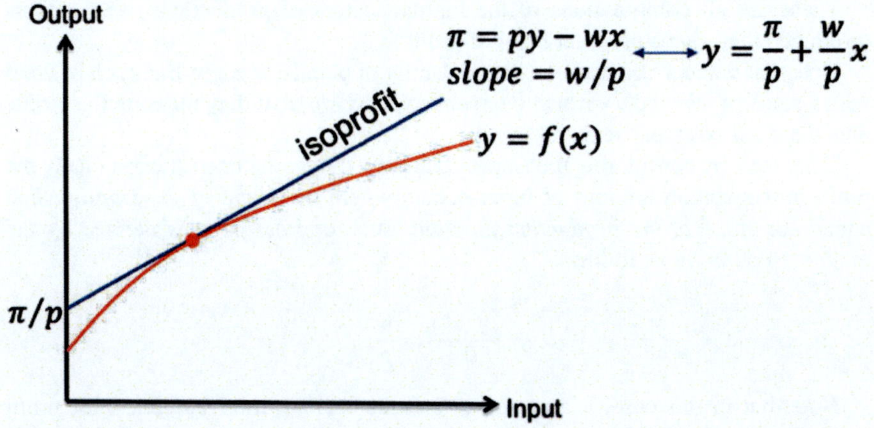

Fig. 1.6 Isoprofit

$$p\frac{\partial f(\boldsymbol{x}^*)}{\partial x_i} = w_i \quad i = 1,2,\ldots,n \tag{1.13}$$

Therefore, the first-order condition states that the value of marginal product of each factor $\left(p\frac{\partial f(\boldsymbol{x}^*)}{\partial x_i}\right)$ must be equal to its price (w_i).

By using the vector notion, the first-order condition can be formalized as follows:

$$p\boldsymbol{D}f(\boldsymbol{x}^*) = \boldsymbol{w}$$

where $\boldsymbol{D}f(\boldsymbol{x}^*)$ is the vector of partial derivatives of production function f with respect to $(x_1, x_2, \ldots, x_n)$ as follows:

$$\boldsymbol{D}f(\boldsymbol{x}^*) = \left(\frac{\partial f(x^*)}{\partial x_1}, \frac{\partial f(x^*)}{\partial x_2}, \ldots, \frac{\partial f(x^*)}{\partial x_n}\right)$$

Assume the two-dimensional case. The profit function is equal to (Varian, 1992):

$$\pi = py - wx$$

By solving for y the profit function, we have a straight-line called *isoprofit line* (as in Fig. 1.6) whose equation is:

$$y = \frac{\pi}{p} + \frac{w}{p}x \tag{1.14}$$

where:

- $\frac{w}{p}$: is the slope of isoprofit and it gives us the *cost for unit of output*
- $\frac{\pi}{p}$: is the vertical intercept of isoprofit and it gives us the *profit per unit of output.*

These are all combinations of the inputs (factors of productions) and outputs (products) that give a constant level of profit π.

Note that when π changes, we have a family of parallel straight-line each of them with a slope of w/p and a vertical intercept equal to π/p, that they measure the profits plus the fixed costs of the firm.

Therefore, by considering the isoprofit line and the production function ($f(x)$), the profit maximization amount of input occurs where the *slope of the isoprofit line* equals the *slope of the production function*. Such optimal point is defined by the *tangency condition* as follows:

$$\frac{\partial f(x^*)}{\partial x} = \frac{w}{p}$$

Note that in this case, it easy to see that the *second-order condition* for profit maximization, that is the second derivative of the production function with respect to the input must be nonpositive, as follows:

$$\frac{d^2 f(x^*)}{dx^2} \leq 0 \tag{1.15}$$

Indeed, the nonpositive condition implies the production function must be locally concave. Usually, it is assumed that the second derivative is strictly negative. It implies that the production function must be concave and at the point of maximal profits the production function must lie below its tangent line at x^*.

By generalizing, for each vector of price (p, w), there will be some optimal choice of factors x^*. The function that gives us:

- the optimal choice of inputs is defined *Demand Function* of the firm: $x(p, w)$
- the optimal choice of production is defined Supply Function of the firm: $y(p, w) = f(x(p, w))$.

Commonly these two functions are well defined and differentiable at least twice. If it is not, we cannot calculate the first and second derivatives.

The right application of these calculus implies that the functions are well defined and derivable. There are some conditions in which it is not possible.

1.3.1 Comparative Statics

The aim of the *Comparative Statistics* is to understand how an economic variable change to the change of its environment. Specifically, the term "comparative" refers to comparing before and after situation and the term "statics" refers to the fact that the comparison must be made after all adjustments have been realized giving the opportunity to compare one equilibrium to another.

In this contest, our problem of comparative statics refers to *how change the firm's choice of inputs and outputs if the prices of inputs and outputs change.*

Consider a simple case. Assume that firm produces only one output by using only one input (x). The profit maximization problem can be formalized as follows (Varian, 1992):

$$\max_{x} pf(x) - wx \tag{1.16}$$

where:

- $pf(x)$: is the total revenue
- wx: is the total cost.

Assume the production function $f(x)$ is differentiable twice.

The *Demand function* $x(p, w)$ must satisfy the first-order and second-order conditions, as follows:

$$pf'(x(p,\ w)) - w \equiv 0 \quad \rightarrow \quad pf'(x(p,\ w)) \equiv w$$

$$pf''(x(p,\ w)) \leq 0$$

Note that these conditions are an identity in p and w. If $x(p, w)$ is the choice able to maximize the profits at (p, w) (by definition), then $x(p, w)$ must satisfy the conditions for profit maximization for all possible values of p and w.

Since the first-order condition is an identity, we can derive it with respect to w as follows:

$$pf''(x(p,\ w))\frac{dx(p,\ w)}{dw} - 1 \equiv 0$$

If we assume that the second derivative $f''(x)$ is not zero, we have a maximum, and then we can get:

$$\frac{dx(p,\ w)}{dw} \equiv \frac{1}{pf''(x(p,\ w))} \tag{1.17}$$

This identity gives two main information about the change in factor demand $x(p, w)$ if the factor prices (w) change. Specifically, the identity states:

1. The higher the curvature of the production function in a neighbourhood of the optimum (the second derivative is large in magnitude), the smaller will be the change in factor demand due to the change in factor prices.
2. Since the second derivative of the production function $f''(x(p, w))$ is negative, then $\frac{dx(p,\ w)}{dw}$ is negative. It implies that the factor demand curve slopes downward.

1.3.2 Weak Axiom of Profit Maximization (WAPM)

Assume a finite number of observations about firm's choices. Denote with $\boldsymbol{p}^t$ the *price vector* and with $\boldsymbol{y}^t$ *net output vectors* for $t = 1, 2, \ldots, T$ (outputs with a positive number and inputs with a negative number). The *supply functions* is equal to ($\boldsymbol{p}^t$, $\boldsymbol{y}(\boldsymbol{p}^t)$) for observations $t = 1, 2, \ldots, T$.

If the firm's aim is to maximize the profit, then the observed net output choice at price $\boldsymbol{p}^t$ must give a profit at least as greater as the profit that at any other net output of the firm could give.

Therefore, denoting with $\boldsymbol{y}^s$ for $s = 1, 2, \ldots, T$, the other choices of the firm, the condition for profit maximization can be formalized as follows (Varian, 1992):

$$\boldsymbol{p}^t\boldsymbol{y}^t \geq \boldsymbol{p}^t\boldsymbol{y}^s \quad \text{for all } t \text{ and } s = 1,2,\ldots,T. \tag{1.18}$$

This condition is called ***Weak Axiom of Profit Maximization (WAPM).***

Assume two observations, t and s, and write WAPM for each one, as follows:

$$1. \boldsymbol{p}^t(\boldsymbol{y}^t - \boldsymbol{y}^s) \geq 0$$
$$2. -\boldsymbol{p}^s(\boldsymbol{y}^t - \boldsymbol{y}^s) \geq 0$$

Adding these two inequalities, we have:

$$\boldsymbol{p}^t(\boldsymbol{y}^t - \boldsymbol{y}^s) - \boldsymbol{p}^s(\boldsymbol{y}^t - \boldsymbol{y}^s) \geq 0$$
$$(\boldsymbol{p}^t - \boldsymbol{p}^s)(\boldsymbol{y}^t - \boldsymbol{y}^s) \geq 0$$

Denoting with $\Delta\boldsymbol{p} = \boldsymbol{p}^t - \boldsymbol{p}^s$ and $\Delta\boldsymbol{y} = \boldsymbol{y}^t - \boldsymbol{y}^s$, and replacing we have:

$$\Delta\boldsymbol{p}\Delta\boldsymbol{y} \geq 0 \tag{1.19}$$

where $\Delta\boldsymbol{p}$ is the changes in factor prices and $\Delta\boldsymbol{y}$ is the change in net outputs.

It implies that the product of change in prices and change in net outputs must be nonnegative. Therefore, if we assume that the firm produces one output (it is measured by a positive number), the supply of that output cannot decrease if its price increases. On the other hand, if we assume that there is one input (it is measured by a negative number), then the demand for that input must not increase if its price increases.

To well-understand consider the following case. Assume that firm have two choices at two different sets of prices:

1. At time t, firm faces prices (p^t, w_1^t, w_2^t) and it makes choices (y^t, x_1^t, x_2^t).
2. At time s, firm faces prices (p^s, w_1^s, w_2^s) and it makes choices (y^s, x_1^s, x_2^s).

Assume that the firm wants to maximize the profit and the production function does not change between the times *s* and *t*. Under these conditions, we have (Varian, 1992):

$$1. p^t y^t - w_1^t x_1^t - w_2^t x_2^t \geq p^t y^s - w_1^t x_1^s - w_2^t x_2^s$$
$$2. p^s y^s - w_1^s x_1^s - w_2^s x_2^s \geq p^s y^t - w_1^s x_1^t - w_2^s x_2^t$$

Based on these two inequalities, profits that the firm realized facing the *t* period prices must be larger than if they used the *s* period plan and vice versa. If either of these inequalities is not respected, firm does not maximize the profits with an unchanging technology.

Assume that WAPM condition is respected. We can derive a useful comparative statics with regard to the behaviour of factor demands and output supplies if prices change.

We can rewrite the second inequalities as follows:

$$-p^s y^t + w_1^s x_1^t + w_2^s x_2^t \geq -p^s y^s + w_1^s x_1^s + w_2^s x_2^s$$

Add this inequality to the first inequality as follows:

$$p^t y^t - w_1^t x_1^t - w_2^t x_2^t - p^s y^t + w_1^s x_1^t + w_2^s x_2^t \geq p^t y^s - w_1^t x_1^s - w_2^t x_2^s - p^s y^s + w_1^s x_1^s + w_2^s x_2^s$$

$$(p^t - p^s) y^t - (w_1^t - w_1^s) x_1^t - (w_2^t - w_2^s) x_2^t \geq (p^t - p^s) y^s - (w_1^t - w_1^s) x_1^s - (w_2^t - w_2^s) x_2^s$$

$$(p^t - p^s) y^t - (w_1^t - w_1^s) x_1^t - (w_2^t - w_2^s) x_2^t - (p^t - p^s) y^s + (w_1^t - w_1^s) x_1^s + (w_2^t - w_2^s) x_2^s \geq 0$$

$$(p^t - p^s)(y^t - y^s) - (w_1^t - w_1^s)(x_1^t - x_1^s) - (w_2^t - w_2^s)(x_2^t - x_2^s) \geq 0$$

By denoting the change in prices $\Delta p = (p^t - p^s)$ and the change in output $\Delta y = (y^t - y^s)$, we have:

$$\Delta p \Delta y - \Delta w_1 \Delta x_1 - \Delta w_2 \Delta x_2 \geq 0$$

The inequality states that the change in the price of output multiplies the change in output minus the change in each factor price multiplies the change in that factor must be nonnegative.

To well-understand consider two cases.

Case 1) Assume that the price of output changes ($\Delta p \neq 0$) but the price of both factors 1 and 2 remains constant ($\Delta w_1 = \Delta w_2 = 0$). In this case, we have:

$$\Delta p \Delta y - \Delta w_1 \Delta x_1 - \Delta w_2 \Delta x_2 \geq 0 \quad \rightarrow \quad \Delta p \Delta y \geq 0$$

It implies that if the price of output increases ($\Delta p > 0$), the change in output must be nonnegative ($\Delta y \geq 0$). Therefore, the profit maximization implies that the supply curve of firm must have a positive (or at least a zero) slope.

Case 2) Assume that the price of factor 1 changes ($\Delta w_1 \neq 0$), while the price of output and factor 2 remain constant ($\Delta p = \Delta w_2 = 0$). In this case it gets:

$$\Delta p \Delta y - \Delta w_1 \Delta x_1 - \Delta w_2 \Delta x_2 \geq 0 \quad \rightarrow \quad - \Delta w_1 \Delta x_1 \geq 0 \quad \rightarrow \quad \Delta w_1 \Delta x_1 \leq 0$$

It implies that if the price of factor 1 increases ($\Delta w_1 > 0$), the demand for factor 1 decreases (or at worst stay the same), so that ($\Delta x_1 \leq 0$). Then, the factor demand curve is a decreasing function of the factor price and then it has a negative slope.

Cost Structure of the Firm 2

2.1 Cost Functions

The term "cost" is one of the most commonly used even if it is also very ambiguous. The cost can be defined as a measurement in monetary terms of the amount of resources used for a specific purpose. Therefore, the term cost requires the presence of three main structural elements:

1. It must be expressed in monetary terms
2. It must measure the use of resources in monetary terms
3. It must be defined with regard to a well-defined cost-object (it can be anything for which monetary measurements of resources used is desired such as direct cost, full cost, opportunity cost, differential cost, etc.)

Generally, the cost curves are used to draw graphically the cost function of a firm which are very useful to study the determination of optimal choices. In fact, cost function is able to:

1. Summarize all information about technology and technological choices available for the firms. Consequently, its behaviour tells us a lot about the nature of the firm's technology
2. Measure the minimum cost of producing a given level of output for some fixed factor prices
3. Describe in a primary way the economic possibilities of the firm

The cost function can be formalized as follows:

$$C(\boldsymbol{w}, Q) \equiv \boldsymbol{wx}(\boldsymbol{w}, Q) \tag{2.1}$$

The identity states that the minimum cost of producing y units of output is the lowest cost to produce y.

P. De Luca, *Corporate Finance*, Springer Texts in Business and Economics,
https://doi.org/10.1007/978-3-031-18300-3_2

The right definition of the function cost requires to distinguish between short run and long run. In the short run only, we can distinguish between:

- *fixed factors* that generate *fixed costs*: they refer to all factors of production that are in fixed amount for the firm and they cannot be changed in their amount used in the period considered. Consequently, these factors of production must be paid even if the firm produces zero output goods.
- *variable factors* that generate *variable costs*: they refer to all factors of production that are in variable amount for the firm and then they can be changed in the amount used in the period considered. Consequently, these factors of production must be paid only if firm produces output goods.

With regard to the distinction between fixed and variable costs in the short run, it is necessary to keep in mind that:

1. Variable costs change when output level (Q) changes, while fixed costs are independent to the level of output of the firm. Cost is fixed with regard to output (Q) only. Therefore, it does not change with changes in output (Q) but it can change for other reasons and specifically it changes in the case of management decisions on the item referenced.
2. The distinction between fixed and variable costs exists only in the short run. In the long run all factors of production can be changed and then all costs are variables by definition. The extreme case is to produce zero units of output at zero costs because it is always possible to go out of business.
3. The short run and the long run are not related to the time. They refer to the firm's production capacity and to the specific problem we are analysing within it. In this sense, the short run is the time period in which it is assumed the same level of firm's production capacity; on the contrary, the long run is the time period in which it is assumed the change of the firm's production capacity. Consequently, the cost is fixed within a defined production capacity and therefore within a defined level of production. Out of the range, increases in output require more production capacity, whose implementation increases fixed costs. Therefore, in the long term by assuming changes in the product capacity, all costs are variable.
4. The long run and short run are always relative concept. Which factors are considered variable and which others are considered fixed depend on the particular problem being analysed.
5. The driver used for the analysis of the cost's behaviour is the volume that measures the level of output. The mean question is to specify what measurement of volume we use. It can be defined on the basis of the production volume, and therefore on the number of products produced, or sale volume and therefore the number of products sold. Commonly, volume is defined in terms of the production volume rather than the sales volume.

2.1.1 Short-Run Cost Functions

In the short run we must distinguish between fixed factors, and then fixed costs, and variable factors and then variable costs.

Denote with:

(a) $\boldsymbol{x}$: the vector of production factors. It is equal to $\boldsymbol{x} = (\boldsymbol{x}_f, \boldsymbol{x}_v)$ where $\boldsymbol{x}_f$ is the vector of fixed factors and $\boldsymbol{x}_v$ is the vector of variable factors.
(b) $\boldsymbol{w}$: the vector of prices (or costs) of production factors. It is equal to $\boldsymbol{w} = (\boldsymbol{w}_f, \boldsymbol{w}_v)$ where $\boldsymbol{w}_f$ is the vector of price (or cost) of the fixed factors and $\boldsymbol{w}_v$ is the vector of price (or cost) of the variable factors.
(c) Q: the output level and then the quantity in units of outputs.

The Short-Run Total Cost (C_S) can be defined as follows:

$$C_S = C(\boldsymbol{w}, Q, \boldsymbol{x}_f) = \boldsymbol{w}_v \boldsymbol{x}_v(\boldsymbol{w}, Q, \boldsymbol{x}_f) + \boldsymbol{w}_f \boldsymbol{x}_f \tag{2.2}$$

This equation can be divided into two terms:

(a) $\boldsymbol{w}_v \boldsymbol{x}_v(\boldsymbol{w}, Q, \boldsymbol{x}_f)$: it is the Short-Run Variable Cost (C_V).
(b) $\boldsymbol{w}_f \boldsymbol{x}_f$: it is the Fixed Cost ($C_F$).

So that the equation can be rewritten as follows:

$$C_S = C_V + C_F \tag{2.3}$$

Note that for Variable and Fixed Costs there is not used the subscript "S" because it is implicit because the distinction between variable and fixed costs exist only in the short run (in the long run all costs are variable).

The Short-Run Marginal Cost (MC_S) is equal to the derivative of Short-Run Total Cost (C_S) with respect to the Q units of output produced, as follows:

$$MC_S = \frac{\partial c(\boldsymbol{w}, Q, \boldsymbol{x}_f)}{\partial Q} = \frac{\partial [\boldsymbol{w}_v \boldsymbol{x}_v(\boldsymbol{w}, Q, \boldsymbol{x}_f) + \boldsymbol{w}_f \boldsymbol{x}_f]}{\partial Q} \tag{2.4}$$

The Short-Run Average Cost (AC_S) is equal to the Short-Run Total Cost (C_S) divided units of output (Q) produced, and it measures the Short-Run Cost per Unit of Output (C_{US}). Formally:

$$AC_S \equiv C_{US} = \frac{C(\boldsymbol{w}, Q, \boldsymbol{x}_f)}{Q} = \frac{\boldsymbol{w}_v \boldsymbol{x}_v(\boldsymbol{w}, Q, \boldsymbol{x}_f) + \boldsymbol{w}_f \boldsymbol{x}_f}{Q} = \frac{\boldsymbol{w}_v \boldsymbol{x}_v(\boldsymbol{w}, Q, \boldsymbol{x}_f)}{Q} + \frac{\boldsymbol{w}_f \boldsymbol{x}_f}{Q} \tag{2.5}$$

where:

(a) The first part is the Short-Run Average Variable Cost (AC_V) and it measures the Short-Run Variable Cost per Unit of Output (C_{VU}):

$$AC_V \equiv C_{VU} = \frac{w_v x_v(w, Q, x_f)}{Q} \tag{2.6}$$

(b) The second part is the Short-Run Average Fixed Cost (AC_F) and it measures the Short-Run Fixed Cost per Unit of Output (C_{FU}):

$$AC_F \equiv C_{FU} = \frac{w_f x_f}{Q} \tag{2.7}$$

Therefore, the Short-Run Average Cost (AC_S) is equal to the sum of Short-Run Average Variable Cost (AC_V) and the Short-Run Average Fixed Cost (AC_F).

In terms of cost per unit of output, the Short-Run Cost per Unit of Output (C_{US}) is equal to the sum of Short-Run Variable Cost per Unit of Output (C_{VU}) and the Short-Run Fixed Cost per Unit of Output (C_{FU}). Formally:

$$AC_S = AC_V + AC_F \leftrightarrow C_{US} = C_{VU} + C_{FU} \tag{2.8}$$

2.1.2 Long-Run Cost Functions

In the long run there is not the distinction between fixed costs and variable costs because all factors are variable and then all costs are variable.

The Long-Run Cost Function depends only on the vector of factor prices (w) and the level of output (Q).

Denote with:

- $x_f(w, Q)$: the optimal choice of the fixed factors.
- $x_v(w, Q) = x_v(w, Q, x_f(w, Q))$: the long-run optimal choice of variable factors.

The Long-Run Total Cost (C_L) can be formalized as follows:

$$C_L = C(w, Q) = w_v x_v(w, Q) + w_f x_f(w, Q) = C(w, Q, x_f(w, Q)) \tag{2.9}$$

The Long-Run Marginal Cost (MC_L) is equal to the derivative of Long-Run Total Cost (C_L) with respect to the (Q) units of output produced, as follows:

$$MC_L = \frac{\partial C(w, Q)}{\partial Q} = \frac{\partial [C(w, Q, x_f(w, Q))]}{\partial Q} \tag{2.10}$$

The Long-Run Average Cost (AC_L) is equal to the Long-Run Total Cost (C_L) divided units of output (Q) produced, and it measures the Long-Run Cost per Unit of Output (C_{UL}). Formally:

$$AC_L \equiv C_{UL} = \frac{C(w, Q)}{Q} = \frac{C(w, Q, x_f(w, Q))}{Q} \tag{2.11}$$

It is relevant to note that the Long-Run Average Cost (AC_L) equals the Long-Run Average Variable Cost because in the long run all costs are variable and consequently, Long-Run Fixed Costs are zero.

2.1.3 Price and Cost Function

Price affects directly the Cost Function. Price of factors can be fixed or variable.
Denote with:

(a) $\boldsymbol{x}$: the vector of production factors, so that $\boldsymbol{x} = (\boldsymbol{x_f}, \boldsymbol{x_v})$ where $\boldsymbol{x_f}$ is the vector of fixed factors, and $\boldsymbol{x_v}$ is the vector of variable factors.
(b) $\boldsymbol{w}$: the vector of prices (or costs) of production factors so that $\boldsymbol{w} = (\boldsymbol{w_f}, \boldsymbol{w_v})$ where $\boldsymbol{w_f}$ is the vector of price (or cost) of the fixed factors, and $\boldsymbol{w_v}$ is the vector of price (or cost) of the variable factors.
(c) Q: the output level and then the quantity in units of outputs.

The main properties of the Cost Function based on the price of factors can be summarized as follows:

1. *Nondecreasing in* w: if $\boldsymbol{w}' \geq \boldsymbol{w}$, therefore $C(\boldsymbol{w}', Q) \geq C(\boldsymbol{w}, Q)$.
   Consider $\boldsymbol{x}$ and $\boldsymbol{x}'$ a cost-minimizing bundles associated with $\boldsymbol{w}$ and $\boldsymbol{w}'$, respectively, so that:
   (a) $\boldsymbol{wx}' \geq \boldsymbol{wx}$ since $\boldsymbol{x}' \geq \boldsymbol{x}$.
   (b) $\boldsymbol{w}'\boldsymbol{x}' \geq \boldsymbol{wx}'$ since $\boldsymbol{w}' \geq \boldsymbol{w}$.

Considering jointly these inequalities, we have $\boldsymbol{w}'\boldsymbol{x}' \geq \boldsymbol{wx}$ as required.

2. Homogeneous of degree 1 in $\boldsymbol{w}$: $C(t\boldsymbol{w}, Q) = tC(\boldsymbol{w}, Q)$ for $t > 0$.
   It implies that multiplying factor prices by a positive scalar ($t > 0$) it does not change the composition of a cost-minimizing bundle, and then costs must rise by exactly a factor of t. Consequently, if $\boldsymbol{x}$ is the cost-minimizing bundle at prices $\boldsymbol{w}$, then $\boldsymbol{x}$ minimizes costs at prices $t\boldsymbol{w}$.

3. Concave in w: $C(tw + (1 - t)w', Q) \geq tC(w, Q) + (1 - t)C(w', Q)$ for $0 \leq t \leq 1$. Assume two cost-minimizing price-factor combinations: (w,x) and (w',x'). Assume that $w'' = tw + (1 - t)w'$ for any $0 \leq t \leq 1$. Then, $C(w'', y) = w''x'' = twx'' + (1 - t)w'x''$. Because x'' is not necessary the lowest way to produce y at prices w' or w, we have $wx'' \geq C(w, y)$ and $w' \cdot x'' \geq C(w', y)$. Therefore, $C(w'', y) \geq tC(w, y) + (1 - t)C(w', y)$.
4. *Continuous in* w: $C(w, Q)$ is continuous as a function of w, for $w \ll 0$.

2.2 Cost Functions in the Short run

To simplify the analysis of the cost curves, assume that the factor prices are fixed.

Under this assumption, the cost function depends on the level of output (Q) only. Consequently, we can define the cost (C) as the function of production output level (Q): $C(Q)$.

The cost curve is always assumed to be monotonic in output: the more you produce, the more is the costs.

By assuming the fixed price of production factors, we can rewrite in simpler way the cost function in the short run.

2.2.1 Short-Run Total Cost Functions

The Short-Run Total Cost (C_S) is equal to:

$$C_S = C(w, Q, x_f) = w_v x_v(w, Q, x_f) + w_f x_f \tag{2.12}$$

Under the assumption of fixed prices of factors, the Short-Run Total Cost (C_S) can be rewritten in simpler way as the sum of the total Variable Costs (C_V) and total Fixed Costs (C_F), as follows:

$$C_s = C_V + C_F \tag{2.13}$$

2.2.2 Short-Run Average Cost Functions

The Short-Run Average Cost (AC_S) measures the Short-Run Cost per Unit of Output (C_{US}) and then it is equal to:

$$AC_S \equiv C_{US} = \frac{c(w, Q, x_f)}{Q} = \frac{w_v x_v(w, Q, x_f) + w_f x_f}{Q} = \frac{w_v x_v(w, Q, x_f)}{Q} + \frac{w_f x_f}{Q} \tag{2.14}$$

Under the assumption of fixed prices of factors, we can rewrite the Short-Run Cost per Unit of Output (C_{US}), in simpler way as follows:

$$AC_S \equiv C_{US} = \frac{C_S}{Q} = \frac{C_V}{Q} + \frac{C_F}{Q} \tag{2.15}$$

where:

(a) The first part is the Short-Run Average Variable Cost (AC_V), and then the Short-Run Variable Cost per Unit of Output (C_{VU}), so that:

$$AC_V \equiv C_{VU} = \frac{C_V}{Q} \tag{2.16}$$

(b) The second part is the Short-Run Average Fixed Cost (AC_F), and it measures the Short-Run Fixed Cost per Unit of Output (C_{FU}), so that:

$$AC_F \equiv C_{FU} = \frac{C_F}{Q} \tag{2.17}$$

where:

(a) AC_F decreases to the increase in output level y so that the Short-Run Average Fixed Cost Curve decreases to the increase in Q. It implies that the Short-Run Fixed Cost per Unit of Output (C_{FU}) decreases to the increase in output (Q).
(b) AC_V it is reasonable to assume that if the production is efficient so that it is possible to realize the scale of output is increased, the Short-Run Average Variable Cost Curve decreases initially and increases in a second moment because if fixed costs are present, they will constrain the production process. In this case, we have a U-shape curve. It implies that the Short-Run Variable Cost per Unit of Output (C_{VU}) first decreases and after increases to the increase in output (Q). It is relevant to note that it is not necessary. Indeed, under the hypothesis of linear approximation, the average variable cost curve increases proportional, more than proportional, less than proportional to the increase in output level Q.

Therefore, the Short-Run Average Cost (AC_S) is equal to the sum of Short-Run Average Variable Cost (AC_V) and the Short-Run Average Fixed Cost (AC_F).

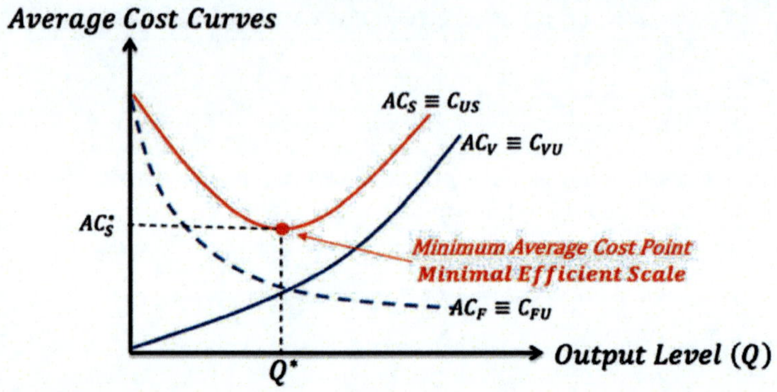

Fig. 2.1 Short-run average cost curves

In terms of cost per unit of output, the Short-Run Cost per Unit of Output (C_{US}) is equal to the sum of Short-Run Variable Cost per Unit of Output (C_{VU}) and the Short-Run Fixed Cost per Unit of Output (C_{FU}), as follows:

$$AC_S = AC_V + AC_F \leftrightarrow C_{US} = C_{VU} + C_{FU} \tag{2.18}$$

Consequently, the Short-Run Average Cost Curve (AC_S) (and then the Short-Run Cost per Unit of Output (C_{US})) is the sum of these two curves:

(a) The Short-Run Average Fixed Cost Curve (AC_F) (and then the Short-Run Fixed Cost per Unit of Output (C_{FU})) that decreases.
(b) The Short-Run Average Variable Cost Curve (AC_V) (and then Short-Run Variable Cost per Unit of Output (C_{VU})) that first decreases and after increases.

Therefore, the Short-Run Average Cost Curve (AC_S) (and then the Short-Run Cost per Unit of Output (C_{US})) has the U-shape.

The level of output at which the Short-Run Average Cost Curve (AC_S) is minimized is the Minimum Average Cost Point and it defines the Minimal Efficient Scale. It can be represented as in Fig. 2.1.

2.2.3 Marginal Cost Function (MC)

The Marginal Cost Function (MC) measures the change in cost for a given change in output (Q). Then it measures a Rate of Changes if we increase the output by one unit: the change in cost divided by a change in output. Therefore, the Marginal Cost Curve MC(Q) measures the cost of producing each additional unit of output as follows:

$$\mathrm{MC}(Q) = \frac{\partial C(Q)}{\partial Q} \tag{2.19}$$

If we assume a change in output level equal to ΔQ (consider ΔQ as being one unit of output), the marginal cost measures the change in our cost due to one more unit of output as follows:

$$\mathrm{MC}(Q) = \frac{\Delta C(Q)}{\Delta Q} = \frac{C(Q + \Delta Q) - C(Q)}{\Delta Q} \tag{2.20}$$

We can rewrite the Marginal Cost in terms of Variable Costs (MC(y)). Indeed, in the short run only the variable costs change to the change in output level, while the fixed costs remain constant and then their derivative is equal to zero. Formally:

$$\mathrm{MC}(y) = \frac{\Delta C_V}{\Delta Q} = \frac{C_V(Q + \Delta Q) - C_V(Q)}{\Delta y} \tag{2.21}$$

The relationship between Marginal Cost Curve (MC) and the Average Cost Curve (AC) can be defined by considering the point of Minimum Average *Cost* (Q^*):

1. To the left of Q^* ($Q \le Q^*$): the Average Cost Curve decreases so that:

$$\frac{d}{dQ}\left(\frac{C}{Q}\right) \le 0 \rightarrow \frac{C'Q - C}{Q^2} \le 0 \rightarrow C' \le \frac{C}{Q} \text{ for } Q \le Q^* \tag{2.22}$$

Therefore, to the left of the minimum average cost point the Marginal Cost is lower than the Average Cost. Then the Marginal Cost Curve must lie below the Average Cost Curve (and then the Average Variable Cost Curve) to the left of the minimum point.

It implies that if we produce in the output range in which the Average Cost Curve is decreasing (because the Average Variable Costs are decreasing), the cost of each additional unit produced is lower than average up to that point. The average goes down by addicting additional units. In this case the lower marginal costs are pushing the average.

2. To the right of Q^* ($Q \ge Q^*$): the Average Cost Curve increases so that:

$$\frac{d}{dQ}\left(\frac{C}{Q}\right) \ge 0 \rightarrow \frac{C'Q - C}{Q^2} \ge 0 \rightarrow C' \ge \frac{C}{Q} \text{ for } Q \ge Q^* \tag{2.23}$$

Therefore, to the right of the minimum point the Marginal Cost is higher than the Average Cost. Then, the Marginal Cost Curve must lie above the Average Cost Curve (and then the Average Variable Cost Curve) to the right of the minimum point.

It implies that if we produce in the output range in which the Average Cost Curve is increasing (because the Average Variable Costs are increasing), the cost of each additional unit produced is greater than average up to that point. The average goes up by addicting additional units. In this case the higher marginal costs are pushing the average.

3. To the level y^* ($Q = Q^*$): both inequalities must hold at output level Q^*. Therefore:

$$C'(Q^*) = \frac{C}{Q^*} \; for \; Q = Q^* \tag{2.24}$$

At the point of Minimum Average Cost, the Marginal Cost is equal to the Average Cost. By considering that the Marginal Cost Curve must lie below the Average Cost Curve (and then the Average Variable Cost Curve) to the left of its minimum point and above it to the right of the minimum point, the Marginal Cost Curve must intersect the Average Cost Curve (and then the Average Variable Cost Curve) at its minimum point.

4. To the level ($Q = 1$): Average Cost and the Marginal Cost have the same value. Indeed, for the first unit of output ($Q = 1$) the Average Cost is equal to the Marginal Cost, as follows:

$$\mathrm{MC}(1) = \frac{[C_V(1) + C_F] - [C_V(0) + C_F]}{1} = \frac{C_V(1) + C_F - C_V(0) - C_F}{1}$$
$$= \frac{C_V(1)}{1} = \mathrm{AC}_V(1) \tag{2.25}$$

This condition implies that:

$$\lim_{Q \to 0} \frac{C}{Q} = \lim_{Q \to 0} C' \tag{2.26}$$

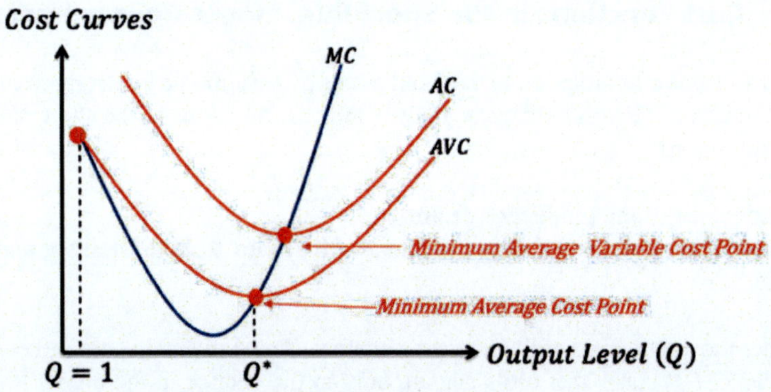

Fig. 2.2 Average cost, average variable cost, and marginal cost in short run

Where the left-hand side is not defined at $Q = 0$. However, this limit is defined. It is possible to compute it by using l'Hopital's rule: the limit of a fraction whose numerator and denominator both approach zero is given by the limit of the derivatives of the numerator and denominator. Therefore:

$$\lim_{Q\to 0}\frac{C}{Q} = \frac{\lim_{Q\to 0}\frac{dC_V}{dQ}}{\lim_{Q\to 0}\frac{dQ}{dQ}} = \frac{C'(0)}{1} \tag{2.27}$$

Based on these relationships, we can summarize as follows:

1. The Average Cost Curve (AC) initially decreases due to declining fixed costs but then it rises due to increasing Average Variable Costs. In fact, the Average Fixed Cost Curve decreases to the increase in output level (Q), while the Average Variable Cost Curve may initially slope down and eventually rise, as long as there are fixed factors that constrain production.
2. The Marginal Cost (MC) and the Average Cost (AC) are the same at the first unit of output.
3. The Marginal Cost Curve passes through the Minimum Average Cost Point of both the Average Variable Cost (AVC) and the Average Cost Curves (AC). In both cases, to the left of the minimum point the Marginal Cost Curve is below the Average Variable Curve and the Average Cost Curve; to the right of the minimum point the Marginal Cost Curve is above the Average Variable Curve and the Average Cost Curve.

We can represent these relationships as in Fig. 2.2.

2.3 Cost Functions in the Short Run: Linear Approximation

We can add a new assumption to the fixed prices by assuming a linear approximation of cost function. Therefore, we can analyse the cost functions in the short run under two assumptions:

1. Fixed prices of the production factors.
2. Linear approximation of cost function, with regard to both variable and fixed costs.

Under the assumption of linear approximation, the relationship between costs and output level (Q) states that costs change only to the change in the output level (Q) without considering any else variables, along a straight-line. The analysis requires the definition of two main parameters:

1. *Relevant Range*: costs move along a straight-line only within a defined range of output level (Q) that is called *Relevant Range*. Consequently, only the Relevant Range must be considered in the analysis because only within it the single straight-line gives a good approximation of the cost behaviour. In this relevant range the cost curves must be able to be approximated by a straight-line.
2. *Relevant Length of the Time Period*: the amount of variable costs is a function of the time period over which cost behaviour is being estimated. If it is one day, few costs can be defined as variable while if it is infinite all costs are variables (normally, it is considered one year). Therefore, it is always necessary to define a relevant length of the time period because only it must be considered in the analysis.

It is necessary always to keep in mind that even if the assumption of linear approximation is useful to simplify calculus, it a very rigid assumption in real world where it is not always easy to distinguish between variable and fixed costs. There are a lot of costs that can be defined as semi-variable costs (or semi-fixed or mixed costs). These costs are characterized by a combination of variable and fixed costs, but they cannot be divided exactly in half. Usually these costs are defined *Sticky Costs* because they can decrease or increase more or less to the decrease or increase of output level and they can change more or less within a specific period of output. The degree of stickiness of cost varies across cost types and firm types.

The Short-Run Total Cost (C_S) is equal to:

$$C_S = C_V + C_F$$

The Short-Run Average Cost (AC_S), and then the Short-Run Cost per Unit of Output (C_{US}), is equal to:

$$\mathrm{AC_S} \equiv C_{\mathrm{US}} = \frac{C_\mathrm{S}}{Q} = \frac{C_\mathrm{V}}{Q} + \frac{C_\mathrm{F}}{Q}$$

where:

(a) The first part is the Short-Run Average Variable Cost ($\mathrm{AC_V}$), and then the Short-Run Variable Cost per Unit of Output (C_{VU}), so that:

$$\mathrm{AC_V} \equiv C_{\mathrm{VU}} = \frac{C_\mathrm{V}}{Q}$$

(b) The second part is the Short-Run Average Fixed Cost ($\mathrm{AC_F}$), and then the Short-Run Fixed Cost per Unit of Output (C_{FU}), so that:

$$\mathrm{AC_F} \equiv C_{\mathrm{FU}} = \frac{C_\mathrm{F}}{Q}$$

2.3.1 Fixed Costs

The Fixed Cost (C_F) remains constant to the change in output (Q), while the Average Fixed Cost ($\mathrm{AC_F}$), and then the Fixed Cost per Unit of Output (C_{FU}), decreases to the increase in output (Q) as well as increases to the decrease in output (Q).

Therefore, the Fixed Cost per Unit of Output changes because the Fixed Cost does not change to the change in output (Q).

$$C_\mathrm{F} = \text{constant} \rightarrow C_{\mathrm{FU}} = \frac{C_\mathrm{F}}{Q} \tag{2.28}$$

We can summarize these relationships as in Fig. 2.3.

2.3.2 Variable Costs

The Variable Cost (C_V) changes proportionally, or more or less proportionally, to the change in output level (Q), because the Average Variable Cost ($\mathrm{AC_V}$), and then the Variable Cost per Unit of Output (C_{VU}), remains constant to the change in output (Q).

Therefore, the Variable Cost changes because the Variable Cost per Unit of Output does not change to the change in output (Q).

$$C_{\mathrm{VU}} = \text{constant} \rightarrow C_\mathrm{V} = C_{\mathrm{VU}} \cdot Q \tag{2.29}$$

We can summarize these relationships as in Fig. 2.4.

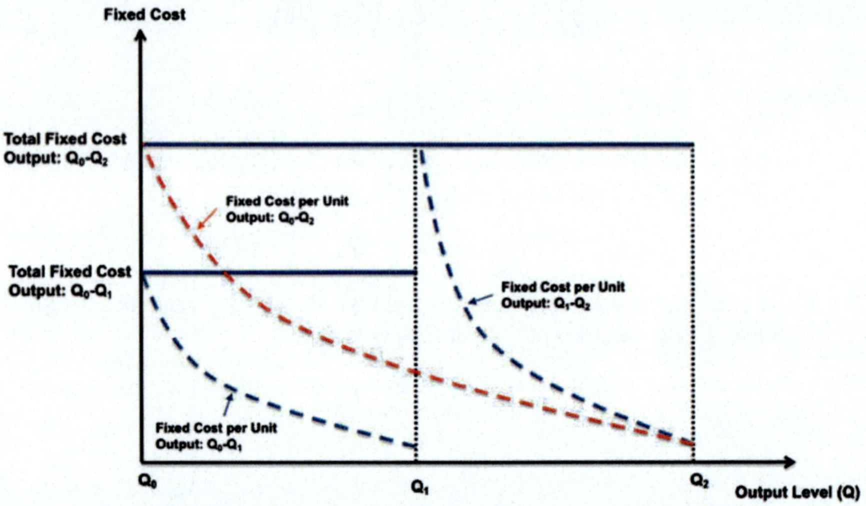

Fig. 2.3 Linear approximation: total fixed cost and fixed cost per unit

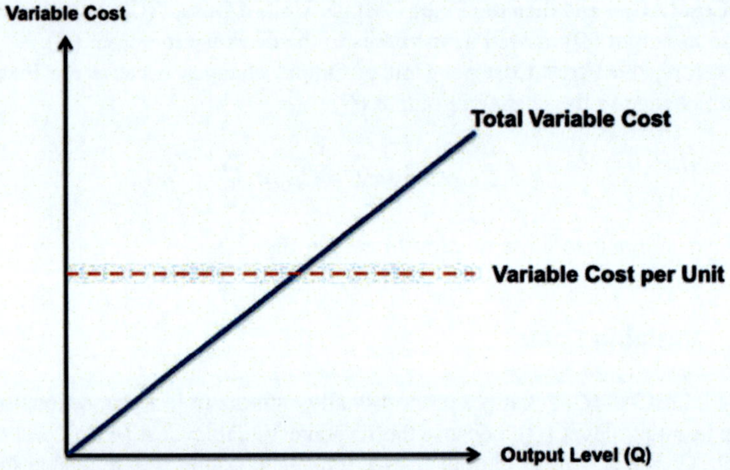

Fig. 2.4 Linear approximation: total variable cost and variable cost per unit

2.3.3 Cost-Output Diagram

Under the assumption of linear approximation of costs, the relationship between output level (Q) and costs can be shown in a Cost-Output Diagram.

Consider the equation of a straight-line ($y = a + b \cdot x$) and substitute:

- the independent variable (x), with the output level (Q)
- the dependent value (y), with the Total Cost (C) at an output level Q

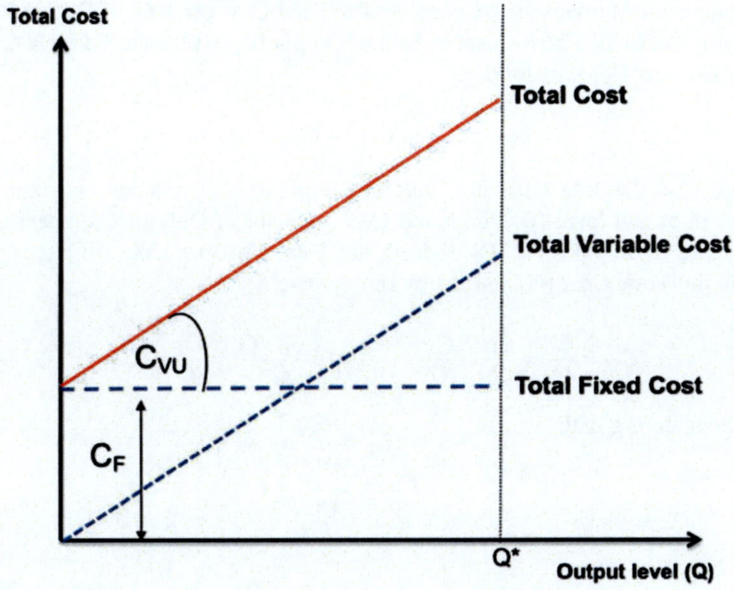

Fig. 2.5 Linear approximation: fixed Cost, variable cost, and total cost

- the vertical intercept (a), with the *Total Fixed Cost* (C_F) at an output level Q
- the slope (b) with the Variable Cost per Unit of Output (C_{VU}) that is the rate of cost change per unit of output.

Therefore, we have:

$$C = C_F + (C_{VU} \cdot Q) \tag{2.30}$$

By considering that:

$$C_V = C_{VU} \cdot Q$$

The equation can be rewritten as follows:

$$C = C_F + C_V \tag{2.31}$$

The equation states that the Total Cost (C) at output level Q is equal to the Total Fixed Costs (C_F) plus the Total Variable Costs (C_V). We can represent this equation as in Fig. 2.5.

The straight-line of Total Cost (C) starts from the vertical intercept defined by the Total Fixed Cost (C_F) and it goes parallel to the straight-line of Total Variable Cost (C_V) because they have the same slope. Consequently, the Total Cost (C) increases to the increase in output (Q) within a defined production capacity ($Q \leq Q^*$).

The question is inverse if we consider the Total Cost per Unit of Output (C_U). In fact, it is equal to the Fixed Cost per Unit of Output (C_{FU}) plus the Variable Cost per Unit of Output (C_{VU}), as follows:

$$C_U = C_{FU} + C_{VU} \tag{2.32}$$

While the Variable Cost per Unit of Output (C_{VU}) remains constant to the increase in output level (Q), the Fixed Cost per Unit of Output (C_{FU}) decreases to the increase in output level (Q). Indeed, the Total Cost per Unit of Output (C_U) is equal to the Total Cost (C) divided by output level (Q):

$$C_U = \frac{C}{Q} = \frac{C_F}{Q} + \frac{C_V}{Q} = \frac{C_F}{Q} + \frac{C_{VU} \cdot Q}{Q} = \frac{C_F}{Q} + C_{VU}$$

By considering that:

$$\frac{C_F}{Q} = C_{FU}$$

We have:

$$C_U = C_{FU} + C_{VU}$$

Therefore,

- the Variable Cost per Unit of Output (C_{VU}) is independent from the output (Q), while the Total Variable Cost (C_V) depends on the output (Q) because: $C_V = C_{VU} \cdot Q$.
- the Total Fixed Cost (C_F) is independent from the output (Q), while the Fixed Cost per Unit of Output (C_{FU}) depends on the output (Q) because: $C_{FU} = C_F/Q$.

We can summarize these relationships as in Fig. 2.6.

Figure 2.6 shows how the Total Cost per Unit of Output (C_U) is parallel to the Fixed Cost per Unit of Output (C_{FU}) because the decrease of the first depends on the decrease of the second.

The Variable Cost per Unit of Output (C_{VU}) represents a constant and therefore it is independent of the output level (Q) and then increases the starting point of the Total Cost per Unit of Output (C_U).

By expanding the production to the output level Q^* and assuming that it is infinite, the Fixed Cost per Unit of Output (C_{FU}) is equal to zero, while the Total Cost per Unit of Output (C_U) is equal to the Variable Cost per Unit of Output (C_{VU}), as follows:

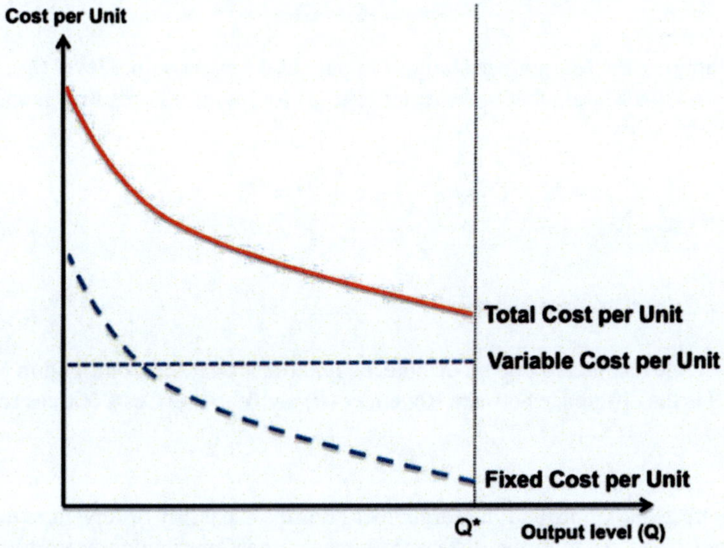

Fig. 2.6 Linear approximation: fixed cost, variable cost, and total cost

$$\lim_{Q \to Q^* = +\infty} C_U = \lim_{Q \to Q^* = +\infty} \left[\frac{C_F}{Q} + C_{VU} \right] = C_{VU}$$

In a real world Q^* is always a well-defined value. Consequently, we have:

$$\lim_{Q \to Q^*} C_U = \lim_{Q \to Q^*} \left[\frac{C_F}{Q} + C_{VU} \right] = \alpha + C_{VU}$$

where the value of α is the Fixed Cost per Unit of Output (C_U) for use of the maximum production capacity. Therefore, it is a function of the quality and characteristics of the production system and managerial skills.

Therefore, the behaviour of the Total Cost (C) and the Total Cost per Unit of Output (C_U) is opposite among them to the increase in output level (Q) within a defined production capacity ($Q \leq Q^*$). Indeed, when the output level (Q) increases within a defined production capacity ($Q \leq Q^*$), the:

(a) Total Cost (C) increases because the Total Fixed Cost (C_F) remains constant while the Total Variable Cost (C_V) increases to the increase in output (Q).
(b) Total Cost per Unit of Output (C_U) decreases because the Variable Cost per Unit of Output (C_{VU}) remains constant, while the Fixed Cost per Unit of Output (C_{FU}) decreases to the increase in output (Q).

Note that the difference between Revenues per Unit of Output (R_U) and Total Cost per Unit of Output (C_U) defines the Margin per Unit of Output (M_U), as follows:

$$M_U = R_U - C_U \tag{2.33}$$

Multiplying the Margin per Unit of Output (M_U) for the output level (Q), it gets the firm's Total Margin that is the firm Profit (π) (or loss if it is negative number) of the firm, as follows:

$$\pi = M_U \cdot Q = R_U \cdot Q - C_U \cdot Q = (R_U - C_U) \cdot Q \tag{2.34}$$

2.3.4 Contribution Margin

The most relevant item based on the linear approximation is the Contribution Margin (CM). It is the difference between Revenues (R) and Variable Costs (C_V) as follows:

$$\text{CM} = R - C_V \tag{2.35}$$

Therefore, the Contribution Margin measures the capability of Revenues to cover the Fixed Costs. In fact, the difference between the Contribution Margin and the Fixed Costs (C_F) defines the firm's Profit (π) (or loss if it is a negative number), as follows:

$$\pi = \text{CM} - C_F = (R - C_V) - C_F \tag{2.36}$$

By distinguishing between Variable and Fixed Costs, the Contribution Margin measures the level of rigidity (or flexibility) of the firm's cost structure.

The Contribution Margin can be analysed in unit terms. The Contribution Margin per Unit of Output (CM_U) is equal to the difference between Revenue per Unit of Output (R_U) and Variable Cost per Unit of Output (C_{VU}), as follows:

$$\text{CM}_U = \text{R}_U - \text{C}_{VU} \tag{2.37}$$

In this case, the Contribution Margin per Unit of Output measures the capability of product price, that is the Revenue per Unit of Product, to cover the Fixed Costs per Unit of Product.

Note that the Contribution Margin per Unit of Output (CM_U) does not depend on the output level (Q), because neither Revenues per Unit of Output (R_U) nor Variable Cost per Unit of Output (C_{VU}) depends on the output level (Q). Consequently, CM_U remains constant to the change in Q.

The Profit per Unit of Output (π_U) (or Loss per Unit of Output if the number is negative) is equal to the difference between the Contribution Margin per Unit of Output (CM_U) and Fixed Costs per Unit of Output (C_{FU}), as follows:

$$\pi_U = \text{CM}_U - C_{FU} = (R_U - C_{VU}) - C_{FU} \tag{2.38}$$

Note that multiplying the Contribution Margin per Unit of Output (CM_U) for the level of Output (Q), it gets the Contribution Margin (CM), as follows:

$$CM_U \cdot Q = R_U \cdot Q - C_{VU} \cdot Q \rightarrow \begin{matrix} CM_U \cdot Q = CM \\ R_U \cdot Q = R \\ C_{VU} \cdot Q = C_V \end{matrix} \rightarrow CM = R - C_V \tag{2.39}$$

Similarly, multiplying the Profit per Unit of Output (π_U) for the level of Output (Q), it gets the firm's Profit (π), as follows:

$$\pi_U \cdot Q = CM_U \cdot Q - C_{FU} \cdot Q \rightarrow \begin{matrix} \pi_U \cdot Q = \pi \\ CM_U \cdot Q = CM \\ C_{FU} \cdot Q = C_F \end{matrix} \rightarrow \pi = CM - C_F \tag{2.40}$$

Two are the main elements of analyses to consider carefully.

First, the Contribution Margin per Unit of Output (CM_U) remains constant per unit of output (Q) because the Variable Cost per Unit of Output (C_{VU}) and the Revenues per Unit of Output (R_U) remain constant per unit of output (Q). Consequently, the Contribution Margin (CM) changes to the change in output (Q) because the Contribution Margin per Unit of Output (CM_U) remains constant per unit of output (Q). Formally:

$$CM = CM_U \cdot Q = (R_U - C_{VU}) \cdot Q \tag{2.41}$$

Second, the Contribution Margin (CM) can increase for the increase in Contribution Margin per Unit of Output (CM_U), in output level (Q), or in both. Formally:

$$CM = f\begin{pmatrix} CM_U & Q \\ + & + \end{pmatrix} \tag{2.42}$$

The increase (decrease) in Contribution Margin due to:

1. increase (decrease) in the level of Output (Q) for the same level of the CM_U, is strictly related to the productivity capacity and its efficient use.
2. increase (decrease) in the Contribution Margin per Unit of Output (CM_U) for the same level of Q, can be realized in two main ways:
   (a) to increase (decrease) the Price per Unit of Output and then Revenues per Unit of Output (R_U) by maintaining the same level of *Variable Cost per Unit of Output* (C_{VU}). If the firm increases R_U, it follows a Price Strategy by requiring a higher price in the market for a structural high quality of its product.
   (b) to decrease (increase) the Variable Cost per Unit of Output (C_{VU}) by maintaining the same level of the Revenues per Unit of Output (R_U). If firm reduces the C_{VU}, it follows a Cost Strategy by reducing in a structural

way the variable costs thanks to a development of a new technologies of product or production process.

2.3.5 Break-Even Point

The linear relationship between costs and output level can be used to define the *Break-Even Point (BEP)*. It defines the equilibrium output level (Q^*) at which the total costs are equal to the total revenues. Consequently, for an output level (Q) realized:

(a) higher than the equilibrium output ($Q > Q^*$), the firm generates profit
(b) lower than the equilibrium output ($Q < Q^*$), the firm generates loss

The amount of profit or loss expected at any level of output is the vertical distance between the points on the total cost and total revenue lines at that output level.

Therefore, at Equilibrium Output level (Q^*), Total Revenues (R) must be equal to Total Cost (C), and the firm Profit (π) is equal to zero, as follows:

$$Q^* : \begin{matrix} R=C \\ \pi=0 \end{matrix} \rightarrow \begin{matrix} R=R_U \cdot Q^* \\ C=C_F + C_V=(C_{VU} \cdot Q^*) \end{matrix} \rightarrow R_U \cdot Q^* = C_F + (C_{VU} \cdot Q^*)$$

and consequently:

$$Q^* = \frac{C_F}{R_U - C_{VU}} \tag{2.43}$$

Note that the denominator of the equation is the Contribution Margin per Unit of Output (CM_U), that is equal to $CM_U = P_U - C_{VU}$. Therefore, the Equilibrium Output (Q^*) is equal to the Fixed Costs (C_F) divided by the Contribution Margin per Unit of Output ($P_U - C_{VU}$). Consequently, if the output level (Q) realized is:

(a) $Q = Q^* \rightarrow R = C \rightarrow \pi = 0$ Equilibrium.
(b) $Q > Q^* \rightarrow R > C \rightarrow \pi > 0$ Profit
(c) $Q < Q^* \rightarrow R < C \rightarrow \pi < 0$ Loss

It is easy to extend the break-even analyses to the case in which the firm defines a Profit Target (π^*). In this case, the output level (Q^{**}) able to realize the profit target is equal to:

$$\pi^* = R - C \rightarrow R = C + \pi^* \rightarrow R_U \cdot Q^{**} = C_F + (C_{VU} \cdot Q^{**}) + \pi^*$$

And then by solving for Q^{**} it gets:

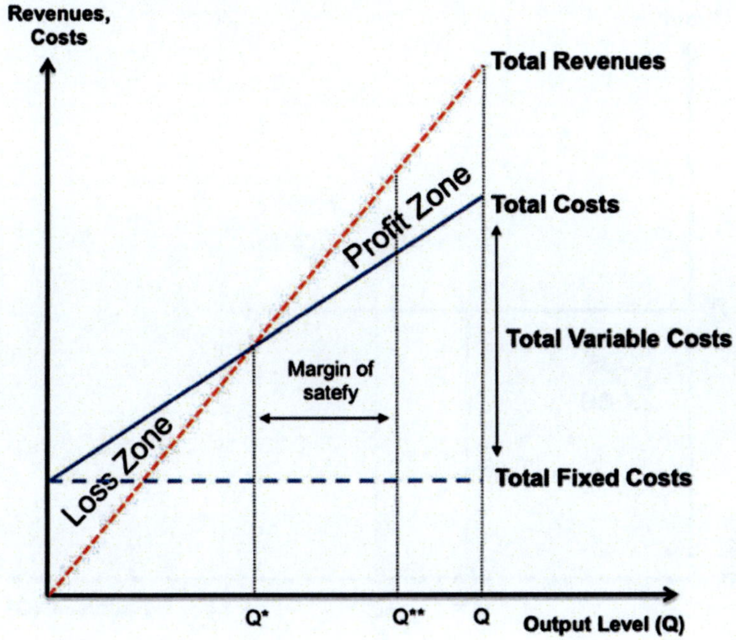

Fig. 2.7 Linear approximation: break-even analysis

$$Q^{**} = \frac{\pi^* + C_F}{R_U - C_{VU}} \tag{2.44}$$

Note that also in this case the denominator of the equation is the Contribution Margin per Unit of Output (CM_U). Therefore, the output level (Q^{**}) to be achieved in order to realize the target Profit (π^*) is equal to the sum between the target Profit (π^*) and the Fixed Costs (C_F) divided up into the Contribution Margin per Unit of Output ($R_U - C_{VU}$).

The BEP analysis can be represented as in Fig. 2.7.

The break-even point can be defined in terms of Contribution Profit. It is based on the Contribution Margin per Unit of Output (CM_U) as shown in Fig. 2.8.

The Figure shows as:

(a) Profit is equal to zero for equilibrium output level (Q^*) that is the output level in which revenues and costs are equal.
(b) The slope is the Contribution Margin per Unit of Output (CM_U).
(c) At zero output the loss is due to the Fixed Costs.

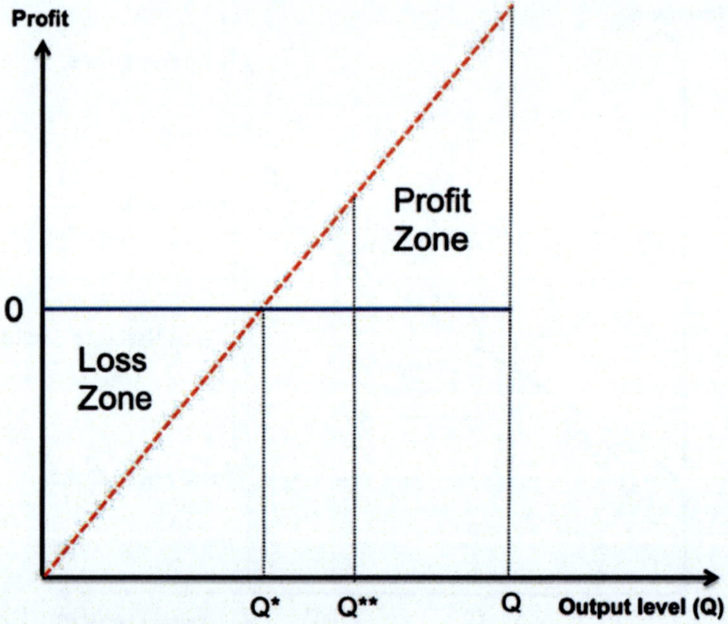

Fig. 2.8 Linear approximation: contribution profit

2.3.6 Product Mix

Relationships previously analysed refer to the case in which the firm produces a single product. In case in which firm produces more than one product, each of them has a Contribution Margin. Therefore, it is necessary to compute the product mix.

We must make a baseline assumption: the proportion of each revenue per product to the total revenues of the firm remains constant over time, so that the product mix remains constant over time. If it is, we can compute the Weighted-Average Contribution Margin of Equivalent Product.

Assume firm produces two products: product A and product B. The Net Income (NI) is equal to the sum of Contribution Margin of Product A ($CM_{(A)}$) and Contribution Margin of Product B ($CM_{(B)}$) less the Fixed Costs (C_F), as follows:

$$NI = CM_{(A)} + CM_{(B)} - C_F$$

Based on the Contribution Margin per Unit of Output of Product A ($CM_{U(A)}$) and Product B ($CM_{U(B)}$) and the output level of Product A ($Q_{(A)}$) and Product B ($Q_{(B)}$), we have:

$$NI = \left[CM_{U(A)} \cdot Q_{(A)} + CM_{U(A)} \cdot Q_{(B)}\right] - C_F$$

By expressing the Contribution Margin per Unit of Output in terms of Revenues per Unit of Output of Product A ($R_{U(A)}$) and Product B ($R_{U(B)}$) and of Variable Cost per Unit of Output of Product A ($C_{VU(A)}$) and Product B ($C_{VU(B)}$), we have:

$$NI = \left[\left(R_{U(A)} - C_{VU(A)}\right) \cdot Q_{(A)} + \left(R_{U(B)} - C_{VU(B)}\right) \cdot Q_{(B)}\right] - C_F$$

Since the *product mix* is defined and well-known, the weighted percentage ($W(\%)$) of each product's output level ($Q_{(A)}; Q_{(B)}$) on total output level ($Q_{(T)}$) can be computed as follows:

$$Q_{(T)} = Q_{(A)} + Q_{(B)} \rightarrow \begin{matrix} W_A = \frac{Q_{(A)}}{Q_{(T)}} \\ W_B = \frac{Q_{(B)}}{Q_{(T)}} \end{matrix}$$

The Equivalent Product (EP) is the basket and then it is defined on the share-part of each product in it. Therefore, it can be considered as a Portfolio of Products.

Obviously, the total output level ($Q_{(T)}$) cannot be existed because it is the sum of different products. It is the output level of the Equivalent Product constructed as a Portfolio of Products.

The Contribution Margin of Equivalent Product ($CM_{(EP)}$) is equal to:

$$CM_{(EP)} = CM_{U(EP)} \cdot Q_{(T)} \quad (2.45)$$

where the Contribution Margin of Equivalent Product per Unit of Output ($CM_{U(EP)}$) is equal to:

$$CM_{U(EP)} = CM_{U(A)} \cdot W_A + CM_{U(B)} \cdot W_B \quad (2.46)$$

Substituting, we have:

$$NI = \left(CM_{U(A)} \cdot W_A \cdot Q_{(T)} + CM_{U(B)} \cdot W_B \cdot Q_{(T)}\right) - C_F$$

$$NI = \left[\left(CM_{U(A)} \cdot W_A + CM_{U(B)} \cdot W_B\right) \cdot Q_{(T)}\right] - C_F$$

$$NI = \left[\left(CM_{U(A)} \cdot W_A + CM_{U(B)} \cdot W_B\right) \cdot Q_{(T)}\right] - C_F$$

$$NI = \left(CM_{U(EP)} \cdot Q_{(T)}\right) - C_F$$

and then:

$$NI = CM_{(EP)} - C_F \quad (2.47)$$

2.3.7 Degree of Operating Leverage

The firm Operating Leverage (OL) is based on the distinction between Variable Costs and Fixed Costs and the correlated concept of Contribution Margin.

The Operating Leverage (OL) measures the reaction of the EBIT to the change in the output level (Q) of goods sold. It is the function of the costs structure by distinguishing the costs in EBIT between Variable Costs and Fixed Costs.

The Operating Leverage (OL) can be measured on the basis of EBIT and output level (Q) of goods sold in a lead-time t_0; t_1 as follows:

$$\mathrm{OL} = \frac{\Delta \mathrm{EBIT}}{\Delta Q} = \frac{\frac{\mathrm{EBIT}_1 - \mathrm{EBIT}_0}{\mathrm{EBIT}_0}}{\frac{Q_1 - Q_0}{Q_0}} = \frac{\mathrm{EBIT}_1 - \mathrm{EBIT}_0}{\mathrm{EBIT}_0} \cdot \frac{Q_0}{Q_1 - Q_0} \tag{2.48}$$

By distinguishing all costs in the EBIT in Fixed Costs and Variable Costs, we can define EBIT on the basis of the Revenue per Unit of Output (R_U), Variable Costs per Unit of Output (C_VU), Total Fixed Costs (C_F), and Output level (Q), as follows:

$$\mathrm{EBIT} = (R_\mathrm{U} - C_\mathrm{VU}) \cdot Q - C_\mathrm{F} = (\mathrm{CM_U} \cdot Q) - C_\mathrm{F} = \mathrm{CM} - C_\mathrm{F}$$

By considering that the Contribution Margin per Unit of Output ($\mathrm{CM_U}$) is independent from the output level (Q), so that it remains constant to the change in Q, we can rewrite the Operating Leverage as follows:

$$\begin{aligned}
\mathrm{OL} &= \frac{[\mathrm{CM_U} \cdot Q_1 - \mathrm{C_F}] - [\mathrm{CM_U} \cdot Q_0 - C_\mathrm{F}]}{\mathrm{CM_U} \cdot Q_0 - C_\mathrm{F}} \cdot \frac{Q_0}{Q_1 - Q_0} \\
&= \frac{\mathrm{CM_U} \cdot Q_1 - C_\mathrm{F} - \mathrm{CM_U} \cdot Q_0 + C_\mathrm{F}}{\mathrm{CM_U} \cdot Q_0 - \mathrm{C_F}} \cdot \frac{Q_0}{Q_1 - Q_0} = \frac{\mathrm{CM_U} \cdot Q_1 - \mathrm{CM_U} \cdot Q_0}{\mathrm{CM_U} \cdot Q_0 - C_\mathrm{F}} \\
&\cdot \frac{Q_0}{Q_1 - Q_0} = \frac{\mathrm{CM_U} \cdot (Q_1 - Q_0)}{\mathrm{CM_U} \cdot Q_0 - C_\mathrm{F}} \cdot \frac{Q_0}{Q_1 - Q_0} = \frac{\mathrm{CM_U} \cdot Q_0}{\mathrm{CM_U} \cdot Q_0 - C_\mathrm{F}}
\end{aligned}$$

and then:

$$\mathrm{OL} = \frac{\mathrm{CM_U} \cdot Q_0}{\mathrm{CM_U} \cdot Q_0 - C_\mathrm{F}} = \frac{\mathrm{CM}}{\mathrm{EBIT}} \tag{2.49}$$

Note that based on this equation, we have:

$$\mathrm{EBIT} = \mathrm{OL} \cdot \mathrm{CM} \tag{2.50}$$

Therefore, the higher the Operating Leverage (OL), the higher the variability of the EBIT to the variations in the output level (Q) of goods sold. Consequently, the EBIT is the function of the Operating Level (and then to the degree of flexibility of the cost structure) and the change in output level (Q). By assuming that the Contribution Margin per Unit of Output does not change (because it does not change

Revenues and Variable Cost per Unit of Output) and the Fixed Cost remains constant, we have that:

(a) The higher Fixed Costs are than Variable Costs, the greater the rigidity of the costs structure. In this case, change in the output level (Q) generates reductions rather than proportional of the EBIT and, all other variables being equal, of the Net Income.
(b) The higher the Variable Costs over Fixed Costs, the greater the flexibility of the costs structure. In this case, change in the output level (Q) generates reductions less than proportional of the EBIT and, all other variables being equal, of the Net Income.

2.4 Cost Curves in the Long run

In the long run all costs are variable by definition. Indeed, while in the short run firm faces factors that are unable to adjust by generating fixed costs, in the long run the firm can choose the level of all factors and then all costs become variable.

Note that short run and long run are not related to the time but to the firm's productivity capacity and to the specific problem that we are analysing within it.

Even if in the long run all costs are variable, however they may still be quasi-fixed factors. Indeed, it may be a feature of the technology that some costs have to be paid to produce any positive level of output. If some factors remain fixed even in the long run, the appropriate long run average cost curve should be U-shaped for the same reasons given in the short-run case.

The Long-Run Cost Curve (C_L) must never lie above any Short-Run Cost Curve (C_S). Indeed, the short-run cost minimization problem can always be considered as a constrained version of the long-run cost minimization problem.

Assume fixed price of factors. Consider a specific fixed factor z and the output level Q. In this case, the Short-Run Cost (C_S) is equal to: $C_s(Q, z)$.

For any given level of output (Q), there is a value of fixed factor that is the optimal level to produce that level of output, that is $z(Q)$.

Therefore, the Long-Run Cost (C_L) of the firm can be defined as follows (Varian, 2014):

$$C_L = C_S(Q, z(Q)) \tag{2.51}$$

Therefore, the Long-Run Cost (C_L) of the firm is the Short-Run Cost (C_S) evaluated at the optimal choice of the fixed factors ($z(Q)$). It happens because firm is allowed to adjust the fixed factor optimally when it produces an output level (Q).

Assume to realize an output level equal to Q^*. The optimal fixed factor to realize this level of output (Q^*) is equal to $z^* = z(Q^*)$. Therefore:

(a) The Short-Run Cost (C_S) for the fixed factor z^* is equal to: $C_S = C(Q, z^*)$
(b) The Long-Run Cost (C_L) is equal to: $C_L = C(Q, z(Q))$.

In the Short-Run Cost (C_S) to produce output level Q must always be at least as large as the Long-Run Cost (C_L) to produce the same level of output Q. It happens because in the short run firm has the fixed factor, while in the long run firm can adjust the fixed factor becoming variable.

Consequently, at the level of output Q^*, we have:

$$C_L \leq C_S(Q, z^*)$$

while at the output level Q^*, where the optimal choice of fixed factor is z^*, we have:

$$C_L = C_S(Q^*, z^*)$$

and then in by considering Q^* and z^*, we have:

$$C(Q^*, z(Q^*)) = C(Q^*, z^*)$$

Therefore, the short-run cost (C_S) is always greater than the long-run cost (C_L) and they are equal at one level of output (Q^*) where the optimal choice of fixed factor is z^*. It implies that firm must be able to do well by adjusting fixed factor at least as by having the fixed factor.

Relationships are the same if we consider the Short-Run Average Cost (AC_S) (and then the Short-Run Cost per Unit of Output (C_{US})) and the Long-Run Average Cost (AC_L) (and then the Long-Run Cost per Unit of Output (C_{UL})). In this case, we have:

$$AC_L \leq AC_S(Q, z^*) \leftrightarrow C_{UL} \leq C_{US}(Q, z^*)$$

$$AC_L = AC_S(Q^*, z^*) \leftrightarrow C_{UL} = C_{US}(Q^*, z^*)$$

Consequently, the Short-Run Average Cost (AC_S) curve always lies above the Long-Run Average Cost (AC_L) curve and they touch at one point that is the output level Q^* where they must be tangent as in Fig. 2.9.

Note that if the Long-Run Cost (C_L) curve and Short-Run Cost (C_S) curve are tangent among them, the long-run Average Cost (AC_L) and the Short-Run Average Cost (AC_S) curve must also be tangent.

Therefore, the Short-Run Average Cost (AC_S) curve always is at least as large as the Long-Run Average Cost (AC_L) curve, and they are the same at the level of output where the long-run demand for the fixed factors equals the amount of the fixed factor. Consequently, the Long-Run Average Cost (AC_L) curve is the lower envelope of the Short-Run Average Cost (AC_S) curves. To well-understand we must consider two cases (Varian, 2014):

Case 1: Assume a continuous level of the fixed factor. If we assume a continuous number of different fixed factors, for each different level of output (Q) has a unique optimal fixed factor (z) associated with it, so that: $z_1 = z(Q_1)$; $z_2 = z(Q_2)$; $z_n = z(Q_n)$. Considering several Short-Run Average Cost (AC_S) curves ($z_1, z_2, z_3, \ldots, z_n$) the

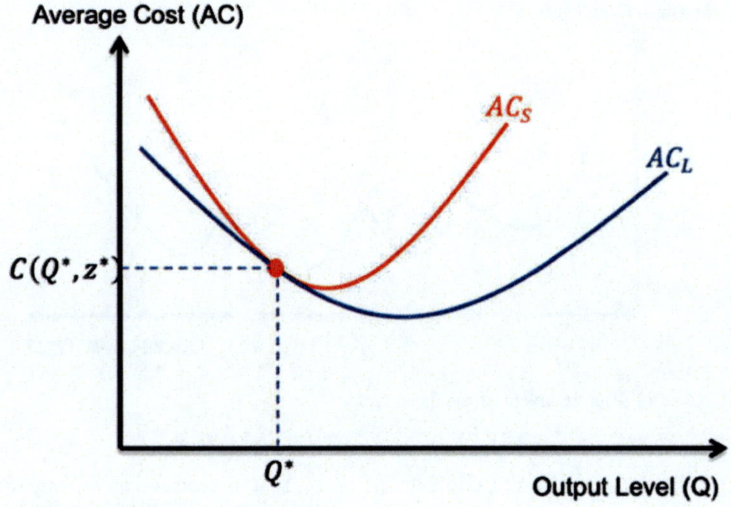

Fig. 2.9 Long-run and short-run cost curves

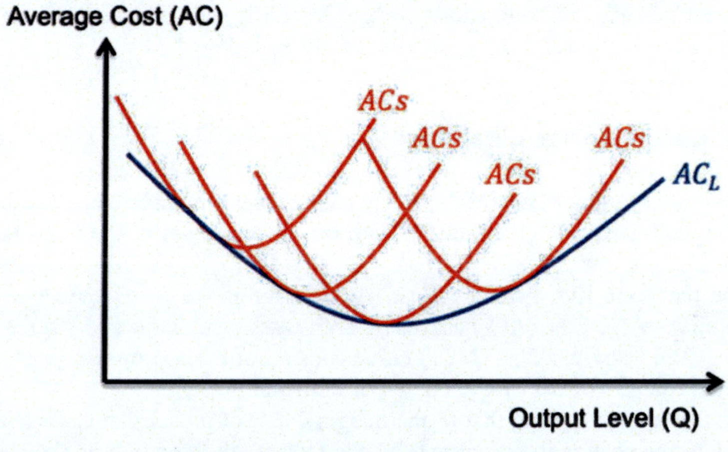

Fig. 2.10 Case of continuous levels of the fixed factor

optimal choice of z to produce the level Q of output will be the choice with the minimum cost of producing Q. The result is that the Long-Run Average Cost (AC_L) curve can be considered as the lower envelope of the Short-Run Average Cost (AC_S) curves, as shown in Fig. 2.10.

Case 2: Assume a discrete level of the fixed factors. If we assume a discrete number of different fixed factors, there are only a few different levels of fixed factor and Average Cost Curves associated with them to choose. Then the Long-Run Average Cost (AC_L) curve is the cost curve obtained by adjusting z optimally.

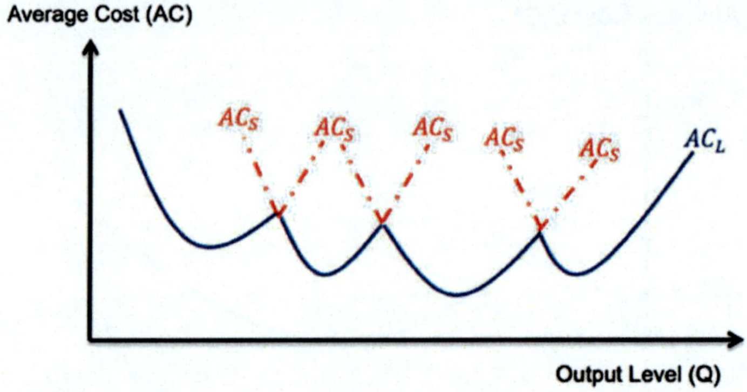

Fig. 2.11 Case of discrete levels of the fixed factor

Assume to have four different choices: z_1, z_2, z_3, z_4 and then we have four different Average Cost Curves associated with them. Since there are only four different z, for any level of output Q, we choose the z that gives us the minimum cost of producing that output level.

The result is that the Long-Run Average Cost (AC_L) curve is the lower envelope of short-run Average Cost (AC_S) curves, as shown in Fig. 2.11.

2.4.1 Long-Run Marginal Cost

The Long-run Marginal Cost (MC_L) at any output level Q must be equal to the Short-Run Marginal Cost (MC_S) associated with the optimal level of the fixed factor to produce Q.

Since the Long-Run Average Cost (AC_L) curve is the lower envelope of the Short-Run Average Cost (AC_S) curves (in both cases continuous and discrete), then the Long-Run Marginal Cost (MC_L) curve consists of the appropriate pieces of the Short-Run Marginal Cost (MC_S) curves as shown in Fig. 2.12.

Note that by considering that (i) the marginal cost of production is the change in cost due to the change in output and (ii) the factors are fixed only in the short run because in the long run the firm can modify them, consequently the Long-Run Marginal Cost (MC_L) is based on two terms: (i) how costs change holding fixed factor plus (ii) how costs changes when the fixed factor can be modified. However, if the fixed factor is chosen optimally, this second term is equal to zero and the Long-Run Marginal Cost (MC_L) is equal to the Short-Run Marginal Cost (MC_S). Formally (Varian, 2014):

$$C \equiv C_S(Q, z(Q))$$

Differentiating with respect to Q, we give:

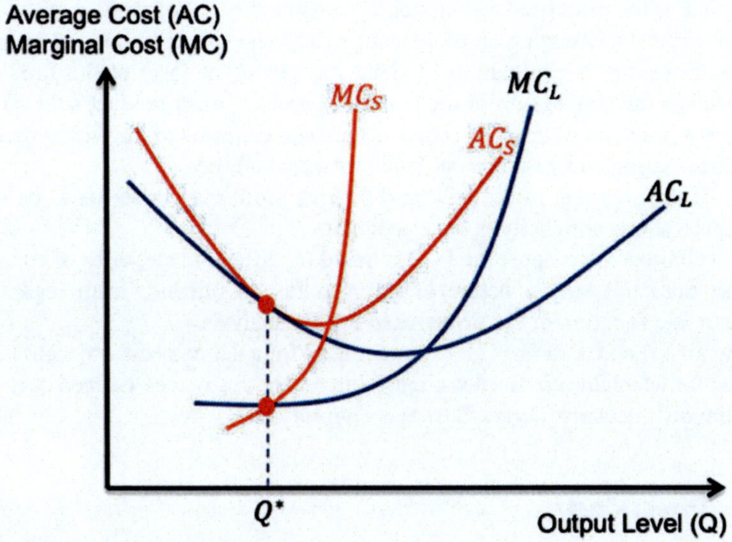

Fig. 2.12 Long-run marginal cost curves

$$\frac{dC}{dQ} = \frac{\partial C_S(Q, z(Q))}{\partial Q} + \frac{\partial C_S(Q, z)}{\partial z} \cdot \frac{\partial z(Q)}{\partial Q}$$

Consider the output level Q^* at with it is associated the optimal fixed factor $z^* = z(Q^*)$. Because the first-order condition must be equal to zero if z^* is the cost-minimizing fixed factor at output level Q^*, we have:

$$\frac{\partial C_S(Q^*, z^*)}{\partial z} = 0$$

and then:

$$\frac{dC(Q^*)}{dQ} = \frac{\partial C_s(Q^*, z^*)}{\partial z} \tag{2.52}$$

2.5 Full Cost of Product

The previous analysis is focused on the firm's cost structure by distinguishing the costs between variable and fixed on the basis of the cost behaviour with respect to the output level (Q) in the short run and long run.

In this contest we want to analyse the cost behaviour with respect to the product of the firm with the main aim to calculate the Full Cost of Product (FCP).

The FCP is the most used techniques to compute the cost of product of the firm in the management accounting and forecasting (business plan and budget) in order to investigate the firm's profitability. Indeed, the profit (or loss) of the firm can be interpreted as the simple sum of the margin of profit of each product sold. Then the wrong determination of the FCP is one of the main elements of the wrong prediction of product margin and, at a general level, firm profitability.

Even if the compute of the FCP and then its profit margin seems to be simple, unfortunately, this simplicity is only apparent.

The technique to compute the FCP is based on different categories of costs. Note that cost does not have a nature of its own. Its classification with regard to its behaviour is a function of the driver used for the analysis.

Generally, the FCP defines all resources used for a defined cost-object that can be anything for which the cost is measured. With regard to any well-defined cost-object, we distinguish between *Direct Cost* and *Indirect Cost*.

2.5.1 Direct Cost

Direct Cost is a cost for which it is always possible to identify a clear and objective causal relationship between the cost and a well-defined cost-object. In this sense, Direct Cost is a cost that is specifically "*traced to*", or "*caused by*", a defined "*cost object*". Consequently, the Direct Cost is "*attributed*" to the cost-object because it is directly charged to it. Therefore, it is always possible to measure directly how much of the cost is attributable to a single cost-object.

The primary cost-objective is the product of the firm. In this case, we can identify three main types of Direct Cost:

(a) ***Direct Material Cost (DMC):*** it is the cost of materials (or raw materials) used in the production and then it can be specifically identified with a product in an economically feasible manner.
The DMC's computation is based on: (1) the Quantity of Material (QM) and (2) the Price of Material per Unit (PM_U) (or Cost of Material per Unit (CM_U)). Formally:

$$DMC = QM \cdot PM_U \tag{2.53}$$

(b) ***Direct Labour Cost (DLC)***: it refers to the earnings of workers who assemble parts and transform them into finished product or operate machines for production. Therefore, it is the cost of labour directly involved in the production activities and then it can be specifically identified with a product in an economically feasible manner.

The DLC's computation is based on: (1) the Quantity of Labour Time (QLT) and (2) the Price of Labour Time per Unit (PLT_U) (Cost of Labour per Unit (CLT_U)). Formally:

$$DLC = QLT \cdot PLT_U \tag{2.54}$$

It is worth noting that labour regulations are normally subject to the law. Therefore, the difference between Direct Labour and Indirect Labour tends to be blurred.

(c) ***Other Direct Cost (ODC)***: it refers to any type of cost activities able to be traced to a single product based on a clear and objective causal relationship identified in an economically feasible manner.
The ODC's computation is based on: (1) the Quantity of Activity (QA) and (2) the Price of Activity per Unit (PA_U) (Cost of Labour per Unit (CA_U)). Formally:

$$ODC = QA \cdot PA_U \tag{2.55}$$

Note that commonly firm tends to consider as Direct Cost only the cost of Direct Material and Direct Labour Costs. However there could be also Other Direct Costs.

2.5.2 Indirect Cost

Indirect Cost is a cost for which it is not possible, or at least not feasible, to define a clear and objective causal relationship between the cost and a well-defined cost-object. Consequently, unlike the Direct Cost, it is not directly traced to each of the cost-object. In this sense, Indirect Cost is a cost "*associated with*", or "*caused by*", two or more "cost-objects jointly".

Assume the product as cost-object the product of the firm. While the Direct Cost is "*attributed*" to the product, the Indirect Cost is "*allocated*" to the product on the basis of the Allocation Rate (or Absorption Rate). Consequently, it is not possible or feasible, to measure directly how much of the cost is attributable to a single product.

Commonly, there are three reasons for which cost is not traced directly to a product: (1) it is not possible; (2) it is possible but do not feasible; (3) management chooses not to do for economic reasons.

2.5.3 Direct–Indirect Costs and Variable–Fixed Costs

Note that it is always wrong the equivalence between Direct Cost and Variable Cost, on the one hand, and between Indirect Cost and Fixed Cost, on the other hand. This confusion occurs because when the cost-object is the product, it is common that Direct Costs are at same times also Variable Costs as well as Indirect Costs are at same time Fixed Costs. Although it seems true, it is wrong to use Direct Costs and Variable Costs as synonyms as well as Indirect Costs and Fixed Costs because it is different to the cost driver. Indeed, Direct–Indirect Cost dichotomy and Variable–Fixed Cost dichotomy are included in a different concept: while the first dichotomy relates to the traceability of costs to specific cost-object (product or cost centre) and therefore it is an accountant's concept, the second dichotomy relates to the behaviour of cost as output level (Q) changes and therefore it is an economist's concept.

2.5.4 Step-Down Order Procedure

Based on the distinction between Direct Costs and Indirect Costs, the Full Cost of Product (FCP) is the sum of Direct Costs *attributed* to the product plus a fair share of Indirect Costs *allocated* to the specific product by using Allocation Rate (or Absorption Rate).

Obviously, the most relevant problem is the right definition in monetary terms of the "*fair-share*" of the Indirect Costs to be allocated to each product.

The most common technique to compute the FCP is the *Step-down Order Procedure*. It requires the preliminary definition of two different cost-objects:

(a) *Cost of Product*: the final cost-object is the product. Therefore, in this case it can be distinguished between Direct Costs and Indirect Costs of product;
(b) *Cost of Centres (Production and Service)*: they are intermediate cost-objects and they are necessary for the application of the Step-down Order Procedure. Therefore, in this case it can be distinguished between Direct Costs and Indirect Costs of Cost of Centre.

Therefore, we have two cost-objects:

1. The product, by distinguishing between Direct Cost of Product and Indirect Cost of Product.
2. The Cost Centre used in the attribution of the Indirect Cost, by distinguishing between Direct Cost of Centre and Indirect Cost of Centre.

The *Step-down order procedure* can be defined in four steps.

Step 1: Identification of Direct Costs and Indirect Costs of Product
In this step, we must recognize all costs of the firm and we must distinguish them in Direct Costs and Indirect Costs of product that is the cost-object in this step.

Therefore, for each specific product it is necessary to identify:

1. *Direct Costs of Product*: they are Direct Material Costs, Direct Labour Costs, and Other Direct Costs. These costs are "*attributed*" to each product.
2. *Indirect Costs of Product*: they must be identified and separated from the Direct Costs. These costs must be "*allocated*" to each product by using Production and Service Cost Centres.

At the end of this step of the process, the entire amount of costs of the firm must be distinguished between Direct Costs and Indirect Costs of product.

Consequently, the sum of Direct Costs and Indirect Costs of product must be equal to the entire amount of the firm's costs.

Step 2: Assignment of Indirect Costs of Product to Production and Service Cost Centres

In this step, it is necessary to assign the entire amount of the Indirect Costs of Product to the Cost Centres. There are two main types of Cost Centres:

1. *Production Cost Centre*: the Centre produces a product or a component of a product.
2. *Service Cost Centre*: the Centre provides services for all firm's activities.

In both cases, note that Product and Service Cost Centres are not identifiable with a specific organizational unit.

These Cost Centres are defined intermediate cost-object because Indirect Costs of product are first accumulated in each Cost Centre and then assigned to each product. Therefore, in this step of process there is a change of cost-object: it is the Cost Centre and not the product that remain the final cost-object.

By considering Cost Centre as the cost-object, we can distinguish between:

1. *Direct Cost of Cost Centre*: it refers to Indirect Costs of product that can be directly *attributed* to a defined Cost Centre on the basis of a clear relationship between the cost and the Cost Centre.
2. *Indirect Cost of Cost Centre*: it refers to Indirect Costs of product that must be *allocated* on the basis of a fair share to each Cost Centre by using different and specific Allocation Rates.

Therefore, each Cost Centre (both Production and Service) is characterized by its Direct Costs plus a fair share of Indirect Costs.

Consequently, the sum of Direct Costs of Cost Centres and the Indirect Costs of Cost Centres must be equal to the entire amount of Indirect Costs of product.

Step 3: Identification of Primary and Secondary Production and Service Cost Centres

In this step, it is necessary to allocate the costs of Production and Service Cost Centres in their Primary and Secondary Cost Centres, respectively.

Specifically, Production Cost Centres must be distinguished between:

1. *Primary Production Cost Centre*: costs assigned to the Production Cost Centre are allocated indirectly through Allocation Rates to the product.
2. *Secondary Production Cost Centre*: costs assigned to the Production Cost Centre are allocated through Allocation Rates to the other Production Cost Centres.

Similar, Service Cost Centres must be distinguished between:

1. *Primary Service Cost Centre*: costs assigned to the Service Cost Centre are allocated through Allocation Rates to the Production Cost Centres that receive the service.
2. *Secondary Service Cost Centre*: costs assigned to the Service Cost Centre are allocated through Allocation Rates to the other Service Cost Centres that receive the service.

Based on these two distinctions, only costs assigned to the Primary Production Cost Centres are allocated through Allocation Rates to the product. Consequently, Secondary Production Cost Centres as well as Primary and Secondary Service Cost Centres are used to allocate with several allocation rate their costs to the Primary Production Cost Centres. Consequently, the entire cost of each Production and Service Cost Centre is the sum of its original cost plus the fair share of costs due to the process.

Therefore, at the end of the process:

(a) The sum of costs allocated in the Primary and Secondary Service Cost Centres must be equal to the total amount of costs allocated in the Service Costs Centres.
(b) The sum of costs allocated in the Primary and Secondary Production Cost Centres must be equal to the total amount of costs allocated in the Production Costs Centres.

Step 4: Computation of the Full Cost of Product

In this last step, we can compute the Full Cost (FCP) for each firm's product. It is equal to the sum of:

(a) *Direct Costs of Product*, with regard to Direct Material Costs, Labour Costs, and Other Direct Costs.
(b) *Indirect Costs of Product* first allocated in the Primary Production Cost Centres, and after allocated to each product on the basis of a specific Allocation Rates. At the end of the process, the cost of each Primary Production Cost Centre is the sum of its original costs assigned plus a fair share of costs due to the Secondary

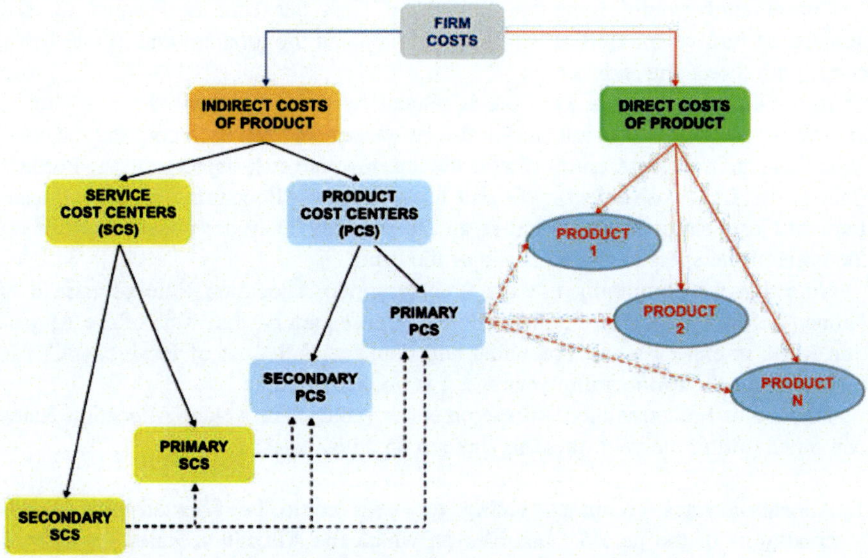

Fig. 2.13 The step-down order procedure to compute the full cost of product

Production Cost Centres and the Primary and Secondary Service Cost Centres. Consequently, the sum of the costs assigned to the Primary Production Cost Centres must be equal to the entire Indirect Production Costs. The *Step-Down Order Procedure* as defined in these four steps can be summarized as in Fig. 2.13.

Note that there are different types of production system. The most common and used is the *Process Cost System*. In this case, they are considered the costs in a well-defined time period. Therefore, all costs included in the Primary Production Cost Centres in the period are allocated to each product in the same time period. Consequently, the Full Cost per Unit of Product is the Average Cost per Unit of Product that is equal to the Full Cost of Product divided by the quantity of products produced during the same time period considered. Therefore, it is not possible to have different costs among a single unit of product.

Consequently, in the period of time considered, multiplying the Cost per Unit of Product for the quantity of product realized, it is obtained the total amount of the firm's costs, both direct and indirect.

It is worth noting that since a time period is considered, it is possible that at the end of the period considered there are several products that have not yet been produced. In this case, it must be used a common unit for the products produced and the products not yet produced. This common unit is the Equivalent Cost per Unit of Product: it is equal to the sum of the inventory at the start of the period and the product produced in the same period, divided by the Equivalent Unit of Product in the time period considered that is equal to the sum of products produced and the products not yet produced.

Consequently, multiplying the Equivalent Cost per Unit of Product for the quantity of Equivalent Unit of Product, it is obtained the total amount of the firm's costs, both direct and indirect.

In the entire process, a key role is played by the *Allocation Rates*. It should express, in as far as is possible, a causal relationship between each cost and the cost-object that are the Cost Centres (that is the intermediate cost-object) and the Product (that is the final cost-object). We can use different Allocation Rates to allocate Indirect Costs either to Cost Centres and to product. They are usually defined on the basis of the specific characteristic of the firm.

Note that we commonly use the Predetermined Allocation Rate because it is defined before the start of the planned year. Consequently, the value of the Allocation Rates is expected and not actual and then the Full Cost of Product (FCP) is estimated for the forthcoming year and it is not actual value.

The use of Predetermined Allocation Rates rather than Actual Allocation Rates computed during the year, presents three main advantages:

1. Allocation rates computed during the year could be affected by peculiar conditions of the period. Variables on which the Allocation Rates are defined could change during the period by generating its fluctuation. Consequently, the Full Cost of Product (FCP) could be misleading because allocation of the Indirect Costs is affected by these fluctuations.
2. The Predetermined Allocation Rate allows for allocation of Indirect Costs of Product at the same time period in which the Direct Costs are attributed to the product.
3. The Predetermined Allocation Rate allows the computation of Forecasted Full Cost of Product and then the variance analysis on the basis of the Actual Full Cost of Product. Indeed, by using the Predetermined Allocation Rates, we use expected costs in planning and the actual costs during the period by computing the difference among them in the variance analysis. It is most important because the analysis of the variance is the most relevant activity in order to measure the difference between forecast and actual for decision making during the year.

The use of the Predetermined Allocation Rates usually requires the use of the Estimated Volume, also called Standard Volume, of the level of activities. It is the estimated level of the activities considered in the period. Usually, by considering a period equal to the year, the monthly standard volume is defined as equal to one-twelfth of the total volume estimated for the forthcoming year.

Obviously, the Cost per Unit of Product is strictly influenced by the relationship between standard volume and the Predetermined Allocation Rates. Indeed, the Cost per Unit of Product is higher if the volume is estimated lower and it is lower if the volume is estimated higher.

The main problem due to the Predetermined Allocation Rates is that the Cost per Unit of Product can include Indirect Costs for activities defined even if these activities have not been carried out. Indeed, the amount of Indirect Costs allocated to the product in a given period on the basis of the standard volume is likely to be different from the amount of Indirect Costs allocated to the product on the basis of actual volume. It occurs because the Indirect Costs assigned to the Cost Centres as well as the actual activity level for the period, are likely to be different from the estimates used when the Predetermined Allocation Rates were calculated. It generates two main phenomena:

(a) *Under-absorbed of Indirect Costs*: the amount of estimated Indirect Costs absorbed by the product are less than the amount of actual Indirect Costs absorbed by product.
(b) *Over-absorbed of Indirect Costs*: the amount of estimated indirect costs absorbed by product exceeds the amount of actual indirect costs absorbed by the product.

The problem of Cross Subsidies is strictly connected with these two phenomena. Generally, if the Indirect Cost structure is quite complex, the use of the Allocation Rates, both predeterminate and actual, leads to understatement of some product costs and overstatement of other product costs.

3 Variance Analysis and Economic Performance

3.1 Variance Analysis: Definition and Aim

The Variance Analysis (VA) measures the firm's economic performance in progress on the basis of the difference between the forecast and actual revenues and costs. Specifically, the variance analysis is based on the difference between revenues and costs:

1. *Forecast* (or *Standard*): it refers to the expected value of revenues and costs. Therefore, it represents what revenues and costs should be. Forecast revenues and costs are defined in financial planning (budget and business plan) with regard to a defined future time-period.
2. *Actual*: it refers to the realized value of revenues and costs in a defined time-period considered. Therefore, it represents what revenues and costs are actual realized.

The main aim of the variance analysis is to allow managers to make decisions in order to achieve their target on the basis of the analysis between the performance forecasted and then expected, and performance actual and then realized in the period considered.

Based on such analysis management can understand relevant questions about the causes of the variances between forecast and actual performance and take appropriate action based on the answers to these questions. Therefore, the variance analysis is focused on a deep understanding of the causes able to generate differences between forecast and actual for the decision-making process at each level of the organization with the main aim to achieve the targets planned.

The variance analysis is based on two main steps.

Step 1: Variance Computation It concerns the right computation of all variances with regard to revenues and costs. Then the aim is to define "*what*" is the amounts of difference between actual and forecast results.

P. De Luca, *Corporate Finance*, Springer Texts in Business and Economics,
https://doi.org/10.1007/978-3-031-18300-3_3

In this contest, it is not relevant if the variance is computed by considering the forecast minus actual or vice versa. Therefore, with regard to the:

(a) *Cost variances*, if: (1) actual cost is lower than the forecast cost, the variance is *favourable*; (2) actual cost is higher than the forecast cost, the variance is *unfavourable*.
(b) *Revenue variances*, if: (1) actual revenue is lower than the forecast revenue, the variance is *unfavourable*; (2) actual revenue is higher than the forecast revenue, the variance is *favourable*.

Therefore, the favourable variance is realized if revenue actual is higher than revenue forecast and cost actual is lower than forecast cost, while the unfavourable variance is realized if revenue actual is lower than revenue forecast and cost actual is higher than forecast cost.

Since revenues less costs define the Net Income, the *favourable variance* makes actual net income higher than forecast net income (because actual revenues are higher than forecast revenues and actual costs are lower than forecast costs), as well as the *unfavourable variance* makes actual net income lower than forecast net income (because actual revenues are lower than forecast revenues and actual costs are higher than forecast costs).

Step 2: Variance Interpretation It concerns the right interpretation of variances in order to make decisions to realign the forecast with the actual revenues and costs. Then the aim is to define "*why*" these variances occurred. Under this aspect, a favourable or unfavourable variance does not imply good or bad performance because it depends on the motivation and logic used in the definition of targets in the planning. Then, it requires the managers valuation according to the defined standard and the actual dynamics and their meaning in the decision-making process and strategies. Note that not all variances computed are under management control and then we must distinguish between variance due to the managers activities and variance out of their control. In both cases, however, it is necessary to understand if the variances computed can be defined operating, due to problem in operating activities and then able to be solved in the operating perspective, or it must be considered strategic by showing problem in the strategy or strategic planning of the firm.

There are three main aspects of variance analysis to keep always in mind:

1. There is not a standard variance analysis. There is not one way to make variance analysis. The depth of the analysis and its complexity is a function of the firm's characteristics and management's needs. The general rule is: (1) to decompose the general variance between forecast and actual revenues and costs in order to well-understand the problem and to make decision to achieve the target; (2) we

can use the variance analysis that are more appropriate to the specific case but the relevance of the outputs must be higher than the cost of the analysis.

2. In any cases, there is not a variance analysis able to measure in perfect way the firm's performance for two main reasons: (1) actual costs are not precisely accurate measure of resources consumed (as shown in the computation of the Full Cost of Product); (2) forecast costs are, at best, only approximate measures of what resources consumption should be under well-defined expected conditions (assumptions play a key role).

3.2 Sales Revenue Variance

The Total Sale Revenues (SR_T) is equal to the Total Quantity of Product (QP_T) sold or to be sold in the period considered multiplied by the Unit Price of Product (PP_U), as follows:

$$SR_T = QP_T \cdot PP_U \tag{3.1}$$

We can decline this equation in the actual and forecast perspectives.

3.2.1 Actual

In the actual perspective, the Total Sale Revenues Actual ($SR_{T(A)}$) is equal to the the Total Quantity of Product Actual ($QP_{T(A)}$) and then really sold in the period considered multiplied by the Unit Price of Product Actual ($PP_{U(A)}$), as follows:

$$SR_{T(A)} = QP_{T(A)} \cdot PP_{U(A)} \tag{3.2}$$

3.2.2 Forecast

In the forecast perspective, the Total Sale Revenues Forecast ($SR_{T(F)}$) is equal to the Total Quantity of Product Forecast ($QP_{T(F)}$) and then to be sold in the period considered multiplied by the Unit Price of Product Forecast ($PP_{U(F)}$), as follows:

$$SR_{T(F)} = QP_{T(F)} \cdot PP_{U(F)} \tag{3.3}$$

3.2.3 Variance Actual Vs Forecast

Based on the actual and forecast data, we can define the Sale Revenues Variance (SRV) as the difference between the Total Sale Revenues Actual ($SR_{T(A)}$) and the Total Sale Revenues Forecast ($SR_{T(F)}$) as follows:

$$\begin{aligned} \text{SRV} &= \text{SR}_{T(A)} - \text{SR}_{T(F)} \\ \text{SRV} &= \left(\text{QP}_{T(A)} \cdot \text{PP}_{U(A)}\right) - \left(\text{QP}_{T(F)} \cdot \text{PP}_{U(F)}\right) \end{aligned} \tag{3.4}$$

Therefore, if:

1. SRV is positive ($\text{SRV} > 0 \rightarrow \text{SR}_{T(A)} > \text{SR}_{T(F)}$), the variance is favourable because the Total Sale Revenues Actual ($\text{SR}_{T(A)}$) is higher than the Total Sale Revenues Forecast ($\text{SR}_{T(F)}$), and then the Total Sale Revenues was higher than expected.
2. SRV is negative ($\text{SRV} < 0 \rightarrow \text{SR}_{T(A)} < \text{SR}_{T(F)}$), the variance is unfavourable because the Total Sale Revenues Actual ($\text{SR}_{T(A)}$) is lower than the Total Sale Revenues Forecast ($\text{SR}_{T(F)}$), and then the Total Sale Revenues was lower than expected.

The Sales Revenue Variance (*SRV*) can be decomposed into two parts: (1) Quantity Component and (2) Price Component. Specifically:

1. Sales Quantity Variance (SQV): it is the quantity component and it is equal to the difference between the Total Quantity of Product Forecast ($\text{QP}_{T(F)}$) to be sold and the the Total Quantity of Product Actual ($\text{QP}_{T(A)}$) and then really sold in the period considered, multiplied by the Unit Price of Product Forecast ($\text{PP}_{U(F)}$), as follows:

$$\text{SQV} = \left(\text{QP}_{T(A)} - \text{QP}_{T(F)}\right) \cdot \text{PP}_{U(F)} \tag{3.5}$$

The use of the price forecast is necessary to isolate the variance related to the quantity. Indeed, if we use the price actual, we have contemporary the variance of the quantity (as possible difference between forecast and actual) and the variance of the price (as possible difference between actual and forecast).

2. Sales Price Variance (SPV): it is the price component of the and it is equal to the difference between the Unit Price of Product Actual ($PP_{U(A)}$) and the Unit Price of Product Forecast ($PP_{U(F)}$) multiplied by the Total Quantity of Product Actual ($QP_{T(A)}$) really sold in the period considered, as follows:

$$\text{SPV} = \left(\text{PP}_{U(A)} - \text{PP}_{U(F)}\right) \cdot \text{QP}_{T(A)} \tag{3.6}$$

We use the quantity of product actual rather than the forecast in order to isolate the variance due to the quantity. Indeed, if we use the quantity forecast, we have contemporary the variance of the quantity (as possible difference between forecast and actual) and the variance of the price (as possible difference between Actual and Forecast).

Therefore, based on these two components, the Total Sale Revenues Variance (SRV) is equal to the sum of the Sales Quantity Variance (SQV) and the Sales Price Variance (SPV) as follows:

$$\begin{aligned} \mathrm{SRV} &= \mathrm{SQV} + \mathrm{SPV} \\ \mathrm{SRV} &= \left[\left(\mathrm{QP}_{T(A)} - \mathrm{QP}_{T(F)}\right) \cdot \mathrm{PP}_{U(F)}\right] + \left[\left(\mathrm{PP}_{U(A)} - \mathrm{PP}_{U(F)}\right) \cdot \mathrm{QP}_{T(A)}\right] \end{aligned} \tag{3.7}$$

3.3 Cost of Material Variance

The Cost of Material per Unit of Product ($\mathrm{CM_{UP}}$) is equal to the Quantity of Material per Unit of Product ($\mathrm{QM_{UP}}$) multiplied by the Unit Price of Material ($\mathrm{PM_U}$), as follows:

$$\mathrm{CM_{UP}} = \mathrm{QM_{UP}} \cdot \mathrm{PM}_U \tag{3.8}$$

The Total Cost of Material (CM_T) in the period considered, is equal to the Cost of Material per Unit of Product ($\mathrm{CM_{UP}}$) multiplied by the Total Quantity of Product (or Output) (QP) in number of units of Product produced in the period:

$$\begin{aligned} \mathrm{CM}_T &= \mathrm{CM_{UP}} \cdot \mathrm{QP} \\ \mathrm{CM}_T &= (\mathrm{QM_{UP}} \cdot \mathrm{PM_U}) \cdot \mathrm{QP} \end{aligned} \tag{3.9}$$

Note that the Quantity of Material per Unit of Product ($\mathrm{QM_{UP}}$) multiplied by the Total Quantity of Product (QP) is the Total Quantity of Material (QM). Therefore, we can compute the Total Cost of Material (CM_T) by multiplying the Total Quantity of Material (QM) for the Unit Price of Material (PM_U), as follows:

$$\mathrm{QM} = \mathrm{QM_{UP}} \cdot \mathrm{QP}$$

$$\mathrm{CM}_T = \mathrm{QM} \cdot \mathrm{PM}_U$$

and then:

$$\mathrm{CM}_T = (\mathrm{QM_{UP}} \cdot \mathrm{QP}) \cdot \mathrm{PM}_U$$

This equation is a simple rearrangement of the previous one.

3.3.1 Forecast

The Cost of Material per Unit of Product Forecast ($\mathrm{CM}_{\mathrm{UP}(F)}$) is equal to the Quantity of Material per Unit of Product Forecast ($\mathrm{QM}_{\mathrm{UP}(F)}$) multiplied by the Unit Price of Material Forecast ($\mathrm{PM}_{U(F)}$):

$$CM_{UP(F)} = QM_{UP(F)} \cdot PM_{U(F)} \tag{3.10}$$

The Total Cost of Material Forecast ($CM_{T(F)}$) in the period considered is equal to the Cost of Material per Unit of Product Forecast ($CM_{UP(F)}$) multiplied by the Total Quantity of Product Actual ($QP_{(A)}$) in number of units of Product produced in the period considered.

$$\begin{aligned} CM_{T(F)} &= CM_{UP(F)} \cdot QP_{(A)} \\ CM_{T(F)} &= \left(QM_{UP(F)} \cdot PM_{U(F)}\right) \cdot QP_{(A)} \end{aligned} \tag{3.11}$$

Note that the Quantity of Material per Unit of Product Forecast ($QM_{UP(F)}$) multiplied by the Total Quantity of Product Actual ($QP_{(A)}$) is the Total Quantity of Material Forecast ($QM_{T(F)}$). Therefore, we can compute the Total Cost of Material Forecast ($CM_{T(F)}$) by multiplying the Total Quantity of Material Forecast ($QM_{T(F)}$) for the Unit Price of Material Forecast ($PM_{U(F)}$), as follows:

$$QM_{T(F)} = QM_{UP(F)} \cdot QP_{(A)}$$

$$CM_{T(F)} = QM_{T(F)} \cdot PM_{U(F)}$$

and then:

$$CM_{T(F)} = \left(QM_{UP(F)} \cdot QP_{(A)}\right) \cdot PM_{U(F)}$$

This equation is the simple rearrangement of the previous one.

3.3.2 Actual

The Cost of Material per Unit of Product Actual ($CM_{UP(A)}$) is equal to the Quantity of Material per Unit of Product Actual ($QM_{UP(A)}$) multiplied by the Unit Price of Material Actual ($PM_{U(A)}$):

$$CM_{UP(A)} = QM_{UP(A)} \cdot PM_{U(A)} \tag{3.12}$$

The Total Cost of Material Actual ($CM_{T(A)}$) in the period considered is equal to the Cost of Material per Unit of Product Actual ($CM_{UP(A)}$) multiplied by the Total Quantity of Product Actual ($QP_{(A)}$) in number of units of Product effectively produced in the period:

$$\begin{aligned} CM_{T(A)} &= CM_{UP(A)} \cdot QP_{(A)} \\ CM_{T(A)} &= \left(QM_{UP(A)} \cdot PM_{U(A)}\right) \cdot QP_{(A)} \end{aligned} \tag{3.13}$$

Note that the Quantity of Material per Unit of Product Actual ($QM_{UP(A)}$) multiplied by the Total Quantity of Product Actual ($QP_{(A)}$) is the Total Quantity of Material Actual ($QM_{T(A)}$). Therefore, we can compute the Total Cost of Material Actual ($CM_{T(A)}$) by multiplying the Total Quantity of Material Actual ($QM_{T(A)}$) for the Unit Price of Material Actual ($PM_{U(A)}$), as follows:

$$QM_{T(A)} = QM_{UP(A)} \cdot QP_{(A)}$$

$$CM_{T(A)} = QM_{T(A)} \cdot PM_{U(A)}$$

and then:

$$CM_{T(F)} = \left(QM_{UP(A)} \cdot QP_{(A)}\right) \cdot PM_{U(A)}$$

This equation is the simple rearrangement of the previous one.

3.3.3 Variance Forecast vs Actual

The Cost of Material Variance (CMV) is equal to the difference between Total Cost of Material Forecast ($CM_{T(F)}$) and the Total Cost of Material Actual ($CM_{T(A)}$) of the product produced in the period considered.

Therefore, the Cost of Material Variance (CMV) is based on the actual quantity of product realized in the period considered. Therefore, it is based on the Quantity of Product Actual ($QP_{(A)}$) in the period considered and the forecast output levels play no role in the analysis. It happens because the Quantity of Product Actual ($QP_{(A)}$) is a certain amount, while the Quantity of Product Forecast ($QP_{(F)}$) is an expected one and then it can be different in the reality by generating variance.

Since both $CM_{T(F)}$ and $CM_{T(A)}$ are based on the Quantity of Product Actual ($QP_{(A)}$) (in number of units), the variance is due to the difference between the Cost of Material per Unit of Product Forecast ($CM_{UP(F)}$) and Actual ($CM_{UP(A)}$) as follows:

$$CMV = CM_{T(F)} - CM_{T(A)} \tag{3.14}$$

Therefore, if:

1. CMV is positive ($CMV > 0 \rightarrow CM_{T(F)} > CM_{T(A)}$), the variance is favourable because the Total Cost of Material Forecast ($CM_{T(F)}$) is higher than the Total Cost of Material Actual ($CM_{T(A)}$), and then the Total Cost of Material was lower than expected.
2. CMV is Negative ($CMV < 0 \rightarrow CM_{T(F)} < CM_{T(A)}$), the variance is unfavourable because the Total Cost of Material Forecast ($CM_{T(F)}$) is lower than the Total Cost of Material Actual ($CM_{T(A)}$), and then the Total Cost of Material was higher than expected.

By considering that:

$$\mathrm{CM}_{T(F)} = \mathrm{CM}_{\mathrm{UP}(F)} \cdot \mathrm{QP}_{(A)} = \left(\mathrm{QM}_{\mathrm{UP}(F)} \cdot \mathrm{PM}_{U(F)}\right) \cdot \mathrm{QP}_{(A)}$$

$$\mathrm{CM}_{T(A)} = \mathrm{CM}_{\mathrm{UP}(A)} \cdot \mathrm{QP}_{(A)} = \left(\mathrm{QM}_{\mathrm{UP}(A)} \cdot \mathrm{PM}_{U(A)}\right) \cdot \mathrm{QP}_{(A)}$$

We have:

$$\begin{aligned} &\mathrm{CMV} = \left(\mathrm{CM}_{\mathrm{UP}(F)} - \mathrm{CM}_{\mathrm{UP}(A)}\right) \cdot \mathrm{QP}_{(A)} \\ &\text{or} \\ &\mathrm{CMV} = \left[\left(\mathrm{QM}_{\mathrm{UP}(F)} \cdot \mathrm{PM}_{U(F)}\right) - \left(\mathrm{QM}_{\mathrm{UP}(A)} \cdot \mathrm{PM}_{U(A)}\right)\right] \cdot \mathrm{QP}_{(A)} \end{aligned} \tag{3.15}$$

Because the Total Cost of Material (both Forecast and Actual) is computed on the basis of the Quantity of Material and the Unit Price of Material, we can decompose the Cost of Material Variance (CMV) into two parts:

1. Material Quantity Variance (MQV): it is the quantity component of the material variance and it is equal to the difference between Total Quantity of Material Forecast ($\mathrm{QM}_{T(F)}$) and Total Quantity of Material Actual ($\mathrm{QM}_{T(A)}$) multiplied by the Unit Price of Material Forecast ($\mathrm{PM}_{U(F)}$), as follows:

$$\mathrm{MQV} = \left(\mathrm{QM}_{T(F)} - \mathrm{QM}_{T(A)}\right) \cdot \mathrm{PM}_{\mathrm{UP}(F)} \tag{3.16}$$

By considering that:

$$\mathrm{QM}_{T(F)} = \mathrm{QM}_{\mathrm{UP}(F)} \cdot \mathrm{QP}_{(A)}$$

$$\mathrm{QM}_{T(A)} = \mathrm{QM}_{\mathrm{UP}(A)} \cdot \mathrm{QP}_{(A)}$$

We have:

$$\begin{aligned} &\mathrm{MQV} = \left(\mathrm{QM}_{\mathrm{UP}(F)} \cdot \mathrm{QP}_{(A)} - \mathrm{QM}_{\mathrm{UP}(A)} \cdot \mathrm{QP}_{(A)}\right) \cdot \mathrm{PM}_{\mathrm{UP}(F)} \\ &\text{or} \\ &\mathrm{MQV} = \left[\left(\mathrm{QM}_{\mathrm{UP}(F)} - \mathrm{QM}_{\mathrm{UP}(A)} \cdot \mathrm{QP}_{(A)}\right) \cdot \mathrm{PM}_{\mathrm{UP}(F)}\right] \end{aligned} \tag{3.17}$$

In this case, we consider the forecast value of the price of material in order to isolate the variance due to quantity. Indeed, if we use the actual value of the price of material instead of its forecast value, we can have contemporary the variance due to the quantity (as possible difference between forecast and actual) and the variance due to the price (as possible difference between forecast and actual).

2. *Material Price Variance* (*MPV*): it is the price component of the material variance and then it is equal to the difference between Unit Price of Material

Forecast ($PM_{U(F)}$) and the Unit Price of Material Actual ($PM_{U(A)}$) multiplied by the Total Quantity of Material Actual ($QM_{T(A)}$), as follows:

$$MPV = \left(PM_{U(F)} - PM_{U(A)}\right) \cdot QM_{T(A)} \tag{3.18}$$

By considering that:

$$QM_{T(A)} = QM_{UP(A)} \cdot QP_{(A)}$$

We have:

$$MPV = \left[\left(PM_{U(F)} - PM_{U(A)}\right) \cdot QM_{UP(A)}\right] \cdot QP_{(A)} \tag{3.19}$$

In this case, we consider the actual value of the quantity of material in order to isolate the variance due to price of Material. Indeed, if we use the Forecast value of the quantity of material instead of its actual value, we can have contemporary the variance due to the price of material (as possible difference between forecast and actual) and the variance due to the quantity of material (as possible difference between forecast and actual).

Therefore, based on these two components, the Cost of Material Variance (CMV) is equal to the sum of the Material Quantity Variance (*MQV*) and the Material Price Variance (*MPV*) as follows:

$$\begin{aligned} CMV &= MQV + MPV \\ CMV &= \left[\left(QM_{T(F)} - QM_{T(A)}\right) \cdot PM_{UP(F)}\right] + \left[\left(PM_{U(F)} - PM_{U(A)}\right) \cdot QM_{T(A)}\right] \end{aligned} \tag{3.20}$$

3.4 Direct Labour Cost Variance

The Direct Labour Cost per Unit of Product (LC_{UP}) is equal to the Direct Labour Time per Unit of Product (LT_{UP}) (usually expressed in hours) multiplied by the Direct Labour Price per Unit of Time (LP_{UT}) that is the standard rate as follows:

$$LC_{UP} = LT_{UP} \cdot LP_{UT} \tag{3.21}$$

The Total Direct Labour Cost (LC_T) in the period considered is equal to the Direct Labour Cost per Unit of Product (LC_{UP}) multiplied by the Total Quantity of Product (QP) in number of units of product produced in the period considered:

$$\begin{aligned} LC_T &= LC_{UP} \cdot QP \\ LC_T &= (LT_{UP} \cdot LP_{UT}) \cdot QP \end{aligned} \tag{3.22}$$

Note that the Direct Labour Time per Unit of Product (LT_{UP}) multiplied by the Total Quantity of Product (QP) is the Total Direct Labour Time (LT_T). Therefore, we can compute the Total Direct Labour Cost (LC_T) by multiplying the Total Direct Labour Time (LT_T) for the Direct Labour Price per Unit of Time (LP_{UT}) as follows:

$$LT_T = LT_{UP} \cdot QP$$

$$LC_T = LT_T \cdot LP_{UT}$$

and then:

$$LC_T = (LT_{UP} \cdot QP) \cdot LP_{UT}$$

This equation is a simple rearrangement of the previous one.

3.4.1 Forecast

The Direct Labour Cost per Unit of Product Forecast ($LC_{UP(F)}$) is equal to the Direct Labour Time per Unit of Product Forecast ($LT_{UP(F)}$) (usually expressed in hours) multiplied by a Direct Labour Price per Unit of Time Forecast ($LP_{UT(F)}$), as follows:

$$LC_{UP(F)} = LT_{UP(F)} \cdot LP_{UT(F)} \tag{3.23}$$

The Total Direct Labour Cost Forecast ($LC_{T(F)}$) in the period considered is equal to the Direct Labour Cost per Unit of Product Forecast ($LC_{UP(F)}$) multiplied by the Quantity of Product Actual ($QP_{(A)}$) in number of units of product produced in the period considered, as follows:

$$\begin{aligned} LC_{T(F)} &= LC_{UP(F)} \cdot QP_{(A)} \\ LC_{T(F)} &= \left(LT_{UP(F)} \cdot LP_{UT(F)}\right) \cdot QP_{(A)} \end{aligned} \tag{3.24}$$

Note that the Direct Labour Time per Unit of Product Forecast ($LT_{UP(F)}$) multiplied by the Total Quantity of Product Actual ($QP_{(A)}$) is the Total Direct Labour Time Forecast ($LT_{T(F)}$). Therefore, we can compute the Total Direct Labour Cost Forecast ($LC_{T(F)}$) by multiplying the Total Direct Labour Time Forecast ($LT_{T(F)}$) for the Direct Labour Price per Unit of Time Forecast ($LP_{UT(F)}$) as follows:

$$LT_{T(F)} = LT_{UP(F)} \cdot QP_{(A)}$$

$$LC_{T(F)} = LT_{T(F)} \cdot LP_{UT(F)}$$

and then:

$$LC_{T(F)} = \left(LT_{UP(F)} \cdot QP_{(A)}\right) \cdot LP_{UT(F)}$$

This equation is a simple rearrangement of the previous one.

3.4.2 Actual

The Direct Labour Cost per Unit of Product Actual ($LC_{UP(A)}$) is equal to the Direct Labour Time per Unit of Product Actual ($LT_{UP(A)}$) (usually expressed in hours) multiplied by a Direct Labour Price per Unit of Time Actual ($LP_{UT(A)}$), as follows:

$$LC_{UP(A)} = LT_{UP(A)} \cdot LP_{UT(A)} \tag{3.25}$$

The Total Direct Labour Cost Actual ($LC_{T(A)}$) in the period considered is equal to the Direct Labour Cost per Unit of Product Actual ($LC_{UP(A)}$) multiplied by the Quantity of Product Actual ($QP_{(A)}$) in number of units of product produced in the period considered, as follows:

$$\begin{aligned} LC_{T(A)} &= LC_{UP(A)} \cdot QP_{(A)} \\ LC_{T(A)} &= \left(LT_{UP(A)} \cdot LP_{UT(A)}\right) \cdot QP_{(A)} \end{aligned} \tag{3.26}$$

Note that the Direct Labour Time per Unit of Product Actual ($LT_{UP(A)}$) multiplied by the Total Quantity of Product Actual ($QP_{(A)}$) is the Total Direct Labour Time Actual ($LT_{T(A)}$). Therefore, we can compute the Total Direct Labour Cost Actual ($LC_{T(A)}$) by multiplying the Total Direct Labour Time Actual ($LT_{T(A)}$) for the Direct Labour Price per Unit of Time Actual ($LP_{UT(A)}$) as follows:

$$LT_{T(A)} = LT_{UP(A)} \cdot QP_{(A)}$$

$$LC_{T(A)} = LT_{T(A)} \cdot LP_{UT(A)}$$

and then:

$$LC_{T(A)} = \left(LT_{UP(A)} \cdot QP_{(A)}\right) \cdot LP_{UT(A)}$$

This equation is a simple rearrangement of the previous one.

3.4.3 Variance Forecast vs Actual

The Direct Labour Cost Variance (DLCV) is equal to the difference between Total Direct Labour Cost Forecast ($LC_{T(F)}$) and Total Direct Labour Cost Actual ($LC_{T(A)}$) in the period considered.

Note that also in this case, we consider the Quantity of Product Actual ($QP_{(A)}$) and then the actual quantity of product realized in the period considered. It happens because the Quantity of Product Actual is a certain value, while the Quantity of Product Forecast is an expected one and then it can be different in the reality by generating variance.

Since both $LC_{T(F)}$ and $LC_{T(A)}$ are based on the Quantity of Product Actual ($QP_{(A)}$) (in number of units produced in the period considered), the variance is due to the difference between the Direct Labour Cost per Unit of Product Forecast ($LC_{UP(F)}$) and Direct Labour Cost per Unit of Product Actual ($LC_{UP(A)}$) as follows:

$$\mathrm{DLCV} = LC_{T(F)} - LC_{T(A)} \tag{3.27}$$

Therefore, if:

1. DLCV is Positive ($\mathrm{DLCV} > 0 \rightarrow LC_{T(F)} > LC_{T(A)}$), the variance is favourable because the Total Direct Labour Cost Forecast ($LC_{T(F)}$) is higher than the Total Direct Labour Cost Actual ($LC_{T(A)}$), and then the Total Direct Labour Cost was lower than expected.
2. DLCV is Negative ($\mathrm{DLCV} < 0 \rightarrow LC_{T(F)} < LC_{T(A)}$), the variance is unfavourable because the Total Direct Labour Cost Forecast ($LC_{T(F)}$) is lower than the Total Direct Labour Cost Actual ($LC_{T(A)}$), and then the Total Direct Labour Cost was higher than expected.

By considering that:

$$LC_{T(F)} = LC_{UP(F)} \cdot QP_{(A)} = \left(LT_{UP(F)} \cdot LP_{UT(F)}\right) \cdot QP_{(A)}$$

$$LC_{T(A)} = LC_{UP(A)} \cdot QP_{(A)} = \left(LT_{UP(A)} \cdot LP_{UT(A)}\right) \cdot QP_{(A)}$$

We have:

$$\begin{gathered} \mathrm{DLCV} = \left(LC_{UP(F)} \cdot LC_{UP(A)}\right) \cdot QP_{(A)} \\ \text{or} \\ \mathrm{DLCV} = \left[\left(LT_{UP(F)} \cdot LP_{UT(F)}\right) - \left(LT_{UP(A)} \cdot LP_{UT(A)}\right)\right] \cdot QP_{(A)} \end{gathered} \tag{3.28}$$

Since the Total Direct Labour Cost (both forecast and actual) is computed on the basis of the Quantity of Time of Direct Labour and the Direct Labour Price per Unit of Time, we can decompose the Direct Labour Cost Variance (DLCV) into two parts:

1. Labour Efficiency Variance (LEV): it is the quantity component of the variance and it is equal to the difference between Total Direct Labour Time Forecast ($LT_{T(F)}$) and Total Direct Labour Time Actual ($LT_{T(A)}$) multiplied by Direct Labour Price per Unit of Time Forecast ($LP_{UT(F)}$) as follows:

$$LEV = \left(LT_{T(F)} - LT_{T(A)}\right) \cdot LP_{UT(F)} \tag{3.29}$$

By considering that:

$$LT_{T(F)} = LT_{UP(F)} \cdot QP_{(A)}$$

$$LT_{T(A)} = LT_{UP(A)} \cdot QP_{(A)}$$

We can explicit further as follows:

$$LEV = \left(LT_{UP(F)} \cdot QP_{(A)} - LT_{UP(A)} \cdot QP_{(A)}\right) \cdot LP_{UT(F)}$$
or
$$LEV = \left[\left(LT_{UP(F)} - LT_{UP(A)}\right) \cdot QP_{(A)}\right] \cdot LP_{UT(F)} \tag{3.30}$$

In this case, we consider the forecast value of the Labour Price per Unit of Time in order to isolate the variance due to quantity. Indeed, if we use the actual value of the Labour Price per Unit of Time instead of its forecast value, we can have contemporary the variance due to the quantity (as possible difference between forecast and actual) and the variance due to the price (as possible difference between forecast and actual).

2. Labour Price Variance (LPV): it is the price component of the variance and it is equal to the difference between Direct Labour Price per Unit of Time Forecast ($LP_{UT(F)}$) and Direct Labour Price per Unit of Time Actual ($LP_{UT(A)}$) multiplied by Total Direct Labour Time Actual ($LT_{T(A)}$) as follows:

$$LPV = \left(LP_{UT(F)} - LP_{UT(A)}\right) \cdot LT_{T(A)} \tag{3.31}$$

By considering that:

$$LT_{T(A)} = LT_{UP(A)} \cdot QP_{(A)}$$

we have:

$$LPV = \left[\left(LP_{UT(F)} - LP_{UT(A)}\right) \cdot LT_{UP(A)}\right] \cdot QP_{(A)} \tag{3.32}$$

In this case, we consider the actual value of the Labour Time per Unit of Product in order to isolate the variance due to price. Indeed, if we use the forecast value of the Labour Time per Unit of Product instead of its actual value, we can have contemporary the variance due to the quantity (as possible difference between forecast and actual) and the variance due to the price (as possible difference between forecast and actual).

Therefore, based on these two components, the Direct Labour Cost Variance (DLCV) is equal to the sum of the Labour Efficiency Variance (LEV) and the Labour Price Variance (LPV) as follows:

$$\begin{aligned} \text{DLCV} &= \text{LEV} + \text{LPV} \\ \text{DLCV} &= \left[\left(\text{LT}_{T(F)} - \text{LT}_{T(A)}\right) \cdot \text{LP}_{\text{UT}(F)}\right] + \left[\left(\text{LP}_{\text{UT}(F)} - \text{LP}_{\text{UT}(A)}\right) \cdot \text{LT}_{\text{T}(A)}\right] \end{aligned} \tag{3.33}$$

3.5 Overhead Costs Variance

The Total Overhead Costs (OC_T) can be distinguished between Total Fixed Overhead Costs (FOC_T) and Total Variable Overhead Costs (VOC_T) in the period considered. Consequently, the Total Overhead Costs (OC_T) is equal to the Total Fixed Overhead Costs (FOC_T) plus the Total Variable Overhead Costs (VOC_T) that are equal to the Variable Overhead Cost per Unit (VOC_U) multiplied by the Quantity

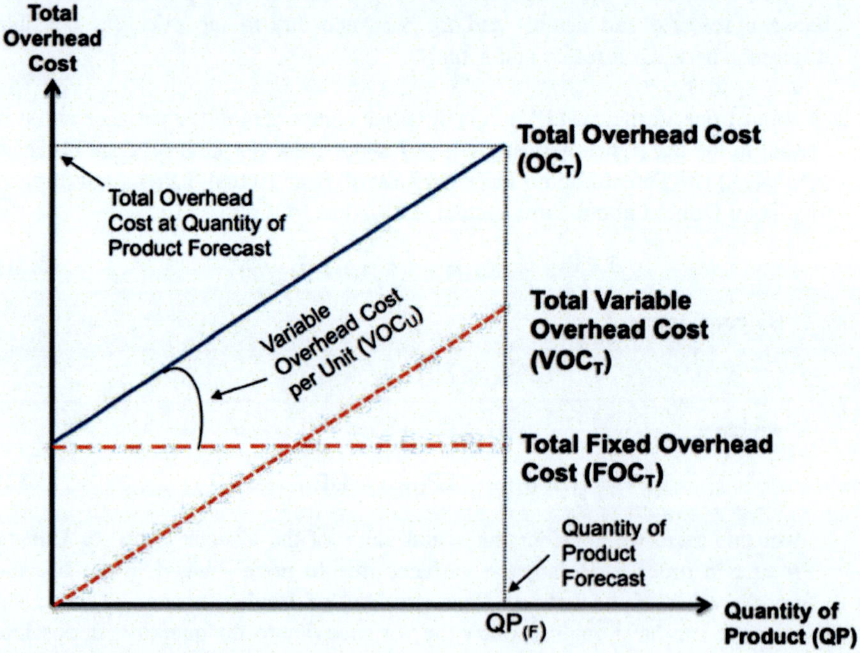

Fig. 3.1 Overhead costs behaviour

of Product (QP). Under the assumption of linear approximation (that is the baseline assumption in this analysis), we have:

$$OC_T = FOC_T + VOC_T = FOC_T + (VOC_U \cdot QP) \tag{3.34}$$

The equation draws a straight-line as shown in Fig. 3.1. It defines the amount of costs expected for each level of volume.

3.5.1 Forecast

In the forecast perspective, the Total Overhead Costs Forecast ($OC_{T(F)}$) is equal to the Total Fixed Overhead Costs Forecast ($FOC_{T(F)}$) plus the Total Variable Overhead Costs Forecast ($VOC_{T(F)}$) that are equal to the Variable Overhead Cost per Unit Forecast ($VOC_{U(F)}$) multiplied by the Quantity of Product Forecast ($QP_{(F)}$), as follows:

$$OC_{T(F)} = FOC_{T(F)} + VOC_{T(F)} = FOC_{T(F)} + \left(VOC_{U(F)} \cdot QP_{(F)}\right) \tag{3.35}$$

3.5.2 Actual

In the actual perspective, the Total Overhead Costs Actual ($OC_{T(A)}$) is equal to the Total Fixed Overhead Costs Actual ($FOC_{T(A)}$) plus the Total Variable Overhead Costs Actual ($VOC_{T(A)}$) that are equal to the Variable Overhead Cost per Unit Actual ($VOC_{U(A)}$) multiplied by the Quantity of Product Actual ($QP_{(A)}$), as follows:

$$OC_{T(A)} = FOC_{T(A)} + VOC_{T(A)} = FOC_{T(A)} + \left(VOC_{U(A)} \cdot QP_{(A)}\right) \tag{3.36}$$

The Total Overhead Costs are allocated to each unit product, through the Predetermined Overhead Rate (POR). It measures the amount of Total Overhead Costs absorbed by each unit product. The Predetermined Overhead Rate is calculated on the basis of the Quantity of Product Forecast (QP_F). Therefore, this rate is computed by dividing the Total Overhead Costs Forecast ($OC_{T(F)}$) estimated to be incurred at the level of the Quantity of Product Forecast (QP_F) divided by this level of production quantity as follows:

$$POR = \frac{OC_{T(F)}}{QP_F} = \frac{FOC_{T(F)} + \left(VOC_{U(F)} \cdot QP_{(F)}\right)}{QP_F} = \frac{FOC_{T(F)}}{QP_F} + \frac{VOC_{U(F)} \cdot QP_F}{QP_F} = FOC_{U(F)} + VOC_{U(F)} \tag{3.37}$$

The equation states that the Predetermined Overhead Rate (POR) is the average overhead cost per unit of product forecast because it is based on the quantity of product forecasted. Indeed, it is equal to the sum of the Variable Overhead Cost per Unit Forecast ($VOC_{U(F)}$) plus the Average Fixed Overhead Cost per Unit Forecast ($FOC_{U(F)}$) at the Quantity of Product Forecast (QP_F).

Two are the main aspect to be considered:

1. The Predetermined Overhead Rate (POR) is computed on the basis of the Quantity of Product Forecast (QP_F) and then on the basis of the level of production (in unit of product) expected during the course of the future period considered (in budget is the year).
2. The Average Fixed Overhead Cost per Unit Forecast ($FOC_{U(F)}$) represents the Fixed Term of the Predetermined Overhead Rate (POR_{FX}) so that $POR_{FX} = FOC_{U(F)}$, while the Variable Overhead Cost per Unit Forecast ($VOC_{U(F)}$) represents the Variable Term of the Predetermined Overhead Rate (POR_V) so that $POR_V = VOC_{U(F)}$. Since the Variable Cost per Unit is constant with respect to the Quantity of Product, the Variable Term of the Predetermined Overhead Rate remains constant. Differently, since Average Fixed Overhead Cost per Unit changes to the change in Quantity of Product, the Fixed Term of the Predetermined Overhead Rate changes to the change in Quantity of Product. Therefore, the Predetermined Overhead Rate changes solely to the change of its Fixed Term.

Based on the Predetermined Overhead Rate (POR) we can calculate the Total Overhead Costs Absorbed (OCA_T). It is equal to the Predetermined Overhead Rate (POR) multiplied by the Quantity of Product Actual (QP_A), as follows:

$$OCA_T = POR \cdot QP_A \tag{3.38}$$

The Total Overhead Costs Variance (OCV_T) is equal to the difference between the Total Overhead Costs Absorbed (OCA_T) and the Total Overhead Costs Actual ($OC_{T(A)}$), as follows:

$$\begin{aligned} OCV_T &= OCA_T - OC_{T(A)} \\ OCV_T &= (POR \cdot QP_A) - OC_{T(A)} \end{aligned} \tag{3.39}$$

Therefore, the Total Overhead Costs Variance (OCV_T) is the difference between the Overhead Costs actually incurred and the Overhead Costs Absorbed by production.

Since each unit of product really produced will be charged with share-part of the Total Overhead Costs on the basis of the Predetermined Overhead Rate, the amount of the Total Overhead Costs Absorbed (OCA_T) by the unit of product produced is the Predetermined Overhead Rate times the number of units of product actual produced.

Therefore, if:

- $OCA_T > OC_{T(A)}$: the Total Overhead Costs Variance is positive and then favourable.

– $OCA_T < OC_{T(A)}$: the Total Overhead Costs Variance is negative and then unfavourable.

The Total Overhead Cost Variance (OCV_T) can be decomposed into two parts: (1) Production Quantity Variance (QPV) and the (2) Spending Variance (SV).

Production Quantity Variance (QPV)

It is due to the difference between the Quantity of Product Actual ($QP_{(A)}$) in unit of product realized in the period considered and the Quantity of Product Forecast ($QP_{(F)}$) that had to be realized in the same period and thus used to calculate the Predetermined Overhead Rate (POR).

Generally, the Production Quantity Variance (QPV) is equal to the difference between the Total Overhead Costs Absorbed (OCA_T) and the Total Overhead Costs Forecast on the basis of the Quantity of Product Actual $\left(OCF_{T(QP_A)}\right)$, as follows:

$$QPV = OCA_T - OCF_{T(QP_A)} \tag{3.40}$$

The Total Overhead Costs Forecast on the basis of the Quantity of Product Actual $\left(OCF_{T(QP_A)}\right)$ is equal to the Total Fixed Overhead Costs Forecast ($FOC_{T(F)}$) plus the Variable Overhead Cost per Unit Forecast ($VOC_{U(F)}$) multiplied by the Quantity of Product Actual ($QP_{(A)}$), as follows:

$$OCF_{T(QP_A)} = FOC_{T(F)} + \left(VOC_{U(F)} \cdot QP_{(A)}\right)$$

By considering that:

$$OCA_T = POR \cdot QP_A$$

Substituting, it gets:

$$QPV = (POR \cdot QP_A) - \left[FOC_{T(F)} + \left(VOC_{U(F)} \cdot QP_{(A)}\right)\right] \tag{3.41}$$

Note that both Absorbed and Forecasted Costs are based on the Quantity of Product Actual ($QP_{(A)}$) in the period considered.

We can define the Production Quantity Variance (QPV) on the basis of the fixed part of the Predetermined Overhead Rate.

Rearrange the equation on the basis of the Quantity of Product Actual (QP_A) as follows:

$$QPV = (POR \cdot QP_A) - FOC_{T(F)} - \left(VOC_{U(F)} \cdot QP_{(A)}\right)$$

$$QPV = QP_A \cdot \left(POR - VOC_{U(F)}\right) - FOC_{T(F)}$$

By considering that the Variable Overhead Cost per Unit is equal to the Variable Term of the Predetermined Overhead Rate (POR_V) so that $VOC_{U(F)} = POR_V$, and by considering that the difference between the Predetermined Overhead Rate (POR) and its Variable Term (POR_V) is the Fixed Term of the Predetermined Overhead Rate (POR_{FX}), we can rewrite the equation as follows:

$$QPV = (QP_A \cdot POR_{FX}) - FOC_{T(F)}$$

By considering that the Total Fixed Overhead Costs Forecast ($FOC_{T(F)}$) is equal to the Average Fixed Overhead Cost per Unit Forecast ($FOC_{U(F)}$) multiplied by the Quantity of Product Forecast ($QP_{(F)}$), and by considering that the Average Fixed Overhead Cost per Unit Forecast ($FOC_{U(F)}$) represents the Fixed Term of the Predetermined Overhead Rate (POR_{FX}) so that $POR_{FX} = FOC_{U(F)}$, so that:

$$FOC_{U(F)} = \frac{FOC_{T(F)}}{QP_{(F)}} \quad \rightarrow \quad FOC_{T(F)} = FOC_{U(F)} \cdot QP_{(F)}$$

$$FOC_{U(F)} = POR_{FX} \quad \rightarrow \quad FOC_{T(F)} = POR_{FX} \cdot QP_{(F)}$$

Substituting, it gets:

$$QPV = (POR_{FX} \cdot QP_A) - (POR_{FX} \cdot QP_F)$$

And then:

$$QPV = POR_{FX} \cdot \left(QP_{(A)} - QP_{(F)}\right) \tag{3.42}$$

The equation states the Production Quantity Variance (QPV) on the basis of the Fixed Part of the Predetermined Overhead Rate. The Production Quantity Variance (QPV) is equal to the Fixed Part of the Predetermined Overhead Rate (POR_{FX}) multiplied by the difference between the Quantity of Product Actual ($QP_{(A)}$) and the Quantity of Product Forecast ($QP_{(F)}$).

Two are the main implication of this equation:

(a) The Production Quantity Variance (QPV) will exist whenever there is a difference between Quantity of Product Forecast and Actual in the period considered.
(b) The Production Quantity Variance (QPV) shows the amount of under-absorbed or over-absorbed Fixed Costs Forecast. Indeed, if all Overhead Costs are Variable Costs they change to the change of quantity production and then the Production Quantity Variance does not exist.

The Total Overhead Costs Absorbed (OCA_T) can be graphically represented by a straight-line starting at zero and with the slope equal to the Predetermined Overhead Rate (POR) as in Fig. 3.2.

Therefore, Forecasted Overhead Costs and Absorbed Overhead Costs will be equal only if the Quantity of Product Forecast ($QP_{(F)}$) is equal to the Quantity of Product Actual ($QP_{(A)}$) for each quantity production level. Specifically, if the:

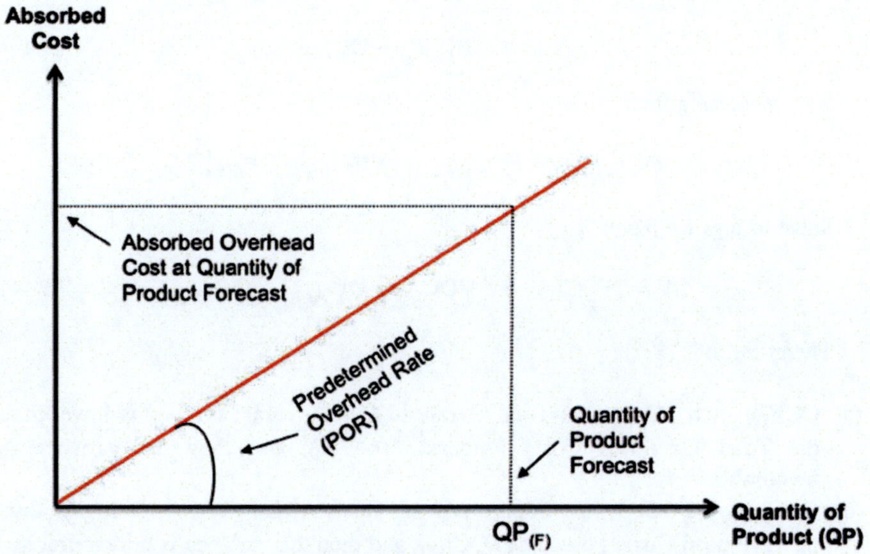

Fig. 3.2 Total overhead costs absorption on the basis of predetermined overhead rate

(a) $QP_{(A)} = QP_{(F)}$: the amount of Total Overhead Costs really absorbed is equal to the amount forecasted at each level of the quantity production.
(b) $QP_{(A)} < QP_{(F)}$: the amount of Total Overhead Costs really absorbed is less than the amount forecasted at that level of quantity production. Consequently, the forecasted overhead costs are under-absorbed (or unabsorbed) by generating an unfavourable variance.
(c) $QP_{(A)} > QP_{(F)}$: the amount of Total Overhead Costs really absorbed is more than the amount forecasted at that level of quantity production. Consequently, the forecasted overhead costs are over-absorbed by generating a favourable variance.

The phenomena of under-absorbed and over-absorbed overhead costs are due to the difference between forecasted and actual (and then really absorbed) overhead costs caused solely by the difference in production quantity between actual and forecast on which is computed the predetermined overhead rate. For this reason, it is defined as production volume variance. Therefore, the favourable or unfavourable variance is caused solely by the fact that the Quantity of Product Actual ($QP_{(A)}$) is different from the Quantity of Product Forecast ($QP_{(F)}$).

Spending Variance (SV)
It is due to difference between the Total Overhead Costs Forecast on the basis of the Quantity of Product Actual $\left(OCF_{T(QP_A)}\right)$ and the Total Overhead Costs Actual ($OC_{T(A)}$) in the period considered, as follows:

$$SV = OCF_{T(QP_A)} - OC_{T(A)} \tag{3.43}$$

By considering that:

$$OCF_{T(QP_A)} = FOC_{T(F)} + \left(VOC_{U(F)} \cdot QP_{(A)}\right)$$

Substituting, we have:

$$SV = \left[FOC_{T(F)} + \left(VOC_{U(F)} \cdot QP_{(A)}\right)\right] - OC_{T(A)} \tag{3.44}$$

Therefore, if:

(a) $OCF_{T(QP_A)} > OC_{T(A)}$: the Total Overhead Costs Actual ($TOC_{(A)}$) is lower than the Total Overhead Costs Forecast ($TOC_{(F)}$), and then the variance is favourable.
(b) $OCF_{T(QP_A)} < OC_{T(A)}$: the Total Overhead Costs Actual ($TOC_{(A)}$) is higher than the Overhead Costs Forecast ($TOC_{(F)}$), and then the variance is unfavourable.

Therefore, the Overhead Cost Variance (OCV) is equal to the sum of Production Quantity Variance (QPV) and the Spending Variance (SV) as follows:

$$OCV = OPV + SV \tag{3.45}$$

We can graphically represent the difference between Overhead Costs Forecasted and Absorbed as in Fig. 3.3.

In Fig. 3.3., the Forecast Line shows the expected (forecast) relationship between Quantity of Product and Total Overhead Costs Forecasted. The Absorption Line shows the relationship between Quantity of Product and the Total Overhead Costs Absorbed. In both cases, we consider the Quantity of Production and not the Quantity of Sales that play no role in the computation of the Overhead Costs as well as in the Direct Material Costs and Direct Labour Costs.

Fig. 3.3. shows a situation in which:

The Quantity of Product Actual ($QP_{(A)}$) is lower than the Quantity of Product Forecast ($QP_{(F)}$).

1. The Total Overhead Costs Actual ($TOC_{(A)}$) is lower than the Total Overhead Costs Forecast ($TOC_{(F)}$) at the level of Quantity of Product Actual ($QP_{(A)}$) but Total Overhead Costs Absorbed (OCA_T) is lower than the Total Overhead Costs Forecasted (OCF_T). Note that the Forecasted Costs are the amount of costs forecasted for the level of Quantity of Product actually attained in the period.
2. The Production Quantity Variance (QPV) is negative and then it is unfavourable because the Total Overhead Costs Absorbed are minus than the Total Overhead Costs Forecasted. Consequently, the Overhead Costs Absorbed is below they

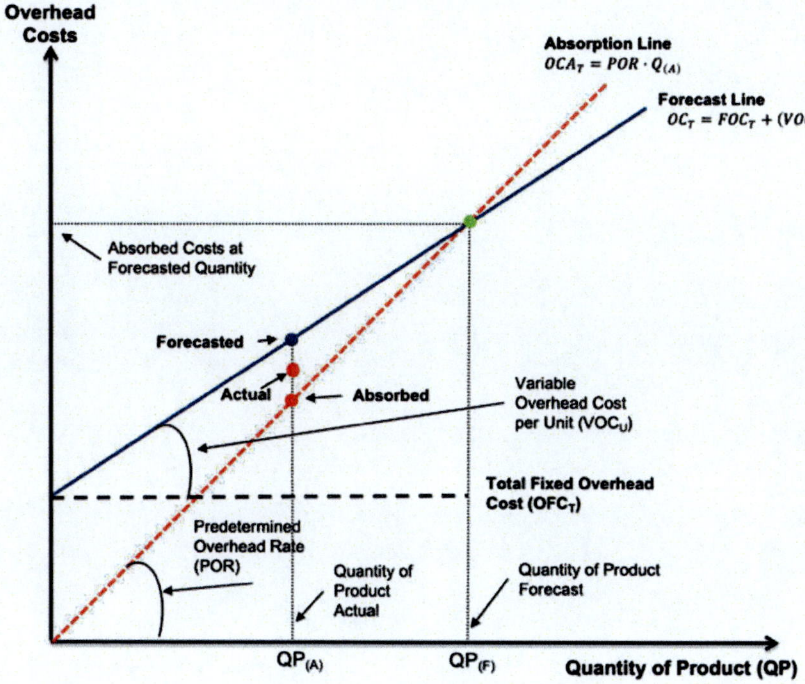

Fig. 3.3 Forecasted and absorbed total overhead costs at various levels of production and costs

would be in the forecast. Note that both Absorbed and Forecasted Cost amounts are based on the Quantity of Product Actual ($QP_{(A)}$) in the period considered.

3. The Spending Variance (SV) is positive and then it is favourable because the amount of Actual Costs is lower than the amount of Forecast Costs.

4 Economic and Financial Dynamic Analysis: Operating Income and Net Income

4.1 Economic and Financial Dynamic Analysis of the Firm

Commonly, the Financial Analysis of the firm is based on the Financial Statements and then it is focused on the past performance of the firm and it uses an accounting approach.

In this contest, the Financial Analysis of the firm is based on the construction, analysis, and valuation of the Economic and Financial Dynamic (EFD) of the firm. The EFD analysis is based on some key economic and financial aggregates able to show clearly, simple and intuitively the effective economic and financial dynamics of the firm over time by considering both the past and the future: it is based on a period of time that starts from 3 or 5 years in the past and goes to 3 or 5 years in the future. Therefore, the EFD considers jointly the historical and forecasted on the basis of the expected future data, with regard to Income, Capital, and Cash-Flows.

Consequently, the EFD shows effects of the strategic and operational decisions on the economic and financial dynamic in an aggregate way by linking the past and the future in an entire period of time.

The main aim of the EFD is to investigate the firm's actual health conditions and its expected capability to create equity value over time in the shareholder's perspective. Consequently, in the EFD analysis the future is more relevant than the past, because the firm's value depends on the future rather than the past.

In this perspective, the EFD must be considered a fundamental tool in the decision-making process. The EFD analysis must allow at all time to develop an:

(a) *Ex ante* analysis and evaluation: on the basis of the expected effects of the strategic and operational decisions on the expected economic and financial dynamic of the firm and then on its expected capability to create value.
(b) *Ex post* analysis and evaluation: on the basis of the real effects of the strategic and operational decisions produced on the actual economic and financial dynamic of the firm and then on the effective value created.

P. De Luca, *Corporate Finance*, Springer Texts in Business and Economics,
https://doi.org/10.1007/978-3-031-18300-3_4

The EFD is based on three Schema of Analysis:

1. Operating and Net Income (ONI)
2. Invested Capital and Capital Structure (ICCS)
3. Free Cash-flow to the Firm and to Equity (FCFE)

While the first (ONI) refers to the analysis of the Economic Dynamic of the firm, the second (ICCS) and the third (FCFE) both refer to the analysis of the Financial Dynamic of the firm.

Note that these Schemes of Analysis are defined based on non-financial companies. Furthermore, they can also be used for financial companies after some changes in their structures.

The consistency of the entire analysis requires that these three Schemes of Analysis:

1. *are strictly related among them*. Therefore, the definition of each one is strictly related to the composition of each other. They are able to show the economic and financial dynamic of the firm over time only if they are analysed simultaneously in a unique way.
2. *must be used on the basis of the same assumptions*. It is fundamental to compare the economic and financial performances of the same firm in different time period, as well as to compare the economic and financial performances of different firms over time.
3. *require coherence between the past and the future data*. The past and forecast economic and financial dynamic must be linked among them. It is necessary in order to simplify the comparison between the past and the future for the same company and between different companies over time.
   The alignment between past and future economic and financial values requires adjustment of the past values. The aim is to obtain *adjusted* (or *normalized*) past values of economic and financial dynamic to well understand the real situation of the company in a stand-alone condition.
   At the end of the adjustment process, it should be simple to understand the actual effective economic and financial conditions of the firm, where they came from and in which way they can evolved in the future as consequences of the probable effects on them of the strategic choices.
4. *strategic perimeter of the firm's core-business*. The necessary connection between the past and the expected future data requires a clear definition of the firm's core-business perimeter and its evolution over time. It is necessary to distinguish in each year the operating activities and non-operating activities. In the analysis of the historical EFD, the use of non-operating activities it is necessary to well define the perimeter of the core-business of the firm in order to measure clearly its operating performance in terms of Income, Invested Capital, and Free Cash-flows. In the analysis of the forecast EFD, we focus on the planning of the operating activities. Therefore, Non-Operating are not

planning because if it is they must be considered Operating and not anymore Non-Operating by increasing the core-business perimeter.

In the EFD analysis, we follow a financial approach rather than accounting approach based on the analysis of the Financial Statements in a past perspective. Consequently:

1. We do not consider any accounting problems regard the Financial Statements (Balance Sheet, Income Statement, and Statement of Cash-Flows) is considered known.
2. Even if we use information derived from the accounting, we do not analyse them to verify their validity with regard to the accounting correctness of the single number, but only we use them for the decision-making process. Therefore, it is not relevant the right computation of each specific historical economic and financial item on the basis of accounting rule, but it is relevant to well-understand the dynamic of some key economic and financial aggregates of the firm over time.
3. We are interested much more in the Cash-Flows rather than the Income. The analysis of the firm's health conditions and the estimation of its capability to create value are strictly related to the dynamic of Cash-Flows over time.
4. The Schema of Analysis used (ONI, ICCS, FCFE) must not be confused with the schemas usually used in the accounting analysis of financial statements: neither the terminology nor the logic of analysis is strictly related to the accounting rules. The choice about the right allocation of each item in each of the three schemes of analysis is not neutral but it is realized by considering the most clear and useful representation of the economic and financial dynamic over time in a strategic perspective.
5. The reference time is the future and not the past. The main aim is to investigate the firm's capability to create value over time. The company's value is based on the expected future cash-flows and then the future is the only reference time. The past analysis is useful to well-understand the effective actual economic and financial conditions of the firm and to link them to the forecast economic and financial dynamic as a consequence of expected effects of the strategic choices.
6. If the future is the reference time, a key role is played by the assumptions. The quality of assumptions requires that each assumption: (1) must be clearly defined in its perimeter and in its computation structure; (2) must be clearly related to the others on the basis of a well-defined relationship. Therefore, each assumption must be individually reliable and coherent with each other.

4.2 Operating Income and Net Income: Scheme of Analysis

The starting point of the Economic and Financial Dynamic (EFD) analysis of the firm is the economic dynamic analysis. It is based on the analysis of the Operating Income and Net Income (ONI) and its aim is to investigate the firm capability to create profit.

It is a high-level analysis of the economic dynamic of the firm over time. It shows in a synthetic way the existence of a real long-run competitive advantage of the firm on the basis of revenues, costs, and margins. We can say that firm has a real long-run competitive advantage only if its economic dynamic shows results better than its competitors for a long-time period.

The scheme of analysis used is reported in Table 4.1.

The analysis scheme (ONI) used highlights the main items able to show in a synthetic and simple way the firm's capability to generate Operating and Net Income.

Preliminarily, it can be useful to solve a terminology problem. In this context, in order to homogenize the analysis with respect to other parts of the book, we will use an economic terminology rather than accounting one and then we use the term cost rather than expense.

The scheme of analysis used groups all revenues and costs in four sections: Operating section; Financial section; Non-Operating section; Taxation section.

4.2.1 Operating Section

It groups all revenues and costs strictly related to the operating activities of the firm on the basis of its core-business.

The main problem is the right definition of the firm's core-business. In this context, it is a strategic matter rather than accounting one. Consequently, the perimeter of the core-business of the firm can change over time both in the short run and long run on the basis of the firm's strategic choices. In this contest, it is relevant to well define the business in which the firm wants to compete. They can change over time because the firm can decide to enter in new business or to go out of existing business. Then, the perimeter of the core-business changes by following the firm's strategic choices.

The key to the analysis is the Operating Income. The main focus is to investigate the firm's capability to generate Operating Income over time because it is the result of the core-business activities.

There are three main economic aggregates that we must investigate in the Operating section: (1) Gross Profit (GP); (2) Earnings Before Interest, Taxes, Depreciation, and Amortization (EBITDA); (3) Earnings Before Interest and Taxes (EBIT).

All costs grouped in this section are operating because they are strictly related to the core-business of the firm. However, we can distinguish three main types of operating costs:

1. *First level of Operating Costs*: they refer all operating costs grouped in the Gross Profit (GP). These operating costs: (1) are *Cash*, because they have financial effects as well as economics one; (2) refer to *Market structure*, because they are

Table 4.1 Scheme of analysis ONI

	Historical data			Forecast data		
	$t_{(-n)}$	$t_{(-2)}$	$t_{(-1)}$	$t_{(1)}$	$t_{(2)}$	$t_{(n)}$
Net operating revenues (NOR)						
(Direct materials cost)						
(Direct production services cost)						
(Direct labour cost)						
Cost of goods sold (COGS)						
Gross profit (GP)						
(Personnel cost)						
(Research and development cost)						
(Marketing and sales cost)						
(Logistic cost)						
(Advisory cost)						
(Leasing and rent cost)						
(General and administrative cost)						
Operating costs (cash)						
EBITDA						
(Amortization of intangible operating assets)						
(Depreciation of tangible operating assets)						
(Impairment of operating assets)						
(Accruals to provisions)						
Operating costs (no-cash)						
EBIT						
(Interest on debt)						
(Other financial costs on debt)						
Financial revenues						
Net financial costs						
EBT-operating (EBT_{Op})						
Non-operating and non-current operating revenues						
(Non-operating and non-current operating costs)						
(Amortization of intangible non-operating assets)						
(Depreciation of tangible non-operating assets)						
(Impairment of non-operating assets)						
Non-operating revenues and costs						
EBT						
Income taxes						
(Taxes)						
NET INCOME (NI)						
Earnings per share of common stock (EPS)						

strictly related to the characteristics of the market in which firm competes rather than its structure.

2. *Second level of Operating Costs*: they refer all operating costs grouped in the EBITDA and below the Gross Profit (GP). These operating costs: (1) are *Cash*,

Table 4.2 Operating costs

Operating costs structure		
First level	1. Operating 2. Cash 3. Market's structure	GROSS PROFIT
Second level	1. Operating 2. Cash 3. Firm's structure	EBITDA
Third level	1. Operating 2. Non-cash 3. Firm's structure	EBIT

because they have financial effects as well as economics one; (2) refer to *Firm structure*, because they are strictly related to the characteristics of the firm and its way to compete in the business.

3. *Third level of Operating Costs*: they refer all operating costs grouped in the EBIT and below the EBITDA. These operating costs: (1) are *Non-Cash*, because they do not have financial effects but only economic one; (2) refer to *Firm structure*, because they are strictly related to the characteristics of the firm and its way to compete in the business.

We can summarize differences between these three types of operating costs as in Table 4.2.

These three levels of operating costs define the Firm's Operating Cost Structure and consequently the relationships among the GP, EBITDA, and EBIT.

4.2.2 Non-Operating Section

It groups all revenues and costs related to the non-operating activities and then out of the firm's core-business.

The problem of the core-business perimeter definition of the firm is a strategic choice of managers. Then, it can change over time both in the short run and long run on the basis of the firm's strategic valuations.

The existence of non-operating revenues and costs leads to the identification of the EBT-Operating (EBT_{OP}) in the EBT. Obviously, if there are not non-operating revenues and costs, the EBT-Operating is equal to the EBT.

In this section are grouped:

1. *Non-Operating Revenues and Costs*: they refer to all revenues and costs related to activities out of the firm's core-business.
2. *Non-Current Operating Revenues and Costs*: they refer to all revenues and costs related to the firm's core-business but non-current because they are valuated as one-off. Consequently, they are unable to be repeated over time because they are strictly related to occasional and not structural both exogenous and endogenous causes.

3. *Amortization, Depreciation, and Impairment of Non-Operating Assets*: they refer all costs strictly related to investments in non-operating assets.

The relevance of the Non-Operating Section is much more in the historical analysis than the forecast analysis.

In the historical analysis Non-Operating Section plays a fundamental role. It allows the adjustment process in order to align the past data and forecast data with the aim to highlight the operating activities.

In the forecast analysis the Non-Operating Section should be not considered because:

(a) it is not possible to estimate the one-off. Therefore, it is not possible to forecast Non-Current Operating Revenues and Costs.
(b) if firm decides to invest in non-operating activities, they become operating activities by definition. In this case, these investments define a new business area by modifying the perimeter of the core-business. The consequence is that the past Non-Operating Revenues and Costs become in the future perspective Operating Revenues and Costs. It implies that the investments in assets need to develop a new business area are new Operating CapEx ($CAPEX_{OP}$) as well as the Accounts Receivable and Payables are grouped in Operating NWC (NWC_{OP}), as we will show.

Consequently, in the forecast analysis there are not:

(a) *Non-Operating Revenues and Costs*, with regard to both Non-Operating and Non-Current Operating Revenues and Costs and Amortization, Depreciation, and Impairment of Non-Operating Assets. Consequently, the EBT-Operating (EBT_{OP}) is equal to EBT.
(b) *Surplus Assets*, with regard to both investments in Non-Operating CapEx (with regard to investments in Tangible, Intangible, and Financial Non-Operating Assets) and in Non-Operating Net Working Capital (with regard to investments in Non-Operating Receivables and Payables). Therefore, Net Operated Invested Capital (NOIC) is equal to the Invested Capital (IC).
(c) *Cash-Flow from Surplus Assets,* and then there are not cash-flows from Non-Operating Revenues and Costs, cash-flows from Non-Operating CapEx ($CAPEX_{NOP}$), cash-flows from Non-Operating Net Working Capital (NWC_{NOP}).

However, it is always possible to use the Non-Operating Section in the forecast analysis. It can be done only in specific and well-defined cases in which Non-Operating Revenues and Costs must be considered.

4.2.3 Financial Section

It groups all financial revenues and costs related to the capital management. Commonly, in non-financial firms:

(a) *Financial costs* refer mainly to the interest on financial debts and other financial costs related to it.
(b) *Financial revenues* refer mainly to the dividend received from share owned in other companies and interest on bank deposits.

Operating and Financial sections are the most relevant to evaluate the firm's capability to generate profit stable and sustainably over time on the basis of its core-business. Indeed, even if the Operating section is the most relevant to realize the core-business's activities, commonly firm requires financial debt. The financial section measures the cost of financial debts and the firm's capability to face debt obligations.

4.2.4 Taxes Section

It groups all taxes both operating and corporate. Even if commonly taxes are considered entirely in this part, a deep analysis should require the right definition of taxes arising from each of the three sections (Operating, Non-Operating, Financial) by operating the tax splitting. In practice, the tax splitting is difficult and it is high the risk to contaminating the economic aggregates making the analysis less effective.

4.3 Gross Profit (GP)

The Gross Profit (GP) (also called Gross Margin) is the difference between revenues generated from selling products (goods or service) and the related direct production costs. In our scheme, it is equal to the difference between Net Operating Revenues (NOR) and the Cost of Goods Sold (COGS).

4.3.1 Net Operating Revenues

The Net Operating Revenues (NOR) is the total amount of revenues of goods and services sold strictly related to the firm's core-business. The NOR is the sum of three main items: (a) Net Sales Revenues, (b) Change in Inventories of Finished Goods and Work in Progress, and (c) Other Operating Revenues.

Net Sales Revenue (NSR)

Net Sales Revenue (NSR) is equal to the Sales Revenue (SR) less the sum of Sales Returns, Sales Refunds, and Sales Discounts.

It is possible to start the analysis from the Sales Revenue or directly from the Net Sales Revenue. It depends on the relevance of the Sales Returns, Refunds, and Discounts in the firm's business. If:

- they are strategic costs for the firm, because they are related to a relevant part of the business such as commercial policy or logistic activities, they must be showed and analysed separately. Then, we must start the analysis from the Sales Revenue
- they are not strategic costs for the firm, they cannot be showed and analysed separately, and then we can start the analysis from the Net Sales Revenue (NSR) directly

Net Sales Revenues (NSR) are the starting point of the analysis both historical and forecast. They influence direct and indirect all other variables that are strictly related from them. Also, they are the most difficult to planning because they depend both on the market and the firm's activities.

Sale Revenues (SR) are based on the following variables that must be considered with regard to the past and in the future:

1. Price per Unit of Product (P_{UP})
2. Quantity of Product (Q_P)
3. Product mix, if the firm sells more than one Product (P_{MIX})

Note that in this contest and following, the use of term "Product" refers to the Goods and Services sold by the firm.

The Sale Revenue (SR) is equal to the Price per Unit of Product (P_{UP}) multiplied by the Quantity of Product produced (Q_P) as follows:

$$SR = P_{UP} \cdot Q_P \tag{4.1}$$

If we have more than one Products, the Total Sales Revenues (SR_T) is equal to the sum of Sale Revenues of each Product (SR_i), as follows:

$$SR_T = \sum_{i=1}^{n} SR_i \tag{4.2}$$

The weight of i-th Product (WP_i) in the Product Mix can be defined on the basis of the weight of its Sale Revenues (SR_i) in the Total Sale Revenues (SR_T) as follows:

$$WP_i = \frac{SR_i}{SR_T} \tag{4.3}$$

The NSR can be forecasted by following two main methods used to make estimation about sales:

1. *Statistical method* based on the market analysis and the application of forecasting models.
2. *Judgemental method* based on opinions of salespersons built on their knowledge of market and customers.

While small firms tend to use the second method only, large firms usually used the two methods jointly: by the first, firm defines a first-step estimation; by the second, firm rearranges the estimation and defines the target of sales to be achieved.

Sales Discounts, Returns, Allowances, and Refunds can be defined as commercial costs and they are strictly related to the Sale Revenues. Usually, these costs represent a percentage of the Sales Revenues.

Change in Inventories of Finished Goods and Work in Progress

In this contest, it is useful to distinguish between Net Sales (NS) and Changes in Inventories in order to well analyse the trend of Sales and to avoid the accounting policies about inventories. Indeed, if the:

- Ending value > Beginning value, there is an increase and then the sign is plus (+)
- Ending value < Beginning value, there is a decrease and then the sign is minus (−).

Other Operating Revenues

It refers to the other operating revenue that we want to distinguish from the Sales for a well defined purpose of the firm for itself and carried at cost, and eventually other operating revenues related to the sales that we want to distinguish from them for a well-defined specific purpose.

We can summarize the Net Operating Revenues (NOR) as in Table 4.3.

If the firm competes in more than one Strategic Business Area (SBA), the Net Sales must be distinguished between each of them. In this case, total amount of Net Sales (NS) is equal to the sum of them for each SBA as follows:

Table 4.3 Net operating revenues (NOR)

Gross sale revenues (GSR)
(Sales returns, allowances, and refunds)
(Sales discounts)
Net sales (NS)
Ending inventories of finished goods and work in progress
(Beginning inventories of finished goods and work in progress)
Change in inventories of finished goods and work in progress
Production for own use
Others operating revenues related to the sales
Other operating revenues (NS)
Net operating revenues (NOR)

$$NS = \sum_{i=1}^{n} NS_{SBAi} \tag{4.4}$$

Too often, the maximization of revenues (either in terms of volume or value) is considered a primary objective for the firm especially in the case of SMEs companies. The increase in revenues is a necessary condition but unfortunately not sufficient condition for the firm's growth.

Because Revenues are not the Profit, it is possible that the increase in revenues generate loss for the firm. It happens when the strategy of the firm is focused on the revenues only without any analysis of the economic and financial dynamic overall. More specifically, if sales generate revenues but not profit margins, or even negative profit margins, the increase in sales generates an increase in costs higher than the increase in revenues and consequently increase in loss for the firm. This type of revenues can be defined *doped revenues* because the increase in revenues is realized at the expenses of profit margins. These revenues are bought on the market giving up profit margins. This type of strategy can be realized to acquire market shares but it is more expensive. Obviously, it is short-signed by definition and even if it is applied, it can be done only in the short-run period. Generally, if the firm pursues sales maximization as its main overriding long-run target, it can generate sales in loss that can lead to the firm default.

Note that the losses generated by the doped revenues increase the debt level in order to cover the financial needs related to the Net Working Capital. It implies that the Capital Structure goes in structural disequilibrium because the debt is not used to finance investments in operating asset with return in terms of EBITDA in the medium-long run.

Based on these considerations, we can say that revenues must be realized with profit margins, and the real growth of the firm must always be measured on the basis of the increase in margin profits accompanied with a Capital Structure optimized and stable over time. Specifically, the increase in profits can be achieved by: (1) increasing the revenues to a greater level than costs, or (2) reducing the costs structurally for equal or decreasing revenues lower than the cost reduction.

4.3.2 Cost of Goods Sold

The Cost of Goods Sold (COGS) (also called Cost of Sales) is the cost of goods or services sold. These costs represent the *first-level operating costs*: costs strictly operating, cash and related to the structure of the market in which the firm competes.

The COGS is the sum of three main items: (1) Direct Materials Cost, (2) Direct Production Services Cost, and (3) Direct Labour Cost.

Direct Materials Cost is equal to the total amount of costs for raw materials, parts and products used for the product production. It is the most relevant direct cost of product because it is strictly related to its realization. It is equal to the sum of *Net*

Table 4.4 Cost of materials

Purchase cost of materials
(Returns, allowances, and discounts)
Other related cost of materials
Net purchase cost of materials
Beginning inventories of materials
(Ending inventories of materials)
Change in inventory of materials
Cost of materials

Purchase Cost of Materials (equal to the purchase cost of materials, plus other related cost, minus good returns, allowances, and discounts) plus the *Change in Inventory of Materials* (if the Ending value > Beginning value, there is an increase and then the sign is minus (−); if the Ending value < Beginning value, there is a decrease and then the sign is plus (+)), as summarized in Table 4.4.

Direct Production Services Cost refers to the cost of outsourcing for production services. These costs refer to all services purchased from an outside firm which are strictly related to the realization of product. These costs came from the Make-or-Buy choices. At any given time, a firm realizes certain activities with its own resources, and it pays outside firms to realize other certain activities. Generally, all firm's activities can be realized in outsourcing. In this contest, we consider only production services and all of them potentially can be realized in outsourcing. To decide which production activities realized in outsourcing there are two main reasons to consider: (1) the differential costs, by giving in outsourcing all production activities that can be realized with a lower cost; (2) the strategic relevance of the production activities, by giving in outsourcing only non-strategic activities. By considering jointly these two reasons, we can say that the outsourcing can involve productions activities that are not strategic for the firm and able to be realized at lower cost.

These costs can be considered *direct cost of product* because for each product it is necessary to acquire a defined level of production service from outside firms in order to produce.

Direct Labour Cost refers to the cost of workers strictly related to the production of goods to be sold.

Note that the Direct Labour Cost requires management accounts that are internal to the firm and strictly reserved. Then its amount is not available for external analysts. Then this cost is usually not considered by external analysts in the compute of the Cost of Goods Sold to avoid to alter the value and then the mining of the GP in the comparing analysis. If we do not consider the Direct Labour Cost, it is included in the Personnel Cost.

4.3.3 Gross Profit and Contribution Margin

All costs grouped in GP are Direct Costs of Product because they are strictly related to the product. Indeed, they are specifically *traced to*, or *caused by*, the cost-object that is the product. By considering the behaviour of costs on the basis of the output of products, these costs tend to be *Variable Costs*. Therefore, they vary directly and proportionately with volume of product and, in this case the GP is equal to the Contribution Margin (CM) of the firm. However, it is always possible that not all costs grouped in the GP are variable costs by including fixed costs. In this case, the GP is different from the CM.

4.3.4 Gross Profit Margin

The GP Margin measures the weight of GP on the Net Operating Revenues (NOR) as follows:

$$\text{GP Margin} = \frac{\text{GP}}{\text{NOR}} \text{ in\%} \tag{4.5}$$

Note that the GP Margin measures indirectly the weight of the Cost of Goods Sold (COGS) on Net Operating Revenues (NOR) as follows:

$$\begin{aligned} &\text{COGS Margin} = \frac{\text{COGS}}{\text{NOR}} \text{ in \%} \\ &\text{COGS Margin} = 100\% - \text{GP Margin} \end{aligned} \tag{4.6}$$

The GP measures the share-part of Operating Revenues able to cover all other operating (cash and non-cash), financial, non-operating costs and taxes. Therefore, it is a key point in the analysis of the Operating Income because it measure the firm's performance in the business in comparison with the market's profitability.

Commonly, all firms that compete in the same market are characterized by the same medium-level of GP Margin. It happens because the most relevant part of costs computed in the GP, that we have defined first level of operating costs, has in media the same weight on the Net Operating Revenues of all firms in the market. In this sense, we can say that each market has an own medium-level of GP Margin that measures the market's profitability.

The market's profitability is strictly related to the competition level on the basis of inverse relationship: higher the competition, lower the market's profitability and then lower the medium-level of GP Margin of firms in the market; on the contrary, lower the competition, higher the market's profitability and then higher the medium-level of the GP Margin of firms in the market.

Commonly, if the market is characterized by a medium-level of GP equal to 50–60%, it can be considered a profitable market; for a value below the 40% the market can be considered not profitable.

Defined the medium-level of the GP Margin in the market, the firm's capability to compete can be measured by comparing its structural level of GP Margin with the medium-level of GP Margin of the market. The firm has a competitive advantage at level of GP Margin only if its structural level of GP Margin is higher than the medium-level of the market. Note that this difference must be structural. It implies that the higher level of GP Margin must be stable, continuous, and sustainable over time and not occasional. It must be the result of a different way of staying in the market by the firm with respect to its competitors. On the contrary, if the firm has not a competitive advantage at level of GP Margin, his structural level of GP Margin will be in line with the medium-level of the market.

The increase of GP higher than the medium-level of the market can be realized on the basis of innovation. Generally, the innovation can be concerned about the product, the process, or both. If there is innovation, a higher level of GP with respect to competitors is due to the increase in operating revenues higher than the increase in related costs. It is relevant to note that the innovation able to increase the GP level is built on the increase in Operating CapEx (CAPEX_{OP}). If it is not, probably the increase in GP is not structural but due to a specific and one-off cause.

Note that the competitive advantage can be at level of GP Margin or EBITDA Margin. It is possible that the firm has a GP Margin in line with market, but a level of EBITDA higher than competitors. In this case, the firm has a competitive advantage at level of EBITDA rather than at level of GP Margin.

Finally, consider that if firm competes in more than one business (Strategic Business Area (SBA)), it can be useful to distinguish the GB for each SBA (GP_{SBA}) and the total GP of the firm (GP_F) is equal to their sum as follows:

$$\text{GP}_F = \sum_{i=1}^{n} \text{GP}_{\text{SBA}i} \tag{4.7}$$

4.4 EBITDA

The EBITDA (Earnings Before Interest, Taxes, Depreciation, and Amortization) is equal to the difference between Gross Profit (GP) and all operating costs cash. These costs represent the *second-level operating costs*: costs strictly operating, cash and related to the firm's structure.

The EBITDA is the Operating Income strictly related to the Operating Costs Cash because it does not consider the Operating Costs Non-Cash.

All Operating Costs (Cash) can be grouped into two main groups: *Discretionary Costs* and *Committed Costs*. While the first costs can be defined each year, the second costs have effects for more than 1 year because they cannot be changed easily.

All these costs are strictly related to the firm capability to generate operating revenues.

Therefore, in the analysis of both historical and forecast, it must always be considered the relationship between these costs and their operating revenues. In this contest it is not relevant the amount of each cost, but the relationship direct or indirect with the revenues: if the cost is able to push direct or indirect the revenues, and if the increase in revenue is higher than the increase in costs, the Profit Margin increases. It implies as consequences that the cost structure must always be coherent with the dynamic of revenues, and if it is not the entire forecasting process can be defined unrealistic.

In this sense, one of the most relevant errors in the forecasting is to define an increasing dynamic of revenues and a flat dynamic of cost structure. It is unrealistic because the increase in revenues is pushed by a cost structure and investment in assets. Without them, it is not possible to expect the increase in revenues.

4.4.1 Personnel Cost

Personnel Cost groups three types of costs: (1) Cost of Salaries; (2) Cost of Social Security and Taxes; (3) and Cost of Fringe Benefits.

Note that the word *wages* refers to the compensation of employees who are paid on a piece-rate, hourly, daily, or weekly basis, whereas the word *salaries* refers to compensation expressed in the long term.

Generally, the Personnel Cost plays a key role in the analysis of EBITDA because it is usually one of the most relevant Operating Costs (Cash).

The Personnel Cost must be investigated on the basis of three main aspects:

1. *Amount*: its weight can be defined on the basis of its amount on Net Operating Revenues (NOR) and Gross Profit (GP). Then, the higher the weight, the less the sustainability over time in case of NOR's reduction.
2. *Variability*: it is a fixed cost by definition in the short run. Therefore, its amount is flat with respect to the dynamic of operating revenues in the short run. Consequently, it is less sustainable in case of NOR's reduction.
3. *Productivity*: it must be investigated on the basis of its return in terms of operating revenues and firm's profitability. The employees' productivity is the main variable to analyse in order to evaluate the sustainability of the entire Personnel Cost over time. Indeed, every amount of Personnel Cost is sustainability over time if it is able to increase the operating revenues and the firm's profitability in a more proportional way. Therefore, the higher the productivity of employees, more than proportional is the increase in operating revenues and in profitability and more the Personnel Cost is sustainability over time.

Note that the Personal Cost is one of the more relevant indicators of the skills' level in the firm. Generally, higher the skills, higher the Personal Cost. In this sense, a medium-low level of the Personal Cost indicates a low skills' level in the firm with relevant to consequence in terms of firm's capability to compete in the market.

There must always be considered in the analysis, both historical and forecast, between the personal level in terms of skills and the operating revenues. Generally, the higher the personal's skills, the hither the operating revenues and the profitability margin.

The employees' productivity can be measured on the basis of simple ratios. Among these, three are the main:

1. *Revenue per Employee*: it is equal to the ratio between Net Operating Revenues (NOR) and the Number of Employees (usually, it is applied by considering the mean of number of employees in a defined time period) as follows:

$$\text{Revenues per Employee} = \frac{\text{Net Operating Revenues (NOR)}}{\text{Number (mean) of Employess}} \text{ in number of time} \quad (4.8)$$

2. *Added Value per Employee*: it is equal to the ratio between Added Value (AV) and the Number of Employees (usually, it is applied by considering the mean of number of employees in a defined time period) as follows:

$$\text{Added Value per Employee} = \frac{\text{Added Value (AV)}}{\text{Number (mean)of Employess}} \text{ in number of time} \quad (4.9)$$

3. *Personnel Cost per Employee*: it is equal to the ratio between total Personnel Cost and the Number of Employees (usually, it is applied by considering the mean of number of employees in a defined time period) as follows:

$$\text{Personnel Cost per Employee} = \frac{\text{Personnel Cost}}{\text{Number (mean) of Employess}} \text{ in number of time} \quad (4.10)$$

4.4.2 Research and Development (R&D) Cost

It is strictly related to the firm's engagement in innovation of production processes, goods, and services. It groups all costs related to the R&D that are not included in the investment in Operating CapEx and then subject to the depreciation and amortization process.

We can say that the higher these costs, the higher the amount of resources invested in innovation and then the higher the probability to develop, or to defence, over time a competitive advantage in the business with positive effect on GP.

Indeed, these costs are strictly related to the firm's capability to increase the GP higher than competitors. General, an innovation can be in:

1. *Production process*: in this case, the innovation lead to a new way to produce the same product (goods and services) but a lower cost or with higher quality. In the first case, there is a reduction of cost of product, while in the second case there is an increase in the price of product. In both cases, there is an increase in GP.
2. *Product (goods and services) realization*: in this case, the innovation lead to a new product (goods and service). The aim of this new product can be the reduction of its cost or the increase of its quality and then its price. In both cases, the GP increases.

Based on these considerations, the only way for the firm to obtain a GP higher than the level of its business (in media) and then higher than its competitors, is to realize an innovation in the production process or in the realization of product (goods and services). By following this reasoning, the firm can decide to enter in a business with a low level of GP (in media) only if it has developed an innovation of the production process or product in a such way to have a competitive advantage by obtaining a GP higher than competitors.

The relevance of R&D Cost can be measured in terms of:

1. *Weight of these costs* on Net Operating Revenues (NOR), as follows:

$$\text{R\&D Margin} = \frac{\text{R\&D Costs}}{\text{NOR}} \text{ in\%} \tag{4.11}$$

   In order to well define the cost structure of the firm, it is useful to measure the weight of R&D Costs in terms of GP because it gives the coverage to these costs, and in terms of EBITDA because these costs define it, as follows:

$$\begin{aligned} \text{R\&D Margin} &= \frac{\text{R\&D Costs}}{\text{GP}} \text{ in \%} \\ \text{R\&D Margin} &= \frac{\text{R\&D Costs}}{\text{EBITDA}} \text{ in \%} \end{aligned} \tag{4.12}$$

2. *Total amount of these costs* independently to their weight on NOR. Commonly, innovations, both of process and product, require a certain critical mass in terms of resources to be committed constantly over time for their effectively realization. Consequently, independently to their weight on NOR, it is necessary to evaluate if the total amount of these costs is enough to push over time innovation in a strongly or weakly way.

4.4.3 Marketing and Sales (M&S) Cost

It is strictly related to the firm's engagement in strategic marketing, sales, and after-sales. These costs are relevant for the right positioning of the firm in the market.

Generally, these costs are strictly related to the increase of NOR and then the GP. Indeed, these costs are focused on the increase of quantity of product sold and/or the increase in price if the firm follows a price advantage.

Note that in these costs can be related to two main types of activities:

1. Activities that are well-defined in their technical aspects, timing of realization, and external firm that will realize them. In this case, the cost for each activity is well-defined in the amount and timing.
2. Activities that are not yet well-defined in all aspects at the time of planning. In this case, managers define a total amount of cost to bear.

The relevance of M&S Cost can be measured in terms of:

1. *Weight of these costs* on Net Operating Revenues (NOR), as follows:

$$\text{M\&S Margin} = \frac{\text{M\&S Costs}}{\text{NOR}} \text{ in\%} \tag{4.13}$$

In order to well define the cost structure of the firm, it is useful to measure the weight of M&S Costs in terms of GP because it gives the coverage to these costs, and in terms of EBITDA because these costs define it, as follows:

$$\begin{aligned} \text{M\&S Margin} &= \frac{\text{M\&S Costs}}{\text{GP}} \text{ in \%} \\ \text{M\&S Margin} &= \frac{\text{R\&D Costs}}{\text{EBITDA}} \text{ in \%} \end{aligned} \tag{4.14}$$

2. *Total amount of these costs* independently to their weight on NOR. Commonly, a right positioning of the firm in the market and the right definition and maintaining of relationship with customers require a certain critical mass in terms of resources to be committed constantly over time for their effective realization. Consequently, it is necessary to evaluate if the total amount of these costs is enough to push the firm in the market in a strongly or weakly way.

4.4.4 Logistic Cost

It refers to all logistic activities of the firm. Logistic activities can be realized by the firm directly, or by outside and specialized firms in outsourcing. The choice is based on the strategic relevance of these activities for the business of the firm.

The Logistic Cost involves two types of costs:

1. Cost related to the machinery and equipment of logistic in the firm.
2. Cost related to the delivery and distribution services.

In both cases, the relevance of these costs can be measured in terms of weight on Net Operating Revenues (NOR) as follows:

$$\text{Logistic Costs Margin} = \frac{\text{Logistic Costs}}{\text{NOR}} \text{ in\%} \tag{4.15}$$

Also in this case, in order to well define the cost structure of the firm, it is useful to measure the weight of these costs in terms of GP because it gives the coverage to these costs, and in terms of EBITDA because these costs define it, as follows:

$$\begin{aligned} \text{Logistic Costs Margin} &= \frac{\text{Logistic Costs}}{\text{GP}} \text{ in \%} \\ \text{Logistic Costs Margin} &= \frac{\text{Logistic Costs}}{\text{EBITDA}} \text{ in \%} \end{aligned} \tag{4.16}$$

4.4.5 Advisory Cost

It refers to all advisory activities. It is relevant to note that the amount of this cost is strictly related to the quality of the firm's advisors. Generally, the higher the cost of advisor, the higher its expertise and its capability to solve firm's problem by helping to increase its performance.

Note that this cost should not consider as a cost in itself, but more as investment one. Indeed, more than the amount the cost in itself, it is relevant in its return in terms of contribution to the increase of firm's performance. Therefore, the impact of this cost on NOR, GP and EBITDA should decrease over time because the increase in them should always be higher than the increase in the cost itself.

Forcing the reasoning, we can say that the advisors add up to the managers and employees in defining the amount and quality of the human capital available for the firm.

Therefore, the relevance of these costs can be measured on their weight on Net Operating Revenues (NOR), GP, and EBITDA as follows:

$$\begin{aligned} \text{Advisory Costs Margin} &= \frac{\text{Advisory Costs}}{\text{NOR}} \text{ in \%} \\ \text{Advisory Costs Margin} &= \frac{\text{Advisory Costs}}{\text{GP}} \text{ in \%} \\ \text{Advisory Costs Margin} &= \frac{\text{Advisory Costs}}{\text{EBITDA}} \text{ in \%} \end{aligned} \tag{4.17}$$

4.4.6 Leasing and Rent (L&R) Cost

It refers to the rent and leasing of assets used by firm to make its business.

Rent cost simply refers to the cost borrowed assets for the other firms. The most common and relevant cost of rent concerns the firm's headquarters and industrial warehouse.

More relevant is the leasing. Generally, firm needs of property, plant, and equipment for the realization of business activities. Leasing is an alternative to purchase these assets. Indeed, in the leasing the owner retains title to the asset and the firm pays for the use of the asset through the leasing payment. It is the cost of leasing for the firm.

Note that when firm lease of asset (property, plant, or equipment) the leases generally exceed 1 year. Consequently, the choice to lease generates a multi-year cost for the firm.

Also in this case, we can measure the weight of the Rent and Leasing (R&L) Cost on Net Operating Income (NOR) and EBITDA, as follows:

$$\begin{aligned} \text{R\&L Costs Margin} &= \frac{\text{R\&L Costs}}{\text{NOR}} \text{ in } \% \\ \text{R\&L Costs Margin} &= \frac{\text{R\&L Costs}}{\text{EBITDA}} \text{ in } \% \end{aligned} \tag{4.18}$$

4.4.7 General and Administrative (G&A) Cost

It refers to utilities, stationary, and all other operating costs cash that are not explicated before. Note that, if it groups costs that are considered relevant for the firm, they must be explicated out of this block.

Therefore, the relevance of these costs on Net Operating Revenues (NOR) and EBITDA usually is low.

$$\begin{aligned} \text{G\&A Costs Margin} &= \frac{\text{G\&A Costs}}{\text{NOR}} \text{ in } \% \\ \text{G\&A Costs Margin} &= \frac{\text{G\&A Costs}}{\text{EBITDA}} \text{ in } \% \end{aligned} \tag{4.19}$$

All costs grouped between GP and the EBITDA are *Indirect Costs of Product* because they are not strictly related to the product. They are not directly *traced to*, or *caused by*, the cost-object that is the product. Therefore, they are associated with two or more cost objects jointly. Indeed, the nature of an indirect cost is such that it is not possible, or at least not feasible, to measure directly how much of the cost is attributable to a single cost-object.

By considering the behaviour of costs on the basis of the output of products, these costs tend to be Fixed Costs. Indeed, all these types of cost do not vary directly and proportionately with volume of product. Note that these costs are fixed and cash because they have financial effects in terms of cash-out or accounting payables.

4.4.8 EBITDA Margin

The first analysis of the EBITDA is based on its Margin with regard to the Net Operating Revenues (NOR) as follows:

$$\text{EBITDA Margin} = \frac{\text{EBITDA}}{\text{NOR}} \text{ in\%} \tag{4.20}$$

The EBITDA is the measurement of the Operating Income by considering only Operating Costs Cash because they have financial effects in terms of cash-out or accounting payables. Therefore, it measures the firm's capability to cover all Operating Costs Cash with Operating Revenues by generating a margin of profit. Two are the main consequences:

1. It does not consider the Operating Costs Non-Cash. It implies that it does not consider the accounting policy with regard to the amortization, depreciation, accruals, and changes in value of assets.
2. It is the first items of the cash-flows and it approximates the firm's capability to create operating cash-flows with its core-business. Note that we say "approximate" because revenues and costs can not generate cash-in and cash-out immediately, but operating receivables and payables with relative effects in terms of cash-flows.

The operating costs positioned between the Gross Profit (GP) and the EBITDA are defined as the *second-level operating costs*. They are strictly related to the firm's structure and choices. Therefore, these costs are very different among the firms that compete in the same market.

Generally, these costs tend to absorb between 30% and 70% of the Gross Profit. If they are equal or lower than 30% over time, the firm can be considered as high-performing.

Note that if the market is characterized by a high level of competition and if the firm does not have a defined competitive advantage, these costs tend to be high. The closer it gets to 100% of the GP the worse the firm's conditions.

The EBITDA can be increased by reducing the Operating Costs (Cash) for the same level of GP or by increasing the Operating Costs much less than the increase in GP due to the increase in Net Operating Revenues.

Innovation reduces the firm's Operating Costs. In this case, the innovation has not effect on GP but directly on EBITDA.

As for the GP, also in this case, if there is an innovation there should be an increase in amortization and depreciation amount related to the increase in Operating CapEx. If it is not, probably the increase in EBITDA is not structural but due to a specific cause and then one-off by definition.

4.5 EBIT

The EBIT (Earnings Before Interest and Taxes) is equal to the difference between Net Operating Revenues (NOR) and all Operating Costs Cash and Non-Cash. These costs define the *third-level operating costs*: costs strictly operating, non-cash, and related to the firm's structure.

By considering all Operating Costs (first, second, and third levels), the EBIT measures the firm's capability to remunerate all factors of production. Therefore, it measures the firm's capability to manage its core-business in a profitable way.

4.5.1 EBIT Margin

The first analysis of the EBIT is based on its Margin with regard to the Net Operating Revenues (NOR) as follows:

$$\text{EBIT Margin} = \frac{\text{EBIT}}{\text{NOR}} \text{ in\%} \tag{4.21}$$

The distance between EBITDA and EBIT can be depended on three main reasons as follows. In any case, it is worth noting that the difference between EBITDA and EBIT is relevant in the economic perspective only. Indeed, in the financial perspective they are equal because Operating Costs Non-Cash do not affect cash-flows.

Amortization and Depreciation

Depreciation of Tangible Operating Assets and Amortization of Intangible Operating Assets refer to the processes of reduction in value of Operating assets over time. Note that they are considered only the depreciation and amortization costs related to the Operating Assets. Indeed, these investments in assets are strictly related to the core-business of the firm and then they should increase the EBITDA over time by pushing up the operating revenues and/or by reducing the operating costs.

The distance between the EBITDA and EBIT due to the amortization and depreciation measures investments in Operating Assets of the firm. Therefore, the higher the investments in Operating CapEx ($CAPEX_{OP}$), the greater the amortizations and depreciations amount, and then the greater the distance between EBITDA and EBIT. In a dynamic perspective, the reduction of this distance over time due to lower amortization and depreciation indicates the reduction of the firm's investments in $CAPEX_{OP}$. It implies the reduction of the firm's capability to compete in the business in the medium and long run. The natural consequence is the reduction over time of the firm's market share, its Operating and Net Income and then its capability to create equity value.

Impairment of Operating Assets

Impairment losses are computed based on the value of Cash Generating Units (CGUs). They are the smallest identifiable group of assets that generates cash inflows from continuing use. Therefore, firm must define a number of independent CGUs and allocate assets for each one. Each year we have to compute the recoverable value of the CGUs in order to define if there is a decrease or increase in value. If the recoverable value is lower than the carrying amount, we have an impairment loss to be recognized. Impairment is first allocated to goodwill (if any) and then among other assets. If the value of GCU increases again, the impairment can be reversed on all assets and goodwill.

The recoverable value is defined as the highest of:

1. the *value in use*: it is equal to the present value of the future expected cash-flows to be realized from the asset.
2. the *net selling price*: it is equal to the amount obtainable from the sale of an asset net to the cost of disposal.

The distance between EBITDA and EBIT due to the impairment losses measures the reduction of Operating Income due to the decrease in value of operating assets. The decrease in the value of assets in Operating CapEx ($CAPEX_{OP}$) implies the decrease in value of Equity and being equal all other conditions, the increase of Financial Debt weight in the Capital Structure.

Accruals to Provisions

Provisions refer to future cost that are set aside in anticipation. Therefore, additions to provisions reduce the Net Income in the year in which they are set aside and not in the year the corresponding cost will actually be incurred.

Consequently, additions to provisions are equivalent to an anticipation of costs.

The distance between EBITDA and EBIT due to the accruals to provisions measures the risks undertaken by the firm in time. In a dynamic perspective, relevance is mainly due to:

1. the probability that they are not enough to cover future costs if they will be executed
2. the fact that they do not impact positively the GP and/or EBITDA by pushing for their increase over time.

4.5.2 Net Operating Profit After Taxes (NOPAT)

By using tax splitting and therefore by distinguishing between Operating and Corporate Taxes (the first are due to the operating activities, while the second are due to the non-operating and financial activities), EBIT is equal to NOPAT *(Net*

Operating Profit After Taxes). Otherwise, if tax splitting is not used and operating taxes as well as corporate taxes are considered jointly in the tax area, EBIT is the operating income before taxes, while the NOPAT is the operating income after taxes.

The NOPAT is more useful in the financial analysis even if usually it is not directly computed on the basis of analytical schemes used.

The NOPAT is equal to the difference between EBIT and Taxes relate the operating activities. By denoting with t_o the mean Operating Corporate Tax Rate, the NOPAT is equal to:

$$\text{NOPAT} = \text{EBIT} \cdot (1 - t_o) \tag{4.22}$$

Therefore, the main problem concerns the right computation of t_o. It implies the tax splitting by distinguishing between the sections of operating, financial, and non-operating and considering only the taxes concerning the operating section.

The right computation of NOPAT is fundamental to compute the Economic Value Added (EVA).

4.6 EBT-Operating

If the firm is characterized by Non-Operating Revenues and Costs, it is useful to distinguish between EBT (Earnings Before Taxes) the EBT-Operating (EBT_{OP}). It measures the part of the EBT strictly related to the operating activities only. Consequently, the EBT_{OP} by measuring the operating results net to the financial results, it is considered the debtholders' remunerations in terms of financial costs on debt.

Obviously, if there are not Non-Operating Revenues and Costs, the EBT_{OP} is equal to the EBT and then no distinction must be made.

In this contest, we assume there are Non-Operating Revenues and Costs and then we distinguish between EBT_{OP} and EBT.

The EBT-Operating (EBT_{OP}) is equal to the difference between the EBIT and Net Financial Costs that refer to all Financial Costs related to the Financial Debt less the Financial Revenues.

The total amount of Financial Costs related to the debt can be distinguished in two parts: (1) Interest on debt and the (2) Other Financial Costs on Debt. This distinction is useful to well define the amount of Interest on debt in order to compute its weight on the financial debt amount. The total amount of Financial Costs is more relevant because it is strictly related to the amount of Financial Debt in the Capital Structure.

Financial Revenues in the non-financial firms tend to be low relevant. They refer revenues come from positive value of bank accounts or investments in Operating Financial Assets.

4.6.1 EBT-Operating Margin

The EBT_{OP} must be considered in its value and its margin as a percentage of Net Operating Revenues (NOR) as follows:

$$EBT_{OP}\ \text{Margin} = \frac{EBT_{OP}}{NOR}\ \text{in}\% \tag{4.23}$$

By assuming that in non-financial firms the Financial Revenues are not relevant, the distance between EBIT and EBT_{OP} is due to the Cost of Financial Debt. Therefore, the higher the distance, the higher the weight of Financial Costs and then it is reasoned to assume the weight of the Financial Debt in the Capital Structure.

The distance between EBIT and EBT_{OP} measures the financial risk related to the EBIT capability to cover the Cost on Financial Debt in order to the EBIT to cover the Cost on Debt. Note that the lower the distance between the EBIT and the Cost of Debt, the higher the financial risk because the higher the probability that firm is not able to cover the Cost of Debt. While the EBIT fluctuates over time due to the dynamics of revenues and costs, the cost of debt is a fixed cost (until defined conditions) and then it is flat. Consequently, the lower the distance between EBIT and Cost of Debt, the higher the probability that a reduction in revenues implies the reduction of EBIT in a such way that it is not able to cover the Cost of Debt.

4.7 EBT and Net Income

The distinction between EBT-Operating (EBT_{OP}) and the EBT comes from the presence of Non-Operating Revenues and Costs. Indeed, if there are not, the EBT_{OP} is equal to EBT.

Therefore, the distance between EBT_{OP} and EBT is measured by the Non-Operating Revenues and Costs. The main aim of the EBT, and then the distinction between EBT_{OP} and EBT, is to "keep clear" the EBT_{OP} by grouping only Operating Revenues and Costs.

Therefore, the EBT groups:

1. *Non-Operating Revenues and Costs*: they are revenues and costs related to activities considered out of the core-business perimeter.
2. *Non-Current Operating Revenues and Costs*: they are revenues and costs related to activities in the core-business perimeter but considered one-off. These revenues and costs come from the adjustment process need to align the past data and forecast data in financial planning.
3. *Non-Operating Financial Revenues*: they are revenues related to investments in financial assets that are non-operating. Generally, they are dividends came from participations that are not considered strategic and then that are out of the core-business perimeter.

4. *Amortization, Depreciation, and Impairment of Non-Operating Assets*: they are related to the Intangible and Tangible Non-Operating Assets.

4.7.1 EBT Margin

The EBT must be considered in its value and its margin as a percentage of Net Operating Revenues (NOR) as follows:

$$\text{EBT Margin} = \frac{\text{EBT}}{\text{NOR}} \text{ in\%} \tag{4.24}$$

Commonly, the distance between EBT_{OP} and EBT tends to be not relevant and then the EBT_{OP} Margin and EBT Margin tend to be the same. If it is not, there are a relevant weight of Non-Operating activities. It may be due to:

1. The adjustment process of historical data for the alignment with forecast data in financial planning. In this case, the adjustment process is necessary to highlight the real value and weight of the historical Operating Income with regard to all its parts (GP, EBITDA, EBIT) in order to align it with the forecasting in financial planning.
2. The relevant weight of investments in non-operating assets. In this case, the problem concerns the right definition of the core-business perimeter. Two are the possible reasons: (1) the first, these investments refer to strategic business area (SBA) that they will enter in the future in the core-business perimeter, and then in the financial planning will be considered operating; (2) the second, these investments must be dismissed because really out of the core-business perimeter today and in the future.

4.7.2 Net Income

Net Income (NI) is the difference between EBT and all Income Taxes. Therefore, the Net Income (NI) is the difference between all revenues and costs and then it measures the wealth created or destroyed by the firm in a defined time period. Specifically, if:

1. Net Income is negative: costs are higher than revenues, we have a *Loss* and then we destroy wealth.
2. Net Income is positive: revenues are higher than costs, we have *Profit* and then we create wealth.

To keep always in mind that wealth and cash are two different concepts, and it is necessary to well-distinguish between them always in the analysis.

4.7.3 Net Income Margin

The Net Income (NI) must be considered in its value and its margin as a percentage of Net Operating Revenues (NOR). The Net Income Margin, also called E-Margin, is equal to:

$$\text{NI Margin} = \frac{\text{NI}}{\text{NOR}} \text{ in\%} \tag{4.25}$$

Note that to sterilize the tax burden, it is useful to measure the firm's performance in terms of EBT rather than the Net Income. It allows for a comparison of different firms in different countries and periods and therefore subject to different tax rules.

4.7.4 Earnings per Share (EPS)

One of the most indicator of the firm's performance for investors in equity is the Earnings per Share (EPS) in its two main forms: basic and diluted.

The *Basic Earnings per Share* is a measurement of the firm's per share performance over a period of time. It is equal to the Net Income of the year divided the number of shares of common stock outstanding during the same period of time. Recall that Treasury Stock is not considered to be stock outstanding.

$$\text{EPS}_{\text{Basic}} = \frac{\text{Net Income of the year}}{\text{Number of Shares of Common Stock Outstanding in the year}} \tag{4.26}$$

If the number of shares of common stock outstanding fluctuates within a year, then it is considered the weighted average number of shares outstanding.

The *Diluted Earnings per Share* consider the potential dilutive common stock shares. It reflects the potential dilution of earnings per share that could occur if contracts and securities were exercised or converted into common stock. Potentially dilutive common stock shares include stock options, warrants, and convertible security such as convertible preferred stock and convertible debt.

5 Economic and Financial Dynamic Analysis: Invested Capital and Capital Structure

5.1 Invested Capital and Capital Structure: Scheme of Analysis

The second step of the Economic and Financial Dynamics (EFD) analysis of the firm is the analysis of the financial dynamic. It is based on two parts:

(a) Invested Capital (IC) and Capital Structure (CS) analysis.
(b) Free Cash-flow to the Firm (FCFF) and Free Cash-flow to Equity (FCFE) analysis.

In this chapter, we analyse the first part, while the second will be analysed in the next chapter.

The aim of the analysis of the Invested Capital and Capital Structure of the firm is to investigate how the capital is invested in operating and non-operating activities of the firm and how these investments are financed.

The Invested Capital (IC) defines the amount of capital invested in firm activities, while the Capital Structure (CS) defines the sources of capital used to finance these activities.

The main aim of the analysis is to highlight the main items able to show immediately the firm's condition about sources of capital used and its investments in operating and non-operating activities.

The scheme of analysis used is characterized by a clear separation between:

1. Financial Assets-Liabilities and Non-Financial Assets-Liabilities
2. Operating and Surplus (that are Non-Operating) Assets-Liabilities, with regard to Non-Financial Assets-Liabilities.

There are two main implications of these separations:

1. First, they allow for definition of the investments directly in firm's assets, both operating and surplus as well as relative capital sources.

P. De Luca, *Corporate Finance*, Springer Texts in Business and Economics,
https://doi.org/10.1007/978-3-031-18300-3_5

2. Second, they allow for an assessment of variations in the assets-liabilities directly in terms of changes in cash-flows.

The Analysis Scheme used is shown in Table 5.1.

5.1.1 Invested Capital (IC)

The Invested Capital (IC) is the total amount of investments in the firm's activities both fixed and working.

In this context, we distinguish the firm's activities in:

1. *Operating*: they refer to all activities related to the firm's core-business. Therefore, in this case, the capital is invested in the Operating Assets (Tangible, Intangible, and Financial) and Operating Working Capital. The total amount of investments in Operating activities is defined as Net Operating Invested Capital (NOIC). It is equal to the Operating Capital Expenditures ($CAPEX_{OP}$), plus Operating Net Working Capital (NWC_{OP}) less Provisions (PS), as follows:

$$NOIC = CAPEX_{OP} + NWC_{OP} - PS \tag{5.1}$$

2. *Non-Operating*: they refer to all activities out of the firm's core-business. Therefore, in this case, the capital is invested in the Non-Operating Assets (Tangible, Intangible, and Financial) and Non-Operating Working Capital. The total amount of investments in Non-Operating activities is defined as Surplus Assets (SA). It is equal to the Non-Operating Capital Expenditures ($CAPEX_{NOP}$) plus Non-Operating Net Working Capital (NWC_{NOP}), as follows:

$$SA = CAPEX_{NOP} + NWC_{NOP} \tag{5.2}$$

Therefore, the Invested Capital (IC) is equal to:

$$IC = NOIC + SA$$

$$IC = [CAPEX_{OP} + NWC_{OP} - PS] + [CAPEX_{NOP} + NWC_{NOP}] \tag{5.3}$$

Nota that:

1. If the firm invests in core-business only, there are not Surplus Assets (SA) and the Invested Capital (IC) is equal to the Net Operating Invested Capital (NOIC), so that: IC = NOIC.
2. If we do not distinguish between Operating Assets and Surplus Assets, the Invested Capital (IC) is equal to the total amount of investments in Capital Expenditures (CapEx) (both Operating and Non-Operating) plus total

Table 5.1 Scheme of analysis ICCS

	Historical analysis			Forecast analysis		
	$t_{(-n)}$	$t_{(-2)}$	$t_{(-1)}$	$t_{(1)}$	$t_{(2)}$	$t_{(n)}$
Operating tangible assets						
Operating intangible assets						
Operating financial assets						
Permanent inventories						
Operating capital expenditures ($CAPEX_{OP}$)						
Trade receivables						
(trade payables)						
Trade working capital (TWC)						
Inventories						
Other operating receivables						
(other operating payables)						
Non-trade working capital (NTWC)						
Operating net working capital (NWC_{OP})						
(provisions for risks and charges)						
(Provision) (PS)						
Net operating invested capital (NOIC)						
Non-operating tangible assets						
Non-operating intangible assets						
Non-operating financial assets						
Non-operating capital expenditures ($CAPEX_{NOP}$)						
Non-operating receivables						
(non-operating payables)						
Non-operating net working capital (NWC_{NOP})						
Surplus assets (SA)						
Invested capital (IC)						
Share capital						
(Treasury share)						
Retained earnings						
Net profit/(loss)						
Equity (E)						
Long-term financial debts						
Long-term debt (D_{LT})						
Short-term financial debts						
(short-term financial credits)						
(marketable securities)						
(cash and cash equivalents)						
Short-term debt (D_{ST})						
Debt (D)						
Capital structure (CS)						

investments in Net Working Capital (NWC) (both Operating and Non-Operating) less Provisions (PS) as follows:

$$IC = CAPEX_{OP} + CAPEX_{NOP} + NWC_{OP} + NWC_{NOP} - PS$$

$$IC = CAPEX + NWC - PS$$

3. The definition of core-business is strictly related to the firm's strategy and not accounting rules as we discussed in the previous chapter. Therefore, the perimeter of firm's core-business can change over time on the basis of its business strategies. In this sense, it is possible that many Non-Operating activities become over time Operating and vice versa. It depends on the firm's decisions about the business in which it competes and in which it will enter.
4. Surplus Assets (SA) can be considered a "residual configuration" because it groups all items that cannot be considered as operating. It can be useful in the historical analysis because it is used to keep clean and highlight operating activities. In the perspective analysis, it has null or at least very little relevance because we forecast only operating activities of the firm.

5.1.2 Capital Structure (CS)

The Capital Structure (CS) is the total amount of capital sources invested in the firm's activities, both Operating (Net Operating Invested Capital (NOCI)) and Non-Operating (Surplus Assets SA)).

Two are the main source of capital: Equity (E) and Debt (D).

The main difference between Equity and Debt is related to their different level of risk that implies a different expected return by investors and then different cost of capital for the firm.

We can define Equity as a source of capital characterized by:

(a) *Heterogeneity*: it can be internal arising from self-financing, or external deriving from the emission of new shares.
(b) *Long run*: it is stable over time in the capital structure and it is used to fund long-term company activities.
(c) *Full riskiness*: the stockholders bear the risk of firm's default (as well as debtholders) but also the probability of "non-congruity" of expected return due to the volatility of dividends and capital gains.
(d) *Variable and uncertain remuneration*: the dividends paid by the firm to its stockholders are uncertain in their amount and time of achievement.
(e) *Direct and indirect refund*: the return for stockholders is realized through dividends paid by the firm and capital gain (or capital loss) paid by the capital

market through the selling of their stocks on the basis of difference between sales price and the buy price.

Similarly, we can define Debt as a source of capital characterized by:

(a) *Homogeneity*: it is an external source of capital.
(b) *Short and long run*: it can be a long-term debt, and then it is a stable source of capital in the capital structure, or a short-term debt.
(c) *Limited riskiness*: the debtholders bear the only risk of firm's default. If it does not happen, the obligations on debts must be paid regardless of the firm's performance. Note that in the case of firm's default, bondholders must be paid before stockholders.
(d) *Fixed and certain remuneration:* the interest on debt for bondholders is certain in the amount and in time of achievement.
(e) *Direct refund:* the company must reimburse the principal at maturity.

Note that the Debt is the Net Financial Debt and it is computed on the basis of the Net Financial Position (NFP) so that:

$$\text{Net Debt or Net Financial Debt } (D) \equiv \text{Net Financial Position (NFP)} \tag{5.4}$$

Based on this identity, Debt (D) and Net Financial Position (NFP) will be used interchangeably in the text because they mean the same thing.

Therefore, the Capital Structure (CS) is equal to Equity (E) plus Debt (D) as follows:

$$\text{CS} = \text{Equity } (E) + \text{Net Debt } (D) \tag{5.5}$$

The Debt (D) can be distinguished between the Long-term Debt (D_{LT}) (or Long-term Net Financial Position (NFP_{LT})) and Short-term Debt (D_{ST}) (or Short-term Net Financial Position (NFP_{ST})), as follows:

$$D = D_{\text{LT}} + D_{\text{ST}} \quad \text{or equivalently} \quad \text{NFP} = \text{NFP}_{\text{LT}} + \text{NFP}_{\text{ST}} \tag{5.6}$$

The distinction between Long-term Debt (D_{LT}) and Short-term Debt (D_{ST}) is fundamental to define the amount of Long-term source of Capital (C_{LT}) and Short-term source of Capital (C_{ST}). Indeed, the:

1. Long-term source of capital (C_{LT}) is equal to the sum of Equity (E) plus Long-Term Debt (D_{LT}), so that: $C_{\text{LT}} = E + D_{\text{LT}}$.
2. Short-term source of capital (C_{ST}) is equal to the Short-Term Debt (D_{ST}), so that: $C_{ST} = D_{ST}$.

The Capital Structure must be defined on the basis of the financial need of the firm to finance its activities. The definition of the amount of Equity and Debt depends on the definition of the "optimum" Capital Structure.

Generally the level of debt is planned on the basis of two main perspectives:

1. In the immediate time and short run, debt level is defined on the basis of the financial needs of the firm that are not covered by the Equity.
2. In the medium and long run, its level must be defined on the basis of the "optimum" debt level able to maximize the firm's value. Therefore, over time the debt level must follow a dynamic towards an optimum level as defined.

5.1.3 Identity Condition

In this context, the baseline identity condition states that the total amount of Invested Capital (IC) must be equal to the total amount of Capital Structure (CS) as follows:

$$\text{Invested Capitsal (IC)} = \text{Capital Structure (CS)} \tag{5.7}$$

By considering the composition of Invested Capital (IC) and the Capital Structure (CS), the identity condition can be defined as follows:

$$[(\text{CAPEX}_{\text{OP}} + \text{NWC}_{\text{OP}}) - \text{PS}] + (\text{CAPEX}_{\text{NOP}} + \text{NWC}_{\text{NOP}}) = E + (D_{\text{LT}} + D_{\text{ST}}) \tag{5.8}$$

5.2 Capital Expenditures

Capital Expenditure (CapEx) refers to all investments in Assets (Tangible, Intangible, and Financial) both Operating and Non-Operating.

Investments in CapEx are strictly related to the strategic vision of the firm. They play a key role in the future firm's capability to compete in the market in a profitability way for two main reasons:

1. They have effect in the medium–long term by pushing on the increase of revenues and the decrease of operating costs by realizing innovation in product and in the production process. Consequently, a good investments planning should increase the EBITDA over time. If it is not, the investments plan can be considered ineffective with relevant to negative effects on the firm's performance in the future.
2. They immobilize capital over time with the consequence that it is not possible to change the investments plan in a fast and simple way. If the market moves in different way respect to the firm's forecast, the investment plan must be re-defined. In this case the main and relevant problem is the re-conversation of the assets in place and their production capacity. Usually, it is not either simple or faster.

Strictly related to the investments plan, there are the amortization and depreciation costs related to the tangible and intangible assets to be considered and their impact on the EBIT. Their amount is defined on the basis of two variables:

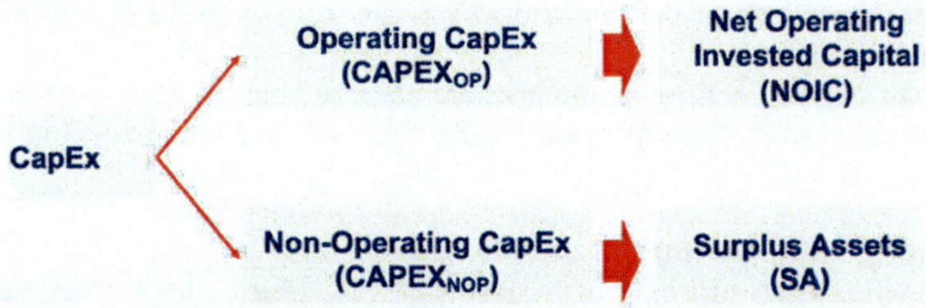

Fig. 5.1 Operating and non-operating CAPEX

1. The amount of invested capital in assets
2. The expected usage-life of the asset defined on the basis of the number of years.

Generally, we can say that a good CapEx has two main effects:

1. In the short run, there is an increase in depreciation and amortization with the reduction of EBIT for the same value of the EBITDA, with the decrease in Operating and Net Income.
2. In the medium and long run, there is an increase in EBITDA more than higher than the reduction of EBIT due to the amortization and depreciation processes with a general increase in Operating and Net Income.

In our scheme of analysis, we distinguish between:

1. *Operating Assets,* that define the Operating Capital Expenditure, or simpler Operating CapEx ($CAPEX_{OP}$): it is the total amount of investments in Operating Tangible, Intangible, and Financial Assets of the firm, and then they are grouped in Net Operating Invested Capital (NOIC).
2. *Non-Operating* Assets, that define the Non-Operating Capital Expenditure, or simpler Non-Operating CapEx ($CAPEX_{NOP}$): it is the total amount of investments in Non-Operating Intangible, Tangible, and Financial Assets of the firm, and then they are grouped in Surplus Assets (SA).

We can schematically represent the difference between Operating CapEx ($CAPEX_{OP}$) and Non-Operating CapEx ($CAPEX_{NOP}$) as in Fig. 5.1.

5.2.1 Operating CapEx ($CAPEX_{OP}$)

The $CAPEX_{OP}$ is the sum of investments in Operating Tangible, Intangible, and Financial Assets plus the Permanent Inventory that is related to the firm's core-business activities.

All investments in Operating Tangible, Intangible, and Financial Assets are considered Operating CapEx only if they are strictly related to the core-business of the firm. It implies that their main functions are to push-up the firm's Operating Income over time.

On the contrary, if these investments are not related to the firm's core-business, they are considered Non-Operating CapEx and then they are grouped in Surplus Assets.

Operating Tangible and Intangible Assets

They refer to assets that have a physical value (Tangibles, such as land, building, machinery, equipment, etc.) and assets that have an intangible value (Intangibles, such as brands, patents, copyright, etc.). They are the engine of the firm. It implies that without a right level of investments continuity over time, sooner or later the firm will be unable to face competition by losing market shares and therefore revenues and profits. Note that they are net to their amortization and depreciation funds.

Operating Financial Assets

They refer to investments in shares in other companies and financial credit over other companies that are considered strategic for the firm's business. They are included in the $CAPEX_{OP}$ only if they are considered strategic by the firm because they are related, direct or indirect, to the core-business. The definition of strategic depends on the strategic plan of the firm and then its qualification can change over time. Therefore, a specific share in other companies can be considered strategic this last year but not this year.

Permanent Inventories

They refer to inventories of raw materials, semi-finished and finished products, goods for resale that can be considered stable over time in order to guarantee production activity and to satisfy customer requirements in time. The level of stable inventories can be considered as investment because it requires immobilized capital. Therefore, part of the inventories that in monetary value must be stable in the firm for the needs of the business can be approximated to an investment in tangible assets and therefore it is included in the Operating CapEx ($CAPEX_{OP}$).

5.2.2 Non-Operating CapEx ($CAPEX_{NOP}$)

The Non-Operating CapEx ($CAPEX_{NOP}$) is the sum of investments in Non-Operating Tangible, Intangible, and Financial Assets related to firm's non-core business activities. Their definition is the same of Operating Tangible, Intangible, and Financial Assets. The only difference is that these types of investments are related to non-core business activities of the firm.

Firm can invest in activities out of its strictly core-business. It could be for simple investment opportunities or the beginning of a diversification process not well defined yet. It is possible that these investments are non-core today but they will be core in the next future. In this case, when it happens these investments will be reallocated in the Operating CapEx.

Therefore, in the forecast analysis, usually Operating CapEx only is considered. The Surplus Assets deriving from investment in tangible, intangible, and financial non-operating assets are not considered. However, it is possible to introduce them in the planning. It happens when we know just now of their future existence with regard to a specific case.

5.3 Net Working Capital

The Net Working Capital (NWC) refers to the firm's investments in working capital arising from repetitive operations (cycle of buying, processing, sales). It is the capital required in the short term to run the business day by day for the firm. Indeed, it is defined as Working Capital because it reflects the cash required to cover financing shortfalls arising from day-to-day activities.

The Net Working Capital (NWC) is the function of the time of operating credits and debts related to the revenues and costs. Therefore, revenues and costs that do not go in cash immediately define credits and debts. Consequently, there is a strict relationship between: revenues and costs, credits and debts, and the cash. Note that in cash must be considered not only the revenues and costs that go to cash directly, but also the credits and debts related to the past revenues and costs that go to cash.

It is relevant to note that the cash considered is related to the movements of revenues and costs, on the one hand, and credits and debts related to these, on the other hand. On the contrary, the change in the total amount of cash at the end of the period considered it is used to define the Free Cash-Flow to Equity and it must be considered as invested capital and not a source of capital.

In our Analysis Scheme, we distinguish between current assets and liabilities arising from the firm's activities and financial current assets and liabilities. Consequently, we group inventory, account receivables and payables in Net Working Capital (NWC), while financial debt, financial credit, cash and equivalents in the Net Financial Position (NFP).

Therefore, in our scheme, the right definition of the Net Working Capital (NWC) implies the contemporary definition of the Net Financial Position (NFP). Indeed, while the NFP includes only Financial Credit and Debt, the NWC includes all other Non-Financial Credit and Debt related to the firm's activities that they can be Operating or Non-Operating but, in any case, never financial as shown in Fig. 5.2.

Similarly to the CapEx, in our Analysis Scheme we distinguish between:

(a) Operating Net Working Capital (NWC_{OP}): it is the total amount of investments in Operating Account Receivables plus Inventories less Operating Account Payables. These Operating Accounting Receivables and Payables are related to the Operating Revenues and Costs and then they are strictly related to the firm's core-business. Consequently, the NWC_{OP} is included in the Net Operating Invested Capital (NOIC).

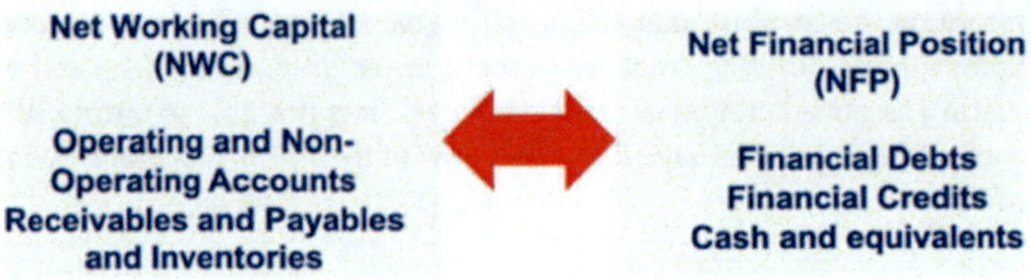

Fig. 5.2 Net working capital (NWC) and net financial position (NFP)

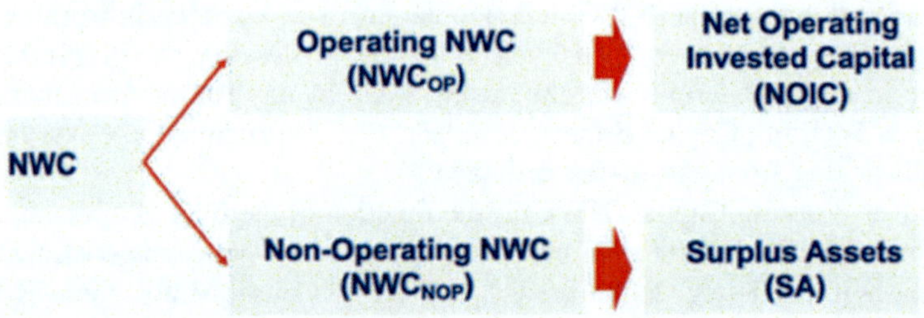

Fig. 5.3 Operating and non-operating NWC

(b) Non-Operating Net Working Capital (NWC_{NOP}): it is the total amount of investments in Non-Operating Account Receivables less Account Payables of the firm. In this case, these Non-Operating Account Receivables and Payables are related to Non-Operating Revenues and Costs and the they are not related to the firm's core-business. Consequently, the NWC_{NOP} is included in Surplus Assets (SA).

We can schematically represent the difference between Operating NWC (NWC_{OP}) and Non-Operating NWC (NWC_{NOP}) as in Fig. 5.3.

5.3.1 Operating Net Working Capital (NWC_{OP})

The Operating Net Working Capital (NWC_{OP}) includes the total amount of Operating Account Receivables and Payables, and Inventories. Therefore, it is the amount of Operating Credits and Debts related to the Operating Revenues and Costs that have not yet translated in cash-in and cash-out. Similar, the Inventory refers to the value of products that have not sold yet and then they are not translated in cash-in.

The NWC_{OP} can be distinguished in two parts:

1. *Trade Working Capital (TWC)*: it is the difference between Trade Receivables Net (TR_n) and Trade Payables (TP):

$$TWC = TR_n - TP \tag{5.9}$$

The Trade Receivables refer to the amount of: (a) credit from customers for goods purchased but not paid yet and (b) prepayments to suppliers for supplies paid but not received yet. Obviously the most relevant part is the first, the credit sales for which the firm has yet to receive payment. The credit that the firm grants to its customers is called Trade Credit.

The Trade Payables refer to amounts of: (a) debt to suppliers for supplies received but not paid yet and (b) prepayment by customers for goods paid but not received yet. Also, in this case, the most relevant part is the first, the debt sales for which the firm has not yet paid for the supplies received. The debt that suppliers grant to firm is called Trade Debt.

Therefore, the TWC is strictly related to the Revenues for sales and Costs of supplier because Trade Receivables and Payables arising from trade activities of the business with customers and suppliers. Note that Trade Receivables are "net" to the relative funds for doubtful accounts.

2. *Non-Trade Working Capital (NTWC)*: it is equal to Inventories (S) plus Other Operating Receivables (OOR) less Other Operating Payables (OOP):

$$NTWC = S + OOR - OOP \tag{5.10}$$

The Inventories (of raw materials, semi-finished and finished products, goods for resale) refer to the value of the inventories in a time t. The Other Operating Receivables and Payables refer all credit and debt strictly related to the operating activities that are not Trade (and then they are not grouped in TWC), they are not non-operating (and then they are not grouped in NWC_{NOP}), and they are not financial (and then they are not grouped in Net Financial Position).

Therefore, the Operating Net Working Capital (NWC_{OP}) is equal to the sum of Trade Working Capital (TWC) and Non-Trade Working Capital (NTWC) as follows:

$$\begin{aligned} NWC_{OP} &= TWC + NTWC \\ NWC_{OP} &= (TR_n - TP) + (S + OOR_n - OOP) \end{aligned} \tag{5.11}$$

5.3.2 Non-Operating Net Working Capital (NWC_{NOP})

The Non-Operating Net Working Capital (NWC_{NOP}) groups two different types of credits and debts:

1. *Non-Operating Receivables and Payables (NOR)*: they are all receivables related to Non-Operating Revenues and Non-Current Operating Revenues.

2. *Non-Operating Payables (NCOP)*: they are all payables related to Non-Operating Costs and Non-Current Operating Costs.

Based on the definition of Non-Operating Receivables and Payables, on the one side, and of Operating Non-Current Operating Receivables and Payables, on the other side, the Non-Operating Working Capital (NWC_{NOP}) is equal to:

$$\begin{aligned} & NWC_{NOP} = (NOR_n - NOP) + (NCOR_n - NCOP) \\ & \text{or equivalently :} \\ & NWC_{NOP} = NOR_n + NCOR_n - NOP - NCOP \end{aligned} \tag{5.12}$$

5.3.3 Net Working Capital Management

Generally, the level of Net Working Capital (NWC) is due to the length of time between when cash goes out of a firm at the beginning of the production process and when it comes back in after the selling of production. Therefore, it is strictly related to the:

1. *Operating cycle:* the length of time between when firm pays cash to purchase its initial inventories (all materials and products need to the production process) and when the firm sales products.
2. *Cash cycle*: the length of time between when the firm pays cash to purchase its initial inventory (all materials and products need to the production process) and when the firm receives cash from the sale of products.

In perfectly competitive market, the amounts of Trade Receivables and Trade Payables are irrelevant for the firm's performance and value. Consequently, it is not relevant to manage the NWC. But in reality, product markets are rarely perfectly competitive. In presence of market friction there are some costs and benefits associated to the NWC and then firm must manage it because NWC has direct and relevant effects on its cash-flow. Generally, we can say that the higher the NWC, the more the short-term capital needs to cover the firm's daily operations. Specifically, the longer is a Cash cycle, the more the NWC, and the more cash needs to cover the firm's daily operations. Indeed, the NWC's increase generates cash-out and then the reduction in Free Cash-flows; on the contrary, the NWC's decrease generates cash-in and then the increase in Free Cash-flows. Also, we must notice that the level of investment in NWC differs from firm to firm not only on the basis of the capability to manage the NWC but also because this level is strictly related to the industry characteristics and standards.

Trade Receivables Management

Firm must define its credit policy. It concerns the way by which the firm offers credit to its customers and after monitors the Trade Receivables on an ongoing basis.

Therefore, the firm must decide its credit policy by defining:

1. *Credit standards*: firm must define its credit standards. This is the first step of the credit policy. Commonly, firm needs to assess the credit risk of each customer before deciding if to grant credit. Therefore, the key decision is how much credit risk to assume. To this decision is linked the amount of money that firm ties up in its receivables. Generally, we can say that a restrictive policy due to high credit standard can generate a low level of sales volume and small level of trade receivables; on the contrary, a less restrictive policy due to a low credit standard can generate a high level of sales volume but also a high level of trade receivables.
2. *Credit terms*: firm must decide its credit terms. It is the second step of the credit policy. The key decision concerns the length of the period before payment must be made (called the net period) and to choose whether to offer a discount to encourage early payments. Also, if the firm offers a discount, it must determine the discount percentage and the discount period.
3. *Credit monitoring*: firm must decide its credit monitoring. It is the third step of credit policy. It concerns who firm must monitor its trade receivables in order to understand if its credit policy is working effectively. To do it, firm can use main tools. Among these, two are the main: (a) Accounts Receivable Days (also called Average Collection Period*)*, that is the average number of days that it takes a firm to collect on its sales. The firm compares this number to the credit terms to evaluate the effectiveness of the credit policy. Note that the firm should also analyse the trend in the accounting receivable days over time; (b) Ageing Schedule, that is the categorization of trade receivables on the basis of the number of days they have been on the book. It can be prepared by considering the number of receivables or the amount in money of them outstanding.
4. *Collection policy*: firm must decide its collection policy. It is the fourth and last step of the credit policy. The key decision concerns what the firm must to do if the customer is paying late. This decision can range from to sending a polite letter of inquiry, to charging interest on payments over a specific period, to threatening legal action at the first or second late payment.

Trade Payables Management

Generally, we can say that firm should pay on the latest day allowed. Indeed, firm should strive to keep its money working for it as long as possible. Obviously, it should be done without developing bad relationship with its suppliers or, even worst, by generating an unethical practice.

To do this, firm must monitor its Trade Payables to ensure that it is making its payments at an optimal time. A good method is to calculate the Trade Payable Days outstanding (is the Trade Payables expressed in terms of the number of days of cost of goods sold) and compare it to the credit terms.

Inventory Management

Commonly firm needs inventory to operate in its business for several reasons. First, firm needs to hold inventories because it must minimize the risk that the firm will not be able to obtain inputs need to the production process by avoiding stock-outs. Second, firm needs to hold inventories because factors such as seasonality in demand mean that customers purchases do not perfectly match the most efficient production cycle.

Note that we can distinguish between: a) the level of inventories that firm must maintain over time for the need of the business called Permanent Inventories; b) the level of inventories that changes continuosly over time generating revenues called Non-Permanent Invetory or simply Inventories. The Permanent Inventories can be considered as a Invested Capital in asset because a defined level of them must be maintained in the firm over time by immobilizing capital needs to cover its value. Consequently, they are grouped in the Operating CapEx. Differently the level of Inventories (Non-Permanent Inventories) changes during the year and they do not require to immobilize capital. Consequently, they are grouped in the Operating Net Working Capital.

Note that all Inventories (Permanent and Non-Permanent) generate operating costs (Acquisition costs, with regard to the costs of the inventories itself; Order costs, with regard to the costs of placing an order; Carrying costs, with regard to the costs of storage and obsolescence) and it absorbs cash-flows.

Indeed, the increase in inventories imply costs for the space, capital immobilized because we do not sales product and, the it increases the cash-out.

Consequently, the main objective of the inventory management is to define the inventory policy of the firm by balancing costs and benefits associated with inventory.

With regard to the sign, the Operating Net Working Capital (NWC_{OP}) can be:

1. *Positive*: it means that the firm does not finance the current operating activities (Operating Receivables plus Inventories) with the current operating liabilities (Operating Payables). It happens when the firm pays suppliers before customers paid it so that the cash-out coming before cash-in. This condition can be considered ordinary because the NWC_{OP} is capital employed.
   The positive value of NWC_{OP} is an investment for the firm and it must be covered by the Capital Structure. By considering that the financial needs generated by the NWC_{OP} is short term, it must be covered by the short-term financial debt and, more generally, with short-term Net Financial Position.
2. *Negative*: it means that the firm finances the current operating activities (Operating Receivables plus Inventories) with the current operating liabilities (Operating Payables). It occurs when the firm pays suppliers after customers paid it so that the cash-in coming before cash-out. This condition can be considered anomalous because it means that the NWC_{OP} is a source of capital rather than capital employed. Therefore, this a special case that must be analysed very carefully. Indeed, if it is a result of a specific firm's commercial policy based on its contractual force and it is applied under defined limit in general condition of a good financial conditions of the firm, it is an advantage because it is able to reduce financial needs of the firm with positive effects on the Net Financial

Position by reducing the short-term financial debts, and on the EBT-Operating by reducing the cost of financial debt.
Differently, if it is due to the firm's difficulty to pay suppliers in a more general condition of financial tension, then it is one of the most relevant signs of financial difficulties of the firm. In this case, the cash-out is structurally greater than cash-in by generating a relevant need of financial resources and the firm is unable to obtain new financial debt because the leverage is already very high.

Similar considerations can be done about the Non-Operating Net Working Capital (NWC_{NOP}) even if with low relevance by considering that it should be not relevant in the total Net Working Capital management. Similar to the NWC_{OP}, the NWC_{NOP} can be:

1. *Positive*: it means that the firm is not able to finance the total amount of Non-Operating and Operating Non-Current Receivables with the Non-Operating and Operating Non-Current Payables. In this case, the positive value of NWC_{NOP} implies that it must be covered with Short-term Net Financial Position with consequent increase of Short-term Financial Debt.
2. *Negative*: it means that the firm is able to finance the total amount of Non-Operating and Operating Non-Current Receivables with the Non-Operating and Operating Non-Current Payables. It implies that there is not increase in Short-term Net Financial Position.

5.4 Provisions (PS)

Provisions (PS) refer to funds accrued for risks and charges, employees and taxes. They refer to the amount of costs accrued but not paid, that will be paid in the future for execution of the reference event.

They are obligations deriving directly from the operating area. It includes:

1. *Provision for employees*: it represents costs achieved but not liquidated yet due to legal constraints. Therefore, they are part of the operating costs with deferred payments. It is a debt for the firm because it refers to payment matured for the employees but that will be paid in the future.
2. *Provision for taxes*: it refers to taxes in firm activities matured but not yet liquidated. If there is contemporaneity between tax maturity and tax payment, there are no provisions. It is a debt for the firm because it refers to the payments matured that will be paid in the near future.
3. *Provision for risks and charges*: it refers to the costs accrued for firm activities executed but whose negative effects will be in the future. Therefore, they represent costs deriving from firm's activities. It is a debt for the firm because they refer to payments that probably will be made in the future based on current events.

Two main considerations are needed:

1. Provisions are a debt for the firm. Therefore, they can be grouped in the source of capital. In this contest, we consider Provisions in Invested Capital (IC) with a negative sign. It allows us: (a) to define the Capital Structure based only on the two main capital sources: Equity and Financial Debt. Consequently, the Invested Capital (IC) is financed by Equity and Debt; (b) to maintain a strict definition of Operating Net Working Capital (NWC_{OP}) based on Receivables, Payables, and Inventories. Note that in a large definition, Provisions can be grouped in (NWC_{OP}).
2. Provisions can be grouped in Operating Net Working Capital (NWC_{OP}) and specifically in the Non-Trade Working Capital (NTWC). In this contest, we want to use a strict determination of NWC and then Provisions are considered separately.

5.5 Equity Capital

The Stockholders' Equity, or simpler Equity (E), refers to the personal sources of the firm. It is the capital source supplied by the firm's owners.

There are two main forms of Equity:

1. *Capital invested by the shareholders*: it can be realized by initial share capital and its increase in later times and in different ways by distinguishing the increase in money and the increase realized by accounting movements.
2. *Self-financing*: it is due to Retained Earning related to the profit generated by the firm and not distributed to shareholders in dividends and used to finance the firm's activities.

The firm's Equity is equal to the *Share Capital* plus *Retained Earnings* and less *Treasury Share*.

5.5.1 Book Value and Market Value of Equity

It is necessary to distinguish between the *Book Value* and the *Market Value* of Equity.

Equity Book Value is the difference between the firm's assets (current assets plus long-term assets) and liabilities (current liabilities plus long-term liabilities):

$$\text{Equity Book Value} = \text{Total Assets} - \text{Total Liabilities} \tag{5.13}$$

Market Equity Value is equal to the number of shares outstanding times the firm's market price per share:

$$\text{Equity Market Value} = \text{Shares outstanding} * \text{Market Price per Share} \tag{5.14}$$

The Market Value of Equity refers to the Market Value of Stock in the capital market and then it represents the firm's Market Capitalization (or simpler, Market Cap).

Note that the market value of the stock depends to the investors' expactiations about the firm future performance. The past is relevant only if it is useful to built the expectations about the future performance.

Based on the Market Value of Equity it is possible to measure indirectly the firm's Enterprise Value (or Total Enterprise Value or TEV) that measures the value of the business itself. Therefore, it measures the value of the underlying assets, unencumbered by debt and separate from any cash and marketable securities (cash equivalents), as follows:

$$\text{Enterprise Value} = \text{Market Value of Equity} + \text{Debt} - \text{Cash and Equivalents} \tag{5.15}$$

The difference between Book Value and Market Value of Equity is mainly due to two main reasons:

1. Many assets listed on the balance sheet are valued based on their historical cost rather than their market value today. It implies that the market value today of an asset may be different, and often it is, from its book value. It implies a difference between Book Value of Equity and its Market Value.
2. Many firm's valuable assets are not captured on the balance sheet (such as expertise of employees and managers, firm's reputation, the value of future research and development activities, etc.). These assets are more relevant in terms of firm's market value but they do not appear on the balance sheet. It implies a difference between Book Value of Equity and its Market Value.

The relationship between Book Value and Market Value of Equity can be defined on the basis of the Market-to-Book Ratio as follows:

$$\text{Market to Book Ratio} = \frac{\text{Market Value of Equity}}{\text{Book Value of Equity}} \tag{5.16}$$

The Equity Book Value, even if accurate from an accounting perspective, is often an inaccurate assessment of the Market Value of the firm's equity. Just consider that it is not unusual that successful firms: (1) are able to borrow in excess of the book value of their assets because creditors think that the market value of the firm's assets is far higher than the book value; (2) investors are willing to pay for equity an amount higher than its book value.

Therefore, for the performing firms the Market-to-Book Ratio exceeds 1. Usually firms with low Market-to-Book Ratios are classified as Value Stock, and firms with high Market-to-Book Ratios are classified as Growth Stocks.

5.5.2 Financial Independence

The firm's capitalization measures its Financial Independence of the firm from the Financial Debt. By considering that the Capital Structure is equal to the sum of Equity and Debt, the capitalization level of the firm can be measured by considering the weight of Equity in the Capital Structure as follows:

$$\text{Equity to Capial Ratio} = \frac{\text{Equity}}{\text{Equity} + \text{Net Debt}} \text{ in\%} \tag{5.17}$$

With regard to the relationship between Equity and Debt in the Capital Structure, we say that the firm is Capitalized if the weight of Equity in the Capital Structure is high as well as we say that the firm is Sub-Capitalized if its weight is low. Commonly, we can say that:

1. Higher the weight of Equity in the Capital Structure, lower the weight of Debt, and higher the level of capitalization.
2. Lower the weight of Equity in the Capital Structure, higher the weight of Debt, and lower the level of capitalization, or in inverse terms, higher the level of Sub-Capitalization. In this case, the firm is Sub-Capitalized.

We can evaluate the level of firm's capitalization on the basis of four main reasons:

1. *Financial Independence*: the capitalization implies financial independence for the firm. On the contrary, sub-capitalization implies financial dependence for the firm.
2. *Impact on EBIT*: the capitalization implies low cost of financial debt with a consequence of a small pression on EBIT for the coverage of interest on debt. On the contrary, sub-capitalization of the firm implies a high cost of financial debt with a consequence of high pression on EBIT for the coverage of interest on debt.
3. *Impact on Free Cash-flow to the Firm (FCFF)*: the capitalization implies low pression on FCFF in order their capability to cover debt obligation in terms of cash-out related to the interest on debt and part of debt reimbursement. On the contrary, sub-capitalization generates high pressure on FCFF because we need high level of it for face debt obligations with regard the cash-out related the interest on debt and the reimbursement of debt.

4. *Financial flexibility*: the capitalization implies financial feasibility because firm can increase debt level if it is necessary in order to face adverse market conditions. On the contrary, sub-capitalization generates financial rigidity because firm cannot increase the debt level, just high, to face adverse market conditions.

Based on these considerations, someone might think that the best condition can be all Equity in the Capital Structure. It is not true. Indeed, the Over-Capitalization is a problem as well as the Sub-Capitalization. Two are the main problems related to the Over-Capitalization:

1. Equity is much expensive than debt. Therefore, if we use all equity in the Capital Structure, we will have the highest cost of capital. The use of debt reduces the cost of capital.
2. In order to remunerate the Equity, the FCFE will be constantly high. It implies a high pression on dividend with consequently reduction of the self-financing to cover the investments in operating activities of the firm.

The right ratio between Equity and Debt in the Capital Structure is one of the most relevant and difficult questions to analyse. We will do following in the book.

5.6 Debt Capital

Preliminary, it is necessary to solve a terminological problem. The Debt (D) in the Capital Structure is the Net Financial Debt (NFD) and it is computed as the Net Financial Position (NFP). Consequently, in this contest is valid the following identity:

$$\text{Debt } (D) \equiv \text{Net Financial Debt (NFD)} = \text{Net Financial Position (NFP)} \quad (5.18)$$

Consequently, we will use Debt (D), Net Financial Debt, and Net Financial Position (NFP) interchangeably because they mean the same thing. In any case, we will always define the Capital Structure of the firm as the sum of Equity (E) and Debt (D).

The Net Financial Position (NFP) requires necessarily the contemporary construction of the Net Working Capital (NWC). Indeed, in the Net Financial Position (NFP) can be grouped only Financial Debts and Credits where the Operating and Non-Operating Debts and Credits are grouped, respectively, in Operating Net Working Capital (NWC_{OP}) and in Non-Operating Net Working Capital (NWC_{NOP}).

The Debt (D) can be distinguished between the Long-term Debt (D_{LT}) (or Long-term Net Financial Position (NFP_{LT})) and Short-term Debt (D_{ST}) (or Short-term Net Financial Position (NFP_{ST})), so that:

$$D = D_{LT} + D_{ST} \quad \text{or} \quad NFP = NFP_{LT} + NFP_{ST}$$

The Debt (*D*) (Net Financial Position (NFP)) is equal to Financial Debts (FD) (both long–medium term and short term) minus Financial Credit (FC), Marketable Assets (MA), and Cash (*C*) (by including also Cash Equivalents):

$$D = \mathrm{FD} - (\mathrm{FC} + \mathrm{MA} + \mathrm{CE}) \tag{5.19}$$

Note that in no-financial firms, usually the Financial Credit tends to be irrelevant as well as the Marketable Assets. Therefore, the Debt (or Net Financial Position) is generally equal to the difference between Financial Debt and Cash.

With regard to the Cash, firm must define the level of cash to hold as an asset. In a perfect capital markets, firm can raise new capital in each moment at fair rate so that it never be short of cash. Unfortunately, in the real world, the capital markets are not perfect. Consequently, liquidity has a cost and there are transaction costs. Three are the main motivation to hold cash:

1. *Transactions balance*: firm must be able to face its day-to-day needs. Consequently, firm must have an amount of cash able to pay its near-time liabilities in time. The level of this amount of cash is strictly related to the total amount of current liabilities and relative time of payment. Therefore, the more the amount of liabilities must be paid in the short run, the larger the amount of cash for transactions balance.
2. *Precautionary balance*: firm must be able to face uncertainty associated with its cash-flows. Consequently, firm must maintain an amount of cash able to counter the uncertainty surrounding its future cash in any moment. The level of this amount of cash is strictly related to degree of uncertainty surrounding a firm's cash-flows. Therefore, the more uncertain cash-flow are, the larger the amount of cash for the precautionary balance.
3. *Compensating balance*: firm must hold an amount of cash due to the requirement of the bank as compensation for service that the bank performs. Usually, compensating balance is deposited in accounts that either earn no interest or pay a very low interest rate.

To hold cash has advantages and disadvantages, on the other hand there are disadvantage. To held excess level of cash is not an optimal condition. Indeed, to hold a cash is an asset. Consequently, it is an investment in an asset that it has not any returns. Also, the increase in cash has negative effect on the cash-flow because they decrease.

Finally, note that to hold cash has relevant effects on cash-flows. Indeed, the increase in cash decreases the cash-flows as well as its decrease increases the cash-flows.

Based on these considerations, it is necessary to define an "optimal level of cash" to be hold by the firm. Commonly, risky firms and firms with high-growth opportunities tend to hold a high level (relatively) of cash as asset. On the contrary, firms with low level of risk and then easy access to capital markets and firms with low opportunities tend to hold a low level (relatively) of cash as asset.

The Debt (D) (or Net Financial Position (NFP)) can be divided into two parts:

1. *Long-term Debt* (D_{LT}) (or Long-term Net Financial Position (NFP_{LT})) with regard to the total amount of medium- and long-term financial debt.
2. *Short-term Debt* (D_{ST}) (or Short-term Net Financial Position (NFP_{LT})) is equal to the difference between Short-term Financial Debt (including the part of Long-term Financial Debt that must be paid in the year) and the sum of Short-term Financial Credits, Marketable Assets, and Cash and Cash Equivalents.

Therefore, we have:

$$D = D_{LT} + D_{ST} \tag{5.20}$$

The Debt (D) (or Net Financial Position (NFP)) can be:

1. *Positive*, when $D > 0$: in this case, the Debt has the same sign in the Capital Structure and then it is a source of capital. It means that the Financial Debt is greater than the sum of Financial Credit, Marketable Assets, and Cash and Cash Equivalents. This is the ordinary condition because the Debt (D) is a source of capital.
2. *Negative*, when $D < 0$: in this case, the Debt has the inverse sign in the Capital Structure and then it is not a source of capital but invested capital. It means that Financial Debt is lower than the sum of Financial Credit, Marketable Assets, and Cash and Cash Equivalents. This is an unordinary condition because the Debt (D) is a Net Cash and it is an invested capital rather than a source of capital.

5.6.1 Firm Leverage

The firm's Leverage measures the Financial Dependence of the firm from the Financial Debt. By considering that the Capital Structure is equal to the sum of Equity and Debt, the Leverage (L) of the firm can be measured by considering the weight of Debt in the Capital Structure as follows:

$$\text{Debt to Capital Ratio} = \frac{\text{Net Debt}}{\text{Equity} + \text{Net Debt}} \text{ in\%} \tag{5.21}$$

It is also possible to measure the Leverage direct on the basis of the ratio between Equity and Debt as follows:

$$\text{Debt to Equity Ratio} = \frac{\text{Net Debt}}{\text{Equity}} \text{ in number of time} \tag{5.22}$$

Note that the Equity can be measured in terms of book value or market value. By considering that Debt is measured on the basis of book value, it is useful to measure Equity in the same terms.

If we consider that the Financial Debt should be used by firm to invest in operating assets able to increase the firm's Enterprise Value, we can measure the Leverage on the basis of the relationship between Debt and Enterprise Value as follows:

$$\text{Debt to Enterprise Value Ratio} = \frac{\text{Net Debt}}{\text{Enterprise Value}} \text{ in\%} \tag{5.23}$$

5.6.2 Financial Debt Sustainability

The Financial Debt sustainability depends on the firm's capability to face debt obligations in terms of Cost of Debt and Debt reimbursement on the basis of its timing defined.

Degree of Financial Leverage

The Degree of Financial Leverage (DFL) measures the financial risk of the firm on the basis of the EBIT capability to bear the Interest on Debt. Generally, the greater the amount of Financial Debt in the Capital Structure, the higher its risk, the higher are the Interest on Debt and the lower is the firm's ability to cover it.

Assume that difference between EBIT and EBT_{OP} is due to the Interest on Debt (I_D) only so that $EBT_{OP} = EBIT - I_D$, and assume that in the period considered ($t_0 - t_1$) the Interest on Debt is the same. The Degree of Financial Leverage (DFL) in the period considered is equal to:

$$DFL = \frac{\Delta(\%)EBT_{OP}}{\Delta(\%)EBIT} = \frac{\frac{EBT_{OP_{(1)}} - EBT_{OP_{(0)}}}{EBT_{OP_{(0)}}}}{\frac{EBIT_1 - EBIT_0}{EBIT_0}} = \frac{EBT_{OP_{(1)}} - EBT_{OP_{(0)}}}{EBT_{OP_{(0)}}} \cdot \frac{EBIT_0}{EBIT_1 - EBIT_0}$$

and then:

$$DFL = \frac{(EBIT_1 - I_D) - (EBIT_0 - I_D)}{EBIT_0 - I_D} \cdot \frac{EBIT_0}{EBIT_1 - EBIT_0}$$

$$= \frac{EBIT_1 - EBIT_0}{EBIT_0 - I_D} \cdot \frac{EBIT_0}{EBIT_1 - EBIT_0} = \frac{EBIT_1 - EBIT_0}{EBIT_0 - I_D} \cdot \frac{EBIT_0}{EBIT_1 - EBIT_0}$$

and then:

$$DFL = \frac{EBIT}{EBIT - I_D} \tag{5.24}$$

Note that we can define the relationship between the change in value of EBT and EBIT on the basis of DFL as follows:

$$\Delta(\%)EBT_{OP} = DFL \cdot \Delta(\%)EBIT \tag{5.25}$$

Therefore, DFL measures the effects of Interest on Debt on EBT dynamic: the higher the DFL, the greater the amount of Interest on Debt due to leverage, the lower is the ability of EBIT to cover it and the higher the probability of the firm's default.

Consequently, the greater the DFL, the higher is the variability of the EBT and Net Income to the variances of the Volume of goods sold.

Interest Coverage Ratio (ICR)

The firm's capability to face Cost of Debt can be measured on the basis of Interest Coverage Ratio (ICR).

Remember that the Cost of Debt has both economic and financial relevance. Indeed, it is a cost that impacts on economic dynamic, and at same times it is a cash-out that impacts on financial dynamic. Consequently, the Interest Coverage Ratio must consider the impact of the Cost of Debt on EBIT with regard to the economic dynamic and on Free Cash-flow to the Firm (FCFF) with regard to the financial dynamic, as follows:

$$ICR_{(EBIT)} = \frac{\text{EBIT}}{\text{Cost of Debt}} \text{ in number of times} \tag{5.26}$$

and:

$$ICR_{(FCFF)} = \frac{\text{FCFF}}{\text{CashOut of Cost of Debt}} \text{ in number of times} \tag{5.27}$$

In both cases, we measure the number of times in which the EBIT and FCFF cover the Cost of Debt: higher the value ratios, higher the EBIT and FCFF to cover the Cost of Debt and then lower is the firm's risk. We can summarize the effects of the ICR value on the EBIT and FCFF as in Table 5.2:

It is necessary to always keep in mind that:

1. EBIT and FCFF are different in their value. Therefore, it is always possible that the ICR on EBIT and on FCFF are different among them (es. $ICR_{(EBIT)} > 1$ and contemporary $ICR_{(FCFO)} < 1$ and vice versa). Consequently, it is necessary always to measure the firm's capability to cover Cost of Debt on the basis of both economic and financial dynamics.

Table 5.2 ICR value and its effects on EBIT and FCFF

ICR	EBIT	FCFF
ICR > 1	It is able to cover the cost of debt in economic dynamic	It is able to cover the cost of debt in financial dynamic
ICR < 1	It is not able to cover the cost of debt in economic dynamic	It is not able to cover the cost of debt in financial dynamic
ICR = 1	It is entirely used to cover the cost of debt in economic dynamic	It is entirely used to cover the cost of debt in financial dynamic

2. EBIT and even more the FCFF are characterized by a high volatility. Therefore, it could be useful to consider a mean of EBIT and FCFF of the last 2–3 years rather than a value of the year in order to stabilize the ratio's dynamic.

The Debt Service Cover Ratios (DSCR)

The firm's capability to face debt obligations with regard to the share-part of debt to reimburse in the year and the total Cost of Debt in the year can be measured on the basis of Debt Service Cover Ratio (DSCR). In this case, we consider all debt obligations and not only its cost. The DSCR is equal to:

$$\text{DSCR} = \frac{\text{Free Cash} - \text{flow to the Firm (FCFF)}}{\text{CashOut Costs of Debt} + \text{Debt to Reimburse in the year}} \text{ in number of times} \tag{5.28}$$

Therefore, the DSCR measures the number of times in which the FCFF covers the cash-out due to the Cost of Debt and the share-parts of Debt reimbursement in the year: the higher the DSCR value, the higher the FCFF to cover debt obligations and then lower is the firm's risk.

The DSCR can be:

1. $DSCR > 1$: in this case, the FCFF is able to cover the cash-out related to the debt obligations in the year.
2. $DSCR < 1$: in this case, the FCFF is unable to cover the cash-out related to the debt obligations in the year.
3. $DSCR = 1$: in this case, the entire FCFF is used to cover cash-out related to the debt obligations in the year.

5.7 Relationship between Invested Capital and Capital Structure

The Matching Principle states that long-term investments must be covered by long-term sources of capital as well as short-term investments are covered by short-term sources of capital. This is the equilibrium condition. Therefore, the equilibrium relationship between Invested Capital (IC) and Capital Structure (CS) must be realized jointly in the short run and long run. These two relationships are strictly related among them so that the equilibrium condition requires that both must satisfy contemporary.

These principles can be violated by following two main policies:

1. *Aggressive financing policy*: it occurs when firm financed its permanent Net Working Capital (NWC) needs with shortest-term debt. It implies the continuous renegotiation of a new loan for the firm. It involves two main problems:

(a) *additional transaction costs*, and it will carry whatever market interest rate exists at the time by exposing the firm to the interest rate risk; (b) *financial distress costs*, if the firm is not able to refinance its debt in a timely manner or a reasonable rate by exposing the firm to the funding risk. We can define ultra-aggressive financing policy when firm uses the short-term sources of capital to finance investments in CapEx.

2. *Conservative financing policy*: it occurs when firm finances its short-term needs with long-term debt. In this case, firm uses long-term sources of capital to finance its Net Working Capital. This policy implies excess cash that leads to the inefficient use of capital because there is a high probability that managers use this cash in a non-productive manner by investing in project with negative or null net present value.

5.7.1 Relationship in Long Run

In the long run the equilibrium relationship between Invested Capital (IC) and Capital Structure (CS) requires that long-term investments in CapEx (both Operating (CAPEX_{OP}) and Non-Operating ($\text{CAPEX}_{\text{NOP}}$)) must be covered by long-term sources of capital equal to the sum of Equity (E) and long-term Debt (D_{LT}). Therefore:

$$\text{Long Term Investments} = \text{Long Term Capital}$$

and then:

$$\begin{aligned} \text{CAPEX}_{\text{OP}} + \text{CAPEX}_{\text{NOP}} &= E + D_{\text{LT}} \\ (\text{CAPEX}_{\text{OP}} + \text{CAPEX}_{\text{NOP}}) &= (E + D_{\text{LT}}) \end{aligned} \quad (5.29)$$

We can measure this relationship by the First-Level Structure Margin (SM_{L1}) as follows:

$$\text{First Level Structure Margin } (\text{SM}_{L1}) = \frac{E + D_{\text{LT}}}{\text{CAPEX}_{\text{OP}} + \text{CAPEX}_{\text{NOP}}} \quad (5.30)$$

Therefore, if:

1. $SM_{L1} = 1$, it implies that $(\text{CAPEX}_{\text{OP}} + \text{CAPEX}_{\text{NOP}}) = (E + \text{NFD}_{\text{LT}})$ and then $(\text{CAPEX}_{\text{OP}} + \text{CAPEX}_{\text{NOP}}) - (E + \text{NFD}_{\text{LT}}) = 0$. There is an *equilibrium in the long run* between Invested Capital (IC) and Capital Structure (CS). The long-term sources of capital are able to cover long-term investments in a perfect manner.
2. $SM_{L1} < 1$: it implies that $(\text{CAPEX}_{\text{OP}} + \text{CAPEX}_{\text{NOP}}) > (E + D_{\text{LT}})$ and then $(\text{CAPEX}_{\text{OP}} + \text{CAPEX}_{\text{NOP}}) - (E + D_{\text{LT}}) > 0$. There is *non-equilibrium in the long run* between Invested Capital (IC) and Capital Stricture (CS). The long-term sources of capital are not able to cover long-term investments by requiring also the use of the short-term debt.

3. $SM_{L1} > 1$: it implies that ($CAPEX_{OP}$ + $CAPEX_{NOP}$) < (E + D_{LT}) and then ($CAPEX_{OP} + CAPEX_{NOP}$) − ($E + D_{LT}$) < 0. There is *non-equilibrium in the long run* between Invested Capital (IC) and Capital Structure (CS). The long-term sources of capital are higher than as required to cover the long-term investments and then they are used to cover also short-term investments in Net Working Capital (NWC).

We can measure the level of self-covered of Investments by considering the First-Level Structure Margin Strictly on Equity $\left(SM_{L1}^{E}\right)$ by considering the ratio between only Equity and CapEx as follows:

$$\text{First Level Structure Margin on Equity } \left(SM_{L1}^{E}\right) : \frac{E}{CAPEX_{OP} + CAPEX_{NOP}} \tag{5.31}$$

It shows as part of CapEx is covered by Equity only. Therefore, if:

1. $SM_{L1}^{E} = 0$, all investments in CapEx are covered by Financial Debt
2. $SM_{L1}^{E} = 1$, all investments in CapEx are covered by Equity
3. $SM_{L1}^{E} > 1$, not only all investments in CapEx are covered by Equity, but it is higher than the total needs required by investments.

5.7.2 Relationship in Short Run

In the short run the equilibrium relationship between Invested Capital (IC) and Capital Structure (CS) requires that short-term investments in Net Working Capital (both in Operating (NWC_{OP}) and Non-Operating (NWC_{NOP})) must be covered by short-term sources of capital that are equal to the short-term Net Financial Position (NFP_{ST}). Therefore:

$$\text{Short Term Investments} = \text{Short Term Capital}$$

and then:

$$\begin{gathered} NWC_{OP} + NWC_{NOP} = D_{ST} \\ (NWC_{OP} + NWC_{NOP}) = D_{ST} \end{gathered} \tag{5.32}$$

We can measure this relationship by the Second-Level Structure Margin (SM_{L2}) as follows:

$$\text{Second Level Structure Margin } (SM_{L2}) = \frac{D_{ST}}{NWC_{OP} + NWC_{NOP}} \tag{5.33}$$

Therefore, if:

1. $SM_{L2} = 1$: it implies that (NWC_{OP} + NWC_{NOP}) = NFD_{ST} and then (NWC_{OP} + NWC_{NOP}) − $D_{ST} = 0$. There is an *equilibrium in the short run* between Invested Capital (IC) and Capital Structure (CS). The short-term sources of capital are able to cover short-term investments in a perfect manner.
2. $SM_{L2} < 1$: it implies that (NWC_{OP} + NWC_{NOP}) > D_{ST} and then (NWC_{OP} + NWC_{NOP}) − $D_{ST} > 0$. There is *non-equilibrium in the short run* between Invested Capital (IC) and Capital Stricture (CS). The short-term sources of capital are not able to cover short-term investments by requiring also the use of the long-term funds by using Equity and long-term financial debt.
3. $SM_{L2} > 1$: it implies that (NWC_{OP} + NWC_{NOP}) < D_{ST} and then (NWC_{OP} + NWC_{NOP}) − $D_{ST} < 0$. There is *non-equilibrium in the short run* between Invested Capital (IC) and Capital Structure (CS). The short-term sources of capital are higher than as required to cover the short-term investments and then they are used to cover also long-term investments in CapEx.

6 Economic and Financial Dynamic Analysis: Free Cash-Flow to the Firm and Free Cash-Flow to Equity

6.1 Free Cash-Flow to the Firm and Free Cash-Flow to Equity: Scheme of Analysis

The analysis of the Free Cash-Flow to the Firm (FCFF) and the Free Cash-Flow to Equity (FCFE) is the second part of the analysis of the Financial Dynamic of the firm. It is the most relevant part of the entire Economic and Financial Dynamic (EFD) analysis because it summarizes all economic and capital movements in terms of cash-flows that they are the most relevant object of analysis by investors.

Generally, the aim of the Cash-flows analysis is to investigate how the operating and non-operating activities of the firm with regard to both economic and capital elements are able to create or destroy Cash-Flows.

The definition of FCFF and FCFE is based on the items related to the Operating and Net Income, on the one side, and the items related to the Invested Capital and Capital Structure, on the other side, as reported in the Scheme of Analysis used as in Table 6.1.

The Free Cash-Flow to the Firm (FCFF) refers to the sum of Cash-flows arising from:

1. Cash-flow from Operating Activities (CFOA).
2. Cash-flow from Surplus Assets (CFSA).

Therefore, the FCFF refers to the cash-flows of the firm by considering both Operating and Non-Operating Activities.

Differently, Free Cash-Flow to Equity (FCFE) refers to the sum of cash-flows arising from:

1. Cash-flow from Equity (CFE)
2. Cash-flow from Debt with regard to the Debt (remember that it is computed on the basis of the Net Financial Position) and the cost of debt (CFD)
3. Cash-flow from Taxes (CFT)

P. De Luca, *Corporate Finance*, Springer Texts in Business and Economics,
https://doi.org/10.1007/978-3-031-18300-3_6

Table 6.1 Scheme of analysis CFFE

	Historical analysis			Forecast analysis		
	$t_{(-n)}$	$t_{(-2)}$	$t_{(-1)}$	$t_{(1)}$	$t_{(2)}$	$t_{(n)}$
EBITDA						
(increase)/decrease—Operating tangible assets						
(increase)/decrease—Operating intangible assets						
(increase)/decrease—Operating financial assets						
(increase)/decrease—Permanent inventories						
(increase)/decrease—Operating capital expenditures ($CAPEX_{OP}$)						
(increase)/decrease—Trade receivables						
Increase/(decrease)—Trade payables						
(increase)/decrease—Trade working capital (TWC)						
(increase)/decrease—Inventories						
(increase)/decrease—Other operating receivables						
Increase/(decrease)—Other operating payables						
(increase)/decrease—Non-trade working capital (NTWC)						
(increase)/decrease—Operating net working capital (NWC_{OP})						
(decrease)—Provisions for risks and charges						
(decrease)—Provisions (PS)						
Cash-flow from operating activities (CFOA)						
Non-operating and non-current operating revenues						
Financial revenues						
(non-operating and non-current operating costs)						
Non-operating revenues and costs						
(increase)/decrease—Non-operating receivables						
Increase/(decrease)—Non-operating payables						
(increase)/decrease—Non-operating net working capital (NWC_{NOP})						
(increase)/decrease—Non-operating tangible assets						
(increase)/decrease—Non-operating intangible assets						
(increase)/decrease—Non-operating financial assets						
(increase)/decrease—Non-operating capital expenditures ($CAPEX_{NOP}$)						
Cash-flow from surplus assets (CFSA)						
Free cash-flow to the firm (FCFF)						
Increase/(decrease)—Share capital in money						
(increase)/decrease—Share buy-backs						
Increase/(decrease)—Equity (E)						
Cash-flow from equity (CFE)						
Increase/(decrease)—Long-term financial debts						
(increase)/decrease—Long-term financial credits						

(continued)

Table 6.1 (continued)

	Historical analysis			Forecast analysis		
	$t_{(-n)}$	$t_{(-2)}$	$t_{(-1)}$	$t_{(1)}$	$t_{(2)}$	$t_{(n)}$
Increase/(decrease)—Long-term debt (D_{LT})						
Increase/(decrease)—Short-term financial debts						
(increase)/decrease—Short-term financial credits						
(increase)/decrease—Marketable securities						
(increase)/decrease—Cash and cash equivalents						
Increase/(decrease)—Short-term debt (D_{ST})						
Increase/(decrease)—DEBT (D)						
(interest on debt)						
(other financial costs on debt)						
Cost of DEBT						
Cash-flow from DEBT (CFD)						
(taxes)						
Cash-flow from taxes (CFT)						
Free cash-flow to equity (FCFE)						

Table 6.2 Analysis scheme (CFFE) summarized

Cash-flow from operating activities (CFOA)
Cash-flow from surplus assets (CFSA)
Free cash-flow to the firm (FCFF)
Cash-flow from equity (CFE)
Cash-flow from debt (CFD)
Cash-flow from taxes (CFT)
Free cash-flow to equity (FCFE)

Therefore, the FCFF are the cash-flows available for investors in equity and debt, and the payments to the State for taxes.

We can summarize the scheme of analysis as in Table 6.2.

Since Equity and Debt are the two sources of capital, if the:

1. *FCFF is positive*: we can choose to reduce the Debt or to distribute Dividends. In this last case, the Debt remains constant and the FCFE is a positive number. This number represents the free cash-flows after having covered all firm requirements and therefore they are designed to pay the shareholders in terms of dividends.
2. *FCFF is negative*: it implies that we must to cover the financial need by choosing between Equity or Debt or both by increasing their value. Indeed, the negative number of the FCFE represents the amount of capital that firm's need to cover its financial need as computed on the basis of cash-flows.

6.2 Cash-In and Cash-Out

The definition of cash-flows based on the items related to the Operating and Net Income, on the one side, and the items related to the Invested Capital and Capital Structure, on the other side, must be considered in a different way.

Items related to Operating Income and Net Income must be considered with regard to their value in the same year of the cash-flows computation and with the same sign. Therefore, for the definition of cash-flow in time t_1 revenues and costs must be considered at the same time t_1 as follows:

1. *Revenues*: all different types of revenues (Operating, Non-Operating, and Financial) generate cash-in.
2. *Costs (Cash)*: all types of costs (Operating, Non-Operating, Financial, and Taxes) generate cash-out.
3. *Costs (Non-Cash)*: all types of Amortization, Depreciation, and Impairment of Operating and Non-operating Assets plus charge to Provisions must not be considered because they have only an economic meaning without effects on cash-flows.

Differently, items grouped in Invested Capital and Capital Structure must be considered with regard to their changes between two different time periods. Therefore, for the definition of the cash-flow in time t_1 we must consider the change of the item between t_0 and t_1.

For cash-flows computation, each item of Invested Capital and Capital Structure must be considered according to the movements in terms of cash-flow regardless of their nature, as summarized in the following.

6.2.1 Credits

They refer to Trade Receivables, Other Operating Receivables, Non-Operating Receivables, and Financial Credits (both short and long term). Cash-flows movements are reported in Table 6.3 as follows:

Table 6.3 Credits

Credits	Movements	Cash-in or cash-out	Cash-flow
1. Trade receivables 2. Other operating receivables 3. Non-operating receivables 4. Financial credits (short and long term)	Increase (↑) Decrease (↓)	Cash-out Cash-in	Decrease (↓) Increase (↑)

6.2.2 Debts

They refer to Trade Payables, Other Operating Payables, Non-Operating Payable, and Financial Debts (both short and long term). Cash-flows movements are reported in Table 6.4 as follows:

6.2.3 Inventories

They refer to both Permanent Inventories and Inventories. Cash-flows movements are reported in Table 6.5 as follows:

6.2.4 Tangible and Intangible Assets

They refer to Operating Tangible and Intangible Assets and Non-Operating Tangible and Intangible Assets. The baseline equation is the following:

$$\text{Asset}_{t1} - (\text{Asset}_{t0} - \text{Impairment}_{t1} - \text{Depreciation or Amortization or}_{t1}) = 0 \tag{6.1}$$

Denote with: A, Assets; IP, Impairment; DA, Depreciation and Amortization. The cash-flows movements can be summarized as in Table 6.6 as follows:

Table 6.4 Debts

Debts	Movements	Cash-in or cash-out	Cash-flow
1. Trade payables 2. Other operating payables 3. Non-operating payables 4. Financial debts (short and long term)	Increase (↑)	Cash-in	Increase (↑)
	Decrease (↓)	Cash-out	Decrease (↓)

Table 6.5 Inventories

Inventory	Movements	Cash-in or cash-out	Cash-flow
1. Permanent inventories 2. Inventories	Increase (↑)	Cash-out	Decrease (↓)
	Decrease (↓)	Cash-in	Increase (↑)

Table 6.6 Tangible and intangible assets

Tangible and intangible assets (operating and non-operating)	Movements	Cash-in or cash-out	Cash-flow
$A_{t1} > (A_{t0} - IP_{t1} - DA_{t1})$ $(Eq > 0)$	Increase (↑)	Cash-out	Decrease (↓)
$A_{t1} < (A_{t0} - IP_{t1} - DA_{t1})$ $(Eq < 0)$	Decrease (↓)	Cash-in	Increase (↑)
$A_{t1} = (A_{t0} - IP_{t1} - DA_{t1})$ $(Eq = 0)$	None	None	None

6.2.5 Financial Assets

They refer to Operating Financial Assets, Non-Operating Financial Assets, and Marketable Securities. The baseline equation is the following:

$$\text{Financial Asset}_{t1} - (\text{Financial Asset}_{t0} - \text{Impairment}_{t1}) = 0 \qquad (6.2)$$

Denote with: FA, Financial Assets; IP, Impairment. The cash-flows movements can be summarized as in Table 6.7 as follows:

It is worth noting that if the increase of Financial Asset is due to a reassessment of the asset, there is no cash-out but the increase of a Reserve in Equity. In this case, this Reserve is not considered in the determination of Dividends. Similarly, if the decrease of Financial Assets is due to the reduction in value, there is no cash-out but operating no-cash costs. In these cases, the movements of the Financial Assets.

6.2.6 Provisions

They refer to Provisions for Risks and Charges. The baseline equation is the following:

$$\text{Provision}_{t1} - (\text{Provision}_{to} + \text{Accruals}_{t1}) = 0 \qquad (6.3)$$

Denote with: PS, Provisions; AC, Accruals to Provisions. The cash-flows movements can be summarized as in Table 6.8 as follows:

Table 6.7 Financial assets and marketable securities

Financial assets (operating and non-operating) and marketable securities	Movements	Cash-in or cash-out	Cash-flow
$FA_{t1} > (FA_t - IP_{t1})$ $(Eq > 0)$	Increase (↑)	Cash-out	Decrease (↓)
$FA_{t1} < (FA_t - IP_{t1})$ $(Eq < 0)$	Decrease (↓)	Cash-in	Increase (↑)
$FA_{t1} = (FA_t - IP_{t1})$ $(Eq = 0)$	None	None	None

Table 6.8 Provisions

Provisions	Movements	Cash-in or cash-out	Cash-flow
$PS_{t1} < (PS_{t0} + AC_{t1})$ $(Eq < 0)$	Decrease (↑)	Cash-out	Decrease (↓)
$PS_{t1} = (PS_t + AC_{t1})$ $(Eq = 0)$	None	None	None

6.2.7 Equity

The Equity changes only if there is an increase or decrease of Share Capital in money or there is an increase or decrease of Treasury Share due to Share Buy-back. Cash-flows movements are summarized in Table 6.9 as follows:

6.2.8 Liquidity

It refers to Cash and Cash Equivalents. Cash-flows movements are summarized in Table 6.10 as follows:

Note that the movements of Liquidity, and therefore its effects on Net Financial Position and Free Cash-flow to Equity, refer to the amount of capital that the firm wants to invest in Liquidity as measured at the end of the period analysed. Therefore, all movements on liquidity used to balance all other movements on items that generate cash-in and cash-out, must be considered transitory.

6.3 Free Cash-Flow to the Firm

The Free Cash-Flow to the Firm (FCFF) refers to all cash-flows (cash-in and cash-out) related to all firm's activities, both operating and non-operating, the cost of debt and taxes. Specifically, FCFF is the sum of:

1. *Cash-Flow from Operating Activities (CFOA)*: it is equal to the EBITDA plus the change in value of Operating Capex ($CAPEX_{OP}$), Operating Net Working Capital (NWC_{OP}), and the decrease of Provisions (PS) if there are.
2. *Cash-Flow from Surplus Assets (CFSA)*: it refers to Non-Operating Activities and thus it is equal to Non-Operating Revenues and Costs plus the change in value of Non-Operating Net Working Capital (NWC_{NOP}) and the change in value of Non-Operating Capex ($CAPEX_{NOP}$).

Table 6.9 Equity

Equity	Movements	Cash-in or cash-out	Cash-flow
Share capital in money	Increase (↑)	Cash-in	Increase (↑)
	Decrease (↓)	Cash-out	Decrease (↓)
Treasury share	Increase (↑)	Cash-out	Decrease (↓)
	Decrease (↓)	Cash-in	Increase (↑)

Table 6.10 Liquidity

Liquidity	Movements	Cash-in or cash-out	Cash-flow
1. cash	Increase (↑)	Cash-out	Decrease (↓)
2. cash equivalents	Decrease (↓)	Cash-in	Increase (↑)

1. Cash-Flow From Operating Activities (CFOA)
The CFOA is equal to the EBITDA plus the change in value of Operating Capex ($CAPEX_{OP}$), change in value of the Operating Net Working Capital (NWC_{OP}), and decrease of Provisions (PS) if there are.

6.3.1 EBITDA

The value of EBITDA is the starting point. Operating Revenues and Costs must be considered in the same t-time of the cash-flows analysis and with the positive sign for revenues and negative sign for costs. Therefore, the EBITDA of the year referencing the analysis must be considered.

Note that all Operating Revenues and Costs are grouped in the EBIT. However, costs group between EBITDA and EBIT are defined Operating Costs Non-Cash because they have an economic relevance but not a financial one. In fact, they have no effects on cash-flows. Consequently, in cash-flow analysis, the EBIT is equal to EBITDA. It implies that we can start directly from EBITDA or, indirectly from EBIT and summing it all Operating Costs Non-Cash.

We consider the EBITDA the starting point. Therefore, we must consider all revenues and costs related to the operating activities of the firm as reported in Table 6.11.

6.3.2 Operating CapEx

The change in value of Operating CapEx ($CAPEX_{OP}$) is due to investments in Operating Intangible, Tangible, and Financial Assets need to the firm's core-business activities plus the Permanent Inventory. The increase in $CAPEX_{OP}$ reduces the CFOA and then the FCFF as well as the decrease in $CAPEX_{OP}$ increases the CFOA and then FCFF as reported in Table 6.12.

The aim of investment in Operating CapEx is to increase the EBITDA over time and then the FCFF. Therefore, the FCFF reduction due to investment in $CAPEX_{OP}$ should be more than compensate in a defined future time by the increase in EBITDA. Indeed, the investments in $CAPEX_{OP}$ should be operated with the aim of increasing Revenues or decreasing Costs and in both cases in a stable way. Whenever neither the increase in Revenues nor decrease in Costs is realized over time, the investment policy in $CAPEX_{OP}$ of the firm must be considered bankruptcy doubtless.

Table 6.11 EBITDA

Items	Cash-in/cash-out	CFOA	FCFF
Operating revenues	Cash-in	Increase (↑)	Increase (↑)
(operating costs)	Cash-out	Decrease (↓)	Decrease (↓)

Table 6.12 Operating CapEx

Items	Increase/ decrease	$CAPEX_{OP}$	Cash-in/ cash-Out	CFOA	FCFF
Operating tangible assets	Increase (↑)	Increase (↑)	Cash-out	Decrease (↓)	Decrease (↓)
	Decrease (↓)	Decrease (↓)	Cash-in	Increase (↑)	Increase (↑)
Operating intangible assets	Increase (↑)	Increase (↑)	Cash-out	Decrease (↓)	Decrease (↓)
	Decrease (↓)	Decrease (↓)	Cash-in	Increase (↑)	Increase (↑)
Operating financial assets	Increase (↑)	Increase (↑)	Cash-out	Decrease (↓)	Decrease (↓)
	Decrease (↓)	Decrease (↓)	Cash-in	Increase (↑)	Increase (↑)
Permanent inventory	Increase (↑)	Increase (↑)	Cash-out	Decrease (↓)	Decrease (↓)
	Decrease (↓)	Decrease (↓)	Cash-in	Increase (↑)	Increase (↑)
Operating CAPEX ($CAPEX_{OP}$)		**Increase (↑)**	**Cash-out**	**Decrease (↓)**	**Decrease (↓)**
		Decrease (↓)	**Cash-in**	**Increase (↑)**	**Increase (↑)**

6.3.3 Operating Net Working Capital (NWC_{OP})

The change in Net Working Capital, both Operating and Non-Operating, generates cash-flows that is needed to run the firm on a day-to-day basis.

The change in value of Operating Net Working Capital (NWC_{OP}) produces effects on CFOA and then on FCFF and it can be decomposed as follows:

1. *Trade Working Capital (TWC)* equals to the difference between Trade Receivables and Trade Payables.
2. *Non-Trade Working Capital (NTWC)* equals to Inventories plus Other Operating Receivables less the Other Operating Payables.

Their effects on CFOA and FCFF are reported in Table 6.13.

The NWC_{OP} is a function of the Operating Income with regard to the Operating Revenues and Costs and their time of cash-in and cash-out. Therefore, investments in NWC_{OP} refer to the investments in Trade Receivables and Payables, Other Operating Receivables and Payables, and Inventories. Specifically, Trade Receivables and Payables as well as Other Operating Receivables and Payables refer to the Operating Revenues and Costs that they do not generate cash-in and cash-out yet. The Inventories refer to the goods not yet sold.

Specifically:

Table 6.13 Operating net working capital

Items	Increase/ decrease	NWC_{OP}	Cash-in/ cash-out	CFOA	FCFF
Trade receivables	Increase (↑)	Increase (↑)	Cash-out	Decrease (↓)	Decrease (↓)
	Decrease (↓)	Decrease (↓)	Cash-in	Increase (↑)	Increase (↑)
Trade payables	Increase (↑)	Decrease (↓)	Cash-in	Increase (↑)	Increase (↑)
	Decrease (↓)	Increase (↑)	Cash-out	Decrease (↓)	Decrease (↓)
Trade working capital (TWC)	**Increase (↑)**	**Increase (↑)**	**Cash-out**	**Decrease (↓)**	**Decrease (↓)**
	Decrease (↓)	**Decrease (↓)**	**Cash-in**	**Increase (↑)**	**Increase (↑)**
Other operating receivables	Increase (↑)	Increase (↑)	Cash-out	Decrease (↓)	Decrease (↓)
	Decrease (↓)	Decrease (↓)	Cash-in	Increase (↑)	Increase (↑)
Other operating payables	Increase (↑)	Decrease (↓)	Cash-in	Increase (↑)	Increase (↑)
	Decrease (↓)	Increase (↑)	Cash-out	Decrease (↓)	Decrease (↓)
Inventories	Increase (↑)	Increase (↑)	Cash-out	Decrease (↓)	Decrease (↓)
	Decrease (↓)	Decrease (↓)	Cash-in	Increase (↑)	Increase (↑)
Non-trade working capital (NTWC)	**Increase (↑)**	**Increase (↑)**	**Cash-out**	**Decrease (↓)**	**Decrease (↓)**
	Decrease (↓)	**Decrease (↓)**	**Cash-in**	**Increase (↑)**	**Increase (↑)**
Operating net working capital (NWC_{OP})		**Increase (↑)**	**Cash-out**	**Decrease (↓)**	**Decrease (↓)**
		Decrease (↓)	**Cash-in**	**Increase (↑)**	**Increase (↑)**

1. Sales Revenues produce Trade Receivables while Costs of Goods Sold generate Trade Payables. The difference between them defines the Trade Working Capital (TWC) that is the first part of the NWC_{OP}. Therefore, if Trade Receivables are greater than Trade Payables, the TWC increases, by increasing the NWC_{OP} and reducing FCFF; otherwise, if the Trade Receivables are lower than Trade Payables, the TWC decreases, by decreasing the NWC_{OP} and increasing FCFF.
2. Other Operating Revenues and Costs generate Other Operating Receivables and Payables. The sum of Other Operating Receivables and Payables and Inventories defines the Non-Trade Working Capital (NTWC) that is the second part of the NWC_{OP}. Therefore, if the Other Operating Receivables plus Inventories are greater than the Other Operating Payables, the NTWC increases, by increasing

the NWC_{OP} and reducing FCFF; otherwise, if the Other Operating Receivables plus Inventories are lower than the Other Operating Payables, the NTWC decreases, by decreasing the NWC_{OP} and increasing FCFF.

We can generalize by saying that:

1. The higher the NWC_{OP}, the higher the sum of Receivables and Inventories than Payables, and therefore the higher the cash-out.
2. The lower the NWC_{OP}, the higher the Payables than the sum of Receivables and Inventories, and therefore the higher the cash-in.

The NWC_{OP} measures the resources invested in operating activities. Therefore, assuming equal revenues, the higher the NWC_{OP}, the higher the cash-out and then the greater the financial needs. Indeed, Receivables and Inventories increase and the lack of cash-in with their displacement in the future time increases the financial needs to cover the cash-out.

Finally, note that the change in NWC_{OP} is not related only to the current EBITDA but also past EBITDA. Indeed, Receivables and Payables are related to the Operating Revenues and Costs both current and past.

6.3.4 Decrease of Provisions (PS)

The Provisions (PS) can decrease only. Indeed, their increase is due to the charges that have only an economic impact and not financial one. Indeed, charges have not financial effects, as reported in Table 6.14.

We can summarize the movements of CFOA on FCFF as reported in Table 6.15 as follows:

2. ***Cash-Flow From Surplus Assets (CFSA)*** The CFSA refers to the Non-Operating activities of the firm and then it is equal to Non-Operating Revenues and Costs plus the change in value of Non-Operating Net Working Capital (NWC_{NOP}) and the change in value of Non-Operating CapEx ($CAPEX_{NOP}$).

Table 6.14 Provisions

Items	Increase/ decrease	Provisions (PS)	Cash-in/ cash-out	CFOA	FCFF
Provisions for risks and charges	Increase (↑)	Increase (↑)	No effect	No effect	No effect
	Decrease (↓)	Decrease (↓)	Cash-out	Decrease (↓)	Decrease (↓)
Provisions (PS)		**Increase (↑)**	**No effect**	**No effect**	**No effect**
		Decrease (↓)	**Cash-out**	**Decrease (↓)**	**Decrease (↓)**

Table 6.15 Movements of CFOA and FCFF

	Increase/ decrease	Cash-in/ cash-Out	CFOA	FCFF
EBITDA				
Operating revenues	N/A	Cash-in	Increase (↑)	Increase (↑)
Operating costs	N/A	Cash-out	Decrease (↓)	Decrease (↓)
Change in operating Capex ($CAPEX_{OP}$)	Increase (↑)	Cash-out	Decrease (↓)	Decrease (↓)
	Decrease (↓)	Cash-in	Increase (↑)	Increase (↑)
Change in operating net working capital (NWC_{OP})	Increase (↑)	Cash-out	Decrease (↓)	Decrease (↓)
	Decrease (↓)	Increase (↑)	Increase (↑)	Increase (↑)
Provisions (PS)	Increase (↑)	No effect	No effect	No effect
	Decrease (↓)	Cash-out	Decrease (↓)	Decrease (↓)

Table 6.16 Non-operating revenues and costs

Items	Cash-in/cash-out	CFSA	FCFF
Non-operating revenues	Cash-in	Increase (↑)	Increase (↑)
Non-operating costs	Cash-out	Decrease (↓)	Decrease (↓)

6.3.5 Non-Operating Revenues and Costs

Non-Operating Revenues and Costs must be considered with the relative sign. Therefore, while Non-Operating Revenues are cash-in and then increase the cash-flows, the Non-Operating Costs are cash-out and then decrease the cash-flows. The effects on Non-Operating Revenues and Costs on CFSA and FCFO are reported in Table 6.16 as follows:

6.3.6 Non-Operating Net Working Capital (NWC_{NOP})

The change in value of Non-Operating Net Working Capital (NWC_{NOP}) produces effects on CFSA and then on FCFF due to Non-Operating Receivables and Non-Operating Payables, as reported in Table 6.17 as follows:

Table 6.17 Non-operating net working capital

Items	Increase/ decrease	NWC_{NOP}	Cash-in/ cash-out	CFSA	FCFF
Non-operating receivables	Increase (↑)	Increase (↑)	Cash-out	Decrease (↓)	Decrease (↓)
	Decrease (↓)	Decrease (↓)	Cash-in	Increase (↑)	Increase (↑)
Non-operating payables	Increase (↑)	Decrease (↓)	Cash-in	Increase (↑)	Increase (↑)
	Decrease (↓)	Increase (↑)	Cash-out	Decrease (↓)	Decrease (↓)
Non-operating net working capital (NWC_{NOP})		**Increase (↑)**	**Cash-out**	**Decrease (↓)**	**Decrease (↓)**
		Decrease (↓)	**Cash-in**	**Increase (↑)**	**Increase (↑)**

Table 6.18 Non-operating CapEx

Items	Increase/ decrease	$CAPEX_{NOP}$	Cash-in/ cash-out	CFSA	FCFF
Non-operating tangible assets	Increase (↑)	Increase (↑)	Cash-out	Decrease (↓)	Decrease (↓)
	Decrease (↓)	Decrease (↓)	Cash-in	Increase (↑)	Increase (↑)
Non-operating intangible assets	Increase (↑)	Increase (↑)	Cash-out	Decrease (↓)	Decrease (↓)
	Decrease (↓)	Decrease (↓)	Cash-in	Increase (↑)	Increase (↑)
Non-operating financial assets	Increase (↑)	Increase (↑)	Cash-out	Decrease (↓)	Decrease (↓)
	Decrease (↓)	Decrease (↓)	Cash-in	Increase (↑)	Increase (↑)
Non-operating capex ($CAPEX_{NOP}$)		**Increase (↑)**	**Cash-out**	**Decrease (↓)**	**Decrease (↓)**
		Decrease (↓)	**Cash-in**	**Increase (↑)**	**Increase (↑)**

6.3.7 Non-Operating CapEx ($CAPEX_{NOP}$)

The change in value of Non-Operating CapEx ($CAPEX_{NOP}$) is due to the investments in Non-Operating Intangible, Tangible, and Financial Assets. The increase in $CAPEX_{NOP}$ reduces the CFSA and then the FCFF as well as the decrease in $CAPEX_{NOP}$ increases the CFSA and then the FCFF as reported in Table 6.18.

We can summarize the movements of CFSA on FCFO as in Table 6.19.

Table 6.19 Movements of CFSA and FCFF

	Increase/ decrease	Cash-in/ cash-out	CFSA	FCFF
NORC				
Non-operating revenues	N/A	Cash-in	Increase (↑)	Increase (↑)
Non-operating costs	N/A	Cash-out	Decrease (↓)	Decrease (↓)
Non-operating net working capital (NWC_{NOP})	Increase (↑)	Cash-out	Decrease (↓)	Decrease (↓)
	Decrease (↓)	Cash-in	Increase (↑)	Increase (↑)
Non-operating Capex ($CAPEX_{NOP}$)	Increase (↑)	Cash-out	Decrease (↓)	Decrease (↓)
	Decrease (↓)	Cash-in	Increase (↑)	Increase (↑)

6.4 Free Cash-Flow to Equity

The Free Cash-Flow to Equity (FCFE) is equal to the sum of:

1. *Cash-Flow from Equity (CFE)*: it refers only to the increase or decrease in money of share capital and the use of money for shares buy-backs.
2. *Cash-Flow from Debt (CFD)*: it refers to the cash-flows related to the Net Financial Position and the Cost of Debt.
3. *Cash-Flow from Taxes (CFT)*: it is related to the cash-flows for taxes both operating and corporate.

1. Cash-Flow from Equity

Equity refers to the shareholders source of capital. Equity can be increased through new share capital in money, shares buy-backs, and self-financing by earnings retained. Among these, the last (self-financing) has no effects on cash-flows as reported in Table 6.20.

Two are the main considerations:

- First, Equity must be repaid by dividends. The FCFE are dividends for shareholders. Therefore, the equity remuneration is residual because it is achieved after the repayment of all production factors only in the case of specific conditions.
- Second, if there is an increase of Equity in money, it is due to the necessity of recapitalization of the firm or to reduce the Debt. In both cases, the FCFE is equal to zero. It would be unusual to ask for a paid capital increase and then distribute dividends.

Table 6.20 Cash-flow from equity

Items	Increase/ decrease	Equity (E)	Cash-in/ cash-out	CFE	FCFE
Share capital in money	Increase (↑)	Increase (↑)	Cash-in	Increase (↑)	Increase (↑)
	Decrease (↓)	Decrease (↓)	Cash-out	Decrease (↓)	Decrease (↓)
Share buy-backs	Increase (↑)	Decrease (↓)	Cash-out	Decrease (↓)	Decrease (↓)
	Decrease (↓)	Decrease (↓)	Cash-in	Increase (↑)	Increase (↑)
Self-financing by earnings retained	Increase (↑)	Increase (↑)	No effect	No effect	No effect
	Decrease (↓)	Decrease (↓)	No effect	No effect	No effect
Cash-flow from equity (E)		**Increase (↑)**	**Cash-in**	**Increase (↑)**	**Increase (↑)**
		Decrease (↓)	**Cash-out**	**Decrease (↓)**	**Decrease (↓)**

2. Cash-Flow from Debt

Remember that Debt refers to Financial Debt and it is computed by the Net Financial Position. Therefore, it is equal to the Financial Debts (both long run and short run) less the sum of Financial Credits, Marketable Securities, Cash and Cash Equivalents.

We can distinguish between the Long-Term Debt (D_{LT}) and Short-Term Debt (D_{ST}). The change in value of Debt produces effects on FCFE as reported in Table 6.21.

Specific reasoning must be reserved to investments in Cash and Cash Equivalents. It refers to the amount of cash that a firm decides to maintain. Therefore, it is capital invested because it is an investment decision. Indeed, it is grouped in the Net Financial Position with negative sign (where debt has a positive sign) by reducing its value.

It is necessary to distinguish between:

- The temporary movements of Cash, that they are due to the effect of cash-in and cash-out used to balance the movements of other items.
- The investment in Cash that defines the level of liquidity that company wants to maintain over time. Only this type can be considered as a proper investment.

In cash-flow terms, it can be considered as a cash-out. Therefore, the increase in Cash is a cash-out and then it reduces the FCFE; otherwise, the decrease in Cash is a cash-in and then it increases the FCFE.

Finally note that if there is an increase in Debt it is generally due to cover the financial needs related to the FCFO. It will be unusual if the increase in Debt is used to have a FCFE. In this case, the firm distributes dividends by using Debt.

Table 6.21 Cash-flow from debt

Items	Increase/ decrease	NFP and cost of debt	Cash-in/ cash-out	CFD	FCFE
Long-term financial debt	Increase (↑)	Increase (↑)	Cash-in	Increase (↑)	Increase (↑)
	Decrease (↓)	Decrease (↓)	Cash-out	Decrease (↓)	Decrease (↓)
Long-term financial credit	Increase (↑)	Decrease (↓)	Cash-out	Decrease (↓)	Decrease (↓)
	Decrease (↓)	Increase (↑)	Cash-in	Increase (↑)	Increase (↑)
Long-term debt (D_{LT})	**Increase (↑)**	**Increase (↑)**	**Cash-in**	**Increase (↑)**	**Increase (↑)**
	Decrease (↓)	**Decrease (↓)**	**Cash-out**	**Decrease (↓)**	**Decrease (↓)**
Short-term financial debt	Increase (↑)	Increase (↑)	Cash-in	Increase (↑)	Increase (↑)
	Decrease (↓)	Decrease (↓)	Cash-out	Decrease (↓)	Decrease (↓)
Short-term financial credits	Increase (↑)	Decrease (↓)	Cash-out	Decrease (↓)	Decrease (↓)
	Decrease (↓)	Increase (↑)	Cash-in	Increase (↑)	Increase (↑)
Marketable securities	Increase (↑)	Decrease (↓)	Cash-out	Decrease (↓)	Decrease (↓)
	Decrease (↓)	Increase (↑)	Cash-in	Increase (↑)	Increase (↑)
Cash and cash equivalents	Increase (↑)	Decrease (↓)	Cash-out	Decrease (↓)	Decrease (↓)
	Decrease (↓)	Increase (↑)	Cash-in	Increase (↑)	Increase (↑)
Short-term debt (D_{ST})	**Increase (↑)**	**Increase (↑)**	**Cash-in**	**Increase (↑)**	**Increase (↑)**
	Decrease (↓)	**Decrease (↓)**	**Cash-out**	**Decrease (↓)**	**Decrease (↓)**
DEBT (D)		**Increase (↑)**	**Cash-in**	**Increase (↑)**	**Increase (↑)**
		Decrease (↓)	**Cash-out**	**Decrease (↓)**	**Decrease (↓)**
(interest on debt)			Cash-out	Decrease (↓)	Decrease (↓)
(other financial costs on debt)			Cash-out	Decrease (↓)	Decrease (↓)
Cost of DEBT		**Increase (↑)**	**Cash-in**	**Increase (↑)**	**Increase (↑)**
		Decrease (↓)	**Cash-out**	**Decrease (↓)**	**Decrease (↓)**

(continued)

Table 6.21 (continued)

Items	Increase/ decrease	NFP and cost of debt	Cash-in/ cash-out	CFD	FCFE
Cash-flow from DEBT		**Increase (↑)**	**Cash-in**	**Increase (↑)**	**Increase (↑)**
		Decrease (↓)	**Cash-out**	**Decrease (↓)**	**Decrease (↓)**

Table 6.22 Cash-flow from taxes

Items	Cash-in/cash-out	CFT	FCFE
(taxes)	Cash-out	Decrease (↓)	Decrease (↓)
Cash-flow from taxes	Cash-out	Decrease (↓)	Decrease (↓)

3. Cash-Flow from Taxes (CFT)

The CFT refers to the cash-flows due to the taxes both operating and corporate as reported in Table 6.22 as follows.

7 Financial Ratios

7.1 Return on Investment

In the Asset Side perspective, we measure the return on invested capital in the firm's assets by using three main financial ratios: (1) Return on Investment (ROI); (2) Return on Operating Invested Capital (ROIC); and (3) Return on Assets (ROA).

7.1.1 Return on Investment (ROI)

The Return on Investment (ROI) is equal to the ratio between Operating Income and Invested Capital (IC).

By considering that the Invested Capital refers to investments in assets, it is useful to measure the Operating Income in terms of EBIT in order to consider the amortization and depreciation process related to the Operating CapEx. Therefore, the ROI is equal to:

$$\mathrm{ROI} = \frac{\mathrm{EBIT}}{\text{Invested Capital (IC)}} \text{ in\%} \quad (7.1)$$

Note that the ROI can be used if there are not Non-Operating Activities or at least they are not relevant in amount. In this case, all investments are in Operating activities and the Invested Capital (IC) is equal to the Net Operating Invested Capital (NOIC).

On the contrary, if there are Non-Operating Activities we can use the ROIC rather than the ROI.

The ROI can be decomposed on the basis of two main ratios:

(a) *Return on Sales (ROS)* that measures the relationship between Sales Revenues (SR) and Operating Income (EBIT) as follows:

P. De Luca, *Corporate Finance*, Springer Texts in Business and Economics,
https://doi.org/10.1007/978-3-031-18300-3_7

$$\text{ROS} = \frac{\text{EBIT}}{\text{SR}} \text{ in\%} \tag{7.2}$$

(b) *Turnover of Invested Capital (TIC)* that measures the relationship between Sales Revenues (SR) and Invested Capital (IC) as follows:

$$\text{TCI} = \frac{\text{SR}}{\text{IC}} \text{ in\%} \tag{7.3}$$

On the basis of ROS and TIC, the ROI is equal to:

$$\text{ROI} = \text{ROS} \cdot \text{TCI} = \frac{\text{EBIT}}{\text{SR}} \cdot \frac{\text{SR}}{\text{IC}} = \frac{\text{EBIT}}{\text{IC}} \tag{7.4}$$

7.1.2 Return on Operating Invested Capital (ROIC)

If the firm invests in both Operating and Non-Operating activities, the Net Operating Invested Capital (NOIC) measures investments in Operating activities only, while the Invested Capital (IC) measures the total amount of investments in Operating and Non-Operating activities.

In this case, we can measure the return on Operating Income by considering the Net Operating Invested Capital (NOIC) rather than Invested Capital (IC). Therefore, we measure the Return on Operating Invested Capital (ROIC) rather than ROI as follows:

$$\text{ROIC} = \frac{\text{EBIT}}{\text{Net Opearating Invested Capital (NOIC)}} \text{ in\%} \tag{7.5}$$

As in case of ROI, the ROIC can be decomposed on the basis of ROS and TCI. The only difference refers to the TCI because the firm invests in Operating and in Non-operating activities. Consequently, it is necessary to consider the Net Operating Invested Capital (NOIC) rather than the Invested Capital (IC) as follows:

$$\text{ROIC} = \text{ROS} \cdot \text{TCI} = \frac{\text{EBIT}}{\text{SR}} \cdot \frac{\text{SR}}{\text{NOIC}} = \frac{\text{EBIT}}{\text{NOIC}} \tag{7.6}$$

We can consider the relationship between Gross Profit (GP) and investments in operating activities. In this case, we can compute the ROIC in terms of GP as follows:

$$\text{ROIC}_{\text{GP}} = \frac{\text{Gross Profit (GP)}}{\text{Net Operating Capital Invested (NOCI)}} \text{ in\%} \tag{7.7}$$

7.1.3 Return on Assets (ROA)

The Return on Assets (ROA) measures the return on Operating Income of the investments in Operating CapEx ($CAPEX_{OP}$) only as follows:

$$ROA = \frac{EBIT}{Opearating\ Capex\ (CAPEX_{OP})}\ in\% \tag{7.8}$$

We can consider the relationship between Gross Profit (GP) and the Operating CapEx by determining the ROA in terms of GP as follows:

$$ROA_{GP} = \frac{Gross\ Profit\ (GP)}{Opearating\ Capex\ (CAPEX_{OP})}\ in\% \tag{7.9}$$

It is worth noting that in all cases (ROI, ROIC, and ROA), the increase of ratios is not necessarily good news. The increase in ratios can be due to the decrease in CapEx consequently to the amortization and depreciation process of tangible and intangible assets. In this case, if we maintain constant the numerator of the ratio (Operating Income or Gross Profit), the reduction of the denominator due to the amortization and depreciation process will increasing the ratio. It is not a good condition because it is related to the reduction in operating investments.

Most of all, the decrease of investments in assets implies the reduction of future capabilities of the firm to compete in the business and, subsequently a future reduction in Operating Income.

Otherwise, the increase of ratios due to the development of technologies indicates an increase of the future capabilities of the firm to compete in the business and, subsequently a future increase in the Operating Income.

7.2 Operating Income Growth Rate

Preliminarily consider that the Growth Rate (g) with regard to a defined time period can be measured in two main ways. Consider a defined amount of Earnings (Er). The Growth Rate of Earnings (Er) over time can be measured on the basis of:

1. Percentage changes in a time period t_0; t_1 (for example, year-to-year, month-to-month, week-to-week, etc.) as follows:

$$g_t = \frac{Er_{t_1} - Er_{t_0}}{Er_{t_0}} = \frac{Er_{t_1}}{Er_{t_0}} - 1 \tag{7.10}$$

2. Compounding effects (CAGG—*Compound Annual Growth Rate*) in a time period t_0; t_n. Denote with Er_{t_n} the ending value of Earnings and then its value at the end of the period considered; Er_{t_0} the beginning value of Earnings and then its value at the start of the period considered; n the number of unit time (year, month, week, etc.) of the period considered. The CAGG is equal to:

$$g_t = \left(\frac{\mathrm{Er}_{t_n}}{\mathrm{Er}_{t_0}}\right)^{\left(\frac{1}{n}\right)} - 1 \tag{7.11}$$

Both measurements of Growth Rate have problems. The first considers the percentage changes in each period but ignores its compounding effects. The second considers the compounding effects by considering the beginning value and the ending value but it ignores what goes on between the start and the end of the period considered. Finally, both measurements contain problems if the amount of item considered (in this case Earnings) is negative because they are meaningless.

The Growth Rate in Operating Income (g_{OI}) can be defined on the basis of two variables: (1) the Investment Rate (IR) and (2) the Return on Operating Invested Capital (ROIC).

The Investment Rate (IR) measures the percentage of Operating Income reinvested in the operating assets. It can be defined on the basis of Operating CapEx ($\mathrm{CAPEX_{OP}}$), Net Working Capital (NWC), and the EBIT, as follows:

$$\mathrm{IR} = \frac{\mathrm{CAPEX_{OP}} + \mathrm{NWC}}{\mathrm{EBIT}} \tag{7.12}$$

The Growth Rate (g_{OI}) is equal to the product between the Return on Operating Invested Capital (ROIC) and the Investment Rate (IR), as follows:

$$g_{\mathrm{OI}} = \mathrm{IR} \cdot \mathrm{ROIC} \quad \Rightarrow \quad \begin{aligned} \mathrm{IR} &= \frac{g_{\mathrm{OI}}}{\mathrm{ROIC}} \\ \mathrm{ROIC} &= \frac{g_{\mathrm{OI}}}{\mathrm{IR}} \end{aligned} \tag{7.13}$$

Therefore, defined a level of Growth Rate (g_{OI}) to be achieved, it gets:

- the higher the ROIC, the lower can be the Investment Rate (IR)
- the lower the ROIC, the higher can be the Investment Rate (IR).

We can define the IR in terms of Dividends (Div). In order to simplify the analysis without loss of significance, assume that Earnings (Er) can be used as dividends less a part reinvested in the operating assets of the firm. In this case, Dividends (Div) are equal to:

$$\mathrm{Div} = \mathrm{Er} \cdot (1 - \mathrm{IR})$$

and by substituting it gets:

$$\mathrm{Div} = \mathrm{Er} \cdot \left(1 - \frac{g_{\mathrm{OI}}}{\mathrm{ROIC}}\right) \tag{7.14}$$

The equation states the relationship between Growth Rate (g_{OI}), ROIC, and Dividend (Div). Specifically, it shows the key role played by the ROIC:

1. The higher the ROIC, the lower the Investment Rate (IR) must be to achieve the defined level of Growth Rate (g_{OI}) and, other conditions being equal, the higher Dividends will be.
2. The lower the ROIC, the higher the Investment Rate (IR) must be to achieve the defined level of Growth Rate (g_{OI}) and, other conditions being equal, the lower the Dividends will be.

Two are the mean aspects to be considered:

1. First, with equal cost of capital, the higher the dividends and then the higher the value of firm based on the discounted dividend models.
2. Second, because the value creation is the difference between the Return on Invested Capital and the Cost of Capital, the higher the ROIC than the Cost of Capital, the higher the value creation. Therefore, if the ROIC is higher than the Cost of Capital, the Growth implies the value creation for the firm. On the contrary, if the ROIC is lower than the Cost of Capital, the Growth implies the value destruction for the firm. Obviously, if the ROIC is equal to the Cost of Capital, the firm value is neither created nor destroyed by the Growth.
   Therefore, being other conditions equal, a high ROIC is always positive; the same cannot be said of Growth Rate because it is only good if the ROIC is higher than the Cost of Capital. Indeed, a firm with high ROIC and low Growth Rate may have a similar or even greater value than a firm with higher Growth Rate but low ROIC. Therefore, a firm with a high ROIC can increase its value by increasing its Growth Rate rather than its ROIC. Otherwise, a firm with a low ROIC can generate more value by focusing on the increase of its ROIC rather than on the increase of the Growth Rate. It implies that if a firm has a high ROIC it should focus on improving Growth Rate; otherwise, if a firm has a low ROIC it should focus on improving ROIC before improving Growth Rate.

7.3 Return on Equity

In the Equity Side perspective, we measure the return on invested capital in the firm's equity by using two main financial ratios: (1) Return on Equity (ROE); (2) Total Return on Shareholders (TRS).

7.3.1 Return on Equity (ROE)

The Return on Equity (ROE) is one of the most popular and most commonly used. It is the true bottom-line measure of firm's performance in terms of equity. It measures the return on Equity (E) on the basis of Net Income (NI) as follows:

$$\text{ROE} = \frac{\text{Net Income (NI)}}{\text{Equity }(E)} \text{ in\%} \tag{7.15}$$

There is a relevant relationship between ROE, ROI, and Leverage (L). Based on this relationship, ROE can be defined on the basis of ROI and Leverage (L).

Assume that the firm invests only in the Operating activities so that there are not Non-Operating activities. In this case, it gets:

1. The total amount of Invested Capital (IC) is equal to the Net Operating Invested Capital (NOIC) because there is not Surplus Assets (SA). It implies that the Return on Investment (ROI) is equal to the Return on Operating Invested Capital (ROIC).
2. The Net Income (NI) is equal to the EBIT less the Interests on Debt (I_D) and Taxes (T). If we assume that the total amount of the Cost of Financial Debt is equal to the Interest on Debt, we have:

$$\text{NI} = \text{EBIT} - I_D - T$$

By considering the marginal tax rate (t_c) on EBT, we have:

$$T = \text{EBT} \cdot t_c = (\text{EBIT} - I_D) \cdot t_c$$

Substituting, it gets:

$$\text{NI} = (\text{EBIT} - I_D) \cdot (1 - t_c) \tag{7.16}$$

Now consider that:

(a) $\text{ROE} = \frac{\text{NI}}{E}$, so that $\text{NI} = \text{ROE} \cdot E$.
(b) $\text{ROI} = \frac{\text{EBIT}}{\text{IC}}$, so that $\text{EBIT} = \text{ROI} \cdot \text{IC}$.
(c) The Interest on Debt (I_D) is equal to the Cost of Debt (K_D) multiplied by the amount of Debt (D) in Capital Structure, so that $I_D = D \cdot K_D$.
(d) The total amount of Capital Structure (CS) is equal to the total amount of Invested Capital (IC) by definition, so that CS = IC. Since the Capital Structure (CS) is equal to the sum of Equity (E) plus Debt (D), $\text{CS} = E + D$, we can define the Invested Capital (IC) as the sum of Equity and Debt, so that: $\text{IC} = E + D$.

By replacing in the equation, we have:

$$\text{ROE} \cdot E = (\text{ROI} \cdot \text{IC} - D \cdot K_D) \cdot (1 - t_c)$$

$$\begin{aligned} \text{ROE} \cdot E &= [\text{ROI} \cdot (E + D) - D \cdot K_D] \cdot (1 - t_c) \\ &= [\text{ROI} \cdot E + D \cdot (\text{ROI} - K_D)] \cdot (1 - t_c) \end{aligned}$$

Dividing first and second terms by Equity (E), it gets:

$$\text{ROE} \cdot E \cdot \frac{1}{E} = \{[\text{ROI} \cdot E + D \cdot (\text{ROI} - K_D)] \cdot (1 - t_c)\} \cdot \frac{1}{E}$$

and then:

$$\text{ROE} = \left[\text{ROI} + \frac{D}{E} \cdot (\text{ROI} - K_D)\right] \cdot (1 - t_c) \tag{7.17}$$

The equation states the relationship between ROE, ROI, and Leverage (L) as measured by Debt-Equity Ratio (D/E).

Specifically, equation states the multiple effects of Debt on ROE. This effect can be positive or negative. It depends on the relationship between the ROI and the Cost of Debt (K_D), on the one hand, and the amount of Debt (D) in the Capital Structure, on the other hand.

Specifically, the Financial Leverage (FL) can be defined as follows:

$$\text{FL} = L \cdot (\text{ROI} - K_D) \tag{7.18}$$

Therefore if:

1. *ROI > K_D, the Financial Leverage (FL) is positive*. The Debt invested in the firm generates a return on investment (ROI) greater than its Cost of Debt (K_D). In this case, the increase in ROE is due to the ROI in an unlevered case plus the positive Leverage (L) effects. Consequently, other conditions being equal, the greater the Leverage (L), the higher the ROE because the Leverage (L) is a positive multiplier. The shareholders achieve earnings created from Debt. They benefit from the positive difference between ROI and K_D.
2. *ROI < K_D, the Financial Leverage (FL) is negative*. The Debt invested in the firm generates a return on investment (ROI) lower than its Cost of Debt (K_D). In this case, the decrease in ROE is due to the ROI in unlevered case plus the negative Leverage (L) effects. Consequently, other conditions being equal, the greater the Leverage (L), the lower the ROE because the Leverage (L) is a negative multiplier. The shareholders claim losses arising from debt. Their loss is due to the negative difference between ROI and K_D.

7.3.2 Total Return on Shareholders (TRS)

If the firm is listed in capital market, a measurement largely used is the Total Return on Shareholders (TRS). While the ROE is an account measure, TRS is based on the stock price. Indeed, TRS combines the amount that shareholders gain through any increase in the share price over a given period with the sum of dividends paid to them over the period. Specifically, TRS is equal to the Percentage Change in Share Price (ΔSP) plus the Dividend Yield (DY) in a given period as follows:

$$\text{TRS} = \Delta\text{SP} + \text{DY} \tag{7.19}$$

The Percentage Change in Share Price (ΔSP) measures the change in Share Price (SP) of the firm. Denote with SP_c the current share price and SP_p the purchase share price. The Percentage Change in Share Price (ΔSP) is equal to:

$$\Delta\text{SP} = \frac{\text{SP}_c - \text{SP}_p}{\text{SP}_p} \text{ in\%} \tag{7.20}$$

The Dividend Yield (DY) measures the annual Dividend per Share paid by the firm to its shareholders expressed as a percentage of its share price. Therefore, the Dividend Yield is equal to Dividend per Share (DPS) (current Dividend per Share (DPS_c)) divided by purchase Share Price (SP_p), as follows:

$$\text{DY} = \frac{\text{DPS}_c}{\text{SP}_p} \text{ in\%} \tag{7.21}$$

Note that if dividends are paid on a quarterly basis, we have to annualize the Dividend Yield by computing the Implied Dividend Yield (IDY) as follows:

$$\text{IDY} = \frac{\text{Most Recent Quarterly DPS} \times 4}{\text{Current SP}}$$

Therefore, the TRS can be explicated as follows:

$$\text{TRS} = \frac{\text{SP}_c - \text{SP}_p}{\text{SP}_p} + \frac{\text{DPS}_c}{\text{SP}_p} = \frac{\text{SP}_c - \text{SP}_p + \text{DPS}_c}{\text{SP}_p} \tag{7.22}$$

It is possible to decompose the TRS in a different way (Koller et al., 2015).

The Percentage Change in Share Price (ΔSP) can be expressed in terms of Percent Increase in Earnings (ΔEr) and the Percentage Change in a Price-to-Earnings Ratio (Δ(*P*/Er)) as follows:

$$\Delta\text{SP} = \Delta\text{Er} + \Delta\left(\frac{P}{\text{Er}}\right)$$

Note that there is an additional cross-term that reflects the interaction of the share price change and the *P*/Er change, but it is generally small and therefore it can be ignored in this context.

The Percentage Increase in Earning (ΔEr) can be broken down into Percent Increase in Revenues (Δ*R*) and in the Percent Change in Profit Margin (ΔPM) where the Profit Margin is equal to the Earnings divided by Revenues (PM = Er/*R*). Consequently, it measures the weight of costs indirectly. Therefore, we have:

$$\Delta\text{Er} = \Delta R + \Delta\text{PM} \quad \rightarrow \quad \Delta\text{Er} = \Delta R + \Delta\left(\frac{\text{Er}}{R}\right)$$

Note that also in this case there is an additional cross-term that reflects the interaction of these two effects, but it is small and then it can be omitted in this context allowing to focus on the key point.

Based on the explicating definition of ΔEr we can rewrite ΔSP as follows:

$$\Delta \mathrm{SP} = \Delta R + \Delta \mathrm{PM} + \Delta\left(\frac{P}{\mathrm{Er}}\right) \tag{7.23}$$

The Dividend Yield (DY) is equal to the Dividend per Share (DPS) (current DPS) divided by the Share Price (SP) (purchase SP) as defined previously.

In order to simplify the analysis without any loss of significance, it is possible to assume that all revenues immediately generate cash-in and all costs immediately generate cash-out. It implies that there is no Net Working Capital (NWC). It also assumes that there are no other cash movements other than investments. Under these assumptions, it is possible to define Dividend per Share (DPS) on the basis of Earning (Er), growth rate (g_n), and ROIC as follows:

$$\mathrm{DPS} = \mathrm{Er} \cdot \left(1 - \frac{g_n}{\mathrm{ROIC}}\right)$$

The Share Price (SP) can be defined on the basis of Earnings (Er) and the Price-Earning ratio as an identity as follows:

$$\mathrm{SP} = \mathrm{Er} \cdot \left(\frac{P}{\mathrm{Er}}\right)$$

Therefore, the Dividend Yield can be defined as follows:

$$\mathrm{DY} = \frac{\mathrm{DPS}}{\mathrm{SP}} = \frac{\mathrm{Er} \cdot \left(1 - \frac{g_n}{\mathrm{ROIC}}\right)}{\mathrm{Er} \cdot \left(\frac{P}{\mathrm{Er}}\right)} = \frac{1 - \frac{g_n}{\mathrm{ROIC}}}{\frac{P}{\mathrm{Er}}} = \left(1 - \frac{g_n}{\mathrm{ROIC}}\right) \cdot \left(\frac{\mathrm{Er}}{P}\right)$$

and rearranging:

$$\mathrm{DY} = \left(\frac{\mathrm{Er}}{P}\right) - \left(\frac{g_n}{\mathrm{ROIC}} \cdot \frac{\mathrm{Er}}{P}\right) \tag{7.24}$$

where:

1. The first term $\left(\frac{\mathrm{Er}}{P}\right)$ is the inverse of the Price-to-Earnings ratio and it is usually called the Earnings Yield (EY) or Zero Growth Return. It represents the return an investor would earn if the firm do not grow or improve its profit margin and if it paid out all its earnings in dividends. Its share price would remain constant.
2. The second term $\left(\frac{g_n}{\mathrm{ROIC}} \cdot \frac{\mathrm{Er}}{P}\right)$ represents the part of its earnings yield that the firm must reinvest each year to achieve its growth at its level of ROIC.

On the basis of the explicating equations of ΔSP and DY, we can define TRS as follows:

$$\mathrm{TRS} = \Delta\mathrm{SP} + \mathrm{DY}$$

$$\mathrm{TRS} = \Delta R + \Delta\mathrm{PM} + \Delta\left(\frac{P}{\mathrm{Er}}\right) + \left(\frac{\mathrm{Er}}{P}\right) - \left(\frac{g_n}{\mathrm{ROIC}} \cdot \frac{\mathrm{Er}}{P}\right)$$

And rearranging we have:

$$\mathrm{TRS} = \Delta R - \left(\frac{g_n}{\mathrm{ROIC}} \cdot \frac{\mathrm{Er}}{P}\right) + \Delta\mathrm{PM} + \left(\frac{\mathrm{Er}}{P}\right) + \Delta\left(\frac{P}{\mathrm{Er}}\right) \tag{7.25}$$

Where:

1. $\Delta R - \left(\frac{g_n}{\mathrm{ROIC}} \cdot \frac{\mathrm{Er}}{P}\right)$: it is the value generated from revenue growth net of the capital required to grow at the firm's projected ROIC.
2. $\Delta\mathrm{PM}$: it is the impact of the change in profit margin.
3. $\left(\frac{\mathrm{Er}}{P}\right)$: it is what TRS would have been, without any growth and profit margin improvements often called the Earning Yield or Zero Growth Return.
4. $\Delta\left(\frac{P}{\mathrm{Er}}\right)$: it is the changes in shareholders' expectations on company performance, measured by the change in its (P/Er) or other multiple earnings.

In TRS a key role is played by investors' expectations. Note that a firm whose TRS has consistently outperformed the market will reach a point in which it will no longer be able to satisfy expectations reflected in its share price. From that point onwards, TRS will be lower than it was in the past, even if the firm may still be creating value.

7.4 Net Income Growth Rate

The expected growth rate in Net Income (g_{NI}) can be defined on the basis of two variables: (1) Retention Rate on Net Income (RR) and (2) Return on Equity (ROE).

The Retention Rate on Net Income (RR) measures the percentage of earnings retained by the firm. It is equal to the ratio between Retained Earnings (RE) and Net Income (NI) as follows:

$$\mathrm{RR} = \frac{\mathrm{RE}}{\mathrm{NI}} \tag{7.26}$$

The Growth Rate (g_{NI}) is equal to the product between the Retention Ratio on Net Income (RR) and the Return on Equity (ROE):

$$g_{NI} = RR \cdot ROE \quad \Rightarrow \quad \begin{array}{l} RR = \dfrac{g_{NI}}{ROE} \\ ROE = \dfrac{g_{NI}}{RR} \end{array} \tag{7.27}$$

Therefore, defined a level of Growth Rate (g_{NI}) to be achieved, it gets:

1. The higher the ROE, the lower can be the Retention Ratio (RR).
2. The lower the ROE, the higher can be the Retention Ratio (RR).

Generally, the relationship between Retention Ratio (RR), Return on Equity (ROE), and expected growth rate on Net Income (g_{NI}) is characterized by a direct proportion: if the company has a high Retention Ratio and a high Return on Equity, it will have a high Growth Rate.

Note that if we assume a constant Equity over time, the Growth Rate (g_{NI}) it is equal to the Growth of Earnings per Share (g_{ES}) as follows:

$$g_{ES} \equiv g_{NI} = RR \cdot ROE \tag{7.28}$$

On the contrary, if we remove this assumption, g_{NI} can be different from g_{ES}. Indeed, if the company issues new equity, and if the new investments increase the Net Income, the increase in the Earnings per Share is not the same because the shares are changed. In this case, the relationship between Net Income and Earnings per Share must be modified.

We can consider two main extensions.

The first extension is based on the ROE. The ROE can be substituted in the equation by considering the joint effects of ROI and Leverage:

$$ROE = [ROI + L \cdot (ROI - K_D)] \cdot (1 - t_c)$$

By replacing it gets:

$$g_{NI} = RR \cdot ROE = RR \cdot [[ROI + L \cdot (ROI - K_D)] \cdot (1 - t_c)] \tag{7.29}$$

In this case, the effects on Growth Rate of ROI and Leverage (L) can be analysed.

The second extension is based on the Retention Rate on Net Income (RR). It is possible to substitute RR with the Equity Reinvestment Rate (ER). It can be defined on the basis of equity reinvested in the business in form of Operating CapEx ($CAPEX_{OP}$), Net Working Capital (NWC), Debt reimbursement (DR), as follows:

$$ER = \frac{CAPEX_{OP} + NWC + DR}{NI} \tag{7.30}$$

Based on ER, the Growth Rate is equal to:

$$g_{\mathrm{NI}} = \mathrm{ER} \cdot \mathrm{ROE} = \left(\frac{\mathrm{CAPEX}_{\mathrm{OP}} + \mathrm{NWC} + \mathrm{DR}}{\mathrm{NI}} \right) \cdot \mathrm{ROE} \tag{7.31}$$

If we consider these two extensions jointly, it gets:

$$\begin{aligned} g_{\mathrm{NI}} &= \mathrm{ER} \cdot \mathrm{ROE} \\ &= \left(\frac{\mathrm{CAPEX}_{\mathrm{OP}} + \mathrm{NWC} + \mathrm{DR}}{\mathrm{NI}} \right) \cdot [[\mathrm{ROI} + L \cdot (\mathrm{ROI} - K_D)] \cdot (1 - t_c)] \end{aligned} \tag{7.32}$$

Investment Analysis Rules

8

8.1 Investment Decisions

An investment refers to the purchase of long-lived asset or simpler asset that can be tangible, intangible, or financial.

The investment is defined in terms of dynamic of cash-in (inflows) and cash-out (outflows) related to the asset: cash-out is committed today is realized in the expectation of receiving cash-in in the future time that are in form of cash earnings generated by the use of the asset that represent jointly:

- a return *of* the investment: is the repayment of the principal
- a satisfactory return *on* the investment: is the cash-in of interest payments received over the life of the investment.

If in the future the cash-in related to the cash earnings exceed the cash-out due to the initial investment, the investment is recovered (return of investment) and that some profit is earned (return on investment). Therefore, we can consider the investment as the purchase of an excepted future stream of cash-in.

Investments in the firm's assets can be done for several reasons. Among these, the main are the following:

1. *Replacement*: the aim of investment is to replace existing asset with more efficient one. In this case, the future expected cash-in are related to the cost saving deriving from lower operating costs, or the increase in profits due to the additional volume produced by the new asset, or both.
2. *Expansion*: the aim of investment is to build or acquire a new asset. In this case, the future expected cash-in are the cash profits from the goods and service produced thanks to the increase in productivity capacity due to the new asset.
3. *Cost reduction*: the aim of investment is to buy asset to perform an operation now done manually. The future expected cash-in are saving resulting from lower operating costs.

P. De Luca, *Corporate Finance*, Springer Texts in Business and Economics,
https://doi.org/10.1007/978-3-031-18300-3_8

4. *Specific asset*: the aim of investment is to purchase specific asset for a specific purpose. In this case, the choice often turns on which assets are expected to give the largest return on the investment.
5. *New Product*: the aim of investment is to produce a new product to add to the line. In this case, the choice turns on whether the expected cash-in from the sale of the new product are large enough to warrant the investment in asset and to cover the operating costs required by new product.

In these cases, and generally in all cases in which firm decides to make investments we can use several tools of investment analysis. Among these, the most used are:

1. Net Present Value (NPV)
2. Internal Rate of Return (IRR)

These methods are usually used jointly in the analysis of the investment in firm's asset.

8.2 Net Present Value (NPV)

All investments are characterized by two types of amounts:

1. The first is the cash-out due for the acquisition of the asset that it is usually made in a lump sum at the beginning of the project. The time in which the investment is realized it is usually defined "Today" or "Time Zero" for analytical purpose.
2. The second is the stream of cash-in expected as the result from the investment over a period of future years.

These two cash-flow streams, cash-out and cash-in, cannot be compared directly because they are related to different times. To make a valid comparison, we must bring the amounts involved to equivalent values at the same point in time that is the Time Zero. Therefore, we must convert the stream of the expected future cash-in to their present value equivalents and then to compare them to the initial cash-out of the investment. This process is called discounting. The baseline concept of the Present Value (PV) is that a dollar received in the future is less valuable than a dollar received today.

The rate at which the expected future cash-in is discounted is called the Discount Rate. The difference between the Present Value (PV) of the expected future cash-in and the cash-out of the investment is called the Net Present Value (NPV). The NPV is the baseline instrument to evaluate the profitability of an investment.

The Present Value (PV) of the future expected cash-in $\left(\overline{\mathrm{CI}}_t\right)$ discounted at Interest Rate (i) is equal to:

$$\mathrm{PV} = \sum_{t=1}^{n} \frac{\overline{\mathrm{CI}_t}}{(1+i)^t} \tag{8.1}$$

Assume a growth rate (g_n) in each period considered. In this case, the Present Value (PV) is equal to:

$$\mathrm{PV} = \frac{\mathrm{CI}_0}{(1+i)^1} + \frac{\mathrm{CI}_0(1+g_n)^1}{(1+i)^2} + \frac{\mathrm{CI}_0(1+g_n)^2}{(1+i)^3} + \ldots + \frac{\mathrm{CI}_0(1+g_n)^{n-1}}{(1+i)^n}$$

If we assume that the growth rate (g_n) is constant over time, and then equal in each period considered, the equation can be generalized as follows:

$$\mathrm{PV} = \sum_{t=1}^{\infty} \frac{\mathrm{CF}_0(1+g_n)^{t-1}}{(1+i)^t} \tag{8.2}$$

With regard to the growth rate (g_n) and the discount interest rate (i), if:

- $g_n > i$: the expected cash-in $(\overline{\mathrm{CI}_t})$ grow faster than they are discounted, and then the Present Value (PV) increases over time.
- $g_n < i$: the expected cash-in $(\overline{\mathrm{CI}_t})$ grow slower than they are discounted, and then the Present Value (PV) decreases over time.

Based on the Present Value (PV) of the future expected cash-in, we can measure the Net Present Value (NPV) of the investment: it is equal to the difference between the Present Value (PV) of future expected cash-in $(\overline{\mathrm{CI}_t})$ and the cash-out (CO) (it is a negative number) as follows:

$$\mathrm{NPV} = \mathrm{CO}_{(t_0)} + \sum_{t=1}^{n} \frac{\overline{\mathrm{CI}_t}}{(1+i)^t} \tag{8.3}$$

If the investment is characterized by several cash-out (CO_t) in different future time (they are negative numbers), we have to compute the present value of the cash-out. In this case, even the cash-out are future and then expected, they are certain in the amount and in the time of realization. Consequently, we can discount them at the Risk-free Rate ($i = R_f$), as follows:

$$\mathrm{NPV} = \sum_{t=0}^{n} \frac{\mathrm{CO}_t}{(1+R_f)^t} + \sum_{t=1}^{n} \frac{\overline{\mathrm{CI}_t}}{(1+i)^t} \tag{8.4}$$

The NPV is an amount. Consequently, if:

(a) NPV is positive $\left(\mathrm{NPV} > 0 \rightarrow \sum_{t=0}^{n} \frac{\mathrm{CO}_t}{(1+R_f)^t} < \sum_{t=1}^{n} \frac{\overline{\mathrm{CI}_t}}{(1+i)^t}\right)$, the investment is profitable and it is all the more profitable the higher its positive number.

(b) NPV is negative $\left(\text{NPV} < 0 \rightarrow \sum_{t=0}^{n} \frac{\text{CO}_t}{(1+R_f)^t} > \sum_{t=1}^{n} \frac{\text{CI}_t}{(1+i)^t}\right)$, the investment is not profitable and it is all the less profitable the higher its negative number.

Considering that the amount of investments is known and then there are known the cash-out (CO_t), the right application of the Net Present Value (NPV) requires the right definition of the three variables: (1) period of investment (t), (2) expected cash-in $\left(\overline{\text{CI}_t}\right)$, and (3) the Discount Interest Rate (i).

Investment Period (t)

The investment period defines the economic life of the investment. It is the number of years (t) in which the investment is expected to generate cash-in. Economic life can rarely be estimated exactly. Nevertheless, it is important that the best possible estimate is made, because the economic life has a significant effect on the compute of the Net Present Value (NPV).

If we expected cash-in for an indefinitely long period, the economic life it is usually set at a specified maximum number of years that it usually is 10, 15, or 20.

In any case, to the increase of the years we have two main problems:

(a) The uncertainty of cash-in estimates increases to the increase of the years considered.
(b) The present value of cash-in for distant years is so low that the amount of these cash-in has no significant effect on the compute.

Expected Cash-in $\left(\overline{\text{CI}_t}\right)$

They are the result of the investment. Generally, the earnings from an investment is the additional amounts of expected cash-in due to the investment as compared with what the cash-in would be if the investment were not made.

One of the problems concern the inflation: if we expected the increase of inflation in the future years, the question is whether future cash-in should therefore be restated in terms of current (time zero) purchasing power before discounting them. Since the Discount Interest Rate already includes an inflation component, he expected cash-in must be considered at a nominal value.

Discount Interest Rate (i)

The Discount Interest Rate (i) is the sum of two parameters:

1. *Price of time*: it is measured on the basis of the Risk-free rate ($R_{f.}$)
2. *Premium risk*: it is related to the risk of investment (P_r) with regard to the effective realization of the future expected cash-in.

Therefore, expected future cash-in $\left(\overline{\text{CI}_t}\right)$ must be discount at an interest rate equal to the sum of Risk-free Rate (R_f) and the Premium risk (P_r) so that:

$$i = R_f + P_r \quad (8.5)$$

The Discount Interest Rate (i) represents the Cost of Capital for the firm. In this case, the Discount Interest Rate measures the risk of the entire firm and then the average risk related to all investments of the firm and not to the specific investment considered.

In this contest, we consider that the Discount Interest Rate (i) measures the only risk of the investment. Therefore, it measures the risk related to the likely realization of the expected cash-in stream of the investment.

The Discount Interest Rate (i) has a direct impact on the Net Present Value (NPV). The higher (lower) the Discount Interest Rate (i), the lower (higher) the Present Value (PV) of the future expected cash-in streams $(\overline{CI_t})$ and then the lower (higher) the Net Present Value (NPV) of the investment.

Note that the risk related to future expected cash-in can be considered on the basis of two different and alternative approaches:

(a) *Risk is considered in the estimation of Cash-in*: in this case, the expected future Cash-in $(\overline{CI_t})$ are "adjusted" on the basis of the probability of their future realization and the interest rate measures only the price of time, so that $i = R_f$.
(b) *Risk is considered in the Discount Interest Rate* (i): in this case, the expected future Cash-in $(\overline{CI_t})$ are not adjusted for the probability of their achievement and then the interest rate measures the price of time plus the premium risk, so that: $i = R_f + P_r$.

8.3 Internal Rate of Return (IRR)

The Internal Rate of Return (IRR) is the interest rate at which we discount the future expected cash-in to obtain the initial cash-out. Then, the IRR is the discount interest rate of the expected future Cash-in stream $(\overline{CI_t})$ at which the cash-out (CO_t) are equal to the present value of expected Cash-in, and then the Net Present Value (NPV) is equal to zero. Formally:

$$\text{IRR} : \text{NPV} = 0 \quad \rightarrow \quad CO_t = \sum_{t=1}^{n} \frac{\overline{CI_t}}{(1 + \text{IRR})^t} \quad (8.6)$$

If the investment is characterized by several cash-out (CO_t) in different future time, we need to compute the present value of the cash-out. In this case, even the cash-out are future and then expected, they are certain in the amount and in the time even if they refer to the future, we can be discounted at the Risk-free Rate (R_f). In this contest, the IRR is the discount interest rate of the expected Cash-in $(\overline{CI_t})$ that makes the Net Present Value (NPV) equal to zero, as follows:

$$\text{IRR}:\text{NPV}=0 \quad \rightarrow \quad \sum_{t=1}^{n} \frac{\text{CO}_t}{(1+R_f)^t} = \sum_{t=1}^{n} \frac{\overline{\text{CI}_t}}{(1+\text{IRR})^t} \tag{8.7}$$

In both cases, the IRR is the equilibrium discount interest rate because it makes the Net Present Value (NPV) equal to zero. Denote with NPV = 0, if:

(a) IRR > IRR*: the NPV is negative and the investment is not profitable. Therefore, the higher the IRR, the less profitable is the investment.
(b) IRR < IRR*: the NPV is positive and the investment is profitable. Therefore, the lower the IRR, the more profitable is the investment.

Therefore, while the Net Present Value (NPV) measures the profitability of the investment on the basis of absolute number, the Internal Rate of Return (IRR) measures the profitability of the investment on the basis of the discount interest rate.

To well-understand, assume an investment that requires an initial Cash-out equal to the amount A and expected Cash-in $\left(\overline{\text{CI}_t}\right)$ stream for 3 years, so that:

$$A = \sum_{t=1}^{3} \frac{\overline{\text{CI}_t}}{(1+\text{IRR}^*)^t} \quad \rightarrow \quad A = \frac{\overline{\text{CI}_1}}{(1+\text{IRR}^*)^1} + \frac{\overline{\text{CI}_2}}{(1+\text{IRR}^*)^2} + \frac{\overline{\text{CI}_3}}{(1+\text{IRR}^*)^3}$$

The computation of the value of the IRR* can be realized by using the Newton's algorithm.

Set α equal to:

$$\alpha = \frac{1}{1+\text{IRR}}$$

so that we can rewrite the equation as follows:

$$A = \overline{\text{CI}_1} \cdot \alpha + \overline{\text{CI}_2} \cdot \alpha^2 + \overline{\text{CI}_3} \cdot \alpha^3$$

$$A - \overline{\text{CI}_1} \cdot \alpha - \overline{\text{CI}_2} \cdot \alpha^2 - \overline{\text{CI}_3} \cdot \alpha^3 = 0$$

Define the function $F(\alpha)$ as follows:

$$F(\alpha) = A - \overline{C_1} \cdot \alpha - \overline{C_2} \cdot \alpha^2 - \overline{C_3} \cdot \alpha^3 \quad \rightarrow \quad F(\alpha) = 0$$

A polynomial of degree n can have n solutions. By using a well-known theorem (if in a polynomial of degree n the coefficient signs change one time, than the polynomial has one solution real and positive also if it is of degree n), it is possible to say that IRR exists and is one.

The aim is to find the zero of the function $F(\alpha)$ and therefore the value of α at which it is done.

The first derivative of the function $F(\alpha)$ with respect to the variable α is equal to:

$$\frac{\partial F(\alpha)}{\partial \alpha} = -\overline{C_1} - 2\alpha\overline{C_2} - 3\alpha^2\overline{C_3}$$

Note that by considering a generic α_s, the first derivative can be approximated to the incremental ratio as follows:

$$\frac{\partial F(\alpha_s)}{\partial \alpha_s} \simeq \frac{F(\alpha_{s+1}) - F(\alpha_s)}{\alpha_{s+1} - \alpha_s}$$

and then:

$$\lim_{\alpha_{s+1} \to \alpha_s} \frac{F(\alpha_{s+1}) - F(\alpha_s)}{\alpha_{s+1} - \alpha_s} = \frac{F(\alpha_s)}{\alpha_s} = \frac{\partial F(\alpha_s)}{\partial \alpha_s}$$

We have to find the IRR able to have the function $F(\alpha)$ equal to zero. Therefore, it is possible to assume $F(\alpha_{s+1}) = 0$ that is the objective value. Indeed, in our case, only for one value of α the function $F(\alpha)$ is equal to zero, so that we can assume that $F(\alpha_{s+1}) = 0$:

$$\frac{\partial F(\alpha_s)}{\partial \alpha_s} = \frac{-F(\alpha_s)}{\alpha_{s+1} - \alpha_s}$$

and by solving for α_{s+1}, it gets:

$$\alpha_{s+1} = \alpha_s - \frac{F(\alpha_s)}{\frac{\partial F(\alpha_s)}{\partial \alpha_s}}$$

by denoting the first derivative as $\frac{\partial F(\alpha_s)}{\partial \alpha_s} = F'(\alpha_s)$, we can simplify as follows:

$$\alpha_{s+1} = \alpha_s - \frac{F(\alpha_s)}{F'(\alpha_s)} \tag{8.8}$$

The equation states the relationship between α_{s+1} and α_s. It is a numerical algorithm able to define interactively the value of IRR which makes the function $F(\alpha) = 0$. The procedure can be summarized as follows:

Step 1: assign to a α any arbitrary value (a number) α_1 so that $\alpha = \alpha_1$. In this case, it gets:

$$\alpha_1 = \frac{1}{1 + \mathrm{IRR}_1}$$

By considering that α_1 is a number, it is possible to compute the IRR_1 as follows:

$$\mathrm{IRR}_1 = \frac{1}{\alpha_1} - 1$$

Step 2: introduce the value (number) α_1 in the function $F(\alpha)$ and verify if it reaches a value near to zero $F(\alpha) \simeq 0$ by using a convergence criterion as follows:

$$\text{if } |F(\alpha)| < \varepsilon \text{ then } F(\alpha) \simeq 0$$

where ε is a positive value (number) small enough to make that the $F(\alpha)$ is near to zero.

Therefore, by introducing the value (number) of α_1 in the function, if $|F(\alpha_1)| < \varepsilon$ the value of α_1 satisfies the convergence criterion and therefore $F(\alpha_1) \simeq 0$. Therefore, the corresponding interest rate IRR_1 is the IRR^* sought. On the contrary, if $F(\alpha_1) \neq 0$, we move onto step 3.

Step 3: calculate the first derivative of the function $F(\alpha_1)$ in the point α_1 as follows:

$$\frac{\partial F(\alpha_1)}{\partial \alpha_1} = -\overline{C_1} - 2\alpha_1\overline{C_2} - 3\alpha_1^2\overline{C_3}$$

Step 4: calculate the new value (number) α_2 on the basis of the α_1 as follows:

$$\alpha_2 = \alpha_1 - \frac{F(\alpha_1)}{F'(\alpha_1)}$$

where $F'(\alpha_1) = \frac{\partial F(\alpha_1)}{\partial \alpha_1}$

Step 5: introduce the value (number) α_2 in the function $F(\alpha)$ and if the convergence criterion is respected, so that:

$$\text{if } |F(\alpha_2)| < \varepsilon \text{ then } F(\alpha_2) \simeq 0$$

the α_2 is correct and the corresponding IRR_2 is the IRR^* sought and the procedure is closed. On the contrary, if $F(\alpha_2) \neq 0$, we move onto step 3 again with the definition of the first derivative of the function with α_2 $F'(\alpha_2)$, and the new definition of the α_3 in step 4 and its validation in step 5. The procedure continues interactively until the convergence criterion is respected in step 5.

Part II

Risk and Return in the Capital Markets

Mean-Variance Portfolio Analysis 9

9.1 Portfolio Expected Return

The mean-variance approach is the most widely used in the portfolio selection (Markowitz, 1952; Tobin, 1958).

The portfolio selection is based on two variables:

1. Expected value of the portfolio return ($\overline{R_P}$)
2. Variance of the expected portfolio returns (σ_P^2) measuring the portfolio's risk.

The efficient portfolio must satisfy the Pareto optimal condition. In this sense, it is not possible to improve one objective without worsening the other. Consequently, the investor prefers the portfolio able to *maximize its expected return* for a given level of variance or to *minimize its variance* for a given level of expected return.

The mean-variance approach to the problem of portfolio selection is characterized by two main advantages: first, it does not require specification about probability distribution; second, it is simple and intuitive because it is only based on the mean and variance. Consequently, the portfolio selection in the mean-variance approach can be considered solely a problem of definition of the weights to be assigned to each asset in the portfolio because the statistical characteristics of each asset (mean, variance, and covariance) are known. The main limit is that this approach neglects a lot of relevant information about distribution probability.

The portfolio expected return is equal to the weighted average of the expected return of assets in the portfolio. The weight applied to each asset's expected return is equal to the fraction of wealth invested in it with respect to total wealth invested in the portfolio.

The analysis of the portfolio expected return can be realized by considering first a portfolio of two assets only and by generalizing to a portfolio of N assets after.

P. De Luca, *Corporate Finance*, Springer Texts in Business and Economics,
https://doi.org/10.1007/978-3-031-18300-3_9

9.1.1 Portfolio of Two Assets

Consider a portfolio of two assets only: Asset 1 and Asset 2. Assume the total wealth invested in the portfolio is equal to w where the wealth invested in the Asset 1 is equal to w_1 and the wealth invested in the Asset 2 is equal to w_2. The weight of Asset 1 and Asset 2 is equal to α_1 and α_2, respectively, as follows:

$$w = w_1 + w_2 \quad \rightarrow \quad \alpha_1 = \frac{w_1}{w}; \alpha_2 = \frac{w_2}{w} \quad \rightarrow \quad \alpha_1 + \alpha_2 = 1 \tag{9.1}$$

We use the term *expected value* $E(.)$ to refer an average and we use a bar over a symbol to indicate the expected value. Therefore, we can indicate the expected value of j-th asset alternatively as $\overline{R_j}$ or $E(R_j)$.

Before to start the analysis, it is useful to always keep in mind two main properties of expected value:

1. The expected value of the sum of two returns is equal to the sum of the expected value of each return, so that: $E(R_1 + R_2) = \overline{R_1} + \overline{R_2}$.
2. The expected value of a constant C times a return is equal to the constant times the expected return, so that: $E[C(R_1)] = C\overline{R_1}$.

Therefore, if the expected return of Asset 1 and Asset 2 is $\overline{R_1}$ and $\overline{R_2}$, respectively, on the basis of their weights (α_1 and α_2), the expected return of the portfolio $\overline{R_P}$ is equal to:

$$\overline{R_P} = \alpha_1 \overline{R_1} + \alpha_2 \overline{R_2} \tag{9.2}$$

The equation states as the expected return on the portfolio $\left(\overline{R_P}\right)$ is a simple weighted average of the expected returns on the individual assets. The weights applied to each return is the fraction of the portfolio invested in that asset and they add to 1.

The equation can be deeply understood if we rearrange it on the basis of two assumptions:

- *Assumption 1).* Define the constraint in terms of α and $(1 - \alpha)$ and assign to α the wealth invested in the Asset 2 so that $\alpha = \alpha_2$ and assign to $(1 - \alpha)$ the wealth invested in Asset 1 so that $\alpha_1 = 1 - \alpha$.
- *Assumption 2).* Define the Asset 2 riskier than Asset 1. Consequently, the variance and mean of the Asset 2 are greater than Asset 1 (on the basis of the direct relationship between risk and return: the higher risk, the higher return).

We can formalize the two assumptions as follows:

$$\text{Assumption 1}: \begin{array}{l} \alpha_2 = \alpha \\ \alpha_1 = 1 - \alpha \end{array} \quad \rightarrow \quad \alpha + (1 - \alpha) = 1$$

Assumption 2 : Asset 2 is riskier than Asset 1 $\rightarrow$ $\begin{array}{c}\sigma_2^2 > \sigma_1^2\ (\sigma_2 > \sigma_1)\\ \overline{R_2} > \overline{R_1}\end{array}$ (9.3)

On the basis of these two assumptions, we can rearrange the equation as follows:

$$\overline{R_P} = (1-\alpha)\overline{R_1} + \alpha\,\overline{R_2}$$

and then:

$$\overline{R_P} = \overline{R_1} + \alpha\left(\overline{R_2} - \overline{R_1}\right) \tag{9.4}$$

The equation states that:

1. There is a linear relationship between the portfolio expected return $\left(\overline{R_P}\right)$ and the assets' expected returns of the two assets $\left(\overline{R_1};\overline{R_2}\right)$.
2. The slope of the straight-line $\left(\overline{R_2} - \overline{R_1}\right)$ is always positive because Asset 2 is riskier than Asset 1 and consequently $\overline{R_2} > \overline{R_1}$ on the basis of direct relationship risk-return.
3. The distance between the expected returns of the two assets, as measured by the difference $\left(\overline{R_2} - \overline{R_1}\right)$, is a constant because the statistical characteristics of the assets are known.
4. The portfolio expected return $\left(\overline{R_P}\right)$ is the function of the wealth (α) and then of wealth invested in the riskier asset (Asset 2); consequently, the higher the wealth (α) invested in Asset 2, the higher the portfolio expected return.
5. The weights assigned to the two assets ($\alpha_1; \alpha_2$ and then $\alpha; 1 - \alpha$) are the only unknown variables. Consequently, the definition of the optimal portfolio can be defined as the choice of the weights to assign to the two assets.

Graphically, the equation draws a straight-line in the plan $\left(\alpha;\overline{R_P}\right)$ as in Fig. 9.1. It is relevant to note that the value of α can change between 0 and 1 or over 0 and 1, on the basis of short selling. Specifically, if the short selling is:

1. *Allowed*: the value of α changes beyond zero and over one ($\alpha < 0; \alpha > 1$). Specifically:
   a) $\alpha < 0$: short selling of Asset 2 and buying of Asset 1. It is a risk hedging because Asset 2 is riskier than Asset 1.
   b) $\alpha > 1$: short selling of Asset 1 and buying of Asset 2. It is a speculative operation because Asset 2 is riskier than Asset 1.
2. *Not allowed*: the value of α can change between 0 and 1 ($0 \leq \alpha \leq 1$). Specifically:
   a) $\alpha = 0$: wealth is invested only in the Asset 1.
   b) $\alpha = 1$: wealth is invested only in the Asset 2 (riskier asset).

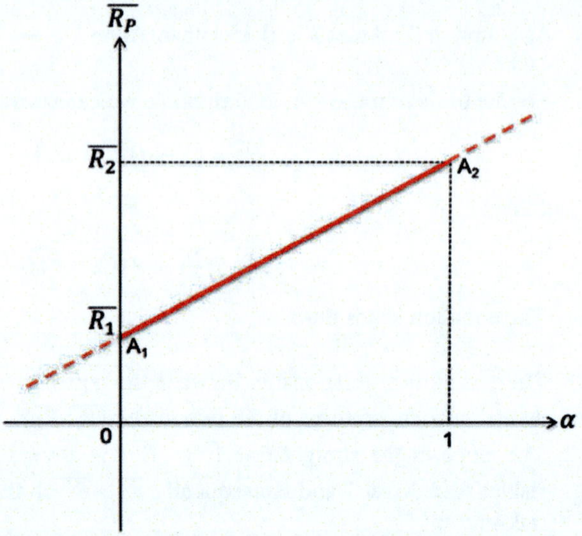

Fig. 9.1 Portfolio expected return as a function of wealth invested in the riskier asset (α)

9.1.2 Portfolio of *N* Assets

We can generalize by considering a portfolio of N assets. The portfolio expected return $\left(\overline{R_P}\right)$ is equal to the weighted average of the expected returns of the assets in portfolio. Their weights are equal to the part of wealth invested in each one. Specifically, by considering a total wealth invested in the portfolio (w) the weight of k-th assets (α_k) is equal to part of wealth invested in it (w_k) on total wealth, as follows:

$$\alpha_k = \frac{w_k}{w}$$

The portfolio expected return $\left(\overline{R_P}\right)$ is equal to:

$$\overline{R_P} = E\left(\sum_{k=1}^{n} \alpha_k R_k\right)$$

By considering that the expected value of the sum of various returns is the sum of the expected values and the expected value of a constant C times a return is equal to the constant times the expected return, we have:

$$\overline{R_P} = \sum_{k=1}^{n} \alpha_k E(R_k)$$

and then:

$$\overline{R_P} = \sum_{k=1}^{n} \alpha_k \overline{R_K} \qquad (9.5)$$

9.2 Portfolio Variance: Two Assets

The portfolio variance measures the variance of the expected portfolio return. It cannot be simply computed on the basis of weighted average variance of the assets in the portfolio. It depends on the covariance, and therefore correlations between the expected return of all assets in the portfolio considered in a pair.

Similar to the analysis of the portfolio expected return, the analysis of the portfolio variance can be realized by considering first a portfolio of two assets only and by generalizing to a portfolio of N assets after.

Consider a portfolio of two assets only: Asset 1 and Asset 2. Their returns are R_1 and R_2 and their weights in the portfolio are α_1 and α_2, respectively.

By considering that the variance of Asset 1 and Asset 2, respectively, is:

$$\sigma_1^2 = E\left(R_1 - \overline{R_1}\right)^2$$

$$\sigma_2^2 = E\left(R_2 - \overline{R_2}\right)^2$$

the variance of portfolio $\left(\sigma_P^2\right)$ is equal to the expected value of the squared deviations of the return on the portfolio from the mean return on the portfolio, as follows:

$$\sigma_P^2 = E\left(R_p - \overline{R_P}\right)^2$$

and then:

$$\sigma_P^2 = E\left[\alpha_1 R_1 + \alpha_2 R_2 - \left(\alpha_1 \overline{R_1} + \alpha_2 \overline{R_2}\right)\right]^2$$

By solving, we have:

$$\sigma_P^2 = E\left[\alpha_1\left(R_1 - \overline{R_1}\right) + \alpha_2\left(R_2 - \overline{R_2}\right)\right]^2$$

$$\sigma_P^2 = E\left[\left(\alpha_1\left(R_1 - \overline{R_1}\right)\right)^2 + \left(\alpha_2\left(R_2 - \overline{R_2}\right)\right)^2 + 2\left(\alpha_1\left(R_1 - \overline{R_1}\right)\right)\left(\alpha_2\left(R_2 - \overline{R_2}\right)\right)\right]$$

$$\sigma_P^2 = E\left[\alpha_1^2\left(R_1 - \overline{R_1}\right)^2 + \alpha_2^2\left(R_2 - \overline{R_2}\right)^2 + 2\alpha_1\alpha_2\left(R_1 - \overline{R_1}\right)\left(R_2 - \overline{R_2}\right)\right]$$

Since (a) the expected value of the sum of the returns is equal to the sum of the expected value of each return and (b) the expected value of the return for a constant is equal to the constant for the expected value of the return, we have:

$$\sigma_P^2 = \alpha_1^2 E\left[\left(R_1 - \overline{R_1}\right)^2\right] + \alpha_2^2 E\left[\left(R_2 - \overline{R_2}\right)^2\right] + 2\alpha_1\alpha_2 E\left[\left(R_1 - \overline{R_1}\right)\left(R_2 - \overline{R_2}\right)\right]$$

The first and the second term are the variance of the Asset 1 (σ_1^2) and Asset 2 (σ_2^2), respectively, and the last term is the covariance of the two assets $(\sigma_{12} = E[(R_1 - \overline{R_1})(R_2 - \overline{R_2})])$. Therefore, we can rewrite the equation as follows:

$$\sigma_P^2 = \alpha_1^2\sigma_1^2 + \alpha_2^2\sigma_2^2 + 2\alpha_1\alpha_2\sigma_{12} \tag{9.6}$$

The covariance plays a key role in the portfolio's variance. It measures how returns on assets move together. Indeed, if two assets have positive or negative deviations at similar times, the covariance is a large positive number; on the contrary, if they have the positive and negative deviations at dissimilar times, the covariance is negative. Finally, if the positive and negative deviations of the two assets are unrelated, the covariance tends to be zero.

It is useful to standardize the covariance by defining the last term of the equation in terms of correlation coefficient. It is useful because, while the covariance indicates the presence or absence of a linear relationship between the variables, the correlation coefficient measures the intensity of this relationship. The correlation coefficient (ρ_{12}) is equal to the ratio between covariance (σ_{12}) and the product of the standard deviation of two assets $(\sigma_1\sigma_2)$, as follows:

$$\rho_{12} = \frac{\sigma_{12}}{\sigma_1\sigma_2}$$

By dividing the covariance between the two assets (σ_{12}) by the product of the standard deviation of each asset $(\sigma_1\sigma_2)$ we have a variable, the correlation coefficient (ρ_{12}), with the same properties as the covariance but with range of -1 to $+1$. Therefore, the correlation coefficient does not change the properties of the covariance but simply scales it to have a value between -1 and $+1$ $(-1 < \rho_{12} < +1)$ so that:

1. $\rho_{12} = +1$: the two assets move in perfect union in the same direction.
2. $\rho_{12} = -1$: the two assets move perfectly together but in exactly opposite direction.
3. $\rho_{12} = 0$: the movements of the two assets are independent among them.

Therefore, we can express the covariance in terms of correlation coefficient as follows:

$$\sigma_{12} = \rho_{12}\sigma_1\sigma_2$$

Based on the correlation coefficient, we can rewrite the portfolio variance as follows:

$$\sigma_P^2 = \alpha_1^2\sigma_1^2 + \alpha_2^2\sigma_2^2 + 2\alpha_1\alpha_2\rho_{12}\sigma_1\sigma_2 \tag{9.7}$$

To well-understand the portfolio variance we can rearrange it on the basis of two assumptions defined for the analysis of the portfolio expected return as follows:

- *Assumption 1)*: $\alpha_2 = \alpha$ and then $\alpha_1 = 1 - \alpha$, so that $\alpha + (1 - \alpha) = 1$.
- *Assumption 2)*: Asset 2 is riskier than Asset 1 so that $\sigma_2^2 > \sigma_1^2$ and then $(\sigma_2 > \sigma_1)$ and consequently $\overline{R_2} > \overline{R_1}$.

On the basis of these two assumptions, the portfolio variance can be redefined as follows:

$$\sigma_P^2 = \alpha^2\sigma_2^2 + (1-\alpha)^2\sigma_1^2 + 2\alpha(1-\alpha)\sigma_{12} \tag{9.8}$$

and in terms of correlation coefficient (ρ_{12}) we have:

$$\sigma_P^2 = \alpha^2\sigma_2^2 + (1-\alpha)^2\sigma_1^2 + 2\alpha(1-\alpha)\rho_{12}\sigma_1\sigma_2 \tag{9.9}$$

The portfolio variance can be divided into two parts:

1. The first part is related to the square of the wealth invested in each asset multiplied by the relative variance. By considering that the statistical characteristics of each asset are known, the only choice of investor is the weight of wealth to invest in each one. Therefore, this part measures the weighted risk on the basis of the variance of each asset.
2. The second part is related to the correlation (or the covariance) among the expected returns of the two assets, multiplied by their respective weight and standard deviation. The key role is played by coefficient correlation. Indeed, the second part can increase or decrease the risk as defined in the first part, on the basis of the sign of the correlation coefficient.

It can be useful to explicate the portfolio variance as follows:

$$\sigma_P^2 = \alpha^2\sigma_2^2 + \sigma_1^2 + \alpha^2\sigma_1^2 - 2\alpha\sigma_1^2 + 2\alpha\rho_{12}\sigma_1\sigma_2 - 2\alpha^2\rho_{12}\sigma_1\sigma_2$$

The first derivative of the portfolio variance (σ_P^2) with respect to α (the wealth invested in the Asset 2 that is the riskier asset) is equal to:

$$\frac{\partial\sigma_P^2}{\partial\alpha} = 2\alpha\sigma_2^2 + 2\alpha\sigma_1^2 - 2\sigma_1^2 + 2\rho_{12}\sigma_1\sigma_2 - 4\alpha\rho_{12}\sigma_1\sigma_2$$

and then:

$$\frac{\partial\sigma_P^2}{\partial\alpha} = \alpha\sigma_2^2 + \alpha\sigma_1^2 - \sigma_1^2 + \rho_{12}\sigma_1\sigma_2 - 2\alpha\rho_{12}\sigma_1\sigma_2 \tag{9.10}$$

We can obtain the stationary point by placing the first derivative equal to zero and by solving for α as follows:

$$\frac{\partial\sigma_P^2}{\partial\alpha} = 0 \quad \rightarrow \quad \alpha\sigma_2^2 + \alpha\sigma_1^2 - \sigma_1^2 + \rho_{12}\sigma_1\sigma_2 - 2\alpha\rho_{12}\sigma_1\sigma_2 = 0$$

$$\alpha = \frac{\sigma_1^2 - \rho_{12}\sigma_1\sigma_2}{\sigma_2^2 + \sigma_1^2 - 2\rho_{12}\sigma_1\sigma_2} \tag{9.11}$$

The second derivative with respect to α is equal to:

$$\frac{\partial^2 \sigma_P^2}{\partial \alpha^2} = \sigma_2^2 + \sigma_1^2 - 2\rho_{12}\sigma_1\sigma_2 \tag{9.12}$$

The sign of the second derivative and the position of α are both the function of the sign of the correlation coefficient (ρ_{12}). Consider the two extreme cases:

(a) positive correlation ($\rho_{12} = +1$)
(b) negative correlation ($\rho_{12} = -1$).

9.2.1 Case 1: Portfolio of Two Assets—Perfect Positive Correlation

In case of perfect positive correlation ($\rho_{12} = +1$), the sign of the second derivative is positive as follows:

$$\frac{\partial^2 \sigma_P^2}{\partial \alpha^2} = \sigma_2^2 + \sigma_1^2 - 2\sigma_1\sigma_2 = (\sigma_2 - \sigma_1)^2 \quad \rightarrow \quad \frac{\partial^2 \sigma_P^2}{\partial \alpha^2} > 0 \tag{9.13}$$

The second derivative is always positive because σ_2 is higher than σ_1 since the Asset 2 is riskier than the Asset 1 so that $\sigma_2 > \sigma_1$.

Therefore, the curve is convex and the stationary point defined is a minimum point of the curve. Consequently, α is the part of wealth to be invested in the riskier asset (Asset 2) to minimize the portfolio variance and therefore portfolio risk.

The position of α with regard to its abscissa is the function of the sign of the correlation coefficient. In this case, α is negative as follows:

$$\alpha = \frac{\sigma_1^2 - \rho_{12}\sigma_1\sigma_2}{\sigma_2^2 + \sigma_1^2 - 2\rho_{12}\sigma_1\sigma_2}$$

and then for $\rho_{12} = +1$, it gets:

$$\alpha = \frac{\sigma_1^2 - \sigma_1\sigma_2}{\sigma_2^2 + \sigma_1^2 - 2\sigma_1\sigma_2} = \frac{-\sigma_1(\sigma_2 - \sigma_1)}{(\sigma_2 - \sigma_1)^2} = -\frac{\sigma_1}{(\sigma_2 - \sigma_1)} \quad \Rightarrow \quad \alpha < 0 \tag{9.14}$$

Since $\sigma_2 - \sigma_1 > 0$ because $\sigma_2 > \sigma_1$ (Asset 2 is riskier than Asset 1), the ratio is always negative.

The negative sign of α ($\alpha < 0$) implies that in case of positive correlation ($\rho_{12} = +1$) between the expected returns of the two assets, the portfolio variance is minimized by a negative value of investment in the riskier asset that can be achieved only by short selling. We can represent it as in Fig. 9.2.

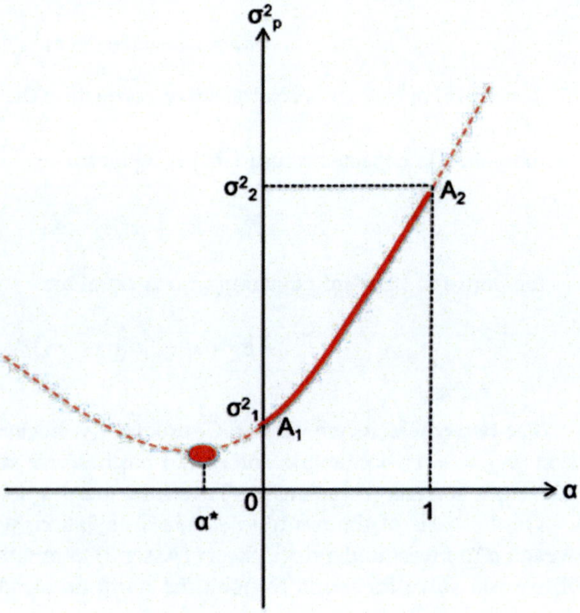

Fig. 9.2 Portfolio variance of two assets with positive correlation

We can shift from the variance to the standard deviation of the portfolio (σ_P). The standard deviation is the square root of the variance.

In case of perfect positive correlation ($\rho_{12} = +1$), the portfolio's variance is equal to:

$$\sigma_P^2 = \alpha^2\sigma_2^2 + (1-\alpha)^2\sigma_1^2 + 2\alpha(1-\alpha)(+1)\sigma_1\sigma_2$$

and then:

$$\sigma_P^2 = \alpha^2\sigma_2^2 + (1-\alpha)^2\sigma_1^2 + 2\alpha(1-\alpha)\sigma_1\sigma_2$$

Since the term in square brackets has the form of $x^2 + 2xy + y^2$ that is equal to $(x + y)^2$, we can rewrite the portfolio's variance as follows:

$$\sigma_P^2 = [\alpha\sigma_2 + (1-\alpha)\sigma_1]^2$$

or in equivalent terms:

$$\sigma_P^2 = [\sigma_1 + \alpha(\sigma_2 - \sigma_1)]^2$$

The difference between σ_2 and σ_1 is always positive ($(\sigma_2 - \sigma_1) > 0$) because Asset 2 is riskier than Asset 1 so that $\sigma_2 > \sigma_1$. Then the argument of the square is always positive. Since the standard deviation of the portfolio (σ_P) is equal to the positive square root of the variance, we can shift directly from the portfolio's variance to its standard deviation as follows:

$$\sigma_P = \sigma_1 + \alpha(\sigma_2 - \sigma_1) \tag{9.15}$$

Therefore, in case of perfect positive correlation the ($\rho_{12} = +1$):

- the portfolio expected return $(\overline{R_P})$ is equal to:

$$\overline{R_P} = \overline{R_1} + \alpha(\overline{R_2} - \overline{R_1})$$

- the portfolio standard deviation (σ_P) is equal to:

$$\sigma_P = \sigma_1 + \alpha(\sigma_2 - \sigma_1)$$

The two equations are similar. Consequently, in case of perfect positive correlation ($\rho_{12} = +1$), both return and risk of portfolio are simply linear combinations of the return and risk of each asset. Therefore, there is not diversification effect.

On the basis of the portfolio standard deviation, we can define the amount of wealth α to invest in the riskier asset (Asset 2) to minimize the portfolio risk. To do it, we can solve for α and to point the portfolio standard deviation equal to zero ($\sigma_P = 0$), as follows:

$$\alpha = \frac{\sigma_P - \sigma_1}{\sigma_2 - \sigma_1}$$

$$\sigma_P = 0 \quad \rightarrow \quad \alpha = \frac{-\sigma_1}{\sigma_2 - \sigma_1} \quad \rightarrow \quad \alpha < 0 \tag{9.16}$$

Since $(\sigma_2 - \sigma_1) > 0$ because Asset 2 is riskier than Asset 1 so that $\sigma_2 > \sigma_1$, the denominator is always positive and then α is negative ($\alpha < 0$). It implies that the portfolio with minimum risk can be achieved by short sales only.

On the basis of the α we can define the portfolio expected return $(\overline{R_P})$ as follows:

$$\overline{R_P} = \overline{R_1} + \alpha(\overline{R_2} - \overline{R_1}) = \overline{R_1} + \left(\frac{\sigma_P - \sigma_1}{\sigma_2 - \sigma_1}\right)(\overline{R_2} - \overline{R_1})$$

and rearranging, it gets:

$$\overline{R_P} = \overline{R_1}\left[1 - \left(\frac{\sigma_P - \sigma_1}{\sigma_2 - \sigma_1}\right)\right] + \overline{R_2}\left(\frac{\sigma_P - \sigma_1}{\sigma_2 - \sigma_1}\right)$$

and:

$$\overline{R_P} = \left[\overline{R_1} - \sigma_1\left(\frac{\overline{R_2} - \overline{R_1}}{\sigma_2 - \sigma_1}\right)\right] + \sigma_P\left(\frac{\overline{R_2} - \overline{R_1}}{\sigma_2 - \sigma_1}\right) \tag{9.17}$$

The equation has three relevant implications:

1. Since Asset 2 is riskier than the Asset 1, it implies that $\sigma_2 - \sigma_1 > 0$ and $\overline{R_2} - \overline{R_1} > 0$ and then $\frac{\overline{R_2} - \overline{R_1}}{\sigma_2 - \sigma_1} > 0$.

2. The portfolio expected return $\left(\overline{R_P}\right)$ is a linear function of the portfolio standard deviation (σ_P) where the statistical characteristics of the two assets $\left(\overline{R_1};\sigma_1;\overline{R_2};\sigma_2\right)$ are known.
3. It draws a straight-line in the plan $\left(\sigma_P;\overline{R_P}\right)$ with intercept equal to $\left[\overline{R_1}-\sigma_1\left(\frac{\overline{R_2}-\overline{R_1}}{\sigma_2-\sigma_1}\right)\right]$ and the positive slope equal to $\left(\frac{\overline{R_2}-\overline{R_1}}{\sigma_2-\sigma_1}\right)$. Then, with an increase of α, and then the part of the wealth invested in the riskier asset (Asset 2), the portfolio's risk increases linearly. All possible assets combinations cannot present a risk higher than the risk represented by the line between the two assets.

Consequently, all combinations of two assets that are perfectly correlated and lie on a straight-line in a risk and return space as in Fig. 9.3.

9.2.2 Case 2: Portfolio of Two Assets—Perfect Negative Correlation

In case of perfect negative correlation ($\rho_{12} = -1$), the second derivative is positive as follows:

$$\frac{\partial^2\sigma_P^2}{\partial\alpha^2}=\sigma_2^2+\sigma_1^2+2\sigma_1\sigma_2=(\sigma_2+\sigma_1)^2 \quad\rightarrow\quad \frac{\partial^2\sigma_P^2}{\partial\alpha^2}>0 \tag{9.18}$$

The second derivative is always positive because the two standard deviations are always positive by definition. Also in this case, the curve is convex and the stationary point defined is a minimum point of the curve. Consequently, α is the part of wealth to be invested in the riskier asset (Asset 2) to minimize the portfolio variance and therefore portfolio risk.

The position of α with regard to its abscissa is the function of the sign of the correlation coefficient. In this case, α is positive as follows:

$$\alpha=\frac{\sigma_1^2-\rho_{12}\sigma_1\sigma_2}{\sigma_2^2+\sigma_1^2-2\rho_{12}\sigma_1\sigma_2}$$

and then for $\rho_{12} = -1$, it gets:

$$\alpha=\frac{\sigma_1^2+\sigma_1\sigma_2}{\sigma_2^2+\sigma_1^2+2\sigma_1\sigma_2}=\frac{\sigma_1(\sigma_2+\sigma_1)}{(\sigma_2+\sigma_1)^2}=\frac{\sigma_1}{(\sigma_1+\sigma_2)} \quad\Rightarrow\quad \alpha>0 \tag{9.19}$$

Therefore, in case of negative correlation ($\rho_{12} = -1$) between the expected returns of the two assets, the portfolio variance is minimized by a positive value of investment in the riskier asset ($\alpha > 0$) as shown in Fig. 9.4.

We can shift from the variance to the standard deviation of the portfolio.

In case of perfect negative correlation ($\rho_{12} = -1$), the portfolio's variance is equal to:

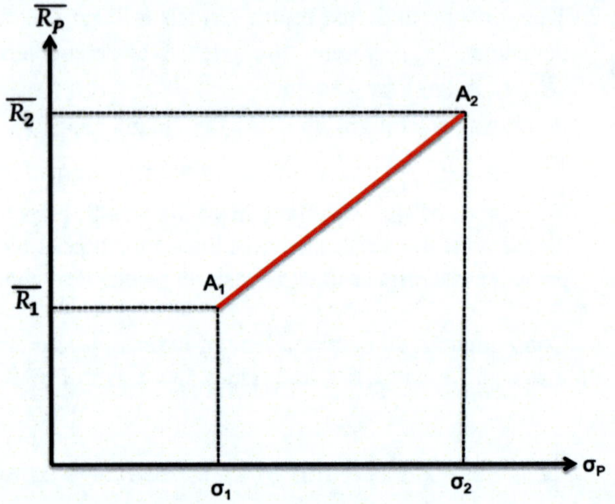

Fig. 9.3 Standard deviation and expected return of the portfolio of two assets in the case of positive correlation

$$\sigma_P^2 = \alpha^2\sigma_2^2 + (1-\alpha)^2\sigma_1^2 + 2\alpha(1-\alpha)(-1)\sigma_1\sigma_2$$

and then:

$$\sigma_P^2 = \alpha^2\sigma_2^2 + (1-\alpha)^2\sigma_1^2 - 2\alpha(1-\alpha)\sigma_1\sigma_2$$

Since the term in square brackets has the form $x^2 - 2xy + y^2$ that is equal to $(x - y)^2$, we can rewrite the portfolio's variance as follows:

$$\sigma_P^2 = [\alpha\sigma_2 - (1-\alpha)\sigma_1]^2$$

or in equivalent terms:

$$\sigma_P^2 = [\alpha(\sigma_1 + \sigma_2) - \sigma_1]^2$$

In this case, it is not possible to move from the portfolio variance (σ_P^2) to its standard deviation (σ_p) directly because the argument under the square is a function of the part of wealth invested in the riskier asset (Asset 2) and of the distance between the standard deviation of the two assets. Since the standard deviation of the portfolio (σ_P) is equal to the positive square root of the variance, we can use the absolute values to shift from the portfolio's variance to its standard deviation as follows:

$$\sigma_p = |\alpha(\sigma_1 + \sigma_2) - \sigma_1| \quad \rightarrow \quad \sigma_P = \begin{cases} \alpha(\sigma_1 + \sigma_2) - \sigma_1 & \text{if} \quad \alpha(\sigma_1 + \sigma_2) - \sigma_1 > 0 \\ \sigma_1 - \alpha(\sigma_1 + \sigma_2) & \text{if} \quad \alpha(\sigma_1 + \sigma_2) - \sigma_1 < 0 \end{cases} \tag{9.20}$$

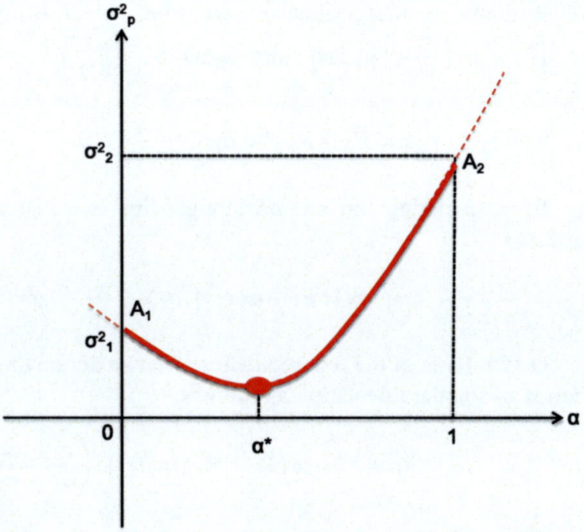

Fig. 9.4 Portfolio variance of two assets with negative correlation

We have two straight-lines: one increasing (if positive) and the other decreasing (if negative). They define the different level of the portfolio standard deviation (σ_P) to the change of part of wealth (α) invested in the riskier asset (Asset 2).

By considering the first straight-line, we can compute α as follows:

$$\sigma_P = \alpha(\sigma_1 + \sigma_2) - \sigma_1 \quad \rightarrow \quad \alpha = \frac{\sigma_P + \sigma_1}{\sigma_1 + \sigma_2} \tag{9.21}$$

On the basis of the α computation, we can define the portfolio expected return in terms of standard deviation as follows:

$$\overline{R_P} = \overline{R_1} + \alpha\left(\overline{R_2} - \overline{R_1}\right) = \overline{R_1} + \left(\frac{\sigma_P + \sigma_1}{\sigma_1 + \sigma_2}\right)\left(\overline{R_2} - \overline{R_1}\right)$$

and rearranging:

$$\overline{R_P} = \overline{R_1}\left[1 - \left(\frac{\sigma_P + \sigma_1}{\sigma_2 + \sigma_1}\right)\right] + \overline{R_2}\left(\frac{\sigma_P + \sigma_1}{\sigma_2 + \sigma_1}\right)$$

and:

$$\overline{R_P} = \left[\overline{R_1} + \sigma_1\left(\frac{\overline{R_2} - \overline{R_1}}{\sigma_1 + \sigma_2}\right)\right] + \sigma_P\left(\frac{\overline{R_2} - \overline{R_1}}{\sigma_1 + \sigma_2}\right) \tag{9.22}$$

The equation states that:

1. The portfolio's expected return $\left(\overline{R_P}\right)$ is a linear function of its standard deviation (σ_P).

2. It draws a straight-line in the plan $(\sigma_P; \overline{R_P})$ with interception equal to $\left[\overline{R_1} + \sigma_1\left(\frac{\overline{R_2}-\overline{R_1}}{\sigma_1+\sigma_2}\right)\right]$ and slope equal to $\left(\frac{\overline{R_2}-\overline{R_1}}{\sigma_1+\sigma_2}\right)$.
3. The slope is positive because $\overline{R_2} - \overline{R_1} > 0$ since Asset 2 is riskier than Asset 1 so that $\sigma_2 > \sigma_1$ and $\overline{R_2} > \overline{R_1}$ and then $\frac{\overline{R_2}-\overline{R_1}}{\sigma_1+\sigma_2} > 0$.

By considering the second straight-line, we can compute the value of α as follows:

$$\sigma_P = \sigma_1 - \alpha(\sigma_1 + \sigma_2) \quad \rightarrow \quad \alpha = \frac{\sigma_1 - \sigma_P}{\sigma_1 + \sigma_2} \tag{9.23}$$

On the basis of the α computation, we can define the portfolio expected return in terms of standard deviation as follows:

$$\overline{R_P} = \overline{R_1} + \alpha\left(\overline{R_2} - \overline{R_1}\right) = \overline{R_1} + \left(\frac{\sigma_1 - \sigma_P}{\sigma_1 + \sigma_2}\right)\left(\overline{R_2} - \overline{R_1}\right)$$

and rearranging:

$$\overline{R_P} = \overline{R_1}\left[1 - \left(\frac{\sigma_1 - \sigma_P}{\sigma_1 + \sigma_2}\right)\right] + \overline{R_2}\left(\frac{\sigma_1 - \sigma_P}{\sigma_1 + \sigma_2}\right)$$

and:

$$\overline{R_P} = \overline{R_1} + \sigma_1\left(\frac{\overline{R_2} - \overline{R_1}}{\sigma_1 + \sigma_2}\right) - \sigma_P\left(\frac{\overline{R_2} - \overline{R_1}}{\sigma_1 + \sigma_2}\right) \tag{9.24}$$

The equation states that:

a) The portfolio's expected return $(\overline{R_P})$ is a linear function of its standard deviation (σ_P).
b) It draws a straight-line in the plan $(\sigma_P; \overline{R_P})$ with interception equal to $\left(\overline{R_1} + \sigma_1\left(\frac{\overline{R_2}-\overline{R_1}}{\sigma_1+\sigma_2}\right)\right)$ and slope equal to $\left(\frac{\overline{R_2}-\overline{R_1}}{\sigma_1+\sigma_2}\right)$.
c) The slope is negative because $\overline{R_2} - \overline{R_1} > 0$ since Asset 2 is riskier than Asset 1 so that $\sigma_2 > \sigma_1$ and $\overline{R_2} > \overline{R_1}$ and then $\frac{\overline{R_2}-\overline{R_1}}{\sigma_1+\sigma_2} > 0$.

By considering these two straight-lines in the plan $(\sigma_P; \overline{R_P})$, the relationship between risk and return of the portfolio in case of perfect negative correlation $(\rho_{12} = -1)$ among the expected returns of the two assets can be represented as in Fig. 9.5.

Note that:

1. The point in which the two straight-lines have the same value of ordinate $(\overline{R^*})$, the portfolio risk is equal to zero. Indeed, for a portfolio with zero standard

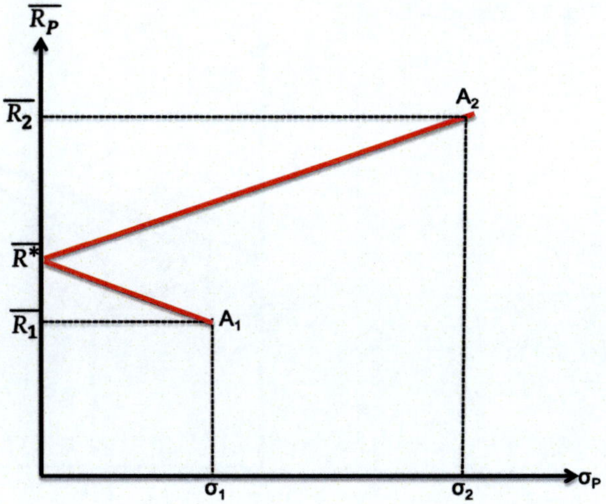

Fig. 9.5 Standard deviation and return of the portfolio of two assets in the case of negative correlation ($\rho_{1,2} = -1$)

deviation ($\sigma_P = 0$), the part of wealth (α) invested in the riskier asset (Asset 2) is positive ($\alpha > 0$) and it is the same for the two straight-lines as follows:

$$\sigma_P = 0 \rightarrow \begin{array}{l} \alpha(\sigma_1 + \sigma_2) - \sigma_1 = 0 \rightarrow \alpha = \frac{\sigma_1}{\sigma_1 + \sigma_2} \\ \sigma_1 - \alpha(\sigma_1 + \sigma_2) = 0 \rightarrow \alpha = \frac{\sigma_1}{\sigma_1 + \sigma_2} \end{array} \rightarrow \alpha > 0 \qquad (9.25)$$

2. The minimization of the portfolio standard deviation can be achieved for a positive value of the wealth (α) invested in the riskier asset (Asset 2): $0 < \alpha^* < 1$.

9.2.3 Correlation Coefficient Between −1 and +1

The analysis of the two cases shows that in the plan standard deviation—expected return $\left(\sigma_P; \overline{R_P}\right)$, the two extreme cases, perfect positive correlation ($\rho_{12} = +1$) and negative positive correlation ($\rho_{12} = -1$) define a space in which we have all possible curves for each level of coefficient correlation $-1 < \rho_{12} < +1$, as in Fig. 9.6.

Therefore if we invest a part of wealth (α) in the riskier asset (Asset 2), the portfolio's risk lower than the case to invest all wealth in the lower risk asset (Asset 1). This is the effect of diversification process. Note that the diversification does not have a value. It is a general concept that acquires value only by defining the target of risk and portfolio return. The trade-off between risk and return is the optimality mean-variance problem.

Figure 9.6 shows two main insight always to keep in mind:

Fig. 9.6 Portfolios for the $-1 \leq \rho_{12} \leq +1$

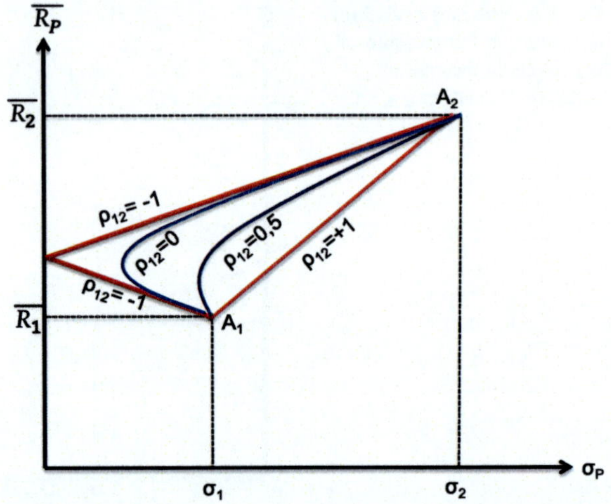

1. The lower the correlation coefficient (closer to -1) between the two assets in portfolio, all other elements remain equal, the higher the diversification.
2. Combinations of two assets can never have more risk than that we found on a straight-line connecting the two assets. Therefore, out of the space defined in risk-return plan $\left(\sigma_P; \overline{R_P}\right)$ there are not all other possible portfolios. We can move along the straight-line (for $\rho_{12} = +1; \rho_{12} = -1$) and in the space delimitated by these two straight-lines only.

The main problem in the diversification is to define a part of wealth (α) to invest in riskier asset (Asset 2) able to obtain the minimum portfolio risk. To do this, it can be useful to move from the plan $\left(\sigma_P; \overline{R_P}\right)$ to the plan $(\sigma_P; \alpha)$ in order to show the right position of α able to minimize the portfolio's risk as in Fig. 9.7.

It is relevant to note that the correlations between the assets' expected returns tend to be: (1) different from zero, because all assets are affected by economic dynamics, and (2) more positive than negative. Generally, in capital markets the correlation between the assets' expected returns tend to be higher than zero and lower than 1 ($0 < \rho_{12} < +1$).

Specifically, the correlation coefficient changes between the range:$-1 \leq \rho_{12} \leq +1$. Theoretically the effects of diversification start for a $\rho_{12} < +1$ and they increase gradually until $\rho_{12} = -1$. The smaller the correlation, the more the curve bends; the greater inclination of the curve is achieved for $\rho_{12} = -1$.

Unfortunately, in capital markets, the cases $\rho_{12} = -1$ is only theoretical (Ross et al., 2015). More generally, the two cases of $\rho_{12} = +1; \rho_{12} = -1$ represent a theoretical hypothesis and they are useful to draw a space in which all portfolios can be found as a function of the correlations between the assets' expected returns according to the changes of α.

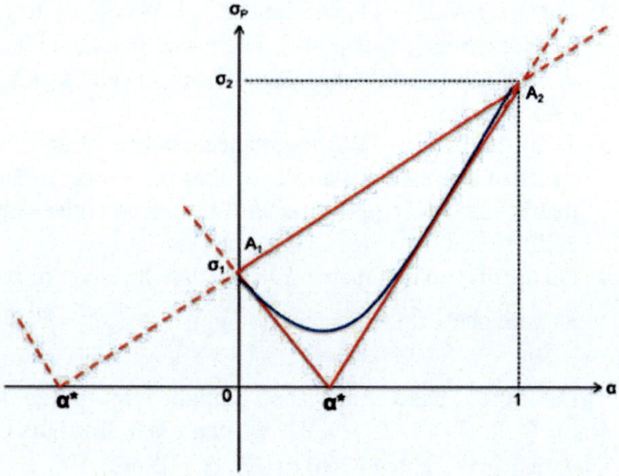

Fig. 9.7 Portfolio's standard deviation function of α

In the absence of short sales the diversification effect is greater as the lower the level of correlation between the asset's expected returns ($\rho \approx 0$). Specifically, we have:

$$0 < \rho_{12} \leq \frac{\sigma_1}{\sigma_2} \tag{9.26}$$

with $\frac{\sigma_1}{\sigma_2}$ very small. Indeed, the higher it is, and therefore the closer it gets to 1, the lower the effects of diversification.

9.3 Portfolio Variance: *N* Assets

The analysis of portfolio of two assets can be generalized by considering a portfolio of *N* assets.

In this case, the covariance, and therefore the correlation, between the expected returns of the assets must be computed by considering the assets in pairs.

The portfolio variance $\left(\sigma_P^2\right)$ can be measured by using the Covariance Matrix (C), as follows:

$$C = \begin{bmatrix} \sigma_{1,1} & \sigma_{1,2} & \cdots & \sigma_{1,n} \\ \sigma_{2,1} & \sigma_{2,2} & \cdots & \sigma_{2,n} \\ \cdots & \cdots & \cdots & \cdots \\ \sigma_{n,1} & \sigma_{n,2} & \cdots & \sigma_{n,n} \end{bmatrix} \tag{9.27}$$

Note that:

1. The generic term σ_{kj} indicates the covariance between the expected returns of the k-th asset (I_k) and the j-th asset (I_j) in portfolio, so that: $\sigma_{kj} = E[(I_k - \mu_k)(I_j - \mu_j)]$.

2. There are $N(N-1)$ covariances: it is necessary to compute covariance between pairs of assets (i-th and j-th). Therefore, the first index (i) can assume N value (one of each asset), while the second index (j) can assume a value of $(N-1)$ because $i \neq j$.
3. There are $[N(N-1)]/2$ covariances: the covariance between i and j is equal to the covariance between j and i, so that $\sigma_{i,j} = \sigma_{j,i}$. The main diagonal divides the matrix into two equal parts and we can consider only one so that $\rho_{i,j} = [N(N-1)]/2$.
4. On the diagonal of matrix $k = j$ so that the covariance σ_{kk} for each k-asset, is equal its variance $\left(\sigma_k^2\right)$: $\sigma_{kk} = E[(I_k - \mu_k)(I_k - \mu_k)] = E\left[(I_k - \mu_k)^2\right] = \sigma_k^2$.

On the basis of the weight of each asset in the portfolio $\left(\alpha_k = \frac{w_k}{w} \text{ for } k = 1, 2, \ldots, n\right)$, we can move from the Covariance Matrix (C) to the Covariance Weighted Matrix (C_α), as follows:

$$C_\alpha = \begin{bmatrix} \alpha_1\alpha_1\sigma_{11} & \alpha_1\alpha_2\sigma_{12} & \ldots & \alpha_1\alpha_n\sigma_{1n} \\ \alpha_2\alpha_1\sigma_{21} & \alpha_2\alpha_2\sigma_{22} & \ldots & \alpha_2\alpha_n\sigma_{2n} \\ \ldots & \ldots & \ldots & \ldots \\ \alpha_n\alpha_1\sigma_{n1} & \alpha_n\alpha_2\sigma_{n2} & \ldots & \alpha_n\alpha_n\sigma_{nn} \end{bmatrix} \tag{9.28}$$

and by using the correlation coefficient $\left(\rho_{kj} = \frac{\sigma_{kj}}{\sigma_k\sigma_j}\right)$, we can move from the Covariance Weighted Matrix (C_α) to the Correlation Matrix (C_ρ) as follows:

$$C_\rho = \begin{bmatrix} 1 & \rho_{12} & \ldots & \rho_{1n} \\ \rho_{21} & 1 & \ldots & \rho_{2n} \\ \ldots & \ldots & \ldots & \ldots \\ \rho_{n1} & \rho_{n2} & \ldots & 1 \end{bmatrix} \tag{9.29}$$

On the basis of Covariance Weighted Matrix (C_α) the portfolio variance $\left(\sigma_P^2\right)$ and the portfolio standard deviation are the following:

$$\sigma_P^2 = \sum_{k=1}^{n}\sum_{j=1}^{n} \alpha_k\alpha_j\sigma_{kj} \quad \rightarrow \quad \sigma_P = \sqrt{\sum_{k=1}^{n}\sum_{j=1}^{n} \alpha_k\alpha_j\sigma_{kj}} \tag{9.30}$$

Or in terms of correlation coefficients, we have:

$$\sigma_P^2 = \sum_{k=1}^{n}\sum_{j=1}^{n} \alpha_k\alpha_j\rho_{kj}\sigma_k\sigma_j \quad \rightarrow \quad \sigma_P = \sqrt{\sum_{k=1}^{n}\sum_{j=1}^{n} \alpha_k\alpha_j\rho_{kj}\sigma_k\sigma_j} \tag{9.31}$$

For greater understanding of the diversification effects, it is possible to divide the equation of portfolio variance into two parts. By introducing the condition $j \neq k$, it is possible to distinguish between the sum of variance and the sum of covariance as follows:

$$\sigma_P^2 = \sum_{k=1}^{n} \alpha_k^2 \sigma_k^2 + \sum_{k=1}^{n} \sum_{\substack{j=1 \\ j \neq k}}^{n} \alpha_k \alpha_j \sigma_{kj} \tag{9.32}$$

where:

1. The first term is the variance of each asset multiplied by the square of its investment. Then the first part of the portfolio's variance is the sum of the variances on the individual assets times the square of the proportion invested in each. It refers to the sum of the n terms square of the matrix.
2. The second term is the covariance between the expected return of the assets in portfolio considering them as a pair (the covariance between each pair). Each covariance is multiplied by twice the product of the weights of the two assets according to the symmetry of the matrix. Therefore, it refers to the sum of the $N(N-1)$ triangle of the matrix (while k can assume N value, since $j \neq k$, j can assume $(N-1)$ value). Note that without the condition $j \neq k$, it gets the variance. Indeed, for $j = k$ it results in the variance as for the matrix symmetry we have $\alpha_{i,j} = \alpha_{j,i}\ \forall\ i, j;\ i \neq j$.

In Eq. (9.32), the second term plays a key role in the diversification process. Indeed, the portfolio variance is the function of the covariance between the expected returns of the assets considered in a pair rather than the variance of the expected return of each asset.

Therefore, the risk of each asset is not related to its variance but to the change in the portfolio variance that it creates as the function of the covariance between its expected returns and the expected returns of the other assets in portfolio.

It is relevant to note that the concept of diversification is not defined in itself. It is not possible to define a general role able to indicate the reduction of the portfolio's risk to the increase of assets.

The absolute relevance of covariance rather than variance in the portfolio variance computation can be easy proof.

Assume a portfolio of all n risky assets in the market and equal investment in each of n assets.

Assume to invest a total wealth (w) in the portfolio is equal to 1 ($w = 1$) and assume to invest the same part of wealth in each asset so that the weight (α_k) of each asset in portfolio is the same and equal to $\alpha_k = 1/n$ ($k = 1, 2, \ldots, n$). The portfolio's variance is equal to:

$$\sigma_P^2 = \sum_{k=1}^{n}\left(\frac{1}{n}\right)^2 \sigma_k^2 + \sum_{k=1}^{n}\sum_{\substack{j=1\\ j\neq k}}^{n}\left(\frac{1}{n}\right)\left(\frac{1}{n}\right)\sigma_{kj}$$

Consider that:

- $\left(\frac{1}{n}\right)^2 = \left(\frac{1}{n}\right)\left(\frac{1}{n}\right)$
- multiply and divide $\left(\frac{1}{n}\right)\left(\frac{1}{n}\right)$ by $(n-1)$, so that $\left(\frac{1}{n}\right)\left(\frac{1}{n}\right)\left(\frac{n-1}{n-1}\right) = \left(\frac{n-1}{n}\right)\left(\frac{1}{n(n-1)}\right)$.

Substituting, we have:

$$\sigma_P^2 = \sum_{k=1}^{n}\left(\frac{1}{n}\right)\left(\frac{1}{n}\right)\sigma_k^2 + \sum_{k=1}^{n}\sum_{\substack{j=1\\ j\neq k}}^{n}\left(\frac{n-1}{n}\right)\left(\frac{1}{n(n-1)}\right)\sigma_{kj}$$

$$\sigma_P^2 = \sum_{k=1}^{n}\left(\frac{1}{n}\right)\left(\frac{\sigma_k^2}{n}\right) + \sum_{k=1}^{n}\sum_{\substack{j=1\\ j\neq k}}^{n}\left(\frac{n-1}{n}\right)\left(\frac{\sigma_{kj}}{n(n-1)}\right)$$

and then:

$$\sigma_P^2 = \left(\frac{1}{n}\right)\sum_{k=1}^{n}\left(\frac{\sigma_k^2}{n}\right) + \frac{(n-1)}{n}\sum_{k=1}^{n}\sum_{\substack{j=1\\ j\neq k}}^{n}\left(\frac{\sigma_{kj}}{n(n-1)}\right)$$

Both terms in the brackets are averages. Specifically, the:

1. $\sum_{k=1}^{n}\left(\frac{\sigma_k^2}{n}\right)$ is the *average variance* $\left(\overline{\sigma}_k^2\right)$ of assets in the portfolio. The term is the summation of variance divided by the number of variances in portfolio. Note as to the increase in n the average variance decreases: as n becomes extremely large, the variance of the portfolio approaches to zero.
2. $\sum_{k=1}^{n}\sum_{\substack{j=1\\ j\neq k}}^{n}\left(\frac{\sigma_{kj}}{n(n-1)}\right)$ is the *average covariance* $\left(\overline{\sigma}_{kj}\right)$. There are n values of k and $(n-1)$ values of j. There are $(n-1)$ values of j because j cannot be equal to k $(j \neq k)$ so that there is one less value of j than k. Therefore, in total there are $n(n-1)$ covariance terms. Consequently, the term is the summation of covariance divided by the number of covariances in portfolio.

Therefore, we can rewrite the portfolio's variance as follows:

$$\sigma_P^2 = \left(\frac{1}{n}\right)\overline{\sigma}_k^2 + \frac{(n-1)}{n}\overline{\sigma}_{kj}$$

and then:

$$\sigma_P^2 = \left(\frac{1}{n}\right)\overline{\sigma}_k^2 + \left(1 - \frac{1}{n}\right)\overline{\sigma}_{kj}$$

or equivalently:

$$\sigma_P^2 = \left(\frac{1}{n}\right)\left(\overline{\sigma}_k^2 - \overline{\sigma}_{kj}\right) + \overline{\sigma}_{kj}$$

In order to measure the contribution of variance and covariance to the portfolio variance, we can consider the infinite increase of n asset in portfolio. In this case, the contribution to the portfolio variance of the variance term is null and remain the only covariance term, as follows:

$$\lim_{n\to\infty}\left[\left(\frac{1}{n}\right)\overline{\sigma}_k^2 + \left(1 - \frac{1}{n}\right)\overline{\sigma}_{kj}\right] = \overline{\sigma}_{kj}$$

Indeed:

1. $\lim_{n\to\infty}\left[\left(\frac{1}{n}\right)\overline{\sigma}_k^2\right] = 0$, so that the contribution to the portfolio's variance of the variance of the individual assets goes to zero as the number of assets in portfolio (n) gets very large.
2. $\lim_{n\to\infty}\left[\left(1 - \frac{1}{n}\right)\overline{\sigma}_{kj}\right] = \overline{\sigma}_{kj}$, so that the contribution of the covariance terms approaches the average covariance as the number of assets in portfolio (n) gets very large.

Therefore, the individual risk of the asset can be diversified away, while the contribution to the total risk related to the covariance cannot be diversified away. Indeed, the contribution to the portfolio's variance of the variance of each asset is null while the contribution of the covariance goes to the average covariance. Consequently, the only relevant term for the portfolio's variance is the covariance between the expected returns of the assets considered in a pair while the specific risk of each asset (as measured by its variance) is diversified.

9.4 Asset Marginal Contribution to the Portfolio

The Asset Marginal Contribution refers to the marginal contribution of the asset to the portfolio. Consequently, the introduction of the k-th asset in the portfolio requires the analysis of the:

1. Asset marginal contribution to portfolio return ($PR_{MC(k.)}$)
2. Asset marginal contribution to portfolio variance ($PV_{MC(k)}$)
3. Asset marginal contribution to portfolio standard deviation ($PSD_{MC(k)}$).

9.4.1 Asset Marginal Contribution to the Portfolio Return

The k-th asset marginal contribution to the portfolio return ($PR_{MC(k)}$) measures the k-th asset's marginal contribution to the expected return of the portfolio by increasing or decreasing it.

It is computed on the basis of the partial derivative of the portfolio expected returns $\left(\overline{R_P}\right)$ with respect to the k-th asset's weight (α_k) in the portfolio.

By considering that the portfolio expected return is equal to:

$$\overline{R_P} = \sum_{i=1}^{n} \alpha_i \overline{R_i} \quad i = 1,2,3,\ldots,n$$

and by considering that of terms involved in the summation, only one is α_k so that each of the other terms ($\alpha_i \neq \alpha_k$) is a constant, it gets:

$$PR_{MC(k)} = \frac{\partial \overline{R_P}}{\partial \alpha_k} = \frac{\partial}{\partial \alpha_k}\left[\sum_{i=1}^{n} \alpha_i \overline{R_i}\right] = \frac{\partial}{\partial \alpha_k}\left[\alpha_k \overline{R_k}\right] = \overline{R_k}$$

so that:

$$PR_{MC(k)} = \frac{\partial \overline{R_P}}{\partial \alpha_k} = \overline{R_k} \tag{9.33}$$

The marginal contribution of the k-th asset to the portfolio return is equal to its expected return $\left(\overline{R_k}\right)$. Consequently, by introducing the k-th asset in the portfolio its expected return $\left(\overline{R_P}\right)$ changes on the basis of the value of the k-th asset expected return $\left(\overline{R_k}\right)$.

9.4.2 Asset Marginal Contribution to Portfolio Variance

The k-th asset's marginal contribution to the portfolio variance ($PV_{MC(k)}$) measures the k-th asset's marginal contribution to the risk of portfolio (on the basis of its variance) by increasing or decreasing it. It is computed on the basis of the partial derivative of the portfolio variance $\left(\sigma_P^2\right)$ with respect to the k-th asset's weight (α_k).

By considering that the portfolio variance is equal to:

$$\sigma_P^2 = \sum_{i=1}^{n} \alpha_i^2 \sigma_i^2 + \sum_{i=1}^{n} \sum_{\substack{j=1 \\ j \neq i}}^{n} \alpha_i \alpha_j \sigma_{ij}$$

we have:

$$PV_{MC(k)} = \frac{\partial \sigma_P^2}{\partial \alpha_k} = \frac{\partial}{\partial \alpha_k} \left[\sum_{i=1}^{n} \alpha_i^2 \sigma_i^2 + \sum_{i=1}^{n} \sum_{\substack{j=1 \\ j \neq i}}^{n} \alpha_i \alpha_j \sigma_{ij} \right]$$

To solve easier this derivative, it can be useful to divided it in the two parts.

The partial derivative of the first term is simple. Of all terms involved in the summation, only one is α_k and then all others ($\alpha_i \neq \alpha_k$) are constant. Therefore:

$$\frac{\partial}{\partial \alpha_k} \left[\sum_{i=1}^{n} \alpha_i^2 \sigma_i^2 \right] = \frac{\partial}{\partial \alpha_k} \left[\alpha_k^2 \sigma_k^2 \right] = 2 \alpha_k \sigma_k^2$$

The partial derivative of the second term can be solved by considering that α_k is computed twice: when $i = k$ and when $j = k$.

For $i = k$, it gets:

$$\sum_{i=1}^{n} \sum_{\substack{j=1 \\ j \neq i}}^{n} \alpha_i \alpha_j \sigma_{ij} = \alpha_k \sum_{\substack{j=1 \\ j \neq k}}^{n} \alpha_j \sigma_{kj} \quad \Rightarrow \quad \frac{\partial}{\partial \alpha_k} \left[\alpha_k \sum_{\substack{j=1 \\ j \neq k}}^{n} \alpha_j \sigma_{kj} \right] = \sum_{\substack{j=1 \\ j \neq k}}^{n} \alpha_j \sigma_{kj}$$

For $j = k$, it gets:

$$\sum_{i=1}^{n} \sum_{\substack{j=1 \\ j \neq i}}^{n} \alpha_i \alpha_j \sigma_{ij} = \alpha_k \sum_{\substack{i=1 \\ i \neq k}}^{n} \alpha_i \sigma_{ik} \quad \Rightarrow \quad \frac{\partial}{\partial \alpha_k} \left[\alpha_k \sum_{\substack{i=1 \\ i \neq k}}^{n} \alpha_i \sigma_{ik} \right] = \sum_{\substack{i=1 \\ i \neq k}}^{n} \alpha_i \sigma_{ik}$$

The two derivatives are equal among them. Indeed: (a) i and j are simply summation indicators and therefore it does not matter which one is used, and (b) the covariance matrix is symmetric so that $\sigma_{ij} = \sigma_{ji}$; $\sigma_{ik} = \sigma_{ki}$; $\sigma_{kj} = \sigma_{jk}$. Therefore, by using the same summation indicator (i or j is indifferent), it gets:

$$\sum_{\substack{j=1\\j\neq k}}^{n} \alpha_j\sigma_{kj} = \sum_{\substack{i=1\\i\neq k}}^{n} \alpha_i\sigma_{ik} \quad \leftrightarrow \quad \sum_{\substack{j=1\\j\neq k}}^{n} \alpha_j\sigma_{kj} + \sum_{\substack{j=1\\j\neq k}}^{n} \alpha_j\sigma_{kj}$$

Consequently, the partial derivative of the second term is equal to:

$$\frac{\partial}{\partial\alpha_k}\left[\sum_{i=1}^{n}\sum_{\substack{j=1\\j\neq i}}^{n} \alpha_i\alpha_j\sigma_{ij}\right] = \sum_{\substack{j=1\\j\neq k}}^{n} \alpha_j\sigma_{kj} + \sum_{\substack{j=1\\j\neq k}}^{n} \alpha_j\sigma_{kj} = 2\sum_{\substack{j=1\\j\neq k}}^{n} \alpha_j\sigma_{kj}$$

Summing the derivatives of the first and the second terms, the partial derivative of the portfolio variance is equal to:

$$\frac{\partial}{\partial\alpha_k}\left[\sum_{i=1}^{n}\alpha_i^2\sigma_i^2 + \sum_{i=1}^{n}\sum_{\substack{j=1\\j\neq i}}^{n} \alpha_i\alpha_j\sigma_{ij}\right] = 2\alpha_k\sigma_k^2 + 2\sum_{\substack{j=1\\j\neq k}}^{n} \alpha_j\sigma_{kj}$$

Summing the terms, and therefore by introducing the first term in the summation dropping the constraint ($j \neq k$) it gets:

$$2\alpha_k\sigma_k^2 + 2\sum_{\substack{j=1\\j\neq k}}^{N} \alpha_j\sigma_{kj} = 2\sum_{j=1}^{n} \alpha_j\sigma_{kj}$$

Therefore, the k-th asset's marginal contribution to the portfolio variance is equal to:

$$\mathrm{PV}_{\mathrm{MC}(k)} = \frac{\partial\sigma_P^2}{\partial\alpha_k} = 2\sum_{j=1}^{n} \alpha_j\sigma_{kj} \tag{9.34}$$

The marginal contribution of the k-th asset to the portfolio variance is equal to its effect of covariance between its expected returns and the expected returns of all other assets considered in pair. Consequently, by introducing the k-th asset in the portfolio its variance $\left(\sigma_P^2\right)$ changes on the basis of the covariance between the k-th asset and all other assets.

Consequently, while the variance of asset is not relevant, its marginal contribution is relevant to the portfolio variance.

9.4.3 Asset Marginal Contribution to Portfolio Standard Deviation

The k-th asset's marginal contribution to the portfolio standard deviation ($PSD_{MC(k)}$) measures the k-th asset's marginal contribution to the risk of portfolio (on the basis of its standard deviation) by increasing or decreasing it. It is computed on the basis of the partial derivative of the portfolio standard deviation (σ_P) with respect to the k-th asset's weight (α_k).

The portfolio standard deviation is equal to:

$$\sigma_P = \sqrt{\sigma_P^2} = \sqrt{\sum_{i=1}^{n} \alpha_i^2 \sigma_i^2 + \sum_{i=1}^{n} \sum_{\substack{j=1 \\ j \neq i}}^{n} \alpha_i \alpha_j \sigma_{ij}} = \left(\sum_{i=1}^{n} \alpha_i^2 \sigma_i^2 + \sum_{i=1}^{n} \sum_{\substack{j=1 \\ j \neq i}}^{n} \alpha_i \alpha_j \sigma_{ij} \right)^{\frac{1}{2}}$$

The partial derivative with respect to the k-th asset's weight (α_k) is equal to:

$$PSD_{MC(k)} = \frac{\partial \sigma_P}{\partial \alpha_k} = \frac{\partial}{\partial \alpha_k} \left[\left(\sum_{i=1}^{n} \alpha_i^2 \sigma_i^2 + \sum_{i=1}^{n} \sum_{\substack{j=1 \\ j \neq i}}^{n} \alpha_i \alpha_j \sigma_{ij} \right)^{\frac{1}{2}} \right]$$

$$= \left(\frac{1}{2}\right) \left(\sum_{i=1}^{n} \alpha_i^2 \sigma_i^2 + \sum_{i=1}^{n} \sum_{\substack{j=1 \\ j \neq i}}^{n} \alpha_i \alpha_j \sigma_{ij} \right)^{-\frac{1}{2}} \left(2\alpha_k \sigma_k^2 + 2 \sum_{\substack{j=1 \\ j \neq k}}^{n} \alpha_j \sigma_{kj} \right)$$

$$= \frac{\left(\frac{1}{2}\right) \left(2\alpha_k \sigma_k^2 + 2 \sum_{\substack{j=1 \\ j \neq k}}^{n} \alpha_j \sigma_{kj} \right)}{\left(\sum_{i=1}^{n} \alpha_i^2 \sigma_i^2 + \sum_{i=1}^{n} \sum_{\substack{j=1 \\ j \neq i}}^{n} \alpha_i \alpha_j \sigma_{ij} \right)^{\frac{1}{2}}} = \frac{\left(\frac{1}{2}\right) \left(2 \sum_{j=1}^{n} \alpha_j \sigma_{kj} \right)}{\sigma_P} = \frac{\sum_{j=1}^{n} \alpha_j \sigma_{kj}}{\sigma_P}$$

Therefore, the marginal contribution of the k-th asset to the portfolio standard deviation is equal to:

$$\text{PSD}_{\text{MC}(k)} = \frac{\partial \sigma_P}{\partial \alpha_k} = \frac{\sum_{j=1}^{n} \alpha_j \sigma_{kj}}{\sigma_P}$$

By considering that:

$$\sigma_{\text{kP}} = \sum_{j=1}^{n} \alpha_j \sigma_{kj}$$

the marginal contribution of the k-th asset to the portfolio standard deviation can be rewritten also as follows:

$$\text{PSD}_{\text{MC}(k)} = \frac{\partial \sigma_P}{\partial \alpha_k} = \frac{\sigma_{kP}}{\sigma_P} \tag{9.35}$$

The marginal contribution of the k-th asset to the portfolio standard deviation is equal to the ratio between the covariance between the portfolio expected return and the k-th asset's expected return and the portfolio standard deviation. Therefore, it measures the change in the covariance for a unit of portfolio risk as measured in terms of standard deviation.

Efficient Frontier 10

10.1 Portfolio of Two Risky Assets

The construction of the efficient frontier is the first step of the analysis. We will develop the analysis by considering three main cases:

- *Case 1*) Portfolio of two risky assets
- *Case 2*) Portfolio of *n* risky assets
- *Case 3*) Portfolio of *n* risky assets and one free-risk asset.

Note that the efficient frontier has a different form as a consequence of the short sales. However, the analysis of the efficient frontier when the short sales are allowed can be interpreted as an extension of the analysis when they are not allowed (Elton et al., 2013). Therefore, in the analysis, we assume that the short sales are allowed and we will specify the effects if they are not allowed.

We start the analysis assuming two assets in portfolio: Asset 1 and Asset 2. Their weight (α_i) is equal to the part of wealth invested in it (w_i) on total wealth invested in the portfolio (w). Therefore, the weight of Asset 1 and Asset 2 is, respectively: $\alpha_1 = w_1/w$ and $\alpha_2 = w_2/w$. Consequently, all possible portfolios can be realized by changing the weight of each asset.

To simplify the analysis, we re-introduce these two baseline assumptions of previous chapter:

Assumption 1: Asset 2 is riskier than Asset 1. It implies that:

(a) The variance (and standard deviation) of Asset 2 is higher than Asset 1: $\sigma_2^2 > \sigma_1^2 \rightarrow \sigma_2 > \sigma_1$.
(b) The expected return of Asset 2 is higher than Asset 1 (on the basis of relationship between risk and return): $\overline{R_2} > \overline{R_1}$.

P. De Luca, *Corporate Finance*, Springer Texts in Business and Economics,
https://doi.org/10.1007/978-3-031-18300-3_10

Assumption 2: define the part of wealth invested in each asset in terms of α *and* $1-\alpha$. Specifically assume that:

(a) The part of wealth invested in Asset 2 is equal to α so that: $\alpha_2 = \alpha$.
(b) The part of wealth invested in Asset 1 is equal to $1-\alpha$ so that: $\alpha_1 = 1-\alpha$.

Based on these two assumptions, by changing α it changes the part of wealth invested in the riskier asset (Asset 2). Therefore, by considering that there are two assets in portfolio, by changing α it is possible to obtain all possible combinations of the two assets.

It is relevant to note that the value of α is the function of short sales. Specifically:

1. If short selling is not allowed: the value of α is between 0 and 1 so that: $0 \leq \alpha \leq 1$.
2. If short selling is allowed: the value of α may exceed $1 (a > 1)$ by acquiring a short position on Asset 1 and acquiring Asset 2; similarly, the value of α may exceed $0\ (a < 0)$ by acquiring a short position on Asset 2 and acquiring the Asset 1.

In the previous chapter, we have analysed the expected return $\left(\overline{R_P}\right)$ and the variance of the portfolio $\left(\sigma_P^2\right)$.

In case of two risky assets in portfolio, the expected return of portfolio $\left(\overline{R_P}\right)$ is equal to:

$$\overline{R_P} = (1-\alpha)\overline{R_1} + \alpha\,\overline{R_2} = \overline{R_1} + \alpha\left(\overline{R_2} - \overline{R_1}\right) \tag{10.1}$$

And the variance of the portfolio $\left(\sigma_P^2\right)$ is equal to:

$$\sigma_P^2 = \alpha^2\sigma_2^2 + (1-\alpha)^2\sigma_1^2 + 2\alpha(1-\alpha)\rho_{12}\sigma_1\sigma_2 \tag{10.2}$$

The first and the second derivatives of the portfolio's variance are equal to:

$$\frac{\partial \sigma_P^2}{\partial \alpha} = \alpha\sigma_2^2 + \alpha\sigma_1^2 - \sigma_1^2 + \rho_{12}\sigma_1\sigma_2 - 2\alpha\rho_{12}\sigma_1\sigma_2$$

$$\frac{\partial^2 \sigma_P^2}{\partial \alpha^2} = \sigma_2^2 + \sigma_1^2 - 2\rho_{12}\sigma_1\sigma_2$$

Since the second derivative is always positive (for $\rho_{12} = +1$ and $\rho_{12} = -1$), the portfolio's variance draws a convex curve. The minimum point of the curve is obtained by putting the first derivative equal to zero as follows:

$$\frac{\partial \sigma_P^2}{\partial \alpha} = 0 \quad \rightarrow \quad \alpha\sigma_2^2 + \alpha\sigma_1^2 - \sigma_1^2 + \rho_{12}\sigma_1\sigma_2 - 2\alpha\rho_{12}\sigma_1\sigma_2 = 0$$

and solving for α, we have:

$$\alpha = \frac{\sigma_1^2 - \rho_{12}\sigma_1\sigma_2}{\sigma_2^2 + \sigma_1^2 - 2\rho_{12}\sigma_1\sigma_2} \tag{10.3}$$

The value of α indicates the amount of wealth to be invested in the riskier asset (Asset 2) to minimize the portfolio's variance.

In case of perfect positive correlation ($\rho_{12} = +1$), the portfolio's variance $\left(\sigma_P^2\right)$ is equal to:

$$\sigma_P^2 = \alpha^2\sigma_2^2 + (1-\alpha)^2\sigma_1^2 + 2\alpha(1-\alpha)\sigma_1\sigma_2 = [\sigma_1 + \alpha(\sigma_2 - \sigma_1)]^2 \tag{10.4}$$

and the minimum point of the curve is obtained for a negative value of α:

$$\alpha = \frac{\sigma_1^2 - \sigma_1\sigma_2}{\sigma_2^2 + \sigma_1^2 - 2\sigma_1\sigma_2} = -\frac{\sigma_1}{(\sigma_2 - \sigma_1)} \quad \Rightarrow \quad \alpha < 0 \tag{10.5}$$

The portfolio's standard deviation (σ_P) is equal to:

$$\sigma_P = \sigma_1 + \alpha(\sigma_2 - \sigma_1) \tag{10.6}$$

By solving for α, and putting the standard deviation of the portfolio equal to zero ($\sigma_P = 0$) we have:

$$\alpha = \frac{\sigma_P - \sigma_1}{\sigma_2 - \sigma_1}$$

$$\sigma_P = 0 \quad \rightarrow \quad \alpha = \frac{-\sigma_1}{\sigma_2 - \sigma_1} \tag{10.7}$$

Introducing the value of α in the portfolio's expected return $\left(\overline{R_P}\right)$, we have:

$$\overline{R_P} = \left[\overline{R_1} - \sigma_1\left(\frac{\overline{R_2} - \overline{R_1}}{\sigma_2 - \sigma_1}\right)\right] + \sigma_P\left(\frac{\overline{R_2} - \overline{R_1}}{\sigma_2 - \sigma_1}\right) \tag{10.8}$$

In case of perfect negative correlation ($\rho_{12} = -1$), the portfolio's variance $\left(\sigma_P^2\right)$ is equal to:

$$\sigma_P^2 = \alpha^2\sigma_2^2 + (1-\alpha)^2\sigma_1^2 - 2\alpha(1-\alpha)\sigma_1\sigma_2 = [\alpha(\sigma_1 + \sigma_2) - \sigma_1]^2 \tag{10.9}$$

and the minimum point of the curve is obtained for a positive value of α:

$$\alpha = \frac{\sigma_1^2 + \sigma_1\sigma_2}{\sigma_2^2 + \sigma_1^2 + 2\sigma_1\sigma_2} = \frac{\sigma_1}{(\sigma_1 + \sigma_2)} \quad \Rightarrow \quad \alpha > 0 \tag{10.10}$$

The portfolio's standard deviation (σ_P) is equal to:

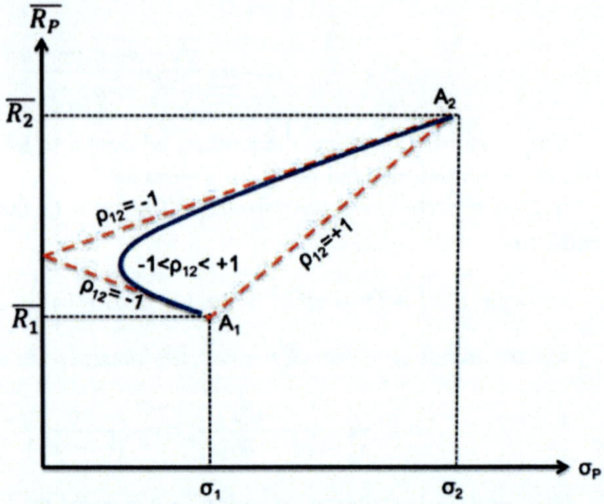

Fig. 10.1 Positive and negative correlation in the plan standard deviation—expected return $(\sigma_P; \overline{R_P})$

$$\sigma_P = |\alpha(\sigma_1 + \sigma_2) - \sigma_1| \quad \rightarrow \quad \sigma_P = \begin{cases} \alpha(\sigma_1 + \sigma_2) - \sigma_1 & \text{if } \alpha(\sigma_1 + \sigma_2) - \sigma_1 > 0 \\ \sigma_1 - \alpha(\sigma_1 + \sigma_2) & \text{if } \alpha(\sigma_1 + \sigma_2) - \sigma_1 < 0 \end{cases} \tag{10.11}$$

By solving the first and the second straight-lines for α, we have:

$$\text{First Straight Line}: \quad \alpha = \frac{\sigma_P + \sigma_1}{\sigma_1 + \sigma_2}$$

$$\text{Second Straight Line}: \quad \alpha = \frac{\sigma_1 - \sigma_P}{\sigma_1 + \sigma_2} \tag{10.12}$$

Introducing the value of α deriving from the first and second straight-lines in the portfolio's expected return $(\overline{R_P})$, we have:

$$\text{First Straight Line}: \quad \overline{R_P} = \left[\overline{R_1} + \sigma_1\left(\frac{\overline{R_2} - \overline{R_1}}{\sigma_1 + \sigma_2}\right)\right] + \sigma_P\left(\frac{\overline{R_2} - \overline{R_1}}{\sigma_1 + \sigma_2}\right)$$

$$\text{Second Straight Line}: \quad \overline{R_P} = \overline{R_1} + \sigma_1\left(\frac{\overline{R_2} - \overline{R_1}}{\sigma_1 + \sigma_2}\right) - \sigma_P\left(\frac{\overline{R_2} - \overline{R_1}}{\sigma_1 + \sigma_2}\right) \tag{10.13}$$

In the plan standard deviation—expected return $(\sigma_P; \overline{R_P})$, the two cases of positive correlation ($\rho_{12} = +1$) and negative correlation ($\rho_{12} = -1$) define a space in which we have all possible curves for each level of coefficient correlation $-1 < \rho_{12} < +1$, as shown in Fig. 10.1.

Note that, by working with the historical data, the statistical characteristics of assets (mean, variance, standard deviation, and then covariance and correlation among them) are well-known and defined. It implies that in the space delimited by the straight-lines there is only one curve because we have only one value of the correlation coefficient. To have a different curve, we must change the correlation coefficient and this implies the change of assets in portfolio.

Therefore, we can make only one choice: the amount of wealth α to be invested in the riskier asset (Asset 2). Thus, by changing the value of α we have all possible portfolios on the basis of the two assets. All these portfolios must lie along on the straight-lines (in case of $\rho_{12} = +1$ and $\rho_{12} = -1$) or along the single curve defined for the specific value of ρ_{12} (for $-1 < \rho_{12} < +1$).

For each value of correlation coefficient (for $-1 < \rho_{12} < +1$), by changing the value of α we can position all portfolios along the curve in the space standard deviation—expected return $\left(\sigma_P; \overline{R_P}\right)$, by solving the system of two equations:

$$\begin{cases} \overline{R_P} = \overline{R_1} + \alpha\left(\overline{R_2} - \overline{R_1}\right) \\ \sigma_P^2 = \alpha^2\sigma_2^2 + (1-\alpha)^2\sigma_1^2 + 2\alpha(1-\alpha)\rho_{12}\sigma_1\sigma_2 \end{cases} \tag{10.14}$$

By solving the portfolio's expected return $\left(\overline{R_P}\right)$ for α, we have:

$$\alpha = \frac{\overline{R_P} - \overline{R_1}}{\overline{R_2} - \overline{R_1}}$$

Substituting the value of α in the portfolio's variance $\left(\sigma_P^2\right)$, we have:

$$\sigma_P^2 = \left(\frac{\overline{R_P} - \overline{R_1}}{\overline{R_2} - \overline{R_1}}\right)^2 \sigma_2^2 + \left(1 - \frac{\overline{R_P} - \overline{R_1}}{\overline{R_2} - \overline{R_1}}\right)^2 \sigma_1^2 + 2\left(\frac{\overline{R_P} - \overline{R_1}}{\overline{R_2} - \overline{R_1}}\right)\left(1 - \frac{\overline{R_P} - \overline{R_1}}{\overline{R_2} - \overline{R_1}}\right)\rho_{12}\sigma_1\sigma_2$$

$$\sigma_P^2 = \left(\frac{\overline{R_P} - \overline{R_1}}{\overline{R_2} - \overline{R_1}}\right)^2 \sigma_2^2 + \left(\frac{\overline{R_2} - \overline{R_1} - \overline{R_P} + \overline{R_1}}{\overline{R_2} - \overline{R_1}}\right)^2 \sigma_1^2 + 2\left(\frac{\overline{R_P} - \overline{R_1}}{\overline{R_2} - \overline{R_1}}\right) \times \left(\frac{\overline{R_2} - \overline{R_1} - \overline{R_P} + \overline{R_1}}{\overline{R_2} - \overline{R_1}}\right)\rho_{12}\sigma_1\sigma_2$$

$$\sigma_P^2 = \left(\frac{\overline{R_P} - \overline{R_1}}{\overline{R_2} - \overline{R_1}}\right)^2 \sigma_2^2 + \left(\frac{\overline{R_2} - \overline{R_P}}{\overline{R_2} - \overline{R_1}}\right)^2 \sigma_1^2 + 2\left(\frac{\overline{R_P} - \overline{R_1}}{\overline{R_2} - \overline{R_1}}\right)\left(\frac{\overline{R_2} - \overline{R_P}}{\overline{R_2} - \overline{R_1}}\right)\rho_{12}\sigma_1\sigma_2$$

$$\sigma_P^2 = \left(\frac{\overline{R_P} - \overline{R_1}}{\overline{R_2} - \overline{R_1}}\right)^2 \sigma_2^2 + \left(\frac{\overline{R_2} - \overline{R_P}}{\overline{R_2} - \overline{R_1}}\right)^2 \sigma_1^2 + 2\left(\frac{\overline{R_P}\,\overline{R_2} - \overline{R_P}^2 - \overline{R_1}\,\overline{R_2} + \overline{R_1}\,\overline{R_P}}{\left(\overline{R_2} - \overline{R_1}\right)^2}\right)\rho_{12}\sigma_1\sigma_2$$

$$\sigma_P^2 = \frac{1}{\left(\overline{R_2} - \overline{R_1}\right)^2} \times \left[\left(\overline{R_P} - \overline{R_1}\right)^2 \sigma_2^2 + \left(\overline{R_2} - \overline{R_P}\right)^2 \sigma_1^2 + 2\left(\overline{R_P R_2} - \overline{R_P^2} - \overline{R_1 R_2} + \overline{R_1 R_P}\right)\rho_{12}\sigma_1\sigma_2\right]$$

$$\sigma_P^2 = \frac{1}{\left(\overline{R_2} - \overline{R_1}\right)^2}\left[\overline{R_P^2}\sigma_2^2 + \overline{R_1^2}\sigma_2^2 - 2\overline{R_1 R_P}\sigma_2^2 + \overline{R_2^2}\sigma_1^2 + \overline{R_P^2}\sigma_1^2 - 2\overline{R_P R_2}\sigma_1^2 + 2\overline{R_P R_2}\rho_{12}\sigma_1\sigma_2 - 2\overline{R_P^2}\rho_{12}\sigma_1\sigma_2 - 2\overline{R_1 R_2}\rho_{12}\sigma_1\sigma_2 + 2\overline{R_1 R_P}\rho_{12}\sigma_1\sigma_2\right]$$

$$\sigma_P^2 = \frac{1}{\left(\overline{R_2} - \overline{R_1}\right)^2}\left[\overline{R_P^2}\left(\sigma_2^2 + \sigma_1^2 - 2\rho_{12}\sigma_1\sigma_2\right) - 2\overline{R_P}\left[\overline{R_1}\sigma_2^2 + \overline{R_2}\sigma_1^2 - \rho_{12}\sigma_1\sigma_2\left(\overline{R_2} + \overline{R_1}\right)\right] + \overline{R_1^2}\sigma_2^2 + \overline{R_2^2}\sigma_1^2 - 2\overline{R_1 R_2}\rho_{12}\sigma_1\sigma_2\right]$$

by placing:

- $A = \sigma_2^2 + \sigma_1^2 - 2\rho_{12}\sigma_1\sigma_2$
- $B = 2\left[\overline{R_1}\sigma_2^2 + \overline{R_2}\sigma_1^2 - \rho_{12}\sigma_1\sigma_2\left(\overline{R_2} + \overline{R_1}\right)\right]$
- $C = \overline{R_1^2}\sigma_2^2 + \overline{R_2^2}\sigma_1^2 - 2\overline{R_1 R_2}\rho_{12}\sigma_1\sigma_2$

it gets the portfolio variance on the basis of its expected return as follows:

$$\sigma_P^2 = \frac{1}{\left(\overline{R_2} - \overline{R_1}\right)^2}\left[A\overline{R_P^2} - B\overline{R_P} + C\right] \tag{10.15}$$

By considering that $\overline{R_2} - \overline{R_1} > 0$, we can shift from portfolio's variance to its standard deviation (σ_P) as follows:

$$\sigma_P = \frac{1}{\left(\overline{R_2} - \overline{R_1}\right)}\sqrt{A\overline{R_P^2} - B\overline{R_P} + C} \tag{10.16}$$

Therefore, in the plan standard deviation—expected return $\left(\sigma_P; \overline{R_P}\right)$ the equation draws a parabola with its axis parallel to the vertical axis and concave upwards. Indeed, A is always positive as follows:

Fig. 10.2 The frontier of all portfolios

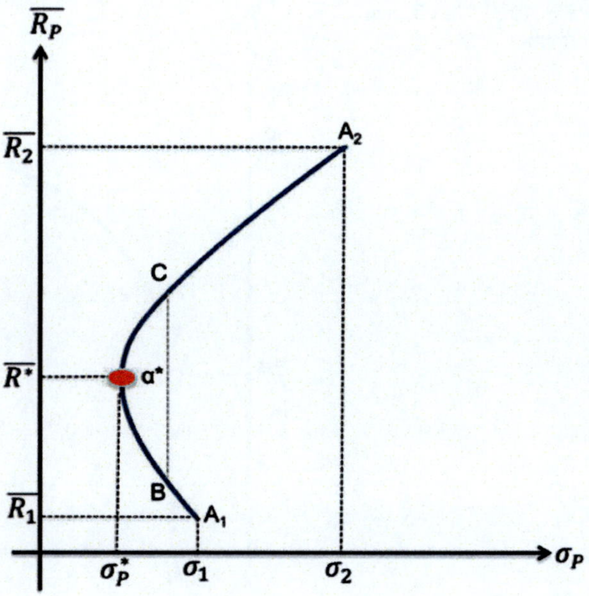

$$A = \sigma_2^2 + \sigma_1^2 - 2\rho_{12}\sigma_1\sigma_2$$

$$\rightarrow \quad \begin{array}{l} \rho_{12} = +1 \rightarrow A = (\sigma_2 - \sigma_1)^2; \sigma_2 > \sigma_1 \rightarrow A > 0 \\ \rho_{12} = -1 \rightarrow A = (\sigma_2 + \sigma_1)^2; \rightarrow A > 0 \\ \rho_{12} = 0 \rightarrow A = \sigma_2^2 + \sigma_1^2; \rightarrow A > 0 \end{array}$$

In the plan expected return-standard deviation $\left(\sigma_P; \overline{R_P}\right)$ the curve represents the *frontier of all portfolios* by changing the value of α as shown in Fig. 10.2.

Note that if:

1. *Short selling is allowed*: for a negative value of ($\alpha < 0$), the portfolio A_1 is exceeded through the short sales of Asset 2 and acquiring Asset 1; similarly, for a positive value of α ($\alpha > 1$), portfolio A_2 is exceeded through the short sales of Asset 1 and acquisition of Asset 2. Therefore, in this case, α can be $\alpha < 0$ and $\alpha > 1$. So that the efficient portfolios move along the curve A_1A_2 and they can over A_1 and A_2 by short selling.
2. *Short selling is not allowed*: the curve is delimited by the portfolios composed of Asset 1 only (portfolio A_1 for $\alpha = 0$) and only by Asset 2 (portfolio A_2 for $\alpha = 1$). Therefore, in this case, α can move between 0 and 1 ($0 \leq \alpha \leq 1$). In this case, all efficient portfolios are positioned along the curve A_1A_2 and they are obtained by combining two assets by changing α.

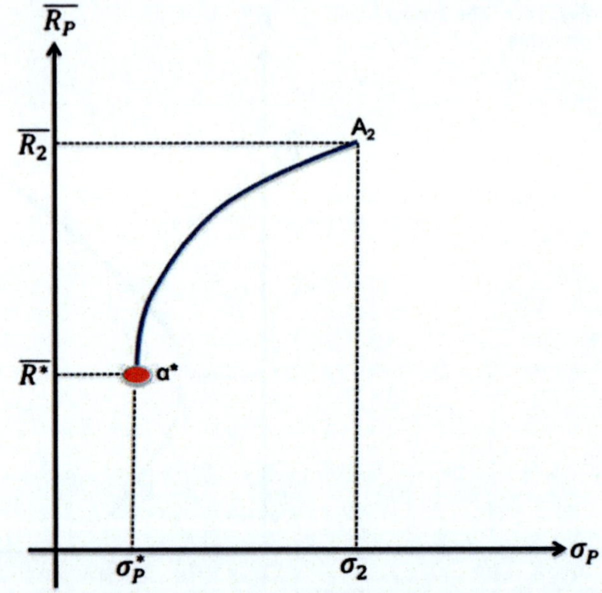

Fig. 10.3 The efficient frontier

The curve A_1A_2 represents the *frontier of minimum variance portfolio* for each defined level of portfolio expected return $(\overline{R_P})$. Consequently, having defined the level of the portfolio expected return, by moving along the curve by changing α, it is possible to minimize the portfolio standard deviation (σ_P) and then the risk.

On the frontier of all portfolios, we can distinguish between two types of portfolio:

1. *Dominated portfolios*: they are all portfolios located on the curve lower branch.
2. *Dominant portfolios*: they are all portfolios located on the curve upper branch.

The dominant portfolios are characterized by a higher expected return for equal level of risk with respect to the dominated portfolios: in Fig. 10.2, the portfolio C dominates the portfolio B.

The point α^* indicates the *minimum variance portfolio*. It is the portfolio with minimum risk obtained by investing a part of wealth in the riskier asset (Asset 2) equal to α^*. The point α^* is the transaction point on the curve from dominated portfolios to dominant portfolios. Indeed, from α^* while the curve lower branch is convex while the curve upper branch is concave and it is called *efficient frontier* because it contains all efficient portfolios. Only these portfolios can be defined as Pareto optimality. In Fig. 10.3 the frontier of efficient portfolios is defined by part of curve $(\alpha^*; A_2)$.

Note that the subset of the *frontier of all portfolios* is larger than the *efficient frontier*. In this sense, it is sufficient to analyse the portfolio C and portfolio B in Fig. 10.2: both portfolios are located on the curve and thus on the frontier of minimum variance portfolios. However, only the portfolio *C* can be defined efficient because for the same variance $\left(\sigma_C^2 = \sigma_B^2\right)$ its expected return is higher than the portfolio *B* $\left(\overline{R_C} > \overline{R_B}\right)$ and then the portfolio *C* dominates the portfolio *B*. Consequently, both portfolios are positioned on the frontier but only portfolio *C* is positioned on the frontier of efficient portfolios.

Defined the frontier of efficient portfolios, note that:

1. *Above the efficient frontier*: represents portfolios that cannot be obtained on the basis of the statistical characteristics of the assets in portfolios.
2. *Below the efficient frontier*: represents portfolios that are not efficient and therefore they are dominated by the portfolios positioned on the efficient frontier.

Consequently, the efficient frontier represents the solution of the optimization problem in the mean-variance criteria. The efficient portfolios show the lower variance for the same expected return level or, equivalently, the higher return for the same variance level.

10.2 Portfolio of *N* Risky Assets

The result is similar to the case of two assets even if the analysis is more complex.

It is necessary to distinguish between two hypotheses: short sales allowed or not allowed. In this contest, we consider the case in which the short sales are allowed (that is the common case).

In this context, the definition of the efficient portfolio can be defined in terms of constrained optimization problem, on the basis of the minimization of variance or the maximization of expected return as follows:

$$\begin{cases} \min\limits_{\boldsymbol{\alpha} \in \mathbb{R}^n} \sigma_P^2(\boldsymbol{\alpha}) \\ \sum\limits_{k=1}^{n} \alpha_k = 1 \end{cases} \tag{10.17}$$

where the first is the objective equation to be minimized where $\boldsymbol{\alpha}$ is a vector: $\boldsymbol{\alpha} = \{\alpha_1, \alpha_2, \ldots, \alpha_k\}$ and the second equation is the constraints.

In extended form, we have:

$$\begin{cases} \min\limits_{\boldsymbol{\alpha} \in \mathbb{R}^n} \sum\limits_{i=1}^{N} \alpha_i^2 \sigma_i^2 + \sum\limits_{i=1}^{N} \sum\limits_{\substack{j=1 \\ j \neq i}}^{N} \alpha_i \alpha_j \sigma_{ij} \\ \sum\limits_{i=1}^{n} \alpha_i = 1 \end{cases} \tag{10.18}$$

By using the Lagrange multiplier $(\mathcal{L})$, we have:

$$\mathcal{L}=\sum_{i=1}^{N}\alpha_i^2\sigma_i^2+\sum_{i=1}^{N}\sum_{\substack{j=1\\ j\neq i}}^{N}\alpha_i\alpha_j\sigma_{i,j}-\lambda\left(\sum_{i=1}^{n}\alpha_i-1\right)$$

By considering that:

$$\frac{\partial}{\partial\alpha_k}\sum_{i=1}^{N}\alpha_i=\alpha_k$$

$$\frac{\partial\sigma_P^2}{\partial\alpha_k}=\frac{\partial}{\partial\alpha_k}\left[\sum_{i=1}^{n}\alpha_i^2\sigma_i^2+\sum_{i=1}^{n}\sum_{\substack{j=1\\ j\neq i}}^{n}\alpha_i\alpha_j\sigma_{ij}\right]=2\sum_{j=1}^{n}\alpha_j\sigma_{kj}$$

the first derivative of the Lagrange multiplier with respect to α_k and λ is equal to:

$$\frac{\partial\mathcal{L}}{\partial\alpha_k}=2\sum_{j=1}^{n}\alpha_j\sigma_{kj}-\lambda=\sum_{j=1}^{n}\alpha_j\sigma_{kj}-\frac{1}{2}\lambda$$

$$\frac{\partial\mathcal{L}}{\partial\lambda}=\sum_{i=1}^{n}\alpha_i-1$$

Placing the first derivatives with respect to α_k and λ equal to zero, we have:

$$\begin{cases}\sum_{j=1}^{n}\alpha_j\sigma_{kj}-\frac{1}{2}\lambda=0\\ \sum_{i=1}^{n}\alpha_i-1=0\end{cases}\tag{10.19}$$

Note that the condition $\frac{\partial\mathcal{L}}{\partial\lambda}=0$ is always by definition because $\sum_{i=1}^{n}\alpha_i=1$ and then we cannot consider. Therefore, by solving we have the coordinate of the minimum variance portfolio.

To well-understand we can find the portfolio with minimum variance with respect to a defined level of portfolio's expected return $\left(\overline{R_0}\right)$. In this case, under the assumption of short sales allowed, we have to introduce a new constraint in the constrained optimization problem as follows:

$$\begin{cases} \min_{\boldsymbol{\alpha}\in\mathbb{R}^n} \sigma_P^2(\boldsymbol{\alpha}) \\ \overline{R_P}(\boldsymbol{\alpha}) = \overline{R_0} \\ \sum_{k=1}^{n} \alpha_k = 1 \end{cases} \tag{10.20}$$

where the first is the objective equation to be minimized, the second and the third equations are the constraints, and $\boldsymbol{\alpha}$ is a vector: $\boldsymbol{\alpha} = \{\alpha_1, \alpha_2, \ldots, \alpha_k\}$. By explicating, it gets:

$$\begin{cases} \min_{\boldsymbol{\alpha}\in\mathbb{R}^n} \sum_{i=1}^{N} \alpha_i^2\sigma_i^2 + \sum_{i=1}^{N} \sum_{\substack{j=1 \\ j\neq i}}^{N} \alpha_i\alpha_j\sigma_{ij} \\ \sum_{i=1}^{n} \alpha_i\overline{R_i} = \overline{R_0} \\ \sum_{i=1}^{n} \alpha_i = 1 \end{cases} \tag{10.21}$$

By using the Lagrange multiplier ($\mathcal{L}$), we have:

$$\mathcal{L} = \sum_{i=1}^{N} \alpha_i^2\sigma_i^2 + \sum_{i=1}^{N} \sum_{\substack{j=1 \\ j\neq i}}^{N} \alpha_i\alpha_j\sigma_{i,j} - \lambda'\left(\sum_{i=1}^{n} \alpha_i\overline{R_i} - \overline{R_0}\right) - \lambda''\left(\sum_{i=1}^{n} \alpha_i - 1\right)$$

and then:

$$\frac{\partial \mathcal{L}}{\partial \alpha_k} = 2\sum_{j=1}^{n} \alpha_j\sigma_{kj} - \lambda'\overline{R_k} - \lambda'' = \sum_{j=1}^{n} \alpha_j\sigma_{kj} - \frac{1}{2}\lambda'\overline{R_k} - \frac{1}{2}\lambda''$$

$$\frac{\partial \mathcal{L}}{\partial \lambda'} = \sum_{i=1}^{n} \alpha_i\overline{R_i} - \overline{R_0}$$

$$\frac{\partial \mathcal{L}}{\partial \lambda''} = \sum_{i=1}^{n} \alpha_i - 1$$

and placing first derivatives equal to zero, it gets:

$$\begin{cases} \sum_{j=1}^{n} \alpha_j \sigma_{kj} - \frac{1}{2}\lambda' \mu_k - \frac{1}{2}\lambda'' = 0 \\ \sum_{i=1}^{n} \alpha_i \overline{R_i} - \overline{R_0} = 0 \\ \sum_{i=1}^{n} \alpha_i - 1 = 0 \end{cases} \tag{10.22}$$

Therefore, we have a system of $n + 2$ equations: n unknown of equation $(\alpha_1, \alpha_2, \alpha_3, \ldots, \alpha_n)$ and λ' and λ''. Denote with $\alpha_{i(\overline{R_0})}$ and then $\alpha_{1(\overline{R_0})}, \alpha_{2(\overline{R_0})}, \ldots, \alpha_{n(\overline{R_0})}$ the solution corresponding to the choice level of $\overline{R_0}$, we have the corresponding coordinates of the with minimum variance as follows:

$$\overline{R_0} = \sum_{i=1}^{n} \alpha_{i(\overline{R_0})} \overline{R_i}$$

$$\sigma_0^2 = \sum_{i=1}^{N} \left(\alpha_{i(\overline{R_0})}\right)^2 \sigma_i^2 + \sum_{i=1}^{N} \sum_{\substack{j=1 \\ j \neq i}}^{N} \alpha_{i(\overline{R_0})} \alpha_{j(\overline{R_0})} \sigma_{ij} \tag{10.23}$$

10.3 Portfolio of *N* Risky Assets and One Riskless Asset

We can simplify the analysis introducing a riskless asset (F) in the portfolio of N risky asset by using the separation theorem (Elton et al., 2013).

Assume investors can lend and borrow unlimited amount of funds at the same free-risk rate R_F. In this case, we can consider lending at a risk-free rate as investing in an asset with a certain outcome such as short-term government bond while borrowing at a risk-free rate such as selling such a security short. In this way, we can lend and borrow at the same riskless rate.

Assume investors want to hold part of the wealth α in portfolio of risky assets A and either $(1 - \alpha)$ lending or borrowing by holding the risk-free rate R_F. Therefore, we can consider all combinations of portfolio of risky asset (A) and the riskless asset (F). The expected return of the portfolio $\left(\overline{R_P}\right)$ derived by the combination of risk-free asset (R_F) and the expected return of the portfolio of risky assets $\left(\overline{R_A}\right)$ as follows:

$$\overline{R_P} = \alpha \overline{R_A} + (1 - \alpha) R_F \quad \leftrightarrow \quad \overline{R_P} = R_F + \alpha\left(\overline{R_A} - R_F\right) \tag{10.24}$$

Note that since the risky asset requires an expected return $\left(\overline{R_A}\right)$ higher than the riskless asset (R_F) by definition $\left(\overline{R_A} > R_F\right)$, their difference is always positive

$\left(\overline{R_A} - R_F > 0\right)$ and it measures the Risk Premium (δ_k) that is the extra-return expected by investors for the risk burden:

$$\delta_A = \overline{R_A} - R_F \qquad \delta_A > 0 \tag{10.25}$$

The variance of the portfolio $\left(\sigma_P^2\right)$ is equal to:

$$\sigma_P^2 = \alpha^2\sigma_A^2 + (1-\alpha)^2\sigma_F^2 + 2\alpha(1-\alpha)\rho_{\mathrm{AF}}\sigma_A\sigma_F$$

Since the return of the riskless asset is certain $\left(\overline{R_F} \equiv R_F\right)$, the variance (and then the standard deviation) of the return on this asset must be zero $\left(\sigma_F^2 = 0; \sigma_F = 0\right)$ as well as the covariance (and then the correlation) between A and F must be equal to zero ($\rho_{\mathrm{AF}} = 0$). Therefore, the variance and the standard deviation of the portfolio are the function of the asset A only as follows:

$$\sigma_P^2 = \alpha^2\sigma_A^2$$

$$\sigma_P = \alpha\sigma_A \tag{10.26}$$

By solving the standard deviation for α, we have:

$$\alpha = \frac{\sigma_P}{\sigma_A} \tag{10.27}$$

Substituting the value of α in the portfolio's expected return $\left(\overline{R_P}\right)$, we have:

$$\overline{R_P} = \left(1 - \frac{\sigma_P}{\sigma_A}\right)R_F + \left(\frac{\sigma_P}{\sigma_A}\right)\overline{R_A}$$

and rearranging, we have:

$$\overline{R_P} = R_F + \left(\frac{\sigma_P}{\sigma_A}\right)\left(\overline{R_A} - R_F\right)$$

or equivalently:

$$\overline{R_P} = R_F + \sigma_P\left(\frac{\overline{R_A} - R_F}{\sigma_A}\right) \tag{10.28}$$

This equation draws a straight-line with intercept R_F and slope $\left[\left(\overline{R_A} - R_F\right)/\sigma_A\right]$ in the plan standard deviation-expected return $\left(\sigma_P; \overline{R_P}\right)$ as shown in Fig. 10.4. The slope is the Sharpe Ratio (π) for the portfolio of risky asset (A):

$$\frac{\overline{R_A} - R_F}{\sigma_A} = \frac{\delta_A}{\sigma_A} = \pi_A \tag{10.29}$$

It measures the *cost of capital for unit of risk* or equivalently, the *unit price for risk*. By using the Sharpe index (π), the portfolio expected return is equal to:

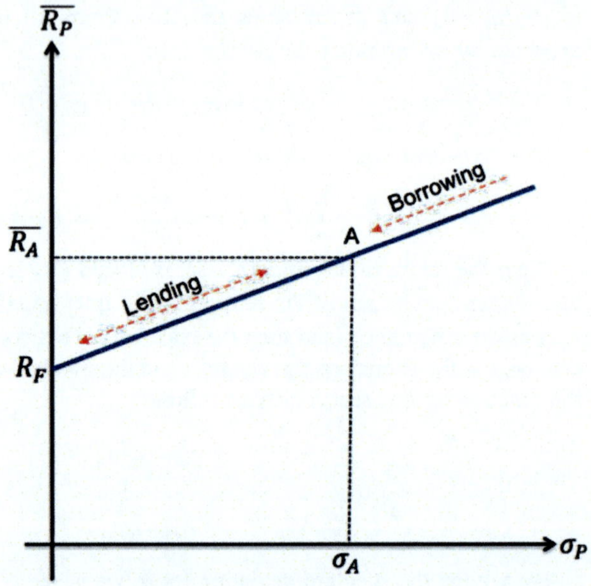

Fig. 10.4 Portfolio of *N* risky assets and one riskless asset

$$\overline{R_P} = R_F + \sigma_P \pi_A \tag{10.30}$$

All combinations of riskless lending or borrowing (*F*) with the portfolio of risky asset (*A*) lie on a straight-line as represented in Fig. 10.4. Note that the line passes through the point *A* $(\sigma_A; \overline{R_A})$. Even if this point has not special properties in this analysis, it distinguishes two parts:

- to the left of the point *A*, we have combinations of lending and portfolio *A*
- to the right of the point *A*, we have combinations of borrowing and portfolio *A*.

Now consider the straight-line and the efficient frontier jointly as in Fig. 10.5.

All portfolios of risky assets (*A*, *B*, *C*) on the efficient frontier are combined with riskless asset (*F*) at which we are lending and borrowing. By combining the portfolio of risky asset *A* with riskless asset (*F*), we can hold combinations along the straight-line R_FA, as well as combining the portfolio *B* with *F* we can hold combinations along the straight-line R_FB, as well as com combining the portfolio *C* with *F* we can hold combinations along the straight-line R_FC. The combinations along the straight-line R_FB are superior to combinations along the straight-line R_FA because they offer greater return for the same level of risk. For the same reason, the combinations along the straight-line R_FC are superior to combinations along the straight-line R_FB. The point *C* is the tangency point between the efficient frontier and the straight-line passing through the point R_F. Therefore, it is not possible to rotate the straight-line

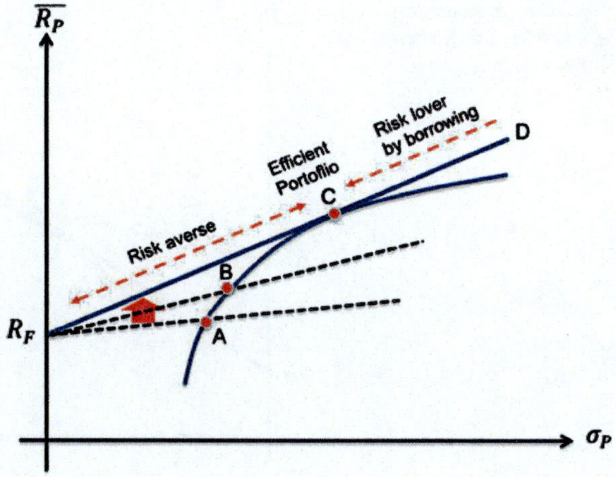

Fig. 10.5 Straight-line and efficient frontier

further because by the definition of efficient frontier there are no portfolio lying above the straight-line passing through R_F and C.

Therefore, for all investors the efficient portfolio is the portfolio C (portfolios A and B are dominated by the portfolio C). If investors can lend and borrow at the same risk-free rate, there is a single portfolio of risky assets (C) that is preferred to all other portfolios. In this case, the efficient frontier is the entire length of the ray extending through R_F and C. Different points along this ray are different amounts of borrowing and/or lending in combination with the optimum portfolio of risky assets C. Remember that the line R_FC is the line with the greatest slope.

Investors who are very risk averse would select the portfolio along the segment R_FC by combining the riskless asset (F) and the portfolio of risky asset (C). On the contrary, investors who are much more tolerant of risk would hold portfolios along the segment CD by borrowing funds and by placing their capital plus the capital borrowed in portfolio of risky asset C. Therefore, the portfolio C represents a solution of the portfolio problem because it is the optimum portfolio of risky assets.

Now consider a more restrictive assumption. In the case just analysed the investor can lend and borrow at the same free-risk rate. If we modify this assumption, the shape of efficient frontier changes.

Consider the two following cases.

Case 1) Assume that investors can lend at the risk-free rate (buy government bonds) but they cannot borrow at this same rate. Under this assumption, the efficient frontier becomes R_FCD. Even if certain investors would decide to hold portfolios of risky assets located between C and D, any investor who held some riskless asset place all remaining funds in the risky portfolio C.

Case 2) Assume that investors can lend at one rate R_F but they borrow at different rate R'_F where probably $R'_F > R_F$. Under this assumption, where the borrowing

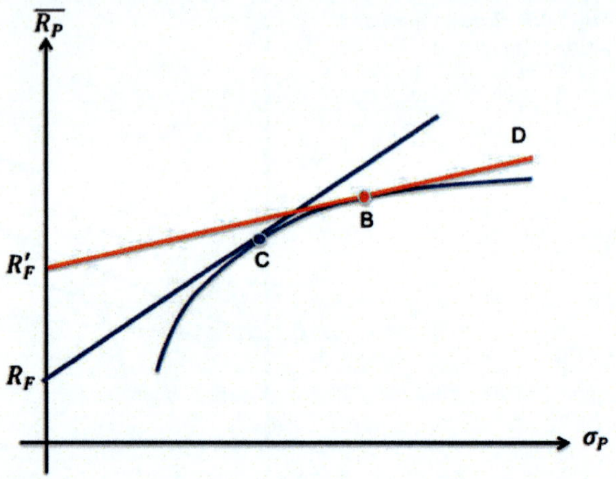

Fig. 10.6 Investors can lend at rate R_F but they borrow at different rate R'_F where $R'_F > R_F$

rate (R'_F) is different and higher than the lending rate (R_F), the efficient frontier changes and it becomes R_FCBD as in Fig. 10.6.

However, if the difference between R_F and R'_F is small, the assumption of lending and borrowing at the same risk-free rate could provide a good approximation.

10.4 Determination of the Efficient Frontier

To determine the efficient frontier, we can consider several assumptions. In this contest, we assume that the short sales are allowed and we will consider two cases (Elton et al., 2013):

- *case 1)* investors can borrow and lend at a risk-free rate ($R_{F,}$)
- *case 2)* investors cannot borrow and lend at a risk-free rate (R_F).

10.4.1 Case 1) Short Sales Allowed and Riskless Lending and Borrowing

Assume that the (1) short sales allowed and (2) investors can borrow and lend at the riskless rate of interest (R_F).

This is the simplest case to derive the efficient set. Indeed, the existence of a riskless lending and borrowing rate implies that there is only one risk-free rate (R_F) and then there is a single portfolio of risky assets that is preferred to all other portfolios: it is the tangent point between the straight-line and the efficient frontier.

We have analysed as the efficient frontier is the entire length of the line extending through R_F and C. All different points along the line R_FC are the different amounts of borrowing and/or lending in combination with the optimum portfolio of risky assets C.

Because the line R_FC is the line with the greatest slope, and by considering that the slope of the straight-line connecting a riskless asset (where the intercept is the risk-free rate) and a risky portfolio is equal in this case to $\frac{\overline{R_P}-R_F}{\sigma_P}$, (that is the Sharpe Ratio), then we can determine the efficient set by finding that portfolio able to maximize that slope under the constrain that the sum of the weights is equal to 1, as follows:

$$\begin{cases} \max\limits_{\alpha_i} \theta = \dfrac{\overline{R_P}-R_F}{\sigma_P} \\ \sum\limits_{i=1}^{N} \alpha_i = 1. \end{cases} \tag{10.31}$$

where the first is the objective function to be maximized and the second is the constraint.

To avoid the Lagrange multiplier $(\mathcal{L})$, the constraint can be replaced in the equation to be maximized (see Elton et al., 2013). It is possible to multiply both terms of the constraint for risk-free rate (R_F) as follows:

$$R_F \sum_{i=1}^{N} \alpha_i = R_F \quad \rightarrow \quad \sum_{i=1}^{N} (\alpha_i R_F) = R_F$$

By considering that the portfolio's expected return $\left(\overline{R_P}\right)$ and its standard deviation (σ_P) are equal to:

$$\overline{R_P} = \sum_{i=1}^{N} \alpha_i \overline{R_i}$$

$$\sigma_P = \sqrt{\sum_{i=1}^{N} \alpha_i^2 \sigma_i^2 + \sum_{i=1}^{N} \sum_{\substack{j=1 \\ j \neq i}}^{N} \alpha_i \alpha_j \sigma_{i,j}} = \left(\sum_{i=1}^{N} \alpha_i^2 \sigma_i^2 + \sum_{i=1}^{N} \sum_{\substack{j=1 \\ j \neq i}}^{N} \alpha_i \alpha_j \sigma_{i,j} \right)^{\frac{1}{2}}$$

and by substituting the constraint in the equation to be maximized, we have:

$$\theta = \frac{\overline{R_P} - R_F}{\sigma_P} = \frac{\sum_{i=1}^{N} \alpha_i \overline{R_i} - \sum_{i=1}^{N} (\alpha_i R_F)}{\left(\sum_{i=1}^{N} \alpha_i^2 \sigma_i^2 + \sum_{i=1}^{N} \sum_{\substack{j=1 \\ j \neq i}}^{N} \alpha_i \alpha_j \sigma_{i,j} \right)^{\frac{1}{2}}}$$

$$= \frac{\sum_{i=1}^{N} \alpha_i \left(\overline{R_i} - R_F \right)}{\left(\sum_{i=1}^{N} \alpha_i^2 \sigma_i^2 + \sum_{i=1}^{N} \sum_{\substack{j=1 \\ j \neq i}}^{N} \alpha_i \alpha_j \sigma_{i,j} \right)^{\frac{1}{2}}}$$

and then:

$$\theta = \frac{\overline{R_P} - R_F}{\sigma_P} = \frac{\sum_{i=1}^{N} \alpha_i \left(\overline{R_i} - R_F \right)}{\left(\sum_{i=1}^{N} \alpha_i^2 \sigma_i^2 + \sum_{i=1}^{N} \sum_{\substack{j=1 \\ j \neq i}}^{N} \alpha_i \alpha_j \sigma_{i,j} \right)^{\frac{1}{2}}} \tag{10.32}$$

In this case, the constrain is included into the objective function so that the objective function maximized as in an unconstrained problem.

Therefore, we have to derive the objective function to be maximized (θ) with respect to the weight of the k-th asset (α_k).

To simplify we can rewrite the objective function as follows:

$$\theta = \left[\sum_{i=1}^{N} \alpha_i \left(\overline{R_i} - R_F \right) \right] \left[\sum_{i=1}^{N} \alpha_i^2 \sigma_i^2 + \sum_{i=1}^{N} \sum_{\substack{j=1 \\ j \neq i}}^{N} \alpha_i \alpha_j \sigma_{i,j} \right]^{\left(-\frac{1}{2}\right)}$$

We have the product of two functions:

$$F_1 = \left[\sum_{i=1}^{N} \alpha_i \left(\overline{R_i} - R_F\right)\right]; \quad F_2 = \left[\sum_{i=1}^{N} \alpha_i^2 \sigma_i^2 + \sum_{i=1}^{N} \sum_{\substack{j=1 \\ j \neq i}}^{N} \alpha_i \alpha_j \sigma_{i,j}\right]^{\left(-\frac{1}{2}\right)}$$

The derivative of the first function with respect to α_k is equal to:

$$\frac{\partial F_1}{\partial \alpha_k} = \frac{\partial}{\partial \alpha_k}\left[\sum_{i=1}^{N} \alpha_i \left(\overline{R_i} - R_F\right)\right] = \overline{R_k} - R_F$$

Indeed, the expression involves a lot of terms that do not contain α_k and only one that contain α_k. Since the derivation is with respect to α_k, all those terms that do not contain α_k are equal to zero because they are constants and the only term involving α_k is equal to $\alpha_k\left(\overline{R_i} - R_F\right)$ and its derivative with respect to α_k is equal to $\overline{R_k} - R_F$.

The derivative of the second function with respect to α_k is more complex. Before to start remember the computation of the asset marginal contribution to the portfolio's variance, where:

$$\frac{\partial}{\partial \alpha_k}\left[\sum_{i=1}^{n} \alpha_i^2 \sigma_i^2\right] = \frac{\partial}{\partial \alpha_k}\left[\alpha_k^2 \sigma_k^2\right] = 2\alpha_k \sigma_k^2$$

$$\frac{\partial}{\partial \alpha_k}\left[\sum_{i=1}^{n} \sum_{\substack{j=1 \\ j \neq i}}^{n} \alpha_i \alpha_j \sigma_{ij}\right] = 2 \sum_{\substack{j=1 \\ j \neq k}}^{n} \alpha_j \sigma_{kj}$$

so that:

$$\frac{\partial}{\partial \alpha_k}\left[\sum_{i=1}^{n} \alpha_i^2 \sigma_i^2 + \sum_{i=1}^{n} \sum_{\substack{j=1 \\ j \neq i}}^{n} \alpha_i \alpha_j \sigma_{ij}\right] = 2\alpha_k \sigma_k^2 + 2 \sum_{\substack{j=1 \\ j \neq k}}^{n} \alpha_j \sigma_{kj}$$

Consequently, the derivative of the second function is equal to:

$$\frac{\partial F_2}{\partial \alpha_k} = \frac{\partial}{\partial \alpha_k}\left[\sum_{i=1}^{N}\alpha_i^2\sigma_i^2 + \sum_{i=1}^{N}\sum_{\substack{j=1\\ j\neq i}}^{N}\alpha_i\alpha_j\sigma_{i,j}\right]^{\left(-\frac{1}{2}\right)}$$

$$= \left(-\frac{1}{2}\right)\left(\sum_{i=1}^{n}\alpha_i^2\sigma_i^2 + \sum_{i=1}^{n}\sum_{\substack{j=1\\ j\neq i}}^{n}\alpha_i\alpha_j\sigma_{ij}\right)^{\left(-\frac{1}{2}-1=-\frac{3}{2}\right)}\left(2\alpha_k\sigma_k^2 + 2\sum_{\substack{j=1\\ j\neq k}}^{n}\alpha_j\sigma_{kj}\right)$$

Knowing the derivative of the first function ($\partial F_1/\partial \alpha_k$) and the second function ($\partial F_2/\partial \alpha_k$), the derivative of the objective function with respect to α_k ($\partial \theta/\partial \alpha_k$) is equal to:

$$\frac{\partial \theta}{\partial \alpha_k} = \frac{\partial}{\partial \alpha_k}\left[\left[\sum_{i=1}^{N}\alpha_i\left(\overline{R_i} - R_F\right)\right]\left[\sum_{i=1}^{N}\alpha_i^2\sigma_i^2 + \sum_{i=1}^{N}\sum_{\substack{j=1\\ j\neq i}}^{N}\alpha_i\alpha_j\sigma_{i,j}\right]^{\left(-\frac{1}{2}\right)}\right]$$

$$= \left[\sum_{i=1}^{N}\alpha_i\left(\overline{R_i} - R_F\right)\right]$$

$$\times\left[\left(-\frac{1}{2}\right)\left(\sum_{i=1}^{n}\alpha_i^2\sigma_i^2 + \sum_{i=1}^{n}\sum_{\substack{j=1\\ j\neq i}}^{n}\alpha_i\alpha_j\sigma_{ij}\right)^{\left(-\frac{3}{2}\right)}\left(2\alpha_k\sigma_k^2 + 2\sum_{\substack{j=1\\ j\neq k}}^{n}\alpha_j\sigma_{kj}\right)\right]$$

$$+\left[\left(\overline{R_k} - R_F\right)\left[\sum_{i=1}^{N}\alpha_i^2\sigma_i^2 + \sum_{i=1}^{N}\sum_{\substack{j=1\\ j\neq i}}^{N}\alpha_i\alpha_j\sigma_{i,j}\right]^{\left(-\frac{1}{2}\right)}\right]$$

Set the derivative equal to zero $\left(\frac{\partial \theta}{\partial \alpha_k} = 0\right)$ to find the stationary point, as follows:

$$\left[\left[\sum_{i=1}^{N}\alpha_i\left(\overline{R_i}-R_F\right)\right]\left[\left(-\frac{1}{2}\right)\left(\sum_{i=1}^{n}\alpha_i^2\sigma_i^2+\sum_{i=1}^{n}\sum_{\substack{j=1\\j\neq i}}^{n}\alpha_i\alpha_j\sigma_{ij}\right)^{\left(-\frac{3}{2}\right)}\left(2\alpha_k\sigma_k^2+2\sum_{\substack{j=1\\j\neq k}}^{n}\alpha_j\sigma_{kj}\right)\right]\right]$$

$$+\left[\left(\overline{R_k}-R_F\right)\left[\sum_{i=1}^{N}\alpha_i^2\sigma_i^2+\sum_{i=1}^{N}\sum_{\substack{j=1\\j\neq i}}^{N}\alpha_i\alpha_j\sigma_{i,j}\right]^{\left(-\frac{1}{2}\right)}\right]=0$$

Multiplying both terms by

$$\left(\sum_{i=1}^{n}\alpha_i^2\sigma_i^2+\sum_{i=1}^{n}\sum_{\substack{j=1\\j\neq i}}^{n}\alpha_i\alpha_j\sigma_{ij}\right)^{\frac{1}{2}}$$

we have:

$$\left[\left[\sum_{i=1}^{N}\alpha_i\left(\overline{R_i}-R_F\right)\right]\left[\left(-\frac{1}{2}\right)\left(\sum_{i=1}^{n}\alpha_i^2\sigma_i^2+\sum_{i=1}^{n}\sum_{\substack{j=1\\j\neq i}}^{n}\alpha_i\alpha_j\sigma_{ij}\right)^{\left(-\frac{3}{2}\right)}\left(2\alpha_k\sigma_k^2+2\sum_{\substack{j=1\\j\neq k}}^{n}\alpha_j\sigma_{kj}\right)\right]\left(\sum_{i=1}^{n}\alpha_i^2\sigma_i^2+\sum_{i=1}^{n}\sum_{\substack{j=1\\j\neq i}}^{n}\alpha_i\alpha_j\sigma_{ij}\right)^{\frac{1}{2}}\right]$$

$$+\left[\left(\overline{R_k}-R_F\right)\left[\sum_{i=1}^{N}\alpha_i^2\sigma_i^2+\sum_{i=1}^{N}\sum_{\substack{j=1\\j\neq i}}^{N}\alpha_i\alpha_j\sigma_{i,j}\right]^{\left(-\frac{1}{2}\right)}\left(\sum_{i=1}^{n}\alpha_i^2\sigma_i^2+\sum_{i=1}^{n}\sum_{\substack{j=1\\j\neq i}}^{n}\alpha_i\alpha_j\sigma_{ij}\right)^{\frac{1}{2}}\right]=0$$

and then:

$$\left[\left[\sum_{i=1}^{N}\alpha_i\left(\overline{R_i}-R_F\right)\right]\left[\left(-\frac{1}{2}\right)\left(\sum_{i=1}^{n}\alpha_i^2\sigma_i^2+\sum_{i=1}^{n}\sum_{\substack{j=1\\j\neq i}}^{n}\alpha_i\alpha_j\sigma_{ij}\right)^{\left(-\frac{3}{2}+\frac{1}{2}=-\frac{2}{2}=-1\right)}\left(2\alpha_k\sigma_k^2+2\sum_{\substack{j=1\\j\neq k}}^{n}\alpha_j\sigma_{kj}\right)\right]\right]$$

$$+\left[\left(\overline{R_k}-R_F\right)\right]=0$$

and:

$$\left[\left[\sum_{i=1}^{N}\alpha_i\left(\overline{R_i}-R_F\right)\right]\left[\left(-\frac{1}{2}\right)\frac{\left(2\alpha_k\sigma_k^2+2\sum_{\substack{j=1\\j\neq k}}^{n}\alpha_j\sigma_{kj}\right)}{\left(\sum_{i=1}^{n}\alpha_i^2\sigma_i^2+\sum_{i=1}^{n}\sum_{\substack{j=1\\j\neq i}}^{n}\alpha_i\alpha_j\sigma_{ij}\right)}\right]\right]$$
$$+\left[\left(\overline{R_k}-R_F\right)\right]=0$$

$$\left[\left[\sum_{i=1}^{N}\alpha_i\left(\overline{R_i}-R_F\right)\right]\left[\left(-\frac{1}{2}\right)\frac{2\left(\alpha_k\sigma_k^2+\sum_{\substack{j=1\\j\neq k}}^{n}\alpha_j\sigma_{kj}\right)}{\left(\sum_{i=1}^{n}\alpha_i^2\sigma_i^2+\sum_{i=1}^{n}\sum_{\substack{j=1\\j\neq i}}^{n}\alpha_i\alpha_j\sigma_{ij}\right)}\right]\right]$$
$$+\left[\left(\overline{R_k}-R_F\right)\right]=0$$

$$\left[\left[\sum_{i=1}^{N}\alpha_i\left(\overline{R_i}-R_F\right)\right]\left[-\frac{\left(\alpha_k\sigma_k^2+\sum_{\substack{j=1\\j\neq k}}^{n}\alpha_j\sigma_{kj}\right)}{\left(\sum_{i=1}^{n}\alpha_i^2\sigma_i^2+\sum_{i=1}^{n}\sum_{\substack{j=1\\j\neq i}}^{n}\alpha_i\alpha_j\sigma_{ij}\right)}\right]\right]+\left[\left(\overline{R_k}-R_F\right)\right]=0$$

Rearranged, we have:

$$\left[-\left(\frac{\sum_{i=1}^{N}\alpha_i(\overline{R_i}-R_F)}{\sum_{i=1}^{n}\alpha_i^2\sigma_i^2+\sum_{i=1}^{n}\sum_{\substack{j=1\\j\neq i}}^{n}\alpha_i\alpha_j\sigma_{ij}}\right)\left(\alpha_k\sigma_k^2+\sum_{\substack{j=1\\j\neq k}}^{n}\alpha_j\sigma_{kj}\right)\right]+\left[(\overline{R_k}-R_F)\right]=0$$

Denote with λ:

$$\lambda=\frac{\sum_{i=1}^{N}\alpha_i(\overline{R_i}-R_F)}{\sum_{i=1}^{n}\alpha_i^2\sigma_i^2+\sum_{i=1}^{n}\sum_{\substack{j=1\\j\neq i}}^{n}\alpha_i\alpha_j\sigma_{ij}}$$

and replacing, we have:

$$-\lambda\left(\alpha_k\sigma_k^2+\sum_{\substack{j=1\\j\neq k}}^{n}\alpha_j\sigma_{kj}\right)+\left[(\overline{R_k}-R_F)\right]=0$$

and then, we have:

$$\frac{\partial\theta}{\partial\alpha_k}=-\left(\lambda\alpha_k\sigma_k^2+\sum_{\substack{j-1\\j\neq k}}^{n}\lambda\alpha_j\sigma_{kj}\right)+\left[(\overline{R_k}-R_F)\right]=0 \qquad (10.33)$$

In our case, to find the maximum of the function, we take the derivative with respect to each variable α_i (for $i=1,2,3,\ldots,n$) and set it equal to zero. The solution of the maximization problem requires to find the solution of the system of simultaneous equations as follows:

$$\begin{cases} \dfrac{\partial \theta}{\partial \alpha_1} = 0 \\ \dfrac{\partial \theta}{\partial \alpha_2} = 0 \\ \dots \\ \dots \\ \dfrac{\partial \theta}{\partial \alpha_n} = 0 \end{cases}$$

Based on the derivative of the function θ with respect to α_k, the derivative of the function θ with respect to each α_i, is equal to:

$$\frac{\partial \theta}{\partial \alpha_i} = -\left(\lambda\alpha_1\sigma_{1,i} + \lambda\alpha_2\sigma_{2,i} + \lambda\alpha_3\sigma_{3,i} \dots + \lambda\alpha_i\sigma_i^2 + \dots + \lambda\alpha_{n-1}\sigma_{n-1,i} + \lambda\alpha_n\sigma_{n,i}\right) + \overline{R_k} - R_F = 0$$

We can simplify the derivative. Since in equation λ is a constant (it is equal to: $\lambda = \left(\overline{R_P} - R_F\right)/\sigma_P^2$), then each α_i is multiplied by a constant. Therefore, we can define a new variable: $Z_i = \lambda\alpha_i$. Substituting, we have:

$$\frac{\partial \theta}{\partial \alpha_k} = -\left(Z_1\sigma_{1,i} + Z_2\sigma_{2,i} + Z_3\sigma_{3,i} \dots + Z_i\sigma_i^2 + \dots + Z_{n-1}\sigma_{n-1,i} + Z_n\sigma_{n,i}\right) + \overline{R_k} - R_F = 0$$

and then:

$$Z_1\sigma_{1,i} + Z_2\sigma_{2,i} + Z_3\sigma_{3,i} \dots + Z_i\sigma_i^2 + \dots + Z_{n-1}\sigma_{n-1,i} + Z_n\sigma_{n,i} = \overline{R_k} - R_F$$

Therefore, we have one equation for each value of i = 1, 2, 3, …, n. Consequently, we have a system of simultaneous equations as follows:

$$\begin{cases} Z_1\sigma_1^2 + Z_2\sigma_{12} + Z_3\sigma_{13} + \dots + Z_n\sigma_{1n} = \overline{R_1} - R_F \\ Z_1\sigma_{12} + Z_2\sigma_2^2 + Z_3\sigma_{23} + \dots + Z_n\sigma_{2n} = \overline{R_2} - R_F \\ Z_1\sigma_{13} + Z_2\sigma_{23} + Z_3\sigma_3^2 + \dots + Z_n\sigma_{3n} = \overline{R_3} - R_F \\ \dots \\ Z_1\sigma_{1n} + Z_2\sigma_{2,n} + Z_3\sigma_{3,n} + \dots + Z_n\sigma_n^2 = \overline{R_n} - R_F \end{cases} \tag{10.34}$$

Therefore, the optimum portfolio is the one that solves this system of simultaneous equations.

The optimum part of wealth to be invested in i-th asset is obtained by solving the equation for the sum of the Z_i as follows:

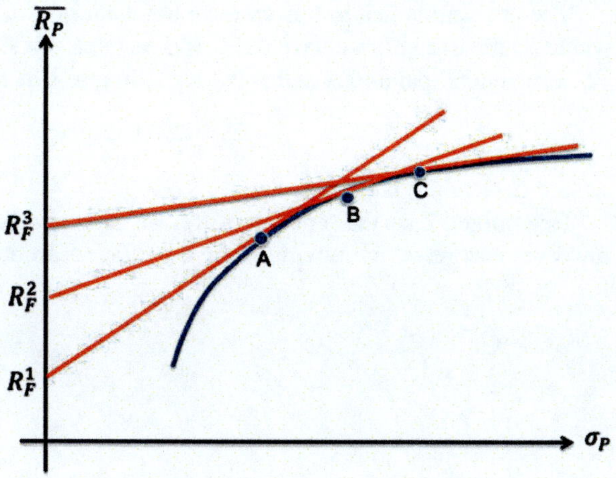

Fig. 10.7 Riskless rates and optimum portfolios

$$\alpha_i = \frac{Z_i}{\sum_{i=1}^{n} Z_i} \tag{10.35}$$

Defined optimum amount to invest in each asset α_i (for $i = 1, 2, 3, \ldots, n$) we can compute the portfolio's expected return and variance.

10.4.2 Case 2) Short Sales Allowed and No Riskless Lending and Borrowing

Assume that the (1) short sales allowed but (2) investors cannot borrow and lend at the riskless rate of interest (R_F).

In this case, we have several risk-free rates and then we have several optimum portfolios one for each tangent point. Assume to have three riskless lending and borrowing rates $R_F^1; R_F^2; R_F^3$. At each one level correspond one optimum portfolio A, B,C given by the tangent point between the straight-line passing $R_F^1; R_F^2; R_F^3$ and tangent to the efficient frontier as showed in Fig. 10.7.

Consider the system of simultaneous equations in the previous case (Case 1):

$$\begin{cases} Z_1\sigma_1^2 + Z_2\sigma_{12} + Z_3\sigma_{13} + \ldots + Z_n\sigma_{1n} = \overline{R_1} - R_F \\ Z_1\sigma_{12} + Z_2\sigma_2^2 + Z_3\sigma_{23} + \ldots + Z_n\sigma_{2n} = \overline{R_2} - R_F \\ Z_1\sigma_{13} + Z_2\sigma_{23} + Z_3\sigma_3^2 + \ldots + Z_n\sigma_{3n} = \overline{R_3} - R_F \\ \ldots \\ Z_1\sigma_{1n} + Z_2\sigma_{2,n} + Z_3\sigma_{3,n} + \ldots + Z_n\sigma_n^2 = \overline{R_n} - R_F \end{cases}$$

The problem is that in this case we have not one value of R_F but more than one value (in the example we have three riskless rates: $R_F^1; R_F^2; R_F^3$). A solution is to leave R_F as a general parameter and solve for Z_i in terms of R_F as follows:

$$Z_i = C_{oi} + C_{1i}R_F \tag{10.36}$$

where C_{oi} and C_{1i} are constants.

Determined Z_i as the function of R_F, we can vary R_F to determine the amount to invest in each asset by moving along the efficient frontier.

11 Optimum Portfolio

11.1 Expected Utility Theorem

The mean-variance approach does not define the optimum portfolio for each investor. The efficient frontier is defined by all efficient portfolios among them the investor must choices on the basis of its preference about risk. This choice depends on the investor's behaviour and preference about the risk. The definition of the degree of risk aversion of investor is out of the data input of mean-variance approach.

The choice of optimum portfolio for the investor can be made on the basis of the *theory of expected utility*: defined the utility function of the investor, the choice of optimum portfolios among the efficient portfolios (on the efficient frontier) is the one able to maximize the investor's expected utility.

The theory of the choices under uncertainty in financial markets defines the behaviour of rational investor who have to decide under uncertainty.

The choice under certainty condition is characterized by a well-defined bidirectional relationship between decisions to be made and their effects in terms of outcomes. It implies that when the decision is made, its outcome is known, as well as, if the outcome is known, we can know the decision made. Consequently, if it is not necessary to distinguish between decisions and outcomes, we can choose the outcome that we want to realize and then we automatically know the decision to be taken.

The choice under certainty requires that the outcomes are ordinated on the basis of the individual's preferences by considering the constraints. Indeed, among decisions that satisfy the constraints, the best outcome for individual is the highest in its scale of preference. Since there is a bidirectional relationship between decision and outcomes, the choosing of the best outcome implies the choice of the decision to be made.

The choice under uncertainty condition implies that there is not the bidirectional relationship between decisions and their effects in terms of outcomes. For any decision we have infinite outcomes because between them there is the random

P. De Luca, *Corporate Finance*, Springer Texts in Business and Economics,
https://doi.org/10.1007/978-3-031-18300-3_11

variable called States of Nature (*SN*). It implies that it is not possible to define the decision to be made on the basis of the preference about its outcomes.

The relationship between decision (*D*), states of nature (*SN*), and the outcomes (*Y*) can be defined as follows:

$$Y = p(D; SN)$$

Therefore, any outcome (*Y*) is the function (p) of a decision (*D*) made and the state of nature (*SN*) realized. Denote with:

- a_i (for $i = 1, 2, 3, \ldots, n$) the set of decisions and each of them belongs to the set of possible decisions (*D*) so that $a_i \in D$.
- s_{nj} (for $j = 1, 2, 3, \ldots, n$) the states of nature that will could be realized and each of them belongs to the set of possible states of nature (*SN*) so that $sn_j \in SN$.
- $y_{i,\,j}$ (for $i = 1, 2, 3, \ldots, n$; $j = 1, 2, 3, \ldots, n$) the outcomes related to the i-th decision (a_i) when the *j*-th state of nature (s_j) is realized.

Under the assumption of no correlation between the set of possible decisions (*D*) and the set of possible states of nature (*SN*), so that each decision (a_i) can never affect the state of nature (sn_j), we have:

$$y_{i,j} = p\left(a_i; sn_j\right)$$

where $y_{i,\,j}$ is a real number associated with each pair $p(a_i; s_{nj})$.

If we assign a probability π_s ($s = 1, 2, 3, \ldots S$) to each state of nature (sn_j) that could be achieved, so that $\sum_{s=1}^{n} \pi_s = 1$, we have:

$$y_{i,j} = p\left(a_i; \pi_s\left(sn_j\right)\right) \tag{11.1}$$

Therefore, the outcome ($y_{i,\,j}$) is the result of the combination between decision made (a_i) and the probability (π_s) associated with the state of nature (sn_j) expected. Consequently, we can associate a probability distribution to each decision where this probability can be estimated based on the relative frequencies or purely subjective. *It implies that the choice between different decisions (a_i) becomes the choice between different probability distributions associated to the possible outcomes of decisions.* Therefore, the investor's preferences are expressed according to the probability distribution associated with the decision. In other words, the investor's choice refers to the probability distribution associated with the decision.

We can use the theory of expected utility to make decision under uncertainty. It is based on two main pillars:

1. The *probability distribution* associate to each decision: for each decision we have to define a finite number of possible outcomes and associate to each one its probability of realization. Consequently, each decision is characterized by a probability distribution with regard to the probability associate to its finite

number of possible outcomes. If we denote with p a generic probability distribution and with $p(x_i)$ the probability assigned to the generic outcome x_i, we have two main conditions: (1) $0 < p(x_i) < 1$ and (2) $\sum_{i=1}^{n} p(x_i) = 1$.
Since each decision is defined in terms of probability distribution associated to its outcomes, the choice between different decisions becomes the choice between different probability distributions. Thus, the preference about decisions becomes the preference about the probability distribution associated to its outcomes. The preference are used to ordinary the probability distribution so that the best distribution is positioned at the top in the scale of preference while the worst at the bottom of the scale. If we have two probability distributions, p and q, three are the possible cases: (1) the probability distribution p is *strictly preferred* to the probability distribution q ($p \succ q$); (2) the probability distribution p is *weakly preferred* to the probability distribution q ($p \succcurlyeq q$); and (3) the probability distribution p is *indifferent* in preference term to the probability distribution q ($p \sim q$). Therefore, the decision P is preferred to the decision Q only if the probability distribution p is preferred to the probability distribution ($p \succ q$).
2. The *utility function* defined on the basis of each outcome: decisions are evaluated on the basis of the expected utility ($E[U(x)]$) rather than their expected value ($E(x)$). The best decision is the one that maximizes the expected utility and thus the decision with the higher expected utility.

The use of the expected utility to represent the preferences in the choice under uncertainty requires that the preferences about the probability distribution must respect specific axioms relate to the individual behaviour and then his preference on the probability distribution. Then, if and only if the probability distributions respect these specific axioms, they can be represented by using expected utility.

Specifically, if the individual behaviour respects these axioms, we can say that a decision A is preferred to a decision B if and only if the decision A has higher expected utility than the decision B.

The use of the theory of the utility function (so that the utility function is used to represent and order the investor's preferences and the preferred decision is the one able to maximize the expected utility) implies that the problem of choice under uncertainty is assimilated to the problem of choice under certainty so that we can use the same analytical tools.

Formally, by considering the probability distribution associated to each decision and the utility function to be used, the utility of the i-th decision (a_i) can be defined as follows:

$$E[U(a_i)] = \pi_1 U(y_{a_i,sn_1}) + \pi_2 U(y_{a_i,sn_2}) + \ldots + \pi_S U(y_{a_i,sn_n})$$
$$= \sum_{i=1}^{n} \pi_i U(y_{a_i,sn_n}) \tag{11.2}$$

where:

- a_i: is the i-th decision (for $i = 1, 2, \ldots, n$) among the possible ones ($a \in D$)
- $U(.)$: is the utility function used
- $y_{a_i,sn}$: are the outcomes arising from the joint combination between the i-th decision (a_i) and the s-th state of nature (for $sn = 1, 2, \ldots, S$)
- π_i: is the probability associated to each state of nature (for $i = 1, 2, \ldots, n$).

Therefore, the decision A is preferred to the decision B, only if the expected utility of the decision A is greater than the decision B:

$$\mathrm{A} \succ \mathrm{B} \leftrightarrow \sum_{i=1}^{n} \pi_i U(y_{a_i,sn_n}) > \sum_{i=1}^{n} \pi_i U(y_{b_i,sn_n}) \tag{11.3}$$

11.1.1 Axiomatic Theory

The preferences can be represented by expected utility only if they respect well-defined axioms about the individual's behaviour.

Generally, economists usually make some assumptions to define the consistency of consumers' preferences. These assumptions define the consumers' behaviour and the way by which the preference relations work. Some assumptions about preference relations are: so fundamental that we usually refer to them as *"axioms" of consumer theory*. If the consumers' behaviour about preference relations respects these assumptions (axioms), we can say that consumers' preferences are consistent.

In this contest, we use the axiomatic approach to define the baseline properties of the rational behaviour of the investor. It implies that the investor's behaviour can be defined rational only if it respects these axioms. Only in this case, the investor's preferences can be classified on the basis of the utility functions. Therefore, it is the axiomatic approach to guarantee the coherence and the rigorous nature of the theory of decisions under uncertainty.

Therefore, if investor's behaviour is aligned to axioms, saying that "decision A is preferred to the decision B" is the same as saying "decision A has a greater expected utility than the decision B". Consequently, the decision A is preferred to the decision B if and only if the first has a greater expected utility than the second. In this sense, the expected utility is a numerical representation of the preferences.

Therefore, if investor's behaviour is in line with these axioms, then it is possible to use the utility function ($U(.)$). They are used to describe and order the investor's preferences only. Then, the value of the utility function, in absolute terms, is not relevant.

11.1.2 Axiom 1: Consistent—Completeness and Transitivity

Preferences must be *complete*. Given two probability distributions, it is always possible for investor to choose the one he prefers or to express his indifference to the choice.

Assuming two probability distribution, p e q, we have:

$$p \succcurlyeq q \text{ or } q \succcurlyeq p \text{ or } p \sim q \tag{11.4}$$

Also, preferences must be *transitive*. If the distribution of probability p is preferred, at least to the probability distribution q, and if, in turn, the probability distribution q is preferred at least to the probability distribution r, then the probability distribution p is preferred at least to the probability distribution r, as follows:

$$p \succcurlyeq q \text{ and } q \succcurlyeq r \quad \Rightarrow \quad p \succcurlyeq r \tag{11.5}$$

If preferences are complete and transitive, they are consistent. Preferences must be consistent because they allow the best choice for each investor on the basis of its own preferences. Therefore, this axiom is fundamental for the maximization of the preferences by giving the opportunity to make the optimal choice for investor on the basis of its preferences.

11.1.3 Axiom 2: Monotonicity

Preferences must be *monotonic* because the *more is always better*. If two distributions of probability are associated with the same outcomes, the decision to be made is the one that provides the best outcomes with the highest level of probability.

Assume two distributions (δ): the first providing the best result (δ_m) with certainty and the second providing the worst result (δ_p) with certainty. Denote with α and β the probability (both between 0 and 1) and use the symbols o and $\bigoplus$ to indicate how the distributions are made. We have:

$$\alpha \, o \, \delta_m \bigoplus (1-\alpha) \, o \, \delta_p \succcurlyeq \beta \, o \, \delta_m \bigoplus (1-\beta) \, o \, \delta_p \quad \Leftrightarrow \quad \alpha \geq \beta \tag{11.6}$$

Therefore, given two deterministic distributions (δ_m and δ_p), the preference is a function of the probability (α and β) of execution and their combination.

11.1.4 Axiom 3: Continuity

Preferences must be *continuous* because the function must be derivable at least twice.

Given two positions, it must be always possible to construct an intermediate position in function of the investor's preference.

Denote with r the distributions that assigns probability 1 to the result x so that $r = \delta_x$, with α the probability between 0 and 1, and with P the set of probability distribution.

Consider the following two alternatives:

- Alternative 1: achieving a defined result with certainty that is assumed to be equal to δ_x.
- Alternative 2: achieving a probability distribution $[\alpha\ o\ \delta_m \bigoplus (1 - \alpha)\ o\ \delta_p]$ resulting in the distributions to achieve the best result (δ_m) and the worst result (δ_p) both with certainty.

In this case, we have:

$$\forall r \in P \exists \alpha \in [0, 1] : r \sim \alpha\, o\, \delta_m \bigoplus (1 - \alpha)\, o\, \delta_p \tag{11.7}$$

The relationship states that:

1. If the probability α is close to 1, the investor prefers the second alternative. In this case, the probability distribution provides a higher probability of achieving the result equal to the best result of the distribution δ_m.
2. If the probability α is close to 0, the investor prefers the first alternative. In this case, the probability distribution provides a higher probability of achieving the result equal to the worst result of the degenerate distribution δ_p.

Therefore, given the two positions it is always possible to define an intermediate position based on a specific investor's preference operating through the mixture. It is always possible define a value of α able to make the investor indifferent between the probability distribution and the certain consequence.

11.1.5 Axiom 4: Independence

The probability distribution p is indifferent to the probability distribution q if any other probability distribution r is considered and the probability α between 0 and 1, we have:

$$\alpha\, o\, p \bigoplus (1 - \alpha)\, o\, r \sim \alpha\, o\, q \bigoplus (1 - \alpha)\, o\, r \tag{11.8}$$

Each of the two terms of the relationship can be considered as a particular probability distribution: with probability α it is obtained the probability distribution p (left side of the relationship) or the probability distribution q (right side of the relationship), while with residual probability $(1 - \alpha)$ is obtained the probability distribution r for both terms.

The difference between the two sides of the relationship ($[\alpha\ o\ p \bigoplus (1 - \alpha)\ o\ r]$ and $[\alpha\ o\ q \bigoplus (1 - \alpha)\ o\ r]$) is due to the probability distributions p and q. Consequently, the indifference between the two terms implies the indifference between p and q. It implies that there is not change to the preference between two probability distributions when an additional random element is introduced if it is added in the same manner in both probability distributions.

Note that if p and q are indifferent among them, the probability distribution p can be replaced by the probability distribution q, obtaining a new probability distribution that is equivalent (for this reason this axiom is also defined axiom of substitutability).

11.1.6 Axiom 5: Reduction

For investor's preference the only final probability associated to the effect is relevant.

Given the two distributions (δ), the first that generates the best result with certainty (δ_m) and the second that generates the worst result with certainty (δ_p), and using α and β to indicate the probability including between 0 and 1, we have:

$$\alpha\ o \left[\beta\ o\ \delta_m \bigoplus (1-\beta)\ o\ \delta_p\right] \bigoplus (1-\alpha)\ o\ \delta_p \sim \gamma\ o\ \delta_m \bigoplus (1-\gamma)\ o\ \delta_p \quad (11.9)$$

The $\gamma = \alpha\beta$ is the total probability to obtain δ_m. Indeed, for investor is indifferent to obtain δ_m at one time with probability γ, or twice with probability α and β.

11.2 Investor Behaviour About Risk

The investors behaviour about the risk can be analyzed by introducing three main baseline assumptions strictly derived by the axioms:

1. We measure the investment decision in terms of wealth as defined in monetary terms (w). It implies that the money is the only argument of the utility function $U(w)$. This assumption is restrictive and implies three main consequences: (1) *mono-dimensional outcomes* because the outcome can be shown through a number on the real number line; (2) *homogeneous behaviour of investors*; and (3) monotonicity of the expected utility function.
2. The utility function $U(w)$ must be *continuous* and at least *twice-differentiable*.
3. *Non-satiation of investor*. It can be expressed saying that "*more is always preferred to less*". Therefore, more wealth $(w + 1)$ is always preferred to less wealth (w). This property implies a restriction to the utility function. Indeed, the

Table 11.1 Fair gamble

Option 1: invest		Option 2: not invest	
Outcome	Probability	Outcome	Probability
€2	½	€1	1
€0	½		

utility must increase as wealth increases. Consequently, the first derivative of utility function (*U*(.)) with respect to wealth (*w*) must be always positive ($U'(w) > 0$) so that:

$$U(w_2) > U(w_1) \quad \forall w_2 > w_1 \quad \rightarrow \quad U'(W) > 0$$

Towards risk the investor can be *averse* (*risk aversion*), *neutral* (*risk neutrality*), or seek risk (*risk seeking*).

Note that the investor's behaviour towards risk (risk aversion, risk neutrality, risk seeking) is defined in terms of a *fair gamble*.

Assume the following fair gamble of Table 11.1

In both cases, assume that investor would have to pay €1 to undertake this investment.

The option 1 (invest) has an expected value equal to 1€ $\left[(€2)\left(\frac{1}{2}\right) + (€0)\left(\frac{1}{2}\right) = €1\right]$. In this case, the expected value is equal to the cost of investment (for this reason is called fair gamble).

The option 2 (not invest) has a certain value equal to €1 because it is the wealth that investor does not invest. The behaviour of investor about the investment depends on he is risk averse, risk neutral, or risk lover.

11.2.1 Risk Aversion

In case of risk aversion, investor rejects a fair gamble because €1 for certain will be preferred to an equal chance to be an outcome equal to €2 or €0. Investor rejects the fair gamble because the disutility of the loss is greater than the utility of an equivalent gain. Indeed, investor prefers money with certainty rather than engage in a fair gamble with the same expected value.

The assumption of risk aversion implies a restriction to the utility function. In this case, the second derivative of utility function (*U*(.)) with respect to wealth (*w*) must be negative: $U''(w) < 0$. Since the investor prefers not to invest, then the expected utility of not investing must be higher than the expected utility of investing. Considering the fair gamble, we have:

$$U(1) > \left(\frac{1}{2}\right)U(2) + \left(\frac{1}{2}\right)U(0)$$

If we multiply both sides by 2, we have:

$$2U(1) > 2\left(\frac{1}{2}\right)U(2) + 2\left(\frac{1}{2}\right)U(0)$$

$$U(1) + U(1) > U(2) + U(0)$$

and then:

$$U(1) - U(0) > U(2) - U(1)$$

In both sides of expression, we have an increase of one-unit. But if the investor is risk averse, the one-unit change from 0 to 1 is more valuable and then it is preferred than one-unit change from 1 to 2.

A utility function in which the additional unit increase is less valuable than the last unit increase is characterized by a negative second derivative. Therefore, the rejection of a fair gamble (assumption of risk aversion) implies the negative second derivative of the utility function.

We can generalize as follows. If $U(w_i)$ is the utility based on the utility function and $E[U(w_i)]$ is the expected utility, and p_i are the probability associated to any wealth outcome w_i so that $\sum_{i=1}^{n} p_i = 1$, we have:

$$E[U(w_i)] = \sum_{i=1}^{n} p_i U(w_i)$$

In case of risk aversion, the second derivative is negative ($U''(w) < 0$), so that:

$$E[U(w)] < U[E(w)] \tag{11.10}$$

Assume two values of wealth (w): w_1 that can be realized with probability p_1 and w_2 can be realized with probability $(1 - p_1)$, respectively. In this case, we have:

$$E[U(w_i)] = \sum_{i=1}^{n} p_i U(w_i) \quad \rightarrow \quad E[U(w)] = p_1 U(w_1) + (1 - p_1) U(w_2)$$

and

$$U[E(w)] = U[p_1 w_1 + (1 - p_1) w_2]$$

Therefore, substituting we have:

$$p_1 U(w_1) + (1 - p_1) U(w_2) < U[p_1 w_1 + (1 - p_1) w_2] \tag{11.11}$$

It implies the concave shape of the function $U(w)$, as shown in Fig. 11.1.

In *Part A)* of Fig. 11.1, the point A_1 coordinates are $(w_1, U(w_1))$, while the coordinates of the point A_2 are $(w_2, U(w_2))$. The coordinates of the point A^* are:

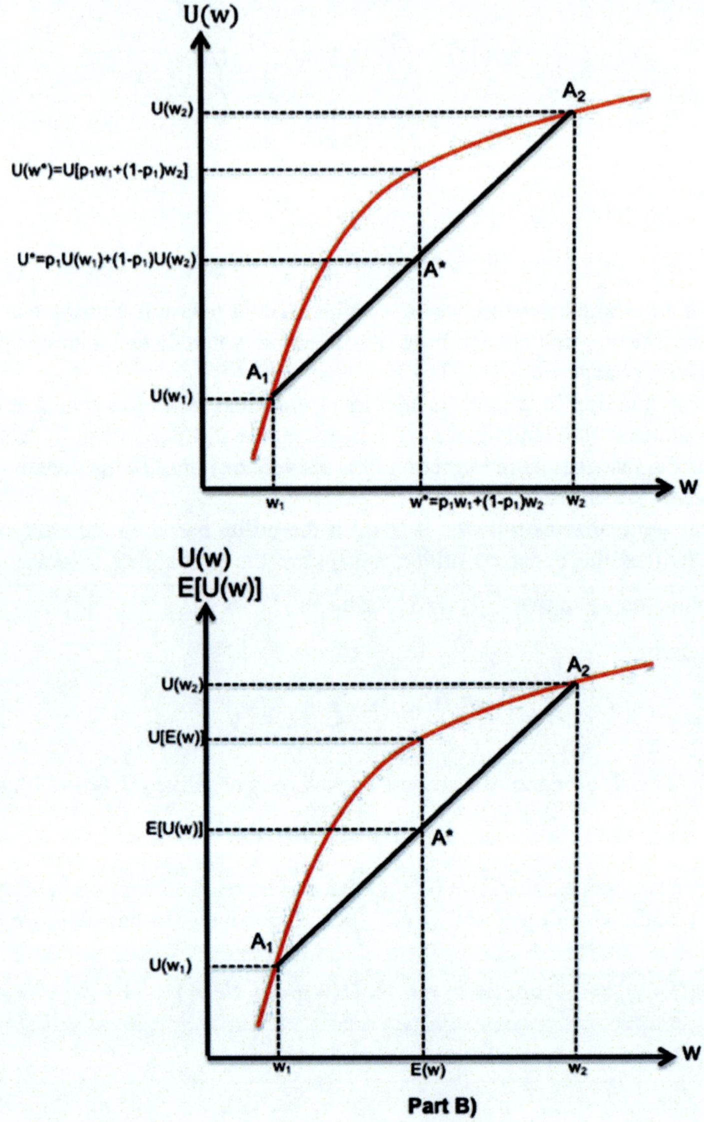

Fig. 11.1 Risk aversion and the concave shape of the utility function

$$w^* = p_1 w_1 + (1 - p_1) w_2$$

$$U^* = p_1 U(w_1) + (1 - p_1) U(w_2)$$

Therefore, point A^* is positioned on the segment A_1A_2. If the utility function $U(w)$ is concave, for $w = w^*$ the function has an ordinate ($U(w^*)$) that is greater than the point A^* ordinate that is (U^*). It is because the curve is positioned above the segment A_1A_2, and then $p_1U(w_1) + (1 - p_1)U(w_2) < U[p_1w_1 + (1 - p_1)w_2]$.

In *Part B)* of Fig. 11.1, the coordinates of the point A_1 are (w_1; $U(w_1)$), while the coordinates of the point A_2 are (w_2; $U(w_2)$).

Considering the probability distribution (p), and associating the portability p_1 to the realization of A_1 and the probability $(1 - p_1)$ to the realization of A_2, the coordinates of the point A^* on the segment A_1A_2 are:

$$A^* \equiv (E(w); E[U(w)])$$

Since the curve is positioned above the segment A_1A_2, we have:

$$E[U(w)] < U[E(w)]$$

Therefore, in the case of risk aversion, the utility function is:

(a) strictly increasing and therefore the first derivative is positive ($U'(w) > 0$).
(b) concave and therefore the second derivative is negative ($U''(w) < 0$).

Note that a risk-averse investor is also said to have a diminishing marginal utility of wealth. Therefore, each additional unit of wealth adds less to utility, the higher the initial level of wealth and then in mathematical terms it implies that $U''(w) < 0$. The degree of risk aversion is given by the concavity of the utility function and it is equivalent to the size of $U''(w)$.

11.2.2 Risk Seeking

In case of risk seeking, investor accepts a fair gamble by preferring the chance to be an outcome equal to €2 or €0 rather than to maintain its wealth equal to €1 if he does not invest. Therefore, investor accepts the fair gamble because the utility of the equivalent gain is greater than the disutility of the loss.

The assumption of risk seeking implies a restriction to the utility function. In this case, the second derivative of utility function ($U(.)$) with respect to wealth (w) must be positive: $U''(w) > 0$. Since the investor prefers to invest, the expected utility of investing must be higher than the expected utility of not investing. Considering the fair gamble, we have the opposite situation of the assumption of risk aversion. Indeed, we have:

$$U(1) < \left(\frac{1}{2}\right)U(2) + \left(\frac{1}{2}\right)U(0)$$

In this case, by multiplying both sides by 2 and rearranging we have:

$$U(1) - U(0) < U(2) - U(1)$$

Therefore, if the investor is risk seeking, the increase of one-unit form 1 to 2 is more valuable (and then it is preferred) to the increase of one-unit from 0 to 1.

A utility function in which the additional one-unit increase is more valuable than the last one-unit is characterized by a positive second derivative. Therefore, the acceptance of a fair gamble (assumption of risk seeking) implies a positive second derivative of the utility function.

We can generalize as follows. In the case of a risk seeking, the second derivative of the utility function is positive ($U''(w) > 0$), so that:

$$E[U(w)] > U[E(w)] \tag{11.12}$$

By considering that:

$$E[U(w)] = p_1 U(w_1) + (1 - p_1) U(w_2)$$

and

$$U[E(w)] = U[p_1 w_1 + (1 - p_1) w_2]$$

Substituting, it gets:

$$p_1 U(w_1) + (1 - p_1) U(w_2) > U[p_1 w_1 + (1 - p_1) w_2] \tag{11.13}$$

It implies that the convex shape of the function $U(w)$, as shown in Fig. 11.2.

In *Part A)* of Fig. 11.2, the coordinates of the point A_1 are $(w_1, u(w_1))$, the point A_2 are $(w_2, u(w_2))$, and the point A^* positioned on the segment A_1A_2 are:

$$w^* = p_1 w_1 + (1 - p_1) w_2$$

$$U^* = p_1 U(w_1) + (1 - p_1) U(w_2)$$

If the utility function $U(w)$ is convex, for $w = w^*$ the function has an ordinate $(U(w^*))$ that is lower than the point A^* ordinate that is (U^*). This is because the curve is positioned below the segment A_1A_2, and therefore $p_1U(w_1) + (1 - p_1)U(w_2) > U[p_1w_1 + (1 - p_1)w_2]$.

In *Part B)* of Fig. 11.2, the coordinates of point A_1 are $(w_1; U(w_1))$ and the point A_2 are $(w_2; U(w_2))$.

Considering the probability distribution (p), and associating probability p_1 to the realization of A_1 and the probability $(1 - p_1)$ to the realization of A_2, the coordinates of point A^* on the segment A_1A_2 are:

$$A^* \equiv (E(w); E[U(w)])$$

Since the curve is positioned below the segment A_1A_2, we have:

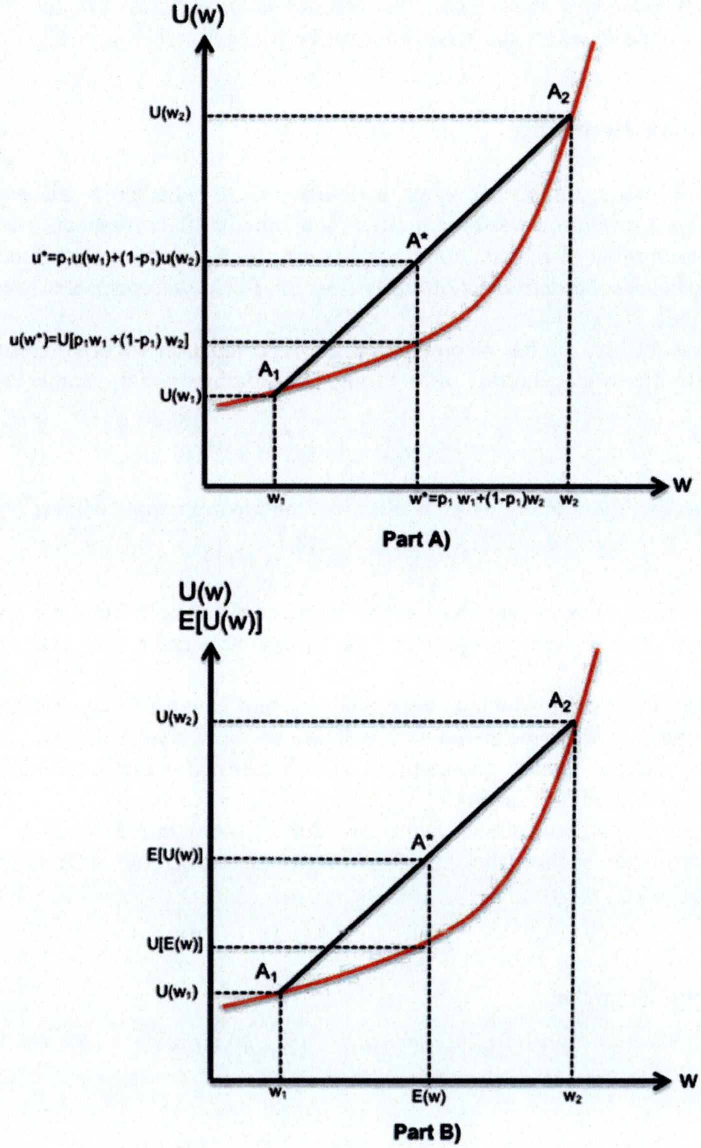

Fig. 11.2 Risk seeking and the convex shape of the utility function

$$E[U(w)] > U[E(w)]$$

Therefore, in the case of risk seeking, the utility function is:

(a) strictly increasing and therefore the first derivative is positive ($U'(w) > 0$)
(b) convex and therefore the second derivative is negative($U''(w) > 0$).

11.2.3 Risk Neutrality

In case of risk neutrality, investor is indifferent to whether a fair gamble is undertaken. Therefore, investor is indifferent to whether the investment was made.

The assumption of risk neutrality implies a restriction to the utility function. In this case, the second derivative of utility function ($U(.)$) with respect to wealth (w) must be null: $U''(w) = 0$.

Because the investor has no preference, the expected utility of not investing must be equal to the expected utility of investing. Considering the fair gamble, we have:

$$U(1) = \left(\frac{1}{2}\right)U(2) + \left(\frac{1}{2}\right)U(0)$$

In this case, by multiplying both sides by 2 and rearranging we have:

$$U(1) - U(0) = U(2) - U(1)$$

In both sides of expression, we have an increase of one-unit. But if the investor is risk neutral, the one-unit change from 0 to 1 is valuable and equals to the one-unit change from 1 to 2.

A utility function in which an additional one-unit is valuable equal than the last one-unit increase is characterized by a null second derivative. Therefore, the indifference to the fair gamble (assumption of risk neutrality) implies a null second derivative of the utility function.

We can generalize as follows. In the case of risk neutral (or indifferent to risk), the second derivative of the utility function is equal to zero ($U''(w) = 0$). In this case, we have:

$$E[U(w)] = U[E(w)] \tag{11.14}$$

By considering that:

$$E[U(w)] = p_1 U(w_1) + (1 - p_1)U(w_2)$$

and

$$U[E(w)] = U[p_1 w_1 + (1 - p_1)w_2]$$

Substituting, it gets:

$$p_1 U(w_1) + (1 - p_1)U(w_2) = U[p_1 w_1 + (1 - p_1)w_2] \tag{11.15}$$

It implies the linearity of the function $U(w)$, as shown in Fig. 11.3.

Therefore, in the case of risk neutrality, the utility function is:

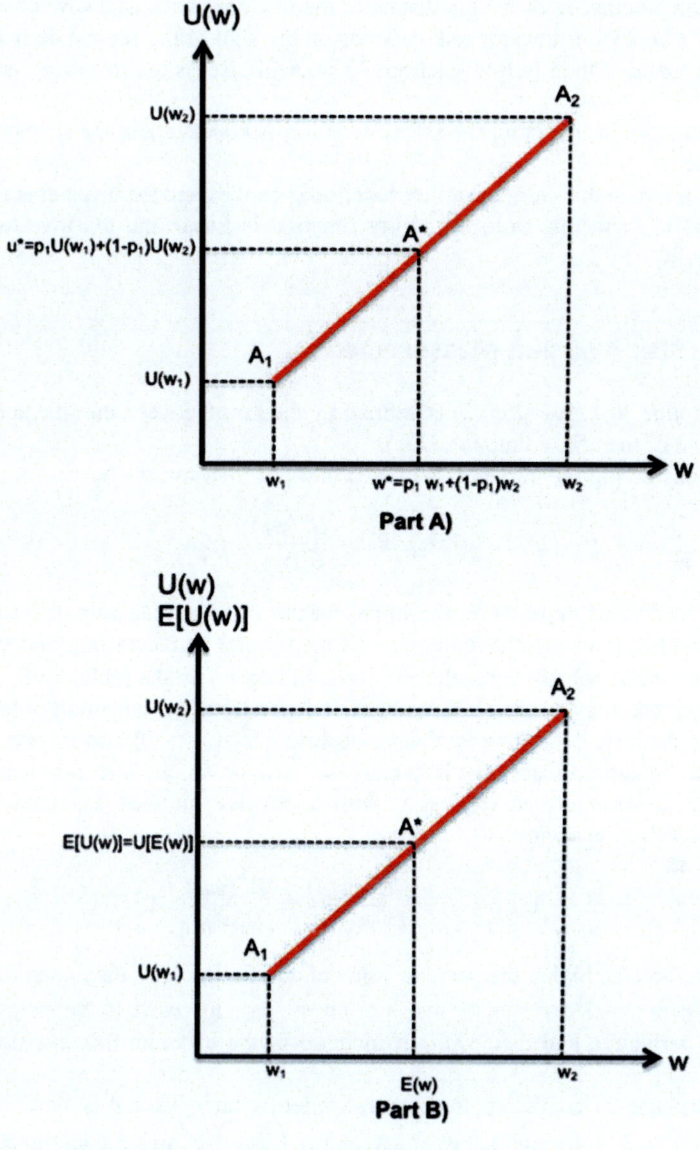

Fig. 11.3 Risk neutral and the linearity of the utility function

(a) strictly increasing and therefore the first derivative is positive ($U^{'}(w) > 0,$)
(b) linear and therefore the second derivative is null ($U^{''}(w) = 0$).

We can summarize by saying that since the first derivative is always positive, the investor's behaviour towards risk depends on the sign of the second derivative and then the shape of their utility function. As we will discuss the following, we have:

- $U''(w) < 0$: in this case, the utility function is concave and the investor is risk averse
- $U''(w) > 0$: in this case, the utility function is convex and the investor is risk lover
- $U''(w) = 0$: in this case, the utility function is linear and the investor is risk neutrality.

11.3 Risk Aversion Measurement

The *Absolute Risk Aversion* (λ) is defined by the ratio between the first and second derivative of the utility function $U(w)$.

By considering the initial level of wealth w_0 of investor, we have:

$$\lambda_{(w_0)} = -\frac{U''(w_0)}{U'(w_0)} \tag{11.16}$$

The coefficient depends on the initial wealth w_0. Consequently, the coefficient $\lambda_{(w_0)}$ can change to the change in w_0 and then it can be increasing, decreasing, or remain constant (when the coefficient does not depend on the initial level of wealth w_0). When the coefficient is not constant, it depends on the same unit of wealth.

Since the first derivative is always positive ($U'(w_0) > 0$) and in case the risk aversion the second derivative is negative ($U''(w_0) < 0$), the sign minus preceding the ratio is necessary to express it with a positive number. Consequently, the coefficient $\lambda_{(w_0)}$ is positive as follows:

$$\lambda_{(w_0)} = -\frac{(-U''(w_0))}{U'(w_0)} = \frac{U''(w_0)}{U'(w_0)} > 0 \tag{11.17}$$

Therefore, the higher the positive value of coefficient $\lambda_{(w_0)}$, the higher the degree of the absolute risk aversion of investor. Indeed, $\lambda_{(w_0)}$ increases to the increase of the second derivative and then with an increase in the absolute risk aversion of the investor.

We can use the coefficient to comparative terms: an investor A is more risk averse than investor B if the coefficient of investor A $\left(\lambda^A_{(w_0)}\right)$ is higher than the coefficient of the investor B $\left(\lambda^B_{(w_0)}\right)$ for each level of wealth (w_0):

$$\lambda^A_{(w_0)} > \lambda^B_{(w_0)}$$

Note that the coefficient $\lambda_{(w_0)}$ does not change in the case of linear transformation of the utility function ($U(w_0)$). Therefore, by considering a utility function $V(w_0)$:

$$V(w_0) = aU(w_0) + b$$

we have:

$$\lambda^V_{(w_0)} = -\frac{V''(w_0)}{V'(w_0)} = -\frac{aU''(w_0)}{aU'(w_0)} = -\frac{U''(w_0)}{U'(w_0)} = \lambda^U_{(w_0)}$$

The *Absolute Risk Tolerance* $\tau_{(w_0)}$ is the inverse of the Absolute Risk Aversion $\lambda_{(w_0)}$:

$$\tau_{(w_0)} = \frac{1}{\lambda_{(w_0)}} = -\frac{U'(w_0)}{U''(w_0)} \tag{11.18}$$

Also, in this case, the value of the coefficient is positive since the first derivative is positive and the second derivative is negative in case of risk aversion of investor.

By considering that the coefficient of the absolute risk tolerance $\left(\tau_{(w_0)}\right)$ is the inverse of the coefficient of absolute risk aversion $\left(\lambda_{(w_0)}\right)$, it implies that the higher the risk aversion of the investor, the lower the risk tolerance.

In comparative terms, if the investor *A* is more tolerant to the risk rather than the investor *B*, the coefficient of the investor *A* $\left(\tau^A_{(w_0)}\right)$ is higher than the coefficient of the investor *B* $\left(\tau^B_{(w_0)}\right)$, for each level of wealth (w_0):

$$\tau^A_{(w_0)} > \tau^B_{(w_0)}$$

If we multiply the ratio between the second and the first derivative for the initial level of wealth (w_o) we have the *Relative Risk Aversion* (ρ) as follows:

$$\rho_{(w_0)} = -w_o\frac{U''(w_0)}{U'(w_0)} \tag{11.19}$$

Similarly, to the coefficient $\lambda_{(w_0)}$, the coefficient $\rho_{(w_0)}$ depends on the initial level of wealth (w_0) and then it can be increasing, decreasing, or remain constant (when the coefficient does not depend on the initial level of wealth w_0).

Since the first derivative is always positive ($U'(w_0) > 0$) and in case the risk aversion the second derivative is negative ($U''(w_0) < 0$), the sign minus preceding the ratio is necessary to express it with a positive number. Consequently, the coefficient $\rho_{(w_0)}$ is positive as follows:

$$\rho_{(w_0)} = -w_o\frac{(-U''(w_0))}{U'(w_0)} = w_o\frac{U''(w_0)}{U'(w_0)} > 0 \tag{11.20}$$

Therefore, the higher the positive value of coefficient $\rho_{(w_0)}$, the higher the degree of relative risk aversion of investor. Indeed, $\rho_{(w_0)}$ increases to the increase of the second derivative.

We can use the coefficient $\rho_{(w_0)}$ in comparative terms. Indeed, if the investor *A* is more relative risk averse than the investor *B*, the coefficient of the investor *A* $\left(\rho^A_{(w_0)}\right)$ is higher than the coefficient of the investor *B* $\left(\rho^B_{(w_0)}\right)$, for each level of wealth (w_0), as follows:

$$\rho^A_{(w_0)} > \rho^B_{(w_0)}$$

Similarly to the coefficient of absolute risk aversion $\left(\lambda_{(w_0)}\right)$, the coefficient of relative risk aversion $\left(\rho_{(w_0)}\right)$ does not change in case of linear transformation of the utility function ($U(w_0)$). Therefore, by considering a utility function $V(w_0)$:

$$V(w_0) = aU(w_0) + b$$

we have:

$$\rho^V_{(w_0)} = -w_o \frac{V''(w_0)}{V'(w_0)} = -w_o \frac{aU''(w_0)}{aU'(w_0)} = -w_o \frac{U''(w_0)}{U'(w_0)} = \rho^U_{(w_0)}$$

The *Relative Risk Tolerance* ($\mathcal{T}$) is the inverse of Relative Risk Aversion as follows:

$$\mathcal{T}_{(w_0)} = \frac{1}{\rho_{(w_0)}} = -\frac{1}{w_o} \frac{U'(w_0)}{U''(w_0)} \tag{11.21}$$

Also, in this case, the value of the coefficient is positive since the first derivative is positive and the second derivative is negative in case of risk aversion of the investor.

By considering that the coefficient of the relative risk tolerance $\left(\mathcal{T}_{(w_0)}\right)$ is the inverse of the coefficient of relative risk aversion $\left(\rho_{(w_0)}\right)$, it implies that the higher the risk aversion of the investor, the lower the risk tolerance.

In comparative terms, if the investor *A* is more tolerant to the risk rather than the investor *B*, the coefficient of the investor *A* $\left(\mathcal{T}^A_{(w_0)}\right)$ is higher than the coefficient of the investor *B* $\left(\mathcal{T}^B_{(w_0)}\right)$, for each level of wealth (w_0):

$$\mathcal{T}^A_{(w_0)} > \mathcal{T}^B_{(w_0)}$$

11.3.1 Utility Functions

The investor's preference changes with a change in wealth. Coefficients of absolute and relative risk aversion, $\lambda_{(w_0)}$ and $\rho_{(w_0)}$, show how the investor's risk preferences change with changes in wealth around the initial local level of wealth.

We can define the problem in a simple way by asking what percentage is invested in risky assets as wealth changes. Specifically, if the wealth of investor increases and investor invests:

1. the same percentage of the wealth in risky assets, investor's behaviour is characterized by Constant Relative Risk Aversion.
2. a greater percentage of the wealth in risky assets, the investor's behaviour is characterized by a Decreasing Relative Risk Aversion.
3. a smaller percentage of the wealth in risky assets, the investor's behaviour is characterized by a Increasing Relative Risk Aversion.

It implies a restriction to the utility function because we have to choose a utility function able to ordinate the preferences on the basis of investor's behaviour about the risk when the wealth change. Despite the restrictions due to the investor's behaviour, the number of potential utility function is relevant.

We can make simple example by considering the power, logarithmic, and negative exponential utility functions.

Power

The utility function $U(w)$ can be defined as follows:

$$U(w) = \frac{1}{a}(w)^a$$

where: $w > 0$ and a is a arbitrary constant whose value must be $a < 1$; $a \neq 0$.

The first and second derivatives with respect to the initial wealth w_0 are, respectively:

$$U'(w_0) = \frac{1}{a} a {w_0}^{a-1} = {w_0}^{a-1}$$

$$U''(w_0) = (a-1){w_0}^{a-2}$$

The absolute risk aversion $\left(\lambda_{(w_0)}\right)$ and the relative risk aversion $\left(\rho_{(w_0)}\right)$ are, respectively:

$$\lambda_{(w_0)} = -\frac{U''(w_0)}{U'(w_0)} = -\left[\frac{(a-1){w_0}^{a-2}}{{w_0}^{a-1}}\right] = -\left[\frac{(a-1){w_0}^{a-1}{w_0}^{-1}}{{w_0}^{a-1}}\right] = -\left[\frac{a-1}{w_0}\right] = \frac{1-a}{w_0}$$

$$\rho_{(w_0)} = -w_0\frac{U''(w_0)}{U'(w_0)} = -w_0\left(\frac{a-1}{w_0}\right) = 1-a$$

The absolute risk aversion $\lambda_{(w_0)}$ decreases to the increase in the initial level of wealth (w_0). The relative risk aversion ($\rho_{(w)}$), on the contrary, is constant because it does not depend on the initial level of wealth w_0. For this reason, this type of utility function is classified in the groups *CRRA (Constant Relative Risk Aversion)*

Logarithmic

The utility function $U(w)$ can be defined as follows:

$$U(w) = a\ln(w) + b$$

where: $w > 0$ and a, b are arbitrary constants.

The first and second derivatives with respect to the initial wealth w_0 are, respectively:

$$U'(w_0) = a\frac{1}{w_0} = a{w_0}^{-1}$$

$$U''(w_0) = a(-1){w_0}^{-2} = -a{w_0}^{-2}$$

The absolute risk aversion $\left(\lambda_{(w_0)}\right)$ and the relative risk aversion $\left(\rho_{(w_0)}\right)$ are, respectively:

$$\lambda_{(w_0)} = -\frac{U''(w_0)}{U'(w_0)} = -\left[\frac{-a{w_0}^{-2}}{a{w_0}^{-1}}\right] = {w_0}^{-1} = \frac{1}{w_0}$$

$$\rho_{(w_0)} = -w_0\frac{U''(w_0)}{U'(w_0)} = -w_0\left[\frac{-a{w_0}^{-2}}{a{w_0}^{-1}}\right] = -w_0\left[-{w_0}^{-1}\right] = -w_0\left[-\frac{1}{w_0}\right] = 1$$

Therefore, the absolute risk aversion ($\lambda_{(w)}$) decreases to the increase in wealth (w_0). The Relative Risk Aversion ($\rho_{(w)}$) is constant and then it does not change to the change in wealth (w_0). For this reason, this function is classified according to function groups *CRRA (Constant Relative Risk Aversion)*.

Negative Exponential

The utility function $U(w)$ can be defined as follows:

$$U(w) = a\left(1 - e^{-\frac{w}{a}}\right)$$

where $a > 0$. The value of a represents the superiorly limited of the exponential function. The parameter a is the upper extremity and therefore it represents the maximum potentiality. Indeed, the function for $U(w) = a$ has a horizontal asymptote:

$$\lim_{w\to+\infty}[U(w)] = \lim_{w\to+\infty}\left[a\left(1 - e^{-\frac{w}{a}}\right)\right] = a(1 - e^{-\infty}) = a\left(1 - \frac{1}{e^{\infty}}\right) = a(1 - 0) = a$$

The first and second derivatives with respect to the initial wealth w_0 are, respectively:

$$U'(w_0) = a\left(-\left(-\frac{1}{a}\right)e^{-\frac{w_0}{a}}\right) = a\left(\frac{1}{a}e^{-\frac{w_0}{a}}\right) = e^{-\frac{w_0}{a}}$$

$$U''(w_0) = \left(-\frac{1}{a}\right)e^{-\frac{w_0}{a}}$$

The absolute risk aversion $\left(\lambda_{(w_0)}\right)$ and the relative risk aversion $\left(\rho_{(w_0)}\right)$ are, respectively:

$$\lambda_{(w_0)} = -\frac{U''(w_0)}{U'(w_0)} = -\left[\frac{\left(-\frac{1}{a}\right)e^{-\frac{w_0}{a}}}{e^{-\frac{w_0}{a}}}\right] = \frac{1}{a}$$

$$\rho_{(w_0)} = -w_0\frac{U''(w_0)}{U'(w_0)} = -w_0\left[\frac{\left(-\frac{1}{a}\right)e^{-\frac{w_0}{a}}}{e^{-\frac{w_0}{a}}}\right] = -w_0\left(-\frac{1}{a}\right) = w_0\frac{1}{a}$$

Therefore, the absolute risk aversion $\left(\lambda_{(w_0)}\right)$ is constant and then it does not change to the change in wealth (w_0) while the relative risk aversion $\left(\rho_{(w_0)}\right)$ increases to the increase in wealth (w_0). Therefore, this type of utility function is classified into the group of functions *CARA* (*Constant Absolute Risk Aversion*).

11.4 Expected Utility and the Mean-Variance Approach

The efficient frontier defines all efficient portfolios among them the investor must choices on the basis of its preference. Indeed, the mean-variance approach does not define the optimum portfolio for each investor. This choice depends on the investor's behaviour about the risk. The definition of the degree of risk aversion of investor is out of the data input of mean-variance approach.

The choice of optimum portfolio for investor can be made by using the expected utility theory: defined the utility function of investor, the choice of optimum portfolios among the efficient portfolios (on the efficient frontier) is the one able to maximize the expected utility of investor.

To do it, it is necessary that the expected utility must be defined in terms of mean and variance. Only in this case, the choice based on the expected utility is compatible with the mean-variance approach based on which are defined the efficient portfolios on the efficient frontier among them investor choices its optimum portfolio.

Generally, we can say that mean-variance approach gives us results that are coherent with the expected utility theory only under two conditions: (1) the portfolio's returns follow a normal distribution or/and (2) the investor uses a quadratic utility function. One of these two conditions must be verified to apply the expected utility theory to the optimum portfolio choice of the investor in the mean-variance approach.

11.4.1 Portfolio's Returns Follow a Normal Distribution

This condition is the most commonly used. Assume that independently from the utility function used, the return of N assets in portfolio follows a normal distribution.

The portfolio's return is equal to the sum of returns of all assets in it each of them weighted on the basis of the wealth invested in it. If the return of each asset follows a normal distribution, then the portfolio's return follows a normal distribution.

If the portfolio's returns follow a normal distribution $N(\mu; \sigma^2)$, the entire probability distribution depends only on mean and variance.

The main problem is that the asset's return usually does not follow a normal distribution. To solve the problem, we use the central limit theorem. It states that in many situations when independent random variables are summed up, their properly normalized sum tends towards a normal distribution even if the original variables are not normally distributed. In our case, the approximation depends on three elements:

1. The degree of correlation among the returns of asset in portfolio: the smaller the correlation, the better the approximation.
2. The number of assets in portfolio: the higher the number of assets in portfolio, the better the approximation.
3. The extent to which the distribution of the returns of each assets approximates the normal distribution.

These elements have relevant effect on the assumption of the normal distribution of the portfolio's returns. Indeed:

1. It is difficult to define ex ante if the approximation to the normal distribution can be reasonable.
2. If assumed valid the approximation to the normal distribution, it implies constraints to the expected utility theory. First, the utility function used must be defined for the same interval of a variable normally distributed and then between $-\infty$ and $+\infty$. It implies problem because some utility functions are not defined for negative value (such as the logarithmic). Therefore, we cannot use any utility functions but only those able to respect the constraint.
3. If we use a utility function able to respect the constrain, the question is if it is reasonable to assume that expected return can have negative value able to increase towards a very high value (theoretically towards $-\infty$). On the contrary, it is reasonable to assume a limit to a negative value of the expected return given by the default condition after a certain negative value.

11.4.2 Quadratic Utility Function

The quadratic utility function can be formalized as follows:

$$U(w) = w - \frac{1}{2}aw^2 \quad \text{where } a > 0$$

The concavity of the utility function is ensured by the positivity of the parameter *a*.

The first and second derivatives with respect to the initial wealth (w_0) are, respectively:

$$U'(w_0) = 1 - aw_0$$

$$U''(w_0) = -a$$

Since $a > 0$ by assumption, the second derivative is negative ($U''(w_0) < 0$) and then the function is concave. Note that the concavity of the function is immediately determined by considering the negative sign of the coefficient *a*/2.

The coordinates of the vertex of the parable are equal to:

$$V = \left(-\frac{b}{2a}; -\frac{\Delta}{4a}\right) \quad \text{where} \Delta = b^2 - 4ac$$

so that:

$$-\frac{b}{2a} = -\frac{1}{2\left(-\frac{a}{2}\right)} = \frac{1}{a}$$

$$-\frac{\Delta}{4a} = -\frac{1}{4\left(-\frac{a}{2}\right)} = \frac{1}{2a}$$

and then:

$$V = \left(\frac{1}{a}; \frac{1}{2a}\right)$$

Since the first derivative must be always positive ($U'(w_0) > 0$) we have to consider only the ascending branch of the parabola where the first derivative is positive ($U'(w_0) > 0$) and not also the down branch where the first derivative is negative ($U'(w_0) < 0$). Consequently, we must reduce the domain (D) of the function to $D = \left[0; \frac{1}{a}\right]$ by considering the value of wealth between 0 and $\frac{1}{a}$ because only in its domain the function has increasing trend as shown in Fig. 11.4.

The *Absolute Risk Aversion* (λ) and *Relative Risk Aversion* (ρ) are, respectively:

Fig. 11.4 Quadratic utility function

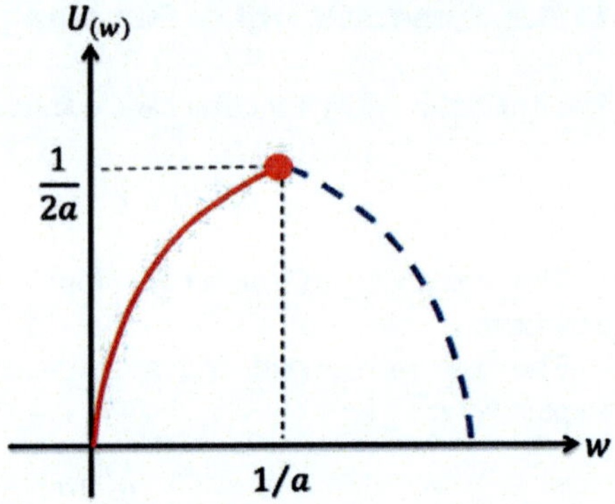

$$\lambda_{(w_0)} = -\frac{U''(w_0)}{U'(w_0)} = -\frac{-a}{1-aw_0} = \frac{a}{1-aw_0}$$

$$\rho_{(w_0)} = -w_o\frac{U''(w_0)}{U'(w_0)} = w_o\frac{a}{1-aw_0}$$

Note that by considering only the ascending branch of the parabola, we have $w < \frac{1}{a}$ and then both $\lambda_{(w_0)}$ and $\rho_{(w_0)}$ are positive. Indeed, in the dominion $D = \left[0; \frac{1}{a}\right]$ the first derivative of the Absolute Risk Aversion is positive as follows:

$$\lambda'_{(w_0)} = \frac{a^2}{(1-aw_0)^2}$$

Therefore, in the domain considered $D = \left[0; \frac{1}{a}\right]$ the risk aversion increases to the increase in wealth (w_0) by considering the positive sign of its first derivative $\left(\lambda'_{(w_0)}\right)$.

This is the weakness point of the quadratic utility function. Indeed, to the increase in wealth (w_0) the investor's increases its risk aversion and it seems to be a counter-intuitive result.

The advantage of the quadratic utility function is that it is coherent with the mean-variance criteria. Indeed, this utility function can be expressed in terms of mean and variance only and then it allows for compatibility between the utility function approach and the mean-variance approach. It implies that the investor whose preferences are represented by a quadratic utility function, can chooses according to criteria coherent with mean and variance approach.

We can prove it by considering a utility function and expanding it on the basis of Taylor's series. Remember that the Taylor's series of a function is an infinite sum of terms that are expressed in terms of the function's derivatives at a single point. Consider the function $f(x)$ in the neighbourhood of the point $\overline{x}$. It is defined as follows:

$$f(x) = f(\overline{x}) + f'(\overline{x})(x-\overline{x}) + \frac{1}{2}f''(\overline{x})(x-\overline{x})^2 + \frac{1}{3!}f'''(\overline{x})(x-\overline{x})^3 + \ldots$$

Therefore, by considering the utility function $U(w)$ in the neighbourhood of the point $E(w) = \overline{w}$, we have:

$$U(w) = U(\overline{w}) + U'(\overline{w})(w-\overline{w}) + \frac{1}{2}U''(\overline{w})(w-\overline{w})^2 + \frac{1}{3!}U'''(\overline{w})(w-\overline{w})^3 + \ldots$$

By considering the expected utility, we have:

$$E[U(w)] = U(\overline{w}) + U'(\overline{w})E(w-\overline{w}) + \frac{1}{2}U''(\overline{w})E(w-\overline{w})^2 + \frac{1}{3!}U'''(\overline{w})E(w-\overline{w})^3 + \ldots$$

By considering that:

$$E(w-\overline{w}) = E(w) - \overline{w} = 0$$

$$E(w-\overline{w})^2 = \sigma^2$$

we have:

$$E[U(w)] = U(\overline{w}) + \frac{1}{2}U''(\overline{w})\sigma^2 + \frac{1}{3!}U'''(\overline{w})E(w-\overline{w})^3 + \ldots$$

Now consider the quadratic utility function as defined previously:

$$U(w) = w - \frac{1}{2}aw^2 \quad \text{where } a > 0$$

Note that for the quadratic utility function the derivatives from the third on are all null. Therefore, we can consider only the first two terms of the Taylor's series.

Passing to the expected value, we have:

$$E[U(w)] = E(w) - \frac{1}{2}aE(w^2)$$

By considering that:

$$E(w) = \overline{w}$$

And the variance can be written as $\sigma^2 = \overline{w}^2 - [E(w)]^2$ so that $[E(w)]^2 = \sigma^2 + \overline{w}^2$, substituting we have:

$$E[U(w)] = \overline{w} - \frac{1}{2}a\left(\sigma^2 + \overline{w}^2\right) \tag{11.22}$$

Therefore, the expected utility of the function ($E[U(w)]$) depends only on mean ($\overline{w}$) and variance (σ^2). It is coherent with the mean-variance approach because investor choices on the basis of mean and variance only.

Note that by considering that the first derivative is positive ($U'(w) > 0$) because the function must be monotonic and the second derivative is negative ($U''(w) < 0$) because the investor is risk adverse, the first and second derivatives of the quadratic utility functions are the following:

$$U'(w) = 1 - aw > 0$$

$$U''(w) = -a < 0$$

By considering that $a > 0$ and we have to consider only the ascending branch of the function so that $w < \frac{1}{a}$, the first derivative is positive $U'(w) > 0$ and the second derivative is negative.

By considering the expected value, we have:

$$E[U'(w)] = 1 - a\overline{w} > 0$$

$$E[U''(w)] = -a < 0$$

The expected value of the first derivative is also positive because the mean of the positive value is positive by definition.

We have the same result if we consider the derivatives of $E[U(w)] = \overline{w} - \frac{1}{2}a(\sigma^2 + \overline{w}^2)$ with respect to $\overline{w}$ and σ^2 as follows:

$$\frac{\partial}{\partial \overline{w}}[E[U(w)]] = 1 - a\overline{w} > 0$$

$$\frac{\partial}{\partial \sigma^2}[E[U(w)]] = -a < 0$$

Therefore, investor prefers portfolio with higher expected return (if we consider the expected return) and lower variance (if we consider the risk).

Despite the quadratic utility function gives us a criterion of investor's preference aligned to the mean-variance approach, it shows three main limits:

1. If the mean-variance approach is valid for all investors, it implies that all investors represent their preference on the basis of the quadratic utility function only and not others. But it is little reasonable.
2. The quadratic utility function is a parabola with a maximum point for $w = \frac{1}{a}$. It implies that before this point the first derivative of the utility function is positive ($U'(w) > 0$) while after it the first derivative is negative ($U'(w) < 0$). It implies that only the ascending branch of the parabola respects the assumption of monotonicity must be considered, while the down branch must not be considered because it

does not respect the assumption. Consequently, the validity interval of the quadratic utility function must be restricted to the value between 0 and $\frac{1}{a}$ by reducing the domain of the function to $D = \left[0; \frac{1}{a}\right]$.

3. By considering the absolute and relative risk aversion, in the domain $D = \left[0; \frac{1}{a}\right]$, the investor's risk aversion increases to the increase in the level of wealth (w_0). It is a counter-intuitive result because the risk aversion should reduce to the increase in wealth.

11.5 Selection of Optimal Portfolio

Assume the respect of one of the two main conditions (the portfolio's returns follows a normal distribution or/and the investor uses a quadratic utility function). In this case, the utility function can be expressed in terms of mean $\left(\overline{R_P}\right)$ and standard deviation (σ_P) of portfolio's return so that. Specifically, the expected utility must be an increasing function of $\overline{R_P}$ and a decreasing function of σ_P. It implies that we can apply the risk-return analysis.

It could be useful a briefly introduction to the Risk-Return analysis.

Generally, the choice under uncertainty is characterized by multidimensional goals. The maximization of the expected utility reduces the complexity of the choice problem because it allows to pass from multidimensional goals to a one global goal. It allows to synthetize all possible elements able to influence the investor's preference about the choice.

Usually, maximization of the expected utility can be defined on the basis of two main objectives: the maximization of profit and the minimization of risk.

By considering an investor with a concave utility function $U(w)$, the risk of w ($\Phi(w)$) can be measured as follows:

$$\Phi(w) = U[E(w) - E[U(w)]] \tag{11.23}$$

If the investor is risk adverse, this difference can never be negative. Therefore, we have:

$$E[U(w)] = U[E(w)] - \Phi(w) \tag{11.24}$$

Consequently, the maximization of the expected utility is realized by balancing the maximization of profit ($U[E(w)]$) and the minimization of the risk ($\Phi(w)$). Note that by considering that the utility function $U(w)$ is monotonic by increasing for w, the profit maximization becomes simple the maximization of $E(w)$. Therefore, the two criterions of choices are: the maximization of expected value of w $\left(\max\limits_{w} E(w)\right)$ and the minimization of the risk $\left(\min\limits_{w} \Phi(w)\right)$.

Consider a defined value of w and denote with m its expected value, so that $m = E(w)$, and with φ the risk of w so that $\varphi = \Phi(w)$. Denote with U the expected utility of the function $U(w)$ so that $U = E[U(w)]$. In the plan risk-expected value (φ, m), we can represent each financial position P on the basis of risk and expected value.

By considering that:

$$E[U(w)] = U[E(w)] - \Phi(w)$$

by substituting, we have:

$$U(\varphi, m) = U(m) - \varphi \tag{11.25}$$

It implies that for each point P (that represent an uncertain financial position w) it will correspond a value of the function $U(P)$. Consequently, the expected utility will be represented in the three-dimensional space (φ, m, U).

Assume that the utility function $U(w)$ is derivable twice at least.

The partial derivative $U(\varphi, m)$ with respect to m is equal to:

$$\frac{\partial}{\partial m}[U(\varphi,\ m)] = U'(m)$$

Therefore, the partial derivative is positive. It implies that the expected utility U is an increasing function of m. For a defined level of risk, and then for the same value of φ, investor prefers the point with a high value of m.

The partial derivative $U(\varphi, m)$ with respect to φ is equal to:

$$\frac{\partial}{\partial m}[U(\varphi,\ m)] = -1$$

Therefore, the partial derivative is negative. It implies that for a defined level of expected value, and then for the same value of m, investor prefers the point with a low value of φ.

In Fig. 11.5, the point A_2 is preferred to the point A_1 ($A_2 \succ A_1$) because it has the high expected value m for the same level of risk φ, as well as the point B_2 is preferred to the point B_1 ($B_2 \succ B_1$) because it has the low level of risk φ for the same level of expected value m.

The position A_1 and B_1 are not be able comparable. It happens because we have considered separately the two objectives of the maximization of the expected value m and the minimization of the risk φ.

A complete representation of the investor's preference can be realized only by considering jointly the two objectives of the expected value m and the minimization of the risk φ by using the utility function $U(\varphi, m)$.

For a defined level of expected utility $\overline{U}$ the indifference curves are defined by the equation:

$$U(\varphi, m) = \overline{U} \tag{11.26}$$

By considering that $U(\varphi, m) = U(m) - \varphi$, we have:

Fig. 11.5 Indifference curves in the plan risk-expected value (φ, m)

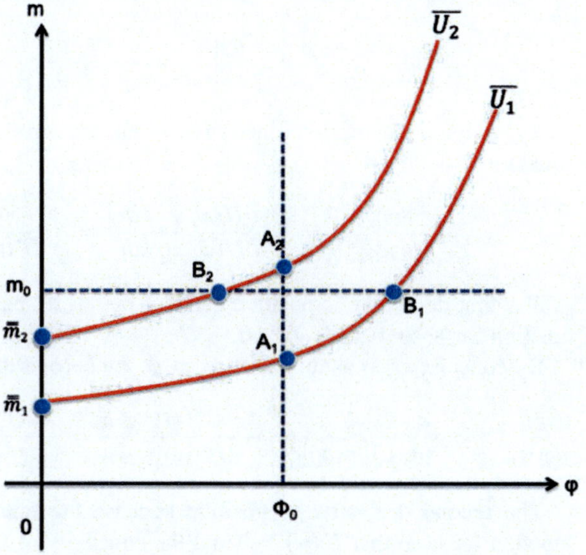

$$U(m) - \varphi = \overline{U}$$

and then:

$$U(m) = \overline{U} + \varphi \tag{11.27}$$

By considering the inverse function of $U(x)$, we have:

$$m(\varphi) = U^{-1}(\varphi + \overline{U})$$

and the solution $\bar{\bar{m}} = U^{-1}(\overline{U})$ of equation:

$$U(0, \bar{\bar{m}}) = \overline{U} \tag{11.28}$$

is the ordinate of the intersection point of the indifference curve $U(\varphi, m) = \overline{U}$ with the vertical axis. Therefore, it is the certain equivalent (a certain wealth) of all points on the indifference curve and then of all uncertain financial position x with expected utility $\overline{U}$.

Consider the implicit function theorem. It states that given a function of two real variables $f(x, y)$ with derivatives $\frac{\partial f}{\partial x}$ and $\frac{\partial f}{\partial y}$, by considering in the plan (x, y) the curve $f(x, y) = k$ with k constant, the derivative of y with respect to x computed along the curve is equal to:

$$\left.\frac{dy}{dx}\right|_{f=k} = -\frac{\partial f/\partial x}{\partial f/\partial y}$$

By applying the implicit function theorem, the derivative of m with respect to φ is equal to:

$$\left.\frac{dm}{d\varphi}\right|_{U=\overline{U}} = -\frac{\partial U(\varphi, m)/\partial\varphi}{\partial U(\varphi, m)/\partial m} = -\frac{-1}{U'(m)} = \frac{1}{U'(m)}$$

The first derivative is positive because the utility function $U(w)$ is an increasing function for w so that $U'(w) > 0$.

By considering m as the function of φ, the second derivative is equal to:

$$\left.\frac{d^2m}{d\varphi^2}\right|_{U=\overline{U}} = \frac{d}{d\varphi}\frac{1}{U'[m(\varphi)]} = -\frac{U''(m)}{[U'(m)]^2}\frac{dm}{d\varphi} = -\frac{U''(m)}{[U'(m)]^2}\frac{1}{U'(m)} = -\frac{U''(m)}{[U'(m)]^3}$$

The second derivative is positive because the function $U(w)$ is an increasing function for w so that $U'(w) > 0$ and the concavity of $U(w)$ so that $U''(w) < 0$.

Based on the first and second derivative, the indifference curves in the plan (φ, m) are functions increasing and convex of φ. Since $U(\varphi, m)$ increases to the increase of m and decrease of φ, by moving up and to the left in the plan (φ, m) we find indifference curves corresponding to an increase value of expected utility as shown in Fig. 11.5. Note that points A_2 and B_2 are indifferent among them because they have the same expected utility $\overline{U_2}$ that is greater than the expected utility $\overline{U_1}$. Also note that $\overline{\overline{m}}_2$ as a certain position and then it is not risk. Therefore, it is the certain equivalent of the risky position represented by the points A_2 and B_2 and all other points along the same indifference curve.

The problem of the maximization of the expected utility requires the definition of a constrain on variables φ and m. Indeed, if we do not introduce limitation about expected value of w (and then m) and the level of risk (φ), it will be always exist the trivial solution $\varphi = 0$ and $m = \infty$.

We can define the frontier opportunities the point with the minimum risk respect all others with the same level of excepted value of w and then the same level of m. Then, for a defined level of m (m_0) and then for a defined level of the expected value of w, so that $E(w) = m_0$, the opportunity frontier is the solution of the system:

$$\begin{cases} \min\limits_{x} \Phi(w) \\ E(w) = m_0 \end{cases} \tag{11.29}$$

where the first is the equation objective and the second is the constraint.

Therefore, fixed the level of m_0 the frontier opportunities are represented by the point P to the right of which all other points along the horizontal line $m = m_0$ are positioned. All these points at the right are dominated by the point P because they are

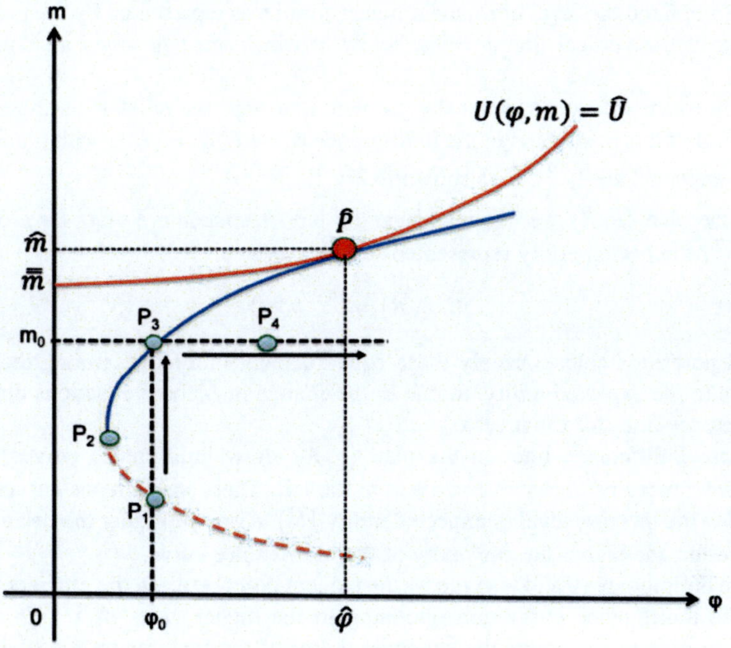

Fig. 11.6 Efficient frontier and the maximization of expected utility

characterized by a high level of risk for the same level of expected value. In Fig. 11.6, the point P_3 is the frontier opportunity and it dominates the point P_4.

By solving the system for all possible value of m_0 we find all opportunities frontier.

We can define efficient opportunity each position on the frontier opportunity that is able to maximize the expected value with respect to all others with the same level of risk (φ). Therefore, for a defined level of risk ($\Phi(w)$) so that defined $\Phi(w) = \varphi_0$, the efficient opportunity is the solution of the system:

$$\begin{cases} \max\limits_{x} E(w) \\ \Phi(w) = \varphi_0 \end{cases} \tag{11.30}$$

where the first is the equation objective and the second is the constraint.

All efficient opportunities define corresponding to all possible value of φ_0 define the efficient frontier. The efficient frontier is represented by an increasing function by construction as shown in Fig. 11.6. The continuous line of the curve defines the dominant positions, while the dashed line the corresponding dominated positions. In Fig. 11.6, the point P_3 dominates the point P_1 because P_3 is characterized by a higher level of expected value for the same level of risk φ_0 with respect to the point P_1.

Therefore, fixed the level of φ_0 the efficient frontier is represented by the point P to the top of the vertical line $\varphi = \varphi_0$ below at which are positioned all dominated points.

Defined the efficient frontier the problem is to find the point $\widehat{P}$ on the efficient frontier that it is positioned in the indifference curve $U(\varphi, m) = \widehat{U}$ with higher level of the expected utility $\left(\widehat{U}\right)$ as shown in Fig. 11.6.

In the plan $\left(\sigma, \overline{R}\right)$ we can introduce the indifference curve of U for a defining level $\overline{U}$ of expected utility represented so that we have:

$$U\left(\sigma, \overline{R}\right) = \overline{U}, \quad \sigma \geq 0 \tag{11.31}$$

All portfolios able to satisfy these equations are: indifferent among them with respect to the expected utility, to that to the change in $\overline{U}$ these equations define the indifference lines for the investor.

These indifference lines in the plan $\left(\sigma, \overline{R}\right)$ draw indifference curves convex (upward concavity) that moves up and to the left. These indifference curves correspond to the increase level of expected utility $\left(\overline{U}\right)$. Also, the higher the risk aversion of investor, the higher the convexity of the indifference curve.

The optimum portfolio is given by the tangent point between the efficient frontier and the indifference curve corresponding to the higher value of $\overline{U}$. This is the portfolio able to maximize the expected utility of the investor on the basis of its preferences as expressed by the utility function $U\left(\sigma, \overline{R}\right)$. Since the tangent point is one, the optimum portfolio is one.

We can graphically show this point as in Fig. 11.7. By considering the indifference curves drawn in green, the optimum portfolio for investor is defined by the point $\widehat{P_1}$ positioned on the efficient frontier and tangent to the utility function $\overline{U'}$.

If investors that have the same efficient frontier but they are characterized by different degree of risk aversion, they are characterized by indifference curves with different convexity. Therefore, they select different optimum portfolios able to maximize their respective expected utility that they are placed on the same efficient frontier. In Fig. 11.7, the two optimum portfolios are $\widehat{P_1}$ and $\widehat{P_2}$ placed on the same efficient frontier but different utility maximization $\overline{U'}$ and $\overline{U''}$, respectively.

In rigorous terms, by denoting with $U\left(\sigma, \overline{R}\right)$ the utility function that indicates the indifference curve at the expected utility $\overline{U}$, the abscissa of the point $\widehat{\sigma}$ of maximum expected utility is determined on the basis of the system of two equations in the unknown σ and $\overline{U}$ as follows:

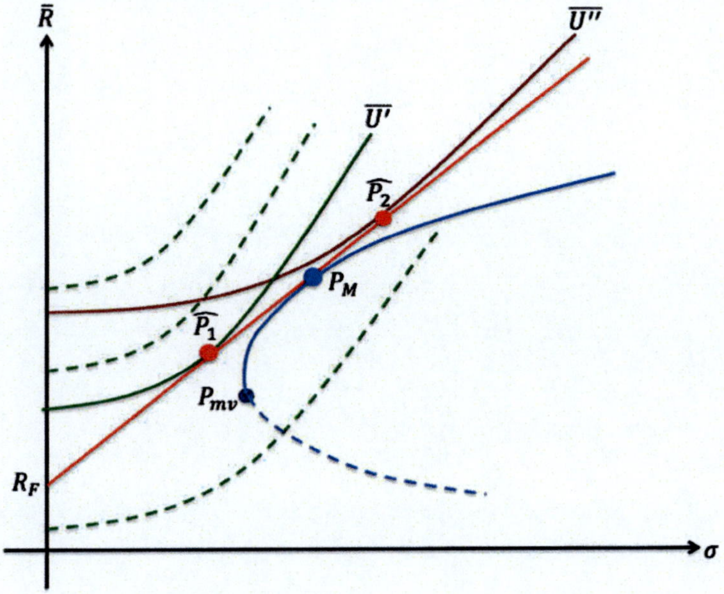

Fig. 11.7 Indifference curves and portfolio choices

$$\begin{cases} U(\sigma, \overline{U}) = R_F + \pi_M \sigma \\ \dfrac{\partial U(\sigma, \overline{U})}{\partial \sigma} = \pi_M \end{cases} \tag{11.32}$$

where:

1. The first equation defines the tangent point between the indifference curve and the efficient frontier.
2. The second equation states that at the point of tangency the indifference curve must have the same slope of the efficient frontier.

Note that π_M is the Sharpe Index and it is equal to: $\pi_M = \frac{\overline{R_M} - R_F}{\sigma_M}$.

Single Index Model

12

12.1 Structure of the Model

The research about portfolio theory (core of the theory was presented in a pioneering paper by Markowitz in 1956) was focusing on two main directions: the first concerns a simplification of the amount and type of input data needed for portfolio's analysis; the second concerns the simplification of the computational procedure needed to determine the optimal portfolio.

In this contest, we restrict the analysis to the problem of simplifying the inputs of the portfolio analysis by focusing on the analysis to the *Single Index Model (SIM)*. It is the most widely used simplification of the portfolio analysis.

Note that in this contest, we use the notion of assets rather than stocks to maintain the homogeneity in all parts of the book. However, they will be used interchangeably.

The Single Index Model (SIM) assumes one common factor, the single index, on which the movement of all assets depend.

By applying the portfolio's theory, for N assets in portfolio, we need to estimate the correlation between each possible pair of assets. Then to estimate the correlation ρ_{ij} for all pairs of assets i and j, the first index i can take on N values, one for each asset, while the second index j can take on $(N - 1)$ value because it must be $i \neq j$. It implies that we have $N(N - 1)$ correlation coefficients. Since the correlation coefficient between assets i and j is the same as that between assets j and i, we have to estimate $[N(N - 1)]/2$ total correlations.

The use of a single index greatly simplified the problem of the estimation of correlation matrix.

The SIM is based on empirical evidence: usually, when the market increases, as indicated by the positivity of some indexes, the majority of the assets increase their price; on the contrary, when the market decreases, as indicated by the negativity of some indexes, the majority of the assets decrease their price. It leads us to believe that price of assets is connected between them, because they respond to the same common factor. Consequently, a measure of the correlation between the assets can

P. De Luca, *Corporate Finance*, Springer Texts in Business and Economics,
https://doi.org/10.1007/978-3-031-18300-3_12

be obtained indirectly by considering the relationship between each asset's expected returns with the defined index's expected returns.

The *i*-th asset's return (R_i) can be defined as follows:

$$R_i = F_i + \beta_i R_m \tag{12.1}$$

where:

- F_i: is the part of the asset's return that is completely independent from the market index. It is a random variable.
- R_m: is the rate of return of the market index that is a random variable. Note it indicates the return the investor would earn by holding a portfolio with a composition identical to the index.
- β_i: is a constant and it measures the sensibility of the asset's returns (R_i) to the change in the market index returns (R_m). Therefore, it measures how sensitive an asset's return is to the return in the market. Then, it is a measurement of the expected change in the R_i due to the change in R_m. A value of $\beta_i = 2$ means that the returns of *i*-th asset increase (decrease) by 2% if the market increases (decreases) by 1%.

Therefore, the equation states that the asset's return is the sum of two parts:

- the first (F_i) is independent of the market,
- the second ($\beta_i R_m$) is dependent on the market, as it is represented by the market index defined, on the basis of a sensibility coefficient.

The component F_i can be divided into two parts, as follows:

$$F_i = f_i + e_i$$

where:

- the first part (f_i) denotes the expected value of F_i and can be defined as "*anticipated term*".
- the second part (e_i) denotes the random (uncertain) element and then the residual term of F_i and it can only be known at the end of the period.

Expectations on the value of the assets in the starting time (t_0) is the function of the information reflected in the price through the component f_i. Therefore, f_i is a component of the asset's price in t_0.

The component e_i is a random variable. The opinion on it usually reflects the investors risk behaviour. Its introduction in the price is mainly due to the investors' risk aversion. Therefore, they require a risk premium to invest in risky assets. This premium risk is the largest return required by investors and it can be translated in a price discount.

The return of *i*-th asset is equal to:

$$R_i = f_i + \beta_i R_m + e_i \quad (i = 1, 2, 3, \ldots, N) \tag{12.2}$$

where both e_i that R_m are random variables.

By construction, we have:

1. The expected value of e_i is equal to zero:

$$E(e_i) = 0 \tag{12.3}$$

2. e_i that R_m are random variables and then they have a probability distribution and a mean and variance (and then standard deviation), so that:

$$\sigma_{e_i}^2 = E[e_i - E(e_i)]^2 = E(e_i - 0)^2 = E(e_i)^2 \quad \text{and then } \sigma_{e_i} = \sqrt{\sigma_{e_i}^2}$$

$$\sigma_m^2 = E(R_m - E(R_m))^2 \quad \text{and then } \sigma_m = \sqrt{\sigma_m^2} \tag{12.4}$$

Now we can introduce two main assumptions.

Assumption 1: the random variables e_i and R_m are uncorrelated. Therefore, there is no correlation between e_i and R_m as follows:

$$\text{Cov}(e_i R_m) = E[(e_i - E(e_i))(R_m - E(R_m))] = E[e_i(R_m - E(R_m))] = 0 \tag{12.5}$$

It implies that the two random variables e_i and R_m are independent among them. Specifically, the accuracy of the equation to describe the asset's return is independent from the market index.

Assumption 2: each asset is only correlated to the market index and not among them. It implies non-correlation between the random elements (residual) e_i and e_j of the *i*-th asset and *j*-th asset for each value of *i* and *j*. By remembering that $E(e_i)$ and $E(e_j)$ are equal to zero by construction, we can formalize the assumption as follows:

$$E\left[(e_i - E(e_i))(e_j - E(e_j))\right] = E(e_i e_j) = 0 \tag{12.6}$$

The assumption ensures that the returns of assets are connected with the market index's returns only, and not among them. Consequently, the returns of all assets move in the same direction because they move with the same common factor as represented by the market index, not because they are related among them. Therefore, the assets move together only because of a common co-movement with the market.

By combining these two assumptions, the SIM is based on the simple concept that asset prices move together only because of common movement with the market as represented by market index.

Note that the second is the key assumption of the SIM. On the basis of it that the SIM can be considered as a special case of the Market Model. Indeed, while SIM assumes the covariance of the assets to the same market index only ($E(e_i e_j) = 0$), the Market Model assumes a correlation between expected returns of the assets in portfolio $E(e_i, e_j) \neq 0$. Therefore, the Market Model is characterized by a less restrictive form than the SIM.

The change in assumption of Market Model about the relationship among the expected returns of assets in portfolio does not lead to the simple expressions of portfolio risk as in the SIM. Then the Market Model reduces the complexity of the pure portfolio's theory less than the SIM.

Therefore, while in the SIM the R_m is the expected returns of the market index, in the Market Model the R_m represents the expected returns of the portfolio built by the investor. Specifically, the expected returns of assets in portfolio are related among them, and therefore the investor has to define the portfolio by choosing the assets to be held on the basis of their expected returns and the correlations with the other assets owned. Consequently, the beta of the i-th asset changes as a function of the choice of the assets in portfolio.

12.2 Portfolio Expected Return and Variance

Based on SIM, the i-th asset's expected return $E(R_i)$ is equal to:

$$E(R_i) = E(f_i + e_i + \beta_i R_m) \rightarrow E(R_i) = E(f_i) + E(e_i) + E(\beta_i R_m)$$

By considering that f_i and β_i are constant, and $E(e_i) = 0$, we have:

$$E(R_i) = f_i + \beta_i E(R_m)$$

By denoting the $E(R) = \overline{R}$, we have:

$$\overline{R_i} = f_i + \beta_i \overline{R_m} \tag{12.7}$$

The i-th asset's variance (σ_i^2) is equal to:

$$\sigma_i^2 = E(R_i - E(R_i))^2 = E\left(R_i - \overline{R_i}\right)^2$$

By substituting R_i and $\overline{R_i}$ with relative equations, we have:

$$\sigma_i^2 = E\left[(f_i + e_i + \beta_i R_m) - \left(f_i + \beta_i \overline{R_m}\right)\right]^2$$

and then:

$$\sigma_i^2 = E\left[f_i + e_i + \beta_i R_m - f_i - \beta_i \overline{R_m}\right]^2 = E\left[e_i + \beta_i\left(R_m - \overline{R_m}\right)\right]^2$$
$$= E\left[(e_i)^2 + \left(\beta_i\left(R_m - \overline{R_m}\right)\right)^2 + 2e_i\beta_i\left(R_m - \overline{R_m}\right)\right]$$

By considering that β_i it is constant, we have:

$$\sigma_i^2 = E(e_i)^2 + \beta_i^2 E\left[\left(R_m - \overline{R_m}\right)\right]^2 + 2\beta_i E\left[e_i\left(R_m - \overline{R_{m.}}\right)\right]$$

By considering that: $\sigma_{ei}^2 = E(e_i)^2$; $\sigma_m^2 = E(R_m - \overline{R_m})^2$; $E[e_i(R_m - \overline{R_m})] = 0$, we have:

$$\sigma_i^2 = \sigma_{ei}^2 + \beta_i^2 \sigma_m^2 \tag{12.8}$$

The covariance between the *i*-th asset and the *j*-th assets is equal to:

$$\sigma_{i,j} = E[(R_i - E(R_i))(R_j - E(R_j))] = E[(R_i - \overline{R_i})(R_j - \overline{R_j})]$$

Substituting R_i, $\overline{R_i}$, R_j, $\overline{R_j}$ with relative equations, we have:

$$\sigma_{i,j} = E\{[(f_i + e_i + \beta_i R_m) - (f_i + \beta_i \overline{R_m})][(f_j + e_j + \beta_j R_m) - (f_j + \beta_j \overline{R_m})]\}$$

and then:

$$\begin{aligned}\sigma_{i,j} &= E\{[f_i + e_i + \beta_i R_m - f_i - \beta_i \overline{R_m}][f_j + e_j + \beta_j R_m - f_j - \beta_j \overline{R_m}]\}\\ &= E\{[e_i + \beta_i(R_m - \overline{R_m})][e_j + \beta_j(R_m - \overline{R_m})]\}\\ &= E\left[e_i e_j + e_i\beta_j(R_m - \overline{R_m}) + e_j\beta_i(R_m - \overline{R_m}) + \beta_i\beta_j(R_m - \overline{R_m})^2\right] = E(e_i e_j)\\ &+ E[e_i\beta_j(R_m - \overline{R_m})] + E[e_j\beta_i(R_m - \overline{R_m})] + E\left[\beta_i\beta_j(R_m - \overline{R_m})^2\right]\end{aligned}$$

and considering that β_i and β_j are constant, we have:

$$\sigma_{i,j} = E(e_i e_j) + \beta_j E[e_i(R_m - \overline{R_m})] + \beta_i E[e_j(R_m - \overline{R_m})] + \beta_i\beta_j E\left[(R_m - \overline{R_m})^2\right]$$

and by considering that: $E(e_i) = 0$, $\sigma_m^2 = E(R_m - \overline{R_m})^2$, $E[e_i(R_m - \overline{R_m})] = 0$, and $E(e_i e_j) = 0$, we have:

$$\sigma_{i,j} = \beta_i \beta_j \sigma_m^2 \tag{12.9}$$

On the basis of the expected return, variance and covariance of *i*-th and *j*-th assets, we can estimate the expected return and variance of portfolio.

Based on the expected return, variance and covariance of assets, we can compute the portfolio's expected return and variance.

The portfolio's expected return $(\overline{R_P})$ is equal to:

$$\overline{R_P} = \sum_{i=1}^{N} \alpha_i \overline{R_i}$$

By considering that $\overline{R_i} = f_i + \beta_i \overline{R_m}$, we have:

$$\overline{R_P} = \sum_{i=1}^{N} \alpha_i \left(f_i + \beta_i \overline{R_m}\right)$$

and then:

$$\overline{R_P} = \sum_{i=1}^{N} \alpha_i f_i + \sum_{i=1}^{N} \alpha_i \beta_i \overline{R_m} \tag{12.10}$$

The portfolio's variance $\left(\sigma_P^2\right)$ is equal to:

$$\sigma_P^2 = \sum_{i=1}^{N} \alpha_i^2 \sigma_i^2 + \sum_{i=1}^{N} \sum_{\substack{j=1 \\ j \neq i}}^{N} \alpha_i \alpha_j \sigma_{i,j}$$

by considering that $\sigma_i^2 = \sigma_{ei}^2 + \beta_i^2 \sigma_m^2$ and $\sigma_{i,j} = \beta_i \beta_j \sigma_m^2$, substituting we have:

$$\sigma_P^2 = \sum_{i=1}^{N} \alpha_i^2 \left(\sigma_{e_i}^2 + \beta_i^2 \sigma_m^2\right) + \sum_{i=1}^{N} \sum_{\substack{j=1 \\ j \neq i}}^{N} \alpha_i \alpha_j \beta_i \beta_j \sigma_m^2$$

and then:

$$\sigma_P^2 = \sum_{i=1}^{N} \alpha_i^2 \beta_i^2 \sigma_m^2 + \sum_{i=1}^{N} \sum_{\substack{j=1 \\ j \neq i}}^{N} \alpha_i \alpha_j \beta_i \beta_j \sigma_m^2 + \sum_{i=1}^{N} \alpha_i^2 \sigma_{e_i}^2 \tag{12.11}$$

The portfolio's standard deviation (σ_P) si equal to:

$$\sigma_P = \sqrt{\sum_{i=1}^{N} \alpha_i^2 \beta_i^2 \sigma_m^2 + \sum_{i=1}^{N} \sum_{\substack{j=1 \\ j \neq i}}^{N} \alpha_i \alpha_j \beta_i \beta_j \sigma_m^2 + \sum_{i=1}^{N} \alpha_i^2 \sigma_{e_i}^2} \tag{12.12}$$

Therefore, the SIM estimates the expected return $\left(\overline{R_P}\right)$ and variance $\left(\sigma_P^2\right)$ of portfolio on the basis of:

- three variables for each i-th asset: f_i, β_i and σ_i^2
- two variables for the market index: $\overline{R_m}$ and σ_m^2.

We have $3N + 2$ terms: f_i, β_i, σ_i^2 for each i-th asset for $i = 1, 2, 3, \ldots, N$, plus 2 terms of index market that are its expected return $\overline{R_m}$ and its variance σ_m^2 tha rae the same for all N assets. Then we can estimate expected return and variance (and standard deviation) of any portfolio by estimating f_i, β_i and σ_i^2 of each asset and the expected return $\overline{R_m}$ and variance σ_m^2 of market index that represents the market.

Consequently, by assuming that the prices of assets move together only because of common movement with the market (as represented by the market index) and they move together only because of a common co-movement with market index, the SIM reduces the number of correlations to be estimated from the $[N(N-1)]/2$ required by the pure portfolio theory, to $3N+2$.

12.3 Asset Contribution to the Portfolio's Risk

The contribution of the i-th asset to the portfolio's risk is the function of its beta β_i that measures the sensitivity of the asset to market movements.

To prove it, define the portfolio's beta (β_P) as a weighted average of the beta (β_i) of assets in portfolio (for $i = 1, 2, 3, \ldots N$) where the weights are the fraction of wealth invested in each asset (α_i), as follows:

$$\beta_P = \sum_{i=1}^{N} \alpha_i \beta_i$$

In a similar way, we can define the portfolio's anticipated term (f_P) as follows:

$$f_P = \sum_{i=1}^{N} \alpha_i f_i$$

By considering that the portfolio's expected return $\left(\overline{R_P}\right)$ is equal to:

$$\overline{R_P} = \sum_{i=1}^{N} \alpha_i f_i + \sum_{i=1}^{N} \alpha_i \beta_i \overline{R_m}$$

substituting, we have:

$$\overline{R_P} = f_P + \beta_P \overline{R_m}$$

On the basis of the equation, if the portfolio P is considered the market portfolio M, therefore it contains the same assets in the market in the same proportion. Consequently, their expected returns must be equal: $\overline{R_P} = \overline{R_m}$. This result can be realized if and only if $f_P = 0$ and $\beta_P = 1$:

$$\begin{matrix} f_P = 0 \\ \beta_P = 1 \end{matrix} \quad \rightarrow \quad \overline{R_P} = \overline{R_m}$$

It implies that the beta coefficient of the market must be equal to 1 and the i-th asset can be defined more or less risky than the market if the β_i is higher or lower than β_P, respectively. Specifically, if $\beta_i > \beta_P = 1$, the i-th asset is more risky than the market, as well as $\beta_i < \beta_P = 1$ is less risky than the market.

Now the problem is to well-understand the contribution of i-th asset to the portfolio's risk. To measure it, consider the portfolio's variance:

$$\sigma_P^2 = \sum_{i=1}^{N} \alpha_i^2 \beta_i^2 \sigma_m^2 + \sum_{i=1}^{N} \sum_{\substack{j=1 \\ j \neq i}}^{N} \alpha_i \alpha_j \beta_i \beta_j \sigma_m^2 + \sum_{i=1}^{N} \alpha_i^2 \sigma_{e_i}^2$$

If we remove the constraint $j \neq i$ we can define the variance without distinguishing between variance and covariance and then the first summation must be considered in the double summation as follows:

$$\sigma_P^2 = \sum_{i=1}^{N} \sum_{j=1}^{N} \alpha_i \alpha_j \beta_i \beta_j \sigma_m^2 + \sum_{i=1}^{N} \alpha_i^2 \sigma_{e_i}^2$$

By considering that:

$$\sum_{i=1}^{N} \alpha_i \beta_i = \beta_P; \quad \sum_{j=1}^{N} \alpha_j \beta_j = \beta_P$$

we have:

$$\sigma_P^2 = \beta_P^2 \sigma_m^2 + \sum_{i=1}^{N} \alpha_i^2 \sigma_{e_i}^2$$

Assume that investor decides to invest an equal amount of wealth in each of N assets so that the weight of each of i-th asset is equal to $\alpha_i = \frac{1}{N}$. The portfolio's variance is equal to:

$$\sigma_P^2 = \beta_P^2 \sigma_m^2 + \sum_{i=1}^{N} \left(\frac{1}{N}\right)^2 \sigma_{e_i}^2$$

That we can rewrite as follows:

$$\sigma_P^2 = \beta_P^2 \sigma_m^2 + \frac{1}{N} \left[\sum_{i=1}^{N} \frac{1}{N} \sigma_{e_i}^2 \right] = \beta_P^2 \sigma_m^2 + \frac{1}{N} \left[\sum_{i=1}^{N} \frac{\sigma_{e_i}^2}{N} \right]$$

Where $\sum_{i=1}^{N} \frac{\sigma_{e_i}^2}{N}$ is the average residual risk $\overline{\sigma}_{e_i}^2$, so that:

$$\sigma_P^2 = \beta_P^2 \sigma_m^2 + \frac{1}{N} \overline{\sigma}_{e_i}^2$$

To the increase of asset in portfolio (N increases) the relevance of the average residual risk $\left(\overline{\sigma}_{e_i}^2\right)$ reduces drastically. By considering an infinite number of asset in portfolio the average residual risk $\overline{\sigma}_{e_i}^2$ is null and the portfolio's risk is the function of β_P as follows:

$$\lim_{N \to \infty} \frac{1}{N} \overline{\sigma}_{e_i}^2 = 0$$

and then:

$$\sigma_P^2 = \beta_P^2 \sigma_m^2$$

Since all are positive terms, we can pass from portfolio's variance (σ_P^2) to its standard devation (σ_P) directly, as follows:

$$\sigma_P = \beta_P \sigma_m$$

By considering that $\beta_P = \sum_{i=1}^{N} \alpha_i \beta_i$, substituting we have:

$$\sigma_P = \left(\sum_{i=1}^{N} \alpha_i \beta_i \right) \sigma_m \tag{12.13}$$

Since σ_m is the same for each i-th asset, the equation states that the i-th asset's marginal contribution to the portfolio's risk is the function of its coefficient beta (β_i) only. This is the same result of the diversification process.

Therefore, the SIM requires the estimation of the beta of each i-th asset (β_i) that we consider to introduce in the portfolio.

The common method is to estimate the future beta on the basis of the past beta. Then, we use the historical beta to estimate the future beta of each i-th asset (β_i). The best technique is the regression analysis.

The return of i-th asset is equal to:

$$R_i = f_i + \beta_i R_m + e_i$$

We assume that this equation is valid in each moment in time even if in reality the value of f_i, β_i and $\sigma_{e_i}^2$ can change over time. Therefore, we assume constant their value, we can use the regression analysis. By applying the Ordinary Least Square (OLS), we have:

$$\beta_i = \frac{\sum_{t=1}^{n} \left[\left(R_i - \overline{R_i} \right) \left(R_m - \overline{R_m} \right) \right]}{\sum_{t=1}^{n} \left(R_m - \overline{R_m} \right)^2} = \frac{\mathrm{Cov}(R_m; R_i)}{\mathrm{Var}(R_m)} = \frac{\sigma_{(mi)}}{\sigma_m^2}$$

and

$$f_i = \overline{R_i} - \beta_i \overline{R_m} \tag{12.14}$$

Obviously, the estimate is subject to error and therefore, the estimated β_i and f_i could not be equal to their real values that existed in the period. Also, β_i and f_i are not perfectly stationarity over time.

12.4 Determination of the Optimum Portfolio

The SIM is able to reduce the complexity of the portfolio's analysis without losing accuracy in the forecast of covariances and correlations between assets. The index models have characterized by another advantage: they allow to develop a very easy system for the computation of the optimum portfolios. Also, usually the methods of portfolio selection make it very clear why stock does enter into optimum portfolio or does not. Indeed, each index model leads to a unique ranking of assets, so that if an asset enters in the optimal portfolio, then any other higher-ranked asset must also enter the portfolio. At the same time, if an asset does not enter in the optimal portfolio, then any other lower-ranked asset does not enter in the portfolio.

In this contest, we analyse the methods for selecting optimal portfolios if we use the SIM to forecast the covariance structure of asset's returns.

The method is based on two steps (Elton et al., 2013):

- first, we define the ranking criteria necessary to order assets for selection of the optimal portfolio.
- second, we define the technique for employing the ranking for forming the optimum portfolio.

The method of the determination of the optimal portfolio must be applied under different assumptions:

1. Short sales allowed or not allowed.
2. Limited or unlimited borrowing and lending at the riskless rate.

In this contest, we limit the analysis to the case in which the short sales are allowed and the investor can lend and borrow at the free-risk rate (R_F).

The index to rank assets is Excess Return to Beta *(ERB)* ratio as follows:

$$\text{ERB} = \frac{\overline{R_i} - R_F}{\beta_i} \tag{12.15}$$

The numerator is the difference between the expected return of *i*-th asset $\left(\overline{R_i}\right)$ and the return of riskless asset as measured by the risk-free rate (R_F) and then it measures the additional return that investor expects to receive from the investment in stocks rather than in riskless asset.

The denominator is the beta of the *i*-th asset and it measures the sensitivity of the *i*-th asset's returns (R_i) to the change in the market index returns (R_m) and then it measures the non-diversifiable market risk and then the risk that investors must bear by investing in stocks rather than in riskless asset.

Therefore, the index of Excess Return to Beta ratio measures the additional return on the i-th asset $\left(\overline{R_i} - R_F\right)$ per unit of non-diversifiable risk (β_i).

The applying of the ERB ratio is simple. If a stock is considered desirable on the basis of the ERB ratio, its ranking represents the minimum that any stock must have for its inclusion in the optimal portfolio. Therefore, all stocks with higher ratio will be included in the optimal portfolio as well as all stocks with lower ratio will be not included in the portfolio.

Note that by using the SIM, the stock is included or excluded depending only on the size of its excess return to beta ratio.

The desirable level of the ERB ratio on the basis of which to rank all stocks are defined Cutoff Rate (C). Therefore, the optimum portfolio is composed by all stocks whose ERB ratio is higher than the Cutoff defined. Then the i-th asset can enter in the portfolio only if its ERB is higher than Cutoff rate as follows:

$$\frac{\overline{R_i} - R_F}{\beta_i} > C \quad \text{stock is selected}$$

$$\frac{\overline{R_i} - R_F}{\beta_i} < C \quad \text{stock is rejected}$$

The value of Cutoff Rate (C) is compounded from the characteristics of all the securities included in the optimum portfolio. Denote C_i the possible candidate of C. The value of C_i is calculating if all i securities are assumed to belong to the optimal portfolio. Since securities are ranked from highest to lowest ERB, if a particular security belongs in the optimal portfolio, consequently all higher-ranked securities are included in the optimal portfolio. We have found the optimum C_i, and it is C only if all securities used in the computation of C_i have a ERB above C_i as well as all securities that have ERB below C_i are not used in the computation of C_i.

In a portfolio of i stocks, we have:

$$C_i = \frac{\sigma_m^2 \sum_{j=1}^{i} \frac{\left(\overline{R_j} - R_F\right)\beta_j}{\sigma_{e_i}^2}}{1 + \sigma_m^2 \sum_{j=1}^{i} \left(\frac{\beta_j^2}{\sigma_{e_i}^2}\right)} \tag{12.16}$$

where σ_m^2 is the variance of the market index and $\sigma_{e_i}^2$ is the variance of stock's movement that is not associated with the movement of the market index.

13 Capital Asset Pricing Model: Standard Form

13.1 Baseline Assumptions

The Capital Asset Pricing Model (CAPM) is the most common and the easiest of the equilibrium models. It was developed independently by Sharpe (1964), Lintner (1965a, b), Mossin (1966). Indeed, we commonly refer to the Sharpe–Lintner–Mossin form of general equilibrium relationship in the capital markets in discussing the standard CAPM. The CAPM is one of the most relevant contribution to understand how capital markets function.

In this contest, we consider the standard form of CAPM while in the next chapter we will discuss the main non-standard form of CAPM.

The main baseline assumptions of the standard CAPM can be summarized as follows:

1. *No transaction costs:* there are no frictions and costs in buying or selling of any asset on market. They are not considered because while their introduction in model adds complexity, the benefits are not so relevant.
2. *Infinite divisibility of any asset:* each asset can be divided without any limitations. Then, each asset and for each quantity, is tradable. Investor can take any position in an investment, regardless of the size of wealth and portfolio.
3. *Marketability of all assets*: all assets are marketable and, consequently any asset can be sold and bought on the market.
4. *No personal income taxes:* there is not difference in the earning from obligations, dividends, and capital gains.
5. *Investor is price-taker:* no one investor can affect the price of the asset on market by buying or selling. Any asset price is defined on the basis of demand and supply aggregate of all investors' decisions simultaneously.
6. *Mean-variance approach in the portfolio choices:* portfolio choices are based on the mean-variance approach and then investors' decisions are always made on the basis of the expected return and standard deviation only.

P. De Luca, *Corporate Finance*, Springer Texts in Business and Economics,
https://doi.org/10.1007/978-3-031-18300-3_13

7. *Homogeneity of expectations:* it has three main consequences. First, all investors consider the mean and variance of returns by using the same mean-variance approach and all investors define the relevant period in the same manner. Second, all investors have the same information and expectations about the statistical characteristics of the assets with regard to the expected returns, variance and correlation matrix based on the correlation structure between all pairs of stock. Third, all investors define the relevant period in the same manner and then the investment time is equal for all investors.
8. *Short sales are allowed illimited*: there are no restrictions on short selling. Consequently, investors can sell short any number of any assets in a given period of time.
9. *Lending and borrowing at the risk-free rate illimited:* investors can lend or borrow at the same risk-free rate.

These assumptions are rigid and sometimes highly restrictive. In any cases, it is not relevant how realistic they are but how much the model based on them is able to explain the reality.

The *standard* CAPM be derived in several forms involving different degrees of rigour and mathematical complexity. In this context, we follow two main approaches (Elton et al., 2013):

(a) *Intuitive approach*: it is based on the economic intuition.
(b) *Rigorous approach*: it is based on a simple mathematical form.

13.2 Intuitive Approach to CAPM

The intuitive approach to generate the CAPM is based on the economic intuition (Elton et al., 2013).

Assume that short sales are allowed and assume that investors can lend and borrow at the risk-free rate. Each investor defines the efficient frontier as shown in Fig. 13.1.

Any investor requires a portfolio of risky assets (M) regardless of their risk preferences. This portfolio lies at the tangent point between the efficient frontier of risky assets and a *straight-line* with intercept equal to the risk-free rate.

Therefore, any investor satisfies the own risk preferences by combining the portfolio M (portfolio of risky assets) with lending or borrowing at a risk-free rate.

Because all investors have homogeneous expectations, they all face the same efficient frontier. Also, they have the same straight-line because there is one risk-free rate on market (and therefore it is the same for all investors). It implies that all investors have the same efficient frontier and straight-line, and then they have the same tangent point between them. Because all investors hold the same risky portfolio (M), in equilibrium condition it must be the market portfolio. This portfolio holds all risky assets in the market and each asset is held in the same proportion of market on

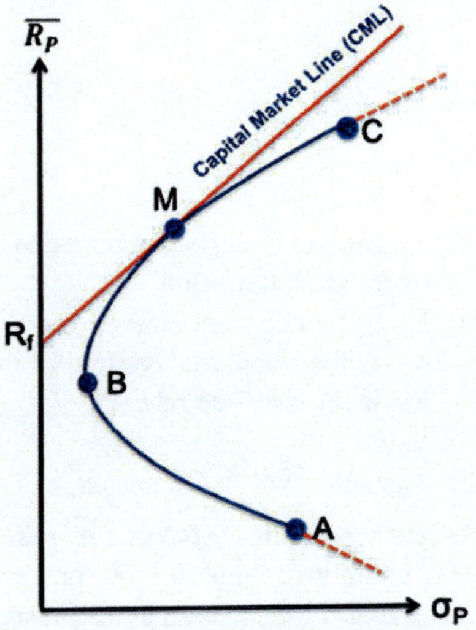

Fig. 13.1 The capital market line

the basis of the ratio between the market value of the asset and the total market value of all risky assets.

Therefore, all investors hold combination of two portfolios only: the market portfolio (M) and the riskless asset. It is called *two mutual fund theorem*. Based on it all investors are satisfied with a market fund plus the opportunity to lend or borrow at risk-free rate.

The straight-line with intercept equal to the risk-free rate and tangent to the efficient frontier by defining the market portfolio (M), is defined Capital Market Line (CML) in the plan standard deviation-expected return $\left(\sigma_p; \overline{R_P}\right)$. All efficient portfolios will be positioned along the CML and non-efficient assets or portfolios are positioned below the CML. There are not non-efficient portfolios above the CML because the statistical characteristics of the assets unchanged and they are always the same. Consequently, the market portfolio (M) is the portfolio on the efficient frontier obtained from the tangent between the efficient frontier and the straight-line with interception equal to the risk-free rate.

Therefore, investors hold a combination of a portfolio of risky assets that is the market portfolio (M) and a risk-free asset. Then, each investor can satisfy its risk preferences by considering the market fund and the opportunity to lend and borrow at the same risk-free asset rate (R_F).

Note that the risk-free rate (R_F) is a theoretical construction only. An investment riskless does not exist by definition. The risk-free rate (R_F) does not measure the risk but the price of time. For its computation, it is assumed equal to the return of a government bond a country whose default risk is so lower to be assumed equal to zero.

The equation of the *CML* is equal to:

$$\overline{R_{ep}} = R_F + \left(\frac{\overline{R_M} - R_F}{\sigma_M}\right)\sigma_{ep} \tag{13.1}$$

where:

- ep: denotes the efficient portfolio, and then $\overline{R_{ep}}$ is its expected return, while σ_{ep} is its standard deviation,
- $\overline{R_M}$ is the expected market return
- σ_M: is the standard deviation of market portfolio
- R_F: is the risk-free rate.

The ratio $\left(\frac{\overline{R_M} - R_F}{\sigma_M}\right)$ is the slope of the CML and it is the market price of risk for all efficient portfolios (note that it is the Sharpe ratio). Indeed, it is equal to the market risk premium $\left(\overline{R_M} - R_F\right)$ per one unit of market risk (σ_M). Consequently, it is the extra-return we can earn by increasing the level of risk (σ_M) on an efficient portfolio by one unit.

Therefore, while the first term (R_F) is the risk-free rate and it measures the price of time, the second term $\left(\left(\frac{\overline{R_M} - R_F}{\sigma_M}\right)\sigma_{ep}\right)$ is the market price of risk multiplied by the total amount of risk in a portfolio and it measures the return required as the function of the risk.

Therefore, the CML's states that the Expected Return on efficient portfolio $\left(\overline{R_{ep}}\right)$ is equal to the Price of Time (R_F) plus the Price of Risk $\left(\frac{\overline{R_M} - R_F}{\sigma_M}\right)$ multiplied by the amount of Risk on an efficient portfolio (σ_{ep}) (the risk is defined as the standard deviation of expected return on any efficient portfolio).

Note that this equation states only the expected return of efficient portfolios positioned along the CML. It does not describe the expected returns of non-efficient portfolios or individual assets.

From the equilibrium relationship for efficient portfolios as defined by the CML, we can derive the equilibrium relationship for any asset or portfolio efficient or inefficient. This relationship is represented by the Security Market Line (SML) in the plan beta-expected return $\left(\beta; \overline{R}\right)$. We can derive the SML as follows.

If the portfolio is well-diversified, the beta coefficient measures the systemic risk of asset that is the only relevant because the specific risk of asset tends to go to zero thanks to the diversification process. The market portfolio, hold by all investors, is well-diversified by definition. Therefore, the only relevant characteristics of an asset are the expected return $\left(\overline{R}\right)$ and beta (β). Indeed, all decisions are based on risk and return.

We can represent all efficient portfolios on a straight-line in the beta-return space $\left(\beta; \overline{R}\right)$ as in Fig. 13.2.

Each point outside of the straight-line generates an opportunity of riskless arbitrage: prices move until the point is positioned on the straight-line. Indeed, two

Fig. 13.2 Portfolios in the plan beta-expected return

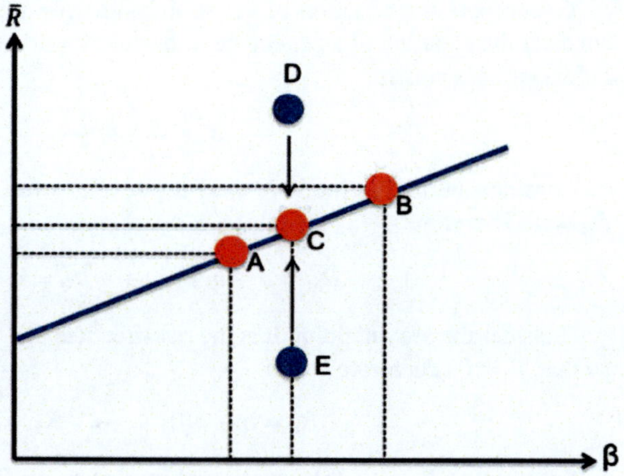

assets or portfolios that are equivalent cannot sell at different prices. In Fig. 13.2, the point D (asset or portfolio) is characterized by the same risk of the point C but it has higher expected return. Point D generates an opportunity of arbitrage: we can sell short the point C to buy the point D. Similarly, the point E has the same risk of the point C but it has a lower expected return. Point E generates an arbitrage opportunity: we can sell short the point E to buy the point C. In both cases, prices move until the point D goes down and the point E goes up to the straight-line where there is the point C.

Therefore, all portfolios must lie along a straight-line in the beta-expected return space. If any portfolio is positioned above or below that straight-line, there is arbitrage opportunity able to move the prices until all portfolios converge towards the straight-line.

Note that the point C can be considered one of the possible combinations between points A and B. Indeed, every combination between two points on the straight-line generates a new point on it.

Now the main problem concerns the definition of the equation of this straight-line in the beta-return space $(\beta; \overline{R})$. The simplest way is to use the Euclid's postulate: a straight-line segment can be drawn joining any two points. Then between two points can pass one and only one straight-line. In our case, the definition of two points is simple:

1. The first point is the market portfolio (M). In CAPM all investors hold the market portfolio because all portfolios must lie on the straight-line. Because the market portfolio groups all assets on market, its beta is equal to 1. Therefore, the market portfolio has beta equal to 1 and expected return equal to $\overline{R_M}$.
2. The second point is the risk-free rate. Because it does not measure the systemic risk but the price of time, its beta is equal to zero. Indeed, it is the interception on the vertical axis. Therefore, the intercept has beta equal to 0 and certain return equal to R_F.

To compute the equation of the straight-line passing between these two points, consider the equation of a general straight-line: $y = a + bx$. By considering a generic k-th asset, it becomes:

$$\overline{R_k} = a + b\beta_k$$

Consider the first point. It is market portfolio whose beta is equal to 1 so that: $\beta_M = 1$. Therefore:

$$\overline{R_M} = a + b(1) \quad \rightarrow \quad \overline{R_M} = a + b$$

Consider the second point. It is the risk-free rate and then the beta is equal to zero so that: $\beta = 0$. Therefore:

$$R_F = a + b(0) \quad \rightarrow \quad R_F = a$$

Substituting $R_F = a$, the equation of market return (R_M) is equal to:

$$\overline{R_M} = R_F + b$$

And by solving for b, it gets:

$$b = \overline{R_M} - R_F$$

By substituting $a = R_F$ and $b = \overline{R_M} - R_F$, in the equation of the straight-line, we have:

$$\overline{R_k} = R_F + \beta_k\left(\overline{R_M} - R_F\right) \tag{13.2}$$

This is the equation of the Security Market Line (SML) and it represents one of the most relevant in the field of finance. This equation defines the expected return for all assets and portfolios of assets whether they are efficient or not. This equation is the most commonly used form to write the CAPM model. The SML can be represented as in Fig. 13.3.

Note that both R_M and R_F are not related to the specific assets considered. It implies that the difference among assets is due to the coefficient beta that measures the asset's systematic risk.

The relationship between the expected return and beta is linear. Because $\overline{R_M}$ and R_F are independent from assets, the expected return of asset is the linear function of its beta. Therefore, the expected return of asset is the function of its systemic risk only and the specific risk is irrelevant. It implies that investor cannot expect an expected return function of the asset's specific risk.

By considering that the beta of k-th asset can be defined as follows:

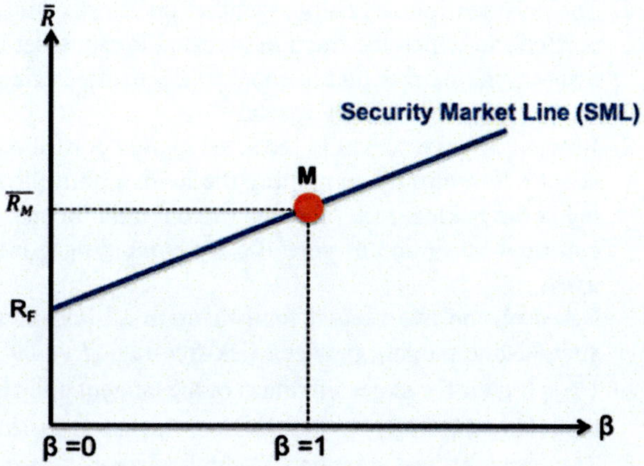

Fig. 13.3 The security market line (SML)

$$\beta_K = \frac{\sigma_{kM}}{\sigma_M^2}$$

Substituting, we have:

$$\overline{R_K} = R_F + \left(\frac{\sigma_{kM}}{\sigma_M^2}\right)\left(\overline{R_M} - R_F\right)$$

Rearranging we can write the SML equation in this new form:

$$\overline{R_K} = R_F + \left(\frac{\overline{R_M} - R_F}{\sigma_M}\right)\left(\frac{\sigma_{kM}}{\sigma_M}\right) \tag{13.3}$$

where:

- $\left(\frac{\overline{R_M} - R_F}{\sigma_M}\right)$ is the Sharpe ratio and it is the market price of risk.
- $\left(\frac{\sigma_{kM}}{\sigma_M}\right)$ is the marginal contribution to the portfolio's standard deviation due to the introduction of the *k*-th asset in the portfolio. Therefore, it measures the impact of the *k*-th asset on the risk of the market portfolio. Then, it is the amount of systemic risk of the *k*-th asset.

In this different form, the SML states that the expected return of any *k*-th asset or portfolio $\left(\overline{R_K}\right)$ is equal to Price of Time (R_F) plus the Market Price of Risk $\left(\frac{\overline{R_M} - R_F}{\sigma_M}\right)$ multiplied by the Amount of Risk of the *k*-the asset $\left(\frac{\sigma_{kM}}{\sigma_M}\right)$.

The main points states by the CAPM can be summarized as follows:

1. The only portfolio of risky asset that investors own is the market portfolio: it is a portfolio in which the fraction invested in any asset is equal to the weight of this asset on the market that is equal to the market value of the asset divided by the market value of all risky assets.
2. Because all investors hold the same market portfolio, they satisfy their preference about risk-return by combining the market portfolio with the lending or borrowing at the riskless rate. The two mutual fund theorem states that all investors can construct an optimum portfolio by combining a market fund with the riskless asset.
3. Based on the two mutual fund theorem all investors hold a portfolio along the straight-line passing between risk-free rate (R_F) and the market expected return $\left(\overline{R_M}\right)$ (that is the expected return of the tangent point between the straight-line and the efficient frontier) in the standard deviation-expected return $\left(\sigma; \overline{R}\right)$ space.
4. This straight-line is called Capital Market Line (CML) and it describes all efficient portfolios only and it is represented by the equation:

$$\overline{R_{\text{ep}}} = R_F + \left(\frac{\overline{R_M} - R_F}{\sigma_M}\right)\sigma_{\text{ep}}$$

This equation states that the expected return on an efficient portfolio $\left(\overline{R_{\text{ep}}}\right)$ is equal to the price of time (R_F) plus the market price of risk $\left(\frac{\overline{R_M} - R_F}{\sigma_M}\right)$ multiplied by the amount of risk on an efficient portfolio (σ_{ep}).

5. The CML defines the equilibrium relationship for efficient portfolios only. Based on CML we can derive the equilibrium relationship for any asset or portfolio efficient or inefficient. This relationship is represented by the Security Market Line (SML) and it is represented by the equation:

$$\overline{R_k} = R_F + \beta_k\left(\overline{R_M} - R_F\right) \quad \text{or} \quad \overline{R_K} = R_F + \left(\frac{\overline{R_M} - R_F}{\sigma_M}\right)\left(\frac{\sigma_{kM}}{\sigma_M}\right)$$

Note that the SML describes the equilibrium return on all portfolios as well as all securities. This equation states that the expected return of any asset or portfolio (efficient or inefficient) $\left(\overline{R_K}\right)$ is equal to the Price of Time (R_F) plus the Market Price of Risk $\left(\frac{\overline{R_M} - R_F}{\sigma_M}\right)$ multiplied by the amount of risk of the k-th asset $\left(\frac{\sigma_{kM}}{\sigma_M}\right)$ that measures the impact of the k-th asset on the risk of market portfolio.

6. In both CML and SML, the risk-free rate (R_F) and the market expected return $\left(\overline{R_M}\right)$ are not related to the assets considered. Consequently, the difference between the expected return of two different assets is related to their risk only. It implies that two assets with the same systemic risk could not offer different returns.

7. The SML, as well as the CML, states a linear relationship between expected return and risk. Specifically, the expected return is a linearly increasing function of risk, and more precisely of the systemic risk because investor does not receive any return for specific risk (eliminated through diversification process). The coefficient beta measures systemic risk of the asset. It implies that the higher the coefficient beta, the higher the expected return.
8. The CAMP is a general equilibrium model. Therefore, to say that the asset with the higher coefficient beta should achieve greater expected returns, it does not mean that it must always be true in all periods. Even if it is reasonable in the long term, in the short term it is possible that the higher coefficient beta may generate a low return and, in this possibility, lies a source of the risk. Also, the standard CAPM model explains the behaviour of asset's return and it does not explain the behaviour of individual investors. Indeed, just think that generally individual investors hold nonmarket and commonly very small portfolios.

13.3 Rigorous Approach to CAPM

The CAPM can be derived on the basis of a rigorous approach in several ways. In this context, we consider one of the most easy (Elton et al., 2013).

It is more relevant the rigorous approach because it allows to incorporate modifications of the assumptions of the standard CAPM.

Assume that short sales are allowed and investors can lend or borrow an unlimited at the risk-free rate (R_F).

Consider the slope of the straight-line passing through the free-risk rate (the intercept on the vertical axis) and a risky portfolio. The optimal portfolio is the one that maximizes this slope under constraint of short sales allowed, as follows:

$$\begin{cases} \max \theta = \dfrac{\overline{R_P} - R_F}{\sigma_P} \\ \sum\limits_{i=1}^{n} \alpha_i = 1 \end{cases} \tag{13.4}$$

Instead of using the method of Lagrangian multipliers to solve the system, we can consider the constrain directly in the function to maximize by passing from a constrained maximization problem to an unconstrained maximization problem (Elton et al., 2013). In this sense, the risk-free rate (R_F) can be rewritten as R_F times 1, so that:

$$\begin{matrix} R_F = 1 \cdot R_F \\ \sum\limits_{i=1}^{n} \alpha_i = 1 \end{matrix} \quad \rightarrow \quad R_F = \left(\sum_{i=1}^{n} \alpha_i \right) R_F = \sum_{i=1}^{N} (\alpha_i R_F)$$

The portfolio's expected return, its variance and standard deviation are, respectively:

$$R_P = \sum_{i=1}^{n} \alpha_i R_i$$

$$\sigma_P^2 = \sum_{i=1}^{N} \alpha_i^2 \sigma_i^2 + \sum_{i=1}^{N} \sum_{\substack{j=1 \\ j \neq i}}^{N} \alpha_i \alpha_j \sigma_{ij}$$

$$\sigma_P = \sqrt{\sum_{i=1}^{N} \alpha_i^2 \sigma_i^2 + \sum_{i=1}^{N} \sum_{\substack{j=1 \\ j \neq i}}^{N} \alpha_i \alpha_j \sigma_{ij}} = \left[\sum_{i=1}^{N} \alpha_i^2 \sigma_i^2 + \sum_{i=1}^{N} \sum_{\substack{j=1 \\ j \neq i}}^{N} \alpha_i \alpha_j \sigma_{ij} \right]^{\frac{1}{2}}$$

Substituting, we have:

$$\theta = \frac{\overline{R_P} - R_F}{\sigma_P} = \frac{\sum_{i=1}^{n} \alpha_i \overline{R_i} - \sum_{i=1}^{n} \alpha_i R_F}{\left[\sum_{i=1}^{N} \alpha_i^2 \sigma_i^2 + \sum_{i=1}^{N} \sum_{\substack{j=1 \\ j \neq i}}^{N} \alpha_i \alpha_j \sigma_{ij} \right]^{\frac{1}{2}}}$$

and then:

$$\theta = \left[\sum_{i=1}^{n} \alpha_i \left(\overline{R_i} - R_F \right) \right] \left[\sum_{i=1}^{N} \alpha_i^2 \sigma_i^2 + \sum_{i=1}^{N} \sum_{\substack{j=1 \\ j \neq i}}^{N} \alpha_i \alpha_j \sigma_{ij} \right]^{-\frac{1}{2}}$$

Remembering that:

$$\frac{\partial}{\partial \alpha_k} \left[\sum_{i=1}^{n} \alpha_i \left(\overline{R_i} - R_F \right) \right] = \overline{R_K} - R_F$$

$$\frac{\partial}{\partial \alpha_k} \left[\sum_{i=1}^{N} \alpha_i^2 \sigma_i^2 \right] = 2 \alpha_k \sigma_k^2$$

$$\frac{\partial}{\partial \alpha_k}\left[\sum_{i=1}^{N}\sum_{\substack{j=1\\ j\neq i}}^{N}\alpha_i\alpha_j\sigma_{ij}\right]=2\sum_{\substack{j=1\\ j\neq k}}^{N}\alpha_j\sigma_{kj}$$

the derivative of the function θ with respect to α_k is equal to:

$$\frac{\partial}{\partial \alpha_k}\left(\left[\sum_{i=1}^{n}\alpha_i\left(\overline{R}_i-R_F\right)\right]\left[\sum_{i=1}^{N}\alpha_i^2\sigma_i^2+\sum_{i=1}^{N}\sum_{\substack{j=1\\ j\neq i}}^{N}\alpha_i\alpha_j\sigma_{ij}\right]^{-\frac{1}{2}}\right)$$

$$=\left\{\left[\sum_{i=1}^{N}\alpha_i\left(\overline{R}_i-R_f\right)\right]\left[\left(-\frac{1}{2}\right)\left(\sum_{i=1}^{N}\alpha_i^2\sigma_i^2+\sum_{i=1}^{N}\sum_{\substack{j=1\\ j\neq i}}^{N}\alpha_i\alpha_j\sigma_{ij}\right)^{-\frac{3}{2}}\right.\right.$$

$$\left.\left.\left(2\alpha_k\sigma_k^2+2\sum_{\substack{j=1\\ j\neq k}}^{N}\alpha_j\sigma_{kj}\right)\right]\right\}$$

$$+\left\{\left[\left(\sum_{i=1}^{N}\alpha_i^2\sigma_i^2+\sum_{i=1}^{N}\sum_{\substack{j=1\\ j\neq i}}^{N}\alpha_i\alpha_j\sigma_{ij}\right)^{-\frac{1}{2}}\right]\left[\overline{R_K}-R_f\right]\right\}$$

To solve the problem we derive the function θ with respect to each k-th asset and set it equal to zero. Generally, pointing the first derivative equal to zero, we have:

$$\frac{\partial}{\partial \alpha_k}=\left\{\left[\sum_{i=1}^{N}\alpha_i\left(\overline{R}_i-R_f\right)\right]\left[\left(-\frac{1}{2}\right)\left(\sum_{i=1}^{N}\alpha_i^2\sigma_i^2+\sum_{i=1}^{N}\sum_{\substack{j=1\\ j\neq i}}^{N}\alpha_i\alpha_j\sigma_{ij}\right)^{-\frac{3}{2}}\right.\right.$$

$$\left(2\alpha_k\sigma_k^2+2\sum_{\substack{j=1\\j\neq k}}^{N}\alpha_j\sigma_{kj}\right)]\}$$

$$+\left\{\left[\left(\sum_{i=1}^{N}\alpha_i^2\sigma_i^2+\sum_{i=1}^{N}\sum_{\substack{j=1\\j\neq i}}^{N}\alpha_i\alpha_j\sigma_{ij}\right)^{-\frac{1}{2}}\right]\left[R_K-R_f\right]\right\}=0$$

multiplying the derivative by $\left[\left(\sum_{i=1}^{N}\alpha_i^2\sigma_i^2+\sum_{i=1}^{N}\sum_{\substack{j=1\\j\neq i}}^{N}\alpha_i\alpha_j\sigma_{ij}\right)^{\frac{1}{2}}\right]$, we have:

$$\left\{\left[\sum_{i=1}^{N}\alpha_i\left(\overline{R}_i-R_f\right)\right]\left[\left(-\frac{1}{2}\right)\left(\sum_{i=1}^{N}\alpha_i^2\sigma_i^2+\sum_{i=1}^{N}\sum_{\substack{j=1\\j\neq i}}^{N}\alpha_i\alpha_j\sigma_{ij}\right)^{-\frac{3}{2}}\right.\right.$$

$$\left.\left.\left(2\alpha_k\sigma_k^2+2\sum_{\substack{j=1\\j\neq k}}^{N}\alpha_j\sigma_{kj}\right)\right]\left[\left(\sum_{i=1}^{N}\alpha_i^2\sigma_i^2+\sum_{i=1}^{N}\sum_{\substack{j=1\\j\neq i}}^{N}\alpha_i\alpha_j\sigma_{ij}\right)^{\frac{1}{2}}\right]\right\}$$

$$+\left\{\left[\left(\sum_{i=1}^{N}\alpha_i^2\sigma_i^2+\sum_{i=1}^{N}\sum_{\substack{j=1\\j\neq i}}^{N}\alpha_i\alpha_j\sigma_{ij}\right)^{-\frac{1}{2}}\right]\left[\left(\sum_{i=1}^{N}\alpha_i^2\sigma_i^2+\sum_{i=1}^{N}\sum_{\substack{j=1\\j\neq i}}^{N}\alpha_i\alpha_j\sigma_{ij}\right)^{\frac{1}{2}}\right]\left[\overline{R_K}-R_f\right]\right\}$$

$$=0$$

and then:

$$\left[\sum_{i=1}^{N} \alpha_i(\overline{R_i} - R_f)\right]$$
$$\times \left[\left(-\frac{1}{2}\right)\left(\sum_{i=1}^{N} \alpha_i^2\sigma_i^2 + \sum_{i=1}^{N} \sum_{\substack{j=1 \\ j\neq i}}^{N} \alpha_i\alpha_j\sigma_{ij}\right)^{-1}\left(2\alpha_k\sigma_k^2 + 2\sum_{\substack{j=1 \\ j\neq k}}^{N} \alpha_j\sigma_{kj}\right)\right]$$
$$+ \left[\overline{R_K} - R_f\right] = 0$$

and then:

$$\frac{\left[\sum_{i=1}^{N} \alpha_i(R_i - R_f)\right]\left[\left(-\frac{1}{2}\right)\left(2\alpha_k\sigma_k^2 + 2\sum_{\substack{j=1 \\ j\neq k}}^{N} \alpha_j\sigma_{kj}\right)\right]}{\left(\sum_{i=1}^{N} \alpha_i^2\sigma_i^2 + \sum_{i=1}^{N} \sum_{\substack{j=1 \\ j\neq i}}^{N} \alpha_i\alpha_j\sigma_{ij}\right)} + \left[\overline{R_K} - R_f\right] = 0$$

and then:

$$\frac{\left[\sum_{i=1}^{N} \alpha_i(\overline{R_i} - R_f)\right]\left[(-1)\left(\alpha_k\sigma_k^2 + \sum_{\substack{j=1 \\ j\neq k}}^{N} \alpha_j\sigma_{kj}\right)\right]}{\left(\sum_{i=1}^{N} \alpha_i^2\sigma_i^2 + \sum_{i=1}^{N} \sum_{\substack{j=1 \\ j\neq i}}^{N} \alpha_i\alpha_j\sigma_{ij}\right)} + \left[\overline{R_K} - R_f\right] = 0$$

and then:

$$-\left(\frac{\sum_{i=1}^{N} a_i\left(\overline{R_i}-R_f\right)}{\sum_{i=1}^{N} a_i^2\sigma_i^2+\sum_{i=1}^{N}\sum_{\substack{j=1\\ j\neq i}}^{N} a_i a_j\sigma_{ij}}\right)\left(a_k\sigma_k^2+\sum_{\substack{j=1\\ j\neq k}}^{N} a_j\sigma_{kj}\right)+\left(\overline{R_K}-R_f\right)=0$$

Defining λ as:

$$\lambda=\frac{\sum_{i=1}^{N} a_i\left(R_i-R_f\right)}{\sum_{i=1}^{N} a_i^2\sigma_i^2+\sum_{i=1}^{N}\sum_{\substack{j=1\\ j\neq i}}^{N} a_i a_j\sigma_{ij}}=\frac{R_P-R_F}{\sigma_P^2}$$

and substituting constant λ, we have:

$$-\lambda\left(a_k\sigma_k^2+\sum_{\substack{j=1\\ j\neq k}}^{N} a_j\sigma_{kj}\right)+\left(\overline{R_K}-R_f\right)=0$$

and then:

$$\left(\lambda a_k\sigma_k^2+\sum_{\substack{j=1\\ j\neq k}}^{N} \lambda a_j\sigma_{kj}\right)=\left(\overline{R_K}-R_f\right)$$

Considering this equation with regard to each asset, a system of simultaneous equations is achieved, as follows:

$$\left(\lambda a_1\sigma_{1k}+\lambda a_2\sigma_{2k}+\lambda a_3\sigma_{3k}+\ldots+\lambda a_k\sigma_k^2+\ldots+\lambda a_{N-1}\sigma_{N-1k}+\lambda a_N\sigma_{Nk}\right)$$
$$=\overline{R_K}-R_F$$

and then:

$$\lambda\left(a_1\sigma_{1k}+a_2\sigma_{2k}+a_3\sigma_{3k}+\ldots+a_k\sigma_k^2+\ldots+a_{N-1}\sigma_{N-1k}+a_N\sigma_{Nk}\right)=\overline{R_K}-R_F$$

Therefore, by deriving the function θ with regard to each asset in the portfolio and each equation is set equal to zero, we have a set of simultaneous equations.

This equation is valid for each asset, and there is one such equation for each asset in the market. Under assumption of the homogeneous expectations, all investors select the same optimum portfolio. Then in equilibrium this portfolio must held all assets in the same percentage that they have on the market. Because the weight of each asset in this portfolio is equal to its weight in the market, then the portfolio reproduces the market composition with regard to the assets and their weight.

Considering α'_i is the weight of i-asset in the market, the market expected return is equal to:

$$\overline{R_M} = \sum_{i=1}^{N} \alpha'_i \overline{R_i}$$

And considering that the covariance between the expected return of the market and the expected return of the k-th asset is equal to:

$$\sigma_{KM} = E\left[\left(R_K - \overline{R_K}\right)\left(R_M - \overline{R_M}\right)\right] = \left[\left(R_K - \overline{R_K}\right)\left(\sum_{i=1}^{N} \alpha'_i R_i - \sum_{i=1}^{N} \alpha'_i \overline{R_i}\right)\right]$$

$$= E\left[\left(R_K - \overline{R_K}\right)\left(\sum_{i=1}^{N} \alpha'_i \left(R_i - \overline{R_i}\right)\right)\right]$$

and solving:

$$\sigma_{KM} = E\left[\alpha'_1\left(R_K - \overline{R_K}\right)\left(R_1 - \overline{R_1}\right) + \alpha'_2\left(R_K - \overline{R_K}\right)\left(R_2 - \overline{R_2}\right) + \ldots\right.$$

$$\left. + \alpha'_k\left(R_K - \overline{R_K}\right)\left(R_k - \overline{R_k}\right) + \ldots + \alpha'_N\left(R_K - \overline{R_K}\right)\left(R_N - \overline{R_N}\right)\right]$$

$$= \alpha'_1 E\left[\left(R_K - \overline{R_K}\right)\left(R_1 - \overline{R_1}\right)\right] + \alpha'_2 E\left[\left(R_K - \overline{R_K}\right)\left(R_2 - \overline{R_2}\right)\right] + \ldots$$

$$+ \alpha'_k E\left[\left(R_K - \overline{R_K}\right)^2 + \ldots + \alpha'_N E\left[\left(R_K - \overline{R_K}\right)\left(R_N - \overline{R_N}\right)\right]\right]$$

and then:

$$\sigma_{KM} = \alpha'_1 \sigma_{1K} + \alpha'_2 \sigma_{2K} + \ldots + \alpha'_{N-1} \sigma_{N-1K} + \alpha'_N \sigma_{NK}$$

The left-side member of the equation is equal to:

$$\lambda\left(\alpha_1 \sigma_{1K} + \alpha_2 \sigma_{2K} + \alpha_3 \sigma_{3K} + \ldots + \alpha_K \sigma_K^2 + \ldots + \alpha_{N-1} \sigma_{N-1K} + \alpha_N \sigma_{NK}\right) = \lambda \sigma_{KM}$$

And then the equation can be rewritten as follows:

$$\lambda\sigma_{KM} = \overline{R_K} - R_F$$

This equation must be true for each k-th asset. It implies that the equation must be true for each portfolio and therefore also for the market portfolio. In fact, since this equation holds for each asset, it must also hold for the market because expected return on the market portfolio is a weighted average of the expected return on individual assets. Therefore, we have:

Particularly for the market portfolio the relationship is the following:

$$\sigma_{MM} = \sigma_M^2 \quad \rightarrow \quad \lambda\sigma_M^2 = \overline{R_M} - R_F$$

and therefore:

$$\lambda = \frac{\overline{R_M} - R_F}{\sigma_M^2}$$

By substituting λ, we have:

$$\frac{\overline{R_M} - R_F}{\sigma_M^2}\sigma_{KM} = \overline{R_k} - R_F$$

and solving by R_k:

$$\overline{R_k} = R_F + \frac{\overline{R_M} - R_F}{\sigma_M^2}\sigma_{KM}$$

or in equal form:

$$\overline{R_k} = R_F + \left(\overline{R_M} - R_F\right)\frac{\sigma_{KM}}{\sigma_M^2}$$

Considering that:

$$\beta_k = \frac{\sigma_{KM}}{\sigma_M^2}$$

we have:

$$\overline{R_k} = R_F + \beta_k\left(\overline{R_M} - R_F\right)$$

That is the equation of the Security Market Line (SML).

13.4 CAPM in Terms of Prices

The CAPM is an equilibrium model of the capital market in terms of expected returns and prices (Elton et al., 2013).

Because the price of any asset is the function of its expected return over time, we can define the CAPM in terms of prices.

Denote with P_i the current price of i-the asset and with $\overline{Y_i}$ the expected price of the i-th asset in the future (next year) and then it is the market value including the future dividends that will pay. The expected return of the i-th asset $(\overline{R_i})$ is equal to:

$$\overline{R_i} = \frac{\overline{Y_i} - P_i}{P_i} = \frac{\overline{Y_i}}{P_i} - 1$$

Denote with P_M the current price of the market portfolio (all assets included) and with $\overline{Y_M}$ the expected price of the market portfolio in the future (next year) and then it is the market value including the future dividends that will pay. The expected return of the market $(\overline{R_M})$ is equal to:

$$\overline{R_M} = \frac{\overline{Y_M} - P_M}{P_M} = \frac{\overline{Y_M}}{P_M} - 1$$

Based on the SML, the expected return of the i-th asset $(\overline{R_i})$ is equal to:

$$\overline{R_i} = R_F + \left(\frac{\sigma_{iM}}{\sigma_M^2}\right)\left(\overline{R_M} - R_F\right)$$

Substituting $\overline{R_i}$ and $\overline{R_M}$ with their equations, and by defining the covariance and variance with regard to their expected returns, it gets:

$$\frac{\overline{Y_i}}{P_i} - 1 = R_F + \left(\frac{\sigma_{(R_iR_M)}}{\sigma^2_{(R_M)}}\right)\left(\frac{\overline{Y_M}}{P_M} - 1 - R_F\right)$$

The covariance between the expected returns of the i-th asset and the expected returns of the market portfolio $(\sigma_{(R_iR_M)})$ is equal to:

$$\begin{aligned}
\sigma_{(R_iR_M)} &= E\left[\left(R_i - \overline{R_i}\right)\left(R_M - \overline{R_M}\right)\right] \\
&= E\left[\left(\frac{Y_i - P_i}{P_i} - \frac{\overline{Y_i} - P_i}{P_i}\right)\left(\frac{Y_M - P_M}{P_M} - \frac{\overline{Y_M} - P_M}{P_M}\right)\right] \\
&= E\left[\left(\frac{Y_i}{P_i} - 1 - \left(\frac{\overline{Y_i}}{P_i} - 1\right)\right)\left(\frac{Y_M}{P_M} - 1 - \left(\frac{\overline{Y_M}}{P_M} - 1\right)\right)\right] \\
&= E\left[\left(\frac{Y_i}{P_i} - \frac{\overline{Y_i}}{P_i}\right)\left(\frac{Y_M}{P_M} - \frac{\overline{Y_M}}{P_M}\right)\right] = E\left[\left(\frac{Y_i - \overline{Y_i}}{P_i}\right)\left(\frac{Y_M - \overline{Y_M}}{P_M}\right)\right] \\
&= E\left[\frac{1}{P_i}\left(Y_i - \overline{Y_i}\right)\frac{1}{P_M}\left(Y_M - \overline{Y_M}\right)\right] = \frac{1}{P_i}\frac{1}{P_M}E\left[\left(Y_i - \overline{Y_i}\right)\left(Y_M - \overline{Y_M}\right)\right] \\
&= \frac{1}{P_i}\frac{1}{P_M}\sigma_{(Y_iY_M)}
\end{aligned}$$

and then:

$$\sigma_{(R_i R_M)} = \frac{1}{P_i}\frac{1}{P_M}\sigma_{(Y_i Y_M)} \tag{13.5}$$

where $\sigma_{(Y_i Y_M)}$ is the covariance between the future expected price of the i-th asset and the market portfolio.

Similarly, the variance of the market portfolio expected returns $\left(\sigma^2_{(R_M)}\right)$ is equal to:

$$\sigma^2_{(R_M)} = E\left[\left(R_M - \overline{R_M}\right)^2\right] = E\left[\left(\frac{Y_M - P_M}{P_M} - \frac{\overline{Y_M} - P_M}{P_M}\right)^2\right]$$

$$= E\left[\left(\frac{Y_M}{P_M} - 1 - \left(\frac{\overline{Y_M}}{P_M} - 1\right)\right)^2\right] = E\left[\left(\frac{Y_M}{P_M} - \frac{\overline{Y_M}}{P_M}\right)^2\right]$$

$$= E\left[\left(\frac{1}{P_M}\right)^2\left(Y_M - \overline{Y_M}\right)^2\right] = E\left[\frac{1}{P_M^2}\left(Y_M - \overline{Y_M}\right)^2\right] = \frac{1}{P_M^2}\sigma^2_{(Y_M)}$$

and then:

$$\sigma^2_{(R_M)} = \frac{1}{P_M^2}\sigma^2_{(Y_M)} \tag{13.6}$$

where $\sigma^2_{Y_M}$ is the variance of the future price of the market portfolio.

Substituting the covariance and variance in the equation, we have:

$$\frac{\overline{Y_i}}{P_i} - 1 = R_F + \left(\frac{\overline{Y_M}}{P_M} - 1 - R_F\right)\frac{\frac{1}{P_i}\frac{1}{P_M}\sigma_{(Y_i Y_M)}}{\frac{1}{P_M^2}\sigma^2_{(Y_M)}}$$

Adding 1 to both terms, we have:

$$\frac{\overline{Y_i}}{P_i} - 1 + 1 = R_F + \left(\frac{\overline{Y_M}}{P_M} - 1 - R_F\right)\frac{\frac{1}{P_i}\frac{1}{P_M}\sigma_{(Y_i Y_M)}}{\frac{1}{P_M^2}\sigma^2_{(Y_M)}} + 1$$

Denote $r_F = 1 + R_F$ and substituting, we have:

$$\frac{\overline{Y_i}}{P_i} = r_F + \left(\frac{\overline{Y_M}}{P_M} - r_F\right)\frac{\frac{1}{P_i}\frac{1}{P_M}\sigma_{(Y_i Y_M)}}{\frac{1}{P_M^2}\sigma^2_{(Y_M)}}$$

Multiplying both term for P_i, we have:

$$P_i\frac{\overline{Y_i}}{P_i} = \left[r_F + \left(\frac{\overline{Y_M}}{P_M} - r_F\right)\frac{\frac{1}{P_i}\frac{1}{P_M}\sigma_{(Y_i;\, Y_M)}}{\frac{1}{P_M^2}\sigma^2_{(Y_M)}}\right]P_i$$

and then:

$$\overline{Y_i} = r_F P_i + \left(\frac{\overline{Y_M} - r_F P_M}{P_M}\right) \frac{\frac{1}{P_i}\frac{1}{P_M}\sigma_{(Y_i Y_M)} P_i}{\frac{1}{P_M^2}\sigma^2_{(Y_M)}} = r_F P_i + \left(\frac{\overline{Y_M} - r_F P_M}{P_M}\right) \frac{\frac{1}{P_M}\sigma_{(Y_i Y_M)}}{\frac{1}{P_M^2}\sigma^2_{(Y_M)}}$$

$$= r_F P_i + \left(\frac{\overline{Y_M} - r_F P_M}{P_M}\right) \frac{\sigma_{(Y_i Y_M)}}{\frac{1}{P_M}\sigma^2_{(Y_M)}} = r_F P_i + \left(\frac{\overline{Y_M} - r_F P_M}{P_M}\right) P_M \frac{\sigma_{(Y_i Y_M)}}{\sigma^2_{(Y_M)}} = r_F P_i$$

$$+ \left(\overline{Y_M} - r_F P_M\right) \frac{\sigma_{(Y_i Y_M)}}{\sigma^2_{(Y_M)}}$$

Solving for P_i, we have:

$$P_i = \frac{1}{r_F}\left[\overline{Y_i} - \left(\overline{Y_M} - r_F P_M\right)\frac{\sigma_{(Y_i Y_M)}}{\sigma^2_{(Y_M)}}\right] \tag{13.7}$$

The equation shows how the current price of the i-th asset (P_i) is the function of its expected price $\left(\overline{Y_i}\right)$ less an amount for risk $\left(\left(\overline{Y_M} - r_F P_M\right)\frac{\sigma_{(Y_i Y_M)}}{\sigma^2_{(Y_M)}}\right)$. This difference is discounted to r_F in order to obtain the present value of the net result. Note that the difference $\left[\overline{Y_i} - \left(\overline{Y_M} - r_F P_M\right)\frac{\sigma_{(Y_i Y_M)}}{\sigma^2_{(Y_M)}}\right]$ can be considered as the certainty equivalent of the future cash payment. Because it is a certain value, we can discount it at the risk-free rate (r_F) to determine its present value.

Note that we can write the equation in a different form as follows:

$$P_i = \frac{1}{r_F}\left[\overline{Y_i} - \left(\frac{\overline{Y_M} - r_F P_M}{\sigma_{(Y_M)}}\right)\frac{\sigma_{(Y_i; Y_M)}}{\sigma_{(Y_M)}}\right] \tag{13.8}$$

In this case, the expected price $\left(\overline{Y_i}\right)$ is reduced by the market price of risk $\left(\frac{\overline{Y_M} - r_F P_M}{\sigma_{(Y_M)}}\right)$ multiplied by the amount of risk $\left(\frac{\sigma_{(Y_i Y_M)}}{\sigma_{(Y_M)}}\right)$. Obviously also in this case this difference can be considered the certainty equivalent and then it can be discounted at the risk-free rate (r_F) to determine its present value.

Capital Asset Pricing Model: Non-standard Form

14

14.1 Zero-Beta CAPM

The CAPM may be descriptive of the equilibrium returns on a macro level, but it is not to micro level with regard to the individual investor behaviour. Indeed, most investors hold portfolio of risky assets that is different from the market portfolio.

The introduction in the model of more realistic assumptions could help to understand better the investor behaviour.

In the economic and financial literature have been examined the effects of modifying most assumptions of the CAPM model. In this chapter, we consider briefly on any of them.

It is important to keep in mind that in each of the following cases analysed, we change only the assumptions considered while all other standard assumptions remain equal. The aim is to analyse the effect due to the change of the only assumption considered on the CAPM.

One of the most relevant assumption of the standard form of the CAPM is that investors can lend and borrow unlimited amount of money at the free-risk rate of interest.

This assumption is very unrealistic. Even if it is to assume that investors can lend unlimited amount of money at the free-risk rate, it is not realistic to assume that investors can borrow at the same riskless rate. Indeed, we can consider the lending assumption equivalent to the case in which investors buy government bond that is equal in maturity to their single investment period horizon. The rate of return offered by this bond is a theoretical proxy of the free-risk rate and it is the same for all investors.

Assume that investors cannot lend and borrow at the risk-free rate and maintain equal all other assumptions of the CAPM standard form.

Under the assumption of no riskless lending and borrowing, the derived non-standard form of the CAPM is considered the second most widely used general equilibrium model and it is called *zero-beta version of the CAPM* or simply *zero-beta CAPM*.

P. De Luca, *Corporate Finance*, Springer Texts in Business and Economics,
https://doi.org/10.1007/978-3-031-18300-3_14

Similar to the standard form of the CAPM also in this case, we can analyse the problem by following two main approaches: intuitive approach and rigorous approach (Elton et al., 2013). In both cases, the reasoning is similar as analysed to derive the standard form of CAPM.

14.1.1 Intuitive Approach

Based on the previous chapters, we know that:

(a) The systemic risk of the asset is the only measure of its risk. Thanks to diversification process, the unsystemic risk (or specific risk) of the asset is essentially null.
(b) The rate of return of the asset is the function of its systemic risk only. Indeed, unsystemic risk does not require rate of return.
(c) Two assets with the same systemic risk must offered the same rate of return.

We can formalize these three main points, in the space beta-expected return $(\beta; \overline{R})$ as in Fig. 14.1.

All assets must be positioned along the straight-line. If it is not, the asset positioned above (point *C*) or below (point *E*) the straight-line will be characterized by the same systemic risk (β) of the asset that lie on the straight-line (point *D*) but they offer higher expected return in the first case (*C* has higher expected return than *D*) or lower in the second case (*E* has a lower expected return than *D*). Therefore, in both cases of *E* and *D* there will be price adjustments until they offer the same return. In fact, investor could purchase *C* and sell *D* short or purchase *D* and sell *E* short by having in both cases higher expected return with the same level of systemic risk.

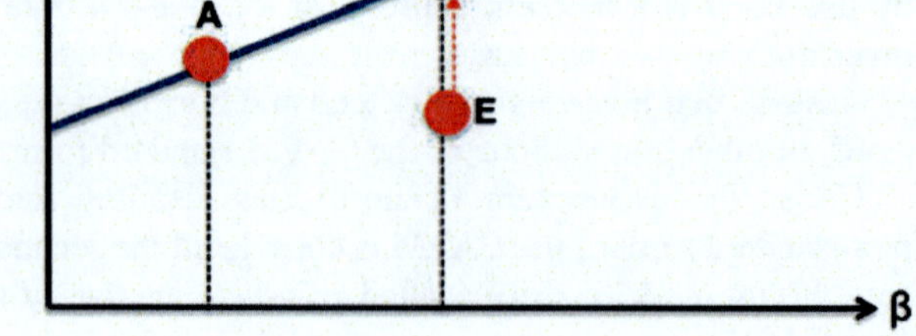

Fig. 14.1 Portfolios in beta-expected return space

Therefore, these opportunities do not exist in equilibrium because all portfolios and assets must lie along a straight-line.

Three are the main consequences of this reasoning:

(a) First, because all investors hold the market portfolio in equilibrium, and in equilibrium no investor sells any asset short, then the elimination of the assumptions of unlimited short sales in the standard form of CAPM with the introduction of the prohibition of short selling does not have impact on the model because it cannot change the equilibrium. Therefore, the CAPM standard form can be derived independently of whether short sales are allowed or not allowed.

(b) Second, if assets or portfolios lie on the straight-line in the beta-expected return space, then all combinations of them (assets or portfolios) would lie on the same straight-line. In Fig. 14.1, if we consider *A* and *D* two risky portfolios, all positive combinations among them lie on the same straight-line in the segment *A–D*.

(c) Third, one portfolio that lies along the straight-line must be the market portfolio. Indeed, if it is not there would exist two assets with the same systemic risk and different return. It is not possible because in equilibrium two assets with the same systemic risk must offer the same return.

The straight-line can be defined on the basis of two points. Then it is enough to find two points. The first point can be the market portfolio where the beta is equal to 1. The second point can be the portfolio where the straight-line cuts the vertical axis and then where the beta is equal to zero.

The equation of the straight-line in the beta-expected return space is equal to:

$$\overline{R} = a + b(\beta)$$

Denote with $\overline{R_Z}$ the expected return of the portfolio where the straight-line cuts the vertical axis and then with beta equal to zero. The expected return is equal to:

$$\overline{R_Z} = a + b(0) \quad \rightarrow \quad \overline{R_Z} = a$$

Denote with $\overline{R_M}$ the expected return of market portfolio whose beta is equal to 1. The expected return is equal to:

$$\overline{R_M} = a + b(1)$$

By considering that $\overline{R_Z} = a$, and substituting we have:

$$\overline{R_M} = \overline{R_Z} + b(1) \quad \rightarrow \quad \overline{R_M} - \overline{R_Z} = b$$

Considering them together and denote with $\overline{R_K}$ and β_K the expected return and beta (systemic risk) of the *k*-th asset or portfolio. The equation of the expected return on any *k*-th asset or portfolio is equal to:

Fig. 14.2 Security market line in the Zero-Beta CAPM

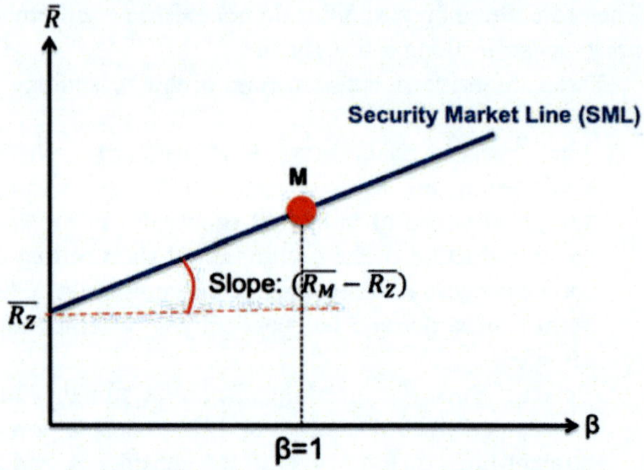

$$\overline{R_K} = \overline{R_Z} + \beta_K\left(\overline{R_M} - \overline{R_Z}\right) \tag{14.1}$$

This equation defines the general equilibrium, and then the Security Market Line (SML) in the Zero-Beta CAPM. It can be represented as in Fig. 14.2.

14.1.2 Rigorous Approach

Consider the space standard deviation-expected return $\left(\sigma; \overline{R}\right)$. Before the introduction of the riskless rate of interest the market portfolio lies on the efficient frontier. Introducing the riskless rate of interest, the entire efficient frontier can be traced finding the tangent point between the efficient frontier and the straight-line passing through the riskless rate on the vertical axis. It implies that corresponding to the riskless rate there is only one point on the efficient frontier and vice versa. Indeed, in the market there is one unique riskless rate.

Note that varying the risk-free rate we have a different tangent point on the efficient frontier. It implies that, in all cases but one, what we call the riskless rate is an artificial construct we use to obtain one point on the efficient frontier.

Define R_F' the risk-free rate if we assume that investors can lend and borrow unlimited amount of money at the same riskless rate. At this risk-free rate R_F' they hold the market portfolio (CAPM standard form). In this case, the investors face the investment opportunity set as shown in Fig. 14.3.

Similar to the derivation of the CAPM standard, the investor faces a set of simultaneous equations; one of these is equal to:

$$\lambda\left(\alpha_1\sigma_{1k} + \alpha_2\sigma_{2k} + \alpha_3\sigma_{3k} + \ldots + \alpha_k\sigma_k^2 + \ldots + \alpha_{N-1}\sigma_{N-1k} + \alpha_N\sigma_{Nk}\right) = \overline{R_K} - R_F'$$

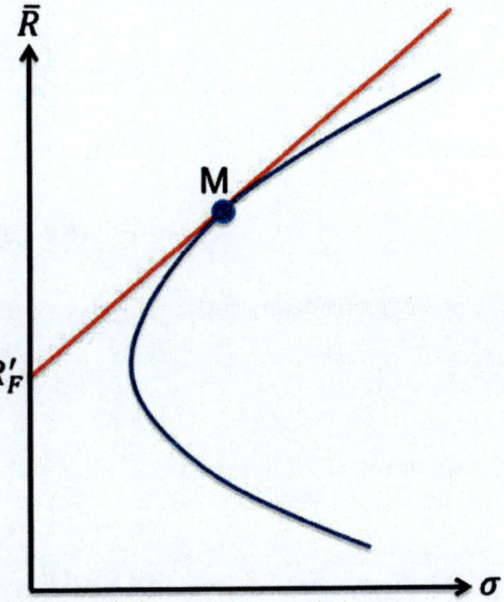

Fig. 14.3 Investors set of opportunities if they can lend and borrow unlimited amount at the riskless rate R'_F

Since the left-hand side of equation is the covariance between the return on k-th asset and the return on the market portfolio (see derivation of the CAPM standard), we have:

$$\lambda \text{cov}\left(\overline{R_K R_M}\right) = \overline{R_K} - R'_F$$

and then:

$$\overline{R_K} = R'_F + \lambda \text{cov}\left(\overline{R_K R_M}\right)$$

Since this equation holds for each asset, it must also hold for the market because expected return on the market portfolio is a weighted average of the expected return on individual assets. Therefore, we have:

$$\overline{R_M} = R'_F + \lambda \text{cov}\left(\overline{R_M R_M}\right)$$

Because the covariance between $\overline{R_M}$ with itself is equal to the variance $\text{cov}\left(\overline{R_M R_M}\right) = \text{var}\left(\overline{R_M}\right)$, substituting we have:

$$\overline{R_M} = R'_F + \lambda \sigma_M^2$$

so that:

$$\lambda = \frac{\overline{R_M} - R'_F}{\sigma_M^2}$$

Substituting the value of λ in the equation, we have:

$$\overline{R_K} = R'_F + \frac{\overline{R_M} - R'_F}{\sigma_M^2} \text{cov}\left(R_K R_M\right)$$

and then:

$$\overline{R_K} = R'_F + \left(\overline{R_M} - R'_F\right) \frac{\text{cov}\left(R_K R_M\right)}{\sigma_M^2}$$

and by considering that:

$$\beta_K = \frac{\text{cov}\left(R_K R_M\right)}{\sigma_M^2}$$

we have:

$$\overline{R_K} = R'_F + \beta_K\left(\overline{R_M} - R'_F\right) \tag{14.2}$$

It is fundamental to note that a riskless asset with a return equal to R'_F does not exist. Indeed, R'_F is a theoretical construction only. There is not asset able to eliminate completely the systemic risk ($\beta = 0$). In fact, the minimum variance portfolio on the efficient frontier can tend to vertical axis but it can never touch it. There are, however, assets and portfolios that give a return of R'_F and they lie along the solid segment $R'_F - C$ and then between Z (that is the less risky asset or portfolio on efficient frontier) and C as in Fig. 14.4.

Any asset or portfolio that has an expected return equal to R'_F must have a beta equal to zero. In fact, if we assume that a k-th asset or portfolio has expected return equal to $\overline{R_K} = R'_F$, it implies that the covariance $\text{cov}\left(\overline{R_K R_M}\right) = \text{cov}\left(R'_F \overline{R_M}\right) = 0$ and then the $\beta = 0$. Therefore, portfolios along the line $Z - C$ are zero-beta portfolios.

We can express the equilibrium by considering the least risky zero-beta portfolio. The portfolio Z is the minimum-variance zero-beta portfolio and it has the least total risk and its expected return is equal to $\overline{R_Z}$. Because $R'_F = \overline{R_Z}$, the Security Market Line (SML) is defined by the following equation:

$$\overline{R_K} = \overline{R_Z} + \beta_K\left(\overline{R_M} - \overline{R_Z}\right) \tag{14.3}$$

The analysis of the minimum-variance zero-beta portfolio (Z) states two main evidences:

First, the expected return on the minimum-variance zero-beta portfolio $\left(\overline{R_Z}\right)$ must be lower than the expected return on the market portfolio $\left(\overline{R_M}\right)$ so that: $\overline{R_M} > \overline{R_Z}$. The proof is simple and can be verified geometrically on Fig. 14.4. Because the market portfolio (M) is positioned on the efficient segment of the frontier above the minimum variance, the slope of the tangent line to M passing for the vertical axis must be positive. It implies that the expected return decreases by moving from the market portfolio (M) towards the vertical axis. Because $\overline{R_Z}$ is the

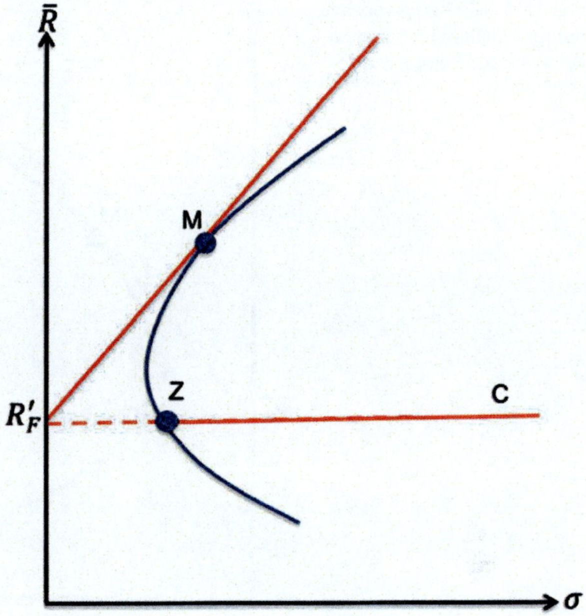

Fig. 14.4 Assets and portfolios with return equal to R'_F

intercept of this tangent line and the vertical axis, it must have a return less than $\overline{R_M}$.

Second, the minimum-variance zero-beta portfolio is not efficient. Denote with *S* the portfolio with minimum variance possible. This portfolio lies on the efficient frontier and then it can be obtained by combining the market portfolio (*M*) and the minimum-variance zero-beta portfolio (*Z*). The variance of portfolio *S* is equal to the sum of the variance of portfolios *M* and *Z* (weighted by the respective investment weights α and $(1 - \alpha)$) only because the covariance between *M* and *Z* is null (*Z* is zero-beta), as follows:

$$\sigma_S^2 = \alpha_Z^2 \sigma_Z^2 + (1 - \alpha_Z)^2 \sigma_M^2 \tag{14.4}$$

The computation of the weights of portfolio *Z* (that is α_Z) and *M* (that is $(1 - \alpha_Z)$) able to minimize the variance of the portfolio *S*, we can derive the variance of the portfolio *S* $\left(\sigma_S^2\right)$ with respect to α_Z and set is equal to zero, as follows:

$$\frac{\partial \sigma_S^2}{\partial \alpha_Z} = 2\alpha_Z \sigma_Z^2 - 2\sigma_M^2 + 2\alpha_Z \sigma_M^2$$

Setting the derivative equal to zero, and solve for α_Z we have:

$$2\alpha_Z \sigma_Z^2 - 2\sigma_M^2 + 2\alpha_Z \sigma_M^2 = 0$$

Fig. 14.5 Minimum variance portfolio, minimum-variance zero-beta portfolio, market portfolio

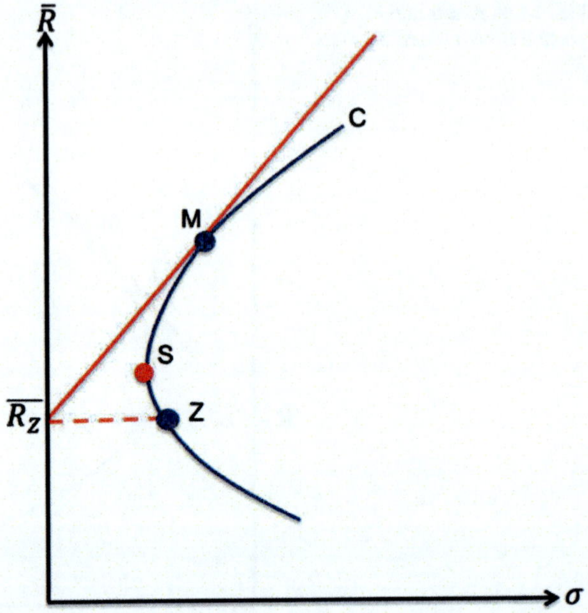

$$2\alpha_Z\left(\sigma_Z^2+\sigma_M^2\right)=2\sigma_M^2$$

$$\alpha_Z=\frac{\sigma_M^2}{\sigma_Z^2+\sigma_M^2} \tag{14.5}$$

Since σ_Z^2 and σ_M^2 are positive numbers, then the minimum variance portfolio (S) must be built by combining with positive weights the market portfolio (M) and the minimum-variance zero-beta portfolio (Z). Since $\overline{R_M}>\overline{R_Z}$, portfolio S obtained by combining portfolios M and Z with positive weights must have a higher expected return than portfolio Z so that: $\overline{R_S}>\overline{R_Z}$. Therefore, the portfolio S has been characterized by higher expected return and smaller variance (it is the minimum variance portfolio by definition) than the portfolio Z. The main consequence is that the minimum-variance zero-beta portfolio (Z) cannot be positioned on the efficient portion of the efficient frontier (from the minimum variance to above). We can summarize these positions as in Fig. 14.5.

In Fig. 14.5, the efficient frontier is the part of the frontier SMC. All efficient portfolios are positioned along the SMC and all investors hold these portfolios (portfolios along the line $\overline{R_Z}M$ do not exist). Therefore, no investors choose to hold the portfolio Z only, because it is not efficient portfolio.

If investors want to hold portfolios offering an expected return:

(a) Between $\overline{R_S}$ and $\overline{R_M}$, they combine of the minimum-variance zero-beta portfolio (*Z*) and the market portfolio (*M*). Consequently, we use the two mutual fund theorem: investors can satisfy their expectation by transactions the market portfolio and the minimum-variance zero-beta portfolio.
(b) Higher than $\overline{R_M}$, by choosing a portfolio to the right of the market portfolio (*M*), they hold a portfolio constructed by selling portfolio *Z* short and buying the market portfolio *M*.

Note that if we consider all investors in an aggregate dimension, to say that they hold market portfolio, it implies that the sum of long and short positions on portfolio *Z* must be equal to zero.

14.1.3 Riskless Lending and No Riskless Borrowing

It is reasonable to assume that investors can lend to the riskless rate but they cannot borrow at the riskless rate. In fact, investors can invest in government bonds that have maturity equal to their time horizon and whose risk is so lower to be considered null by obtaining a return equal to the riskless rate.

In this contest, assume that investors can lend at the risk-free rate but they cannot borrow at the riskless rate and we maintain equal all other assumptions of the CAPM standard form.

Under this assumption, investors can lend at the risk-free rate, and the set of opportunities that they face can be represented as in Fig. 14.6.

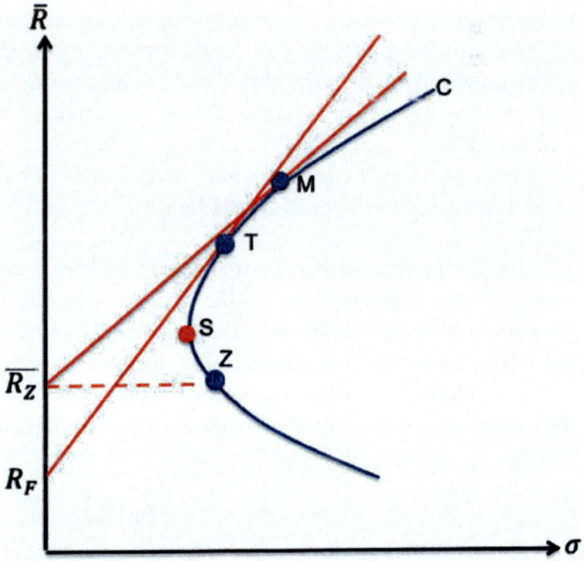

Fig. 14.6 Investors opportunity set with riskless lending but not borrowing

In this case, all combinations of risky portfolio and riskless asset must lie on the straight-line passing through the risk-free rate asset (R_F) and tangent to the efficient frontier at T: the line R_FT.

Therefore, under the assumption of no lending and borrowing at the riskless rate, investors hold portfolios along the efficient frontier SMC. By introducing the possibility for investors to lend at the riskless rate, investors can hold portfolio constructed by combining the riskless asset and risky portfolio (T) along the line R_FT.

Note that portfolio T is always below and to the left to the market portfolio M and it implies that $\overline{R_Z} > R_F$.

The portfolio T is below and to the left of the market portfolio M because any investor can choose to hold a portfolio of investments to the right of T on the efficient frontier STC. By considering that market portfolio (M) is an average of the portfolios held by all investors, it must be a combination of specific investor's portfolio on the efficient frontier STC to the right of the portfolio T and the portfolio T. Therefore, market portfolio M must lie to the right of T.

Now consider that $\overline{R_Z}$ is the intersection of the vertical axis and the line tangent at M as well as R_F is the intersection of the vertical axis and the line tangent at T. Because M lies above T the slope of the efficient frontier at M is less than at T, and then the line tangent at M must intersect the vertical axis above the line tangent at T. The consequence is that $\overline{R_Z}$ must be greater than R_F and then $\overline{R_Z} > R_F$.

Therefore, under the assumption that investors can lend at the riskless rate but they cannot borrow at riskless rate, the efficient frontier is given by the straight-line R_FT and the curve TMC. Not all combinations of efficient portoflios are efficient. Combinations of portfolio from the line R_FT and the portfolio from the curve TMC are dominated by a portfolio lying along the curve TMC. Indeed, note that:

a) Portfolio T can be constructed by combining portfolio Z and M.
b) Portfolios along the line R_FT are constructed by combining the portfolio T (that is the combination of portfolios Z and M) and the riskless asset (R_F).
c) Portfolios along the segment TM are constructed by combining the portfolios Z and M.
d) Portfolios along the segment MC are constructed by selling the portfolio Z short and investing in the portfolio M long.

Therefore, investors can always satisfy their expectation by holding, in long or short position, combinations of the: market portfolio (M), the minimum-variance zero-beta portfolio (Z), and the riskless asset (R_F). Note we pass from the two mutual fund theorem to the three mutual fund theorem.

By considering that the market portfolio (M) is still the efficient portfolio, and then there are not modification to the analysis developed previously. Then for each k-th asset contained in the market portfolio, the expected return $\left(\overline{R_K}\right)$ is equal to:

$$\overline{R_K} = \overline{R_Z} + \beta_K\left(\overline{R_M} - \overline{R_Z}\right)$$

14.2 Tax CAPM

Taxes are not considered in the standard form of the CAPM. It implies that investors are indifferent to receive capital gains or dividends and all investors hold the same portfolio of risky assets.

Assume the introduction of taxes on dividends and capital gains and maintain equal all other assumptions of the CAPM standard form.

Investors must consider the expected return-risk profile of their portfolios after taxes. It has a relevant consequence. Even if homogeneous expectation about before-tax expected return, the efficient frontier after-tax for each investor will be different. Consequently, the portfolio selected by each investor could be different because taxes can produces heterogeneous after-tax expectations, the introduction of taxes produces heterogeneous after-tax expectations. Therefore, while the before-tax expectations about returns are homogeneous, the after-tax expectations are heterogeneous.

We can derive the general equilibrium pricing equation for all assets and portfolios by considering taxes on dividends and capital gain (Elton et al., 2013).

Consider any investor's portfolio P different from market portfolio M. For any k-th asset in the portfolio P the equilibrium expected return $\overline{R_K}$ is equal to:

$$\overline{R_K} = \overline{R_{0P}} + \frac{\sigma_{KP}}{\sigma_P^2}\left(\overline{R_P} - \overline{R_{0P}}\right) \tag{14.6}$$

where $\overline{R_{0P}}$ is the expected return on the minimum variance portfolio that is uncorrelated with portfolio P. Note that by assuming riskless lending and borrowing unlimited (we change only the assumption with regard to the taxes in the standard form of the CAPM being all other assumptions equal), there is the riskless rate R_F, and then we can substitute $\overline{R_{0P}}$ with R_F.

By considering taxes, investors try to find equilibrium in terms of after-tax returns. We have:

$$\overline{R_{Ki}^A} = R_{Fi}^A + \frac{\operatorname{cov}\left(\overline{R_{Ki}^A}, \overline{R_{Pi}^A}\right)}{\operatorname{var}\left(\overline{R_{Pi}^A}\right)}\left(\overline{R_{Pi}^A} - R_{Fi}^A\right) \tag{14.7}$$

where the superscript A on each variable evidence that it is after-tax term and the subscript i refers to i-th investor.

Denote with:

- δ_K: the dividend yield (dividends divided by price) of on k-th stock
- t_{di}: the i-th stockholder's marginal tax rate on interest and dividends
- t_{gi}: the i-th stockholder's marginal tax rate on capital gains
- α_K: the amount of i-th stockholder wealth invested in risky assets
- α: the sum of all wealth invested in risky assets so that: $\alpha = \sum_{K=1}^{n} \alpha_K$.

We have:

$$\overline{R_{Ki}^{A}} = \left(\overline{R_K} - \delta_K\right)\left(1 - t_{gi}\right) + \delta_k(1 - t_{di}) = \overline{R_K}\left(1 - t_{gi}\right) - \delta_K\left(t_{di} - t_{gi}\right)$$

$$R_{Fi}^{A} = R_F(1 - t_{di})$$

Assume that the expected dividends are predictable enough to be approximated as certain. Under this assumption, we have:

$$\operatorname{cov}\left(\overline{R_{Ki}^{A}}\,\overline{R_{Pi}^{A}}\right) = \operatorname{cov}(R_K R_P i)\left(1 - t_{gi}\right)^2$$

$$\operatorname{var}\left(\overline{R_{Pi}^{A}}\right) = \sigma_{Pi}^2\left(1 - t_{gi}\right)^2$$

Therefore, substituting we have:

$$\overline{R_K}\left(1 - t_{gi}\right) - \delta_K\left(t_{di} - t_{gi}\right) = R_F(1 - t_{di}) + \frac{\operatorname{cov}(R_K R_{Pi})\left(1 - t_{gi}\right)^2}{\sigma_{Pi}^2\left(1 - t_{gi}\right)^2}\left(\overline{R_{Pi}^{A}} - R_{Fi}^{A}\right)$$

and then:

$$\left(\overline{R_K} - R_F\right)\left(1 - t_{gi}\right) - \left(\delta_K - R_F\right)\left(t_{di} - t_{gi}\right) = \frac{\overline{R_{Pi}^{A}} - R_{Fi}^{A}}{\sigma_{Pi}^2}\operatorname{cov}(R_K R_{Pi})$$

Define λ_K as follows:

$$\lambda_K = \frac{\overline{R_{Pi}^{A}} - R_{Fi}^{A}}{\sigma_{Pi}^2} \cdot \frac{1}{\left(1 - t_{gi}\right)}$$

Dividing through by (1 − t_{gi}) and multiplying through by α_K, and dividing through by λ_K, we have:

$$\frac{\alpha_K}{\lambda_K}\left(\overline{R_K} - R_F\right) - \left(\delta_K - R_F\right)\frac{\left(t_{di} - t_{gi}\right)}{\left(1 - t_{gi}\right)}\frac{\alpha_K}{\lambda_K} = \alpha_K \operatorname{cov}(R_K R_{Pi})$$

We can sum this equation for all investors and dividing by $\alpha = \sum_{K=1}^{n} \alpha_K$ we have:

$$\left(\overline{R_K} - R_F\right)\frac{\sum_{K=1}^{n}\frac{\alpha_K}{\lambda_K}}{\sum_{K=1}^{n}\alpha_K} - \left(\delta_K - R_F\right)\left[\frac{\sum_{K=1}^{n}\frac{\left(t_{di} - t_{gi}\right)\alpha_K}{\left(1 - t_{gi}\right)\lambda_K}}{\sum_{K=1}^{n}\alpha_K}\right] = \frac{\left(\sum_{K=1}^{n}\alpha_K\right)\operatorname{cov}(R_K R_{Pi})}{\sum_{K=1}^{n}\alpha_K}$$

Because:

$$R_M = \frac{\sum_{K=1}^{n} \alpha_K R_{\text{Pi}}}{\sum_{K=1}^{n} \alpha_K}$$

then:

$$\frac{\left(\sum_{K=1}^{n} \alpha_K\right) \text{cov}(R_K R_{\text{Pi}})}{\sum_{K=1}^{n} \alpha_K} = \text{cov}(R_K R_M)$$

Denote with:

$$H = \frac{\sum_{K=1}^{n} \alpha_K}{\sum_{K=1}^{n} \frac{\alpha_K}{\lambda_K}}$$

$$\tau = H \left[\frac{\sum_{K=1}^{n} \frac{(t_{\text{di}} - t_{\text{gi}})\alpha_K}{(1 - t_{\text{gi}})\lambda_K}}{\sum_{K=1}^{n} \alpha_K} \right]$$

Therefore, the tax factor τ is a complex function of the investor's tax rates and wealth. It should be a positive number.

Substituting, we have:

$$(\overline{R_K} - R_F) - (\delta_K - R_F)\tau = H\text{cov}(R_K R_M)$$

and then:

$$\overline{R_K} = R_F + (\delta_K - R_F)\tau + H\text{cov}(R_K R_M)$$

Because this equation must hold for any asset or portfolio, it must hold for the market portfolio. Therefore, we have:

$$(\overline{R_M} - R_F) - (\delta_M - R_F)\tau = H\text{cov}(R_M R_M)$$

$$(\overline{R_M} - R_F) - (\delta_M - R_F)\tau = H\sigma_M^2$$

where δ_M is the dividend yield of the market portfolio (M).

Solving for H, we have:

$$H = \frac{(\overline{R_M} - R_F) - (\delta_M - R_F)\tau}{\sigma_M^2}$$

Substituting, we have:

$$\overline{R_K} = R_F + (\delta_K - R_F)\tau + \frac{(\overline{R_M} - R_F) - (\delta_M - R_F)\tau}{\sigma_M^2} \mathrm{cov}(R_K R_M)$$

or:

$$\overline{R_K} = R_F + \beta_K\left[(\overline{R_M} - R_F) - (\delta_M - R_F)\tau\right] + (\delta_K - R_F)\tau \tag{14.8}$$

That is the equation of the equilibrium if we consider taxes.

Note that if the dividends are taxed on average at a higher rate than capital gain, τ is positive. Then the expected return $(\overline{R_K})$ is an increasing function of dividend yield. It is reasonable because the larger the fraction return paid in the form of dividends, the highest the taxes that investors have to pay, and then the higher the pretax expected return required by investor.

Note that in the last term, we have subtract R_F to the dividend yield the R_F. It is to consider the tax treatment of interest on lending and borrowing since the interest payments are taxed at the same rate of dividends.

Finally note that in the standard form of CAPM the only variable associated to the k-th asset that affect its expected return is the coefficient beta. In this case, k-th asset is affected by its beta and its dividends yield. It implies that the equilibrium must be defined in the three-dimensional space (R_K, β_K, δ_K) rather than the two-dimensional space (R_K, β_K) as in the standard form.

14.3 Consumption CAPM

Cochrane (2001) generalizes CAPM to a multiperiod economy with a paradigm for asset pricing based on a consumption-based intertemporal equilibrium model that bypasses the standard development through the single-period theory that lead to the standard CAPM. Obviously, in this contest, we want to give only a very brief introduction by considering few and main essential elements of this approach.

This approach defines the investor's problem in terms of wealth allocation to maximize the utility of consuming both now and in the future. It implies that the investor faces an intertemporal choice problem that we can formalize in the form:

$$\text{Max } E_t\left[\sum_{J=0}^{\infty} \delta^j U(C_{t+j})\right] \tag{14.9}$$

where:

- C_{t+j} is the future consumption
- δ is a subjective discount factor applied to future consumption.

By considering the budget constraint, the first-order conditions for the maximization problem implies that:

$$U'(C_t) = \delta^j E_t\left[\left(1 + R_{i,t+j}\right)U'\left(C_{t+j}\right)\right] \tag{14.10}$$

for all i-assets and j-periods into the future.

Dividing through by the marginal utility of consumption today ($U'(C_t)$), we have:

$$\frac{U'(C_t)}{U'(C_t)} = \frac{\delta^j E_t\left[\left(1 + R_{i,t+j}\right)U'\left(C_{t+j}\right)\right]}{U'(C_t)}$$

and then:

$$1 = E_t\left[\left(1 + R_{i,t+j}\right)m_{t,j}\right] \tag{14.11}$$

where $m_{t,\,j}$ is the ***intertemporal marginal rate of substitution*** and it is equal to:

$$m_{t,j} = \delta^j \frac{U'\left(C_{t+j}\right)}{U'(C_t)} \tag{14.12}$$

It can be interpreted as a stochastic discount factor: it takes an asset with uncertain per dollar future payoff €$(1 + R_{i,\,t+j})$ back to the present value to be valued at €1.

If there is a riskless asset in economy with return $R_{F,\,t+j}$, we have:

$$1 = E_t\left[\left(1 + R_{F,t+j}\right)m_{t,j}\right]$$

$$1 = \left(1 + R_{F,t+j}\right)E_t\left[m_{t,j}\right]$$

$$E_t\left[m_{t,j}\right] = \frac{1}{\left(1 + R_{F,t+j}\right)} \tag{14.13}$$

The equation states that the expected value of the stochastic discount factor ($E_t[m_{t,\,j}]$) is equal to the discount factor that we use when the future payments are certain $\left(\frac{1}{\left(1+R_{F,t+j}\right)}\right)$.

Therefore, the intertemporal equilibrium model provides a simple way to value all financial assets. Indeed, the asset price is determined on the basis of the expected value of the growth of a dollar invested discounted on the basis of the stochastic discount factor equals the value of a dollar today.

We can rise in a simple way to a beta pricing model. If we do not consider the time subscripts, we have:

$$1 = E[(1+R_i)m] = E(1+R_i)\overline{m} + \sigma_{\text{im}}$$

Substituting:

$$\overline{m} = \frac{1}{(1+R_F)}$$

we have:

$$\overline{R_i} = R_F - \frac{\sigma_{\text{im}}}{\overline{m}} = R_F + \beta_{i,m}\lambda_m$$

and then:

$$\overline{R_i} = R_F + \beta_{i,m}\lambda_m \tag{14.14}$$

where:

- $\beta_{i,m} = \frac{\sigma_{\text{im}}}{\sigma_m^2}$ is the beta of the asset on this stochastic discount factor m
- $\lambda_m = -\frac{\sigma_m^2}{\overline{m}}.$

The main problem is that the stochastic discount factor m is not observable. However, there are several techniques to estimate it.

Part III

Money, Interest Rates and Bond Market

Demand for Money, Supply of Money, and Equilibrium Interest Rate

15

15.1 Monetary Base

Central Banks (CBs) are the government authorities in charge of monetary policy and then they play a key role in the financial markets.

While most central banks in the world share many common features and goals, however there are a number of differences in the structure and policy tools that each central bank adopts.

In this contest, we limit to give some basic concepts. Our aim is to understand what are the main effects of CBs choices on the financial markets and firms.

The balance sheet of a Central Bank (CB) can be represented in the simpler way as in Table 15.1:

Liabilities
They are composed by:

1. *Currency in circulation (CC)*: it is the total amount of currency in the people's hands. Currency is issued by CB.
2. *Reserves (RS)*: they refer to the deposits of banks at the CB. Reserves consist of deposits at the CB plus currency that is physically held by banks (called vault cash because it is stored in bank vaults). Banks can demand payment on them at any time and the CB is called to satisfy the obligation. Consequently, Reserves represent an asset for banks and a liability for the CB.

The total amount of Reserves can be divided into two parts:

P. De Luca, *Corporate Finance*, Springer Texts in Business and Economics,
https://doi.org/10.1007/978-3-031-18300-3_15

Table 15.1 Central bank assets and liabilities

Central bank (CB)	
Assets	Liabilities
Securities Loans to financial institutions	Currency in circulation Reserves

a) *Required Reserve (RR)*: it is the reserve that the CB requires banks to hold. The amount of this reserve is computed on the basis of each Checkable Deposit (*D*) on the basis of the *Required Reserve Ratio* (rr), so that $\text{RR} = \text{rr} \cdot D$. Consequently, the total amount of Required Reserve (RR) equals the Required Reserve Ratio (rr) times the total amount of Checkable Deposits (*D*). If $\text{rr} = 0.10$ the CB requires a Required Reserve equal to 10 cents for each euro deposit. Note that the rr is expressed as a fraction: $10 = 1/0.10$;
b) *Excess Reserve (ER)*: it is the additional reserves that banks choose to hold.

Therefore, it gets:

$$\text{Reserves (RS)} = \text{Required Reserves (RR)} + \text{Excess Reserves (ER)}$$

The sum of Currency in Circulation (CC) and Reserves (RS) defines the CB's Monetary Liabilities:

$$\text{CB Monetary Liabilities} = \text{Currency in Circulation (CC)} + \text{Reserves (RS)}$$

The sum of the CB's Monetary Liabilities and the Government Securities' Monetary Liabilities (for example, the U.S. Treasury currency in circulation, primarily coins) defines the Monetary Base also called High-Powered Money:

$$\text{Monetary Base} = \text{CB Monetary Liabilities} \\ + \text{Government Securities Monetary Liabilities}$$

However, since the weight of Government Securities on the Monetary Base is usually low, it is common to refer to the Monetary Base by considering only the CB's Monetary Liabilities, as follows:

$$\text{Monetary Base (MB)} \approx \text{CB Monetary Liabilities} = \text{Currency in Cirulation (CC)} \\ + \text{Reserves(RS)}$$

Consequently, the Monetary Base (MB) is equal to Currency in circulation (CC) plus Reserves (RS) as follows:

$$\text{MB} = \text{CC} + \text{RS} \tag{15.1}$$

Assets

They are composed by:

1. *Securities*: they include the Government Securities and other securities in unusual and specific circumstances. Purchasing securities is the primary way by which the CB provides reserves to the banks.

Table 15.2 Bank's balance sheet

Bank	
Assets	Liabilities
Reserves Loans Bonds	Checkable deposits

2. *Loans to financial institutions:* they include loans to banks and other financial institutions. These loans are defined as Discount Loans (or borrowing from the CB or borrowed reserves). The interest rate on these loans charged to banks is called Discount Rate. Note that in normal conditions, CB makes loans only to the bank institutions. Making loans to banks and other financial institutions is the second way by which CB can provide reserves to the banking system.

It is relevant to note that CB's Assets are relevant for two main reasons:

1. Changes in the Assets lead to the change in Reserves and consequently in Monetary Base and then Monetary Supply.
2. These assets (Government Securities and Loans) earn higher interest rate than the liabilities.

The CB works through the bank system. Therefore, to well-understand it can be useful to consider a brief and simple scheme of Balance Sheet of Bank, as in Table 15.2.

Liabilities includes the funds received from people and firms and then what the bank owes to them. At any point in time, people and firms can write checks, use a debit card, or withdraw funds up to the full amount of their account balance. Consequently, bank's liabilities are equal to the total amount of Checkable Deposits. Note that Bank's liabilities are money and it is what makes Banks special respect to the other financial intermediaries.

Assets include Bonds and Loans to people and firms made and Reserves that Bank hold partly in cash and partly in account at the Central Bank, for three main reasons:

1. First, every day cash-in (due to the deposits of people and firms in their checking accounts) and cash-out (due to withdraw of people and firms from their checking accounts) can be different in their amount. Consequently, bank must keep cash on hand.
2. Second, every day people and firm with accounts in different banks write checks among them. Consequently, the bank must keep cash on hand to settle positions with other banks.
3. Third, bank must keep a reserve in some proportion of Checkable Deposits.

The CB has the complete control of the Monetary Base (MB) through two main tools:

Table 15.3 The open market purchase (OMP)

Bank		Central bank	
Assets	Liabilities	Assets	Liabilities
(−) Securities (+) Reserves		(+) Securities	(+) Reserves

Table 15.4 Open market sales (OMS)

Bank		Central bank	
Assets	Liabilities	Assets	Liabilities
(+) Securities (−) Reserves		(−) Securities	(−) Reserves

1. Open Market Operations
2. Lending to Financial Institutions

1. *Open Market Operations*

The primary way by which the CB can change the Monetary Base is through its Open Market Operations. Two are the main:

(a) *Open Market Purchase (OMP)*: the CB purchases bonds. The OMP increases the Monetary Base because it increases the amount of Reserves in CB. Indeed, the OMP implies a reduction in Securities and an increase in Reserves in the banking system (and then it does not change the total amount of assets) and, the increase in Securities and Reserves in the CB because it pays for the bonds with Reserves. We can summarize these movements as in Table 15.3.

Consequently, the OMP increases the Monetary Base by an amount equal to the amount of the purchase.

(b) *Open Market Sales (OMS)*: the CB sales bonds. The OMS decrease the Monetary Base because it decreases the amount of Reserves in CB. Indeed, the OMP implies an increase in Securities and a decrease in Reserves in the banking system (and then it does not change the total amount of assets) and, the decrease in Securities and Reserves in the CB because it sells bonds by reducing the Reserves. We can summarize these movements as in Table 15.4.

Consequently, the OMS decreases the Monetary Base by an amount equal to the amount of the sales.

Note that CB purchases and sales bonds through primary dealers that are government securities dealers who operate out of private banking institutions.

2. *Lending to Financial Institutions*

The CB can make loans to financial institution.

Table 15.5 CB lends to the banks

Bank		Central bank	
Assets	Liabilities	Assets	Liabilities
(+) Reserves	(+) Loans	(+) Loans	(+) Reserves

Table 15.6 Bank reduces its borrowing

Bank		Central bank	
Assets	Liabilities	Assets	Liabilities
(−) Reserves	(−) Loans	(−) Loans	(−) Reserves

Table 15.7 Shifting from deposits to currency

Bank		Central bank	
Assets	Liabilities	Assets	Liabilities
(−) Reserves	(−) Checkable deposits		(+) Currency in circulation (−) Reserves

If the CB lends to the bank system, it increases the amount of its Loans and then Reserves. In this case, the CB increases its monetary liabilities and then the Monetary Base by the same amount. We can summarize these movements as in Table 15.5.

If the CB does not lend to the bank system and banks pay off a loan from the CB by reducing its borrowing, the CB reduces the amount of its Loans and then Reserves. In this case, the CB decreases its monetary liabilities, and then it decreases the Monetary Base by the same amount. We can summarize these movements as in Table 15.6.

Note that if a bank shifts from deposits to currency, it will affect its Reserves without any impact on the Monetary Base. Indeed, if the depositors in the bank want to hold more currency, they reduce the amount of their checkable deposits in exchange of currency. In the bank there is the reduction of Reserves and the Checkable Deposits while in the CB there is a reduction in Reserves but an equal increase in the Currency in circulation without effects on the total liabilities and then on the Monetary base. We can summarize these movements as in Table 15.7.

These two main tools to control the Monetary Base (MB) by the CB are different.

The Open Market Operations (both Open Market Purchase (OMP) and Open Market Sale (OMS)) are completely controlled by the CB because is the CB to place orders with dealers in bond markets.

On the contrary, the Lending to Financial Institutions is not completely controlled by CB because in this case the amount of borrowing is defined by banking system and not by CB. The CB can set the Discount Rate (the interest rate on loans to banks) but the decision about the amount of loans lies with the bank only that plays a key role.

Therefore, by focusing on the control Monetary Base (MB) by the CB, it can split into two parts:

1. *Nonborrowed Monetary Base* (MB_n): it is the amount of Monetary Base (MB) created by Open Market Operations and then the part of MB under the full control of the CB.
2. *Borrowed Reserves* (*BR*): it is the amount of Monetary Base (MB) created by Loans to Financial Institutions and then the part of MB that is not completely controlled by the CB.

Therefore, the Monetary Base (MB) is equal to:

$$\mathrm{MB} = \mathrm{MB}_n + \mathrm{BR} \tag{15.2}$$

Obviously, it implies that the Monetary Base under the full control of the CB is equal to:

$$\mathrm{MB}_n = \mathrm{MB} - \mathrm{BR} \tag{15.3}$$

15.2 Deposit Multiplier

The Multiple Deposit Creation implies that if the CB supplies the banking system with €1 of additional Reserves, their deposits increase by a multiple of this amount.

The Deposit Multiplier (DM) is equal to the inverse of the Required Reserve Ratio (rr) as follows:

$$\mathrm{DM} = \frac{1}{\mathrm{rr}} \tag{15.4}$$

The Simple Deposit Multiplier Formula equation is used to compute Multiple Creation of Deposits (MCD) as follows:

$$\Delta D = \frac{1}{\mathrm{rr}} \cdot \Delta \mathrm{RS} \tag{15.5}$$

Therefore, if the Reserves (ΔRS) increase of €1 million and the Required Reserve Ratio (rr) is equal to 0.10, the change in Checkable Deposits (ΔD) is equal to €10 million. Consequently, the Multiple Deposit Creation (MDC) with an increase in Reserves (ΔRS) of €1 million with a Required Reserve Ratio equal to 0.10 (rr), is equal to €10 million.

We can derive the equation of Simple Deposit Multiplier Formula in an easy way. Assume that banks do not hold on to any Excess Reserves (ER). By considering that total amount of Reserves (RS) is equal to the Required Reserves (RR) plus the Excess Reserves (ER), and by assuming that the Excess Reserves (ER) are equal to zero, the total amount of Reserves (RS) is equal to the Required Reserves (RR) only.

Since the total amount of Required Reserve (RR) is equal to the Required Reserve Ratio (rr) times the total amount of Checkable Deposits (D), the total amount of Reserves (RS) is equal to:

$$\text{RS} = \text{RR} + \text{ER} = \text{rr} \cdot D + \text{ER}$$

$$\text{for ER} = 0 \rightarrow \text{RS} = \text{RR} \rightarrow \text{RS} = \text{rr} \cdot D$$

and solving for Checkable Deposits (D), it gets:

$$D = \frac{1}{\text{rr}} \cdot \text{RS}$$

Assuming the change (Δ) in both sides of this equation, it gets:

$$\Delta D = \frac{1}{\text{rr}} \cdot \Delta\text{RS}$$

We can derive the Simple Deposit Multiplier Formula in a more formal way by considering the change in Checkable Deposits (ΔD) as follows:

$$\Delta D = \Delta\text{RS} \cdot 1 + \Delta\text{RS} \cdot (1 - \text{rr}) + \Delta\text{RS} \cdot (1 - \text{rr}) \cdot (1 - \text{rr}) + \Delta\text{RS} \cdot (1 - \text{rr}) \cdot (1 - \text{rr}) \cdot (1 - \text{rr}) + \ldots$$

$$\Delta D = \Delta\text{RS} \cdot 1 + \Delta\text{RS} \cdot (1 - \text{rr}) + \Delta\text{RS} \cdot (1 - \text{rr})^2 + \Delta\text{RS} \cdot (1 - \text{rr})^3 + \ldots + (1 - \text{rr})^n$$

$$\Delta D = \Delta\text{RS} \cdot \left[1 + (1 - \text{rr}) + (1 - \text{rr})^2 + (1 - \text{rr})^3 + \ldots + (1 - \text{rr})^n\right]$$

By using the formula for the sum of an infinite series, it gets:

$$\Delta D = \frac{1}{1 - (1 - \text{rr})} \cdot \Delta\text{RS} = \frac{1}{\text{rr}} \cdot \Delta\text{RS}$$

The equation of the Simple Deposit Multiplier shows that:

1. If the Required Reserve Ratio is less than 1 ($\text{rr} < 1$), it implies that €1 of Reserves can support more than €1 of Deposits, by generating the Deposit Multiplier. The lower the Required Reserve Ratio (rr), the higher the Simple Deposit Multiplier. Assume that banks do not want to hold Excess Reserve ($\text{ER} = 0$). The total amount of Reserves (RS) is equal to the Required Reserves (RR) and then to the Required Reserve Ratio (rr) multiplied by Checkable Deposits (D), so that $\text{RS} = \text{RR} = \text{rr} \cdot D$. Assume that $\text{rr} = 0.10$ and $D =$ €1.500. The amount of Reserve (RS) is equal to $\text{RS} = 0.10 \cdot$ €1.500 = €150. Therefore, the amount of Checkable Deposits of €1.500 is supported by a total amount of Reserve equal to €150. In inverse terms, we need to hold a Reserve equal to €150 to support Checkable Deposits equal to €1.500. Consequently, the Reserve (RS) can support ten times this amount in Checkable Deposits (D) thanks to the Multiple Deposit Creation.

2. We can examine the banking system as a whole rather than one bank at a time. Indeed, the single bank cannot by itself generate Multiple deposit expansion. By considering the entire banking system the Deposit Creation will stop when the total amount of Excess Reserves (ER) in the banking system is equal to zero. Therefore, the equilibrium in the banking system will be achieved when the total amount of Required Reserves equals the total amount of Reserves (RS = RR). Consequently, if the increase in Checkable Deposits (*D*) is less than it must be if RS = RR, the total amount of Excess Reserves is not equal to zero and they still exist somewhere in the banking system.
3. If banks decide to use their Excess Reserve (ER) by purchasing Securities, there are not effects on the deposit creation. Consequently, when banks choose to use its Excess Reserves to make loans or to purchase securities, the effect on deposits is the same.

Note that in any case, the Deposit Creation can never be realized in a so mechanical way as described. Indeed, the entire model is based on two main rigid baseline assumptions:

a) *Assumption 1: Banks do not want to hold Excess Reserves* (*ER* = 0). It implies that banks make loans for the entire amount of Checkable Deposits less the Required Reserves. But if banks decide to hold Excess Reserves (ER $\neq$ 0), no deposits will be made in other banks and this stop the deposit creation process. Therefore, if banks choose to hold Excess Reserves, the full expansion of deposits predicted by the basic model of multiple deposit creation does not occur.

Consequently, the effective level of the Multiple Deposit Creation depends also by the banks regarding the amount of Excess Reserves to hold.

b) *Assumption 2: Borrowers do not want to hold currency and they use the total amount of loan*. It implies that they write checks and then they deposit at other banks the loan received. But if borrowers decide to hold currency, then less multiple expansion occurs overall, and money supply does not increase by the amount predicted by the model of multiple deposit creation. Indeed, currency does not lead to multiple deposit expansion and the choice to hold currency stop the deposit creation process. Consequently, the effective level of the Multiple Deposit Creation depends also by the depositors' behaviour about how much currency to hold.

Therefore, the effective level of the Multiple Deposit Creation depends from the behaviour of three players:

1. *Central Bank (CB)*, with regard to the decision about the Required Reserves (RS) and then the level of the Required Reserve Ratio (rr). More it is, less is the process of the deposit expansion.

2. *Bank System*: with regard to their decision about the amount of Excess Reserves (ER) to hold. More it is, less is the process of the deposit expansion.
3. *Depositors*: with regard to their decisions about the amount of currency to hold. More it is, less is the process of the deposit expansion.

Based on behaviour of CB, Bank system, and Depositors we can identify factors able to affect the Money Supply.

To well-understand the single effect of each factor, we can look at changes in each of them in turn holding the others constant.

1. *Changes in the Nonborrowed Monetary Bases (MB_n): Money Supply is positively related to the Nonborrowed Monetary Bases (MB_n).*
   (a) *Open Market Purchase (OMP) of CB*: purchase bonds increase Securities and then Reserves that it increases the Monetary Base. Consequently, there is an expansion of the Multiple Deposit Creation and the Money Supply rises.
   (b) *Open Market Sale (OMS) of CB*: sale bonds decrease Securities and then Reserves that it reduces the Monetary Base. Consequently, there is a reduction of the Multiple Deposit Creation and the Money Supply falls.

2. *Changes in Borrowed Reserves (BR): Money Supply is positively related to the level of Borrowed Reserves (BR).*
   (a) *CB increases Loans to bank system*: it increases the amount of the Loans and then Reserves and then it increases the Monetary Base. Consequently, there is an expansion of the Multiple Deposit Creation and the Money Supply rises.
   (b) *CB decreases Loans to bank system*: it decreases the amount of Loans and Reserves and then it decreases the Monetary Base. Consequently, there is a reduction of the Multiple Deposit Creation and then the Money Supply falls.

3. *Changes in the Required Reserve Ratio (rr): Money Supply is negatively related to the Required Reserve Ratio (rr).*
   (a) *CB increases the Required Reserve Ratio*: it implies an increase in Required Reserves (RR) and then a reduction in the Multiple Deposit Creation. Consequently, the Monetary Supply falls.
   (b) *CB decreases the Required Reserve*: it implies a reduction of the Required Reserves (RR) and then an expansion of the Multiple Deposit Creation. Consequently, the Monetary Supply rises.

4. *Changes in the Excess Reserve (ER): Money Supply is negatively related to the amount of Excess Reserve (ER).*
   (a) *Bank System increases the Excess Reserve*: Reserves are not used to make loans. It implies a reduction in the Multiple Deposit Creation and the Money Supply falls.

Table 15.8 Factors that affect the money supply

Player	Variable	Relationship (variable vs money supply)	Change in variable	Multiple deposit creation	Money supply
Central bank (CB)	1) Nonborrowed monetary base (MB_n)	Positively	Increase (↑)	Increase (↑)	Increase (↑)
			Decrease (↓)	Decrease (↓)	Decrease (↓)
Central bank (CB)	2) Required reserve ratio (rr)	Negatively	Increase (↑)	Decrease (↓)	Decrease (↓)
			Decrease (↓)	Increase (↑)	Increase (↑)
Bank system	3) Borrowed reserves (BR)	Positively	Increase (↑)	Increase (↑)	Increase (↑)
			Decrease (↓)	Decrease (↓)	Decrease (↓)
Bank system	4) Excess reserves (ER)	Negatively	Increase (↑)	Decrease (↓)	Decrease (↓)
			Decrease (↓)	Increase (↑)	Increase (↑)
Depositors	5) Currency holdings (*C*)	Negatively	Increase (↑)	Decrease (↓)	Decrease (↓)
			Decrease (↓)	Increase (↑)	Increase (↑)

(b) *Bank System decreases the Excess Reserve*: Reserves are used to make loans. It implies an increase in the Multiple Deposit Creation and the Money Supply rises.

5. *Changes in Currency Holdings (C): Money Supply is negatively related to Currency in circulation (CC)*
   (a) *Depositors increase the Currency holding*: checkable deposits are converted into currency. It implies a reduction in the Multiple Deposit Creation and then the Money Supply falls.
   (b) *Depositors decrease the Currency holding*: checkable deposits are not converted into currency. It implies an expansion in the Multiple Deposit Creation and then the Money Supply rises.

We can summarize impacts of variables on the Money Supply as in Table 15.8.

15.3 Money Multiplier

The process of Money Supply is based on the Money Multiplier (m): it defines how much the Money Supply changes for a given change in the Monetary Base (MB).

The relationship between Money Supply (M), Money Multiplier (m), and Monetary Base (MB) can be formalized as follows:

$$M = m \cdot \text{MB}$$

$$M = m \cdot (\text{MB}_n + \text{BR}) \tag{15.6}$$

Therefore, the Money Multiplier (m) indicates how much of the Money Base is transformed into the Money Supply. In other terms, the Money Multiplier (m) tells us how much the Money Supply (M) changes in response to a given change in the Monetary Base (MB) both Nonborrowed Monetary Base (MB_n) and Borrowed Reserves (BR).

The Money Multiplier (m) is typically larger than 1. It implies that a €1 change in the Monetary Base (MB) typically leads to more than a €1 change in Money Supply (M). For this reason, the Monetary Base is also called High-Powered Money.

We can derive the Money Multiplier (m) in the following manner.

Consider that:

1. The Monetary Base (MB) is equal to the sum of Currency in Circulation (CC) and Reserves (RS), so that: MB = CC + RS.
2. The total amount of Reserves (RS) in the bank system is equal to the sum of Required Reserves (RR) and Excess Reserves (ER), so that: RS = RR + ER.
3. The total amount of Required Reserves (RR) is equal to the Required Reserve Ratio (rr) times the amount of Checkable Deposits (D), so that: RR = rr $\cdot$ D.

Based on these relationships, it gets:

$$\text{MB} = \text{CC} + \text{RS}$$

$$\text{RS} = \text{RR} + \text{ER} = (\text{rr} \cdot D) + \text{ER}$$

$$\text{MB} = \text{CC} + (\text{rr} \cdot D) + \text{ER}$$

Assume that the amount of Currency in Circulation (CC) and Excess Reserve (ER) grow proportionally with Checkable Deposits (D). In this case, we can define two ratios:

1. Currency Ratio (c), equal to the Currency in Circulation (CC) divided by Checkable Deposits (D) as follows:

$$c = \frac{\text{CC}}{D} \tag{15.7}$$

2. Excess Reserve Ratio (er), equal to the Excess Reserve (ER) divided by Checkable Deposits (D) as follows:

$$\text{er} = \frac{\text{ER}}{D} \tag{15.8}$$

Because we have assumed that the Currency in Circulation (CC) and Excess Reserve (ER) grow proportionally with Checkable Deposits (D), the Currency Ratio (c) and Excess Reserve Ratio (er) are constant.

Consequently, we can define Checkable Deposits (D) and Excess Reserve (ER) on the basis of their ratios (that are both constant) as follows:

$$\text{CC} = c \cdot D; \;\; \text{ER} = \text{er} \cdot D$$

Substituting, it gets:

$$\text{MB} = (c \cdot D) + (\text{rr} \cdot D) + (\text{er} \cdot D) = D \cdot (c + \text{rr} + \text{er})$$

By solving for Checkable Deposits (D), we have:

$$D = \frac{1}{(c + \text{rr} + \text{er})}\text{MB}$$

Consider the definition $M1$ of Money Supply. It defines M equal to the Currency in Circulation (CC) plus Checkable Deposits (D). If we use the $M1$ definition of Money Supply, so that $M = M1$, and by considering that $\text{CC} = c \cdot D$, it gets:

$$M = \text{CC} + D = c \cdot D + D = D(1 + c)$$

By solving for Checkable Deposits (D), it gets:

$$D = \frac{1}{(1 + c)}M$$

Substituting, it gets:

$$\frac{1}{(1 + c)}M = \frac{1}{(c + \text{rr} + \text{er})}\text{MB}$$

and solving for M, it gets:

$$M = \frac{(1 + c)}{(c + \text{rr} + \text{er})}\text{MB}$$

By considering that:

$$M = m \cdot \mathrm{MB}$$

Therefore, the *Money Multiplier* (*m*) is equal to:

$$m = \frac{1 + c}{c + \mathrm{rr} + \mathrm{er}} \tag{15.9}$$

The equation states that the Money Multiplier (*m*) is the function of the behaviour of Central Bank (CB), Bank system, and Depositors. Indeed, it depends on:

1. *Required Reserve Ratio (rr) set by the CB*. Between rr and Monetary Supply (*M*) there is a *negatively relationship*: the increase in rr reduces the Money Multiplier (*m*) and the Monetary Supply (*M*) falls; otherwise, the decrease in rr increases the Money Multiplier (*m*) and the Monetary Supply (*M*) rises.
2. *Excess Reserves Ratio (er) set by Banks*. Between er and Monetary Supply (*M*) there is a *negatively relationship*: the increase in er reduces the Money Multiplier (*m*) and the Monetary Supply (*M*) falls; otherwise, the decrease in er increases the Money Multiplier (*m*) and the Monetary Supply (*M*) rises.
3. *Currency Ratio (c) set by Depositors*. The relationship between *c* and Monetary Supply (*M*) is ambiguous because it is in numerator and denominator. If *c* increases, there is a shifting from Deposit to Currency. In general terms, it should lower the overall amount of multiple expansion and then the Money Supply.

15.4 Equilibrium Interest Rate: Currency Only

In this contest, the aim of the analysis is to determine the Equilibrium Interest Rate.

Money in economy consisted of Currency in Circulation, supplied by Central Bank (CB), plus Checkable Deposits supplied by (private) banks.

In order to well-understand what determines the interest rate in an economy, we can divide the analysis into two steps:

- In the first step (this paragraph), we will consider only the Currency in Circulation (this paragraph)
- In the second step (next paragraph), we will consider both Currency in Circulation and Checkable Deposits.

15.4.1 The Demand for Money

Assume only two assets, money and bond, and assume there is only one type of bond.

Money is used for transaction but it does not pay interest. There are two main types of money:

(a) *Currency*: in form of coins and bills.
(b) *Checkable Deposits*: bank deposits on which it is possible to write checks or use debt card.

Bond cannot be used for transactions but it pays an interest rate. Assume there is only one type of bond. It implies there is only one interest rate.

People define the level of money and bond to hold on the basis of two main variables:

1. *Level of transactions*: people hold an amount of money enough to cover their needs without to have to sell their bonds. Consequently, the higher the level of transactions, the higher the amount of money that people want to hold. It reduces the amount of bond.
2. *Level of interest rate on bond*: people hold bond to earn interest rate. Consequently, the higher the interest rate, the higher the amount of bond that people want to hold. It reduces the amount of money in hand.

The Demand for Money (M^D) defines the amount of money people and firms want to hold. Then, it is equal to the sum of demands for money by the people and firms.

The Demand for Money (M^D) is the function of two variables:

1. *Overall level of transactions in the economy*: it is commonly defined proportional to the Nominal Income. It is the income measured in money terms and it is usually denoted by €*Y*. Nominal Income has a positive effect on Demand for Money: an increase in the level of Nominal Income increases the Demand for Money.
2. *Level of interest rate* (i): it has a negative effect on Demand for Money because if interest rate increases, people want to hold bond by reducing the amount of money in hand. Consequently, an increase in the interest rate decreases the Demand for Money.

The relationship between Demand for Money (M^D), Nominal Income (€*Y*), and Interest Rate (i) can be formalized as follows:

$$M^D = €YL(\underset{(-)}{i}) \tag{15.10}$$

where L is a decreasing function of interest rate (i) as denoted by the sing minus (−) under the i.

Therefore, the equation states that the Demand for Money (M^D) is equal to Nominal Income (€*Y*) times a decreasing function ($L_{(-)}$) of interest rate (i). Consequently, the Demand for Money increases to the increase in Nominal Income and decrease in Interest Rate. These relationships can be shown as in Fig. 15.1.

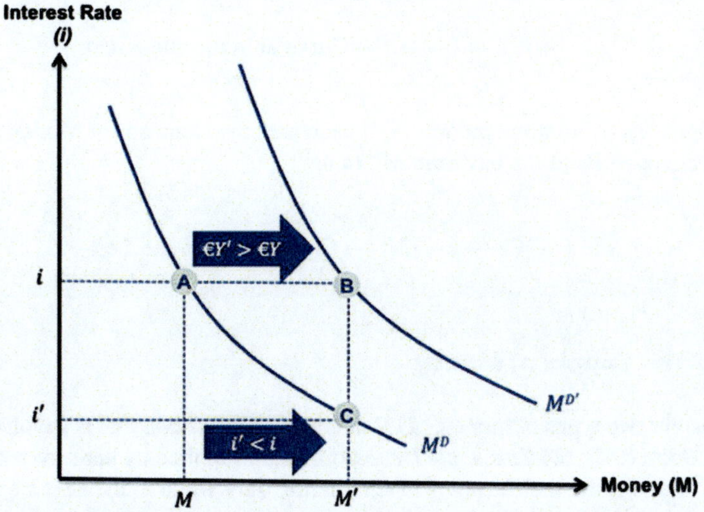

Fig. 15.1 Demand for money

The Demand for Money curve (M^D) is defined on the basis of Interest Rate for a given level of Nominal Income and on the basis of the Nominal Income for a given level of Interest Rate.

Consequently, the curve is downward slope. Indeed, for a defined level of Nominal Income (€Y):

1. The lower the Interest Rate (i), the higher the amount of money that people want to hold, and then the higher the Demand for Money (M^D). It implies that we move downward along the curve:

$$\overline{€Y}: \ (-)i \rightarrow (+)M^D \rightarrow \text{Downward along the curve} \tag{15.11}$$

2. The higher the Interest Rate (i), the higher the amount of bond people want to hold, the lower the amount of money required, and then the lower the Demand for Money (M^D). It implies that we move upward along the curve:

$$\overline{€Y}: \ (+)i \rightarrow (-)M^D \rightarrow \text{Upward along the curve} \tag{15.12}$$

Also, the curve can shift on the rightward or leftward. Indeed, for a defined level of Interest Rate (i):

1. An increase in Nominal Income (€Y) increases the Demand for Money (M^D) and the curve shifts to the right from M^D to M_1^D:

$$\bar{i}: \ (+)€Y \rightarrow (+)M^D \rightarrow \text{Curve shifts to the Right} \tag{15.13}$$

2. A decrease in Nominal Income (€Y) decreases the Demand for Money (M^D)and the curve shifts to the left from M^D to M_2^D:

$$\bar{i}: \ (-)€Y \rightarrow (-)M^D \rightarrow \text{Curve shifts to the Left} \tag{15.14}$$

15.4.2 The Supply of Money

We consider two types of money: *(1) Currency in Circulation* that is supplied by the Central Bank (CB); *(2) Checkable Deposits* that are supplied by bank system. In this contest, we consider the Currency in Circulation only while in the next step we will consider also the Checkable Deposits.

Assume that the amount of money defined by the Central Bank (CB) is equal to M. Consequently, the Supply of Money (M^S) is equal to:

$$M^S = M \tag{15.15}$$

The way the Central Bank (CB) changes the Supply of Money by the Open Market Operations by operating in the open market of bonds with Open Market Purchase (OMP) and Open Market Sales (OMS).

Note that in bond markets the bond prices is determined and the interest rates is determined indirectly on the basis of the price. There is an inverse relationship between price and interest rate: if price increases, interest rate decreases; otherwise, if price decreases, interest rate increases.

Specifically, if the Central Bank (CB) wants to:

(a) *increase the amount of money in the economy*: the CB intervenes with an *expansionary open market operation*. It buys bonds and pays by creating money by expanding the Supply of Money. In other words, by buying the bonds in exchange for money that it created, the CB increases the money supply. If CB buys bonds, the Demand for Bond (B^D) increases, the Prices of Bond (P_B) increases and conversely the Interest Rate (i) decreases.

$$\text{CB Buys Bond} \rightarrow (\uparrow)B^D \rightarrow (\uparrow)P_B \rightarrow (\downarrow)i \tag{15.16}$$

(b) *decrease the amount of money in the economy*: the CB intervenes with *contractionary open market operation*. It sells bonds and removes from circulation the money received in exchange for the bonds by contracting the Supply of Money. In other words, by selling the bonds in exchange for money held by householders, the CB reduces the money supply.

If CB sells bonds, the Demand for Bond (B^D) decreases, the Prices of Bond (P_B) decrease and conversely the Interest Rate (i) increases.

$$\text{CB Sells Bond} \rightarrow (\downarrow)B^D \rightarrow (\downarrow)P_B \rightarrow (\uparrow)i \tag{15.17}$$

Therefore, the monetary policy of the CB affects interest rates indirectly. By buying and selling bonds in exchange for money, the CB affects the price of bonds and conversely the Interest Rates on bonds.

15.4.3 Equilibrium Interest Rate

The equilibrium point requires that the Demand for Money (M^D) is equal to the Supply of Money (M^S), as follows:

$$M^S = M^D \tag{15.18}$$

By considering that:

- $M^S = M$
- $M^D = €YL(i)$
  $(-.)$

It gets:

$$M = €YL(i) \quad (-) \tag{15.19}$$

The equation states that for a given level of Nominal Income ($€Y$), the Interest Rate (i) plays the key role. Based on Interest Rate people define the amount to hold in Money and in Bond. Consequently, to reach the equilibrium point, the Interest Rate must be at such level that people are willing to hold an amount of money equal to the existing money supply M as shown in Fig. 15.2.

Therefore, the Demand for Money (M^D) defines a Demand Curve with downward sloping for a given level of Nominal Income ($€Y$). Consequently, the higher Interest Rate (i), the lower the Demand for Money.

The Supply of Money (M^S) defines a Supply Curve that is a vertical line. Therefore, the Supply of Money is equal to an amount (M) that is independent from the Interest Rate (i).

The equilibrium point (A) occurs when the Demand Curve meets the Supply Curve. The interest corresponding to the equilibrium point defines the *Equilibrium Interest Rate* (i^*). Therefore, the Equilibrium Interest Rate is reached when the Demand for Money is equal to the Supply of Money.

The Equilibrium Interest Rate (i^*) can change on the basis of changes in Demand and Supply Curves.

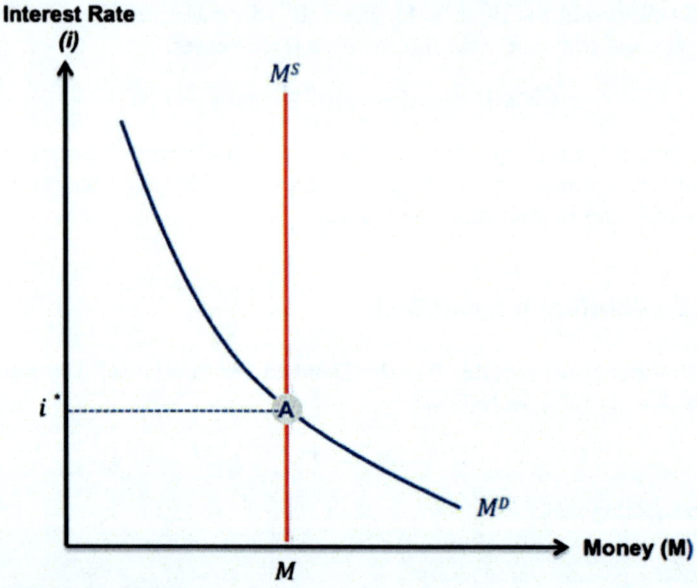

Fig. 15.2 Equilibrium interest rate

Changes in Demand Curve for a Given Supply of Money

For a given and constant Supply of Money $\left(\overline{M^S}\right)$, change in Nominal Income (€Y) affects the Interest Rate (i) and the Demand Curve shifts. Consider Fig. 15.3. Therefore, if:

(a) *Nominal Income increase* (from €Y to €Y_1): it increases the level of transactions and then the amount of money required by people to hold. The Demand for Money (M^D) increases and the Demand Curve shifts to the right from M^D to M_1^D at each level of interest rate.
The equilibrium point moves up from the point A to B and then the Equilibrium Interest Rate increases moving up from i_A to i_B. It happens because at the initial level of i_A, the Demand for Money is higher than the Supply of Money $\left(M^D > \overline{M^S}\right)$, so that the increase in Interest Rate decreases the amount of money that people want to hold and the Demand for Money decreases.
We can summarize these relationships by saying that for a given Supply of Money, an increase in Nominal Income (€Y) leads to an increase in the Interest Rate (i).

(b) *Nominal Income decrease* (from €Y to €Y_2): it decreases the level of transactions and then the amount of money required by people to hold. The Demand for Money (M^D) decreases and the Demand Curve shifts to the left from M^D to M_2^D at each level of interest rate.

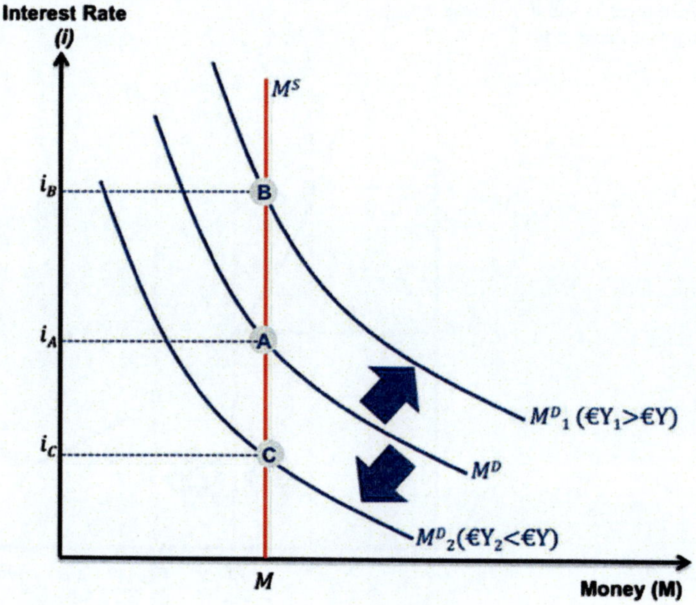

Fig. 15.3 Changes in demand curve for a given supply of money

The equilibrium point moves down from the point A to C and then the Equilibrium Interest Rate decreases moving down from i_A to i_c. It happens because at the initial level of i_A, the Demand for Money is lower than the Supply of Money $\left(M^D < \overline{M^S}\right)$, so that the *decrease* in Interest Rate increases the amount of money that people want to hold and the Demand for Money increases.

We can summarize these relationships by saying that for a given Supply of Money, a decrease in Nominal Income (€Y) leads to a decrease in the Interest Rate (i).

Changes in Supply Curve for a Given Demand for Money

For a given and constant Demand of Money $\left(\overline{M^D}\right)$, change in the amount of money supplied by Central Bank (CB) affects the Interest Rate and the Supply Curve shifts. Consider Fig. 15.4. Therefore, if:

a) *Supply of Money increase* (from M to M_1): the Supply Curve shifts to the right (from M^S to M_1^S) at each level of interest rate. The equilibrium point moves down from A to C and then the Equilibrium Interest Rate decreases moving down from i_A to i_C. It happens because at the initial level of i_A, the Demand for Money is higher than the Supply of Money $\left(\overline{M^D} > M^S\right)$, so that the decrease in the Interest Rate increases the Demand for Money until it meets the Supply of Money

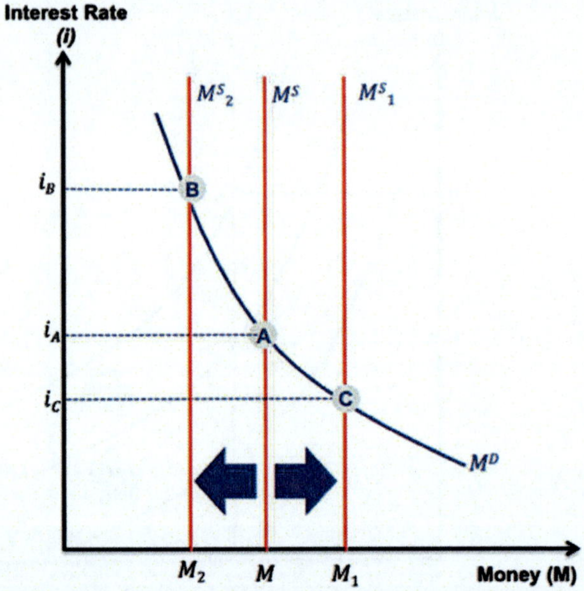

Fig. 15.4 Changes in supply curve for a given demand for money

increased by the Central Bank. We can summarize these relationships by saying that for a given Demand for Money, an increase in the Supply of Money by the Central Bank (CB) leads to a decrease in the Interest Rate (i).

b) *Supply of Money decreases* (from M to M_2): the Supply Curve shifts to the left (from M^S to M_2^S) at each level of interest rate. The equilibrium point moves up from A to B and then the Equilibrium Interest Rate increases by moving up from i_A to i_B. It happens because at the initial level of i_A, the Demand for Money is lower than the Supply of Money $\left(\overline{M^D} < M^S\right)$, so that the increase in the Interest Rate decreases the Demand for Money until it meets the Supply of Money decreased by the Central Bank. We can summarize these relationships by saying that for a given Demand for Money, a decrease in the Supply of Money by the Central Bank (CB) leads to an increase in the Interest Rate (i).

It is relevant to note that commonly the Central Bank (CB) thinks in terms of Interest Rate that it wants to achieve and then moves the Supply of Money with the main purpose to achieve it. In this perspective, we can say that the Interest Rate is not the result of the process, but the entire process is realized to achieve its defined level.

15.5 Equilibrium Interest Rate: Currency and Checkable Deposits

In this second step of the analysis, we introduce the Checkable Deposits. Consequently, all money in economy consisted of Currency in Circulation, supplied by Central Bank (CB), plus Checkable Deposits supplied by (private) banks.

Therefore, now our problem is to understand what determines the interest rate in an economy by considering both Currency in Circulation and Checkable Deposits.

15.5.1 The Demand for Money

The Demand for Money (M^D) is the function of the demand for Currency by people plus demand for Reserves by banks. Consequently, it implies two main decisions:

1. *First decision*: people decide how much money want to hold. It depends on the level of interest rate on bonds. People decide to hold money the higher the level of transaction and the lower the interest rate on bond. Therefore, it gets:

$$M = €YL\underset{(-)}{(i)}$$

2. *Second decision*: people decide how much of this money they want to hold in Currency and how much in Checkable Deposits. Currency is more convenient for small transactions as well as checks are more convenient for large transactions. Note that the larger the amount of Checkable Deposits, the larger the amount of reserves the banks must hold for precautionary and for regulatory. Assume that people hold a part of money (c) in Currency and the rest part $(1 - c)$ in Checkable Deposits. Therefore, the Demand for Currency (C^D) and the Demand for Checkable Deposits (D^D) are the following:

$$C^D = c \cdot M^D$$

$$D^D = (1 - c) \cdot M^D$$

The Demand for Checkable Deposits (D^D) leads to a demand by banks for Reserves (R). Therefore, the Required Reserve (RR) is equal to the Reserve Ratio (rr) that is the amount of reserves banks hold per euro of Checkable Deposits, multiplied by the total dollar amount of Checkable Deposits (D), as follows:

$$\mathrm{RR} = \mathrm{rr} \cdot D$$

If people want to hold Checkable Deposits equal to D^D, the banks must hold reserves equal to R^D so that:

$$R^D = \text{rr} \cdot D^D$$

Therefore, the Demand for Reserves by Banks (R^D) is equal to:

$$R^D = \text{rr} \cdot (1 - c) \cdot M^D$$

Therefore, the Demand for Central Bank Money (H^D) is equal to the sum of the Demand for Currency (C^D) and the Demand for Reserves (R^D), so that:

$$H^D = C^D + R^D$$

$$H^D = c \cdot M^D + \text{rr} \cdot (1 - c) \cdot M^D$$

$$H^D = [c + (1 - c) \cdot \text{rr}] \cdot M^D$$

$$H^D = [c + (1 - c) \cdot \text{rr}] \cdot €YL(\underset{(-)}{i})$$

and then

$$H^D = [c + (1 - c) \cdot \text{rr}] \cdot €YL(\underset{(-)}{i}) \tag{15.20}$$

15.5.2 The Supply of Money

The Supply of Central Bank Money (H^S) is under the control of the Central Bank (CB). It can change the amount of Supply of Money through Open Market Operations (Open Market Purchase (OMP) and Open Market Sales (OPS)).

15.5.3 The Equilibrium Interest Rate

In the equilibrium condition the Supply of Central Bank Money (H^S) must be equal to the Demand for Central Bank Money (H^D), so that:

$$H^S = H^D$$

and then:

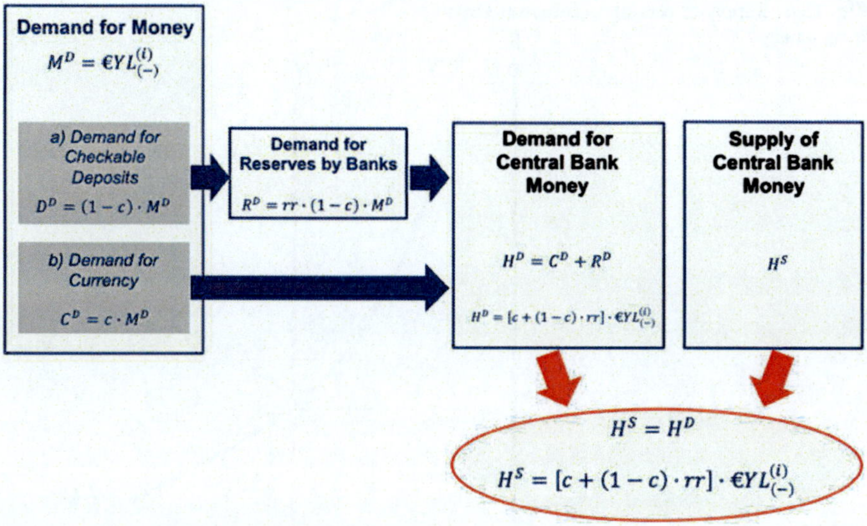

Fig. 15.5 Equilibrium condition

$$H^S = [c + (1-c) \cdot rr] \cdot €YL\underset{(-)}{(i)} \tag{15.21}$$

The entire process can be represented as in Fig. 15.5.

The equation states that the Supply of Central Bank Money (H^S) is equal to the factor of proportionality ($c + (1 - c) \cdot rr$) of the total Demand for Money $\left(€YL\underset{(-)}{(i)}\right)$.

Usually, the Supply of Central Bank Money (H^S) is positioned between the two extreme cases:

(a) People want to hold only Currency: in this case, $c = 1 \rightarrow H^S = €YL^{(i)}_{(-)}$. Consequently, banks do not play any role in the Supply of Money.

(b) People want to hold only Checkable Deposits: in this case, $c = 0 \rightarrow H^S = rr \cdot €YL^{(i)}_{(-)}$. Consequently, banks play a key role in the Supply of Money.

The Equilibrium Interest Rate is the level at which the Demand for Central Bank Money (H^D) is equal to the Supply of Central Bank Money (H^S). Consequently:

1. A decrease in Central Bank Money leads to an increase in interest rate.
2. An increase in Central Bank Money leads to a decrease in interest rate.

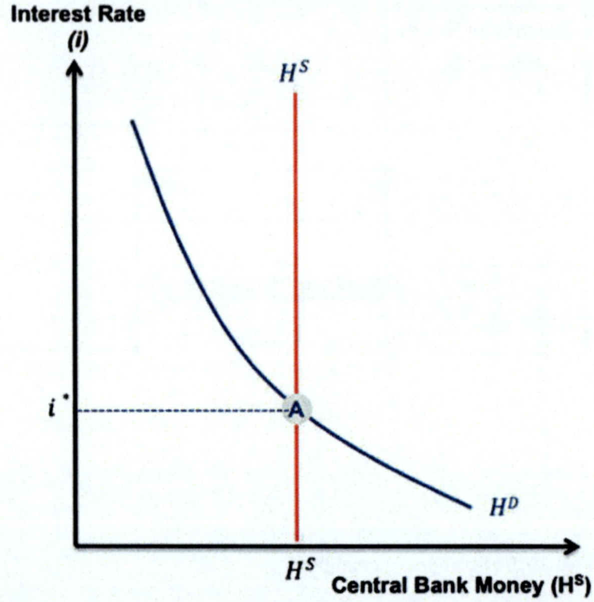

Fig. 15.6 Supply of central bank money

The equilibrium condition can be represented as in Fig. 15.6.

Note that Central Bank (CB) controls the Interest Rate (i) indirectly by changing the amount of Currency. Consequently, if the CB wants to:

1. *Increase the Interest Rate* (i): it decreases the amount of Central Bank Money and then the Supply of Central Bank Money (H^S) shifts to the left.
2. *Decrease the Interest Rate* (i): it increases the amount of Central Bank Money and then the Supply of Central Bank Money (H^S) shifts to the right.

The Interest Rate (i) cannot go below the zero (this constrain is known as Zero Lower Bound). If Interest Rate (i) is down to zero, the monetary policy cannot decrease it further. Therefore, the monetary policy no longer works and the economy fall in the Liquidity Trap.

Indeed, if the Interest Rate (i) is equal to zero, people define the amount of money to hold on the basis of transactions and for the residual part of their wealth they are completely indifferent to held money or bonds because they pay the same interest rate, namely zero.

Note that if the Interest Rate is equal to zero, also banks are indifferent to hold reserves or bonds because they both pay zero interest rate.

The Liquidity trap can be represented as in Fig. 15.7.

In Fig. 15.6 before the point B, the decrease in Interest Rate pushes people to hold money and not bonds, and the Demand for Money increases. When the Interest Rate is equal to zero, people want to hold an amount of money at least equal to the point B. In any case people are willing to hold even more money, point C, because they are

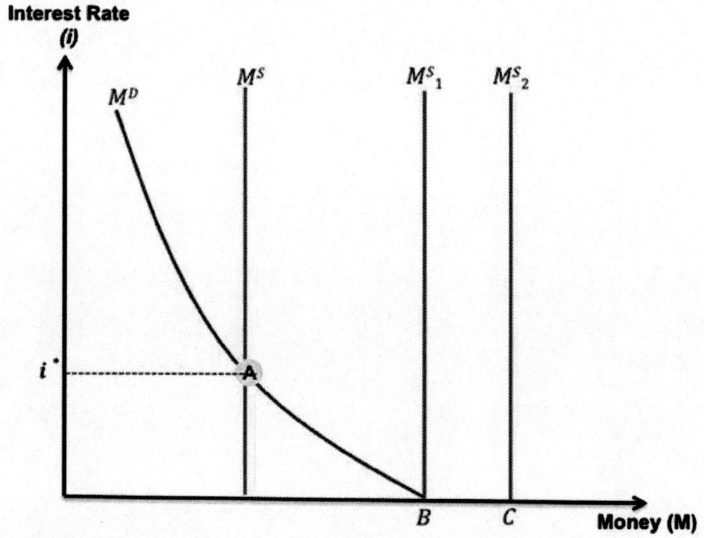

Fig. 15.7 Liquidity trap

indifferent between money and bonds. Consequently, the Demand for Money becomes horizontal after the beyond point *B*.

Obviously, the increase in Supply of Money from M_1^S to M_2^S shifts the equilibrium point from point *B* to point *C*. In both cases, the equilibrium Interest Rate is equal to zero. Therefore, the increase of Supply of Central Bank Money has no effect on Interest Rate which remains equal to zero.

16 Behaviour of Interest Rates

16.1 Government Bonds

All types of Bonds are characterized by some common elements. Commonly, each type of bond can be defined on the basis of five main elements:

1. *Two players*: (a) the *issuer or borrower*, that is the organization (firm or government) that issues the bond; (b) the *lender or bondholder*, that is the investor in debt.
2. *Face value* (or *par value* or *principal*): It is the amount that issuer has to pay back to the bondholder at the bond maturity.
3. *Price:* It is the amount of money that the bondholder has to pay today to buy the bond.
4. *Coupon:* It is the amount of money that bondholder receives by issuer as interest payments. The interest rate is defined in percentage of the face value, it is implicit and it is equal to the difference between the invested capital and the face value and coupon paid by issuer.
5. *Maturity date*: It is the time in which the issuer has to pay back the face value of the bond. Commonly, the maturity can range from as little as 1 day to as long as 30 years.

Bonds can be grouped into three main categories on the basis of their structural characteristics:

1. **Bonds with a Defined Face Value and Fixed Coupon.**
   They are called *Fixed-Income Securities* because it is well known the amount of cash that bondholders get back if they keep the bond until maturity.
   The coupon can be constant or variable during the period of maturity (*step-up*, if the coupon increases over time, or *step-down*, if the coupon decreases over time) but in any cases well-defined at the time of emission of the bond.
   There are two main types of this bond:

P. De Luca, *Corporate Finance*, Springer Texts in Business and Economics,
https://doi.org/10.1007/978-3-031-18300-3_16

(a) *Coupon Bond (CB)* (or *Fixed-coupon bond*): The bond must be repaid by the borrower to the lender by paying a fixed interest rate, the *coupon payment*, every year until the maturity date when the defined final amount, that is the *face value* or *par value*, is repaid. The coupon rate is the amount of money of the yearly coupon payment expressed as a percentage of the face value of the bond: if a coupon payment is equal to 100 € and the face value is equal to 1.000 €, the coupon rate is equal to 100 €/1000 € = 0.10 = 10%. The maturity is medium–long term and it goes from 3–5 year to 10–15 or 30 years. Coupons are normally constant and they are paid twice a year (generally every 6 months).

(b) *Zero-Coupon Bond (ZCB) (or Discount bond):* The bond must be repaid at the face value by the borrower to the lender at maturity in one solution. In this case, the bond is bought at a price below its face value (in this sense at a discount), but the face value is repaid at maturity date: a discount bond with face value equal to 1.000 € might be bought at 950 €, but the owner would be repaid the face value of 1.000 €. Consequently, unlike the Coupon Bond, the Discount bond does not make any interest payments and it just pays off the face value. The maturity is short-term and it goes from 3–6 months to 12 months.

2. **Bonds with Defined Face Value and Coupon "Unknown"**

For these bonds the amount of the coupon will be known at the maturity or at least at a later time following emission. It happens because the coupon is the function of a specific market parameter. Two are the main types of this bond:

(a) *Floater*: The coupon is direct function of another bond's yield. If we link the coupon to Zero-Coupon Bond (ZCB) and considering a defined percentage of coupon ($\alpha\%$), it can take on this form:

$$\text{Coupon} = \alpha\% + \text{ZCB yield to 12 months}$$

(b) *Reverse floater*: The coupon is inverse function of another bond's yield. In this case it is not enough to link the coupon to Zero-Coupon Bond (ZCB) and define a percentage of coupon ($\alpha\%$). Indeed, if we consider only these two parameters, it is possible that the value of coupon is negative but it can never be done. Therefore, we must define an inferior limit equal to zero as follows:

$$\text{Coupon} = \text{Max}[0; (\alpha\% - \text{ZCB yield to 12 months})]$$

3. **Bonds with Face Value and Coupon "Unknown"**

For these bonds the amount of the coupon and/or the reimbursement value will be known at the maturity or at least at a later time following emission. It happens because they are the function of a specific market parameter. Two are the main types of this bond:

(a) *Real index bonds*: The bond coupon and/or reimbursement value are the function of a specific market parameter different from the Interest Rate. In this sense, the market parameter could be the Inflation Rate. In this case, the bond could take on the following form:

$$\text{Coupon and reimbursment value} = \alpha\% \cdot 100 \cdot (1 + \text{Inflation Rate})$$

(b) *Structural Bonds*: These bonds are based on the other types of assets. The most common are:
- *Callable Bond*: It is based on the Coupon Bond and the acquisition of a Call Option on the Coupon Bond by the issuer: *Callable Bond = Coupon Bond − Call Option*
- *Puttable Bond*: It is based on the Coupon Bond and the acquisition of a Put Option on the Coupon Bond by bondholder: *Puttable Bond = Coupon Bond + Put Option*
- *Convertible Bond*: It is based on the Coupon Bond and the acquisition of an Option to convert the bond in stock by bondholder: *Convertible Bond = Coupon Bond + Call Option.*

16.1.1 Bond Rating

When we consider the bond's risk, the quality and reliability of the issuer is the most relevant because it is the main assurance for investor of being paid.

The issuer's reliability is always valuated by Rating Agency on the basis of its performance both past and expected. Rating Agency (the most known are Moody's, Standard & Poors (S&P), and Fitch) issue a Bond Rating for each issuer. It is a synthetic judgement about the issuer's reliability and therefore the quality of the bonds issued. In Table 16.1 is reported an example of the classification of bond rating.

Therefore, not all bonds are inherently safer than stocks and certain types of bonds can be just as risky, if not riskier in certain conditions, than stocks. The general rule states that the lower the grade of the bond, the higher the risk of investment and therefore the higher must be the return offered by the issuer to the investors in the bond.

Table 16.1 Bond rating

Moody's	S&P	Fitch	Grade	Risk
Aaa	AAA	AAA	Investment	Highest quality
Aa	AA	AA	Investment	High quality
A	A	A	Investment	Strong
Baa	BBB	BBB	Investment	Medium grade
Ba,B	BB,B	BB,B	Junk	Speculative
Caa/Ca/C	CCC/CC/C	CCC/CC/C	Junk	Highly speculative
C	D	D	Junk	In default

16.2 Price, Interest Rate, and Yield to Maturity

It is necessary to introduce a distinction between the primary market and secondary market. The bonds are issued in the primary market and underwritten by bondholders. Bonds can be held by bondholders until their maturity, or they can decide to sell the bonds owned to another investor. In this second case, bond is sold before its maturity date in the secondary market or open market. In the open market, the price of bond changes on a daily basis and then it can fluctuate just like any other traded security.

The Face Value is not the price of the bond. The Face Value of the bond is the amount of money that will be paid at the maturity date (T) and it is conventionally defined in 100 monetary units. The Price of the bond is the amount of money that investor pays to buy the bond at the start-time (t).

By considering the time period (τ) (where $\tau = T - t$), the Price (P) is the monetary units that the investor pays today (t) in order to receive the Face Value (FV) of 100 monetary units at the maturity date in time (T), as follows:

$$P = \frac{\text{FV}}{(1+i)^{\tau}} = \frac{100}{(1+i)^{\tau}} \tag{16.1}$$

If the bond is traded at a:

(a) Price *above* its Face Value ($P > \text{FV}$), it is sold at a premium.
(b) Price *below* its Face Value ($P > \text{FV}$), it is sold at a discount.

The Interest Rate (i) paid by bond is obtained indirectly on the basis of the Price (P) defined at time t. Indeed, on the basis of the Bond Price (P) at the start of the period (t) and Face Value equal to 100 units in money (FV = 100), the Interest Rate (i) paid by Bond at maturity date (T), is equal to:

$$(1+i)^{\tau} = \frac{\text{FV}}{P(t,T)} \quad \rightarrow \quad [(1+i)^{\tau}]^{\frac{1}{\tau}} = \left(\frac{\text{FV}}{P(t,\ T)}\right)^{\frac{1}{\tau}} \quad \rightarrow \quad 1+i = \left(\frac{\text{FV}}{P(t,\ T)}\right)^{\frac{1}{\tau}}$$

and then:

$$i = \left(\frac{\text{FV}}{P(t,\ T)}\right)^{\frac{1}{\tau}} - 1 \tag{16.2}$$

By considering Price (P) and Interest Rate (i), three are the main notion to keep in mind:

1. Price and Interest Rate provide the same information. Indeed, defined one of them we have the other.

2. There is an inverse relationship between Price and Interest Rate: the higher the Interest Rate, the lower the Price, as well as the lower the Interest Rate, the higher the Price.
3. There is an inverse relationship between maturity period and the price on the basis of the Interest Rate: the higher the maturity period, the lower the Price as well as the lower the maturity period, the higher the Price.

The most important instrument to compute Interest Rate is the Yield to Maturity. It is usually considered the most accurate measure of Interest rates.

The Yield to Maturity (YTM) indicates the earns of debtholder by keeping the bond until maturity by receiving all of the payments.

The Yield to Maturity (YTM) of the Bond is the Interest Rate (i) that makes equal the Price of Bond today (P) with the present value of its future cash flow payments PV(CFP), as follows:

$$\text{Yield to Maturity (YTM)} \equiv i \quad \rightarrow \quad P = \sum_{t=1}^{\tau} \frac{\text{CFP}_t}{(1+i)^t} \tag{16.3}$$

where τ is the maturity of the bond and it is equal to the difference between the start of the period (t) and the end of the time period (T), so that $\tau = T - t$.

The Yield to Maturity (YTM) states that Bond Price and Interest Rate are negatively related, so that if the Interest Rate rises, the Price of bond falls and vice versa.

For period equal to 1 year ($\tau = T - t = 1$), the Yield to Maturity (YTM) is the Interest Rate (i) that equals the bond Price (P_t) at the t-time (today) and the present value of the bond Price (P_T) at the T-time as follows:

$$P_t = \frac{P_T}{(1+i)}$$

and then, the for a period equal to 1 year the Yield to Maturity (YTM) is equal to:

$$i = \left(\frac{P_T}{P_t}\right) - 1 \tag{16.4}$$

Note that in this case, the Yield to Maturity (YTM) is equal to the simple interest rate. Therefore, the term i is used to denote both the Yield to Maturity and the simple interest rate. Finally, note that it is an equality and then it can be solved for each variable given the others.

For period higher than 1 year ($\tau = T - t > 1$) the Yield to Maturity (YTM) is the Interest Rate (i) that equals the bond Price (P_t) at the t-time (today) and the present value of the bond Price (P_T) at the T-time as follows:

$$P_t = \frac{P_T}{(1+i)^{\tau}}$$

and then, the Yield to Maturity (YTM) is equal to:

$$i = \left(\frac{P_T}{P_t}\right)^{\frac{1}{\tau}} - 1 \quad (16.5)$$

If Bond pays coupons in the period considered $\tau = T - t$, we must consider their value in P_T. Consequently, P_T is equal to the price of the bond in T-time plus the sum of all payments received in the time period τ ($\tau = T - t$). Therefore, if:

(a) Coupons received during the time period (τ) are reinvested until the T-time on the basis of a compound interest rate, P_T is equal to:

$$P_T = c_{t1}(1+i)^{T-t_1} + c_{t2}(1+i)^{T-t_2} + \ldots + c_T(1+i)^{T-T=1} + P \quad (16.6)$$

where c_t are the payments received in a time between the start of the period (t) and the end of the period (T) so that $t \leq t_n \leq T$ and i the interest rate used in the compound interest rule.

(b) Coupons received are not invested in the time period (τ), only the payments received are considered and P_T is equal to:

$$P_T = c_{t1} + c_{t2} + \ldots + c_T + P \quad (16.7)$$

16.3 Supply, Demand, and Equilibrium in Bond Market

The analysis of supply and demand in the bond market is strictly based on the relationship between Bond Price and Interest Rate. This relationship is negative:

(a) If the Price of bond rise, interest rate fall.
(b) If the Price of bond fall, interest rate rise.

To well focus the attention on the relationship between Bond Price and Interest Rate, it is necessary to assume constant and known all other economic variables.

Therefore, based on the inverse relationship between Price and Interest Rate and by assuming all other economic variables known and constant, we can derive the Demand Curve for Bonds (B^D) and the Supply Curve for Bonds (B^S).

Denote with: p the bond Price, i the Interest Rate, YTM the Yield to Maturity, Q_B^D the quantity of bonds demanded, and Q_B^S the quantity of bond suppled.

16.3.1 Demand Curve of Bond

Based on the inverse relationship between Price (p) and Interest Rate (i) and by assuming all other economic variables known and constant:

(a) If the Price decreases, the Interest Rate increases, and the quantity demanded of bond increases. Indeed, if Interest Rate increases, the Yield to Maturity increases and investors demand more bonds. Also, if the Price decreases, the investor's return increases.
(b) If the Price increases, the Interest Rate decreases, and the quantity demanded of bond decreases. Indeed, if Interest Rate decreases, the Yield to Maturity decreases and investors demand less bonds. Also, if the Price increases, the investor's return decreases.

We can summarize these relationships as follows:

$$\begin{array}{ccccccc} p\,(\downarrow) & \rightarrow & i\,(\uparrow) & \rightarrow & \text{YTM}\,(\uparrow) & \rightarrow & Q_B^D\,(\uparrow) \\ p\,(\uparrow) & \rightarrow & i\,(\downarrow) & \rightarrow & \text{YTM}\,(\uparrow) & \rightarrow & Q_B^D\,(\downarrow) \end{array} \tag{16.8}$$

Therefore, the Demand Curve for Bonds (B^D) has usual a downward slope: the lower the bond Price, the higher the Interest Rate, the higher the Quantity demanded of bonds by investors because the higher the yield to maturity.

16.3.2 Supply Curve

Based on the inverse relationship between Price (p) and Interest Rate (i) and by assuming all other economic variables known and constant:

(a) If the Price decreases, the Interest Rate increases, and the quantity supplied of bond decreases. Indeed, if the Interest Rate increases, it is costlier to borrow by issuing bond.
(b) If the Price increases, the Interest Rate decreases, and the quantity supplied of bond increases. Indeed, if the interest rate decreases, it is less costly to borrow by issuing bond.

We can summarize these relationships as follows:

$$\begin{array}{lllll} p\,(\uparrow) & \rightarrow & i\,(\downarrow) & \rightarrow & Q_B^S\,(\uparrow) \\ p\,(\downarrow) & \rightarrow & i\,(\uparrow) & \rightarrow & Q_B^S\,(\downarrow) \end{array} \tag{16.9}$$

The Supply Curve for Bonds (B^S) has usual upward slope: the higher the bond Price, the lower the Interest Rate, the higher the quantity supplied of bonds by borrowers because the lower is the cost of borrow by issuing bonds.

16.3.3 Market Equilibrium

The relationships between bond Price (p), Interest Rates (i), and the Demand $\left(Q_B^D\right)$ and Supply $\left(Q_B^S\right)$ of Bond can be summarized as follows:

Price of Bond	Interest Rate	Quantity of Bond Demanded	Quantity of Bond Supply
$p\,(\downarrow)$	$i\,(\uparrow)$	$Q_B^D\,(\uparrow)$	$Q_B^S\,(\downarrow)$
$p\,(\uparrow)$	$i\,(\downarrow)$	$Q_B^D\,(\downarrow)$	$Q_B^S\,(\uparrow)$

More detailed, by denoting with K_B the cost of capital of bond and R_B the expected return of bond, the relationships can be represented as follows:

$$p\,(\uparrow) \rightarrow i\,(\downarrow) \rightarrow \begin{array}{lll} K_B\,(\downarrow) & \rightarrow & Q_B^S\,(\uparrow) \\ R_B\,(\downarrow) & \rightarrow & Q_B^D\,(\downarrow) \end{array}$$

and:

$$p\,(\downarrow) \rightarrow i\,(\uparrow) \rightarrow \begin{array}{lll} K_B\,(\uparrow) & \rightarrow & Q_B^S\,(\downarrow) \\ R_B\,(\uparrow) & \rightarrow & Q_B^D\,(\uparrow) \end{array} \tag{16.10}$$

The Market Equilibrium is reached when the Supply Curve for Bonds (B^S) and the Demand Curve for Bonds (B^D) are equal among them. Therefore, the equilibrium point is reached when the Quantity of Bonds Demanded $\left(Q_B^D\right)$ equals the Quantity of Bonds Supplied $\left(Q_B^S\right)$.

$$B^D = B^S \quad \leftrightarrow \quad Q_B^D = Q_B^S \tag{16.11}$$

The equilibrium point can be represented as Fig. 16.1.

On the vertical axis is indicate the Price (p). Each Price on the vertical axis corresponds to a defined value of Interest Rate (i). The dynamic of interest rate is opposite to the price: while price increases on the vertical axis, the interest rate decreases on the same vertical axis. On the horizontal axis it indicates the Quantity of Bonds.

The price (p^*) (and in inverse term, the interest rate (i^*)) at which the Quantity Demanded of bond $\left(Q_B^D\right)$ equals the Quantity Supplied $\left(Q_B^S\right)$, is the Market Equilibrium. It is defined Market-Clearing Price if it is defined in terms of price, or the Market-Clearing Interest Rate if it is defined in terms of interest rate.

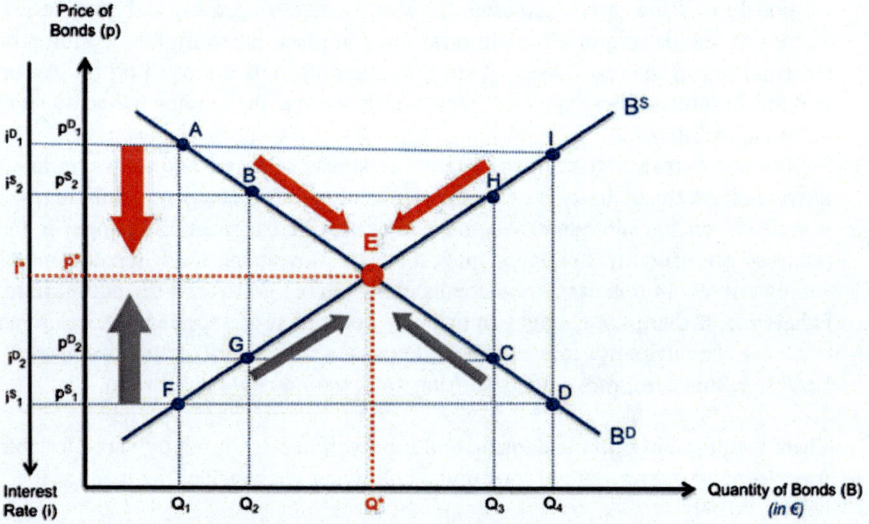

Fig. 16.1 Supply, demand, and equilibrium in bond market

The market moves toward its equilibrium. Indeed, if:

(a) *The bond price is higher than the equilibrium price* ($p > p^*$): The interest rate is lower than the equilibrium interest rate ($i < i^*$), the quantity supplied is higher than quantity demand ($B^S > B^D$). Indeed, if the interest rate is low, the cost of debt is low for the borrower and, consequently, the expected return is low for lender (investor). Therefore, borrowers sell more bonds than lenders want to buy. This situation defines a condition of Excess Supply. Indeed, the quantity of bonds supplied (Q_4 at point I) is greater than the quantity of bonds demanded (Q_1 at point A). In this condition, the price of bonds will fall until it is equal to the equilibrium price ($p = p^*$).

(b) *The bond price is lower than the equilibrium price* ($p < p^*$): The interest rate is higher than the equilibrium interest rate ($i > i^*$), the quantity supplied is lower than quantity demand ($B^S < B^D$). Indeed, if the interest rate is high, the cost of debt is high for the borrower and, consequently, the excepted return is high for lender (investor). Therefore, lenders want to buy more bonds than borrowers are willing to sell. This situation defines a condition of Excess Demand. Indeed, the quantity of bonds supplied (Q_1 at point *F*) is lower than the quantity of bonds demanded (Q_4 at point *D*). In this condition, the price of bonds will increase until it is equal to the equilibrium price ($p = p^*$).

The analysis of the supply and demand diagram highlights three main elements:

1. The diagram can be drawn for any type of bonds and it shows as at each level of bond price correspond a defined level of interest rate on the basis of inverse

relationship (if the price increases, the interest rate decreases, and vice-versa). Therefore, the definition of equilibrium price implies indirectly the definition of the equilibrium interest. Consequently, the definition of the equilibrium can be realized in terms of both price or interest rate because they define the same level of bonds quantity.
2. Supply and demand are defined in terms of stocks of assets and not in terms of flows. Indeed, the quantity is defined in terms of amounts at a given point in time.
3. If there are changes in quantity demanded or supplied as result of changes in the price (or, equivalently, in interest rate), there are movements along the demand or supply curves. In this case, movements along curves go toward the equilibrium. Otherwise, if there are changes in quantity demanded or supplied at each given price (or, equivalently, interest rate), there is a shift in the demand or supply curves. In this case, movements shifting go toward a new equilibrium.

There are possible shifts in demand and supply of bonds caused by variables able to affect price or interest rate of the bonds. Following we consider the main of them (Mishkin, 2019).

16.4 Shift in the Demand Curve for Bonds

The main variables able to affect the Demand Curve for Bonds with consequent its shifting to the right or to the left, are (Mishkin, 2019): (1) wealth; (2) expected Interest Rate; (3) expected return of alternative assets; (4) expected Inflation; (5) risk; (6) liquidity.

We analyze each of them buy considering constant all others and all other variables in the economy.

1. **Wealth**

   In the business cycle expansion, the increase in income and wealth makes more resources available to investment in any asset. The quantity of assets demanded rises. Consequently, there is always a positive relationship between Wealth and Demand of Asset: holding everything else constant, an increase in Wealth (W) rises the Quantity of Asset Demanded $\left(Q_{\mathrm{A}}^{\mathrm{D}}\right)$ by increasing the Demand of Asset (D_{A}). On the contrary, a decrease in Wealth falls the Quantity of Asset Demanded by decreasing the Demand of Asset. We can summarize this relation as follows:

$$W\uparrow(\downarrow)\ \rightarrow\ Q_{\mathrm{A}}^{\mathrm{D}}\uparrow(\downarrow)\ \rightarrow\ D_{\mathrm{A}}\uparrow(\downarrow) \tag{16.12}$$

In bond market the rise in wealth increases the Demand for Bonds at each Price level (or interest rate) as well as the fall in wealth decreases the demand for bonds at each level price (and interest rate). Therefore, in case of:

(a) *Business cycle expansion*: The increase of Income and Wealth (W) increases the Quantity of Bonds Demanded $\left(Q_B^D\right)$ and the Demand Curve for Bonds (B^D) shifts to the right at each at each level price (and interest rate).

$$W \uparrow \quad \rightarrow \quad Q_B^D \uparrow \quad \rightarrow \quad B^D \text{ shifts to the right} \tag{16.13}$$

(b) *Business cycle recession*: The decrease of Income and Wealth (W) decreases the Quantity of Bonds Demanded $\left(Q_B^D\right)$ and the Demand Curve for Bonds (B^D) shifts to the left at each bond price (and interest rate).

$$W \downarrow \quad \rightarrow \quad Q_B^D \downarrow \quad \rightarrow \quad B^D \text{ shifts to the left} \tag{16.14}$$

Note that there is a strictly relationship between Wealth and propensity to save. Indeed, if people:

(a) Save more, wealth increases, the demand for bonds rises, and consequently the demand curve for bonds shifts to the right.
(b) Save less, wealth decreases, demand for bonds fall, and consequently the demand curve for bonds shifts to the left.

2. **Expected Interest Rate**
For any asset the demand increases if its expected return is higher than alternative asset for the same time period and level of risk. There is a positive relationship between Expected Return and Demand of Asset: holding everything else constant, an increase in Expected Return $\left(R_A^E\right)$ of the asset compared with an alternative asset, raises the Quantity of Asset Demanded $\left(Q_A^D\right)$ by increasing the Demand of Asset (D_A). On the contrary, a decrease in Expected Return falls the Quantity of Asset Demanded by decreasing the Demand of Asset.

$$R_A^E \uparrow (\downarrow) \quad \rightarrow \quad Q_A^D \uparrow (\downarrow) \quad \rightarrow \quad D_A \uparrow (\downarrow) \tag{16.15}$$

In bond market is relevant to note that the interest rate and the Yield to Maturity (that is the expected return) are identical only for a 1-year holding period. For the time period greater than 1 year, they may be different.

By assuming a period time greater than 1 year and by assuming a constant value of expected return of all alternative assets and inflation rate, if:

(a) The future Expected Interest Rates (I_E) increases, the Expected Return for long-term Bonds $\left(R_B^E\right)$ decreases, the Quantity of Bonds Demanded $\left(Q_B^D\right)$ falls and the Demand Curve for Bonds (B^D) shifts to the left at each level price (and interest rate).

$$I_E \uparrow \quad \rightarrow \quad R_B^E \downarrow \quad \rightarrow \quad Q_B^D \downarrow \quad \rightarrow \quad B^D \text{ shifts to the left} \tag{16.16}$$

Indeed, if the future interest rates are expected to be higher than initially considered, the long-term bond prices would be expected to fall more than originally anticipated. In this case, the consequently lower expected return today would fall the quantity of bonds demanded at each bond price and interest rate.

Therefore, higher Expected future Interest Rates lower the Expected Return for long-term Bonds and, consequently, lower the Quantity of Bonds Demanded with shift of the Demand Curve for Bonds to the left.

(b) the future Expected Interest Rates (I_E) decreases, the Expected Return for long-term Bonds $\left(R_B^E\right)$ increases, the Quantity of Bonds Demanded $\left(Q_B^D\right)$ rises, and the Demand Curve for Bonds (B^D) shifts to the right at each level price (and interest rate).

$$I_E \downarrow \quad \rightarrow \quad R_B^E \uparrow \quad \rightarrow \quad Q_B^D \uparrow \quad \rightarrow \quad B^D \text{ shifts to the right} \tag{16.17}$$

Indeed, if the future interest rates are expected to be lower than initially considered, the long-term bond prices would be expected to rise more than originally anticipated. In this case, the consequently higher expected return today would rise the quantity of bonds demanded at each bond price and interest rate.

Therefore, lower Expected future Interest Rates, the higher the Expected Return for long-term Bonds and, consequently, the higher the Quantity of Bonds Demanded with shift to the Demand Curve for Bonds to the right.

3. **Expected return of alternative assets**
   By removing the assumption of constant value of expected returns of alternative assets (as indicated in the case 2), the changes in the expected return of alternative assets can change the demand for bonds by shifting the demand curve. Indeed, if:
   (a) The Expected Return of alternative Assets $\left(R_A^E\right)$ increases while the Expected Return on Bonds $\left(R_B^E\right)$ held constant, the Quantity of Bonds Demanded $\left(Q_B^D\right)$ falls and the Demand Curve for Bonds (B^D) shifts to the left at each level price (and interest rate).

$$\begin{matrix} R_A^E \uparrow \\ R_B^E \text{ Constant} \end{matrix} \rightarrow Q_B^D \downarrow \rightarrow B^D \text{ shifts to the left} \qquad (16.18)$$

Indeed, if the stock market is expected to increase in the future, the price of stocks increases and expected returns on stocks and capital gains will rise. If expected return on bonds held constant, people will prefer stocks to the bonds, and the quantity of bond demanded falls.

(b) the Expected Return of alternative Assets $\left(R_A^E\right)$ decreases while the Expected Return on Bonds $\left(R_B^E\right)$ held constant, the Quantity of Bonds Demanded $\left(Q_B^D\right)$ rises, and the Demand Curve for Bonds (B^D) shifts to the right at each level price (and interest rate).

$$\begin{matrix} R_A^E \downarrow \\ R_B^E \text{ Constant} \end{matrix} \rightarrow Q_B^D \uparrow \rightarrow B^D \text{ shifts to the right} \qquad (16.19)$$

Indeed, if the stock market is expected to decrease in the future, the price of stocks decreases and expected returns on stocks and capital gains will fall. If expected return on bonds is held constant, people will prefer bonds to the stocks, and the quantity of bonds demanded rises.

4. **Expected Inflation**

By removing the assumption of constant inflation rate (as indicated in the case 2), the changes in inflation rate can change the demand for bonds by shifting the demand curve. Indeed, if:

(a) The Expected Rate of Inflation (π_E) increases, the Expected Return on Bonds $\left(R_B^E\right)$ decreases, the Quantity of Bonds Demanded $\left(Q_B^D\right)$ falls and the Demand Curve for Bonds (B^D) shifts to the left at each level price (and interest rate).

$$\pi_E \uparrow \rightarrow R_B^E \downarrow \rightarrow Q_B^D \downarrow \rightarrow B^D \text{ shifts to the left} \qquad (16.20)$$

Indeed, inflation rate has effects on real assets by changing the price. An increase in the expected inflation leads to higher prices of real assets in the future by increasing their expected returns. Also, the rise in expected inflation reduces the real interest rate on bonds and then their expected returns. Therefore, the quantity of bonds demanded falls and the demand curve for bonds shifts to the left.

(b) The Expected Rate of Inflation (π_E) decreases, the Expected Return on Bonds $\left(R_B^E\right)$ increases, the Quantity of Bonds Demanded $\left(Q_B^D\right)$ rises, and the Demand Curve for Bonds (B^D) shifts to the right at each level price (and interest rate).

$$\pi_E \downarrow \quad \rightarrow \quad R_B^E \uparrow \quad \rightarrow \quad Q_B^D \uparrow \quad \rightarrow \quad B^D \text{ shifts to the right} \tag{16.21}$$

Indeed, an decrease in the expected inflation leads to lower prices of real assets in the future by decreasing their expected returns. Also, the fall in expected inflation increases the real interest rate on bonds and then their expected returns. Therefore, the quantity of bonds demanded rises and the demand curve for bonds shifts to the right.

5. **Risk**

   The degree of risk or uncertainty is associated to any asset because its return is expected by definition. If the risk of the asset is higher than compared assets for the same level of expected return, investors prefer the alternative assets and the demand for the asset falls.

   There is always a negative relationship between Risk and Demand of Asset: holding everything else constant, an increase in Risk of the Asset (RS_A) compared with alternative assets, decreases the Quantity of Asset Demanded $\left(Q_A^D\right)$ by decreasing the Demand of Asset (D_A).

$$RS_A \uparrow (\downarrow) \quad \rightarrow \quad Q_A^D \downarrow (\uparrow) \quad \rightarrow \quad D_A \downarrow (\uparrow) \tag{16.22}$$

In the bond market, the risk of bond is associated to the price volatility. Indeed, the increase in the volatility of the bond price increases its risk and the demand falls. On the contrary, the reduction of the volatility of the bond price reduces its risk and the demand rises.

Therefore, if:

(a) The Risk of Bonds (RS_B) increases, the Quantity of Bonds Demanded $\left(Q_B^D\right)$ falls and the Demand Curve for Bonds (B^D) shifts to the left at each level price (and interest rate).

$$RS_A \uparrow \quad \rightarrow \quad Q_B^D \downarrow \quad \rightarrow \quad B^D \text{ shifts to the left} \tag{16.23}$$

(b) The Risk of Bonds (RS_B) decreases, the Quantity of Bonds Demanded $\left(Q_B^D\right)$ rises and the Demand Curve for Bonds (B^D) shifts to the right at each level price (and interest rate).

$$RS_A \downarrow \quad \rightarrow \quad Q_B^D \uparrow \quad \rightarrow \quad B^D \text{ shifts to the right} \tag{16.24}$$

6. **Liquidity**

   For any asset, it is relevant how quickly it can be converted into cash at low cost. Asset is liquid if it can be converted into cash quickly and at low cost in the market in which it is traded.

The liquidity of the asset is relevant because higher its liquidity higher the probability to sell and to buy it in the market.

The liquidity of the assets is the function of the development of the financial markets in which they are traded. Generally, higher the number of players (buyers and sellers), higher the liquidity of the assets in the market.

There is always a positive relationship between Liquidity and Demand of Asset: holding everything else constant, an increase in Liquidity of the Asset (L_A) increases the Quantity of Asset Demanded $\left(Q_A^D\right)$ by increasing the Demand of Asset (D_A).

In the bond market, the liquidity of the bond is associated to the level of simplicity, quickly and cost to sell and buy it: more is simple and quick and less is the cost, then the higher the bond liquidity.

Therefore, if:

(a) The Liquidity of Bonds (L_B) increases, the Quantity of Bonds Demanded $\left(Q_B^D\right)$ rises and the Demand Curve for Bonds (B^D) shifts to the right at each level price (and interest rate).

$$L_B \uparrow \quad \rightarrow \quad Q_B^D \uparrow \quad \rightarrow \quad B^D \text{ shifts to the right} \tag{16.25}$$

(b) The Liquidity of Bonds (L_B) decreases, the Quantity of Bonds Demanded $\left(Q_B^D\right)$ falls and the Demand Curve for Bonds (B^D) shifts to the left at each level price (and interest rate).

$$L_B \downarrow \quad \rightarrow \quad Q_B^D \downarrow \quad \rightarrow \quad B^D \text{ shifts to the left} \tag{16.26}$$

We can summarize these movements as in Fig. 16.2.

16.5 Shift in the Supply Curve for Bonds

The main variables able to affect the Supply Curve for Bonds with consequent its shifting to the right or to the left are (Mishkin, 2019): (1) expected profitability of investment opportunity; (2) expected inflation; (3) government budget deficit (with regard to the bonds issue by States).

We analyze each of them buy considering constant all others and all other variables in the economy.

1. **Expected profitability of investment opportunities**
   Consider a firm. If it has a lot of profitable investments opportunities, it has more willing to issue bond in order to acquire the financial resources need to finance these investments. Therefore, in case of business cycle expansion, the economy grows rapidly and the profitable investment opportunities greatly increase. In this case, the Quantity of Bond Supplied increases for each level of price (and interest rate). Therefore, in case of:

   Generally, in the case of:

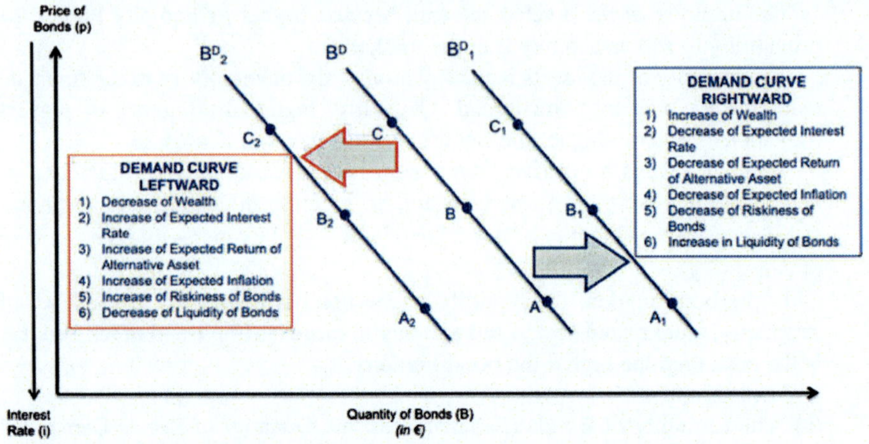

Fig. 16.2 Variables that affect the Demand Curve for Bonds

(a) *Business cycle expansion:* The increase in Expected Profitability Investment Opportunities (IO_E) increases the Quantity of Bond Supplied (Q^S_B) and the Supply Curve (B^S) shifts to the right at each bond price (and interest rate).

$$IO_E(\uparrow) \rightarrow Q^S_B(\uparrow) \rightarrow B^S \text{ shifts to the right} \tag{16.27}$$

(b) *Business cycle recession:* The decrease in Expected Profitability Investment Opportunities (IO_E) decreases the Quantity of Bond Supplied (Q^S_B) and the Supply Curve (B^S) shifts to the left at each bond price (and interest rate).

$$IO_E(\downarrow) \rightarrow Q^S_B(\downarrow) \rightarrow B^S \text{ shifts to the left} \tag{16.28}$$

2. **Expected Inflation**
The inflation rate has relevant effect on the real interest rate that is the most accurately measurement of bonds cost.

Indeed, the real interest rate is equal to the difference between nominal interest rate and the expected inflation rate.

Therefore, for each level of interest rate (and then price), if the expected inflation rate increases, the real cost of bond falls, and the quantity of bonds supplied increases.

Generally, if the:

(a) *Expected inflation* (π_E) *increases*: The real Cost of Bond (K_B) falls, the Quantity of Bonds Supplied $\left(Q_B^S\right)$ increases, and Supply Curve (B^S) shifts to the right for each interest rate (and bond price).

$$\pi_E(\uparrow) \rightarrow K_B(\downarrow) \rightarrow Q_B^S(\uparrow) \rightarrow B^S \text{ shifts to the right} \tag{16.29}$$

(b) *Expected inflation* (π_E) *decreases*: The real Cost of Bond (K_B) raises, the Quantity of Bonds Supplied $\left(Q_B^S\right)$ decreases, and Supply Curve (B^S) shifts to the left for each interest rate (and bond price).

$$\pi_E(\downarrow) \rightarrow K_B(\uparrow) \rightarrow Q_B^S(\downarrow) \rightarrow B^S \text{ shifts to the left} \tag{16.30}$$

3. **Government Budget Deficit**
The Government bonds are issued by State to finance their government deficit caused by expenditures greater than revenues.
The government activities can influence the movements of bond supply in several ways. Indeed, higher the deficit, higher the quantity of bonds issued by increasing the quantity of bond supplied at each level of price (and interest rate). Therefore, in case of:
(a) *Government deficit*: Higher is the deficit (D_G) more the expenditures are greater than revenues, higher the issue of bond by government to cover the gap. Therefore, the Quantity of Bond Supplied $\left(Q_B^S\right)$ increases and the Supply Curve (B^S) shifts to the right at each bond price (and interest rate).

$$D_G(\uparrow) \rightarrow Q_B^S(\uparrow) \rightarrow B^S \text{ shifts to the right} \tag{16.31}$$

(b) *Government surplus*: Higher is the surplus (D_S) more the revenues are greater than expenditures, lower the issue of bond by government. Therefore, the Quantity of Bond Supplied $\left(Q_B^S\right)$ decreases and the Supply Curve (B^S) shifts to the left at each bond price (and interest rate).

$$D_G(\downarrow) \rightarrow Q_B^S(\downarrow) \rightarrow B^S \text{ shifts to the left} \tag{16.32}$$

We can summarize these movements as in Fig. 16.3.

16.6 Expected Inflation and Business Cycle Effects on Demand and Supply of Bond

Expected Inflation and Business Cycle affect both Demand and Supply of Bond. Therefore, it can be useful to analyze for each of them their effects on Demand and Supply jointly.

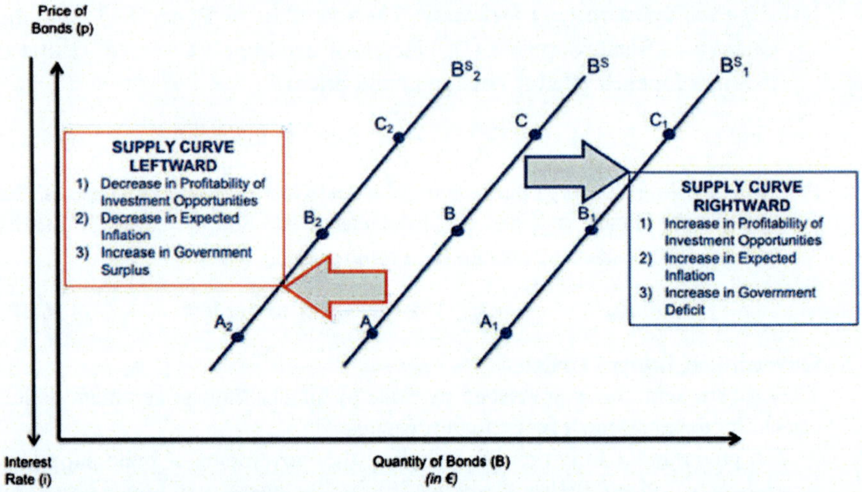

Fig. 16.3 Variables that affect the Supply Curve for Bonds

16.6.1 Expected Inflation

The inflation rate has effect on real interest. The increase in inflation rate increases the nominal interest rate and reduces the real interest rate; similarly, the decrease in inflation rate reduces the nominal interest rate and increases the real interest rate.

Case 1: Expected Inflation Rises
In this case, the:

1. *Demand curve shifts to the left*: The increase in the expected inflation reduces the expected return on bonds relative to real assets (whose expected return decrease due to the increase of prices) for any level of bond price and interest rate. It generates the fall of the demand for bonds and the demand curve shifts to the left at each level of price and interest rate;
2. *Supply curve shifts to the right*: The increase in the expected inflation reduces the real interest rate and then the real cost of borrowing for any given nominal rate. It generates the rises of supply of bonds and the supply curve shifts to the right at each level of price and interest rate.

The jointly movement of the demand and supply curves shifts the equilibrium point characterized by a lower price level. Then, the equilibrium price falls. By considering the negative relationship between interest rate and price, if the equilibrium price falls the equilibrium interest rate rises. Consequently, if the expected Inflation (π_E) rises, expected Prices (P_E) will fall and expected Interest Rate (I_E) will rise:

$$\pi_{\mathrm{E}}(\uparrow) \quad \rightarrow \quad P_{\mathrm{E}}(\downarrow) \quad \rightarrow \quad I_{\mathrm{E}}(\uparrow) \tag{16.33}$$

Therefore, when expected inflation rises, interest rates rise. It is called Fisher effect because the economist Irving Fisher was the first to point out the relationship of expected inflation to interest rates.

Note that by changing the price equilibrium, it is possible that the equilibrium quantity changes in turn. Indeed, the equilibrium quantity of bonds can remain the same or can change by increasing or decreasing. It depends on the size of the shifts in demand and supply curves.

Case 2: Expected Inflation Falls
In this case, the:

1. *Demand curve shifts to the right*: The decrease in the expected inflation increases the expected return on bonds relative to real assets (whose expected return decrease due to the decrease of prices) for any level of bond price and interest rate. It generates the rise of the demand for bonds and the demand curve shifts to the right at each level of price and interest rate.
2. *Supply curve shifts to the left*: The decrease in the expected inflation increases the real interest rate and then the cost of borrowing for any given nominal rate. It generates the fall of supply of bonds and the supply curve shifts to the left at each level of price and interest rate.

The jointly movements of demand and supply curves (in a direction opposite to the case of inflation increases) lead to a rise in the equilibrium price and a fall of equilibrium interest rate on the basis of Fisher effect. Indeed, if the expected Inflation (π_{E}) falls, expected Prices (P_{E}) will rise, and expected Interest Rate (I_{E}) will fall:

$$\pi_{\mathrm{E}}(\downarrow) \quad \rightarrow \quad P_{\mathrm{E}}(\uparrow) \quad \rightarrow \quad I_{\mathrm{E}}(\downarrow) \tag{16.34}$$

We can summarize the Inflation Rate effects on the Demand and Supply of Bond as in Fig. 16.4.

16.6.2 Business Cycle

The business cycle has relevant effects on both demand and supply of bonds. Generally, in a case of business cycle expansion, the economy growth and then income and wealth increase as well as increase the profitability investment opportunities.

Otherwise, in case of business cycle recession, the economy does not grow or grow at low level. Consequently, the income decreases and then the investment opportunities decrease.

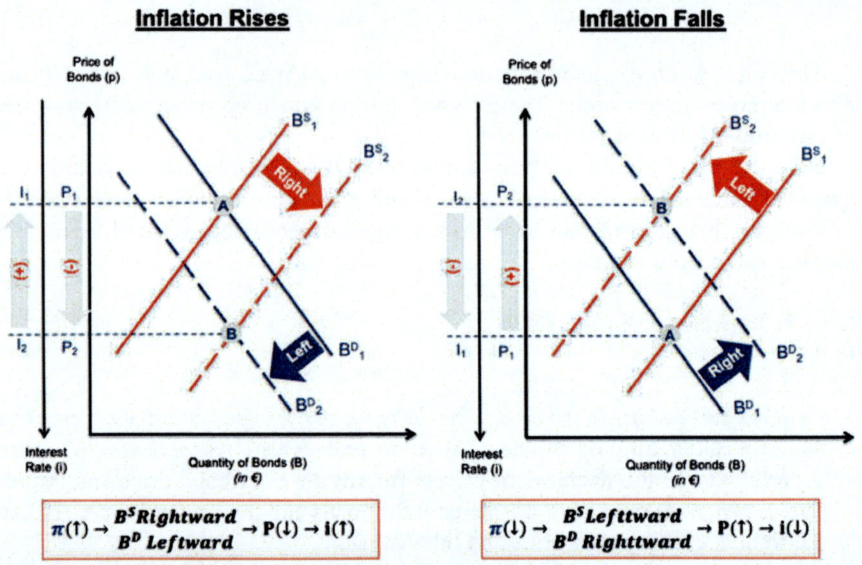

Fig. 16.4 Inflation rate effects on Demand and Supply of Bond

Case 1: Business Cycle Expansion

In this case, the income and wealth increase and increase the profitability investment opportunities. It impacts on demand and supply curves of bonds as follows:

1. *Demand curve shifts to the right*: In the business cycle expansion, income and wealth growth and the demand for bonds rises and the demand curve shifts to the right at each level price and interest rate.
2. *Supply curve shifts to the right*: In the business cycle expansion, the profitable investment opportunities growth and the firm are willing to borrow by issuing bonds for finance their activities. Then, the quantity of bonds that firm wants to sell increases at a given bond price. Consequently, the quantity of bonds supplied increases and the supply curve shifts to the right at each level of price and interest rate.

The jointly movements of demand and supply curves can lead to a new equilibrium point. Given that both the supply and demand curve shift to the right, it is not possible to define if the new price equilibrium rise or fall (and inversely fall or rise the new equilibrium interest rate). It depends on the size of the shift of the two curves. Indeed, if:

1. *Supply curve shifts to the right more than Demand curve*: The equilibrium price falls and the equilibrium interest rate rises.
2. *Demand curve shifts to the right more than Supply curve*: The equilibrium price rises and the equilibrium interest rates falls.

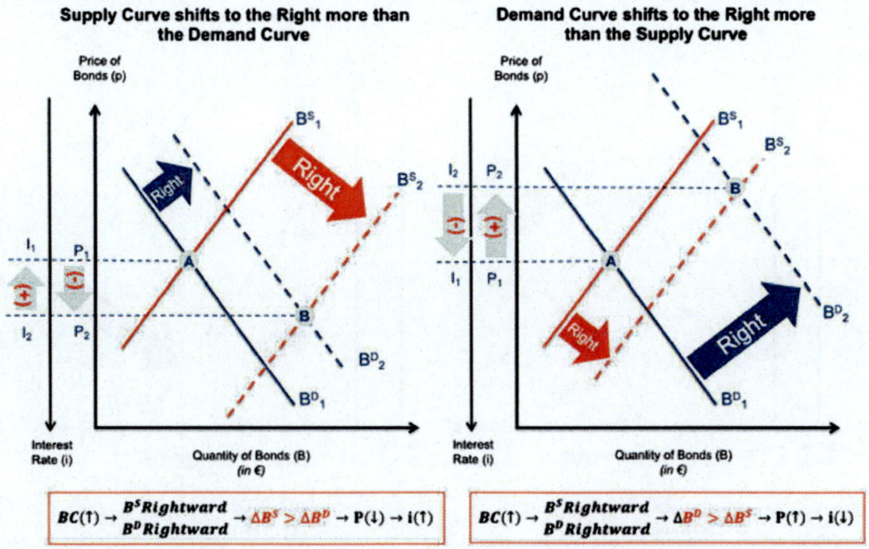

Fig. 16.5 Business cycle expansion effects on Demand and Supply of Bonds

We can be summarized as follows:

$$\text{BC}(\uparrow) \rightarrow \begin{matrix} w(\uparrow) \rightarrow B^{\text{D}}\text{Rightward} \\ \text{IO}(\uparrow) \rightarrow B^{\text{S}}\text{Rightward} \end{matrix} \rightarrow \text{if} \begin{matrix} \Delta B^{\text{S}} > \Delta B^{\text{D}} \rightarrow P(\downarrow) \rightarrow I(\uparrow) \\ \Delta B^{\text{D}} > \Delta B^{\text{S}} \rightarrow P(\uparrow) \rightarrow I(\downarrow) \end{matrix} \tag{16.35}$$

These two different cases can be represented as in Fig. 16.5.

However, it is more common that the interest rate tends to rise during a business cycle expansion. It implies that the shift in the supply curve is greater than the shift in the demand curve.

Case 2: Business Cycle Recession

In this case, income and wealth fall and decrease the profitability investment opportunities. It impacts on demand and supply curves of bonds as follows:

1. *Demand curve shifts to the left*: In the business cycle recession, the income and wealth decrease and the demand for bonds fall and the demand curve shifts to the left at each level price and interest rate;
2. *Supply curve shifts to the left*: In the business cycle recession, the profitable investment opportunities fall and the firms reduce the issue of bonds because the debt increases their default risk. Consequently, the quantity of bonds supplied decreases and the supply curve shifts to the left at each level of price and interest rate.

Also in this case, the jointly movements of demand and supply curves can lead to a new equilibrium point that depend on the size of the two movements. Indeed, both

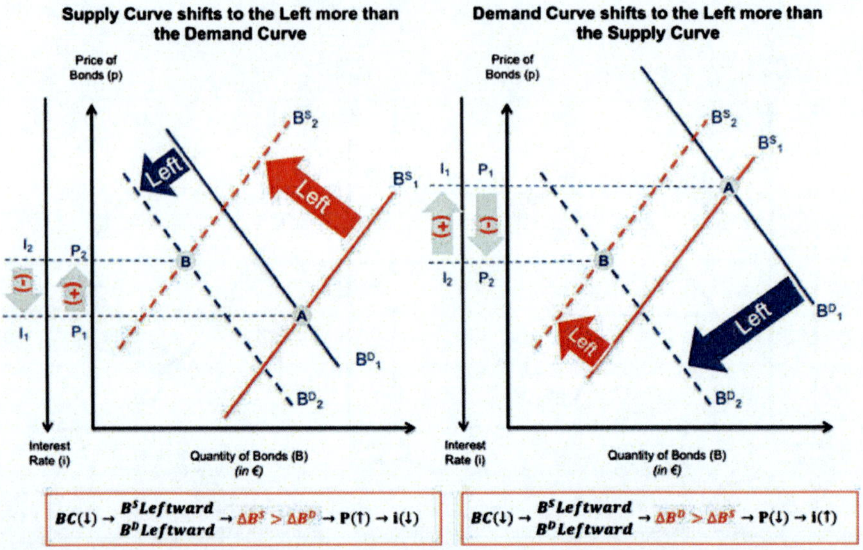

Fig. 16.6 Business cycle recession effects on Demand and Supply of Bonds

the supply and demand curve shift to the left. Consequently, it is not possible to define if the new price equilibrium rises or falls (and inversely falls or rises the new equilibrium interest rate). Generally, if:

1. *Supply curve shifts to the left more than Demand curve*: The equilibrium price rises and the equilibrium interest rate falls.
2. *Demand curve shifts to the left more than Supply curve*: The equilibrium price falls and the equilibrium interest rate rises.

We can be summarized as follows:

$$\mathrm{BC}(\downarrow)\rightarrow \begin{array}{l} w(\downarrow)\rightarrow B^{\mathrm{D}}\text{Leftward} \\ \mathrm{IO}(\downarrow)\rightarrow B^{\mathrm{S}}\text{Leftward} \end{array} \rightarrow \text{if} \begin{array}{l} \Delta B^{\mathrm{S}} > \Delta B^{\mathrm{D}} \rightarrow P(\uparrow)\rightarrow I(\downarrow) \\ \Delta B^{\mathrm{D}} > \Delta B^{\mathrm{S}} \rightarrow P(\downarrow)\rightarrow I(\uparrow) \end{array} \tag{16.36}$$

These two different cases can be represented as in Fig. 16.6.

However, also in this case, it is more common that the interest rate tends to fall during a business cycle recession.

If firms expected that the economy does not increases, they reduce their investments because they think that there will not profitable investment opportunities. It reduces the issue of bonds, and the supply curve shifts to the left. The leftward shift of the supply curve for bonds leads to a further decrease in interest rate (by increasing the bond price). The low level of interest rate is not necessarily a good thing. It could generate the increase of money in the financial system and pushes the investors to acquire more risk to obtain an enough return.

Risk and Term Structure of Interest Rates 17

17.1 Risk Structure of Interest Rates

In the previous chapter, we have considered one interest rate. Unfortunately, there are a lot of bonds on which interest rates are different. It requires to understand the relationships among the various interest rates in order to decide which bonds to purchase and which ones to sell. Two are the mains:

1. The *Risk Structure of Interest Rates*: It refers to the relationship among interest rates on bonds characterized by the same Maturity and different Risk Premium.
2. The *Term Structure of Interest Rates*: It refers to the relationship among interest rates on bonds characterized by the same Risk Premium and different Maturity.

We start with the analysis of the Risk Structure of interest rates. In this case, we refer to the relationship among interest rates on bonds characterized by the same Maturity and different Risk Premium.

The Risk Premium of Bond (RP_B) can be considered as the increase in interest rate necessary to attract investors to acquire the bond. Then the Risk Premium (RP_B) is the function of two main variables:

1. *Default Risk of Bond* (DR_B): It measures the probability of default of the bond's issuer. The default occurs if the issuer of bond (government or firm) is unable or unwilling to pay interests when promised or pay off the face value when at bond maturity.
   There is a positive relationship between Default Risk and Risk Premium: the higher the Default Risk of the bond, the higher its Risk Premium, so that:

$$DR_B \uparrow (\downarrow) \rightarrow RP_B \uparrow (\downarrow) \tag{17.1}$$

P. De Luca, *Corporate Finance*, Springer Texts in Business and Economics,
https://doi.org/10.1007/978-3-031-18300-3_17

2. *Liquidity Risk of Bond* (LR_B): It measure the effective possibility to convert bond into money quickly and at a low cost in the bond market. Generally, the higher the speed and lower the cost to convert into money the bond in the market, higher the level of liquidity of the bond. Obviously, the lower the Liquidity Risk of the bond, the higher its desirable on bond market.
   There is a positive relationship between Liquidity Risk and Risk Premium: the higher the Liquidity Risk, the higher its Risk Premium, so that:

$$LR_B \uparrow (\downarrow) \rightarrow RP_B \uparrow (\downarrow) \tag{17.2}$$

Note that the Liquidity Risk can be interpreted in positive terms as Liquidity of the bond (L_B). In this case, the higher the Liquidity of the bond, the lower is the Liquidity Risk. In this case there is a negative relationship between Liquidity of the bond and Risk Premium: the higher the Liquidity of the bond, the lower the Risk Premium, so that:

$$L_B \uparrow (\downarrow) \rightarrow RP_B \downarrow (\uparrow) \tag{17.3}$$

Denoting with (+) the positive relationship and with (−) the negative relationship, we can summarize these relationships as follows:

$$RP_B = f\begin{pmatrix} DR_B & ; & LR_B \\ (+) & & (+) \end{pmatrix} \leftrightarrow RP_B = f\begin{pmatrix} DR_B & ; & L_B \\ (+) & & (-) \end{pmatrix} \tag{17.4}$$

Considering the risk of bond on of its default probability and liquidity, we can say that the higher the default risk and the lower the liquidity, the higher the bond risk; the lower the default risk and the higher the liquidity, the lower the bond risk.

The Government Bond is a bond issued by State. If the bond is issued by a Government that is considered so solid that the level of risk is very low to be approximated null, it is defined Risk-free Bond.

All bonds with a risk higher than the Risk-free bonds are defined Risky Bonds (typically the Corporate Bonds) and they have to pay higher interest rates. Note that the Risk-free bond can be only one. Indeed, each other bonds, both government bonds or company bonds, with interest rate higher than it, must pay a Risk Premium.

The Risk Premium is the difference (defined *spread*) between the interest rate on risky bond and Risk-free bond, both the same maturity. Therefore, the Risk Premium measures the additional interest rate people must earn to be willing to hold the risky bond. Then, the higher the bond's Default Risk, the higher its Risk Premium.

To well-understand consider Fig. 17.1.

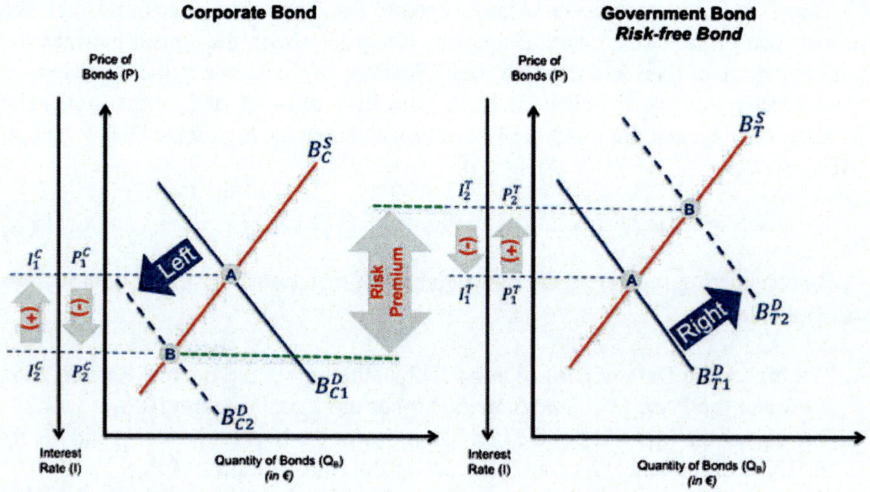

Fig. 17.1 Risk premium on bond

Assume two bonds: a Corporate Bond (C) that is a risky bond, and a Government Bond (T) that we can consider a Risk-free bond. Assume these two bonds present the same risk and maturity. Consequently, they have the same Equilibrium Price $\left(P_1^C = P_1^T\right)$ and then the same Equilibrium Interest Rate $\left(I_1^C = I_1^T\right)$. Therefore, in this case there is no spread between the interest rates of these two bonds and then there is not Risk Premium (RP).

Now assume that the Corporate Bond (C) becomes riskier rather than the Government Bond (T) due to the worsening of the company's fundamentals. In this case:

1. *Corporate Bond*: The quantity required decreases, the demand falls and the demand curve shifts to the left (from B_{C1}^D to B_{C2}^D). The equilibrium price falls from P_1^C to P_2^C and then the equilibrium interest rate rises from I_1^C to I_2^C (on the basis of the negative relationship between price and interest rate).
2. *Government Bond*: The quantity of bond required increases, the demand rises, and the demand curve shifts to the right (from B_{T1}^D to B_{T2}^D). The equilibrium price rises from P_1^T to P_2^T and then the equilibrium interest rate falls from I_1^T to I_2^T (on the basis of the negative relationship between price and interest rate).

The difference between the interest rate on Corporate Bond $\left(I_2^C\right)$ and the interest rate on Government Bond $\left(I_2^T\right)$ is called Spread (Sp) and it measures the Risk Premium (RP):

$$\mathrm{Sp} \equiv \mathrm{RP} = I_2^C - I_2^T \tag{17.5}$$

Therefore, if the interest rate of the Corporate Bond rises (the price falls) while the interest rate of the Government Bond falls (the price rises), the spread between the two interest rates rises and then the Risk Premium of Corporate Bond increases.

Generally, we can say that the higher the Risk of bond (RK_B), the higher the Interest Rate (I_B) and the lower the Price (P_B), and then the higher the Risk Premium (RP_B), so that:

$$RK_B \uparrow (\downarrow) \rightarrow I_B \uparrow (\downarrow) \leftrightarrow P_B \downarrow (\uparrow) \rightarrow RP_B \uparrow (\downarrow) \tag{17.6}$$

By considering separately the two variables of risk, default risk and liquidity, we can say that:

1. The higher the Default Risk of bond (DR_B), the higher the Interest Rate (I_B) and the lower the Price (P_B), and then the higher the Risk Premium (RP_B).
2. The higher the Liquidity of the bond (L_B), lower the Interest Rate (I_B) and higher the Price of the bond (P_B), and then lower the Risk Premium (RP_B).

We can summarize as follows:

$$\begin{matrix} DR_B \uparrow (\downarrow) \\ L_B \downarrow (\uparrow) \end{matrix} \rightarrow I_B \uparrow (\downarrow) \rightarrow P_B \downarrow (\uparrow) \rightarrow RP_B \uparrow (\downarrow) \tag{17.7}$$

17.2 Term Structure of Interest Rates

The Term Structure of Interest Rates refers to the relationship among interest rates on bonds characterized by the same Risk Premium and different Maturity.

The plot of the yield on bonds with same Risk Premium but different terms of Maturity, is called Yield Curve and it describes the Term Structure of Interest Rates for types of bonds.

The Yield Curves can be classified on the basis of their shape:

1. *Upward-sloping curve:* In this case, the Yield Curve slopes upward. Therefore, the long-term interest rates are above short-term interest rates. It can be considered the most common case.
2. *Downward-sloping curve* (or *Inverted Curve*): In this case, the Yield Curve slopes downward. Therefore, the long-term interest rates are below short-term interest rates. It is opposite to the common case, and the Yield Curve is defined Inverted.
3. *Flat curve*: In this case the Yield Curve is flat. Therefore, the long-term and short-term interest rates are the same.

Obviously, Yield Curve can take on different shapes at different times by passing from upward slope to downward slope or vice versa.

In this contest we consider briefly two main theories that try to explain the term structure of interest rates and then the relationships among interest rates on bonds of different maturities: (1) expectations theory, (2) the liquidity premium theory.

We can evaluate these theories on the basis of three main empirical facts (Mishkin, 2019):

1. *Empirical fact 1*: Interest rates on bonds of different maturities tend to move together over time.
2. *Empirical fact 2*: If short-term interest rates are low, yield curves are more likely to have an upward slope. Inversely, if the short-term interest rates are high, yield curves are more likely to have a downward slope and become inverted.
3. *Empirical fact 3*: Yield curves almost always slope upward.

17.2.1 Expectations Theory

The Expectations Theory of the term structure interest rates states that the interest rate on a long-term bond is equal to the average of the short-term interest rates that investors expect to occur over the life of the long-term bond. It implies that the Expectations Theory predicts that the interest rates on bonds of different maturities differ because we expected that the short-term interest rates will have different values at future date.

Assume that investors expect that the short-term interest rates will be 8% on average over the coming 5 years. Consequently, the interest rate on bonds with 5 years to maturity will be 8% too. Assume that the short-term interest rates are expected to increase in the after 5-year period so that the average short-term interest rate over the coming 10 years is 10%. In this case, the interest rate on 10 years bonds will be 10% and then it will be higher than the interest rate on 5-year bonds.

The basline assumption of the theory is that bonds with different maturities are perfect substitutes. It implies that investors that acquire bonds do not prefer bonds of one maturity over another. They will not hold any quantity of a bond if its expected return is less than that of another bond with a different maturity. If bonds with different maturities are perfect substitutes, then the expected returns on them must be equal.

We can formalize the Expectations Theory by saying that the interest rate on an *n*-period bonds (i_{nt}) is equal to:

$$i_{nt} = \frac{i_t + i^e_{t+1} + i^e_{t+2} + \ldots + i^e_{t+(n-1)}}{n} \tag{17.8}$$

where:

- n: is the bond maturity.
- i_{nt}: is the *n*-period interest rate.

- i_t: is today's (in time t) interest rate on one-period bond.
- i^e_{t+1}: is interest rate on a one-period bond expected for next period (in time $t + 1$).
- $i^e_{t+(n-1)}$: is the interest rate on a one-period bond expected for $n - 1$ period (in time $t + (n - 1)$).

Therefore, the n-period interest rate (i_{nt}) equals the average of the one-period interest rates expected to occur over the n-period life of the bond.

Assume that the 1-year interest rate over the next 5 years is expected to be 3%, 5%, 7%, 8%, 9%. Therefore, the interest rate on:

- Two-year bond is equal 4% $\left(\frac{3\%+5\%}{2}\right)$.
- Three-year bond is equal to 5% $\left(\frac{3\%+5\%+7\%}{3}\right)$.
- Four-year bond is equal to 5.75% $\left(\frac{3\%+5\%+7\%+8\%}{4}\right)$.
- Five-year bond is equal to 6.4% $\left(\frac{3\%+5\%+7\%+8\%+9\%}{5}\right)$.

The Expectations Theory is able to explain why the term structure of interest rates, as represented by Yield Curve, changes at different times. Indeed, when:

1. *Yield curve is upward-sloping*: The Expectation Theory states that short-term interest rates are expected to rise, on average, in the future. In this case, the long-term rate is currently higher than the short-term rate because the average of the future short-term rates is expected to be higher than the current short-term rate. This is the most common case.
2. *Yield curve is downward-sloping*: The Expectation Theory states that short-term interest rates are expected to fall, on average, in the future. In this case, the long-term rate is currently lower than the short-term rate because the average of the future short-term rates is expected to be lower than the current short-term rate. In this case, we say that the Yield Curve is Inverted.
3. *Yield curve is flat*: The Expectation Theory states that short-term interest rates are not expected to change, on average, in the future. In this case, the long-term rate is aligned with the short-term rate because the average of the future short-term rates is not expected to change than the current short-term rate.

The Expectations Theory is able to explain Empirical facts 1 and 2 but not the 3. Indeed:

1. If short-term interest rates increase today, generally they will tend to be higher in the future. The increase in short-term rates will raise investors' expectations of future higher short-term rates. Since the long-term rates are the average of expected future short-term rates, then a raise in short-term rates implies a raise of long-term rates. The consequence is that the short-term and long-term interest rates move together.
   Therefore, the theory explains the empirical fact 1.

2. If short-term interest rates are low, investors expect they will increase toward a normal level in the future. It implies that the average of future expected short-term interest rates is high relative to the current short-term interest rate. Since the long-term rates are the average of expected future short-term rates, then the long-term interest rates will be higher than current short-term interest rates. Consequently, the Yield Curve will have the common upward slope.
   Inversely, if short-term interest rates are high, investors expect them to come back down. Since the long-term rates are the average of expected future short-term rates, then they will be lower than current short-term rates. Consequently, the Yield Curve will slope downward and become inverted.
   Therefore, the theory explains the empirical fact 2.
3. The upward slope of the Yield Curve implies that short-term interest rates are expected to rise in the future. In this case, the long-term interest rates (that are the average of the future expected short-term interest rates) are expected will be higher than the current short-term interest rates. Unfortunately, short-term interest rates are just as likely to fall and to rise. Consequently, the Yield Curve can be upward slope as well as downward slope.
   Therefore, the theory does not explain empirical fact 3.

17.2.2 Liquidity Premium Theory

The Liquidity Premium Theory of the term structure interest rates states that the interest rate on a long-term bond will equal an average of short-term interest rates expected to occur over the life of the long-term bond plus a Liquidity Premium (also called Term Premium) based on supply and demand for bond.

The baseline assumption of the theory is that bonds of different maturities can be considered substitutes but however not perfect substitutes. Specifically, by saying that bonds of different maturities are:

1. *Substitutes*, it implies that interest rate on one bond does influence the interest rate on a bond with different maturity.
2. *But not perfect substitutes*, it implies that investors tend to prefer one bond maturity over another. Also, since investors are risk averse, they tend to prefer short-term bonds to long-term bonds because the first are characterized by less interest rate risk than the second. The main consequence is that investors must be offered a positive premium, the Liquidity Premium or Term Premium, to induce them to hold longer-term bonds.

Formally, the Liquidity Premium Theory is obtained by modifying the Expectations Theory by adding a positive value of Liquidity Premium, as follows:

$$i_{nt} = \frac{i_t + i^e_{t+1} + i^e_{t+2} + \ldots + i^e_{t+(n-1)}}{n} + l_{nt} \tag{17.9}$$

where l_{nt} is the Liquidity or Term Premium for the *n*-period bond at time *t*.

The equation states that the n-period interest rate (i_{nt}) is equal to the average of the one-period interest rates expected to realize over the n-period life of the bond $\left(\frac{i_t+i^e_{t+1}+i^e_{t+2}+\ldots+i^e_{t+(n-1)}}{n}\right)$ (that is the Expectations Theory), plus a Liquidity Premium or Term Premium (l_{nt}) for the n-period bond at time *t* that is always positive and it rises with the term to maturity (*n*) of the bond.

Consider the previous example. Assume that the one-year interest rate over the next 5 years is expected to be 3%, 5%, 7%, 8%, 9%. Assume that investors prefer to hold short-term bonds so that they require a Liquidity Premium for 1–5-years bonds that is equal to 0%, 0.20%, 0.40%, 0.60%, 0.80%, respectively. It implies that:

- Two-year bond, it is equal to $\frac{3\%+5\%}{2} + 0.20\% = 4.20\%$ (while in Expectations Theory it is equal to $\frac{3\%+5\%}{2} = 4\%$).
- Three-year bond, it is equal to $\frac{3\%+5\%+7\%}{3} + 0.4\% = 5.4\%$ (while in Expectations Theory it is equal to $\frac{3\%+5\%+7\%}{3} = 5\%$).
- Four-year bond, it is equal to $\frac{3\%+5\%+7\%+8\%}{4} + 0.6\% = 6.35\%$ (while in Expectations Theory it is equal to $\frac{3\%+5\%+7\%+8\%}{4} = 5.75\%$).
- Five-year bond, it is equal to $\frac{3\%+5\%+7\%+8\%+9\%}{5} + 0.8\% = 7.2\%$ (while in Expectations Theory it is equal to $\frac{3\%+5\%+7\%+8\%+9\%}{5} = 6.4\%$).

The Liquidity Premium Theory explains all the three empirical facts by solving also the third empirical fact respect to the Expectations Theory. Indeed, the Liquidity Premium Theory add to the Expectations Theory the term of Liquidity Premium, whose value is positive and tend to be increased to the increase in the maturity of bond. Specifically, with regard to the:

- Empirical fact 1, the Theory states that an increase in short-term interest rates indicates that short-term interest rates on average will be higher in the future. In implies that the long-term interest rates will rise by following the short-term interest rates.
- Empirical fact 2, the Theory states that in case of low current short-term interest rates, there are two effects to be considered: (1) investors generally expect that the short-term interest rates will rise toward a normal level, and then the future expected short-term interest rates on average will be higher than the current short-term interest rates. (2) the Liquidity Premium is always positive and it tends to increase to the increase in maturity. The result of these two effects is that the long-term interest rates will be higher than current short-term interest rates, and then the yield curve will slope upward.

  On the contrary, in case of high current short-term interest rates, investors will expect that the short-term interest rates fall down toward a normal level. It implies that the future short-term interest rates expected will be, on average, lower than the current short-term interest rates. Therefore, the long-term interest rates will be lower the current short-term interest rates despite the positive Liquidity Premium. The main consequence is that the yield curve will slope downward by generating ad Inverted Yield Curve.

- Empirical fact 3, the Theory states that the Liquidity Premium is positive term and its value increases to the increase of bond's maturity because investors prefer short-term bonds rather than long-term bond since they are risk averse. Therefore, the long-term interest rates will be above current short-term interest rates and the yield curve will typically slope upward.

Based on the Liquidity Premium Theory, we can use the slope of the Yield Curve to estimate the future movements of the short-term interest rates. Therefore, if the:

1. *Yield Curve rises steeply*: Short-term interest rates are expected to rise in the future.
2. *Yield Curve rises moderately*: Short-term interest rates are not expected to rise or fall in relevant way in the future.
3. *Yield Curve is flat:* Short-term interest rates are expected to fall moderately in the future.
4. *Yield Curve falls generating the Inverted Yield Curve*: Short-term interest rates are expected to fall in the future.

Part IV

Financial Policies and Capital Structure Choices

Firm Financing: Equity and Debt 18

18.1 Shareholders Equity

The company's ownership is represented by the stock certificate. Therefore, the company's owners hold stock certificates that indicate their shares of ownership and they are called *Shareholders' Equity* or *Stockholders' Equity*.

The equity book value is based on three main items: Share Capital, Treasury Shares, and Retained Earnings.

18.1.1 Share Capital

Company can issue Common Stock or Preferred Stock. In both cases, the company can issue a maximum number of shares.

Common Stock

The book value of common stocks is the total shareholders' equity reported on the balance sheet.

Common Stocks are characterized by a residual interest company's profits and assets in case of liquidation. These stocks are below that of all other creditors and preferred stockholders.

The Paid-in Capital, that is the amount invested in the firm by shareholders, can be reported as a single amount or in two pieces by distinguish between:

1. *Common Stock at Par*, that is the amount based on par or stated value of the outstanding common stocks issued. The par value of the common stocks is usually a nominal amount (such as 1 €) and it is different to the par value on a bond or Preferred Stock. It tells us nothing about the proceeds received by the firm upon issuance of the stock.

P. De Luca, *Corporate Finance*, Springer Texts in Business and Economics,
https://doi.org/10.1007/978-3-031-18300-3_18

2. *Additional Paid-In Capital* also called *Other Paid-In Capital*, that is the amount by which the proceeds from issuing Common Stock have exceeded the par value of the Common Stocks issued.

Preferred Stock

Preferred stocks have preference, or priority, over Common Stocks with regard to mainly the following matter:

(a) *Liquidation*: It is defined a minimum amount that must be paid to preferred stockholders before any payments to common stockholders in the event of liquidation, sale, or merger of the firm.
(b) *Seniority*: It is uncommon for investors in later rounds to require the seniority of investors in earlier rounds. If investors in a later round accept stocks with equal priority, they are said to be *pari passu*.
(c) *Participation right*: Convertible stocks without participation rights require that shareholders must choose between require their liquidation preference or converting their stocks to common stock. Differently, participation rights allow to shareholders to receive both the liquidation preference and any payment to common shareholders as they had converted their stocks.
(d) *Anti-Dilution Protection*: In case of down round with a new round of funding realized at a lower price than in the prior one, the anti-dilution protection lowers the price at which shareholders in earlier rounds can convert their stocks to common.
(e) *Board Membership*: Shareholders can negotiate the right to appoint one or more members to the firm's board of directors.

Note that all these provisions are negotiable. Commonly in each funding round, these terms are negotiated on the basis of the relative bargaining power of firm and investors.

Preferred Stocks are commonly issued with a face value, or par, per share, and they pay a stated dividend. In case of firm is liquidated, preferred stockholders are entitled to receive par value for their shares, if exist assets enough after liabilities payment.

Note that Preferred Stock may be cumulative or non-cumulative. If they are cumulative and if the firm is unable to pay the dividend, the unpaid dividends are accumulated and they must be paid before the firm pays dividends on Common Stock.

The Convertible Preferred Stock gives the possibility to be converted into common stock. It is useful for the young firm that issued Preferred Stock because even if the firm does not pay regular cash dividends, it gives the owner the option to convert it into Common Stock.

Therefore, the Share Capital can be summarized as in Table 18.1.

Commonly firm raises capital at different time by Funding Round. Each round is characterized by its own set of shares with special terms and provisions (usually each round is named by securities alphabetically, such as Series A preferred stock, Series

Table 18.1 Share Capital

Common Stock
Common Stock at Par
Additional Paid-In Capital
Preferred Stock
Share Capital

B preferred stock, etc.). It implies that at the end of each funding round, firm has several shares issued. In this case, we must distinguish between:

1. *Pre-money valuation*, that is the value of the prior shares outstanding at the price in the funding round.
2. *Post-money valuation*, that is the value of total shares, by including old and new shares, at the funding round price.

The difference between post-money valuation and pre-money valuation is the Amount Invested by new investors and the Percentage Ownership is the fractional ownership that they hold:

$$\text{Amounted Invested} = \text{Post Money Valuation} - \text{Pre Money Valuation}$$

$$\text{Percentage Ownership} = \frac{\text{Amount Invested}}{\text{Post Money Valuation}} \tag{18.1}$$

18.1.2 Treasury Share

The Treasury Share (also called Treasury Stock or Share buy-backs) refers to the outstanding stock that is repurchased by the issuing firm. The result of the repurchase shares issued is the reduction of the number of outstanding shares on the market.

The are several reasons to repurchase shares. Among them, the main concern:

1. To use shares in the future for several scope such as acquisition, bonus plans, exercise of warrants, and conversion of convertible bonds or preferred stocks.
2. To increase the earnings per share (EPS) and then the market price of stock.
3. To avoid takeover by avoiding that any outsider can accumulate shares.

By accounting point of view, the Treasury Share is reported with a negative sign in the Equity by reducing it. The total amount of Treasury Share is equal to the repurchase cost regardless of its pair value. The amount of Treasury Share is shown in equity until the shares repurchase are cancelled or reissued.

If shares are reissued, if the selling price is higher than the costs, the gain is reported in the Paid-In Capital account; on the contrary, if the selling price is lower than the costs, the loss reduces the Capital-in Paid, and if it is not enough the loss is debited to Retained Earnings. Note that any gain or loss on the share repurchase is not reported in the Income Statement, nor is it used for income tax computation.

18.1.3 Retained Earnings

The Retained Earnings refer to the earnings generated by the firm and reinvested in the firm for future needs of the firm rather than to use for generating dividends for shareholders. Because the earning remains in the company, it increases the amount of the equity book value and then the firm's own recourses to finance its future activities.

The total amount of the Retained Earnings is equal to the cumulative Net Income of the firm since its beginning and not used to generate dividends for shareholders.

Note that the Retained Earnings is the sum of all Reserves account generated by the firm for several use. In this sense, each Reserve account represents a segregated portion of Retained Earnings. Obviously, firm can show for a specific some of Reserves in a separate way. In this case its amount must be subtracted to the total amount of Retained Earnings. In extreme case, if the firm shows all Reserves in separate accounts, the Retained Earnings is equal to zero.

18.2 Stocks Issue

In this context, we do not consider the IPO (it will be analyzed in Chap. 30).

The new shares can be issued with option or without option.

18.2.1 New Shares Issue with Option

The use of call option is the commonly used in the most European countries in which the shareholders have the call option right in case of new issue of shares by the firm.

If firm issues new shares, the right of call option is in-the-money and it is listed in the market for few weeks. Three are the main advantages for the shareholders:

1. They can exercise the call option by writing the new shares issued.
2. They can sell their call option on market.
3. They can expire their call option without using them.

The possibility to sell the call options and their tradable on market, gives to the shareholders that do not want to be involved in the firm's equity increase, the opportunity to compensate in money their dilution in the capital of the company.

Commonly the new shares are offered at a price that is lower than both (i) the current market price and (ii) the theoretical price ex-right (TERP).

Consider the following example. Assume that the company Alfa decides to issue new shares. We can consider three stages:

Table 18.2 New shares issued by Alfa firm

	Pre-equity increase	Equity increase	Post-equity increase
Number of shares issued	12.000.000	5.333.333.333	5.345.333.333
Share price	10.5	0.15	10.5
Theoretical Price Ex-Right (TERP)			0.173
TERP discount			13.4%
Value of Call Option			10.33
Total Market Value	126.000.000	800.000.000	926.000.000

(a) *Before equity increases* (pre-equity increase): The firm Alfa has n.12 million of shares issued and trade on market at the share price of 10.5 € for a total market value of the company equal to 126 million euros.
(b) *Equity increases*: The company issues n.5.333,3 million of new shares at a price per share equal to of 0.15 € by raising new equity for 800 million euros.
(c) *After equity increases*: Under the assumption that there is not information able to change the market share price, the firm's market value is equal to 926 million euros (126 million euros of initial equity plus 800 million euros of new equity) and the total number of shares issued is equal to n.5.345,3 millions (equal to n.12 millions of old shares plus n.5.333,3 millions of new shares). The Theoretical Price Ex-Right (*TERP*) per share after the equity increase is equal to 0.173 € (the firm's market value equal to 926 million euros divided for number of n.5.345,3 million of shares issued on market). It implies that the shareholder of the firm has 1 share whose price is equal to 10.5 €, 1 share whose TERP is equal to 0.173 €, and 1 call option whose value is equal to 10,327 € (it is the difference between the total price of share cum right of call option, equal to 10.5 €, less the TERP equal to 0.173 €. We can summarize the example as in Table 18.2.

If we assume a tradeable call option on market at a market price aligned with its value, the:

(a) *Actual shareholders* can compensate the reduction of value of the share from current price to TERP by monetizing the call option.
(b) *New shareholders* can buy the call option on the market and then to underwrite the increase of equity by paying the shares at the TERP.

Note a timing for the execution of the equity increase plays a key role to avoid the risk that the TERP may be reduced since it become lower than the price of issue of shares during the period of underwrite of new shares. For this reason, the price of issue of new shares is commonly fixed at a discount of TERP with the aim to protect the firm from the risk of an incomplete capital increase. The mining of the discount is the timing need to complete the capital increase with option. In the example, the price of new shares, equal to 0.15 €, is lower than TERP, equal to 0.173 €, with a discount of 13.4%.

To protect firm from the risk that the TERP may reduce since it become lower than the price of issue of new shares during the period of their underwrite, the firm can ask a consortium of banks to guarantee the subscription of the new shares by paying a fee. Therefore, the consortium of banks undertakes to subscript the new shares if the shareholders do not it. In this case, the price of new shares will be defined between the firm and the lead bank of consortium. The price of new shares will be defined at discount on the TERP so that the distance between TERP and the price of new shares is large enough to guarantee to the banks the unlikely of their subscription of the company's new shares by earning the commission fee. Commonly, in this case, the discount on TERP is between 30% and 40% and it is strictly related to the dynamic of financial markets. Specifically, it reflects the market risk and its size is defined on the basis of the three main variables: (i) the stock market volatility in the period considered; (ii) the size of the capital increase with respect to the market capitalization of the company; (iii) the level of medium discount on TERP recently applied on market.

18.2.2 New Shares Issue Without Option

This is the most common way in the USA where the shareholders have not the right of call option if company decides to issue new shares. In this case, new shares are underwritten by investors through the method of book-building.

The price of new shares issued by the company is defined at the end of long process of price discovery that involves institutional investors that are potential buyer of these new shares. The end step of the price discovery process is called book-building in which the placement syndicate records the purchase requests received from institutional investors during the offer in an order book. Closed the offer period, the placement syndicate arranges all the orders collected on the basis of the price and size, and then proposes to the issuing company the price at which all the shares offered may be sold. The issuing company decides whether to accept the price or withdraw the offer of new shares from the market.

A particular procedure is called Accelerated Book-Building (ABB). It refers to the capital increases of small size compared to the market capitalization of the issuing company that are underwritten by the investors in few hours.

Note that it does not make difference between issue of new shares or shares outstanding. Indeed, it is used in the placement of outstanding shares owned by company shareholders.

In the ABB the price of new shares issued or the sell price of outstanding shares, it is commonly defined on the basis of the current market price of shares. Since the market price of shares is based on the trading volumes of daily shares and by considering that the volume of the ABB is higher than the daily traded volumes, the price of new shares is defined at discount with respect to the current market share price. Therefore, because with the in the ABB the company sell in few hours a volume of shares much higher than the daily traded volume, the consequence is that it offers a discount on share price to push investors to buy.

18.3 Private Debt

We can distinguish between private debt and public debt: the first is not publicly traded differently from the second one.

The Private Debt is the most commonly used by the companies, so that its market is large than the Public Debt market.

The most common are the following (Berk & DeMarzo, 2017).

18.3.1 Bank Loans

Bank loans are one of the primary sources of company's financing, especially for small business. It is initiated with a promissory note which is a written statement that indicates the amount of the loan, the date payment is due, and the interest rate.

Three are the main types of bank loans:

1. *Single, End-of-period Payment Loans*: It is the most straightforward type of bank loan. Firm pays interest on the loan and pay back the principal in one lump sum at the end of the loan. The interest rate can be: (i) *fixed*, in this case, a defined rate is defined by the banks at the time in which the loan is underwriter; (ii) *variable*, in this case, the rate varies with regard a specific benchmark rate. The common benchmark rate is the yield on one-year Treasury securities, the prime rate (which is the rate banks charge their most creditworthy customers), the London Inter-Bank Offered Rate (LIBOR) (which is the rate of interest at which banks borrow funds from each other in the London interbank market).
2. *Lines of Credit*: The bank agrees to lend a firm any amount up to a stated maximum. Therefore, the company can draw upon the line of credit whenever it chooses. Commonly, the line of credit can be: (i) *Uncommitted line of credit*: it is an informal agreement because it does not legally bind the bank to provide the funds. Therefore, if the financial condition of the firm remains good, the bank continues to advance the funds; (ii) *Committed line of credit*: it is a formal agreement because it is written and legally binding. The bank is obligated to provide funds to the firm regardless its financial condition if the firm is not in default situation and it respects any restrictions defined in the agreement. The firm pays a commission fee equal to a percentage of the unused portion of the line of credit plus interest on the amount that the firm borrowed; (iii) *Revolving line of credit*: it is a credit commitment of the bank for a time-period of time, typically 2–3 years, and to some limit which the firm can use as needed. A revolving line of credit that is characterized by non-defined maturity is called Evergreen Credit. Commonly banks renegotiate the terms of a line of credit on an annual basis. Banks usually renegotiate the terms of a line of credit on an annual basis.

3. *Bridge Loans*: It is used by the bank to "bridge the gap" until a firm can realize a long-term financing. The bridge loan is commonly used by the firm to finance its plant and equipment costs until it receives a long-term debt or increases its equity. Commonly bridge loans are quoted as discount loans with fixed interest rates. Often bridge loans are quoted as discount loans with fixed interest rates. With a discount loan, firm pays interest at the beginning of the loan period, and the bank deducts interest from the loan proceeds when the loan is made.
4. *Syndicated Bank Loans*: It is a particular case in which a single loan to the firm is funded by a group of banks rather than just a single bank. The lead bank of the syndicate, negotiates the terms of the bank loan. Commonly the syndicated loans are rated as investment grade. A particular form of syndicated is realized when is a single bank to grant the loan to the company to negotiate in a second moment with other small banks the breakdown of the loan that is commonly large size.

Note that firm must pay commission fee as well as interest on loan to the bank. Therefore, the commission fee on loan adds to the interest on loan by increasing the cost of loan. Specifically, the commission fee mainly refers:

1. *Commitment fee*: It is common associated with a committed line of credit. It affects interest rate that the company pays in a such way that we can really consider it an interest charge under another name.
2. *Loan origination fee*: It is a bank charges to cover credit checks and legal fees. The firm pays the fee at the start of the loan, and similar to a discount loan, it reduces the amount of usable proceeds that the firm receives.
3. *Compensating balance requirements*: The bank may require a compensating balance requirement in the loan agreement. in this case, the firm must hold a defined percentage of the loan recevied in an account at the bank. Therefore, it reduces the usable loan proceeds.

18.3.2 Secured Loans

Security Loans are loans collateralized by short-term assets, typically firm's accounts, trade receivables, and inventory. The most common are the following.

Accounts Receivable as Collateral

Firm can use Accounts Receivable, and more specifically Trade Receivables, as security for a loan by pledging or factoring. Specifically:

1. *Pledging of Accounts Receivable*: In this case, the lender (bank or financial company) reviews the invoices that represent the firm's credit sales, and it decides which credit accept as collateral for the loan. The lender lends to the firm a percentage of the value of the accepted invoices (commonly 70%–80%). If the firm's customer does not pay the bill, the lender can require to the firm for the money.

2. *Factoring of Accounts Receivable*: In this case the firm sells its trade receivables to the lender (the factor) that pays to the firm the amount due form its customers at the end of the firm's payment period. The firm's customers are usually instructed to make payments directly to the lender. Firm can borrow a percentage (commonly as much as 80%) of the face value of its receivables from the factor. In this case, the lender charges interest on the loan in addition to the commission fee. Both the interest rate and the commission fee of the factor vary depending on such issues as the size of the firm, the volume of its trade receivables, and the creditworthiness of its customers. A factoring arrangement can be: (i) *with recourse*: in this case, the lender can seek payment from the firm should the firm's customers do not pay their bills; (ii) *without recourse*: in this case, the lender bears the risk of bad-debt losses if the firm's customers do not pay their bills. The factor pays the firm the amount due regardless of whether the factor receives payment from the firm's customers.

Inventory as Collateral

Manufacturing firms can use the inventory as collateral for loan. Three are the main ways:

1. *Floating Lien* (also called *General Lien* or *Blanket Lien*): In this case the inventory is used as collateral for the loan to secure it. The risk for the lender (bank or financial company) is related the reduction of the collateral value dwindles as inventory is sold. The consequence is that the loan may become under-collateralized. To reduce this risk, the lender requires a high interest rate and will loan a low percentage of the inventory's value.
2. *Trust Receipt* (also called *Floor Planning*): In this case, a distinguishable inventory items are held in a trust as security for the loan. If these items are sold by reducing the value oif the distinguishable inventory, the firm gives the proceeds from their sale to the lender in repayment of the loan.
3. *Warehouse Arrangement*: In this case, the inventory used as collateral for the loan is stored in a warehouse that can be: (1) *Public Warehouse*, whose role is storing and tracking the inflow and outflow of the inventory. The lender extends a loan to the firm on the bases of the value of the inventory stored. If firm needs to sell inventory, it requires the permission by the lender and then it returns to the warehouse and retrieves it upon. Consequently, the lender has the tightest control over the inventory; (2) *Field Warehouse*, that is set up in a specific and separate location of the firm, but it is managed by a third party so that the inventory collateralizing the loan is kept apart from the firm's main inventory. In both cases, this is the least risky collateral arrangement from the standpoint of the lender.

18.3.3 Other Types of Loans

There are two other main types of loan are:

1. *Commercial Paper*: It is short term and unsecured debt used by large corporations that is usually a cheaper than a short-term bank loan. Similar to the long-term debt, commercial paper is rated by credit rating agencies. The interest on Commercial Paper is commonly paid by the firm by selling it at an initial discount. The average maturity of Commercial Paper is usually between 30 and 270 days. Commercial Paper is referred to as: (i) *direct paper*, when the firm sells the security directly to investors; (ii) *dealer paper*, when dealers sell the commercial paper to investors in exchange for a commission fee. This fee decreases the proceeds that the issuing firm receives, by increasing the effective cost of the paper.
2. *Private Placements*: It is a bond issued by the company and underwriter by a small group of investors and it is not trade on a public market. Because it is not tradeable on the market, it has characterized by less issued costs and it does not need to be conform to the same standards as public debt. Therefore, it can be tailored on the basis of specific characteristics and need of the company issued.

18.4 Corporate Bond

Corporate Bonds are securities issued by corporations. Similar to the stocks, the issue of a bond requires a public offering memorandum which contain all details of the offer to the investors.

The bond face value or principal amount is denominated in standard increments (for example 1.000 €). The face value of bond does not always correspond to the money effectively raised because of underwriting fees and the possibility that the bond might not sell for its face value when it is offered for sale initially to investors in order to be more attractive.

Most corporate bonds are coupon bonds and coupons are paid in one of 2 years. However, there are corporations that issued zero-coupon bonds. If a coupon bond is issued at a discount, it is called an Original Issue Discount (OID) bond.

Corporate Bonds may be issued with a wide range of maturities. Corporate Bonds with maturities higher than 30 years are called Sleeping Beauty Bonds.

Almost all bonds that are issued are *Registered Bonds*. The company issuer maintains a list of all holders of its bonds. Also, brokers keep informed the firm issuer of any changes in ownership.

There are four many types of Corporate Bonds (Berk & DeMarzo, 2017): (1) *Notes*; (2) *Debentures*; (3) *Mortgage Bonds*; (4) *Asset-backed bonds*. The main difference among them refer to the debt security:

1. Notes and Debentures are *Unsecured Debt*: In case of firm's bankruptcy the bondholders' right is related to only the firm's assets that are not already pledged

as collateral on other debts. The bond's seniority is relevant because more than one debenture might be outstanding, and then it is relevant the bondholder's priority in claiming assets in the event of firm's default. To reduce this risk, most debentures issues contain clauses restricting the company from issuing new debt with equal or higher priority than existing debt.
When the company proceeds to a subsequent debenture issue with a lower priority than its outstanding debt, the new debt is called *subordinated debt* (or *subordinated debentures*). In the event of the firm's default, the firm's asset not pledged as collateral for outstanding bonds cannot be used to pay off the holders of subordinated debentures until more senior debt has been paid off.
2. Mortgage Bonds and Asset-backed bonds are *Secured Debt*: in this case specific assets are pledged as collateral on which bondholders have a direct claim to in the event of firm's bankruptcy. While the Mortgage bonds are secured by real property, the Asset-backed bonds can be secured by any kind of asset.

International bonds can be classified into four main categories:

1. *Domestic bonds*: They are bonds issued by local company and traded in a local market, even if they can be purchased by foreigners.
2. *Foreign bonds*: They are bonds issued by a foreign company in a local market and are intended for local investors and then they are in the local currency.
3. *Eurobonds*: They are international bonds that are not denominated in the local currency of the country in which they are issued. There is not any connection between the physical location of the market in which bonds are traded and the location of the issuing company. These bonds can be denominated in any number of currencies that can be or not be connected to the location of the issuer. Also, their trading is not subject to any particular nation's rules.
4. *Global bonds*: They are bonds that combine characteristics of domestic, foreign, and Eurobonds. These bonds are offered for sale in several different markets simultaneously.

Note that a bond that makes its payment in a foreign currency implies the risk of holding that currency. Therefore, it is priced off the yields of similar bonds in that currency.

Commonly bond agreements contain *Bond Covenants*. They are restrictive clauses in a bond contract that limit the firm from behaviour that may reduce the firm's capability to repay its bonds to the detriment of bondholders. Indeed, managers may put actions able to maximize the benefit for shareholders at the expenses of debtholders. Commonly these covenants concern the dividends payment, the debt level increases, the level of Net Working Capital to avoid policies that lead to an excessive increase of Trade Payables. If the firm fails to live up to any covenant, the bond goes into default.

Note that the stronger the covenants are, the less likely the firm will default on the bond, and then the lower the interest rate required by investors who buy the bond. Therefore, by including more covenants, firm can reduce its cost of borrowing. There is a trade-off between flexibility and cost of borrowing: the higher the covenants, the lower the flexibility, the lower the cost of borrowing. If the reduction in costs of borrowing is higher than the cost due to the reduction of flexibility associated with covenants, then covenants are well accepted by the firm.

Note there is another way to repay bonds. It is called *Sinking Fund*. In this case, firm makes regular payments into a sinking fund administrated by a trustee over the life of the bond in order to repay it on the maturity date. In this way firm can reduce the amount of outstanding debt with a gradual effect on its cash-flows.

The trustee decides which bonds to repurchase. If the bond is trading below their face value, the company repurchases the bond on market; on the contrary, if a bond is trading above its face value, because the bonds are repurchased at par the decision is made by lottery.

If the sinking fund payments are not sufficient to retire the entire debt, the company must make a large payment on the maturity date, called Balloon Payment.

18.4.1 Callable Bonds

Even if the most common way to repay bond by the firm to bondholders is to pay coupon and principal at defined time, there are at least other two main ways (Berk & DeMarzo, 2017): (1) firm can repurchase a fraction of the outstanding bond on market or it can make a tender offer for the entire amount of bond; (2) firm can repay bond by exercising a *call provision*. It gives the firm the right (and not the obligation) to repurchase the outstanding bond at a predetermined price (*call price*) at a specific date or after (*call date*). The bond that contains the right (and not the obligation) of call provision is defined *Callable Bonds*.

Note that firm can always retire one of its bonds early by repurchasing the bond in the open market. Obviously, if the call provision offers a cheaper way to retire the bonds, the firm will not have precedencies to the purchasing the bonds in the open market and call the bonds instead.

In the perspective of the bondholders, when the call is exercised bondholder finds himself in the difficult position of looking for an alternative investment when market rates are lower than bond's coupon rate that bondholder is currently receiving. It is the risk bears by bondholder by holding a callable bond. This is the main reason for which the callable bond is relatively less attractive to the bondholder than the identical non-callable bond. Consequently, a callable bond will trade at a lower price (and therefore a higher yield) than an otherwise equivalent non-callable bond.

18.4.2 Convertible Bonds

Convertible Bonds give to bondholders the option right to convert bonds owned into a fixed number of shares of common stock at any time up to the maturity date for the bond and at ratio called the *Conversion Ratio* (Berk & DeMarzo, 2017).

Convertible Bond can be defined of as a regular bond plus a special type of call option called *warrant*. A warrant is a call option written by the company itself on new shares differently from a regular call option that it is written on existing stock. It implies that when a holder of a warrant exercises it by purchasing stock, the company delivers these stocks by issuing new stocks. For all other elements, a warrant is identical to a call option.

On the maturity date of the bond, the strike price of the embedded warrant in a convertible bond is equal to the face value of the bond divided by the conversion ratio, that is the *Conversion Price*.

It is common that companies issue convertible bonds that are callable. In this case, if the firm calls them, the bondholders can choose to convert rather than let the bonds be called. When the bonds are called, the bondholder faces the same decision as he would face on the maturity date of the bonds: to convert if the stock price exceeds the conversion price and let the bonds be called otherwise.

Note that by calling the bonds, the company forces bondholders to make their decision about to exercise the conversion option earlier than they would. The consequence is that by calling a convertible bond we transfer the remaining time value of the conversion option from bondholders to shareholders.

Capital Structure Choice and Company Value

19

19.1 Modigliani-Miller Propositions

One of the most relevant question in corporate finance concern the capital structure choices and then how a firm should choose the sect of securities to raise capital on market.

The main question concerns the effect of the Capital Structure choices on the Company's Value. The answer to this question is different if we assume perfect capital market or unperfect capital market. In the first case, the Modigliani-Miller Propositions give a clear answer to the question. They statues that under the condition of perfect capital market, the company's value is not affected by the capital structure choices. On the contrary, if we consider market's imperfection, there is a relationship between capital structure choices and the company's value and then we can hypnotize that there is an "optimal" capital structure able to maximize the company's value.

The Modigliani and Miller (MM) Propositions can be considered the starting point of the modern capital structure theory. Their theory was developed over time on the basis of five main works:

1. 1958: "*The Cost of Capital, Corporate Finance and the Theory of Investment*" is the first and the most popular paper. In this work, MM define the well-known Propositions I and II.
2. 1961: "*Dividend Policy, Growth, and the Valuation of Shares*" is the second paper, in which MM try to complete and refine the analysis of the Propositions.
3. 1963: "*Corporate Income Taxes and the Cost of Capital: a Correction*" is the third paper in which MM introduced the corporate taxes and then they redefined the Propositions I and II elaborated in the first paper.
4. 1977: "*Debt and Taxes*" by Miller only, is the fourth paper in which he introduces personal taxes in addition to corporate taxes.

P. De Luca, *Corporate Finance*, Springer Texts in Business and Economics,
https://doi.org/10.1007/978-3-031-18300-3_19

5. 1982: "*Debt, Dividend Policy, Taxes, Inflation and Market Valuation*" by Modigliani only, is the fifth paper in which he revises the version of the Propositions elaborated in 1963.

Among these works, the most relevant are the first and third papers (1958, 1963) in which are defined and revised the Propositions I and II. Indeed, they are the core of their theory.

The Propositions I and II (MM, 1958) are developed under the assumption of perfect capital market. Specifically, the main, stronger and more restrictive assumptions are the following:

1. All physical assets are owned by companies.
2. Company can be financed by equity and debt (note that in a first time, they assume that company can be financed by common stocks only).
   With regard to the Equity, they assume that assets provide stockholders with a flow of profit over time even if it is uncertain and it is not constant.
   With regard to Debt, they assume that all bonds yield a constant income per unit of time, and this income is regarded as certain by all traders regardless of the issuer. Consequently, all bonds are perfect substitutes up to a scale factor.
3. All stocks and bonds are traded in a perfect capital market. Consequently, they must all sell at the same price per dollar's worth of return, or equivalently, they must yield the same rate of return. This rate of return referred to as the rate of interest, or equivalently, as the capitalization rate for sure streams.
4. This stream of earning (and then the stream of earning on any share of common stock) represents a random variable subject to a probability distribution. Therefore: (i) the return of the share is defined equal to the average value over time of the stream of earnings accruing to a given share; (ii) the expected return of the share is defined equal to the expectation of this average value. Consequently, the uncertainty connects with the mean value over time of the stream of earning.
5. Investors agree on the expected return of any share despite the fact that they may have a different probability distribution of the return of any share.
6. Firms are grouped into "equivalent return classes": the return on the shares issued by any company in the same class is proportional to the return on the shares issued by any other company in the same class; the returns on shares as perfectly correlated between them. Therefore, the shares within the same class differ between them by only on one scale factor. The result is that if we consider the ratio between the return and the expected return, the probability distribution of the ratio is the same for all shares within the same class. It implies that there are only two relevant properties of a share: (i) their reference class; (ii) their expected return in the same class.
   This assumption is one of the most relevant of the model because it allows the creation of homogeneous classes of stock.
7. Shares are traded in the perfect capital markets under conditions of atomistic competition.

8. Investor can borrow at the same conditions as the company. Consequently, any investor can reproduce the same company leverage in its portfolio by borrowing on a personal level.

To derive the MM Propositions, it can be useful to follow strictly MM's argumentations sometimes by using the same words and symbols.

Based on the baseline assumptions, under equilibrium condition the price of every share in any given class must be proportional to its expected return. This "*proportionality factor*" for any class is the same for all companies within the class.

Therefore, for the ***jth company in the kth class*** the *Price per Share* (p_j) is the function of its Expected Return per Share (x_j) and the *Proportionality Factor* ($1/p_k$) that is specific for the ***kth class*** in which the *j*th company is included and it is the same for all companies grouped in the same *k*th class:

$$p_j = \frac{1}{p_k} x_j \tag{19.1}$$

The rate p_k can be interpreted as the price that an investor must pay for a dollar's worth of expected return in the *k*th class. Consequently, p_k *is the market rate of capitalization for the expected value of uncertain streams generated by the companies grouped in the kth class* and then it is the *expected rate of return of any share in the kth class*. Consequently, the rate p_k:

1. Is one for each of the *k*-classes.
2. Is a constant for all *j*-firms grouped in the *k*-class, so that it is the same for all companies grouped in the same *k*th class.

Since p_k is one for each *k*th class and it is constant for all *j*-firms grouped in the same *k*th class, the ratio between *Expected Return per Share* (x_j) and the *Price per Share* (p_j) is the same for all *j*-companies grouped in the same *k*th class:

$$p_k = \frac{x_j}{p_j} \tag{19.2}$$

Based on these concepts we will define the MM Propositions I and II as summarized in Table 19.1.

In the following part of the chapter, we will derive these equations and their meaning.

19.2 Proposition I

The Proposition I (1958) statues that in a perfect capital market the market value of any company is independent of its capital structure and is created by capitalizing its expected return at the rate (p_k) for a pure equity stream in the class. Equivalently,

Table 19.1 MM Propositions

	Paper 1958		Paper 1963 "A Correction"
	No Corporate Tax	*Corporate Tax*	*With Corporate Tax*
P.I	$\frac{X_j}{(E_j+D_j)} \equiv \frac{X_j}{W_j} = p_k$	$\frac{(X_j - rD_j)(1-t)+rD_j}{(E_j+D_j)} \equiv \frac{X_j^t}{W_j} = p_k^t$	$W_{\mathrm{L}} = \frac{(1-t)\overline{X}}{p_t} + \frac{tR}{r} = W_{\mathrm{U}} + tD_{\mathrm{L}}$
P. II	$i_j \equiv \frac{X_j - rD_j}{E_j} = p_k + (p_k - r)\frac{D_j}{E_j}$	$i_j \equiv \frac{\pi_j^t}{E_j} = p_k^t + (p_k^t - r)\frac{D_j}{E_j}$	$i_E = p_t + (1-t)(p_t - r)\frac{D}{W_{\mathrm{U}}}$

the average cost of capital to any company is completely independent of its capital structure and is equal to the capitalization rate (p_k) of a pure equity stream of its class.

In other word, the total value of the company is equal to the market value of the total cash-flows generated by its assets and it is not affected by the capital structure choices. Consequently, the total cash-flows paid out to all holders of firm's securities are equal to the total cash-flows generated by the firm with its assets. Then the total firm's assets and its securities must have been the same market value.

Consequently, the Proposition I statues that company Levered Value (W_L) is equal to its Unlevered Value (W_U). This value is the company Market Value (W_j):

$$W_j = W_L = W_U \tag{19.3}$$

By denoting with:

- X_j the expected return of the *j*-company's assets.
- D_j the market value of the debt of the *j*-company.
- E_j is the marker value of the equity of the *j*-company.
- W_j the company Market Value (W_j) that is equal to $E_j + D_j$.
- p_k is the expected rate of return of the stock of the *k*th class of the *j*-company referenced that is constant for all companies within the same *k*th class and it is one for each *k*th class.

We have:

$$W_j = \frac{X_j}{p_k} \rightarrow E_j + D_j = \frac{X_j}{p_k} \tag{19.4}$$

Since p_k is one for each *k*th class and it is constant for all *j*-firms grouped in the same *k*th class, the ratio between *Expected Return* (X_j) and the *company Market Value* (W_j) is the same for all *j*-companies grouped in the same *k*th class:

$$p_k = \frac{X_j}{W_j} = \frac{X_j}{(E_j + D_j)} \tag{19.5}$$

Therefore, p_k *is independent of the specific capital structure of the company and it is the "average cost of capital" of any j-company in the kth class.*

We can proof the Proposition I by considering two companies:

- Company 1: is financed by equity only, and then it is defined Unlevered Firm (F_U).
- Company 2: is financed by equity and debt, and then it is defined Levered Firm (F_L).

Assume that these two companies are grouped in the same *k*th class. Therefore, the Expected Returns of Company 1 (X_1) and Company 2 (X_2) are equal among them. We can define this same level of Expected Return with X so that:

$$X_1 = X_2 = X$$

Consider two different cases.

Case 1
Assume that the value of the Company 2 (W_2) is higher than the value of Company 1 (W_1). Therefore, the value of Levered Company (W_L) is higher than the value of the Unlevered Company (W_U):

$$W_2 > W_1 \rightarrow W_L > W_U$$

Assume that the investor holds shares (e_2) of Company 2 (Levered Company) equal a fraction (α) of the company's total equity (E_2):

$$e_2 = \alpha E_2 \rightarrow \alpha = \frac{e_2}{E_2}$$

Therefore, the return of the investor's portfolio (Y_2) is equal to a fraction (α) of the total return (X) of Company 2 less the interest on debt equal to rate return of debt (r) multiplied by the debt (D), as follows:

$$Y_2 = \alpha(X - rD)$$

Assume that the investor wants to sell his share of Company 2 ($e_2 = \alpha E_2$) and to buy share of the Company 1 $\left(e_1 = \alpha E_1 \rightarrow \alpha = \frac{e_1}{E_1}\right)$. To buy the shares of Company 1, the investor uses the proceeds from the sale of the shares of the Company 2 (αE_2) plus a personal debt subscripted by using new shares of Company 1 as a collateral, so that:

$$\frac{e_1}{E_1} = \frac{\alpha(E_2 + D_2)}{E_1}$$

where $\alpha(E_2 + D_2)$ is the amount invested to buy a fraction of the equity of Company 1.

In this contest, the *key role is played by the assumption that investor can to borrow at the same conditions as the company*. This assumption plays a key role in this contest because:

(a) It allows to the investor can reproduce the same company leverage in its portfolio by borrowing on a personal level.

(b) The Levered company cannot command a premium over an Unlevered company because investors can replace the company leverage into their portfolio directly by borrowing on a personal account.

By considering the interest payments on personal debt (αD), the return of the investor's portfolio (Y_1) is equal to:

$$Y_1 = \frac{\alpha(E_2 + D_2)}{E_1} X - r(\alpha D)$$

Company 1 is financed by equity only. Consequently, the Equity Value (E_1) is equal to the company value (W_1) that it is equal to the company Unlevered Value (W_U):

$$E_1 = W_1 = W_U$$

Company 2 is financed by debt and equity. Consequently, the sum of Equity Value (E_2) and Debt Value (D_2) is equal to the company value (W_2) that it is equal to the company Levered Value (W_L):

$$E_2 + D_2 = W_2 = W_L$$

Based on these equalities, we can rewrite the return of the investor's portfolio (Y_1) in the Company 1, as follows:

$$Y_1 = \frac{\alpha W_2}{W_1} X - r(\alpha D) = \alpha\left(\frac{W_2}{W_1} X - rD\right)$$

The case 1 assumes that the value of Company 2 (W_2) is higher than the value of Company 1 (W_1). It implies that the ratio between W_2 and W_1 is positive:

$$W_2 > W_1 \rightarrow \frac{W_2}{W_1} > 0$$

Consequently, the returns of Portfolio 1 (Y_1) is higher than the return of Portfolio 2 (Y_2):

$$Y_1 = \alpha\left(\frac{W_2}{W_1} X - rD\right) > Y_2 = \alpha(X - rD)$$

Therefore, since the value of Company 2 (Levered Value) is higher than the value of Company 1 (Unlevered Value), the return of Portfolio 1 (Y_1) is higher than the return of Portfolio 2 (Y_2):

$$W_2 > W_1 \rightarrow Y_1 > Y_2$$

We have a condition of arbitrage: the investor sells the shares of Company 2 (with depreciation of E_2 and therefore W_2) and buys shares of Company 1 (with increase of E_1 and therefore W_1). This movement continues until the value of the two firms is aligned in a new equilibrium condition:

$$W_2 = W_1 \rightarrow W_L = W_U$$

Case 2
Assume that the value of Company 1 (W_1) is higher than the value of Company 2 (W_2). Therefore, the value of Unlevered Company (W_U) is higher than the value of the Levered Company (W_L):

$$W_1 > W_2 \rightarrow W_U > W_L$$

Assume that the investor holds shares (e_1) of Company 1 (Unlevered Company) equal a fraction (α) of the company's total equity (E_1):

$$e_1 = \alpha E_1 \rightarrow \alpha = \frac{e_1}{E_1}$$

In this case, the return of the investor's portfolio (Y_1) is equal to:

$$Y_1 = \alpha X \rightarrow Y_1 = \frac{e_1}{E_1} X$$

Assume that the investor decides to exchange his portfolio with another one of the same value equal to e_1 and consisting of e_2 shares of Company 2 and of d bonds. In this context, e_2 and d are given by:

$$e_2 = \frac{E_2}{W_2} e_1; d = \frac{D_2}{W_2} e_1$$

Therefore, the investor's wealth (e_1) is invested in a portfolio consisting of shares of Company 2 (e_2) and bonds (d) proportionally, respectively, to the value of equity on the total levered value (E_2/W_2), and the value of debt on the total levered value (D_2/W_2) of Company 2.

In this contest, the *key role is played by the "undoing" the leverage*. The acquisition of a mixed portfolio of stock of a levered company (Company 2) and bonds in the proportions equal to the value of equity to total levered value (E_2/W_2) and the value of debt on total levered value (D_2/W_2) of the Levered Company (Company 2), respectively, can be regarded as an operation that "undoes" the leverage, providing access to an appropriate fraction of total return of the unlevered company. The undoing the leverage prevents the value of levered companies from being consistently less than those of unlevered companies or, in equivalent terms, it prevents the average cost of capital from being systematically higher for a levered company than for an unlevered company in the same class.

In this case:

(a) The return on shares (R_S) is a fraction (α) of the total return of the stockholders of Company 2. Remember that: (i) fraction α is equal to the shares hold by the investor (e_2) on the total value of the equity of Company 2 (E_2) so that: $\alpha = e_2/E_2$; (ii) the total return of the stockholders of Company 2 is equal to the total return of assets (X) less the rate return (r) on debt (D_2) of Company 2 so that: $X - rD_2$. Therefore:

$$R_S = \alpha(X - rD_2) = \frac{e_2}{E_2}(X - rD_2)$$

(b) The return from the bonds (R_B) is equal to the rate return (r) on bonds (d):

$$R_B = rd$$

Therefore, the the return of the investor's Portfolio 2 (Y_2) is equal to:

$$Y_2 = \frac{e_2}{E_2}(X - rD_2) + rd$$

Substituting e_2 and d with their expressions, we have

$$Y_2 = \frac{\frac{E_2}{W_2}e_1}{E_2}(X - rD_2) + r\frac{D_2}{W_2}e_1$$

And solving, it gets:

$$Y_2 = \frac{E_2}{W_2E_2}e_1(X - rD_2) + r\frac{D_2}{W_2}e_1 = \frac{e_1}{W_2}(X - rD_2) + r\frac{D_2}{W_2}e_1 - \frac{e_1}{W_2}X - \frac{e_1}{W_2}rD_2$$
$$+ r\frac{D_2}{W_2}e_1 = \frac{e_1}{W_2}X - \frac{1}{W_2}e_1rD_2 + \frac{1}{W_2}e_1rD_2 = \frac{e_1}{W_2}$$

Since $e_1 = \alpha E_1$, it gets:

$$Y_2 = \frac{e_1}{W_2} = \frac{\alpha E_1}{W_2}X = \alpha\frac{E_1}{W_2}X$$

Since Company 1 is unlevered, the Equity Value (E_1) is equal to the company value (W_1). Substituting, it gets:

$$Y_2 = \alpha\frac{W_1}{W_2}X$$

The case 2 assumes that the value of Company 1 (W_1) is higher than the value of Company 2 (W_2). It implies that the ratio between W_1 and W_2 is positive:

$$W_1 > W_2 \rightarrow \frac{W_1}{W_2} > 0$$

Consequently, the return of Portfolio 1 (Y_1) is higher than the return of Portfolio 2 (Y_2):

$$Y_2 = \alpha \frac{W_1}{W_2} X > Y_1 = \alpha X$$

Therefore, since the value of Company 1 (Levered Value) is higher than the value of Company 2 (Unlevered Value), the return of Portfolio 2 (Y_2) is higher than the return of Portfolio 1 (Y_1):

$$W_1 > W_2 \text{ and } Y_2 > Y_1$$

We have a condition of arbitrage: the investor sells the shares of Company 1 (with depreciation of E_1 and therefore W_1) and buy a mixed portfolio containing an appropriate fraction of the shares of Company 2 (with increase in E_2 and therefore W_2). This movement continues until the value of the two companies is aligned in new conditions of equilibrium, so that:

$$W_2 = W_1 \rightarrow W_\text{L} = W_\text{U}$$

19.3 Proposition II

The Proposition II (1958) can be defined as following: the expected yield of a stock share is equal to the appropriate capitalization rate (p_k) for a pure equity stream in the class, plus a premium related to financial risk equal to the debt-to-equity ratio times the spread between p_k and r.

Therefore, the Expected Rate of Return of the *j*th company's stock (i_j) in the *k*th class is equal to the Expected Rate of Return of pure equity (p_k) for the *k*th class in which the *j*th company is grouped (it is constant for any company in the *k*th class and it is one for each *k*th class) plus the difference between p_k and the Rate of Return in Debt (r_D) multiplied by the ratio between the market value of Debt (D_j) and Equity (E_j) of the *j*th company. Formally:

$$i_j = p_k + (p_k - r_D)\frac{D_j}{E_j} \tag{19.6}$$

The Equation statues that for all companies in the same kth class, the relation between the Return on stock (i_j) and capital structure (D_j/E_j), will approximate a straight line with slope equal to ($p_k - r_D$) and point of interception equal to p_k.

The market price of any stock is equal to the capitalization of its expected return at the variable rate i_j. Then, the capital structure does not affect the cost of capital because the return on equity is linear function of the relationship between debt and equity.

The expected Rate of Return of the stock of the jth company (i_j) is equal to the ratio by the expected return on assets of the company (X_j) less the Rate of Return on Debt (r_D) multiplied by the Debt amount (D_j) in the capital structure, and the Equity Value of the company (E_j), as follows:

$$i_j = \frac{X_j - r_D D_j}{E_j} \tag{19.7}$$

It is the yield on equity capital.

The Proposition II is a direct consequence of Proposition I. Indeed, we can derive the Proposition II from Proposition I as follow. Remember that from Proposition I, we have:

$$p_k = \frac{X_j}{W_j} = \frac{X_j}{(E_j + D_j)}$$

By solving for the *Expected Return* (X_j), we have:

$$X_j = p_k(E_j + D_j)$$

and substituting:

$$i_j = \frac{X_j - r_D D_j}{E_j} = \frac{p_k(E_j + D_j) - r_D D_j}{E_j} = \frac{p_k E_j + p_k D_j - r_D D_j}{E_j}$$
$$= \frac{p_k E_j + D_j(p_k - r_D)}{E_j} = \frac{p_k E_j}{E_j} + \frac{D_j(p_k - r_D)}{E_j}$$

and then:

$$i_j = p_k + (p_k - r)\frac{D_j}{E_j}$$

that is the Proposition II.

Therefore, the Propositions I and II statues that the company value is function of its business operating activities only, and the capital structure defines the way in which this value is distributed between the investors in equity and debt. Consequently, the capital structure choices are irrelevant both with regard to the company value and its capital cost.

Note that the conclusion of Propositions I and II comply with the *law of preservation of investment value* (Williams, 1938): under the assumption of no corporate taxes, the company value is function of operating cash-flow only. The way by which these cash-flows are distributed among investors in equity and debt it is irrelevant in the perspective of company value. Then, the company's assets cannot be influenced by the composition of capital structure.

Consequently, if the value of the assets is independent of the capital structure choices, the discount rate of the operating cash-flows cannot be influenced by the capital structure choices.

19.4 Proposition I with Corporate Taxes

In the paper of 1958 MM introduced the Corporate Taxes even if their conclusions were revised and modified in the paper of 1963.

In the first version (1958), MM stated that in condition of equilibrium the market value of companies in each class must be proportional to their expected return net of corporate taxes.

Therefore, the Expected Net Income of the *j*th company $\left(X_j^t\right)$ (that is equal to income less corporate taxes) can be defined as follows:

$$X_j^t = (X_j - r_D D_j)(1 - t) + r_D D_j$$

where:

- X_j is the expected income before taxes.
- r_D the rate return of debt.
- D_j the market value of the debt of the *j*-company.
- t the average rate of income corporate tax.

We distinguish two parts of equation:

- The first part, equal to $(X_j - r_D D_j)(1 - t)$ is the Expected Net Income of the shareholders.
- The second part, equal to $r_D D_j$, is the Expected Return of Bondholders.

We can introduce the Expected Net Income of the *j*th company $\left(X_j^t\right)$ in the Propositions I and II.

Remember that the Proposition I statues that:

$$p_k = \frac{X_j}{W_j} = \frac{X_j}{(E_j + D_j)}$$

Substituting, we can rewrite the Proposition I with corporate taxes (1958) as follows:

$$p_k^t = \frac{X_j^t}{W_j} = \frac{(X_j - r_D D_j)(1-t) + r_D D_j}{(E_j + D_j)}$$

where p_k^t is the Expected Rate of Net Return of the *k*th class in which the *j*th company is grouped. It is constant for any companies in the *k*th class, and one for each *k*th class.

Remember that the Proposition II statutes that:

$$i_j = \frac{X_j - r_D D_j}{E_j} = p_k + (p_k - r_D)\frac{D_j}{E_j}$$

Substituting, we can rewrite the Proposition II with corporate taxes (1958) as follows:

$$i_j = \frac{X_j - r_D D_j}{E_j} = p_k + (p_k - r_D)\frac{D_j}{E_j}$$

The Proposition II can be modified as follows:

$$i_j^t = \frac{X_j^t - r_D D_j}{E_j} = \frac{[(X_j - r_D D_j)(1-t) + r_D D_j] - r_D D_j}{E_j} = \frac{(X_j - r_D D_j)(1-t)}{E_j}$$

and then:

$$i_j^t = \frac{(X_j - r_D D_j)(1-t)}{E_j} = p_k^t + (p_k^t - r_D)\frac{D_j}{E_j}$$

where i_j^t is the *yield on equity capital*, and p_k^t is the capitalization rate for net income (income net of corporate taxes) for the *j*th company in the *k*th class. This definition is equivalent to the expected rate of net return of the *k*th class in which is included the *j*-company.

In the second version (1963) MM proposed "*a correction*" by modifying the conclusions which were reached in the original paper (1958). While in the first version (1958), the introduction of the corporate taxes do not change the form and structure of both Proposition I and II, in the second version (1968) the Propositions I and II are modified in their structure.

The ***Proposition I with Corporate Taxes*** *(1963) can be defined as following: the value of the levered company is equal to sum of the unlevered company plus the value of the tax shields due to the interest on debt deducibility.*

Therefore, the leverage plays a key role in the company value. Specifically, the Proposition I with corporate taxes statues that the arbitrage makes values within any class a function not only of expected net returns (after tax returns), but also of the tax rate and degree of leverage. It implies that the tax advantages of debt financing are relevant, and they generate a quantitative difference between levered and unlevered value of the company.

Denote with:

- X the random variable of the long-run average EBIT generated by current assets of the jth company grouped in the kth risk class.
- $\overline{X}$ the expected value of the variable X.
- Z the random variable of the kth class so that it is the same for all companies grouped in the kth class. Therefore, the variable Z is a constant, and it is a drawing from a distribution, say $f_k(Z)$.

Therefore, in the kth class, the variable X can be defined as follows:

$$X = \overline{X}Z$$

and then:

$$Z = \frac{X}{\overline{X}} \leftrightarrow f_k(Z)$$

The random variable of the Net Return (X^t) (after-tax return), can be expressed as function of EBIT (X), the amount of interest on debt (R), the marginal corporate income tax rate (assumed equal to the average) (t) as follows:

$$X^t = (X - R)(1 - t) + R = (1 - t)X + tR$$

Substituting X with its random variable (that is equal for all companies grouped in the same kth class), we have:

$$X^t = (1 - t)\overline{X}Z + tR$$

Since the expected Net Return $\left(\overline{X}^t\right)$ is equal to:

$$\overline{X}^t = (1 - t)\overline{X} + tR$$

it gets:

$$(1 - t)\overline{X} = \overline{X}^t - tR$$

Substituting, we have:

$$X^t = \left(\overline{X}^t - tR\right)Z + tR$$

We can rewrite this equation as follows:

$$X^t = \overline{X}^t \left(1 - \frac{tR}{\overline{X}^t}\right) Z + tR$$

The equation statues that if the tax rate is different from zero, the shape of the distribution of Net Return (X^t) depends on:

(a) The scale of the expected Net Income $\left(\overline{X}^t\right)$ on distribution (*Z*).
(b) The tax rate (*t*).
(c) The degree of leverage according to interest on debt as measured by the ratio between the interests paid (*R*) and the expected Net Income $\left(\overline{X}^t\right)$.

Consequently, in the investors' perspective, the long-run average stream of Net Returns (after-tax returns) is equal to the sum of components:

(a) An uncertain stream equal to $(1-t)\overline{X}Z$: that is all of the expected net returns.
(b) A sure stream equal to tR: that is the extra net return (extra after tax return) due to the tax advantages of debt as function of the deducibility of interest payments on debt. It is usually defined as the tax savings on interest payments.

The first component is the company Unlevered Value (W_U):

$$W_U = \frac{(1-t)\overline{X}}{p_t} \leftrightarrow p_t = \frac{(1-t)\overline{X}}{W_U}$$

where p_t is the rate at which the market capitalizes the expected Net Returns of an unlevered company of size $\overline{X}$ within *k*th class.

The second component is the Value of Tax Shields due to the tax advantages of debt function of deducibility of interest payments on debt.

If we assume that the rate of interest is a constant independent of the debt amount so that:

$$r = \frac{R}{D} \rightarrow D = \frac{R}{r} \rightarrow R = Dr$$

then, the Value of Tax Savings (W_{TS}) is equal to:

$$W_{TS} = \frac{tR}{r} \leftrightarrow r = \frac{tR}{W_{TS}}$$

where *r* is the rate at which the market capitalizes the sure streams generated by tax savings on interest payments.

Therefore, the company Levered Value of size $\overline{X}$ with a permanent level of debt (D_L) in the capital structure, is equal to:

$$W_{\mathrm{L}} = \frac{(1-t)\overline{X}}{p_t} + \frac{tR}{r} = W_{\mathrm{U}} + tD_{\mathrm{L}}$$

Note that $r < p_t$ because the extra after tax earnings (tR) is a sure income while the expected after tax earnings $\left((1-t)\overline{X}\right)$ is uncertain.

Therefore, the company Levered Value (W_{L}) is equal to its Unlevered Value (W_{U}) plus the Value of Tax Savings (W_{TS}) as follows:

$$W_{\mathrm{L}} = W_{\mathrm{U}} + W_{\mathrm{TS}} \tag{19.8}$$

that is the Proposition I with Corporate Taxes.

19.5 Proposition II with Corporate Taxes

The Proposition II with Corporate Taxes (1963) can be defined as following: the cost of equity is positively related to the degree of leverage.

We can derive the Proposition II from the Proposition I as follows.

Remember that:

- $(1-t)\overline{X} = \overline{X}^t - tR$
- $r = \frac{R}{D} \rightarrow \begin{matrix} D = \frac{R}{r} \\ R = Dr \end{matrix}$
- $W_{\mathrm{L}} = \frac{(1-t)\overline{X}}{p_t} + \frac{tR}{r}$

And by substituting it gets:

$$W_{\mathrm{L}} = \frac{(1-t)\overline{X}}{p_t} + \frac{tR}{r} = \frac{\overline{X}^t - tR}{p_t} + tD = \frac{\overline{X}^t - tDr}{p_t} + tD = \frac{\overline{X}^t}{p_t} - \frac{tDr}{p_t} + tD = \frac{\overline{X}^t}{p_t} + tD\left(1 - \frac{r}{p_t}\right) = \frac{\overline{X}^t}{p_t} + tD\left(\frac{p_t - r}{p_t}\right)$$

And then:

$$W_{\mathrm{L}} = \frac{\overline{X}^t}{p_t} + tD\left(\frac{p_t - r}{p_t}\right) \tag{19.9}$$

Solving the Eq. for $\left(\overline{X}^t / W_{\mathrm{L}}\right)$, we have:

$$\frac{\overline{X}^t}{p_t} = W_L - tD\left(\frac{p_t - r}{p_t}\right) \rightarrow \overline{X}^t = W_L p_t - p_t tD\left(\frac{p_t - r}{p_t}\right) \rightarrow \frac{\overline{X}^t}{W_L} = \frac{W_L}{W_L} p_t - \frac{tD(p_t - r)}{W_L}$$

and then:

$$\frac{\overline{X}^t}{W_L} = p_t - t(p_t - r)\frac{D}{W_L} \tag{19.10}$$

The equation states that the after-tax yield is affected by leverage.

Note that we can compute the after-tax yield on equity. It is equal to the ratio between net profit (profit after taxes) and the value of the shares.

Subtracting D from both side of the equation of W_L as follows:

$$W_L = \frac{\overline{X}^t}{p_t} + tD\left(\frac{p_t - r}{p_t}\right) \rightarrow W_L - D = \frac{\overline{X}^t}{p_t} + tD\left(\frac{p_t - r}{p_t}\right) - D$$

Defines $\overline{X}^t$ into its two components of the expected net profit after taxes (π_t) and the interest payments on debt ($R = rD$), so that $\overline{X}^t = \pi_t + rD$. Substituting, we have:

$$W_L - D = \frac{\pi_t + rD}{p_t} + tD\left(\frac{p_t - r}{p_t}\right) - D$$

and solving, we have:

$$W_L - D = \frac{\pi_t}{p_t} + \frac{rD}{p_t} + tD - \frac{tDr}{p_t} - D; W_L - D = \frac{\pi_t}{p_t} + \frac{rD}{p_t}(1 - t) - D(1 - t); W_L - D = \frac{\pi_t}{p_t} + (1 - t)\left(\frac{rD}{p_t} - D\right); W_L - D = \frac{\pi_t}{p_t} - (1 - t)\left(D - \frac{rD}{p_t}\right); W_L - D = \frac{\pi_t}{p_t} - (1 - t)\left(D\left(1 - \frac{r}{p_t}\right)\right)$$

and then:

$$W_L - D = \frac{\pi_t}{p_t} - (1 - t)D\left(\frac{p_t - r}{p_t}\right) \tag{19.11}$$

Because the company levered value (W_L) less debt (D) is equal to the company unlevered value (W_U), so that $W_U = W_L - D$, we have:

$$W_U = \frac{\pi_t}{p_t} - (1-t)D\left(\frac{p_t - r}{p_t}\right)$$

and by solving for π_t, and dividing both terms by W_U, we have:

$$\pi_t = W_U p_t + p_t(1-t)D\left(\frac{p_t - r}{p_t}\right)$$

$$\frac{\pi_t}{W_U} = p_t + (1-t)(p_t - r)\frac{D}{W_U}$$

Because the after-tax yield on equity capital (i_E) is equal to the ratio between expected net profit after taxes (π_t) and the value of shares and therefore the unlevered value of the company (W_U), so that $i_E = \frac{\pi_t}{W_U}$, the equation can be rewritten as follows:

$$i_E = p_t + (1-t)(p_t - r)\frac{D}{W_U} \tag{19.12}$$

The equation statues an increase in the after-tax yield on equity (i_E) as leverage increases which is smaller than the original version of Proposition II by a factor of $(1-t)$. But again, the linear increasing relation of this equation is still fundamentally different from the original in which the cost of equity is completely independent from the leverage. In this case, the cost of equity dependents from leverage.

19.6 Corporate and Personal Taxes

At a later stage, Miller (1977) introduced personal taxes in addition to corporate tax.

By introducing personal taxes, the value of tax savings can be rewritten as follows:

$$W_{TS} = D\left[1 - \frac{(1-t_c)(1-t_e)}{(1-t_d)}\right] \tag{19.13}$$

where: D is the debt level in the capital structure; t_c is the corporate tax rate (in average); t_e is the personal tax rate on equity investor; t_d is the personal tax rate on interest of debt.

We have said that the company levered value (W_L) is equal to the company unlevered value (W_U) plus the value of tax savings (W_{TS}) so that $W_L = W_U + W_{TS}$. Substituting the new definition of the W_{TS}, we can rewritten the equation as follows:

$$W_L = W_U + D\left[1 - \frac{(1-t_c)(1-t_e)}{(1-t_d)}\right] \tag{19.14}$$

In order to demonstrate this equation, assume that company is financed by equity and debt (Ross et al. 1977).

The stockholders' return (r_E) and bondholders' return (r_D) can be defined, respectively, as follows:

$$r_E = (\mathrm{EBIT} - \mathrm{DK_D})(1 - t_c)(1 - t_e)$$

$$r_D = K_D D(1 - t_d)$$

The investor's total return (r_I) is equal to the return on share and return on debt as follows:

$$r_I = r_E + r_D = (\mathrm{EBIT} - \mathrm{DK_D})(1 - t_c)(1 - t_e) + \mathrm{K_D D}(1 - t_d)$$

and rearranging we have:

$$r_I = \mathrm{EBIT}(1 - t_c)(1 - t_e) + \mathrm{DK_D}(1 - t_d)\left[1 - \frac{(1 - t_c)(1 - t_e)}{(1 - t_d)}\right]$$

The first part of equation is the unlevered value of the company (W_U), and then:

$$W_U = \mathrm{EBIT}(1 - t_c)(1 - t_e)$$

The second part of equation, is the value debt D, so that we can write:

$$D \equiv \mathrm{DK_D}(1 - t_d)$$

Substituting, we have the value of levered company as follows:

$$W_L = W_L + D\left[1 - \frac{(1 - t_c)(1 - t_e)}{(1 - t_d)}\right]$$

It is relevant to note that if we assume the same tax rate on debt and equity, so that ($t_d = t_e$), or if we assume that there are equal to zero ($t_d = t_e = 0$), the equation becomes:

$$W_L = W_L + Dt_c$$

that is the Proposition II with corporate taxes only.

If we assume that the personal tax rate is different from zero and the tax rate on equity is different from the tax rate on debt, we have two cases:

(a) $t_e < t_d$: personal taxes on levered company are higher than the unlevered company. Consequently, tax savings is lower than tax savings due to corporate taxes only. Therefore, the lower corporate taxes for the unlevered company are offset by an increase in personal taxes on investors.
(b) $t_e > t_d$: tax savings on unlevered company are higher than the levered company. The tax saving on unlevered company is the higher than tax savings due to

corporate taxes only. Therefore, the levered value of the company is increased by savings due to both corporate and personal taxes.

Also, if:

(a) $(1 - t_d) = (1 - t_c)(1 - t_e)$: there is no tax savings. The tax savings due to corporate taxes is equal to an increase in personal taxes. Consequently, the value of a levered company is equal to the value of an unlevered company in accordance with Proposition I.
(b) $(1 - t_d) < (1 - t_c)(1 - t_e)$: the levered value of the company is lower than its unlevered value ($W_L < W_U$).
(c) $(1 - t_d) > (1 - t_c)(1 - t_e)$: the levered value of the company is higher than its unlevered value ($W_L > W_U$).

19.7 Optimal Capital Structure Theories

MM Propositions I and II of MM are based on perfect capital markets an related very restrictive assumptions that are not feasible in a real world.

The introduction of many variables in the model leads to postulate the relevance of capital structure choices on company value and consequently the existence of the "optimal" capital structure.

Several theories have been developed over time. Among these, there are three main ones:

1. Trade-off theory by including the agency cost of equity and debt.
2. Packing order theory.
3. Market time theory.

While the first and the second define the optimal capital structure on the basis of the balance between benefits and costs related to the debt, the third and the fourth are based on the market conditions.

19.7.1 Trade-Off Theory

The *Trade-off Theory* (Kraus and Litzenberger, 1973) states the optimal capital structure on the basis of the tax advantages and the costs of financial distress related to the debt.

Consequently, the capital structure is a result of the trade-off between benefits and costs related to the debt.

In the framework of trade-off we can consider also the benefits and costs of debt related to the agency theory.

The *agency theory* (Jensen, 1986; Jensen and Meckling, 1976) focuses attention on the debt effects on the relationship between: (i) stockholders and management, and (ii) stockholders and bondholders. In this sense, the capital structure choices have effects on agency cost of equity and debt. Generally, we can say that too much equity can lead to conflicts between managers and stockholders, as well as too much debt can lead to conflicts between stockholders and bondholders.

Debt has a positive effect on *agency cost of equity*. It reduces conflicts between stockholders and management due to the difference in their utility functions, with consequent different behaviour, targets, information (it is reasoning to assume that managers have more information and better quality than stockholders with the creation of asymmetric information) and operating decisions. While the first wants to maximize equity value, the second wants to maximize the firm value because it increases their control of resources, power and compensation.

Usually conflicts are strong if company is able to generate high free cash-flows. In this case, managers can choose to invest in negative -NPV projects or able to increase their visibility and interest by destroying value for the shareholders. Debt is a discipline tool for managers. It increases the company's default risk according to the cash-out related debt obligations, requiring to maximization of efficiency, therefore increasing equity value. The positive effects of debt are clearer for manager-owner who have their personal wealth invested in the company because bankruptcy has a greater impact on their interests.

The existence and the relevance of agency costs of equity are strictly depending of several variables. Among them the most are related to the culture and values of the firm's managers; the way by which firm's managers can exercise their preferences without considering the value maximization in decision making; the monitoring tools and bonding activities; the tools to measure the manager's performance over time; the incentives tools; the existence and implementation of specific behavioural rules or policies; the costs of managers' replacement.

Debt has a negative effect on *agency costs of debt* because it can increase conflicts between stakeholders and bondholders. Equity offers holders residual claims on company cash-flow, while debt offers holders a fixed claim over a borrowing company's cash-flow. The debt increase can push the stakeholders' moral hazard and asset-substitutions are possible.

If the company is financed by equity and debt, bondholders are damaged in the presence of high-risk investments because they support the risk without a premium. Indeed, if the project fails, bondholders bear most of the consequences mainly due to the stockholders limited liability; otherwise, if the project is successful, the bondholders will be paid a fixed amount and stockholders capture most of the gains.

The main problem is that bondholders do not know what type of projects will be chosen by the company (safe projects, risky projects, average safe-risky projects) and then they are not able to align risk and return in terms of debt interest rate in the presence of asset substitutions effects. Indeed, the managers can always choose a risky project to maximize equity value after raising funds from bondholders shifting from lower-risk to higher-risk investments without alignment of debt interest rate to major risk.

For this reason, bondholders try to anticipate the shareholders' opportunistic behaviour by lending less debt or increasing its cost.

19.7.2 Pecking Order Theory

The *pecking order theory* (Baker and Wurgler, 2002; Fama and French, 1998, 2002; Shyam-Sunder and Myers, 1999; Myers, 1984; Myers and Majluf, 1984) is based on the adverse selection and statues that the capital structure is the result of a *source hierarchy*. Therefore, it is not the result of a trade-off between benefits and costs of debt and equity.

The company structure choice of the company is based on source hierarchy:

1. The company initially prefers sources of due to self-finance adapting the dividend policy to the investment opportunities.
2. If external sources are required, the company prefers to resort debt and hybrid instruments.
3. At the end company requires new equity.

Consequently, the internal sources of finance (self-finance) are preferred to external ones, where debt is preferred to equity.

Note that there are two kinds of equity: internal, regarding self-financing, that is at the top of the packing order; external, regarding the new shares issue, that is at the bottom of the packing order.

19.7.3 Market Time Theory

The *market time theory* (Baker and Wurgler, 2002) is based on capital market's imperfections and asymmetric information. It statues that the company's capital structure choices are strictly related to the capital market conditions and it evolves over time as a cumulative outcome of the pasts attempts to time the equity market.

The theory statues that market timing has large and persistent effects on capital structure of the company because the existing capital structure of the company is a cumulative result of the company's past experience, which it has attempted time to time under equity market.

The theory states that there is no optimal capital structure where capital structure is an outcome of various decisions, which have been made over time. Therefore, the market time theory, as well as packing order theory, is structured more on the manager reactions to the environment rather than to a trade-off of specific determinants.

Based on this theory, firm always looks at current conditions in both debt and equity markets and if it needs financing it tends to use whichever market currently looks more favourable. Then, the company tends to exploit temporary fluctuations in the cost of equity related to the cost of other capital forms.

Firms tend to issue equity (instead of debt) when:

1. Market value is high (relative to book value and past market values) and repurchase equity when market value is low. Indeed, the company issues share at

higher prices and repurchases at a lower price. It implies that the low leverage companies are the ones that raised funds when their market valuations were high, as measured by the market-to-book ratio, while high leverage companies are the ones that raised funds when their market valuations were low.
2. The cost of equity is relatively low and repurchase equity when the cost is relatively high.
3. Investors are too enthusiastic about earnings perspectives.
4. .anagers consider the market timing is very relevant in the capital structure choices.

There are two versions of equity market timing that lead to similar capital structure dynamics:

1. The first, is based on the rational managers and investors and adverse selection costs. Based on it, the company tends to announce equity issue in presence of information which may reduce information asymmetry. Consequently, the new share are issued in periods in which the announcement effects tend to be smaller.
2. The second is based on irrational investors and managers and time-varying mispricing or perceptions of mispricing. Managers issue equity when they believe its cost is irrationally low and repurchase equity when they believe its cost is irrationally high.

Payout Policy

20

20.1 Payout Policy: Dividend and Buyback

Firm must decide how to use the free cash-flows generated. The general rules statue that if firm has new positive-NPV (Net Present Value) investment opportunities, it should reinvest these free cash-flows by increasing the firm's enterprise value.

Commonly, firms focused on their growth choice to reinvest the entire amount of free cash-flows generated. On the contrary, firms that are consolidated, mature and profitable tend to distribute a part of their free cash-flows to shareholders.

If firm is able to generate free cash-flows and then excess cash to the firm's need, it can decide to:

1. To *retain* the free cash-flows with the aim to invest in new positive-NPV opportunities or to increase cash reserves.
2. To *payout* the free cash-flows to shareholders by paying dividends or repurchasing shares called buyback.

In Fig. 20.1 are summarized the firm's choices.

This choice is called *payout policy* and it is even more relevant because while the retain of cash-flows and then their reinvestment is aimed to increase the firm's enterprise value, the payout is aimed to increase the firm's equity value.

In this contest, we will focus the analysis on the payout of free cash-flows to shareholders. The payout can be made by dividends or buyback.

20.1.1 Dividends

Dividends are the most commonly way to remunerate the shareholders by the firm. Dividends are paid by reducing the current or accumulated retained earnings of the firm. The decision to pay dividends and their amount is made by the firm's board of directors.

P. De Luca, *Corporate Finance*, Springer Texts in Business and Economics,
https://doi.org/10.1007/978-3-031-18300-3_20

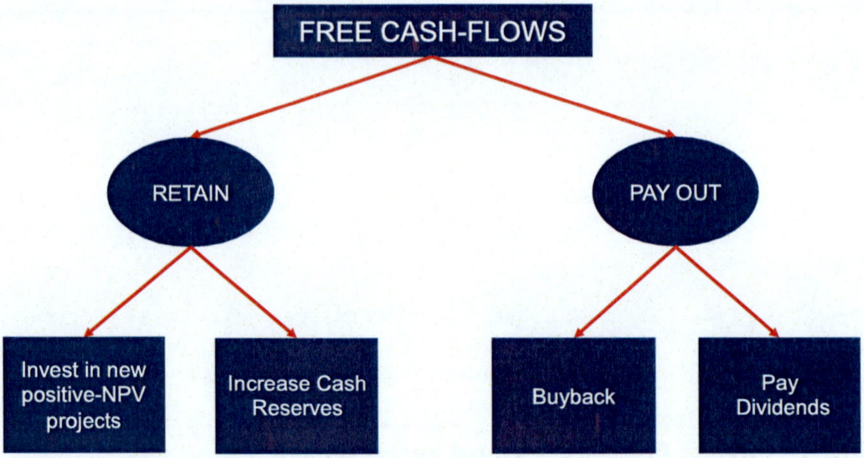

Fig. 20.1 Payout Policy

Note that the date on which the board authorizes the dividends payment is called the *Declaration Date,* and dividend payment becomes a legal obligation for the firm. The firm pays dividends to all shareholders of record on a specific date. This date is called *record date* and it is defined by the board. Because the registration requires three business days, the consequence is that only shareholders that held stocks at least three days prior to the record date will receive the dividends paid by the firm. The date of two business days prior to the record date is called *ex-dividend date,* and anyone who purchases the stocks on or after the ex-dividend date will not receive the dividend by the firm.

The most companies that pay dividends, make it in a regular manner and commonly at quarterly intervals. Generally, firms tend to adjust the amount of their dividends gradually, with little variation in the amount of the dividend from quarter to quarter. Occasionally, a firm may pay a *special dividend* that is usually much larger than a regular dividend.

If dividends are paid by the firm making the stock split or stock dividend by the firm, shareholders will receive additional shares rather than cash.

20.1.2 Buyback

The Buyback or Share Repurchase is an alternative way to pay shareholders. In this case, firm uses cash to buy its shares of its own outstanding stock on market. The shares repurchased are held by the firm in its corporate treasury, and they can be resold on market if the firm needs to raise capital in a future time.

The buyback can be realized in three main ways:

1. *Open Market Repurchase*: It is the most common way. The firm communicates its intention to buy its own shares on open market, and it proceeds to repurchase shares over time like any other investor. To do it firm must follow specific legal rules. Indeed, in any case the firm must not buy its shares in a such way that can be considered manipulative of the share market price.
2. *Tender Offer*: The firm offers to buy shares at a prespecified price during a very short time period that is commonly of few days. The price is usually set at a substantial premium, 10% and 20%, to the current market price.
   Note that the offer often depends on shareholders tendering a sufficient number of shares. Consequently, if shareholders do not tender enough shares, the firm may cancel the offer, and no buyback occurs.
   A specific method is called *Dutch Auction* share repurchase: The firm lists different prices at which it is prepared to buy shares, and shareholders indicate how many shares are willing to sell at each price; then firm pays the lowest price at which it can buy back its desired number of shares.
3. *Targeted Repurchase*: Firm repurchases shares directly from a major shareholder. The purchase price is negotiated directly with the seller of shares.
   The method is well applied if there is a major shareholder that wants to sell a large number of shares but the market is not sufficiently liquid to sustain such a large sale without affecting the price in a relevant manner.
   Under these conditions, the shareholder may be willing to sell its shares back to the firm at a discount to the current market price.
   On the contrary, the major shareholder could be threatening to take over the entire firm and remove its management. In this case, the firm's board could decide to eliminate the threat by buying out the shares of the major shareholder by paying a large premium over the current market price.

Note that while the Open Market Repurchase represents about the 95% of all repurchase transactions, the other two methods are more used if the firm wishes to repurchase a substantial portion of its shares, often as part of a recapitalization process.

Based on these considerations, firm can choice to remunerate its shareholders by paying dividends or repurchasing shares. This choice can be analyzed by considering two contests: perfect capital markets and unperfect capital markets.

20.2 Payout Policy in Perfect Capital Market

Under the baseline assumption of the perfect capital market, Modigliani and Miller (MM) proposition about the payout policy (1961) statues that *in a perfect capital market, holding fixed the investment policy, the firm's choice about of payout policy is irrelevant because it does not affect the market share price and then the firm's value.*

Similar to the capital structure choice, MM statues that the firm value derives from its underlying free cash-flows. The level of free cash-flows determines the level of payout for investors that can be made by dividends or share repurchase indifferently because the choice among them does not matter.

Therefore, for the payout policy choice MM statues the same result of the capital structure choice. Under the baseline assumption of the perfect capital market, the choice between equity and debt does not affect the firm's value as well as the choice between dividends and buyback. Also, in the perspective of investors, in both cases, they can replicate homemade leverage and dividends.

Note that under the assumption of a *perfect capital market, also investors are indifferent to the firm's choice between pay dividends or repurchase shares because they always can replicate either payout method on their own (using homemade dividend) by reinvesting dividends or selling shares.*

We can demonstrate the irrelevance of the choice between dividends and buyback under the assumption of the perfect capital market following a simple example.

Assume the Alfa Firm has already generated 30 million euros in excess cash and it expected to realize free cash-flows equal to 50 million euros per year in perpetuity. Assume that the firm is financed by equity only and then it has no debt. Assume an unlevered cost of capital, and then the cost of equity, equal to 10%. Finally, assume a number shares outstanding equal to ten million.

The firm's enterprise value (EV) is equal to 500 million euros:

$$EV = \frac{\text{ExpFCF}}{K} = \frac{50}{10\%} = 500$$

Adding the initial excess cash, the firm's Total Market Value (TMV) is equal to 530 million euros as follows:

$$TMV = \text{Excess Cash} + EV = 30 + 500 = 530$$

Assume that the firm's board decides to use the initial excess cash, equal to 30 million euros, to remunerate shareholders. The firm can choice between dividends or buyback.

Case 1: Dividends

Assume the firm decides to pay dividends for a total amount of 30 million euros. Because the number of shares outstanding is equal to ten million, the dividend per share is equal to 3 €. Also, the firm decides to anticipate dividend on the future expected free cash-flows, equal to 50 euros per year, by paying a dividend per share equal to 5 € per year thereafter. Consequently, the market price per share is equal to the expected dividend per share discounted to the cost of equity.

Before the ex-dividend date, the stock is traded ***cum-dividend*** ("with" dividend) because anyone who buys the stock in time will be entitled to receive the current dividend:

$$P_{\text{cumDiv}} = \text{Current Dividend} + \frac{\text{Exp(Div)}}{K_E} = 3 + \frac{5}{10\%} = 53$$

After the ex-dividend date, the stock is traded without dividend because the new buyers will not receive the current dividend. In our case, the *market price of stock after the dividend payment (ex-dividend data)* (P_{exDiv}) is equal to

$$P_{\text{exDiv}} = \frac{\text{Exp(Div)}}{K_E} = \frac{5}{10\%} = 50$$

Therefore, the difference between the two prices is the current dividend equal to 3 €.

The market share price fall when a dividend is paid because the reduction in cash due to the dividend payment decreases the firms' market value. Indeed:

1. *Before the dividend payment*, the Total Market Value (TMV) is equal to 530 million euros and by considering the number of shares outstanding equal to n.10 million, the Total Market Value per Share (TMVS) is equal to 53 €.
2. *After the dividend payment*, the Total Market Value (TMV) is equal to 500 million euros and by considering the number of shares outstanding equal to n.10 million, the Total Market Value per Share is equal to 50 €.

The difference is equal to 3 € that is equal to the amount of dividend paid by the firm to its shareholders.

The example shows as although the stock price falls, investors do not incur a loss overall. Indeed:

1. *Before the dividend payment*, the investor's stock was worth 53 €.
2. *After the dividend payment*, the investor's stock is worth 50 € but investor had received 3 € in cash from the dividend for a total value of 53 €.

We can summarize by saying that in a perfect capital market, when dividend is paid, the stock price drops by the amount equal to the dividend paid without loss for investors.

Case 2: Buyback

Assume the firm decides to use the initial excess cash, equal to 30 million euros, to repurchase its own shares on the open market.

Before repurchase shares, the firm's Total Market Value is equal to 530 million euros (in initial excess cash equal to 30 million euros plus enterprise value equal to 500 million euros). Because the number of shares outstanding is equal to n.10 million, the market price per share is equal to 53 €.

At this share market price, the firm repurchases its own shares for a total value equal to 30 million euros. Then the number of shares repurchase is equal to n.566.038 (30 million euros divided by market price per share equal to 53 €). After the share repurchase by the firm, the total amount of its outstanding shares is equal to n.9.433.962 (n.10.000.000 less the shares repurchase equal to n.566.038). The market price per share does not change and remain equal to 53 €. Indeed, the firm's Total Market Value is now equal to 500 million euros and the total shares outstanding are equal to n. 9.433.962. It happens because the fall of the firm's Total Market Value is exactly compensated with the reduction on number of shares outstanding with the consequence of unchanging of the market price of share.

Note that this result does not change even if we consider the future expected dividends, equal to 50 million euros per year in perpetuity. Because the total shares outstanding after the share repurchase is equal to n.9.433.962, the future expected dividend per share is equal to 5.30 €. It implies that the market share price after repurchase (P_{rep}) is equal to 53 € as follows:

$$P_{rep} = \frac{\text{Exp(Div)}}{K_E} = \frac{5{,}30}{10\%} = 53$$

Therefore, if firm decides to repurchase shares rather than to pay dividends, the firm increases its dividends per share in the future in a such manner to compensate shareholders for the dividends they give up today.

We can summarize by saying that in a perfect capital market, the firm's shares repurchase do not affect the stock price that remain the same of the cum-dividend price.

In the reality, the capital markets are not perfect. As discussed about the capital structure choice, we need to introduce others variable that are strictly related to the imperfections existing in capital markets.

Following we consider the main variable able to affect this choice.

20.3 Payout Policy and Taxes

In no-perfect capital market, taxes are an important variable able to influence the firm's choice about payout policy.

Shareholders must pay taxes on: (i) dividends received by the firm and (ii) capital gain realized in case of selling shares.

Generally, when the tax rate on dividends is the higher than the tax rate on capital gains, shareholders will pay lower taxes by investing in a firm whose payout policy is based on shares repurchase rather than dividends.

However, if dividends are taxed at a higher tax rate than capital gains, shareholders will prefer share repurchase to dividends because they can always sell their shares by realizing homemade dividend that will be taxed according to the capital gain tax rate when they decide to realize it.

It implies that firms will have to pay dividends at a higher pre-tax return to offer their investors the same after-tax return as firms that use share repurchase.

In any case, there is always a tax advantage for share repurchase over dividend for investors. Even if we equalize the tax rate on dividends and capital gains, dividends are taxed when firm decides to distribute it to shareholders, while capital gains are taxed when shareholders decide to sell their shares with the main consequence to can plan their taxes.

Even if these considerations seem to statues that the optimal payout policy is to *pay no dividends at all* especially when the dividend tax rate exceeds the capital gain tax rate, dividends remain the most common form of payouts to shareholders.

To well-understand the investor's preferences, we can consider the combined effects of dividend and capital gains taxes to determine an effective dividend tax rate for an investor.

Assume the investor buys a stock before it goes ex-dividend and decides to sell it after the stock goes to ex-dividend. Denoting with *Div* the amount of dividend paid by the stock, and with τ_{Div} the investor's dividend tax rate, the investor's after-tax cash-flow from dividend (CFD_{AT}) is equal to:

$$CFD_{AT} = Div \cdot (1 - \tau_{Div}) \tag{20.1}$$

Since the investor decides to sell the stock after the dividend payment, he will expect to incur in a capital loss. Indeed, the share price before the stock goes ex-dividend [that is the price cum-dividend (P_{cum})] is higher than the share price after the stock goes ex-dividend [that is the price ex-dividend (P_{exDiv})]. Denoting with τ_{CG} the tax rate on capital gain, the investor's after-tax cash-flow from stock sells ($CFCL_{AT}$) is equal to:

$$CFCL_{AT} = (P_{cum} - P_{exDiv}) \cdot (1 - \tau_{CG}) \tag{20.2}$$

Therefore, if:

1. The after-tax dividend is higher than the after-tax capital loss, the investor can earn a profit by trading to obtain the dividend.
2. The after-tax capital loss exceeds the after-tax dividend, the investor benefits by selling the stock just before it goes ex-dividend and buying it afterward, thereby avoiding the dividend.

Note there is an arbitrage opportunity unless the price drop ($P_{cum} - P_{exDiv}$) and dividend are equal to after taxes, as follows:

$$(P_{cum} - P_{exDiv}) \cdot (1 - \tau_{CG}) = Div \cdot (1 - \tau_{Div})$$

Solving for price drop, it gets:

$$P_{cum} - P_{exDiv} = Div \cdot \left(\frac{1 - \tau_{Div}}{1 - \tau_{CG}}\right)$$

and then:

$$P_{cum} - P_{exDiv} = Div \cdot \left(1 - \frac{\tau_{Div} - \tau_{CG}}{1 - \tau_{CG}}\right) \tag{20.3}$$

The ratio $\frac{\tau_{\text{Div}}-\tau_{\text{CG}}}{1-\tau_{\text{CG}}}$ is the *effective dividend tax rate* $\left(\tau^*_{\text{Div}}\right)$ and it measures the additional tax paid by the investor per euro of after-tax capital gains income that is paid by the firm in dividend.

$$\tau^*_{\text{Div}} = \frac{\tau_{\text{Div}} - \tau_{\text{CG}}}{1 - \tau_{\text{CG}}} \tag{20.4}$$

and substituting, it gets:

$$P_{\text{cum}} - P_{\text{exDiv}} = \text{Div} \cdot \left(1 - \tau^*_{\text{Div}}\right)$$

or

$$P_{\text{cum}} - P_{\text{exDiv}} = \text{Div} \cdot \left(\frac{1 - \tau_{\text{Div}}}{1 - \tau_{\text{CG}}}\right) \tag{20.5}$$

Note that if we assume that τ_{Div} and τ_{CG} are equal among them, the effective dividend tax rate $\left(\tau^*_{\text{Div}}\right)$ is equal to zero and it eliminate the tax disadvantage of dividends.

To well-understand assume that the τ_{Div} is equal to 40% and τ_{CG} is equal to 20%. The effective dividend tax rate $\left(\tau^*_{\text{Div}}\right)$ is equal to 25% as follows:

$$\tau^*_{\text{Div}} = \frac{40\% - 20\%}{1 - 20\%} = 25\%$$

By assuming a dividend equal to 1 €, we have:

$$P_{\text{cum}} - P_{\text{exDiv}} = 1 \cdot (1 - 25\%) = 0.75$$

It implies that each 1 € of dividends is worth only 0.75 € in capital gains. Then, there is a significant disadvantage of dividend.

If we assume that both τ_{Div} and τ_{CG} are equal to 20%, we have $\tau^*_{Div} = 0$ by eliminating the tax disadvantage of dividends.

Obviously, the *effective dividend tax rate* $\left(\tau^*_{\text{Div}}\right)$ for an investor depends on taxes rate that investor faces on dividends (τ_{Div}) and capital gain (τ_{CG}). These rates are the function of several variables such as income level, tax jurisdiction, investment horizon.

Taxes affect the firm's choice to retain excess free cash-flows generated or to remunerate shareholders by dividends or shares repurchases.

Consider that an investor must pay taxes on interest, dividend and capital gain.

Assume that the firm has only one asset whose value is 100 € in cash and all investors face the same tax rate. Under these assumptions, consider the following two cases.

Case 1) firm pays its entire cash as an immediate dividend of 100 € and shuts down.

Since the firm pays dividends and shot down, the price ex-dividend is equal to zero ($P_{\text{exDiv}} = 0$). Therefore, the price that investor pay for this firm is equal to the price before the dividend is paid [the price cum-dividend (P_{cum})], that is equal to:

$$P_{\text{cum}} - P_{\text{exDiv}} = \text{Div} \cdot \left(\frac{1 - \tau_{\text{Div}}}{1 - \tau_{\text{CG}}}\right)$$

$$P_{\text{cum}} = 100 \cdot \left(\frac{1 - \tau_{\text{Div}}}{1 - \tau_{\text{CG}}}\right)$$

This is the price that investor pays to the firm and it depends on the tax rate on dividend (τ_{Div}) received and the capital gains tax rate τ_{CG} for the capital loss when the firm shuts down.

Case 2) firm retains the cash equal to 100 € permanently, and invest it in Government bond by using the interest earned equal to the risk-free rate (R_f) to pay dividends to shareholders each year.

The firm must pay corporate taxes at the corporate tax rate of τ_C on the interest earned on government bond, and after it pays dividend (Div) to shareholders that is equal to:

$$\text{Div} = 100 \cdot R_f \cdot (1 - \tau_{\text{C}})$$

The price that investor pays to the firm must consider that the investor's cost of capital is equal to $R_f \cdot (1 - \tau_i)$ where τ_i is the investor's tax rate on interest income.

Therefore, because the investor must pay taxes on the dividends as well, the value of the firm and then the price that investor pay is equal to the price retain (P_{retain}) that it is equal to:

$$P_{\text{retain}} = \frac{\text{Div} \cdot (1 - \tau_{\text{Div}})}{R_f \cdot (1 - \tau_i)} = \frac{100 \cdot R_f \cdot (1 - \tau_{\text{C}}) \cdot (1 - \tau_{\text{Div}})}{R_f \cdot (1 - \tau_i)} = 100 \cdot \frac{(1 - \tau_{\text{C}}) \cdot (1 - \tau_{\text{Div}})}{(1 - \tau_i)}$$

We can compare the equations of the two cases, as follows:

$$P_{\text{cum}} = 100 \cdot \left(\frac{1 - \tau_{\text{Div}}}{1 - \tau_{\text{CG}}}\right) \quad \rightarrow \quad 100 = \frac{P_{\text{cum}}}{\left(\frac{1 - \tau_{\text{Div}}}{1 - \tau_{\text{CG}}}\right)}$$

Substituting in the P_{retain} we have:

$$P_{\text{retain}} = \frac{P_{\text{cum}}}{\left(\frac{1 - \tau_{\text{Div}}}{1 - \tau_{\text{CG}}}\right)} \cdot \frac{(1 - \tau_{\text{C}}) \cdot (1 - \tau_{\text{Div}})}{(1 - \tau_i)}$$

And rearranged, we have:

$$P_{\text{retain}} = P_{\text{cum}} \cdot \frac{(1-\tau_C)\cdot(1-\tau_{\text{Div}})}{(1-\tau_i)} \cdot \left(\frac{1-\tau_{CG}}{1-\tau_{\text{Div}}}\right)$$

$$P_{\text{retain}} = P_{\text{cum}} \cdot \frac{(1-\tau_C)\cdot(1-\tau_{CG})}{(1-\tau_i)}$$

The ratio among the corporate tax rate (τ_C), the investor's taxes rate capital gain (τ_{CG}), and the investor's tax rate on interest income (τ_i), defines the *tax disadvantage of retaining cash* $\left(\tau^*_{\text{retain}}\right)$ as follows:

$$\tau^*_{\text{retain}} = \frac{(1-\tau_C)\cdot(1-\tau_{CG})}{(1-\tau_i)}$$

and substituting, we get:

$$P_{\text{retain}} = P_{\text{cum}} \cdot \left(1-\tau^*_{\text{retain}}\right)$$

where all tax rate in the equation are percentage and then 1 is the 100% in order to define the disadvantage.

Note that the dividend tax rate (τ_{Div}) does not affect the cost of retaining cash because the dividend tax will be paid whether the firm pays the excess free cash-flows immediately or retains them and pays the interest over time.

The equation shows as the cost of retaining cash depends on the combined effects of the corporate and capital gain taxes, compared to the single tax on interest income.

Assume that $\tau_C = 40\%$, $\tau_i = 35\%$, $\tau_{CG} = 20\%$. In this case, the effective tax disadvantage of retained cash is equal to $\tau^*_{\text{retain}} = 26.2\%$. Therefore, after adjusting for investors taxes, the remains a substantial tax disadvantage for the firm to retaining excess cash.

Despite the tax disadvantage to retain cash, companies tend to retain excess free cash-flows generated because they want to be able to grasp all eventually future potential opportunity of investments in positive-NPV projects that they are able to find on market. This is the most relevant reason for companies that need to fund large-scale research and development projects or large acquisitions. To retain excess cash-flows firm can avoid all transaction costs of raising new capital in debt or issuing new equity and relative problems of amount and sources.

Therefore, companies tend to balance the tax costs of holding cash with the potential benefits of not need to raise external funds in the future avoiding transaction costs.

In any cases, there is not benefit to shareholders if firm decides to held excess cash-flow and beyond its future investment or liquidity needs. In addition to the tax cost, there must be considered the agency costs associated with having too much cash. Indeed, managers can use this cash in inefficient ways by investing in negative-NPV projects or waste money to the detriment of shareholders. Generally, dividend as the leverage can reduce opportunistic behaviour by the managers because they reduce the amount of cash in the firm generating a discipline effects on managers.

20.4 Payout Policy and Signaling Theory

Under assumption of the no-perfect capital market, the payout policy plays a key role in a contest of asymmetric information. Because managers have better information than investors regarding the firm future perspectives, the payout policy is commonly considered by investors a relevant signal of the firm conditions and its perspectives.

Theoretically firm can change dividends at any time. In practice companies tend to vary the dividends amount infrequently and tendency they are less volatile than earnings. The practice of a relatively constant dividend policy over time is called *dividend smoothing*. If the dividend policy is changed by the firm, the increase of dividends is much more frequently than their cut.

Companies known that investors tend to prefer stable dividends with sustained growth. Therefore, companies tend to maintain a long-term target level of dividends stable over time. To do it, managers commonly define dividends as a fraction of earnings. However, because mangers do not wish to commit to a dividend that the firm cannot afford to pay out of regular earnings, managers sets dividends at a level it expects to be able to maintain based on the firm's earnings prospects. It implies that dividends raise only if managers are strong expected a long-term sustainable increase in the future level of earnings and decide to cut dividends only as a last resort. Indeed, to cut dividends is costly for the managers in terms of their reputation and the reaction of investors.

Therefore, the firm's choices about dividends are considered by investors a relevant sign for the market because it contains information regarding management's expectation of future earnings. The idea that the dividend policy is able to reflect the managers' thinking about the firm's future expectation of growth and its expected future earnings is called the ***dividend signalling hypothesis***. Based on this hypothesis, if firm decides to:

1. *Increase dividends*, it sends a positive signal to investors regarding managers expectation about firm capability to afford the high dividend level for the foreseeable future.
2. *Cut dividends*, it sends a negative signal that the firm expects low level of earning in the short-term and then it reduces dividends to save cash that must be used for the firm's needs.

Even if an increase of a firm's dividend commonly is considered as a positive signal by investors, however it might be considered as a negative signal. It happens if investors interpreter the increase of dividends as a lack of new positive-NPV investment opportunities for the firm in the future time. In this case, the market stock price decreases rather than increase.

Similarly, a cut of dividends, if it is justified to exploit new positive-NPV investment opportunities, might be considered positive by investors. In this case, the market price increase rather than decrease.

It implies that investors must always interpret firm's dividend policy on the basis of their belief about the information that managers are likely to have. Because managers know that the interpretation can be based on bias and then it can be wrong, their prefer a stable dividend policy over time.

In any case, the dividend signalling hypothesis is based on the same baseline assumption of the use of leverage as a signal to the market about firm's expectation of growth. Similar to dividends, the increase in leverage is considered a positive signal to investors regarding the firm capability to growth in a such manner to afford the future interest payments and the capital reimbursement.

Like dividends, *share repurchase* is able to signal to investors managers' view about firm's growth in the future time. However, there are several important differences between dividends and share repurchase. Among them the main relevant are:

1. First, companies are much less committed to share repurchases than to pay dividends. Also, when firm announces authorization for an open market share repurchase, it concerns the maximum amount firm plans to spend on repurchase and the actual amount spent may be far less. In any case, the firm takes several years to complete the share repurchase.
2. Second, the firm announcement of share repurchase today does not necessarily represent a long-term commitment to repurchase shares. The consequence is that the share repurchase can be considered less of a signal than dividends about the firm's expectation about its future earnings.
3. Third, the effectively cost of a share repurchase depends on the stock market price. Consequently, if managers believe the stock is currently overvalued, the share repurchase is costly to the shareholders. By contrast, repurchasing shares when managers perceive the stock to be undervalued is a positive investment for shareholders.

Consequently, if managers are focused on the maximization of the firm's future share price, they are willing to repurchase shares if they believe the stock to be undervalued. In this sense, share repurchases are considered by investors a credible signal that management believes its share is under-priced. Consequently, investors may react favourably to share repurchase announcement.

20.5 Stock Dividend and Stock Split

Stock dividend and Stock Split are another way to pay dividend to shareholders by firm. In both case the firm does not pay out any cash to shareholders.

The Stock Dividend is used by the firm that wants to retain funds to finance expansion, but it does not want to reduce the dividends distribution. The stock dividend increases shareholder's number of shares by the same percentage: with a 5% of stock dividend, the shareholder who holds 100 shares would receive 5 more shares.

Stock Dividend increases the number of shares outstanding without changing the firm's earnings, its assets, or each shareholder's proportionate equity interest in the firm. Because each shareholder increases its shares by the same proportion, every shareholder's equity in the firm remains unchanged.

With a Stock Split each shareholder receives a multiple of the number of shares hold doubling the total number of shares held before the split. If a firm decides a 10% stock dividend, each shareholder receives one new share of stock for every 10 shares already owned.

In case of the stock dividend is equal or more than 50%, commonly it is called *stock split*. With a 50% stock dividend, each shareholder receives one new share for every two shares owned. It is called 3:2 (*three-for-two* split) stock split because the shareholder of two shares will end up holding three new shares. In case of 100% stock dividend, we have 2:1 stock split (or *two-for-one split*).

Similar to the stock dividend, the stock split has no effect on the firm's value, it does not change the shareholder's proportional interest in the firm, but it increases the number of shares outstanding.

Note that there is a fundamental difference between a *stock split* and a *share issuance*: when firm issues share, the number of shares increases, but the firm also raises cash to add to its existing assets. If the shares are sold at a fair price, the stock price should not change.

In case of stock split, the total market value of the firm's unchanged, but it increases the number of shares outstanding. Consequently, the market price of stock will fall because the same total equity value is divided over a larger number of shares. Indeed, the number of shares is proportionally increased and the price per share is proportionally reduced because there is no change in firm value.

Commonly the stock split is used by firm to maintain its share price in a range on market that is considered attractive to small investors. If the share price rises significantly, it might be difficult for small investors to afford firm's shares (for example in case of 2:1 split if the stock was 100 € par value prior to the split, after the split it becomes automatically 50 €).

Firm tries to make its shares more attractive to small investors because it can increase the demand for and the liquidity of the stock, and in turn it may increase the stock price.

The inverse process to the stock split is the reserve split. Companies do not want their stock price to fall too low. In case it happens, the firm can engage in a reverse split by reducing the number of shares outstanding. Consequently, the share price increases because the firm's value does not change, but the number of shares outstanding is reduced. For example, in a 1:10 reverse split, every 10 shares of stock are replaced with a single share and the share price increases tenfold. Therefore, by combining stock splits and reverse splits, companies can keep their share prices in the range desired.

Stock dividend and stock split increase the number of shares outstanding without changing the firm's earnings, its assets, or each shareholder's proportionate equity interest in the firm. Because they have not effect on the firm's value, they do not change the shareholder's proportional interest in the firm, but they increase the number of shares outstanding, in theory the stock dividend should reduce the market price per share of the stock. The share price reduction should be in inverse proportion to the split. In practice, the share price drops less than the theory predicts. If it happens, the stock dividend increases the value for both the firm and investors.

Cost of Capital

21

21.1 Investor Expected Return and the Firm's Cost of Capital

The Cost of Capital plays a key role in the firm's valuation based on the discounted cash-flow models.

In the Discounted Cash-Flow valuations, the cost of capital is the discounted rates used to discount the future expected cash-flows and it reflects the expected return of investors. Indeed, the core of the entire modern investment theory is based on models that tried to measure the risk in investments and convert them into expected returns.

Specifically, the cost of equity (K_E) reflects the expected return of investor in equity ($E(R_E)$) and thus it incorporates a risk premium for equity risk so that $K_E = E(R_E)$. Similarly, the cost of debt ($E(R_D)$) reflects the expected return of investors in debt (R_D) and it incorporates the default premium for the default risk in the debt, so that $K_D = E(R_D)$.

Therefore, the expected return of investors, both in Equity and Debt, is for the firm's cost of capital, both the cost of equity and the cost of debt.

Therefore, the cost of equity and the cost of debt measure the risk of investors in equity and debt. By considering that the risk of equity.

By considering only these main characteristics, the Risk of Equity (E_{RISK}) is always higher by the Risk on Debt (D_{RISK}), consequently the expected Return on Equity $\left(\overline{R_E}\right)$ is, and it must always be higher than the expected Return on Debt $\left(\overline{R_D}\right)$ and consequently the Cost of Equity (K_E) is and it must always be, higher than the Cost of Debt (K_D). We can summarize these relationships as follows:

$$E_{RISK} \ll D_{RISK} \quad \Rightarrow \quad \overline{R_E} > \overline{R_D} \quad \Rightarrow \quad K_E > K_D \tag{21.1}$$

Note that in this relationship the independent variable is the risk, while the expected rate of return by investors and then the firm's cost of capital is the dependent variable.

In the modern finance, the risk is:

P. De Luca, *Corporate Finance*, Springer Texts in Business and Economics,
https://doi.org/10.1007/978-3-031-18300-3_21

1. *Defined in terms of the distribution of actual returns around an expected return*: This difference is measured by the variance or standard deviation of the distribution. Consequently, the risk comes from the volatility of the distribution of actual returns around the expected return: the greater variance (and then the standard deviation), the greater the risk;
2. *Measured from the perspective of a marginal investor who is well-diversified*: It is one of the most relevant baseline assumptions in the modern finance. It implies that the only risk measured is the market-risk while the firm-specific risk is not considered thanks to the diversification process (see Part 3). On the contrary, the assumption that investor is not well-diversified implies that he or she is exposed to both firm-specific risk and market-risk.

21.2 Cost of Equity

The cost of equity is the rate of return that investor requires to make an equity investment in the firm $\left(\overline{R_{\mathrm{E}}} = K_{\mathrm{E}}\right)$. It implies three main problems:

1. The cost of equity is an implicit cost and then it cannot be observed directly.
2. By assuming that investor in equity is a marginal investor and then well-diversified, the cost of equity varies across equity investors in order to their portfolio.
3. The expected rate of return on investment in equity is different for all investors in equity in the same firm because it depends on the diversification process.

Therefore, to estimate the cost of equity requires to solve these two problems. The first task is to translate the implicit cost into explicit cost, and the second task is to estimate which rate of return the diverse investors in equity will accept as the right expected return in equity investment as a measure of their risk. Note that the risk considered is only the market-risk under the assumption that the investor in equity is well-diversified.

To solve these two points, require to use models that measure the risk in an investment in equity and convert it in an expected return for investors in equity that is the cost of equity for the firm. The most well-known models developed over the years are referred to the Capital Asset Pricing Model (CAPM), Arbitrage Pricing Model (APM), Multifactor Model, and Proxy Model. In this contest, we will use the CAPM approach because it is the commonly used in financial community to measure the market risk.

Based on CAPM, the SML states that the expected return of investment in *i*th asset $\left(\overline{R_{\mathrm{j}}}\right)$ and then the cost of equity of jth firm (K_{Ej}) is calculated on the basis of the risk-free rate (R_f), the beta of the *i*th asset (β_j), and the risk premium for average-risk asset $\left[\overline{R_{\mathrm{m}}} - R_{\mathrm{f}}\right]$, as follows:

$$\overline{R_j} \equiv K_{Ej} = R_f + \beta_j \left[\overline{R_m} - R_f\right] \tag{21.2}$$

In the equation the coefficient beta plays the key role by measuring the entire market risk.

The right application of the model requires the estimation of its three parameters: risk-free rate (R_f), risk premium $\left[\overline{R_m} - R_f\right]$ and coefficient beta (β).

21.3 Risk-Free Rate Estimation

There is not investment with no risk by definition. Therefore, we can obtain a risk-free rate only by doing a restrictive assumption: we assume that an asset with very low level of risk can be considered risk free and we use its expected return as the risk-free rate. Assets with this characteristic are generally issued by governments. Consequently, we associate the risk-free rate to the return of assets issued by government perceived by investors with low default probability: the risk-free rate is estimated equal to the rate on a long-term government bond issued by government with low default probability. To do it, it is relevant that there must not be uncertainty about reinvestment rates. It implies that there are no intermediate cash-flows (example if we want the risk-free rate for a 5-year time period, we have to consider a 5-year zero-coupon bond of the default-free government).

It is relevant to note that by considering that the risk-free rate is not related to the risk, it measures the price of time.

Theoretically, the risk-free rates may be different in each period of the analysis. Usually in practice, we use a duration of the default-free asset (that we use as a risk-free rate) that matches with the duration of the cash-flows in the analysis.

Since the risk-free rate must be measured consistently with the cash-flows, if the cash-flows are estimated at their nominal value (that is the standard condition), the risk-free rate must be nominal and in the same currency in which the cash-flows are estimated.

Therefore, in the choice of the risk-free rate, it is relevant the currency in which the cash-flows are estimated and it is not relevant where the asset or firm is domiciliated. It implies that if we value a Italian firm in dollars, we use a dollar discount rate and then we use the US Treasury Bond rate as the risk-free rate.

Even if the normal rule is to consider the nominal risk-free rate, in case of high and unstable inflation, we can evaluate on the basis of real terms rather than nominal. The real cash-flows are estimated using a real growth rate, and they are discounted at a real rate of discount. Consequently, the risk-free rate must be a real risk-free rate. Since the government bills and bonds are in nominal terms, the standard approach to estimate the real risk-free rate is to subtract the expected inflation rate from the nominal interest rate.

The risk-free rate is estimated on the basis of the return of asset issued by the government. The assumption that government does not default, at least on the local currency borrowing, could be not reasonable in some cases. Indeed, not all governments can be considered default free risk with consequent difficulty to estimate the risk-free rate in their currencies. The problem increases a lot if to the investors' perception about the government capability of defaulting is coupled with the fact that government does not issue long-term bonds denominated in the local currency. This condition is very difficult to estimate the risk-free rate in that currency. To solve the problem, we can compute the risk-free rate in the local currency by following two main approaches:

1. We can look at the largest and safest firms in that market and use the rate that they pay on their long-term borrowings in the local currency as the risk-free rate.
2. We can adjust the local currency government bond rate by the estimated default spread on the bond by using the local currency ratings issued by ratings agencies (for example if the government bond rate in nominal local currency is 11% and then the local currency rating assigned to the government is equal to BBB and it corresponds at a default spread equal to 3%, the risk-free rate is equal to 8%).

21.4 Risk Premium Estimation

The risk premium in the CAPM measures the extra return demanded by investors for invest on risk-assets rather than in riskless-assets.

The risk premium can be estimated by following several approaches. Among them two are the main: (a) *historical premiums* and (b) *implied equity premium*.

21.4.1 Historical Premiums

It is the common approach to estimate the risk premium in financial asset pricing models. It estimates the risk premium on the basis of historical data. The risk premium is estimated on the basis of the difference between average returns on stocks and average returns on risk-free assets over an extended historical time period.

Even if the common thinking of analysts is that the historical premium is the best estimate of the risk premium looking forward, however we can observe differences in the actual premiums used in practice. Three are the main reasons to explain these differences:

1. *Time period referenced*: We can use data going back of 50, 30, 20, or 10 years to estimate the historical risk premium. The general rule is that the shorter time periods used, the greater can be the error in the risk premium estimate.
   To well-understand the problem, assume that the annual standard deviation in stock prices is equal to 20%, and compute the standard error (based on the assumption that annual returns are uncorrelated over time, and then it is likely underestimated) associated with the risk premium for different time periods as in Table 21.1.

Table 21.1 Standard errors in risk premium estimates

Time period (in years)	Annual standard deviation in stock prices	Standard error of risk premium estimate	Variation	
			In value	In %
	20%			
5		$20/\sqrt{5}=8.94\%$		
10		$20/\sqrt{10}=6.32\%$	(2.62%)	(29.29%)
15		$20/\sqrt{15}=5.16\%$	(1.16%)	(18.35%)
20		$20/\sqrt{20}=4.47\%$	(0.69%)	(13.40%)
25		$20/\sqrt{25}=4.00\%$	(0.47%)	(10.56%)
30		$20/\sqrt{30}=3.65\%$	(0.35%)	(8.71%)
35		$20/\sqrt{35}=3.38\%$	(0.27%)	(7.42%)
40		$20/\sqrt{40}=3.16\%$	(0.22%)	(6.46%)
45		$20/\sqrt{45}=2.98\%$	(0.18%)	(5.72%)
50		$20/\sqrt{50}=2.83\%$	(0.15%)	(5.13%)

The table shows that to get a reasonable standard error, we need a very long time periods of historical returns. Generally, the longer the time series, better the risk premium estimation.

2. *Risk-free asset referenced*: If the yield curve is upward-sloping for most of the past decades, the risk premium is larger when it is estimated relative to shorter-term government assets. The risk-free rate used in calculating the risk premium must be consistent with the risk-free rate used to calculate the expected return. Therefore, since the risk-free rate is a long-term default-free government bond rate, thus the risk premium used should be the premium earned by stocks over long-term bonds.
3. *Arithmetic or Geometric Averages used*: It refers to the way by which the average returns on stocks and risk-free assets are calculated. The Arithmetic Average measures the simple mean of the series of annual returns, while the Geometric Average looks at the compounded return as follows:

$$\text{Gemetric Average} = \left(\frac{\text{Value}_N}{\text{Value}_0}\right)^{\left(\frac{1}{N}\right)} - 1$$

Traditionally analysts prefer the Arithmetic Average. It is the best-unbiased estimate of the risk premium if the objective is to estimate the risk premium for the next year and the annual returns are uncorrelated over time.

The Geometric Average is preferred to the Arithmetic Average if the returns on stocks are negatively correlated over time. In this case, the arithmetic average is likely to overstate the premium.

Country Risk Premium

In many emerging markets, usually we have to face two main problems: (1) little historical data; (2) high volatility. If these two conditions are realized, or even one of them, the consequence is to yield a low meaningful estimate of the risk premium.

Therefore, in this case, the risk premium estimation requires before the right estimation of the *Country Risk Premium*. Commonly, analysts estimate the equity risk premium in emerging markets by addicting to the base premium for mature equity market a specific premium for the country risk as follows:

$$\text{Equity Risk Premium} = \text{Base Premium for Mature Equity Market} + \text{Country Risk Premium} \tag{21.3}$$

The first component, the Base Premium for mature Equity Market, is the equity risk premium for a mature market and it is defined on the basis of country characterized by a significant development of the equity market (such as the USA).

The second component, the Country Risk Premium, reflects the extra risk due to the specific market conditions. We can use three main approaches to estimate the Country Risk premium:

1. *Country bond default spreads*: We can consider the rating assigned to a country's debt by a rating agency a approximation of the equity risk. Even if the rating measures the default risk of the country and not the equity risk, however we can use is because the equity risk is affected by many of the factors that drive rating (such as the stability of the country's currency, its budget, its political standing, and so on).
   Note that if we use the default spreads as measures of country risk, we usually add them on to both cost of equity and cost of debt of every firm traded in that country.
2. *Relative Standard Deviation*: We measure the equity risk on the basis of the standard deviation in the stock prices so that the higher the standard deviation, the higher the equity risk. It assumes that the equity risk premium reflects the differences in equity risk, as measured by the volatilities of equities in these markets. Therefore, we can measure the relative standard deviation of one country (Country X) by scale it to the standard deviation of another country (Country Y), as follows:

$$\text{Relative Standard Deviation}_{\text{Country X}} = \frac{\text{Standard Deviation}_{\text{Country X}}}{\text{Standard Deviation}_{\text{Country Y}}} \tag{21.4}$$

Multiplying the Relative Standard Deviation by the Premium used for the Country Y stocks, we have a measure of the total risk premium for any market, as follows:

$$\text{Equity Risk Premium}_{\text{Country X}} = \text{Risk Premium}_{\text{Country Y}} \cdot \text{Relative Standard Deviation}_{\text{Country X}} \tag{21.5}$$

3. *Default spreads plus relative standard deviation*: We compare the volatility of the equity market in a country and the volatility of the country bond used to estimate the spread. It assumes reasonable that the country equity risk premium is larger than the country default risk spread. Therefore:

$$\text{Country Risk Premium} = \text{Country Default Spread} \cdot \left(\frac{\text{Standard Deviation}_{\text{Equity}}}{\text{Standard Deviation}_{\text{Country Bond}}}\right) \tag{21.6}$$

21.4.2 Implied Equity Premiums

The implied equity premium extracts the implicit premium from the current market data. Therefore, it does not require historical data or corrections for country risk.

The baseline assumption is that the overall stock market is correctly priced, and the we can extract the equity premium from the stock price because the current level of the market price is the value.

To well-understand consider one of the simplest valuation models, the Dividend Discounted Modem (DDM) with a constant growth rate:

$$\text{Value} = \frac{\text{Expected Dividends next period}}{\text{Required Return on Equity} - \text{Expected growth rate in dividends}}$$

Under the assumption that the stock market is correctly priced, then the current level of the market is the value. Also, analysts can define directly in a simple way the expected dividends next period and the expected growth rate in the long term. Therefore, the only unknown variable is the Required Return on Equity. By solving the equation for the Required Return on Equity and by subtracting yo it the risk-free rate, we obtain the implied Equity Risk Premium, as follows:

$$\text{Required Return on Equity} = \frac{\text{Expected Dividends next period}}{\text{Value}} - \text{Expected growth rate in dividends}$$

$$\text{Implied Equity Risk Premium} = \text{Required Return on Equity} - \text{RiskFree rate} \quad (21.7)$$

21.5 Beta Estimation

Beta plays a key role in the estimation of the cost of equity based on the asset pricing models. It measured the market risk on the basis that the investor in equity is well-diversified. This assumption is reasonable for publicly traded firm, while it can be not reasonable for private firms.

We can use two main techniques to estimate beta:

1. *Regression Beta*: It is the commonly technique used by analysts to estimate beta for traded firms in the market by assuming that investor in equity is well-diversified.
2. *Fundamental Beta*: It is usually used to estimate beta for private firms no traded in market by assuming that owner of the firm is not diversified.

Note that also for private firm we can use the CAPM approach. In this case, the assumption is that the firm can realize in the short-term objective of sales and profit margin comparable to a large publicly traded firm. Under this assumption, also for the private firm, we can use the market beta and then the cost of equity based on it.

21.5.1 Regression Beta Approach

The regression beta is considered by financial community the conventional approach for traded firms in the market. The baseline assumption is that investor in equity is well-diversified, and then the beta reflects the market risk only where the specific risk of the firm is not considered.

The regression beta is based on the historical data on market prices for firms that have been publicly traded for a length of time. In this case, it is simple to compute returns that an investor would have made on its equity in weekly or monthly intervals over that period. These returns can then be related to returns on a proxy for the market portfolio by obtaining the beta.

In theory, stock returns on assets should be related to returns on a market portfolio that includes all traded assets. In practice, we use a stock index as a proxy for the market portfolio, and the beta is estimated for stocks against the stock index considered.

By using the regression equation, a time period considered, the expected return of *j*th firm can be estimated as follows:

$$\overline{R_j} = \alpha_j + \beta_j \overline{R_m} + e_j \tag{21.8}$$

Applying the Ordinary Least Square (OLS), we have:

$$\beta_j = \frac{\sum_{t=1}^{n} \left[\left(R_j - \overline{R_j}\right)\left(R_m - \overline{R_m}\right) \right]}{\sum_{t=1}^{n} \left(R_j - \overline{R_j}\right)^2} = \frac{\mathrm{Cov}\left(\overline{R_j}, \overline{R_m}\right)}{Var\left(\overline{R_m}\right)} = \frac{\sigma_{\left(\overline{R_j R_m}\right)}}{\sigma^2_{\overline{R_m}}}$$

and:

$$\alpha_j = \overline{R_j} - \beta_j \overline{R_m} \tag{21.9}$$

The value of β_i and α_i, is used to estimate the true value of β_i and α_i that exist for an asset. Obviously, the estimates are subject to error and therefore, the estimated β_i and α_i could not be equal to their real values that existed in the period. Furthermore, β_i and α_i are not perfectly stationary over time.

In the CAPM, investors will keep diversifying until they hold a market portfolio and they will differ only in terms of how much of their wealth they want to invest in this market portfolio and how much in a riskless asset. Consequently, the risk of any asset is related to the risk that it adds to the market portfolio. We can measure the risk added by an asset to the market portfolio by its covariance with that portfolio.

Since the beta of market portfolio is equal to 1 (the covariance of the market portfolio with itself is its variance), assets that are riskier than market portfolio will have beta greater than 1. On the contrary, assets that are lower risk than market portfolio will have beta lower than 1. The riskless asset will have beta equal to 0.

The intercept (α_j) provides simple measures of performance of the investment in the *j*th firm during the period of regression when returns on investment in the j firm are measured against the expected returns on the basis of the CAPM.

Note that the equation of the cost of equity of *j*th firm can be rewritten as follows:

$$K_{E_j} = R_f\left(1 - \beta_j\right) + \beta_j \overline{R_m} \tag{21.10}$$

The difference between the intercept a_j and $R_f(1 - \beta)$ is the Jensen's Alpha (A):

$$A = a_j - R_f\left(1 - \beta_j\right) \tag{21.11}$$

It measures the stock performance of the *j*th firm compared with companies with similar beta during the regression period. If:

- $a_j > R_f(1 - \beta_j)$: the *j*-firm has earned more than companies with a similar beta during the regression period.

- $a_j = R_f(1 - \beta_j)$: the *j*-firm has earned equal the same as companies with a similar beta during the regression period.
- $a_j < R_f(1 - \beta_j)$: the *j*-firm has earned lower than companies with a similar beta during the regression period.

In the setting of regression, the analyst must be made decision about three main aspects:

1. *The length of the estimation period*: long time period is usually preferred to the short time period because it provides more data even if the firm could be changed in its characteristics.
2. *The return interval*: return on stocks are available on an annual, monthly, weekly, daily, and intraday basis. Usually weekly or monthly returns are preferred because they reduce the nontrading bias.
3. *The market index as a proxy of the market portfolio*: the common practice in the choice of market index as a proxy of market portfolio, is to consider the holding of the marginal investor in the firm being analyzed. Therefore, if the marginal investors in a firm hold only domestic stocks, we should use a local index; on the contrary, if the marginal investor is a global investor, we should use a global index.

By setting in different ways these three parameters, we have different estimation of beta. Indeed, betas reported by different estimation services (Standard&Poor's, Morningstar, Bloomberg, etc.) for the same firm can be very different because they set in different way the parameters of regression: different time periods (two years, three years, five years), different return intervals (daily, weekly, or monthly), different market indices, and different post-regression adjustments.

One of the relevant problems in the beta (β_j) estimation by regression model concerns the length of the time period considered. It is due to a normal trade-off: a longer estimation period provides more data, but the firm may have changed in its risk characteristics over time.

There are two main techniques to adjust the regression beta: Blume's technique and Vesicek's technique.

Based on the observation that generally in the long-term period beta tends to converge, on average, to 1, it is possible to modify the past betas to capture the tendency. The Blume's technique (1975) corrects the past betas by measuring this adjustment directly towards 1. It assumes that the adjustment in one period is a good estimate of the adjustment in the next. Specifically, in the second period ($t = 2$) the beta of *i*th asset ($\beta_{i,\,2}$) can be estimated on the basis of the beta in the first period ($\beta_{i,\,1}$) adjusted as follows:

$$\beta_{i,2} = 0.33 + 0.67\beta_{i,1} \tag{21.12}$$

By lowering the high value of beta and raising the low value of beta, the equation pushes all estimated betas towards 1.

Note that if the average beta increased over these two periods, it assumes that average betas will increase over the next period. Obviously, if there are no expectations about this trend, this change in beta represents an undesirable property.

Based on the equation, we can compute the Adjusted Beta (β_A) that is the expected beta. It is equal to the Raw Beta (β_{RB}) (that is the historical beta) considered for 2/3(0.67) plus the Beta of Market Portfolio (β_M) (that is equal 1 by definition) considered for 1/3(0.33), as follows:

$$\beta_A = \beta_{RB}\,(0.67) + \beta_M(0.33) = \beta_{RB}\,(0.67) + 1.00(0.33) \tag{21.13}$$

Differently, the Vesicek's technique (1973) assumes that the adjustment depends on the size of the uncertainty about beta. Consequently, the larger the sampling error, the greater the change in large differences from the average being due to sampling error the greater the adjustment.

The technique adjusts the beta on two main considerations: (i) many sectors are characterized by structurally lower or higher betas than the market, so that the average beta of the sector should be considered rather than the market; (ii) the correction of historical beta to obtain the expected beta should be proportional to the relevance of the standard error of the beta.

Denoting with: β_S the beta of the sector and with $\sigma^2_{\beta_S}$ its variance; β_{MS} the average beta of the sector and with $\sigma^2_{\beta_{MS}}$ its variance; SE^2 the square of the standard error of the historical beta; β_{RB} the Raw Beta that is the historical beta.

The Adjusted Beta (β_A) that measures the expected beta is equal to:

$$\beta_A = \beta_{RB}\,\frac{\sigma^2_{\beta_S}}{\dfrac{\left(\sigma^2_{\beta_S} + SE^2\right) + \left(\sigma^2_{\beta_{MS}} + SE^2\right)}{\left(\sigma^2_{\beta_S}\right) + SE^2}} \tag{21.14}$$

The equation shows that the higher the standard error of the historical beta, the higher the adjustment of the beta of the firm in the estimate process.

21.5.2 Fundamental Beta

The Fundamental Beta can be used to estimate beta for private firms not traded in the market and in case of Initial Public Offering (IPO).

For the firms traded in financial market we usually assume that the investor in equity is well-diversified, so that he bears only market risk. Differently, in case of private firm it is reasonable assume that the owner generally is not diversified by investing all or relevant part of its wealth in the firm and bearing the entire risk: market risk plus firm-specific risk.

This approach estimates the firm's beta on the basis of firm's fundamental decisions about:

1. *Type of Business*: The beta is affected by the business characteristics of the firm. Beta measures the risk of firm relative to the market, so that the higher the sensitive of firm to the business and overall economic conditions, the higher is its beta. Therefore, it is relevant to measure the sensitivity of the firm's performance to the market's movements. Generally, other variables being equal, cyclical companies can be expected to have higher betas than non-cyclical companies.
2. *Degree of Operating Leverage*: It refers to the cost structure of the firm and specifically to the relationship between fixed costs and variable costs on total costs. The higher the fixed costs relative to total costs, the higher the operating leverage. The relationship between beta and operating leverage is due to its effects on operating and net income: the higher the operating leverage, the greater the fixed costs, the higher the volatility of operating and net income due to the volatility of revenues. Therefore, the higher the operating leverage, the higher the variability in operating income due to the fixed costs and then the higher the beta.
3. *Degree of Financial Leverage*: It refers to the capital structure and specifically to the relationship between debt and equity. The higher the debt in the capital structure, the higher the financial leverage. Three are the main effects of high debt: first, the interest on debt are cash-out and contemporary they are a fixed cost by increasing the Operating Leverage; second, interest on debt are tax deductible by generating a tax benefit for the firm; third, increase the default risk of the firm by making riskier both in debt and equity investment in the firm.

   Generally, investors in equity will expect that if leverage increases, they bear increasing amount of risk in the firm, and it leads to higher beta.

Based on these considerations, the firm's beta is determined by fundamental decisions about the business, operating and financial leverage. Note that while the first and second variables define the business risk of the firm, the third variable defines its financial risk. Generally, the financial risk multiplies the underlying business risk. It is the reason by which firms characterized by high business risk should reduce the financial leverage.

Breaking risk down into *business risk* (types of business plus degree of operating leverage) and financial risk (due to the degree of financial leverage), we can say that we tend to have high betas in two situations: firm operates in risky business, or the firm uses a very high leverage in a relatively stable business.

The right application of this approach implies the implementation of a procedure called *Bottom-Up Betas*.

This procedure is based on a specific property of the beta: the beta of two assets put together is equal to a weighted average of the individual asset betas, where their weights are based on their market value. Consequently, the beta for a firm is weighted average of the betas of all the different businesses it is in.

Based on this beta's property, we can estimate the bottom-up beta of the firm on the basis of the following procedure:

- *Step 1)* Identify the business or businesses that characterize the firm whose beta we want to estimate. We can use the breakdown of the operating revenues and operating income of the firm on the basis of the business in which it operates.
- *Step 2)* Estimate the average unlevered betas of other publicly traded firms that operate primarily or only in each of these businesses in which the firm operates. It implies that we have: (1) to define a list of comparable firms; (2) to estimate the betas of each of the comparable firms preferably by using the same common index if it is possible; (3) to compute an unlevered beta for each firm in the comparable firm list by using the debt-to-equity ratio and tax rate for that firm (alternatively we can compute the average beta, debt-to-equity ratio, and tax rate for the sector and unlevered using the averages; (4) to adjust for cash by considering that investments in cash and marketable assets have betas close to zero as follows.

$$\beta_U \text{ corrected for cash} = \frac{\beta_U}{1 - \frac{\text{Cash}}{\text{Firm Value}}}$$

- *Step 3)* Calculate the unlevered beta for the firm. We can consider the weighted average of the unlevered betas of the businesses in which the firm operates by using as weights the right proportion of firm value derived from each business. If we cannot estimate these values, we can use the operating income or operating revenues as weights.
- *Step 4)* Compute the current debt-to-equity ratio for the firm, by using the market values. If it is not possible, we can consider the target debt-to-equity ratio as defined by the firm or the industry typical value of the ratio.
- *Step 5)* Estimate the levered beta for the firm and each of its businesses using the unlevered beta (the bottom-up unlevered beta) and the leverage of the firm. The bottom-up beta reflects changes to a firm's business mix and financial leverage and then it can help to define target in business mix as well as in the financial policy.

The Bottom-Up Beta approach is based on the relationship between beta of levered companies and beta of unlevered companies (Hamada, 1972).

Assume that:

(a) The interest on debt are tax deductions by generating tax savings.
(b) The value of tax shield is based on a constant debt over time.
(c) The discount rate used to estimate the value of tax shield is assumed equal to the cost of debt (K_D). Consequently, the value of the tax shield (W_{TS}) is proportionate to the market value of debt so that: $W_{TS} = D \cdot t_c$.
(d) The debt risk level is very low and then the beta of debt can be assumed equal to zero ($\beta_D = 0$).

Denote with: E_U the equity of unlevered firm; E_L the equity of the levered firm; EBIT the Earnings before tax and interest; t_c the corporate tax rate; I the interest payments on debt; ΔIC the changes in capital invested in the business; β_L the Levered beta for equity in the firm; β_U the Unlevered beta of the firm and then for equity because there is not debt; β_D the beta of Debt; t_c the Marginal tax rate for the firm; D/E: Debt-to-Equity ratio and then the leverage.

The expected return on equity for an unlevered firm $\left(\overline{R_{E_U}}\right)$ and the expected return on equity for a levered firm $\left(\overline{R_{E_L}}\right)$ are equal respectively to:

$$\overline{R_{E_U}} = \frac{\text{EBIT}(1-t_c) - \Delta\text{IC}}{E_U}$$

$$\overline{R_{E_L}} = \frac{\text{EBIT}(1-t_c) - I - \Delta\text{IC}}{E_L}$$

Consider the beta of *j*th firm beta (β_j), and assume that the covariance between expected return on market $\left(\overline{R_m}\right)$ and the components of capital invested in the firm and interests on debt are zero ($\beta_{\Delta IC} = \beta_I = 0$), so that:

$$\beta_j = \frac{\text{Cov}\left(\overline{R_j}, \overline{R_m}\right)}{\text{Var}\left(\overline{R_m}\right)} \rightarrow \begin{array}{l} \beta_U = \dfrac{\text{Cov}\left(\frac{\text{EBIT}(1-t_c)}{E_U}, \overline{R_m}\right)}{\text{Var}(R_M)} \\ \beta_L = \dfrac{\text{Cov}\left(\frac{\text{EBIT}(1-t_c)}{E_L}, \overline{R_m}\right)}{\text{Var}(R_M)} \end{array}$$

The equity, both levered and unlevered, does not have a covariance with market portfolio so that:

$$\beta_U = \frac{\frac{1}{E_U}\text{Cov}\left(\text{EBIT}(1-t_c), \overline{R_m}\right)}{\text{Var}(R_M)} = \frac{\text{Cov}\left(\text{EBIT}(1-t_c), \overline{R_m}\right)}{E_U \text{Var}(R_M)} \rightarrow \beta_U E_U = \frac{\text{Cov}\left(\text{EBIT}(1-t_c), \overline{R_m}\right)}{\text{Var}(R_M)}$$

$$\beta_L = \frac{\frac{1}{E_L}\text{Cov}\left(\text{EBIT}(1-t_c), \overline{R_m}\right)}{\text{Var}(R_M)} = \frac{\text{Cov}\left(\text{EBIT}(1-t_c), \overline{R_m}\right)}{E_L \text{Var}(R_M)} \rightarrow \beta_L E_L = \frac{\text{Cov}\left(\text{EBIT}(1-t_c), \overline{R_m}\right)}{\text{Var}(R_M)}$$

Since:

$$\beta_U E_U = \beta_L E_L$$

it gets:

$$\beta_L = \beta_U \frac{E_U}{E_L}$$

By considering the tax shield, the value of levered firm (W_L) is greater than the value of an unlevered firm (W_U) where the difference is related to the value of tax shield (W_{TS}) as follows:

$$W_L = W_U + W_{TS}$$

By considering that the firm levered value is equal to the value of equity and debt ($W_L = E_L + D$), the firm unlevered value is equal to the equity value ($W_U = E_U$), and the value of the tax shield is proportionate to the market value of debt ($W_{TS} = Dt_c$), and substituting, we have:

$$E_L + D = E_U + Dt_c$$

and by solving by E_U, we have:

$$E_U = E_L + D(1 - t_c)$$

By substituting the unlevered equity (E_U) in the equation $\beta_L = \beta_U \frac{E_U}{E_L}$, it gets:

$$\beta_L = \beta_U \left[\frac{E_L + D(1 - t_c)}{E_L}\right] = \beta_U \left[\frac{E_L}{E_L} + \frac{D(1 - t_c)}{E_L}\right] = \beta_U \left[1 + (1 - t_c)\frac{D}{E_L}\right]$$

and then:

$$\beta_L = \beta_U \left[1 + (1 - t_c)\left(\frac{D}{E}\right)\right]$$

and inverse:

$$\beta_U = \frac{\beta_L}{\left[1 + (1 - t_c)\left(\frac{D}{E}\right)\right]} \tag{21.15}$$

that is the Hamada's equation.

If we consider the debt risk, the beta of debt is not equal to zero ($\beta_D \neq 0$). Remaining equal all other assumptions (a, b, c), the equation can be rewritten as follows:

$$\beta_L = \beta_U \left[1 + (1 - t_c)\frac{D}{E}\right] - \beta_D (1 - t_c)\left(\frac{D}{E}\right)$$

That it can be rearranged as follows:

$$\beta_L = \beta_U + (\beta_U - \beta_D) \cdot (1 - t_c)\frac{D}{E}$$

and inverse:

$$\beta_U = \frac{\beta_L + \beta_D(1 - t_c)\left(\frac{D}{E}\right)}{\left[1 + (1 - t_c)\left(\frac{D}{E}\right)\right]} \tag{21.16}$$

The unlevered beta measures the risk of unlevered firm and therefore the risk function of the firm of its business only. Otherwise, the levered beta is the function of the capital structure choices and then of the financial risk of leverage. Consequently, other variables being equal, an increase in financial leverage increases the levered beta while the unlevered beta does not change. This effect of debt on beta tends to explain why companies operating in the same business, with the same business risk, can have different levered beta as a result of the different capital structure.

21.6 Cost of Debt

The Cost of Debt (K_D) measures the current cost of borrowing funds for the firm. It is the rate of return that investors require to make a debt investment in the firm.

The cost of debt is the function of the *default risk* of the firm that investors perceive: the higher the default risk of the firm perceived by investors, the higher their expected return and then the higher the cost of debt for the firm.

By investing in debt, the interests are fixed at the time of investment, and they represent the promised cash-flow on debt. The worst-scenario for bondholders, is that investor in debt does not receive, with a different degree, the payment of interest and the reimbursement of capital. It happens in case of firm's default.

Since the firm's default risk is the key of the cost of debt, it depends on the specific risk of the firm, differently to the cost of equity that depends on the market risk only by assuming that investor is well-diversified. Indeed, while the risk-return models for equity are based on the effects of the market risk only by assuming a diversified investor (marginal investor), differently models of default risk are based on the effects of firm-specific default risk on promised return for investors in debt.

The expected return for bondholders is equal to the risk-free rate (R_f) plus a premium for default risk of the firm (D_F) that is function of the probability of the firm's incapacity to face debt obligation. Therefore, the cost of debt (K_D) is equal to:

$$R_D = R_f + D_F \tag{21.17}$$

Based on this equation, there is a positive proportional relationship between cost of debt and firm's default risk: the higher the default risk, the higher the return on debt required by investors, and then the higher the cost of debt for the firm.

The firm's default risk is a function of two main variables:

1. *The firm's capability to generate operating cash-flows*: They must be able to face debt obligations in terms of interest in debt and principal repayment. The grater the firm's capability to generate high cash-flows from operating activities relative to debt obligations, the lower default risk. Note this firm's capability to generate operating cash-flows must be evaluated in structural terms over the future time period. It implies that the valuation must be made on the expected return on investments of the firm financed by the debt and its impact on expected operating cash-flows.
2. *The volatility of these operating cash-flows*: The operating cash-flows generated by the firm must be stable over time. The higher the stability in the operating cash-flows, the lower the default risk.

Based on these two conditions, generally firms in predicable and stable business in which they are able to generate high operating cash-flows, will have a low default risk and then low cost of debt.

The firm's default risk can be measured in several way.

The firm's default risk can be measured in a simple way if the firm has long-term bonds outstanding that are widely traded. It is the simpler scenario to measure the default risk. Indeed, if the firm has bonds outstanding that are liquid and trade frequently, the market price of bond can be used to calculate the yield curve that it is used as the cost of debt.

Out of this simple case, one of the most widely measure of the firm's default risk is the bond rating. It is generally assigned by an independent rating agency (such as Standard&Poor's, Moody's and Fitch that are the three most known agency rating). Firms require the rating of bond to the rating agencies because they play a relevant role in financial markets.

The process starts with a firm that requires a rating from bond rating agency. The agency collects information from both publicly available sources, such as financial statements and firm, and makes decisions about rating. If the firm disagrees with the rating assigned, it can present additional information.

Generally, small and private firms are not rated and then there is not rating available to estimate the cost of debt. In this case, two are the common approaches used by analysts:

1. *The use of recent borrowing history*: If the firm borrows money from banks or other financial institutions, we can look at the most recent borrowings made by a firm to deduce the default spreads applied to the firm and use them to estimate the cost of debt.
2. *Estimate a synthetic rating and default spread*: We assign to a firm a synthetic rating by using rating models on the basis of the firm's economic and financial dynamics over time. Specifically, we assign to the firm analysed the same rating of rated firms in the common rating class as defined on the basis of the same economic and financial characteristics. Therefore, we assign the rating by comparison the firm economic and financial conditions to the economic and financial conditions of the firm rated in the same class and we assign their rating. The main

problem is to define the financial ratios to be used for the comparison between the firm analysed and the rated firms.

A more complex approach, requires to use more than one financial ratio. In order to use a multiple financial ratios approach, we can use the Altman Z-Score. It uses five financial ratios as a proxy for default risk. The five ratios used and their weight are based on past history on defaulted firms.

21.7 Weighted Average Cost of Capital

The firm's cost of capital reflects the cost of the financing mix used in the capital structure. Intuitively, the firm's cost of capital is the weighted average of the costs of the different component of financing used by firm to finance its activities.

The most common widely used approach in financial community to estimate the firm's cost of capital is the Weighted Average Cost of Capital (WACC). Based on WACC, the firm's cost of capital (K_F) is equal to the cost of equity (K_E) plus the cost of debt (K_D) weighted on the basis of to equity [$E/(E + D)$] and debt [$D/(E + D)$] in the capital structure and by considering the tax saving due to the fact that interest on debt are tax deductible ($1 - t_c$) as follows:

$$K_F = K_E\left(\frac{E}{E+D}\right) + K_D\left(\frac{D}{E+D}\right)(1 - t_c) \tag{21.18}$$

The right application of the WACC requires to estimate the cost of equity, the cost of debt and the cost of hybrid securities. In this contest, we do not consider specifically the cost of hybrid securities. Since the hybrid securities share some of the characteristics of debt and some of the characteristics of equity, we can break down into their debt and equity components and to estimate them separately.

One of the problems in the WACC apply is the choice of weights. Indeed, we can compute the weight of equity and debt in the capital structure on the basis of their book value or their market value.

The main argument to choose market value is that the cost of capital is a forward-looking measure and it has to capture the cost of raising new capital for the firm. Since new debt and equity have to be raised in the market at prevailing prices, the market value weight is more appropriate. Also, the true value of the firm changes over time on the basis of new information about the firm and the overall condition of economy and financial markets, and then the cost of capital should reflect the market.

On the contrary, the main argument to choose book value is that the book value is not volatile as the market value and then it is more conservative in estimating the cost of capital and debt ratios.

Generally, the use of market value is preferred for the traded firm, while the book value is preferred for private firms.

The Market Value of Equity is equal to the number of shares outstanding times the current stock price. Since it measures the cost of raising funds today, the practice to use average stock process over time or some normalized version of the price is not appropriate.

If the firm is not traded and then there are not shares traded in financial market, the simpler way to estimate the market value of equity is to use the multiple approach by looking at multiples of revenues and operating and net income at which publicly traded firms trade.

The Market Value of Debt is equal to the value of firm's bonds trading in the market. The main problem is that there are very few firms that have all of their debt in the form of bonds outstanding trading in the market. Generally, firms have nontraded debt (such as bank debt) which is specified in book value terms but not market value terms. In this case, we cannot estimate the market value of debt directly by looking at financial markets.

The simpler way to solve the problem is to assume that the book value of the debt is equal to its market value. By refusing this approach, an alternative way is to convert the book value of debt into its market value.

In case of multiple borrowings short- and long-term bonds and bank debt with different terms and interest rates, the simpler solution is to compute the cost of debt by combining all debt and attach the long-term cost of debt to it. In other words, we add the default spread to the long-term risk-free rate and use that rate as the pretax cost of debt.

By applying this approach, the cost of debt is higher than we use the short-term debt. Indeed, the short-term rates tend to be lower than the long-term rates with upward-sloping yield curves. But if we look at the long-term investments because their impact on the firm's value, we want the rate that reflects the cost of long-term borrowing and not short-term borrowing.

In the Cost of Debt estimation, we have to consider the tax advantage due to the fact that interest on debt is tax deductible by generating the tax savings that it reduces the cost of debt.

To estimate the tax advantage, we must use the *marginal tax rate*. It is the tax rate on marginal income (or the last dollar of income). Therefore, we have:

$$\text{After tax cost of debt} = \text{Pretax Cost of debt} \cdot (1 - \text{Marginal tax rate}) \tag{21.19}$$

The marginal tax rate estimation can be problematic and firm tends to use the *effective tax rate* on taxable income that it is equal to taxes paid divided by the net taxable income reported in the financial statement.

The problem is that the marginal tax rate can be different from the effective tax rate. However, we can use the effective tax rate to estimate the marginal tax rate by assuming that they tend to be equal.

Alternatively, the marginal tax rate can be estimated on the basis of the tax rate of the country where firm earns its operating income. If firms realize its operating income in more than one country, the marginal tax rate used should be the average of the different marginal tax rates, weighted by operating income by locale.

Obviously, to obtain the tax advantages of debt, firm must be profitable. Indeed, there is no tax advantage from interest on debt to a firm that has operating losses.

Part V

Valuation

Firm Valuation Approach

22

22.1 The General Equation of Value of the Firm

Firm is able to create value over time if the expected return on invested capital is greater than the cost of capital invested in the firm's activities.

We can formalize these relationships by using an behaviour equation as follows:

$$W_F = W_F\left(R_A^e; K_L^e\right) \qquad (22.1)$$
$$\qquad (+)\,(-)$$

The equation states that the Firm Value (W_F) is a function of expected Return on Invested Capital $\left(R_A^e\right)$ and the expected Cost of Capital of the firm $\left(K_L^e\right)$. Specifically, the Firm Value (W_F) is:

- *Positively* related to the expected Return on Invested Capital $\left(R_A^e\right)$, as indicated by the sign (+) under the variable in the equation. It implies that the increase in R_A^e increases W_F as well as the decrease in R_A^e increases W_F.
- *Negatively* related to the expected Cost of Capital $\left(K_L^e\right)$, as indicated by the sign (–) under the variable. It implies that the decrease in K_L^e increases W_F as well as the increase in K_L^e decreases W_F.

Therefore, the firm's value is the function of its fundamentals and the financial markets for the definition of both variables R_A^e and K_L^e.

Following the financial approach, the equation can be declined in operating terms on the basis of the time, cash-flows and the cost of capital of the firm. In this sense, the firm's value is equal to the present value of expected future cash-flows discounted at the cost of capital of the firm.

Therefore, the firm's value is the function of three main variables:

P. De Luca, *Corporate Finance*, Springer Texts in Business and Economics,
https://doi.org/10.1007/978-3-031-18300-3_22

1. *Time*: The referenced time is always the future. Therefore, the value of the firm is strictly related to future performance.
2. *Cash-flows*: Firm's performances are measured in terms of cash-flows. Specifically, they are considered the expected future cash-flows from operations and to equity.
3. *Cost of capital*: It is used to discount the expected cash-flows, both operating and to equity, and it refers to the cost of capital invested in the firm both in debt and in equity.

Among these variables there are relationships that must be considered in the formalization of models to estimate the firm's value. Therefore, valuation models are based on these variables and on relationships among them.

These variables and relationships among them can be formalized as follows:

$$W_{\mathrm{F}} = \sum_{t=1}^{\infty} \frac{\overline{\mathrm{CF}_t}}{(1+k)^t} \tag{22.2}$$

That is the *General Equation of Firm Value.* The Eq. states that the firm's value (W_{F}) is equal to sum of the expected cash-flows $(\overline{\mathrm{CF}})$ of the firm estimate in each future period (t) discounted at the cost of capital of the firm (k).

Note that both variables, cash-flows and cost of capital, are estimated value. We do not use now and in the future the symbol of estimated value $E[.]$ only to simplify the notion.

The equation states the relationship between firm value, the expected cash-flow and the cost of capital in the time of valuation: the firm's value increases together with an increase in the expected cash-flow and decreases together with an the increase in the cost of capital.

The General equation of Firm Value has a great theoretical relevance but unfortunately it is unable to be applied directly. Two are the main problems to be solved:

1. The definition of the time period.
2. The definition of the valuation perspective.

22.2 Valuation Time Period: Analytical and Synthetical Valuation

The first problem concerns the definition of the valuation time period. In Eq. (22.2) time goes from one year ($t = 1$) to infinite ($t = n$). The problem is usually solved by dividing the valuation time period in two main parts:

1. *The analytic valuation*: It is based on a definite time period that it is equal to 3 or 5 years on the basis of firm characteristics and its market. It defines the *time period of the analytical valuation.*
2. *The synthetical valuation*: It is based on *an* indefinite time period that it goes from the end of time period of analytical valuation to infinity. It represents the *time period of synthetic valuation*. The synthetical valuation is usually realized on the basis of the *Terminal Value (TV)*. Its estimation is a relevant problem in the entire valuation process. We can follow two main approaches:
   (a) *The going concern approach*: It assumes the firm continues to deliver cash-flows in perpetuity. Therefore, the Terminal Value reflects the firm's value after the end of the analytic valuation in perpetuity. This approach is the commonly used in the valuation process because it assumes the indefinite life of the firm. Following we will used this approach to estimate the Terminal Value.
   (b) *The liquidation approach*: It assumes the end of the firm's life at the end of the analytical period. Therefore, the Terminal Value reflects the liquidation value of the firm. It can be estimated at the end of the analytical period on the basis of: (i) the book value of firm's assets adjusted for the inflation during the period or (ii) the earning power of the assets on the basis of the present value of their expected cash-flows. This approach can be considered a special case because different from the first, it assumes the end of the firm's life.

By distinguishing between the analytical and synthetical valuation, we have:

$$W_F = \sum_{t=1}^{n} \frac{\overline{CF}_t}{(1+K)^t} + \frac{TV_n}{(1+K)^n} \tag{22.3}$$

where TV_n indicates the estimation of the Terminal Value at the end ($t = n$) of the period of the analytical valuation.

Therefore, while the first part of the equation estimates the firm's value in a given time period (analytical value of the firm), the second part of the equation estimates the firm's value in an indefinite time period by using the Terminal Value (synthetical value of the firm).

Therefore, Terminal Value (TV) plays a key role in firm's valuation. Specifically, its weight in the estimation of firm value is relevant. If it is high in relevant manner, the entire valuation process can be considered unreliable. We can say that the greater the Terminal Value (TV), the greater the synthetic valuation and the lower the analytic valuation. It implies that much of the estimated value is out of the strategic and financial planning of the firm, then out of the firm's fundamental analysis. In our perspective, the Terminal Value should be less than 40% of firm value.

Following an ongoing approach, we can use two main techniques to estimate the Terminal Value (TV):

1. *Relative Value*: It is based on multiples of earnings, revenues or book value and therefore it is based on relative value. Even if this technique is easy to apply, it has a relevant limit. Multiples are estimated by looking at comparable companies in the business and then it is not based on firm's fundamentals. It implies a dangerous mix between synthetical valuation based on a relative value and the analytical valuation based on firm's fundamentals. This inhomogeneity between the first and the second part of the eq. has a relevant impact on the unreliability of the entire firm's valuation.
2. *Intrinsic Value*: It is based on discounted cash-flow by applying the baseline assumption that the future expected cash-flows will grow at a constant rate in perpetuity. Therefore, assuming a stable growth rate, the Terminal Value can be estimated using a perpetual growth model. Even if this technique is more complex than the relative value, it is based on the firm's fundamentals by eliminating the incoherence between analytical valuation and synthetical valuation and giving homogeneity between the first and second part of equation.
   By following this approach, the Terminal Value can be estimated as follows:

$$\mathrm{TV}_t = \frac{\overline{\mathrm{CFN}_{t+1}}}{K - g_n} \tag{22.4}$$

where:

- $\overline{\mathrm{CFN}_{t+1}}$: is the future normalized expected cash-flow in perpetuity from the first year after the end-time of analytic valuation (t + 1).
- K: is the cost of capital.
- g_n: is the stable growth rate.

Two are the main problem to be solved to apply the TV's equation: (i) the estimation of the stable growth rate (g_n) and (ii) the normalization the expected cash-flows in perpetuity $\left(\overline{\mathrm{CFN}}\right)$. Note that small changes in the estimation of these two variables can imply relevant change in the estimation of Terminal Value and then on the entire firm's valuation.

The common assumption concerns the growth rate is its stability in perpetuity. It implies, among other things, that the firm is characterized by a stable capital structure, low or null excess returns on investments and low reinvestments. Also, the right application of this assumption requires caution because it is very strong restrictions. Particularly, three are the main caveats that must always kept in mind:

1. *The firm cannot grow in perpetuity at a rate higher than the growth rate of the economy referenced.* It implies that the stable growth rate must always be lower or equal to the expected growth rate of the market in which the firm competes or, in general terms, the entire economy. Therefore, if the firm has a domestic dimension, due to internal or external constraints, the expected growth rate of domestic economy represents the limiting value of the expected stable growth

rate of the firm. On the other hand, if the firm has a multinational dimension, or it expects to be so in the future, the expected growth rate in the global economy, or at least in the parts in which the firm operates or wants to operate in the future, represents the limiting value of the expected stable growth rate of the firm.
Also, note that if the valuation is based on nominal value (nominal valuation), the stable growth rate should be nominal and, therefore it should include the expected inflation rate; however, if the valuation is based on real value (real valuation), the stable growth rate should be real and therefore should be lower than nominal one.
Note that by estimating the stable growth rate lower or equal to the growth rate of the economy referenced, it ensures that the stable growth rate will be less than the discount rate.
2. *The period in which the firm is able to sustain a high growth rate before laying down on stable growth rate cannot be defined in a certain way.* Generally, a high growth rate of the firm is the function of its competitive advantage and its related capability to create value over time higher than its competitors. In a strategic perspective, the ability of the firm to sustain a high growth rate for a long period before it will lay down on a stable growth rate is function of two main variables: firstly, the existence of the firm's competitive advantage allowing it to obtain and defend a profitable market position; secondly, the characteristics and competitive dynamics in the market.
3. *The shift from the high growth scenario to the stable growth scenario can be achieved in different ways.* It can be realized by follow: (1) a two-stage model, in which the firm maintains a high growth condition for a period and then it suddenly falls into a stable growth condition abruptly; a three-stage model, in which the firm maintains a high growth condition for a period and then it undergoes a transition period in which it reduces growth gradually towards a stable growth condition. As we will discuss, two-stage and three-stage models represent the basis to estimate the enterprise and equity value.

On the basis of the Terminal Value equation, we can rewrite the firm's value (W_F) as follows:

$$W_F = \sum_{t=1}^{n} \frac{\overline{CF_t}}{(1+K)^t} + \frac{\boxed{\frac{\overline{CFN_{t+1}}}{K-g_n}}}{(1+K)^n} \tag{22.5}$$

and then:

$$W_F = \sum_{t=1}^{n} \frac{\overline{CF_t}}{(1+K)^t} + \frac{\overline{CFN_{t+1}}}{(K-g_n)(1+K)^n} \tag{22.6}$$

The equation has great relevance. It allows to apply the General Equation of Value on the basis of estimation of cash-flows, cost of capital and growth rate.

Obviously, by changing the assumption about the estimation of these variables, it changes the firm value.

It is relevant to note that in the first part of equation, the growth rate (g) is directly considered in the process of forecasting of economic and financial item summarized in the cash-flow for each time period of analytical valuation. Therefore, it is equal to:

$$g = \frac{\mathrm{CF}_t - \mathrm{CF}_{t-1}}{\mathrm{CF}_{t-1}} = \frac{\mathrm{CF}_t}{\mathrm{CF}_{t-1}} - 1$$

Note that while the growth rate g is included in forecasting of cash-flows for each year of the analytical valuation, g_n is the growth rate in a steady condition and then it is the growth at which the cash-flows will grow in perpetuity.

22.3 Valuation Perspective: Equity Side and Asset Side

The second problem relates the application of the General Equation is: the definition of the valuation perspective. Indeed, the right application of the equation requires the identification of: (1) the expected cash-flow to be discounted and (2) the cost of capital used to discount the expected cash-flow.

We can use two perspectives: Equity Side and Asset Side.

22.3.1 Equity Side Perspective

In the *Equity Side* perspective, we estimate the firm's Equity Value (W_{E}). Therefore, cash-flows to be discounted are the expected Free Cash-Flow to Equity ($\overline{\mathrm{FCFE}}$), and the cost of capital used to discount these cash-flows is the Cost of Equity (K_{E}).

Use of the Cost of Equity is due to the nature of the FCFE to be discounted: they are the residual cash-flows after the coverage of the firm's needs and the debt obligations and destined to equity remuneration.

Therefore, in the Equity Side perspective, the Equity Value of the firm is equal to:

$$W_{\mathrm{E}} = \sum_{t=1}^{n} \frac{\overline{\mathrm{FCFE}_t}}{(1+K_{\mathrm{E}})^t} + \frac{\mathrm{TV}_n}{(1+K_{\mathrm{E}})^n} \tag{22.7}$$

By denoting with $\overline{\mathrm{FCFEN}_{t+1}}$ the future normalized expected FCFE in perpetuity from the first year after the end-time of analytic valuation ($t + 1$), and by considering the stable growth rate (g_n), the Terminal Value is equal to:

$$\mathrm{TV}_t = \frac{\overline{\mathrm{FCFEN}_{t+1}}}{K_{\mathrm{E}_{t+1}} - g_n} \tag{22.8}$$

Substituting, it gets:

$$W_E = \sum_{t=1}^{n} \frac{\overline{FCFE_t}}{(1+K_E)^t} + \frac{\left[\frac{\overline{FCFEN_{t+1}}}{K_{E_{t+1}} - g_n}\right]}{(1+K_E)^n} \tag{22.9}$$

and then, in the Equity Side perspective the firm's Equity Value is estimated equal to:

$$W_E = \sum_{t=1}^{n} \frac{\overline{FCFE_t}}{(1+K_E)^t} + \frac{\overline{FCFEN_{t+1}}}{(K_{E_{t+1}} - g_n)(1+K_E)^n} \tag{22.10}$$

22.3.2 Asset Side Perspective

In the *Asset Side* perspective, we estimate the firm's asset value usually called Enterprise Value (W_A).

Therefore, cash-flows to be discounted are the expected Free Cash-Flow from Operations $\left(\overline{FCFO}\right)$, and the cost of capital used to discount these cash-flows is the firm's Cost of Capital (K_A).

Use of the firm's Cost of Capital, is based on both the cost of equity and the cost of debt, is due to the nature of the FCFO to be discounted: they derive from the operating activities of the firm and they are used in remuneration of both equity-holders and debt-holders.

Therefore, in Asset Side perspective, the Enterprise Value of the firm is equal to:

$$W_A = \sum_{t=1}^{n} \frac{\overline{FCFO_t}}{(1+K_A)^t} + \frac{TV_n}{(1+K_A)^n} \tag{22.11}$$

By denoting with $\overline{FCFON_{t+1}}$ the future normalized expected FCFO in perpetuity from the first year after the end-time of analytic valuation (t + 1), and by considering the stable growth rate (g_n), the Terminal Value is equal to:

$$TV_t = \frac{\overline{FCFON_{t+1}}}{K_{A_{t+1}} - g_n} \tag{22.12}$$

Substituting, it gets:

$$W_A = \sum_{t=1}^{n} \frac{\overline{FCFO_t}}{(1+K_A)^t} + \frac{\left[\frac{\overline{FCFON_{t+1}}}{K_{A_{t+1}} - g_n}\right]}{(1+K_A)^n} \tag{22.13}$$

and then, in the Asset Side perspective, the firm's Enterprise Value is estimated equal to:

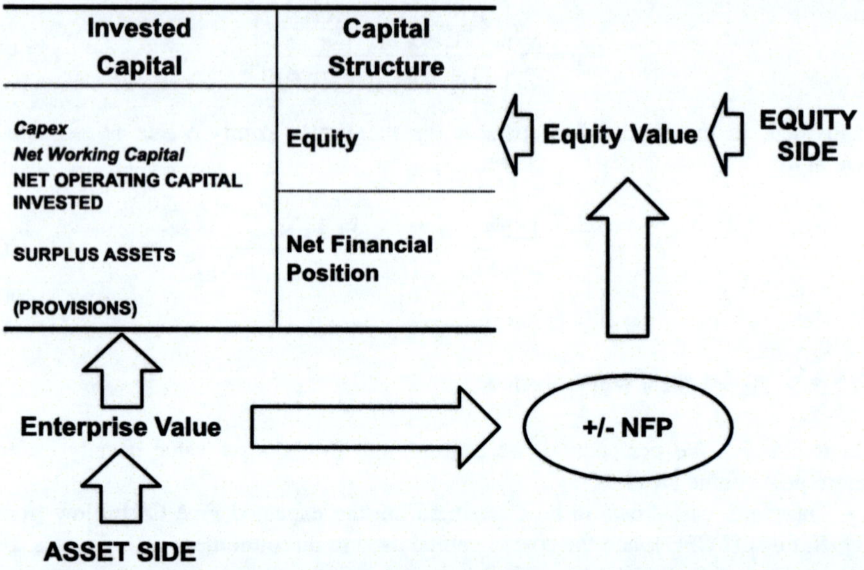

Fig. 22.1 Valuation perspectives: Asset Side and Equity Side

$$W_A = \sum_{t=1}^{n} \frac{\overline{\text{FCFO}_t}}{(1+K_A)^t} + \frac{\overline{\text{FCFON}_{t+1}}}{(K_{A_{t+1}} - g_n)(1+K_A)^n} \tag{22.14}$$

Note that we can estimate the Equity Value (W_E) in indirect way on the basis of the Enterprise Value (W_A). In this case, the Equity Value is equal to the Enterprise Value less the Net Financial Position (NFP) as follows:

$$W_E = W_A - \text{NFP} \tag{22.15}$$

It implies that if there are not financial debt the Equity Value is equal to the Enterprise Value and then there is not the problem of the valuation perspective.

The two valuation perspectives, Asset Side and Equity Side, can be schematically represented as in Fig. 22.1.

There are several models to estimate the Equity Value and the Enterprise Value. In this context, we will follow the financial approach. Therefore, we estimate the *Equity Value* by using:

1. Dividend Discounted Model.
2. Free Cash-Flow to Equity Discounted Model.

Similarly, we estimate the *Firm Value* by using:

1. Free Cash-Flow to the Firm Discounted Model based on Cost of Capital Approach and on Adjusted Present Value Approach.
2. Discounted Economic Profit.

The model of both Equity Value and Enterprise Value will be applied by considering three main scenarios: (1) Constant growth or one-period model; (2) Two-Stage Growth or two-period model: (3) Three-Stage Growth or three-period model.

Obviously, it is possible to use others steps by passing from the three-period model to an n-period model. By moving from the one-period model to three-period model (or *n*-period model), we need more information and we must consider more variables and it implies more complexity in the evaluation process. On the contrary, the use of few variables implies a high level of simplicity but a low level of confidence about the value estimated. The right trade-off between complexity and manageability must be solved on the basis of the information available and the analyst's forecasting skills.

Finally, we will estimate both the Equity Value and the Enterprise Value by using the multiples approach.

Equity Valuation Models 23

23.1 Dividend Discount Model

The shareholder's value is function of two variables:

1. *Expected dividends*, that they are paid by the company during the period the shares are held.
2. *Expected capital gain*, that are paid by the capital markets at the end of the holding period if the selling price is higher than the buying price. The expected stock price in financial markets, is the function of two main variables: (i) company's fundamentals, from which depend on the expected dividends that could be paid by the company; (ii) supply and demand of the stock in financial market based on trading analysis.

Note that in this contest, all expected value are not denoted with bar on the variable to avoid further burdening the notation.

The company's dividend policy is usually measured on the basis of the Dividend Payout Ratio (PR): it is equal to the sum of the dividend (Div) and stock buyback (SB) divided by Net Income (NI), as follows:

$$\mathrm{PR} = \frac{\mathrm{Div} + \mathrm{SB}}{\mathrm{NI}} \tag{23.1}$$

and by considering the Dividend per Share (DPS), the Stock Buyback per Share (SBS) and the Earnings per Share (EPS), we have:

$$\mathrm{PR_S} = \frac{\mathrm{DPS} + \mathrm{SBS}}{\mathrm{EPS}} \tag{23.2}$$

To avoid that the stock buyback could be financed by debt, we can compute the Payout Ratio Adjusted ($\mathrm{PA_A}$) by subtracting the long-term debt (D_{LT}) as follows:

P. De Luca, *Corporate Finance*, Springer Texts in Business and Economics,
https://doi.org/10.1007/978-3-031-18300-3_23

$$PR_A = \frac{\text{Div} + \text{SB} - D_{LT}}{\text{NI}} \tag{23.3}$$

The DDM is based on the expected Dividends (Div). It is relevant to note that they are equal to the expected Free Cash-Flow to Equity (FCFE) used in the Discounted Cash-Flow (DCF). The difference among them refers the way by which they are estimated in the valuation models:

1. Dividends in DDM are estimated on the basis of direct approach by considering directly their growth over time.
2. Free Cash-Flow to Equity (FCFE) used in the Discounted Cash-Flow (DCF) are estimated on the basis of indirect approach by considering indirectly their growth in the economic and financial dynamics and then on the basis of the forecast of each economic and financial item.

The DDM is the simplest model to estimate Equity Value. Three are the main advantages:

1. It is based on an easy economic intuition: dividends are the only cash-flows relevant and tangible for the shareholders.
2. The estimation of dividends requires few assumptions: dividends are estimated by applying a growth rate to the last dividend paid or by considering the historical trend.
3. Dividends are usually assumed stable over time: equity value estimation based on dividends is more stable than the estimation based on cash-flows.

Even if the DDM is a simple model, it has relevant limit due to the strong baseline restrictions. Among them two are the main:

1. Cash generated and used for the company's self-funding, and then do not distributed in dividends, is not considered. It implies that the equity value could be underestimated.
2. Dividends may be paid by issuing new debt or new shares. It implies that share value could be overestimated.

Therefore, on the basis of the trade-off between advantage and disadvantage of the model, the model can be useful in three main cases:

1. Case 1: If the cash-flows generated by the company are lower than dividends paid. In this case, dividends to be paid reduce the managers' opportunity to invest in low-value investments.
2. Case 2: If dividends paid by the company are stable over time. In this case, the estimation of the share value is realistic.

3. Case 3: If the estimation of the Free Cash-Flow to Equity on the basis of the economic and financial dynamics of the company is very complex. In this case, the dividends are the only stable parameter for evaluation in Equity Side.

The *Dividend Discounted Model (*DDM*)* estimates the Equity Value (W_E) equal to the present value of the expected Dividends in the future (Div_t) discounted to the Cost of Equity (K_E), as follows:

$$W_E = \sum_{t=1}^{\infty} \frac{\text{Div}_t}{(1+K_E)^t} \tag{23.4}$$

If we consider the Dividend per Share (DPS_t) the DDM estimates the Equity Value per Share (W_{E_S}) equal to the present value of the expected Dividend per Share (DPS_t) discounted to the Cost of Equity (K_E), as follows:

$$W_{E_S} = \sum_{t=1}^{\infty} \frac{\text{DPS}_t}{(1+K_E)^t} \tag{23.5}$$

Therefore, the DDM is based on three variables: (i) the *expected Dividend* (Div); (ii) the *cost of equity* (K_E), and the time period (t) of valuation.

Even if the equation has a relevant theoretical value, it not directly applicable by requiring the definition of assumptions about variables. On the basis of these assumptions, we can have several versions of the DDM model. Among them the three are the main versions:

1. *Steady-state Growth or Constant Growth model* (DDM_{CG}): The grow of dividends is assumed constant over time indefinitely.
2. *Two-Stage Growth model* (DDM_{2S}): The grow of dividends is assumed to change over time on the basis of two time period: in the first period, the growth is extraordinary for a defined number of years; in the second period, the growth is steady-state in an indefinitely way.
3. *Three-Stage Growth model* (DDM_{3S}): The grow of the dividends is assumed to change over time on the basis of three time period: in the first period, the growth is extraordinary for a defined number of years; in the second period, the growth goes to a long-run steady-state level for a defined number of years; in the third period, the growth is steady-state in an indefinitely way.

In order to simply the DDM's analysis in its three versions, we will consider the Stock Price (P) by assuming that in time $t = 0$,it reflects the equity value per share (W_{E_S}), so that: $W_{E_{S(0)}} = P_0$.

23.2 Discount Dividend Model: Constant Growth

The *Constant Growth DDM* (DDM_{CG}), also called *Single-Period Model* or *One-Period Model* (or Gordon Growth Model), is the simplest version of the DDM. It assumes that dividends will grow at the same growth rate (g_n) into an indefinite future. Therefore, the DDM_{CG} is based on a steady-state growth rate (g_n) of dividends over time.

The DDM_{CG} is based on strong baseline assumptions. Among them three can be considered the main:

1. The company's and its business must be characterized by a dynamic in line with the stable growth rate.
2. The company must maintain a stable dividend policy.
3. The company must earn a stable return on new equity investment over time.

The DDM_{CG} estimates the Equity Value (W_E) of the company on the basis of the expected dividends in the next period (Div_1), the cost of equity (K_E) and a constant growth rate of dividends (g_n), as follows:

$$W_E = \frac{Div_1}{(1+K_E)} + \frac{Div_1(1+g_n)}{(1+K_E)^2} + \frac{Div_1(1+g_n)^2}{(1+K_E)^3} + \frac{Div_1(1+g_n)^3}{(1+K_E)^4} + \ldots + \frac{Div_1(1+g_n)^{n-1}}{(1+K_E)^n}$$

Since the growth rate g_n is assumed constant over time, and by using the formula of the sum of a geometric progression, it gets:

$$W_E = \frac{\frac{Div_1}{(1+K_E)}\left[1-\left(\frac{1+g_n}{1+K_E}\right)^n\right]}{1-\frac{1+g_n}{1+K_E}}$$

Since the growth rate g_n is assumed constant over time, we have:

$$\lim_{n\to\infty}\left(\frac{1+g_n}{1+K_E}\right)^n = \lim_{n\to\infty}\frac{(1+g_n)^n}{(1+K_E)^n} = 0$$

and consequently:

$$W_E = \frac{\frac{Div_1}{1+K_E}}{1-\frac{1+g_n}{1+K_E}} = \frac{\frac{Div_1}{1+K_E}}{\frac{1+K_E-1-g_n}{1+K_E}} = \frac{Div_1}{1+K_E}\cdot\frac{1+K_E}{K_E-g_n} = \frac{Div_1}{K_E-g_n}$$

and then:

$$W_E = \frac{Div_1}{K_E-g_n} \tag{23.6}$$

Therefore the DDM_{CG} states that the company's Equity Value (W_E) is equal to the expected dividend of the next first year of forecast (Div_1) divided by the difference between the Cost of Equity (K_E) and the expected constant growth rate (g_n) over time.

The company's Equity Value (W_E) can be different to the Current Stock Prices (P_0) at least in the short-run. If we assume that the Equity Value (W_E) is equal to the Current Stock Prices (P_0) ($W_E = P_0$), we can use the equation to define directly the Current Stock Prices (P_0) as follows:

$$P_0 = \frac{\text{Div}_1}{K_E - g_n} \tag{23.7}$$

If we assume that the Equity Value is equal to the Current Stock Price ($W_E = P_0$), we can explicit the DDM_{CG} in terms of rate of return (r_E). Solving the equation for the Cost of Equity (K_E), and by considering that the cost of equity (K_E) is the rate of return (r_E) expected by investors in equity, so that $r_E \equiv K_E$, we can rewrite the equation as follows:

$$r_E = \frac{\text{Div}_1}{P_0} + g_n \tag{23.8}$$

We can define the expected returns of investors' in equity (r_E) in terms of:

- Share-part of Earnings Retained (b) by the firm for self-financing;
- Rate of Return on Earn (r) of the new firm's investment (I).

We can define the Earnings (E) in time t as follows:

$$E_t = E_{t-1} + rI_{t-1}$$

If we assume constant the Rate of Return on Earn (r), the firm's new investments are equal to the earnings retained (b) by the firm, so that:

$$E_t = E_{t-1} + rbE_{t-1} = E_{t-1}(1 + rb)$$

We can define the Growth Rate of Earnings (g_E) as follows:

$$g_E = \frac{E_t - E_{t-1}}{E_{t-1}} = \frac{E_{t-1}(1 + rb) - E_{t-1}}{E_{t-1}} = \frac{E_{t-1} + E_{t-1}rb - E_{t-1}}{E_{t-1}} = rb$$

The equation shows that by defining the share-part of earnings retained for self-financing (b) and by assuming constant the rate of return on earn of new investments (r), the growth of earnings (g_E) implies the definition of the growth rate of dividends (g_D). Indeed, on the basis of r and b, if a constant part of earning is used to finance the new investment, the other part is used to pay dividend.

If r and b are assumed constant over time, we can define the constant growth rate g_n in terms of r and b, so that:

$$g_n = rb$$

Consequently, the Current Stock Price (P_0) is equal to:

$$P_0 = \frac{\mathrm{Div}_1}{K_E - rb} \quad (23.9)$$

and the expected returns of investors' in equity r_E, is equal to:

$$r_E = \frac{\mathrm{Div}_1}{P_0} + rb \quad (23.10)$$

Note that in these equations, a key role is played by new future profitability of investment opportunities. The Rate of Return on Earn (r) of the new firm's investment can be expressed as a fraction (α) of the Rate of Return of Investors' in equity (r_E):

$$r = \alpha r_E$$

By considering that:

$$\mathrm{Div}_1 = (1 - b)E_1$$

the expected return of investors in equity (r_E) is equal to:

$$r_E = \frac{\mathrm{Div}_1}{P_0} + rb = \frac{(1 - b)E_1}{P_0} + \alpha r_E b$$

and rearrange, it gets:

$$r_E = \frac{(1 - b)E_1}{(1 - \alpha b)P_0} \quad (23.11)$$

The equation states that:

1. If there are no extraordinary investment opportunities, $\alpha = 1$ and consequently $r_E = E_1/P_0$. Therefore, the Equity-holder requires the inverse of Price-Earnings ratio.
2. If there are extraordinary investment opportunities, $\alpha > 1$ and the investment opportunities are expected to offer a return above the one required by the Equity holders.

The DDM_{CG} is very simple in its logic and application. Unfortunately, its utility is limited. The main problems can be summarized as follows:

1. The model can be used with some utility only if the firm is characterized by a stable growth rate and a stable dividend payout policy over time.
2. By considering the dividend only, the model underestimates the company with the self-financing process.
3. The growth rate of the stable growth has to be less than or equal to the growth rate of the markets referenced. It is unreasonable to assume that the company can grow at a rate greater than the growth rate of the referenced market in the long-term.

23.3 Discount Dividend Model: Two-Stage Growth

The *Two-Stage Growth DDM* (DDM_{2S}), also called *Two-Period Growth Model* is based on two stages of growth:

1. *Extraordinary growth period*: It is the first period (*form* $t = 1$ *to* $t = n$) the growth rate of dividend cannot be considered stable over time. Indeed, it can be higher or lower than the stable growth rate, and then the growth rate is defined "extraordinary" (g_e).
2. *Steady-state growth period*: It is the second period (*from* $t = n + 1$ *to* $t = \infty$) the growth rate of dividend can be considered stable over time, and then the growth rate is defined "stable" (g_n). Note that after a certain number of years, we usually assume a growth rate stable because it is very difficult to estimate it.

In both periods, the discount rate is the Cost of Equity (K_E). In order to distinguish the cost of equity in the two periods, we can denote with $K_{E,\ eg}$ the Cost of Equity in the first period (extraordinary growth period) and with $K_{E,\ st}$ the cost of equity in the second period (constant growth). These two costs of equity, they can be equal ($K_{E,\ eg} = K_{E,\ sg}$) or different ($K_{E,\ eg} \neq K_{E,\ sg}$). It is relevant to note that these two costs of equity refer to the period considered only and not to the growth rate applied to dividends. Therefore, they can be different in the two period only if we expected to change the risk-free rate (R_f) or the return on market (R_m) and then the premium risk on market ($R_m - R_m$) while the coefficient beta does not change.

On the basis of these two periods of time, the Current Stock Price (P_0) can be estimated as follows:

$$P_0 = \left[\frac{\mathrm{Div}_1}{(1 + K_{E,eg})} + \frac{\mathrm{Div}_1(1 + g_e)}{(1 + K_{E,eg})^2} + \frac{\mathrm{Div}_1(1 + g_e)^2}{(1 + K_{E,eg})^3} + \ldots + \frac{\mathrm{Div}_1(1 + g_e)^{n-1}}{(1 + K_{E,eg})^n}\right] + \frac{P_n}{(1 + K_{E,st})^n}$$

where the P_n is the price of stock in the second period (steady-state growth period). It can be estimate on the basis of the one-period model as follows:

$$P_n = \frac{\mathrm{Div}_{n+1}}{K_{\mathrm{E,st}} - g_n}$$

Based on the formula for the sum of a geometric progression, we have:

$$P_0 = \left[\frac{\frac{\mathrm{Div}_1}{(1+K_{\mathrm{E,eg}})}\left[1-\left(\frac{1+g_e}{1+K_{\mathrm{E,eg}}}\right)^n\right]}{1-\frac{1+g_e}{1+K_{\mathrm{E,eg}}}}\right] + \frac{\frac{\mathrm{Div}_{n+1}}{K_{\mathrm{E,st}}-g_n}}{(1+K_{\mathrm{E,st}})^n}$$

By considering that the first part of equation (in brackets) can be rearranged as follows:

$$\frac{\frac{\mathrm{Div}_1}{(1+K_{\mathrm{E,eg}})}\left[1-\left(\frac{1+g_e}{1+K_{\mathrm{E,eg}}}\right)^n\right]}{1-\frac{1+g_e}{1+K_{E,eg}}} = \frac{\frac{\mathrm{Div}_1\left[1-\left(\frac{1+g_e}{1+K_{\mathrm{E,eg}}}\right)^n\right]}{(1+K_{\mathrm{E,eg}})}}{\frac{1+K_{\mathrm{E,eg}}-1-g_e}{1+K_{\mathrm{E,eg}}}} = \frac{\mathrm{Div}_1\left[1-\left(\frac{1+g_e}{1+K_{\mathrm{E,eg}}}\right)^n\right]}{(1+K_{\mathrm{E,eg}})}$$

$$\cdot\frac{(1+K_{\mathrm{E,eg}})}{K_{\mathrm{E,eg}}-g_e} = \frac{\mathrm{Div}_1\left[1-\left(\frac{1+g_e}{1+K_{\mathrm{E,eg}}}\right)^n\right]}{K_{\mathrm{E,eg}}-g_e}$$

We have:

$$P_0 = \mathrm{Div}_1\left[\frac{1-\left(\frac{1+g_e}{1+K_{\mathrm{E,eg}}}\right)^n}{K_{\mathrm{E,eg}}-g_e}\right] + \frac{\frac{\mathrm{Div}_{n+1}}{K_{\mathrm{E,st}}-g_n}}{(1+K_{\mathrm{E,st}})^n}$$

and then:

$$P_0 = \mathrm{Div}_1\left[\frac{1-\left(\frac{1+g_e}{1+K_{\mathrm{E,eg}}}\right)^n}{K_{\mathrm{E,eg}}-g_e}\right] + \frac{\mathrm{Div}_{n+1}}{(K_{\mathrm{E,st}}-g_n)(1+K_{\mathrm{E,eg}})^n} \tag{23.12}$$

We can define the equation on the basis of the current dividend (Div_0). Consider that:

1. Dividend in time $t = n + 1$ (Div_{n+1}) can be expressed in terms of dividend in the first period as follows:

$$\mathrm{Div}_{n+1} = \mathrm{Div}_1(1+g_e)^{n-1}(1+g_n)$$

2. Dividend in time $t = 1$ (Div_1) can be expressed in terms of current dividend (Div_0) as follows:

$$\text{Div}_1 = \text{Div}_0(1 + g_e)$$

Therefore, we have:

$$\begin{aligned}\text{Div}_{n+1} &= \text{Div}_1(1 + g_e)^{n-1}(1 + g_n) = \text{Div}_0(1 + g_e)(1 + g_e)^{n-1}(1 + g_n)\\ &= \text{Div}_0(1 + g_e)^n(1 + g_n)\end{aligned}$$

Substituting, we can rewrite the equation on the basis of the current dividend (Div_0) as follows:

$$P_0 = \text{Div}_0(1 + g_e)\left[\frac{1 - \left(\frac{1+g_e}{1+K_{\text{E,eg}}}\right)^n}{K_{\text{E,eg}} - g_e}\right] + \frac{\text{Div}_0(1 + g_e)^n(1 + g_n)}{(K_{\text{E,st}} - g_n)\left(1 + K_{\text{E,eg}}\right)^n} \quad (23.13)$$

If we do not know the current dividend (Div_0), we can use a approximate procedure. The current dividend can be estimated on the basis of Net Income (NI) and Payout Ratio (PR), as follows:

$$\text{Div} = \text{NI} \cdot \text{PR}$$

Similarly, we can estimate the Dividend per Share (DPS) on the basis of the Earning per Share (EPS) and Payout Ratio per Share (PRS), as follows: DPS = EPS · PRS

On the basis of it, the Current Stock Price (P_0) is equal to:

$$\begin{aligned}P_0 = \text{NI}_0 \cdot \text{PR}_o \cdot (1 + g_e)&\left[\frac{1 - \left(\frac{1+g_e}{1+K_{\text{E,eg}}}\right)^n}{K_{\text{E,eg}} - g_e}\right]\\ &+ \frac{\text{NI}_0 \cdot \text{PR}_o \cdot (1 + g_e)^n(1 + g_n)}{(K_{\text{E,st}} - g_n)\left(1 + K_{\text{E,eg}}\right)^n}\end{aligned} \quad (23.14)$$

Note that there is a strict relationship between the Payout Ratio (PR) and the growth rate (g). Conceptually, if the growth rate is expected to drop drastically in the second period, the payout should be higher in the second period (steady-state growth period) than the first period (extraordinary growth period). A company in steady-state period can pay out more of its earnings in dividends than it can do in the high growth period (first period) in which it needs to self-financing for its investments.

The relationship between Payout Ratio (PR) and growth rate (g) can be expressed on the basis of the ROE.

An approximate measure of self-financing is the Retention Rate (RR) on ROE. The Retention Rate (RR) is equal to 1 less Payout Ratio (PR): RR = 1 − PR.

The growth rate (g) can be approximated as the Retention Rate (RR) and ROE, as follows:

$$g = \text{RR} \cdot \text{ROE} = (1 - \text{PR}) \cdot \text{ROE}$$

By solving for Payout Ratio (PR), it gets:

$$\text{PR} = 1 - \frac{g}{\text{ROE}} \tag{23.15}$$

23.3.1 The DDM$_{2S}$ Based on Dividends Estimation

We can apply the DDM$_{2S}$ on the basis of the estimation of dividends for each year in the first period (Div$_t$), and a constant dividend in the second period (Div$_{n+1}$) as follows:

$$P_0 = \sum_{t=1}^{n} \frac{\text{Div}_t}{\left(1 + K_{\text{E,eg}}\right)^t} + \frac{\frac{\text{Div}_{n+1}}{K_{\text{E,sg}} - g_n}}{\left(1 + K_{\text{E,sg}}\right)^n}$$

and then:

$$P_0 = \sum_{t=1}^{n} \frac{\text{Div}_t}{\left(1 + K_{\text{E,eg}}\right)^t} + \frac{\text{Div}_{n+1}}{\left(K_{\text{E,sg}} - g_n\right)\left(1 + K_{\text{E,sg}}\right)^n} \tag{23.16}$$

We can apply this equation when the growth rate of dividends it is not constant over time and then it is not possible to apply the geometric progression. Indeed, in this case, the growth rate is incorporated in the dividend that we have to discount.

We can divide the equation in two parts:

1. The first part of Equation is the present value of the expected dividends in the first period ($t = 1 \to n$). In this first period (extraordinary growth period) dividends are estimated for each year (Div$_t$) and the growth rate (g_e) is incorporated in the dividend estimation in each year and then it can be different over the years. Therefore, the growth rate can be measured as a variation from 1 year to the next as follows: $g_e = \frac{\text{Div}_{t+1}}{\text{Div}_t} - 1$.
2. The second part of Equation is the present value of the constant dividends in the second period ($t = n + 1 \to \infty$). It this second period (steady-state growth period) the dividends (Div$_{n+1}$) are estimated constant over time, and the growth rate (g_n) is assumed constant in perpetuity.

Also in this case, in both periods the cost of equity is used to discount the expected dividends. It can be assumed equal in the two periods ($K_{\text{E, eg}} = K_{\text{E, sg}}$) or different ($K_{\text{E, eg}} \neq K_{\text{E, sg}}$).

Generally, the DDM$_{2S}$ is useful for the firm characterized by different growth levels between the first and the second period. Specifically, the model can be used if the firm is characterized by a growth rate in the first period higher or lower than the stable growth rate of the second period.

Three are the main problems of the model:

- First, it is difficult to estimate the length of the first period (the extraordinary growth period).
- Second, the growth rate is assumed high in the first period and declining at the end of the first period until a stable level characterizes the second period. Even if we assume this trend, however, it is reasonable to assume that the move from the high growth to stable growth happens gradually over time.
- Third, the model underestimates the value of the firm when it prefers the self-financing to the dividend payout.

23.3.2 Two-Stage Growth DDM with H-Model Specification

A specific version of DDM_{2S} is the *Two-Stage Growth DDM with H-Model Specification* (DDM_{2SH}). The DDM_{2SH} is based on three baseline assumptions:

1. The growth rate (g_a) decreases in a linear manner during the first period (extraordinary growth) characterized by two stages (2H) to reach a stable growth rate during the second period (steady-state).
2. Cost of equity (K_E) is constant over time and it is independent of the growth rate (g).
3. Dividend is assumed constant over time and then in both periods. Also, it is assumed independent of the growth rate (g).

Based on these assumptions, the Current Stock Price (P_0) is equal to:

$$P_0 = \frac{\text{Div}_0(1 + g_n)}{K_E - g_n} + \frac{\text{Div}_0(g_a - g_n)H}{K_E - g_n} \tag{23.17}$$

The DDM_{2SH} allows to exceed the limit of the DDM_{2S} in which the growth rate (g_e) drops drastically from high growth to stable growth. Otherwise, the DDM_{2SH} is characterized by two main problems:

- First, the model assumes a linear decrease of the growth rate (g_a) from a level in perpetuity. Even assuming a fall in the growth rate, it may not be linear. Generally, small differences from the assumption are not relevant to the company value estimation; otherwise, relevant differences have a high impact on this. Therefore, the model can be used for the company characterized by a high growth rate, but with an estimation of its gradual fall mainly due to the growth of the company size and reduction of the competitive advantage.
- Second, the model assumes constant dividends (payout ratio) in both periods. In reality, usually when the growth rate decreases, the payout ratio increases.

Therefore, the model is not appropriate for companies with low dividends or with no dividends.

23.4 Discount Dividend Model: Three-Stage Growth

The *Three-Stage Growth DDM* (DDM_{3S}), also called *Three-Period Growth Model*, is based on three different periods:

1. *Extraordinary growth period*: It is the first period and it is characterized by extraordinary (high or low) growth rate (g_e).
2. *Transitional growth period*: It is the second period and it is characterized by a growth rate (g_{tr}) declining or increasing to reach a stable level.
3. *Steady-state growth period*: It is the third period and it is characterized by a steady-state growth rate (g_n).

The Current Stock Price (P_0) is equal to the sum of present values of expected Dividends (Div) in the extraordinary growth period (first period), transitional growth period (second period) and the steady-state growth period (third period).

On all these three periods, the Cost of Equity (K_E) is used to discount the expected dividends. We can denote with $K_{E,\ eg}$ the cost of equity in the extraordinary growth period (first period), $K_{E,\ tr}$ the cost of equity in the transitional growth period (second period), $K_{E,\ st}$ the cost of equity in the steady-state growth period (third period). They can be assumed equal or different among them.

Also in this case, the three costs of equity refer to the three period considered only and not to the growth rate applied to dividends. Therefore, they can be different among them only if we expected to change the risk-free rate (R_f) or the return on market (R_m) and then the premium risk on market ($R_m - R_m$) while the coefficient beta does not change.

The DDM_{3S} define the Current Stock Price (P_0) as follows:

$$P_0 = \left[\frac{\mathrm{Div}_1}{(1+K_{E,eg})} + \frac{\mathrm{Div}_1(1+g_e)}{(1+K_{E,eg})^2} + \frac{\mathrm{Div}_1(1+g_e)^2}{(1+K_{E,eg})^3} + \ldots + \frac{\mathrm{Div}_1(1+g_e)^{n-1}}{(1+K_{E,eg})^n}\right]$$
$$+ \left[\frac{\mathrm{Div}_{n+1}}{(1+K_{E,tr})^{n+1}} + \frac{\mathrm{Div}_{n+1}(1+g_{tr})^{n+1}}{(1+K_{E,tr})^{n+2}} + \frac{\mathrm{Div}_1(1+g_{tr})^{n+2}}{(1+K_{E,tr})^{n+3}} + \ldots\right.$$
$$\left. + \frac{\mathrm{Div}_1(1+g_{tr})^{m-1}}{(1+K_{E,tr})^m}\right] + \frac{P_m}{(1+K_{E,st})^m}$$

where the P_m is the price of stock in the third period (steady-state growth period). It can be estimated on the basis of the one-period model as follows:

$$P_m = \frac{\mathrm{Div}_{m+1}}{K_{\mathrm{E,st}} - g_n}$$

Based on the formula for the sum of a geometric progression, we have:

$$P_0 = \left[\frac{\frac{\mathrm{Div}_1}{(1+K_{\mathrm{E,eg}})}\left[1-\left(\frac{1+g_e}{1+K_{\mathrm{E,eg}}}\right)^n\right]}{1-\frac{1+g_e}{1+K_{\mathrm{E,eg}}}}\right] + \left[\frac{\frac{\mathrm{Div}_{n+1}}{(1+K_{\mathrm{E,tr}})}\left[1-\left(\frac{1+g_{\mathrm{tr}}}{1+K_{\mathrm{E,tr}}}\right)^m\right]}{1-\frac{1+g_{\mathrm{tr}}}{1+K_{\mathrm{E,tr}}}}\right] + \frac{\frac{\mathrm{Div}_{m+1}}{K_{\mathrm{E,st}}-g_n}}{(1+K_{\mathrm{E,st}})^m}$$

The second part of the equation can be rewritten as follows:

$$\frac{\frac{\mathrm{Div}_{n+1}}{(1+K_{\mathrm{E,tr}})}\left[1-\left(\frac{1+g_{\mathrm{tr}}}{1+K_{\mathrm{E,tr}}}\right)^m\right]}{1-\frac{1+g_{\mathrm{tr}}}{1+K_{\mathrm{E,tr}}}} = \frac{\frac{\mathrm{Div}_{n+1}\left[1-\left(\frac{1+g_{\mathrm{tr}}}{1+K_{\mathrm{E,tr}}}\right)^m\right]}{(1+K_{\mathrm{E,tr}})}}{\frac{1+K_{\mathrm{E,tr}}-1-g_{\mathrm{tr}}}{1+K_{\mathrm{E,tr}}}} = \frac{\mathrm{Div}_{n+1}\left[1-\left(\frac{1+g_{\mathrm{tr}}}{1+K_{\mathrm{E,tr}}}\right)^m\right]}{(1+K_{\mathrm{E,tr}})}$$

$$\cdot\frac{(1+K_{\mathrm{E,tr}})}{K_{\mathrm{E,tr}}-g_{\mathrm{tr}}} = \frac{\mathrm{Div}_{n+1}\left[1-\left(\frac{1+g_{\mathrm{tr}}}{1+K_{\mathrm{E,tr}}}\right)^m\right]}{K_{\mathrm{E,tr}}-g_{\mathrm{tr}}}$$

Therefore, by substituting we have:

$$P_0 = \left[\mathrm{Div}_1\left[\frac{1-\left(\frac{1+g_e}{1+K_{\mathrm{E,eg}}}\right)^n}{K_{\mathrm{E,eg}}-g_e}\right]\right] + \left[\mathrm{Div}_{n+1}\left[\frac{1-\left(\frac{1+g_{\mathrm{tr}}}{1+K_{\mathrm{E,tr}}}\right)^m}{K_{\mathrm{E,tr}}-g_{\mathrm{tr}}}\right]\right] + \frac{\frac{\mathrm{Div}_{m+1}}{K_{\mathrm{E,st}}-g_n}}{(1+K_{\mathrm{E,eg}})^m}$$

and then:

$$P_0 = \left[\mathrm{Div}_1\left[\frac{1-\left(\frac{1+g_e}{1+K_{\mathrm{E,eg}}}\right)^n}{K_{\mathrm{E,eg}}-g_e}\right]\right] + \left[\mathrm{Div}_{n+1}\left[\frac{1-\left(\frac{1+g_{\mathrm{tr}}}{1+K_{\mathrm{E,tr}}}\right)^m}{K_{\mathrm{E,tr}}-g_{\mathrm{tr}}}\right]\right]$$
$$+\frac{\mathrm{Div}_{m+1}}{(K_{\mathrm{E,st}}-g_n)(1+K_{\mathrm{E,eg}})^m} \quad (23.18)$$

23.4.1 The *DDM*$_{3S}$ Based on Dividends Estimation

We can apply the DDM$_{3S}$ on the basis of the estimation of dividends for each year in the first period ($\mathrm{Div}_{t\,=\,1;\,n}$) and the second period ($\mathrm{Div}_{t\,=\,n\,+\,1;\,m}$), and a constant dividend in the third period ($\mathrm{Div}_{m\,+\,1}$), as follows:

$$P_0 = \sum_{t=1}^{n} \frac{\text{Div}_t}{(1+K_{\text{E,eg}})^t} + \sum_{t=n+1}^{m} \frac{\text{Div}_t}{(1+K_{\text{E,tr}})^t} + \frac{\frac{\text{Div}_{m+1}}{K_{\text{E,sg}} - g_n}}{(1+K_{\text{E,st}})^m}$$

and then:

$$P_0 = \sum_{t=1}^{n} \frac{\text{Div}_t}{(1+K_{\text{E,eg}})^t} + \sum_{t=n+1}^{m} \frac{\text{Div}_t}{(1+K_{\text{E,tr}})^t} + \frac{\text{Div}_{m+1}}{(K_{\text{E,sg}} - g_n)(1+K_{\text{E,st}})^m} \quad (23.19)$$

We can apply this equation when the growth rate of dividends it is not constant over time and then it is not possible to apply the geometric progression. Indeed, in this case, the growth rate is incorporated in the dividend that we have to discount.

The Equation can be divided into three parts:

- The first part is the present value of the expected dividends in the first period ($t = 1 \rightarrow n$). It is based on: (i) dividends estimate for each year (Div_t) of the first period and (ii) the growth rate (g_e) that it is incorporated in the dividend estimation in each year and then it can be different over the years. Therefore, the growth rate can be measured as a variation from one year to the next as follows: $g_e = \frac{\text{Div}_{t+1}}{\text{Div}_t} - 1$.
- The second part is the present value of the expected dividends in the second period ($t = n + 1 \rightarrow m$). It is based on: (i) the dividends estimate for each year (Div_t) of the second period and (ii) the growth rate (g_{tr}) that it is incorporated in the dividend estimation in each year and then it can be different over the years. Therefore, the growth rate can be measured as a variation from one year to the next as follows: $g_{tr} = \frac{\text{Div}_{t+1}}{\text{Div}_t} - 1$.
- The third part is the present value of the price in the third period and then at the end of the m-years ($t = m + 1 \rightarrow \infty$). It is based on: (i) the dividends (Div_{m+1}) estimate constant over time and (ii) the growth rate (g_n) that it is assumed constant in perpetuity.

It is worth noting that in all these three periods, the cost of equity is used to discount the expected dividends. It can be assumed equal in the three periods ($K_{\text{E, eg}} = K_{\text{E, tr}} = K_{\text{E, sg}}$) or different ($K_{\text{E, eg}} \neq K_{\text{E, tr}} \neq K_{\text{E, sg}}$).

The $\text{DDM}_{3\text{S}}$ is more flexible than the $\text{DDM}_{2\text{S}}$. It is more useful in a contest characterized by changes in growth rate, risk profile and dividend policy. Also it is useful if the company is characterized by a high growth rate expected to maintain for an initial period after which it is expected to gradually decrease until reaching a stable growth rate.

Note that the pay-out ratio is normally assumed as inverse to the growth rate; in the first period, high growth rate requires a low pay-out ratio, while in the third period a low-stable growth rate is compatible with a high pay-out ratio. In the second period their dynamics are inverted.

23.5 Free Cash-Flow to Equity Discounted Model

The Discounted Cash-Flow (DCF) model is one of the most use to estimate the value. It can be applied in the Equity Side (DCF_{ES}) or Asset Side (DCF_{AS}) perspective. While in the Equity Side perspective, we estimate the Equity Value of the firm, in the Asset Side perspective, we estimate the entire Enterprise Value.

The Discounted Cash-Flow model in Asset Side perspective (DCF_{ES}), is based on the Free Cash-Flow to Equity (FCFE) and the Cost of Equity (K_E).

Since the FCFE are the Dividends paid by company to investors, the fundamental difference between the Dividend Discounted Model (DDM) and the Discounted Cash-Flow model in Equity Side perspective (DCF_{ES}) is due to the different estimation of dividends:

- In DDM expected dividends paid are estimated synthetically on the basis of the past and present without considering the company's fundamentals. In this case, the growth rate incorporates all reasonings about the expected dividends and then it is an input of the model.
- In DCF_{ES} the expected Free Cash-Flow to Equity (FCFE) is estimated analytically on the basis of economic and financial dynamics of the company and then on its fundamental analysis. Therefore, the growth rate is incorporated in all economic and financial items. Consequently, the yearly change of FCFE incorporates the growth rate that is the output of the model.

Therefore, while DDM is based on the growth rate of dividend as input of the model, in the DCF_{ES} the growth rate on FCFE is the output of the entire process of planning in which it is considered the growth rate of each economic and financial item. In this sense, in the DDM the dividends are estimated synthetically, while in the DCF_{ES} the FCFE are estimated analytically on the basis of the company fundamental analysis. For this reason, the DCF_{ES} can be considered more effective than the DDM.

Also, in dividends in the DDM can be estimated by considering also the self-financing needs of the firm. Differently, the FCFE in DCF_{ES} are the cash-flow residual after the coverage of all company's obligations (they are defined "free" for this reason) and distributed to equityholders as dividend. Consequently, there is not cash accumulation (self-financing) in the company.

Finally, dividends in the DDM are estimated positive by definition. A negative amount of dividend is a nonsense if we must consider its forecast development on the basis of a growth rate. It happens because the dividend is estimated in a synthetical way and then problem concern financial requirements are just solved so that the dividend can be at least equal to zero.

Differently, FCFE in the DCF_{ES} can be estimated also negative because they are estimated analytically on the basis of the forecast of economic and financial dynamic of the company. If it happens, their amount represents the company's capital needs and then the amount of the financial requirement.

These fundamental differences imply that the two models, can arrive at a different estimation of the dividends and then a different estimation of the company's equity value even if they are both based on the dividends. If it happens the DCF_{ES} is more effective than the DDM.

Even if the DCF_{ES} can be considered more reliable than the DDM, we must always to keep in mind that the right application of the DCF_{ES} requires a deeply knowledge of the company and its fundamentals. Indeed, the FCFE estimation requires the development of the forecast economic and financial dynamic of the company, and then a lot of information and it is more complex. Since external analysts usually do not have all information need to a deeply analysis of the firm, they prefer the DDM to the DCF_{ES}.

Note that based on this difference, while in DDM we can define a constant growth rate of dividends, and then we can operate on the basis of the geometric progression, in DCF the growth rate is not constant and then we cannot operate in that way unless for the Terminal Value in which we define the constant growth rate.

The DCF_{ES} estimate the Equity Value (W_E) on the basis of the Free Cash-Flow to Equity (FCFE) and the Cost of Equity (K_E), as follows:

$$W_E = \sum_{t=1}^{\infty} \frac{FCFE_t}{(1 + K_E)^t} \tag{23.20}$$

The equation is based on three variables: (1) the *expected Free Cash-Flow to equity (FCFE);* (2) the *cost of equity* (K_E), and (3) the time period (t) of valuation.

Even if the equation has a relevant theoretical value, it is not directly applicability by requiring the definition of assumptions about variables. On the basis of these assumptions, we can use several versions of the DCF_{ES} model. Among them the three are the main versions:

1. *Steady-state Growth or Constant Growth model* ($DCF_{ES\text{-}CG}$): The grow of the company and then the FCFE is assumed constant over time indefinitely.
2. *Two-Stage Growth model* ($DCF_{ES\text{-}2S}$): The grow of the company and then the FCFE is assumed to change over time on the basis of two time period: in the first period, the growth is extraordinary for a defined number of years; in the second period, the growth is steady-state in an indefinitely way.
3. *Three-Stage Growth model* ($DCF_{ES\text{-}3S}$): The grow of the company and then the FCFE is assumed to change over time on the basis of three time period: in the first period, the growth is extraordinary for a defined number of years; in the second period, the growth goes to a long-run steady-state level for a defined number of years; in the third period, the growth is steady-state in an indefinitely way.

23.6 Free Cash-Flow to Equity Discounted Model: Constant Growth

The *Constant Growth DCF in Equity Side perspective* ($DCF_{ES\text{-}CG}$) estimates the Equity Value of the firm on the basis of a constant and stable growth (g_n).

The $DCF_{ES\text{-}CG}$ estimates the Equity Value (W_E) of the company on the basis of the expected Free Cash-Flow to Equity (FCFE) in the next period ($FCFE_1$), the Cost of Equity (K_E) and a constant growth rate (g_n), as follows:

$$W_E = \frac{FCFE_1}{(1+K_E)} + \frac{FCFE_2}{(1+K_E)^2} + \ldots + \frac{FCFE_n}{(1+K_E)^n}$$

By considering that the implicit growth rate of the FCFE are constant over time, we can approximate as follows:

$$W_E = \frac{FCFE_1}{(1+K_E)} + \frac{FCFE_1(1+g_n)}{(1+K_E)^2} + \frac{FCFE_1(1+g_n)^2}{(1+K_E)^3} + \ldots + \frac{FCFE_1(1+g_n)^{n-1}}{(1+K_E)^n}$$

and by using the formula of the sum of a geometric progression, it gets:

$$W_E = \frac{\frac{FCFE_1}{(1+K_E)}\left[1 - \left(\frac{1+g_n}{1+K_E}\right)^n\right]}{1 - \frac{1+g_n}{1+K_E}}$$

Since the growth rate g_n is assumed constant over time, we have:

$$\lim_{n\to\infty}\left(\frac{1+g_n}{1+K_E}\right)^n = \lim_{n\to\infty}\frac{(1+g_n)^n}{(1+K_E)^n} = 0$$

and consequently:

$$W_E = \frac{\frac{FCFE_1}{1+K_E}}{1 - \frac{1+g_n}{1+K_E}} = \frac{\frac{FCFE_1}{1+K_E}}{\frac{1+K_E-1-g_n}{1+K_E}} = \frac{FCFE_1}{1+K_E} \cdot \frac{1+K_E}{K_E - g_n} = \frac{FCFE_1}{K_E - g_n}$$

and then:

$$W_E = \frac{FCFE_1}{K_E - g_n} \tag{23.21}$$

The equation is similar to the Gordon's model for the DDM with constant growth. Consequently, it is characterized by the same limitations.

In this case a further consideration it is necessary with regard to the FCFE. Indeed, different from the DDM_{CS} in this case the growth rate of the FCFE is known only at the end of the process in which we have forecasted each economic and financial item by considering a specific growth rate for each of them.

Consequently, the growth rate of FCFE in the analytical valuation is not constant over time. Differently, in the computation of Terminal Value, in which we have to define in a synthetical way the FCFE stable over time, we can define a stable growth rate and then we can always apply this equation.

23.7 Free Cash-Flow to Equity Discounted Model: Two-Stage Growth

The *Two-Stage Growth DCF in Equity Side perspective* ($DCF_{ES\text{-}2S}$) estimates the Equity Value of the firm on the basis an extraordinary growth rate in the first period until to reach a steady-state growth rate in a second period.

Therefore, the model assumes two different period characterized by different growth rates:

1. *Extraordinary growth period*: It is the first period and it is characterized by higher growth than steady-state growth. This period lasts n years.
2. *Steady-state growth period*: It is the second period and it is characterized by a steady-state growth over time.

On the basis of these two periods, the $DCF_{ES\text{-}2S}$ estimates the company's Equity Value (W_E) equal to the present value of FCFE during the extraordinary growth period (first period) plus the present value of Terminal Value (TV) estimated for the steady-state growth period (second period).

The Cost of Equity (K_E) used to discount the expected FCFE is equal to the $K_{E,\ eg}$ in the first period (extraordinary growth period) and $K_{E,\ st}$ in the second period (Steady-state growth period). They can be equal or different among them.

Formally:

$$W_E = \sum_{t=1}^{n} \frac{\mathrm{FCFE}_t}{(1 + K_{E,eg})^t} + \frac{\mathrm{TV}_n}{(1 + K_{E,st})^n} \tag{23.22}$$

By considering that the growth rate is already considered in the estimation of the FCFE, we can define it in the first period as follows:

$$g = \frac{\mathrm{FCFE}_{t+1}}{\mathrm{FCFE}_t} - 1$$

The *extraordinary growth rate* (g) in the first period is different from *steady-state growth rate* (g_n) of the second period.

To estimate the Terminal Value (TV) we can use the $DCF_{ES\text{-}CG}$ (and then on the basis of Gordon Growth Model in DDM) in which the growth rate is assumed constant over time indefinitely. Therefore, it is equal to.

$$\mathrm{TV}_n = \frac{\mathrm{FCFE}_{n+1}}{K_{\mathrm{E,sg}} - g_n} \tag{23.23}$$

Substituting, it gets:

$$W_{\mathrm{E}} = \sum_{t=1}^{n} \frac{\mathrm{FCFE}_t}{\left(1 + K_{\mathrm{E,eg}}\right)^t} + \frac{\frac{\mathrm{FCFE}_{n+1}}{K_{\mathrm{E,st}} - g_n}}{\left(1 + K_{\mathrm{E,sg}}\right)^n}$$

and then:

$$W_{\mathrm{E}} = \sum_{t=1}^{n} \frac{\mathrm{FCFE}_t}{\left(1 + K_{\mathrm{E,eg}}\right)^t} + \frac{\mathrm{FCFE}_{n+1}}{\left(K_{\mathrm{E,sg}} - g_n\right)\left(1 + K_{\mathrm{E,sg}}\right)^n} \tag{23.24}$$

Therefore, the equation estimates the company's Equity Value (W_{E}) on the basis of two parts:

1. The first part is the present value of the expected FCFE estimated in the first period for each year. Therefore, it represents the "analytical" part of valuation because the expected FCFE is estimated for each year considered.
2. The second part is the present value of expected Terminal Value estimated in the second period from the end of the first period in perpetuity. Therefore, it represents the "synthetical" part of valuation because it is based on the Terminal Value.

23.8 Free Cash-Flow to Equity Discounted Model: Three-Stage Growth

The *Three-Stage Growth DCF in Equity Side perspective* ($\mathrm{DCF}_{\mathrm{ES\text{-}3S}}$) estimates the Equity Value of the company on the basis of three different period characterized by different growth rates:

1. *Extraordinary growth period*: It is the first period and it is characterized by a high growth rate.
2. *Transitional growth period*: It is the second period and it is characterized by a declining growth rate until to reach a stable level.
3. *Steady-state growth period*: It is the third period and it is characterized by a steady-state growth rate.

The company's Equity Value (W_{E}) is equal to the sum of present values of expected FCFE in the extraordinary growth period (first period) in which the growth rate is equal to (g_a), transactional growth period (second period) in which the growth rate is equal to (g_{tr}) and steady-state growth period (third period) in which the growth rate is equal to (g_n).

The Cost of Equity (K_E) used to discount the expected FCFE, is equal to $K_{E,\ eg}$ in the first period, $K_{E,\ tr}$ in the second period and $K_{E,\ st}$ in the third period.

Therefore, the $DCF_{ES\text{-}3S}$ estimates the company's Equity Value (W_E) as follows:

$$W_E = \sum_{t=1}^{n} \frac{FCFE_t}{\left(1 + K_{E,eg}\right)^t} + \sum_{t=n+1}^{m} \frac{FCFE_t}{\left(1 + K_{E,tr}\right)^t} + \frac{TV_m}{\left(1 + K_{E,st}\right)^m} \tag{23.25}$$

Since the growth rate in the first period (g_a) and in the second period (g_{tr}) are incorporated in the estimation of the FCFE, we can compute them as follows:

$$g_a = \frac{FCFE_{t+1}}{FCFE_t} - 1;\ g_{tr} = \frac{FCFE_{t+1}}{FCFE_t} - 1$$

Also in this case, the Terminal Value (TV) can be estimated on the basis of the $DCF_{ES\text{-}CG}$ (and then on the basis of Gordon Growth Model in DDM) in which the growth rate is assumed constant over time indefinitely, as follows:

$$TV_m = \frac{FCFE_{m+1}}{K_{E,st} - g_m} \tag{23.26}$$

Substituting, it gets:

$$W_E = \sum_{t=1}^{n} \frac{FCFE_t}{\left(1 + K_{E,eg}\right)^t} + \sum_{t=n+1}^{m} \frac{FCFE_t}{\left(1 + K_{E,tr}\right)^t} + \frac{\frac{FCFE_{m+1}}{K_{E,st} - g_m}}{\left(1 + K_{E,st}\right)^m}$$

and then:

$$W_E = \sum_{t=1}^{n} \frac{FCFE_t}{\left(1 + K_{E,eg}\right)^t} + \sum_{t=n+1}^{m} \frac{FCFE_t}{\left(1 + K_{E,tr}\right)^t} + \frac{FCFE_{m+1}}{\left(K_{E,st} - g_m\right)\left(1 + K_{E,st}\right)^m} \tag{23.27}$$

Therefore, the model is based on three parts:

1. The first part is the present value of expected FCFE in the first period (from $t = 1$ to $t = n$) and it is characterized by a high growth rate (g_a).
2. The second part is the present value of the expected FCFE in the second period (from $t = n + 1$ to $t = m$) and it is characterized by a transitional growth rate (g_{tr}).
3. The third part is the present value of expected Terminal Value in the third period (from $t = m + 1$ in perpetuity) and it is characterized by a steady-state growth rate (g_n).

While the first and second parts represent the "analytical" part of valuation because in both parts expected FCFE are estimated for each year considered, the third part represents the "synthetical" part of valuation because it is based on the Terminal Value.

Firm Valuation Models

24

24.1 Free Cash-Flow to the Firm Discount Models

The Discounted Cash-Flow (DCF) model can be applied in Asset Side (DCF_{AS}) perspective other than in the Equity Side (DCF_{ES}) perspective as analyzed in the previous chapter. While in the Equity Side perspective, we estimate the Equity Value of the firm, in the Asset Side perspective, we estimate the entire Firm Value. Consequently, while in Equity valuation we consider the perspective of the shareholders only, in the Enterprise valuation, we consider the perspective of all investors in equity and debt of the firm.

Similar to Equity Value estimation, the Firm Value is estimated by following a financial approach on the basis of Cash-Flow Discounted model. Different to the Equity Side perspective, in Asset Side perspective the cash-flow considered are the Free Cash-Flow to the Firm (FCFF) (instead of the Free Cash-Flow to Equity (FCFE) used in Equity Value) and the cost of capital is the Company's Cost of Capital (K_A) (instead of the Cost of Equity (K_E) in Equity Value).

Therefore, the Discounted Cash-Flow model in Asset Side perspective (DCF_{AS}), is based on the Free Cash-Flow to the Firm (FCFF) and the Firm Cost of Capital (K_A).

We can always define a simple relationship between Firm Value and Equity Value. Indeed, the Equity Value can estimate indirectly on the basis of the Firm Value by subtracting to it the value of Net Financial Position. Similarly, the Firm Value can estimate indirectly on the basis of Equity Value by adding to it the value of the Net Financial Position.

However, it is possible, and it usually is, that in both cases, Equity value and Firm Value, the direct valuation is different from the indirect valuation.

Specifically, Equity Value estimated indirectly on the basis of the Firm Value tends to be equal to the Equity value estimated directly only if we introduce consistent assumptions about debt level. Generally, the direct estimation of Equity Value is preferred to indirect one if the company is characterized by a non-optimal debt level (very high or low). In this case, the direct estimation of the Equity Value

P. De Luca, *Corporate Finance*, Springer Texts in Business and Economics,
https://doi.org/10.1007/978-3-031-18300-3_24

based on the FCFE is able to capture well the effects of debt on value rather than the indirect estimation of the Equity value based on the Firm Value.

The DCF_{AS} is characterized by three main problems with respect to the DCF_{ES}:

1. The FCFF's are less intuitive than the FCFE. While the FCFE is the expected dividends that company will pay to the shareholders, the FCFF is an intermediate dimension of cash-flow used to analyze the company's ability to face debt obligations and to pay dividends.
2. The FCFF can hide the real problem of company survival. If the company is characterized by a positive FCFF but a negative FCFE, the focus on FCFF could hide the problem. Indeed, even if the FCFF is positive, the negative value of the FCFE measures the recapitalization need of the company.
3. The estimation of the Company's Cost of Capital requires the evaluation and inclusion of all costs and benefits related to the debt. This procedure requires the use of several assumptions that have a relevant impact on the Firm Value.

The DCF_{AS} can be applied by following two main approaches:

1. *Cost of Capital (CC) approach*: The Firm Value is estimated on the basis of Free Cash-Flow from Operations (FCFF) discounted at a Company's Cost of Capital by considering either the cost of equity and the cost of debt. Following this approach, costs and benefits of debt are considered directly in the Cost of Capital used to discount the future expected FCFF.
2. *Adjusted Present Value (APV) approach*: The Firm Value is estimated by distinguishing and summing three parts: i) the *unlevered value of company*, equal to the present value of the unlevered Free Cash-Flow from Operations (FCFF); ii) the *value of the benefits on debt*, equal to the present value of the tax savings due to the interests on debt; iii) the *value of the default risk* due to the bankruptcy costs as function of leverage. Following this approach, the Firm Value is the sum of these three parts.

Note that these two approaches do not necessarily come up with the same Firm Value. Three are the main reasons:

1. Bankruptcy costs are considered in different ways in the two approaches and the indirect costs due to the bankruptcy are more clearly defined and analyzed in the APV approach than in the CC approach.
2. The tax benefits link to the debt are considered by the APV approach on the basis of the existing debt level. Differently, the CC approach estimates tax benefits only after the definition of the "target" debt level that is the debt level able to "optimize" the capital structure. In this case, the cost of capital is used to define the debt level.
3. The value of tax shield is estimated in the APV approach is equal to the present value of the tax savings. The expected cash-flows of tax savings may be discounted at a rate different from Cost of Debt (such as the Cost of Unlevered

Equity or Cost of Capital). Consequently, by change the discount rate, changes the Firm Value.

Among these two approaches, the Cost of Capital (CC) approach is more useful in the case of ongoing company evaluation characterized by a sustainable capital structure. Differently, the Adjusted Present Value (APV) approach is preferred in transactions based on a non-optimal debt level of the firm and where the debt repayment is negotiated or well known.

Note that in this contest, all expected values are not denoted with bar on the variable to avoid further burdening the notation.

24.2 Free Cash-Flow to the Firm Discount Model: Cost of Capital Approach

The Discounted Cash-Flow Model in Asset Perspective applied by following the Cost of Capital approach ($DCF_{AS(CC)}$) estimates the Firm Value (W_A) equal to the present value of the Free Cash-Flow from Operation (FCFF) discounted to the Company's Cost of Capital (K_A), as follows:

$$W_A = \sum_{t=1}^{\infty} \frac{FCFF_t}{(1 + K_A)^t} \quad (24.1)$$

The Company's Cost of Capital (K_A) is estimated on the basis of the Cost of Equity (K_E) and the Cost of Debt (K_D). Consequently, it represents the expected returns of investors in equity and debt, respectively. Therefore, this approach considers the problem of the debt level choice directly in the cost of capital, whose estimation is a key variable in the model.

The Company's Cost of Capital (K_A) is usually estimated on the basis of the Weighted-Average Cost of Capital (WACC).

The equation has a theoretical value only. Its applications require assumptions about its three variables: 1) the *expected Free Cash-Flow to the Firm (FCFF); 2)* the company Cost of Capital (K_A), and 3) the time period (t) of valuation.

Similar to the Dividend Discounted Model (DDM) and the Discounted Cash-Flow in Equity perspective (DCF_{ES}), on the basis of assumptions concern these three variables, we can use several versions of the $DCF_{AS(CC)}$ model. Among them the three are the main versions:

1. *Steady-state Growth or Constant Growth model* ($DCF_{AS(CC)\text{-}CG}$): The grow of the company and then the FCFF is assumed constant over time indefinitely.
2. *Two-Stage Growth DCF* ($DCF_{AS(CC)\text{-}2S}$): The grow of the company and then the FCFF is assumed to change over time on the basis of two time period: in the first period, the growth is extraordinary for a defined number of years; in the second period, the growth is steady-state in an indefinitely way.

3. *Three-Stage Growth DCF* ($DCF_{AS(CC)\text{-}3S}$): The grow of the company and then the FCFF is assumed to change over time on the basis of three time period: in the first period, the growth is extraordinary for a defined number of years; in the second period, the growth goes to a long-run steady-state level for a defined number of years; in the third period, the growth is steady-state in an indefinitely way.

In all three cases, the same considerations made for the Dividend Discounted Model (DDM) and the Discounted Cash-Flow in Equity perspective (DCF_{ES}) can be directly applied here.

24.2.1 Steady-State Growth Model

The *Constant Growth DCF in Asset Side perspective* ($DCF_{AS(CC)\text{-}CG}$) estimate the Firm Value of the company on the basis of a constant growth rate over time.

The model estimates the Firm Value (W_A) of the company on the basis of the expected Free Cash-Flow to the Firm (FCFF) in the next period ($FCFF_1$), the Cost of Capital (K_A) and a constant growth rate (g_n), as follows:

$$W_A = \frac{FCFF_1}{(1+K_A)} + \frac{FCFF_2}{(1+K_A)^2} + \ldots + \frac{FCFF_n}{(1+K_A)^n}$$

By considering that the growth rate of the FCFF is constant over time, it is possible to approximate as follows:

$$W_E = \frac{FCFF_1}{(1+K_A)} + \frac{FCFF_1(1+g_n)}{(1+K_A)^2} + \frac{FCFF_1(1+g_n)^2}{(1+K_A)^3} + \ldots + \frac{FCFF_1(1+g_n)^{n-1}}{(1+K_A)^n}$$

and by using geometric progression, it gets:

$$W_A = \frac{\frac{FCFF_1}{(1+K_A)}\left[1 - \left(\frac{1+g_n}{1+K_A}\right)^n\right]}{1 - \frac{1+g_n}{1+K_A}}$$

The growth rate g_n is assumed constant over time. Therefore, we have:

$$\lim_{n\to\infty}\left(\frac{1+g_n}{1+K_A}\right)^n = \lim_{n\to\infty}\frac{(1+g_n)^n}{(1+K_A)^n} = 0$$

and consequently:

$$W_A = \frac{\frac{FCFF_1}{1+K_A}}{1 - \frac{1+g_n}{1+K_A}} = \frac{\frac{FCFF_1}{1+K_A}}{\frac{1+K_A-1-g_n}{1+K_A}} = \frac{FCFF_1}{1+K_A}\cdot\frac{1+K_A}{K_A-g_n} = \frac{FCFF_1}{K_A-g_n}$$

and then:

$$W_A = \frac{\text{FCFF}_1}{K_A - g_n} \tag{24.2}$$

Therefore, the Firm Value (W_A) is equal to the present value of di Free Cash-Flow to the Firm in the next year assumed in perpetuity (FCFF_1) discounted at the company's Cost of Capital (K_A) less the growth rate in perpetuity (g_n).

The is similar to the Gordon's model in DDM and its extension to the Discounted Cash-Flow in Equity perspective ($\text{DCF}_{\text{ES-CG}}$) by assuming a constant growth rate.

In this case the FCFF_1, that is the Free Cash-Flow to the Firm in the next following year (in $t = 1$), must be estimated by assuming that it can be realized also in each future year in perpetuity. Also, the estimation of the FCFF_1 is synthetical because it is not based on the analytical estimation. Indeed, it is not the result of the process in which each economic and financial item is estimated, but it is assume synthetically as input of the model. Consequently, the Firm Value is estimated synthetically on the basis of the assumptions with regard to the growth rate and the cost of capital without any analytical estimation of the FCFF.

The right application of the equation requires the respect of two main conditions:

- The expected growth rate in perpetuity (g_n) must be equal or lower than the expected growth rate of the economy or the business of the firm.
- The company characteristics must be assumed constant over time so that the firm can growth in constant way over time. To do this, it is necessary that the company's investments must not be relevant because the growth margin is low. In this sense, we can derive the reinvestment rate on the basis of the stable growth rate and the return on investment in perpetuity. Specifically, the ReInvestment Rate in stable growth condition (IR_{SG}) can be estimated equal to the growth rate in a steady-state condition (g_n) divided by Return on Investment that they are assumed stable over time (ROI_{SG}), as follows:

$$\text{IR}_{\text{GS}} = \frac{g_n}{\text{ROI}_{\text{GS}}} \tag{24.3}$$

24.2.2 Two-Stage Growth Model

The *Two-Stage Growth DCF in Asset Side perspective* ($DCF_{AS(CC)\text{-}2S}$) estimates the Firm Value of the company on the basis of an extraordinary growth rate in the first period until to reach a steady-state growth rate in a second period.

Therefore, the model assumes two different periods characterized by different growth rates:

1. *Extraordinary growth period*: It is the first period and it is characterized by higher growth than steady-state growth. This period lasts n years.

2. *Steady-state growth period*: It is the second period and it is characterized by a steady-state growth over time.

On the basis of these two periods, the $DCF_{AS(CC)\text{-}2S}$ estimates the Equity Value (W_E) of the firm equal to the present value of FCFF during the extraordinary growth period (first period) plus the present value of Terminal Value (*TV*) estimated for the steady-state growth period (second period).

The Cost of Capital (K_A) used to discount the expected FCFF is equal to the $K_{A,\,eg}$ in the first period (extraordinary growth period) and $K_{A,\,st}$ in the second period (Steady-state growth period). Formally:

$$W_A = \sum_{t=1}^{n} \frac{\text{FCFF}_t}{(1 + K_{A,\text{eg}})^t} + \frac{\text{TV}_n}{(1 + K_{A,\text{st}})^n} \tag{24.4}$$

By considering that the growth rate is already considered in the estimation of the FCFF, we can define it in the first period as follows:

$$g = \frac{\text{FCFF}_{t+1}}{\text{FCFO}_t} - 1.$$

The *extraordinary growth rate* (g) in the first period is different from *steady-state growth rate* (g_n) of the second period.

To estimate the Terminal Value (TV), we can use the $DCF_{AS(CC)\text{-}CG}$ (and then on the basis of Gordon Growth Model in DDM) in which the growth rate is assumed constant over time indefinitely. Therefore, it is equal to.

$$\text{TV}_n = \frac{\text{FCFF}_{n+1}}{K_{A,\text{sg}} - g_n} \tag{24.5}$$

Substituting, it gets:

$$W_A = \sum_{t=1}^{n} \frac{\text{FCFF}_t}{(1 + K_{A,\text{eg}})^t} + \frac{\frac{\text{FCFF}_{n+1}}{K_{A,\text{st}} - g_n}}{(1 + K_{A,\text{sg}})^n}$$

and then:

$$W_A = \sum_{t=1}^{n} \frac{\text{FCFF}_t}{(1 + K_{A,\text{eg}})^t} + \frac{\text{FCFF}_{n+1}}{(K_{A,\text{sg}} - g_n)(1 + K_{A,\text{sg}})^n} \tag{24.6}$$

Therefore, the equation estimates the Firm Value (W_A) on the basis of two parts:

1. The first part is the present value of the expected FCFF estimated in the first period for each year. Therefore, it represents the "analytical" part of valuation because the expected FCFF is estimated for each year considered.
2. The second part is the present value of expected Terminal Value estimated in the second period from the end of the first period in perpetuity. Therefore, it

represents the "synthetical" part of valuation because it is based on the Terminal Value.

Note that the Cost of Capital should be different in the two periods ($K_{A,\ eg} \neq K_{A,\ sg}$). Since it is based on the cost of equity and the cost of debt, even if the cost of equity is assumed constant, the cost of debt reflects the choices about capital structure and then it can be changed over time. It is reasonable to assume that the capital structure in the second period characterized by a steady-state condition may be different from the first period characterized by an extraordinary growth.

24.2.3 Three-Stage Growth Model

The *Three-Stage Growth DCF in Asset Side perspective* ($DCF_{AS(CC)\text{-}3S}$) estimates the Firm Value of the company on the basis of three different period characterized by different growth rates:

1. *Extraordinary growth period*: It is the first period and it is characterized by a high growth rate.
2. *Transitional growth period*: It is the second period and it is characterized by a declining growth rate until it reach a stable level.
3. *Steady-state growth period*: It is the third period and it is characterized by a steady-state growth rate.

The company's Firm Value (W_A) is equal to the sum of present values of expected FCFF in the extraordinary growth period (first period) in which the growth rate is equal to (g_a), transactional growth period (second period) in which the growth rate is equal to (g_{tr}) and steady-state growth period (third period) in which the growth rate is equal to (g_n).

The Cost of Capital (K_A) used to discount the expected FCFF, is equal to $K_{A,\ eg}$ in the first period, $K_{A,\ tr}$ in the second period and $K_{A,\ st}$ in the third period.

Therefore, the model estimates the company's Firm Value (W_A) as follows:

$$W_A = \sum_{t=1}^{n} \frac{\text{FCFF}_t}{(1 + K_{A,\text{eg}})^t} + \sum_{t=n+1}^{m} \frac{\text{FCFF}_t}{(1 + K_{A,\text{tr}})^t} + \frac{\text{TV}_m}{(1 + K_{A,\text{st}})^m} \tag{24.7}$$

Since the growth rate in the first period (g_a) and in the second period (g_{tr}) are incorporated in the estimation of the FCFF, we can compute them as follows:

$$g_a = \frac{\text{FCFF}_{t+1}}{\text{FCFF}_t} - 1;\ g_{\text{tr}} = \frac{\text{FCFF}_{t+1}}{\text{FCFF}_t} - 1$$

Also in this case, the Terminal Value (TV) can be estimated on the basis of the $\text{DCF}_{\text{AS(CC)-CG}}$ (and then on the basis of Gordon Growth Model in DDM) in which the growth rate is assumed constant over time indefinitely, as follows:

$$\mathrm{TV}_m = \frac{\mathrm{FCFF}_{m+1}}{K_{A,\mathrm{st}} - g_m} \tag{24.8}$$

Substituting, it gets:

$$W_A = \sum_{t=1}^{n} \frac{\mathrm{FCFF}_t}{\left(1 + K_{A,\mathrm{eg}}\right)^t} + \sum_{t=n+1}^{m} \frac{\mathrm{FCFF}_t}{\left(1 + K_{A,\mathrm{tr}}\right)^t} + \frac{\frac{\mathrm{FCFF}_{m+1}}{K_{A,\mathrm{st}} - g_m}}{\left(1 + K_{A,\mathrm{st}}\right)^m}$$

and then:

$$W_A = \sum_{t=1}^{n} \frac{\mathrm{FCFF}_t}{\left(1 + K_{A,\mathrm{eg}}\right)^t} + \sum_{t=n+1}^{m} \frac{\mathrm{FCFF}_t}{\left(1 + K_{A,\mathrm{tr}}\right)^t} + \frac{\mathrm{FCFF}_{m+1}}{\left(K_{A,\mathrm{st}} - g_m\right)\left(1 + K_{A,\mathrm{st}}\right)^m} \tag{24.9}$$

Therefore, the model is based on three parts:

1. The first part is the present value of expected FCFF in the first period (from $t = 1$ to $t = n$) and it is characterized by a high growth rate (g_a).
2. The second part is the present value of the expected FCFF in the second period (from $t = n + 1$ to $t = m$) and it is characterized by a transitional growth rate (g_{tr}).
3. The third part is the present value of expected Terminal Value in the third period (from $t = m + 1$ in perpetuity) and it is characterized by a steady-state growth rate (g_n).

While the first and second parts represent the "analytical" part of valuation because in both parts expected FCFF are estimated for each year considered, the third part represents the "synthetical" part of valuation because it is based on the Terminal Value.

As discussed in the model on two stage, also in this case the cost of capital may be different across the three periods ($K_{A,\ \mathrm{eg}} \neq K_{A,\ \mathrm{tr}} \neq K_{A,\ \mathrm{st}}$). It is reasonable to assume that the company's capital structure changes over time until it stabilizes during the last period. Therefore, the debt level changes as well as the cost of capital.

24.3 Free Cash-Flow to the Firm Discount Model: Adjusted Present Value Approach

The Discounted Cash-Flow Model in Asset Perspective based on the Adjusted Present Value approach ($\mathrm{DCF}_{\mathrm{AS(APV)}}$).

The Discounted Cash-Flow Model in Asset Perspective applied by following the Adjusted Present Value approach ($\mathrm{DCF}_{\mathrm{AS(APV)}}$) estimates the Firm Value (W_A) by distinguishing between:

1. The *unlevered value*: It is the value of the company without debt.
2. The *leverage net value*: It is the value of the company related to the benefits and costs of debt.

Therefore, the model estimates the Firm Value (W_A) of the firm on the basis of three parts:

1. The Unlevered Value (W_{AU}) of the firm and then the Firm Value without debt.
2. The Value of the Tax Shields (W_{TS}) due to the interests on debt benefits. It is the value of advantage of debt and it is added to the unlevered value.
3. The Value of the Default Risk and Bankruptcy Costs (W_{DB}) related to the debt. It is the value of debt cost and it is subtracted from the unlevered value.

Based on these three parts, the Firm Value (W_A) of the firm is equal to the Unlevered Value (W_{AU}) plus the Value of the Tax Shields (W_{TS}) minus the Value of the Default Risk and Bankruptcy Costs (W_{DB}) related to the debt, as follows:

$$W_A = W_{AU} + W_{TS} - W_{DB} \tag{24.10}$$

Therefore, the model estimates the debt effects, both positive and negative, separately from the unlevered value. Differently, in the Cost of Capital Approach the positive and negative effects of debt are considered directly in the cost of capital used to discount FCFF. Generally, the Cost of Capital (CC) approach is preferred when the debt level is stable over time. This is even more true when the WACC is used as the cost of capital. Differently, when the debt level changes over time, the Adjusted Present Value (APV) approach is more useful to estimate Firm Value.

24.3.1 Unlevered Value

The *Unlevered Firm Value* (W_{AU}) is the first term of model. It measures the Firm Value of the firm financed by equity only. Since there is not debt in the capital structure, the Cost of Capital (K_A) used to discount the expected Free Cash-Flow to the Firm (FCFF) is equal to the Unlevered Cost of Equity (K_{EU}), as follows:

$$K_A = K_{EU}$$

Therefore, the Unlevered Firm Value (W_{AU}) of the firm is equal to:

$$W_{AU} = \sum_{t=1}^{\infty} \frac{FCFF_t}{(1 + K_{EU})^t} \tag{24.11}$$

The application of the equation can be realized on the basis of the three versions analyzed: steady-state growth, two-stage growth and three-stage growth.

Steady-State Growth Scenario

The Unlevered Firm Value (W_{AU}) of the firm is estimated on the basis of a constant growth rate over time (g_n).

The model estimates the Unlevered Firm Value (W_{AU}) of the firm on the basis of the expected Free Cash-Flow to the Firm (FCFF) in the next period ($FCFF_1$), the to the Unlevered Cost of Equity (K_{EU}), and a constant growth rate (g_n), as follows:

$$W_{AU} = \frac{FCFF_1}{(1 + K_{EU})} + \frac{FCFF_2}{(1 + K_{EU})^2} + \ldots + \frac{FCFF_n}{(1 + K_{EU})^n}$$

And by considering that the growth rate of the FCFF is constant over time, we can approximate as follows:

$$W_{AU} = \frac{FCFF_1}{(1 + K_{EU})} + \frac{FCFF_1(1 + g_n)}{(1 + K_{EU})^2} + \frac{FCFF_1(1 + g_n)^2}{(1 + K_{EU})^3} + \ldots + \frac{FCFF_1(1 + g_n)^{n-1}}{(1 + K_{EU})^n}$$

and by using geometric progression, it gets:

$$W_{AU} = \frac{\frac{FCFF_1}{(1+K_{EU})}\left[1 - \left(\frac{1+g_n}{1+K_{EU}}\right)^n\right]}{1 - \frac{1+g_n}{1+K_{EU}}}$$

The growth rate g_n is assumed constant over time. Therefore, it gets:

$$\lim_{n \to \infty} \left(\frac{1 + g_n}{1 + K_{EU}}\right)^n = \lim_{n \to \infty} \frac{(1 + g_n)^n}{(1 + K_{EU})^n} = 0$$

and then we can approximate as follows:

$$W_{AU} = \frac{\frac{FCFF_1}{1+K_{EU}}}{1 - \frac{1+g_n}{1+K_{EU}}} = \frac{\frac{FCFF_1}{1+K_{EU}}}{\frac{1+K_{EU}-1-g_n}{1+K_{EU}}} = \frac{FCFF_1}{1 + K_{EU}} \cdot \frac{1 + K_{EU}}{K_{EU} - g_n} = \frac{FCFF_1}{K_{Eu} - g_n}$$

and then:

$$W_{AU} = \frac{FCFF_1}{K_{EU} - g_n} \tag{24.12}$$

Therefore, the Unlevered Firm Value (W_{AU}) of the firm is equal to the present value of di Free Cash-Flow to the Firm in the next year assumed in perpetuity ($FCFF_1$) discounted at the company's Unlevered Cost of Equity Cost of Capital (K_{EU}) less the growth rate in perpetuity (g_n).

Two-Stage Growth Scenario

The Unlevered Firm Value (W_{AU}) of the firm is estimated on the basis of two periods characterized by different growth rates:

1. *Extraordinary growth period*: It is the first period and it is characterized by higher growth than steady-state growth. This period lasts n years.
2. *Steady-state growth period*: It is the second period and it is characterized by a steady-state growth over time.

On the basis of these two periods, the Unlevered Firm Value of the firm is equal to the present value of FCFF during the extraordinary growth period (first period) plus the present value of Terminal Value (TV) estimated for the steady-state growth period (second period).

In both periods, the Cost of Capital used is the Unlevered Cost of equity (K_{EU}). It is equal to $K_{EU,\ eg}$ in the first period (extraordinary growth period) and $K_{EU,\ st}$ in the second period (Steady-state growth period). Formally:

$$W_{AU} = \sum_{t=1}^{n} \frac{FCFF_t}{\left(1 + K_{EU,eg}\right)^t} + \frac{TV_n}{\left(1 + K_{EU,sg}\right)^n} \tag{24.13}$$

The Terminal Value can estimate by assuming a Steady-State growth rate (g_n) and then it is equal to:

$$TV_n = \frac{FCFF_{n+1}}{K_{EU,sg} - g_n} \tag{24.14}$$

Substituting, it gets:

$$W_{EU} = \sum_{t=1}^{n} \frac{FCFF_t}{\left(1 + K_{EU,eg}\right)^t} + \frac{\frac{FCFF_{n+1}}{K_{EU,sg} - g_n}}{\left(1 + K_{EU,sg}\right)^n}$$

and rearranging:

$$W_{EU} = \sum_{t=1}^{n} \frac{FCFF_t}{\left(1 + K_{EU,eg}\right)^t} + \frac{FCFF_{n+1}}{\left(K_{EU,sg} - g_n\right)\left(1 + K_{EU,sg}\right)^n} \tag{24.15}$$

Therefore, the equation estimates the Unlevered Firm Value (W_{EU}) on the basis of two parts:

3. The first part, is the present value of the expected FCFF estimated in the first period for each year. Therefore, it represents the "analytical" part of valuation because the expected FCFF are estimated for each year considered.
4. The second part, is the present value of expected Terminal Value estimated in the second period from the end of the first period in perpetuity. Therefore, it represents the "synthetical" part of valuation because it is based on the Terminal Value.

Note that the Cost of Capital in the two periods considered can be different ($K_{EU,\ eg} \neq K_{EU,\ sg}$) or equal ($K_{EU,\ eg} = K_{EU,\ sg}$). However, by considering that there is not debt in the capital structure, it is independent from the capital structure and it can change on the basis of changes in market condisions. Therefore, usually they are assumed equal among them.

Three-Stage Growth Scenario

The Unlevered Firm Value (W_{AU}) of the firm is estimated on the basis of three periods characterized by different growth rates:

1. *Extraordinary growth period*: It is the first period and it is characterized by a high growth rate.
2. *Transitional growth period*: It is the second period and it is characterized by a declining growth rate until it reach a stable level.
3. *Steady-state growth period*: It is the third period and it is characterized by a steady-state growth rate.

The company's Unlevered Firm Value (W_{AU}) is equal to the sum of present values of expected FCFF in the extraordinary growth period (first period) in which the growth rate is equal to (g_a), transactional growth period (second period) in which the growth rate is equal to (g_{tr}) and steady-state growth period (third period) in which the growth rate is equal to (g_n).

In all periods, the Cost of Capital used is the Unlevered Cost of equity (K_{EU}). It is equal to $K_{EU,\,eg}$ in the first period, $K_{EU,\,tr}$ in the second period and $K_{EU,\,st}$ in the third period.

Therefore, the Unlevered Firm Value (W_{AU}) of the firm, is equal to:

$$W_{AU} = \sum_{t=1}^{n} \frac{FCFF_t}{(1 + K_{EU,eg})^t} + \sum_{t=n+1}^{m} \frac{FCFF_t}{(1 + K_{EU,tr})^t} + \frac{TV_m}{(1 + K_{EU,st})^m} \quad (24.16)$$

The Terminal Value (TV) can be estimated on the basis of Steady-State growth rate (g_n), and then it is equal to:

$$TV_m = \frac{FCFO_{m+1}}{K_{EU,st} - g_n} \quad (24.17)$$

Substituting, it gets:

$$W_{AU} = \sum_{t=1}^{n} \frac{FCFF_t}{(1 + K_{EU,eg})^t} + \sum_{t=n+1}^{m} \frac{FCFF_t}{(1 + K_{EU,tr})^t} + \frac{\frac{FCFF_{m+1}}{K_{EU,st} - g_m}}{(1 + K_{EU,st})^m}$$

and rearranging it gets:

$$W_{AU} = \sum_{t=1}^{n} \frac{\text{FCFF}_t}{(1+K_{\text{EU,eg}})^t} + \sum_{t=n+1}^{m} \frac{\text{FCFF}_t}{(1+K_{\text{EU,tr}})^t} + \frac{\text{FCFF}_{m+1}}{(K_{\text{EU,st}} - g_n)(1+K_{\text{EU,st}})^m} \tag{24.18}$$

Therefore, the model is based on three parts:

1. The first part, is the present value of expected FCFF in the first period (from $t = 1$ to $t = n$) and it is characterized by a high growth rate (g_a).
2. The second part, is the present value of the expected FCFF in the second period (from $t = n + 1$ to $t = m$) and it is characterized by a transitional growth rate (g_{tr}).
3. The third part, is the present value of expected Terminal Value in the third period (from $t = m + 1$ in perpetuity) and it is characterized by a steady-state growth rate (g_n).

While the first and second parts represent the "analytical" part of valuation because in both parts expected FCFF are estimated for each year considered, the third part represents the "synthetical" part of valuation because it is based on the Terminal Value.

As discussed in the model on two stages, also in this case the cost of capital may be different ($K_{\text{EU, eg}} \neq K_{\text{EU, tr}} \neq K_{\text{EU, st}}$) across the three periods or equal among them ($K_{\text{EU, eg}} = K_{\text{EU, tr}} = K_{\text{EU, st}}$). Also in this case, by considering that there is not debt in the capital structure, they tend to be equal among them rather than different.

The most relevant difference between the Firm Value and the Unlevered Firm Value is due to the Unlevered Cost of Equity.

The main problem concerns the determination of the beta coefficient. In an Unlevered Firm Value, we can consider the Unlevered Beta (β_U) (Hamada, 1972). It can be defined on the basis of:

- Levered Beta (β_L), that is the current beta if the capital structure is based on equity and debt.
- Corporate taxes (t_c), that is the taxes rate.
- Leverage, that is equal to the ratio between debt level and equity (D/E).

On the basis of these three components, the Unlevered Beta (β_U) is equal to:

$$\beta_U = \frac{\beta_L}{1 + (1 - t_c)\frac{D}{E}} \tag{24.19}$$

Based on the Unlevered Beta (β_U), the Unlevered Cost of Equity (K_{EU}) is equal to:

$$K_{\text{EU}} = R_f + \beta_U(R_m - R_f)$$

and then:

$$K_{\text{EU}} = R_f + \frac{\beta_L}{1 + (1 - t_c)\frac{D}{E}}(R_m - R_f) \tag{24.20}$$

24.3.2 Value of Tax Shields

The *Value of the Tax Shields* (W_{TS}) is the second term of the model. It is based on the tax deductibility of the interests on debt. If the interests on debt are tax deductible, they generate a tax savings with positive effects on the cash-flows.

Obviously, the tax shields can be estimated for a given debt level. Consequently, its amount can be estimated only if we have just defined the debt level.

The value of the tax shields is equal to the present value of the expected cash-flow of the tax savings discounted to the appropriate rate on the basis of their risk level.

The cash-flow from tax savings (CF_{TS}) can be estimated equal to the corporate taxed (t_c) multiplies interest on debt (I_D) that is equal to the Cost of Debt (K_D) multiplied by the debt level (D), as follows:

$$\text{CF}_{\text{TS}} = t_c \cdot I_D$$

$$I_D = K_D \cdot D$$

$$\text{CF}_{\text{TS}} = t_c K_D D$$

Denoting with K_{TS} the discount rate of the cash-flow from tax savings (CF_{TS}), the value of the tax shields (W_{TS}) is equal to:

$$W_{\text{TS}} = \frac{t_c K_D D}{K_{\text{TS}}} \tag{24.21}$$

The definition of the K_{TS} is the main problem of the equation. It measures the function of the risk level of the cash-flow from tax savings. Usually, the value of this discount rate is assumed equal to the cost of debt (K_D). The reason for this relationship is that tax shields exist because the debt exist. If the company does not pay interest on debt, there is no cash-flow from tax savings. Therefore, the risk level of cash-flow from tax shields can be assumed equal to the risk level of debt. By assuming that $K_{\text{TS}} = K_D$, the equation can be rewritten as follows:

$$W_{\text{TS}} = \frac{t_c K_D D}{K_D} = t_c D \tag{24.22}$$

24.3.3 Value of Bankruptcy Costs

The *Value of Bankruptcy Costs* (W_{BC}) is the third term of the model. It measures the amount of cost that firm must be coverage in case of its default due to the leverage.

In the case of default, the company has to bear several bankruptcy costs that are direct and indirect. Consequently, the value of default risk can be assumed equal to the bankruptcy direct and indirect costs due to the default.

These costs can be measured for a given debt level. Similar to the tax saving, the value of default risk can be estimated only if we define the debt level.

The value of bankruptcy costs (W_{BC}) is estimated equal to the probability (π_D) of default related to the increase in debt from a given level, multiplied by the expected cash-flow related to the bankruptcy direct and indirect costs (CF_{BC}), as follows:

$$W_{BC} = \pi_D \cdot CF_{BC} \tag{24.23}$$

The main problem of the equation concerns the computation of the variables. Neither the probability of the company's default (π_D) nor the bankruptcy costs (CF_{BC}) can be estimated directly in a simple way. We can follow two main approaches:

1. We can use the bond rating and then we can use it to measure empirically the default probabilities on the basis of its rating.
2. We can use the statistical techniques based on the company's fundamental characteristics.

Note that the direct costs related to the company's default tend to be lower than the indirect costs. Therefore, the indirect costs have much more effect on the company's value than the direct costs. Generally, indirect costs are estimated equal to 25%–30% of company value (Titman, 1984).

24.3.4 Firm Value

The Firm Value (W_A) of the company based on these three components—Unlevered Firm Value (W_{AU}), Value of Tax Shields (W_{TS}) and Value of Bankruptcy Costs (W_{BC})—is equal to:

$$W_A = W_{AU} + W_{TS} - W_{BC} \tag{24.24}$$

Note that while the first part (W_{AU}) can be declined in three growth scenarios, the second part (W_{TS}) and the third part (W_{BC}) of the equation remain the same. Therefore:

(a) in Steady-State growth scenario, we have:

$$W_A = \frac{\text{FCFF}_1}{K_{\text{EU}} - g_n} + t_c D - \pi_D \cdot \text{CF}_{\text{BC}} \tag{24.25}$$

(b) in Two-Stage growth scenario, we have:

$$W_A = \sum_{t=1}^{n} \frac{\text{FCFF}_t}{\left(1 + K_{\text{EU,eg}}\right)^t} + \frac{\text{FCFF}_{n+1}}{\left(K_{\text{EU,st}} - g_n\right)\left(1 + K_{\text{EU,st}}\right)^n} + t_c D - \pi_D \cdot \text{CF}_{\text{BC}} \tag{24.26}$$

(c) in Three-stage growth scenario, we have:

$$W_A = \sum_{t=1}^{n} \frac{\text{FCFF}_t}{\left(1 + K_{\text{EU,eg}}\right)^t} + \sum_{t=n+1}^{m} \frac{\text{FCFF}_t}{\left(1 + K_{\text{EU,tr}}\right)^t} + \frac{\text{FCFF}_{m+1}}{\left(K_{\text{EU,st}} - g_n\right)\left(1 + K_{\text{EU,st}}\right)^m} + t_c D - \pi_D \cdot \text{CF}_{\text{BC}} \tag{24.27}$$

The relationship between the capital structure choices and the company's value can be analyzed more efficiently in an APV approach rather than the cost of capital approach.

The main APV approach advantage with regard to the identification of debt effects on company value through the second and third parts. However, it is not able to define clearly how and in which measure changes in the debt level affect the default risks and the bankruptcy costs. This is the main reason for which the APV approach is commonly used with a given debt level.

24.4 Discounted Economic Profit

The Economic Profit (EP) (also called Economic Value Added (EVA)) is a direct measurement of the company's ability to create value (Koller et al., 2015).

The EP is based on a simple relationship: the company generates value if the return on investments is greater than the cost of capital invested. This positive difference measure is the excess returns and it measures the value created by the company.

In operating terms, by considering the operating activity of the company, the EP is computed on the basis of the Net Operating Invested Capital (NOIC), the Net Operating Profit After Taxes (NOPAT) (also called NOPLAT—Net Operating Profit Less Adjusted Taxes), the Return on Invested Capital (ROIC), and firm's Cost of Capital (K_A), as follows:

$$EP = NOIC \cdot (ROIC - K_A)$$

By considering that:

$$ROIC = \frac{NOPAT}{NOIC}$$

Substituting, it gets:

$$EP = NOIC \cdot \left(\frac{NOPAT}{NOIC} - K_A\right)$$

and then:

$$EP = NOPAT - K_A \cdot NOIC \tag{24.28}$$

The equation measures the EP, the value created by the company in a single period.

By considering an multi-period scenario, we can use the EP to estimate the Firm Value (W_A): it is equal to the Discounted Economic Profit (DEP) as follows:

$$W_A = NOIC_{(t_0)} + \sum_{t=1}^{\infty} \frac{EP_t}{(1+K_A)^t} \tag{24.29}$$

To apply the equation, we can combine the "analytical" and "synthetical" valuation as follows:

$$W_A = NOIC_{(t_0)} + \sum_{t=1}^{n} \frac{EP_t}{(1+K_A)^t} + \frac{PV(EP_n)}{(1+K_A)^n} \tag{24.30}$$

where $PV(EP_n)$ is the present value of the Economic Profit at the end of the analytical time period.

The computation of the $PV(EP_n)$ requires assumption about the growth rate. Also in this case we can assume three scenarios:

24.4.1 Steady-State Growth Rate

Under the assumption of the steady-state growth scenario, the growth rate (g_n) is assumed constant over time and the $PV(EP_n)$ is estimated equal to:

$$PV(EP_n) = \frac{EP_{n+1}}{K_A - g_n}$$

Consequently, by substituting it gets:

$$W_A = \mathrm{NOIC}_{(t_0)} + \sum_{t=1}^{n} \frac{\mathrm{EP}_t}{(1+K_A)^t} + \frac{\frac{\mathrm{EP}_{n+1}}{K_A - g_n}}{(1+K_A)^n}$$

and then:

$$W_A = \mathrm{NOIC}_{(t_0)} + \sum_{t=1}^{n} \frac{\mathrm{EP}_t}{(1+K_A)^t} + \frac{\mathrm{EP}_{n+1}}{(K_A - g_n)(1+K_A)^n} \quad (24.31)$$

The equation shows as the Firm Value (W_A) of the firm is based on three terms:

1. The first term is the Net Operating Invested Capital today and then the amount of investments in assets (in both Capex and Net Working Capital operating) in place.
2. The second term is the present value of the expected Economic Profit in analytical period (from t_1 *to* t_n).
3. The third term is the present value of the expected Economic Profit in steady-state condition (from t_n in perpetuity).

Note that under defined assumptions the DEP can be considered equivalent to the Firm Value (W_A) based on the discounted FCFF (Cost of Capital Approach) (Koller et al., 2015).

Assume that all company's taxes are related to the operating activities only. Under this assumption NOPAT can be assumed equal to the EBITDA less Taxes (T_C) so that: NOPAT = EBITDA − T_C.

Assume there are not investments in Surplus Assets, so that the Net Operating Invested Capital (NOIC) in core-business is equal to the total amount of the Invested Capital (*IC*), so that NOIC = IC.

Consequently, the Return on Invested Capital (ROIC) is equal to the ratio between NOPAT and the Net Operating Invested Capital (NOIC) as follows:

$$\mathrm{ROIC} = \frac{\mathrm{NOPAT}}{\mathrm{NOIC}}$$

The Free Cash-Flow to the Firm (FCFF) is equal to:

$$\mathrm{FCFF} = \mathrm{EBITDA} - \mathrm{OT} + \Delta\mathrm{NOIC}$$

and then:

$$\mathrm{FCFF} = \mathrm{NOPAT} - (\mathrm{NOIC}_{t+1} - \mathrm{NOIC}_t)$$

The change in Net Operating Invested Capital (ΔNOIC) can be approximate on the basis of the Investment Rate (IR). It is a portion of the NOPAT reinvested into the core-business. Consequently, it can be estimated on the basis of the ratio between the Net Operating Invested Capital and the NOPAT as follows:

$$\text{IR} = \frac{\text{NOIC}}{\text{NOPAT}}$$

Based on this relationship, the change in Net Operating Invested Capital (ΔNOIC) can be approximated as follows:

$$\text{NOIC} = \text{IR} \cdot \text{NOPAT}$$

Substituting, it gets:

$$\text{FCFF} = \text{NOPAT} - (\text{NOPAT} \cdot \text{IR}) = \text{NOPAT} \cdot (1 - \text{IR})$$

The growth rate (g) can be estimated on the basis of ROIC and Investment Rate (IR) as follows:

$$g = \text{ROIC} \cdot \text{IR}$$

Consequently, the Investment Rate (IR) is equal to:

$$\text{IR} = \frac{g}{\text{ROIC}}$$

Substituting, it gets:

$$\text{FCFF} = \text{NOPAT} \cdot \left(1 - \frac{g}{\text{ROIC}}\right)$$

Now consider the Firm Value (W_A) based on the Cost of Capital Approach by assuming a steady-state growth rate (g_n) is equal to:

$$W_A = \frac{\text{FCFF}_{(1)}}{K_A - g_n}$$

Substituting the FCFF in the equation, it gets:

$$W_A = \frac{\text{NOPAT}_{(t_1)} \cdot \left(1 - \frac{g_n}{\text{ROIC}}\right)}{K_A - g_n}$$

The NOPAT can be expressed on the basis of ROIC and NOIC as follows:

$$\text{NOPAT}_{(t_1)} = \text{NOIC}_{(t_0)} \cdot \text{ROIC}$$

So that:

$$W_A = \frac{\text{NOIC}_{(t_0)} \cdot \text{ROIC} \cdot \left(1 - \frac{g_n}{\text{ROIC}}\right)}{K_A - g_n}$$

and then:

$$W_A = \text{NOIC}_{(t_0)} \cdot \left(\frac{\text{ROIC} - g_n}{K_A - g_n}\right) \tag{24.32}$$

The equation shows the value drivers. Based on it, the Firm Value (W_A) of the firm is the function of three variables: steady-state growth rate (g_n), the Return on Operating Invested Capital (ROIC) and the company's Cost of Capital (K_A).

The main problem of this equation is that it assumes a constant value over time of all three variables.

We can rewrite the Equation in term of Economic Profit (EP) (Koller et al., 2015). To do this it is necessary to demonstrate that the Firm Value (W_A) based on discounted FCFF is equivalent to the current book value of invested capital plus the present value of future economic profits.

Assume a steady-state scenario. Under this assumption, on the basis of previous consideration, the Firm Value (W_A) is equal to:

$$W_A = \frac{\text{FCFF}_1}{K_A - g_n} = \text{NOIC}_{(t_0)} \cdot \left(\frac{\text{ROIC} - g_n}{K_A - g_n}\right)$$

Add and subtract the Cost of Capital (K_A) in the numerator, as follows:

$$W_A = \text{NOIC}_{(t_0)} \cdot \left(\frac{\text{ROIC} - K_A + K_A - g_n}{K_A - g_n}\right)$$

and separating the fraction in two terms, we have:

$$W_A = \text{NOIC}_{(t_0)} \cdot \left(\frac{\text{ROIC} - K_A}{K_A - g_n}\right) + \text{NOIC}_{(t_0)} \cdot \left(\frac{K_A - g_n}{K_A - g_n}\right) = \text{NOIC}_{(t_0)} + \text{NOIC}_{(t_0)} \cdot \left(\frac{\text{ROIC} - K_A}{K_A - g_n}\right)$$

By considering that:

$$\text{Economic Profit (EP)} = \text{NOIC}_{(0)} \cdot (\text{ROIC} - K_A)$$

substituting, we have:

$$W_A = \text{NOIC}_{(t_0)} + \frac{\text{EP}_{(1)}}{K_A - g_n} \tag{24.33}$$

The equation states that the Firm Value (W_A) is equal to the book value of Net Operating Invested Capita ($\text{NOIC}_{(0)}$) plus the present value of the future economic profit ($\text{EP}_{(1)}$).

Since the second term of the equation is the Discounted FCFF in the steady-state growth, it implies that:

1. If the future economic profits are expected to be zero ($EP_{(1)} = 0$), the Firm Value of the firm is equal to the book value of Net Operating Invested Capital: $W_A = NOIC_{(0)}$. Consequently, the intrinsic value of the Enterprise of the firm is equal to its book value.
2. If the future economic profits are expected less than zero ($EP_{(1)} < 0$), the investments in operating activities of the firm destroy value and then the Firm Value is less than its book value.
3. If the future economic profits are expected higher than zero ($EP_{(1)} > 0$), the investments in operating activities of the firm generate value and then the Firm Value is higher than its book value.

The equation can be generalized (Koller et al., 2015). The general equation of the Firm Value (W_A) of the firm is equal to:

$$W_A = \sum_{t=1}^{\infty} \frac{FCFF_t}{(1+K_A)^t}$$

We can add and subtract the discounted Net Operating Invested Capital $\left(\sum_{t=0}^{\infty} \frac{NOIC_t}{(1+K_A)^t}\right)$ as follows:

$$W_A = \sum_{t=1}^{\infty} \frac{FCFF_t}{(1+K_A)^t} + \sum_{t=0}^{\infty} \frac{NOIC_t}{(1+K_A)^t} - \sum_{t=0}^{\infty} \frac{NOIC_t}{(1+K_A)^t}$$

By considering the starting point $t = 0$, the first cumulative sum becomes $\left(NOIC_{(t_0)} + \sum_{t=1}^{\infty} \frac{NOIC_t}{(1+K_A)^t}\right)$ while the second starts from $t = 1$ to infinity and then it changes each t inside in the second cumulative sum to $t - 1$ $\left(\sum_{t=1}^{\infty} \frac{NOIC_{t-1}}{(1+K_A)^{t-1}}\right)$, as follows:

$$W_A = \sum_{t=1}^{\infty} \frac{FCFF_t}{(1+K_A)^t} + NOIC_{(0)} + \sum_{t=1}^{\infty} \frac{NOIC_t}{(1+K_A)^t} - \sum_{t=1}^{\infty} \frac{NOIC_{t-1}}{(1+K_A)^{t-1}}$$

Multiply and divide the last term by $\frac{1+K_A}{1+K_A}$ as follows:

$$\sum_{t=1}^{\infty} \frac{NOIC_{t-1}(1+K_A)}{(1+K_A)^{t-1}(1+K_A)} = \sum_{t=1}^{\infty} \frac{NOIC_{t-1}(1+K_A)}{(1+K_A)^{t-1+1}} = \sum_{t=1}^{\infty} \frac{NOIC_{t-1}(1+K_A)}{(1+K_A)^t}$$

and then, we have:

$$W_A = NOIC_{(t_0)} + \sum_{t=1}^{\infty} \frac{NOIC_t}{(1+K_A)^t} - \sum_{t=1}^{\infty} \frac{NOIC_{t-1}(1+K_A)}{(1+K_A)^t} + \sum_{t=1}^{\infty} \frac{FCFF_t}{(1+K_A)^t}$$

and:

$$W_A = \text{NOIC}_{(t_0)} + \sum_{t=1}^{\infty} \frac{\text{NOIC}_t - \text{NOIC}_{t-1}(1+K_A) + \text{FCFF}_t}{(1+K_A)^t}$$

and:

$$W_A = \text{NOIC}_{(t_0)} + \sum_{t=1}^{\infty} \frac{\text{NOIC}_t - \text{NOIC}_{t-1} - \text{NOIC}_{t-1} \cdot K_A + \text{FCFF}_t}{(1+K_A)^t}$$

By considering that we can approximate the FCFF as follows:

$$\text{FCFF} = \text{NOPAT} - (\text{NOIC}_t - \text{NOIC}_{t-1})$$

and substituting, we have:

$$W_A = \text{NOIC}_{(t_0)} + \sum_{t=1}^{\infty} \times \frac{\text{NOIC}_t - \text{NOIC}_{t-1} - \text{NOIC}_{t-1} \cdot K_A + \text{NOPAT}_t - (\text{NOIC}_t - \text{NOIC}_{t-1})}{(1+K_A)^t}$$

and:

$$W_A = \text{NOIC}_{(t_0)} + \sum_{t=1}^{\infty} \times \frac{\text{NOIC}_t - \text{NOIC}_{t-1} - \text{NOIC}_{t-1} \cdot K_A + \text{NOPAT}_t - \text{NOIC}_t + \text{NOIC}_{t-1}}{(1+K_A)^t}$$

and:

$$W_A = \text{NOIC}_{(t_0)} + \sum_{t=1}^{\infty} \frac{\text{NOPAT}_t - \text{NOIC}_{t-1} \cdot K_A}{(1+K_A)^t}$$

Considering that:

$$\text{Economic Profit (EP)} = \text{NOPAT}_t - (\text{NOIC}_{t-1} \cdot K_A)$$

substituting, we have:

$$W_A = \text{NCI}_{(t_0)} + \sum_{t=1}^{\infty} \frac{\text{EP}_t}{(1+K_A)^t} \tag{24.34}$$

The equation statues that the Firm Value (W_A) of the firm is equal to the book value of the Net Operating Invested Capital ($\text{NOIC}_{(0)}$) plus the present value of all future economic profits $\left(\sum_{t=1}^{\infty} \frac{\text{EP}_t}{(1+K_A)^t}\right)$. Consequently:

1. If the future economic profits are expected to be zero $\left(\sum_{t=1}^{\infty} \frac{EP_t}{(1+K_A)^t} = 0\right)$, the Firm Value of the company is equal to the book value of its Net Operating Invested Capital. Consequently, the intrinsic value of the Enterprise is equal to the book value.
2. If the future economic profits are expected less than zero $\left(\sum_{t=1}^{\infty} \frac{EP_t}{(1+K_A)^t} < 0\right)$, the investments in operating activities destroy value and then the Firm Value of the company is less than its book value.
3. If the future economic profits are expected higher than zero $\left(\sum_{t=1}^{\infty} \frac{EP_t}{(1+K_A)^t} > 0\right)$, the investments in operating activities create value and then the Firm Value of the company is higher than its book value.

It is relevant to note that the equivalence between Discounted Economic Profit and the Firm Value based on the Discounted FCFF, requires well-defined assumptions (Koller et al., 2015):

1. Use beginning-of-year invested capital instead of average or current-year invested capital.
2. Define invested capital for both economic profit and ROIC using the same value.
3. Use a constant cost of capital as discount rate.

Finally, note that also in this case by using the EP it is possible to move from the Firm Value (W_A) to Equity Value (W_E). In this case, it is necessary to subtract the Net Financial Position (NFP) to the Firm Value as follows:

$$W_E = W_A - \text{PFN}$$

and the, we have:

$$W_{E_{(t_0)}} = \left[\text{NOIC}_{(t_0)} + \frac{\text{EP}_{(1)}}{K_A - g_n}\right] - \text{PFN}_{(t_0)} \tag{24.35}$$

$$W_{E_{(t_0)}} = \left[\text{NOIC}_{(t_0)} + \sum_{t=1}^{\infty} \frac{\text{EP}_t}{(1+K_A)^t}\right] - \text{PFN}_{(t_0)} \tag{24.36}$$

$$W_{E_{(t_0)}} = \left[\text{NOIC}_{(t_0)} + \sum_{t=1}^{n} \frac{\text{EP}_t}{(1+K_A)^t} + \frac{\text{EP}_{n+1}}{(K_A - g_n)(1+K_A)^n}\right] - \text{PFN}_{(t_0)} \tag{24.37}$$

Multiples Valuation

25

25.1 Multiples Approach

The relative valuation estimates the Equity and Firm value of the company on the basis of multiples approach. It is based on the comparison between the company and the current market price of comparable companies.

The basic principle is simple: if two assets are equal among them, then their price in the market must be equal. Consequently, the value of the company we analyze can be estimated based on the market value of other comparable companies whose value is known on the basis of its market price. Generally, the "comparable company" is defined as a company with similar expected cash-flows, growth rate and risk profile in the same business.

The great advantage of the multiple approach is its simply application in estimate the Enterprise and Equity Value. Indeed, it requires few variables and does not require their forecasting.

Generally, the strengths of the multiples approach can be summarized as follows:

1. It requires less time, efforts and information than a direct valuation based on Discounted Cash-Flow Models.
2. It does not require basic assumptions.
3. It is easy to apply and to understand.
4. It is able to reflect the market dynamics more than the direct valuation based on the discounted cash-flow models because the objective is the relative value of the company based on market price and not its intrinsic value.

If these are the main strengths the multiple approach is characterized by weakness too. Indeed, its low level of sophistication implies the existence of several limits that must always be kept in mind in its application. Among these, the main limits of the multiple approach can be summarized as follows:

P. De Luca, *Corporate Finance*, Springer Texts in Business and Economics,
https://doi.org/10.1007/978-3-031-18300-3_25

1. Multiples require "comparable asset". It is a great simplification because there are no two assets, and therefore two companies, that can be defined equal in the market.
2. Multiples can generate an inconsistent valuation of the firm compared with the discounted cash-flow models because it does not consider directly expectations about the future free cash flow and risk.
3. Multiples reflect the market trend, and then the company's value tend to reflects more the market trends rather than its intrinsic value. Consequently, the company's valuation could be overestimated (or underestimated) if the market is overestimated (or underestimated).
4. Multiples could be manipulated in a simple way because they do not based on a clear and robust assumptions.
5. Multiples can be calculated in several way because there is not a single useful manner. Also, if the variable considered (usually EBITDA or EBIT) is negative, we cannot compute the multiple by using these variables.
6. Equity and firm value estimated by using multiples tend to be unstable in the long-run. It implies two main considerations. First, one company may be cheaper than another company today, but not tomorrow. Second, it is not always easy to compare the value of a multiple at different times.
7. Multiples tend to use subjective judgments more than objective parameters.

Even if the multiples approach is easy, however its correct application requires a rigorous procedure to avoid errors in valuation process. This procedure can be defined on the basis of 6 steps:

1. *Find a comparable company*. The "comparable company" can be defined as a company with similar expected cash-flows, growth rate and risk profile in the same business.
2. *Relate the market price with common variables by generating the well-known multiples* (such as net income, EBITDA, EBIT, Capital invested, etc.). It is necessary to standardize the price for comparison.
3. *Define the multiple coherently according to the relationship between numerator and denominator*. If the numerator refers to equity (or enterprise), the denominator has to refer to equity (or enterprise) too.
4. *Define the multiple evenly for all comparable companies. It must be defined in the same way for all comparable companies*. Also, it is useful to understand the companion variable of the multiple in order to measure the sensitivity of the multiple to the company's fundamental changes. Finally, it is necessary to understand the range of the "normal value" of the multiple with regard to the business references.
5. *Adjust the company's value estimated by multiples according to the differences between the company evaluated and the company comparable*.
6. *Understand the statistic characteristics of the distribution of the multiple with regard to the specific business and the market in general*. The first is useful to

understand the position of the company in the business; the second is useful to understand the position of the business in the market.

In this context, we consider multiples derived from the discounted cash flow approach (Discounted Dividend Model (DDM), Discounted Cash-Flow Model (DCF) based on Free Cash-Flow to Equity (DCF_E) and Free Cash-Flow to the Firm (DCF_A)). Consequently, since all these models are based on the expected cash flows (FCFF and FCFE), the expected growth rate and the cost of capital (K_E and K_A), then multiples will be function of the same variables.

In this context, we analyze the following most useful multiplies:

1. Price-to-Earnings (P/E or PE)
2. Price to Earning (PE)-to-Growth (PE/G or PEG)
3. Price-to-Book Value (P/BV or PBV)
4. Price-to-Sales (P/S or PS)
5. Firm value-to-EBITDA (EV/EBITDA)
6. Firm value-to-Book Value (EV/BV)
7. Value of Operating Assets-to-Sales (EV/Sales)

25.2 Price to Earnings

The Price to earnings (PE or P/E) ratio is the most commonly used multiple to estimate Equity Value. Probably it is one of the most popular in the security analysis.

Note that despite the multiple use appears to be simple, several errors are usually made in the application. These errors are mainly due to an unclear relationship with company's fundamentals.

We can use three approaches. The simplest way is to define a measure of earnings: present earnings, normalized earnings, predicted earnings. On the contrary, the most complex way is to investigate and to discuss large numbers of variables that should affect the multiple in order to find which of them really affects the multiple and their weights. The relationship between the multiple and variables identified is usually defined by using a regression analysis and multiple regression analysis. It is worth noting that all models developed over time are able to explain stock price at a given point in time. They are not able to select the appropriate stocks to buy or sell short at the same time. Consequently, models are able to find which variables and their weights are important in the stock price at a given point in time but they cannot identify which stock will be successful. It happens for three main reasons:

1. Market changes constantly. Therefore, the weight of variables change over time, sometimes rapid and drastic.
2. The values of each variable change over time. Even if the market preference on variables remain constant over time, the theoretical value of stock changes because the estimation of the value of variables changes.

3. Models are not able to capture all company fundamentals and their effects on stock price. Consequently, the actual price of stocks can be above or below their theoretical prices.

The PE is equal to the ratio between Market Price per Share (MPS) of the company and its Earnings per Share (EPS):

$$PE = \frac{MPS}{EPS} \tag{25.1}$$

The Market Price per Share (MPS) of the company can be defined in terms of:

(a) *Current* market price
(b) *Mean* market price based on the last quarter or the last year

The Earnings per Share (EPS) of the company can be defined in terms of:

(a) *Current* earnings per share, with regard to the most recent book value earnings
(b) *Trailing* earnings per share, with regard to the book value earnings of the last quarter
(c) *Forward* earnings per share, with regard to the expected book value earnings for the next year

We can define several configurations of the multiples by combining these determinations as follows:

1. *Current or mean* market price / *current* earnings per share (*PE current*): is the ratio between the current market price and the current earnings per share of the company.
2. *Current or mean* market price / *trailing* earnings per share (*PE trailing*): is the ratio between the market price and the earnings per share of the last year.
3. *Current or mean* market price / *forward* earnings per share (*PE forward*): is the ratio between the market price and the expected earnings per share for the next year.

These three configurations of the multiple give three different value. The relationship among them are the following:

$$\text{PE forward} < \text{PE trailing} < \text{PE current}$$

We can investigate the relationship between the multiple P/E and the company's fundamentals. To do this, we can use the Discounted Dividend Model (DDM) in the two versions of 1) steady-state growth scenario and 2) two-stage growth scenario.

25.2.1 Steady-State Growth Scenario

In the *steady-state growth scenario*, the current stock price (P_0) is defined on the basis of the Dividends per Share (DPS) that company will pay in perpetuity, the cost of equity (K_E) and the steady-state growth rate (g_n) as follows:

$$P_0 = \frac{\text{DPS}}{K_E - g_n}$$

If we divide both side by Earnings per Share (EPS), we have:

$$\frac{P_0}{\text{EPS}} = \frac{\frac{\text{DPS}}{K_E - g_n}}{\text{EPS}} \rightarrow \frac{P_0}{\text{EPS}} = \frac{\text{DPS}}{(K_E - g_n)\text{EPS}}$$

The first member of equation is the PE ratio, and then we have:

$$\text{PE} = \frac{\text{DPS}}{(K_E - g_n)\text{EPS}}$$

The Dividends per Share (DPS) can be defined on the basis of Earnings per Share (EPS) and Payout Ratio (PR) as follows:

$$\text{DPS} = \text{EPS} \cdot \text{PR}$$

Note that the expected Dividends per Share (DPS) can be defined on the basis of expected Earnings per Share (EPS) on the basis of the growth rate in a steady-state scenario (g_n), and by applying to it the Payout Ratio (PR), as follows:

$$\text{DPS} = [\text{EPS}(1 + g_n)] \cdot \text{PR}$$

Substituting in the equation, we have:

$$\text{PE} = \frac{[\text{EPS}(1 + g_n)]\text{PR}}{(K_E - g_n)\text{EPS}}$$

and then:

$$\text{PE} = \frac{\text{PR}(1 + g_n)}{K_E - g_n}$$

We can define the Payout Ratio (PR) on the basis of the steady-state growth rate (g_n) and ROE.

In steady-state scenario:

(a) The growth rate (g_n) can be estimated equal to ROE multiply Retention Ratio (RR): $g_n = \text{RR} \cdot \text{ROE}$.
(b) The Retention Ratio (RR) can be defined as 1 less Payout Ratio (PR): $\text{RR} = 1 - \text{PR}$.

Consequently, the Payout Ratio (PR) can be defined as follows:

$$\begin{cases} g_n = \text{RR} \cdot \text{ROE} \\ \text{RR} = 1 - \text{PR} \end{cases} \rightarrow g_n = (1 - \text{PR}) \cdot \text{ROE}$$

and by solving for PR, it gets:

$$\text{PR} = 1 - \frac{g_n}{\text{ROE}}$$

Substituting PR, it gets:

$$\text{PE} = \frac{\left(1 - \frac{g_n}{\text{ROE}}\right)(1 + g_n)}{K_E - g_n} \tag{25.2}$$

The equations statues the relationship between P/E and the company's fundamental in steady-state growth scenario.

25.2.2 Two-Stage Growth Scenario

In *two-stage growth scenario,* the current stock price (P_0) is defined on the basis of the Earnings per Share (EPS) of the company, the growth rate (g_e) and the cost of equity ($K_{E,\ eg}$) in extraordinary growth period that (the first period), the growth rate (g_n) and the cost of equity ($K_{E,\ sg}$) in steady-state growth period (the second period), as follows:

$$P_0 = \frac{\text{EPS} \cdot (1 + g_e) \cdot \text{PR}\left[1 - \frac{(1+g_e)^n}{(1+K_{E,eg})^n}\right]}{K_{E,eg} - g_e} + \frac{\text{EPS} \cdot \text{PR} \cdot (1 + g_e)^n (1 + g_n)}{(K_{E,sg} - g_n)(1 + K_{E,sg})^n}$$

By dividing the first and second member by Earning per Share (EPS), it gets:

$$\frac{P_0}{\text{EPS}} = \frac{\text{EPS} \cdot (1 + g_e) \cdot \text{PR}\left[1 - \frac{(1+g_e)^n}{(1+K_{E,eg})^n}\right]}{\text{EPS}(K_{E,eg} - g_e)} + \frac{\text{EPS} \cdot \text{PR} \cdot (1 + g_e)^n (1 + g_n)}{\text{EPS}(K_{E,sg} - g_n)(1 + K_{E,sg})^n}$$

The first member is the PE ratio, so that:

$$\text{PE} = \frac{\text{PR} \cdot (1 + g_e)\left[1 - \frac{(1+g)^n}{(1+K_{E,eg})^n}\right]}{(K_{E,eg} - g_e)} + \frac{\text{PR} \cdot (1 + g_e)^n (1 + g_n)}{(K_{E,sg} - g_n)(1 + K_{E,sg})^n}$$

By estimating the Payout Ratio (PR) on the basis the growth rate and ROE as follows:

$$PR = 1 - \frac{g_n}{\text{ROE}}$$

and substituting:

$$PE = \frac{\left(1 - \frac{g_n}{\text{ROE}}\right)(1 + g_e)\left[1 - \frac{(1+g_e)^n}{(1+K_{E,eg})^n}\right]}{\left(K_{E,eg} - g_e\right)} + \frac{\left(1 - \frac{g_n}{\text{ROE}}\right)(1 + g_e)^n(1 + g_n)}{\left(K_{E,sg} - g_n\right)\left(1 + K_{E,sg}\right)^n}$$

and rearranging, it gets:

$$PE = \left(1 - \frac{g_n}{\text{ROE}}\right)\left[\frac{(1 + g_e)\left[1 - \frac{(1+g_e)^n}{(1+K_{E,eg})^n}\right]}{\left(K_{E,eg} - g_e\right)} + \frac{(1 + g_e)^n(1 + g_n)}{\left(K_{E,sg} - g_n\right)\left(1 + K_{E,sg}\right)^n}\right] \quad (25.3)$$

The equation statues the relationship between P/E multiple and company's fundamental in the two-stage growth scenario.

25.3 Price to Earning to Growth

The Price to Earning to Growth (PEG or PE/G) ratio is equal to Price to Earnings (PE) divided by the company's expected Growth (G).

The Growth of the company can be estimated on the basis of the growth rate (g) of Earnings per Share, as follows:

$$PEG = \frac{PE}{g} \quad (25.4)$$

Note that we use the growth rate of earnings per share rather than the growth rate of operating income because the consistency requires coherence between the numerator and denominator. Since the numerator is the PE, the denominator requires the growth rate of earnings per share.

We can use the PEG ratio is commonly used by analyst to identify underestimated or overestimated companies in a simple way. Indeed, if the:

- $\frac{PE}{G} < 1$, the PE is less than their expected growth rate (g) and the company is considered undervalued. Therefore, the lower the PE/G, the higher the undervaluation of the company.
- $\frac{PE}{G} > 1$, the PE is more than their expected growth rate (g) and the company is considered overvalued. Therefore, the greater the multiple PE/G, the higher the overvaluation of the company.

The PE multiple has different versions as analyzed previously. Its right configuration depends on the way by which the growth rate is estimated. Therefore, if we use:

- The *current* earnings, we consider the *current* PE.
- The *trailing* earnings, we consider the *trailing* PE.
- *Forward* PE should not be used because the growth may be considered twice.

We can define the relationship between the multiple PEG and company's fundamentals. Also in this case, to do this we can use the Discounted Dividend Model in the two versions of 1) steady-state growth scenario and 2) two-stage growth scenario.

25.3.1 Steady-State Growth Scenario

In the *steady-state growth scenario*, the current stock price (P_0) is defined on the basis of the Dividends per Share (DPS) that company will pay in perpetuity, the cost of equity (K_E) and the steady-state growth rate (g_n) as follows:

$$P_0 = \frac{\text{DPS}}{K_E - g_n}$$

By dividing both side by Earnings per Share (EPS), the first term is the PE ratio. The Dividend per Share (DPS) in the second term can be expressed in terms of Earnings per Share (EPS) and Payout Ratio (PR): DPS = EPS · PR. Consequently, the expected DPS can be expressed on the basis of the expected EPS whose depend on the growth rate (g_n), so that: DPS=[EPS(1 + g_n)] · PR.

Therefore, it gets:

$$\frac{P_0}{\text{EPS}} = \frac{\frac{\text{DPS}}{K_E - g_n}}{\text{EPS}} \rightarrow \text{PE} = \frac{\text{DPS}}{(K_E - g_n)\text{EPS}} \rightarrow \text{PE} = \frac{[\text{EPS}(1 + g_n)]\text{PR}}{(K_E - g_n)\text{EPS}}$$

and then:

$$\text{PE} = \frac{\text{PR}(1 + g_n)}{K_E - g_n}$$

By dividing both terms by the steady-state growth rate (g_n), it gets:

$$\frac{\text{PE}}{g_n} = \frac{\text{PR}(1 + g_n)}{g_n(K_E - g_n)}$$

Where the first member is the multiple PEG:

$$\text{PEG} = \frac{\text{PR}(1+g_n)}{g_n(K_E - g_n)}$$

We can define the Payout Ratio (PR) on the basis of the growth rate (g_n) and ROE:

$$\text{PR} = 1 - \frac{g_n}{\text{ROE}}$$

Substituting, it gets:

$$\text{PEG} = \frac{\left(1 - \frac{g_n}{\text{ROE}}\right)(1+g_n)}{g_n(K_E - g_n)} \tag{25.5}$$

Note that the same result we find directly if we divide the first and second member of the multiple PE for the growth rate (g_n), as follows:

$$\text{PE} = \frac{\left(1 - \frac{g_n}{\text{ROE}}\right)(1+g_n)}{K_E - g_n} \rightarrow \frac{P/E}{g_n} = \text{PEG} = \frac{\left(1 - \frac{g_n}{\text{ROE}}\right)(1+g_n)}{g_n(K_E - g_n)}$$

The equation statues the relationship between multiple PE/G and company's fundamentals in a steady-state growth scenario over time.

25.3.2 Two-Stage Growth Scenario

In *two-stage growth scenario* the current stock price (P_0) is defined on the basis of the Earnings per Share (EPS) of the company, the growth rate (g_e) and the cost of equity ($K_{E,\ eg}$) in extraordinary growth period that (the first period), the growth rate (g_n) and the cost of equity ($K_{E,\ sg}$) in steady-state growth period (the second period), as follows:

$$P_0 = \frac{\text{EPS} \cdot (1+g_e) \cdot \text{PR}\left[1 - \frac{(1+g_e)^n}{(1+K_{E,eg})^n}\right]}{K_{E,eg} - g_e} + \frac{\text{EPS} \cdot \text{PR} \cdot (1+g_e)^n (1+g_n)}{(K_{E,sg} - g_n)(1+K_{E,sg})^n}$$

By dividing both terms of equation by the Earning per Share (EPS), the first term is the multiple PE $\left(\frac{P_0}{\text{EPS}} = \text{PE}\right)$ so that:

$$\text{PE} = \frac{\text{PR} \cdot (1+g_e)\left[1 - \frac{(1+g_e)^n}{(1+K_{E,eg})^n}\right]}{(K_{E,eg} - g_e)} + \frac{\text{PR} \cdot (1+g_e)^n (1+g_n)}{(K_{E,sg} - g_n)(1+K_{E,sg})^n}$$

By dividing both terms of equation by the steady-state growth rate (g_n), the first term is the multiple PEG $\left(\frac{\text{PE}}{g_n} = \text{PEG}\right)$, so that:

$$\text{PEG}=\frac{\text{PR}\cdot(1+g_e)\left[1-\frac{(1+g_e)^n}{(1+K_{E,eg})^n}\right]}{g_n\left(K_{E,eg}-g_e\right)}+\frac{\text{PR}\cdot(1+g_e)^n(1+g_n)}{g_n\left(K_{E,sg}-g_n\right)\left(1+K_{E,sg}\right)^n}$$

By considering that we can define the Payout Ratio (PR) on the basis steady-state growth rate (g_n) and ROE $\left(\text{PR}=1-\frac{g_n}{\text{ROE}}\right)$, and substituting it gets:

$$\text{PEG}=\frac{\left(1-\frac{g_n}{\text{ROE}}\right)(1+g_e)\left[1-\frac{(1+g_e)^n}{(1+K_{E,eg})^n}\right]}{g_n\left(K_{E,eg}-g_e\right)}+\frac{\left(1-\frac{g_n}{\text{ROE}}\right)(1+g_e)^n(1+g_n)}{g_n\left(K_{E,sg}-g_n\right)\left(1+K_{E,sg}\right)^n} \tag{25.6}$$

Note that we can find the same result in directly way if we divide the first and second member of the multiple PE by the steady-state growth rate (g_n) as follows:

$$\frac{\text{PE}}{g_n}=\text{PEG}=\frac{\left(1-\frac{g_n}{\text{ROE}}\right)(1+g_e)\left[1-\frac{(1+g_e)^n}{(1+K_{E,eg})^n}\right]}{g_n\left(K_{E,eg}-g_e\right)}+\frac{\left(1-\frac{g_n}{\text{ROE}}\right)(1+g_e)^n(1+g_n)}{g_n\left(K_{E,sg}-g_n\right)\left(1+K_{E,sg}\right)^n}$$

The equation statues the relationship between the multiple PEG ratio and company's fundamentals in a condition of two-stage growth.

25.4 Price to Book Value

The Price to Book Value (PBV or P/BV) ratio is equal to the ratio between the Equity Market Value, as defined on the basis of the Share Market Price, and the Equity Book Value of the company.

Specifically, it is equal to the Market Price per Share (MPS) of the company divided by its Equity Book Value per Share (EBVS) as follows:

$$\text{PBV}=\frac{\text{MPS}}{\text{EBVS}} \tag{25.7}$$

The *Market Price per Share (MPS)* is the function of the investors' expectation about the company's capability to generate cash-flows on earnings per share in the future. The *Equity Book Value (EBVS)* is equal to the difference between the book value of assets and liabilities.

The multiple PBV is characterized by several advantages:

- The book value is simple to calculate and it is generally a stable variable. Consequently, it is easy to compare with the market price of the company.
- The multiplier is able to allow an immediately valuation about the undervalued or overvalued of the company. Specifically, company with a market price lower than equity book value can be considered undervalued, as well as, company with market price higher than equity book value can be considered overvalued.

- The multiplier allows an easier comparison between companies and for the same company in different time. Obviously, it implies consistent accounting standards across companies compared.
- By considering that it is more likely that company realize a negative earning rather than a negative equity book value, then it is more likely that the PE ratio is meaningless (if the earning is negative) rather than the PBV (if the equity book value is negative).

If these are the main advantages, it is necessary always to keep in mind that the book value is function of the accounting principles. Therefore, the ratio is affected by accounting standards principles and accounting policies applied by the company.

One of the main problems concern the possibility to have several classes of share. To solve the problem, or its major part, we can consider the Total Equity Market Value (EMV) and then the Total Equity Book Value (EBV), as follows:

$$\mathrm{PBV} = \frac{\mathrm{EMV}}{\mathrm{EBV}} \tag{25.8}$$

In order to analyze the PBV ratio, we can find a relationship between the ratio and the company's fundamentals. Also in this case, we can use the Discounted Dividend Model (DDM) in two scenarios:

(a) Steady-state growth over time scenario
(b) Two-stage growth scenario: extraordinary growth in the first period and steady-state growth in the second period

25.4.1 Steady-State Growth Scenario

In the *steady-state growth scenario*, the current stock price (P_0) is defined on the basis of the Dividends per Share (DPS) that company will pay in perpetuity, the cost of equity (K_E) and the steady-state growth rate (g_n) as follows:

$$P_0 = \frac{\mathrm{DPS}}{K_E - g_n}$$

By considering that:

- The Dividends per Share (DPS) is equal to the Earning per Share (EPS) multiplied the Payout Ratio (*PR*) so that: DPS = EPS · PR.
- The ROE can be expressed as the ratio between the Earnings per Share (EPS) and Equity Book Value (EBV), so that: $\mathrm{ROE} = \frac{\mathrm{EPS}}{\mathrm{EBV}} \rightarrow \mathrm{EPS} = \mathrm{ROE} \cdot \mathrm{EBV}$.

substituting, it gets:

$$P_0 = \frac{\mathrm{DPS}}{K_E - g_n} = \frac{\mathrm{EPS} \cdot \mathrm{PR}}{K_E - g_n} = \frac{\mathrm{ROE} \cdot \mathrm{EBV} \cdot \mathrm{PR}}{K_E - g_n}$$

By dividing both terms by Equity Book Value (EBV), we have:

$$\frac{P_0}{\mathrm{EBV}} = \frac{\mathrm{ROE} \cdot \mathrm{EBV} \cdot \mathrm{PR}}{\mathrm{EBV}(K_E - g_n)} = \frac{\mathrm{ROE} \cdot \mathrm{PR}}{(K_E - g_n)}$$

The first member is the PBV multiple. In the second term, we can define the Payout Ratio (PR) on the basis of the growth rate (g_n) and ROE as follows:

$$\mathrm{PR} = 1 - \frac{g_n}{\mathrm{ROE}}$$

Substituting, it gets:

$$\mathrm{PBV} = \frac{\mathrm{ROE} \cdot \mathrm{PR}}{(K_E - g_n)} = \frac{\mathrm{ROE} \cdot \left(1 - \frac{g_n}{\mathrm{ROE}}\right)}{(K_E - g_n)}$$

and then:

$$\mathrm{PBV} = \frac{\mathrm{ROE} - g_n}{K_E - g_n} \tag{25.9}$$

The equation shows the relationship between PBV Ratio and company's fundamentals in steady-state growth scenario over time.

25.4.2 Two-Stage Growth Scenario

In *two-stage growth scenario* the current stock price (P_0) is defined on the basis of the Earnings per Share (EPS) of the company, the growth rate (g_e) and the cost of equity ($K_{E,\,eg}$) in extraordinary growth period that (the first period), the growth rate (g_n) and the cost of equity ($K_{E,\,sg}$) in steady-state growth period (the second period), as follows:

$$P_0 = \frac{\mathrm{EPS} \cdot (1 + g_e) \cdot \mathrm{PR}\left[1 - \frac{(1+g_e)^n}{\left(1+K_{E,eg}\right)^n}\right]}{K_{E,eg} - g_e} + \frac{\mathrm{EPS} \cdot \mathrm{PR} \cdot (1 + g_e)^n (1 + g_n)}{\left(K_{E,sg} - g_n\right)\left(1 + K_{E,sg}\right)^n}$$

By considering that the Earnings per Share (EPS) can be expressed equal the ROE multiplied the Equity Book Value (EBV) (EPS = ROE · EBV), and by dividing both terms by current Equity Book Value (EBV), it gets:

$$\frac{P_0}{\mathrm{EBV}} = \frac{\mathrm{ROE} \cdot \mathrm{EBV} \cdot \mathrm{PR} \cdot (1+g_e) \cdot \left[1 - \frac{(1+g_e)^n}{(1+K_{E,\mathrm{eg}})^n}\right]}{\mathrm{EBV}\left(K_{E,\mathrm{eg}} - g_e\right)} + \frac{\mathrm{ROE} \cdot \mathrm{EBV} \cdot \mathrm{PR} \cdot (1+g_e)^n (1+g_n)}{\mathrm{EBV}\left(K_{E,\mathrm{sg}} - g_n\right)\left(1+K_{E,\mathrm{sg}}\right)^n}$$

$$\frac{P_0}{\mathrm{EBV}} = \frac{\mathrm{ROE} \cdot \mathrm{PR} \cdot (1+g_e) \cdot \left[1 - \frac{(1+g_e)^n}{(1+K_{E,\mathrm{eg}})^n}\right]}{\left(K_{E,\mathrm{eg}} - g_e\right)} + \frac{\mathrm{ROE} \cdot \mathrm{PR} \cdot (1+g_e)^n (1+g_n)}{\left(K_{E,\mathrm{sg}} - g_n\right)\left(1+K_{E,\mathrm{sg}}\right)^n}$$

$$\frac{P_0}{\mathrm{EBV}} = \mathrm{ROE}\left\{\frac{\mathrm{PR} \cdot (1+g_e) \cdot \left[1 - \frac{(1+g_e)^n}{(1+K_{E,\mathrm{eg}})^n}\right]}{\left(K_{E,\mathrm{eg}} - g_e\right)} + \frac{\mathrm{PR} \cdot (1+g_e)^n (1+g_n)}{\left(K_{E,\mathrm{sg}} - g_n\right)\left(1+K_{E,\mathrm{sg}}\right)^n}\right\}$$

The first member is the PBV multiple, so that:

$$\mathrm{PBV} = \mathrm{ROE}\left\{\frac{\mathrm{PR} \cdot (1+g_e) \cdot \left[1 - \frac{(1+g_e)^n}{(1+K_{E,\mathrm{eg}})^n}\right]}{\left(K_{E,\mathrm{eg}} - g_e\right)} + \frac{\mathrm{PR} \cdot (1+g_e)^n (1+g_n)}{\left(K_{E,\mathrm{sg}} - g_n\right)\left(1+K_{E,\mathrm{sg}}\right)^n}\right\} \quad (25.10)$$

The equation statues the relationship between the multiple PBV ratio and company's fundamentals in a condition of two-stage growth.

25.5 Price to Sales

The Price to Sales (PS or P/S) ratio is based on Sales Revenue. Specifically, the multiple estimates the Equity Value (as well as the Firm value) on the basis of the company's ability to generate sales revenue.

Its simplicity generates relevant advantages:

- It can be used to evaluate a young company with negative earnings or for new-economy companies in which its value can be estimated based on the specific sector measures (such as the number of customers, subscribers, web site visitors).
- While the earning can be negative and therefore the ratio is not meaningful, revenues are positive and then the ratio is always meaningful.

- While earnings are heavily affected by accounting standards and then they can be manipulated, revenues are relatively difficult to manipulate.
- Revenue multiples tend to have a low volatility and therefore they are more stable over time.

The main problem of the multiple is that it may assign high value to a company that generates high revenue but low or null margin.

The *Price-to-Sales Ratio (PS)* is equal to the ratio between the *Equity Market Value* (*EMV*) and the *Revenues* (*Rev*) of the company as follows:

$$\mathrm{PS} = \frac{\mathrm{EMV}}{\mathrm{Re\,v}} \tag{25.11}$$

We can investigate the relationship between the multiple and the company's fundamentals. It can be done on the basis of the DDM in two scenarios:

(a) Steady-state growth over time scenario
(b) Two-stage growth scenario: extraordinary growth in the first period and steady-state grow in the second period

25.5.1 Steady-State Growth Scenario

In the *steady-state growth scenario*, the current stock price (P_0) is defined on the basis of the Dividends per Share (DPS) that company will pay in perpetuity, the cost of equity (K_E) and the steady-state growth rate (g_n) as follows:

$$P_0 = \frac{\mathrm{DPS}}{K_E - g_n}$$

The Dividend per Share (DPS) can be explicated on the basis of the Earnings per Share (EPS), steady-state growth rate (g_n) and Payout Ratio (PR) as follows:

$$\mathrm{DPS} = \mathrm{EPS}(1 + g_n) \cdot \mathrm{PR}$$

Substituting, we have:

$$P_0 = \frac{\mathrm{EPS}(1 + g_n) \cdot \mathrm{PR}}{K_E - g_n}$$

We can define the Net Margin on Sales (NMS) the ratio between Earnings (*Er*) and Sales (*S*). Consequently, the Net Margin on Sales per Share (NMSS) is equal to the ratio between Earnings per Share (EPS) and Sales (*S*). Therefore, we can define the Earnings per Share (EPS) as the Net Margin on Sales per Share (NMSS) multiply by Sales (*S*) as follows:

$$\text{NMS} = \frac{\text{Er}}{S} \rightarrow \text{NMSS} = \frac{\text{EPS}}{S} \rightarrow \text{EPS} = \text{NMSS} \cdot S$$

Substituting we have:

$$P_0 = \frac{\text{NMSS} \cdot S \cdot (1 + g_n) \cdot \text{PR}}{K_E - g_n}$$

By dividing both terms by Sales (*S*), we have:

$$\frac{P_0}{S} = \frac{\text{NMSS} \cdot S \cdot (1 + g_n) \cdot \text{PR}}{S \cdot (K_E - g_n)} = \frac{\text{NMSS} \cdot (1 + g_n) \cdot \text{PR}}{(K_E - g_n)}$$

And then:

$$\text{PS} = \frac{\text{NMSS} \cdot (1 + g_n) \cdot \text{PR}}{(K_E - g_n)} \tag{25.12}$$

The equation shows the relationship between PS Ratio and company's fundamentals in steady-state growth scenario over time.

25.5.2 Two-Stage Growth Scenario

In *two-stage growth scenario* the current stock price (P_0) is defined on the basis of the Earnings per Share (EPS) of the company, the growth rate (g_e) and the cost of equity ($K_{E,\ eg}$) in extraordinary growth period (the first period), the growth rate (g_n) and the cost of equity ($K_{E,\ sg}$) in steady-state growth period (the second period), as follows:

$$P_0 = \frac{\text{EPS} \cdot (1 + g_e) \cdot \text{PR} \left[1 - \frac{(1+g_e)^n}{(1+K_{E,eg})^n}\right]}{K_{E,eg} - g_e} + \frac{\text{EPS} \cdot \text{PR} \cdot (1 + g_e)^n (1 + g_n)}{(K_{E,sg} - g_n)(1 + K_{E,sg})^n}$$

By considering that:

$$\text{EPS} = \text{NMSS} \cdot S$$

and substituting, we have:

$$P_0 = \frac{\text{NMSS} \cdot S \cdot (1 + g_e) \cdot \text{PR} \left[1 - \frac{(1+g_e)^n}{(1+K_{E,eg})^n}\right]}{K_{E,eg} - g_e} + \frac{\text{NMSS} \cdot S \cdot \text{PR} \cdot (1 + g_e)^n (1 + g_n)}{(K_{E,sg} - g_n)(1 + K_{E,sg})^n}$$

Dividing both terms by Sales (*S*), we have:

$$\frac{P_0}{S} = \frac{\text{NMSS} \cdot S \cdot (1+g_e) \cdot PR\left[1 - \frac{(1+g_e)^n}{(1+K_{E,\text{eg}})^n}\right]}{S_{(0)}\left(K_{E,\text{eg}} - g_e\right)} + \frac{\text{NMSS} \cdot S \cdot \text{PR} \cdot (1+g_e)^n(1+g_n)}{S_{(0)}\left(K_{E,\text{sg}} - g_n\right)\left(1+K_{E,\text{sg}}\right)^n}$$

$$\frac{P_0}{S} = \frac{\text{NMSS} \cdot (1+g_e) \cdot \text{PR}\left[1 - \frac{(1+g_e)^n}{(1+K_{E,\text{eg}})^n}\right]}{\left(K_{E,\text{eg}} - g_e\right)} + \frac{\text{NMSS} \cdot \text{PR} \cdot (1+g_e)^n(1+g_n)}{\left(K_{E,\text{sg}} - g_n\right)\left(1+K_{E,\text{sg}}\right)^n}$$

$$\frac{P_0}{S} = \text{NMSS}\left\{\frac{(1+g_e) \cdot PR\left[1 - \frac{(1+g_e)^n}{(1+K_{E,\text{eg}})^n}\right]}{\left(K_{E,\text{eg}} - g_e\right)} + \frac{\text{PR} \cdot (1+g_e)^n(1+g_n)}{\left(K_{E,\text{sg}} - g_n\right)\left(1+K_{E,\text{sg}}\right)^n}\right\}$$

And then:

$$PS = NPMS\left\{\frac{(1+g_e) \cdot PR\left[1 - \frac{(1+g_e)^n}{(1+K_{E,eg})^n}\right]}{\left(K_{E,eg} - g_e\right)} + \frac{PR \cdot (1+g_e)^n(1+g_n)}{\left(K_{E,sg} - g_n\right)\left(1+K_{E,sg}\right)^n}\right\} \tag{25.13}$$

The equation statues the relationship between the multiple PS ratio and company's fundamentals in a condition of two-stage growth.

25.6 Firm Value to EBITDA

The Firm Value-to-EBITDA (EV/EBITDA) ratio is one of the most commonly used to estimate the Firm value.

Its main advantage is that it is based on the EBITDA. The use of EBITDA simplifies the analysis because:

- It is usually positive where its negativity can be considered an anomalous condition of the company.
- It has a direct impact on Free Cash Flow and then on the financial dynamic of the company.
- It does not consider the depreciation and amortization process, and then it allows companies comparison with different level of investments.
- It does not consider the effects of leverage, and then it allows companies comparison with different capital structures.

The ***EV/EBITDA*** is equal to the ratio between Firm value (EV) and the EBITDA as follows:

$$\mathrm{EV/EBITDA} = \frac{\mathrm{EV}}{\mathrm{EBITDA}} \tag{25.14}$$

We can investigate the relationship between the multiple and the company's fundamentals. It can be done on the basis of the DDM in two scenarios:

(a) Steady-state growth over time scenario
(b) Two-stage growth scenario: extraordinary growth in the first period and steady-state grow in the second period

25.6.1 Steady-State Growth Scenario

In the *steady-state growth scenario*, the Firm value (W_A) can be defined on the basis of the Free Cash-Flow to the Firm (FCFF), the levered cost of capital of the company (K_A) and the steady-state growth rate (g_n) as follows:

$$W_A = \frac{\mathrm{FCFF}}{K_A - g_n}$$

Note that the Firm value (W_A) in the multiple EV/EBITDA is defined EV so that: $W_A \equiv \mathrm{EV}$.

By considering only the operating activities of the company, the Free Cash Flow From Operations (FCFF) is equal to the Cash Flow From Operating Activities (CFOA) and then it is equal to EBITDA, plus changes in Operating Capex ($\Delta \mathrm{CAPEX_{OP}}$), plus changes in Operating Net Working Capital ($\Delta \mathrm{NWC_{OP}}$), minus cash-out due to negative changes in Provisions (ΔPS), as follows:

$$\mathrm{FCFF} = \mathrm{EBITDA} + \Delta \mathrm{CAPEX_{OP}} + \Delta \mathrm{NWC_{OP}} - \Delta \mathrm{PS}$$

and substituting, we have:

$$\mathrm{EV} = \frac{\mathrm{EBITDA} + \Delta \mathrm{CAPEX_{OP}} + \Delta \mathrm{NWC_{OP}} - \Delta \mathrm{PS}}{K_A - g_n}$$

By dividing both terms by EBITDA, we have:

$$\frac{\mathrm{EV}}{\mathrm{EBITDA}} = \frac{\mathrm{EBITDA} + \Delta \mathrm{CAPEX_{OP}} + \Delta \mathrm{NWC_{OP}} - \Delta \mathrm{PS}}{\mathrm{EBITDA} \cdot (K_A - g_n)}$$

and then:

$$\frac{\mathrm{EV}}{\mathrm{EBITDA}} = \frac{1}{(K_A - g_n)} \cdot \left[1 + \frac{1}{\mathrm{EBITDA}} (\Delta \mathrm{CAPEX_{OP}} + \Delta \mathrm{NWC_{OP}} - \Delta \mathrm{PS})\right] \tag{25.15}$$

The Equation defines the relationship between the multiple EV/EBITDA and the company's fundamentals. Note that the multiple is affected by:

(a) *Depreciation and Amortization process*: If the company derives a greater portion of its EBITDA from depreciation and amortization, it should trade at lower multiples of EBITDA than similar companies.
(b) *Operating Capex and Net Working Capital*: The greater the portion of the EBITDA that needs to be reinvested in the company to generate expected future growth, the lower multiple of EBITDA.
(c) *Cost of Capital*: A company with lower cost of capital should trade at much higher multiples of EBITDA.
(d) *Steady-state growth rate*: The higher the steady-state growth rate, higher the multiple of EBITDA.

We can use the EBIT instead of EBITDA. In this case the multiple becomes EV-to-EBIT (EV/EBIT) as follows:

$$\mathrm{EV/EBIT} = \frac{\mathrm{EV}}{\mathrm{EBIT}} \tag{25.16}$$

Note that the relationship between the multiple EV/EBIT and the company's fundamentals is the same defined for the multiple EV/EBITDA. It happens because in cash-flows perspective, the EBIT is equal to the EBITDA.

25.6.2 Two-Stage Growth Scenario

In *two-stage growth scenario* the Firm value (W_A) is defined on the basis of the Free Cash-Flow to the Firm (FCFF) of the company, the growth rate (g_e) and the levered cost of capital of the company in extraordinary growth period ($K_{A,\ eg}$) (the first period) and in steady-state growth period ($K_{A,\ sg}$) (the second period), the growth rate (g_n) as follows:

$$W_A = \frac{\mathrm{FCFF}(1+g_e)\left[1 - \frac{(1+g_e)^n}{(1+K_{A,eg})^n}\right]}{K_{A,eg} - g_e} + \frac{\mathrm{FCFF}(1+g_e)^n(1+g_n)}{(K_{A,sg} - g_n)(1+K_{A,sg})^n}$$

By considering that:

- $W_A \equiv \mathrm{EV}$
- $\mathrm{FCFF} = \mathrm{EBITDA} + \Delta\mathrm{CAPEX_{OP}} + \Delta\mathrm{NWC_{OP}} - \Delta\mathrm{PS}$

Substituting, we have:

$$\mathrm{EV} = \frac{[\mathrm{EBITDA} + \Delta\mathrm{CAPEX_{OP}} + \Delta\mathrm{NWC_{OP}} - \Delta\mathrm{PS}](1+g_e)\left[1 - \frac{(1+g_e)^n}{(1+K_{A,eg})^n}\right]}{K_{A,eg} - g_e} + \frac{[\mathrm{EBITDA} + \Delta\mathrm{CAPEX_{OP}} + \Delta\mathrm{NWC_{OP}} - \Delta\mathrm{PS}](1+g_e)^n(1+g_n)}{(K_{A,sg} - g_n)(1+K_{A,sg})^n}$$

$$\mathrm{EV} = [\mathrm{EEBITDA} + \Delta\mathrm{CAPEX_{OP}} + \Delta\mathrm{NWC_{OP}} - \Delta\mathrm{PS}] \times \left[\frac{(1+g_e)\left[1 - \frac{(1+g_e)^n}{(1+K_{A,eg})^n}\right]}{K_{A,eg} - g_e} + \frac{(1+g_e)^n(1+g_n)}{(K_{A,sg} - g_n)(1+K_{A,sg})^n}\right]$$

By dividing both terms of equation by EBITDA, we have:

$$\frac{\mathrm{EV}}{\mathrm{EBITDA}} = \left[1 + \frac{1}{\mathrm{EBITDA}}(\Delta\mathrm{CAPEX_{OP}} + \Delta\mathrm{NWC_{OP}} - \Delta\mathrm{PS})\right] \times \left[\frac{(1+g_e)\left[1 - \frac{(1+g_e)^n}{(1+K_{A,eg})^n}\right]}{K_{A,eg} - g_e} + \frac{(1+g_e)^n(1+g_n)}{(K_{A,sg} - g_n)(1+K_{A,sg})^n}\right] \quad (25.17)$$

The Equation shows the relationship between the multiple EV/EBITDA and the company's fundamentals in the two-stage growth scenario.

25.7 Firm Value to Book Value

The Firm Value-to-Book (EV/BV) ratio is equal to the Firm value (EV) of the company and its Book Value (BV) of Equity and Debt that defines the Capital Structure (CS) of the company
as follows:

$$\mathrm{EV/BV} = \frac{\mathrm{EV}}{\mathrm{BV}} \quad (25.18)$$

We can investigate the relationship between the multiple and the company's fundamentals. It can be done on the basis of the DDM in two scenarios:

(a) Steady-state growth over time scenario
(b) Two-stage growth scenario: extraordinary growth in the first period and steady-state grow in the second period

25.7.1 Steady-State Growth Scenario

In the *steady-state growth scenario*, the Firm Value (W_A) can be defined on the basis of the Free Cash-Flow to the Firm (FCFF), the levered cost of capital of the company (K_A) and the steady-state growth rate (g_n) as follows:

$$W_A = \frac{\text{FCFF}}{K_A - g_n}$$

Note that the Firm value (W_A) in the multiple EV/EBITDA is defined EV so that: $W_A \equiv \text{EV}$.

We can define the Free Cash-Flow to the Firm (FCFO) as a part of EBITDA that is the Reinvestment Rate (RR) as follows:

$$\text{FCFF} = \text{EBITDA}(1 - \text{RR})$$

Substituting, we have:

$$\text{EV} = \frac{\text{EBITDA}(1 - \text{RR})}{K_A - g_n}$$

Dividing both terms by the Book Value (BV) of the Invested Capital, we have:

$$\frac{\text{EV}}{\text{BV}} = \frac{\text{EBITDA}(1 - \text{RR})}{\text{BV}(K_A - g_n)}$$

$$\frac{\text{EV}}{\text{BV}} = \frac{\text{EBITDA}(1 - \text{RR})}{\text{BV}(K_A - g_n)} \tag{25.19}$$

The Equation shows the relationship between the multiple and company fundamentals. This equation can be further developed.

The Book Value of Equity and Debt defines the Capital Structure (CS)of the company. The Capital Structure is equal by definition to the Invested Capital (IC), so that: CS = IC.

Assume that there are only operating activities and then the entire capital is invested in the core-business of the company. Under this assumption, we have:

$$\text{ROI} = \frac{\text{EBITDA}}{\text{BV}} \rightarrow \text{EBITDA} = \text{ROI} \cdot \text{BV}$$

Substituting, we have:

$$\frac{\text{EV}}{\text{BV}} = \frac{\text{ROI} \cdot \text{BV} \cdot (1 - \text{RR})}{\text{BV} \cdot (K_A - g_n)} = \frac{\text{ROI}(1 - \text{RR})}{K_A - g_n}$$

In a steady-state growth scenario, the Reinvestment Rate (RR) is equal to the ratio between the steady-state growth rate (g_n) and ROI. Indeed, it is the requirement of the reinvestment to increase the ROI by following the growth rate:

$$g_n = \mathrm{RR} \cdot \mathrm{ROI} \rightarrow \mathrm{RR} = \frac{g_n}{\mathrm{ROI}}$$

Substituting, we have:

$$\frac{\mathrm{EV}}{\mathrm{BV}} = \frac{\mathrm{ROI}\left(1 - \frac{g_n}{\mathrm{ROI}}\right)}{K_A - g_n}$$

and then:

$$\frac{\mathrm{EV}}{\mathrm{BV}} = \frac{\mathrm{ROI} - g_n}{K_A - g_n} \tag{25.20}$$

The Equation defines further the relationship between the multiple *EV*/*BV*and the company's fundamentals.

25.7.2 Two-Stage Growth Scenario

In *two-stage growth scenario* the Firm value (W_A) is defined on the basis of the Free Cash-Flow to the Firm (FCFF) of the company, the growth rate (g_e) and the levered cost of capital of the company in extraordinary growth period ($K_{A,\ eg}$) (the first period) and in steady-state growth period ($K_{A,\ sg}$) (the second period), the growth rate (g_n) as follows:

$$W_A = \frac{\mathrm{FCFF}(1+g_e)\left[1 - \frac{(1+g_e)^n}{\left(1+K_{A,eg}\right)^n}\right]}{K_{A,eg} - g_e} + \frac{\mathrm{FCFF}(1+g_e)^n(1+g_n)}{\left(K_{A,sg} - g_n\right)\left(1+K_{A,sg}\right)^n}$$

By considering that:

- $W_A \equiv \mathrm{EV}$
- $\mathrm{FCFF} = \mathrm{EBITDA}(1 - \mathrm{RR})$

Substituting, we have:

$$\mathrm{EV} = \frac{\mathrm{EBITDA}(1-\mathrm{RR})(1+g_e)\left[1 - \frac{(1+g_e)^n}{\left(1+K_{A,eg}\right)^n}\right]}{K_{A,eg} - g_e} + \frac{\mathrm{EBITDA}(1-\mathrm{RR})(1+g_e)^n(1+g_n)}{\left(K_{A,sg} - g_n\right)\left(1+K_{A,sg}\right)^n}$$

$$EV = EBITDA(1 - RR)\left\{\frac{(1+g_e)\left[1-\frac{(1+g_e)^n}{(1+K_{A,eg})^n}\right]}{K_{A,eg}-g_e}+\frac{(1+g_e)^n(1+g_n)}{(K_{A,sg}-g_n)(1+K_{A,sg})^n}\right\}$$

By dividing both terms by the Book Value of the Invested Capital, we have:

$$\frac{EV}{BV} = \frac{EBITDA(1-RR)}{BV} \times \left\{\frac{(1+g_e)\left[1-\frac{(1+g_e)^n}{(1+K_{A,eg})^n}\right]}{K_{A,eg}-g_e}+\frac{(1+g_e)^n(1+g_n)}{(K_{A,sg}-g_n)(1+K_{A,sg})^n}\right\} \quad (25.21)$$

The Equation shows the relationship between the multiple EV/BV and company's fundamentals. Also in this case, this equation can be further developed.

Remember that the Book Value of Equity and Debt defines the Capital Structure (CS) of the company. The Capital Structure is equal by definition to the Invested Capital (IC) so that CS = IC.

Assume that there are only operating activities and then the entire capital is invested in the core-business of the company. Under this assumption, we have:

$$ROI = \frac{EBITDA}{BV} \rightarrow EBITDA = ROI \cdot BV$$

And substituting, we have:

$$\frac{EV}{BV} = \frac{ROI \cdot BV \cdot (1-RR)}{BV} \times \left\{\frac{(1+g_e)\left[1-\frac{(1+g_e)^n}{(1+K_{A,eg})^n}\right]}{K_{A,eg}-g_e}+\frac{(1+g_e)^n(1+g_n)}{(K_{A,sg}-g_n)(1+K_{A,sg})^n}\right\}$$

$$\frac{EV}{BV} = ROI(1-RR)\left\{\frac{(1+g_e)\left[1-\frac{(1+g_e)^n}{(1+K_{A,eg})^n}\right]}{K_{A,eg}-g_e}+\frac{(1+g_e)^n(1+g_n)}{(K_{A,sg}-g_n)(1+K_{A,sg})^n}\right\}$$

The Reinvestment Rate (RR) must be equal to the growth rate (g_e) to achieve the ROI, so that:

$$g_e = \mathrm{RR} \cdot \mathrm{ROI} \rightarrow \mathrm{RR} = \frac{g_e}{\mathrm{ROI}}$$

Substituting, we have:

$$\frac{\mathrm{EV}}{\mathrm{BV}} = \mathrm{ROI}\left(1 - \frac{g_e}{\mathrm{ROI}}\right)\left\{\frac{(1+g_e)\left[1 - \frac{(1+g_e)^n}{(1+K_{A,eg})^n}\right]}{K_{A,eg} - g_e} + \frac{(1+g_e)^n(1+g_n)}{(K_{A,sg} - g_n)(1+K_{A,sg})^n}\right\}$$

and then:

$$\frac{\mathrm{EV}}{\mathrm{BV}} = (\mathrm{ROI} - g_e) \times \left\{\frac{(1+g_e)\left[1 - \frac{(1+g_e)^n}{(1+K_{A,eg})^n}\right]}{K_{A,eg} - g_e} + \frac{(1+g_e)^n(1+g_n)}{(K_{A,sg} - g_n)(1+K_{A,sg})^n}\right\} \quad (25.22)$$

The Equation is a further relationship between the multiple EV/BV and company's fundamentals.

25.8 Firm Value to Sales Revenue

The Firm Value to Sales (EVS or EV/S) ratio is calculated based on the value of the operating assets to revenues. Specifically, it is equal to the ratio between Firm value (EV) and Sales Revenue (S) as follows:

$$\mathrm{EV}/S = \frac{\mathrm{EV}}{S} \quad (25.23)$$

We can investigate the relationship between the multiple and the company's fundamentals. It can be done on the basis of the DDM in two scenarios:

(a) Steady-state growth over time scenario
(b) Two-stage growth scenario: extraordinary growth in the first period and steady-state grow in the second period

25.8.1 Steady-State Growth Scenario

In the *steady-state growth scenario*, the Firm value (W_A) can be defined on the basis of the Free Cash-Flow to the Firm (FCFF), the levered cost of capital of the company (K_A) and the steady-state growth rate (g_n) as follows:

$$W_A = \frac{\text{FCFF}}{K_A - g_n}$$

Note that the Firm value (W_A) in the multiple EV/EBITDA is defined EV so that: $W_A \equiv \text{EV}$.

We can define the Free Cash-Flow to the Firm (FCFO) as a part of EBITDA that is the Reinvestment Rate (RR) as follows:

$$\text{FCFF} = \text{EBITDA}(1 - \text{RR})$$

Substituting, we have:

$$\text{EV} = \frac{\text{EBITDA}(1 - \text{RR})}{K_A - g_n}$$

Dividing both terms by the Sales Revenue (S), we have:

$$\frac{\text{EV}}{S} = \frac{\text{EBITDA}(1 - \text{RR})}{S\,(K_A - g_n)}$$

We can define the Operating Margin (OM) on the basis of the ratio between EBITDA and Sales Revenue as follows:

$$\text{OM} = \frac{\text{EBITDA}}{S}$$

Substituting, we have:

$$\frac{\text{EV}}{S} = \text{OM}\frac{(1 - \text{RR})}{K_A - g_n} \tag{25.24}$$

The Equation defines the relationship between the EV/S multiple and the company's fundamentals in the steady-state growth scenario.

25.8.2 Two-Stage Growth Scenario

In *two-stage growth scenario* the Firm value (W_A) is defined on the basis of the Free Cash-Flow to the Firm (FCFF) of the company, the growth rate (g_e) and the levered cost of capital of the company in extraordinary growth period ($K_{A,\ eg}$) (the first period) and in steady-state growth period ($K_{A,\ sg}$) (the second period), the growth rate (g_n) as follows:

$$W_A = \frac{\mathrm{FCFF}(1+g_e)\left[1-\frac{(1+g_e)^n}{\left(1+K_{A,\mathrm{eg}}\right)^n}\right]}{K_{A,\mathrm{eg}}-g_e} + \frac{\mathrm{FCFF}(1+g_e)^n(1+g_n)}{\left(K_{A,\mathrm{sg}}-g_n\right)\left(1+K_{A,\mathrm{sg}}\right)^n}$$

By considering that:

- $W_A \equiv \mathrm{EV}$
- FCFF = EBITDA(1 − RR.)

Substituting, we have:

$$\mathrm{EV} = \frac{\mathrm{EBITDA}(1-\mathrm{RR})(1+g_e)\left[1-\frac{(1+g_e)^n}{\left(1+K_{A,\mathrm{eg}}\right)^n}\right]}{K_{A,\mathrm{eg}}-g_e} + \frac{\mathrm{EBITDA}(1-\mathrm{RR})(1+g_e)^n(1+g_n)}{\left(K_{A,\mathrm{sg}}-g_n\right)\left(1+K_{A,\mathrm{sg}}\right)^n}$$

Dividing both terms by Sales Revenue (S), we have:

$$\frac{\mathrm{EV}}{S} = \frac{\mathrm{EBITDA}(1-\mathrm{RR})(1+g_e)\left[1-\frac{(1+g_e)^n}{\left(1+K_{A,\mathrm{eg}}\right)^n}\right]}{S\left(K_{A,\mathrm{eg}}-g_e\right)} + \frac{\mathrm{EBITDA}(1-\mathrm{RR})(1+g_e)^n(1+g_n)}{S\left(K_{A,\mathrm{sg}}-g_n\right)\left(1+K_{A,\mathrm{sg}}\right)^n}$$

and then:

$$\frac{\mathrm{EV}}{S} = \frac{\mathrm{EBITDA}}{S}(1-\mathrm{RR})\left\{\frac{(1+g_e)\left[1-\frac{(1+g_e)^n}{\left(1+K_{A,\mathrm{eg}}\right)^n}\right]}{K_{A,\mathrm{eg}}-g_e} + \frac{(1+g_e)^n(1+g_n)}{\left(K_{A,\mathrm{sg}}-g_n\right)\left(1+K_{A,\mathrm{sg}}\right)^n}\right\}$$

We can define the Operating Margin (OM) on the basis of the ratio between EBITDA and Sales Revenue as follows:

$$\mathrm{OM} = \frac{\mathrm{EBITDA}}{S}$$

Substituting, we have:

$$\frac{\mathrm{EV}}{S} = \mathrm{OM}(1-\mathrm{RR}) \times \left\{\frac{(1+g_e)\left[1-\frac{(1+g_e)^n}{\left(1+K_{E,\mathrm{eg}}\right)^n}\right]}{K_{A,\mathrm{eg}}-g_e} + \frac{(1+g_e)^n(1+g_n)}{\left(K_{A,\mathrm{sg}}-g_n\right)\left(1+K_{A,\mathrm{sg}}\right)^n}\right\} \quad (25.25)$$

The Equation shows the relationship between the EV/*S* multiple and the company's fundamentals in the two-stage growth scenario.

Part VI

Options

Financial Options 26

26.1 Definitions and Basic Elements

Financial Options today are one of the most important traded financial assets on market. They are introduced of publicly traded on the Chicago Board Options Exchange (CBOE) in 1973.

The most common financial options are the *options on shares of stock*. In this contest, we will focus the attention on these.

The *financial option* gives the owner the right but not the obligation to buy (*call option*) or to sell (*put option*) an asset at a defined fixed price (*strike price* or *exercise price*) at some future given date (*expiration date)*.

Therefore, any financial option is essentially a financial contract between two parties:

1. *Option Holder* (or *Option Buyer*): Holds the right to exercise the option and has a *long position* in the contract.
2. *Option Writer* (or *Option Seller)*: Sells the option and has a *short position* in the contract.

Therefore, the Option Holder is in the *long-side* of contract and it has the option to exercise, while the Option Writer is in the *short-side* of contract and it has an obligation to fulfil the contract.

There are two kinds of options:

1. *American options*: They are the most common, and they allow the holder the right to exercise the option on any date up to and including the expiration date.
2. *European options*: They allow the holder the right to exercise the option only on the expiration date and not before.

Note that in both cases, they are traded worldwide independently to the location indicated in the name.

P. De Luca, *Corporate Finance*, Springer Texts in Business and Economics,
https://doi.org/10.1007/978-3-031-18300-3_26

With regard to the price, if the current price of stock is equal to the strike price, the option is defined *at-the-money*. By exercising an option immediately, if:

(a) The payoff is *positive*, the option is said "*in-the-money*". Therefore, are in-the-money: *i)* call options with strike price below than the current stock price; *ii)* put options with strike price above the current stock price.
(b) The payoff is *negative*, the option is said "*out-of-the-money*". Therefore, are out-of-the-money: *i)* call options with strike prices above the current stock price; *ii)* put options with strike prices below the current stock price. Obviously, the owner would not exercise an option if it is out-of-the-money.

Otherwise, if the strike price and the stock price are very far apart, the option is defined "*deep in-the-money*" or "*deep out-of-the-money*".

Because the option (both put and call) is exercise only if there is a gain, then whenever the option is exercised, the short-position loss the gain of the long-position.

The option is costly. When investor sells an option, he gets paid for it. The market price of the option is also called *option premium*. Note that commonly the option contracts are always written on 100 shares of stock while the option prices are quoted on a per-share basis (for the option price per-share equal to € 2.50, the option contract is equal to $€2.50 \cdot 100 = €250$).

26.2 Payoffs and Profit

To determine an option's payoff at the expiration date, we have to consider both the long-position and the short-position (Berk & DeMarzo, 2017).

26.2.1 Investor in Long Position

Consider the investor in long position in both call option and put option.

(A) **Call Option**

The value of the call option (C) is equal to the positive difference between the stock price (S) and the strike price (K):

$$C = (S - K)$$

If the stock price (S) at expiration date is above the strike price (K), the value of the call option (C) is positive: $(S - K) > 0 \rightarrow C > 0$;

On the contrary, if the stock price (S) at expiration date is below the strike price (K), the owner does not exercise the call so that the option is worth nothing: $(S - K) < 0 \rightarrow C = 0$.

Therefore, the value of call option at expiration date is equal to:

$$C = \max(S - K, 0) \tag{26.1}$$

The equation states that the call value is the maximum of the difference between the stock price (S) and the strike price (K) and then ($S - K$), and zero.

Note that *max* is the maximum of the two quantities in the parentheses. It implies that the gain does not have limit because the stock price can always go up while the strike price is fixed.

Assume the investor holds a call option with a strike price (K) equal to € 30: $K = €30$. On the expiration date, consider two scenarios:

(a) The stock price (S) is higher than strike price (K): $(S - K) > 0$. Assume that $S = €35$. In this case, the investor exercises the call by paying €30 (the strike price for the stock) and immediately sells the stock in the market for €35. The difference between the stock price and the strike price, equal to €5 is what the call option is worth.
(b) The stock price (S) is lower than strike price (K): $(S - K) < 0$. Assume that $S = €25$. In this case, investor does not exercise the call option and it is worth nothing.

Therefore, the value of call option (C) is equal to:

$$C = \max(S - 30.0)$$

(B) **Put Option**

The value of the put option (P) is equal to the positive difference between the strike price (K) and the stock price (S):

$$P = (K - S)$$

If the strike price (K) is above the stock price (S) at expiration, the value of the put option (P) is positive: $(K - S) > 0 \rightarrow P > 0$;

On the contrary, if the strike price (K) is below the stock price (S) at expiration date, the owner does not exercise the put so that the option is worth nothing: $(K - S) < 0 \rightarrow P = 0$

Therefore, the value of put option at expiration date is equal to:

$$P = \max(K - S, 0) \tag{26.2}$$

The equation states that the put value is the maximum of the difference between the strike price (K) and the stock price (S) and then ($K - S$), and zero.

Note that *max* is the maximum of the two quantities in the parentheses. It implies that the maximum gain of the put is equal to the strike price that is fixed because the minimum of the stock price is equal to zero.

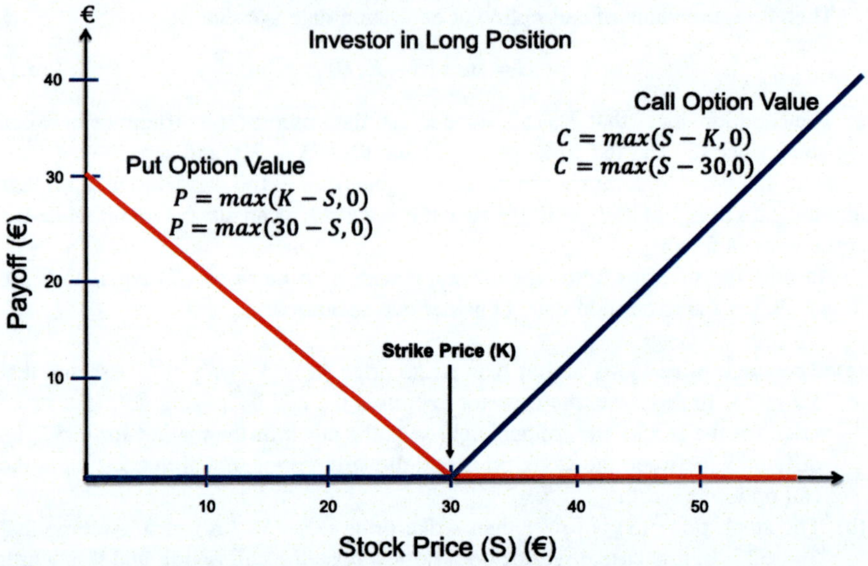

Fig. 26.1 Investor in long position

Assume the investor holds a put option with a strike price (K) equal to € 30: $K = €30$. On the expiration date, consider two scenarios:

(a) The stock price (S) is lower than strike price (K): $(K - S) > 0$. Assume that $S = €25$. In this case, the investor exercises the put by receiving €30 (the strike price for the stock). The difference between the strike price (K) and the stoke price (S), equal to €5 is what the put option is worth.
(b) The stock price (S) is higher than strike price (K): $(K - S) < 0$. Assume that $S = €35$. In this case, the investor does not exercise the put option and it is worth nothing.

Therefore, the value of put option (P) is equal to:

$$P = \max(30 - S, 0)$$

We can represent the value of the both call option (C) and the put option (P) for an investor in a long position as in the Fig. 26.1.

26.2.2 Investor in Short Position

The investor in a short position in the option contract has an obligation because takes the opposite side of the option contract to the investor in the long position that have the right to exercise the option. Consequently, the gain of investor in long position is symmetrically the loss of investor in short position and vice versa.

Note that since the investor in the long position of option can only receive money (because if the option is out-of-the-money the investor will not exercise the option), the investor in the short position can only pay money.

Consider the previous cases in the perspective of the investor in the short position in both call option and put option.

(A) Call Option

Assume a strike price (K) equal to €30 ($K = €30$) of the call option of the investor in long position. At the expiration date, consider the two previous scenarios:

(a) The stock price (S) is higher than the strike price (K) of a call: $(S - K) > 0$. Assume that $S = €35$. In this case, the investor in a long position exercises the call option. The investor in a short position has the obligation to sell the stock at the strike price $K = €30$. Consequently, the investor must purchase the stock at the market price of $S = €35$, by losing the difference between stock price (S) and strike price (K) equal to $-(S - K) = -(€35 - €30) = -€5$.

(b) The stock price (S) is lower than the strike price (K) of a call: $(S - K) < 0$. Assume that $S = €25$. In this case, the investor in a long position will not exercise the call option and then the investor in short position loses nothing and gains the commission fee.

(B) Put Option

Assume a strike price (K) equal to €30 ($K = €30$) of the put option of the investor in long position. At the expiration date, consider the two previous scenarios:

(a) The stock price (S) is lower than the strike price (K) of a put: $(K - S) > 0$. Assume that $S = €25$. In this case, the investor in a long position exercises the put option. The investor in a short position has the obligation to sell the stock at the strike price $K = €30$. Consequently, the investor must purchase the stock at the market price of $S = €25$ by losing the difference between stock price (S) and strike price (K) equal to $-(K - S) = -(€30 - €25) = -€5$.

(b) The stock price (S) is higher than the strike price (K) of a put: $(K - S) < 0$. Assume that $= €35$. In this case, the investor in a long position will not exercise the put option and then the investor in short position loses nothing and gains the commission fee.

Note that in case of Call Option there is no limit to the potential loss for the investor in short position because it depends on the strike price that can always increase. On the contrary, for the put option the investor in the short position has a limit to the gain equal to the strike price because the minimum of the stock price is equal to zero.

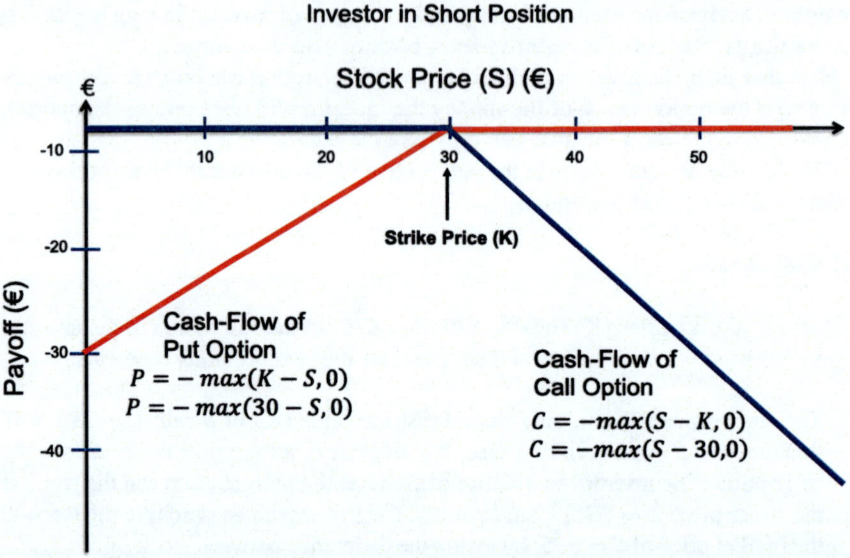

Fig. 26.2 Investor in short position

We can represent the value of the both call option (C) and the put option (P) for investor in a short position as in Fig. 26.2.

26.2.3 Profit for Call and Put Options

Even if the *payout* on a long position can be never negative, the *profit* that investor realizes can be. It happens when at expiration date the payout is less the initial cost to purchase the call option.

Denote with: S the stock price on expiration; K the strike price; P_C is the price of each call option; i the interest rate; nd, the number of days of option expiration (they are considered on the total days per years equal to 365). The profit of call option (π_c) is equal to:

$$\pi_c = \max(S - K, 0) - P_C(1 + i)^{\frac{nd}{365}} \tag{26.3}$$

The profit of the put option follow the same logic of call option. Therefore, by denoting the price of put option (P_P), the profit of put option (π_P) is equal to:

$$\pi_P = \max(K - S, 0) - P_P(1 + i)^{\frac{nd}{365}} \tag{26.4}$$

Assume that the investor purchases a call option at the cost of $P_C = €5$, and the number of days at the expiration date are 45. Assume that investor gets to in debt for the full cost of the call option and pays a year interest rate equal to $i = 2.5\%$. Assume that the strike price (K) is equal to $K = €70$.

Under these assumptions, investor receives a positive payoff if the stock price (S) is higher than strike price (K) and then $S = €71$. However, to realize a profit we must consider all the cost for the call purchasing. In this case, the stock price (S) must be higher than $S = €75.02$. Therefore, the unknown variable of the equation is the stock price (S):

$$\pi_c = \max(S - 70.0) - €5(1 + 2.5\%)^{\frac{45}{365}}$$

Results can be summarized as follows:

- If $S > €70$ there is a positive payoff.
- If $S > €75.02$ there is a profit.
- If $€70 < S < €75.02$ there is a loss.

The equation states that, being other variables equal:

(a) The lower the option price (P_C), the larger is the potential gain. Also, the lower the price of the call (P_C), the lower must be the stock price (S) to make a profit.
(b) The lower strike price (K) requires, the lower must be the stock price (S) to make a profit.

By considering that the short position in a call option is the other side of the long position, symmetrically the profit from a long position is the loss in the short position.

26.3 Call and Put Combinations

Investor can combine call and put options in the portfolio. The most common combination are the following.

26.3.1 Straddle

Assume an investor in a long position with a portfolio of both call and put options with the same strike price (K) and expiration date. This combination of options is called *straddle* and it can be represented as in Fig. 26.3.

Combining the call option (the blue line in Figure) and the put option (the red line in Figure), the investor receives the money until the options do not expire at-the-money: the farther away from the strike price (K) the options are, the more money investor will make.

Therefore, the payoff will be all more positive the greater distance between the stock price (S) and the strike price (K).

With regard to the profit, we must consider that in both cases, the call and put option require to pay a cost. Consequently, the profit (payoff less cost) will be: *i)*

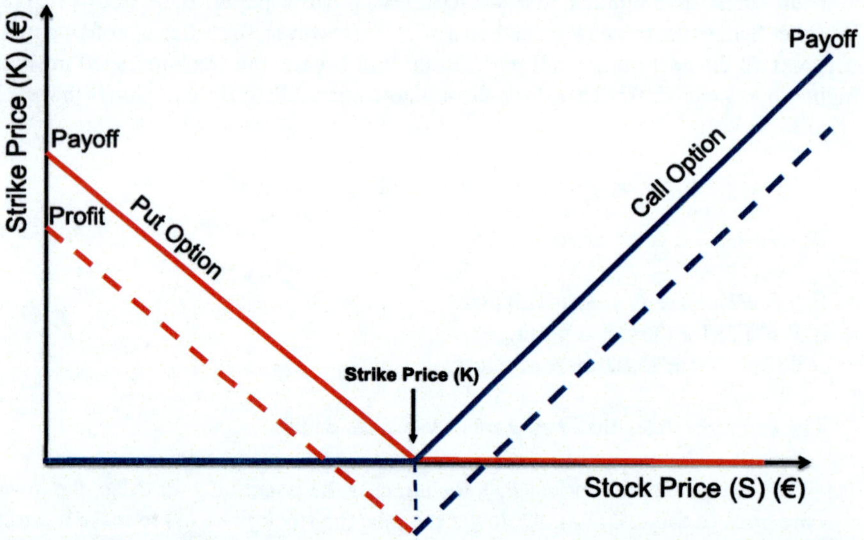

Fig. 26.3 Straddle combination

negative, if the stock prices (*S*) close to the strike price (*K*); *ii)* positive, if the stock price (*S*) is different from the strike price (*K*) and it will be all more positive the greater the distance among them.

The straddle combination is commonly used by investors that expect the stock price (*S*) will be characterized by high volatility by moving up or down significantly and in unexpectable direction. In any cases, investors expect that the stock price (*S*) do not end up near the strike price (*K*).

26.3.2 Stock and Portfolio Insurance

The investor can use a combination of call and put options to insure against a loss.

If the investor wants to purchase a stock and wants to insure this stock against a possible decline of its price, the investor can purchase a put option with a protective aim (called *protective put* for this reason). Therefore, if the stock price: *i)* increases, the investor can make money by sell the stock; *ii)* decreases, the investor exercises the put and sell the stock at the strike price by making money also in this case.

Assume that investor purchase a stock Alfa and wants to insurance against the possibility that the market price of the stock Alfa decreases below ($S <$ €50). Investor purchases a European put option with strike (*K*) equal to $K =$ €50. At the expiration date, if the stock price is: *i)* above €50 ($S >$ €50), investor keep the stock or sell it on the market by making money; ii) stock price is below €50 ($S <$ €50), the investor exercises the put and sell the Alfa stock at the strike price $K =$ €50 by making money. We can represent this case, as in Fig. 26.4.

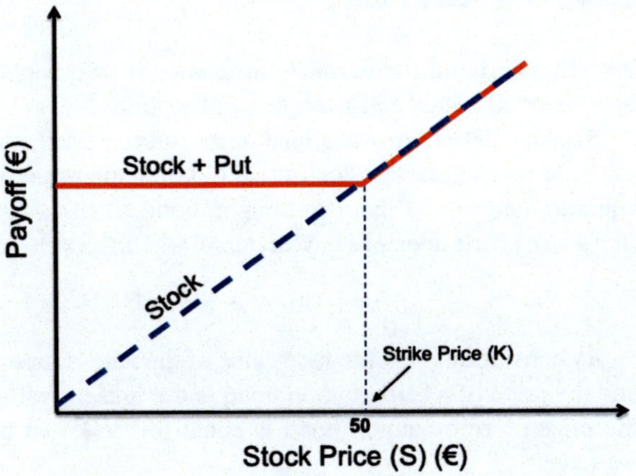

Fig. 26.4 Portfolio Insurance: combination of Stock and European Put Option

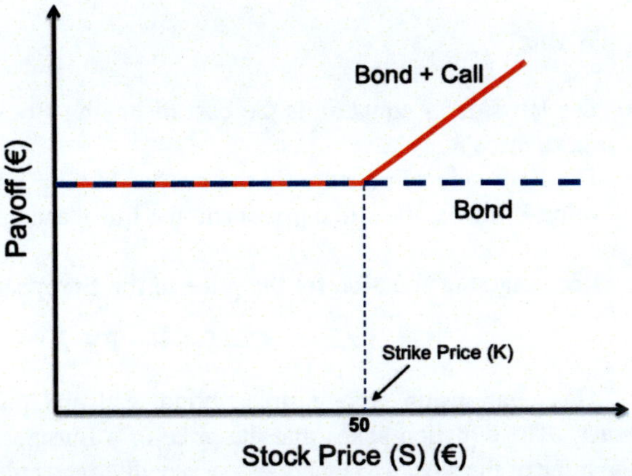

Fig. 26.5 Portfolio insurance: combination of Bond and Call Option

The investor can use the *protective put* to insure against the loss on an entire portfolio of stocks. The combination of a portfolio of stocks and put options is called *portfolio insurance*.

It is possible to achieve at the same result of *portfolio insurance* by using a call option. In this case, the investor combines bonds and a call options rather than stocks and put options.

Assume that the stock Alfa does not pay dividends. Assume investor purchases a riskless zero-coupon bond with face value of €50 and a European call option with a strike price (K) equal to $K = €50$. Therefore, if the stock price (S) of Alfa is: *i)* below €50 ($S < €50$), investor receives the payoff from the bond by making money; *ii)* above €50 ($S > €50$), investor exercises the call and use the payoff from the bond to buy the stock at the strike price $K = €50$ and sell the stock at the market price stock (S) by making money for the difference. In Fig. 26.5 we can represent this situation.

26.4 Put-Call Parity

Investor can build the *portfolio insurance* in two ways: *i)* stocks and European put options or *ii)* bonds and European call options.

Because these two ways lead to the same payoff, then they must have the same price. In this sense, the stock price (S) plus the price of the put option (P) must be equal to the price of the zero-coupon bond (B) plus the price of the call option (C) (for a stock that does not pay dividend), as follows:

$$S + P = B + C \tag{26.5}$$

By considering that the face value of the zero-coupon bond is the strike price (K), and the price of a zero-coupon bond is the present value (PV) of its face value, then the price of zero-coupon bond is equal to $\mathrm{PV}(K)$ so that: $B = \mathrm{PV}(K)$. Rearrange, we have:

$$S + P = \mathrm{PV}(K) + C$$

Where:

- The left side of equation is the cost of buying stock and European put with the strike price K.
- The right side of equation is the cost of buying a zero-coupon bond with face value K (that is the strike price) and the European call option with strike price K.

Rearrange the equation for the price of the European call option (C), we have:

$$C = S + P - \mathrm{PV}(K) \tag{26.6}$$

This relationship among stock, bond, call and put options, is called *put-call parity*. The equation states that the price of a European call option (C) is equal to the price of the stock (S) that does not pay dividends plus the price of identically put option (P) (same strike price and expiration date) less the price of the bond ($\mathrm{PV}(K)$) that goes to maturity on the exercise data of options. Then, the *putt-call parity* gives the price of the European call option in terms of European put, underlying stock and a zero-coupon bond.

The difference between the stock price and the bond price ($S - \mathrm{PV}(K)$) can be defined as the levered position in the stock. Therefore, we can define the call option as a combination of a levered position in the stock plus the insurance against the possibility that the price of stock decrease (that is the price of put option (P)).

Until now we have assumed that the stock does not pay dividends. If we remove this assumption by considering that stock that pays dividends, the put-call parity changes because stock will pay dividend while the zero-coupon bond will not.

By considering the present value of future dividends PV(Div), the *put-call parity* becomes:

$$S + P = \text{PV}(K) + PV(\text{Div}) + C \tag{26.7}$$

where:

- The left side of equation, is the price of the stock and the put option.
- The right side of equation is the price of the zero-coupon bond, the price of call option and the present value of the dividends will be paid by the stock during the period of options.

Rearrange the equation for the price of the European call option (C), we have:

$$C = P + S - \text{PV}(\text{Div}) - \text{PV}(K) \tag{26.8}$$

The equation states that the price of a call option (C) is equal to the price of the stock (S) less the present value of the dividends that the stock will pay during the life of the options, plus the price of put option (P) (same strike price and expiration date) less the price of the bond (PV(K)) that goes to maturity on the exercise data of options. Therefore, the price of call option is equal to a levered position in the stock without dividends (S – PV(Div) – PV(K)) plus the insurance against the possibility the stock price decrease (that is the price of put option (P)).

Note that we can use the equation to estimate the expected present value of the stock dividends during the life of options as follows:

$$\text{PV}(\text{Div}) = P - C + S - \text{PV}(K) \tag{26.9}$$

26.5 European and American Options

To evaluate the difference between American and European options, we have considered two different cases: stocks with no dividend payments and stocks with dividend payments.

Case (1): Stock Pays No Dividends

In the case of a stock pays no dividends prior the expiration date of the options, the price of a European ***call option*** is:

$$C = P + S - \text{PV}(K)$$

The price of the zero-coupon bond (PV(K)) can be written by considering its face that is the strike price (K) less the amount of the discount from face value to account for interest (dis(K)) as follows:

$$\text{PV}(K) = K - \text{dis}(K)$$

Replacing in the equation, we have:

$$C = P + S - K + \text{dis}(K)$$

and then:

$$C = S - K + \text{dis}(K) + P \tag{26.10}$$

where:

1. $S - K$ is the *intrinsic value of the option* that is the value it would have if it expired immediately. Then, the intrinsic value is the amount by which the option is currently in-the-money, or zero if the option is out-of-the-money.
2. $\text{dis}(K) + P$ is the *time value* of the option that is the difference between the current option price and its intrinsic value.

The equation states that if the *time value* is positive, the price of call option is higher than its *intrinsic value*.

In the case of European call options, both terms of the time value are positive before the expiration date. Indeed, by assuming positive interest rates the discount on a zero-coupon bond before the maturity date is positive, as well as the price of put option is also positive before expiration date. Therefore, the European call option always has a positive time value.

With regard to the American call option, by considering that it is worth at least as much as a European call option, it must also have a positive time value before expiration.

Therefore, we can say that the price of any call option on stock pays no dividends always exceeds its intrinsic value.

It implies that it is never optimal to exercise a call option on stock that no pays dividends and it is always better to sell the option. Indeed, if investor exercises an option he gets its intrinsic value, while by selling the option he gets its price that it is greater than its intrinsic value.

With specific regard to an American call option on a stock that no pay dividends, since it is never optimal to exercise the call option early, the right to exercise the call option early is worthless.

Therefore, an American call option on a stock that no pay dividends has the same price of the European call option on the same stock.

The question is different for an American *put option* on stock pays no dividends.

We can rearrange the put-call parity equation to get the price of a European put option as follows:

$$P = K - S + C - \text{dis}(K) \tag{26.11}$$

where:

1. $K - S$ is the Intrinsic Value of the option.
2. $C - \text{dis}(K)$ is the Time Value of the option.

Therefore, in the put option the time value includes a negative term, that is the discount on a bond with face value (dis(K)). It is the opportunity cost of waiting to receive the strike price (K). Indeed, if the strike price (K) is so high that the put option is very deep in-the-money, this discount amount is high and the time value of a European put option is negative. It implies that the price of the European put option is less than its intrinsic value.

With regard to the American put option, it cannot sell for less than its intrinsic value because it opens to arbitrage profits by immediately exercising it. Consequently, the American put option can be worth more than an identical European put option. The difference in value is due to the right to exercise the option early that we have to consider.

Case (2): Stock Pays Dividends

In the case of a stock pays dividends prior the expiration date of the options, the price of a European *call option* is:

$$C = S - K + \text{dis}(K) + P - \text{PV}(\text{Div})$$

where:

1. $S - K$ is the Intrinsic Value of the option.
2. dis(K) + P − PV(Div) is the Time Value of the option.

The sign of the time value is strictly related to the size of the present value of the dividends. If it is large enough, the time value is negative. In this case, the price of call option is less than its intrinsic value.

Since the American call option can never be worth less than its intrinsic value, its price can exceed the price of a European call option.

The optimal time to exercise the American call option is just before the ex-dividend date of the stock in order to capture the dividends paid by the stock.

In the case of European put option its price is equal to:

$$P = K - S + C - \text{dis}(K) + \text{PV}(\text{Div})$$

where:

1. $K - S$ is the Intrinsic Value of the option.
2. C − dis(K) + PV(Div) is the Time Value of the option.

In this case, dividends have a positive effect on the time value of the put option.

Therefore, if a stock pays dividends, investor benefits by waiting for the stock price to drop after it goes ex-dividend before exercising the put option. Thus, it is less likely that a put option on a stock that pays dividends is exercised early.

Option Pricing

27

27.1 Binomial Option Pricing Model

In this contest, we use three main techniques to price option:

1. Binomial Option Pricing Model
2. Black-Scholes formula
3. Risk-neutral probabilities

The *Binomial Option Pricing Model* (Cox et al., 1979; Rendleman & Bartter, 1979) prices the option on the basis of the simplifying assumption: at the end of the next period, the stock price has only two possible values.

27.1.1 Two-State Single-Period Model

In a very simple form, we consider only one period to compute the price of option.

We can value the option by constructing a ***replicating portfolio***. It is a portfolio of other securities that has the same payoffs of the option in the one period. If they have the same payoffs, then they must have the same value.

Consider a stock whose current price is equal to S. Assume that in one-period that it is the next period, the stock price can go up equal to S_u or go down equal to S_d. Assume a one-period risk-free interest rate is equal to R_f and it measures the bond returns.

We can determine the price of an option (C). It will be valued equal to C_u if the stock price goes up ($S \rightarrow S_u$), and C_d if the stock price goes down ($S \rightarrow S_d$).

We can also determine the numbers of shares of stock (ΔS) and the amount in bonds (B) in a such way that the payoff of the replicating portfolio matches the payoff of the option in both cases if the stock goes up or goes down.

The two simultaneous equations with two unknowns, ΔS and B, are the following:

P. De Luca, *Corporate Finance*, Springer Texts in Business and Economics,
https://doi.org/10.1007/978-3-031-18300-3_27

$$S_u \Delta S + (1 + R_f)B = C_u$$
$$S_d \Delta S + (1 + R_f)B = C_d$$

By solving these two equations for the unknown variables, ΔS and B, we get the general formula for the replicating portfolio in the binomial model as follows:

$$\Delta S = \frac{C_u - C_d}{S_u - S_d}$$
$$B = \frac{C_d - S_d \Delta S}{1 + R_f} \tag{27.1}$$

Note that the formula for ΔS can be interpreted as the sensitivity of the option's value to the change in the stock price. Indeed, it is equal to the slope of the line showing the payoff of the replicating portfolio.

The value of B indicates the amount of investment in bond if it is positive (long position), or the borrowing if it is negative (short position).

The value of the portfolio of stocks and bonds must be equal to the value of the call option in every possible state. Therefore, in the up-state the value of portfolio must be equal to C_u (that is the value of the option if $S \rightarrow S_u$), as well as in the down-state, it must be equal to C_d (that is the value of the put if $S \rightarrow S_d$). Therefore, we can check that the portfolio replicates the option as follows:

$$S \rightarrow S_u: \quad S_u \Delta S + (1 + R_f)B = C_u$$
$$S \rightarrow S_d: \quad S_d \Delta S + (1 + R_f)B = C_d$$

On the basis of the replicating portfolio, we can compute the value of the option (C) today as the cost of this portfolio. Therefore, the *Option Price in the Binomial Model* is equal to:

$$C = S\Delta S + B \tag{27.2}$$

These two equations (replicating portfolio and call option price) summarize the binomial option pricing model.

To well understand, assume a *European call option* on a stock pays no dividends during the life of the call option. Note that this is the default assumption if it is not specified differently. Assume that the current stock price is equal to $S = €60$ and the call expires in one period and its strike price (K) is equal to $K = €60$. Assume that in one period the stock price can rise (*up state*) by €15 so that the stock price goes up to €75, or fall (*down state*) so that the stock price goes down to €45. In the first case, the price of call option is equal to €15 ($\max(€75 - €60, €0) = €15$) while in the second case, it is equal to 0 ($\max(€45 - €60, €0) = €0$). Assume that the one-period risk-free rate is equal to 5% and the current price of one bond is equal to €1 so that it will be worth in one period €1.05 (€1 + 5%).

We can summarize all this information on a binomial tree as follows.

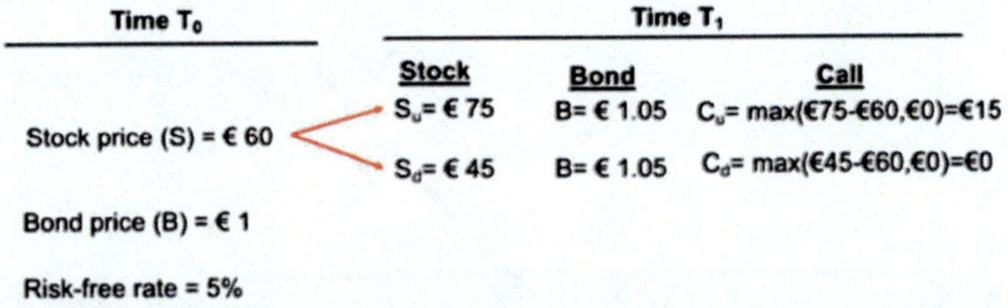

We can replicate this payoff using a portfolio of the stocks and the bonds in order to determine the value of the call option.

Assume to purchase a number of shares of stock equal to ΔS and the investment in bonds is equal to B (in €). The replicating portfolio is equal to:

$$\Delta S = \frac{C_u - C_d}{S_u - S_d} = \frac{15 - 0}{75 - 45} = 0.5$$

$$B = \frac{C_d - S_d \Delta S}{1 + R_f} = \frac{0 - 45 \cdot (0.5)}{1 + 5\%} = -21.43$$

Therefore, in one period the portfolio that matches the value of the call option is defined by *long 0.5 shares of stock* and *short €21.43 worth of bonds* (we borrow €21.43 at a 5% interest rate).

The value of the portfolio of stocks and bonds must be equal to the value of the call option in every possible state. Therefore, in the up-state the value of portfolio must be equal to €15 (that is the value of the call in this state), as well as in the down-state it must be equal to €0 (that is the value of the call in this state). Therefore, we can check that the portfolio replicates the call option as follows:

$$S \rightarrow S_u : \quad S_u \Delta S + (1 + R_f)B = C_u \quad \rightarrow \quad €75 \cdot 0.5 + (1 + 5\%) \cdot -€21.43 = €15$$
$$S \rightarrow S_d : \quad S_d \Delta S + (1 + R_f)B = C_d \quad \rightarrow \quad €45 \cdot 0.5 + (1 + 5\%) \cdot -€21.43 = €0$$

Therefore, the price of the call option today must be equal the current market value of the replicating portfolio. The value of the portfolio today is equal to 0.5 shares at the current stock price of €60 less the amount of bond borrowed (equal to €21.43). Consequently, defined the replicating portfolio, the value of option (C) today is the cost of this portfolio as follows:

$$\text{Call Value} = C = S\Delta S + B = €60 \cdot 0.5 - €21.43 = €8.57$$

The value of the call option today is equal to €8.57.

The use of stock and bond to replicate the payoff of the call option can be represented as in Fig. 27.1. As the function of the future stock price, the payoff of the replicating portfolio is a straight-line with slope equal to $\Delta S = 0.5$ and intercept equal to $PV(B) = 1.05 \cdot (-€21.43) = -€22.5$. This straight-line is different from the broken line representing the payoff of the call option, that is equal to zero below the strike price of ($Z = €60$) and increases 1:1 with the stock price above €60 ($S > €60$).

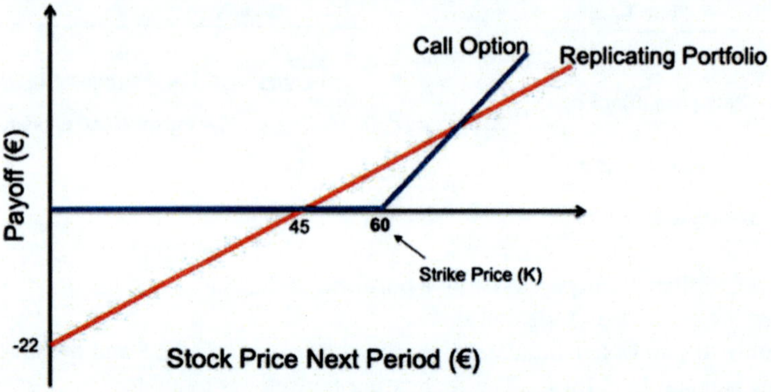

Fig. 27.1 Replicating Portfolio and Call Option in the Binomial Model

Two are the main key elements of the model:

1. The option and the replicating portfolio have the same payoffs given the only in the two outcomes we have assumed possible for the stock price ($S = €75$ and $S = €45$).
2. We have solved for the price of the call option without knowing the probabilities of the states in the binomial tree. Indeed, we do not need to specify the likelihood that the stock goes up versus down. Consequently, we do not need to know the expected return of the stock, that it depends on these probabilities.

We can consider the case of a ***European Put Option***. Assume that the current price stock is equal to $S = €70$, and in one-period it will go up to $S = €82$ or go down to $S = €62$. Assume that the strike price is equal to $S = €70$ and in one-period risk-free rate is equal to 4%. The binomial tree can be represented as follows:

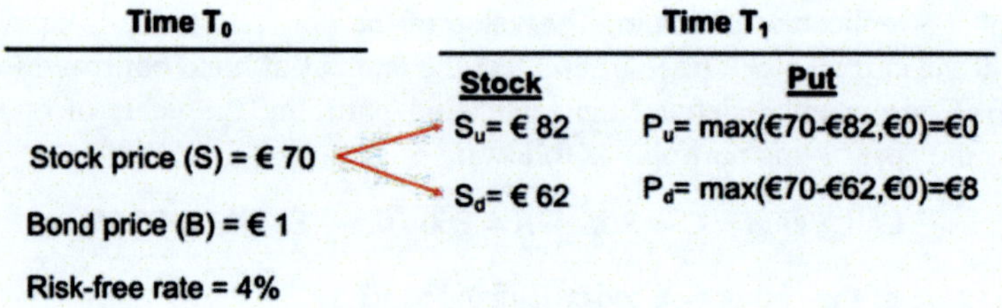

The price of the European Put Option is equal to:

$$\Delta S = \frac{C_u - C_d}{S_u - S_d} = \frac{0 - 8}{82 - 62} = -0.4$$

$$B = \frac{C_d - S_d \Delta S}{1 + R_f} = \frac{8 - 62 \cdot (-0.4)}{1 + 4\%} = \frac{32.8}{1.04} = 31.54$$

Therefore, this portfolio *is short 0.4 shares of stock*, and *long € 31.54 bonds* by investing in the risk-free bond.

The value of the portfolio of stocks and bonds must be equal to the value of the put option in every possible state. Therefore, in the up-state the value of portfolio must be equal to €0 (that is the value of the put in this state), as well as in the down-state it must be equal to €8 (that is the value of the put in this state). Therefore, we can verify that the portfolio replicates the call option as follows:

$$S \rightarrow S_u: \quad S_u \Delta S + (1 + R_f) B = C_u \quad \rightarrow \quad €82 \cdot (-0.4) + (1 + 4\%) \cdot €31.54 = €0$$
$$S \rightarrow S_d: \quad S_d \Delta S + (1 + R_f) B = C_d \quad \rightarrow \quad €62 \cdot (-0.4) + (1 + 4\%) \cdot €31.54 = €8$$

Therefore, the price of the put option today must be equal the current market value of the replicating portfolio. The value of the portfolio today is equal to −0.4 shares at the current stock price of €70, plus the investment in bonds equal to €21.43. Consequently, defined the replicating portfolio, the value of option (C) today is the cost of this portfolio as follows:

$$\text{Put Value} = C = S\Delta S + B = €70 \cdot (-0.4) + €31.54 = €3.54$$

The value of put option today is equal to €3.54.

27.1.2 A Multiperiod Model

The two-State Single-Period Model does not consider that there are many more than two possible outcomes for the stock price in the real world. Therefore, to make the model more realistic, we introduce the possibility of many states and periods.

The fundamental assumption of the binomial model is that in each period, there are only two possible outcomes: the stock price (S) goes up ($S \rightarrow S_u$) or goes down ($S \rightarrow S_d$).

By considering two-period, we have the following binomial tree for the stock price:

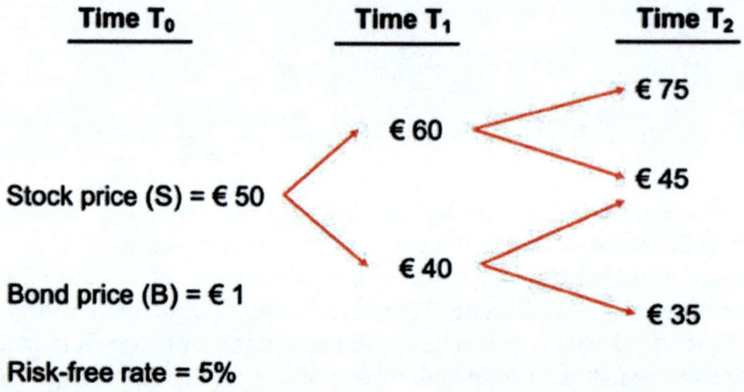

Therefore, by adding an additional period, the number of possible stock prices at the end has increased.

Assume that the strike price is equal to $K = €60$ that expires in two periods and a risk-free rate of interest is equal to 5% for one-year and it will remain constant.

To compute the value of the call option in a multiperiod binomial tree, we start from the end of the tree and work backward.

At time T2 the call option expires and then its value is equal to its intrinsic value.

If the stock price is equal to $S = €60$ at time T1 and it goes up to $S_u = €75$ in time T2, the value of call option is equal to $C_u = €15$; on the contrary, if the stock price goes down $S_d = €45$ in time T2, the call option is equal to $C_d = €0$, as follows:

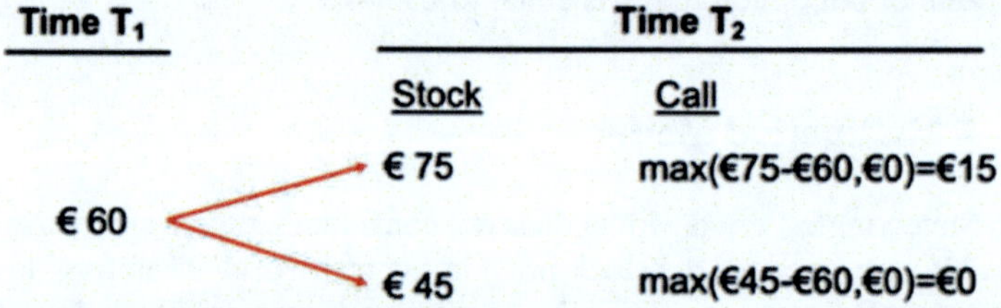

We can compute the replicating portfolio on the basis of $\Delta S = 0.5$ shares of stock and a bond position of $B = -€21.43$. The call value is equal to €8.57.

If the stock price is equal to $S = €40$ in the time T1 and it goes up to $S_u = €45$ in time T2, the value of call option is equal to $C_u = €0$; on the contrary, if the stock price goes down $S_d = €35$ in time T2, the call option is equal to $C_d = €0$, as follows:

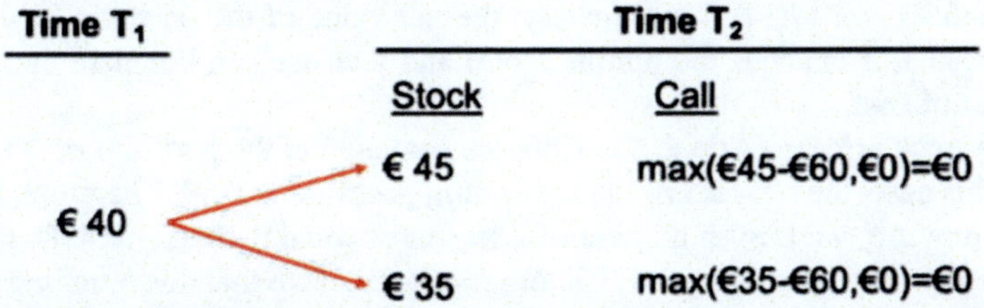

The replicating portfolio on the basis of $\Delta S = 0$ shares of stock and a bond position of $B = 0$. The call value is equal to €0. Therefore, in this case the option is worthless.

Therefore, now we can work backward and determine the value of the call at time T0. The binomial tree is the following:

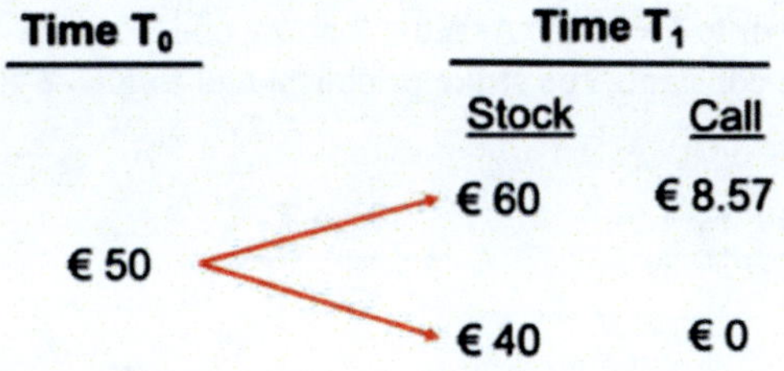

Note that the call option value at the end of the tree (time T1) is the value of the call option one period prior to expiration, and then it is not the final payoffs.

However, we can compute the replicating portfolio at time T0. This is the portfolio whose value match the value of the call option at time T1.

$$\Delta S = \frac{C_u - C_d}{S_u - S_d} = \frac{8.57 - 0}{60 - 40} = 0.4286$$

$$B = \frac{C_d - S_d \Delta S}{1 + R_f} = \frac{0 - 40 \cdot 0.4286}{1 + 5\%} = -\frac{17.14}{1.05} = -16.32$$

The initial value of the call option is equal to the initial cost of this portfolio as follows:

$$\text{Call Value} = C = S\Delta S + B = 50 \cdot 0.4286 - 16.32 = 5.10$$

Therefore, the initial value of the call option at time period T0 is € 5.10.

For this two-period call option, we need to adjust our replicating portfolio at the end of each time period.

We start off long 0.4285 shares of stock and borrow € 16.32 for initial cost of € 5.10. If:

(a) The stock price goes down to S = €40: shares are worth $S\Delta S$ = €40 · 0.4286 = €17.14 and the debt goes up to $B(1 + R_f)$ = 16.32

(1 + 5%) = €17.14. Consequently, the net value of the portfolio is worthless, (note that it matches the option value) and then we can liquidate the portfolio without cost.

(b) The stock price goes up to $S = €60$: the net value of the portfolio rises to € 8.57. In this case, the new ΔS of the replicating portfolio is 0.50. Therefore, to match the new ΔS, we buy an number of new shares equal to $0.50 - 0.4286 = 0.0715$ and pay it by borrowing $0.0715 \cdot €60 = €4.29$. Note that this retrading does not require new money. Indeed, at the end the total debt is equal to $€16.32 \cdot (1 + 5\%) + €4.29 = €21.43$, that it matches the value of B computed earlier.

On the expiration date at time T2, the value of the portfolio €15 if the stock price goes up to €75, and is zero otherwise.

Now consider a *European Put Option*. Assume that the current stock price per share is equal to $S = €50$. In time T1 assumes that the stock price can go up to $S = €70$ or go down to $S = €30$. Assume that the one-year risk-free rate is equal to 4% and it remains constant. The strike price is equal to $K = €70$.

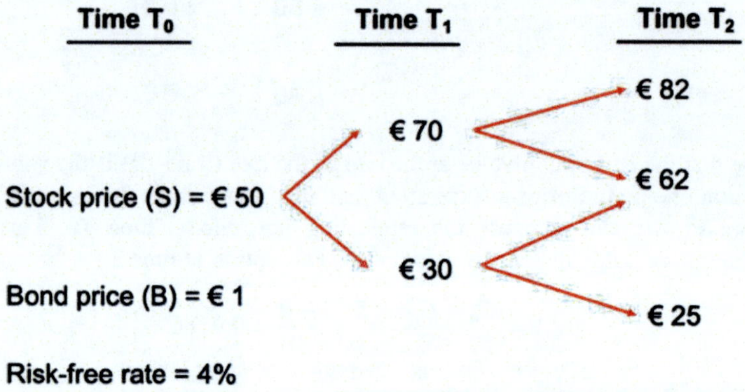

At time T1, if the stock price:

(a) Goes up $S = €70$, the value of the put option is equal to €3.54 as follows:

$$\Delta S = \frac{C_u - C_d}{S_u - S_d} = \frac{0 - 8}{82 - 62} = -0.4$$

$$B = \frac{C_d - S_d \Delta S}{1 + R_f} = \frac{8 - 62 \cdot (-0.4)}{1 + 4\%} = \frac{32.8}{1.04} = 31.54$$

This portfolio is short one share of the stock and it has €31.54 invested in the bond at the rate of return equal to the risk-free rate equal to 4%.

And then the value of put option today is equal to €3.54 as follows:

$$\text{Put Value} = C = S\Delta S + B = €70 \cdot (-0.4) + €31.54 = €3.54.$$

(b) Goes down $S = €30$, at the time T2 the value of put option is equal to €8 if the stock price goes up to $S = €62$ and it is equal to €45 if the stock price goes down to $S = €25$. Therefore, in this case, we have.

$$\Delta S = \frac{C_u - C_d}{S_u - S_d} = \frac{8 - 45}{62 - 25} = -1$$

$$B = \frac{C_d - S_d \Delta S}{1 + R_f} = \frac{45 - 25 \cdot (-1)}{1 + 4\%} = 67.31$$

This portfolio is short one share of the stock and it has €67.31 invested in the bond at the rate of return equal to the risk-free rate equal to 4%.

The value of the put option is the cost of this portfolio, and then:

$$\text{Put Value} = C = S\Delta S + B = 30 \cdot (-1) + €67.31 = €37.31$$

Now we can compute the value of the put option at time T0. The binomial Tree at time T0 is equal to:

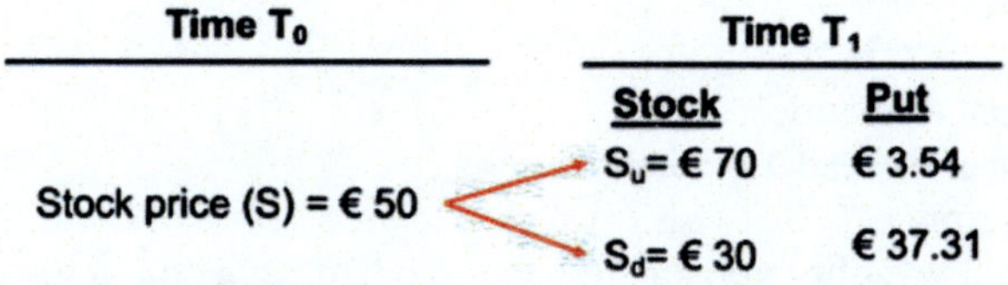

At time T1, the put option will be worth €3.54 if the stock price goes up to $S = €70$ and €37.31 if the stock price goes down to $S = €30$.

Therefore, the replicating portfolio at time T0 is equal to:

$$\Delta S = \frac{C_u - C_d}{S_u - S_d} = \frac{3.54 - 37.31}{70 - 30} = -0.84$$

$$B = \frac{C_d - S_d \Delta S}{1 + R_f} = \frac{37.31 - 30 \cdot (-0.84)}{1 + 4\%} = 60.22$$

This portfolio is short one share of the stock and it has €60.32 invested in the bond at the rate of return equal to the risk-free rate equal to 4%.

The value of a European put option at time T0 is equal to €18.01 as follows:

$$\text{Put Value} = C = S\Delta S + B = 50 \cdot (-0.84) + €60.22 = €18.01$$

27.2 Black-Scholes Option Pricing Model

Robert Merton and Myron Scholes (nobel prize in economics in 1997. Black died two years before the prize was awarded) discovered in 1973, together with Fischer Black the formula to calculate the price of an option. The model is called the *Black-Scholes Option Pricing Model.*

The Black-Scholes formula was derived by Fischer Black and Myron Scholes (1973) building on earlier work by Robert Merton.

Even if the formula itself represents a great contribution to economics, even more important is the technique used by Black, Scholes, and Merton to value options. Two are the main relevant factors of the Black-Scholes formula:

1. It does not require model preferences because it is not based on the unobservable parameters such as investors' preferences.
2. It has contributed to the huge growth in the types of financial securities available in the market because all techniques used to price them can be traced to this formula.

In this chapter, we will focus on the application of the formula only without derive it.

Denote with:

- S: the current stock price.
- T: the number of years left to expiration.
- K: the strike price.
- σ: the annual volatility measured by the standard deviation of the stock's return.
- PV(K): the price of zero-coupon bond. Indeed, the face value of the zero-coupon bond is the strike price (K) on the expiration date of the option, and the price of a zero-coupon bond is the present value (PV) of its face value.
- $N(d)$: the cumulative normal distribution, that is the probability that a normally distributed variable is less than d.

The value at time t of a call option on a stock that does not pay dividends prior to the option's expiration date is given by the formula:

$$C = S \cdot N(d_1) - \mathrm{PV}(K) \cdot N(d_2)$$
$$\text{where :}$$
$$d_1 = \frac{\ln\left[S/PV(K)\right]}{\sigma\sqrt{T}} + \frac{\sigma\sqrt{T}}{2} \quad \text{and} \quad d_2 = d_1 - \sigma\sqrt{T} \tag{27.3}$$

this is the *Black-Scholes Price of a Call Option on a Non-Dividend-Paying Stock.*

Note that the formula requires only five inputs to price the call: the stock price (S), the strike price (K), the exercise date (T), the risk-free interest rate (R_f) to compute the present value of the strike price (PV(K)), and the volatility of the stock price (σ). Among these five inputs, four are directly observable: S, K, T, R_f. Only one parameter, the volatility of the stock price (σ) is not directly observed. It can be estimated by using two main techniques:

1. *Historical date* on daily stock returns. Therefore, the volatility of the stock is estimated on over the past several months. It is considered the most straightforward approach because the volatility trend tends to be persistent. Consequently, the past can provide a reasonable forecast for the stock's volatility in the future.
2. *Current market prices* of traded options. An estimate of stock's volatility that is implied by an options' price is called *implied volatility*. Therefore, the implied volatility from one option is used to estimate the value of other options on the stock with the same expiration date.

We do not need to know the expected return on the stock to compute the option price. The only parameter that we need to forecast is the stock's volatility. Since the stock's volatility is much easier to measure than its expected return, the Black-Scholes formula can be very precise.

Note that the current stock price already reflects its expected return because the market price discounts the value of its future payoffs. Therefore, the Black-Scholes formula depends on the stock's current price, and then indirectly is based on the implicit expected returns.

Finally note that the Black-Scholes formula is derived assuming that a European call option. By considering that an American call option on a stock that no pays dividends has the same price of the European call option, then the Black-Scholes formula can be used to price American or European call options on non-dividend-paying stocks.

To well-understand the Black-Scholes formula consider the following example. Assume a stock price is equal to $S=€6.05$, the strike price is equal to $S=€7$, the volatility of the stock is $\sigma=55\%$ per year, the risk-free rate of interest is equal to $R_F=1\%$ per year, the days left until the expiration date are $T=160$ (by considering 365 days per year).

Based on these data, we have:

$$\text{PV}(K)=\frac{7.00}{(1+1\%)^{\left(\frac{160}{365}\right)}}=€\,6.97$$

$$d_1=\frac{\ln\left[6.05/6.97\right]}{0.55\cdot\sqrt{\frac{160}{365}}}+\frac{0.55\cdot\sqrt{\frac{160}{365}}}{2}=-0.21$$

$$d_2=-0.21-0.55\cdot\sqrt{\frac{160}{365}}=-0.57$$

The $N(d_1)$ and $N(d_2)$ are equal to:

$$N(-0.21) = 0.417 \text{ and } N(-0.57) = 0.284$$

Consequently, the price of call option is equal to:

$$C = 6.05 \cdot 0.417 - 6.97 \cdot 0.284 = € \, 0.54$$

27.2.1 European Put Options

The Black-Scholes formula can be used to calculate the price of European Put Option on stock that no pays dividends, by using the Put-Call Parity. It is equal to:

$$S + P = \text{PV}(K) + C$$

and then:

$$P = C - S + \text{PV}(K)$$

Substituting C, we have:

$$P = [S \cdot N(d_1) - \text{PV}(K) \cdot N(d_2)] - S + \text{PV}(K)$$

And rearranging, we have:

$$P = S \cdot N(d_1) - \text{PV}(K) \cdot N(d_2) - S + \text{PV}(K)$$

$$P = \text{PV}(K)[1 - N(d_2)] - S + S \cdot N(d_1)$$

$$P = \text{PV}(K)[1 - N(d_2)] - S[1 - N(d_1)] \tag{27.4}$$

this is the *Black-Scholes Price of a European Put Option on a Non-Dividend-Paying Stock.*

Assume that: the current stock price is equal to $S = €6.05$; strike price is equal to $K = €6$; free-risk interest rate equal to $R_F = 1\%$ per year; stock volatility is equal to $\sigma = 55\%$ per year, days left to the expiration of the option is equal $T = 185$ (by considering 365 days per year).

Based on these data, we have:

$$\text{PV}(K) = \frac{6.00}{(1 + 1\%)^{\left(\frac{185}{365}\right)}} = € \, 5.97$$

$$d_1 = \frac{\ln[6.05/5.97]}{0.55 \cdot \sqrt{\frac{185}{365}}} + \frac{0.55 \cdot \sqrt{\frac{185}{365}}}{2} = 0.23$$

$$d_2 = 0.23 - 0.55 \cdot \sqrt{\frac{185}{365}} = -0.16$$

The $N(d_1)$ and $N(d_2)$ are equal to:

$$N(0.23) = 0.591 \text{ and } N(-0.16) = 0.436$$

Consequently, the price of put is equal to:

$$P = 5.97 \cdot (1 - 0.436) - 6.05 \cdot (1 - 0.591) = €\,0.89$$

27.2.2 Call Option on Dividend-Paying Stocks

Even if the Black-Scholes formula is applied to option on stock does not pay dividends, we can easily adjust the formula by considering a European option on stock pays dividend.

Two are the main element to keep in mind: first, the owner of the European call option does not receive benefit from the dividend that will be paid prior to the expiration date of the option, second, the stock price drops by the amount of dividend when the stock goes ex-dividend. Consequently, because the final stock price will be lower, dividends decrease the value of a call option.

Denote with S the current price of stock that pay dividends; PV(Div) the present value of any dividends paid prior to the expiration date of the option; S^* the current price of the stock excluding any dividends prior to expiration. We have:

$$S^* = S - \text{PV(Div)}$$

Since the European call option is the right to buy the stock without these dividends, we can use the Black-Scholes formula with S^* in place of S.

Note that if the stock pays a dividend proportional to its stock price, to compute the value of S^* we have to consider the stock's dividend yield until the expiration date (q) as follows:

$$S^* = \frac{S}{(1+q)}$$

Therefore, if the stock pays an annual dividend yield equal to 8% and the stock price is equal to $S = €40$, we have:

$$S^* = \frac{40}{(1+8\%)} = \frac{40}{(1.08)} = €\,37.04$$

27.2.3 Replicating Portfolio

The Replicating Portfolio used in the Binomial Option Pricing Model was discovered by Fischer Black and Myron Scholes while they were deriving their model.

By using the Replicating Portfolio in the Binomial Option Pricing Model the price of a call option (*C*) is given by the price of the replicating portfolio, as follows:

$$C = S\Delta S + B$$

where:

$$\Delta S = \frac{C_u - C_d}{S_u - S_d}$$
$$B = \frac{C_d - S_d \Delta S}{1 + R_f}$$

By comparing this equation to the Black-Scholes formula, we have the shares of stock (ΔS) and the amount in bonds (*B*) in *the Black-Scholes replicating portfolio of a Call Option* as follows:

$$\Delta S = N(d_1)$$
$$B = -\mathrm{PV}(K)N(d_2)$$

Note that *N*(*d*) is the cumulative normal distribution function with a minimum value equal to 0 and maximum value equal to 1. Consequently, ΔS is defined between 0 and 1 as well as *B* is defined between $-K$ and 0.

The ΔS can be interpreted as the change in the price of the option given a €1 change in the price of the stock. Because ΔS is always less than 1, it implies that the change in the call price is always less than the change in the stock price.

To well understand consider the following example. Consider a stock does no pay dividends. Assume that the current stock price is equal to $S = €15$; the stock's return has a volatility equal to $\sigma = 50\%$; the risk-free rate is $R_f = 5\%$; the strike price is equal to $K = €15$ and time is equal to $T = 1$.

We can determine the portfolio to hold today to replicate a one-year at-the-money call option on the stock as follows.

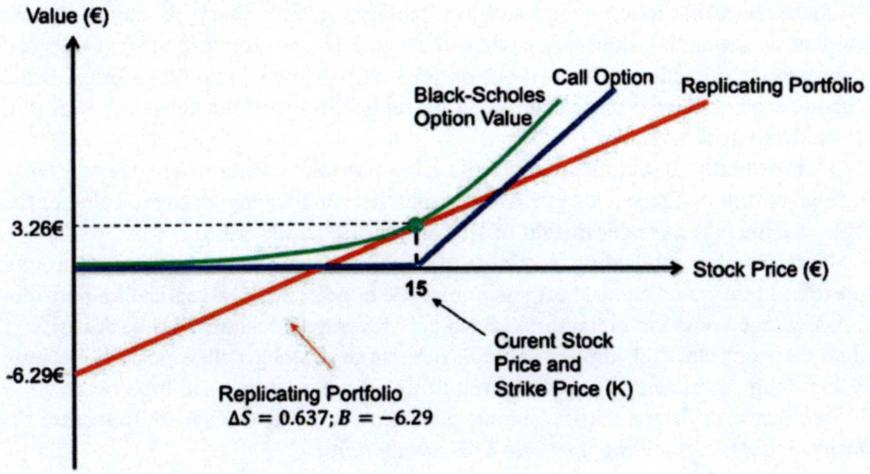

Fig. 27.2 Black-Scholes and Replicating Portfolio for the Call Option

By applying the Black-Scholes formula, we have:

$$\text{PV}(K) = \frac{15}{(1+5\%)} = \frac{15}{(1.05)} € \, 14.29$$

The d_1 and d_2 are equal to:

$$d_1 = \frac{\ln{[10.00/14.29]}}{0.50} + \frac{0.50}{2} = 0.35$$

$$d_2 = 0.35 - 0.50 = -0.15$$

The $N(d_1)$ and $N(d_2)$ are equal to:

$$N(0.35) = 0.637 \text{ and } N(-0.15) = 0.440$$

The replicating portfolio for the option is:

$$\Delta S = N(d_1) = N(0.35) = 0.637$$

$$B = -\text{PV}(K) \cdot N(d_2) = -14.29 \cdot 0.440 = -6.29$$

Therefore, we should buy 0.637 shares of stock and borrow €6.29. The total cost (TC) is equal to €3.26 as follows:

$$\text{TC} = 15 \cdot 0.637 - 6.29 = 3.26$$

This total cost is the Black-Scholes value of the call option. We can summarize as in Fig. 27.2.

Since the Call Option Value and the Replicating Portfolio (with slope ΔS) are tangent at the initial stock price, then the value of the Replicating Portfolio can approximate the value of the call option for small changes to the stock price. If the change in stock price is more than small, the replicating portfolio needs to be updated to maintain accuracy.

Consequently, if we update our replicating portfolio continuously, we can replicate an option on the stock by remaining on a line that is tangent to the value of the option. This is the greater insight of Black, Scholes and Merton.

Note that the replicating portfolio of a call option always consists of a long position in the stock and a short position in the bond. Then, the replicating portfolio is a leveraged position in the stock. Because a leveraged position in a stock is riskier than the stock itself, it implies that call options on a stock with a positive beta are riskier than the underlying stock by requiring a higher returns and high betas.

We can also derive the replicating portfolio for a Put Option. In this case, *the Black-Scholes replicating portfolio of a Put Option* is:

$$\Delta S = -[1 - N(d_1)]$$
$$B = \mathrm{PV}(K)[1 - N(d_2)]$$

In this case, ΔS is defined between -1 and 0, and B is defined between 0 and K. It implies that the replicating portfolio of a put option always consists of a long position in the bond and a short position in the shares of stock. Consequently, the put option on a stock with a positive beta has a negative beta.

27.3 Risk-Neutral Probabilities

In the Binomial Option Pricing Model as well as in the Black-Scholes Option Pricing Model, we do not need to know the probability associate with each possible future stock price to calculate the option price.

Consider the case in which we know these probabilities. In this case, we can calculate the expected payoff of the option and discount it at the appropriate cost of capital. The main problem is to estimate the cost of capital. However, there is a case in which the cost of capital can be precisely estimated. It is the case in which all investors are risk neutral and then all financial assets would have the same cost of capital that is equal to the risk-free rate of interest (R_f).

To well-understand consider the follow example. Assume all investors are risk-neutral on the market. Assume that the stock price today is equal to $S = €60$ and in one-period (for time $t = 1$) it can go up equal to $S_u = €75$ with probability equal to ρ or go down equal to $S_d = €45$ with probability equal to $(1 - \rho)$. The probabilities ρ and $(1 - \rho)$ are called *risk-neutral probabilities*. Assume that the one-period risk-free rate is equal to $R_f = 5\%$ and the strike price is equal to $K = €60$.

The value of the stock today and then its price must equal the present value of the expected price next period discounted at the risk-free rate, as follows:

$$S = \frac{S_u \cdot \rho + S_d \cdot (1 - \rho)}{(1 + R_f)^{t=1}} \tag{27.5}$$

and then:

$$60 = \frac{75\rho + 45(1 - \rho)}{1.05}$$

By solving the equation for ρ, we have:

$$\rho = \frac{S(1 + R_f) - S_d}{S_u - S_d} \tag{27.6}$$

and then:

$$\rho = \frac{60(1.05) - 45}{75 - 45} = 0.6$$

Therefore, we have $\rho = 60\%$ and $(1 - \rho) = 40\%$.

By knowing the probabilities of each states, we can price the call by calculating the present value of its expected payoff next period.

Since the strike price of call option is equal to $K = €60$, it will be worth either €15 or nothing at expiration. Therefore, the present value of the expected payouts is equal to:

$$\text{Call Value} = C = \frac{15 \cdot 60\% + 0 \cdot 40\%}{1.05} = 8.57$$

Note that this is the same value of call option calculated in the previous example in the Binomial Option Pricing Mode: Two-State Single-period Model. It happens because in both the Binomial Option Pricing Model and in the Black-Scholes Option Pricing Model, there is no need of assumption about risk preferences of investors. Consequently, models must work for any set of preferences even including the risk-neutral assumption.

In real world investors are risk-adverse. It implies that ρ is not the actual probability of the stock price increase but it means how the actual probability must be adjusted to keep the stock price the same in a risk-neutral world.

Assume that the effectively probability to stock price equal to $S = €60$ goes up to $S_u = €75$ is equal to $\rho = 75\%$. Consequently, the effectively probability that the stock price goes down to $S_d = €45$ is equal to $(1 - \rho) = 25\%$. In this case, the expected return is equal to:

$$S = \frac{S_u \cdot \rho + S_d \cdot (1-\rho)}{(1+i)} \quad (27.7)$$

and then:

$$60 = \frac{75 \cdot 70\% + 45 \cdot 30\%}{(1+i)}$$

The stock's expected return (i) si equal to:

$$i = \frac{S_u \cdot \rho + S_d \cdot (1-\rho)}{S} - 1 \quad (27.8)$$

and then:

$$i = \frac{75 \cdot 70\% + 45 \cdot 30\%}{60} - 1 = 10\%$$

Therefore, the stock's expected return is equal to 10%.

By considering that the risk-free interest rate is equal to $R_f = 5\%$, it implies that the stock has a risk premium equal to $RP = 5\%$. Therefore, risk-neutral probability that the stock will increase is $\rho = 60\%$ that is less then the true probability that is $\rho = 70\%$.

Therefore, the expected return of the stock in the risk-neutral world is equal to:

$$60 = \frac{75 \cdot 60\% + 45 \cdot 40\%}{(1+i)}$$

where:

$$i = 5\%$$

That is equal to the risk-free rate (R_f).

It is possible to use this result to pricing options. We can compute the risk-neutral probability that makes the stock's expected return equal to the risk-free rate, as follows:

$$\frac{S_u \cdot \rho + S_d(1-\rho) \cdot S_d}{(1+R_f)} = S$$

Solving for R_f, we have:

$$R_f = \frac{\rho S_u + (1-\rho) S_d}{S} - 1 \quad (27.9)$$

And solving for the risk-neutral probability ρ, we have:

$$\rho = \frac{(1+R_f)S - S_d}{S_u - S_d} \quad (27.10)$$

Therefore, we can compute the value of the option by calculating its expected payoff using the risk-neutral probabilities, and discount the expected payoff at the risk-free interest rate.

Part VII

Special Topics

Mergers & Acquisitions

28

28.1 Reasons of the M&A

The competitive success of the company is strictly related to its capability to growth in a structural way over time. The company growth can be realized by following an organic growth process (internal growth process) or by Mergers & Acquisitions (M&A) deal (external growth process).

Even if the choice between is always available, the M&A reveal to be the only realistic way to growth in all cases in which the organic growth process is too much expenses in terms of both costs and time, the M&A is the only realistic way to growth. Consequently, M&A is a fundamental tool for the company to compete in the market by generating and maximizing value over time by following external growth line.

In a narrow perspective, the M&A deals refer to:

1. *Merger*: It refers to the process through two or more companies become a single company. It can be realized in two main ways: *a)* by creating a new company called Newco, that it includes all companies involved in the deal that will cease to exist; *b)* by merger in strict sense, in which a company incorporates the others.
2. *Acquisition*: It refers to buying shares or entire company. The acquisition can be: *a) partial*, if it involves minority or majority shares, or *b) total*, if it involves the entire company that is acquired by another company but they remain distinct. Also, the acquisition can be: *a) horizontal*, if companies involved in the deal are in the same markets; *b) vertical*, if companies operate in the same production or service process by realizing part of product or service; *c) conglomerate*, if companies operate in markets that are different and do not related among them. Finally, acquisition may relate specific part of a company that are company's branches formed by a set of specific assets.

   Note that the acquisition is in the buy-side perspective. In the sell-side perspective, the company sales can be: *a) total*, if it includes all shares of the company, or *b) partial*, if it is involved a part of company's shares than can be minority or

P. De Luca, *Corporate Finance*, Springer Texts in Business and Economics,
https://doi.org/10.1007/978-3-031-18300-3_28

majority. Also, sales may relate specific part of a company that are company's branches formed by a set of specific assets.

The M&A deals are based on a complex process whose key steps are related to *valuation, negotiation, decision*. Each of those phases is characterized by a complex system of variables that are strictly related to the nature and perimeter of the deal and the characteristics of companies involved.

Generally, the design, construction, and realization of the M&A deal requires several high-level competences. It implies that M&A deal involves a team of high-qualified professions in all aspect of the deal.

In this context, we cannot analyze in a deep way all aspects of the M&A. It requires a competence in many several fields that it is not possible to have. Therefore, we will analyze the M&A from the perspective of the Financial Advisor only.

Generally, the M&A can be: *i) Horizontal*, if the target and the bidder company are in the same industry; *ii) Vertical*, if the target buys or sells to the bidder; *iii) Conglomerate*: if the target and the bidder operate in unrelated industries.

In all these cases, the company to make an M&A in order to achieve the following main objectives:

1. *Synergies creation*: The aim is to generate synergies between the companies involved in the deal. These synergies can be realized in terms of: *i)* costs reduction in a structural way, that is the common and easier synergy to achieve, or *ii)* revenues increase, by expanding the company's business in new markets in term of both products and geographic locations.
2. *Economy of scale and scope*: The aim is to reduce the production costs in a structural way. It is also true in case of the company's *overcapacity* with an excess production capacity. In this case, company can acquire one of its competitors to increase the quantity of products produced and sold by reducing the fixed cost per unit.
3. *Vertical integration*: The aim is to control the main stages of the production cycle. More are the number of stages of the entire production process that are integrated, high the level of vertical integration of the company. These stages can be upstream or downstream from the company: in the first case, the company wants the direct control of the inputs of the production, while in the second case, the company wants the direct control of the distribution of products. While the most relevant benefit of the vertical integration is the high level of control and coordination among all stages, the main limit refers to the costs of coordination itself which they are the higher the greater the level of vertical integration.
4. *Expertise*: The aim is to acquire the specific skills and know-how to enter and compete in a business. The creation of this know-how internally to the company can be a very long, complex, and expenses process by requiring high investments and costs. Commonly to acquire an existing company in the business that has all skills need to compete in the market can be a simpler and more efficient solution.
5. *Monopoly gains*: The aim is to acquire one or more firms that are direct competitors in its market in order to reduce the competition and increase profits.

Note that most countries have antitrust laws that limit such policies. Indeed, the drive to generate monopolies by large companies is so relevant that it is essential for nations to have strong and effective antitrust laws to limit this company's strategy.

6. *Efficiency gains*: The aim is to manage the company by increasing its level of efficiency in order to increase the earnings per share. Generally, buyers argue that they can run the target company more efficiently than existing management could by increasing the level of profit. This is one of the most reasons for the hostile takeover. Even if it can be easy to discover companies underperforming, the takeover main problem concerns the resistance to change that could be in the post-takeover stage. It implies that to this type of takeover, it is necessary to try an under performant company with high probability to complete efficiently the post-takeover process.
7. *Diversification of product and business*: The aim is to realize a product or market extension by increasing the offer or/and entering new markets. Thanks to the M&A the company can enter in new business or geographic market by reducing the cost need to create a new position.

The diversification commonly reduces the operating and financial risk level of the company and increase the profitability.

The diversification can be realized also by an industry creation. In this case, the company tries to create a new business by converging two other different sectors.

Note that the diversification of the company leads to an indirect diversification of its shareholders. In the private company, they are commonly under-diversified by investing the great part, if not the entire wealth, in the company. Consequently, the diversification of the company in more than one business can be considered as the shareholders' indirect diversification.

8. *Managerial motives*: Managers tend to prefer to run a large company due to the additional pay and prestige it brings. Then, managers could realize mergers to increase the size of the company to increase their prestige and personal benefits. The great risk is that the merger increases the company's size, but it reduces the company's capability to generate value over time. Even if managers do not try to maximize their personal targets, however, they could be overconfident in their ability and realize deals that destroy value rather than generating it.

Whatever the motivation behind the deal, it is essential that it is clear to management. Deals usually fall because there are not clear the motivation and the potential effects both positive and negative.

Note that even if an M&A deal is realized to create value, it does not mean that each deal is always able to generate value effectively. On the contrary, several empirical studies show as in much cases, the M&A deal fail for several reasons among them the main are two: 1) *asymmetric information*, because companies involve in the deal are characterized by different level and accuracy of information and they use them to obtain an advantage in the deal price by reducing the return of one of the two parts; 2) *failure in integration process*: the post-deal process of integration among the companies involved in the deal is very difficult and is commonly characterized by a high probability that it is not realized as companies expected. The main elements to able to fail the post-merger integration and then the failure of the deal are: *i)* failure of objectives to be achieved to increase the company value; *ii)* unclear roles with the absence of a strong and credible leadership capable of managing the integration process effectively and successfully; *iii)* reduction in performance because people are focused on the deal rather than their tasks and business; *iv)* higher integration costs than planned.

Therefore, we can say that to several successful operations able to create value, they are many others that fail by destroying value.

By following the general rule that states a good investment is able to create value for investors, the M&A deal must be evaluated on the basis of its capability to create value for investors. To evaluate the value creation, we can compare the expected return of the deal $\left(\overline{R_D}\right)$ with the expected return offered by alternative investments $\left(\overline{R_{AI}}\right)$ with the same risk profile, so that:

(a) $\overline{R_D} > \overline{R_{AI}}$, deal creates value
(b) $\overline{R_D} < \overline{R_{AI}}$, deal destroys value
(c) $\overline{R_D} = \overline{R_{AI}}$, deal retains the value

Note that we can interpreter the expected return of alternative investment $\left(\overline{R_{AI}}\right)$ as the *minimum* expected return required by investors to invest, and then the target expected return of investors.

To compute the expected return a key role is played by the deal price based on a good valuation in the perspective of both target's company and bidder.

In the perspective of shareholders of the bidder company, the deal value is strictly related to the expected capability of the target company to create value after the deal as the result of an efficient integration process between companies involved in the deal. In this sense, the main role is played by synergies between companies.

In the perspective of the shareholders of the target company, the deal value is strictly related to the difference between the value realized by selling the shares with the present value of the expected dividends in the future that will be paid by the company if they do not sell shares. Note that we can realize a "variable price" if the shareholders of the target company sell a part of their shares (and not the 100%) but remain in the company with a minority shareholding. In this case, the variable price is linked to the future result of the company (earn-out). It is common when the shareholders of the target are involved in the operating activities as in the case of family business.

Commonly, shareholders of the target company are able to snatch higher prices from the bidder company. Indeed, it is common that the shareholders of target company realize a premium of 20–30% with respect to the value of their shares. It happens for two main reasons: 1) to acquire the control of the target, if the bidder acquires a part of the shares; 2) to push shareholders of the target company to make the deal.

Obviously, the higher the premium paid to the target's shareholders, the lower the return of the bidder's shareholders form the deal.

Therefore, in each deal managers must be able to identify the rational elements of the deal and the expected value they are able to realize effectively with deal. These two elements must always be clear and well-defined. If it is not, there is a high probability that returns in the short and medium terms for the shareholders are lower than they expected because the market is not able to explain the premium usually paid for the deal. It is not uncommon that the premium paid turned out to be so high to make the deal fail.

28.2 Investors Approach

The M&A deal can involve two main types of investors: strategic investor and financial investor. They are characterized by a different objectives, approach and horizon of investment. Specifically:

Strategic Investors follow an industrial perspective in the building and valuation of a deal. Their aim is to increase the company's value (enterprise value) in the medium-long term.

In the Buy-Side M&A, they are interested to increase the company's value by creating or developing the competitive advantage. In this contest the influence of the bidder company on the target company is complete by involving all aspects of the company manage. Because the deal successful is strictly related to the integration of the companies involved, the post-deal phase is one of the most critical of the deal and it is able to determine the deal fail.

In the Sell-Side M&A, we can distinguish two different types of deals: if the company is a private company (such as typically family business), the decision to sell shares is usually linked to a decision to sell the company for several reasons that go from the financial problem to the general transaction. If the company is a public company, the decision to sell shares is strictly related to a strategic valuation of shareholders.

Financial Investors are typically private equity, venture capitalist, hedge funds, Spac and generally all those who professionally manage the capital of others by investing it. They follow a financial perspective in the building and valuation of a deal. Their aim is to manage the risk of the deal and to maximize the capital gains in the short-medium terms (typically in 3–5 years). Indeed, financial investor is a temporary shareholder in the company. Commonly, financial investors accompany the company in a defined phase of its life (start-up, growth, restructuring) and having reached the goal, they leave the capital. In any case, financial investors are not involving in operating activities because usually they do not have specific business skills, by they are focused on the strategic and financial choice and in the manage and control of the company to improve its capability to create value. To do it, financial investors can push for add-on deal that are strategic acquisition for the company as well as sell of non-strategic asset or business.

Since financial investors do not have specific business skill, one of the most relevant decision about the target company is the choice of management. From this choice depends on the company's capability to create value and then the maximization of the capital gains. The relevance of the business skills of the management is one of the most relevant elements to choose the target for the deal. If the management is considered unfit in achievement of the aim, financial investors changes managers after the deal closing.

Financial investors exercise influence of the target company's board and then indirectly (and not directly) on the management.

In the Buy-Side M&A financial investors are focused on company able to realize relevant capital gains when they decide to sell their share. Therefore, it is relevant the capital needs to acquire shares, the evolution of the company and then the increase of its value, the expected return to the selling of the share at the end of the time period of investment.

In the Sell-Side M&A the decision about the exit is strictly related to valuation of the expected return on capital invested.

Generally, financial investors are interested to acquire the control (direct or indirect) of the company because only in this way they can introduce changes in company able to increase rapidly its value in the period-time of the investment.

The use of leverage tends to be high in the deal. Indeed, the choice of the target is also done on the basis of its possibility to increase its debt level.

Note that the deal price tends to be lower in case of financial investors than strategic investors. In case of financial investors, the price is strictly related to the expected price to the exit. Consequently, the higher the price of deal, the lower the value of the deal for investor. Financial investor commonly does not consider the value of synergy or in general strategic advantage due to the deal, because the value of the deal is the function of the capital gain realized at the end of deal. On the contrary, strategic investors are willing to pay higher price if they think to develop in the future a new competitive advantage able to increase in a structural way the company's capability to growth by generating value over time. Then, strategic investors consider the price on the basis of future strategic advantage that thinks to realize.

28.3 The Team of M&A

The design, the construction and the realization of the M&A deal require several high specialist skills by involving a team of professionals with specific and high-level competence. The main players in the team are the following.

28.3.1 Financial Advisor

The Financial Advisor plays a key role. The FA is the register of the deal by coordinating also all other advisors to the close of the deal.

On the basis of the great deal and its value, this role is played by the business bank (for the great deal) or by advisor boutique specialized in M&A for small and medium deal. In all cases, the Financial Advisor must have skills with regard to:

1. *Valuation*, by using all techniques to estimate the value and then the price of the company in the deal.
2. *Deal structure*, by using the best practice to design the deal with the best structure on the basis of the specific conditions and needs of companies involved.
3. *Negotiation skills*, needs to guarantee the interest of company.
4. *Knowledge of the business* of the company, in order to evaluate the effective competitive advantage pre and post-deal. Also, it is necessary to identify the best opportunity of the target companies.
5. *Networking skills*, to develop relationship with CEO of companies and the specialist to build the team for the deal.

General, the Financial Advisor supports the company in all phases of the deal from the start in which the company must evaluate the opportunity to make a deal, in the design of the deal, in the search of company target or bidder, in the building and managing of the team, until into the deal closing.

28.3.2 Legal Advisor

The Legal Advisor is necessary for all types of M&A. Each phase of the deal is characterized by a definition of legal documents among the companies involved in the deal. Among them, the most relevant are:

1. *Non-disclosure agreement (NDA)*: The document is used to formalize the commitment of the companies to treat the information in a confidential manner in order to evaluation of the opportunity of the deal.
2. *Approach Letter*: The document is used to establish the first contact with potential companies interested in the deal, clarifying the reasons and objectives of the deal.
3. *Letter of Intent (LOI)*: The document is used to formalize a general proposal of the bidder at the end of an initial negotiation period, that it is often subject to a series of conditions precedent.
4. *Non-binding offer (NBO)*: The document is used to formalize the essential conditions for a possible agreement between the companies.
5. *Sales and Purchase agreement (SPA)*: The document is used to formalize the final conditions of the agreement between the companies and then to close the negotiation.

All legal documents are focused to protect the interest of the client company, to guarantee the compliance of the deal structure to the law, and to avoid misunderstanding among the companies on all aspects of the deal.

Also, the Legal Advisor must realize the *legal due diligence* in the deal in order to evaluate all legal commitments undertaken by the target company towards third parties. The aim is to map all possible legal risk deriving from the target for the bidder. Note that the result of the legal due diligence is relevant in the negotiation process because it can reduce the price of the deal if there are legal risk arise for the bidder.

28.3.3 Fiscal Advisor

The Fiscal Advisor has to evaluate all fiscal elements related to the deal. Therefore, it plays a relevant role in the phase of deal design in order to evaluate the possible structure of deal. It is not uncommon that the valuation of the fiscal impact on deal is so relevant to fail the deal project even if it has a relevant strategic impact.

The Fiscal Advisor has to realize the *Fiscal Due Diligence* of the target company in order to verify with respect to the fiscal law for the target. The aim is to map the possible risk arising from the target for the bidder.

28.3.4 Transaction Advisor

The Transaction Advisor is an expert auditor specialized in Financial Due Diligence (FDD) and organized by the big audit firms in dedicate team called Transaction Services.

The aim is to verify the consistency of the accounting of the target company and the normalization of the economic and financial historical dynamics. Specifically, with the FDD must:

1. Validate the correct keeping of the accounts
2. Validate historical economic and financial items
3. Identify any risk areas from an accounting point of view
4. Verify the historical economic and financial dynamics of the company in view of its prospective projection

In the Sell-side M&A the company can require the Transaction Service a Vendor Due Diligence (VDD). Even if the VDD is required for the target, the auditor firm can also communicate the result to the potential target company. It can reduce the phase of the Financial Due Diligence by limiting to verify the result of the VDD. The main result of the VDD is to give to all potential companies target a common set of high-quality information about the target for their preliminary evaluation by reducing the time of the deal.

28.3.5 Strategic Advisor

The Strategic Advisor is an expert in the business and his aim is to support the company client in to evaluate the impact of the deal in terms of business strategy. Generally, the role of Strategic Advisor is played by the management consulting firm specialized in strategy.

The Strategic Advisor plays a key role in the evaluation of possibility to make an M&A and in the evaluation of the different construction of the deal. Also, the Strategic Advisor is more relevant in the phase post-deal in which the success of the M&A is related to the integration of companies involved in order to maximize the value of synergies.

Also, the Strategic Advisor must realize the ***Business Due Diligence***. The analysis is focused to well-understand the:

1. Dynamics of business of the target company
2. The position of target with respect to its competitors
3. The possibility to introduce significant improvements able to create value
4. Possibility of consolidation interventions (add-on) through the acquisition of additional companies

This role is more relevant if the deal is realized by financial investor. In this case, financial investor usually does not have the appropriate skills to evaluate the effective potential of the company to create value in its business.

28.4 Buy-Side M&A

The M&A deals involve two parts: bidder company and target company. Because the deal can be closed only if both parts are satisfied, the M&A process must be analyzed in the perspective of the bidder as well as of the target. Consequently, in this contest, we analyze the:

1. *Buy-Side M&A*: The deal is promoted by the bidder company and then we assume its perspective in the analysis.
2. *Sell-Side M&A*: The deal is promoted by the target company and then we assume its perspective in the analysis.

In both cases, the after the decision to evaluate the opportunity to make an M&A, the company should appoint a financial advisory. The financial advisor is fundamental to analyze deeply the reasons and the opportunity to make a deal, and to manage the entire process of M&A.

The M&A deal is a complex process that requires high specialist-skills to analyze and to evaluate all variables to lead to a successful deal. Commonly the main mistakes made by private companies (both small and medium) are: to think that the only variable of the deal is the price, that the price can be defined independently to the quantitative analysis of the company in both historical and expected dynamics; the negotiation process can be realized directly between the entrepreneurs without the support of financial advisors.

We can start by analysing the Buy-Side M&A process. The Sell-Side M&A process is similar except for some aspects that are specific to this procedure.

The Buy-Side process can be decomposed into four main phases: preliminary, exploratory, selection, negotiation, and closing.

28.4.1 Step (1): Preliminary Phase

The aim of this phase is to analyze detailed the reason and the opportunity to make the deal and to define all its strategic elements.

Specifically, the company has to define in very detailed manner the:

1. *Real and effective reasons of the deal*. It is necessary to understand if the deal is: *i)* a solution to a specific need of the company, and then we need to detailed the problem and the reasons by which the deal is the solution; *ii)* an opportunity the company wants to realize, and then we need to detailed the reasons by which it can be considered a real opportunity for the company.
2. *Strategic elements of the deal*. Three are the main aspects to be considered: *i)* the definition of the specific characteristics that potential target company must have in terms of business, products, dimension, economic and financial performance; ii) the definition of the form of deal, in which the main choice concerns the decision to acquire share of the company target, the Stock Deal, or to acquire the target company partially or totally, the Asset Deal; *iii)* the timing of the deal, trying to consider and evaluate all possible variables able to impact on the timing of deal; *iv)* the choose of financial advisor to give the mandate to follow the company in all the entire M&A process by coordinating the advisory team that includes all specialists needed to the deal. Note that the advisory team can be chosen by the financial advisor that use its team, or by the company and then the financial advisor coordinates their works.
3. *Financial cover*. M&A deals are expensive. Therefore, before to start it is necessary to define the total amount of the investments required by the deal and the source of capital that company can use to cover this financial need.

The phase is closed only when the company has defined clearly and detailed the reasons, strategy and financial coverage of the deal.

Note that this phase plays a key role in the entire process of the M&A. Indeed, most of the failure in deals are due to errors in this preliminary phase.

Given the mandate to the financial advisor this and all other phases of the process are commonly developed by the company with the support of financial advisory and the advisory team.

28.4.2 Step (2): Exploratory Phase

The aim of this phase is to identify the possible target companies within a defined business. The analysis is developed on the basis of the specific characteristics that target must have as defined in the previous phase. Commonly the company has not developed relationship with the potential target companies, and then the analysis in this phase is developed on public documents. The information research about the potential target companies concern the financial and economic items, product and service, known-how, market shares, perspective of development, governance, and in general all type of information that are able to lead an evaluation of the deal opportunity. Obviously, the efficiency of the analysis is strictly related to the information available and their accuracy.

Note that the analysis of the target companies in this phase is based on a stand-alone perspective. Then, target companies are considered in their actual structure without considering and evaluating any benefit come from the deal between target and bidder.

The company commonly arrives to identify a rather large number of potential target companies among them are chosen the most interesting by matching their characteristics with the "ideal target" as defined in the preliminary phase. These companies define the list of the potential target companies for the deal.

The first contact is a very delicate moment for which it must be handled very carefully. It has an immediate and direct impact on shareholders, that immediately make valuation about the opportunity of deal, and management that immediately could try to oppose to the deal for fear of losing their position in the company. Consequently, a wrong approach to the potential company target implies the failure of the perspective of the deal immediately.

For this reason, the first approach is commonly realized by the financial advisor who have to develop a negotiation. If the target company is interested, the financial advisor sends the "*Approach Letter*" in which are synthetical summarized: *1)* the profile of the company bidder, *2)* its strategic aim for deal proposed, *3)* the perspective offered to the target company and its shareholders with the deal, *4)* the road map with the formal steps of the deal.

Note that in the first contact, it is fundamental to the success of the first contact that the company and financial advisor strive to highlight all possible elements of value that the deal proposed would bring to the target company and its shareholders.

28.4.3 Step (3): Selection Phase

The aim of this phase is to define a short-list of a limited of potential target companies for the deal and start with their analysis.

Based on the reaction of target companies to the financial advisor contact, the company defines a short-list by including the companies who responded positively to the potential deal.

Defined the short-list of the target companies, the company started with their deep analysis. This analysis is developed on a direct information given to the company by the target companies in order to verify the condition of a possible deal.

The acquisition of information about the company targets requires the underwrite of a document called *Non-Disclosure Agreement* (NDA) in order to guarantee the reservation on all information acquired. The NDA underwrote by the bidder company, contains mainly: *1)* the length of the period (generally between 1 and 3 years) in which each information acquired cannot be divulged; *2)* the obligation for the bidder company to use all information acquired about target company only for the deal with possibility to share these information only with people involved in the deal for whom the same obligations are valid; *3)* the obligation for the bidder company to return all documents received upon a simple request by company target.

In this phase, also the target company has to appoint a financial advisor that follows the entire deal by protecting its interests. After the NDA underwriting, financial advisor of the target company prepares and send to the bidder company a document called *Information Memorandum* in which are summarized the most relevant information about the target company. Specifically, it must contain mainly: 1) the analysis of the business and its threats and opportunities; 2) the analysis of the products' portfolio; 3) the analysis of the governance, the organization structure, the composition of shareholders, the identification of the top managers and the key figure; 4) the assets and their value; 5) the economic and financial performance (with specific regard to the cash-flows) with regard to both historical trend and expected about the future.

On the basis of the Information Memorandum received by the company targets included in the short-list, the bidder company proceeds with their deep analysis.

28.4.4 Step (4): Negotiation and Closing Phase

The aim of this phase is to select the company target in the short-list and to start the negotiation.

Before to start the negotiation, the bidder commonly defines a possible price of the target and the potential range in which it can change.

Commonly the negotiation starts with the indication of terms that are considered fundamental for the deal close for both bidder and target.

In the first phase of negotiation, all terms are formalized in a document called *Letter of Intent (LOI)*. The content of the LOI can vary greatly due to the complexity of the negotiation. In any case it must contain mainly: *1)* the confirmation of the bidder's interest to the negotiation process; *2)* the definition of the price commonly agreed by the parties under the condition that the assumptions made in the preliminary analysis and on which the price is based on correct; *3)* the start and terms of the due diligence by attaching the checklist of document required by advisors; *4)* the definition of the time period for the deal and road-map of all steps with relative timing; *5)* the clear identification and definition of conditions precedent or impeding the close of the deal; 6) the time period in which the LOI is valid; 7) the period of exclusivity in which the target cannot be starting negotiation with other bidders.

After negoitiation of all terms of the LOI, the bidder sends the defined version of the LOI underwritten to the target company for its underwriting.

Generally, all terms reported in the LOI are not binding between companies. However, the LOI can become binding in all terms or specific terms if it is requested specifically by the companies in the LOI itself.

The LOI underwrote by companies it opens a new phase of the negotiation in which the companies deepen the analyzes and the comparison in order to share an agreement on the basis of a defined fundamental points. The main terms of negotiation commonly are: 1) the minimum contents of the analysis in the Due Diligence and its timing; 2) the timing of the negotiation process; 3) the events able to determine the stop temporary o definitively to the negotiation.

This second phase of negotiation all terms are formalized in a new document called *Non-Binding Offer (NBO)*.

The NBO is a structured in the form of a purchase offer but it is not binding. The aim of NBO is to share between bidder and target the terms of the agreement that could be signed at the end of negotiation. The NBO is not binding for the bidder because the due diligence on the target is not realized yet. Indeed, when the NBO is underwritten by the companies, the bidder can start the due diligence (financial, fiscal, legal, and on specific items considered necessary to the successful of the deal) of the target company.

The due diligence is fundamental to indicate all risk for the bidder deriving from the deal. Then it increases the degree of awareness of the bidder about the risk of deal. For this reason, its results are very important for the successful closing of the deal. It is not uncommon that the result of the due diligence leads the bidder to change the offer price or other terms in the NBO and/or to require guarantee to the target for eventually may request by third parties.

The successful of negotiation allows to the *signing* of the binding agreement and the closing of deal.

On the contrary, if the negotiation is not successful, because it is stopped on a specific aspect that it is not solved, the bidder company stops definitively the process and restart the process with another target companies in the short-list.

Timing

The M&A (in both Buy-Side and Sell-side) is a complex process and its timing is not easy to define previously. Commonly, an M&A can be closed in less than one year.

Generally, the timing of the M&A is related to three main phases of the entire process:

The starting phases of the process, in which all activities involve only one part (bidder in buy-side and target in sell-side) to design and structure the deal are the faster and it can be closed in 2 months.

The phases of contact and negotiation, in which the company promoting deal must contact and negotiate with potential targets (Buy-Side) or potential buyers (Sell-Side). This phase is most complex. Three are the main complexity to manage:

1) negotiation involves the players of the companies involved in the deal. It requires time to know the counterpart and the definition of the decision; 2) the preparation of the set of documents is a complex process that requires time proportional to the structural condition of the company; *3)* the deal has relevant and deeply impact on the companies (also high emotional in the family business) by requiring time to understand and manage all possible effects. However, they should close in 3–4 months.

The phases of due diligence, in which the company promoting the deal require on the potential target (Buy-Side) or potential buyer (Sell-Side). This phase is relevant because the results of due diligence can change the terms of the negotiation if risks are identified. This activities, plus final negotiation and closing can require 2–3 months.

28.5 Sell-Side M&A

The Sell-Side M&A process is similar to the Buy-Side M&A process expect for some aspects that are specific of this procedure due to the fact that the deal is promoted from the target company. Indeed, shareholders of the company decide to sell their shares in part, that can be minority or majority, or entire and then they find a buyer company.

The entire process of Sell-Side M&A is different from the Buy-Side M&A in the first part in which it is necessary to identify the buyer company. The other phases are common to both. Therefore, in this contest, we consider only the specific characteristics of the Buy-Side M&A.

After a deep analysis of the reasons and opportunity to make the deal, the first step is to define the way buy which to realize the deal. Two are the most common:

1. *Competitive auction process*. In this case, in a defined time period, all potential buyer companies send their offer to the shareholders of the target company. These offers are evaluated by the shareholders. In order to the number of potential buyer companies that we want to involve, we can choose between:
   (i). *Open auction*, in which we communicate to the entire market the intention to initiate a company sales process. Then, it involves a lot of potential buyers who the target company gives the same information to evaluate the deal. On the basis of the offer received, the target company defines a short-list. The main vantage possibility to maximize the share price because it involved the highest number of potential buyers by generating competition among them. The main problems concern the slowly of the process, the absence of confidentiality and, most relevant, the negative signal to the market in case of no offer from the potential buyers.
   (ii). *Private auction*, in which the decision to sales the company is communicating to a delimited number of selected potential buyers commonly 10–15 among them about 4–5 with high interest. The main advantages concern, the price because the competition between the buyers should increase the price

and the possibility to shift to the open auction if the private auction fails. On the contrary, the main problems concern the slowly of the process and the possibility to exclude buyers with high interest.

2. *Bilateral negotiation*. In this case, all elements of the deal are defined among the companies through the negotiation process. Even if it is common that the negotiation is carried out with one buyer from the first moment, it is possible in a preliminary phase to involve 2 or 3 potential buyers among to choose who with which to develop the negotiation. Therefore, in this case, there is an exclusive negotiation with higher probability to close the deal.
   The main advantages refer to the process that is characterized by fast, high level of confidentiality and flexibility. The main problems refer to the possibility to no-maximize the price, the need to find a buyer interested with high probability to exclude high potential buyers.

All these approaches are characterized by vantage and disadvantage that must be evaluated carefully on the basis of the company's characteristics and needs.

Note that a relevant part in the success of the deal is played by the confidentiality. Indeed, if the deal is known prematurely, there could be several negative reactions from many internal and external players to the companies involved able to lead to the deal failure. Consequently, it is considered a good rule for the company to limit the decision of deal and its first steps to a very small number of people.

Note that if we consider the variable the price, it is intuitively that the higher the number of potential buyers, the higher the price. Indeed, the greater the number of potential buyers, the higher the negotiation power of the target company with the consequence to maximize the share price. Even if it can be considered a general rule, also the private negotiation can lead to the maximization of the price. It happens when the buyer company is well-identify on the basis of strategic valuation about the business development and the growth capability.

In the Sell-Side M&A a key role is played by the set of documents containing all information about the company to give the potential buyers to evaluate the company target and the opportunity to realize the deal.

Three are the main documents that company must prepare:

1. *Blind Profile*: It contains synthetical and anonymous information about the company by highlighted the macro-element of value. In a first phase, it is necessary a strictly control of any information about potential deal to avoid negative reaction by people in both company and potential buyer that are able to make the deal to fail. Consequently, in the *approach letter* is common to use the *blind profile*. The aim is to focus the attention of the potential buyers on the distinctive characteristics of the company (that are not indicated) and macro-elements of its value.
2. *Investment memorandum*: It contains all relevant elements that concern the company target. Specifically, it mainly contains: *1)* the company history, 2) the referenced markets and portfolio of products; *3)* the competitive advantage developed and its vision for the future, *4)* the governance and management

structure; 5) the assets and their value; *6)* the economic and financial performance with regard to both the past and the expected future; *7)* the reasons and aim of the deal proposed. Therefore, this document introduces to the deal by indicating the most relevant element of value of the company target. Commonly it is sent to the potential company buyers after the underwriting of the *Non-Disclosure Agreement* (NDA).

3. *Business and financial plan*: It contains the definition of all elements of the business model and the forecast of its economic and financial dynamic on the basis of a clear definition of the assumptions. Commonly, all quantitative information are formalized in a business plan developed for the future 3–5 years. Also in this case it is sent to the potential company buyers after the underwriting of the *Non-Disclosure Agreement* (NDA).

The set of documents must be comprehensive, accurate, and high reliable. The main aim is to help the potential buyers to evaluate correctly the opportunity of the deal. Since the relevance of these documents, their preparation is commonly demanded by the financial advisor. The main role is to help company to acquire, elaborate, organize and finally present all information about the itself in a manner to satisfy the information need of potential buyers for the evaluation of the deal.

The set of documents preparing is a relevant problem for the private business (small or medium) in which the reporting necessary is not available or it is completely out of the most professional standards. In this contest, it is necessary before to start the deal, to create the set of information with the help of financial advisor.

Commonly in this phase, the financial advisor defines the sell target price of the company and eventually its potential range. It is absolutely necessary that the valuation of the company and then the definition of its potential target price, must be defined in a rigorous way by following the professional models and standards. It is necessary to demonstrate the target price to the buyer in the negotiation process by indicating the models and a clear explanation of the assumptions on the bases the forecast was constructed and then by avoiding that it is the result of the expectation of the shareholders of the company without any rational support. The main risk is to evaluate the target company by the entrepreneur or shareholders in a unobjectively and rational way based only on their wishes. It is not uncommon that the value estimated by the financial advisor is significantly lower than thinking by shareholders with the result of not process with the deal and the search of alternatives.

28.6 Price and Terms of Payment

In the M&A, there is a deep difference between price paid and the value of the company. In the M&A we must consider the intrinsic value of the target company as well as the value of synergies and control premium.

The *Intrinsic value* of the target company is determined on the basis of the financial modelling discussed (see Part x.x). Two are the main techniques used: *i) multiple*, is the simpler because the value of the target company is defined by comparison with comparable companies in the market and with their value estimate in M&A realized; *ii)* discounted cash-flow (DCF), is most complex because the value of the target company is defined on the basis of its fundamentals and the expected economic and financial dynamic over time.

Synergies are the most relevant strategic motivation for the M&A because they are able to increase the value of the company over time. The synergies can be distinguished between two categories: *i) Cost synergies*, when the deal allows to the company the possibility to reduce the level of fixed and variable costs in a structural way. They are simpler to identify and to realize; *ii) Revenue synergies*, when the deal allows to the company to increase the unit price of the quantity of sales.

Note that in the synergies can include a *strategic premium*. If the target company is a strong competitor, its acquisition by the bidder can be motivated by the reduction of competitors in the market. It is more relevant if the target company is characterized by a unique product or market. In this way, the bidder company acquires a strong market position and the opportunity to realize competitive advantage in the market by generating value in a long term.

The *control premium* can be defined as the price that the bidder is willing to paid to obtain the power to manage the target company. Indeed, it is related to the acquisition of the majority of the company's shares that give the control of the company and then the power to manage the company directly or indirectly by appointing people in key role.

Note that if the bidder company acquires minority shares of the target company, the price must be reduced by considering the *minority discount* because it does not acquire the control.

The valuation and pricing of the Control Premium are not easy. Several are the variables involved in the pricing of control premium. Consequently, the control premium paid by investors is highly variable and it depends on the strategic analysis as well as to the development level of the capital market and the law about right votes and corporate governance rules.

The price of the target company, and its possible range, is defined on the basis of the intrinsic value of the company, the valuation and pricing of synergies and control premium. Specifically, the range of the price of the target company must be defined by starting from the intrinsic value that is the current market value in (stand alone value, that it is the value of the target company "as is"), and by summing the synergies value, the control premium and the strategy premium as represented in Fig. 28.1.

The Maximum Price (Pmax) is equal to the value of the company stand-alone that defines the Minimum Price (Pmin), plus the value of Synergies (VS) and plus the Control Premium (CP), as follows:

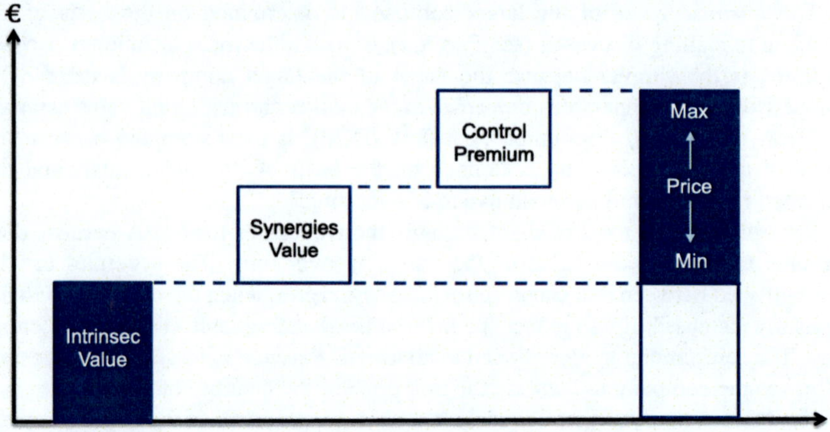

Fig. 28.1 Intrinsic value and price of the firm in M&A

$$Pmax = Pmin + VS + CP \tag{28.1}$$

The *terms of payment* are relevant in the negotiation process because commonly, they are used to find a compromise on the price. The most common way to pay are:

1. *Cash*: The company pays the shareholders of the target by using the cash available. It implies that the company has the financial source need to close the deal. If it is not, the company must increase its the amount of equity, debt or both in combination. The choice of the mix of capital source to finance the deal depends on several elements such as the effectively liquidity available of bidder, the capability to acquire capital in the market, the optimal capital structure post-deal, the company capability to generate cash-flows, the credit rating available, the dividend policy. Note that it is relevant to well-understand the capital structure of the companies, target and bidder, pre-deal as well as post-deal as the result of the deal. Generally, we can say that there is not an optimum choice to finance a deal because it is strictly the function of the characteristics of the companies involved and the aim in terms of capital structure post-deal to achieve.
2. *Shares*: The company offers its shares to the shareholders of the target. There is a shares exchange between the bidder and the target companies. In this case, the main aspects to consider are: 1) the evaluate of both companies in order to define the *exchange ratio* that is the number of bidder shares received in exchange for each target shares; 2) the changes in the governance of the company bidder due to the increase of shareholders; 3) the reduction in shares hold by the old shareholders and then the reduction of the dividend per share.
3. *Convertible bonds*: The company offers to the shareholders of the target a debt instrument that can be converted in equity in the future under a defined condition

of time and events. Shareholders of the target this solution is appreciated if they expected that the value of the bidder will growth in the future.
4. *Defer payment over time*: There is an asymmetric information between the bidder and the target about the target potential growth in the future. Consequently, if the bidder and target disagree on the expectation of the target about the future performance on which the price is determined, companies can use the earn-out. It implies that the shareholders of the target sell only a part of their shares, and they are still involved in the target company for a defined time period in which are defined a set of objectives that the target must realize. Therefore, a part of the price of the deal is paid by the bidder to the target at the achievement of these objectives. In this way, the target can demonstrate the validity of the forecast defined and its value while the bidder has the opportunity to verify this value and to push the management of the target to realize the objectives.

Some reflection deserves the construction of the *exchange ratio*. The stock-swap merger is a positive-NPV investment for the bidder's shareholders only if the price per share of the merged company (that is the price per share of the bidder company after the merger) exceeds the pre-merger price per share of the bidder company.

Denote with:

- W_B: the pre-merger value (or stand-alone value) of the bidder company
- W_T: the pre-merger value (or stand-alone value) of the target company
- W_{SC}: the value of synergies generated by the merger and the control premium of the target company
- N_{SB}: the pre-merger number of shares outstanding of the bidder company
- α_B: the number of shares issued by the bidder to pay the shareholders of the target company
- N_{TS}: the pre-merger number of shares outstanding of the target company
- P_B: the pre-merger price per share of bidder that it is equal to $P_B = \frac{W_B}{N_{SB}}$
- P_{BM}: the post-merger price per share of bidder
- P_T: the pre-merger price per share of the target company.

Because the price per share of the merged company (that is the price per share of the bidder company after the merger) must exceed the pre-merger price per share of the bidder company, it is necessary that:

$$\frac{W_B + W_T + W_{SC}}{N_{SB} + \alpha_B} > \frac{W_B}{N_{SB}} \tag{28.2}$$

where:

(a) The left-side of equation is the post-merger price per share of the bidder company (P_{BM}): it is equal to the total value post-merger of the bidder company (equal to the stand-alone value of bidder pre-merger of bidder and target company plus the value of synergies and control premium created by the deal) divided by the total number of shares outstanding of the bidder company post-merger.

(b) The right-side of equation is the pre-merger price per share of the bidder company (P_B): it is equal to the total value of the bidder company pre-merger divided the its total number of share outstanding pre-merger.

Therefore, we can rewrite the equation on the basis of pre-merger and post-merger price per share of the bidder company as follows:

$$P_{BM} = \frac{W_B + W_T + W_{SC}}{N_{SB} + \alpha_B} > \frac{W_B}{N_{SB}} = P_B$$

We can rearrange the equation in order to find the condition based on the bidder to realize a positive NPV as follows:

$$\frac{W_B + W_T + W_{SC}}{N_{SB} + \alpha_B} > P_B;\ W_T + W_{SC} > P_B(N_{SB} + \alpha_B) - W_B;\ W_T + W_{SC} > P_B N_{SB} + P_B\alpha_B - W_B;$$

$$\frac{W_B}{N_{SB}} = P_B;\ W_B = P_B N_{SB};\ W_T + W_{SC} > W_B + P_B\alpha_B - W_B;\ W_T + W_{SC} > P_B\alpha_B$$

and then:

$$W_T + W_{SC} > P_B\alpha_B \quad (28.3)$$

The equation states that the value of shares offered ($P_B\alpha_B$) by the bidder to the shareholders of the target company must be less than the pre-merger value of the target company plus the value of synergies and control premium generated by the deal.

Considering that the (P_T) the price per share of the target company pre-merger (P_T) is equal to:

$$P_T = \frac{W_T}{N_{TS}}$$

the maximum of the exchange ratio the bidder should offer is equal to:

$$\text{Exchange ratio} = \frac{\alpha_B}{N_{TS}} < \frac{P_T}{P_B}\left(1 + \frac{W_{SC}}{W_T}\right) \quad (28.4)$$

28.7 Takeover Defence

The board of directors of both the bidder and the target companies must approve the deal and they must require the shareholders' vote.

The target company can consider the merger proposed by the bidder company as:

1. *Friendly takeover*: The board of directors of the target company support the merger, negotiates with bidder, and agrees on a price that is ultimately put to a shareholders' vote.
2. *Hostile takeover*: The board of directors of the target compony fights the takeover attempt. To succeed, the bidder must garner enough shares to take control of the target and replace the board of directors. In this case, the acquirer is called *Raider*.

Generally, managers of the target company can oppose the merger proposed for several reasons, the main ones being: *1)* the management of the target company may oppose the deal to protect their own self-interest. That is most relevant if the main reason of the deal is the efficiency gain that bidder think to realize by changing the leadership of the company; *2)* the offer price is considered too low by the board of target company; *3)* in case of stock-swap payment the board of target might believe that bidder's shares are over-valued with the consequence that the value of the bidder is less than the stand-alone value of target.

The target company can use several tools to oppose a hostile takeover. Among them, the most successful are the following.

28.7.1 Poison Pills

A poison pills is the right of existing shareholders of the target company to buy shares in the target itself at a deeply discounted price once certain conditions are realized.

Because shareholders can purchase shares at less than the market price, the rights offering dilutes the value of any shares held by the bidder. Consequently, the dilution makes the takeover so expensive for the shareholders of the bidder that they can decide to not precede buy passing to another deal.

Also, in case of partial takeover, the most poison pills states that if a raider buys more than a defined amount of the shares of the target company but not the total outstanding shares, existing shareholders of the target have the right to buy more shares in the target itself at a discounted price.

Poison pills also increase the bargaining power of the target company in the negotiation process because they make it difficult to complete the takeover without the cooperation of the board of the target company. This bargaining power can allow to the shareholders of the target company to realize a higher premium.

Even if poison pills are very effective in stopping the takeover, they have a relevant negative effect. By adopting poison pills, the company effectively entrenches its management and it renounces to the "market discipline" by making it much more difficult to replace bad managers with consequent high probability to destroy value. It is not uncommon that companies that adopted poison pills have below-average financial performance and their stock price drops.

If the company adopts poison pills, it is harder to take over. If it happens, the shareholders of the target company receive a high premium for their stocks. It implies that the takeover is high costly. Consequently, it is necessary a high expectation of the bidder about the possibility to increase the value of the target company at a such level to justify the investment.

28.7.2 White Knights

If the target company considers inevitable the hostile takeover, it can look for another "friendlier" company that is willing to acquire it. This friendlier company is called ***white knight***. To win the white knight will make a more lucrative offer for the target company than hostile bidder. Managers of the target company maintain control by reaching an agreement with the white knight to retain their positions.

A variant of this scheme is called ***white squire*** defence. In this case, a large investor or company agrees to purchase a substantial block of stocks with special voting rights of the target company. This is effective to prevent a hostile raider from acquiring control of the target company. Obviously, the basic idea is that the white squire itself will not choose to exercise its control rights. The threat is enough.

28.7.3 Golden Parachutes

A golden parachute is a very lucrative severance package of the top managers in case they are fired after the takeover.

The adoption of golden parachute creates value because if it exists managers will be more likely to be receptive to a takeover. Indeed, the existence of golden parachute reduces likelihood of managerial entrenchment.

Commonly the stock price rise on average if companies announce the plan to introduce a golden parachute policy rather than poison pills.

28.7.4 Recapitalization

The company can modify its capital structure by increasing the debt level to make itself less attractive as a target for raiders.

High debt level reduce the target attractivity because in many cases a relevant part of synergy gains that an acquirer anticipates from a takeover is from the possibility to increase leverage as well as the cost structure reduction.

Private Equity, Venture Capital, and Hedge Fund

29

29.1 Private Equity

The most common Private equity definition is an investor who provides equity capital to non-listed companies in stock market with the main aim to develop the company realizing a capital gain (if the sales price of share is higher than its buy price) at the time of investment exit.

On the basis of the size of the target companies, the Private Equity can be distinguished between:

1. *Large buyout fund*: If the value of the target companies is higher than one billion euro. This Private equity are usually global and multi-sectors.
2. *Mid-market Buyout fund*: If the value of the target companies is between 100 million euro and one billion euro. This Private equity are usually multi-country and they can be multi-sectors or focused on a specific sector.
3. *Small buyout fund*: If the value of the target companies is lower than 100 million euro. This Private equity usually operate at country level.

Commonly we distinguish between Private Equity and Venture Capital. The most difference regard the phase of life cycle of the company in which they are usually to invest: the private equity prefers to invest in the development stage of an already structured company, while the venture capital prefers to invest in the early stages of company's life such as start-up.

The main reasons for a private equity investment in a company are common: 1) a complicated generational transition; 2) the entrepreneur decisions to diversify; 3) the company state of crisis; 4) a growth opportunity; 5) misalignment between shareholders' interests; 6) managers decision to become entrepreneur; 7) the company's reorganization with sell of non-strategic activities.

The Private Equity investments can be distinguished in two main categories:

P. De Luca, *Corporate Finance*, Springer Texts in Business and Economics,
https://doi.org/10.1007/978-3-031-18300-3_29

1. *Growth capital* or *expansion capital*: It is the acquisition of *minority* shares with the main aim to support the company as a financial and strategic advisor but without to be involved in the company operating manage.
2. *Buyout*: It is the acquisition of *majority* shares with the aim to acquire the control of the company and manage it. Even if the investor does not enter in the daily operating activities, however, he plays an important role in the company by naming and controlling managers.

All buyout realized by using equity capital by the private equity plus financial debt by the bank are called *Leveraged Buyout (LBO)*.

Since the Private Equity can support different players in the company's acquisition, we can distinguish between different form of buyout on the basis of who effectively realize the deal. The most common are: 1) *Management Buyout (MBO)*; the deal is realized by the managers of the company with the consequence to become their self the entrepreneur; 2) *Management Buy-In (MBI)*, the deal is realized by managers external to the company with consequence to have a new managers in the company after the deal; 3) *Buy-In Management Buyout (BIMBO)*, the deal is realized by internal and external managers to the company jointly; 4) *Management-Employees Buyout (MEBO)*, the deal is realized by the managers and employees of the company jointly; 5) *Family Buyout*, the deal is realized by a member or a part of the family that acquire the shares of the others member of the family.

The Private Equity business is commonly realized in form of Limited Partnership (LP) and the capital is funded from Limited Partners (LPs) that are financial institution (such as pension funds, assurance, banks, family office, endowment, asset manager, etc). The investment of the capital raised is realized by a General Partner (GP) with his/her team of investments. The relationship between LPs and GP must be defined detailed in the fund regulation mainly with regard to rules about:

1. The *duration of the fund*. It is usually defined in ten years (plus two eventually). This period can be distinguished in *investment period* and *divestment period* each of them equal to 5 years long.
2. The *governance the operational rules*. The key figures are:
   (a) *Investment committee*: It makes the investment decisions. It is composed by the senior members of the investment team (called *key men*) and there can be also external members and the committee decides by majority.
   (b) *Advisory board*: It is a committee of some LPs and its aim is to supervise on the correct of the manage on the basis of the compliance with the fund rules.
   (c) *LPs meeting*: It decides about relevant questions such as the change in the fund rules, the change of the GP, the liquidation of the fund.
   (d) *Drawdown and distribution rules*: The drawdown notice is the clause that discipline the timing of the calling capital. The LPs have an irrevocable commitment for the entire duration of the fund to provide the capital in the amount decided at the start of the fund. The GP calls the capital need only at

the moment to deliberate a new investment and for an amount equal to pro-share of the investment on the total capital raised in the fund.

1. The *economic conditions*. The main aim is to align the economic interest of GP and LPs. Three are the main tools used:
   (a) *Management fees*: It refers to a part of the fee for the GP's remuneration (it is the lower part of the entire remuneration while the highest part is the *carried interest*) and the coverage of the annual structure costs. Commonly it is equal to the 2% per year (or lower for the mega funds). The fee is applied on the total amount of the capital raised by the fund in the investment period, and on the cost of shares still in portfolio in the *divestment period*.
   (b) *Carried interest*: It is the most relevant part of the GP's remuneration and it is strictly related to the performance of the fund. It is defined as a percentage (general equal to 20%) of capital gain realized. Commonly, the carried interest is recognized to the GP upon exceeding a defined level of minimum return for LPs called *hurdle rate* (usually equal to 8%). Consequently, the carried interest is paid to the GP only if the LPs have already received the capital initially paid plus the hurdle rate.
   (c) *GP co-investment*: It is common to require to GP to invest in the fund an amount of its own wealth equal to 1%–5% of the total capital of the fund. The main aim is to involve the GP in the risk of downside.
2. *Limits of the fund managements and the protection tools of LPs*. It refers to the rules need to limit the risk for LPs since the decision about investments is made by GP and its investment committee. The most common are:
   (a) *Limit to the risk concentration*: the fund has a limit to invest in a single company to limit the risk. Usually threshold is set equal to 20%–25% of the total capital of the fund.
   (b) *Investment restriction*: the LPs can require limit to the investments in specific countries or sectors.
   (c) *Reporting*: commonly on half-yearly basis (or also quarterly basis), the GP must report to the LPs about the activities developed and the shares in portfolio and their economic and financial performance.

29.2 Phases of the Private Equity Investment

The Private Equity investment can be distinguished in four main phases: *1) Fundraising*; *2) Investment*; *3) Monitoring*; *4) Exit.*

29.2.1 Phase (1): Fundraising

In this phase, the team of investment promotes its investment vehicle with the aim to raise capital need to the fund creation.

Commonly the potential LPs are pension funds, banks, funds of funds (they are funds that rise capital to invest in other funds of private equity rather than to invest directly in the companies), family office, insurance companies, endowment, sovereign and government funds.

Before to raise capital, the promoting team of the Private equity fund must be developed its investment strategy detailed by defining which type of investments they want to realize (minority or majority shares, turnaround, etc.), the size of the fund, the sectors and the countries in which to invest, and so on. The investment strategy must be clear and a distinctive element of the team. Indeed, the investment team and its investment strategy are the key variables in the fundraising.

The track record of the investment team is the best indicator of its ability to perform in the future. It is not uncommon that LPs prefer GPs that invest always in the same type of deal by applying an investment strategy in line with the past because it is synonymous with knowledge, experience, and performance already realized.

The LPs must analyze deeply and detailed the investment team. Commonly LPs meet all member of the team jointly and separately in order to evaluate: their specific experience and track record, their financial and managerial competences, cohesion and harmony as a team, organization of the team, capability to generate investment opportunities.

The phase of fundraising has a duration of approximately 12–18 months and it can be divided into seven main phases:

1. Definition of the market for the capital raising: it implies the identification of which type of LPs to contact. It depends on the investment strategy that the private equity wants to realize.
2. Pre-marketing: it is the choice of the first LPs to involve. It is fundamental to attract other LPs.
3. Construction of the Private Equity: it implies the definition of all technical aspects (legal, fiscal, organization, etc.) concern the fund start.
4. Preparation and Distribution of the Placement Memorandum: the document containing the investment strategy, the target market, the characteristics of the fund, the economic conditions of the fund, the rules of the funds, the team, reporting system, and the track record of the performance realized.
5. Roadshow with potential LPs: among the LPs they are the *gatekeepers*. They are advisors or GP that represent a lot of LPs. A good reception among them is a good marketing instrument by attracting a lot of LPs that consider it a guarantee.
6. Definition of the legal documents: it is defined the fund regulation.
7. Closing: capital is entire raised. The LPs has signed an irrevocable commitment to provide a defined amount of capital and they undertake to honour the capital calling by GP when the investment opportunity is identified.

29.2.2 Phase (2): Investment

The investment is the principal phase of the Private Equity's activity. It is a long and complex process. We can define the investment process in five main steps: 1) *origination*, 2) *analysis*, 3) *execution*, *4) monitoring, 5) exit*.

Step (1): Origination

It refers to the research, identification, and selection of the investment opportunities that must be in line with the investment strategy of the fund. The higher the number of the potential deals identify (the *deal flow*), the easier to find the investment opportunities that are in line with the fund's investment strategy.

The strategy for the origination will be different in order to the investment strategies and the target of the companies. In any case, a good and strong reputation in a sector based on an excellent track record are always the main elements to generate a constant and relevant deal flow.

Step (2): Analysis

The investment opportunities find must be screened in order to analyze their profitability and if they are in line with the investment strategy of the fund.

Only the investment opportunities that pass this screening, are really subject to a deeply and detailed analysis through due diligence. In this case, the investment team studies the company to identify risk and opportunity, strengths and weakness that can have a positive or negative impact on investment. The main analysis refers:

1. *Business model of the company and market analysis*: The aim is to understanding the business model of the company and its ability to perform in referenced market.

Therefore two are the main aspects to be investigated: *1)* the market's structure and its profitability mainly with regard to the size, structure, growth rate, cyclicity, barriers to entry and exit, competitive forces, critical success factors; *2)* the company's business model and its ability to perform in the market referenced mainly with regard to: portfolio products, competitive advantage and its sustainability over time, governance and organizational structure, market share and its potential growth over time.

Note that this analysis is more relevant and deeply if it is realized by a private equity with an industrial approach rather than a private equity with a financial approach.

2. *Governance and management valuation*: The aim is to investigate the adequacy of the governance rules and the quality of the management of the target company with regard to their competence and skills. The right valuation of the managers is a relevant key point because it has direct effect on the success of the deal. Indeed, the success of the deal requires a strictly alignment between company's management and private equity with regard to the definition of the objectives

and the approach used to achieve them. If the valuation of private equity about managers is not satisfactory, private equity can require in a post-deal phase their substitution with the introduction of new managers to company's reinforcement.

3. *Economic and financial performance*: The aim is to analyze the performance of the company with regard to the past and its expectation about the future. The past economic and financial dynamic of the target company is object of due diligence (financial, fiscal, legal, information technology, environmental, etc.) realized by specialized advisors with the main aim to identify potential risk and opportunity. The future expected economic and financial dynamic is forecasted by the target company and formalized in the business plan. It is an important tool to attract investors. However, in the phase of analysis, investors usually prefer to redefine the economic and financial dynamic forecasted by the company with the support of the company's managers to define their own idea about the potentiality of the target company.

Note that since the value of the company is the function of the future performance and not the past one, expectations about the future are more relevant than the past.

4. *Definition and valuation of the exit strategy*: The private equity must define the exit strategy already in the deal building. Private equity is a temporary shareholder of the target company and then it must define the exit jointly to the investment in the company. In the analysis of the potential deal, private equity must evaluate the target company at the start of the investment and at the end of it. Then, for the private equity is fundamental to define before starting the investment the potential growth that target company may realize during the investment period in order to maximize the capital gain. Generally, the value of the deal can be estimate on the basis of this relationship: *i)* the greater the growth of the target company during the investment period, *ii)* the greater its value, *iii)* the higher the capital gain and then the value of the deal.

Step (3): Execution

The investment execution requires the definition of the: 1) price, 2) deal structure, 3) governance.

The *price* is defined on the basis of the business plan and the result of the due diligence of the target company. The most common methodology used by private equity to evaluate the target company and then define the price is multiple. The definition of the price is the result of the balance between risk profile of investment and the fund's expected return on the basis of all variables analyzed and discussed in the negotiation process. The price of deal is defined in the *Share Purchase Agreement (SPA)*.

The *structure of the deal* can be several. A typical deal structure requires the establishment of new company, called Newco. It is a financial vehicle financed by equity supplied by private equity and eventually third parties involved in the investment (also managers and entrepreneur of the target company if they are involved in the deal) and debt, with the aim to acquire the target company. In the second moment, the Newco and the target company will be merged and the equity and debt of the Newco are consolidated in the target company.

Even if the equity and debt are the two sources of capital used to the deal the debt is common higher than equity. The extreme case in the use of the debt is the Leveraged buyout (LBO). In this case, the price of the target company is paid in large part by debt and it is consolidated in the target company itself and repaid by its future cash-flows. In other words, with LBO the target company pays its acquisition.

The use of debt instead of equity to finance the deal is due to the *Leverage effect*: for the same level of the economic and financial expected performance of the target company and for the same price of buying and selling at the end of the investment, the expected return on equity will be greater the higher the debt level respect to equity in financing the deal.

The amount of debt granted is a function of several variables, first of all the characteristic of the target company and its need of investments in asset, stability of the expected cash-flows, shareholders' expected returns, the reputation of both the target company and the private equity.

Even if the private equity tries to optimize the leverage effect by defining the optimum balance between equity and debt to finance the deal, there is not an "optimal" equity-debt ratio for all types of deal. Commonly, the use of debt to finance the deal is generally 50%–60% and it can increase over 60% in a specific period (in the period 2006–2007 in which the use of leverage is maximum and unscrupulous, the level of leverage also reached 90%–95%).

To finance private equity deals, the debt commonly used is provided by banks and debt funds and it is a medium-term debt such as 1) *senior debt*, of a period of 6 year and reimbursement privileged over all other debt instruments. It is the most common debt used; 2) *subordinated debt*, of a period of 6–7 years and reimbursement privileged over equity but subordinated over the senior debt. It can be characterized by equity kicker that is an option to acquire shares in favorable circumstance. To guarantee their interests, the debtholders require the covenants underwriting. These covenants can have a negative form, if they indicate prohibitions and limitations, or positive form if they impose well-defined obligations with regard to actions or informative obligations. In this contest, financial covenants have great relevance. They states the company obligation to maintain some financial ratios in a well-defined range of minimum and maximum value. The most common financial covenants are Financial Debt / EBITDA ratio; Free Cash-Flow from Operations / Debt Obligation (with regard to the cash-out related to the interest on debt plus the reimbursement of debt capital) ratio; EBIT / Interest ratio.

Since one of the most relevant keys in the deal successful is the strictly relationship between management and private equity, the private equity may require to the managers their involving in the deal. Generally, the higher the investment in equity by manager of the target company alongside the private equity, the higher the confidence of the private equity. Two are the main tools: *i) different price of shares issue*: managers can buy the shares issue by the Newco at their nominal value, while the private equity buys these shares at higher price than nominal one; *ii) use of ratchet*: managers can increase their shares in the target company at the achievement of defined performance objectives, at the end of the investment. Thanks to these tools, managers can realize a high return at the end of the investment period of the private equity, and then they are strongly incentivized to maximize the value of target company in that period.

The *definition of the governance* of the target company. It refers to the rules between investors, managers and entrepreneur (if he/she maintain a shares in the target company). It is a key point for the deal closing. It is common that the deal does not close because the parts involved do not agree on the governance that the company will have. Among the most relevant questions concern the definition of the management, the member of the board and other control structure, the property rights, the level of reporting, the indication of the exit strategy of the private equity and relative timing (even if it is defined in the negotiation, the private equity tend always to maintain a high degree of freedom of action).

In any cases, there is not a defined model that can be considered successful in all cases. A general rule is to try to find an equilibrium between the interest of all parts involved in the deal.

The governance and its rules are formalized in the Shareholders Agreement.

29.2.3 Phase (3): Monitoring

This phase refers to the private equity monitoring activity of the target companies in its portfolio during the period of investment.

Acquired the shares of the target companies, the private equity play a role in the governance of the company with the main aim to help managers in the decisions process and evaluation of the results. Indeed, the successful of the deal is strictly related to managers of the target company and private equity to work jointly to achieve the objectives of the business plan defined.

Commonly the private equity requires the appointment of one or more members of the board of directors of the target company. The level involvement of the private equity in the target company activities depends on the approach following. In this sense, we can distinguish between private equity with:

1. *Financial approach*: The private equity is low involved in the company's activities by preferring a role of financial advisor with the aim to optimize the economic and financial dynamic of the company and its capital structure in order to maximize the company's ability to create value. Consequently, the private equity prefers to invest in company with expected high cash-flows to maximize the leverage effect through the optimization of capital structure and the cost structure on which it builds its capital gain. Indeed, the company's capability to generate high cash-flows reduces the debt level and then automatically increase the equity value for the private equity.
2. *Industrial approach*: The private equity is high involved in the company's activities. However, it is not involved in the daily operating activities of the company, but it plays a role of partner helping the company to define the strategy

and its implementation. The main aim is to develop the company and its competitive advantage at the maximum level to achieving a good strategic positioning in the market. Consequently, the private equity is focused on the increase of the company's EBITDA and profitability in the investment period on the basis of which it builds its capital gains.

In any cases, the private equity is not involved in the daily company's operating activities. Its role is to help the company by management reinforcement and its empowerment, competence and skills, strategic and financial vision, with the main aim to push and maximize the process of value creation of the company.

To increase the value of investment the private equity can make policies with regard to three main directrices:

1. *EBITDA increase*: Private equity tends to help the company to increase in a structural way its EBITDA to maximize the company's value over time. In this perspective, the main levers of the value creation are: *i) revenues*, by pushing on the increase of quantity of products sold and/or increase of sale price; *ii) cost structure*, with the optimization of costs in a sustainability way over time; *iii) size increase*, by acquisition of companies following a strategy of buy and build able to consolidate the company's market position.
2. *Deleveraging*: The private equity is focused on the reduction of the debt level of target company during the period of investment. Indeed, by assuming a constant level of the multiple EV/EBITDA, use of cash-flows generated by the company to reduce its debt, increases the equity value.
3. *Multiple arbitrage*: The valuation of the target company is commonly realized by multiple. One of the most commonly used is the EV/EBITDA (Enterprise Value / EBITDA ratio). The private equity maximizes its investment by increasing this multiple during the investment period so that the shares acquired can be sold at higher price. Note that the effective increase or decrease of the multiple is the function not only of the private equity ability to negotiate the entry and exit from the investment and to help the company to increase its performance, but also to the macroeconomic condition. In this sense, consider how in the periods of economic growth, the multiples are higher than their value in the period of recession. Similar, crisis in the debt market can have a negative impact on the leverage to finance the deal and the multiple tend to be lower.

Commonly the most part of deal value with a price of sell higher than the price of buy is generated by the increase of EBITDA primarily, by the deleveraging secondarily, and finally by the multiple arbitrage.

29.2.4 Phase (4): Exit

The time period of the investment for the private equity commonly is 5–6 years. At the end of the period, private equity must maximize the capital gain through the selling of the shares of the target company at a sell price higher than buy price. It requires a definition of a good investment strategy as well as a good exit strategy.

Two main variables to define in the exit strategy: 1) *timing*, with the definition of the best moment to exit; 2) *way*, with the definition of the best way to exit.

Therefore, the private equity must foresee the exit strategy by defining the timing and the way to exit from the investment. The common ways prefer by the private equity to exit are:

1. *IPO*, with the sale of the shares by listing the company.
2. *Buyback*, with the repurchase of the shares by the original shareholder.
3. *Trade sale*, with the sale of the shares to another company with industrial approach.
4. *Secondary buyout*, with the sale of the shares to another private equity.

Note that, even if the question of the exit strategy is discussed in the negotiation process, the private equity tends always to keep a high level of discretionary maintaining the hands free. Indeed, unexpected factors could lead the private equity to modify the exit strategy negotiated to maximize the capital gain.

At the moment of the exit, the valuation of the investment is commonly realized on the basis of two main indicators:

1. *The multiple Cash on Cash (MoM)*: It is the ratio between the capital received at the exit and the capital invested.
2. *Internal Rate of Return (IRR)*: It is the compound annual rate of return (it can be computed as the compound annual growth rate—CAGR). If this rate is lower than the equilibrium rate (the rate able to make the Net Present Value (NPV) equal to zero) the NPV of investment is positive and the deal created value; on the contrary, if this rate is greater than the equilibrium rate, the NPV of investment is negative and the deal destroyed value.

29.3 Venture Capital

Private Equity and Venture Capital are different mainly with regard to the mission, investment approach, referenced market.

Venture Capital (VC) is defined by National Venture Capital Association (in USA), and shared by the European Venture Capital Association o EVCA (in Europe), as the "*money provided by professionals who invest alongside management in young rapidly growing companies that have the potential to develop into significant economic contributors*". Therefore, VC is focused on the companies that are in the early stage (sometimes the company is not even exist, and then it is called *paper company*) and presents high potential growth in the market thanks to a high technological aspect with regard to the process or product. The most sought-after companies are *unicorns*, that are private companies with an implied potential value greater than $ 1 billion.

The VC is fundamental for the company's development in the early for financial resources as well as for the managerial and strategic support to the company.

The development curve of the company in the perspective of the VC is called *hockey-stick curve* and is based on seven main phases:

1. *Seed Financing*: It identifies the state of initial development of the company and it is characterized by the need to financing the research on product and to explore the effective market potential. In this phase, the company realizes and tests prototypes, but there is no production.
2. *Startup*: The capital raised is used to extend the results of the previous phase with regard to both industrial and commercial perspectives. The phase is characterized by the production and testing of advanced versions of the product and market penetration.
3. *Early Development*: This phase is characterized by the start of pre-production. The development of deep business and financial plans and sensitivity analyzes are essential tools to understand whether to continue or exit to the investment.
4. *Expansion*: In this phase, the company has a reasoning estimation of the market penetration, the speed in the achievement of targets defined, and the investments needs are defined in a detailed way.
5. *Profitability*: In this phase, the company realizes the growth of revenues and margins, the reduction of the operating risk level, and a detailed definition of the potential of the company's expansion. In this phase the financial sources are used to support the development of the production and distribution of the products on the markets.
6. *Growth:* In this phase, the company produces profits and cash-flows enough to support its own growth realizing self-financing. Eventual increase in equity through and debt can be realized to push up the company growth faster.
7. *Cash-Out*: It is the phase VC realizes the capital gains with the exit from investment in the company.

The analysis of these phases shows as the VC investment is characterized by a high level of risk. Specific investment structures are needed to manage this high level of risk.

Commonly the investments in VC are realized by using a *closed-end fund* (in the USA for a long time) with the clear separation between *management company* and the *fund*. All investors are identified as the *Limited Partner (LP)* of the fund and they participate in any losses of the fund only limited to the amount of the paid-up capital. Separately there is the *management company* of the equity fund that have own assets. The management of the fund's capital is entrusted to the team of the management company who act in the interests of the LPs.

The relationship between managers and investors is defined in a detailed manner with regard to all elements in a binding document called *Limited Partnership Agreement (LPA)*. Since the rules defined in the LPA must be valid for each investor of the fund, the LPA is negotiated by a few investors, the *lead investors*, for all investors. The lead investors are generally the first investors in the fund and with the most significant shares of the fund.

The rules for remuneration of the managers of the management company are the same of the Private Equity:

1. *Co-investment*: Co-investment of the shareholders of the management company within the fund. The co-investment is equal to approximately 1% of the total amount.
2. *Management fee*: It is used to cover the fixed costs of the management company, including salaries of managers and staff. Since the amount of the management fee reduces the capital available to be invested, it is defined equal to the 2% of the committed capital in the first phase and the capital called up for the investment in the second phase.
3. *Carried interests*: It is the real incentive for management. It is commonly equal to 20% of the profit of the fund net to the *hurdle rate* that is the minimum level of return expected by investors. It implies that if the investors' return is lower than the hurdle rate, there is not carried interest for managers. The hurdle rate is generally fixed equal to 6–8% of IRR (internal rate of return). It is applied to the entire capital committed along the entire period of the fund.

29.4 Venture Capital Valuation Method

In the VC investment, a critical phase is the selection of the target companies. Commonly for 1000 of projects analyzed only 10 (1%) are selected. The investment selection is so difficult because it is a mix of analytical capability and art. Generally, the analytical analysis can help the investor to reduce the number of projects by defining a short-list of 60–70 projects, among them the selection of investments to realize is strictly depend on the VC intuition. The main problem is that while a rigorous analytical analysis can be taught and learned in specialized courses and textbooks, the intuition does not, and it is to make the difference. It implies that a successful of VC is not related only to the amount of capital available to invest, but much more to the quality and capability of the management team.

Commonly the VC prefer to specialize in a defined market. Indeed, a good network and a deep capability to understand the dynamic of the sector or technology are relevant success factors.

Defined a short-list of potential target companies the VC must evaluate them. In this contest, standard method such as the DCF is difficult even if impossible to use. Indeed, the VC investment are characterized by the absence of positive cash-flows during intermediate phases, generation of losses for a several periods, difficulty in the identification of the market and the potential of company's growth, difficult to estimate revenues and profit margins over time. For these and other reasons, the practice in VC has developed a specific *Venture Capital Method* (VCM) to estimate the value of the target company.

The VCM is based on two main pillars:

1. *Estimation of the post-money value at the exit of investment*: It is the Terminal Value (TV) and it incorporates the financial sources invested in the company by the VC and the expectation of the company's growth. Because this value can be obtained only thanks to the VC investment in the company, it is called *post-money value*. It implies that the *pre-money value* is equal to the post-money value less the VC investment in the company. The post-money value is commonly estimated on the basis of multiples with regard to the expected market value at the moment of exit of some main items such as EBITDA, EBIT or Net Earnings. The horizon time of investment must be defined on the basis of the business and financial plan of the company and the dynamic of its market both actual and prospective.
2. *Definition of the discount factor*: The present value of the target company at the moment of the exit requires to define the discount factor. It reflects the risk of VC and commonly it is not estimated on the basis of the CAPM as for DCF method. On the contrary, it is defined by the market practice between 40% and 70% or more on the basis of the stage of the company's development. The high discount rate depends on the composition of the VC's portfolio and the target of expected return (generally equal around 20%). Commonly the portfolio is composed of: 20–30% of investments that give a positive return; 30–40% of investments that return only the capital invested without any return; 30–40% of investments that generate the total loss of investments.
3. *Compute of the VSs shares of the target company*: The number of shares request by the VC is defined on the basis of the post-money value divided the capital invested.

To well-understand the VCM, consider the following example.

Assume that the Venture Capital decides to invest in Alfa Company euro four million. Assume that the period of investment is defined in 5 years, and at the end of this period, the VC estimates that the Alfa company is able to realize an earning of six million stable over time. To estimate the Terminal Value (TV) at the time of exit, the VC uses the multiple Price/Earnings (P/E). Assume that the comparable companies in the market have characterized by a multiple P/E average equal to 15x. Assume that the VC by considering the early-stage of the company applies a discount rate equal to 50%.

Under these assumptions:

1. The Terminal Value of the company is equal to Euro 90 million as follows:

$$TV = \text{Earnings} * \text{Multiple} = 6{,}000{,}000 * 15 = 90{,}000{,}000$$

2. The Post-Money Value is equal to euro 11.8 million, as follows:

$$\frac{TV}{(1+IIR)^5} = \frac{90{,}000{,}000}{(1+50\%)^5} = 11{,}851{,}852$$

3. The Pre-Money Value is equal to 7.8 million, as follows:

$$PreMoneyValue = PostMoneyValue - Investment = 11{,}851{,}852 - 4{,}000{,}000 = 7{,}851{,}852$$

4. The shares amount of Alfa's equity requested by VC is equal to 33.75%, as follows:

$$EquityRequested = \frac{11{,}851{,}852}{4{,}000{,}000} = 33.75\%$$

One of the characteristics of the VC investment is to require several capital investments before to estimate the return and then to estimate the exit. This practice is called *staging,* and the use of more than one round of investments have three main objectives:

1. To reduce the risk for investor by reducing the capital invested before the company shows signals about effective development of the plan.
2. To reduce the capital dilution effect of the company's shareholders by avoiding they can reduce their incentive to the company's development.
3. To allow the entry of new investors in different stages of company's development, enjoying a lower risk profile of the company but paying a higher cost of entry to the benefit of first investor. In this case, we apply the Venture Capital Method in different moments of the investment life.

29.5 Venture Capital Control Tools

In any VC investments (as well as in Private Equity investment) one of the most relevant problems refer to the asymmetric information between the company's managers and VC with regard to the effective growth potential of the company.

Even if it is commonly that VC requites to appoint key people in the board of the company with right of veto or address with reference to particular decisions to control the governance of the target company, the formal control on the governance can be considered limited in their effectiveness for two main reasons:

1. *Limited time*: The VC's management team must follow of companies in the portfolio and then their time for each company is limited. It implies that they cannot be involved efficiently in the operating activities of the company by monitoring and managing effectively all risk factors.
2. *Limited skills*: Even if we assume the direct involving of the VC's team in the company's operating activities, it will be not effectively. Indeed, entrepreneur and managers of the company are characterized by a high competence in their business while the VC's team usually none. Note that if we assume that the VC's team is able to replace effectively the entrepreneur and managers of the company, it implies that their competences are very low and that points questions about the right valuation of the investment.

Therefore, practice has developed several tools that can be used to manage the conflicts between company and VC to avoid inefficient use of capital invested. The common way is to introduce key clauses in the contract with economic impact. The most common key clauses are:

1. *Liquidation preference*: In the event of company's sales, the VC has the right to sell its shares first and at a price based on a multiple of initial investment as defined in the contract at the beginning; until the VC has realized its right, all other shareholders of the company will not receive any payment and then the value of their shares will be equal to zero. This clause is very relevant when the company's performance is low and then the sale price is low. The same mechanism is applied in the case of company's assets liquidation.
   Considering the potential economic effect, this clause is object of heated negotiation. The problem is not the introduction, but the definition of the multiple to use for the value definition to introduce in the contract. Indeed, the higher the multiple and its value, the higher the probability that in case of company's low performance the entire or a relevant part of the company's sale value will be attributed to the VC;
2. *Anti-dilution rights*: In the event of more than one round of investments from the same VC or different VCs, there could be the dilution effect if the last round is realized at lower price than the previous. In this case the VC who subscribed the previous round, would be dilute in the company's equity because it has paid a high price (and therefore a low shares) in the previous round against a low price (and therefore a high shares) of the current round. To avoid the dilution effect, the anti-dilution right states the right of the VC to renegotiate the price paid (and then the number of shares) in the previous round. The realignment of the price can be realized in two ways:
   (a) *Full ratchet*: The price of the shares already subscribed is realigned to the price of the shares negotiated for the new round. Because the second price is lower than the fist, the increase of number of shares is total.
   (b) *Weighted Average*: The realignment price is defined on the basis of the average price of the new and old shares. In this case, the increase of number of shares is partial.

3. *Redemption Rights*: The VC has the right to request to the company the repurchase of its shares after a predefined time period at a predefined price based on a multiple. Therefore, it can be considered as the Put Option that gives to the VC an option to exit from the company in cases there are no other alternatives.
   However, the effectiveness application of this clause is limited. Indeed, it implies that the company has the financial sources to repurchase the shares. But if we assume that commonly the absence of alternative is due to the low performance of the company, it is unlikely that the company has financial sources enough to pay the shares. And even if we assume there are the financial resources, in any case there are always limit imposed by the law in case of company's purchase of its shares;
4. *Tag-along and Drag-along*: The Tag-Along Right the right that allows the minority shareholders to oblige the majority shareholders in event of company's sale, to force the buyer to purchase also the minority shares. It is relevant if the VC is minority shareholders. The Drag-along Right gives the majority shareholders the right to impose the sale to all minority shareholders at the same conditions if this is functional to the sale to a third party.

These and all other key clauses that VC can introduce in the contract, are used as exit strategy in case of the VC investment failure. By considering the nature and the characteristics of the VC investment, these clauses are the common way to exit.

On the contrary, if the VC investment is successful, the exit strategy is commonly represented by an M&A or IPO. The choice depends on the company's valuation and the market dynamics.

29.6 Hedge Fund

Hedge Fund (HF) is grouped in the category of *alternative investments* as well as Private Equity (PE) and Venture Capital (VC) Funds.

The Hedge Fund is a fund with the specific mandate to realize a positive absolute return regardless of financial market trends. Consequently, it must realize positive returns even if the capital markets go down. Then, the hedging against negative yields is one of the main characteristics of the most Hedge Funds even if they are defined speculative.

In the Hedge Fund, we must distinguish between *i)* the fund and *ii)* the management company.

The fund is a collective investment vehicle, commonly a Limited Partnership (LP), which invests private capital. They are collective investment funds, typically open-ended funds, although closed-end funds may be present, intended for institutional investors and highly qualified investors.

Investors in HF are typically characterized by a high level of competence in finance, high personal wealth and a vision of a long period. They are usually institutional investors (typically endowment, family office and funds of funds) and private qualify investors defined High Net Worth Individuals (HNWI). Commonly the minimum investment amount requires is so high to be considered a barrier to entry for the retail investors.

Note that investors in HF must respect two main constraints in order to receive the reimbursement of the capital invested:

1. *Look-up period*: The investment can be reimbursed only after a defined period (usually 12 months to the start of the investment). At the end of this period, the investor can redeem his investment by following the redemption procedure.
2. *Redemption date*: The capital redemption procedure provides for only a few windows each year (commonly the first or last day of the month or quarter and coincide with the NAV publication) and a notification period (commonly from 30 to 60 days).

The *management company* has the mandate to manage the fund. Therefore, the fund gives a mandate to a management company that invests the fund's capital by following its own investment strategies in order to achieve the objective of positive return regardless of the performance of the financial markets. To achieve this objective, the management company has characterized by a wide flexibility in terms of instruments, techniques and investment strategies.

Following we use the HF by denoting the fund plus the management company.

29.6.1 The Team and Fees

The success of the HF depends completely on the ability of its investment team. The size of the team can vary on the basis of investment strategies. The key figures are:

1. *Chief Investment Officer (CIO)*: He/she is the investment manager of the HF and he/she decides the investment strategies. The CIO decides the asset class in which to invest, the timing, the amount of investment for each of them, the hedging of risk. Also, the CIO coordinates the entire team. Consequently, the CIO is the most relevant person of the HF in a way that commonly the entire HF identifies with the person of CIO. Note that the CIO is the main shareholder of the management company and it is the key person in the fundraising of capital. The relevance of the person of CIO is so much that to his person is link the clause of "key man": it states the possibility of investors to with draw from the investment if the CIO leaves the management company.
2. *Portfolio Managers (PM)*: They are the senior member of the team. They manage a portfolio or a its part. They report directly to the CIO and they coordinate the analysts. Their remuneration is strictly function of the return of their investments.
3. *Analysts*: They are responsible for the analysis of assets in portfolio and the potential new investments. They can have competence in a specific sectors or markets, or they can be generalist by following all markets.
4. *Trading desk*: They are responsible for the execution of the buy or sell orders of assets in portfolio. They monitor the flows on the financial markets in order to

define the timing and the amount of buying and selling. The trading desk reports directly to the CIO because it is an activity complementary to the investment.
5. *Chief Risk Officer (CRO)*: He/she has the responsability of the risk management. In the limit cases, the CRO can require to sell the fund's positions or require hedging strategies even if the CIO is disagreed. It can be considered, even if improperly, a controller of the CIO by representing a source of reassurance for investors. For this reason, the relationship between CIO and CRO is complex and each HF defines the relative rules in order to put the CRO in the best conditions to exercise independent judgment.
6. *Chief Operating Officer (CCO)*: He/she has the responsability of coordination and optimization of all operating activities. Its role is fundamental for the CIO gives him the possibility to focus on the investment only.

All staff functions (such as IT, administration, legal, investor relator) can be internal or external. It depends on the size of the fund. The higher the size, the high the number of staff functions internal to the HF.

The HF's remuneration is based on two main commissions:

1. *Management fee*: It is equal to 1%–2% of the capital and it is computed on Net Asset Value (NAV) (it is the sum of the counter values of all the assets in the portfolio) monthly or quarterly frequency. This fee is used to cover the fixed cost of the management company included the salaries of the team.
2. *Performance fee*: It is equal to 10%–30% and it is computed on the capital gains realized in a defined time period (generally equal to the solar year). This fee is the bonus for the team and then it is the real incentive for the team to realize positive returns.

These commissions are paid by the fund to the management company. To avoid moral hazard by the team link to the performance fee (by assuming a fee equal to 20%, in case of capital gain the investors receive the 80% while the team the 20%; on the contrary, in case of capital loss, the investors bears the 100% of the loss while the team lose nothing), investors require that the team invest a relevant part of their personal wealth in the fund. So that the team is push not only to realize positive performance but also to preserve the capital invested without losing it.

29.6.2 Investment Strategy

The Investment Strategy is focused to realize a positive absolute return regardless of financial market trends. To do it, the HF has a great flexibility in choice of asset class and in their risk/return profile. Also, they have no restriction in the use of leverage, short selling, level of risk constraints and level of portfolio's concentration with the possibility to invest in few companies with high level of concentration. Therefore, they are different from the traditional mutual funds.

Two are the main variables of the investment strategy: *i)* leverage and *ii)* short selling.

Specifically, Hedge Funds have not limit to the ***leverage***. Commonly they invest much more they have in capital with the aim to increase the fund's return. Then, the leverage can be higher than 100% over the assets managed by the fund. It can be realized in two main ways: *1)* borrowing money from the *prime broker* (this activity is carried out by investment banks and the main services offered to Hedge Funds refer to the stock lending and loans); 2) through derivative. Commonly HFs use both to increase leverage over the 100%.

To analyze the performance of the HF that use the leverage in a strongly way, it is common to compute the unlevered return of the fund in order to distinguish between: performance and the leverage.

The *Short Selling* is the most tools used by the HFs to protect the market risk. It allows to realize positive returns in case of financial markets go down.

HFs have several options to reduce their *net market exposure* that is equal to the difference between Long exposure less short exposure divided by Net Asset Value (NAV):

$$\text{Net Market Exposure} = \frac{\text{Long Exposure} - \text{Short Exposure}}{\text{Net Asset Value (NAV)}}$$

The short selling commonly involve:

1. Derivative instruments on indices (overlay) such as the derivative instruments on futures indices because they are traded on all major markets.
2. Stocks of a specific company. Among all possible strategies one of the most commonly used is the *Equity Long/Short strategy*. It is based on a deeply fundamental quantitative analysis of the company. The investment team try to identify company under valuated (or over valuated) by the market and for which the team expected a higher (or lower) performance than the market's performance. Note that always more often the distance between intrinsic value of the company and its price in the market is filled by the HFs through their activism in the company.

For the short selling transactions, the stock loan is guaranteed to Hedge Funds by Prime Brokers. The HF must first check the availability of the security by its Prime Broker before to short sell it. The Prime Broker is an intermediary between the owner of the stock and the HF. Indeed, the commission pays by HF to the Prime Broker is, in turn, pays in a part by Prime Broker to the effective lender of the stocks.

Initial Public Offering 30

30.1 Reasons of IPO

The Initial Public Offering (IPO) refers to the listing of company's shares on a regulated capital market. By the IPO the company raises equity capital by listing its shares to be traded by all investors on a recognized stock exchange and becoming public company.

Note that the IPO is not the only moment in which the company goes on market to acquire capital need to its growth. Company can return to equity markets by offering new shares for sale. This type of offering is called a *Seasoned Equity Offering (SEO)*. In this case, we follow many of the same steps of the IPO. The main difference is that in this case a market price of stock already exists, so the price-setting process typical of the IPO, in this case, is not necessary.

With regard to the shares of company offered, we can distinguish between:

1. *Primary offering*: The offer concerns a large block of shares for sale to the public for the first time by the company. Therefore, shares sold in IPO are new shares that raise new capital.
2. *Secondary offering*: The offer concerns existing shares sold by current shareholders as a part of their exit strategy. Therefore, shares sold are not new shares and then they do not raise new capital.

Company must have specific requirements for listing. Commonly, they are defined in three main directives:

1. *Size*: The company must be characterized by a minimum level of revenues, EBITDA, net income, and the valuation must allow shares offering higher than a defined amount in order to guarantee the liquidity of the shares in the market after the IPO to be attractive for investors.
2. *Equity story*: The company must have an equity story able to attract investors. Basic elements of the equity story are: *i)* a growing market and a position leader in

P. De Luca, *Corporate Finance*, Springer Texts in Business and Economics,
https://doi.org/10.1007/978-3-031-18300-3_30

it, *ii)* a well-defined and performing business model able to generate and defend a competitive advantage, *iii)* a management team with high profile, effective governance rules and a business strategy able to push the company growth after the listing, *iv)* an expected future economic and financial dynamic able to support the company's growth with investments and by paying dividend to shareholders.

3. *Timing*: It represents a particular aspect because a good IPO implies that the financial markets are in a phase of stability and receptively to the listing of new company. The number and value of IPO are also related to the dynamic of financial markets.

The IPO has relevant advantages at different levels:

1. In the company's perspective, the listing allows to increase the equity capital by expanding the shareholders, obtaining the financial sources need to finance the company's internal growth or external one through M&A.
2. In the shareholders' perspective, the company listing allows to monetize their investment in the company by selling their shares in any moment on the basis of the share price on the market and gives the opportunity to investors to diversify. On the contrary, one of the most limit is due to the loss of direct control of the entrepreneur.
3. In the managers' perspective, the company listing allows to the increase of their reputation in the market, the possibility to benefice of stock option programs and the opportunity to attract talents.

The main disadvantage of IPO is the high cost. It is mainly due to the *Underpricing*. On average IPOs tend to be underpricing because the stock price at the end of the first day tends to be substantially higher than the IPO price. Three are the main reasons: 1) investments banks, to control their risk set the issue price in a way that the average first-day return is positive; 2) investors, that if there are able to buy stock from investment banks at the IPO price know that can gain from the first-day underpricing; 3) if the IPO goes well, the demand for stocks at issue price is higher and the allocation of stocks for each investor is rationed; on the contrary, if the IPO does not go well, the demand at issue price is weak and all initial orders are filled completely. This form of adverse selection is called *winner's curse*: you get all the shares requested when demand is low and the IPO is more likely to perform low.

To the underpricing, we have to sum the *spread* that is the discount below the issue price at which the underwriter purchases the shares from the issuing company that is a percentage of the issue price.

30.2 Preparation of the IPO

The IPO is a complex process. By considering a European IPO, we can define the IPO process in three main phases: 1) *Preparation of the IPO*; 2) *Investor education*; 3) *offer period*.

Note that in Europe in the phases *1)* and *3)* is not possible to discuss about the estimation on the expected future net income of the company because the company cannot spread it. Only in the phase *2)* financial analysists discuss with investors about their estimation on the expected future net income of the company. On the contrary, in the USA there is not this phase *2)* because the first report about financial analysts estimation can be released only 40 days after the IPO.

The preparation of the IPO opens with the appoints the *advisor team*. Two are the key roles in the entire process of IPO:

- *Financial advisor*, that represents the needs and interests of the company. The main aims of the financial advisor are: 1) to define the structure of the IPO; 2) to coordinate the advisor team (legal, fiscal, auditors, etc.); 3) to build the financial modelling; 4) to support the company in the writing of its equity story and the presentation to the financial analysts and investors; 5) to assure that the company due diligence is complete and well done; 6) to support the company in the negotiation process with banks and investors for the stocks placement and subscription agreement;
- *Coordinator of the placement syndicate* is an investment bank or more investment banks that must place stocks of the company with institutional and private investors. If the company does not appoint the financial advisor, the coordinator coordinates the work of the advisor team and to manage the entire process of the IPO. Even if it is always possible, it is relevant to note that this choice could be not efficiently. Because bank place more IPO in the same place, there may be generate conflict interest between the bank and company. To avoid this risk, it is fundamental that the company appoints a financial advisor able to dialogue and negotiate all the fundamental steps with banks and investors in order to guarantee the total protection of the company's interests.

The company, with its advisor team, defines mainly the *timing*, the *equity story*, the *financial models* and the *IPO preliminary prospectus*.

30.2.1 Timing

The timing is defined in the *kick-off meeting* between the company, the financial advisor and eventually all advisory team. Commonly the entire IPO process requires a period of 5–6 months. Note that by considering the holiday periods (both in winter and summer), the market practice and the need to publish quarterly data not earlier than a defined number of days (usually 135) from the date of the offer to receive the comfort letter from the auditors, in the year there are only few defined periods in which we can listing the company. Commonly: *i)* between January and mid-February, by using the financial data of the 9 months of the previous year; *ii)* between April and July, by using the financial data of the December of the previous year; *iii)* after mid-May by using the financial data of the previous March; *iv)* between September and October, by using the financial data of the previous June.

Also considering the financial markets volatility, companies usually prefer the period between April and July in order to have a longer period in which to look for the right time to listing.

30.2.2 Equity Story

The equity story is a presentation of the company by including the main elements that characterized the company such as: 1) the potential growth of the referencing market and its position leader in it; 2) the efficient and effective business model and its capability to generate and defend a competitive advantage; 3) a good governance and a skilled, experienced and well-motivated management team able to push the company's growth over time; 4) the expected growth in the first years after the IPO; 4) an future expected economic and financial dynamic able to support the company's growth generating cash-flows enough to support investments and a dividend policy in line with investors expectation.

The company's equity story must be coherent with the position of the company regarding comparable companies.

Commonly the equity story must be detailed for the financial analysts and in the IPO prospectus, while in the presentation to potential investors, it is summarized and focused on its most important aspect to attract their attention.

30.2.3 Financial Model

The financial model of the company is fundamental for two main reasons:

1. To well-understand the economic and financial dynamic of the company with regard to the historical data and the expected future data.
2. To evaluate the company in order to define the price. Even if in the IPO the most used method is the multiples of comparable companies, the model based on the fundamental analysis of the company such as the DCF is used to define the range of possible price. Also, it is fundamental to analyze the effect of dilution due to the IPO and then to rearrange the capital structure.

The Financial Model allows to well-understand the quantitative dynamic of the company over time to evaluate its capability to perform in the market by generating value. Also, it allows scenario-analysis by simulating the effects of alternative scenario and to test several assumptions on the expected economic and financial dynamic over time and their effects on the company's ability to create value.

Financial Model must always be built on reliable data. Specifically, with regard to:

1. The *historical data*, a deep due diligence is necessary to assure that all economic and financial data are well-evaluate without significant error or omissions.

2. The *expected future data*, the economic and financial dynamic must be built on a well-defined and detailed assumptions for each variable considered as well as in their systemic dynamic.

30.2.4 IPO Prospectus

It is written by the company's legal advisors (that have the responsibility of all legal documents need to the entire IPO process) and discussed with the other members of the advisory team before being send to the Authority for their comments. The main elements of the IPO prospectus are commonly: 1) the summary, 2) the risk factors; 3) the company description; 4) the offer description; 5) the use of the proceeds of the offer; 6) the dividend policy; 7) the capital structure of the company; 8) the main economic and financial data of the company; 9) the shareholders of the company; 10) the company's board and the management team and a description of the workface; 11) the taxation of financial instruments; 12) transactions with related parties; 13) the conditions for subscribing to the offer; 14) a section containing the last three annual reports and any interim reports. Note that prospectus cannot include expected future elements of economic and financial dynamic.

30.2.5 Pilot-Fishing

Before to formalize the IPO, it is common that company and its advisors meet a significant number of major institutional investors (commonly coordinators of IPO select 10–15 investors) that are considered opinion leader and able to make significant order in the order book and then they are fundamental for the success or failure of IPO in order to verify their opinion and interest to the company.

This step is called *pilot-fishing* (or *anchor marketing*) and commonly it is realized before the presentation to the financial analysts, or in any case before the publication of their report about the company and relative disclosure to investors.

The main aim of the company and its advisors is to acquire the first indications and humors from the market about its IPO, even if the price is not discussed.

30.3 Pricing of the IPO

The pricing of the IPO is based on the second phase (investment education) and third phase (offer period).

The second phase refers to the investment education.

In this phase, the financial analysts of the bank or banks coordinator of the placement consortium:

1. Publish their report about the company. It contains the description of the company and the main economic and financial data, but it does not include

recommendation or target price (note that in the USA, the publication of this report is not permitted).
2. Meet investors (commonly in 2–3 weeks) in order to receive regard possible valuation of the company and their interest to participate to the IPO.

In the meantime that company's managers, advisors and IPO coordinators prepare the presentation for the roadshow, the due diligence is closed and the eventually comments of the Authority are included in the IPO prospectus.

Based on the feedback received by investors, advisors define a potential price range.

The last phase refers to the *offer period*. It opens with two main acts: 1) the preliminary IPO prospectus send to potential investors with indication of price range; 2) the roadshow of the company's managers with potential investors to present the company trying to involve them in the IPO. During the roadshow (commonly 2 weeks) company acquires the intention of investors to be involved in the IPO and the price they are interested to buy that are included in the order book. At the end of the roadshow, the order book is closed.

Specifically, the stock price of the company in IPO is defined on the basis of a procedure defined *price discovery*. Investors define the stock price on the basis of the company characteristics and comparable companies listing in the market by applying multiples on expected revenues, EBITDA, net income as estimated by financial analysts.

The ending phase of the price discovery is the *book-building*. The coordinators of the placement syndicate of the IPO record the purchase requests from investors that they have received during the offer period in an order book. At the end of offering period, coordinators order all the orders collected on the basis of price and size by proposing to the company a possible stock price at which all the shares offered can be sold. The company decides whether to accept the stock price or not by withdrawing the IPO (even if this it is not common because the IPO preparation require several months and all players involved have a clear idea about the possible price). Note that coordinators tend to define the price at a discount of 10–15% with respect to the expected stock price trade in the market post-IPO. It is used to involve investors in IPO. Indeed, the discount applied allows investors to gain in IPOs if the stocks are traded at a higher price after the IPO. Company may not agree on this discount, if the managers think to be best than competitors and then the investors should pay the maximum price. However, if the company plans to return to the market in the future to raise more funds from investors, it will be more willing to discount the price for the possible future involvement of these investors in the subsequent offers.

The allocation of company stocks to investors included in the order book is defined by coordinators of IPO on the basis of several criteria such as: 1) quality of investor, 2) size of order, 3) date of placing the order (the priority is assigned to investors that are first in the order book), 4) expectation about the duration of the investment, preferring investors who will not sell their stocks after the first few weeks.

Therefore, at the end of this phase there is the definition of the offer, the allocation of the stocks and the start of trading on the stock exchange of the listed security.

References

Agarwal, V., & Taffler, R. J. (2007). Twenty-five years of the Taffler Z-score model: Does it really have predictive ability? *Accounting and Business Research, 37*(4), 285–300.

Aghion, P., & Bolton, P. (1992). An incomplete contracts approach to financial contracting. *The Review of Economic Studies, 59*(3), 473–494.

Alexander, G. (1976). The derivation of efficient sets. *Journal of Financial and Quantitative Analysis, XI*(5), 817–830.

Alexander, G. (1977a). Mixed security testing of alternative portfolio selection models. *Journal of Financial and Quantitative Analysis, XII*(4), 817–832.

Alexander, G. (1977b). An algorithmic approach to deriving the minimum-variance zero-beta portfolio. *Journal of Financial Economics, 4*(2), 231–236.

Alexander, G. (1978). A reevaluation of alternative portfolio selection models applied to common stock. *Journal of Financial and Quantitative Analysis, XIII*(1), 71–78.

Alexander, G. J. (1980). Applying the market model to long-term corporate bonds. *Journal of Financial and Quantitative Analysis, XV*(5), 1063–1080.

Alexander, G. J., & Benston, P. G. (1982). More on beta as a random coefficient. *Journal of Financial and Quantitative Analysis, XVII*(1), 27–36.

Alexander, G. J., & Chervany, N. L. (1980). On the estimation and stability of Beta. *Journal of Financial and Quantitative Analysis, XV*(1), 123–138.

Allen, F., & Michaely, R. (2003). Payout policy. In G. Constantinides, M. Harris, & R. Stulz (Eds.), *Handbook of the economics of finance: Corporate finance* (Vol. 1A). Elsevier.

Altaman, E. (1969). Bankrupt firm's equity securities as an investment alternative. *Financial Analysts Journal, 25*(4), 129–133.

Altman, E. I. (1968). Financial ratios, discriminant analysis and the prediction of corporate bankruptcy. *Journal of Finance, 23*(4), 589–609.

Altman, E. I. (1987). *Investing in junk bonds: Inside the high yield debt market*. Wiley.

Altman, E. I., Haldeman, R. G., & Narayanan, P. (1977). ZETAM analysis: A new model to identify bankruptcy risk of corporations. *Journal of Banking and Finance, 1*(1), 29–54.

Altman, E. I., Hartzell, J., & Peck, M. (1995). *Emerging markets corporate bonds: A scoring system*. Salomon Brothers.

Amihud, Y., & Lev, B. (1981). Risk reduction as a managerial motive for conglomerate mergers. *Bell Journal of Economics, 12*, 605–6017.

Anderson, M. C., Banker, R., & Janakiraman, S. (2003). Are selling, general and administrative costs "sticky"? *Journal of Accounting Research, 41*, 47–63.

Anthony, R. N., Hawkins, D. F., & Merchant, K. A. (2011). *Accounting: Text and cases* (13th ed.). McGraw-Hill.

Arditti, F., & Pinkerton, J. (1978). The valuation and cost of capital of the levered firm with growth opportunities. *Journal of Finance, XXXIII*(1), 54–73.

P. De Luca, *Corporate Finance*, Springer Texts in Business and Economics,
https://doi.org/10.1007/978-3-031-18300-3

Arrow, K. (1965). *"The theory of risk aversion", Aspects of the theory of risk-bearing (Lecture 2)*. Yrjs Jansson Foundation.

Arrow, K. (1971). *Essays in the theory of risk-bearing*. Markham.

Arrow, K. (1984). *Individual choice under certainty and uncertainty, collected papers of Kenneth J. Arrow* (Vol. 3). Belknap Press.

Arzac, E., & Bawa, V. (1977). Portfolio choice and equilibrium in capital markets with safety-first investors. *Journal of Financial Economics, 4*(3), 277–288.

Asquith, P., Mullins, D., & Wolff, E. (1989). Original issue high yield bonds: aging analysis of defaults, exchanges and calls. *Journal of Finance, 44*, 923–953.

Atrill, P., & McLaney, E. (2018). *Management accounting for decision makers* (9th ed.). Pearson.

Back, K. E. (2017). *Asset pricing and portfolio choice theory* (2nd ed.). Oxford University Press.

Baker, M., & Wurgler, J. (2002). Market timing and capital structure. *Journal of Finance, 57*, 1–32.

Balduzzi, P., Elton, E. J., & Green, T. C. (2001). Economic news and the yield curve: Evidence from the US Treasury Market. *Journal of Financial and Quantitative Analysis, 36*, 523–543.

Bancel, F., & Mittoo, U. R. (2004). Cross-country determinants of capital structure choice: A survey of european firms. *Financial Management, 33*(4), 103–132.

Baninoe, R. (2010). *Corporate bankruptcy prediction and equity returns in the UK*. Cranfield School of Management, Cranfield University.

Banker, R. D., Kaplan, R. S., Young, S. M., & Atkinson, A. A. (2000). *Management accounting*. Pearson College.

Bao, J. (2009). *Structural models of default and the cross section of corporate bond yield spreads, Working Paper*, MIT.

Barclay, M. J., & Holderness, C. G. (1989). Private benefits of control in public corporations. *Journal of Financial Economics, 25*, 371–374.

Barney, J. (1991). Firm resources and sustained competitive advantage. *Journal of Management, 17*, 99–120.

Baron, D. (1975). Firm valuation, corporate taxes, and default risk. *Journal of Finance, XXX*(5), 1251–1264.

Bawa, V., & Lindenburg, E. (1977). Capital market equilibrium in a mean-lower partial moment framework. *Journal of Financial Economics, 5*, 189–200.

Bawa, V. S., Brown, S. J., & Klein, R. W. (1979). *Estimation risk and optimal portfolio choice*. North Holland.

Beaver, W. H. (1966). Financial ratios as predictors of failure. *Journal of Accounting Research, 4*(3), 179–192.

Beaver, W. H. (1968). Alternative accounting measures as predictors of failure. *Journal of Accounting Research, 6*(1), 113.

Beaver, W., & Morse, D. (1978). What determines price-earnings ratios? *Financial Analysts Journal, 34*(4), 65–76.

Beaver, W., Kettler, P., & Scholes, M. (1970). The association between market determined and accounting determined risk measures. *The Accounting Review, 45*, 654–682.

Beck, T., Demirgüç-Kunt, A., & Maksimovic, V. (2002). *Financing patterns around the world: The role of institutions*. World Bank Policy Research Working Paper 2905.

Beidelman, C. (1971). Pitfalls of the price-earnings ratio. *Financial Analysts Journal, 27*(4), 86–91.

Benartzi, S., Michaely, R., & Thaler, R. (1997). Do changes in dividends signal the future or the past? *Journal of Finance, 52*, 1007–1034.

Benninga, S. (2014). *Financial modeling* (4th ed.). MIT Press.

Benninga, S., & Protopapadakis, A. (1991). The stock market premium, production and relative risk aversion. *The American Economic Review, 81*(3), 591–599.

Bergh, D. D. (1995). Size and relatedness of units sold. *Strategic Management Journal, 16*, 221–240.

Berk, J., & DeMarzo, P. (2017). *Corporate finance* (4th ed.). Pearson Education.

Berkowitz, D., Pistor, D., & Richard, J. F. (2003). Economic development, legality, and the transplant effect. *European Economic Review, 47*, 165–195.

Bernstein, P. L. (1973). What rate of return can you "reasonably" expect? *Journal of Finance, XXVIII*(2), 272–282.
Bernstein, S., Giroud, X., & Townsend, R. (2016). The impact of venture capital monitoring. *Journal of Finance, 17*(4), 1591–1622.
Bertsekas, D. (1974). Necessary and sufficient conditions for existence of an optimal portfolio. *Journal of Economic Theory, 8*(2), 235–247.
Bethel, J. E., & Liebeskind, J. (1993). The effects of ownership structure on corporate restructuring. *Strategic Management Journal, 14*, 15–31.
Bhagat, S., Bolton, B., & Subramanian, A. (2011). Manager characteristics and capital structure: Theory and evidence. *Journal of Financial and Quantitative Analysis, 46*, 1581–1627.
Bhatia, U. (1988). Predicting corporate sickness in India. *Studies in Banking and Finance, 7*, 57–71.
Bhimani, A., Horngren, C. T., Datar, S. M., & Rajan, M. (2015). *Management and cost accounting* (6th ed.). Pearson.
Bing, R. (1971). Survey of practitioners' stock evaluation methods. *Financial Analysts Journal, 27*(3), 55–69.
Black, F. (1972). Capital market equilibrium with restricted borrowing. *Journal of Business, 45*(3), 444–455.
Black, F. (1976). The dividend puzzle. *Journal of Portfolio Management, 2*, 5–8.
Black, F., & Cox, J. C. (1976). Valuing corporate securities: Some effects of bond indenture provisions. *Journal of Finance, 31*, 351–367.
Black, F., & Scholes, M. (1973). The pricing options and corporate liabilities. *Journal of Political Economy, 81*, 637–654.
Black, F., & Scholes, M. (1974). The effects of dividend yield and dividend policy on common stock prices and returns. *Journal of Financial Economics, 1*, 1–22.
Blanchard, O. (2017). *Macroeconomics* (7th ed.). Pearson.
Blume, M. E. (1970). Portfolio theory: A step toward its practical application. *The Journal of Business, 43*(2), 152–1573.
Blume, M. W. (1975). Betas and their regression tendencies. *The Journal of Finance, 30*(3), 785–795.
Blume, M. K. J., & Kraft, A. (1977). Determinants of common stock prices: A time series analysis. *Journal of Finance, XXXII*(2), 417–425.
Bonnes, J. C. A., & Jatusipitak, S. (1972). On relations among stock price behaviour a d changes in the capital structure of the firm. *Journal of Financial and Quantitative Analysis, VII*(4), 1967–1982.
Booth, L., Aivazian, V., Demirgüç-Kunt, A., & Maksimovic, V. (2001). Capital structure in developing countries. *Journal of Finance, 55*, 87–130.
Borch, K. (1969). Equilibrium, optimum and prejustices in capital markets. *Journal of Financial and Quantitative Analysis, IV*(1), 4–14.
Bower, J. L. (2001). Not all M&As are alike, and that matters. *Harvard Business Review, 79*(3), 92–101.
Bower, D., & Bower, S. R. (1970). Test of a stock valuation model. *Journal of Finance, XXV*(2), 483–492.
Boyd, J., & Jagannathan, R. (1994). Ex-dividend price behavior of common stocks. *Review of Financial Studies, 7*, 711–741.
Brace, A., Gatarek, D., & Musiela, M. (1997). The market model of interest rate dynamics. *Mathematical Finance, 7*(2), 127–147.
Brander, J., & Lewis, T. (1986). Capital structure and product market behaviour: The limited liability effect. *American Economic Review, 76*, 956–970.
Brav, A., Geczy, C., & Gompers, P. (2000). Is the abnormal return following equity issuances anomalous? *Journal of Financial Economics, 56*, 209–249.
Brav, A., Graham, J., Harvey, C., & Michaely, R. (2005). Payout policy in the 21st century. *Journal of Financial Economics, 77*, 483–527.

Brealey, R. A., Myers, S. C., & Allen, F. (2016). *Principles of corporate finance* (12th ed.). McGraw-Hill.

Breeden, D. (1979). An intertemporal asset pricing model with stochastic consumption and investment opportunities. *Journal of Financial Economics, 7*(3), 265–296.

Breeden, D., & Litzenberger, R. (1978). Prices of state-contingent claims implicit in option prices. *Journal of Business, 51*, 621–651.

Brennan, M. (1970). Taxes, market valuation and corporation financial policy. *National Tax Journal, 23*, 417–427.

Brennan, M. J. (1971). Capital market equilibrium with divergent borrowing and lending rates. *Journal of Financial and Quantitative Analysis, VI*(5), 1197–1205.

Brennan, M. J., & Kraus, A. (1976). The geometry of separation and myopia. *Journal of Financial and Quantitative Analysis, XI*(2), 171–193.

Brennan, M. J., & Schwartz, E. S. (1977). Convertible bonds: Valuation and optimal strategies for call and conversion. *Journal of Finance, 32*, 1699–1715.

Brennan, M. J., & Schwartz, E. S. (1980). Conditional predictions of bond prices and returns. *Journal of Finance, 35*(2), 405–416.

Brennan, M. J., & Schwartz, E. S. (1982). Bond pricing and market efficiency. *Financial Analyst Journal, 38*(5), 49–56.

Brenner, M., & Subrahmanyam, M. (1978). Portfolio selection in an economy with marketability and short sales restrictions. *Journal of Finance, XXXIII*(2), 589–601.

Brounen, D., De Jong, A., & Koedijk, K. (2006). Capital structure policies in Europe: Survey evidence. *Journal of Banking and Finance, 30*, 1409–1442.

Brown, S., & Barry, C. (1985). Differential information and security market equilibrium. *Journal of Financial and Quantitative Analysis, 20*, 407–422.

Brumelle, S. (1974). When does diversification between two investments pay? *Journal of Financial and Quantitative Analysis, IX*(3), 473–483.

Bruner, R. F. (2004). *Applied mergers and acquisitions*. Wiley Finance.

Buffet, M., & Clark, D. (2008). *Warren buffet and the interpretation of financial statements*. Simon & Schuster.

Buser, S. (1977). Mean-variance portfolio selection with either a singular or non-singular variance-covariance matrix. *Journal of Financial and Quantitative Analysis, XII*(3), 436–461.

Campbell, J. Y. (1986). A defense of traditional hypotheses about the term structure of interest rates. *Journal of Finance, 41*(1), 183–193.

Campbell, R. M. (2015). *Microeconomics: Principles, problems, and policies*. McGraw-Hill.

Campbell, J., & Shiller, R. (1989). The dividend price ratio and expectation of future dividends and discount factors. *Review of Financial Studies, 1*, 195–228.

Canner, N. (1997). An asset allocation puzzle. *American Economic Review, 87*(1), 181–193.

Carhart, M. (1997). On persistence in mutual fund performance. *Journal of Finance, 52*, 661–692.

Carleton, W. T., & Cooper, I. A. (1976). Estimation and uses of the term structure of interest rates. *Journal of Finance, 31*, 1067–1083.

Carlson, M., Fisher, A., & Giammarino, R. (2004). Corporate investment and asset price dynamics: Implications for the cross-section of returns. *Journal of Finance, 59*(6), 2577–2603.

Case, K. E., Ray, C. F., & Oster, S. E. (2016). *Principles of microeconomics* (19th ed.). Pearson.

Cass, D., & Stiglitz, J. (1970). The structure of investor preferences and asset returns, and separability in portfolio allocation: A contribution to the pure theory of mutual funds. *Journal of Economic Theory, 2*(2), 122–160.

Castellani, G., De Felice, M., & Moriconi, F. (2005). *Manuale di Finanza 2. Teoria del portafoglio e mercato azionario*. Il Mulino.

Cesari, R. (2012a). *Introduzione alla finanza matematica. Concetti di base, tassi e obbligazioni* (2nd ed.). McGraw-Hill.

Cesari, R. (2012b). *Introduzione alla finanza matematica. Mercati azionari, rischi, e portafogli* (2nd ed.). McGraw-Hill.

Chamberlain, G., & Rothschild, M. (1983). Arbitrage, factor structure, and mean-variance analysis on large asset markets. *Econometrica, 51*, 1281–1304.

Chambers, D. R., Carleton, W. T., & Waldman, D. W. (1984). A new approach to estimation of the term structure of interest rates. *Journal of Financial and Quantitative Analysis, 19*(3), 233–252.

Chan, A., & Thomson, H. E. (1988). Jump-diffusion and the term structure of interest rates. *Journal of Finance, 43*(1), 155–174.

Chan, L. K. C., Karceski, J., & Lakonishok, J. (1999). On portfolio optimization: Forecasting covariances and choosing the risk model. *Review of Financial Studies, 12*, 263–278.

Chance, D. M. (1990). Default risk and the duration of zero coupon bonds. *Journal of Finance, 45*(1), 265–274.

Chen, A. (1977). Portfolio selection with stochastic cash demand. *Journal of Financial and Quantitative Analysis, XII*(2), 197–213.

Chen, N. (1998). Risk and return of value stock. *Journal of Business, 71*(4), 501–535.

Chen, H., & Ritter, J. (2000). The seven percent solution. *Journal of Finance, 55*(3), 1105–1131.

Chen, A., Jen, F., & Zionts, S. (1971). The optimal portfolio revision policy. *Journal of Business, 44*(1), 51–61.

Chen, A., Kim, H., & Kon, S. (1975). Cash demands, liquidation costs and capital market equilibrium under uncertainty. *Journal of Financial Economics, 2*(3), 293–308.

Chen, N., Roll, R., & Ross, S. (1986). Economic forces and the stock market. *Journal of Business, 59*, 386–403.

Chen, L., Lesmond, D. A., & Wei, J. (2007). Corporate yield spreads and bond liquidity. *Journal of Finance, 62*, 119–149.

Chevalier, J., & Scharfstein, D. (1996). Capital markets imperfections and countercyclical markups: Theory and evidence. *American Economic Review, 86*, 703–725.

Chiang, E. P. (2013). *Core microeconomics* (3rd ed.). Worth Publishers.

Choe, H., Masulis, R., & Nanda, V. (1993). Common stock offerings across the business cycle: Theory and evidence. *Journal of Empirical Finance, 1*(1), 3–31.

Claessens, S., & Klapper, L. F. (2005). Bankruptcy around the world: Explanations of its relative use. *American Law and Economics Review, 7*(1), 253–283.

Cochrane, J. (2001). *Asset pricing*. Princeton University Press.

Cohen, K., & Pogue, J. (1967). An empirical evaluation of alternative portfolio selection models. *Journal of Business, 46*, 166–193.

Comment, R., & Jarrell, G. (1991). The relative signaling power of dutch-auction and fixed-price self-tender offers and open-market share repurchases. *Journal of Finance, 46*, 1243–1271.

Comment, R., & Schwert, G. W. (1995). Poison or placebo: Evidence on the deterrence and wealth effects of modern antitakeover measures. *Journal of Financial Economics, 39*(1), 3–43.

Connor, G. (1984). A unified beta pricing theory. *Journal of Economic Theory, 34*, 13–31.

Connor, G., & Korajczyk, R. (1993). A test for the number of factors in an approximate factor model. *Journal of Finance, 48*, 1263–1291.

Constantinides, G. M. (1980). Admissible uncertainty in the intertemporal asset pricing model. *Journal of Financial Economics, 8*(1), 71–87.

Cook, D., Krigman, L., & Leach, J. (2004). On the timing and execution of open market repurchases. *Review of Financial Studies, 17*, 463–498.

Copeland, T. (1979). Liquidity changes following stock splits. *Journal of Finance, 34*, 115–141.

Copeland, T., Weston, F., & Shastri, K. (2004). *Financial theory and corporate policy* (4th ed.). Addison-Wesley.

Cowen, T., & Tabarrok, A. (2014). *Modern principles of microeconomics* (3rd ed.). Worth Publishers.

Cox, J., Ross, S., & Rubinstein, M. (1979). Option pricing, a simplified approach. *Journal of Financial Economics, 7*, 229–263.

Cox, J. C., Ingersoll, J. E., & Ross, S. (1980). An analysis of variable rate loan contracts. *Journal of Finance, 35*(2), 389–404.

Cox, J. C., Ingersoll, J. E., & Ross, S. A. (1985). A theory of the term structure of interest rates. *Econometrica, 53*(2), 385–407.

Cremers, M., Driessen, J., & Maenhout, P. (2008). Explaining the level of credit spreads: Option implied jump risk premia in a firm value model. *Review of Financial Studies, 21*, 2209–2242.

Cuthbertson, K., & Nitzsche, D. (2014). *Quantitative financial economics: Stocks, bonds and foreign exchange* (2nd ed.). Wiley.

Dalal, A. J. (1983). On the use of a covariance function in a portfolio model. *Journal of Financial and Quantitative Analysis, XVIII*(2), 223–228.

Dallocchio, M., & Salvi, A. (2004). *Finanza d'azienda*. Egea.

Dallocchio, M., Tzivelis, D., & Vinzia, A. (2011). *Finanza per la crescita sostenibile*. Egea.

Dallocchio, M., Lucchini, G., & Pirrone, C. (2021). *Mergers and acquisitions* (2nd ed.). Egea.

Damodaran, A. (2012). *Investment valuation: tools and techniques for a determining the value of any assets* (3rd ed.). Wiley.

Damodaran, A. (2015). *Applied corporate finance* (4th ed.). Wiley.

Dasgupta, S., & Titman, S. (1998). Pricing strategy and financial policy. *Review of Financial Studies, 4*, 705–737.

De Jong, A., Kabir, R., & Nguyen, T. T. (2008). Capital structure around the world: The roles of firm and country specific determinants. *Journal of Banking and Finance, 32*, 1954–1969.

De Luca, P. (2015). The debt choices of the firms in developed countries: Evidence from G-7. *International Journal of Economics and Finance, 7*(4), 122–134.

De Luca, P. (2017). Debt level and the firm levered cost of capital. *International Journal of Economics and Financial Issues, 7*(5), 475–484.

De Luca, P. (2018). *Analytical corporate valuation* (pp. 1–469). Springer.

Demirgüç-Kant, A., & Maksimovic, V. (1998). Law, finance, and firm growth. *Journal of Finance, 53*, 2107–2137.

Demirgüç-Kant, A., & Maksimovic, V. (1999). Institutions, financial markets and firm debt maturity. *Journal of Financial Economics, 54*, 295–336.

Diamond, D. W. (1989). Reputation acquisition in debt markets. *Journal of Political Economy, 97*, 828–862.

Drury, C. (2016). *Management accounting for business* (6th ed.). Thomson Learning.

Duffie, D. (2001). *Dynamic asset pricing theory* (3rd ed.). Princeton University Press.

Duffie, D., & Singleton, K. (1999). Modeling term structures of defaultable bonds. *Review of Financial Studies, 12*(4), 197–226.

Dunbar, C. (2000). Factors affecting investment banks initial public offering market share. *Journal of Financial Economics, 55*(1), 3–41.

Dybving, P. H. (1984). Short sales restrictions and kinks of the mean variance frontier. *Journal of Finance, 39*(1), 239–244.

Dyck, A., & Zingales, L. (2004). Control premium and the effectiveness of corporate governance system. *Journal of Applied Finance, 16*, 51–72.

Eckbo, B. E., Masulis, R., & Norli, O. (2001). Seasoned public offerings: Resolution of the new issues puzzle. *Journal of Financial Economics, 56*(2), 251–291.

Edwards, F., & Goetzmann, W. (1994). Short horizon inputs and long horizon portfolio choice. *Journal of Portfolio Management, 20*(4), 76–81.

Elliott, B., & Elliott, J. (2013). *Financial accounting and reporting* (16th ed.). Pearson.

Elton, E., & Gruber, M. (1970). Marginal stockholder tax rates and the clientele effect. *Review of Economics and Statistics, 52*, 68–74.

Elton, E. J., & Gruber, M. J. (1971a). Valuation and the cost of capital for regulated industries. *Journal of Finance, XXVI*(3), 661–670.

Elton, E. J., & Gruber, M. J. (1971b). Dynamic programming applications in finance. *Journal of Finance, XXVI*(2), 473–505.

Elton, E. J., & Gruber, M. J. (1973). Asset selection with changing capital structure. *Journal of Financial and Quantitative Analysis, VIII*(3), 459–474.

Elton, E. J., & Gruber, M. J. (1974). Portfolio theory when investment relatives are lognormally distributed. *Journal of Finance, XXIX*(4), 1265–1273.
Elton, E. J., & Gruber, M. J. (1976). Valuation and the asset selection under alternative investment opportunities. *Journal of Finance, XXXI*(2), 525–539.
Elton, E. J., & Gruber, M. J. (1977). Risk reduction and portfolio size: An analytical solution. *Journal of Business, 50*(4), 415–496.
Elton, E. J., Gruber, M. J., & Urich, T. (1978). Are betas best? *Journal of Finance, XIII*(5), 1375–1384.
Elton, E. J., Gruber, M. J., Agrawal, D., & Mann, C. (2001). Explaining the rate spread on corporate bonds? *Journal of Finance, LVI*(1), 247–279.
Elton, E. J., Gruber, M. J., & Spitzer, J. (2006). Improved estimates of correlation coefficients and their impact on the optimum portfolios. *European Financial Management, 12*(3), 303–318.
Elton, E. J., Gruber, M. J., Brown, S. J., & Goetzmann, W. N. (2013). *Modern portfolio theory and investment analysis* (9th ed.). Wiley.
Eom, Y. H., Helwege, J., & Huang, J. Z. (2004). Structural models of corporate bond pricing: An empirical analysis. *Review of Financial Studies, 17*, 499–544.
Epps, T. W. (1981). Necessary and sufficient conditions for the mean-variance portfolio model with constant risk aversion. *Journal of Financial and Quantitative Analysis, XVI*(2), 169–176.
Fama, E. (1968). Risk, return, and equilibrium: Some clarifying comments. *Journal of Finance, 23*, 29–40.
Fama, E. (1970). Multi-period consumption investment decision. *American Economic Review, 60*, 163–164.
Fama, E. (1971). Risk, return and equilibrium. *Journal of Political Economy, 79*(1), 30–55.
Fama, E. (1976a). *Foundations of finance*. Basic Books.
Fama, E. (1976b). Forward rates as predictors of future sport rates. *Journal of Financial Economics, 3*, 361–377.
Fama, E. (1981). Stock return, real activity, inflation and money. *American Economic Review, 71*, 545–565.
Fama, E. (1984a). The information in the term structure. *Journal of Financial Economics, 13*(4), 509–528.
Fama, E. (1984b). Term premiums in bond returns. *Journal of Financial Economics, 13*(4), 529–546.
Fama, E. (1998). Determining the number of priced state variable in the ICAPM. *Journal of Financial and Quantitative Analysis, 33*(2), 271–231.
Fama, E., & French, K. (1993). Common risk factors in the return on stocks and bonds. *Journal of Financial Economics, 33*, 3–56.
Fama, E., & French, K. (1998). Taxes, financing decisions, and firm value. *Journal of Finance, 53*, 819–843.
Fama, E., & French, K. (2001). Disappearing dividends: Changing firm characteristics or lower propensity to pay? *Journal of Financial Economics, 60*, 3–43.
Fama, E., & French, K. (2002). Testing trade-off and pecking order predictions about dividends and debt. *Review of Financial Studies, 15*, 1–33.
Fama, E., & James, M. B. (1973). Risk, return, and equilibrium: empirical tests. *Journal of Political Economy, 38*, 607–636.
Fama, E., MacBeth, J., & Schwert, G. (1977). Asset returns and inflation. *Journal of Financial Economics, 5*, 115–146.
Fama, E., MacBeth, J., & Schwert, G. (1979). Inflation, interest and relative prices. *Journal of Business, 52*, 183–209.
Fan, J., Titman, S., & Twite, G. (2012). An international comparison of capital structure and debt maturity choices. *Journal of Financial and Quantitative Analysis, 47*, 23–56.
Farrell, J. (1974). *The multi-index model and practical portfolio analysis*. The Financial Analysts Research Foundation Occasional Paper, No. 4.

Farre-Mensa, J., Michaely, R., & Schmalz, M. (2014). Payout policy. *Annual Review of Financial Economics, 6*, 75–134.

Fishburn, P. C., & Kochenberger, G. A. (1979). Two-piece von Neumann-Morgenstern utility functions. *Decision Sciences, 10*(4), 503–518.

Fisher, I. (1930). *The theory of interest*. Macmillan.

Foster, E. (1970). Price-earnings ratio and corporate growth: A revision. *Financial Analysts Journal, 26*(4), 115–118.

Fraine, H. G., & Mills, R. H. (1961). The effect of default and credit deterioration on yields of corporate bonds. *Journal of Finance, 16*, 423–433.

Francis, J. C. (1975). Intertemporal differences in systemic stock price movements. *Journal of Financial and Quantitative Analysis, 10*(2), 205–219.

Frank, M. Z., & Goyal, V. K. (2003). Testing the pecking order theory of capital structure. *Journal of Financial Economics, 67*, 217–248.

Frank, M. Z., & Goyal, V. K. (2009). Capital structure decisions: Which factors are reliably important? *Financial Management, 38*, 1–37.

Frankel, R., & Lee, C. M. C. (1998). Accounting valuation, market expectation, and cross-sectional stock returns. *Journal of Accounting and Economics, 25*, 283–319.

Friend, I., & Hasbrouck, J. (1988). Determinants of capital structure. *Research in Finance, 7*, 1–19.

Friend, I., & Westerfield, R. (1980). Co-skewness and capital assets pricing. *The Journal of Finance, 35*(4), 897–914.

Fuller, R. J., & Farrell, J. L. (1987). *Modern investments and security analysis*. McGraw-Hill.

Fuller, R. J., & Hsia, C. C. (1984). A simplified common stock valuation model. *Financial Analysts Journal, 40*(5), 49–56.

Garrison, R. H., Noreen, E. W., & Brewer, P. C. (2014). *Managerial accounting* (15th ed.). McGraw-Hill.

Gompers, P., & Lerner, J. (1999). *The venture capital cycle*. MIT Press.

Gonedes, N. J. (1973). Evidence on the information content of accounting numbers: Accounting-based and market-based estimates of systemic risk. *Journal of Financial and Quantitative Analysis, 8*, 407–443.

Gordon, M. (1962). *The investment, financing, and valuation of the corporation*. Richard D. Irwin.

Graham, J. R. (1999). Do personal taxes affect corporate financing decisions? *Journal of Public Economics, 73*, 41–73.

Graham, J. R. (2000). How big are the tax benefits of debt? *Journal of Finance, 55*, 1901–1941.

Graham, B., & Dodd, D. (1940). *Security analysis*. McGraww-Hill Book Company.

Graham, J. R., & Harvey, C. R. (2001). The theory and practice of corporate finance: Evidence from the field. *Journal of Financial Economics, 60*, 187–243.

Graham, B., Dodd, D., & Cottle, S. (1962). *Security analysis principles and techniques* (4th ed.). McGraw-Hill.

Gravelle, H., & Rees, R. (1992). *Microeconomics* (2nd ed.). Longman.

Grossman, S., & Hart O. (1982). Corporate finance structure and managerial incentives. In *The economics of information and uncertainty*. National Bureau of Economic Research, Inc.

Grossman, S., & Shiller, R. (1982). Consumption correlatedness and risk measurement in economies with non-traded assets and heterogeneous information. *Journal of Financial Economics, 10*, 195–210.

Grossman, S., Melino, A., & Shiller, R. (1985). Estimating the continuous-time consumption-based asset-pricing model. *Journal of Business and Economic Statistic, 5*, 315–328.

Grullon, G., & Ikenberry, D. (2000). What do we know about stock repurchase? *Journal of Applied Corporate Finance, 13*(1), 31–51.

Grullon, G., & Michaely, R. (2002). Dividends, share repurchases, and the substitution hypothesis. *Journal of Finance, 57*, 1649–1684.

Grullon, G., Michaely, R., & Swaminathan, B. (2002). Are dividend changes a sign of firm maturity? *Journal of Business, 75*, 387–424.

Guiso, L., Jappelli, T., & Terlizzese, D. (1996). Income risk, borrowing constraints, and portfolio choice. *The American Economic Review, 86*(1), 158–172.

Gupta, V. (2013). A unified credit risk model for predicting default. *Prajnam, 42*(3), 2015–2045.

Hagerman, R., & Kim, H. (1976). Capital asset pricing with price level change. *Journal of Financial and Quantitative Analysis, XI*(3), 381–391.

Hakansson, N. (1970). An induced theory of the firm under risk: The pure mutual fund. *Journal of Financial and Quantitative Analysis, V*(2), 155–178.

Hall, G. C., Hutchinson, P. J., & Michaelas, N. (2004). Determinants of the capital structures of European SMEs. *Journal of Business Finance and Accounting, 31*, 711–728.

Hamada, R. S. (1972). The effect of the firm's capital structure on the systemic risk of common stocks. *Journal of Finance, 27*(2), 435–452.

Hamel, G., & Prahalad, C. (1990). The core competence of the corporation, *Harvard Business Review*, May–June, pp. 1–15.

Handa, P., Kothari, S. P., & Wasley, C. (1989). The relationship between the return interval and betas: Implications for the size effect. *Journal of Financial Economics, 23*(1), 79–101.

Hansen, R. (2001). Do investment banks compete in IPOs?: The advent of the 7% plus contract. *Journal of Financial Economics, 59*(3), 313–346.

Hansen, L., & Singleton, K. (1982). Generalized instrumental variables estimation of nonlinear rational expectations models. *Econometrica, 50*, 1269–1286.

Harris, R. S., & Pringle, J. J. (1985). Risk-adjusted discount rates-extensions from the average-risk case. *Journal of Financial Research, 8*(3), 237–244.

Harris, M., & Raviv, A. (1991). The theory of capital structure. *Journal of Finance, 1*, 297–355.

Hart, O., & Moore, J. (1995). Debt and seniority: An analysis of the role and hard claims in constraining management. *American Economic Review, 85*(3), 567–585.

Haugen, R., & Kumar, P. (1974). The traditional approach to valuing levered-growth stocks: A clarification. *Journal of Financial and Quantitative Analysis, IX*(6), 1031–1044.

Haugen, R., & Pappas, J. L. (1971). Equilibrium in the pricing of capital assets, risk-bearing debt instruments, and the question of optimal capital structure. *Journal of Financial and Quantitative Analysis, VI*(3), 943–953.

Hawkins, D. (1977). Toward an old theory of equity valuation. *Financial Analysts Journal, 33*(6), 48–53.

Healy, P., & Palepu, K. (1988). Earnings information conveyed by dividend initiations and omissions. *Journal of Financial Economics, 21*, 149–176.

Heap, S., Lyons, B., Hollis, M., Sugden, R., & Weale, A. (1992). *The theory of choice: A critical guide*. Blackwell.

Heath, D., Jarrow, R., & Morton, A. (1992). Bond pricing and the term structure of interest rates: A new methodology for contingent claims valuation. *Econometrica, 60*(1), 77 105.

Heckerman, D. (1972). Portfolio selection and the structure of capital asset prices when relative prices of consumption goods may change. *Journal of Finance, XXVII*(1), 47–60.

Heron, R., & Lie, E. (2006). One the use of poison pills and defensive payouts by takeover targets. *Journal of Business, 79*(4), 1783–1807.

Hicks, J. R. (1939). *Value and capital* (2nd ed.). Clarendon Press.

Hill, R. (1976). An algorithm for counting the number of possible portfolios given linear restrictions on the weights. *Journal of Financial Economics, XI*(3), 479–487.

Hill, N. C., & Stone, B. K. (1980). Accounting betas, systematic operating risk, and financial leverage: A risk-composition approach to the determinants of systemic risk. *Journal of Financial and Quantitative Analysis, XV*(3), 595–638.

Hilliard, J. E. (1980). Asset pricing under a subset of linear risk tolerance functions and log-normal market returns. *Journal of Financial and Quantitative Analysis, XV*(5), 1041–1062.

Hillier, D., Ross, S., Westerfield, R., Jaffe, J., & Jordan, B. (2016). *Corporate finance* (3rd ed.). McGraw-Hill.

Hirshleifer, J., & Riley, J. G. (1992). *The analytics of uncertainty and information*. Cambridge University Press.

Ho, T., & Lee, S. (1986). Term structure movements and pricing interest rate contingent claims. *Journal of Finance, 41*(5), 1011–1029.
Holderness, C., & Pontiff, J. (2016). Shareholders nonparticipation in valuable rights offerings: New findings for an old puzzle. *Journal of Financial Economics, 120*(2), 252–268.
Hoskisson, R. E., Johnson, J. R. A., & Moesel, D. D. (1994). Corporate divestiture intensity in restructuring firms: effects of governance, strategy and performance. *Academy of Management Journal, 37*, 1207–1238.
Hovakimian, A. (2006). Are observed capital structures determined by equity market timing? *Journal of Financial and Quantitative Analysis, 41*, 221–243.
Huang, J. Z., & Huang, M. (2012). How much of the corporate-treasury yield spread is due to credit risk? *The Review of Asset Pricing Studies, 2*(2), 153–202.
Hull, J., & White, A. (1990). Pricing interest-rate derivative securities. *The Review of Financial Studies, 3*(4), 573–592.
Ikenberry, D., Lakonishok, J., & Vermaelen, T. (1995). Market underreaction to open market share repurchase. *Journal of Financial Economics, 39*, 181–208.
Ingersoll, J. E. (1987). *Theory of financial decision making*. Rowman&Littlefield Pub Inc.
Jacob, N. (1974). A limited-diversification portfolio selection model for the small investor. *Journal of Finance, XXIX(3)*, 847–856.
Jarrow, R. (1980). Heterogeneous expectations, restrictions and short sales, and equilibrium asset prices. *The Journal of Finance, 35*(5), 1105–1114.
Jarrow, R., & Turnbull, M. T. (1995). *Pricing derivatives on financial securities subject to credit risk, 50*(1), 53–85.
Jennings, E. (1971). An empirical analysis of some aspects of common stock diversification. *Journal of Financial and Quantitative Analysis, VI*(2), 797–813.
Jensen, M. C. (1986). Agency cost of free cash flow, corporate finance and takeovers. *American Economic Review, 76*, 323–329.
Jensen, M. C., & Meckling, W. (1976). Theory of the firm: Managerial behavior, agency costs, and ownership structure. *Journal of Financial Economics, 3*, 305–360.
Johnson, R. (1967). Term structure of corporate bond yields as a function of risk of default. *Journal of Finance, 22*, 313–345.
Johnson, K., & Shannon, D. (1974). A note of diversification and the reduction of dispersion. *Journal of Financial Economics, 1*(4), 365–372.
Jones-Lee, M. W. (1971). Some portfolio adjustment theorems for the case of non-negativity conditions on security holdings. *Journal of Finance, XXVI*(3), 763–775.
Joy, M., & Jones, C. (1970). Another look at the value of P/E ratios. *Financial Analysts Journal, 26*(4), 61–64.
Julio, B., & Ikenberry, D. (2004). Reappearing dividends. *Journal of Applied Corporate Finance, 16*, 89–100.
Jung, K., Kim, Y. C., & Stulz, R. M. (1996). Timing, investment opportunities, managerial discretion, and security issue decision. *Journal of Financial Economics, 42*, 159–185.
Kalay, A. (1982). The ex-dividend day behavior of stock prices: A reexamination of the clientele effect. *Journal of Finance, 37*, 1059–1070.
Kalay, A., & Michaely, R. (2000). Dividends and taxes: A reexamination. *Financial Management, 29*, 55–75.
Kaplan, R., & Atkinson, A. A. (1998). *Advanced Management Accounting* (3rd ed.). Prentice Hall.
Kaplan, S., & Ruback, R. (1995). The valuation of cash flow forecast: An empirical analysis. *The Journal of Finance, 4*, 1059–1093.
Kim, J., Ramaswamy, K., & Sundaresan, S. (1993). Does default risk in coupons affect the valuation of corporate bonds?: A contingent claims model. *Financial Management*, Autumn, 177–131.
Klemkosky, R., & Martin, J. (1975). The effect of market risk on portfolio diversification. *Journal of Finance, X(1)*, 147–153.
Koller, T., Goedhart, M., & Wessels, D. (2015). *Valuation* (6th ed.). Wiley.

Korajczyk, R. A., & Levey, A. (2003). Capital structure choice: Macroeconomic conditions and financial constraints. *Journal of Financial Economics, 68*, 75–109.

Korajczyk, R. A., Lucas, D., & McDonald, R. (1991). The effects of information releases on the pricing and timing of equity issue. *Review of Financial Studies, 4*, 685–708.

Korajczyk, R. A., Lucas, D., & McDonald, R. (1992). Equity issue with time-varying asymmetric information. *Journal of Financial and Quantitative Analysis, 27*, 397–417.

Koski, J., & Michaely, R. (2000). Prices, liquidity, and the information content of trades. *Review of Financial Studies, 13*, 659–696.

Kraus, A., & Litzenberger, R. H. (1973). A state-preference model of optimal financial leverage. *Journal of Finance, 28*, 911–922.

Kraus, A., & Litzenberger, R. (1975). Market equilibrium in a multi-period state preference model with logarithmic utility. *Journal of Finance, XXX*(5), 1213–1227.

Kreps, D. M. (1979). A representation theorem for "preference for flexibility". *Econometrica, 47*(3), 565–577.

Kreps, D. M. (1990). *A course in microeconomic theory*. Princeton University Press.

Kreps, D. M. (2012). *Microeconomic foundations I: Choice and competitive markets*. Princeton University Press.

Kroll, Y., & Levy, H. (1992). Further tests of the separation theorem and the capital asset pricing model. *The American Economic Review, 82*(3), 664–670.

Krugman, P., & Wells, R. (2018). *Microeconomics* (5th ed.).

Kryzanowski, L., & To, M. C. (1983). General factor models and structure of security returns. *Journal of Financial and Quantitative Analysis, 18*, 31–52.

Kumar, R. G., & Kumar, K. (2012). A comparison of bankruptcy models. *International Journal of Marketing, Financial Services and Management Research, 1*(4), 76–86.

La Porta, R. (1996). Expectations and the cross section of stock returns. *Journal of Finance, 51*, 1715–1742.

La Porta, R., Lopez-De-Silanes, F., Shleifer, A., & Vishny, R. W. (1997). Legal determinants of external finance. *Journal of Finance, 52*, 1131–1150.

La Porta, R., Lopez-De-Silanes, F., Shleifer, A., & Vishny, R. W. (1998). Law and finance. *Journal of Political Economy, 106*, 1113–1155.

La Porta, R., Lopez-de-Silanes, F., Shleifer, A., & Vishny, R. W. (1999). The quality of government. *Journal of Law, Economics, and Organization, 15*, 222–279.

La Porta, R., Lopez-de-Silanes, F., Shleifer, A., & Vishny, R. W. (2002). Investor protection and corporate valuation. *Journal of Finance, 57*, 1147–1170.

Lakonishok, J., & Lev, B. (1987). Stock splits and stock dividends: Why, who and when. *Journal of Finance, 42*, 913–932.

Landskroner, Y. (1977a). Nonmarketable assets and the determinants of the market price of risk. *Review of Economics and Statistics, LIX*(4), 482–514.

Landskroner, Y. (1977b). Intertemporal determination of the market price of risk. *Journal of Finance, XXXII*(5), 1671–1681.

Lane, P. J., Cannella, A. A., Jr., & Lubatkin, M. H. (1998). Agency problems as antecedents to unrelated mergers and diversification: Amihud and lev reconsidered. *Strategic Management Journal, 19*, 555–578.

Latane, H., Tuttle, D., & Young, A. (1971). How to choose a market index. *Financial Analysis Journal, 27*(4), 75–85.

Ledoit, O., & Wolf, M. (2003). Improved estimation of the covariance matrix of stock returns with an application to portfolio selection. *Journal of Empirical Finance, 10*(5), 603–624.

Lehari, D., & Levy, H. (1977). The capital asset pricing model and the investment horizon. *Review of Economics and Statistics, LIX*(1), 92–1904.

Leland, H. E., & Toft, K. B. (1996). Optimal capital structure, endogenous bankruptcy, and the term structure of credit spreads. *The Journal of Finance, 51*, 987–1019.

Lennox, C. (1999). Identifying failing companies: A re-evaluation of the logit, probit, and DA approaches. *Journal of Economics and Business, 15*, 347–364.

Levy, R. A. (1971). On the short-term, stationary of Beta coefficients. *Financial Analysis Journal, 27*(5), 55–62.

Levy, H. (1973). The demand for assets under condition of risk. *Journal of Finance, XXVIII*(1), 79–81.

Levy, R. A. (1974). Beta coefficients as predictors of return. *Financial Analysts Journal, 30*(1), 61–69.

Levy, H. (1984). Measuring risk and performance over alternative investment horizons. *Financial Analysis Journal, 40*(2), 61–67.

Lewis, A. L. (1988). A simple algorithm for the portfolio selection problem. *Journal of Finance, 43*(1), 71–82.

Lintner, J. (1956). Distribution of incomes of corporations among dividends. *Retained Earnings and Taxes, American Economic Review, 49*, 97–113.

Lintner, J. (1965a). The valuation of risk assets and the selection of risky investments in stock portfolios and capital budgets. *Review of Economics and Statistics, 47*(1), 13–37.

Lintner, J. (1965b). Security prices, risk, and maximal gains from diversification. *Journal of Finance, 20*(4), 587–615.

Lintner, J. (1969). The aggregation of investor's diverse judgments and preferences in purely competitive security markets. *Journal of Financial and Quantitative Analysis, IV*(4), 347–400.

Lintner, J. (1970). The market price of risk, size of market and investor's risk aversion. *The Review of Economics and Statistics, 52*(1), 87–99.

Lintner, J. (1971). The effect of short selling and margin requirements in perfect capital markets. *Journal of Financial and Quantitative Analysis, VI*(5), 1173–1195.

Litzenberg, R., & Ronn, E. (1986). A utility based model of common stock return. *Journal of Finance, 41*, 67–92.

Litzenberger, R., & Budd, A. (1970). Corporate investment criteria and the valuation of risk assets. *Journal of Financial and Quantitative Analysis, V*(4), 385–419.

Litzenberger, R., & Ramaswamy, K. (1979). The effects of personal taxes and dividends on capital asset prices: Theory and empirical evidence. *Journal of Financial Economics, 7*, 163–165.

Logue, D., & Merville, L. (1972). Financial policy and market expectations. *Financial Management, 1*, 37–44.

Long, J. (1974). Stock prices, inflation, and the term structure of interest rates. *Journal of Financial Economics, 1*(2), 131–170.

Loughran, T., & Ritter, J. (1995). The new issues puzzle. *Journal of Finance, 50*, 23–51.

Lucas, R. (1978). Asset prices in an exchange economy. *Econometrica, 46*, 1429–1445.

Lucas, D., & MacDonald, R. (1990). Equity issues and stock price dynamics. *Journal of Finance, 45*, 1019–1043.

Lyandres, E., Sun, L., & Zhang, L. (2008). The new issues puzzle: Testing the investment-based explanation. *Review of Financial Studies, 21*(6), 2825–2855.

Malatesta, P., & Walkling, R. (1988). Poison pill securities: Stockholder wealth, profitability and ownership structure. *Journal of Financial Economics, 20*(1), 347–376.

Malkiel, B. (1963). Equity yields, growth, and the structure of share prices. *American Economic Review, 53*, 1004–1031.

Malkiel, B. (1966). *The term structure of interest rates*. Princeton University Press.

Malkiel, B., & Cragg, J. (1970). Expectations and the structure of share price. *American Economic Review, LX*(4), 601–617.

Mankiw, N. G. (2016). *Principles of microeconomics* (8th ed.). South-Western Publishing.

Markowitz, H. (1952). Portfolio selection. *The Journal of Finance, 7*(1), 77–91.

Markowitz, H. (1956). The optimization of a quadratic function subject to linear constraints. *Naval Research Logistics, 3*(1–2), 111–133.

Markowitz, H. (1959). *Portfolio selection: Efficient diversification of investment*. Wiley.

Markowitz, H. (1976). Markowitz revisited. *Financial Analysts Journal, 32*(4), 47–52.

Markowitz, H. (2014). *The theory and practice of rational investing. Risk-return analysis* (Vol. I). McGraw-Hill.

Markowitz, H. (2016). *The theory and practice of rational investing. Risk-return analysis* (Vol. II). McGraw-Hill.

Marsh, P. (1982). The choice between equity and debt: An empirical study. *Journal of Finance, 37*, 121–144.

Martin, J., & Klemkosky, R. (1975). Evidence of heteroscedasticity in the market model. *Journal of Business, 48*(1), 81–86.

Massari, M., & Zanetti, L. (2008). *Valutazione. Fondamenti teorici e best practice nel settore industriale e finanziario*. McGraw-Hill.

Mayers, D. (1973). Nonmarketable assets and the determination of capital asset prices in the absence of a riskless asset. *Journal of Business, 46*(2), 258–267.

Mayers, D. (1976). nonmarketable assets, market segmentation and the level of asset prices. *Journal of Financial and Quantitative Analysis, XI*(1), 1–37.

McCulloch, J. H. (1971). Measuring the term structure of interest rate. *Journal of Business, 44*, 19–31.

McCulloch, J. H. (1975). An estimate of the liquidity premium. *Journal of Political Economy, 83*, 95–119.

Mellen, C. M., & Evans, F. C. (2010). *Valuation for M&A, building value in private companies*. Wiley.

Merton, R. (1972). An analytic derivation of the efficient portfolio frontier. *Journal of Financial and Quantitative Analysis, VII*(4), 1851–1872.

Merton, R. (1973). An intertemporal capital asset pricing model. *Econometrica, 41*(5), 867–888.

Merton, R. (1974). On the pricing of corporate debt: The risk structure of interest rates. *Journal of Finance, 29*(2), 449–470.

Meyers, S. (1973). A re-examination of market and industry factors in stock price behavior. *Journal of Finance, VIII*(3), 695–705.

Miles, J. A., & Ezzell, J. R. (1980). The weighted average cost of capital. *Perfect Capital Markets, and Project Life: A Clarification, 15*(3), 719–730.

Miller, M. H. (1977). Debt and taxes. *Journal of Finance, 32*(2), 261–275.

Miller, M. H., & Scholes, M. (1978). Dividends and taxes. *Journal of Financial Economics, 6*, 333–364.

Milne, F., & Smith, C. (1980). Capital asset pricing with proportional transaction cost. *Journal of Financial and Quantitative Analysis, XV*(2), 253–266.

Mishkin, F. S. (2019). *The economics of money, banking, and financial markets* (12th ed.). Pearson.

Modigliani, F. (1982). Debt, dividend policy, taxes, inflation and market valuation. *Journal of Finance, 37*(2), 255–273.

Modigliani, F., & Miller, M. H. (1958). The cost of capital, corporate finance and the theory of investment. *American Economic Review, 48*, 261–297.

Modigliani, F., & Miller, M. H. (1961). Dividend policy, growth, and the valuation of shares. *The Journal of Business, 34*(4), 411–433.

Modigliani, F., & Miller, M. H. (1963). Corporate income taxes and the cost of capital: A correction. *American Economic Review, 53*, 433–443.

Modigliani, F., & Pogue, J. (1974a). An introduction to risk and return. *Financial Analysists Journal, 30*(2), 68–80.

Modigliani, F., & Pogue, J. (1974b). An introduction to risk and return: Part II. *Financial Analysists Journal, 30*(3), 69–86.

Modigliani, F., & Sutch, R. (1966). Innovations in interest rate policy. *American Economic Review, LVI*, 178–197.

Molodovsky, N., May, C., & Chottinger, S. (1965). Common stock valuation. *Financial Analysts Journal, 21*, 104–123.

Morellec, E. (2004). Can managerial discretion explain observed leverage ratios? *Review of Financial Studies, 17*, 257–294.

Morellec, E., & Schurhoff, N. (2010). Dynamic investment and financing under personal taxation. *Review of Financial Studies, 23*, 101–146.

Mossin, J. (1966). Equilibrium in a capital asset market. *Econometrica, 34*(4), 768–783.

Mossin, J. (1968). Optimal multiperiod portfolio policies. *Journal of Business, 41*(2), 215–229.

Myers, S. C. (1974). Interactions of corporate financing and investment decisions – Implications for capital budgeting. *The Journal of Finance, 29*(1), 1–25.

Myers, S. C. (1977). Determinants of corporate borrowing. *Journal of Financial Economics, 5*, 147–175.

Myers, S. C. (1984). The capital structure puzzle. *Journal of Finance, 39*, 575–592.

Myers, S. C. (2001). Capital structure. *Journal of Economic Perspectives, 15*, 81–102.

Myers, S. C. (2003). Financing of corporations. In G. Constantinides, M. Harris, & R. Stulz (Eds.), *Handbook of the economics of finance* (pp. 215–253). Elsevier.

Myers, S. C., & Majluf, N. S. (1984). Corporate financing and investment decision when firms have information that investors do not have. *Journal of Financial Economics, 13*, 187–221.

Nayak, S., & Prabhala, N. (2001). Disentangling the dividend information in splits: A decomposition using conditional event-study methods. *Review of Financial Studies, 14*, 1083–1116.

Nelson, C. R., & Siegel, A. F. (1985). *Parsimoneous modeling of yield curves for U.S. Treasury Bills*. NBER Working Paper, No. 1594.

Nevona, T. (2003). The value of corporate voting rights and control: A cross-country analysis. *Journal of Financial Economics, 68*, 325–351.

Noe, T. (1988). Capital structure and signalling game equilibria. *Review of Financial Studies, 1*, 331–356.

Noe, T., & Rebello, M. J. (1996). Asymmetric information, managerial opportunism, financing, and payout policies. *Journal of Finance, 51*, 637–660.

Oded, J. (2005). Why do firms announce open-market repurchase programs? *Review of Financial Studies, 18*, 271–300.

Officer, R. R. (1973). The variability of the market factor of the New York Stock Exchange. *Journal of Business, 46*(3), 434–453.

Ohlson, J. (1975). Portfolio selection in a log-stable market. *Journal of Financial and Quantitative Analysis, X*(2), 285–298.

Ohlson, J. A. (1980). Financial ratios and the probabilistic prediction of bankruptcy. *Journal of Accounting Research, 18*(1), 109–131.

Pagano, M., Panetta, F., & Zingales, L. (1998). Why do companies go public? An empirical analysis. *Journal of Finance, 53*, 27–64.

Pearson, C. A., & Titman, S. (2008). Empirical capital structure: A review. *Foundations and Trends in Finance, 3*, 1–93.

Perloff, J. (2016). *Microeconomics: Theory and applications with calculus* (4th ed.). Pearson.

Pettit, R. R., & Westerfield, R. (1972). A model of capital asset risk. *Journal of Financial and Quantitative Analysis, VII*(2), 1649–1668.

Pindyck, R. S., & Rubinfeld, D. L. (1992). *Microeconomics* (9th ed.). Pearson.

Pogue, G., & Solnik, B. (1974). The market model applied to European common stocks: Some empirical results. *Journal of Financial and Quantitative Analysis, IX*(6), 917–944.

Porter, M. E. (1985). *Competitive advantage. Creating and sustaining superior performance*. Free Press.

Pratt, J. W. (1964). Risk aversion in the small and in the large. *Econometrica, 32*(1/2), 122–136.

Pye, G. (1973). Lifetime portfolio selection in continuous time for a multiplicative class of utility functions. *American Economic Review, LXIII*(5), 1013–1020.

Rabinovitch, R., & Owel, J. (1978). Non-homogeneous expectations and information in capital asset market. *Journal of Finance, XXXIII*(2), 575–587.

Rajan, R. G., & Zingales, L. (1995). What do we know about capital structure: some evidence from international data. *Journal of Finance, 50*, 1421–1460.

Rajan, R. G., & Zingales, L. (1998). Financial dependence and growth. *American Economic Review, 88*, 559–587.

Rajan, R. G., & Zingales, L. (2003). The great reversals: The politics of financial development in the twentieth century. *Journal of Financial Economics, 69*, 559–586.